FISKE
GUIDE TO
COLLEGES

2004

Also by Edward B. Fiske

Fiske Guide to Getting into the Right College with Bruce G. Hammond

Smart Schools, Smart Kids: Why Do Some Schools Work? with Sally Reed and R. Craig Sautter

Get Organized! with Phyllis Steinbrecher

Using Both Hands: Women and Education in Cambodia

When Schools Compete: A Cautionary Tale with Helen F. Ladd

FISKE
GUIDE TO
COLLEGES

2004

EDWARD B. FISKE

former Education Editor of
The New York Times
with Robert Logue
and
The *Fiske Guide to Colleges* Staff

SOURCEBOOKS, INC.®
NAPERVILLE, ILLINOIS

Published by Sourcebooks, Inc.
P.O. Box 4410
Naperville, Illinois 60567-4410
(800) 432-7444
FAX: (630) 961-2168
www.sourcebooks.com

ISBN 1-4022-0060-9
Twentieth Edition

Your comments and corrections are welcome.
Please send them to:

The Fiske Guide to Colleges
P.O. Box 287
Alstead, NH 03602
Fax: (603) 835-7859
Email: editor@fiskeguide.com

Printed and bound in the United States of America
DR 10 9 8 7 6 5 4 3 2 1

To Sunny

Contents

Index by State ix

Index by Price xiii

The Best Buys of 2004 xvi

Introduction xvii
   Fiske Guide to Colleges—and How to Use It xvii
   What Is the *Fiske Guide to Colleges*? xvii
   How the Colleges Were Selected xviii
   How the *Fiske Guide* Was Compiled xviii
   The Format xix
   Best Buys xix
   Statistics xx
   SAT and ACT Scores xx
   Scholarship Information xxi
   Ratings xxii
      Academics xxii
      Social Life xxii
      Quality of Life xxiii
   Overlaps xxiii
   If You Apply… xxiii
   Consortia xxiv
   Moving Forward xxiv

Sizing Yourself Up xxv
   Develop Your Criteria xxv
   Keep an Open Mind xxvi

Fiske's Sizing-Yourself-Up Survey xxvii
   Sizing Up the Survey xxviii
   Putting It All Together xxviii

A Guide for Preprofessionals xxxi
   Architecture xxxi
   Art/Design xxxi
   Business xxxi
   Communications/Journalism xxxii
   Engineering xxxii
   Film/Television xxxiii

Performing Arts—Music xxxiii

Performing Arts—Drama xxxiii

Performing Arts—Dance xxxiii

Environmental Studies xxxiv

International Studies xxxiv

Learning Disabilities xxxv

Fiske Guide to Colleges 2004 1

Consortia 745

Index 751

Acknowledgments 755

About the Author 757

Notes 758

Index by State

The colleges in this guide are listed alphabetically and cross-referenced for your convenience. Below is a list of the selected colleges grouped by state. Following this listing, you will find a second listing in which the colleges are categorized by the yearly cost of attending each school.

Alabama
Alabama, University of, 3
Auburn University, 41
Birmingham-Southern College, 62

Arizona
Arizona, University of, 27
Arizona State University, 29
Prescott College, 509

Arkansas
Arkansas, University of, 31
Hendrix College, 305

California
California, University of–Berkeley, 88
California, University of–Davis, 91
California, University of–Irvine, 93
California, University of–Los Angeles, 95
California, University of–Riverside, 98
California, University of–San Diego, 100
California, University of–Santa Barbara, 103
California, University of–Santa Cruz, 105
California Institute of Technology, 108
Claremont McKenna College (Claremont Colleges), 146
Deep Springs College, 205
Harvey Mudd College (Claremont Colleges), 148
Mills College, 416
Occidental College, 474
Pacific, University of the, 493
Pepperdine University, 501
Pitzer College (Claremont Colleges), 150
Pomona College (Claremont Colleges), 152
Redlands, University of, 524
San Francisco, University of, 574
Santa Clara University, 576
Scripps College (Claremont Colleges), 155
Southern California, University of, 592
Stanford University, 599
Whittier College, 715

Colorado
Colorado College, 169
Colorado, University of–Boulder, 171
Colorado School of Mines, 174
Denver, University of, 212

Connecticut
Connecticut, University of, 179
Connecticut College, 182
Fairfield University, 242
Trinity College, 644
Wesleyan University, 702
Yale University, 740

Delaware
Delaware, University of, 207

District of Columbia
American University, 19
Catholic University of America, The, 132
George Washington University, 261
Georgetown University, 264
Howard University, 324

Florida
Eckerd College, 233
Florida, University of, 245
Florida Institute of Technology, 247
Florida State University, 249
Miami, University of, 401
New College of Florida, 435
Rollins College, 552
Stetson University, 618

Georgia
Agnes Scott College, 1
Clark College (Atlanta University Center), 34
Emory University, 237
Georgia, University of, 267
Georgia Institute of Technology, 269
Morehouse College (Atlanta University Center), 34
Morris Brown College (Atlanta University Center), 34
Oglethorpe University, 476
Spelman College (Atlanta University Center), 36

Hawaii
Hawaii, University of–Manoa, 303

Idaho
Albertson College, 6

Illinois
Chicago, University of, 139
DePaul University, 215
Illinois, University of–Urbana-Champaign, 326
Illinois Institute of Technology, 329
Illinois Wesleyan University, 332
Knox College, 360
Lake Forest College, 365
Northwestern University, 465
Principia College, 515
Wheaton College, 708

Indiana
DePauw University, 217
Earlham College, 230
Indiana University, 334
Notre Dame, University of, 468
Purdue University, 519
Rose-Hulman Institute of Technology, 554
Wabash College, 682

Iowa
Cornell College, 187
Grinnell College, 278
Iowa, University of, 337
Iowa State University, 339

Kansas
Kansas, University of, 352

Kentucky
Centre College, 135
Kentucky, University of, 354

Louisiana
Louisiana State University, 376
Loyola University–New Orleans, 378
Tulane University, 655
Xavier University of Louisiana, 738

Maine
Atlantic, College of the, 38
Bates College, 53
Bowdoin College, 69
Colby College, 163
Maine, University of–Orono, 382

Maryland
Goucher College, 276
Hood College, 317
Johns Hopkins University, The, 346
Maryland, University of–College Park, 391
St. John's College, 559
St. Mary's College of Maryland, 567

Massachusetts
Amherst College, 21
Babson College, 45
Boston College, 64
Boston University, 66
Brandeis University, 69
Clark University, 157
Emerson College, 235
Gordon College, 274
Hampshire College, 291
Harvard University, 296
Holy Cross, College of the, 314
Massachusetts, University of–Amherst, 395
Massachusetts Institute of Technology, 398
Mount Holyoke College, 427
Northeastern University, 463
Smith College, 584

Tufts University, 652
Wellesley College, 697
Wheaton College, 710
Williams College, 723
Worcester Polytechnic Institute, 736

Michigan
Albion College, 8
Alma College, 15
Calvin College, 111
Hope College, 319
Kalamazoo College, 349
Michigan, University of, 405
Michigan State University, 408

Minnesota
Carleton College, 124
Gustavus Adolphus College, 284
Macalester College, 380
Minnesota, University of–Morris, 418
Minnesota, University of–Twin Cities, 420
St. John's University, and St. Benedict, College of, 562
St. Olaf College, 569

Mississippi
Millsaps College, 413

Missouri
Missouri, University of–Columbia, 422
Saint Louis University, 572
Truman State University (formerly Northeast Missouri State University, 650
Washington University in St. Louis, 694

Montana
Montana Tech of the University of Montana, 425

Nebraska
Nebraska, University of–Lincoln, 432

New Hampshire
Dartmouth College, 196
New Hampshire, University of, 437

New Jersey
Drew University, 222
New Jersey, The College of, 440
New Jersey Institute of Technology, 442

Princeton University, 511
Rutgers University, 556
Stevens Institute of Technology, 620

New Mexico
New Mexico, University of, 444
New Mexico Institute of Mining and Technology, 446
St. John's College, 559

New York
Alfred University, 10
Bard College, 47
Barnard College (Columbia University), 50
Clarkson University, 159
Colgate University, 166
Columbia College, 176
Cooper Union, 185
Cornell University, 189
Fordham University, 252
Hamilton College, 286
Hartwick College, 294
Hobart and William Smith Colleges, 310
Houghton College, 322
Ithaca College, 341
Manhattanville College, 384
New School University–Eugene Lang College, 448
New York University, 451
Rensselaer Polytechnic Institute, 529
Rochester, University of, 547
Rochester Institute of Technology, 549
St. Lawrence University, 564
Sarah Lawrence College, 579
Skidmore College, 581
SUNY–Albany, 604
SUNY–Binghamton University, 606
SUNY–Buffalo, 609
SUNY–Geneseo, 611
SUNY–Purchase College, 613
SUNY–Stony Brook, 615
Syracuse University, 630
Union College, 659
Vassar College, 670
Wells College, 700

North Carolina
Davidson College, 200
Duke University, 226
Guilford College, 281
North Carolina, University of–Asheville, 453

North Carolina, University of–Chapel Hill, 456
North Carolina, University of–Greensboro, 458
North Carolina State University, 461
Wake Forest University, 684

Ohio
Antioch College, 24
Case Western Reserve University, 129
Cincinnati, University of, 142
Dayton, University of, 202
Denison University, 210
Hiram College, 307
Kenyon College, 357
Miami University, 403
Oberlin College, 471
Ohio State University, 478
Ohio University, 481
Ohio Wesleyan University, 483
Wittenberg University, 728
Wooster, The College of, 733

Oklahoma
Oklahoma, University of, 485
Tulsa, University of, 657

Oregon
Lewis and Clark College, 373
Oregon, University of, 488
Oregon State University, 490
Reed College, 527
Willamette University, 717

Pennsylvania
Allegheny College, 12
Bryn Mawr College, 81
Bucknell University, 83
Carnegie Mellon University, 127
Dickinson College, 219
Drexel University, 224
Franklin and Marshall College, 254
Gettysburg College, 272
Haverford College, 300
Lafayette College, 362
Lehigh University, 370
Muhlenberg College, 430

Pennsylvania, University of, 495
Pennsylvania State University, 499
Pittsburgh, University of, 504
Susquehanna University, 623
Swarthmore College, 625
Ursinus College, 662
Villanova University, 675
Washington and Jefferson College, 689

Rhode Island
Brown University, 77
Rhode Island, University of, 532
Rhode Island School of Design, 534

South Carolina
Charleston, College of, 137
Clemson University, 161
Furman University, 257
Presbyterian College, 507
South Carolina, University of, 589
Wofford College, 731

Tennessee
Rhodes College, 537
South, University of the (Sewanee), 587
Tennessee, University of–Knoxville, 633
Vanderbilt University, 667

Texas
Austin College, 43
Baylor University, 55
Dallas, University of, 193
Rice University, 539
Southern Methodist University, 594
Southwestern University, 597
Texas, University of–Austin, 635
Texas A&M University, 637
Texas Christian University, 640
Texas Tech University, 642
Trinity University, 647

Utah
Brigham Young University, 74
Utah, University of, 665

Vermont
Bennington College, 60
Marlboro College, 386
Middlebury College, 411
Vermont, University of, 672

Virginia
George Mason University, 259
Hampden-Sydney College, 289
Hollins University, 312
James Madison University, 344
Mary Washington College, 393
Randolph-Macon Woman's College, 521
Richmond, University of, 542
Sweet Briar College, 628
Virginia, University of, 677
Virginia Polytechnic Institute and State University, 680
Washington and Lee University, 692
William and Mary, College of, 720

Washington
Evergreen State College, The, 240
Puget Sound, University of, 517
Washington, University of, 687
Whitman College, 712

West Virginia
West Virginia University, 706

Wisconsin
Alverno College, 17
Beloit College, 57
Lawrence University, 368
Marquette University, 389
Ripon College, 544
Wisconsin, University of–Madison, 726

Canada
British Columbia, University of, 115
McGill University, 117
Queen's University, 119
Toronto, University of, 123

Index by Price

PUBLIC COLLEGES AND UNIVERSITIES

Inexpensive—$

Alabama, University of–Tuscaloosa, AL, 3
Auburn University, AL, 41
British Columbia, University of, Canada, 115
Charleston, College of, SC, 137
Delaware, University of, DE, 207
Florida State University, FL, 249
George Mason University, VA, 259
Kentucky, University of, KY, 354
McGill University, Canada, 117
Mary Washington College, VA, 393
Montana Tech of the University of Montana, MT, 425
Nebraska, University of–Lincoln, NE, 432
New College of Florida, FL, 435
New Mexico, University of, NM, 444
New Mexico Institute of Mining and Technology, NM, 446
North Carolina, University of–Asheville, NC, 453
North Carolina, University of–Chapel Hill, NC, 456
North Carolina, University of–Greensboro, NC, 458
North Carolina State University, NC, 461
Ohio State University, OH, 478
Oklahoma, University of, OK, 485
Oregon, University of, OR, 488
South Carolina, University of, SC, 589
Truman State University, MO, 650
Utah, University of, UT, 665
William and Mary, College of, VA, 720

Moderate—$$

Arizona State University, AZ, 29
Arkansas, University of, AR, 31
Clemson University, SC, 161
Colorado, University of–Boulder, CO, 171
Colorado School of Mines, CO, 174
Evergreen State College, The, WA, 240

Georgia, University of, GA, 267
Hawaii, University of–Manoa, HI, 303
Illinois, University of–Urbana-Champaign, IL, 326
Iowa, University of, IA, 337
Iowa State University, IA, 339
James Madison University, VA, 344
Kansas, University of, KS, 352
Louisiana State University, LA, 376
Massachusetts, University of–Amherst, MA, 398
Michigan State University, MI, 408
Minnesota, University of–Twin Cities, MN, 420
Missouri, University of–Columbia, MO, 422
New Jersey, The College of, NJ, 440
Purdue University, IN, 519
Queen's University, Canada, 119
SUNY–Albany, NY, 604
SUNY–Binghamton University, NY, 606
SUNY–Buffalo, NY, 609
SUNY–Geneseo, NY, 611
SUNY–Purchase College, NY, 613
SUNY–Stony Brook, NY, 615
Tennessee, University of–Knoxville, TN, 633
Texas A&M University, TX, 637
Texas Tech University, TX, 642
Toronto, University of, Canada, 123
Virginia, University of, VA, 677
Virginia Polytechnic Institute and State University, VA, 680
West Virginia University, WV, 706
Wisconsin, University of–Madison, WI, 726

Expensive—$$$

Arizona, University of, AZ, 27
California, University of–Berkeley, CA, 88
California, University of–Davis, CA, 91
California, University of–Irvine, CA, 93
California, University of–Riverside, CA, 98

California, University of–San Diego, CA, 100
California, University of–Santa Barbara, CA, 103
Cincinnati, University of, OH, 142
Connecticut, University of, CT, 179
Indiana University, IN, 334
Maryland, University of–College Park, MD, 391
New Jersey Institute of Technology, NJ, 442
Ohio University, OH, 481
Oregon State University, OR, 490
Pennsylvania State University, PA, 499
Pittsburgh, University of, PA, 504
Rhode Island, University of, RI, 532
Rutgers—The State University of New Jersey, NJ, 556
Washington, University of, WA, 687

Very Expensive—$$$$

California, University of–Los Angeles, CA, 95
California, University of–Santa Cruz, CA, 105
Florida, University of, FL, 245
Georgia Institute of Technology, GA, 269
Maine, University of–Orono, ME, 382
Miami University, OH, 403
Michigan, University of, MI, 405
Minnesota, University of–Morris, MN, 418
New Hampshire, University of, NH, 437
New Jersey Institute of Technology, NJ, 442
St. Mary's College of Maryland, MD, 567
Texas, University of–Austin, TX, 635
Vermont, University of, VT, 672

PRIVATE COLLEGES AND UNIVERSITIES

Inexpensive—$

Albertson College, ID, 6
Albion College, MI, 8
Alma College, MI, 15
Alverno College, WI, 17
Atlantic, College of the, ME, 38
Austin College, TX, 43
Baylor University, TX, 55
Brigham Young University, UT, 74
Calvin College, MI, 111
Centre College, KY, 135
Cooper Union, NY, 185
Dallas, University of, TX, 193
Deep Springs College, CA, 205
Gordon College, MA, 274
Goucher College, MD, 276
Gustavus Adolphus College, MN, 284
Hampshire College, MA, 291
Hendrix College, AR, 305
Hope College, MI, 319
Houghton College, NY, 322
Howard University, DC, 324
Illinois Institute of Technology, IL, 329
Manhattanville College, NY, 384
Millsaps College, MS, 413
Morehouse College (Atlanta
   University Center), GA, 34
Ohio Wesleyan University, OH, 483
Presbyterian College, SC, 507
Principia College, IL, 515
Rhodes College, TN, 537
Rice University, TX, 539
Ripon College, WI, 544
St. John's University and College of
   St. Benedict,, MN, 562
Santa Clara University, CA, 576
Southwestern University, TX, 597
Spelman College (Atlanta University
   Center), GA, 36
Stevens Institute of Technology, NJ, 620
Texas Christian University, TX, 640
Tulsa, University of, OK, 657
Washington and Lee University, VA,
   692
Wells College, NY, 700
Wheaton College, IL, 708
Xavier University of Louisiana, LA, 738

Moderate—$$

Agnes Scott College, GA, 1
Alfred University, NY, 10
Allegheny College, PA, 12
Antioch College, OH, 24
Beloit College, WI, 55
Birmingham–Southern College, AL, 62
California Institute of Technology,
   CA, 108
Case Western Reserve University, OH,
   129
Catholic University of America, The,
   DC, 132
Cornell College, IA, 187
Dayton, University of, OH, 202
DePaul University, IL, 215
DePauw University, IN, 217
Eckerd College, FL, 233
Florida Institute of Technology, FL, 247
Furman University, SC, 257
Grinnell College, IA, 278
Guilford College, NC, 281
Hampden-Sydney College, VA, 289
Hiram College, OH, 307
Hollins University, VA, 312
Hood College, MD, 317
Illinois Wesleyan University, IL, 332
Ithaca College, NY, 341
Kalamazoo College, MI, 349
Knox College, IL, 360
Lake Forest College, IL, 365
Lewis and Clark College, OR, 373
Macalester College, MN, 380
Marlboro College, VT, 386
Marquette University, WI, 389
Muhlenberg College, PA, 430
Oglethorpe University, GA, 476
Pacific, University of the, CA, 493
Prescott College, AZ, 509
Randolph-Macon Woman's College,
   VA, 521
Richmond, University of, VA, 542
Rochester Institute of Technology,
   NY, 549
St. John's College, MD, 559
St. John's College, NM, 559
St. Olaf College, MN, 569
Saint Louis University, MO, 572
South, University of the (Sewanee),
   TN, 587
Southern Methodist University, TX,
   594
Stetson University, FL, 618
Susquehanna University, PA, 623
Sweet Briar College, VA, 628
Trinity University, TX, 647
Wabash College, IN, 682
Washington and Jefferson College,
   PA, 689
Wittenberg University, OH, 728
Wofford College, SC, 731
Wooster, The College of, OH, 733

Expensive—$$$

Amherst College, MA, 21
Bucknell University, PA, 83
Carleton College, MN, 124
Carnegie Mellon University, PA, 127
Clark University, MA, 157
Clarkson University, NY, 159
Connecticut College, CT, 179
Denison University, OH, 210
Dickinson College, PA, 219
Drexel University, PA, 224
Earlham College, IN, 230
Emerson College, MA, 235
Fordham University, NY, 252
Franklin and Marshall College, PA,
   254
Gettysburg College, PA, 272
Hartwick College, NY, 294
Kenyon College, OH, 357
Lafayette College, PA, 362
Lawrence University, WI, 368
Lehigh University, PA, 370
Loyola University–New Orleans, LA,
   378
Miami, University of, FL, 401
Mills College, CA, 416
New School University–Eugene Lang
   College, NY, 448
Northeastern University, MA, 463
Puget Sound, University of, WA, 517
Redlands, University of, CA, 524
Reed College, OR, 527
Rhode Island School of Design, RI,
   534
Rochester, University of, NY, 547
Rose-Hulman Institute of Technology,
   IN, 554
St. Lawrence University, NY, 564
San Francisco, University of, CA, 574
Scripps College (Claremont Colleges),
   CA, 155
Smith College, MA, 584
Syracuse University, NY, 630
Union College, NY, 659

Ursinus College, PA, 662
Whitman College, WA, 712
Whittier College, CA, 715
Willamette University, OR, 717
Williams College, MA, 723

Very Expensive—$$$$

American University, DC, 19
Babson College, MA, 45
Bard College, NY, 47
Barnard College (Columbia University), NY, 50
Bates College, ME, 53
Bennington College, VT, 60
Boston College, MA, 64
Boston University, MA, 66
Bowdoin College, ME, 69
Brandeis University, MA, 73
Brown University, RI, 77
Bryn Mawr College, PA, 81
Chicago, University of, IL, 139
Claremont McKenna College (Claremont Colleges), CA, 146
Colby College, ME, 163
Colgate University, NY, 166
Colorado College, CO, 169
Columbia College (Columbia University), NY, 176
Cornell University, NY, 189
Dartmouth College, NH, 196

Davidson College, NC, 200
Denver, University of, CO, 212
Drew University, NJ, 222
Duke University, NC, 226
Emory University, GA, 237
Fairfield University, CT, 242
George Washington University, DC, 261
Georgetown University, DC, 264
Hamilton College, NY, 286
Harvard University, MA, 296
Harvey Mudd College (Claremont Colleges), CA, 148
Haverford College, PA, 300
Hobart and William Smith Colleges, NY, 310
Holy Cross, College of the, MA, 314
Johns Hopkins University, The, MD, 346
Massachusetts Institute of Technology, MA, 398
Middlebury College, VT, 411
Mount Holyoke College, MA, 427
New York University, NY, 451
Northwestern University, IL, 465
Notre Dame, University of, IN, 468
Oberlin College, OH, 471
Occidental College, CA, 474
Pennsylvania, University of, PA, 495
Pepperdine University, CA, 501

Pitzer College (Claremont Colleges), CA, 150
Pomona College (Claremont Colleges), CA, 152
Princeton University, NJ, 511
Rensselaer Polytechnic Institute, NY, 529
Rollins College, FL, 552
Sarah Lawrence College, NY, 579
Skidmore College, NY, 581
Southern California, University of, CA, 592
Stanford University, CA, 599
Swarthmore College, PA, 625
Trinity College, CT, 644
Tufts University, MA, 652
Tulane University, LA, 655
Vanderbilt University, TN, 667
Vassar College, NY, 670
Villanova University, PA, 675
Wake Forest University, NC, 684
Washington University in St. Louis, MO, 694
Wellesley College, MA, 697
Wesleyan University, CT, 702
Wheaton College, MA, 710
Worcester Polytechnic Institute, MA, 736
Yale University, CT, 740

The Best Buys of 2004

Following is a list of forty-four colleges and universities
that qualify as Best Buys based on the quality of the
academic offerings in relation to the cost of attendance.

Public

University of British Columbia (Canada)
University of Colorado–Boulder
University of Illinois–Urbana-Champaign
University of Iowa
University of Kansas
Mary Washington College
McGill University (Canada)
University of Minnesota–Twin Cities
New College of Florida
The College of New Jersey
University of North Carolina–Asheville
University of North Carolina–Chapel Hill
University of Oregon
Queen's University (Canada)
SUNY–Binghamton
SUNY–Buffalo
SUNY–Stony Brook
Texas A&M University
University of Toronto (Canada)
University of Virginia
College of William and Mary
University of Wisconsin–Madison

Private

Brigham Young University
California Institute of Technology
Case Western Reserve University
Centre College
Cooper Union
University of Dallas
Deep Springs College
Grinnell College
Hampshire College
Illinois Institute of Technology
Illinois Wesleyan University
Macalester College
Manhattanville College
Ohio Wesleyan University
Presbyterian College
Rhodes College
Rice University
St. John's College (MD and NM)
St. Olaf College
University of the South (Sewanee)
Washington and Lee University
Xavier University of Louisiana

Introduction

THE *FISKE GUIDE TO COLLEGES*—AND HOW TO USE IT

The 2004 edition of the *Fiske Guide to Colleges* is a revised and updated version of a book that has been a best-seller since it first appeared two decades ago and is universally regarded as the definitive college guide of its type. Features of the new edition include:

- Updated write-ups on more than three hundred of the country's best and most interesting colleges and universities
- A section titled "Sizing Yourself Up," with a questionnaire that will help you figure out the kind of school that is best for you
- A Guide for Preprofessionals that lists colleges and universities strong in nine preprofessional areas
- A list of schools with strong programs for students with learning disabilities
- Designation of the forty-four schools that constitute this year's Best Buys
- Statistical summaries that give you the numbers you need, but spare you those that you do not
- Authoritative rankings of each institution by academics, social life, and quality of life
- The unique If You Apply... feature, which summarizes the vital information that you need about each college's admission policies—including deadlines and essay topics
- A section on the top Canadian universities in response to the fact that a growing number of students and families in the United States have become aware of the educational bargains that are lurking just across the border to the north. These Canadian universities offer first-rate academics—easily the equivalent of the flagship public institutions in the U.S.—but at a fraction of the cost.

Picking the right college—one that will coincide with your particular needs, goals, interests, talents, and personality—is one of the most important decisions that any young person will ever make. It is also a major investment. Tuition and fees alone now run at least $3,500 at a typical public university and $17,500 at a typical private college, and the tab at the most selective and expensive schools tops $27,500. Obviously, a major investment like that should be approached with as much information as possible.

That's where the *Fiske Guide to Colleges* fits in. It is a tool to help you make the most intelligent educational investment you can.

WHAT IS THE *FISKE GUIDE TO COLLEGES?*

The *Fiske Guide to Colleges* mirrors a process familiar to any college-bound student and his or her family. If you are wondering whether to consider a particular college, it is logical to seek out friends or acquaintances who go there and ask them to tell you about their experiences. We have done exactly that—but on a far broader and more systematic basis than any individual or family could do alone.

In using the *Fiske Guide*, some special features should be kept in mind:

- The guide is *selective*. We have not tried to cover all four-year colleges and universities. Rather, we have taken more than three hundred of the best and most interesting institutions in the nation—the ones that students most want to know about—and written descriptive essays of one thousand to twenty-five hundred words about each of them.
- Since choosing a college is a matter of making a calculated and informed judgment, this guide is also *subjective*. It makes judgments about the strengths and weaknesses of each institution, and it contains a unique set of ratings of each college or university on the basis of academic strength, social life, and overall quality of life. No institution is right for every student. The underlying assumption of the *Fiske Guide* is that each of the colleges chosen for inclusion is the right place for some students but not a good bet for others. Like finding the right husband or wife, college admissions is a matching process. You know your own interests and needs; the *Fiske Guide* will tell you something about those needs that each college seems to serve best.

• Finally, the *Fiske Guide* is *systematic*. Each write-up is carefully constructed to cover specific topics, from the academic climate and the makeup of the student body to the social scene, in a systematic order. This means that you can easily take a specific topic, such as the level of academic pressure or the role of fraternities and sororities on campus, and trace it through all of the colleges that interest you.

HOW THE COLLEGES WERE SELECTED

How do you single out "the best and most interesting" of the more than twenty-two hundred four-year colleges in the United States? Obviously, there are many fine institutions that are not included. Space limitations simply require that some hard decisions be made.

The selection was done with several broad principles in mind, beginning with academic quality. Depending on how you define the term, there are about 175 "selective" colleges and universities in the nation, and by and large these constitute the best institutions academically. All of these are included in the *Fiske Guide*. In addition, an effort was made to achieve geographical diversity and a balance of public and private schools. Special efforts were made to include a good selection of three types of institutions that seem to be enjoying special popularity at present: engineering and technical schools, those with a religious emphasis, and those located along the Sunbelt, where the cost of education is considerably less than at its northern counterparts. This current edition also includes several colleges that in recent years have significantly increased their academic quality and appeal to students.

Finally, in a few cases we exercised the journalist's prerogative of writing about schools that are simply interesting. The tiny College of the Atlantic, for example, would hardly qualify on the basis of superior academic program or national significance, but it offers an unusual and fascinating brand of liberal arts within the context of environmental studies. Likewise, Deep Springs College, the only two-year school in the *Guide*, is a unique institution of intrinsic interest.

HOW THE *FISKE GUIDE* WAS COMPILED

Each college or university selected for inclusion in the *Fiske Guide to Colleges* was sent a packet of questionnaires. The first was directed to the administration and covered topics ranging from their perception of the institution's mission to the demographics of the student body. Administrators were also asked to distribute a set of questionnaires to a cross-section of students.

The questions for students, all open-ended and requiring short essays as responses, covered a series of topics ranging from the accessibility of professors and the quality of housing and dining facilities to the type of nightlife and weekend entertainment available in the area. By and large, students responded enthusiastically to the challenge we offered them. The quality of the information in the write-ups is a tribute to their diligence and openness. American college students, we learned, are a candid lot. They are proud of their institutions—but also critical in the positive sense of the word.

Other sources of information were also employed. Administrators were invited to attach to their questionnaires any catalogs, in-house research, or other documents that would contribute to an understanding of the institution and to comment on their write-up in the last edition. Also, staff members have visited many of the colleges, and in some cases, additional information was solicited through published materials, telephone interviews, and other contacts with students and administrators.

The information from these various questionnaires was then collated by a staff of journalists and freelance writers and edited by Edward B. Fiske, former Education Editor of the *New York Times*.

THE FORMAT

Each essay covers certain broad subjects in roughly the same order. They are as follows:

Academics	**Housing**
Campus setting	**Food**
Student body	**Social life**
Financial aid	**Extracurricular activities**

Certain subtopics are covered in all of the essays. The sections on academics, for example, always discuss the departments (or, in the case of large universities, schools) that are particularly strong or weak, while the sections on housing contain information on whether the dorms are coed or single-sex and how students get the rooms they want. Other topics, however, such as class size, the need for a car, or the number of volumes in the library, are mentioned only if they constitute a particular strength or weakness at that institution.

We paid particular attention to the effect of the twenty-one-year-old drinking age on campus life. Also, we noted efforts some schools' administrations have been making to change or improve the social and residential life on campuses by such measures as banning fraternities and constructing new athletic facilities.

BEST BUYS

One of the lesser-known facts of life about higher education in the U.S. is that price and quality do not always go hand in hand. The college or university with the jumbo price tag may or may not offer a better education than the institution across town with much lower tuition. The relationship between the cost paid by the consumer and the quality of the education is affected by factors ranging from the size of an institution's endowment to judgments by college officials about what the market will bear.

In the face of today's skyrocketing tuition rates, students and families in all economic circumstances are looking for ways to get the best value for their education dollar. Fortunately, there are some bargains to be found in higher education; it just takes a bit of shopping around with a little guidance along the way.

Since its inception nearly two decades ago, the *Fiske Guide* has featured an Index by Price that groups public and private institutions into four price categories, from inexpensive to very expensive. Now we have gone one step further: we have combined the cost data with academic and other information about each college and university, and have come up with forty-four institutions—twenty-two public and twenty-two private—that offer remarkable educational opportunities at a relatively modest cost. We are calling them Best Buys, and they are indicated by a Best Buy graphic next to the college name. (A list of the 2004 Best Buys appears on page xvi.)

All of our Best Buys fall into the inexpensive or moderate price category, and most have four- or five-star academic ratings. But there are bargains to be found among all levels and types of institutions. For example, some of the best values in American higher education are public colleges and universities that have remained relatively small and offer the smaller classes and personalized approach to academics that are typically found only in expensive private liberal arts colleges. Several of these are included as Best Buys.

STATISTICS

At the beginning of each write-up are basic statistics about the college or university—the ones that are relevant to applicants. These include the address, type of location (urban, small town, rural, etc.), enrollment, male/female ratio, SAT or ACT score ranges of the middle 50 percent of the students, percentage of students receiving need-based financial aid, relative cost, whether or not the institution has a chapter of Phi Beta Kappa, the number of students who apply and the percentage of those who are accepted, the percentage of accepted students who enroll, the number of freshmen who graduate within six years, and the number of freshmen who return for their sophomore year. For convenience, we include the telephone number of the admissions office and the school's website and mailing address.

Unlike some guides, we have intentionally not published figures on the student/faculty ratio because colleges use different—and often self-serving—methods to calculate the ratio, thus making it virtually meaningless.

A word about several of these items:

> You will sometimes encounter the letters "N/A." In most cases, this means that the statistic was not available. In other cases, however, such as schools that do not require standardized tests, it means "not applicable." The write-up should make it clear which meaning is the relevant one.
>
> We have included information on whether the school has a chapter of Phi Beta Kappa because this academic honorary society is a sign of broad intellectual distinction. Keep in mind, though, that even the very best engineering schools, because of their relatively narrow focus, do not usually qualify under the society's standards.
>
> Tuition and fees are constantly increasing at American colleges, but for the most part, the cost of various institutions in relation to one another does not change. Rather than put in specific cost figures that would immediately become out of date, we have classified colleges into four groups ranging from inexpensive ($) to very expensive ($$$$) based on estimated costs of tuition, fees, and housing for the 2002–2003 academic year. Separate scales were used for public and private institutions, and the ratings for the public institutions are based on cost for residents of the state; out-of-staters should expect to pay more. If a public institution has a particularly low or high surcharge for out-of-staters, this is noted in the essay. The categories are defined as follows:

	PUBLIC	PRIVATE
$$$$	More than $16,000	More than $34,000
$$$	$14,000–$16,000	$30,000–$34,000
$$	$11,000–$14,000	$26,000–$30,000
$	Less than $11,000	Less than $26,000

> We also include an index that groups colleges by their relative cost (see Index by Price pages xiii–xv).

SAT and ACT SCORES

A special word needs to be said about SAT and ACT scores. Some publications follow the practice of giving the median or average score registered by entering freshmen. Such figures, however, are easily misinterpreted as thresholds rather than averages. Many applicants forget that if a school reports average SAT-Verbal scores of 500, this means that, by definition, about half of the students scored below this number and half scored above. An applicant with a 480 would still have lots of company.

To avoid such confusion, we report the range of scores of the middle half of freshmen—or, to put it another way, the scores achieved by those in the twenty-fifth and seventy-fifth percentiles. For example, that college where the SAT-Verbal average was 500 might have a range of 440 to 560. So if you scored within this range, you would have joined the middle 50 percent of last year's freshmen. If your score was above 560, you would have been in the top quarter and could probably look forward to a relatively easy time; if it was below 440, you would have been struggling along with the bottom quarter of students.

The reporting of ranges rather than a single average is an increasingly common practice, but some colleges do not calculate ranges. These are indicated by "N/A." Keep in mind, as well, that score ranges (and averages, for that matter) are misleading at colleges such as Bates, Bowdoin, and Union, which do not require test scores from all applicants. These are indicated by "N/R."

Unfortunately, another problem that arises with SAT and ACT scores is that, in their zeal to make themselves look good in a competitive market, some colleges and universities have been known to be less than honest in the numbers they release. They inflate their scores by not counting certain categories of students at the low end of the scale, such as athletes, certain types of transfer students, or students admitted under affirmative-action programs. Some colleges have gone to such extremes as reporting the relatively high math scores of foreign students, but not their relatively low verbal scores. Aside from the sheer dishonesty of such practices, they can also be misleading. A student whose own scores are below the twenty-fifth percentile of a particular institution needs to know whether his profile matches that of the lower quarter of the student body as a whole or whether there is an unreported pool of students with lower scores.

Even when dealing with a range rather than a single score, keep in mind that standardized tests are an imprecise measure of academic ability, and comparisons of scores that differ by less than 50 or 60 points on a scale of 200 to 800 have little meaning. According to the laws of statistics, there is one chance in three that the 550 that arrived in the little envelope from ETS should really be at least 580 or no more than 520. On the other hand, median scores offer some indication of your chances to get into a particular institution and the intellectual level of the company you will be keeping—or, if you prefer, competing against. Remember, too, that the most competitive schools have the largest and most sophisticated admissions staffs and are well aware of the limitations of standardized tests. A strong high-school average or achievement in a field such as music will usually counteract the negative effects of modest SAT or ACT scores.

SCHOLARSHIP INFORMATION

Since the first edition of the *Fiske Guide to Colleges* appeared, the problems of financing college have become increasingly critical, mainly because of the rising cost of education and a shift from grants to loans as the basis for financial-aid packages.

In response to these developments, many colleges and universities have begun to devise their own plans to help students pay for college. These range from subsidized loan programs to merit scholarships that are awarded without reference to financial need. Most of these programs are aimed at retaining the middle class.

We ask each college and university to tell us what steps it has taken to help students pay their way, and their responses are incorporated in the write-ups. Also indicated is whether a candidate's inability to pay the full tuition, room, and board charges is a factor in admissions decisions. Some colleges advertise that they are "need blind" in their admissions, meaning that they accept or reject applicants without reference to their financial situation and then guarantee to meet the "demonstrated need" of all students whom they accept. Others say they are need blind in their admissions decisions, but do not guarantee to provide the financial aid required of all those who are accepted. Still others agree to meet the demonstrated need of all students, but they package their offers so that students whom they really want receive a higher percentage of their aid in the form of outright grants than in repayable loans.

"Demonstrated need" is itself a slippery term. In theory, the figure is determined when students and families fill out a needs-analysis form, which leads to an estimate of how much the family can afford to pay. Demonstrated need is then calculated by subtracting that figure from the cost at a particular institution. In practice, however, various colleges make their own adjustments to the standard figure.

Students and parents should not assume that because their family has even a six-figure income they are automatically disqualified from some kind of subsidized financial aid. In cases of doubt, they should fill out a needs-analysis form to determine their eligibility. Whether they qualify or not, they are also eligible for a variety of awards made without regard to financial need.

Inasmuch as need-based awards are universal at the colleges in this guide, the awards generally singled out for special mention in the write-ups in the *Fiske Guide to Colleges* are the merit scholarships. We have not mentioned awards of a purely local nature—restricted to residents of a particular county, for example—but all college applicants should search out these awards through their guidance offices and the bulletins of the colleges that are of interest to them. Similarly, we have not duplicated the information on federally guaranteed loan programs that is readily available through both high-school and college counseling offices, but we cite novel and often less-expensive variants of the federal loan programs that are offered by individual colleges.

For more information on the ever-changing financial-aid scene, we suggest that you consult the companion book to this guide, *Fiske Guide to Getting into the Right College*.

RATINGS

Much of the controversy that greeted the first edition of the *Fiske Guide to Colleges* revolved around its unique system of rating colleges in three areas: academics, social life, and quality of life. In each case, the ratings are done on a system of one to five, with three considered normal for colleges included in the *Fiske Guide*. If a college receives a rating higher or lower than three in any category, the reasons should be apparent from the narrative description of that college.

Students and parents should keep in mind that these ratings are obviously general in nature and inherently subjective. No complex institution can be described in terms of a single number or other symbol, and different people will have different views of how various institutions should be rated in the three categories. They should not be viewed as either precise or infallible judgments about any given college. On the other hand, the ratings are a helpful tool in using this book. The core of the *Fiske Guide* is the essays on each of the colleges, and the ratings represent a summary—an index, if you will—of these write-ups. Our hope is that each student, having decided on the kind of configuration that suits his or her needs, will then thumb through the book looking for other institutions with a similar set of ratings.

The categories are defined as follows.

Academics ✍

This is a judgment about the overall academic climate of the institution, including its reputation in the academic world, the quality of the faculty, the level of teaching and research, the academic ability of students, the quality of libraries and other facilities, and the level of academic seriousness among students and faculty members.

Although the same basic criteria have been applied to all institutions, it should be evident that an outstanding small liberal arts college will by definition differ significantly from an outstanding major public university. No one would expect the former to have massive library facilities, but one would look for a high-quality faculty that combines research with a good deal of attention to the individual needs of students. Likewise, public universities, because of their implicit commitment to serving a broad cross-section of society, might have a broader range of curriculum offerings but somewhat lower average SAT scores than a large private counterpart. Readers may find the ratings most useful when comparing colleges and universities of the same type.

In general, an academics rating of three pens suggests that the institution is a solid one that easily meets the criteria for inclusion in a guide devoted to the top 10 percent of colleges and universities in the nation.

An academics rating of four pens suggests that the institution is above average even by these standards and that it has some particularly distinguishing academic feature, such as especially rich course offerings or an especially serious academic atmosphere.

A rating of five pens for academics indicates that the college or university is among the handful of top institutions of its type in the nation on a broad variety of criteria. Those in the private sector will normally attract students with combined SAT scores of at least 1300, and those in the public sector are invariably magnets for the top students in their states. All can be assumed to have outstanding faculties and other academic resources.

For the 2004 edition, in response to the suggestion that the range of colleges within a single category has been too broad, we have introduced some half-steps into the ratings.

Social Life ☎

This is primarily a judgment about the amount of social life that is readily available. A rating of three telephones suggests a typical college social life, while four telephones means that students have a better-than-average time socially. It can be assumed that a college with a rating of five is something of a party school, which may or may not detract from the academic quality. Colleges with a rating below three have some impediment to a strong social life, such as geographic isolation, a high percentage of commuting students, or a disproportionate number of nerds who never leave the library. Once again, the reason should be evident from the write-up.

Quality of Life ★

This category grew out of the fact that schools with good academic credentials and plenty of social life may not, for one reason or another, be particularly wholesome places to spend four years. The term "quality of life" is one that has been gaining currency in social science circles, and, in most cases, the rating for a particular college will be similar to the academic and/or social ratings. The reader, though, should be alert to exceptions to this pattern. A liberal arts college, for example, might attract bright students who study hard during the week and party hard on weekends, and thus earn high ratings for academics and social life. If the academic pressure is cut-throat rather than constructive, though, and the social system is manipulative of women, this college might get an apparently anomalous two stars for quality of life. By contrast, a small college with modest academic programs and relatively few organized social opportunities might have developed a strong sense of supportive community, have a beautiful campus, and be located near a wonderful city—and thus be rated four stars for quality of life. As in the other categories, the reason can be found in the essay to which the ratings point.

OVERLAPS

Most colleges and universities operate within fairly defined "niche markets." That is, they compete for students against other institutions with whom they share important characteristics, such as academic quality, size, geographical location, and the overall tone and style of campus life. Not surprisingly, students who apply to College X also tend to apply to the other institutions in its particular niche. For example, "alternative" colleges such as Bard, Bennington, Hampshire, Marlboro, Oberlin, Reed, and Sarah Lawrence share many common applications, as do those with an evangelical flavor, such as Calvin, Hope, and Wheaton (IL).

As a service to readers, we ask each school to give us the names of the five colleges with which they share the most common applications, and these are listed in the Overlaps section at the end of each writeup. We encourage students who know they are interested in a particular institution to check out the schools with which it competes—and perhaps then check out the "overlaps of the overlaps." This method of systematic browsing should yield a list of fifteen or twenty schools that, based on the behavior of thousands of past applicants, would constitute a good starting point for the college search.

IF YOU APPLY...

An extremely helpful feature is the If You Apply... section at the end of each write-up. This is designed for students who become seriously interested in a particular college and want to know more specifics about what it takes to get in.

This section begins with the deadlines for early admissions or early decision (if the college has such a program), regular admissions, and financial aid. If the college operates on a rolling-admissions basis—making decisions as the applications are received—this is indicated.

If You Apply... gives a snapshot of the institution's financial-aid policies. It indicates whether the college or university guarantees to meet the demonstrated need of applicants and, if so, the percentage of students whose financial need is actually met. The phrase "guarantees to meet demonstrated need" means that the institution for all practical purposes makes every effort possible to come up with the aid for which all of its students qualify.

Colleges have widely varying policies regarding interviews, both on campus and with alumni, so we indicate whether each of these is required, recommended, or optional. We also indicate whether reports from the person doing the interview are used in evaluating students or whether, as in many cases, the interview is seen only as a means of conveying information about the institution and answering applicants' questions.

This section also tells what standardized tests—SAT, ACT, or achievement—are required, and whether applicants are asked to write one or more essays. In the latter case, the topics are given.

The admissions policies of most colleges are fairly similar, at least among competing clusters of institutions. In some cases, however, a school will have its own special priorities. Some don't care that much about test scores. Others are looking for students with special talent in math or science, while others pay special attention to personal characteristics such as leadership in extracurricular activities. We asked each institution to tell us if its admission policies are in any ways "unique or unusual," and their answers are reported.

CONSORTIA

Many colleges expand the range of their offerings by banding together with other institutions to offer unusual programs that they could not support on their own. These options range from foreign-study programs around the world to semesters at sea, and keeping such arrangements in mind is a way of expanding the list of institutions that might meet your particular interests and needs. The final section of the *Fiske Guide* describes sixteen of these consortia and lists the member institutions.

MOVING FORWARD

Students will find the *Fiske Guide* useful at various points in the college-selection process—from deciding whether to visit a particular campus to selecting among institutions that have accepted them. To make it easy to find a particular college, the write-ups are arranged in alphabetical order in the index. Indexes by state and price can be found on pages ix and xiii, respectively.

While most people are not likely to start reading at Agnes Scott and keep going until they reach Yale (though some tell us they do), we encourage you to browse. This country has an enormously rich and varied network of colleges and universities, and there are dozens of institutions out there that can meet the needs of any particular student. Too many students approach the college-selection process wearing blinders, limiting their sights to local institutions, the pet schools of their parents or guidance counselors, or to ones they know only by possibly outdated reputations.

But applicants need not be bound by such limitations. Once you have decided on the type of school you think you want—a small liberal arts college, an engineering school, or whatever—we hope you will thumb through the book looking for similar institutions that might not have occurred to you. One way to do this is to look at the overlaps of schools you like and then check out those schools' overlaps. Many students have found this worthwhile, and quite frankly, we view the widening of students' horizons about American higher education as one of the most important purposes of the book. Perhaps the most gratifying remark we hear comes when a student tells us, as many have, that she is attending a school that she first heard about while browsing through the *Fiske Guide to Colleges*.

Picking a college is a tricky business. But given the current buyer's market, there is no reason why you should not be able to find the right college. That's what the *Fiske Guide to Colleges* is designed to help you do. Happy college hunting.

Sizing Yourself Up

The college search is a game of matchmaking. You have interests and needs; the colleges have programs to meet those needs. If all goes according to plan, you'll find the right one and live happily ever after——or at least for four years. It ought to be simple, but today's admissions process resembles a high-stakes obstacle course.

Many colleges are more interested in making a sale than they are in making a match. Under intense competitive pressure, many won't hesitate to sell you a bill of goods if they can get their hands on your tuition dollars. Guidance counselors generally mean well, but they are often under duress from principals and trustees to steer students toward prestigious schools regardless of whether the fit is right. Your friends won't be shy with advice on where to go, but their knowledge is generally limited to a small group of hot colleges that everyone is talking about. National publications rake in millions by playing on the public's fascination with rankings, but a close look at their criteria reveals distinctions without a difference.

Before you find yourself spinning headlong on this merry-go-round, take a step back. This is your life and your college career. What are you looking for in a college? Think hard, and don't answer right away. Before you throw yourself and your life history on the mercy of college-admissions officers, you need to take some time to objectively and honestly evaluate your needs, likes and dislikes, strengths and weaknesses. What do you have to offer a college? What can a college do for you? Unlike the high-school selection process, which is usually predetermined by your parents' property lines, income level, or religious affiliation, picking a college isn't a procedure you can brush off on dear ol' Mom and Dad. You have to take some initiative. You're the best judge of how well each school fits your personal needs and academic goals.

We encourage you to view the college-selection process as the first semester in your higher education. Life's transitions often call forth extra energy and focus. The college search is no exception. For the first time, you'll be contemplating a life away from home that can unfold in any direction you choose. Visions of majors and careers will dance in your head as you sample various institutions of higher learning, each with hundreds of millions of dollars in academic resources; it is hard to imagine a better hands-on seminar in research and matchmaking than the college search. The main impact, however, will be measured by what you learn about yourself. Piqued by new worlds of learning and tested by the competition of the admissions process, you'll be pushed as never before to show your accomplishments, clarify your interests, and chart a course for the future. More than one parent has watched in amazement as an erstwhile teenager suddenly emerged as an adult during the course of a college tour. Be ready when your time comes.

DEVELOP YOUR CRITERIA

One strategy is to begin the search with a personal inventory of your own strengths and weaknesses and your "wish list" for a college. This method tends to work well for compulsive list-makers and other highly organized people. What sorts of things are you especially good at? Do you have a list of skills or interests that you would like to explore further? What sort of personality are you looking for in a college? Mainstream? Conservative? Offbeat? What about extracurriculars? If you are really into riding horses, you might include a strong equestrian program in your criteria. The main problem won't be thinking of qualities to look for—you could probably name dozens—but rather figuring out what criteria should play a defining role in your search. Serious students should think carefully about the intellectual climate they are seeking. At some schools, students routinely stay up until 3:00 A.M. talking about topics like the value of deconstructing literary texts or the pros and cons of free trade. These same students would be viewed as geeks or weirdos on less cosmopolitan campuses. Athletes should take a hard look at whether they really want to play college ball, and if so, whether they want to go for an athletic scholarship or play at the less-pressured Division III level. Either way, intercollegiate sports require a huge time commitment.

Young women have an opportunity all to themselves—the chance to study at a women's college. The *Fiske Guide* profiles fourteen such campuses, a vastly underappreciated resource on today's higher-education scene. With small classes and strong encouragement from faculty, students at women's colleges move on to graduate study in significantly higher numbers than their counterparts at coed schools, especially in the natural sciences.

Males seeking an all-male experience will find two options in the *Fiske Guide*, Hampden-Sydney College and Wabash College.

Students with a firm career goal will want to look for a course of study that matches their needs. If you want to major in aerospace engineering, your search will be limited to schools that have the program. Outside of specialized areas like this, many applicants overestimate the importance of their anticipated major in choosing a college. If you're interested in a liberal arts field, your expected major should probably have little to do with your college selection. A big purpose of college is to develop interests and set goals. Most students change their intentions regarding a major at least two or three times before graduation, and once out in the working world, they often end up in jobs bearing no relation to their academic specialty. Even those with a firm career goal may not need as much specialization as they think at the undergraduate level. If you want to be a lawyer, don't worry yourself looking for something labeled prelaw. Follow your interests, get the best liberal arts education available, and then apply to law school.

Naturally, it is never a bad idea to check out the department(s) of any likely major, and occasionally your choice of major will suggest a direction for your search. If you're really into national politics, it may make sense to look at some schools in or near Washington, D.C. If you think you're interested in a relatively specialized field, say, oceanography, then be sure to look for some colleges that are a good match for you and also have programs in oceanography. But for the most part, rumors about top-ranked departments in this or that should be no more than a tie-breaker between schools you like for more important reasons. There are good professors (and bad ones) in any department. You'll have plenty of time to figure out who is who once you've enrolled. Being undecided about your career path as a senior in high school is often a sign of intelligence. Don't feel bad if you have absolutely no idea what you're going to do when you "grow up." One of the reasons you'll be paying megabucks to the college of your choice is the prospect that it will open some new doors for you and expand your horizons. Instead of worrying about particular departments, try to keep the focus on big-picture items like, What's the academic climate? How big are the freshman classes? Do I like it here? and Are these my kind of people?

KEEP AN OPEN MIND

The biggest mistake of beginning applicants is hyper-choosiness. At the extreme is the "perfect-school syndrome," which comes in two basic forms.

In one category are the applicants who refuse to consider any school that doesn't have every little thing they want in a college. If you're one who begins the process with a detailed picture of Perfect U. in mind, you may want to remember the oft-quoted advice, "Two out of three ain't bad." If a college seems to have most of the qualities you seek, give it a chance. You may come to realize that some things you thought were absolutely essential are really not that crucial after all.

The other strain of perfect-school syndrome is the applicant who gets stuck on a "dream" school at the beginning and then won't look anywhere else. With those twenty-two hundred four-year colleges out there (not counting those in Canada), it is just a bit silly to insist that only one will meet your needs. Having a first choice is OK, but the whole purpose of the search is to consider new options and uncover new possibilities. A student who has only one dream school—especially if it is a highly selective one—could be headed for disappointment.

As you begin the college search, don't expect any quick revelations. The answers will unfold in due time. Our advice? Be patient. Set priorities. Keep an open mind. Reexamine priorities. Again, be patient.

To get the ball rolling, move on to the Sizing-Yourself-Up Survey.

FISKE'S SIZING-YOURSELF-UP SURVEY

With apologies to Socrates, knowing thyself is easier said than done. Most high-school students can analyze a differential equation or a Shakespearean play with the greatest of ease, but when it comes to cataloging their own strengths, weaknesses, likes, and dislikes, many draw a blank. But self-knowledge is crucial to the matching process at the heart of a successful college search. The thirty-item survey below offers a simple way to get a handle on some crucial issues in college selection—and what sort of college may fit your preferences.

In the space beside each statement, rate your feelings on a scale of 1 to 10, with 10 = Strongly Agree, 1 = Strongly Disagree, and 5 = Not Sure/Don't Have Strong Feelings. (For instance, a rating of 7 would mean that you agree with the statement, but that the issue is a lower priority than those you rated 8, 9, or 10.) After you're done, read on to Grading Yourself to find out what it all means.

Size

_____ 1) I enjoy participating in many activities.

_____ 2) I would like to have a prominent place in my community.

_____ 3) Individual attention from teachers is important to me.

_____ 4) I learn best when I can speak out in class and ask questions.

_____ 5) I am undecided about what I will study.

_____ 6) I want to earn a Ph.D. in my chosen field of study.

_____ 7) I learn best by listening and writing what I hear.

_____ 8) I would like to be in a place where I can be anonymous if I choose.

_____ 9) I prefer devoting my time to one or two activities rather than many.

_____ 10) I want to attend a college that most people have heard of.

_____ 11) I am interested in a career-oriented major.

_____ 12) I like to be on my own.

Location

_____ 13) I prefer a college in a warm or hot climate.

_____ 14) I prefer a college in a cool or cold climate.

_____ 15) I want to be near the mountains.

_____ 16) I want to be near a lake or ocean.

_____ 17) I prefer to attend a college in a particular state or region.

_____ 18) I prefer to attend a college near my family.

_____ 19) I want city life within walking distance of my campus.

_____ 20) I want city life within driving distance of my campus.

_____ 21) I want my campus to be surrounded by natural beauty.

Academics and Extracurriculars

_____ 22) I like to be surrounded by people who are free-thinkers and nonconformists.

_____ 23) I like the idea of joining a fraternity or sorority.

_____ 24) I like rubbing shoulders with people who are bright and talented.

_____ 25) I like being one of the smartest people in my class.

_____ 26) I want to go to a prestigious college.

_____ 27) I want to go to a college where I can get an excellent education.

_____ 28) I want to try for an academic scholarship.

_____ 29) I want a diverse college.

_____ 30) I want a college where the students are serious about ideas.

Grading Yourself

Picking a college is not an exact science. People who are total opposites can be equally happy at the same college. Nevertheless, particular types tend to do better at some colleges than others. Each item in the survey is designed to test your feelings on an important issue related to college selection. Sizing Up the Survey (below) offers commentary on each item.

Taken together, your responses may help you construct a tentative blueprint for your college search. Statements 1–12 deal with the issue of size. Would you be happier at a large university or a small college? Here's the trick: add the sum of your responses to questions 1–6. Then make a second tally of your responses to 7–12. If the sum of 1–6 is larger, you may want to consider a small college. If 7–12 is greater, then perhaps a big school would be more to your liking. If the totals are roughly equal, you should probably consider colleges of various sizes.

Statements 13–21 deal with location. The key in this section is the intensity of your feeling. If you replied to No. 13 with a 10, does that mean you are going to look only at schools in warm climates? Think hard. If you consider only schools within a certain region or state, you'll be eliminating hundreds of possibilities. By examining your most intense responses—the 1s, 2s, 9s, and 10s—you'll be able to create a geographic profile of likely options.

Statements 22–30 deal with big-picture issues related to the character and personality of the college that may be in your future. As before, pay attention to your most intense responses. Read on for a look at the significance of each question.

Sizing Up the Survey

1. **I enjoy participating in many activities.** Students at small colleges tend to have more opportunities to be involved in many activities. Fewer students means less competition for spots.

2. **I would like to have a prominent place in my community.** Student-council presidents and other would-be leaders take note: it is easier to be a big fish if you're swimming in a small pond.

3. **Individual attention from teachers is important to me.** Small colleges generally offer more one-on-one with faculty both in the classroom and the laboratory.

4. **I learn best when I can speak out in class and ask questions.** Students who learn from interaction and participation would be well-advised to consider a small college.

5. **I am undecided about what I will study.** Small colleges generally offer more guidance and support to students who are undecided. The exception: students who are considering a preprofessional or highly specialized major.

6. **I want to earn a Ph.D. in my chosen field of study.** A higher percentage of students at selective small colleges earn a Ph.D. than those who attend large institutions of similar quality.

7. **I learn best by listening and writing what I hear.** Students who prefer lecture courses will find more of them at large institutions.

8. **I would like to be in a place where I can be anonymous if I choose to be.** At a large university, the supply of new faces is never-ending. Students who have the initiative can always reinvent themselves.

9. **I prefer devoting my time to one or two activities rather than many.** Students who are passionate about one activity—say, writing for the college newspaper—will often find higher quality at a bigger school.

10. **I want to attend a college that most people have heard of.** Big schools have more name recognition because they're bigger and have Division I athletic programs. Even the finest small colleges are relatively anonymous among the general public

11. **I am interested in a career-oriented major.** More large institutions offer business, engineering, nursing, etc., though some excellent small institutions do so as well (depending on the field).

12. **I like to be on my own.** A higher percentage of students live off campus at large schools, which are more likely to be in urban areas than their smaller counterparts.

13. I prefer a college in a warm or hot climate. Keep in mind that the Southeast and the Southwest have far different personalities (not to mention humidity levels).

14. I prefer a college in a cool or cold climate. Consider the Midwest, where there are many fine schools that are notably less selective than those in the Northeast.

15. I want to be near the mountains. You're probably thinking Colorado or Vermont, but don't zero in too quickly. States from Maine to Georgia and Arkansas to Arizona have easy access to mountains.

16. I want to be near a lake or ocean. Oceans are only on the coasts, but keep in mind the Great Lakes, the Finger Lakes, etc. Think about whether you want to be on the water or, say, within a two-hour drive.

17. I prefer to attend a college in a particular state or region. Geographical blinders limit options. Even if you think you want a certain area of the country, consider at least one college located elsewhere just to be sure.

18. I prefer to attend a college close to home. Unless you're planning to live with Mom and Dad, it may not matter whether your college is a two-hour drive or a two-hour plane ride.

19. I want city life within walking distance of my campus. Check out the neighborhood(s) surrounding your campus. Urban campuses—even in the same city—can be wildly different.

20. I want city life within driving distance of my campus. Unless you're a hardcore urban-dweller, a suburban perch near a city may beat living in the thick of one. Does public transportation or a campus shuttle help students get around?

21. I want my campus to be surrounded by natural beauty. A college viewbook will take you only so far. To really know if you'll fall in love with the campus, visiting is a must.

22. I like to be surrounded by free-thinkers and nonconformists. Plenty of schools cater specifically to students who buck the mainstream. Talk to your counselor or browse *The Fiske Guide to Colleges* to find some.

23. I like the idea of joining a fraternity or sorority. Greek life is strongest at mainstream and conservative-leaning schools. Find out if there is a split between Greeks and non-Greeks.

24. I like rubbing shoulders with people who are bright and talented. This is perhaps the best reason to aim for a highly selective institution, especially if you're the type who rises to the level of the competition.

25. I like being one of the smartest people in my class. If so, maybe you should skip the highly selective rat race. Star students get the best that a college has to offer.

26. I want to go to a prestigious college. There is nothing wrong with wanting prestige. Think honestly about how badly you want a big-name school and act accordingly.

27. I want to go to a college where I can get an excellent education. Throw out the *U.S. News* rankings and think about which colleges will best meet your needs as a student.

28. I want to try for an academic scholarship. Students in this category should consider less-selective alternatives. Scholarships are more likely if you rank high in the applicant pool.

29. I want a diverse college. All colleges pay lip service to diversity. To get the truth, see the campus for yourself and take a hard look at the student-body statistics in the *Guide*'s write-ups.

30. I want a college where students are serious about ideas. Don't assume that a college necessarily attracts true intellectuals mercly because it is highly selective. Some top schools are known for their intellectual climate—and others for their lack of it.

Putting It All Together

We hope the survey will help you get started on a thorough self-assessment that will continue throughout the college search. After thinking about your priorities, the time is right to begin looking at the colleges. Hundreds of them await!

Use the state-by-state index to search geographically if you like, or simply browse to find those that interest you. When you find a likely candidate, look to the Overlaps at the end of the article to find additional possibilities.

A Guide for Preprofessionals

The lists that follow include colleges and universities with unusual strength in each of nine preprofessional areas: engineering, architecture, business, art/design, drama, music, dance, communications/journalism, and film/television. In order to make the lists as useful as possible, we have included some schools that do not receive full-length write-ups in the *Fiske Guide*. Moreover, while the lists are suggestive, they are by no means all-inclusive, and there are other institutions in the *Fiske Guide to Colleges* that offer fine programs in these areas. Nevertheless, we hope the lists will be a starting place for students interested in these fields. We also recommend that you shop for a school that will allow you to combine preprofessional training with an adequate dose of liberal arts. For that matter, you might consider a double major (or minor) in a liberal arts field to complement your area of technical expertise. If you allow yourself to get too specialized too soon, you may end up as tomorrow's equivalent of the typewriter repairman. In a rapidly changing job market, nothing is so practical as the ability to read, write, and think.

ARCHITECTURE

Private Universities Strong in Architecture
Carnegie Mellon University
Columbia University
Cooper Union
Cornell University
Howard University
Lehigh University
Massachusetts Institute of Technology
University of Notre Dame
Princeton University
Rensselaer Polytechnic Institute
Rice University
Tulane University
Washington University in St. Louis

Public Universities Strong in Architecture
University of California–Berkeley
University of Cincinnati
Georgia Institute of Technology
University of Illinois–Urbana-Champaign
University of Kansas
Miami University (OH)
University of Michigan
State University of New York–Buffalo
University of Oregon
Pennsylvania State University
University of Texas–Austin
Virginia Polytechnic Institute and State University
University of Washington

A Few Arts-Oriented Architecture Programs
Barnard College
Bennington College
Pratt Institute
Rhode Island School of Design
Wellesley College
Yale University

ART/DESIGN

Top Schools of Art and Design
Art Center College of Design
California Institute of the Arts
Cooper Union
Maryland Institute, College of Art
Massachusetts College of Art
Moore College of Art and Design
Museum of Fine Arts, Boston
North Carolina School of the Arts
Otis Institute of Art and Design
Parsons School of Design
Pratt Institute
Rhode Island School of Design
School of the Art Institute of Chicago
School of Visual Arts

Major Universities Strong in Art and Design
Boston University
Carnegie Mellon University
University of Cincinnati
Cornell University
Harvard University
University of Michigan

New York University
University of Pennsylvania
University of Rochester
Washington University in St. Louis
University of Washington

Small Colleges and Universities Strong in Art and Design
Alfred University
Bard College
Brown University
Furman University
Hollins College
Hope College
Kenyon College
Lake Forest College
Manhattanville College
State University of New York–Purchase
Randolph-Macon Woman's College
University of North Carolina–Greensboro
Scripps College
Skidmore College
Smith College
Williams College

BUSINESS

Private Universities Strong in Business
Carnegie Mellon University
Case Western Reserve University
Emory University

Georgetown University
Howard University
Massachusetts Institute of
  Technology
New York University
University of Notre Dame
University of Pennsylvania
Rensselaer Polytechnic Institute
University of Richmond
University of Southern California
Southern Methodist University
Tulane University
Wake Forest University
Washington University in St. Louis

Public Universities Strong in Business

University of Arizona
University of California–Berkeley
University of Florida
University of Illinois–Urbana-
  Champaign
Indiana University
Miami University (OH)
University of Michigan
State University of New
  York–Albany
University of North
  Carolina–Chapel Hill
University of Vermont
University of Virginia
College of William and Mary
University of Washington

Small Colleges and Universities Strong in Business

Babson University
Bucknell University
Claremont McKenna College
DePauw University
Fairfield University
Franklin and Marshall College
Gettysburg College
Hendrix College
Lehigh University
Lewis and Clark College
Morehouse College
Ohio Wesleyan College
Skidmore College
Trinity University (TX)
Washington and Lee University

COMMUNICATIONS/ JOURNALISM

Major Universities Strong in Communications/Journalism

American University
Boston University
University of California–Los Angeles
University of Florida
University of Georgia
University of Illinois–Urbana-
  Champaign
Indiana University
University of Michigan
University of Missouri–Columbia
University of North
  Carolina–Chapel Hill
Northwestern University
Ohio University
University of Southern California
Stanford University
Syracuse University

ENGINEERING

Technical Institutes

California Institute of Technology
Colorado School of Mines
Cooper Union
Florida Institute of Technology
Georgia Institute of Technology
Harvey Mudd College
Illinois Institute of Technology
Massachusetts Institute of
  Technology
New Mexico Institute of Mining
  and Technology
Rensselaer Polytechnic Institute
Rochester Institute of Technology
Rose-Hulman Institute of
  Technology
Stevens Institute of Technology
Worcester Polytechnic Institute

Private Universities Strong in Engineering

Carnegie Mellon University
Case Western Reserve University
Columbia University
Cornell University
Duke University
The Johns Hopkins University

Northwestern University
University of Notre Dame
University of Pennsylvania
Princeton University
University of Southern California
Stanford University
Tufts University
Tulane University
Vanderbilt University
Washington University in St. Louis

Public Universities Strong in Engineering

University of California–Berkeley
University of California–
  Los Angeles
Clemson University
University of Illinois–Urbana-
  Champaign
Iowa State University
University of Michigan
Michigan State University
State University of New
  York–Buffalo
Pennsylvania State University
Purdue University
Rutgers—The State University of
  New Jersey
Texas A&M
University Virginia Polytechnic
  Institute and State University
University of Washington

Small Colleges and Universities Strong in Engineering

Brown University
Bucknell University
Calvin College
Clarkson University
Dartmouth College
Lafayette College
Lehigh University
University of the Pacific
University of Redlands
Rice University
Smith College
Swarthmore College
Trinity College (CT)
Tuskegee University
Union College

FILM/TELEVISION

Major Universities Strong in Film/Television

Arizona State University
Boston University
University of California–
  Los Angeles
University of Cincinnati
University of Florida
University of Kansas
University of Michigan
New York University
Northwestern University
Pennsylvania State University
University of Southern California
University of Texas–Austin

Small Colleges and Universities Strong in Film/Television

Bard College
Beloit College
Brown University
Evergreen State University
Hampshire College
Hofstra University
Ithaca College
State University of New
  York–Purchase
Occidental College
Pitzer College
Pomona College
Sarah Lawrence College

PERFORMING ARTS— MUSIC

Major Universities Strong in Music

Boston University
University of California–
  Los Angeles
Carnegie Mellon University
Case Western Reserve University
University of Cincinnati
University of Colorado–Boulder
Harvard University
Indiana University
Ithaca College
University of Miami (FL)
University of Michigan

University of Nebraska–Lincoln
New York University
Northwestern University
Rice University
University of Southern California
Vanderbilt University
Yale University

Small Colleges and Universities Strong in Music

Bard College
Bennington College
DePauw University
Illinois Wesleyan University
Lawrence University*
Manhattanville College
Mills College
Oberlin College*
St. Mary's College of Maryland
St. Olaf College
Sarah Lawrence College
Skidmore College
Smith College
Stetson University
Wesleyan University
Wheaton College (IL)
*Has a conservatory

PERFORMING ARTS— DRAMA

Major Universities Strong in Drama

Boston College
Boston University
University of California–
  Los Angeles
Carnegie Mellon University
The Catholic University of America
DePaul University
Fordham University
Indiana University
New York University
Northwestern University
University of North
  Carolina–Chapel Hill
University of Southern California
Southern Methodist University
Syracuse University
University of Washington
Yale University

Small Colleges and Universities Strong in Drama

Bennington College
Connecticut College
Ithaca College
Kenyon College
Lawrence University
Macalester College
State University of New
  York–Purchase
Princeton University
Rollins College
Sarah Lawrence College
Skidmore College
Vassar College
Whitman College

PERFORMING ARTS— DANCE

Major Universities Strong in Dance

Arizona State University
University of California–Irvine
University of California–
  Los Angeles
Case Western Reserve University
Florida State University
Hope College
Indiana University
New York University
Ohio University
Southern Methodist University
University of Texas–Austin
University of Utah
Washington University in St. Louis

Small Colleges and Universities Strong in Dance

Amherst College
Barnard College
Bennington College
Connecticut College
Dartmouth College
Goucher College
Kenyon College
Princeton University
Sarah Lawrence College
Smith College
State University of New
  York–Purchase

ENVIRONMENTAL STUDIES

Allegheny College
College of the Atlantic
Bowdoin College
University of California–Davis
University of California–Santa Barbara
Colby College
University of Colorado–Boulder
Dartmouth College
Deep Springs College
The Evergreen State College
Middlebury College
University of New Hampshire
University of North Carolina–Greensboro
Oberlin College

Prescott College
St. Lawrence University
Tulane University
University of Vermont
University of Washington
University of Wisconsin–Madison

INTERNATIONAL STUDIES

American University
Austin College
Claremont McKenna College
Colby College
Connecticut College
Dartmouth College
Dickinson College
Georgetown University
George Washington University

Goucher College
Hiram College
The Johns Hopkins University
Kalamazoo College
Lewis and Clark College
Macalester College
University of Massachusetts–Amherst
Middlebury College
Occidental College
Princeton University
Reed College
St. Olaf College
Sweet Briar College
Tufts University
College of William and Mary

Learning Disabilities

Services for students with learning disabilities have proliferated in recent years. Following is a list of major universities and small colleges with strong support for such students.

Major Universities with Strong Support for Students with Learning Disabilities

American University
University of Arizona
University of California–Berkeley
Clark University
University of Colorado–Boulder
University of Denver
DePaul University
University of Georgia
Hofstra University
Purdue University
Rochester Institute of Technology
Syracuse University
University of Vermont
University of Virginia

Small Colleges with Strong Support for Students with Learning Disabilities

Bard College
Curry College
Landmark College
Loras College
Lynn University
Marist College
Mercyhurst College
Mitchell College
Muskingum College
University of New England
St. Thomas Acquinas College (NY)
Southern Vermont College
Westminister College (MO)
West Virginia Wesleyan College

FISKE GUIDE TO COLLEGES 2004

Agnes Scott College

141 East College Avenue, Atlanta/Decatur, GA 30030

Combines the tree-lined seclusion of Decatur with the bustle of Atlanta. More money in the bank than most Ivy League schools, and enrollment is up 50 percent since 1990. Small classes, sisterhood, and a more exciting location than the Sweet Briars of the world.

Agnes Scott College, founded in 1889, continues to be the South's leading women's institution. Academically challenging across the board, this liberal arts college is highly acclaimed for its science and mathematics programs. With a commitment to higher education and a caring atmosphere, most students agree that Agnes Scott is "special because of the attention it lavishes on its students." Outward expansion has brought about the development of new facilities, programs, and a closer connection to the opportunities of nearby Atlanta.

The school, comprised of a combination of Gothic and Victorian architecture, is located on one hundred acres of beautifully wooded Georgia landscape nestled in a historic district of Decatur. Donated rare shrubs, bushes, trees, and gardens decorating the campus and one of the largest per-student endowments in the country are evidence of the school's strong alumni support. A $125 million capital improvement campaign has resulted in expansion and renovation of McCain Library, a new campus center, a new building for the Campbell Science Hall, a new parking struc-

"All professors know students by name, not by social security number."

ture, a newly purchased apartment complex, a newly purchased property for the Offices of Telecommunications and Facilities, a renovated dining hall, and a new Public Safety office.

The relationship between professors and students at Agnes Scott is a close one. "All professors know students by name, not by social security number," a freshman says. Academic and career counseling staff "work hard to ensure that the students can make informed decisions," a biology major says. Some of ASC's best departments include English, psychology, biology, history, and economics. The nationally acclaimed foreign language department has had a number of its German majors named Fulbright scholars in recent years. The fine and performing artists have their own modern facility, and the scientists have their own expanded observatory. Creative writers get the chance to rub elbows with real-life practitioners each spring, when the college sponsors a writers' festival. Would-be Heideggers can philosophize at ASC's own regional Undergraduate Philosophy Conference, or those more inclined to science can attend the Spring Annual Research Conference. There also are internship programs for entrepreneurs.

Agnes Scott is primarily a liberal arts college. First-year students are required to take two semesters of English composition and reading. In addition, everyone must take at least one course each in a variety of areas, including literature, math, historical studies and classical civilization, and fine arts. They must also complete a foreign language through the intermediate level

"They say we have dorm rooms like palaces."

and two semesters of physical education and science. ASC is affiliated with the Presbyterian Church, and one course in religion and philosophical thought is mandatory. The average class size is fifteen, and students are lavished with personal attention from the faculty. The downside of ASC's size is that some courses are taught only every other year, and scheduling conflicts are sometimes a problem.

Website: www.agnesscott.edu
Location: Urban
Total Enrollment: 885
Undergraduates: 869
Male/Female: 0/100
SAT Ranges: V 540–680
   M 530–620
ACT Range: 23–29
Financial Aid: 66%
Expense: Pr $ $
Phi Beta Kappa: Yes
Applicants: 709
Accepted: 74%
Enrolled: 31%
Grad in 6 Years: 89%
Returning Freshmen: 75%
Academics: ✍ ✍ ✍
Social: ☎ ☎
Q of L: ★ ★ ★ ★
Admissions: (404) 471-6285
Email Address: admission @agnesscott.edu

Strongest Programs:
   German
   Astrophysics
   English
   Psychology
   Biology/Biochemistry

The popular Return to College program enables women of any age to complete an interrupted degree in the same classes as traditional students, and the Atlanta Semester Program concerns the issues of women, leadership, and social change. Those with an international bent can go abroad under the auspices of the Global Awareness Program or the Global Connections Program, which gives students a semester of cross-cultural study before sending them out to all corners of the world. "The study-abroad program is terrific," says a junior. Southerners who want a taste of the California lifestyle can spend a semester at all-female Mills College in Oakland, California, while engineers and architects may complete their degrees in a 3–2 program with Georgia Tech or in a 3–4 program with Washington University in St. Louis. The library has about 211,000 volumes, online access to digital library resources, and a cozy spot on the main floor where students can curl up in front of a fireplace. As part of the Atlanta Regional Consortium for Higher Education, Agnes Scott shares facilities and resources with twenty other Atlanta-area schools through a cross-registration program.

The student body hails mainly from the Southeast, with about half being native Georgians. Most students share conservative upbringings but champion many liberal causes. "With an active, but not overpowering, lesbian population, we are politically correct," says a political science major. A sophomore notes that "feminism, political correctness, and social consciousness are major issues at ASC." Seventy-nine percent of the students are from public high schools, and African-Americans, Hispanics, and Asian-Americans make up 31 percent of the student body. "Agnes Scott women are leaders, thinkers, mothers, daughters, and much more," shares a senior. An honor system, which is strictly enforced by the Honor Court student judiciary, allows for self-scheduled exams and unmonitored tests and is frequently cited as the cornerstone of the college. Agnes Scott awards merit scholarships based on academic performance, demonstrated leadership, or musical ability.

Linked by tree-lined brick walks, dorms at Agnes Scott are large and spacious. "They say we have dorm rooms like palaces," gushes a freshman. Ninety-one percent of students live on campus. Three older dorms, prized for their high ceilings and hardwood floors, still wear their original and impressive Victorian facades. Freshmen are assigned to two of six dorms which tend to be more "chummy" or a modern apartment complex. The students can grab a bite at the snack bar or dine in the newly expanded and renovated dining hall.

ASC women tend to spend their weekends "trying to meet guys" at monthly TGIFs (a euphemism for beer blasts). Every October, students invite the men of their choice to a formal dance known as Black Cat. The dance follows a weeklong festival of class competitions that marks the end of the new-student orientation period. Other quaint old traditions survive, such as throwing anyone recently engaged into the alumnae pond. Seniors who have been accepted into graduate schools or found jobs climb the stairs of the college's bell tower to ring the bell, sharing their good news. But for the most part, those looking for fun travel to Georgia Tech. The "Agnes Scott Convent" has no sororities, but with only eight hundred or so students, the college itself is a close-knit sisterhood. Alcohol policies are covered under the honor code, but some underage students still find a way to drink. "The policies and enforcement are not so strict that people can't get around them," a senior says.

"There's a homey feel without all the boredom."

There is a college-run shuttle and taxi service to Emory and other locations in the Atlanta area. The city's public transportation is also convenient to campus and lures students to the symphony or to the High art museum, as well as to haunts traditionally more popular with males. All in all, the bustling city of Atlanta is a "big plus" to this little college in Decatur. "There's a homey feel without all the boredom" of a small town, a psychology major says. Varsity sports are improving with the school's inclusion in NCAA Division III and the addition of cross-country, soccer, volleyball, softball, swimming, and basketball as intercollegiate sports. The tennis team is definitely a standout. Intramural activities are popular and include the standard roundup of sports plus a few more exotic ones, such as studio dance.

The phrase "I am woman, hear me roar" fits perfectly into the mantra at ASC, which revolves around independence, intellectual growth, and strong voices for smart women. Small classes encourage quick thinking, while a host of off-campus internship and study opportunities make it easy to explore new ideas. "Students come to this school to better themselves," explains a freshman. "Scott graduates become leaders."

If You Apply To ➤ **Agnes Scott:** Early decision: Nov. 15. Regular admissions: Mar. 1. Financial aid: May 1. Campus interviews: recommended, evaluative. Alumni interviews: optional, informational. SATs or ACTs: required. SAT IIs: optional. Accepts the Common Application and electronic applications. Essay question: significant experience or risk; issues of concern; significant person; influence of a fictional or historical character, or art work; topic of choice.

University of Alabama

Box 870132, Tuscaloosa, AL 35487-0166

Roll, Tide, Roll says it all. Not exactly a hotbed of intellectual energy, 'Bama has been left in the dust by University of Georgia and its Hope Scholarship. Look for pockets of excellence in the professional programs, the Blount Undergraduate Initiative, and honors programs.

Tuscaloosa, Alabama only looks like a place where time stands still. Sure, the city's landmarks include those that have largely faded from view in other Southern towns: well-preserved antebellum homes, down-home Dreamland barbecue, and world-renowned blues music. And devotion to the University of Alabama and its powerful football team, the Crimson Tide, remains as strong as ever. But Tuscaloosa has also grown to include the only Mercedes-Benz plant outside of Germany and a modern trolley service, which connects the 'Bama campus to the city's thriving downtown. A pro-education governor and school president Andrew Sorensen are working to boost diversity, shift the focus from athletics to academics, and use new technology and facilities to re-invigorate the state's first university, which dates to 1831.

'Bama's one thousand-acre campus combines classical, revival-style buildings (several of which survived the 1865 burning of the university by Union troops) with modern structures. One of the most stunning in the South, the campus wraps around a shaded quadrangle, the home of the main library and "Denny Chimes," a campanile carillon that rings the Westminster Chimes on the quarter hour. A new student-services center, women's softball stadium and the Alabama Institute for Manufacturing Excellence have been added in recent years, as has a landscaped walkway called the Crimson Promenade.

The University of Alabama is organized into eight undergraduate colleges and schools, which together offer 215 degree programs. The Culverhouse College of Commerce and Business offers strong programs in marketing, information systems, and accounting; finance and marketing are the second- and third-most popular majors on campus (following public relations). Alston Hall, an imposing classroom-administrative

Website: www.ua.edu
Location: Small city
Total Enrollment: 19,130
Undergraduates: 15,201
Male/Female: 47/53
SAT Ranges: V 490–610
  M 490–610
ACT Range: 21–26
Financial Aid: N/A
Expense: Pub $
Phi Beta Kappa: Yes
Applicants: 7,864
Accepted: 79%
Enrolled: 30%
Grad in 6 Years: 61%
Returning Freshmen: 82%
Academics: ✍ ✍ ✍
Social: ☎ ☎ ☎
Q of L: ★ ★ ★
Admissions: (205) 348-5666
Email Address:
  admissions@ua.edu

(Continued)

Strongest Programs:
Communications
Dance
Management Information
    Systems
Marketing
Engineering
Athletic Training
Theater
Psychology
English

Professors teach lectures and many seminar courses, and UA is home to the Carnegie Foundation's 2001–02 National Professor of the Year, Cornelius Carter.

On the weekends, much of 'Bama's social life revolves around the Greek system. Participation has been steady in recent years, despite administrators' efforts to weaken it by prohibiting fraternities and sororities from having parties on campus.

building, provides state-of-the-art instructional technology for budding tycoons. Online databases in the Bruno Business Library and Bashinsky Computer Center offer search and retrieval of information from a wide variety of sources. The College of Communication and Information Sciences has one of the country's top-ten journalism schools, while respected programs in the College of Human Environmental Sciences include nutrition and hospitality management. The School of Music is a regional standout, attracting guest artists like Jean-Pierre Rampal and Midori. Students also give high marks to programs in engineering and advertising.

Students who receive academic scholarships, or who score at least 28 on the ACT or at least 1240 on the SAT may enroll in the Honors Program, which features smaller classes, better professors, and the opportunity to write a senior thesis. Additionally, twenty talented students of any major—mostly engineers—may participate in the Computer-Based Honors Program, which pays them to develop software programs in their field of study. The Blount Undergraduate Initiative is a living-learning program within the College of Arts and Sciences, where freshmen are housed with a faculty director and fellows. Other innovative offerings include 'Bama's Weekend College, the continuing-education division, which has attracted a large undergraduate following, and the May interim term, when students focus on one course in-depth.

"Course difficulty varies by department and instructor."

About 20 percent of Alabama freshmen take part in the Arts and Sciences Mentoring Program, which pairs them with faculty mentors who ease the adjustment to college through informal counseling and enrichment activities, such as concerts, movies, or lectures. All students may also enroll in the two-credit Academic Potential Seminar, which covers self-assessment, motivation, personal responsibility, time management, memory, textbook reading, note-taking, and test preparation. The only course 'Bama requires students to take during the first year on campus is a two-term English composition sequence. Before graduation, students must also take courses in writing, natural sciences, math, humanities and social sciences, and either two semesters of a foreign language or one of computer science.

While UA's core curriculum has been streamlined, and the math requirement has been reduced, don't expect to party all the time and still pass, students say. "If students want to be mediocre, they can," says a journalism and Spanish major. "If they want to compete and succeed, there are plenty of opportunities and rigorous programs. Course difficulty varies by department and instructor." Professors teach lectures and many seminar courses, and UA is home to the Carnegie Foundation's 2001–02 National Professor of the Year, Cornelius Carter. "I have never had a teaching assistant, except in laTucson," says an international studies major. "I've had graduate teaching assistants that are better than the actual professors," adds a public relations major.

Seventy-nine percent of 'Bama's students are homegrown, 21 percent hail from elsewhere in the U.S., and 5 percent are international, from more than ninety countries. Alabama leads Southern flagship universities with almost 17 percent minority enrollment: nearly 15 percent African-American, 1 percent Asian-American, and just shy of 1 percent Hispanic. "Racism and homosexuality often occupy editorial pages in the campus newspaper," says a senior. "Greek versus non-Greek issues are also very big, especially around Homecoming and Student Government Association elections," partially because the black and white Greek systems remain separate. 'Bama awards athletic scholarships in eleven women's sports and nine men's sports, as well as 434 merit scholarships, ranging from $150 to $7,956 per semester.

Most Alabama students live in off-campus apartments in the Tuscaloosa area; only 28 percent remain in campus residence halls, where options range from apartment-style living to private rooms and suites. "The dorms are comfortable and well-maintained, though not perfect," says a senior. "Some years, housing is tighter than others. Usually they find you a room, just not always where you wish to be." Sixteen percent of men pledge fraternities and 21 percent of women join sororities, and they may live in chapter houses. Six dorms have cafeterias, as does the student union. 'Bama's campus is safe, thanks to visible school police, though "most students feel nervous about the areas just off campus at night," one student says. Students may use a free school escort service, 348-RIDE, to reach their destinations after dark.

On the weekends, much of 'Bama's social life revolves around the Greek system. Participation has been steady in recent years, despite administrators' efforts to weaken it by prohibiting fraternities and sororities from having parties on campus. Those under twenty-one can't have alcohol in the dorms—or elsewhere, for that matter, per state law—but a senior says, "Many underage drinkers, who probably started in high school, continue to find ways to get served." Those who don't go Greek, or who don't wish to drink, will find everything from the Society for Creative Anachronism (medievalists) to Bible study groups. City Fest, featuring music, food, beer, and a German theme, is a popular annual event, as is Capstone, a Saturday dedicated

"Even the professors and administrators are very attentive and kind."

to community service. Road trips to New Orleans (for Mardi Gras and Greek weekend formals), Atlanta, Nashville, Birmingham, and the Gulf Coast and Florida beaches are popular, too.

Legendary coach Bear Bryant is long gone, and the program that he once led has been rocked by a series of scandals involving sexual favors, hard partying, and recruiting violations that have landed the football team on NCAA probation. Nevertheless, the annual Auburn-Alabama game—the Iron Bowl, one of the most intense rivalries in college sports—is the highlight of the school year. Alabama competes in Division I-A, and the gymnastics team brought home an NCAA championship in 2002. Football, baseball, and men's basketball also attract fans, as does the women's softball team.

In part because the recent athletic scandals have made Alabama something of an academic laughingstock, administrators are no longer satisfied with being a purely athletic and social school. (In fact, they brag, the school's debate team has won fourteen national championships—two more than the football team!) 'Bama is emphasizing technology, merit scholarships, global perspectives, and undergraduate research to raise its academic profile. UA wants to make what happens in the classrooms and laboratories, rather than the results of the weekend's gridiron contests, the university's top priority. What won't change, students hope, is the welcoming atmosphere. "Even the professors and administrators are very attentive and kind," says a senior.

Alabama built a national reputation on the strength of its football program, but the school's debate team has won fourteen national championships—two more than the football team!

Overlaps

Auburn, University of Georgia, Florida State, University of Tennessee, University of Florida

If You Apply To ➤

'Bama: Rolling admissions: July 1. Housing: Mar. 1. Meets demonstrated need of 98%. Campus interviews: recommended, evaluative. Alumni interviews: recommended, informational. SATs or ACTs: required. SAT IIs: optional. Accepts the Common Application and electronic applications. No essay question.

Albertson College

Caldwell, Idaho 83605

Got a map? You'll need a sharp eyes to spot Albertson, the *Fiske Guide*'s only liberal arts school (along with Colorado College) in the interior of the Mountain West. Innovative programs include Leadership Studies and the Center for Experiential Learning.

Albertson College of Idaho, the state's oldest four-year university, offers students an opportunity to earn a solid liberal arts education through small classes in a small town. Its strengths are natural sciences and traditional liberal arts, but the college is placing a new focus on technology, education, and interdisciplinary courses. Outside class, the school's scenic environment allows sports and nature enthusiasts to experience the playground that is so much of this unspoiled state.

The college is located in the small town of Caldwell where the atmosphere is calm and serene. For those looking for a little excitement, the state capitol of Boise is a short drive from campus. Also nearby are some of Idaho's most scenic locations such as beautiful mountains, deserts, and whitewater rivers. The school, originally a Presbyterian college, first planted roots in downtown Caldwell in 1891 and then moved to its present site in 1910, where its twenty-one buildings now inhabit forty-three acres. For more than eighty years, it was called the College of Idaho. But officials changed the college's name to honor the Albertson family, which gave $13.5 million for new facilities. The McCain Center, a $3 million student union, features a snack bar, coffee shop, student theater, movie theater, and outdoor eating area. New offices and labs are planned in order to accommodate the growing student population.

> **"The teaching quality at Albertson, on a 10-point scale, is an 11.5."**

Most classes at Albertson have twenty-five or fewer students, and all are taught by full professors. "The teaching quality at Albertson, on a 10-point scale, is an 11.5," one junior raves. Students agree its small size is the school's strongest asset, allowing students to usually get into the classes they want. "Teaching is incredible and outstanding," says one senior. Students appreciate being able to get to know their professors. "I love it because there's a real sense of community, it's so small. Professors are on a first-name basis," says a junior.

The school's academic schedule is composed of twelve-week semesters, spring and fall, separated by a six-week winter session, during which students can assist professors with research, take an internship, volunteer, or travel abroad. Offerings run from "creative writing and backcountry skiing in the Sawtooth Mountains" to "history of art in London." The general-education requirements include natural sciences, writing, mathematics, physical education, and cultural diversity. Freshmen go through a first-year program that includes a specialized curriculum and intensive two-semester writing course. First-year students demonstrating leadership potential are invited to a series of seminars to draw them into the leadership studies program, a business minor. The two libraries have 178,000 volumes and are accessible twenty-four hours a day online.

Biology, English, and history are among the majors recommended by students, and preprofessional majors, such as premed, prevet, and prelaw are also popular and strong. Weaker departments are the smaller ones, such as foreign languages, music, business, and education. To improve business offerings, the school is revising the curriculum and increasing internship opportunities. Students can choose such specializations as sports and fitness-center management. It has also overhauled education and is adding a five-year master's degree program. The college cooperates with Columbia University, the University of Idaho, Boise State University, and Washington University in St. Louis to offer a five-year course of study in engineering. The new Center for Experiential Learning coordinates out-of-classroom experiences, such as international education and service learning. For those who want to venture abroad (physically or mentally), the International Education Program offers several options, including attending a foreign university, traveling overseas during the summer and winter breaks, and taking international studies on campus. Travel has really taken off, with 25 percent of students accepting opportunities to such places as Cuba, Greece, and Germany. Advising is available to help students make good academic choices. "Advisors are incredible. They are always willing to help sort out your academic program," says a senior majoring in politics and economics.

The school's price tag is lower than that of most private colleges. It offers 474 merit scholarships ranging from $500 to $16,700, as well as 174 athletic scholarships in Albertson sports. Not surprisingly, some of those scholarship dollars are set aside for skiers. Seventy-six percent of the students are from Idaho; 82 percent are white. Only 2 percent hail from foreign nations. "PC is an issue," says a junior. "Our campus is concerned about environmental issues and we're evenly divided between conservatives and liberals."

Fifty-six percent of students live on campus. Each room in the five residence halls has individual heating and cooling and hookups for Internet access, and each hall has a computer lab. Dorms are "decent-sized, not any better or worse than a typical college," a junior comments. The college recently implemented a round-the-clock escort system.

Nineteen percent of men and women participate in the Greek system, which dominates campus social life. Annual social highlights include Winterfest and Spring Fling and Homecoming Week. Games against rival Northwest Nazarene also attract attention. Caldwell, with 24,000 people, is not a great spot for college students. "Finals breakfasts" offer something for bleary-eyed students to look forward to during finals week. At midnight on Tuesday, faculty and staff cook breakfast for students. Nearby Boise is a popular destination for shopping, dining, cultural events, and volunteering. Many students take advantage of hiking, kayaking, and skiing in the surrounding area, and many hit the road during a weeklong break taken every six weeks.

Basketball is a crowd-pleaser, and the team has made Albertson students proud, chalking up victories in NAIA Division II competition. The women's team was a runner-up in 2001. The men's baseball team won the 1999 NAIA Division II national championship and competed in the conference World Series in 2002. The women's ski team competed for the national championship during the 1999–2000 season. For those who enjoy the game but might not make the team, there is an active intramurals program, including Frisbee football,

"Our campus is concerned about environmental issues and we're evenly divided between conservatives and liberals."

volleyball, basketball, and softball, and the large J.A. Albertson Activities Center. Beyond sports, extracurricular activities include Bible study, choir, student government, an environmental club, and a rejuvenated Hispanic club.

Albertson College has much to offer the "Yotes" (translation: "We are the coyotes.") They enjoy a solid liberal arts education and personal academic attention on a campus striving to keep its offerings on the cutting edge.

The college cooperates with Columbia University, the University of Idaho, Boise State University, and Washington University in St. Louis to offer a five-year course of study in engineering.

First-year students demonstrating leadership potential are invited to a series of seminars to draw them into the leadership studies program, a business minor.

Overlaps

Boise State, University of Idaho, Linfield, Gonzaga, Willamette

Albertson: Early action: Nov. 15. Regular admission: June 1. Does not guarantee to meet demonstrated need. Campus interviews: recommended, informational. Alumni interviews: optional, informational. SATs or ACTs: required. SAT IIs: optional. Accepts the Common Application and electronic applications. Essay question: fictional character, sentimental possession, important issue.

Albion College

Albion, MI 49224

Next to evangelical Hope and Calvin and out-there Kalamazoo, Albion is Michigan's middle-of-the road liberal arts college. Think Gerald Ford, the moderate Republican president who is the namesake of Albion's signature Institute for Public Service. Future doctors, lawyers, and business-people will be well served.

Website: www.albion.edu
Location: Small town
Total Enrollment: 1,548
Undergraduates: 1,548
Male/Female: 45/55
SAT Ranges: V 510–640
   M 520–630
ACT Range: 22–27
Financial Aid: 60%
Expense: Pr $
Phi Beta Kappa: Yes
Applicants: 1,297
Accepted: 87%
Enrolled: 40%
Grad in 6 Years: 72%
Returning Freshmen: 86%
Academics: ✍ ✍ ✍
Social: ☎ ☎
Q of L: ★ ★ ★
Admissions: (800) 858-6770
Email Address:
   admissions@albion.edu

Strongest Programs:
   Economics & Business
   Ford Institute for Public
      Service
   Environment Institute
   Premed
   Prelaw

Albion is a small, private college in Michigan whose motto is, "Liberal arts at work." The school's motto emphasizes the importance Albion places on combining learning with hands-on experience. Students at Albion often participate in leadership and service learning seminars. And when the work is through, students here enjoy a close-knit social life. "The people are the biggest reason I have enjoyed Albion College," admits a senior. Another student says, "Since Albion is a small school, it gives each student personal attention in every aspect of their education while having all of the advantages of a larger school due to all the resources available to the students."

Founded in 1835 by the Methodist Church, Albion is located near the banks of the Kalamazoo River. In addition to its newer Georgian-style architecture, the college has retained and restored several of its nineteenth-century buildings. The campus is spacious with statuesque oaks and a beautiful nature center. Robinson Hall, the campus centerpiece, houses myriad departments, including the Ford Institute for Public Service, the Gerstacker Liberal Arts Program in Professional Management, and the Anna Howard Shaw Women's Center. The campus continues to expand with the addition of the Ferguson Student Services Building.

> **"The people are the biggest reason I have enjoyed Albion College."**

Academically, Albion is as sound as its buildings. It was the first private college in Michigan to have a Phi Beta Kappa chapter (1940) and has produced three Rhodes Scholars. On their journey to becoming Rhodes Scholars, students are required to take core courses distributed among humanities, natural sciences, social sciences, fine arts, and math. They must also satisfy requirements in environmental science and gender and ethnicity studies. Freshmen must take first-year seminars designed to provide a "stimulating learning environment" in a small-class setting, while seniors participate in a capstone experience.

Albion's most distinguishing feature is the emphasis placed on citizenship and service. The Gerald R. Ford Institute for Public Service takes a unique approach for future civic leaders. Students participate in a simulation of city government in which they play the roles of community leaders. Visiting speakers include senators and congressmen, governors and state legislators, and interest-group representatives. The premedical and prelaw programs draw dedicated undergrads, and the English and economics departments are well respected. Another option is the Summer Research Program, which allows students to remain on campus during the summer to work with faculty members on different projects.

The academic climate at Albion is described as competitive but not cut-throat. One student says, "We are competitive with other colleges and strive for the best in ourselves, but we are supportive of each other and the college." Top-notch academic and career counseling and low student/faculty ratios keep students on track and motivated. Class size varies, but the average class is under twenty-five students. Professors are interested in students' academic performance and their emotional well-being. While "the courses are carefully prepared and the professors expect diligence from the students, the professors really care and take an interest in the students" and it is not "uncommon to have class at a professor's house with pizza and holiday cookies." The professors seem to know the secret to motivating college students— feed them and they will work! Teaching assistants are used for tutoring, not teaching. Albion's libraries feature computer facilities, an inter-

Albion was the first private college in Michigan to have a Phi Beta Kappa chapter (1940) and has produced three Rhodes Scholars.

"We are competitive with other colleges and strive for the best in ourselves, but we are supportive of each other and the college."

library loan service, a listening lab for language or music study, and a helpful staff. If you can't find what you need at Albion's libraries, weekly bus trips to the University of Michigan libraries in Ann Arbor provide access to even more resources.

Albion continues to attract an ambitious, involved group of students. Michigan residents make up 90 percent of the student population. Eighty-five percent are Caucasian, 2 percent African-American, and 1 percent Hispanic. Up to now, there has been little deviation from the white, upper-middle-class norm. In an effort to change this, a new host-family program matches minority students with families from within the community. There are a number of merit scholarships available, based on academic records, extracurricular involvement, and demonstrated leadership abilities. There are no athletic scholarships.

Eighty-nine percent of Albion students call the residence halls home, which are comfortable and well-maintained. The majority of the freshman class inhabits Wesley Hall, which is described as "beautiful and full of heritage." During their sophomore year, many students move to Seaton or Whitehouse halls; seniors enjoy new, apartment-style housing called The Mae. Dorms are coed by hall or floor, and the information each student provides in their Housing Request Form is used to assign rooms and roommates. One student claims, "The dorms are extremely well maintained and have maintenance boards located on every floor so that the students can voice their concerns. Most of the concerns are taken care of by the next day." Other housing options include apartment annexes and fraternity houses. Sororities do not have houses; they hold their meetings in lodges. Two large dining rooms feed campus residents on an "eat all day" meal plan.

Forty percent of Albion men and women belong to one of the school's six national fraternities and seven sororities. Greek parties draw large crowds, composed of Greeks and non-Greeks, making them a primary part of many students' social lives. Controlling the alcoholic intake of students has become a priority of the administration. Students say "underage drinking does happen" but the college "has strict consequences if caught." Those who insist on imbibing can do it at Gina's or Cascarelli's, popular bars in town.

Road trips are a big part of weekends for many students. Ann Arbor, East Lansing, and Canada are frequent destinations. A well-run Union Board organizes all sorts of activities—films, lectures, plays, comics, and concerts—to keep students occupied in their spare time. Several students report that the town movie theatre shows "free movies if you show a valid student ID!"

Still, students complain that there are not many social outlets available at Albion. Students focus some of their energy on work for groups supported by the Student Volunteer Bureau; in fact, half of the students volunteer on a regular basis. They are

The College's Foundation for Undergraduate Research, Scholarship, and Creative Activity is providing students with funding for the summer so that they can remain on campus and work with faculty members on different research projects.

very involved in the community, including "city clean-up day, Habitat for Humanity, and volunteering at nursing homes and schools." Some traditional events that offer a nice break from academics are the Briton Bash, a fair that familiarizes students with clubs and organizations, and the Day of Woden, which is a picnic held in the spring on the last day of class.

"Free movies if you show a valid student ID!"

The varsity football team has won nine conference championships in the past decade. Recently, the women's soccer team brought home the Conference MIAA Championship. Men's track, baseball, and golf, along with women's swimming, also receive a lot of attention on campus. Hope College is a hated rival, as is Alma College.

At Albion, professors are accessible and interested, and academics are challenging without being overwhelming. Students agree that the "small campus with friendly students, caring faculty, and kind staff members" make this college a special place.

If You Apply To ➤ **Albion:** Early decision: Nov. 15. Financial aid: Feb. 15. Does not guarantee to meet demonstrated need. Campus interviews: recommended, evaluative. Alumni interviews: optional, informational. SATs or ACTs: required. SAT IIs: optional. Accepts the Common Application and electronic applications. Essay question.

Alfred University

Alumni Hall, Saxon Drive, Alfred, NY 14802-1205

Talk about an unusual combination—Alfred combines a nationally renowned college of ceramics, a school of art and design, an engineering program, and a business school wrapped up in a university of just more than two thousand students. It takes elbow-grease to pry coastal types to the hinterlands of western New York.

Website: www.alfred.edu
Location: Rural
Total Enrollment: 2,400
Undergraduates: 2,000
Male/Female: 50/50
SAT Ranges: V 480–610
    M 510–610
ACT Range: 24–28
Financial Aid: 90%
Expense: Pr $ $
Phi Beta Kappa: No
Applicants: 1,935
Accepted: 75%
Enrolled: 35%
Grad in 6 Years: 79%
Returning Freshmen: 88%
Academics: 🏛 🏛 🏛
Social: ☎ ☎ ☎
Q of L: ★ ★ ★

When you think of ceramics, what comes to mind? Sculptures or semiconductors? Either way, Alfred University has a top-notch program to satisfy your educational needs. This small school boasts highly respected programs in art and design, as well as ceramic engineering. Innovation not only shapes the curriculum, but also has a profound effect on campus life. Small classes and friendly competition support this diversity while encouraging individuals to succeed. With just under 2,500 students, Alfred isn't a bustling academic factory; it's a quiet, cloistered, self-described "educational village" in a tiny town wholly dedicated to the "industry of learning."

Alfred's campus consists of a charming, close-knit group of modern and Georgian brick buildings, along with a stone castle. The Kanakadea Creek runs right through campus, and the town of Alfred consists of two colleges (the other is the Alfred State College) and a main street with one stoplight. There are a few shops and restaurants, but certainly no malls, parking lots, or tall buildings. Recent campus construction includes renovations of labs and classrooms in Binns-Merrill Hall and Kanakadea Hall.

"All the profs are down to earth and very approachable."

The university and its students share a no-nonsense approach to education. Although prospective students apply directly to one of four colleges and declare a tentative major, half of all requirements for a bachelor's degree are earned in the liberal arts college. Requirements are quite different in each school. However, the mix usually includes coursework in oral and written communication, foreign language and culture, social sciences, history, literature, philosophy, and religion.

Alfred, though private, is actually the "host" school for the New York State College of Ceramics, which is a unit of the state university system and comes with a public-university pricetag. Ceramic engineering (the development and refinement of ceramic materials) is the undisputed king of the academic castle and the program that brings Alfred international recognition. The school is the site of a great deal of superconductivity research, as well as the Ceramic Corridor, a research project involving Corning Enterprises. In fact, students talk about the excellence of the ceramic engineering program regardless of their personal majors or interests, and the clay artists often earn the fond nickname "cement heads." The art department, with its programs in ceramics, glass, printmaking, sculpture, video, and teacher certification, is also highly regarded. The School of Art and Design offers a graphic design major in which students use electronic and computer equipment. The business administration school also gets good reviews from students and provides undergraduates with work experience through a small-business institute where students have real clients.

"Financial aid is great. Without it, I would not be here."

Many majors also offer a co-op program that alternates semesters of work and study. "It is competitive enough to make you work hard, but not enough to drive you to suicide," says one ceramic engineering major. Recently, health planning and management has moved from a major to a career emphasis within the College of Business. The major in foreign language and culture sponsors trips abroad, and exchange programs are available in England, Germany, Italy, France, Japan, China, and the Czech Republic. The Track II program enables students to design their own interdisciplinary majors with personal guidance from top faculty members.

Whatever their major, all students enjoy very small classes (average size is eighteen students), and the quality of teaching is described as very high. "All the profs are down to earth and very approachable," explains a senior. Most classes are taught by full professors, with graduate students and teaching assistants helping out only in lab sessions. The university stresses its commitment to helping undergrads plan their future, and the academic-advising and career-planning services are strong enough for Alfred to deliver on its promise. Students say faculty members really want to see them succeed, both in class and in the "real world." "Professors are very involved with the students and clearly interested in teaching," brags one junior.

"I feel that there is a cloning process going on at schools across America," opines one student. "Students look alike, act alike, think alike, and dress alike. Alfred is a refreshing exception to this rule." Nearly two-thirds of the students at Alfred are from New York State, and 25 percent graduated from high school in the top 10 percent of their class. Students are mostly white and from public schools. Minority enrollment is growing: 6 percent are African-American, 6 percent are Hispanic, and 4 percent are Asian-American. Students praise the financial-aid packages they receive. "Financial aid is great. Without it, I would not be here," says a junior. The university is holding freshman tuition steady under the "Alfred Plan." Outstanding students can apply for many merit scholarships ranging from $2,500 to a full ride, and National Merit finalists receive Alfred's Award of Merit. There are no athletic scholarships.

No one seems to mind the two-year on-campus residency requirement, since the rooms are large and comfortable, and the dorms are equipped with lounges, kitchens, and laundry facilities; some even boast such extras as computers and saunas. Upperclassmen have a choice of coed-by-floor dorms, with single rooms, suites, or apartments. Freshmen enjoy their own housing divided into doubles. The favorite freshman dorm is Barresi. Seventy-five percent of all students choose to live

(Continued)
Admissions: (800) 541-9229
Email Address:
admwww@alfred.edu

Strongest Programs:
Ceramic Engineering
Art
Business
Sciences
Psychology
English

Ceramic engineering (the development and refinement of ceramic materials) is the undisputed king of the academic castle and the program that brings Alfred international recognition.

on campus, but some juniors and about half of the seniors opt to live off campus. The school has two dining halls and a choice of six meal plans. Freshmen and sophomores are required to subsist on cafeteria cuisine, which features an enormous variety of regular buffets, plus a salad bar, a deli line, and daily international lines. Campus security is good, according to most. "This town is very safe," says one female student. "I do not even think twice about walking around at night."

Alfred's location in the Finger Lakes region, almost two hours from Buffalo and an hour and a half from Rochester, is isolated. Social life is difficult due to the rural atmosphere, but the Student Activities Board brings many events to campus, including musicians, comedians, lecturers, and movies. Favorite road trips are to Letchworth and Stony Brook state parks, and to Ithaca, Rochester, Buffalo, and Toronto. Many students are skiing, hunting, camping, and rock-climbing enthusiasts. Friendly games of hackeysack, Frisbee, football, softball, and other sports can often be found somewhere on campus. Fraternities and sororities, which had been attracting a declining proportion of students in recent years and facing repeated sanctions, were eliminated last year following the death of a fraternity member near the campus. The alcohol policy is enforced on the campus, but students say it is not impossible to get alcohol. "The alcohol policies are very strict for freshmen, but after freshmen year, they don't work very well," says a sophomore.

"This town is very safe."

Because Alfred shares the town with Alfred State University, the dominant student population makes Alfred a good college town. "This town is dead when college is not in session," observes a communications major. The downtown scene provides students with an adequate number of movie theaters and eateries. Every spring brings the annual Hot Dog Weekend, a big fund-raising event that fills Main Street with game booths, bands, and lots and lots of hot dog stands. Alfred's Division III Saxons are ominous opponents on the football, soccer, and lacrosse fields, and alpine skiing, equestrian, and men's swimming have all won spots in the top ten nationally.

If you want to spend four years concentrating on your ABCs (that's arts, business, or ceramic engineering), then small, secluded Alfred University is a good choice. But bring your heavy coat and gloves, because upstate New York winters can be brutal.

Overlaps

SUNY–Geneseo, Rochester Institute of Technology, Syracuse, Ithaca, Clarkson

If You Apply To ➤

Alfred: Early decision: Dec. 1. Regular admissions: Feb. 1. Financial aid and housing: May 1. Campus interviews: recommended, evaluative. Alumni interviews: optional, informational. SATs or ACTs: required. SAT IIs: recommended. Accepts the Common Application and electronic applications. Essay question: favorite family or cultural tradition; take a standard piece of paper and be creative; build a webpage and send us the address; contributions to Alfred.

Allegheny College

520 North Main Street, Meadville, PA 16335

An unpretentious cousin to more well-heeled places like Dickinson and Bucknell. Draws heavily from the Buffalo-Cleveland-Pittsburgh area. The college's powerhouse athletic teams clean up on Division III competition. If you've ever wondered what lake-effect snow is, you'll find out here.

Allegheny College is a down-to-earth Eastern liberal arts school boasting a rich history of academic excellence in an intimate setting. Administrators here understand the importance of providing students with real-world experience to complement their classroom work. The school's innovative May term offers time for internships or other off-campus work and study. Allegheny's small size means students don't suffer from lack of attention, and despite the heavy workload, anyone struggling academically will get help before the situation becomes dire. "There are great one-on-one relationships between students and professors," says a sophomore.

Tucked away in tiny Meadville, Pennsylvania, ninety miles north of Pittsburgh, lies Allegheny's seventy-two-acre campus. Founded in 1815, nestled in the Norman Rockwell–esque rolling hills of northwestern Pennsylvania, the campus is home to traditional, ivy-covered buildings and redbrick streets, as well as new apartment-style housing for upperclassmen and a new facility for the communication arts department. A $14.5 million science complex supports already-strong programs, and students who wish to pump iron can visit the new fitness center. The college also owns a 182-acre outdoor recreational facility and a 283-acre nature preserve.

Students at Allegheny work hard and do well, as evidenced by the fact that 32 percent of a recent senior class immediately went on to graduate or professional school. "Allegheny is a very challenging institution, however, I would not describe it as a highly competitive school," says an English and political science major. The school's strongest programs are environmental studies, economics, psychology, neuroscience, and biology, administrators say, while students give high marks to English, too. The critical languages such as sign language, Italian, Asian, and Classical language programs are weaker. Programs in sociology/anthropology and education have been dropped, although Allegheny now offers a co-

"If it's your passion to be an activist, there are plenty of organizations to get involved with."

op education program with Pittsburgh's Chatham College. There is a new minor in values, ethics, and social action, and new majors in biochemistry, applied computing, and art and technology. Other co-op programs include a 3–2 option leading to double BS degrees in engineering, a Physicians Shortage Program with Jefferson College, and a linkage program with MCP Hahneman University School of Medicine. The college also has an articulation agreement with the University of Pittsburgh Graduate School of Education. The Allegheny College Center for Experiential Learning (ACCEL) is a clearinghouse for internship opportunities, service learning, and overseas study.

Allegheny has two fifteen-week semesters each year, and its general education requirements keep students busy. Freshmen take the first seminar in their first semester, and the second seminar in their second. Sophomores have a writing and speaking seminar, while juniors take a seminar in their major field, and seniors complete an intensive capstone project in their major. All students must take courses in each of three major divisions (humanities and the natural and social sciences) and must finish a minor in a subject area outside their major. Despite Allegheny's small size—81 percent of courses have fewer than thirty students—most of those enrolled graduate in four years, although it can be tough to get into communication arts courses, students say.

Students praise Allegheny's faculty for their passion, knowledge, and accessibility. A senior says, "Whenever I need help with an assignment, I feel extremely comfortable talking to my professors." You won't find a TA at the lectern in any Allegheny classroom, and the college's honor code allows students to take unproctored exams. Off campus, Allegheny offers study in several U.S. cities or abroad, an on-campus independent-study option, and semester internships or "externships" (a chance to observe a professional at work during the winter vacation). There's also a

Website: www.allegheny.edu
Location: Small city
Total Enrollment: 1,879
Undergraduates: 1,879
Male/Female: 47/53
SAT Ranges: V 540–650
    M 540–640
ACT Range: 23–28
Financial Aid: 74%
Expense: Pr $ $
Phi Beta Kappa: Yes
Applicants: 2,530
Accepted: 79%
Enrolled: 24%
Grad in 6 Years: 71%
Returning Freshmen: 88%
Academics: ✍ ✍ ✍
Social: ☎ ☎ ☎
Q of L: ★ ★ ★
Admissions: (800) 521-5293
    or (814) 332-4351
Email Address:
    admiss@allegheny.edu

Strongest Programs:
    Environmental Science
    Economics
    Psychology
    Neuroscience
    Biology

The Allegheny College Center for Experiential Learning (ACCEL) is a clearinghouse for internship opportunities, service learning, and overseas study.

The campus offers more than two hundred computer workstations, which *The Chronicle of Higher Education* calls "staggering," given the institution's small size and limited technical resources.

three- or four-week Experiential Learning term following spring semester for study abroad and internships not available during the year. The library holds more than 670,000 volumes and the campus offers more than two hundred computer workstations, which *The Chronicle of Higher Education* calls "staggering," given the institution's small size and limited technical resources.

Sixty-six percent of Allegheny's students hail from Pennsylvania, and sizable contingents come from nearby Ohio, New York, and New England. While Allegheny isn't a terribly diverse campus—minority students make up only 7 percent of the total—the school is committed to increasing awareness of and appreciation for diversity. "Some people aren't politically conscious or aware at all. However, if it's your passion to be an activist, there are plenty of organizations to get involved with," comments one senior. Merit scholarships are available, ranging from $500 to $15,000.

Ten residence halls and twenty houses (including TV and study rooms) accommodate undergraduates in relative style and comfort with a variety of living situations: all-freshmen dorms; coed and single-sex halls; small houses; and single, double, and triple rooms and suites.

"There is a mix of on- and off-campus social life."

Dorms are "clean and of reasonable size," says a senior, and "there is no trouble getting a room," says a sophomore. Housing is guaranteed for four years, and 75 percent of students stay on campus. The most popular dorm is the new, townhouse-style College Court complex, which holds eighty students in suites with four single bedrooms each. Students want more variety in food services and more parking, since cars are a necessity for trips to the factory outlets in nearby Grove City, Pennsylvania, or the bright lights of Pittsburgh, Buffalo, or Cleveland. Officers from campus security are available twenty-four hours a day, but they aren't much needed. "Meadville is a safe, quite town," says a senior.

Greek organizations draw 17 percent of the men and 30 percent of the women, and provide a great deal of nightlife. Three fraternities have their own houses, while the four sororities are relegated to special dorm suites. There are also two campus theater series, two-dollar movies on Wednesday nights, and comedians, ventriloquists, and live bands provided by the center for student activities. Large-scale philanthropic events like Make a Difference Day and the Month of Service, in March, are also popular. "There is a mix of on- and off-campus social life," says a junior. College policy states that students must be twenty-one to have or consume alcohol on campus. Homecoming, Springfest (a day full of bands, activities, and food), and Winter Carnival break up the monotony of studying for exams.

Downtown Meadville, lovingly referred to as Mudville, is a ten-minute walk from campus and has a four-screen movie theater and several community playhouses, as well as schools, hospitals, children's homes, animal shelters, and other organizations that benefit from the more than 26,000 hours of service students contribute each year. "The students do a lot of volunteer work and help immensely throughout the community," says an economics major. When more time in Meadville is too much to bear, students hit the road. Nearby state parks at Conneaut Lake and Lake Erie offer water-skiing and boating in warm weather and cross-country skiing in the winter.

As for Allegheny traditions, there's the somewhat-suspect "13th Plank" ritual, which states that all freshman women must be kissed on the thirteenth plank of the campus bridge by an upperclassman to be considered a "true Allegheny coed." Of course, a group of freshman men steal the plank every year at the beginning of the first semester to prevent that from happening. Athletics play a big role in Allegheny life, although there are no athletic scholarships, and the recent addition of a $13 million sports and fitness complex gave students new reason to cheer. The baseball team made it to the Division III World Series in 2000, and the women's basketball and soccer teams are very popular.

Overlaps
Penn State, University of Pittsburgh, Washington and Jefferson, Dickinson, Gettysburg

Allegheny College boasts a rich history of academic excellence in an intimate setting, augmented by a new emphasis on extracurricular experiences designed to produce well-rounded alumni. The campus's natural beauty and the genuine affection students feel for it and for each other remain unchanged. Indeed, the Allegheny experience "urges you to be well rounded and grow as a person, not just as a student," proclaims a proud junior.

Alma College

Alma, MI 48801

The college that put the Alma back in alma mater. As friendly a campus as you'll find, Alma combines the liberal arts with distinctive offerings in health-related fields. Diversity is an issue and few out-of-staters enroll. If central Michigan drives you stir-crazy, join the hordes who go abroad.

Alma College may be located in Michigan's lower peninsula, but its reach extends around the world. Students here get a liberal arts education with lots of close, personal attention. But they also expand their learning around the globe, participating in everything from the U.S. mission to the United Nations to the reclamation of a Jewish cemetery in Poland. The annual Highland Festival features kilt-wearing bagpipers and competitions and has led some to dub the school "Scotland, USA." "For the most part we are all looking for a small, personal college where we can get the best education," a freshman says.

Alma's twenty-five Prairie-style buildings of red brick and limestone surround a scenic central mall. "The campus has lots of trees and open places to sit," says one student. Administrators are looking at how best to expand toward the Pine River, because the current campus is bounded by residential neighborhoods, making it difficult to find room for new academic, athletic, and living facilities. The Evergreen Planning Task Force is working with a campus designer to plan Alma's layout for the twenty-first century.

> "The campus has lots of trees and open places to sit."

Academics at Alma are demanding, "but faculty support is amazing," says a senior. "It is somewhat competitive. The courses are very challenging," says a sophomore chemistry major. Students must demonstrate proficiency in communication, computation, and foreign language, and must complete sixteen credits in each of three areas: arts and humanities, social sciences, and natural sciences. In addition, students must complete a comprehensive series of English courses. Anthropology has been added to the sociology major, and there's now a minor in new media studies, while the peacemaking and conflict resolution minor was dropped. Computer science and math were split into two different departments. Weaker departments include modern languages, philosophy, economics, and religious studies.

The top major is business administration, followed by education and biology. The popular exercise and health science major prepares students for health-related

Website: www.alma.edu
Location: Rural
Total Enrollment: 1,371
Undergraduates: 1,371
Male/Female: 41/59
ACT Range: 22–27
Financial Aid: 78%
Expense: Pr $
Phi Beta Kappa: Yes
Applicants: 1,237
Accepted: 80%
Enrolled: 32%
Grad in 6 Years: 75%
Returning Freshmen: 85%
Academics: ✍ ✍ ✍
Social: ☎ ☎ ☎
Q of L: ★ ★ ★
Admissions: (800) 321-ALMA
Email Address:
  admissions@alma.edu

Strongest Programs:
  Biology
  Business Administration
  Communications
  Education
  English

(Continued)
Exercise and Health Science
History
Psychology

professions, including wellness intervention programs, public health, and rehabilitation therapies. Alma's Service Learning Program links classroom instruction with community service and lets students work with nonprofit economic-development organizations or with educational, environmental, and health agencies. The annual Honors Day features presentations of scholarly work from nearly 10 percent of the student body, and teachers are demanding higher achievement from students. A new project strives to help students find their calling in life. Freshmen begin with a seven-day seminar that includes readings, discussions, and research, and introduces them to computer resources, on-campus life, and extra-curricular activities.

> **"The classes are small enough for the teachers to know your name."**

Despite Alma's small size, one of the college's selling points is its wide variety of study-abroad opportunities. During the one-month spring term, students enroll in a single intensive course, which often includes off-campus study. Past programs have involved Pacific Rim work in Australia, language and culture in Paris, and archaeological fieldwork in Israel. Alma also offers foreign study programs in Australia, Bolivia, Ecuador, England, France, Germany, New Zealand, Peru, Scotland, and Spain.

Back on campus, Alma's professors win praise. "The teachers aren't condescending or too lofty for us," says an English major. "They have students over to dinner for Shakespeare discussions and often act as academic and more personal career advisors." Adds a psychology major: "The classes are small enough for the teachers to know your name, and many teachers challenge you in ways you would never believe." Ninety-six percent of Alma's classes have fifty or fewer students, and 73 percent have twenty-five or less. Students say graduating in four years is seldom a problem, except for education majors, who may need a ninth semester to complete their student teaching.

The Alma-Albion rivalry keeps students interested in Scots athletics, where the softball team is a perennial Michigan Intercollegiate Athletic Association champion.

Ninety-five percent of Alma students are from Michigan, and minorities comprise 7 percent of the student body. "The administration is trying to recruit more people of diverse backgrounds, more international students and out-of-staters," reports a junior. "We do have issues regarding equality for all—male, female, African-American, Hispanic, Asian, white. Everyone has to do their part." The "Bursting the Bubble" weekend, centered on Martin Luther King Jr. day, promotes diversity. Brainy types can vie for an unlimited number of merit scholarships that range from $200 to full tuition.

Eighty-five percent of Alma's students live on campus in the "comfortable," "somewhat spacious" dorms. Only fifty seniors may live off campus, creating what one freshman called a "horrible situation." Dorms "are maintained pretty well, although they're all getting pretty old," says a psychology major. Freshmen are assigned rooms in single-sex and coed dorms (some coed by room, others by floor), while upperclassmen play the lottery and usually end up in suites. Two international houses, a multicultural house, and fraternities and sororities—33 percent of men and 22 percent of women go Greek—round out the housing options. Everyone buys fourteen or nineteen meals a week and chows down at the all-you-can-eat Commons or at Joe's Place, a snack bar.

> **"There is always either a party, a hall or dorm activity, a movie event—and it all takes place on campus."**

Alma students may live in a small town, but "we know how to relax and have fun," says a senior. Near campus, students find a movie theater, bowling alley, and three bars, while on-campus social life is dominated by Greeks. "Social life is what you make it," says a junior. "There is always either a party, a hall or dorm activity, a movie event—and it all takes place on campus," thanks to the student-run Union Board. The campus alcohol policy (no one under twenty-one can drink) has little effect, students say. Underage students caught imbibing are written up and fined, but "no matter where you go, you can find a way to buy" alcohol if you want it, says a premed student.

Town-gown relations at Alma are strong, students say. Students, including Greek and other organizations, work with Big Brothers/Big Sisters, local hospitals and schools, the Red Cross, the Women's Aid Shelter, and the Masonic Home. The annual Highland Festival features ubiquitous bagpipers and Scottish dancing; for members of the school's marching band, who strut in kilts stitched from MacPherson tartan, every performance might as well be a festival. Almost all Alma students welcome St. Paddy's Day with Irish Pub, a thunderous celebration sure to rouse the leprechauns for a celebratory toast. "The best road trip is to go twenty miles away to Mt. Pleasant or Saginaw, East Lansing—basically anywhere your car will take you," says a psychology major. Ski slopes are an hour away, and for warm-weather diversions, students hit the "pits," old gravel pits filled with water and surrounded by beaches. The Alma-Albion rivalry keeps students interested in Scots athletics, where the softball team is a perennial Michigan Intercollegiate Athletic Association champion.

Alma students can delve into the arts, sciences, business, or another culture and leave well prepared for today's job market. Accessible professors and the small size create a close-knit, at-home feel. "Everyone is very fun loving and the atmosphere is a comfortable place to want to be," says a freshman.

The world is the classroom for Alma students, who have the opportunity to participate in formal study programs in ten foreign countries.

Overlaps

Michigan State, Central Michigan, Grand Valley State, Albion, University of Michigan

If You Apply To > — **Alma:** Rolling admissions. Early action: Nov. 1. Housing: May 1. Meets demonstrated need of 92%. Campus interviews: recommended, informational. No alumni interviews. SATs or ACTs: required (ACT preferred). SAT IIs: optional. Accepts electronic applications. Optional essay question: creatively introduce yourself.

Alverno College

3401 South 39th Street, P.O. Box 343922, Milwaukee, WI 53234-3922

At last, a college that evaluates students on what they can do rather than how well they can memorize. Forget oval-blackening; students here show mastery in their chosen fields. Practical and hands-on, Alverno is at its best in preprofessional programs. Only women need apply.

At Alverno College, you can forget about striving for an A. That's because this small Roman Catholic women's college emphasizes ability-based learning instead of letter grades. Students are required to show "mastery" in a range of liberal arts courses, as well as demonstrated ability in eight broad areas: communications, analysis, problem solving, values in decision making, social interaction, global perspectives, effective citizenship, and aesthetic responsiveness. Students move through interdisciplinary progressive levels toward a degree by being "validated" in these areas. For example, a course in sociology might contribute to validation in communication and social interaction, as well as in making independent value judgments. The learning environment isn't competitive, though the ability-based method can "create a lot of work requiring much thought," says a professional communications major. As one senior puts it: "We learn in a way that gives us a cutting edge."

Alverno is located in a quiet, well-kept residential area. The parklike forty-six-acre campus is just fifteen minutes from downtown Milwaukee and a ten-minute

Website: www.alverno.edu
Location: Suburban
Total Enrollment: 1,952
Undergraduates: 1,779
Male/Female: 0/100
ACT Range: N/A
Financial Aid: 89%
Expense: Pr $
Phi Beta Kappa: No
Applicants: 511
Accepted: 80%
Enrolled: 50%
Grad in 6 Years: 57%

(Continued)

Returning Freshmen: 78%

Academics: ✍ ✍ ✍

Social: ☎

Q of L: ★ ★ ★ ★

Admissions: (414) 382-6100

Email Address:
admissions@alverno.edu

Strongest Programs:
Nursing
Education
Business and Management
Psychology
Biology
Professional Communication
Interdisciplinary Arts and
Humanities

walk from shops and restaurants. Its three main academic buildings, of 1950s and '60s vintage, feature brick and stone exteriors and stained-glass windows. The Teaching, Learning, and Technology Center houses 73,000 square feet of science labs, multimedia production areas, and computer facilities.

Alverno is really two colleges rolled into one. There is a regular weekday program that attracts mostly traditional college-age women, the majority of whom are from Milwaukee. The Weekend College allows women, most of them older with full-time jobs, to earn a degree in four years by attending classes every other weekend. Students in the weekday college may earn credit by spending four to eight hours a week in internships related to their field of study. First-year students take an orientation seminar, and introductory courses in the arts and humanities, science, psychology and sociology, communications, and math. The student body is diverse—in age, ethnic background, and religion. "It would be very hard to make generalizations," one junior says. Religious studies aren't required, but for those who seek it, a Catholic liturgy is available on a daily basis.

Alverno's business and management programs are well established. "The level of professionalism that Alverno students have compared to those at other colleges or universities is amazing," one junior says. Students praise the professional communications and teacher education programs and its strong nursing program. Newer majors include computer studies, global studies, and community leadership and development. One art education major says the art department "has produced some of the best art instructors, local artists, and art therapists that Milwaukee has to offer." The library holds 350,000 titles, and for major research projects students can use the online library/media center catalog made available through a consortial arrangement with five Milwaukee colleges. Bali, Paris, Tokyo, and London are just a few of the places where students have taken advantage of the school's study-abroad program.

Many professors at Alverno teach all levels of classes, so "there is no distinct difference" in the quality of teaching for freshmen or seniors, one international business major says. The instructors don't generally focus on publishing research—usually a major element of professors' job security at other schools. "The faculty and staff really care whether you are successful," says a social science major. "They want to see you achieve and are willing to go over and beyond to make sure you do." Academic counseling and individual attention run throughout students' academic careers to keep them on track. "We couldn't have more help," one junior says.

"We learn in a way that gives us a cutting edge."

Many students are older than the typical college age and quite a few have children. There are dozens of student groups and cultural groups, like Women of Color, active on campus. Students and faculty often engage in roundtable discussions to look at political or social issues, according to a sophomore. With so many different kinds of people on campus, the college "is open-minded to all views but does not allow hate or anything that might hurt any specific group," one senior says. The vast majority of the students receive financial aid, and merit scholarships ranging from $2,100 to $5,800 are awarded based on a personal evaluation of each incoming student.

There are no letter grades at Alverno. Instead, students move through four levels of mastery in eight broad areas, ranging from communications to citizenship to analysis.

A three-day orientation program serves freshmen, transfer, resident, and commuter students. The majority of students are commuters, though there are a limited number of dorm rooms. Students say the residence halls offer clean, spacious rooms with fully equipped lounges, laundry, and cooking facilities available on each floor. "Dorms are comfortable and well maintained every day, including weekends," says one junior. Male visitors are allowed, but they must sign in and be out by midnight on weekdays and 2:00 A.M. on weekends.

Most of the social life takes place off campus at local clubs, bars, coffee bars, and nearby colleges, but the student union, called the Pipeline, frequently offers on-campus activities. The campus also has an on-site day-care center, a fitness center, and a jogging track, and sponsors dance and theater groups. "Milwaukee is a thriving city of the arts—visual, theatrical, and performance—not to mention the festivals that go on every year," says one art education major. There are also myriad parks and shopping centers, a Performing Arts Center, professional sports teams, ethnic festivals, and free outdoor concerts.

Students look forward to the annual Rotunda Ball and homecoming festivities.

"We couldn't have more help."

When it comes to alcohol on campus, the combination of strict policies and a generally low amount of drinking means Alverno is rarely the home of the *Animal House* booze fest.

Alverno competes in Division III and fields varsity basketball, volleyball, softball, soccer, and cross-country teams. Intramurals are popular as well. Nonsporting annual events include Student Seminar Day, which allows students and faculty to change places so that students can "share their experiences" with the Alverno community.

Attending a school like Alverno promises an experience far afield in some ways from the traditional college world. The lack of grades and emphasis on real-world applications builds confidence in one's actual ability to perform, rather than ability to score an A. Students and faculty are often on a first-name basis from the start and build relationships that help students find their "own unique style of learning," one senior says. It's a method that obviously works.

> The campus has an on-site day-care center, a fitness center, and a jogging track, and sponsors dance and theater groups.

Overlaps

Milwaukee Area Technical College, University of Wisconsin, Cardinal Stritch, Carroll

---

If You Apply To ≫

Alverno: Rolling admissions. Does not guarantee to meet demonstrated need. Campus interviews: optional, informational. No alumni interviews. ACTs: required. Accepts the Common Application and electronic applications. Essay question: recent activities and/or work history, academic goals and abilities, and most important reason for applying to Alverno.

American University

4400 Massachusetts Avenue NW, Washington, DC 20016-8001

If the odds are against you at Georgetown and you can't see yourself on GW's non-campus, welcome to American University. The allure of AU is simple: Washington, D.C. American has a nice campus in a nice neighborhood with easy access to the Metro. About a third smaller than GW.

In 2001, the women's lacrosse team was nationally ranked in turnovers caused per game, while the women's volleyball and men's soccer teams won Patriot League championships, and men's swimming took the Colonial Athletic Association title.

No one in Washington, D.C., wants to admit to having clawed his way to the top, but if you're a student at American University, there's no getting around it: your mascot, an eagle named Clawed, is everywhere. And as it goes in real estate, where the name of the game is location, location, location, the same is true for AU. The school boasts outstanding programs in political science and government, international studies, and journalism because of its proximity to the nation's capital. Just outside the classroom door, real-world internships prepare students for careers as reporters, diplomats, lobbyists, and policymakers. "Students here aren't just going to college," one explains. "They're working in Congress, government agencies, and businesses."

Website: www.american.edu
Location: Urban
Total Enrollment: 10,694
Undergraduates: 5,851
Male/Female: 38/62
SAT Ranges: V 550–660
 M 550–650
ACT Range: 24–29
Financial Aid: 63%
Expense: Pr $ $ $ $
Phi Beta Kappa: Yes
Applicants: 10,355

(Continued)

Accepted: 68%

Enrolled: 20%

Grad in 6 Years: 72%

Returning Freshmen: 85%

Academics: ✍ ✍ ✍ ½

Social: ☎ ☎ ☎

Q of L: ★ ★ ★

Admissions: (202) 885-6000

Email Address:
   afa@american.edu

Strongest Programs:
   International Studies
   Political Science/Government
   Justice, Law, and Society
   Studio Art
   Premed

AU's eighty-four acre residential campus is located in the northwest corner of Washington, D.C., just minutes from downtown; free shuttle buses transport students to the nearby subway station. There's a mix of classical and modern architecture and flower gardens alongside the parking lots. The quads have numerous sitting areas for reflection and study. The University Center has been renovated, with offices for student clubs, casual lounges, and a wireless cybercafe. By spring 2003, the three hundred seat Greenberg Theater is slated to open. AU is also installing new radios and base stations that will boost the strength of cell-phone signals, especially in the dorms, ensuring that wireless phone and Internet service is always available.

> **"Students here aren't just going to college. They're working in Congress, government agencies, and businesses."**

All AU undergraduates must demonstrate competency in writing and English, either through two courses or an exam; for math or statistics, it's one semester of class or placing out through a test. The required general education program draws thirty credit hours from five areas: the creative arts, traditions that shape the Western world, international and intercultural experience, social institutions and behavior, and the natural sciences. The requirements are typically completed during the first two years, so that students can study abroad or participate in an internship or co-op—of which there are many, thanks to the school's relationships with more than nine hundred private, nonprofit, or government institutions. The school also uses these connections in its Washington Semester* program, which attracts a wide range of majors.

In the classroom, AU has outstanding programs in political science and government, international studies, and history. An honors program offers the top 15 percent of entering students small seminars, special sections of many courses, and designated floors in the residence halls, plus specialized work in the major and a senior capstone experience. The B.A. in arts and cultural management and B.S. in accounting have been dropped, but accounting has been added under the B.S. in business administration. New programs include a combined B.S./M.S. in physics and computing, and a new minor in applied physics. Overall, courses are "somewhat rigorous," says a sophomore. "The course material itself is not hard; it is the teachers' expectations that are challenging."

On the quality of teaching, students' opinions are mixed. American has a reputation for bringing in adjunct professors who are well known outside academia, which "is good since they have real experience and good contacts, but bad because they are never around," one student says. Freshmen are taught by professors, but often they are non-tenured assistants or visitors, who leave after a year or two, "making it hard to make connections," says an international relations and Spanish major. "The quality of teaching that I have received is poor, in comparison to what I had been expecting." AU's career center offers counseling and a career fair. Students must meet with academic advisors before registering for classes, though that's often difficult because of everyone's busy schedules, one student says. AU does offer significant support services for students with disabilities, whether physical or learning-related.

AU is installing new radios and base stations that will boost the strength of cell-phone signals, especially in the dorms, ensuring that wireless phone and Internet service is always available.

AU prides itself on drawing students from every state and more than 140 foreign countries; just 12 percent hail from the District of Columbia. Six percent of the student body is African-American, just over 4 percent is Hispanic, and about the same fraction is Asian-American. Unlike many college campuses where apathy reigns, AU is very active politically—after all, this is Washington, D.C., and causes are what the city is all about. AU's price tag is a hefty $33,444 a year, but the school offers 776 merit scholarships, ranging from $500 to full tuition. It also provides scholarships in ten women's and nine men's sports.

About two-thirds of AU's students, mostly freshmen and sophomores, live on campus. The dorms are air-conditioned—a must during D.C.'s muggy early fall and late spring—with kitchens and laundry facilities on each floor, and carpeting and built-in furniture in the rooms. "Housing draw is difficult, since it not only goes by current dorm status, but also by credits, making it more difficult for those with fewer credits," says a sophomore. "You will most likely get a room, just not where you desire." Students say they generally feel safe on campus, noting that public-safety officers are visible, and that AU is adding more blue-light emergency telephones.

AU prides itself on drawing students from every state and more than 140 foreign countries; just 12 percent hail from the District of Columbia.

Most social life at AU revolves around campus-related functions, such as room and frat parties; 15 percent of men and 18 percent of women go Greek, though the women lament that the bottom-heavy male-female ratio is "a little ridiculous." The immediate area around AU—called Tenleytown—has restaurants and shops but little true nightlife. While greater D.C. certainly has its share of clubs and bars, they're largely off-limits to students under twenty-one. Students of legal age may imbibe at AU's Tavern; otherwise, the campus is officially dry. Each year, Family Weekend brings games, rides, and popular bands to campus, along with a carnival on the quad. Homecoming and Founder's Week are also campus favorites. D.C. also has plenty of monuments, museums, and other attractions

"You just jump on the Metro to get anywhere in the city."

to keep students occupied—with the added bonus that they're free of charge. "You just jump on the Metro to get anywhere in the city," says a communication major. Popular road trips include Baltimore, Annapolis, and the Ocean City shore, and nearby amusement parks.

American competes in Division I, but sports are an afterthought for most students. There's no football team, but students are enthusiastic about Eagles basketball, where games against Bucknell and the Naval Academy top the schedule. In 2001, the women's lacrosse team was nationally ranked in turnovers caused per game, while the women's volleyball and men's soccer teams won Patriot League championships, and men's swimming took the Colonial Athletic Association title. Women's tennis brought home a Patriot League championship in 2002.

Students agree that location is what makes AU special. "Because of the location, AU has many programs and cool political speakers and opportunities," a senior points out. The school appeals to career-minded individuals who can make good grades and job contacts in a city where advantages—and distractions—are plentiful.

Overlaps
George Washington, Syracuse, NYU, Boston University, University of Maryland

---

If You Apply To >

American: Early decision: Nov. 15. Regular admissions: Feb. 1. Financial aid: Nov. 15 (early decision), Mar. 1 (regular admissions). Does not guarantee to meet demonstrated need. Campus and alumni interviews: recommended, informational. SATs: required. SAT IIs: recommended. Accepts the Common Application and electronic applications. Essay question: cover story for a national news magazine on Jan. 1, 2025, an event or individual instrumental in shaping who you are, or a sample of creative or fiction writing produced for a class.

Amherst College

Amherst, MA 01002-5000

Original home to the well-rounded, superachieving, gentle-person jock. Compare to Williams, Middlebury, and Colby. Not Swarthmore, not Wesleyan. Amherst has always been the king in its category—mainly because there are four other major institutions in easy reach to add diversity and depth.

At Amherst College, the focus isn't on racking up high-grade point averages. Instead, students focus on becoming people who base their thinking on a strong

Website: www.amherst.edu

(Continued)

Location: Small town
Total Enrollment: 1,631
Undergraduates: 1,631
Male/Female: 51/49
SAT Ranges: V 660–760
　M 660–750
ACT Range: 27-33
Financial Aid: 47%
Expense: Pr $ $ $
Phi Beta Kappa: Yes
Applicants: 5,175
Accepted: 19%
Enrolled: 44%
Grad in 6 Years: 94%
Returning Freshmen: 97%
Academics: ✍ ✍ ✍ ✍ ✍
Social: ☎ ☎ ☎
Q of L: ★ ★ ★ ★
Admissions: (413) 542-2328
Email Address:
　admission@amherst.edu

Strongest Programs:
　English
　Psychology
　Political Science
　History
　Economics
　Dance

foundation in the liberal arts. Emphasizing "freedom to explore," the spotlight here is on learning, not competing for grades. "Special topics classes, interdisciplinary majors, open curriculum—and close contact with professors" make Amherst special, says a senior. While there is little time left for partying or playing games, a weekly student-sponsored keg bash, known as TAP, and any athletic contest against archrival Williams will draw students away from their books.

Amherst's 964 acres overlook the picturesque town of Amherst and the Pioneer Valley, and offer a panoramic view of the Holyoke Range and the Pelham Hills. On campus, a plot of open land housing a wildlife sanctuary and a forest shares space with academic and residential buildings and athletic fields and facilities. While Amherst's predominant architectural style remains nineteenth-century academia—red brick is key—everything from a "pale yellow octagonal structure to a garish, modern new dorm" can be found here. Amherst looks like a college is supposed to look, with trees and paths winding through the buildings to offer long, contemplative walks. Of course, the flip side is snowy winters that don't end soon enough when spring break has come and gone. An academic building was recently converted into the Appleton Dormitory for first-year students, while a facility adjacent to campus was renovated into a multidenominational religious center.

Amherst's curriculum emphasizes education as a process or activity rather than a form of production. There is no core program and there are no distribution requirements; to graduate, students must only take a first-year seminar, declare a major at the end of sophomore year, fulfill departmental program requirements, pass the requisite number of electives, and perform satisfactorily on comprehensive exams in their major field. First-year seminars, taught by two or more professors, help foster interdisciplinary approaches across topics. Of this approach to education, administrators say, "A student should be free at this stage to make choices—even foolish choices." Says an anthropology major, "Amherst students seem to me to be more competitive with their own personal performances than with each other. Students are likely to collaborate when given the chance."

The most popular majors—English, economics, psychology, political science, history, and biology, and what Amherst calls its unique "law, jurisprudence, and social thought" course—are top-notch, and students may mix and match among these subjects to form dual-degree programs. (About one-third of students pursue double majors, and a few even triple major, administrators report.) Students may create their own courses of study from Special Topics classes if the subject of their interest is not available. The dance program is also strong, although it requires courses at each school in the Five College Consortium.* Chemistry and physics are "ridiculously difficult," cautions a senior, especially for those without strong backgrounds or a desire to go on to medical school. Smaller departments, such as women's and gender studies, anthropology, and sociology have fewer majors but aren't necessarily weak, students say. To house all these programs, Amherst has spent millions of dollars over the past few years renovating facilities, upgrading technological capabilities, and improving spaces for study, exhibits, performances, and sports.

> **"Amherst students seem to me to be more competitive with their own personal performances than with each other."**

On such a small campus without graduate students, interaction with professors is constant and friendly. Even as freshmen, students can become involved in a professor's research. "Professors are here because they want to teach at a liberal arts college and interact with students," a senior says. "They're here to teach and be our friends." In fact, Amherst believes teaching is a professor's highest priority, more important even than research, students insist. "This is, bar none, the best, most intensive, most committed teaching I've ever experienced," says a music major.

In addition to being one of the Five Colleges—the others are Smith, Mount Holyoke, the University of Massachusetts at Amherst, and Hampshire—Amherst also belongs to the Maritime Studies Program* and the Twelve College Exchange.* With three other liberal arts colleges and a major state university a brief shuttle-bus ride away, cross-registration in any one of a host of fields—like basic accounting at UMass or "something experimental" at Hampshire—is a godsend about the middle of sophomore year. All-female Smith and Mount Holyoke also add to the social life (especially for Amherst men), and numerous cultural and artistic events at the other schools are open to Amherst students. Each year, about one-third of the junior class spends a semester or year abroad; in the past two years, students enrolled in seventy-two programs in thirty-five countries, ranging from a math program in Budapest to analyzing architecture in Rome. Amherst also has a program in Kyoto, Japan, where one of the college's Colonial-style buildings has been duplicated.

Amherst is working hard to shake off its image as a homogenous, elitist, and male-dominated school, although economic diversity is still a concern, says a senior: "Many students feel that the social scene revolves around money and those with money. However, there's currently a group—FACE—that's addressing classes issues; the group has wide campus support from those from all backgrounds." The college dealt a major blow to the old-boy network when it

"This is, bar none, the best, most intensive, most committed teaching I've ever experienced."

abolished fraternities in the mid-'80s, and students from public high schools now account for 55 percent of the student body. Minority enrollment includes 9 percent African-Americans, 8 percent Hispanics, and 11 percent Asian-Americans, sizable fractions for a school of this size. "Amherst students are very actively political," says a junior. "The Democrats and Republicans each host events." One history/French major doesn't see it that way: "The campus is quite liberal, and I think it might be difficult to be a conservative at Amherst."

Housing at Amherst is guaranteed for four years, and 98 percent of students live on campus. Of freshman housing, a philosophy major says, "Army barracks would be an improvement. Fortunately, they're upgrading." Another students says, "Upperclass residences are first-rate, often in large Victorian mansions" that once belonged to the frats, complete with ballrooms, pianos, hardwood floors, and stained-glass windows. "Sophomore housing sucks (many triples)," says a senior. "However, juniors and seniors typically live in fantastic singles," often in the apartment-style social dorms. Everyone who lives on campus, and anyone else who wants to, eats in Valentine Hall, which includes a central serving station and five dining rooms. Students are trying to secure more meal-plan options; the only one now available is all-you-can-eat.

The legacy of beer-drenched partying at Amherst lingers even after the demise of the frats. "The college wants us to remain safe, so policies toward alcohol are relaxed to ensure that people remain on campus when they party instead of driving elsewhere and getting in trouble. It's pretty easy to get alcohol underage," says a senior. Thursday Night TAP (The Amherst Party), complete with kegs, dancing, and security monitors, is the place to see and be seen, with popular theme nights such as Madonna TAP and Motown TAP. Not that everyone has to drink plain-old beer to have fun, as one junior describes: "My friends and I organized 'anti-parties' in our substance-free dorm. The college paid for our root-beer keg."

While much of Amherst's social life takes place on campus, the four other schools in the area also provide diversions. The biggest party of the year, thrown in February, is Casino Night, which includes gambling with real money. The weekend-long Bavaria festival in the spring offers a pig roast and big-wheel joust, while a lip-sync contest that offers winners first pick in room draw usually attracts hilarious entries. The relatively new Campus Center includes outdoor terraces, a formal living room, a game room, a snack bar, a small theater, and a student-run co-op coffeehouse, open three nights a week, with live entertainment. Amherst is located in "the quintessential college town, full of academics, old hippies, small shops, and cheap restaurants," says an interdisciplinary studies major. "The town is also much more diverse than usual in western Massachusetts. There are large Vietnamese, Cambodian, and Puerto Rican populations." For the many outdoorsy types, good skiing in Vermont is not far, and Boston (an hour and a half) and New York (almost four) are close enough to be convenient road-trip destinations. Amherst's idyllic setting seems to bring out the athlete in everyone.

> **"The quintessential college town, full of academics, old hippies, small shops, and cheap restaurants."**

Sports are taken seriously, both varsity and intramurals, and the admissions office frankly acknowledges that seventy-five spots in each year's freshman class are reserved for student-athletes who are recruited by coaches and who may or may not meet the academic standards demanded of other admits. Amherst competes in Division III, but the strong baseball team takes on Division I opponents as well. In the 2001–2002 year, Amherst women's soccer teams were NESCAC champions, and the women's cross-country team was ECAC champion, while the men placed second. The women's swimming team came in second in the NESCAC, and men's and women's lacrosse teams were NESCAC semi-finalists. Any showdown with archrival Williams is inevitably the biggest game of the season, drawing fans from all corners of campus.

Combine a lack of restrictive requirements with a cadre of professors who are focused on teaching, and it becomes clear why students here so love their institution. "Students enjoy an unprecedented level of independence," says a senior, which prepares them well for whatever challenges they undertake after graduation.

Overlaps

Harvard, Brown, Yale, Stanford, Princeton

If You Apply To ➤ **Amherst:** Early decision: Nov. 15. Regular admissions: Dec. 31. Guarantees to meet demonstrated need. No campus or alumni interviews. SATs or ACTs: required. SAT II: required (any three). Accepts the Common Application and electronic applications. Essay question: one Common Application question and one of student's choice.

Antioch College

795 Livermore Street, Yellow Springs, OH 45387

Part Goth, part granola, and part anarchist—with plenty of none-of-the-above mixed in—Antioch is a haven for square pegs. Yet Antioch offers something very practical: the chance for sixteen-week co-op experiences interspersed with academic study. March and protest, then get a job. Cool.

Website:
www.antioch-college.edu
Location: Rural
Total Enrollment: 682
Undergraduates: 682
Male/Female: 38/62

Come to Yellow Springs, Ohio, and you may think you've stepped out of a time machine. But no, you haven't spun back to 1969—you're simply at Antioch College, where the humanistic messages of that generation are still taken to heart and put into action. The students, many of them products of "alternative" high schools, discuss feminism, gay rights, and nuclear proliferation over vegetarian meals, and they are more likely to take road trips to Washington for an environmental rally than to show up at a neighboring school's fraternity party.

Founded in 1852 by abolitionist and social reformer Horace Mann, Antioch remains a haven for outspoken and independent students who thrive under the rigors of a refreshingly nontraditional education. Antioch pioneered the idea that students should alternate time in the classroom with jobs in the "real world," and this idea has remained the foundation for Antioch's unique approach to training students. Under the college's famed co-op program, students spend nearly half of their college years out in the "real world," be it selling fresh-squeezed orange juice on a street corner in California, studying Buddhism in India, or working in a *Fortune 500* company in New York City.

Antioch does not use standardized test scores for admission. In classes, written faculty evaluations take the place of grades, and students are required to submit self-evaluations of their class performance. "Antioch is for the independent learner," notes a junior. A senior adds, "The academic program is reading intensive, discussion-based, and covers a wide range of topics."

In completing Antioch's thirty-two-credit general education program, students spend their first year pursuing a core of courses that blends the traditional liberal arts with examination of the "social, historical, philosophical, and economic" nature of work. In addition, there are distribution requirements in the humanities, social and behavioral sciences, natural sciences, and cultural studies. Physical education is also required. Students report that the academic climate is laid-back yet rigorous. Because classes are usually no larger than twenty, students must always be prepared to participate. Close relationships often develop between students and faculty; representatives of both groups sit on several of the influential governing committees, including the administrative council, the housing board, and the community council. Each student is also assigned a co-op advisor to help with the nearly continuous job hunt, and a network of alumni offering jobs is one major resource that students can depend on in their search. "Academic advisors range from very helpful to practically useless," says a senior. "The trick is to make sure your advisor is knowledgeable about *your* field of study." You can't miss, though, with the career counselors, says the same student. "It's not just counseling, it's cooperative education that teaches you more about yourself than you could imagine. It's the best reason to come to Antioch."

"Antioch is for the independent learner."

Antioch's trimester system lasts fifteen weeks, with co-op terms lasting sixteen weeks. The college helps place students in co-op programs, and credit is earned after the student completes a paper or project demonstrating what he or she learned during the co-op experience. Antioch's mission lies in its "commitment to undergraduate experiential learning and to preparing students to face the challenges and opportunities of the twenty-first century." In order to receive a "cross-cultural" experience, Antioch has all students spend three to twelve months in a significantly different cultural environment. In addition to those offered by the school, study-abroad options are available through the Great Lakes College Association.* There is a downside to this: students blame the high attrition rate on the rigors of the co-op program. One student explains that "students often move every three or six months because of co-op—this is both financially and emotionally draining." Friendships and involvement in extracurricular activities at the Yellow Springs campus often suffer because of the on-again, off-again attendance schedules. But the co-op program wouldn't have been there for so long if it didn't have its fans such as this senior, who says, "The co-op program is amazing; it's the reason to come to Antioch. It's made me as confident and clear about my life goals as can be."

Antioch's traditional academic programs are somewhat uneven. Although there are only eight official majors, each allows for concentration in a more specialized

(Continued)

SAT Ranges: N/A
ACT Range: N/A
Financial Aid: 91%
Expense: Pr $ $
Phi Beta Kappa: No
Applicants: 502
Accepted: 82%
Enrolled: 5%
Grad in 6 Years: 45%
Returning Freshmen: 78%
Academics: ✍ ✍ ✍
Social: ☎ ☎
Q of L: ★ ★ ★ ★
Admissions: (937) 769-1100
Email Address: admissions@ antioch-college.edu

Strongest Program:
Cooperative Education

Being different may be the only thing Antioch students have in common, and diversity is a given on this campus.

Antioch remains a haven for outspoken and independent students who thrive under the rigors of a refreshingly nontraditional education.

area. The major in physical sciences has traditionally been strong, especially with its heavily stocked research laboratory. Concentrations in political science, psychology, and many of the arts offerings are also established strongholds. Environmental and life sciences is excellent, in part because of the proximity of a one thousand-acre forest preserve, Glen Helen, and a nature museum. Students complain mostly about the history department. The communications program benefits from a major public radio station operated by Antioch, which gives students experience in the broadcasting field.

Being different may be the only thing Antioch students have in common, and diversity is a given on this campus. "Antioch students are all individuals," says a sophomore, who describes his peers as "liberal-minded, politically aware, and very

"The co-op program is amazing; it's the reason to come to Antioch."

active." Twenty-eight percent of the students come from Ohio; the rest hail from points throughout the nation.

Four percent of students are African-American, 2 percent are Asian-American, and 5 percent are Hispanic. A variety of merit scholarships are renewable for four years.

Ninety-five percent of the students are housed on campus in apartment-style dorms. "To get financial aid, you have to live on campus," says one resident. In contrast to the college's democratic creed, room assignments are determined by the whim of "a much-courted administrator." Coed and single-sex dorms are available, and all come equipped with kitchens. Everyone is guaranteed on-campus housing if they want it, and students can choose from a number of special options that include a quiet hall, a moderate-noise hall, and even a substance-free hall, which bars smoking and drinking. The Spalt International Center, just a few years old, houses sixty students in foreign language living/learning halls. Seven- and nineteen-meal-a-week plans are available at the Caf, which features vegetarian entrées, a salad bar, and a popcorn machine.

In order to receive a "cross-cultural" experience, Antioch has all students spend three to twelve months in a significantly different cultural environment.

Without Greek organizations, social life tends to be rather spontaneous and limited to on-campus activities. Drinking is said to be less of a problem among students than among the high-school students who make the scene at campus parties. There is a student coffeehouse, which "is the best hangout space," while stargazers frequently congregate on the roof of the science building. Each fall, a three-day blues festival hits town. "Community Day" is actually two days a year where everyone takes the day off to mellow out and relax. Many student organizations, including the Anarchist Study Group and Third World Alliance, draw widespread student interest. A noteworthy tradition on this untraditional campus is the Quasi-Prom, an annual dance put on by the Lesbian/Gay Center.

Traditionally considered taboo, varsity sports have nevertheless enjoyed a rousing comeback, thanks to the women's rugby team. Gym classes are offered in kayaking, rafting, and horseback riding. Camelot, a one hundred-lap bicycle race, is an

"We are here to educate ourselves about social and political injustices so that we can change our world."

annual event: a team of two races around a muddy track while the audience slings yogurt, mud, and "anything else that isn't hard" at them. The

one thousand-acre nature preserve ("the glen") across the street "lets you forget the boring flatlands of Ohio." Behind the glen is John Bryan State Park. A nearby reservoir is a popular place for swimming and windsurfing, and Clifton Gorge offers rock climbing.

The town of Yellow Springs is "a bubble of liberalism in Bible Belt Southern Ohio," according to one student. The town hosts a variety of health-food stores, a pizza joint that makes its pies with whole-wheat crust, and an assortment of bars and restaurants. Yellow Springs may become limiting for some students, but that problem is usually solved by the next co-op trimester.

For those who think cooperative education would be a "far out" experience, Antioch offers a unique opportunity to discover themselves in both the working world and among the college's bright, opinionated, and cooperative student body. Horace Mann once implored his students to "be ashamed to die until you have won some victory for humanity." The Antioch community takes this message to heart. "We are here to educate ourselves about social and political injustices so that we can change our world," says a health and human development major.

If You Apply To ➤ **Antioch:** Recommended deadline of Feb. 1 for summer or fall regular admissions. Financial aid: Mar. 1. Housing: July 1. Does not guarantee to meet demonstrated need. Campus interviews: recommended, informational. No alumni interviews. SATs: optional. SAT IIs: optional. Essay question: important experience; significant personal, local, or national issue; or portfolio. Looks for independent, self-directed students who are willing to take risks.

University of Arizona

Robert L. Nugent Building, Tucson, AZ 85721

Tucson is an increasingly popular destination, and it isn't just because of the UA basketball team. A well-devoted honors program attracts top students, as do excellent programs in the sciences and engineering. Bring plenty of shorts and sunscreen.

With a campus that's encircled by mountain ranges and the beautiful Sonoran Desert, lined with palm trees and cacti, and set against a backdrop of stunning Tucson sunsets, it's no surprise that students at the University of Arizona love to hang out at the mall. Of course, we're not referring to the shopping center but to a huge grassy area in the middle of campus where nearly 35,000 Wildcats gather between classes. Judging by numbers alone, that's enough people to fill a medium-sized town. But students are quick to point out that UA has a strong sense of community and offers a genuinely friendly campus. "Nobody else has a huge central meeting place like we do," says a senior marketing major. "I always see familiar and friendly faces around the mall area." With all the natural beauty that surrounds them, many Wildcats simply purr through four satisfying years.

Architecturally, the UA campus distinguishes itself from the city's regiment of adobe buildings with a design that seems a study in the versatility of red brick. Old Main, the university's first building, is into its second century, but others verge on high-tech science facilities. Hard hats and heavy machinery have become commonplace on campus; recent construction includes a new student union, facilities for first-year students and learning-disabled students, the Athletic Hall of Fame and weight training facility, a residence hall, and a 1,300-space parking structure.

Sciences are unquestionably the school's forte—the astronomy department is among the nation's best, helped by those clear night skies. Students have access not only to leading astronomers, but also to the most up-to-date equipment, including a huge 176-inch telescope operated jointly by the university and the Smithsonian. A $28-million aerospace and mechanical engineering building has a state-of-the-art subsonic wind tunnel and rocket-combustion test facility. The history and English departments are standouts, as are several of the social science programs. Eager shutterbugs can pore through photographer Ansel Adams's personal collection, and the Center for Creative Photography offers one of the leading photographic collections in the world. Students in the popular business and public administration school

Website: www.arizona.edu
Location: Urban
Total Enrollment: 34,488
Undergraduates: 26,404
Male/Female: 47/53
SAT Ranges: V 480–600
 M 490–620
ACT Range: 19–27
Financial Aid: 70%
Expense: Pub $ $ $
Phi Beta Kappa: Yes
Applicants: 17,889
Accepted: 80%
Enrolled: 35%
Grad in 6 Years: 54%
Returning Freshmen: 78%
Academics: ✐ ✐ ✐ ½
Social: ☎ ☎ ☎ ☎
Q of L: ★ ★ ★ ★
Admissions: (520) 621-3237
Email Address:
 appinfo@arizona.edu

Strongest Programs:
 Management Information
  Systems
 Nursing

(Continued)
Astronomy
Pharmacy
Creative Writing
Aerospace Engineering

Sciences are unquestionably the school's forte—the astronomy department is among the nation's best, helped by those clear night skies.

can pick racetrack management as their area of expertise, while interested anthropology students can delve into garbage research. Two new programs are optics and public health. Areas getting low marks from students are the language programs and the journalism department.

Under the core curriculum, students take ten general-education courses in common. They fall under the broad categories of arts, humanities, traditions and cultures, natural sciences, and individuals and societies. In addition, almost everyone gets a healthy dose of freshman composition, math, and foreign language. Academic competition, according to most students, is left up to both the individual and the specific concentration. "The courses can range in difficulty from somewhat challenging to impossible," explains one senior. The University Honors Center offers one of the nation's largest and most selective honors programs (students must maintain a GPA of 3.5 to remain in the program). In addition to offering two hundred honors courses per year, the center features smaller classes, personalized advising, special library privileges, and great research opportunities. The Undergraduate Biology Research Program also has a national reputation. Teaching is well regarded, with some freshman courses taught by graduate students. "Each of the professors and TAs have something special to bring to the classes and show an exceptional amount of enthusiasm," a sophomore says.

One student describes his peers as "go-getters" who "bleed red and blue." Despite tougher admission standards, the administration cites a sharp increase in freshman applications over the past few years, especially out-of-staters, who constitute 28 percent of the student body. In addition to various merit scholarships, all the athletic scholarships allowed by the NCAA are available. Hispanics account for 15 percent of the enrollment, African-Americans for 3 percent, and Asian-Americans for 6 percent. A diversity action council, a newly developed student minority advisory committee, and cultural resource centers help students deal with race-relation issues. An active and popular student government runs a free legal service and a tenants' complaint center, and the university has instituted many programs to help those with learning disabilities.

"I always see familiar and friendly faces around the mall area."

Dorm rooms tend to be small but well maintained, the major problem being getting a room rather than living comfortably in it. "It's important to send your housing application in early," advises a veteran. Only 20 percent of undergraduates live in the dorms, while most upperclassmen flock to the abundant and inexpensive apartments near the school. The best way to enjoy the excellent food service at the student union's seven restaurants is to use the university-issued All Aboard credit card, which helps students take advantage of the wealth of different gustatory options and frees them from carrying cash.

Despite the high percentage of off-campus residents, students stream back onto campus on weekends for parties, sports, and cultural events. Fifteen percent of the men and women belong to fraternities or sororities. The campus is technically alcohol free, though some question whether the frats have realized that yet. Still, most social life takes place off campus. There are a lot of different dance clubs around town, and some do have after hours for underaged people. Those who feel they must go elsewhere need only head to the Mexican town of Nogales (one hour away), where there is no drinking-age limitation. Many students are content remaining in Tucson because it offers "the most incredible sunrises and sunsets, and delightful temperatures year-round."

One of the UA's most time-honored traditions is Spring Fling, described as the largest student-run carnival in the country.

One of the UA's most time-honored traditions is Spring Fling, described as the largest student-run carnival in the country. Athletics is also somewhat of a tradition here. The basketball Wildcats have been among the nation's leaders in recent years.

Division I football and baseball enjoy national prominence, generate lots of money for other men's and women's sports teams, and provide great weekend entertainment, especially when the opposing team is big-time rival Arizona State. UA's battle cry "Bear Down!" frequently heard at sporting events, dates back to the 1930s, where a campus football hero, fatally injured in a car crash, whispered his last message to his teammates: "Tell them, tell them to bear down." More than sixty years years later, the enigmatic slogan still appears on T-shirts and in a gym on the central campus.

"The most incredible sunrises and sunsets, and delightful temperatures year-round."

The University of Arizona offers a wide variety of academic opportunities and enough diversions to make it no place for those who need coddling or individual guidance. As for the spectacular weather, prospective students are warned to honestly evaluate how it will affect their ability to concentrate. UA is the place to go to engage in the pursuit of truth, knowledge, and a good tan.

Overlaps

Arizona State, Northern Arizona, UCLA, University of Colorado, UC-Santa Barbara

If You Apply To ➢

Arizona: Regular admissions: Apr. 1. Financial aid: Feb. 14. Housing: Mar. 1. Campus interviews: optional, informational. No alumni interviews. SATs or ACTs: required. SAT IIs: optional. Accepts electronic applications. No essay question.

Arizona State University

Box 870112, Tempe, AZ 85287-0112

Want to get lost in the crowd? ASU is the biggest university in the Southwest—apologies to UCLA. No matter how appealing the thought of forty-four thousand new faces, you'd better find the right program to get a good education. Try the professional schools and the honors college.

You've no doubt heard about the postcard that reads, "Weather beautiful, wish you were here." Though this usually applies to some remote vacation spot, it could just as well apply to Arizona State University. Perennial sunshine and balmy afternoons make for a gorgeous academic setting. Add solid academics, top-notch facilities, and caring faculty to the mix, and you can see why students at ASU seem so pleased. Says a student, "If you want something at ASU, you will be able to find it."

The ASU campus is a beautiful blend of palm-lined walkways, desert landscapes, and public art displays. Campus architecture ranges from the decidedly modern to turn-of-the-century historic, including the newly renovated Old Main with its Territorial Romanesque style. The campus is officially listed as an arboretum, and ASU groundskeepers tend to more than 115 species of trees that thrive in Arizona's arid climate. A newly completed residence hall houses approximately 250 freshmen students.

Despite all the pleasant outdoor diversions, ASU students definitely find time to study, and some report the academic climate is challenging. A fifth of the students enter the college of business administration, which is one of the largest in the country and ranks second in placing graduates in the Big Four accounting firms. Business is ASU's most popular major, followed by psychology and communication. There are eight undergraduate schools: business, liberal arts and sciences, engineering

Website: www.asu.edu
Location: Urban
Total Enrollment: 45,693
Undergraduates: 33,191
Male/Female: 48/52
SAT Ranges: V 490–600
  M 500–610
ACT Range: 20–26
Financial Aid: 40%
Expense: Pub $ $
Phi Beta Kappa: Yes
Applicants: 18,129
Accepted: 86%
Enrolled: 40%
Grad in 6 Years: 48%
Returning Freshmen: 76%
Academics: ✐ ✐ ✐
Social: ☎ ☎ ☎ ☎ ☎

(Continued)

Q of L: ★★★★★

Admissions: (480) 965-7788

Email Address:

ugradinq@asu.edu

Strongest Programs:

Accountancy

Planetary Science

Engineering

Business

Anthropology

Journalism

Geology

The Walter Cronkite School of Journalism and Telecommunication finished fourth in the Hearst annual writing competition, and Cronkite makes it a point to visit the campus to lecture every year.

Anthropology is a strong department, and Donald C. Johnson, the discoverer of the 3.2-million-year-old fossil skeleton named Lucy, has moved his Institute of Human Origin to the ASU campus.

and applied sciences, architecture and environmental design, education, fine arts, nursing, and public programs (justice studies, leisure studies, communication, social work, and public affairs). The fine arts program features outstanding facilities, an innovative child drama program, and nationally recognized programs in art, music, and dance. Engineering programs, especially microelectronics, robotics, and computer-assisted manufacturing, are sure bets; the facility for high-resolution microscopy allows students to get a uniquely close-up view of atomic structures.

ASU students also can specialize across several disciplines. For example, specialization in computer sciences and technology crosses the business, engineering, education, and liberal arts and sciences colleges. The brightest students attend the three-year-old Barrett Honors College, which gives them a challenging living/learning experience that culminates in a senior thesis. There are also undergraduate research apprenticeship programs offered in numerous areas. Students who want to leave ASU for a semester or a year may choose to experience London, Latin America, Germany, or numerous other domestic and foreign special programs.

In the liberal arts, the sciences (including solar energy, physical science, geology, and biology) and social sciences are strong and boast first-class facilities, notably the largest university-owned meteorite collection in the world. Planetary science is out of this world; students have the opportunity to collaborate on projects with NASA. Anthropology is a strong

"If you want something at ASU, you will be able to find it."

department, and Donald C. Johannson, the discoverer of the 3.2-million-year-old fossil skeleton named Lucy, has moved his Institute of Human Origin to the ASU campus. The less technically minded may enjoy the interdisciplinary opportunities in such areas as film studies, urban planning, and Islamic studies. The Walter Cronkite School of Journalism and Mass Communications finished fourth in the Hearst annual writing competition, and Cronkite makes it a point to visit the campus to lecture every year. Among the social sciences, psychology is the standout. Students cite the statistics and sociology departments as weak.

Under the general studies program, all students must meet core requirements by choosing courses from five disciplines—literacy and critical inquiry, numeracy, humanities and fine arts, social and behavioral sciences, and natural sciences—as well as from three awareness areas: global, historical, and U.S. cultural diversity. The more than thirty-three thousand undergrads register for class using the "Intouch" telephone system. Students can usually get into a full class if they need to with a

"ASU has quite a mellow and laid-back attitude."

faculty override. With ASU's size also come charges of delays and trouble finding the answers to everyday questions. Despite this, students maintain that ASU is a "user-friendly" campus. The library, a noteworthy facility, contains more than 3.1 million volumes, 4.1 million microforms, and almost 30,000 magazine subscriptions.

Arizona State's admissions policy says out-of-state students must either rank in the top quarter of their class or have a 3.0 GPA, cumulative SAT score of 1110, or ACT of 24 in order to enjoy automatic admission. Nearly a quarter of each freshman class comes from out of state, including many Chicagoans fleeing miserable winters. In-state students need to be in the top quarter of their class or have a 3.0 GPA, as well as a total SAT score of 1040 or an ACT of 22. ASU offers hundreds of athletic scholarships and more than one thousand merit scholarships to qualified students. Of the student body, Hispanics make up the largest minority group at 11 percent, while African-Americans and Asian-Americans combine for 8 percent. While social and political issues touch on everything from race to gender to religious freedom, overall, "ASU has quite a mellow and laid-back attitude," reports a communication major.

The coed dorms are generally well maintained and spacious, but they can accommodate only a small percentage of the student body, and there is a waiting list. "Rooms fill up quickly!" warns a senior. Because returning students receive priority, prospective freshmen should return their housing applications to be ensured a room. Those who get into campus housing are especially pleased to be placed in one of the three residence halls that boast their own swimming pools and volleyball courts.

Many students own cars, and the university has three parking structures to alleviate the parking crunch. A car also puts Colorado mountains, California beaches, Vegas slots, and real Mexican food all within a day's reach. The Grand Canyon is also a popular road trip. Although small in numbers (9 percent of the men and 7 percent of the women), the Greeks have some say on campus, and there are plenty of Greek and non-Greek parties to go around for those who aren't road-tripping on the weekends. "ASU houses more than four hundred clubs and organizations," says a student. "There is

> **"ASU houses more than four hundred clubs and organizations."**

definitely something for everyone." The ban on alcohol for students under twenty-one is strictly enforced on campus and, according to a former Resident Assistant, "many underage students are able to get alcohol...however, if caught, our judge is not lenient."

ASU football and basketball fans turn out in droves to cheer on various Division I Sun Devil teams, and the "Fork 'em Devils!" rallying cry often reverberates around campus. The football team really gave them something to cheer about in 1997 when they played in the Rose Bowl. The men's baseball, wrestling, badminton, archery, and gymnastics teams and the men's and women's golf teams are national powerhouses. Intramurals alone feature more than sixty different sports.

Despite the university's massive size, the atmosphere at Arizona State is not overbearing. In fact, ASU students praise all the resources provided to them and revel in the "diversity of opportunity," as one student calls it, including nationally recognized undergraduate programs. For those attending this sun-drenched university, ASU offers a "devil" of a good time.

A fifth of the students enter the college of business administration, which is one of the largest in the country and ranks second in placing graduates in the Big Four accounting firms.

Overlaps

University of Arizona, Northern Arizona, San Diego State, UCLA, University of Colorado

If You Apply To ➤

ASU: Rolling admissions. Financial aid: Feb. 15. Guarantees to meet demonstrated need. Campus interviews: optional, informational. No alumni interviews. SATs or ACTs: required. SAT IIs: optional. Accepts electronic applications. No essay question.

University of Arkansas

200 Hunt Hall, Fayetteville, AR 72701

University of Arkansas rates in the second tier of Southern public universities alongside Alabama, LSU, and Ole' Miss. With traditional strength in agriculture, U of A has also developed programs in business, engineering, and other professional fields. U of A's highest-ranked program takes the field on Saturday afternoons.

If you're planning to attend the University of Arkansas, you'd better start practicing your wildest and craziest hog call. Although this behavior might seem silly at some universities, it's practically mandatory when the pride and joy of this university, the Razorbacks, play. But the school is about much more than hog cheers and crazy

Website: www.uark.edu
Location: Small city
Total Enrollment: 15,752

(Continued)
Undergraduates: 12,818
Male/Female: 52/48
SAT Ranges: V 500–640
   M 510–640
ACT Range: 22–28
Financial Aid: 44%
Expense: Pub $ $
Phi Beta Kappa: Yes
Applicants: 4,470
Accepted: 89%
Enrolled: 89%
Grad in 6 Years: 45%
Returning Freshmen: 82%
Academics: ✍ ✍ ✍
Social: ☎ ☎ ☎ ☎
Q of L: ★ ★ ★
Admissions: (501) 575-5346
Email Address:
   uofa@uark.edu

Strongest Programs:
   Marketing
   Finance
   Accounting
   Psychology
   Information Systems
   Elementary Education
   Business Administration
      Management

In April of 2002, the school received a $300 million donation from the Walton Family Charitable Support Foundation. This is the largest gift ever donated to a public university.

Arkansas is prime Bible Belt territory, so vocal fundamentalist groups are in no short supply.

school spirit. U of A students perform research, travel abroad, and claim top fellowships while studying fields ranging from poultry science to creative writing and translation. "I feel that students here are well balanced in social, academic, and psychological aspects," observes one junior.

The campus is nestled among the mountains, lakes, and streams of the Ozark in the extreme northwest corner of the state. Its architecture has been characterized as "mismatched towers," with walkways connecting the modern concrete and WPA-vintage buildings. A bit of Hollywood Boulevard–style nostalgia can be found on the Senior Walk; the concrete sidewalk is engraved every year with the name of every student who made it through to graduation. The focal point of the campus is the stately brick Old Main building, which used to house the entire university. In April of 2002, the school received a $300 million donation from the Walton Family Charitable Support Foundation, the largest gift ever donated to a public university. The money will be divided and $200 million will be used to establish a university-wide

> "I feel that students here are well balanced in social, academic, and psychological aspects."

undergraduate honors college. The remaining $100 million will go to the graduate school. Many facilities are being renovated and expanded, and recently completed projects include the indoor track facility, Razorback Stadium, and the poultry lab. Current renovations include Carnall Hall, the U of A Innovation Center, and the health facility.

Established as a land-grant institution in 1871, the University of Arkansas has since expanded its scope of educational responsibilities from solely agricultural and mechanical arts to a broad spectrum of academic offerings in eight colleges and professional schools. If you are of the fowl-mooded type, you may want to roost in the school's Poultry Health Center, one of the nation's laboratories for the containment and research of poultry epidemics. Undergraduate research is encouraged, but it isn't the only game in town; U of A offers more than 150 undergraduate degree programs. The Dale Bumpers College of Agriculture Food and Life Sciences offers directed study and internships at the Scottish Agricultural College in Edinburgh, Scotland, while business administration students take advantage of study-abroad options around the globe. The university boasts a fine English department and a history department strong in Southern history. Doctoral programs were recently added in anthropology and microelectronics. The most popular major is psychology, followed by childhood education, finance, computer information systems, and marketing. Some programs which were not meeting the university's standards have recently been dropped. These include bachelors' degrees in botany, microbiology, and zoology.

Every student must take the required university core curriculum, which includes courses in English, math, science, social studies, and electives. Arts and sciences students must also achieve proficiency in a foreign language. The honors program gives undergraduates a chance for independent study, self-designed courses, and individual research. "I would describe the academic climate as moderately competitive," says an apparel studies major. The quality of teaching varies, depending on the teacher.

Students at the U of A are of the small-town, 1950s Main Street variety. Arkansas residents make up 88 percent of the student body. Six percent of the students are African-American, 2 percent are Hispanic, and another 3 percent are Asian-American. The university is striving to increase diversity and improve race relations and is also taking steps to make the transition to college easier for all freshmen. Arkansas is prime Bible Belt territory, so vocal fundamentalist groups are in no short supply. Campus dress ranges from upscale to down-home, though the Greeks are known for wearing "ties, oxfords, and dresses," presumably not all at once.

Approximately seven hundred merit scholarships are available, ranging from $525 to $15,146. The university also gives out athletic scholarships to 240 bristling young Razorbacks in a wide variety of sports.

Forty percent of undergrads and more than three-quarters of freshmen live in on-campus housing, which is abundant and relatively well maintained. All the dorms are single-sex, except one that is coed by floor. Students recommend Gregson and Holcombe halls for freshmen. Dining facilities are adequate—a few prize salad bars are to be found on campus for those willing to seek them out. The twenty-five Greek societies (19 percent of the women and 14 percent of the men join) are the most prominent social presence on campus, to the dismay of many. Campus-sponsored activities include theme parties, such as Casino Night or Holiday on the Hill, but a crackdown on campus drinking has stanched the flow of alcohol. For entertainment off campus, George's and José's are popular weekend night-spots. Fayetteville is a quiet, reasonably crime-free town that provides most of the necessities of student life. Bluegrass festivals, craft fairs, and good fishing are among the regional charms. "Most students have a great social life," one student reports. "Events take place regularly both on and off campus."

"The awesome school spirit makes this school a special place."

And then there are sports, which bring an influx of visitors. "The Hogs rule" is how one student describes sports' role on campus. There are Razorback logos on T-shirts, napkins, book covers, license plates, and on game day, on the cheeks of ecstatic fans. The school's indoor track, outdoor track, and cross-country teams boast a coach who has won more NCAA championships than any coach in the history of the NCAA. The basketball and cross-country teams boast recent conference championships as well. A well-equipped recreation center provides more than adequate facilities for less serious jocks of both sexes.

Students flock here to get a solid education at a bargain price while reveling in the spirit of the South. "The awesome school spirit makes this school a special place," proclaims one sophomore.

Overlaps

University of Oklahoma , Arkansas State, University of Central Arkansas, Oklahoma State, Hendrix

If You Apply To ➤

Arkansas: Rolling admissions. Early action: Nov. 15. Does not guarantee to meet demonstrated need. Campus interviews: optional, evaluative. Alumni interviews: optional, informational. SATs or ACTs: required. SAT II: recommended. Accepts the Common Application. Essay question: Meaning of leadership, personal experience, future plans.

Atlanta University Center

Atlanta is viewed as the preeminent city in the country for bright, talented, and successful African-Americans. It became the capital of the civil rights movement in the 1960s—the town whose leaders said was "too busy to hate"—and today it is a place where middle-class African-Americans can savor "the African-American experience."

At the heart of this extraordinary culture is the Atlanta University Center, the largest African-American educational complex in the world, replete with its own central library and central computing center. The seven component institutions have educated generations of African-American leaders. The Reverend Martin Luther King Jr. went to Morehouse College; his grandmother, mother, sister, and daughter went to Spelman College. Graduates spread across the country in a pattern that developed when these were among the best of the few colleges to which talented African-Americans could aspire. Even now, when the options are almost limitless, alumni continue to send their children back for more.

The center consists of three undergraduate colleges (Morris Brown, Morehouse, and Spelman) and three graduate institutions (Clark Atlanta University, the Interdenominational Theological Seminary, as well as the Morehouse College of Medicine) on adjoining campuses in the center of Atlanta three miles from downtown. Students at these affiliated schools can enjoy the quiet pace of their beautiful magnolia-studded campuses or plunge into all the culture and excitement of this most dynamic of Deep South cities. The six original schools—all but the medical school—became affiliated in 1929, using the model of California's Claremont Colleges, but they remain fiercely independent. Each has its own administration, board of trustees, and academic specialties, and each maintains its own dorms, cafeterias, and other facilities. There is cross-registration among the institutions (Morehouse students, for example, go to Spelman for drama and art courses) and with Georgia State and Emory University as well. The governing body of the consortium, the Atlanta University Center, Inc., administers a center-wide dual-degree program in engineering in conjunction with Georgia Tech—and it runs campus security, a student crisis center, and a joint institute of science research. There is also a center-wide service of career planning and placement where recruiters may come and interview students from all six of the institutions.

Dating and social life at the coeducational institutions tend to take place within the individual schools, though Morehouse, a men's college, and Spelman, a women's college, maintain a close academic and social relationship. The Morehouse-Spelman Glee Club takes its abundance of talent around the nation, and its annual Christmas concert on the Spelman campus is a standing-room-only event.

Morehouse and Spelman (see full write-ups) constitute the Ivy League of historically African-American colleges. The following are sketches of the other two institutions offering undergraduate degrees.

Clark Atlanta University. (www.cau.edu)

Formed by the consolidation of Clark College, a four-year liberal arts institution, and Atlanta University, which offered only graduate degrees, CAU is a comprehensive coeducational institution that offers undergraduate, graduate, and professional degrees. The university draws on the former strengths of both schools, offering quality programs in the health professions, public policy, and mass communications (including print journalism, radio and television production, and filmmaking). Graduate and professional programs include education, business, library information studies, social work, and arts and sciences. Undergraduate enrollment: 4,000.

Morris Brown College. (www.morrisbrown.edu)

An open-admission, four-year undergraduate institution that is related to the African Methodist Episcopal Church. Its most popular programs are education and business administration. Students receive considerable personal attention, and those arriving with poor academic preparation are provided with special help. Morris Brown also offers evening courses for employed adults, as well as a program of co-op work-study education. Only a small percentage of Morris Brown graduates continue their formal education beyond the baccalaureate. Enrollment: 600 men/870 women.

Morehouse College

830 Westview Drive, Atlanta, GA 30314

Along with sister school Spelman, Morehouse is the most selective of the historically black schools. Alumni list reads like a Who's Who of African-American leaders. Best known for business and popular 3–2 engineering program with Georgia Tech. Built on a Civil War battlefield, Morehouse is a symbol of the new South.

Website:
www.morehouse.edu
Location: Urban

Founded in 1867, Morehouse College has the distinction of being the nation's only historically African-American, four-year, liberal arts college for men. If its sister school, Spelman, was once the "Vassar of African-American society," Morehouse was the Harvard or Yale, attracting male students from the upper echelons of society around the country. Top students come to Morehouse because they want an institution with a strong academic program and a supportive atmosphere in which to cultivate their success-orientation and leadership skills without facing the additional barriers they might encounter at a predominantly white institution. "Morehouse is a college of young, assertive, ambitious black men," says a psychology major. Notable alumni include the Reverend Martin Luther King Jr., Samuel L. Jackson, Spike Lee, and Dr. Louis Sullivan, current president of the Morehouse School of Medicine and former U.S. Secretary of Health and Human Services.

Located near downtown Atlanta, the sixty-one-acre Morehouse campus is home to thirty-five buildings, including the Martin Luther King Jr., International Chapel. In a little more than a decade, the college has enriched its academic program, conducted a successful multimillion-dollar national fund-raising campaign, increased student scholarships and faculty salaries, doubled its endowment, improved its physical plant, and acquired additional acres of land.

The general education program includes not only sixty-eight semester hours in four major disciplines (humanities, natural sciences, math, and social sciences), but also the study of "the unique African and African-American heritage on which so much of our modern American culture is built." In fact, appreciation of this culture

"Many students are here to get a greater understanding of their heritage and to promote it."

is one of the college's main drawing cards. "Many students are here to get a greater understanding of their heritage and to promote it," attests one student. The academic climate at the House can get intense, with students learning and challenging themselves for the sake of learning and not just to bust a curve. "Morehouse offers an academic structure that is both competitive and rigorous," states a freshman. Counseling, including career counseling, is considered quite strong.

Undergraduate programs include the traditional liberal arts majors in the humanities and social and natural sciences. While the sciences have been traditionally strong at Morehouse, business courses have risen in prominence. The college has obtained accreditation of the undergraduate business department by the American Assembly of Collegiate Schools of Business, and current students are linked to graduates who serve as mentors in the ways of the business world. The most popular major is business administration. Engineering, which trails shortly behind in popularity, is actually a 3–2 program in conjunction with Georgia Tech and other larger universities. The school also runs a program with NASA that allows students to engage in independent research. Programs that receive less favorable reviews from students are English, art, and drama, and the administration admits that physical education and some of the

"Drinking is not a big deal here."

humanities offerings could use some strengthening. Study-abroad options include programs offered through the Associated Colleges of the South consortium.* The school also offers courses and additional resources as a member of the Atlanta Regional Consortium for Higher Education.* Newer options include a major in applied physics and minors in public health sciences and telecommunications.

Sixty-seven percent of Morehouse students come from outside the state, with a sizable number from New York and California. Sixty-seven percent graduated in the top quarter of their high-school class. More than six hundred merit scholarships are available, many providing full tuition. There are 121 scholarships for athletes in football, basketball, track, soccer, and tennis.

There's limited housing, leaving half of the student body to find their own off-campus accommodations. For freshmen, students recommend Graves Hall, the college's oldest building, built in 1889. Those who do get campus housing sometimes wish they hadn't. Complaints range from "too small" to "not well-maintained."

(Continued)

Total Enrollment: 2,970
Undergraduates: 2,970
Male/Female: 100/0
SAT Ranges: V 440–680
  M 470–680
ACT Range: 19–32
Financial Aid: N/A
Expense: Pr $
Phi Beta Kappa: Yes
Applicants: 2,079
Accepted: 75%
Enrolled: 36%
Grad in 6 Years: 63%
Returning Freshmen: 83%
Academics: ✍ ✍ ✍
Social: ☎ ☎ ☎ ☎
Q of L: ★ ★ ★ ★
Admissions: (404) 215-2632
  or (800) 851-1254
Email Address: admissions@
  morehouse.edu

Strongest Programs:
  Economics
  Business
  Biology
  Political Science
  Psychology

While the sciences have been traditionally strong at Morehouse, business courses have risen in prominence.

Most upperclassmen live off campus. The meal plan at Morehouse is mandatory for students living on campus, and draws its share of complaints.

Morehouse's Homecoming, the centerpiece of Spike Lee's movie, *School Daze*, is a joint effort between Morehouse and Spelman. The queen elected by Morehouse men has traditionally been a Spelman woman, as are the cheerleaders and majorettes. The four fraternities, which sign up a very small percentage of the students, hold popular parties; "drinking is not a big deal here," most students concur. Going out on the town in Atlanta is a popular evening activity, and on-campus football games, concerts, movies, and religious programs all draw crowds. In its early years, Morehouse left much to be desired in the area of varsity sports, but it now competes well in NCAA Division II. Track, cross-country, tennis, basketball, football, and soccer are all strong, but it is the strong intramural program that allows students a chance to become the superstars they know is lurking within them. During football season, Morehouse men road-trip to follow the games at Howard, Hampton, and Tuskegee universities.

Morehouse is well equipped to serve the modern heirs of a distinguished tradition. Morehouse students don't just attend Morehouse. They become part of what amounts to a network of "Morehouse Men," who share the bonds of having had the Morehouse experience, and graduates find previous alumni stand ready and willing to help them with jobs and other needs.

Overlaps

Clark Atlanta, Howard, Georgia Tech, Hampton

If You Apply To ➤

Morehouse: Early action: Nov. 1. Regular admissions: Feb. 15. Financial aid: Apr. 1. Does not guarantee to meet demonstrated need. Campus and alumni interviews: recommended, informational. SATs or ACTs: required. SAT IIs: optional. Essay question: greatest influence on your life; why Morehouse?

Spelman College

350 Spelman Lane, Atlanta, GA 30314

The Wellesley of the black college world. Reputation draws students from all corners of the country. Unusually strong in the sciences with particular emphasis on undergraduate research. Wooded Atlanta campus offers easy access to urban attractions.

Website: www.spelman.edu
Location: Urban
Total Enrollment: 2,065
Undergraduates: 2,065
Male/Female: 0/100
SAT Ranges: V 490–590
    M 470–560
ACT Range: 20–24
Financial Aid: 86%
Expense: Pr $
Phi Beta Kappa: No
Applicants: 3,266
Accepted: 53%
Enrolled: 33%

As one of only two surviving African-American women's colleges in the United States, Spelman College is far and away the most prestigious. And it's certainly found a friend in comedian Bill Cosby. His $20 million gift helps keep tuition low and quality academics available. Cosby is not alone in his generosity; Spelman recently completed a campaign that raised what is said to be the largest amount ever raised by a historically African-American university. These contributions—as well as a strong academic department—are sure to produce promising young African-American women who will become leaders in fields ranging from science to the arts.

Founded in 1881 by two Caucasian women from New England (it was named after John D. Rockefeller's mother-in-law, Mrs. Harvey Spelman), the school was traditionally the starting point for teachers, nurses, and other African-American female leaders. Today's emphasis is on getting Spelman grads into the courtrooms, boardrooms, and engineering labs. Honing women for leadership is the main mission, and that nurturing takes place on a classic collegiate-green thirty-two-acre campus with a $140 million endowment.

These are heady times for Spelman. Although the college finds itself competing head-on with the Seven Sisters and other prestigious and predominantly Caucasian institutions that are eager to recruit talented African-American women, the college is holding its own. Students still flock here for that something special that the predominantly Caucasian schools lack: an environment with first-rate academics where African-American women can develop self-confidence and leadership skills before venturing into a world where they will once again be in the minority.

The college offers a well-rounded liberal arts curriculum that emphasizes the importance of critical and analytical thinking and problem solving. Usually by the end of sophomore year, students are expected to complete thirty-four credit hours of core requirements, including English composition, foreign language, health and physical education, mathematics, African diaspora and the world, African-American women's studies, and computer literacy. In addition, freshmen are required to take First Year Orientation, and sophomores must take Sophomore Assembly. Spelman's liberal arts program introduces students to the principal branches of learning, specifically languages, literature, English, the natural sciences, humanities, social sciences, and fine arts.

"If there is any place that a student can be academically enriched, it is here."

Spelman's established strengths lie in the natural sciences (especially biology) and the humanities, both of which have outstanding faculties. Over the last decade, the college has greatly strengthened its offerings in math and the natural sciences; extensive undergrad research programs provide students with publishing opportunities, and many end up attending grad school to become researchers. Many students have discarded the popular majors of the early '70s—education and the fine arts—in favor of premed and prelaw programs, and these programs remain strong. The dual-degree program in engineering (in cooperation with Georgia Tech) is also a standout. The Women's Research and Resource Center specializes in African-American women's studies and community outreach to African-American women.

Individual attention is the hallmark of a Spelman education. About 70 percent of the faculty have doctorates, and many are African-American and/or female—and thus excellent role models, ones the students find very accessible. One political science major reports that the majority of instructors are "very well learned. Their lectures are tactful and effective," and she is "often challenged to put forth the best effort." Except for some of the required courses, classes are small; most have fewer than twenty-five students. Students who want to spread their wings can venture abroad through a variety of programs, or try one of the domestic exchange arrangements with Wellesley, Mount Holyoke, Vassar, or Mills. The school also offers courses and additional resources as a member of the Atlanta Regional Consortium for Higher Education.*

Spelman's reputation continues to attract African-American women from all over the country, including a high proportion of alumnae children. Three-quarters of the students come from outside Georgia. Students represented here include high achievers looking for a supportive environment and those women with high potential who performed relatively poorly in high school. Only 4 percent of the student body are not African-American. Spelman does not guarantee to meet the financial need of all those admitted, but it does offer 120 merit scholarships worth up to $18,015. There are no athletic scholarships.

"No alcohol on campus—period."

Fifty-seven percent of students live on campus, and housing is "well kept and quite comfortable," reports a mathematics major. Because Spelman is an old school and it has tried to keep up the original buildings, most of the dorms are relatively

(Continued)
Grad in 6 Years: 75%
Returning Freshmen: 91%
Academics: ✍ ✍ ✍
Social: ☎ ☎ ☎ ☎
Q of L: ★ ★ ★ ★ ★
Admissions: (800) 982-2411
Email Address:
  admiss@spelman.edu

Strongest Programs:
  Biology
  Engineering
  Natural Sciences
  Premed
  Prelaw

Extensive undergrad research programs provide students with publishing opportunities, and many end up attending grad school to become researchers.

old. But that certainly can add to the school's historical charm, and students report having little trouble in getting a room. There are eleven dorms, and students recommend that freshmen check out the Howard Harreld dorm. The meal plan is mandatory for campus-dwellers.

Largely because of the Atlanta University Center, students also have plenty of chances for social interaction with other nearby colleges. "Students mingle in the student centers of all four schools all the time, especially on Fridays," a veteran explains. "Atlanta is a great college town!" gushes one junior. "If there is any place that a student can be academically enriched, it is here." Spelmanites do take advantage of the big-city nightlife; they attend plays, symphonies, and the hot Atlanta nightclubs such as Ethiopian Vibrations, Fat Tuesdays, and Lenoxx. Sororities are present but only in small numbers—3 percent of the students go Greek. The attitude on drinking leans toward the conservative. Says one student, "No alcohol on campus—period." The most anticipated annual events include sisterhood initiation ceremonies and the Founders Day celebration. Although varsity sports are not the highlight here, the school boasts fine volleyball, basketball, and tennis teams. Synchronized swimming is the specialty, however. Athletic facilities are poor, but there are several organized intramurals, including flag football and bowling.

Spelman College has spent a century furthering the education and opportunities of African-American women. It has adapted its curriculum to meet the career aspirations of today's youth, built up its bankroll, and successfully met the challenge posed by affirmative action in other universities. Still an elite institution in African-American society, Spelman is staking its future on its ability to provide a unique kind of education that allows its graduates to compete with anyone.

Overlaps

Clark Atlanta, Howard, Hampton, Georgia State, Florida A&M

If You Apply To ➤

Spelman: Early action: Nov. 15. Regular admissions: Feb. 1. Housing: May 1. Does not guarantee to meet demonstrated need. Campus interviews: optional, informational. No alumni interviews. SATs or ACTs: required. SAT IIs: optional. Accepts the Common Application. Essay question: personal statement reflecting achievements, interests, personal goal; or issue of personal, local, or national concern. Seeks women who are active in school, church, or community.

College of the Atlantic

105 Eden Street, Bar Harbor, ME 04609

In the conservative world of today, COA is as out-there as it gets. A haven for communal, vegetarian types who would rather save the world than make a buck. Cozy is an understatement; with less than three hundred students, it is the second-smallest institution in the *Fiske Guide*.

Website: www.coa.edu
Location: Small town
Total Enrollment: 263
Undergraduates: 260
Male/Female: 41/59
SAT Ranges: V 570–670
   M 550–640
ACT Range: 25–29
Financial Aid: 70%

The College of the Atlantic attracts rugged individualists troubled by the same harmful effects of job automation—pollution, environmental damage, troubled inner cities—that so-worried the founders of this "mission-oriented" school. Today, the tiny college's curriculum is focused on human ecology—the study of the relationship between humans and their natural and social environments. The goal, says a senior, is "to educate people to do something good with their lives—to make the little corner of their world, wherever they end up, a little better off."

The twenty-six-acre campus, covered in lush flowers, vegetable gardens, and lawns, sits on the island of Mount Desert, along the shoreline of Frenchman Bay and adjacent to the magnificent Acadia National Park. In addition, the college has recently acquired two offshore island research centers and an eighty-six-acre organic farm.

Most courses focus on a single aspect of human's relationship to the world. Instead of traditional academic departments, the school has three broad resource areas: environmental science, arts and design, and applied human studies. A course on creativity, for instance, might pair a scientist and a poet to examine parallels in scientific and artistic thought. Many students choose to concentrate on more narrowly defined topics within human ecology, such as marine studies, biological and environmental sciences, public policy, visual and performing arts, environmental design, or education. With advisors and resource specialists, each student designs an individual course of study drawing from different programs. A student studying elementary education describes the draw of that department as "a nontraditional, rigorous program that looks at teaching/being an educator from many different perspectives."

Given COA's location, the natural sciences are stellar, with excellent instruction in ecology, zoology, and marine biology. The arts are catching up, with a more formal video and performance art program created in recent years. "Students work very hard and participate enthusiastically, but not aggressively," says a junior. Allied Whale, the school's marine study arm, offers hands-on research opportunities, while another course prepares exhibits for the college's natural history museum. COA also offers more than ninety

"Students work very hard and participate enthusiastically, but not aggressively."

courses in human studies, with significant concentrations in literature, philosophy, economics, history, law, and anthropology. Unusual offerings include study on an organic farm and in a taxidermy lab.

Student life at COA is intense and semi-communal, beginning with a rugged five-day wilderness orientation preceding first trimester. Before graduating, students must also complete a ten-week off-campus internship, participate in a student-run problem-solving workshop, and support at least one "campus-building" activity, such as the student government or newspaper. Requirements are few: freshmen take a human ecology course and a writing course, and juniors write a human-ecology essay, expanding it during the following year until it grows into their senior project, a major independent work.

Some departments only have a professor or two. Since the student body is small, they can become close to faculty members. "The professors are all called by their first name and have a more personal relationship with students than at traditional colleges," says a student. In lieu of grades, students receive in-depth, written evaluations of their work, although they may request grades as well. They must reciprocate with an evaluation of the course and their

"The professors are all called by their first name and have a more personal relationship with students than at traditional colleges."

performance in it. The unusual advising system, a three-person student-faculty team chosen by the advisee, further promotes close contact between students and professors.

Students attracted to the quirky College of the Atlantic and its unique curriculum are often bright and idealistic; many worked with Americorps or traveled the world before beginning school. COA is predominantly Caucasian, with African-American, Hispanics, and Asian-Americans comprising 5 percent of the student body. However, a sizable number of international students attend COA. The college's governance system gives students and administrators almost equal voices in how it's run; anyone may voice concerns or vote on policy-change proposals or the hiring of

(Continued)

Expense: Pr $
Phi Beta Kappa: No
Applicants: 233
Accepted: 80%
Enrolled: 34%
Grad in 6 Years: 44%
Returning Freshmen: 90%
Academics: ✍ ✍ ✍
Social: ☎ ☎
Q of L: ★ ★ ★
Admissions: (800) 528-0025 or (207) 288-5015
Email Address: inquiry@ecology.coa.edu

Strongest Programs:
  Education
  Environmental Studies
  Organic Agriculture
  Land Use Management
  Visual and Performing Arts
  Public Policy/Law
  Marine Biology

Student life at COA is intense and semi-communal, beginning with a rugged five-day wilderness orientation preceding first trimester.

A course on creativity might pair a scientist and a poet to examine parallels in scientific and artistic thought.

new faculty at the All College Meeting. "Political issues are spoken of all the time, and many share deep concerns about what is right and wrong," says a student.

Forty percent of students—freshmen, international students, and upper-class resident advisors—live on campus, while the balance find cozy, inexpensive apartments or houses in the nearby town of Bar Harbor. Campus-dwellers may choose from small cooperative houses with five to twenty students or a fairly new dorm with space for sixty students, "which looks like a beautiful ski chalet," says one resident. The college provides fifteen meals during the week, including vegetarian alternatives, but students fend for themselves on weekends.

Though the tiny tourist town of Bar Harbor is packed with visitors during the summer, it shuts down in the winter. "We have the bare necessities—bank, bookstore, grocery stores, video store, movie theater, and a few restaurants," says a senior. Students get to know the townspeople through the required forty hours of community service. "People do lots of stuff for local organizations, including work on farms, parks, the downeast AIDS network, and the YMCA," writes a

"People do lots of stuff for local organizations."

student. On weekends, few students leave campus, since Portland, the nearest urban center, is three hours away. Campus social functions revolve around nature and the seasons, including biking, hiking, boating, cross-country skiing, skating, and rock climbing, often in Acadia National Park. Some students take road trips to Canada. Not surprisingly for a school that cultivates its "tree-hugger" and "granola" image, there are no fraternities or sororities. Students kick back at off-campus house parties, which are generally alcohol free. There's no drinking on campus, and it's tough for underage students to get served in town. COA's new men's and women's soccer teams, known as the Blackflies and nicknamed the "Swarm," have already earned strong student support.

The College of the Atlantic is a place where Earth Day really is a cause for celebration, where students ride nude through the cafeteria and on nearby streets during Bike Week, and where everyone from students to trustees jumps into frigid Frenchman Bay on the first Friday of the first week of classes, trying to swim from the school's docks to Bar Island. "Everyone who's not swimming stands on shore and cheers them on," a senior reports. "About a dozen and a half make it there and back. A few get hypothermia."

The long snowy winters and shrunken winter population make for an atmosphere that is cozy to some, dreary to others. But students appreciate the rich curriculum and tight community found at COA, a school still committed to helping those who want to help the world.

Overlaps

Colby, Marlboro, Hampshire, Colorado, Barnard

If You Apply To ➤

COA: Early decision: Dec. 1, Jan. 10. Regular admissions: Mar. 1. Financial aid: Feb. 15. Housing: May 1. Does not guarantee to meet demonstrated need. Campus interviews: recommended, evaluative. Alumni interviews: optional, evaluative. SAT I or ACT: optional. SAT IIs: optional. Accepts the Common Application and electronic applications. Essay question: does your academic record accurately reflect your ability and potential?; most rewarding nonacademic experience; how COA fits with your goals; and an essay on any topic (four suggested topics are provided). Looks for students committed to improving the quality of life on Earth.

Auburn University

202 Mary Martin Hall, Auburn, AL 36849

Sweet Home Alabama, where the skies are so blue and the spirit of football lasts year-round. Auburn was once called Alabama Polytechnic, and today AU's programs in engineering, agriculture, and the health fields are still among its best.

Auburn University is more than football. True, it is home to more than twenty thousand football-crazy students. But beyond its impressive and renowned team, Auburn is known for its successful agricultural and technical fields. Auburn offers courses in many other strong departments as well on this campus that positively drips with Southern charm and beauty.

"On the rolling plains of Dixie, 'neath its sun-kissed sky," goes Auburn's alma mater, and that's not all. Huge mossy trees, lush lawns, and majestic colonnades grace the nearly two thousand sprawling acres, though most of the "mellow" red-brick Georgian and modern academic buildings are grouped in a compact central location. The town of Auburn, whose namesake is depicted in an Oliver Goldsmith poem as the "loveliest village of the plain," grew amid miles of forest and farmland largely to serve the university.

As a public land-grant institution, Auburn's traditional academic strengths have been in the agricultural sciences. Architecture, business, and engineering are also excellent. Pharmacy and veterinary medicine are highly regarded, as are the biological sciences; the premed major is popular, as are psychology, civil engineering, mechanical engineering, and education. Auburn also offers a freshwater fisheries program that ranks among the strongest offered anywhere.

The university's common core of courses requires six semester hours of composition; six semester hours each of history, literature, and social science; three semester hours each of philosophy and fine arts; three semester hours of math; and eight semester hours of a lab science. There is an optional (and popular) freshman seminar called the Auburn Experience, which serves as an introduction to university resources and transition into the college environment. Whereas engineering and premed are intense, many other areas are fairly casual. Some say that overall it gets easier as you go along. "The first two years, when you are completing the core classes, are competitive," says a senior. "Once you get into your major classes, it gets a little more laid back." The co-op option, which provides pay and credits in several professional fields, is increasingly popular, as is the campus ROTC program. An honors program offers greater academic challenge to those who want it. The faculty receives praise from students. Grad students teach about 10 percent of classes. Students describe professors as "extremely knowledgeable" and "interesting."

Two-thirds of the undergraduates are homegrown Alabamians and 51 percent graduated in the top quarter of their high-school class. African-Americans account for 8 percent of the undergraduates. The conservative tone of this Bible Belt campus fosters many Christian groups, and Auburn is home to one of the largest branches of the Campus Crusade for Christ movement in the United States. Each year, the school awards over 1,500 merit scholarships and offers hundreds of athletic scholarships and its own need-based loan program.

Fourteen of Auburn's twenty-five dorms have been renovated, but only 16 percent of the students reside in them. Visiting hours are restricted to weekends. The best dorms for women are on the quad; for guys, it's the Carolyn Draughon Village

> **"The first two years, when you are completing the core classes, are competitive."**

Website: www.auburn.edu
Location: Small town
Total Enrollment: 22,469
Undergraduates: 18,922
Male/Female: 51/49
SAT Ranges: V 490–600
  M 510–610
ACT Range: 21–26
Financial Aid: 28%
Expense: Pub $
Phi Beta Kappa: Yes
Applicants: 13,645
Accepted: 83%
Enrolled: 36%
Grad in 6 Years: 68%
Returning Freshmen: 81%
Academics: ✍ ✍
Social: ☎ ☎ ☎
Q of L: ★ ★ ★
Admissions: (334) 844-4080
  (800) AUBURN9 (in Alabama)
Email Address:
  admissions@auburn.edu

Strongest Programs:
  Agriculture
  Architecture
  Engineering
  Pharmacy
  Veterinary Medicine
  Prehealth Programs
  Fisheries
  Education

Extension. Twenty-one percent of the men join fraternities, and 35 percent of the women join sororities, which have space in the choicest dorms. Freshmen must request housing when they apply for admission and compete on a first-come, first-served basis with returning students. There are five cafeterias and several snack bars on campus; fraternity men have the option of eating in their houses. Once they set aside their books, Auburn students revel in old school traditions such as football rivalries and tailgating parties.

Seldom are students so bored by their bucolic surroundings that they have to hightail it out of town the minute their last Friday class ends, but they do enjoy supporting their football team, no matter where the destination. Reports one fan, "The best trips are to college football games—away." The Greek system plays a major role in keeping the social scene lively, but "by no means does not being Greek mean not being social," says one socialite. Plays, concerts, pep rallies, parties, carnivals, battles of the bands, comedians, and traditional festivities such as the Burn the (Georgia) Bulldogs Parade are available to give the mind a vacation from studying for a few hours. Once a year, these students, in the spirit of Southern hospitality, celebrate Hey Day, when everyone wears a name tag and walks around saying, "Hey!" The proximity of I-85 is very convenient, putting Montgomery (where Auburn has a branch campus) just an hour away, and Atlanta, Birmingham, and the inviting Gulf Coast beaches just a couple of hours farther off.

"The best trips are to college football games—away."

Auburn is traditionally a football powerhouse; 86,000 screaming fans turn Auburn into the state's fourth-largest city on home Saturdays, and the time-honored rallying cry, "Warrrrr Eagle!" reverberates through the stadium every time an Auburn back runs to daylight. A popular pastime centers on composing catchy slogans for football rallies and parades. Whenever there's a football victory, one can be sure that Toomer's Corner (in downtown Auburn) is going to be rolled with toilet paper. Of the Auburn vs. Alabama game, a sophomore says, "Nothing like it. One hundred fifty thousand people gather for the game, but only about half get into the stadium. Everyone gets ready for the game at least a week in advance. Fans arrive and camp out in trailers and Winnebagos a full two weeks before the game." Although swimming and track draw nowhere near the rabid crowds of their pigskin-crazy peers, these sports produce teams that are just as impressive. Auburn's resurgent men's basketball team is now drawing record crowds. Intramurals are popular, especially among Greeks, who compete for the coveted All-Sports trophy every year.

Students affirm that Auburn's history, tradition, and high spirits make the feeling of genuine warmth contagious. An aerospace engineering student says, "Students at Auburn seem to care about each other. Every Auburn man or woman wants to see his fellow student succeed, and they go about their college career helping each other through difficult courses."

Overlaps

Florida State, University of Georgia, University of Tennessee, Mississippi State, Georgia Tech

If You Apply To >

Auburn: Early decision: Nov. 1. Regular admissions: Aug. 1. Does not guarantee to meet demonstrated need. Campus and alumni interviews: optional, informational. SATs or ACTs: required. SAT IIs: optional. Accepts electronic applications. No essay question.

Austin College

900 North Grand Avenue, Sherman, TX 75020-4440

The second-most famous institution in Texas with Austin in its name. Half the size of Trinity (TX), runs neck-in-neck with Southwestern to be the leading Texas college under two thousand students. Combines the liberal arts with strong programs in business, education, and the health fields.

Only an hour away from the ten-gallon hats and gleaming skyscrapers of Dallas is Austin College, a small but warm institution where students know their professors personally and take advantage of a broad array of majors. With about 1,200 undergraduates, no one is just a number at Austin. Professors here even serve their students breakfast at 10:00 P.M. the night before finals. It's just another example of the personal style that is typical of this charming Southern institution.

Austin's sixty-five-acre campus is located in a residential area outside the city of Sherman. The campus is designed in the traditional quadrangle style and hosts beige sandstone buildings, tree-lined plazas, decorative fountains, and an impressive seventy-ton sculptured solstice calendar. Dorms are conveniently located approximately two hundred yards from most classrooms, which eases the pain of first-period classes. The new 81,000-square-foot Wright Campus Center features space for a snack bar, post office, bookstore, game room, and dining room, and also houses facilities for student organizations.

Austin College challenges its students, but the atmosphere is far from cut-throat. One psychology major analyzes the situation this way: "The students are competitive with themselves, instead of with each other." But classes are not a breeze. "Austin is definitely an academically intensive institution with a student body of future leaders," says a physics/computer science double major. The core curriculum begins with a fresh-man seminar called Communi-cation/Inquiry. Each professor

"Very open-minded and liberal compared to other institutions in the South."

who teaches the course becomes the mentor for the twenty freshmen in his or her class. Next is a three-course sequence on the Heritage of Western Culture. Then comes a slew of optional courses in eight categories, including formal reasoning, language and written expression, and historical or social perspectives. Two-thirds of all classes have twenty-five students or fewer, and no class has more than a hundred. Students report that they rarely have problems getting the classes they want, but sometimes it's necessary to plan early.

Preprofessional areas are Austin College's specialties. When it comes time to apply to grad school, premed and predental students at this little college have one of the highest acceptance rates of any Texas school, and aspiring lawyers also do well. AC's five-year teaching program grants students both a bachelor's and a master's degree. Science and education receive high marks from students, as do international studies and political science. Business is among the school's most popular majors. The Jordan Language House boards forty-eight students studying French, German, Japanese, and Spanish, along with a native speaker of each language. Students can also earn a double major or combine three of the school's twenty-six majors into an interdisciplinary degree. A cooperative engineering program links the college with other schools, and a number of minors—some interdisciplinary—have been added, such as environmental studies and gender studies.

A January term option lets students take an "experiential learning" course, usually outside their major, on a pass/fail basis. An international studies concentration

Website:
  www.austincollege.edu
Location: Small town
Total Enrollment: 1,261
Undergraduates: 1,227
Male/Female: 43/57
SAT Ranges: V 550–640
  M 550–650
ACT Range: 23–29
Financial Aid: 60%
Expense: Pr $
Phi Beta Kappa: Yes
Applicants: 1,004
Accepted: 80%
Enrolled: 39%
Grad in 6 Years: 72%
Returning Freshmen: 86%
Academics: ✍ ✍ ✍
Social: 🕿 🕿 🕿
Q of L: ★ ★ ★
Admissions: (903) 813-3000
Email Address: admission@
  austincollege.edu

Strongest Programs:
  Health Sciences
  The Austin Teacher Program
  International Studies
  Religion
  Philosophy

provides opportunities to study abroad. The college also offers its students independent study, directed research, junior year abroad, and departmental honors programs. The Leadership Institute is open to just fifteen students of each entering class, and five more can get in after their first year. Participating students enjoy a suite of privileges, from study abroad options to working with mentors outside the college. Austin also provides three research areas located in Grayson County: the Barry Buckner Biology Preserve, the Lee Harrison Bratz Field Laboratory, and the Clinton and Edith Sneed Environmental Research Area.

Eighty-nine percent of Austin students hail from the Lone Star State. Hispanics and African-Americans comprise 7 and 5 percent of the student body, respectively, and Asian-Americans make up 8 percent. Hot political issues include abortion and homosexuality, and one junior reports that the campus is "very open-minded and liberal compared to other institutions in the South." Austin has been tied to the Presbyterian Church in the United States since 1849; this affiliation manifests itself

"The concepts of learning, leadership, and lasting values are stressed."

in the emphasis on values in the core courses, participation in service activities, and limited residence-hall visitation hours. Students are beginning to chafe under that latter rule, one student says. AC offers 250 merit scholarships, ranging from $500 to just over $16,000.

As for dorm life, there are six residence halls, and 74 percent of undergraduates live in this traditional dorm housing. (Only juniors and seniors are permitted to live in apartment-style buildings owned by the college.) One sophomore says the dorms are "better than your average state school," but a junior notes that Luckett Hall is usually not that clean. One AC dorm is coed, one houses language studies students, two are men-only, and two are women-only. Dean (the only coed residence hall) seems to be a popular choice for freshmen, despite (or perhaps because of) its reputation as being loud and social. Others say Clyce is the best bet for freshman women, and Luckett for freshman men. Residence hall access is computerized, and security officers are on duty 24 hours a day. Nearly all students take advantage of the three-meal-a-day plan, though not all take advantage of the all-you-can-eat option. Then there's the Pouch Club, an on-campus joint that serves beer and wine for those students 21 and over.

"Most of the social life is either on or near campus, with the Greeks taking the lion's share of credit. Twenty-one percent of the men and 19 percent of the women belong to fraternities and sororities, but the Greeks are not school-funded and are not allowed to advertise off-campus parties without the college's permission. Not everyone depends on the Greek system for a good time. Students get an eyeful during the Baker Bun Run, in which the men of Baker Hall strip to their boxers and cavort around the campus on the Monday night before finals. Students can have alcohol in dorm rooms only if they are twenty-one or older, and school policy prohibits booze at campus organization events. Popular weekend excursions are the drive to Dallas or to the college's twenty-eight-acre recreational spot on Lake Texoma (a half-hour north). Some students say having a car is an absolute must. "Sherman is not a great college town," a psychology major laments. "The population is rather elderly and there's little nightlife."

Even without athletic scholarships, varsity sports are generating increasing support. The school's teams compete in Division III, and the women's basketball, soccer, and volleyball teams have each won recent championships.

At Austin, the teachers are inspiring and the atmosphere familial. "The concepts of learning, leadership, and lasting values are stressed," a sophomore says. Notes another, "It's easy to adjust to, and the closely interacting faculty and students make it a good place."

Overlaps

University of Texas, Texas A&M, Baylor, University of North Texas, Texas Tech

If You Apply To ➢

Austin: Early decision: Dec. 1. Early action: Jan. 15. Regular admissions: Mar. 1. Financial aid: Apr. 1. Housing: May 1. Campus and alumni interviews: recommended, evaluative. SATs or ACTs: required. SAT IIs: optional. Accepts the Common Application and electronic applications. Essay question: political, social, or economic issue of personal concern; significance of a "defining moment" in your life.

Babson College

Babson Park, MA 02457-0310

The only college in the *Fiske Guide* devoted entirely to business. Only fourteen miles from College Student Mecca, a.k.a. Boston, and tougher to get into now than at any time in its history. The only college in Massachusetts where it is possible to be a Republican with head held high.

The budding business leaders who choose Babson College know that nothing is as valuable as hands-on experience. Sure, they complain about the demanding workload and the dull social life. But how many other undergrads get school funding to start businesses during freshman year, or hone stock-picking skills by managing part of their college's endowment? The school's "reputation, faculty, and networking capabilities" make Babson special, says a senior.

Founded in 1919, Babson sits on a 370-acre campus near the sedate Boston suburb of Wellesley. The tract features open green spaces, gently rolling hills, and heavily wooded areas. The atmosphere is one of peace and tranquility, with trees gently shading buildings, and parking lots relatively hidden. Architectural styles vary but are mainly neo-Georgian and modern. Recent additions include the Sorenson Center for the Arts, Reynolds Student Center, and Blank Center for Entrepreneurship.

The college's general education requirements emphasize field experience. The curriculum focuses on competency in five areas: rhetoric; numeracy; ethics and social responsibility; international and multicultural perspectives; and leadership, teamwork and creativity. The three-course Integrated Management Core (IMC) helps students develop sound managerial decision-making skills. Freshmen are required to take composition, quantitative methods, history and society,

> "Intermediate and some advanced liberal arts classes are too cursory and act as curriculum filler."

law, speech, statistics, arts and humanities, economics, and the Foundation Management Experience. In the FME, working in groups of thirty, first-years get $3,000 in seed money to launch, manage, and liquidate a business, with profits going to charity. Last year, the class donated $31,830.

All Babson students major in business and then select a concentration, such as entrepreneurial studies, finance, marketing, management information systems, or accounting. The entrepreneurial studies program brings prominent venture capitalists and entrepreneurs to campus for how-to lectures. "Course loads are challenging," says a sophomore. "There are many, many brilliant students that are competing with you for the select few As distributed." Students say the management department is excellent but warn that fine arts or sciences courses are likely to be weak. "Intermediate and some advanced liberal arts classes are too cursory and act as curriculum filler," says a senior.

In the classroom, Babson relies on the case-study approach, where students address specific business situations in groups or as officers of pseudo-corporations.

Website: www.babson.edu
Location: Suburban
Total Enrollment: 3,328
Undergraduates: 1,719
Male/Female: 60/40
SAT Ranges: V 560–650
  M 610–680
Financial Aid: N/A
Expense: Pr $ $ $ $
Phi Beta Kappa: No
Applicants: 3,127
Accepted: 35%
Enrolled: 37%
Grad in 6 Years: 81%
Returning Freshmen: 89%
Academics: ✍ ✍ ✍
Social: ☎ ☎
Q of L: ★ ★ ★
Admissions: (781) 239-5070
  or (800) 488-3696
Email Address:
  ugradadmission@
  babson.edu

Strongest Programs:
  Entrepreneurial Studies
  Finance
  Marketing

In the Foundation Management Experience, working in groups of thirty, first-years get $3,000 in seed money to launch, manage, and liquidate a business, with profits going to charity. Last year, the class donated $31,830.

Most courses have less than sixty students per section; the average is twenty-six. Even though upperclassmen get priority in registration, students say it's not hard to get into required courses. However, says a freshman, "getting specific professors or times can be hard"—and so can getting certain elective or science courses, adds a sophomore. Professors teach all courses, and many are former operating executives who "bring so much real-life experience to the classroom," says a senior. A junior disagrees, saying that while most professors are very knowledgeable, "it can be hard to learn from them as they do not teach very well." Babson's use of the case method, more typically employed by MBA programs, means there are many group projects. For these, students take advantage of more than 250 workstations in the computer center's five labs—except for the twenty-four-hour quiet lab, where talking is not allowed.

Babson remains largely white and wealthy, despite administrators' efforts to diversify. African-Americans comprise 3 percent of the student body, Hispanics 4 percent, and Asian-Americans 8 percent. About a quarter of Babson's undergrads are Massachusetts's natives, and 20 percent come from abroad. "Students are intense, competitive, and sheltered," says a senior. They're also "very driven and goal-oriented," a classmate adds. "They compete against one another for the best grades and only have business on their minds, all the time." Forget about dressing down for class, says a sophomore. "Students are very rich, have BMWs, and wear expensive clothes," she says. "Informal clothing—like wearing pajamas at the dining hall—is not as common."

Babson guarantees housing for four years, and 85 percent of undergraduates live on campus, resulting in high demand for singles and suites. Dorms are air-conditioned and carpeted, and most upper-class rooms have their own bathrooms,

"The dorms range from very comfortable to shoe boxes."

says a senior. "Getting the room you want can be hard, especially as an underclassman," says a freshman—thanks to a lottery where standing is based on credits earned. "Housing is pretty expensive for what you get," says a junior. "The dorms range from very comfortable to shoe boxes." Most halls are coed, but one dorm is reserved for men, and floors and wings of other buildings are reserved for women. Every Wednesday is gourmet night at the dining hall, and the menu may include fresh lobster, Italian specialties, or turkey with all the trimmings.

Social life at Babson "is lackluster, due to workload, stress, and general discontent," says a burned-out senior. "Things are improving, but the mentality has been ingrained." The Campus Activities Board brings in comedians and organizes parties, as do Greek organizations, which attract 13 percent of the women and 13 percent of the men. If you're caught with booze while underage, it's three strikes and you're out, says a sophomore. (Fines of $75 each for underage drinking and open containers have helped cut down on illegal imbibing but haven't curbed it entirely. In fact, some enterprising students recently worked up T-shirts parodying the school motto, "Always Thinking," as "Always Drinking.") Those over twenty-one may shoot pool and relax with a beer at the campus pub. Two miles from campus, a subway stop gives students access to the greater Boston area, where they participate in mandatory first-year volunteer projects. For those with wheels, the clubs and bars of Boston beckon, as do the beaches of Cape Cod and Martha's Vineyard, and the ski slopes of Vermont and New Hampshire. New York City and Montreal are popular weekend getaways.

The town of Wellesley is "a commuter town for the very wealthy," says a junior. It's a town that "would likely prefer not to host a college," says a senior—which is unfortunate, since it has two. (Wellesley College is the other; it's not uncommon for Babson students to socialize with Wellesley women.) Babson students look forward to Alumni Weekend (great networking opportunities), Spring and Winter

In the classroom, Babson relies on the case-study approach, where students address specific business situations in groups or as officers of pseudo-corporations.

Weekends, and Babson Founders Day, where classes are cancelled so that everyone can celebrate entrepreneurship.

While making money may be the most competitive "sport" at Babson, the Beavers participate in NCAA Division III athletics, too. The baseball and men's basketball teams won conference championships in 2002, and the men's golf and women's tennis teams also brought home titles recently. Matches against archrival Bentley and annual soccer games against Brandeis and Colby are most popular among spectators. Intramural sports are also a big draw.

Babson encourages students to develop their management skills with hands-on experience outside the classroom. Despite its total focus on all things financial, or maybe because of that, Beavers graduate able to juggle multiple projects, budget their time, and—for those who think it's important—make their own fun. For many, the first step up the corporate ladder occurs in the halls of Babson College.

Overlaps

Boston College, Bentley, Boston University, NYU, University of Pennsylvania.

If You Apply To ➤ **Babson:** Early decision and early action: Dec. 1. Regular admissions: Feb. 1. Financial aid: Feb. 15. Campus and alumni interviews: recommended, evaluative. SATs or ACTs: required. SAT IIs: recommended (writing and math Ic or IIc). Accepts the Common Application and electronic applications. Essay questions: why Babson, and how it will help you achieve personal and career goals; and personal statement, which may cover a significant experience or achievement, issue of concern, influential person, fictional character, historical figure or creative work, or a topic of student's choice.

Bard College

Annandale-on-Hudson, NY 12504

Welcome to Nonconformity-Central-on-Hudson, the only major U.S. institution where en masse cross-dressing on Parents' Weekend is a time-honored tradition. More selective than Hampshire and with a better male-female ratio than Sarah Lawrence, Bard is an up-and-comer among the nontraditional liberal arts colleges.

The first class at Bard College, founded in 1860, consisted of twelve men studying to enter the seminaries of the Episcopal Church. They would no doubt be surprised at the eclectic mix of students that now populate Bard, a hotbed of artsy intellectualism. The professors are highly praised and the courses are rigorous but don't fuel intense competition. "Bard is a place where I feel free to think and learn and make mistakes," a film major says. Adds a math major: "It's a very unique and intellectual community."

Bard was once known mainly as a school for the performing arts, and creative types have long flocked to its lovely campus, which occupies six hundred well-landscaped acres in New York's Washington Irving country. The hodgepodge of architectural styles leaves each ivy-covered brick building with a character all its own, especially the dorms, which come in every variety, from cottages in the woods to one Russian Colonial–style dorm. Construction has completed on a $40 million performing arts center designed by renowned architect Frank O. Gehry. Other recent improvements include a multi-use campus center, a new sixty-eight-student dorm, and renovation of the main dining hall.

> "Bard is a place where I feel free to think and learn and make mistakes."

Students can get a taste of Bard's individualized approach to higher education before they are even admitted if they choose to participate in a daylong

Website: www.bard.edu
Location: Rural
Total Enrollment: 1,515
Undergraduates: 1,343
Male/Female: 44/56
SAT Ranges: V 650–720
  M 590–690
Financial Aid: 60%
Expense: Pr $ $ $ $
Phi Beta Kappa: No
Applicants: 2,970
Accepted: 44%
Enrolled: 30%
Grad in 6 Years: 70%
Returning Freshmen: 86%
Academics: ✍ ✍ ✍ ✍
Social: ☎ ☎ ☎
Q of L: ★ ★ ★ ★
Admissions: (845) 758-7472

(Continued)
Email Address:
admission@bard.edu

Strongest Programs:
Film
Visual and Performing Arts
Humanities
Literature
Creative Writing
Languages

seminar/interview known as the Immediate Decision Plan, after which they receive an immediate acceptance or denial. Freshmen show up three weeks before classes start for the unique, required Workshop in Language and Thinking, organized around the quaint notion that good writing and clear thinking are necessary tools for higher learning. Designed to "provide a balanced encounter between classical and progressive traditions," Bard's general education requirements include a year-long multidisciplinary freshman seminar. At the end of their second year, all students write their educational autobiography and declare a major program of study. These are presented before a board of professors in the relevant area and discussed with the student. Junior year includes a tutorial in preparation for the senior project, and during senior year students do the project, equivalent to an undergraduate dissertation—an original work that could materialize in the form of a critical analysis of literature, a portfolio of artwork, a dance, a novel, or a research project. Ninety-five percent of classes have twenty-five or fewer students.

Students agree that the academic climate is intense and classes are rigorous, but say students rarely compete with each other. "We are encouraged to challenge ourselves. You must be self-motivated," says a junior. Independent studies and tutorials are the soul of the curriculum. Students have the opportunity to

"We are encouraged to challenge ourselves. You must be self-motivated."

draw up their own course description, find a professor to sponsor it, and produce a custom-designed program. Bard also makes a point of recognizing visual and performing arts as equals among academic disciplines, and all faculty members are full professors. A political studies major describes professors as "phenomenal, friendly, approachable, knowledgeable, and willing to help."

With distinguished authors such as John Ashbery, Mona Simpson, Chinua Achebe, and Bradford Morrow teaching seminars in creative writing, it is no wonder that some students feel the best divisions at the school are literature and writing. Natural sciences and physics are surprisingly good for their size, and the distinguished-scientist scholars program offers full tuition to the top students in the Division of Natural Science and Mathematics. Students say that the history and dance departments need improvement. A new collaborative program with Rockefeller University allows Bard undergrads to study at this premier science research institution. Students also complain about inadequate library resources—only 190,000 volumes, slim for the amount of research that success at Bard requires.

Bard offers combined programs with other schools in engineering, architecture, city planning, social work, public health, business and public administration, forestry, and environmental science. Students can take part in special Bard programs in China, Greece, India, Senegal, and South Africa, and study language in France, Germany, Italy, or Mexico. The winter field period comes at the end of December and lasts six weeks: a chance to take in-depth courses on or off campus, pursue internships, travel, or just experience life while remaining a student. A few of the research opportunities include the summer Archaeology Field School and a science scholars program that carries a $1,500 stipend for summer research.

Diversity, be it racial, ideological, or even regarding fashion, is a hallmark at Bard. "There is no one way of describing a Bardian—you'll find every type of person here," a junior says. Three percent of students are African-American, 4 percent Hispanic, and 3 percent Asian-American. Most students are from out of state, and 30 percent attended private school. In terms of political correctness, "Half the people make it an issue, the other half make an issue of rebelling against it," an art major sighs. A recent pig roast protested widespread vegetarianism. Hot debate issues range from gay rights to racism, biodevastation, and abortion. In terms of dress code, according to one student, "There are those who wear Izods and flannel nighties,

Bard is virtually devoid of dedicated jocks. "Athletics is definitely not a popular activity," says one student. But another notes, "there are plenty of pseudo-jocks and intellectuals in good shape."

those with nose clips and purple hair. You see everything from Arab robes to three-piece suits." Although Bard does not guarantee financial aid for all four years, 60 percent of the students receive some form of financial assistance. Bard offers up to twenty merit scholarships of $500 to $26,900. Under Bard's unique Excellence and Equal Cost program, high-school students in their class's top ten can apply to Bard at the cost of their state university's tuition. Admission to this program is not automatic; about two hundred students vie for forty spots.

Freshmen are required to live on campus in dorms, which range from cabins on stilts in a ravine to converted mansions. "Housing at Bard is all about luck," a sophomore says. One student boasts, "My room has four diamond-paneled bay windows that face west with sunsets like a Monet painting. It has oak walls, carved ceilings, and its own bathroom with a marble shower." The room draw system can be chaotic, driving about a quarter of the students to rent rooms off campus. That option can be less expensive, but it does require transportation. All residential students eat on campus, and food quality has improved with a new food service.

Social life at Bard is far from an endless party, but Bardians enjoy films, concerts (a lot of indie rock and hip hop), dances, student art exhibits, and lectures, as well as local coffee shops. There are no fraternities or sororities on campus. Bard's Winter Carnival raises money to fight world hunger while offering a weekend of outdoor winter games, an auction of faculty memorabilia, and a formal dance. Drag Race, which happens on Parents' Weekend, is a cross-dressing, performance-based extravaganza bearing the theme "Dress in Drag or Don't Dress At All."

In athletics, although soccer, tennis, cross-country, fencing, basketball, squash, and women's volleyball are popular, Bard is virtually devoid of dedicated jocks. "Athletics is definitely not a popular activity," says one student. But another notes "there are plenty of pseudo-jocks and intellectuals in good shape." There's always Ultimate Frisbee in the fall, and intramural softball competition is "a staple

"There is no one way of describing a Bardian—you'll find every type of person here."

in the spring," for which most majors—and faculty and staff—form teams. Nearby, there are five miles of trails through the woods along the Hudson that are perfect for myriad outdoor activities, from raspberry picking to skiing, jogging, or hiking.

Having a car on this lovely but rural campus does much to prevent occasional attacks of claustrophobia. Some students say Bard's hometown of Annandale-on-Hudson is "in the woods." But the town is less than twenty miles away from great shopping in Woodstock and within striking distance of ski slopes in the Catskills or Berkshires. Plus, New York City is just a two-hour Amtrak ride away. Students also cite the Upstate Films movie theater in Rhinebeck as one of the best cinematic experiences around.

Over the last two decades, this small school has carved out a significant niche for itself in higher education, mainly due to the iconoclastic vision of its president, Leon Botstein (known to everyone simply as Leon) who, when not running the college, can often be found conducting the London Symphony.

Students at Bard have the unique opportunity to decide what they want to learn and how they want to learn it and the ways to use that information after college. The environment is warm and students have a great deal of freedom to mold their educations. "Bard is special because of the open-minded atmosphere," says one sophomore, who adds slyly, "You can get away with anything. But in a good way."

In terms of dress code, according to one student, "There are those who wear Izods and flannel nighties, those with nose clips and purple hair. You see everything from Arab robes to three-piece suits."

Overlaps
NYU, Vassar, Oberlin, Reed, Wesleyan

Barnard College

3009 Broadway, New York, NY 10027-6598

With applications running double what they were ten years ago, Barnard has eclipsed Wellesley as the nation's most popular women's college. Barnard women are a little more artsy and a little more city-ish than their female counterparts at Columbia College. Step outside and you're on Broadway.

Website: www.barnard.edu
Location: Urban
Total Enrollment: 2,261
Undergraduates: 2,261
Male/Female: 0/100
SAT Ranges: V 630–710
  M 620–700
ACT Range: 26–30
Financial Aid: 55%
Expense: Pr $ $ $ $
Phi Beta Kappa: Yes
Applicants: 4,074
Accepted: 33%
Enrolled: 40%
Grad in 6 Years: 85%
Returning Freshmen: 93%
Academics: 🖉 🖉 🖉 🖉 🖉
Social: ☎ ☎ ☎
Q of L: ★ ★ ★
Admissions: (212) 854-2014
Email Address:
  admissions@barnard.edu

Strongest Programs:
  English
  Psychology
  Political Science
  Economics
  History
  Art History
  Sociology

Among the din of taxi cabs and sidewalk crowds of New York City is Barnard College, a small women's school dedicated to endowing its students with a firm liberal arts education. Intellectual breadth and a sense of women's contributions and experiences are emphasized, while course-sharing with Columbia University allows Barnard students to enjoy a wide span of academic settings that create an intense, personalized education. The student body is an eclectic mix of women, but all have a few traits in common: they're independent, opinionated, and have a yen for city life.

The tiny campus, dwarfed by its Manhattan surroundings, consists of architecturally diverse buildings that are notably more modern than Columbia's. Although Barnard is situated in one of the most cosmopolitan cities in the world, lawns, trees, and other greenery abound on the campus itself. Springtime sunbathers on the lawn can look through a lovely brass fence onto Broadway and, across the street, Columbia. First-year students share an orientation program with Columbia, where they are mixed together, put into small groups, and led around campus and the city. Students can also enjoy COOP, a preorientation backpacking expedition.

Barnard offers the intimate attention of a small, independent women's college and the resources of a major research university. English, psychology, political science, economics, history, and the cut-throat premed program are particularly strong subjects. While the courseload is challenging and rigorous, a political science major says it is a "caring and accessible environment." The experimentally oriented psychology department is excellent, and the women's studies program also ranks high, although majors in this field must have a concentration in another department as well. Barnard students must trek across the street if they want to major in computer science, though the school has upgraded several classrooms into state-of-the-art teaching facilities with multimedia capabilities. The school also has made major improvements to the animal research facilities and new greenhouse. In most subject areas, Columbia's departments have more offerings, and with cross-registration Barnard students can take full advantage of them. Many students cite the low faculty-student ratio and preponderance of classes taught by full professors as one of the more appealing aspects of the school. "You get the support of a small school with the benefits of a major Ivy League institution," a senior says.

Barnard also offers several interdisciplinary majors unique within the university, including a new program in Jewish studies, as well as medieval and Renaissance studies and urban affairs. An arts program offers women the chance to concentrate on their particular specialty—dance, music, theater, visual arts, or writing—while completing a program in liberal arts. Thanks to a reciprocal agreement between the schools, music students can also take classes at Juilliard and the Manhattan School of Music.

The school's curriculum requirements are designed to reflect the changing nature of our technological society and the fact that more and more of its graduates are going into law, business, and other professions rather than academic careers. The curriculum includes a traditional freshman writing course and a freshman seminar taught by a senior faculty member on some broad theme like "the modern idea of freedom" or "the rise of possessive individualism." Other requirements include courses in areas such as Reason and Value, Cultures in Comparison, Quantitative and Deductive Reasoning, and Literature. While these requirements guarantee Barnard grads intellectual breadth, the mandatory senior thesis project or comprehensive examination ensures them of academic depth. To add to their academic career, Barnard's students can take graduate courses throughout the university and sign up for a variety of dual-degree programs. A joint-degree program with the Jewish Theological Seminary is also available.

The Senior Scholars program enables academically advanced students to substitute a single extensive research project for a semester or year of classes, and ten especially able students of any class are awarded stipends of $2,500 to be spent on an independent project under the Centennial Scholars program. While Barnard's 195,000-volume library accommodates both "lookers and gabbers" and the more studious, the many gaps in the collection are easily filled by the Columbia University library system's whopping six million volumes.

Barnard professors enjoy the proximity of a research institution almost as much as undergraduates do, and each year one-third of the full-time faculty teaches in the graduate departments throughout the university. But students, not research, are given top priority by faculty members. "Professors really make an effort to get to know students and help them excel in or even find their interests," an upperclasswoman says. First-year students can have access to top professors, and upper-level seminars guarantee intimate access once you're seriously into a subject. Students call the career-counseling services "one of the best parts of the academic program."

"You get the support of a small school with the benefits of a major Ivy League institution."

Ninety-seven percent of Barnard students are from the top quarter of their high-school class. Asian-Americans make up 21 percent of the student body, while African-Americans and Hispanics make up another 11 percent. Thirty-five percent are natives of New York, and there are plenty of wealthy East-Siders. A hefty 44 percent went to private schools. As would be expected at a women's school, feminism looms large on campus, but it doesn't take over. Other big issues include socially responsible investing, human rights, the Middle East conflict, and the unionization of teaching assistants. Barnard is also one of the most politically liberal colleges in the nation, and students are seldom shy to rally and protest. The annual Take Back the Night rally, for example, draws thousands of women.

Barnard now competes head to head with Columbia in admissions. A large percentage of the women who are accepted decide to enroll, which shows that Barnard is still the first choice of many students, though the cross-street rivalry doesn't appear to be dying down any time soon. In general, women looking for a more traditional college experience should head for Columbia, while those seeking a more "go your own way" atmosphere might do better at Barnard.

Barnard's housing has come a long way since the college was primarily a commuter school, and with New York's notorious rent prices, demand for on-campus housing remains high. Eighty-eight percent of all Barnard students live on campus, though the housing is reported as "no frills." "It's a great deal compared with finding

Thanks to a reciprocal agreement between the schools, music students can also take classes at Juilliard and the Manhattan School of Music.

Requirements include courses in Reason and Value, Cultures in Comparison, Quantitative and Deductive Reasoning, and Literature.

an apartment on your own," reports an economics major. The college guarantees housing. In addition to the eighteen-story Barnard dormitory tower, the college has one dorm complex and five off-campus apartment buildings. Two coed dorms are shared with Columbia, though as Columbia women increase in number, there is less and less space. Barnard has dedicated a great deal of resources to upgrading heat and air-conditioning systems, elevators, and windows in the residence halls. Lest anyone attempt to exist on a diet of coffee, de Beauvoir, and Derrida, students who reside in Barnard's on-campus dorms must buy a full meal plan, and the meal cards can be used at Columbia's John Jay cafeteria. Though in the city, Barnard students say they generally feel safe on campus, and many take advantage of the campus security van that will tote them from dorm to dorm at night if they feel unsafe.

While Barnard has had difficulty in the past trying to keep its students on campus on the weekends, this is certainly not a problem anymore, even with the best of New York nightlife right outside the school's gates. "Social life takes place both on and around campus and all over New York City," says an economics major. One senior laughs, "Barnard doesn't have a whole lot of traditions that made it past the tumultuous '60s and '70s," so the newly revived Greek games are extra popular with both students and locals.

> "Social life takes place both on and around campus and all over New York City."

Midnight Breakfast takes place the night before finals begin—the deans and administrators serve up breakfast in the gym. Certainly Barnard students have much to choose from; on any given night there are movies, lectures, and readings by female poets. Women in the arts are celebrated in the annual Winterfest. You don't need a car in New York City—the extensive public transportation system (including your own two feet) will take you shopping in SoHo, museum-hopping in midtown, and star-gazing on Broadway.

Female athletes from both sides of Broadway compete on joint teams. The fencing team is strong, as are archery and basketball. Other strong teams include tennis, volleyball, and cross-country. Barnard women are welcome to take advantage of Columbia's marvelous gym and the numerous coed intramurals. Spectator sports evoke little interest.

Barnard won't provide raucous frat-boy-infested beer bashes. There are too many other things to do in New York City, from seeking out sleek clubs to relishing the renowned museums and slice of every culture the world has to offer. The independent, open-minded women of Barnard know how to have fun and take advantage of a small liberal arts school and its Ivy League partner. As an environmental science major says, it's a place where "students can make things happen."

Overlaps

NYU, Columbia University, Wellesley, Cornell, UC-Berkeley

If You Apply To ➤ **Barnard:** Early decision: Nov. 15. Regular admissions: Jan. 1. Financial aid: Feb. 1. Guarantees to meet demonstrated need. Campus interviews: recommended, evaluative. Alumni interviews: optional, evaluative. ACTs or SATs and SAT IIs: required (writing or literature and two others). Accepts the Common Application. Essay question: describe an experience that shaped you; a person who influenced you; an idea that matters to you.

Bates College

23 Campus Avenue, Lewiston, ME 04240

Bowdoin got rid of its frats, Bates never had them, and therein hangs a tale. With its long-held tradition of egalitarianism, Bates is a kindred spirit to Quaker institutions such as Haverford and Swarthmore. A month-long spring term helps make Bates a leader in study abroad.

Bates College has a long history of taking risks to provide a haven for those seeking guidance and knowledge. Founded by abolitionists in 1855, this small school offers a wealth of programs at home and abroad that provide students with a well-rounded liberal arts education. Selective and unconventional, Bates attracts many of the nation's brightest minds.

The Bates campus features an intriguing mix of Georgian and Federal buildings and Victorian homes, all spread out over grassy lawns. The campus seems to be an oasis in the New England industrial city of Lewiston. Situated near Boston (about two and a half hours) and Maine's picturesque coast, Lewiston

"Even my calculus teacher made class entertaining."

is an old mill town that provides plenty of internships and part-time jobs, a distinct vocational advantage not always found at such small colleges. "Almost all second-through sixth-graders at a nearby elementary school have mentors from Bates," one freshman notes.

True to its ancestry, this very selective school remains open-minded academically as well. SAT scores are not required of applicants, and a unique 4–4–1 calendar saves some of the most interesting, unconventional learning experiences for the end of the school year. But don't think Bates is home to the easy A. "Courses are very rigorous," a sophomore says. "Once you start getting to upper-level classes, be ready to hit the books." Professors make the hard stuff fun. "Even my calculus teacher made class entertaining," one student raves.

Bates features a traditional liberal arts curriculum that is as strong as the pressure to achieve within it. Students cite chemistry, biology, physics, and geology as solid in the sciences, and English, history, psychology, and economics as standouts on the humanities side. Weaker departments include art and theater. The philosophy program appears to be rising steadily as student interest in such courses as Contemporary Moral Disputes climbs. The music and art departments benefit from the Olin Arts Center, which houses a performance hall, gallery, recording studio, art studios, and practice rooms. Bates also boasts a rhetoric program and a national-level debate team that is great for prelaw students. These academic offerings are enhanced by a challenging independent studies program, the junior year abroad for top scholars, and the Washington Semester.*

A fall semester study abroad program is open to first-year students (in fact, preference is given

"It feels like Bates got all the rich, smart, and popular kids from high school."

to new students) and includes home stays with families and tours throughout the country. Fall semester programs have included study in France, Ecuador, and Japan.

The 4–4–1 calendar at Bates is also conducive to studies abroad at the end of the college year, and trips to China, India, or South America are there for the taking. While the spring short-term courses may be more relaxed, students nonetheless find them worthwhile. After all, what could be more valuable than the ever-popular Philosophy of Star Trek? Or how about Cult and the Community, which led two students to a five-week tour with the Grateful Dead? One student cites an Arts and

Artists course, which took him to several major U.S. cities, as having greatly influenced his view of the art world. While only two short-term courses are required for graduation, many students take more. In addition, students have access to the ten-college Venture Program* and the American Maritime Studies Program at Mystic Seaport*—two unusual and attractive options for students seeking real-world experience. Students also benefit from the Ladd Library, with more than five hundred thousand volumes, an all-night study room, a typing room, and "an audio room with everything from Bach to Bruce Springsteen."

Eighty-three percent of the students come from outside Maine, many from Massachusetts, Connecticut, and New York. Many students decry the lack of diversity on campus—it's 84 percent Caucasian—but administrators are working hard to change that. "It feels like Bates got all the rich, smart, and popular kids from high school," a freshman says. True to form for this crunchy locale, environmental issues are hot at Bates. Students also are involved in fighting for equal rights for women, homosexuals, and marginalized groups in society. The college guarantees to meet the demonstrated need of almost all students, but no athletic or merit scholarships are awarded.

All but 10 percent of the student popular reside on campus, and they are spread out among student centers, upperclass dorms, and charming old Victorian houses. Maid service once a week makes living in Bates housing an even more pleasant experience. Housing space has been tight, but is guaranteed. There is a lottery. Smith, once an all-freshmen dorm, is reportedly

> **"Bates has a strong sense of community, and students here look out for one another socially and academically."**

loud and lots of fun. Upperclassmen who want singles will probably have to settle for the single-sex dorms or houses. All boarders eat in the Commons, where they enjoy near-restaurant-quality food. A few adventurous or penurious souls take to cheaper off-campus living as one way to beat the increasing cost of education.

Most students don't stray far from campus to find their weekend hangouts because there's simply not much to do in Lewiston. Campus parties are hardly dry affairs, considering the college isn't draconian in its policies. "As long as the party isn't too loud or destructive, they won't bother to break it up," a freshman says. Getting served at local bars isn't an impossible feat, but drinking on campus can seem that way. "College policies are strict regarding campus-wide events," a sophomore says, "but dorm parties still rock." Other social activities at Bates are far more wholesome. There's the annual Winter Carnival, with ice skating, snow sculpting, and a semiformal dance. And there's the Puddle Jump on St. Patrick's Day, when "students of Irish descent and all those who want to be Irish for the day cut a hole in the ice on Lake Andrews and jump in," a student explains. Leaving Lewiston can be a relief, especially when the driveable destinations include Portland, Boston (and Fenway Park), and Montreal. Skiing is a common passion, and excellent slopes, including Sugar Loaf, are just more than an hour away.

Most students stick around when their varsity teams—especially basketball, football, and lacrosse—are playing, despite their unexceptional records. The Bates teams that do excel are the women's volleyball, the men's and women's ski, the men's and women's lacrosse, and the men's and women's cross-country. As for rivalries, Colby or Bowdoin fans should tread lightly at Bates. The intramural program, organized by the students and supervised by faculty members, is "strong and spirited," complete with lively dorm rivalries.

So it's cold up there, and Lewiston isn't exactly hopping with activity. But Batesies are a dedicated bunch: dedicated to taking advantage of enthusiastic professors, camaraderie, and the gorgeous scenery of New England. "Bates has a strong sense of community, and students here look out for one another socially and academically," says a political science major. One freshman is sold. "It's a fun place," the student says. "People just seem happy here."

If You Apply To ➢	**Bates:** Early decision: Nov. 15, Jan. 1. Regular admissions and financial aid: Jan. 15. Guarantees to meet demonstrated need. Campus and alumni interviews: recommended, evaluative. SATs and ACTs: optional. SAT IIs: optional. Accepts the Common Application and electronic applications. Essay question: Why Bates? Encourages applicants to send additional material.

Baylor University

Waco, TX 76798

Come to Baylor and Mom can rest easy. Baylor is Southern Baptist, which means less of the debauchery that is prevalent at most schools. Dad will like it, too: Baylor happens to be one of the least expensive private universities in the country. The football team is still praying to beat UT.

Baylor University's Baptist heritage remains an anchor of campus life, but students and faculty at this Texas institution are also looking forward, aiming to become one of America's elite universities. The school's 2012 Vision plan includes twelve strategic imperatives, such as lowering the student-teacher ratio, and building 1,600 new residence-hall beds to house half of the student body on campus within a decade. One thing that won't change is the sense of community that students say makes the school a special place. "Baylor offers students a unique opportunity to grow academically, socially, physically, and most of all spiritually, thereby developing the whole person," says a history and environmental studies major.

The 432-acre Baylor campus, nicknamed Jerusalem on the Brazos, abuts the historic Brazos River near downtown Waco, Texas (population: 110,000). The architectural style emphasizes the gracious tradition of the Old South, and the central part of campus, the quadrangle, was built when Baylor moved from Independence, Texas, in 1886. Recent new additions include an NCAA-regulation baseball and softball complex along with tennis courts and related facilities. Baylor's campus is smack-dab in the middle of Texas, midway between Dallas and Austin, about one hundred miles from each.

> **"Baylor offers students a unique opportunity to grow academically, socially, physically, and most of all spiritually."**

Waffling on what to study? Not to worry. Except for those in the school of music, all freshmen enter the college of arts and sciences, where they complete the Baylor Interdisciplinary Core, with "interlinking basic courses that share themes," explains an education major. After the core, students pursue their majors—in arts and sciences or one of Baylor's five other schools: business, education, engineering and computer sciences, music, and nursing. All students also take two religion courses and two semesters of Chapel Forum, a series of lectures and meetings on various issues or Christian testimonies. In the fall of 2002, the Honors College began to oversee the Honors Program (which offers opportunities for course integration and independent research), the University Scholars Program (which waives most distribution requirements), the Core, and the new Great Texts of the Western Tradition program. Students may major or minor in Great Texts, an interdisciplinary program exploring "the richness and diversity of the Western intellectual heritage."

Website: www.baylor.edu
Location: Center city
Total Enrollment: 14,221
Undergraduates: 12,190
Male/Female: 44/56
SAT Ranges: V 530–630
  M 540–650
ACT Range: 22–27
Financial Aid: N/A
Expense: Pr $
Phi Beta Kappa: Yes
Applicants: 7,986
Accepted: 79%
Enrolled: 44%
Grad in 6 Years: 71%
Returning Freshmen: 85%
Academics: ✍ ✍ ✍
Social: ☎ ☎ ☎
Q of L: ★ ★ ★
Admissions: (254) 710-3435
Email Address: Admission_ Serv_Office@baylor.edu

Strongest Programs:
Premed
Communications/Speech
  Pathology
Education
Accounting
Biology
Psychology

Biology is Baylor's most popular major, followed by psychology, teacher education, journalism, and forensic science (the school has the only such program in Texas). The business school's programs in accounting, professional selling (one of only two worldwide), and entrepreneurship also draw praise. More unusual options include church-state studies and museum studies, and institutes focusing on environmental studies and childhood learning disorders. The archeology and geology departments benefit from fossil- and mineral-rich Texas prairies. An increasing number of Baylor students are traveling on study-abroad programs, which send them to England, Mexico, Costa Rica, Brazil, and many other countries. A European studies semester in the Netherlands is especially popular.

One of Baylor's greatest strengths is the sense of campus community, fostered by the emphasis on Christianity and by the administration's efforts to focus faculty members on teaching, rather than on research and other activities outside the classroom, students say. Baylor also strives to keep classes small—students say most have fifty or fewer enrolled—which can make it difficult to fulfill requirements on time. "Many people don't graduate in four years without summer school," says a sophomore. The level of rigor varies with the course, a classmate adds: "The basic classes are laid-back. The major classes are more in-depth and difficult." Professors teach most courses, but not all instructors are of equal quality, cautions a speech communication major: "Finally, in my fourth semester here, do I have those great teachers you always hear about."

Baylor students are largely middle- to upper-middle-class Christians. Eighty-one percent are Texans, and most "are more conservative than the rival institutions around our area," says a Spanish major. "It is a bit conformist," agrees another student. "Here, 'different' isn't always so cool."

"The basic classes are laid-back. The major classes are more in-depth and difficult."

Minorities total nearly one-fifth of the student body, with Hispanics the largest group at 7 percent, Asian-Americans at 6 percent, and African-Americans at 5 percent. Important issues include environmentalism and animal rights, says one student, adding that "many oppose" a new club formed by homosexual students.

As might be expected on a conservative and religious campus like Baylor's, dorms are single-sex and have restrictive visitation privileges, which can be frustrating. The "very comfortable and well-kept" halls have lounges, computer labs, and gyms, and house 30 percent of the student body—mainly freshmen, says a sophomore. Upperclassmen look off campus for cheaper housing with private rooms and fewer rules, says a junior. Those who've moved out of the dorms appreciate the presence of twenty fully commissioned police officers patrolling the area on bikes and in patrol cars. "Waco is not a safe town, but I feel safe on campus," says a speech communication major.

Fifteen percent of Baylor's men and 17 percent of the women belong to a fraternity or sorority, providing a party scene for those who want it, and community-service outlets for those who don't participate in the school-sponsored Steppin' Out service days that occur once a semester. Easy road trips include Dallas, Austin, San Antonio, Bryan/College Station, and beaches at Galveston, South Padre Island, and Corpus Christi. Most destinations are within two-and-one-half hours' drive, students say, making a set of wheels a big help, if not a necessity. "Waco gets boring," laments a sophomore. "Some weekends there is nothing to do but go out to eat." Alcohol isn't served on campus or at campus-sponsored events, "but you can find it off campus," says a senior. "Baylor strictly looks down on alcohol consumption," adds a junior. But "if you desire to drink, it is not hard to get."

Highlights of Baylor's social calendar include the annual Halloween Monster Bash (complete with a scary ghost story told by the university president), and the

Dia del Oso (Day of the Bear), when classes are cancelled for a day in April in favor of a campus-wide carnival. The Fiesta on the River, organized by the Residence Hall Association, lets student-run organizations set up booths to raise funds for the causes they support. The school also has the largest collegiate homecoming parade in the nation.

When it comes to football, remember: you're in Texas. Freshmen wear team jerseys to games and take the field before the players, then sit together as a pack. "It's a very awesome part of the freshman experience," one student says. The men's tennis and golf teams recently captured Big 12 titles, while women's track and field also draws fans. For weekend warriors, the McLane Student Life Center offers the tallest rock-climbing wall in Texas. The university maintains a small marina for swimming and paddle boating, and several lakes with good beaches are nearby. Generally, though, religious groups are more popular than the intramural sports program, with chapters of Campus Crusade for Christ and the Fellowship of Christian Athletes very much alive and well.

For all its emphasis on conservative, traditional Christianity, Baylor also recognizes that it must remain open to new ways of thinking to achieve its goal of becoming a top-tier university by 2012. Not long ago, Baylor's president took a step in that direction by giving his wife a whirl in public, signaling an end to the school's unwritten but long-standing ban on dancing. Students and alumni alike recognize that while traditional moral values have a place here, and no doubt always will, there's no other constant except change—in Baylor's case, for the better.

Overlaps

University of Texas, Texas A&M, Texas Tech, Rice, Texas Christian

If You Apply To >
Baylor: Rolling admissions. Does not guarantee to meet demonstrated need. SATs or ACTs: required. Campus and alumni interviews: optional. Accepts electronic applications. Essay question: How your value system would help you succeed as a Baylor student and throughout your lifetime. Looks for students who want a "Christian education with academic excellence."

Beloit College

700 College Street, Beloit, WI 53511

Tiny Midwestern college known for free-thinking students and international focus. Has steered back toward the mainstream after its heyday as an alternative school in the '60s and '70s. Wisconsin location makes Beloit easier to get into than similar schools in sexier places.

Beloit College, that bastion of '60s and '70s liberalism tucked away in unlikely Wisconsin, is moving back toward the mainstream by increasing the size of its student body and boosting academic rigor. The school encourages study abroad and immersion in other cultures and languages to foster tolerance and understanding; just one in five undergraduates comes from in state. "It seems like everyone goes somewhere, and this adds a great dynamic to the campus," says a sophomore.

Beloit's forty-acre campus is a northeastern-style oasis an hour's drive from Madison and Milwaukee. Academic and administrative buildings sit on one side of campus, with residence halls on the other. Two architectural themes dominate, says one student: "1850s Colonial and obtuse 1930s buildings." In 2001, the college's Turtle Creek Bookstore opened in downtown Beloit, three blocks from campus. A cozy coffee bar and a patio for relaxing, reading, or studying augment the typical

Website: www.beloit.edu
Location: Small city
Total Enrollment: 1,273
Undergraduates: 1,273
Male/Female: 41/59
SAT Ranges: V 580–690
M 540–650
ACT Range: 24–29
Financial Aid: 74%
Expense: Pr $ $
Phi Beta Kappa: Yes

(Continued)

Applicants: 1,529
Accepted: 66%
Enrolled: 32%
Grad in 6 Years: 69%
Returning Freshmen: 93%
Academics: ✍ ✍ ✍
Social: ☎ ☎ ☎
Q of L: ★ ★ ★ ★
Admissions: (800) 356-0751
Email Address:
    invent@beloit.edu

Strongest Programs:
    Anthropology
    Biology
    Chemistry
    Economics
    English
    Geology
    Psychology
    Theatre Arts

Among more unusual
options are the Museum
Studies minor and the
Rhetoric and Discourse
major, which asks students
to reflect on current
nonfiction writing while
producing their own prose.

stacks of textbooks. A new dorm opened in the fall of 2002, offering apartment-style living for forty-eight seniors.

All Beloit freshmen complete a First Year Initiative seminar, led by a faculty member who becomes their advisor until the major declaration the following year. Past FYI topics include "Russian-American Relations in a Post-Communist World" and "Colonizing Mars: Science Fact and Fiction." Beloit's Sophomore Year Program extends FYI with a retreat, Exploration Week, and the charting of a Comprehensive Academic Plan for the final two years, which often includes internships, research, and off-campus study. Eighty percent of the student body conducts some type of independent project, and the annual Student Symposium lets them present findings in a campus-wide forum.

All students must also complete three writing courses, at least two units in each of three subject areas (natural science and math, social sciences, and arts and humanities), and a unit of interdisciplinary studies, such as "Campus Protest in the '60s." Students are likewise required to complete at least two units involving a different culture or language. The academic climate is challenging but not cutthroat. "We'll lend a student notes if he was sick, and we often form informal study groups before exams," says a freshman. "This does not mean we are lazy," adds a classmate. "Kids party hard when they have time, but often Friday nights are first spent in the library."

> **"Kids party hard when they have time, but often Friday nights are first spent in the library."**

As might be expected at a small college, teaching is the faculty's first priority, and the vast majority of classes have twenty-five or fewer students. "I know all my professors by their first names, and have even had dinner over at their houses," brags a political science major. Anthropology is the most popular major, followed by English language and literature, biology, economics, and psychology, which students say are among Beloit's best departments. Among more unusual options are the Museum Studies minor and the Rhetoric and Discourse major, which asks students to reflect on current nonfiction writing while producing their own prose. Physics is Beloit's one weak spot, students and administrators say; education majors should be prepared to spend an extra semester on campus because of complexities related to certification.

Students need not worry about a lack of options for satisfying Beloit's experiential learning and global diversity requirements. The college's Venture Grants program offers $500 to $1,500 for "entrepreneurial, self-testing activities" that benefit the community; one recent awardee traveled to the Dominican Republic to learn traditional dances, and another started an information-technology consulting business. For those who tire of small-town life, an exchange program sends five Beloit students and a faculty member to China's Fudan University, and brings their counterparts to Beloit. Other options include student teaching in Britain or Australia and studying marine biology at the University of the French Pacific in Tahiti. Half of Beloit's students study abroad through the college's World Affairs Center, where destinations include African and South American nations. The Center for Language Studies complements Beloit's own foreign-language programs with intensive summer study in Chinese, Japanese, Russian, Hungarian, and English as a second language. Beloit is also a member of the Associated Colleges of the Midwest* consortium, increasing students' choices.

> **"People for the most part are pretty accepting of each other."**

Beloit's alternative programs and educational strengths attract an independent and diverse student body, including 10 percent from outside the United States. African-Americans, Hispanics, and Asian-Americans each comprise 4 percent of the total. Students get riled up about women's issues—"to shave or not to shave is the final question," quips a sophomore—as well as the environment, domestic violence, homosexuality, and world peace. "People for the most part are pretty accepting of each other," says a political science major. "Just don't wear any glaringly large brand-name clothing."

Ninety-three percent of Beloit students live on campus, where the rooms get high marks but the food leaves much to be desired. Chapin, Aldrich, Haven, and Wood are the best residence halls, according to one freshman; Haven, Wood, and 815 boast new carpeting, furniture, and central air-conditioning and heat. Four fraternities attract 15 percent of the men, and two sororities draw 5 percent of the women; members may live in their chapter houses. Specialty houses are also organized around themes like foreign languages, music, or the outdoors.

Movies, dances, and parties at the frats and special-interest houses tie up many Friday and Saturday nights here, and some students lament the "Beloit Bubble" that results from the campus-focused social life. Two all-campus festivals liven up the calendar: the Folk and Blues Fall Music Festival brings jazz,

> "There are organizations on campus that are working to help the college and community interact more."

Half of Beloit's students study abroad through the college's World Affairs Center, where destinations include African and South American nations.

reggae, folk, and blues bands to campus, while on Spring Day, classes are canceled in favor of concerts, and everyone kicks back to enjoy the (finally!) warmer weather. The school's alcohol policy is lax, students say. "You can't be served in town, but you can always find an older student to buy for you," explains a freshman. "You will never get in trouble for drinking unless you are really dumb and really hurt yourself or others."

Having wheels here will definitely raise your social standing, as they make it easier to take off for Chicago or the college town of Madison, also easily reached through a cheap local bus service. It's no wonder students want to get away, says a political science major: "Beloit is rather lacking in every aspect." That said, the town has basic necessities, such as a few bars (check out the excellent burgers at Hanson's Pub, says a junior), a bowling alley, a movie theater, and a Wal-Mart. "There are organizations on campus that are working to help the college and community interact more," says an economics and management major.

Sports at Beloit are played more for fun than glory. Among the school's Division III squads, standouts include women's track, volleyball, soccer, and swimming, and men's baseball, football, track, and soccer, especially against rival Ripon College. Intramural Ultimate Frisbee had more than two hundred participants on fifteen teams last year, says a geology and art major.

Beloit is a bundle of contradictions: a small liberal arts college in the heart of Big Ten state university country, where the academic program has an East Coast rigor but the lack of competition between students reflects the free-and-easy spirit of the Midwest.

Beloit is a bundle of contradictions: a small liberal-arts college in the heart of Big Ten state university country, where the academic program has an East Coast rigor but the lack of competition between students reflects the free-and-easy spirit of the Midwest. The school tends to draw students seeking their own path, motivated to learn from each other and from their professors. "Beloit students want to be here," says one. "There are less eccentric kids now, which is really too bad, because that's why I came. It is still a haven for different thinking, though."

Overlaps
Oberlin, Macalester, Grinnell, Lawrence, Knox.

If You Apply To ➤ | **Beloit:** Early action: Nov. 15, Dec. 15. Rolling admissions: Feb. 1. Financial aid: Mar. 1. Housing: May 1. Guarantees to meet demonstrated need. Campus interviews: recommended, informational. Alumni interviews: optional, informational. SATs or ACTs: required. SAT IIs: optional. Accepts the Common Application and electronic applications. Essay question: How you heard about Beloit, factors that have led you to apply, and topic of your choice.

Bennington College

Bennington, VT 05201

Known for top-notch performing arts and lavish attention to every student. Arts programs rely heavily on part-time faculty who are practitioners in their field. Less competitive than Bard and Sarah Lawrence, comparable to Hampshire. Enrollment is robust after a dip in the '90s.

Website:
www.bennington.edu
Location: Rural
Total Enrollment: 730
Undergraduates: 588
Male/Female: 31/69
SAT Ranges: V 560–680
M 510–640
Financial Aid: 61%
Expense: Pr $ $ $ $
Phi Beta Kappa: No
Applicants: 719
Accepted: 65%
Enrolled: 25%
Grad in 6 Years: 82%
Returning Freshmen: 79%
Academics: ✍ ✍ ✍
Social: ☎ ☎ ☎
Q of L: ★ ★ ★ ★
Admissions: (800) 833-6845
Email Address: admissions@
bennington.edu

Strongest Programs:
Literature
Writing
Music
Dance
Architecture
Sciences

The first principle of life at Bennington College is learning by practice—that's about the only thing that hasn't been tweaked or adjusted since the school began in 1932. Faculty members teach in their own disciplines, and in groups linking scholars, artists, and scientists with similar interests. As the first school in the nation to grant the arts equal status with other disciplines, Bennington offers a novel, participatory, and hands-on learning approach. "It's vibrant; it's a place to be totally immersed in discovery and pursuing your passions," says a senior. "It's a place for someone who doesn't want his or her choices made by default." And besides, there's a treehouse—and milk and cookies served at every meal. Who says going to college means growing up?

Bennington sits on 550 acres at the foot of Vermont's Green Mountains. The campus was once an active dairy farm, and a converted barn houses the main classroom and administrative spaces. But don't let the quaint, New England setting fool you. The Dickinson Science Building offers high-tech equipment for intensive study of chemistry, biology, environmental science, and genetics. It's

"It's vibrant; it's a place to be totally immersed in discovery and pursuing your passions."

also home to a media lab dedicated to the learning of foreign languages, including Chinese, French, German, Italian, Japanese, Russian, and Spanish. At the Community Farm, students work with full-time farmers to cultivate ninety varieties of vegetables and conduct intensive agro-ecological studies. Recent campus additions include three new student houses, which were featured in the February 2002 issue of *Architectural Record* magazine.

Owing to its focus on experiential learning, Bennington's academic structure is far different from that of a typical college or university. Each student designs a major, and, rather than grades, all students—except premed and prevet—get written comments from instructors twice a term. There are few academic requirements, aside from the mandate to complete a seven-week internship each January and February, in a field related to academic or career interests, in a location of the student's choice. Professors will know your name and probably more, since each advises fewer than a dozen students, with whom he or she must meet weekly. "I work in the ecology department with a great professor, and also roof his house on the weekends, or have breakfast with his family," says a writing major. Even without grades, students push themselves to learn, grow, and achieve, says an architecture major: "Academic rigor operates off of personal challenge, not structured fear."

Absent academic departments, the Core Faculty works together to provide students with a well-rounded academic foundation. Since the school's size limits standard course offerings, more than 175 tutorials fill in the gaps. The most popular area of study is visual and performing arts, followed closely by multidisciplinary or interdisciplinary studies, including such unlikely combinations as biology and set design. Another popular program, English language and literature, now focuses on creative writing supervised by working poets, novelists, short-story writers, essayists, and playwrights, rather than critical analysis of existing work.

Bennington's "fluid and free-form" climate appeals to certain types of students, mostly liberal and typically those who "stumped high-school teachers," says a junior. "Smarter and more stimulating than the grade-grubbers, we were the kids that teachers lent their personal books to." Just five percent are from Vermont; nearly 12 percent hail from abroad. Together, African-Americans, Hispanics, and Asian-Americans account for 5 percent of the student body. "Activism is becoming more and more common," enthuses a senior. The Student Action Network sponsors political events and protests on and off campus, centered on issues such as pacifism, globalization, and workers' rights.

Since Bennington lacks traditional departments, requirements, and even tenure for professors, it's probably not a surprise that the school also lacks dorms. Most students live in one of the college's eighteen coed houses; fifteen are white New England

There are few academic requirements, aside from the mandate to complete a seven-week internship each January and February, in a field related to academic or career interests, in a location of the student's choice.

"Academic rigor operates off of personal challenge, not structured fear."

clapboard, and three are more modern. Each house holds twenty-five to thirty people, with an elected chairperson to govern house affairs. "There's little trouble finding a house that suits your personality and habits," says a sophomore. The houses boast "comfortable, spacious rooms, nice windows, and actual architecture rather than cinder-block cells," says a senior. Most houses also have common rooms with working fireplaces; the college sees to it that cords of wood are delivered to keep them running. Freshmen and sophomores share rooms—those of the opposite sex may live together if both parties request it—and juniors and seniors are guaranteed singles. Those frustrated with college food service or their own cooking will find hearty, inexpensive meals at the nearby Blue Benn Diner.

Most houses also have common rooms with working fireplaces; the college sees to it that cords of wood are delivered to keep them running.

Although the vibe on Bennington's campus is liberal, sophisticated, and cosmopolitan, the neighboring town—four miles away—is far more conservative, typical of rural New England. "Town? What town?" quips a junior. "Oh, you mean the Wal-Mart and the Gas 'n' Guns store?" There isn't mush else in town aside from two movie theaters and a bowling alley, a sophomore says. Students are trying to mend the town-gown rift through volunteer work in local schools and homeless shelters, and with adopt-a-grandparent and Big Brother Big Sister programs. The social life centers on rehearsals, performances, films, and lectures. "There's always plenty to do and a

"There's little trouble finding a house that suits your personality and habits."

variety of 'scenes,'" adds a literature and social sciences major. "It does, however, become incestuous here at times. It's a good idea to take trips to Boston or NYC for a little anonymity every now and then." Road trips to Montreal, Albany (an hour away), and Burlington, Vermont, are also popular.

Given Bennington's rugged location, hiking, rock climbing, caving, camping, and canoeing—at least in the warmer months—keep students moving. In May, the annual Sunfest brings bands to campus for a day of outdoor concerts and a picnic lunch. During Parents' Weekend, Transvestite Night livens things up. Ski slopes beckon in the winter, when the college turns part of its huge Visual and Performing Arts complex into an indoor roller rink for the Rollerama party. "Imagine several hundred pairs of roller skates, a disco ball, at least half of the student body, and lots of '80s music," says a writing and literature major. "Lots of people wear costumes." Another tradition is the midnight breakfast during finals week. The blaring of fire-truck sirens tells weary students to head to the dining hall, where professors and the college president serve up French toast. Sports aren't a big focus, but the college does compete in an intramural coed soccer league composed of Northeastern colleges.

Bennington's emphasis on self-direction, field work, and personal relationships with professors sets it apart even from other liberal arts colleges of similar (small) size. Crossing disciplines is encouraged, and forget about taking the road less traveled;

Overlaps
Bard, Oberlin, Sarah Lawrence, Hampshire, Reed

each student here charts his or her own course. Perhaps that's because the school is less than a century old—young for a college, notes a sophomore: "It's been in a constant state of experimentation and reevaluation since it began, and I think this will continue."

Birmingham–Southern College

Box A18, Birmingham, AL 35254

One of the deep South's best liberal arts colleges. The vast majority of students come from Alabama and the surrounding states. At 1,407 students, B-S is roughly the same size as Rhodes (TN) and Millsaps (MS). Strong fraternity system and a throwback to the way college used to be.

Website: www.bsc.edu
Location: Urban
Total Enrollment: 1,407
Undergraduates: 1,316
Male/Female: 42/58
SAT Ranges: V 560–650
    M 530–640
ACT Range: 24–29
Financial Aid: 42%
Expense: Pr $ $
Phi Beta Kappa: Yes
Applicants: 1,007
Accepted: 92%
Enrolled: 39%
Grad in 6 Years: 74%
Returning Freshmen: 86%
Academics: ✍ ✍ ✍
Social: ☎ ☎ ☎
Q of L: ★ ★ ★
Admissions: (205) 226-4696
Email Address:
    admission@bsc.edu

Strongest Programs:
    Biology
    English
    Business
    Humanities

Birmingham-Southern College is a throwback to way college used to be. BSC stresses service, effectively preserving the school's image as a strong liberal arts institution with its own brand of community involvement and conservative values. More than half the student body participates in community service through Southern Volunteer Services, as well as claiming active membership in fraternities and sororities. Caring and attentive faculty add to a sense of commitment to both personal and community growth. Says a junior: "'Southern has this incredible atmosphere in which students meet great friends, delve into different areas of academics, become involved in the community, and feel proud of their school."

Known as the Hilltop because of its hilly environment, BSC is the result of the 1918 merger of two smaller colleges: Birmingham College and Southern University. The campus, a green and shady oasis in an urban neighborhood, contains a pleasing hodgepodge of traditional and modern architecture, all surrounded by a security fence that controls access and increases security. Recent additions include the $27 million Elton B. Stephens Science Center, which offers one hundred thousand square feet of learning space, as well as new dorms, and a renovated gymnasium and theatre.

The academic climate at BSC is described as rigorous by most. "Students can generally handle the workload," says a junior, "but must remain dedicated and diligent in their studies to succeed." Each student is assigned a faculty member who serves as his or her academic advisor from freshman convocation to graduation, an arrangement that students praise for its effectiveness. Equal praise goes out to faculty in the classrooms, where 80 percent of classes have fewer than twenty-five students. "The professors at Southern are very interested in the students and provide a very good learning environment," reports a political science major. Half of the students go on to professional or graduate school.

"Students can generally handle the workload, but must remain dedicated and diligent in their studies to succeed."

English is one of the school's strongest programs, and premeds cite the strong biology program as a major drawing card. The Stephens Science Laboratory gives this program, as well as the chemistry and physics departments, a further boost. About a quarter of the students major in business, a division that includes programs ranging from accounting to international issues. The art, drama, dance, and music programs are all among the best in the South. A recent group of students traveled to Florida to help conceptual artist Christo wrap an island, while back at 'Southern, students stage several major productions each year, often including American and world premieres.

All liberal arts majors must complete a general education program that includes courses in writing, mathematics, a foreign language, and seven different liberal arts areas. BSC, a member of the Associated Colleges of the South* consortium, also offers a wide variety of special programs. The January term allows students to explore new areas of study from cooking lessons to travel in China. In addition, this extensive program focuses on-campus energies into culturally diverse opportunities via project experiences, social activities, ethnic food fairs, and many other projects. The international studies program offers students the chance

"The rooms are not large, but more than adequate,"

to study abroad in several different countries, and the honors program allows twenty-five exceptional first-year students to take small seminars with one or more professors. The most recent curricular change was the addition of the Expanded Paradigm, an enhancement for the liberal arts program. This concept was awarded a $100,000 Hewlett Foundation grant to fund course expansions and development. America's Project is a cohesive, multidisciplinary program that examines the society, culture, and history of North, South, and Central America as a whole.

Seventy-five percent of the students are homegrown Alabamians, and practically all the rest hail from Deep South states, many with family ties to 'Southern. Though moderate by Alabama standards, the student body is quite conservative. Thirty-eight percent of the students belong to the Methodist Church, and the school chaplain heads the personal counseling program. Despite their geographic homogeneity, students of color do exist at BSC: 6 percent are African-American, 1 percent are Hispanic, and 3 percent are Asian-American. "Birmingham-Southern is a conservative Southern school," says a student. "There is not a great amount of mixing of ideas, but there is no obvious racism, homophobia, or anything of the sort." There is an honor code at BSC that students take very seriously. In addition to need-based awards, BSC offers various merit scholarships to 85 percent of students, with grants ranging from $1,000 to $28,000. National Merit Scholars who list 'Southern as their first choice receive an automatic scholarship of $500 to $2,000, and up to ten get full-tuition awards. Athletes compete for scholarships in fourteen sports.

Eighty-five percent of the students live on campus, including many of those whose families reside in Birmingham. Coed housing hasn't filtered down to 'Southern yet, so all seven dorms are single-sex, with a variety of visitation policies, depending on student preferences. North Hall and New Mens are generally the most desired men's residences, while Margaret Daniel is the preferred choice for women. "The rooms are not large,

"It's a small unique campus, where the strongest friendships grow."

but more than adequate," says a student. The school is working on building a new fraternity row with six houses. Campus security is quite visible and students praise its effectiveness in keeping the campus safe.

Fifty-four percent of the men and 60 percent of the women are members of Greek organizations, which means that much of the social activity at BSC revolves around the Greek system. "Fraternity row is always hoppin' for Greeks and independents," says one socializer. "We often have jazz and blues bands on Sunday afternoon on the Dorm Quad, and the SGA sponsors fall and spring concert weekends as well," a history major reports. As for alcohol, it's not allowed on the quad,

Students take advantage of what the city of Birmingham has to offer in the way of nightlife—cultural events, bars, and the rather bohemian (at least for Alabama) South Side.

The new $27 million Elton B. Stephens Science Center offers one hundred thousand square feet of learning space for BSC's plethora of science majors.

and elsewhere it must be in an opaque container, a policy most students find reasonable. The biggest social event of the year is Southern Comfort, a four-day festival that is "always a wild time," notes one satisfied customer. Another popular music celebration is E-Fest. When social opportunities on campus dry up, many students take advantage of the shuttle to Birmingham for the city's nightlife—cultural events, bars, and the rather bohemian (at least for Alabama) South Side. Road trips to Auburn, Nashville, and Atlanta are popular, and beaches and mountains are less than five hours away.

In a state where the late Bear Bryant of 'Bama is practically a saint, BSC is a school without a football team. Men's basketball partially fills the void, as does the baseball team, which at one point had twenty winning seasons in a row. The men's soccer team is also top-notch, and both the men's and women's tennis teams are of championship caliber. Beyond that, however, "women's sports are virtually nonexistent," one student complains. Intramurals are popular, though dominated by the Greeks.

BSC is proud of its close ties to the Deep South, and its ever-expanding academic challenges that keep students on their intellectual toes. In the meantime, the close relationships between faculty and students ensures that nobody at 'Southern is ever left out in the cold. "It's a small unique campus," says a freshman, "where the strongest friendships grow."

If You Apply To ➤   **'Southern:** Rolling admissions. Does not guarantee to meet demonstrated need. Campus interviews: recommended, evaluative. No alumni interviews. SATs or ACTs: required. SAT IIs: optional. Accepts the Common Application and electronic applications. Essay questions: topic of interest; two pages of autobiography; choose fictional characters from literature as TV guests.

Boston College

140 Commonwealth Avenue, Devlin Hall, Room 208, Chestnut Hill, MA 02167

Many of the students clamoring for a spot at Boston College are surprised to learn that it is affiliated with the Roman Catholic church. Set on a quiet hilltop at the end of a "T" (subway) line, BC's location is solid gold. A close second in the pecking order among true-blue Catholics.

Boston College is a study in contrasts. Academics are well respected, but so are the athletic teams. The environment is safely suburban, but barely twenty minutes from Boston, the hub of the collegiate Eastern seaboard. The Jesuit influence on the college, the largest Roman Catholic school in the country, really does provide a guiding spirit for campus life, but the social opportunities still seem endless. If you're looking for the best of all possible worlds, you just might find it here.

Don't let the name fool you. Boston College is actually a university with nine schools and colleges. It has two campuses: the main campus at Chestnut Hill and the Newton campus a mile and a half away. The dominant architecture of the main campus (known as "the Heights") is Gothic Revival, with modern additions over the past few years, including new dining-hall facilities and Fulton Hall for the Carroll School of Management. There's lots of grass and trees, not to mention a large, peaceful reservoir (perfect to jog around) right in the front yard.

The college's mission is to "educate skilled, knowledgeable, and responsible leaders within each new generation." To accomplish this goal, the Core Curriculum requires not only literature, science, history, philosophy, social science, and theology, but also writing, mathematics, the arts, and the study of other cultures, in addition to specific requirements set by each undergraduate school. "Core Curriculum forces you to take classes you might not want to take but end up enjoying," says a senior. Students in arts and sciences must also show proficiency in a modern foreign language or classical language before graduation. Freshmen are required to take a writing workshop, in which each student develops a portfolio of personal and academic writing and reads a wide range of texts. Seniors participate in the University Capstone program, a series of seminars aiming to give a "big-picture" perspective to the college experience.

The climate here is challenging. A senior says, "The courses are rigorous but intellectually stimulating." A junior adds, "In general, other students and all teachers are very supportive and motivated." Professors are described as "phenomenal" and "unbelievable." The Jesuits on BC's faculty (about sixty out of nine hundred) exert an influence out of proportion to their numbers. "The philosophy, theology, and ethics departments are the most important in setting the tone of the campus, because they keep the students encouraged to be open minded," says a freshman. Another student says, "Our teachers are dedicated to students and scholarly research, and they are easily accessible through regular office hours." Registration is made painless through a computerized system, and students report that getting required classes is "never much of a problem."

The schools of arts and sciences, management, nursing, and education award bachelor's degrees. In the College of Arts and Sciences—the largest undergraduate division—English, biology, and psychology are popular. Future Massachusetts politicians will benefit from the strong political science program. Outside the traditional classroom, at the Boston College Museum of Art in Devlin Hall, students find exhibitions, lectures, and gallery tours. The Music Guild sponsors professional concerts throughout the year, and music students emphasizing performance can take advantage of facilities equipped with Steinways and Yamahas. Theater majors find a home in the six hundred-seat E. Paul Robsham Theater Arts Center, which produces eight student-directed productions each year.

> "Core Curriculum forces you to take classes you might not want to take but end up enjoying."

Students searching for out-of-the-ordinary offerings will be happy at BC. The student-run PULSE program provides participants with the opportunity to fulfill their philosophy and theology requirements while engaging in social service fieldwork at any of about thirty-five Boston organizations. Perspectives, a four-part freshman program, attempts to illustrate how great thinkers from the past have made us who we are. There's also a Freshman-Year Experience program, which offers seminars and services to help students adjust to college life and take advantage of the school and the city. An honors program allows students to work at a more intensive pace and requires a senior thesis.

Thirty percent of BC students come from the greater Boston area, and Catholics comprise about 80 percent of the student body. Blacks now constitute 4 percent of the student body, while Asian-Americans make up another 8 percent, and Hispanics 5 percent. According to a marketing major, BC's "biggest problem is the lack of minorities on campus." Still, the Jesuit appeal for tolerance means that students can find support and interaction even when approaching hot-button issues that Catholicism will not condone.

Housing is plush compared to most colleges. When students are admitted, they are notified whether they will get on-campus housing for three or four years, and most juniors with three-year guarantees live off campus or study abroad that year. The city of Boston has a fairly reliable bus and subway system to bring distant residents

(Continued)
Grad in 6 Years: N/A
Returning Freshmen: N/A
Academics: ✍ ✍ ✍ ½
Social: ☎ ☎ ☎ ☎
Q of L: ★ ★ ★
Admissions: (617) 552-3100
Email Address: N/A

Strongest Programs:
  Chemistry
  Music
  Art
  Drama

The Jesuit appeal for tolerance means that students can find support and interaction even when approaching hot-button issues that Catholicism will not condone.

Although the Doug Flutie era is over, football games remain a big draw—the annual contest with Notre Dame is jokingly referred to as the "Holy War."

to campus; if students want to drive to school, there's a lottery for parking stickers. Another lottery system determines where on-campus residents hang their hats. Freshman dorms are described as "not great and not very modern," but accouterments in upper-class suites include private baths, dishwashers, and full kitchens. Students pay in advance for a certain number of dining hall meals, served a la carte.

BC students are serious about their work, but not excessively so. There is time and plenty of places to party. Yet BC's reputation as a hard-core party school is diminishing, now that no kegs or cases of beer are allowed on campus grounds. Those of legal age can carry in only enough beer for personal consumption. Bars in Boston ("The best city!" gushes a freshman, when asked how Boston rates as a college town) are a big draw because it's easier to get served there. On weekends, especially in the winter, the mountains of Vermont and New Hampshire beckon outdoorsy types who like to hike and ski. The campus is replete with sporting events, movies, festivals, concerts, and plays. And as far as social life is concerned, "BC is not a dating school," laments one lonesome student. As at other Jesuit institutions, there is no Greek system at BC.

"The courses are rigorous but intellectually stimulating."

Athletic events become social events too, with tailgate and victory parties common. Although the Doug Flutie era is over, football games remain a big draw—the annual contest with Notre Dame is jokingly referred to as the "Holy War." The football program has been recognized for achieving the highest graduation rate in the College Football Association, and the women's field hockey team made it to the quarterfinals of the NCAA Tournament. The Silvio O. Conte Forum Sports Arena is well attended, and BC meets fierce competition from Big East rivals Georgetown, Syracuse, Pitt, Villanova, and Miami. Students even get the day off from classes to line the edge of campus and cheer Boston Marathon runners up "Heartbreak Hill." Intramural sports are huge here, and students rave about BC's marvelous recreational complex.

BC students spend four years fine-tuning the art of the delicate balance, making old-fashioned morals relevant to life in the twenty-first century, and finding time for fun while keeping an eye on their academic averages.

Overlaps

Georgetown, Notre Dame, Boston University, Harvard, Penn

If You Apply To ➤

BC: Early action: Nov. 1. Regular admissions and housing: Jan. 1, Jan. 15. Financial aid: Feb. 1. No campus or alumni interviews. SATs or ACTs: required. SAT IIs: required (English, math, and one other). Apply to particular schools or programs. Meets demonstrated need of 94%. Essay question: why Boston College; a flash of revelation you have had; how a piece of art impacted you; or an important issue facing today's teens.

Boston University

121 Bay State Road, Boston, MA 02215

One of the nation's biggest private universities, but easy to miss amid the bustle of the city. Boston's Back Bay neighborhood is the promised land for hordes of students nationwide seeking a funky, artsy, youth-oriented urban setting that is less in-your-face than New York City.

Website: www.bu.edu
Location: Center city

Boston University is shouldering up to the more competitive institutions, becoming more selective and adding creative programs to its academic menu. For a private college, BU is mammoth, and its variety of programs and location in the world's best college town make BU attractive to students from across the nation. BU seems to offer something for everyone, from aspiring actors, musicians, print and television reporters, and film directors to doctors, dentists, and hotel concierges. Between cheering at hockey games, exploring bustling Boston on the T, and burning the midnight oil to succeed in competitive classes, students here keep happily busy.

Like its East Coast counterparts, George Washington University and NYU, the BU campus is practically indistinguishable from the city that surrounds it. This may be the quintessential college town, but be warned that the campus is anything but bucolic; a six-lane thoroughfare, Commonwealth Avenue, runs through the middle of the school's property, and BU's hodgepodge of nondescript high-rises and large Gothic buildings is woven into the city streets alongside fast-food restaurants and shops. A measure of relief from the urban bustle is available on the tree-lined side streets, which feature quaint Victorian brownstones.

John Silber, the pugilistic president and Kant scholar who helped build BU's academic reputation from 1971 through 1996, is back at the helm and is once again provoking controversy among students and faculty members, this time with talk of larger classes and a smaller payroll. The new Photonics Center serves students and faculty in chemistry, physics, biology, medicine, and engineering, and includes a curriculum laboratory where professors translate current projects into coursework, lectures, and student experiments. Students looking to attend law, business or medical school after graduating from

"Students definitely work hard, but I don't feel competition among classmates."

BU will find solid preprofessional offerings in the school's College of Arts and Sciences, the largest undergraduate college, which also has an outstanding psychology department. The College of Communication combines theory and hands-on training, some by adjunct professors whose day jobs are with major television networks, and houses the nation's only center for the study of political disinformation. The School of Theatre Arts is strong, while the School of Music benefits from its own concert hall, the Tsai Performance Center, in which members of the Boston Symphony Orchestra teach. A dance minor has been added and the School of Theatre Arts has instituted a freshman core for the performance and design production programs. The Sargent College of Health and Rehabilitation Sciences offers a nutritional science program with options in nutritional sciences and dietetics.

The School of Management, already viewed as one of BU's top programs, now has a four-year honors program, while the College of Engineering has its own robotics and biomedical engineering lab. Companies seeking to employ School of Hospitality Administration alumni are supporting scholarships for their future workers, and hospitality students may now find internships in Belgium and London as well as stateside. By invitation only, serious liberal arts students can enroll in the College of Arts and Sciences honors program. Also intriguing is the University Professors program, which begins with a two-year integrated core of courses focusing on major authors and central themes of Western thought. As juniors and seniors, students in the program create individualized, interdisciplinary courses of study, unbounded by neat departmental divisions. The College of General Studies provides an alternative path into BU; after a two-year introduction to college academics, successful students may transfer into one of the school's other divisions. CGS offers "personal relationships with the professors," reports a business administration student, and a well-rounded liberal arts degree. BU also offers seven- and eight-year programs admitting qualified students to both an undergraduate program and medical or dental school.

Each of BU's schools sets its own general education requirements, but all students must take the two-semester Freshman Writing Program, theme-oriented seminars limited to eighteen students each with readings from the classics, natural and

(Continued)

Total Enrollment: 27,756
Undergraduates: 17,602
Male/Female: 39/61
SAT Ranges: V 600–680
   M 610–690
ACT Range: 26–30
Financial Aid: 49%
Expense: Pr $ $ $ $
Phi Beta Kappa: Yes
Applicants: 27,562
Accepted: 48%
Enrolled: 27%
Grad in 6 Years: 72%
Returning Freshmen: 89%
Academics: ✍ ✍ ✍ ✍
Social: ☎ ☎ ☎ ☎
Q of L: ★ ★ ★
Admissions: (617) 353-2300
Email Address:
   admissions@bu.edu
international admissions:
   intadmis@bu.edu

Strongest Programs:
   University Professors
      Program
   Accelerated Medical/Dental
      Program
   Art and Design
   Music
   Department of Physics,
      Astronomy, Economics,
      and Anthropology
   Biomedical Engineering
   Music
   Film

social sciences, and the arts and humanities. Students laud psychology classes, and there is said to be a certain amount of anxiety on the part of some non-science types when faced with heavy chemistry and biology coursework. BU offers study abroad and exchange programs in countries including France, Spain, the United Kingdom, Ecuador, Greece, Israel, and Italy, as well as the Sea Semester,* a program welcoming students from many schools to live and study on a cruise ship. Students who wish to work abroad may vie for internships in locales as diverse as Australia and Moscow.

The academic climate at BU requires students to hit the books, but is relaxed enough that they don't hit one another. "Students definitely work hard, but I don't feel competition among classmates," says a junior. Amazingly for such a large school, administrators claim that 86 percent of courses taken by freshmen have twenty-five or fewer students. Perhaps that's why those seeking admission to a course taught by Nobel laureate Elie Wiesel must sign up a year in advance. There are large lecture classes for introductory classes, although smaller workshop sections, often led by graduate students, are offered in subjects like English. Students say full professors teach most courses, and rate the quality of instruction as "very good" and "superior." Academic advisors are very involved in the registration process adds a psychology major, who simultaneously laments "all the red tape" at the university.

Diversity here extends from academics to the student body, of which a sizable majority is female. About 68 percent of BU students hail from outside Massachusetts, and 9 percent come from foreign countries. Although BU has a local reputation as a rich kids' school, 72 percent of students attended public high schools, and minorities comprise 19 percent of the total. In a school this size, there is room for all types. Students are "very much into fashion," says a psychology major. "Basically, it's very diverse," adds a junior. The student body's diversity is even reflected in response to the question of whether social issues are important here. "PC is an issue," says one junior, while another says, "I don't know. I hate politics." Financial aid is praised by many, including a math major who raves, "It's fabulous. It cost less for me to come here than my state school." Nearly four thousand merit scholarships are available to qualified applicants.

"It's fabulous. It cost less for me to come here than my state school."

BU's diversity extends to on-campus housing, which is guaranteed for four years, although a sophomore cautions that once you move off campus, it's difficult to get decent dorm accommodations again, and more than one student gripes about overly strict security and overnight-guest policies. Sophomores typically move into smaller dorms or three-story university-owned brownstones on the side streets, although a junior says most of them, too, end up cramped into small rooms in "enormous cement buildings." Upperclassmen compete in separate lotteries for special-interest floors or rooms in other dorms, some of which feature Macintosh computer labs. Thirty-two percent of undergraduates live off campus. Flexible meal plans are available, including kosher food at Hillel and one dining hall serving vegetarian and vegan fare.

Social life consists mainly of parties on campus, and bars and nightclubs (many just around the corner from the dorms) off campus. Parties at neighboring colleges are an option, too, and owing to Boston's heavily Irish heritage, St. Patrick's Day is an occasion for revelry as well. Fenway Park, home of the Boston Red Sox, is a short walk across Kenmore Square, while the Green Line of the Boston subway system squiggles through the center of the campus and puts the city at students' fingertips. "The area supports its college students and has activities geared toward it." Three percent of the men and 4 percent of the women go Greek. Drinking is fairly common, though BU strictly enforces liquor laws in dorms and Boston's college-town reputation keeps bartenders and stores on the lookout for underage drinkers with fake IDs. "Campus is like a prison," grumps an underage junior. "No under twenty-one years old can drink." The Splash party in September, Homecoming in October, and Spring Thaw in April round out the social calendar.

The annual Beanpot hockey tournament, which pits BU, Boston College, Harvard, and Northeastern against one another, is the athletic highlight of the school year, and one that BU, with a championship hockey team, often wins. Most any game against archrival BC also draws a crowd. The Head of the Charles regatta, which starts at

> "The area supports its college students and has activities geared toward it."

BU's crew house and is usually held in October, draws college crews from across the country, while the city's Boston Marathon is also a celebrated event. BU has brought home half a dozen American East Championships since 2001. The women's field hockey, men's and women's soccer, and men's and women's basketball teams are also popular. Sadly for pigskin fans, there's no football team. The college offers a full range of athletic scholarships.

With 283 degree programs, almost four hundred clubs and organizations, nearly thirty thousand peers and a campus centered in a major city to distract them from their chosen course of study, BU students must work hard to stay focused. When they take a break, Boston's rich cultural resources and social events beckon just outside their dorm-room doors. Many types mix comfortably here, thus the popularity of the T-shirt "Be You."

Overlaps

NYU, Boston College, Northeastern, George Washington, Tufts

If You Apply To ➤ | **BU:** Early decision: Nov. 1. Regular admissions: Jan. 1 (Dec. 1 for some programs and scholarships). Financial aid: Feb. 15. Housing: May 1. Meets demonstrated need of 64%. Campus interviews: optional, informational (required, evaluative for some programs). Alumni interviews: optional, informational. SATs or ACTs: required. SAT IIs: required (vary by program). Apply to particular school or program. Accepts the Common Application and electronic applications.

Bowdoin College

Brunswick, ME 04011

Rates with Amherst, Williams, and Wesleyan for liberal arts excellence and does not require SAT I. Bowdoin has strong science programs, and outdoor enthusiasts benefit from proximity to the Atlantic coast. Smaller than some of its competitors, with less overt competition among students.

Bowdoin College, alma mater of the great American poets Longfellow and Hawthorne, takes pride in tradition. Upon matriculation, new students sign their names in a book on Hawthorne's very desk. Since its 1794 founding, Bowdoin has been dedicated to making nature, art, friendship and the world of books integral to the student experience. The school has developed a reputation for excellence in practically every academic pursuit. It's a "quiet place" that ranks among the best liberal arts colleges in the country—and besides that, students say, it serves amazing food.

Bowdoin's compact campus covers two hundred acres in Brunswick, Maine, the state's largest city, with a patchwork of pine groves and athletic fields. Hidden in the trees are 115 buildings, in styles ranging from German Romanesque, Colonial, Medieval, and neoclassical to neo-Georgian, modern, and postmodern. Former fraternity houses have been renovated to house academic and administrative functions after the phase-out of Greek groups. Two new college houses opened recently.

Website: www.bowdoin.edu
Location: Medium-size town
Total Enrollment: 1,635
Undergraduates: 1,635
Male/Female: 51/49
SAT Ranges: V 640–730
M 640–710
Financial Aid: 40%
Expense: Pr $ $ $ $
Phi Beta Kappa: Yes
Applicants: 4,536
Accepted: 24%

(Continued)
Enrolled: 42%
Grad in 6 Years: 90%
Returning Freshmen: 94%
Academics: ✍ ✍ ✍ ✍ ✍
Social: ☎ ☎ ☎
Q of L: ★ ★ ★
Admissions: (207) 725-3100
Email Address:
admissions@bowdoin.edu

Strongest Programs:
Biology
Chemistry
Anthropology
Sociology
Economics
English
Government
Environmental Studies

The school has its own Coastal Studies Center, and offers coursework in Arctic studies (its mascot is the polar bear).

The college has added majors in Latin American studies and Eurasian and East European studies, and incorporates service learning into courses across the curriculum.

Bowdoin is notable for its strength in the sciences, which "take advantage of Bowdoin's surroundings," says a biology and music major. "Biology, environmental science, and geology really use Maine's resources, such as nearby beaches." The school has its own Coastal Studies Center, and offers coursework in Arctic Studies (its mascot is the polar bear), as well as opportunities for Arctic archeological research in Labrador or ecological research at the Kent Island Scientific Station in Canada. Premeds of all persuasions will find top-of-the-line lab equipment and outstanding faculty; the field of microscale organic chemistry was developed and advanced here. About 60 percent of juniors and seniors conduct independent study projects with one or more faculty members, often publishing their results. Students also praise the art history and English departments, and say programs in government and economics are deservedly popular. The philosophy department suffers

"Many times, I've enjoyed professors so much that I've taken other classes solely because they teach them."

from a small teaching staff, says a junior, and the physics department is notoriously difficult. The college has added majors in Latin American Studies and Eurasian and East European Studies, and incorporates community service into various courses.

You won't find monster classes at Bowdoin; 95 percent of freshmen courses have fifty students or fewer. Professors "are the real deal," says a history and government major. "They care about teaching." A senior Spanish major has been disappointed by a class "maybe once or twice," she says. "Many times, I've enjoyed professors so much that I've taken other classes solely because they teach them." Teaching assistants offer only extra help, not primary instruction, says a math major. A junior cautions, however, that "visiting professors are all too common, and their quality varies substantially."

While the quality of instruction may vary, students agree that Bowdoin's academics are uniformly rigorous. There isn't much competition for grades, though; the focus is on learning. "There is room for each student to be as much of an over achiever or as much of a slacker as she wants to be," says a freshman. To graduate, students must complete thirty-two courses, including two each in natural sciences and math, social and behavioral sciences, humanities and fine arts, and non-Eurocentric studies. Freshmen have their choice of more than seventy seminars, each limited to sixteen students, which emphasize improved reading and writing skills. Before school begins, about 70 percent of the entering class takes pre-orientation trips that teach

"The college's goal regarding alcohol seems to be just to keep people safe."

them about the people and landscape of Maine, such as hiking, canoeing, and sea kayaking. Recently, Bowdoin also offered a community-service experience in Brunswick for students less interested in the outdoors.

Fourteen percent of Bowdoin students hail from Maine; even out-of-staters are generally hard-working, fun-loving, athletic, and attired in preppy duds from J. Crew, Abercrombie and Fitch, or L.L. Bean (the catalog giant's 24/7 factory store is just down the road in Freeport). Students "tend to be serious about academics and their education, but not to the point of excess," says a history and government major. "The typical prep-school kid prevails," agrees a junior. African-Americans and Hispanics each constitute 3 percent of the student body, and Asian-Americans make up 7 percent. Bowdoin was the first U.S. institution to make SAT scores optional in the admissions process, shifting the emphasis to a student's whole body of work.

Eighty-eight percent of Bowdoin students live on campus in spacious dorms or apartments, where freshmen get double or triple rooms, and everyone else takes his or her chances in the annual lottery. (Those who choose to join social houses, which have taken the place of sororities and fraternities, may escape the lottery by living with these groups.) Bowdoin's liberal housing options include coed suites with four bedrooms adjoining a common living room. Off-campus accommodations along the shore are popular with seniors thanks to low, off-season rates. Dining service "is fabulous," says a junior, with lobster bakes, a Thanksgiving feast, Chinese New Year and Mardi Gras celebrations, and a "just like home" dinner, with winning parents' recipes.

With the demise of the Greeks, social life at Bowdoin revolves around the social houses—at least for freshmen, says a senior. Older students typically go to house parties in friends' rooms or off-campus digs, where "there always seems to be more than enough alcohol," despite the school's limits on the number of kegs permitted on any given night. Crime isn't a major issue, so college police keep busy requiring students to register parties where alcohol will be served. They remain lax, however, about monitoring under age drinking, students say. "The college's goal regarding alcohol seems to be just to keep people safe," says a freshman. The Campus Activities Board books large concerts, comedy and novelty acts, and smaller cultural and theatrical events throughout the year, says an art history major. Homecoming, Ivies Weekend (one last blast of fun before spring finals, with bands and jumping bubbles set up in the quad), and the BearAIDS benefit concert are eagerly anticipated annual events.

Students say Brunswick (pop. 22,000) isn't a typical college town, though it is "quaint and charming all the same." The outlet-store-filled town of Freeport is fifteen minutes away, while the city of Portland is just a bit farther. A shuttle program takes students to nearby cities like Boston, which is less than three hours' drive, and ski bums will find several resorts within an eighty-mile radius. Habitat for Humanity and various mentoring programs are helping to build bridges between local residents and students, who've been criticized for living in the "Bowdoin Bubble." For those who get really stir-crazy, study abroad programs are available in more than one hundred nations, including warm ones like Ecuador. On campus, "there aren't enough warm months," complains a math major. "Be ready for those winter jackets!"

> **"We are so well taken care of and are fed so well that it is as if we are at summer camp."**

The winter months also bring out school spirit, with any sporting event against Colby—especially hockey games—inspiring excitement. "Each winter, the Farley Ice Arena will be shaking with the enthusiastic stomping and yelling of Bowdoin students and locals," says a junior. In recent years, the men's cross-country and women's basketball, ice hockey, and field hockey teams have brought home conference championships. Athletic facilities include a sixteen-lane swimming pool, a two hundred-meter track, tennis courts, exercise rooms, and a fitness center with free weights and Cybex stations.

Bowdoin is a friendly, intimate school where students are open to learning from each other and from their surroundings. "My friends from home joke that there must be a group of Bowdoin employees who spend their time thinking up cute and creative twists to decorations and activities," says a freshman. "We are so well taken care of and are fed so well that it is as if we are at summer camp." Though some will bristle at the bitter Maine winters, many will find the academic climate here warm and hospitable.

About 70 percent of the entering class takes pre-orientation trips that teach them about the people and landscape of Maine, such as hiking, canoeing, and sea kayaking. Last year, Bowdoin also offered a community-service experience in Brunswick for students less interested in the outdoors.

Overlaps

Dartmouth, Williams, Middlebury, Brown, Amherst

If You Apply To >

Bowdoin: Early decision: Nov. 15. Regular admissions: Jan. 1. Financial aid: Feb. 15. Guarantees to meet demonstrated need. Campus and alumni interviews: recommended, evaluative. SATs or ACTs: optional (SATs preferred). SAT IIs: optional. Accepts the Common Application and electronic applications. Essay question: impactful secondary teacher; your greatest challenge; influential work of art, book, activity, or experience. Places less emphasis on test scores than do comparable colleges.

Brandeis University

Waltham, MA 02454-9110

Founded in 1948 by Jews who wanted an elite institution to call their own. Now down to 55 percent Jewish and seeking top students of all faiths. Academic specialties include the natural sciences, the Middle East, and Jewish studies. Competes with Tufts in the Boston area.

Website: www.brandeis.edu
Location: Suburban
Total Enrollment: 4,882
Undergraduates: 3,081
Male/Female: 44/56
SAT Ranges: V 620–710
   M 620–720
Financial Aid: 56%
Expense: Pr $ $ $ $
Phi Beta Kappa: Yes
Applicants: 6,653
Accepted: 41%
Enrolled: 27%
Grad in 6 Years: 84%
Returning Freshmen: 93%
Academics: ✍ ✍ ✍ ✍
Social: ☎ ☎ ☎
Q of L: ★ ★ ★
Admissions: (781) 736-3500
Email Address:
   sendinfo@brandeis.edu

Strongest Programs:
   Neuroscience
   Biochemistry
   East Asian Studies
   Politics
   Psychology
   English
   Near Eastern and Judaic
     Studies
   Biology

Brandeis University was founded to provide educational opportunities to those otherwise discriminated against, and has always had a reputation for intense progressive thought. Now, it's also being recognized as a rising star among research institutions. The only nonsectarian Jewish-sponsored college in the nation, Brandeis continues its struggle to maintain its Jewish identity while attracting a well-rounded, eclectic group of students.

Set on a hilltop in a pleasant residential neighborhood nine miles west of Boston, Brandeis's attractively landscaped 270-acre campus boasts many distinctive buildings. The music building, for example, is shaped like a grand piano; the theater looks like a top hat. The Carl and Ruth Shapiro Admissions Center, built in a stunning "international style," welcomes and informs campus visitors. Construction of the $22 million Shapiro Campus Center is in progress, and a two hundred-room residence hall is scheduled for completion in 2003.

At Brandeis, biochemistry, chemistry, neuroscience, and physics are top-notch, benefiting from the $41.5 million Volen Natural Center for biological, cognitive, and computational research. Several other departments, including English, history, theater arts, music, and political science offer nationally ranked graduate programs. Dedicated premeds are catered to hand and foot, with special advisors, internships,

> **"Brandeis takes its academic integrity seriously."**

and their own Berlin Premedical Center, with specialized laboratories designed to provide would-be MDs with research opportunities. Psychology, biology, and economics are the most popular majors here; prelaw and premed students dominate. Grad school acceptance rates are impressive; 80 percent of those who apply to medical school are accepted.

With the largest faculty in the field outside of Israel, the university is virtually unrivaled in Near Eastern and Judaic studies; Hebrew is a Brandeis specialty. The school's East Asian Studies Program gives students a broad yet intimate knowledge of the history, politics, economics, art, and language of the major areas of East Asia. A wide variety of interdisciplinary programs, including Latin American, medieval, Russian, peace, and women's studies, add spice to the academic menu. Brandeis also maintains a commitment to the creative arts, with strong theater offerings and a theory-based music program founded by the late Leonard Bernstein. Students rave about the natural sciences—biology, chemistry, physics—but a senior says anthropology and sociology could "use some help." The great majority of classes have nineteen or fewer students.

The Brandeis core curriculum is rooted in a commitment to developing strong writing, foreign language, and quantitative reasoning skills and an interdisciplinary and cross-cultural perspective. Newly approved interdepartmental programs include Internet studies, which enables students to study the evolution of the Internet and its political, economic, cultural, and artistic ramifications, and Social Justice and Social Policy, in which students study theoretical approaches to social justice. Brandeis also offers "Tutorials," in which four to eight sophomore and juniors engage in close interaction with a faculty member while addressing such topics as "Cuba: a Critical Study in History, Culture, and Literature" and "Does Character Matter? Honesty in Social Relationships and Public Discourse".

The student body at Brandeis is 25 percent in-staters and heavily bicoastal otherwise, with sizable numbers of New York, New Jersey, and California residents. The group is also very bright; 95 percent graduated in the top quarter of their high-school class, and professors want them to keep working hard. Students say the academic climate here is intense. "Brandeis takes its academic integrity seriously," notes a creative writing and English major. "Our programs are highly competitive and professors here expect great things from their students. Classes here are designed to challenge, and they do." There is an out, though; the Flex 3 option allows students to take three classes one semester if an especially rough course is required, and five the next, to stay on track for four-year graduation.

Though more than half the student body is Jewish, there are three chapels on campus—Catholic, Jewish, and Protestant—built so that the shadow of one never crosses the shadow of another. It's an architectural symbol that students say reflects the realities of the campus community. African-Americans make up 3 percent of the student body, Hispanics 2 percent, and Asian-Americans 10 percent. "Everyone at Brandeis wants others, even those different from them, to feel accepted and comfortable," says a senior. Gays and lesbians have an established presence, and throw some of the liveliest parties. The unofficial fraternities and sororities that have colonized at Brandeis are clamoring for recognition from the school. Other hot-button issues include political correctness, rape awareness, and environmental causes. As might be expected, "The major political issues deal more with the Middle East than any American social or political issues," says a senior.

Even with one of the highest tuition rates in the country, Brandeis does not guarantee to meet each student's full demonstrated need, but help is generally available to those who apply on time. The level of support remains fairly constant over four years, students report. The university also offers more than seven hundred merit scholarships, in amounts from $10,000 to $27,000. The six-day freshman-orientation program is one of the most extensive in the nation, including a broad spectrum of events, such as a Boston Harbor cruise and special programs for minority, international, commuter, and transfer students.

As befits its mold-breaking heritage, Brandeis is the only school in the nation where you can live in a replica of a Scottish castle with pie-shaped rooms and stairways leading to nowhere. More pedestrian housing options include traditional quadrangle dormitories, where freshmen and sophomores live in doubles, and juniors live in singles. "North Quad is the

"There's a lot of fun things to do in Waltham. You just have to look for them."

newest area and very well maintained," reports a junior. "On the other side of campus is Mossel, a quad with a very peaceful pond in the middle." The Foster Living Center, or the "Mods," are coed, university-owned town houses reserved for seniors. According to a junior, "Ziv Quad, with its air-conditioning and modern suites, is the hope of many sophomores." Freshmen and sophomores are guaranteed housing, while upperclassmen play the lottery each spring. Eighty-two percent of students live on campus, and the rest find affordable off-campus housing nearby. Brandeis boasts the best college food in the Boston area, as well as the most appetizing setups, students say, thanks to a decision to outsource dining services. Campus meal tickets buy lunch or dinner in a fast-food joint, the pub, a country store, a kosher dining hall with vegetarian selections, or the Boulevard, a cafeteria where "the salad bars are huge."

Social life at Brandeis offers lots of options for those ready to relax. There are 207 campus clubs to keep students busy, but "Brandeis is not the type of school

Though the student body at Brandeis is 55 percent Jewish, there are three chapels on campus—Catholic, Jewish, and Protestant—built so that the shadow of one never crosses the shadow of another.

Brandeis is the only school in the nation where you can live in a replica of a Scottish castle with pie-shaped rooms and stairways leading to nowhere.

The athletic program gets a boost from its membership in the University Athletic Association, a neo–Ivy League for high-powered academic institutions.

where there are parties at every corner," a student adds. Weekends begin on Thursday, with live entertainment at the on-campus Stein pub. Students can party at will in the dorms so long as they don't get too rambunctious, but suites are officially "dry" unless a majority of the residents are over twenty-one. Major events on the campus calendar include a Tropics Night dance (where beachwear is required in February), the massive Bronstein Weekend festival just before spring finals, and the "Screw Your Roommate" dance, where dormies set up their roommates on blind dates. Also well attended are the Homecoming soccer match and the annual lacrosse tilt against cross-town rival Bentley College. The possibilities for off-campus diversion are nearly infinite, thanks to the proximity of Boston and Cambridge, which are accessible by the free Brandeis shuttle bus or a nearby commuter train. (A car is more trouble than it's worth.) And what about Waltham, Brandeis's host town? "We have a hugely successful volunteer/community-service program called the Waltham Group," says a senior. But, quips a history major, "Waltham is a blue-collar town containing a university of students with champagne backgrounds and caviar aspirations." Another student sees it differently: "There's a lot of fun things to do in Waltham. You just have to look for them."

Though the school does not field a football team, Brandeis has developed strong men's baseball, basketball, tennis, soccer, track, and cross-country squads, and women's basketball, track and cross-country, and fencing squads, all of which have taken regional championships in recent years. The athletic program gets a boost from its membership in the University Athletic Association, a neo–Ivy League for high-powered academic institutions such as the University of Chicago, Johns Hopkins, and Carnegie Mellon. Brandeis's sports facilities include the seventy thousand-square-foot Gosman Sports and Convocation Center, reportedly the largest multipurpose indoor athletic facility in the East.

Few private universities have come as far as Brandeis in just fifty years, evolving from a bare 270-acre site with the leftovers of a failed veterinary school to a modern research university of more than one hundred buildings and a $406-million endowment. Landscaping, dining services, health services, and the campus computer network have all been dramatically improved in the past few years, students say, adding to their feelings of pride in the school. One student sums it up this way: "Brandeis is not only an awesome place to get an education, it's also an open, accepting place where anyone can feel at home."

Overlaps

Tufts, Brown, Harvard, University of Pennsylvania, Boston University

If You Apply To ➤

Brandeis: Early decision: Jan. 1. Regular admissions and financial aid: Jan. 31. Does not guarantee to meet demonstrated need. Campus and alumni interviews: recommended, evaluative. SATs or ACTs: required. SAT IIs: required (writing and two others). Accepts the Common Application and electronic applications. Essay question: significant experience or achievement with special meaning; issue of personal, local, national, or international concern; or influential person.

Brigham Young University

ASB A153, Provo, UT 84602

From the time they are knee-high, Mormons in all corners of the country dream about coming to BYU. Most men and some women do a two-year stint as a missionary. The atmosphere is generally mild-mannered and conservative—and goes absolutely bonkers for its sports teams.

You don't have to be a Mormon to attend Brigham Young University, but it helps. The school's strong bond with the Church of Jesus Christ of Latter-Day Saints means that "religion is a part of our everyday life," says a junior. "It's easy to find good, clean fun." A sense of the spiritual pervades most everything at BYU, where faith and academia are intertwined, and life is governed by a strict code of ethics, which covers everything from dating to academic dishonesty. Most students say the school's commitment to church values is the reason they chose BYU in the first place. "Coming here takes a commitment to follow certain rules, which are enforced," says a junior. "Those that complain are usually those who don't follow the rules."

Mormon values of prosperity, chastity, and obedience are strongly in evidence on BYU's 638-acre campus, where the utilitarian buildings, like everything else, are "clean, modern, and orderly." The campus sits 4,600 feet above sea level, between the shores of Utah Lake and Mount Timpanogos, and offers breathtaking sunsets and easy access to magnificent skiing, camping, and hiking areas. Days begin early; church bells rouse students at 6 A.M. with the first four bars of the church hymn "Come, Come Ye Saints." (The same bells also peal every hour throughout the day.) Recent construction includes the Miller Park Building, an addition to the Harold B. Lee Library, the University Parkway Center, and a student health center.

The church's influence continues when students set their schedules; they must take one religion course per term to graduate, and offerings include, of course, study of the Book of Mormon. Students must also complete an extensive general education program that includes work in arts and fine arts, English, history, math, biological or physical sciences, social sciences, education, health and human performance, and foreign languages (there more than fifty to choose from). "The coursework here ranges from fairly challenging to quite demanding, especially in the upper-division classes," says an English major. "While at least half of the students are pretty competitive, there is a healthy population who aren't."

BYU has more full-time students than any other church-sponsored university in the U.S. Academic offerings run the gamut from the basic liberal arts to novelties such as range management, travel and tourism, and clothing and textiles. Programs in the sciences are especially strong, as are accounting and music. Weak spots include interior design, animal science, and social work, administrators say. The study-abroad program offers travel to Vienna, London, Jerusalem, and elsewhere at relatively low cost. An honors program, open to highly motivated students, offers small seminars and allows students more interaction with professors, who are addressed as "Brother" or "Sister." "Most of my professors—some in dance, one in physical science, and another in the history department—have been excellent, even inspiring, on a daily basis," says a junior.

"Coming here takes a commitment to follow certain rules, which are enforced."

About half of the courses taken by BYU freshmen have fifty or fewer students, and 15 percent—mostly introductory lectures—have more than one hundred. Telephone registration helps students sign up with a minimum of headaches, but even so, they report difficulty in getting into courses in some departments, including art, dance, and international studies. "Professors are usually quite obliging and cooperate beautifully with students who need to enroll in their classes—even when they're full," says a history major. Still, only 71 percent of students graduate within six years, because 80 percent of the men and 12 percent of the women interrupt their studies—typically after the freshman year—to serve two years as a missionary.

Thirty percent of BYU students are from Utah, another quarter hail from California and Idaho, and about 5 percent are from abroad, who speak more than seventy different languages and testify to the effectiveness of the far-ranging Mormon

Website: www.byu.edu
Location: City outskirts
Total Enrollment: 32,771
Undergraduates: 29,815
Male/Female: 50/50
ACT Range: 24–29
Financial Aid: 30%
Expense: Pr $
Phi Beta Kappa: No
Applicants: 10,293
Accepted: 66%
Enrolled: 79%
Grad in 6 Years: 71%
Returning Freshmen: 91%
Academics: ✍ ✍ ✍
Social: ☎ ☎ ☎
Q of L: ★ ★ ★ ★
Admissions: (801) 422-2507
Email Address:
admissions@byu.edu

Strongest Programs:
Accounting
Law
Economics
Engineering
Music
Languages
Chemistry
Education

Days begin early; church bells rouse students at 6 A.M. with the first four bars of the church hymn "Come, Come Ye Saints."

missionary effort. Despite the heavy international presence, BYU's campus remains largely white—only 4 percent of students are Asian-American or Pacific islanders, 3 percent are Hispanic, and less than 1 percent are African-American. "Students at BYU are happy and ambitious," says a history major. "Most students have extremely high moral standards, and don't drink, smoke, or do drugs. They're very clean-cut." Politics doesn't get much attention on campus, reports a junior, "except regarding the Provo dance ordinance." More important, says a music education major, are issues within the student "wards," or mini-congregations, involving marriage, family, and the proper way to prepare for and raise children. Tuition for church members is $770 lower than that for nonmembers, because Mormon families contribute to the university through their tithes.

Twenty percent of BYU students—primarily freshmen—live in the single-sex residence halls, where the Freshman Academy program allows them to take courses and eat meals with fellow dorm-dwellers and professors. Upperclassmen typically opt for nearby off-campus apartments, which are also single-sex (remember the honor code?). To promote a more intimate social life, the campus is broken into geographic "wards," and then again into smaller "home evening groups" of about fifteen students. "It's an effective way of shrinking the big-university atmosphere," a student explains. There are no fraternities and sororities to provide housing or parties, which is just fine with most students here. "We willingly abstain from alcohol," says a recent graduate. "No one wants it, or even cares about it." Clubs and organizations focus on everything from astronomy and bagpipes to zoology and folk dancing.

"Students at BYU are happy and ambitious."

Whether it's work with the homeless or disabled, dances, concerts, plays or sporting events, most of BYU's social life is organized through or linked to the church. Students visit patients at hospitals and care centers, perform at local festivals, and build and refurbish houses. The town of Provo, about forty-five miles south of Salt Lake City, satisfies students' basic needs, but a better bet is the mall in Orem, accessible by bus. For those with wheels, the best road trips include Las Vegas, Park City, Lake Powell and national parks in southern Utah for skiing, hiking, or camping. Dating is common, within the church's bounds of propriety. In accordance with Mormon beliefs, alcohol is banned, as are soda and other caffeinated drinks. Campus traditions include Tuesday-morning devotional prayers, and the Fall and Spring Fling festivals.

Physical fitness is big here, and the intramural facilities rate as some of the country's best, with indoor and outdoor jogging tracks; courts for tennis, racquetball, and handball; plus a pool and golf course. Also important are varsity sports; the church philosophy of obedience has worked wonders for Cougar teams. The BYU football team has a national reputation, and annual contests with the University of Utah or Utah State transform the mild-mannered BYU student body into the gracious but raucous BY Zoo (hence their nickname, "Zoobies"). One of the most popular course offerings at BYU is ballroom dancing, partly because many participants aspire to join BYU's award-winning dance team. The soccer, women's cross-country, and men's volleyball teams have also brought home championships recently.

"We willingly abstain from alcohol. No one wants it, or even cares about it."

To most Americans, BYU probably seems like a step back in time—a "clean-scrubbed complacency farm," in one student's words. But what appears artificial and isolated to some may be just what the elder ordered for young members of the Church of Latter-Day Saints. BYU's caring faculty and its emphasis on moral and upright living have helped this Mormon institution endure.

If You Apply To ➤

BYU: Rolling admissions: Feb. 15. Financial aid: June 30. Housing: No deadline; first-come, first-served. Does not guarantee to meet demonstrated need. Campus and alumni interviews: optional, informational. ACTs: required. SAT IIs: optional. Accepts electronic applications. Essays: additional information the admissions committee should consider; life experience that has strengthened your character. Looks for college prep courses versus overall GPA.

Brown University

45 Prospect Street, Providence, RI 02912

To today's stressed-out students, the thought of taking *every* course pass/fail is a dream come true. In fact, nobody does, but the pass/fail option, combined with Brown's lack of distribution requirements, gives it the freewheeling image that students love. Bashed by conservatives as a hotbed of political correctness.

With a growing number of applications and an overwhelming number of happy students, Brown University finds itself a perennial "hot college." Students not only receive the prestige and quality of an Ivy League education, but they have a chance to explore their creative sides at a liberal arts college that does not emphasize grades and preprofessionalism, and shuns required courses. This unique environment has drawn both praise and criticism over the years, but Brown students say they thrive on this discussion and on lively debate. "The freedom of shaping one's own education is both frightening and exhilarating, since the possibilities for good and ill are almost endless," says one student.

Located atop College Hill on the east side of Providence, Brown's 140-acre campus affords an excellent view of downtown Providence that is especially pleasing at sunset. Campus architecture is a composite of old and new—plenty of grassy lawns surrounded by historic buildings that offer students refuge from the city streets beyond. One student describes it as a "melting pot of architecture's finest. We

> **"The freedom of shaping one's own education is both frightening and exhilarating."**

have a building that resembles a Greek temple [and] buildings in the Richardsonian tradition." The neighborhoods that surround the campus lie within a national historic district and boast beautiful tree-lined streets that are full of ethnic charm.

Brown's faculty has successfully resisted the notion that somewhere in their collective wisdom and experience lies a core of knowledge that every educated person should possess. As a result, aside from completing courses in a major, the only university-wide requirements for graduation are to demonstrate writing competency and complete the thirty-course minimum satisfactorily. (The assumption is that students will take four courses a term for a total of thirty-two in four years.) Freshmen have no requirements. Those with interests in interdisciplinary fields will enjoy Brown's wide range of concentrations that cross departmental lines and cover everything from cognitive science to public policy. Indeed, there are bona fide departments in cognitive and linguistic sciences and media and modern culture. Students can also create their own concentration from the array of goodies offered. Brown also offers group independent-study projects, a popular alternative for students with the gumption to take a course they have to construct primarily by themselves. Particularly adventurous students can choose to spend time in one of Brown's fifty-seven study-abroad programs (including Brazil, Great Britain, France, Tanzania, Japan, Denmark, and Egypt). Closer to home, students can cross-register with Rhode Island School of Design, which is also located on College Hill, or participate in the Venture Program.*

Website: www.brown.edu
Location: City center
Total Enrollment: 7,782
Undergraduates: 5,500
Male/Female: 47/53
SAT Ranges: V 640–750
    M 650–750
ACT Range: 27–32
Financial Aid: 38%
Expense: Pr $ $ $ $
Phi Beta Kappa: Yes
Applicants: 14,612
Accepted: 17%
Enrolled: 60%
Grad in 6 Years: 93%
Returning Freshmen: 96%
Academics: ✑ ✑ ✑ ✑ ✑
Social: ☎ ☎ ☎ ☎
Q of L: ★ ★ ★ ★ ★
Admissions: (401) 863-2378
Email Address:
    admission_undergraduate@
    brown.edu

Strongest Programs:
    History
    Geology
    Computer Science
    Religious Studies
    Film and Television
    Engineering
    Art and Design
    Writing
    International Relations

Students can take their classes one of two ways: either for marks of A, B, C, or No Credit; or Satisfactory/No Credit. The NC is not recorded on the transcript, while the letter grade or Satisfactory can be supplemented by a written evaluation from the professor. A habit of NCs, however, lands students in academic hot water. Any fewer than seven courses passed in two consecutive semesters makes for an academic "warning" that does find its way onto the transcript, and means potential dismissal from the university.

Among traditional departments, history and geology are some of the university's best, and students also praise computer science, religious studies, and applied math. Other top-notch programs include comparative literature, classics, modern languages, and the writing program in the English department. Among the sciences, engineering and the premed curriculum are standouts. Future doctors can try for a competitive eight-year liberal medical education program where students can earn an MD without having to sacrifice their humanity. The political science department is said to be rapidly improving, as is the international relations concentration. Sociology, psychology, and math, however, still receive thumbs down from students. Scientific technology–related fields have very good facilities, including an instructional technology center, while minority issues are studied at the Center for Race and Ethnicity.

Brown prides itself on undergraduate teaching and considers skill in the classroom as much as the usual scholarly credentials when making tenure decisions.

"Students are self-motivated, study often, and learn a great deal."

Younger professors can receive fellowships for outstanding teaching, and the administration's interest in interdisciplinary instruction and imaginative course design help cultivate high-quality instruction. The advising system reflects the administration's commitment to treat students as adults. The lack of a set of predetermined requirements is supposed to challenge students, so "no one is going to tell you what to take." The advising system pairs each freshman with a professor and a peer advisor, and resident counselors in the dorms are also available to lend an ear. "As an Asian, I have an Asian advisor as well as a woman's peer counselor, a resident counselor, a minority counselor, and a head counselor who lived on my floor in the dorm," reports one well-counseled student. Sophomores utilize special advising resources, upperclassmen are assigned an advisor in their concentration, and a pool of interdisciplinary faculty counselors is on hand for general academic advising problems.

Brown offers more than one hundred freshman courses via the Curricular Advising Program (CAP), and the professors in these courses officially serve as academic advisors for their students' first year. This program receives mixed reviews, but some professors are highly praised by students for their abilities and availability. "They are very casual about open office hours, and welcome students to pop in for a chat." Upper-level classes are usually in the teens, CAP courses are limited to twenty, and only 13 percent of introductory lectures have more than fifty students. Especially popular courses are usually jammed with students, and often there aren't enough teaching assistants to staff them effectively. Some popular smaller courses, especially writing courses in the English department and studio art courses, can be nearly impossible to get into, although the administration claims that perseverance makes perfect—in other words, show up the first day and beg shamelessly. Compared with the other Ivies, Brown's academic climate is relatively casual, or at least seems to be. "Students are self-motivated, study often, and learn a great deal, because they want to do the work, not compete with others," one student says.

"Brown is ideally suited to two kinds of people," offers one student, "someone who wants to sample many different departments before deciding what they want to do…and someone who wants to examine a certain area in their studies and not worry about core requirements." With a small percentage of the students hailing from Rhode Island, geographical diversity is one of Brown's hallmarks. Brown is one of the few remaining hotspots of student activism in the nation; nary has a semester passed without at least one demonstration about the issue of the day. Students of color account for 29 percent of the population, and foreigners make up another 9 percent. Minorities rarely miss an opportunity to speak out on issues of concern. The gay and lesbian community is also prominent. "They throw the best dances on campus," says one science major. Ninety-seven percent of students were in the top quarter of their high-school class, and 40 percent hail from private or parochial schools.

Brown admits 95 percent of the students on a need-blind basis, and although it doesn't offer athletic or academic merit scholarships, it does guarantee to meet the full demonstrated need of everyone who is admitted. "The most contentious issue is making Brown a need-blind institution," says one student. The administration has launched a worldwide capital campaign to enhance the endowment and the alumni consciousness to eventually provide need-blind admissions for all students. Fifteen Starr National Service scholarships, ranging from $1,000 to $2,000, are also awarded each year to students who devote a year or more to volunteer public-service jobs. About 120 other "academically superlative" students, called University Scholars, will find their financial-aid package sweetened with extra grant money.

Students can take their classes one of two ways: either for marks of A, B, C, or No Credit; or Satisfactory/No Credit. The NC is not recorded on the transcript, while the letter grade or Satisfactory can be supplemented by a written evaluation from the professor.

Freshmen arrive on campus a few days before everyone else for orientation, which includes a trip to Newport, and there is also a Third World Transition Program. About half the freshmen are assigned to one of the eight coed Keeney Quad dorms, in "loud and rambunctious" units of thirty to forty with several sophomore or junior dorm counselors. The other half live in the quieter Pembroke campus dorms or in a few other scattered locations. After the freshman year, students seeking on-campus housing enter a lottery. The lottery is based on seniority, and sometimes the leftovers for sophomores can be a little skimpy, though there are some special houses set aside to give them a chance at some decent rooms.

The dorms themselves are fairly nondescript. "There are no fireplaces or engraved wood trim a la Princeton," observes one student, but nevertheless there are many options from which to choose, including apartment-like suites with kitchens, three sororities, two social dorms, and three coed fraternities. Brown guarantees housing all four years, and a dorm with suites of singles ensures that there is room for all. A significant number of upperclassmen get "off-campus permission." Places nearby are becoming more plentiful and more expensive as the area gentrifies. Brown's food service, which gets high marks from students for tastiness and variety, offers meal plans ranging from seven to twenty meals a week. Everyone on a meal plan gets a credit

"I feel safer here than I do at home."

card that allows the student to do what students at every other school only wish they could: use the meal ticket for nocturnal visits to snack bars should they miss a regular meal in one of Brown's two dining halls. Campus security is described as "very good." Says a junior, "I feel safer here than I do at home."

Providence is an old industrial city that recently underwent a renaissance. It is still the butt of student jokes—"Be prepared to wear your proletarian disguise," cautions one—but extensive renovations of the downtown area have had a positive impact. Providence is Rhode Island's capital, so many internship opportunities in state government are available, as are a few good music joints, lively bars, and a number of fine, inexpensive restaurants. For the couch-potato set, there are plenty of good things right in the neighborhood. "Downtown is a ten-minute walk, but why bother when you can buy anything from Cap'n Crunch to cowboy boots on Thayer Street, which runs through the east side of campus?" a philosophy concentrator explains. For a change of scenery, many students head to Boston or the beaches of Newport, each an hour away.

The few residential Greek organizations are generally considered much too unmellow for Brown's taste (only 10 percent of the men and 2 percent of the women sign up), and hence freshmen and sophomores are their chief clientele. The nonresidential black fraternities and sororities serve a more comprehensive student-life function. Tighter drinking rules have curtailed campus drinking somewhat. The university sponsors frequent campus-wide parties, and plays, concerts, and special events abound. Funk Nite every Thursday night at the Underground, a campus pub, draws a mixed bag of dancing fools. The biggest annual bash of the year is Spring Weekend, which includes plenty of parties, and a big-name band. Strong theater and dance programs, daily and weekly newspapers, a skydiving club, political organizations, "even a Scrabble club and a successful croquet team," represent just a few of the ways Brown students manage to keep themselves entertained. One other is the campus student center, which has been thoroughly renovated. For those interested in community outreach—and there are many at Brown who are—the university's nationally recognized public-service center helps place students in a variety of volunteer positions. The Brown Community Outreach, in fact, is the largest student organization on campus.

Brown isn't an especially sports-minded school, but a number of teams nevertheless manage to excel. Of the thirty-six varsity teams, recent Ivy League champions include men's and women's crew, men's soccer, and women's ice hockey. The football team, once

"You get four years of choice."

noted for "choking" in big games, gained new respect thanks to a strong showing in the 1998 Ivy League championship. Athletic facilities include an Olympic-size swimming pool and an indoor athletic complex with everything from tennis courts to weight rooms. There's also a basketball arena for those trying to perfect their slam dunks. The intramural program is solid, mixing fun with competitiveness.

Ever since the days of Roger Williams, Rhode Island has been known as a land of toleration, and Brown certainly is a twentieth-century embodiment of this tradition. The education offered at this university is decidedly different from that provided by the rest of the Ivy League, or for that matter, by most of the country's top universities. Brown is content to gather a talented bunch of students, offer a diverse and imaginative array of courses, and then let the undergraduates, with a little help, make sense of it all. It takes an enormous amount of initiative, maturity, and self-confidence to thrive at Brown, but most students feel that they are up to the challenge. "You get four years of choice," says one student. "Deal with it."

Overlaps

Harvard, Yale, Stanford, Cornell University, Princeton

If You Apply To ➤

Brown: Early action: Nov. 1. Regular admissions: Jan. 1. Financial aid: Jan. 20. Guarantees to meet demonstrated need. Campus and alumni interviews: optional, evaluative. SATs or ACTs: required. SAT IIs: required (any three). Essay question: personal statement in your own handwriting.

Bryn Mawr College

101 North Merion Avenue, Bryn Mawr, PA 19010-2899

BMC has the most brainpower per capita of the elite women's colleges. Politics range from liberal to radical. Do Bryn Mawrters take themselves a little too seriously? The college still benefits from ties to nearby Haverford, though the relationship is not as close as in the days when Haverford was all men.

Leafy suburban enclaves are a dime a dozen around Philadelphia. But only one is home to Bryn Mawr College, a top-notch liberal arts school. On this campus, students find a range of academic pursuits from archeology to film studies to physics, and a diverse yet community-oriented student body. Founded in 1885, Bryn Mawr has evolved into a place that prepares students for life and work in a global environment. Although students here abide by a strict academic honor code and participate in a host of loopy and long-standing campus traditions, they remain doggedly individualistic.

Bryn Mawr's lovely campus is a path-laced oasis, peaceful and self-contained. Just a twenty-minute train ride to downtown Philadelphia, Bryn Mawr provides a country setting with a vital and exciting city nearby. The predominant architecture is collegiate Gothic, a style that Bryn Mawr introduced to the United States. Ten of Bryn Mawr's buildings are listed in the National Register of Historic Places. The M. Carey Thomas Library, which was named after the school's first dean and second president, a pioneer in women's education, is also a National Historic Landmark. Variations on the collegiate Gothic theme include a sprinkling of modern buildings, such as Louis Kahn's slate-and-concrete residence hall and the redbrick foreign language dormitory. A new Multicultural Center and construction is underway on buildings that will house student activities. All of this is set among trees (many carefully labeled with Latin and English names) and lush green hills, perfect for an afternoon walk, bike ride, or jog.

Students don't discuss their grades out of respect for their academic honor code, but they freely admit that they work hard. "Students are very self-motivated and only compete with themselves," says a romance languages major. Most departments are strong, especially the sciences, classics, archaeology, art history, and the foreign languages, including Russian and Chinese. The fine arts department, however, is cited as weaker than most because of its small size. Mawrters who want to do serious work in music, art, photography, or astronomy hike over to Haverford, Bryn Mawr's nearby partner in the "bi-college" system. Bryn Mawr handles the theater, dance, creative writing, geology, art history, Italian, and Russian programs for the two colleges, and the departments of German and French are joint efforts. Bryn Mawr also offers a rich variety of special programs. Approximately one third of students study overseas during their junior year. Projects include fieldwork in the Aleutian Islands with the Anthropology Department and studying Viennese architecture with the Growth and Structure of Cities Department.

> **"All professors make themselves available and love to talk to students and answer questions."**

The general education requirements include two classes in each of the three divisions (social sciences, natural sciences, and the humanities), one semester of "quantitative" work, an intermediate level of competency in a foreign language, and the requirements of a major. Students are also required to take eight half-semesters of physical education and must also pass a swimming test. In addition, all freshmen

Website: www.brynmawr.edu
Location: Suburban
Total Enrollment: 1,756
Undergraduates: 1,333
Male/Female: 1/99
SAT Ranges: V 620–710
   M 590–670
ACT Range: 27-30
Financial Aid: 57%
Expense: Pr $ $ $ $
Phi Beta Kappa: No
Applicants: 1,522
Accepted: 60%
Enrolled: 37%
Grad in 6 Years: 80%
Returning Freshmen: 89%
Academics: ✍ ✍ ✍ ✍ ✍
Social: ☎ ☎ ☎
Q of L: ★ ★ ★
Admissions: (800) BMC-1885
Email Address:
   admissions@brynmawr.edu

Strongest Programs:
   Archaeology
   Growth and Structure of
      Cities
   Physics
   Mathematics
   Art History
   Classics
   Foreign Languages

are required to take two College Seminars to develop their critical thinking, writing, and discussion skills.

The quality of teaching at Bryn Mawr is unquestionably high. "Because of the close faculty-student ratio, students get a lot of opportunities to work closely with professors," a Russian major says. A political science major raves that "all professors make themselves available and love to talk to students and answer questions."

Freshmen are initiated to the Bryn Mawr experience during Customs Week, which includes a variety of seminars and workshops as well as a tour of the campus and town. To help first-year students acclimate, Bryn Mawr has developed the OWLS (Orientation Workshop Leaders) program, which begins during orientation and continues throughout the first year. A wide range of topics, from going home for the first time to the honor code and dealing with stress, are discussed by first-year and upper-class students, administrative staff, and faculty. For those looking ahead to see what the steep tuition will buy in the long term, the campus has a career resource center that offers information on interviewing and building a résumé. It also brings recruiters to campus, offers mock interviews, and keeps students posted on internships.

"Almost all rooms have nice perks: hardwood floors, a window seat, a nice view, a bay window."

The student body is fairly diverse—African-Americans make up 4 percent, Hispanics 3 percent, and Asian-Americans 15 percent. To encourage diversity and harmony on campus, freshmen can take an intensive four-hour session during orientation on pluralism, which teaches students to examine assumptions about class, race, and sexual orientation. "Every type of person is seen and accepted here," says an economics major. "Everyone from BMW princesses to militant vegan lesbians."

Even though the much-prized fireplaces do not operate, housing at Bryn Mawr is "beautiful," says one student. "Almost all rooms have nice perks: hardwood floors, a window seat, a nice view, a bay window," a student says. Seventy percent of the rooms are singles. The college has added dining halls to two dorms, and the rooms have high-speed Internet access. Dorms have quotas for students from all four classes, so freshmen mix freely with upperclassmen. Though housing is a little tighter than it was a few years ago, it is still guaranteed for four years, and most students can expect singles after freshman year. All those who live on campus—95 percent of the student body—must subscribe to the twenty-meal-a-week plan, and most seem to really like it. In fact, the food service has even received a national award from *Restaurants and Institutions Magazine*.

Bryn Mawr is located on suburban Philly's wealthy Main Line (named after a railroad), and the campus is two blocks from the train station. "The people who live here are yuppies with BMWs," a sophomore notes. "Bryn Mawr equals suburbia."

"There is a general feeling of empowerment and camaraderie here."

Shopping at national chain stores is nearby, and there are cute places to eat, but, like college students around the world, Mawrters duck out of town and head to the city for nightlife. The twenty-minute train ride provides students with easy access to cultural attractions, as well to social and academic events at the nearby University of Pennsylvania. "We really have the best of both worlds," a junior says.

The social life at Bryn Mawr is, well, different due to the fact that it is basically a women's college. There are no sororities and little pressure to "go with any flow," a student says. Of course, party opportunities abound off campus at Swarthmore, Haverford, or Penn. What social life there is at Bryn Mawr generally includes Haverford men who, one junior gripes, "regress to apes when drunk." Top road trips include New York, Atlantic City, the Jersey shore, and even Hershey Park.

Tradition is a very important part of the social scene on campus. The Elizabethan-style May Day festivities are held the Sunday after classes end in May. Everyone wears white, eats strawberries, and watches Greek plays. Students are known to skinny-dip in the fountains and drink champagne on the lawn. The presentation of lanterns and class colors to incoming freshmen on Lantern Night, and regal pageants, such as Parade Night, Hell Week, and Step-Sings, fill life with a Gothic sense of wonder and school spirit. Says a student, "They play a big role in uniting all four classes and give students a role in the greater history of the college." As for athletics, cross-country, volleyball, and field hockey are competitive. And, of course, there's always the champion badminton team.

Bryn Mawr is a study in dichotomy: the campus is in suburbia, but steps from a major city. The academic foundation is based on the liberal arts, but science majors are enormously popular. The students are independent but revel in college traditions. The result is overwhelmingly positive. "There is a general feeling of empowerment and camaraderie here," a junior says. "We are incredibly diverse yet we have a strong sense of community and unity." Taken together, it all means that Bryn Mawr is one unique place.

If You Apply To ➤ **Bryn Mawr:** Early decision: Nov. 15, Jan. 15. (application and financial aid). Regular admissions, financial aid: Jan. 15. Housing: June 1. Guarantees to meet demonstrated need. Campus and alumni interviews: recommended, informational. SATs: required. SAT IIs: required (English and two others). Accepts the Common Application and electronic applications. Essay question: significant experience, achievement, or risk; issue of concern to you; significant person; fictional character, historical figure, or creative work that influenced you; topic of your choice.

Bucknell University

Lewisburg, PA 17837

Bucknell, Colgate, Hamilton, Lafayette—all a little more conservative than the Ivy schools and nipping at their heels. Bucknell is the biggest of this bunch and the only one with engineering. (Perhaps Lehigh is a better comparison.) The central Pennsylvania campus is isolated but one of the most beautiful in the nation.

Bucknell University's idyllic central-Pennsylvania location and strong programs in business, engineering, and the natural sciences continue to make it a top destination for hordes of hardworking, hard-partying students. The school has a preprofessional bent, but small classes and caring faculty members mean you'll be more than just a number. In the classroom, students work hard, though they focus on learning rather than grades. And when the weekend comes, watch out—Bucknellians definitely know how to let off steam. "Bucknell's rural setting provides the perfect atmosphere for the 'college experience,'" says a management major. "The professors are approachable and always willing to help. Students are active and involved in the campus and community. You would be hard-pressed to find a student who just studies. We do it all here!"

In addition to being comfortable and friendly, Bucknell is physically beautiful. Located on a hill just south of Lewisburg, Pennsylvania, the campus overlooks the scenic Susquehanna River valley, and features a landscape of leafy nooks and grassy expanses of playing fields. Greek Revival architecture dating from the nineteenth century provides a picture-book setting, blended with modern residential complexes,

Website: www.bucknell.edu
Location: Rural
Total Enrollment: 3,587
Undergraduates: 3,430
Male/Female: 51/49
SAT Ranges: V 590–680
    M 610–690
ACT Range: 25–30
Financial Aid: 55%
Expense: Pr $ $ $
Phi Beta Kappa: Yes
Applicants: 8,043
Accepted: 39%
Enrolled: 29%
Grad in 6 Years: 86%

(Continued)

Returning Freshmen: 94%

Academics: ✍ ✍ ✍ ✍

Social: ☎ ☎ ☎ ☎

Q of L: ★ ★ ★

Admissions: (570) 577-1101

Email Address:
    admissions@bucknell.edu

Strongest Programs:
    Humanities
    English
    Music
    Theater
    Psychology
    Engineering and Natural
        Sciences
    International Relations

a magnificent science center and a performing arts center. The $9 million O'Leary Psychology and Geology Building and the first phase of a $31.5 million recreation and athletics center opened in 2002. The rec center includes an Olympic-sized pool and 15,000-square-foot fitness facility. A four thousand-seat gymnasium and $5 million art building are also planned.

All freshmen in Bucknell's College of Arts and Sciences start with Interdisciplinary Foundation seminars, designed to strengthen research, computing, and writing skills. Arts and Sciences distribution requirements include four courses in the humanities, two in social sciences, and three in natural sciences and mathematics. Two of these courses must address "broadened perspectives" on the natural and fabricated world, and on human diversity. All students enrolled in the College of Engineering have a common first semester, including a special course that exposes them to all five engineering disciplines. Along with major-related requirements, each student completes a capstone project during senior year, and must demonstrate competence in writing in order to graduate. Arts and Sciences students complete at least thirty-two credits in their four years, while engineering students complete at least thirty-four.

After fulfilling Bucknell's many requirements, students select from a variety of courses, including the popular Management 101, where students create and sell a product and donate their profits to charity. Thirty-seven percent of each graduating class studies abroad. The school has its own programs in England, France, and Barbados, led by Bucknell professors, and through relationships with other colleges and universities, students may travel to more than sixty other nations, ranging from Japan and Sweden to China, Argentina and Australia. Independent research projects often pair students and professors with common interests. The two-summer Institute of Leadership in Technology and Management, for example, allows engineering and business students to learn new ways to solve problems while enhancing critical thinking, teamwork, and communication skills. On-campus study the first summer is followed by an off-campus internship during the second.

"Bucknell is definitely a school with an academic priority."

Back on campus, courses taken by freshmen rarely have more than fifty students, and the emphasis is on classroom discussion. "Bucknell is definitely a school with an academic priority," says an international relations major. Courses are rigorous, but not cut-throat. "The main goals seem to be learning and growth," says a junior. "The expectations of my professors are always reasonable. They are open to working with a student's busy schedule." Programs in economics, engineering, management, and biology get especially high marks from students, who are close to professors. Faculty members "are at Bucknell because they love it and the students that attend," says a junior. "I have chatted one-on-one over lunch or coffee with several of my professors, and feel like I've been able to develop good relationships with them," says an art history and French major.

Bucknell students tend to be ambitious and goal-oriented, says an economics major. "They all wear J. Crew, Banana Republic, or Abercrombie and Fitch clothes, and listen to the Dave Matthews Band," sighs a chemistry major. "There is very little variation." Two-thirds come from Pennsylvania, and most are white, with African-Americans and Hispanics each accounting for 3 percent of the total, and Asian-Americans 5 percent. Key social and political issues include increasing campus diversity and whether or not to go Greek. (Ten fraternities and seven sororities attract 38 percent of the men and 43 percent of the women.) "Students here tend to use their four years wisely, and make the most of them," one student says. "The activities offered on campus allow students to develop as well-rounded individuals."

All first-year students must live in the dorms, and housing is guaranteed for four years, so 87 percent of the student body stays on campus. Residence halls have laundry

The $9 million O'Leary Psychology and Geology Building and the first phase of a $31.5 million recreation-and-athletics center opened in 2002.

facilities, lounges with cable TV, study areas, and rooms are wired for Internet access and voicemail. "Dorms are nice—especially the newer ones, which are like four-star hotels," says a junior. "The older ones have new furniture, and have a lot of character." Seniors who want to move off campus must apply for the privilege, which is a hassle, so more than three hundred upperclassmen live in five college-owned apartment buildings. About 25 percent of each entering class affiliates with one of the six intellectually focused "colleges": Environmental, Global, Social Justice, Humanities, Arts, and Society and Technology. Some upperclassmen live in the colleges, too, but most enter a lottery based on seniority for rooms in traditional dorms.

Social life at Bucknell is centered on campus, where "we have more than 120 clubs and organizations, and new ones are springing up all the time," one student says. Activities and Campus Events books comedians, performers, and speakers, while the non-alcoholic, school-run Uptown nightclub offers dancing 'til dawn. The school sponsors road trips to Washington, Baltimore, Philadelphia, and New York City, and movie theaters and malls offer diversion closer to home. "There is always more to do than time allotted!" says

"Students here tend to use their four years wisely, and make the most of them."

a junior. In 1999, Bucknell implemented a ten-point program to reduce alcohol abuse, which stresses education and counseling, alternative social programming, and stricter sanctions. Violations related to underage drinking have point values, and students who accumulate eight points must take a leave of absence. Alcohol-related incidents fell 32 percent during the 2001-02 academic year, and it's getting more difficult for the underage to be served, especially at fraternity parties, students say. For those who choose not to imbibe, the substance-free organization C.A.L.V.I.N. and H.O.B.B.E.S. moved into a former fraternity house in the fall of 1995. The meaning of the longest acronym ever seen? Creating a Lively, Valuable, Ingenious, and New Habit of Being at Bucknell and Enjoying Sobriety.

Even as the focus of socializing shifts away from drinking, students still look forward to annual traditions like Homecoming, Parents' Weekend and the springtime House Party Weekend, planned by the Greeks, with food, music, and fun for all. The black-tie Chrysalis Ball, the last weekend of April, is open to faculty, staff, students, and alumni. At graduation, the whole university community gathers under a huge tent to fete new alumni. Town-gown relations between Bucknell and the quaint, beautiful town of Lewisburg are good. The town is "our little secret," says a junior. "There are many nice shops, restaurants, bars, and resources." Community-service opportunities include work at the local

"There are many nice shops, restaurants, bars, and resources."

hospital and projects organized by B.I.S.O.N., Bucknellians In Service to Our Neighbors. For those seeking more excitement, parties and concerts at Penn State's main campus are just an hour away, and the nearby town of Bloomsburg offers ethnic eateries with Indian and Thai cuisine.

A six-time winner of the Patriot League Presidents Cup for overall athletic excellence, Bucknell boasts recent championships in men's and women's cross-country, women's indoor and outdoor track, women's volleyball, and men's lacrosse and baseball. Two new women's teams are water polo and golf. Bucknell's biggest rivalries are with Lafayette and Lehigh, though these aren't a tremendous focus.

Penn State students may go to school in "Happy Valley," but that nickname might be better applied to Bucknell's Lewisburg campus. Bucknellians are a content, tight-knit group whose biggest complaints are the rain, the reliance on old-fashioned paper and pencil to register for classes, and the lack of parking, which should be remedied by next year. "Everyone is here for each other, and works hard in every regard to make it a better place," says a junior. "The students are the voice of the school."

Overlaps

Colgate, Lehigh, Boston College, Lafayette, Cornell University

If You Apply To ➤	**Bucknell:** Early decision: Nov. 15. Regular admissions, financial aid, and housing: Jan. 1. Does not guarantee to meet demonstrated need. Campus interviews: recommended, evaluative. Alumni interviews: optional, evaluative. SATs or ACTs: required. Accepts the Common Application and electronic applications. Essay question: significant experience or achievement; issue of personal, local, or national concern; influential person, fictional character, historical figure, or creative work; or topic of choice.

California Colleges and Universities

California's three-tiered system of colleges and universities has long been viewed as a model of excellence by other public higher-education institutions nationwide and even around the world. Many have attempted to emulate its revered status, which offers a wealth of educational riches including world-class research universities, enough Nobel Prize winners to fill a seminar room, and colleges on the cutting edge of everything from film to viticulture. Underlying the creation of this remarkable system was a commitment to the notion that all qualified Californians, whatever their economic status, were entitled to the benefits of a college education. In pursuing this ideal, California led the nation in opening up access to higher education for African-Americans, Hispanics, and other previously disenfranchised groups.

Unfortunately, in the early 1990s, this golden dream started fading due to the state's recession, population growth, and many other contributing factors. As a result, California's public universities and colleges received reduced tax support, student charges and user's fees shot up, student/faculty ratios increased, fewer classes were offered, and, in some cases, entire academic programs were eliminated. Although it still remained relatively lower than most states, tuition started to climb. The good news is that California has made a brave attempt to counteract this quandary despite an unprecedented budget deficit in 2002–2003, and total enrollment swelling to sixty thousand students over the next decade. Tuition increases are a likelihood on the horizon.

The system is composed of the nine combined research and teaching units of the University of California (UC), with a tenth campus, UC Merced, expected to open in 2004 with one thousand students, and twenty-three state universities and colleges (CSUC), including the newest CSU campus at Channel Islands, that focus on undergraduate teaching. It also includes 106 two-year community colleges that offer both terminal degrees and the possibility of transferring into four-year institutions.

Admissions requirements to the three tiers and the institutions within them vary widely. Community colleges are open to virtually all high-school graduates. The top third of California high-school graduates (as measured statewide by a combination of SAT scores and grade-point average) may attend units of the state university and college system; all applicants must have taken a course in the fine or performing arts to be considered for admission. In the past, students in the top 12.5 percent of their class have been eligible to attend the University of California. In-state students graduating in the top 4 percent of their high-school class will be guaranteed admission to the UC system, although not to a particular campus. The 4 percent proposal is part of a plan to broaden the representation of California applicants and to give more weight to GPA and SAT II subject tests. Out-of-state students continue to face ferocious competition for a limited number of spots, and still pay more.

Although one university system, the nine campuses each offer a full range of academic programs, and each has its own distinctive character. In recent years, UC has moved from relying primarily on statistical academic information to a "comprehensive review" that takes into consideration not only course work and test scores but also leadership, special talent, and the educational opportunities available to each student. Despite state laws that prohibit the university from considering race in admission, the system remains dedicated to achieving a diverse student body. The university offers a number of outreach programs designed to assist low-income or educationally disadvantaged students who have promising academic potential with admissions and support services.

To apply for admission to the University of California, complete the electronic application available at UC's PATHWAYS Application Center or submit the printed version to UC's Undergraduate Application Processing Service. Prospective students may apply to as many as eight UC campuses using the same application form. It should be noted that UC does not base admission on the applicant's campus choice, so students cannot request a campus preference. However, it is possible to be accepted at more than one school; in that case, the applicant is free to choose between those campuses. Each of the major undergraduate UC campuses receives a full-length summary in the following pages.

The California State University and College System is totally separate from the University of California; in fact, the two institutions have historically competed for funds as well as students. The largest system of senior higher education in the nation, Cal State focuses on undergraduate education; while its members can offer master's degrees, they can award doctorates only in collaboration with a UC institution. Research in the state-university system is severely restricted, a blow to Cal State's national prestige but a big plus for students. Unlike UC, where the mandate to publish or perish is alive and well, teachers in the state system are there to teach. Cal State's biggest problem is the success of UC, and its frequent lament—"Anywhere else we'd be number one"—is not without justification.

The twenty-three-campus system caters to more than 350,000 students a year. And while most of the campuses serve mainly commuters, Chico, Humboldt, Monterey Bay, San Luis Obispo, and Sonoma stand out as residential campuses. While a solid liberal arts education is offered, the stress is usually on career-oriented professional training. Size varies dramatically, from about thirty thousand students at San Diego and Long Beach to fewer than six thousand at several other branches like San Marcos, Channel Islands, and Monterey Bay. Each campus has its own specific strengths, although in most cases a student's choice of school is dictated by location rather than by academic specialties. For those with a wider choice, some of the more distinctive campuses are profiled below.

Chico (enrollment: 14,983), situated in the beautiful Sacramento Valley, draws a large majority of its students from outside a one hundred-mile radius. The on-campus undergraduate life is strong and the social life is great. Bakersfield (5,594) and San Bernardino (12,000) boast residential villages along with more conventional dorms. The former is in a living/learning center with affiliated faculty members; the latter has its own swimming pool. California Polytechnic at San Luis Obispo is the toughest state university to get into. It provides excellent training in the applied branches of such fields as agriculture, architecture, business, and engineering. Enrollment: 16,735. Fresno, located in the Verdant Central Valley, has the only viticulture school in the state outside of Davis, and undergraduates can work in the school winery. Yosemite, Kings Canyon, and Sequoia national parks are nearby. Enrollment: 18,113.

San Diego State is the biggest and balmiest of the campuses, and since it has a more residential and outdoorsy, campus-oriented social scene, it appeals more to traditional-age undergraduates. "You could go for the weather alone—some do," says one former student. Contrasted with other state schools, athletics are very important, and the academic offerings are almost as oriented to the liberal arts as at its UC neighbor at San Diego. Enrollment: 30,776.

Humboldt State is perched at the top of the state near the Oregon border in the heart of the redwoods. Humboldt's forestry and wildlife departments have national reputations, and the natural sciences are, in general, strong. Students have the run of excellent laboratory facilities and Redwood National Park. Most in-staters come here to get away from Los Angeles and enjoy the rugged coastline north of San Francisco. Enrollment: 7,475.

California Maritime Academy, located thirty miles northeast of San Francisco with six hundred students, specializes in marine transportation, engineering, and maritime technology, and requires summer cruises on the *T.S. Gold Bear*. Monterey Bay, one mile from the beach with three thousand students, 65 percent of whom live on campus, offers an interdisciplinary focus with global perspective and opportunities for internships.

To apply to California State University, complete either the electronic application available at their website, which will be routed to the campus of the applicant's choice, or the paper application, which should be mailed to the admissions office of the campus to which the applicant is applying. It should be noted that Cal Poly and San Diego State require electronic applications. The prospective student can list a first and alternate campus choice on the application. If the first choice can't accommodate the applicant, it automatically sends the application to the alternate campus. However, for competitive campuses and programs, it is wiser to send separate applications to avoid delays.

Mention Berkeley and even down-to-earth students get stars in their eyes. Students who come here want the biggest and best of everything, though sometimes that ideal runs head-long into budget cuts, tuition increases, and housing shortages. Never mind. Berkeley is where the action is.

Website: www.berkeley.edu
Location: Urban
Total Enrollment: 31,347
Undergraduates: 22,705
Male/Female: 49/51
SAT Ranges: V 580–710
    M 620–730
ACT Range: N/A
Financial Aid: 48%
Expense: Pub $ $ $
Phi Beta Kappa: Yes
Applicants: 31,108
Accepted: 27%
Enrolled: 43%
Grad in 6 Years: 83%
Returning Freshmen: 94%
Academics: ✎ ✎ ✎ ✎ ✎
Social: ☎ ☎ ☎ ☎
Q of L: ★ ★ ★
Admissions: (510) 642-3175
Email Address:
    ouars@uclink4.berkley.edu

Strongest Programs:
    Engineering
    Architecture
    Business
    Theoretical Physics
    Molecular and Cell Biology
    Political Science
    English

If you want a quick indicator of Berkeley's academic prowess, look no farther than the parking lot. The campus is dotted with spots marked "NL"—spots reserved for resident Nobel laureates. The last time anyone counted, Berkeley boasted seven Nobel Prize winners, 140 Guggenheim fellows, and a bevy of Pulitzer Prize recipients, MacArthur fellows, and Fulbright scholars. Is it any wonder that this radical institution of the '60s still maintains the kind of reputation that makes the top private universities take note? Engineering, architecture, and business are a few of the best of the fine programs at this mother of UC schools. The social climate is not as explosive as it once seemed to be, but don't expect anything tame on today's campus. Flower children and granola chompers still abound, as do fledgling Marxists, young Republicans, and body-pierced activists.

Spread across 1,200 scenic acres on a hill overlooking San Francisco Bay, the Berkeley campus is a parklike oasis in a small city. The sometimes startlingly wide variety of architectural styles ranges from the stunning classical amphitheater to the modern University Art Museum draped in neon sculpture. Large expanses of grass dot the campus and are just "perfect for playing Frisbee or lying in the sun." The oaks along Strawberry Creek and the eucalyptus grove date back to Berkeley's beginnings nearly 130 years ago.

Like everything else, the academic side of Berkeley can be overwhelming. With more than twenty-two thousand undergraduate overachievers crammed into such a small space, it is no wonder that the academic climate is about as intense as you can get at a public university. "Everyone was the top student in his or her high-school class so they can't settle for anything less than number one," says one student. A classmate concedes that "it can be a stressful environment, especially during the first years." Another says tersely, "Expect very little sleep." Some introductory courses,

> **"Everyone was the top student in his or her high-school class so they can't settle for anything less than number one."**

particularly in the sciences, have as many as eight hundred students, and professors, who must publish or perish from the university's highly competitive teaching ranks, devote a great deal of time to research. After all, Berkeley has made a large part of its reputation on its research and graduate programs, many of which rank among the best in the nation.

And while the undergraduate education is excellent, students take a gamble with the trickle-down theory, which holds out the promise that the intellectual might of those in the ivory towers will drip down to them eventually. As a political science major explains, "This system has allowed me to hear outstanding lectures from amazing professors who write the books we read, while allowing far more personal attention by the graduate-student instructors." Another student opines, "It's better to stand fifty feet from brilliance than five feet from mediocrity." Evidence of such gravitation is seen in the promising curriculums designed specifically for freshmen and sophomores that include interdisciplinary courses in writing, public speaking, and the history of civilization, and an offering of small student seminars (enrollment is limited to fifteen) taught by regular faculty. Despite these attempts at catering to undergraduates, the sheer number of students at Berkeley makes it difficult to treat each student as an individual. As a result, such things as academic counseling suffer. "Advising? You mean to tell me they have advising here?" asks one student.

Each college or school has its own set of general education requirements, which are generally not extensive, and many can be fulfilled through advanced-placement exams in high school. All students, however, must take English composition and literature, and one term each of American history and American institutions. Also, undergrads have an American Cultures requirement for graduation—an original approach (via courses offered in several departments) to comparative study of ethnic groups in the United States.

Most of the departments here are noteworthy, and some are about the best anywhere (like engineering and architecture). Sociology, mathematics, physics, chemistry, history, and English are just a handful of the truly dazzling departments. Engineering is also strong, and Berkeley offers a 3-2 engineering program with UC–Santa Cruz. The biological sciences department integrates several undergraduate majors in biochemistry, biophysics, botany, zoology, and others into more interdisciplinary programs such as integrative biology and molecular and cell biology. The College of Natural Resources has streamlined its eight departments into four, and established an Institute for Natural Resource Systems.

Special programs abound at Berkeley, though it's up to the student to find out about them. "Our class enrollment system is much like playing a low-risk lottery," opines one undergrad. "Maybe you'll win, or maybe you won't. If anything, adding courses will definitely toughen up any person." Students may study abroad on fellowships at one of fifty centers around the world, or spend time in various internships around the country. If all you want to do is study, the library system, with more than eight million volumes, is one of the largest in the nation and maintains open stacks. The system consists of the main library (Doe-Moffitt) and more than twenty branch libraries, one of which (Bancroft) houses rare books and Western Americana.

Forty-five percent of the student population is Asian-American, 4 percent African-American, and 9 percent Hispanic. The Coalition for Excellence and Diversity in Mathematics, Science and Engineering, which provides women and minorities with undergraduate mentors in these fields, received the Presidential Award for Excellence in Science, Mathematics, and Engineering in 1998. The university also provides a variety of other programs

"It's better to stand fifty feet from brilliance than five feet from mediocrity."

to promote diversity, including Project DARE (Diversity Awareness through Resources and Education), the Center for Racial Education, and a Sexual Harassment Peer Education Program. Despite Berkeley's liberal reputation, the recent trend is away from the legacy of the free-speech movement. Business majors and fraternity members increasingly outnumber the young Communists and peaceniks, though the school does boast a large number of Peace Corps volunteers.

The main issue concerning every group on campus? Cost. In the past few years, outrageous fee hikes and severe budget cuts had some students wondering if a first-rate, affordable education had gone the way of the dinosaurs. In addition, the passage of Proposition 1A will provide $2.5 billion to California public higher-education institutions for new facilities or renovations of older ones, some of which will assist Berkeley in its effort of the seismic rehabilitation of many of its structures.

Though dorms have room for only a quarter of the students, freshmen are guaranteed housing for their first year. After that, the Community Living Office is a good resource for finding an apartment in town. Many students live a couple of

Berkeley is a quintessential college town ("kind of a crazy little town"), and of course, there's always the people-watching; where else can an individual meet people trying to convert pedestrians to strange New Age religions or revolutionary political causes on every street corner?

Just about everyone turns out for the "Big Game," where the favorite activity on the home side of the bleachers is badmouthing the rival school to the south: Stanford.

miles off campus, where "apartments are cheaper," says one student. About two-thirds of the university's highly prized dorm rooms are reserved for freshmen, and the few singles go to resident assistants. Doubles are likely to become crowded triples, albeit at a reduced fee. Losers in the May lottery automatically go on a long waiting list to vie for rooms in subsequent monthly lotteries. In the absence of a mandatory meal plan, everybody eats "wherever and whenever they wish," including in the dorms.

Though the housing shortage can get you down, the beautiful California weather will probably take your mind off it in time. The BART subway system provides easy access to San Francisco, by far one of the most pleasant cities in the world and a cultural and countercultural mecca. The Bay Area boasts myriad professional sports teams, including the Oakland A's and the San Francisco 49ers. From opera to camping, San Francisco has a wide variety of activities to offer. Get yourself a car, and hike in Yosemite National Park, ski and gamble in Nevada, taste wine in the Napa Valley, or visit the aquarium at Monterey. But be advised that a car is only an asset when you want to go out of town—students warn that parking in Berkeley is difficult, to say the least.

"Social life at UC–Berkeley is killer!" exclaims one geography major. Weekends are generally spent in Berkeley, hanging out at the many bookstores, coffeehouses, and sidewalk cafés, heading to a fraternity or sorority party, or taking advantage of the many events right on campus. Berkeley is a quintessential college town ("kind of a crazy little town," opines one anthropology major), and of course, there's always the people-watching; where else can an individual meet people trying to convert pedestrians to strange New Age religions or revolutionary political causes on every street corner? Nearby Telegraph Avenue is famous (infamous?) for such antics every weekend. More than three hundred student groups are registered on campus, which ensures that there is an outlet for just about any interest and that no one group will ever dominate campus life.

"At Berkeley, it is worse to be dull than odd."

Despite all this activity, many students use the weekend to catch up on studying. Greeks have become more popular, with 9 percent of the men and 6 percent of the women in a fraternity or sorority. Varsity athletics have always been important, with strengths in the men's gymnastics and crew teams. A surge in popularity for the basketball team probably has to do with its great performance in the PAC 10. And just about everyone turns out for the "Big Game," where the favorite activity on the home side of the bleachers is badmouthing the rival school to the south: Stanford. Intramurals are popular, and the personal fitness craze is fed by an extensive recreational facility and gorgeous weather year-round.

The common denominator in the Berkeley community is academic motivation, along with the self-reliance that emerges from trying to make your mark among upward of twenty-two thousand peers. Beyond that, the diversity of town and campus makes an extraordinarily free and exciting college environment for almost anyone. "It makes one feel free to dress, say, think, or do anything and not be chastised for being unorthodox," explains a student. "At Berkeley, it is worse to be dull than odd."

Overlaps

UCLA, Stanford, UC–San Diego, UC–Davis, Harvard

If You Apply To ➤ | **Berkeley:** Regular admissions: Nov. 30. Financial aid: Mar. 2. Guarantees to meet demonstrated need of in-state students. No campus or alumni interviews. SATs or ACTS: required. SAT IIs: required (writing, math I or II, and one other). Essay question: personal statement. Apply to particular school or program.

agree that the homey campus dwellings provide a good experience for freshmen, though finding a room can be a challenge. "If you really want on-campus housing," warns a student, "you need to make sure you meet the deadlines." Newly added housing, including those with academic themes and ones especially for fraternities and sororities, opens more rooms for students, but most opt to move off campus after their first year. Currently, 70 percent of freshmen live off campus—many on the beach—giving the campus a commuter-school atmosphere. One student laments, "You have to find the social life on this campus. It won't find you."

Still, the Greek scene is vigorous. There are eighteen sororities and eighteen fraternities, and each has something going on every weekend. As for booze, UCI is a dry campus and students say finding a drink on campus without proper ID is difficult. Irvine touts many festivals that seem to attest to a celebration of diversity: the Rainbow festival (cultural heritage), Asian Heritage week, Black History month, Cinco de Mayo, and rush week. The one event that brings everybody out is the daylong Wayzgoose, when the campus is transformed into a medieval fair complete with mimes, jugglers, and performers dressed up in medieval costumes.

> **"If you really want on-campus housing, you need to make sure you meet the deadlines."**

But if life on campus is slow, life off campus is not. That's because the campus is located just fifty miles from L.A., five miles from the beach, and a little more than an hour from the ski slopes. Catalina Island, with beaches and hiking trails, is a quick boat trip off Newport Harbor; Mexico is two hours away. While some students treasure the quiet setting of Irvine, others lament its "lackluster, homogeneous communities." Notes one student, "UCI and the city of Irvine seem like completely different entities; the former is slightly liberal while the latter is ultraconservative."

Irvine fields twenty athletic teams and competes in Division I of the NCAA. Tennis and cross-country are perennial Big West powerhouses, and men's water polo has been ranked in the top five nationally for twenty-three of the last thirty-one years. There is no football team, but intramurals are extremely popular, as is the five thousand-seat multipurpose gym.

What lures students to UCI is its top-name professors, innovative academic programs, and the chance to be a part of its cutting-edge research. For the students who come here prepared to keep their heads buried in a book for a few years, the ultimate reward will be an exceptional education.

Students may be overwhelmed by the size of most classes. Even seniors find their classes packed with one hundred undergrads, which leaves little time for personal attention.

Overlaps

UCLA, UC–San Diego, UC–Santa Barbara, UC–Berkeley, University of Southern California

If You Apply To ➤ **Irvine:** Regular admissions: Nov. 30. Financial aid and housing: May 1. No campus or alumni interviews. SATs or ACTs: required. SAT IIs: required (English composition, math, and one other). Accepts electronic applications. Essay question: autobiographical statement.

UC–Los Angeles

1147 Murphy Hall, 405 Hillgard Avenue, Los Angeles, CA 90095

Tucked into exclusive Beverly Hills with the beach, the mountains, and chic Hollywood hangouts all within easy reach. Practically everything is offered here, but the programs in arts and media are some of the best in the world. More conservative than Berkeley and nearly as difficult to get into.

Website: www.ucla.edu
Location: Urban
Total Enrollment: 36,890
Undergraduates: 25,011
Male/Female: 45/55
SAT Ranges: V 560–680
   M 610–720
ACT Range: 23–29
Financial Aid: 51%
Expense: Pub $ $ $ $
Phi Beta Kappa: Yes
Applicants: 37,794
Accepted: 29%
Enrolled: 38%
Grad in 6 Years: 80%
Returning Freshmen: 96%
Academics: ✍ ✍ ✍ ✍ ✍
Social: ☎ ☎ ☎
Q of L: ★ ★ ★
Admissions: (310) 825-3101
Email Address:
   ugadm@saonet.ucla.edu

Strongest Programs:
   Music
   Film and Television
   Communications
   Premed
   Drama
   Engineering
   Dance
   Political Science

As befits a university next door to Hollywood, the School of Film, Theater, and Television is first-rate, and its students have the opportunity to study in Verona, Italy, with the Theater Overseas program.

With stellar programs in music, film and television, journalism/communication, dance, and drama, you'd think UCLA was some kind of incubator for truly talented and gifted people. Or with alumni such as Kareem Abdul-Jabbar, Troy Aikman, and Arthur Ashe, maybe UCLA's some sort of farm that grows superstar athletes. Well, UCLA is all that and more. A superb faculty, a reputation for outstanding academics, and a powerful athletics program make this university the ultimate place to study. "There are endless opportunities and unlimited resources because of the size of this university," says an English major. "There's nothing you can't do at UCLA."

UCLA's prime location—sandwiched between two glamorous neighborhoods (Beverly Hills and Bel Air) and a short drive away from Hollywood, the Sunset Strip, and downtown Los Angeles—makes it appealing for students who want more from their college experience than what classes alone can offer. The university's beautifully landscaped 419-acre campus features a range of architectural styles, with Romanesque/Italian Renaissance as the dominant motif, providing only one of a number of reasons students also enjoy staying on campus. A wealth of gardens—botanical, Japanese, and sculpture—adds a touch of quiet elegance to the campus. Planned facilities include additional student apartments, a physics and astronomy building, and the Luck Center, which will house research activities in orthopedics and related fields.

Strong programs abound at UCLA, and many are considered among the best in the nation. The School of Engineering and Applied Science, especially electrical engineering, is generally regarded as the leading department. As befits a university next door to Hollywood, the School of Film, Theater, and Television is first-rate, and its students have the opportunity to study in Verona, Italy, with the Theater Overseas program. The dance and drama departments are excellent, and the popular music department offers a course in jazz studies. The biological sciences are also highly regarded; new majors include plant biology, marine biology, ecology, and behavior and evolution. Research opportunities abound at UCLA, and the university ranks seventh in the nation in federal funding for research. In the Student Research Program, more than 1,400 undergrads work side by side with professors on cutting-edge research. Students say that the math department doesn't add up to the sum total of its parts.

Freshmen are encouraged to participate in a three-day summer orientation, which provides workshops, counseling, and a general introduction to the campus and community. During their first two years, most students take required core classes that are sometimes jammed with three hundred to four hundred people. But administrators are quick to point out that nearly two-thirds of all undergraduate classes have fewer than fifty students. Savvy students come to UCLA with advanced courses in their high-school backgrounds and test out of the intro courses. First-year students are required to take a course involving quantitative reasoning unless they hit 600 or higher on their math SAT, and English composition requirements should also be met during the freshman year. Lab science and a language requirement are also required for a liberal arts degree.

"There's nothing you can't do at UCLA."

Simply getting into classes here can be a big challenge. Students register by phone in a sequence of two scheduled "passes" based on their class standing. UCLA's academic environment is extremely intense. "Depending on your major, the courses can be very time-consuming," says a senior. The faculty is also impressive. "My professors have been dynamic and inspirational and genuinely interested in the student's success," says an English major. On the other hand, there is a widespread sense here that undergraduate teaching is often sacrificed on behalf of scholarly research. "Some professors considered their research primary and teaching their students secondary," says a mechanical engineering major. The UCLA library ranks in the top ten of all research libraries, public or private, and actually consists of the College Library and nine specialized libraries containing more than 7.2-million volumes. The campus newspaper, the *Daily Bruin*, is the third-largest daily in all of Los Angeles.

"We have some very interesting and eccentric students at our school," says a freshman. "Most are social, trendy, and tanned." In 1995, Proposition 209 abolished admissions decisions based on affirmative action in California. At this time, Asian-Americans account for 38 percent of UCLA's student population, Hispanics make up 14 percent, African-Americans 4 percent, and Native Americans 1 percent. "Affirmative action and minority representation are the largest political issues on campus," says a sophomore.

"We have some very interesting and eccentric students at our school."

UCLA has several student-run newsmagazines as alternatives to the *Daily Bruin*, including the feminist *Together* and the Asian-American newsmagazine *Pacific Ties*. UCLA is also one of the few universities in the nation with a gay fraternity and a lesbian sorority. These groups, as well as GALA (Gay and Lesbian Association) and *TenPercent*, have helped foster a rising feeling of empowerment among the campus's gay and lesbian students and faculty.

Freshmen are guaranteed housing, but for everyone else it's strictly a waiting list. "Dorm life is awesome!," says one student. "It spawns lifelong friendships." Overcrowding is a concern, though future housing construction should give students a bit more elbow room. The campus is philosophically divided into North and South. North attracts more liberal arts aficionados, while those in math and science tend to favor South. Fifteen dining halls, restaurants, and snack bars serve average meals.

Freshmen are encouraged to participate in a three-day summer orientation, which provides workshops, counseling, and a general introduction to the campus and community.

UCLA has won a nation-leading number of collegiate championships, including eighty-six NCAA titles, and has produced more than 250 Olympians. The men's football, basketball, baseball, and tennis teams are the undeniable superstars as are the women's gymnastic and water-polo teams. Beating USC is the name of the game in any sport; UCLA fans regard their intracity rivals with passionate feelings. ("Bruins are forever, but a Trojan is good only once.")

If you would rather be a doer than a watcher, the opportunities awaiting you are superb. "UCLA has an awesome social setting!" exclaims a junior. "Since we're based right here in L.A., there's too much to do." The hopping Westwood suburb, which borders the university, has at least fifteen movie theaters and scores of restaurants, but the shops cater to the upper class. UCLA's Ocean Discovery Center, located on the Santa Monica Pier, is an innovative, hands-on ocean classroom for students and the public. The beach is five miles away, and the mountains are only a short drive. Although public transportation is cheap, it's also inconvenient, making a car almost a necessity for going outside of Westwood. Unfortunately, parking is expensive and difficult to obtain. The easiest solution is to live close to campus and bike it.

"UCLA has an awesome social setting!"

With all the attractions of the City of Angels at its doorstep, the campus tends to empty out on the weekends (except when the football Bruins have a home game). Eleven percent of the men and 10 percent of the women join one of UCLA's fifty fraternities and sororities. The university's alcohol policy is similar to that of other UC schools—open consumption is a no-no. But according to one student, "It is extremely easy for undergrads to be served, especially at fraternities." Top-name entertainers, political figures, and speakers of all kinds come to the campus; film and theater presentations are frequent, and the air is thick with live music, usually every week.

Overlaps

UC–San Diego,
UC–Berkeley,
UC–Santa Barbara,
UC–Irvine, USC

A leading research center, UCLA's broad range of innovative academic programs, distinguished faculty members, and outstanding athletics make it one of the most prestigious universities in the nation. In order to make the most of this university, a student must have stamina, self-reliance, and willpower.

UC–Riverside

Riverside, CA 92521

While multitudes of students throng other UC campuses, Riverside offers a more personal touch. A unique biomedical studies program is a major drawing card. The town of Riverside is not—but it is an hour from L.A. Without big-time athletics or a marquee location, Riverside is rarely a first choice.

Website: www.ucr.edu
Location: City outskirts
Total Enrollment: 14,429
Undergraduates: 12,714
Male/Female: 46/54
SAT Ranges: V 450–570
  M 490–620
ACT Range: 18–24
Financial Aid: 60%
Expense: Pub $ $ $
Phi Beta Kappa: Yes
Applicants: 16,950
Accepted: 82%
Enrolled: 24%
Grad in 6 Years: 64%
Returning Freshmen: 84%
Academics: ✍ ✍ ✍ ½
Social: ☎ ☎
Q of L: ★ ★ ★
Admissions: (909) 787-3411
Email Address:
  discover@pop.ucr.edu

Strongest Programs:
  Biomedical Sciences
  Dance
  History
  Political Science
  Creative Writing

Lacking the big-name reputation and booming athletic programs of the other UC schools, UC–Riverside has chosen to place its emphasis on something that not all institutions consider to be an important component of higher education: the student. Riverside offers one of the lowest student/faculty ratios in the UC system, strong programs with personalized attention, and a sense of academic community that seems to have been forgotten at other UC schools. "Students are well taken care of and get personal attention," says one satisfied senior. Though part of the UC system, UC–Riverside is a breed apart.

Located sixty miles east of Los Angeles, UCR is surrounded by mountains on the outskirts of the city of Riverside. The beautifully landscaped campus consists of mainly modern architecture, with a 160-foot bell tower (forty-eight-bell carillon)

> "Students are well taken care of and get personal attention."

marking its center. Wide lawns and clusters of oaks are spread out over 1,200 acres, creating "a veritable botanical garden," where students and faculty enjoy relaxing between classes. New facilities include a science library, fine arts building, and entomology building.

Years ago, researchers at UC–Riverside decided the regular orange had too many seeds and was hard to peel, so they perfected the navel orange. Riverside still specializes in the plant sciences, but all the sciences, as well as math, statistics, and computer science, are excellent. The biomedical sciences program, unique in California, is UCR's most prestigious and demanding course of study, and its students can earn a seven-year BS/MD with UCLA. Other notable majors include Asian studies, women's studies, and creative writing. One of the few undergraduate environmental engineering programs is at UCR, as is a doctoral program in dance history and theory. Academic weaknesses include psychology and some languages. The University Honors Program offers exceptional students further academic challenges, in addition to extracurricular activities and special seminars for participating freshmen. A moratorium on entry of new students has been imposed in the Conservation Biology major.

All students are required to meet extensive "breadth requirements" that include courses in English composition, natural sciences and math, humanities and social sciences, and ethnicity, as well as fluency in a foreign language. In addition, students are required to take American History and Institutions, must fulfill a unit requirement, and also must meet a minimum residence requirement of three-quarters. Students do not encounter much difficulty in getting the courses they want. "Underclassmen have more of a struggle for classes that may be popular with upperclassmen," explains a biology major. The library has an impressive 1.5 million volumes, and what Riverside doesn't have can probably be found at UCLA's massive collections; a daily shuttle bus runs students back and forth to the UCLA campus.

Research is an institutional priority for faculty, but unlike those at other UC schools, Riverside professors dedicate much of their time and attention to their students. Plus, UCR has a tradition of undergraduate and faculty interaction with a wide range of undergraduate research grants available during the academic year. "The teachers at UCR are superb," says one student. "They present material through the latest technological devices and are very knowledgeable about their subjects." This may be why one in six graduates goes on to get a Ph.D. to become faculty members themselves.

"The teachers at UCR are superb."

Ninety-nine percent of the UCR student body are from California, mainly the L.A., San Diego, and Bay areas. Ninety-four percent of the students graduated in the top tenth of their public high-school class. Asian-Americans account for 40 percent of the students, and Hispanics and African-Americans 22 percent and 6 percent, respectively. As part of the UC commitment to diversity, Riverside upholds policies prohibiting sexual harassment, hazing, and physical and verbal abuse, and supports a Women's Resource Center as well as programs in ethnic studies. A senior English major declares, "There is not necessarily a distinct separation among the minority groups, but definitely a separation between them and the Caucasians on campus." Numerous merit scholarships, ranging from $3,856 to $10,000, are doled out every year, as well as athletic scholarships in baseball, softball, basketball, tennis, volleyball, track and field, and water polo. National Merit Scholars are guaranteed a $750 award each year they attend, and scholarships are available for engineering students.

Unlike those at other UC schools, Riverside professors dedicate much of their time and attention to their students.

Housing is a breeze—reasonably priced and reasonably easy to obtain. Thirty percent of the students live in the well-maintained dorms, where freshmen and continuing dorm residents are guaranteed a spot. Twenty-eight percent of the students live in off-campus apartments, and another third commute from home. Dorms, all of which are coed, are clean and comfortable, and provide a social context as well as a living atmosphere. Social life is relatively tame, since so many of the students commute. The administration claims "a quiet atmosphere, conducive to serious study"; students say it's boring but friendly. "Social life is quite dull," says a senior. "The campus is quiet after 5:00 P.M." Fraternities lure 3 percent of the men, and sororities 3 percent of the women. The groups usually hold campus-wide parties once a quarter. "Any campus with 10 fraternities does its share of partying," observes a math major. But "it is becoming harder for undergrads under 21 to drink," says a theater major. And in general there is "no wild party action here," reports one slightly disappointed student. A campus hangout known as the Barn has live bands, comedy nights, and movies. Every Wednesday the campus can enjoy a "nooner," where live bands play during lunch. "We're not on the beach and don't have a football team, so we don't have jocks and air-headed blondes," reports one serious student. Scots Week is a festival of athletic and other activities; clubs vie to see who can stage the best prank, and individuals engage in a pie-eating/throwing contest.

"Social life is quite dull. The campus is quiet after 5:00 P.M."

Homecoming is also a big to-do, and sports generate a considerable amount of interest at UCR. Both the male and female karate teams are among the best in the

Scots Week is a festival of athletic and other activities; clubs vie to see who can stage the best prank, and individuals engage in a pie-eating/throwing contest.

nation, and the men's basketball consistently performs at championship levels. Men's tennis and cross-country are also strong contenders. Among women's sports, the national championship volleyball team draws big crowds. For weekend athletes, intramurals are a popular antidote to too many hours in the library. People have been known to camp outside the sign-up office for a night in order to make sure their team gets a place in the intramural league.

Most students agree with a physics major who says, "The thing I like least about Riverside is the city of Riverside," which is "an hour from everywhere, in the middle of nowhere." A suburb is about the nicest thing it gets called, but the weather is wonderful three seasons a year (the smog is terrible in the summertime). Near the campus there are a few bars and nightclubs, but farther down the road lies a run-down neighborhood. Luckily, Los Angeles, Palm Springs, the beaches, and (if you go for horned toads, Gila monsters, and rattlers) the desert are all within an hour's drive of the campus. Big Bear and Mountain High ski resorts are also within easy reach.

All in all, coming to Riverside is a trade-off. Some students complain that course offerings are limited, and others that the school lacks history, tradition, and culture. But the intimate, personalized style is unique in the UC system and especially cherished by the homesick. Academics are serious and demanding, but on-campus social life and extracurriculars are on a strictly do-it-yourself basis. It can't do what Berkeley or UCLA does, but then it doesn't try. Comparing Riverside to schools ten times its size really doesn't work; it's a little like comparing apples and, well, navel oranges.

Overlaps

UC–Irvine, UCLA, UC–San Diego, UC–Santa Cruz, UC–Santa Barbara

If You Apply To ➤ **Riverside:** Regular admissions: Nov. 30. Financial aid: Mar. 2. Housing: June 1. Guarantees to meet demonstrated need. No campus or alumni interviews. SATs or ACTs: required. SAT IIs: required (writing, math, and one other). Accepts electronic applications. Essay question: personal statement.

UC–San Diego

9500 Gilman Drive, Department 0021-A, La Jolla, CA 92093-0021

Applications have doubled in the past ten years at this seaside paradise. UCSD now rivals better-known Berkeley and UCLA as the Cal campus of choice for top students. Five undergraduate colleges break down UCSD to a more manageable size. Best known for science and engineering.

Website: www.ucsd.edu
Location: Suburban
Total Enrollment: 19,918
Undergraduates: 16,230
Male/Female: 48/52
SAT Ranges: V 550–650
M 590–690
ACT Range: 22–27
Financial Aid: 51%
Expense: Pub $ $ $

Some say that looking good is better than feeling good, but at UC–San Diego, they're doing a lot of both. Set against the serene beauty of La Jolla's beaches, students catch as much relaxation time as they do study time. But it's not all fun and games around this campus. The research star of the UC system, UCSD's faculty is rated number one nationally among public institutions in science productivity. And within each of the five undergraduate colleges, a system that offers undergraduates more intimate settings, students are honing their minds with the classics and the cutting edge in academics. Sure, San Diegans tend to be more mellow than the average Southern Californian, and UCSD students follow suit. But beneath the frown-free foreheads and bright smiles, UCSD's bubbling with intellectual energy and the healthy desire to be at the top of the UC system.

San Diego's tree-lined campus sits high on a bluff overlooking the Pacific in the seaside resort of La Jolla. Each of the five colleges has its own flavor, but the predominant architectural theme is contemporary, with a few out-of-the-ordinary structures, including a library that looks like an inverted pyramid. Another tinge of the postmodern is the nation's largest neon sculpture, which wraps around one of the high-rise academic buildings and consists of seven-foot-tall letters that spell out the seven virtues superimposed over the seven vices.

UCSD's programs in science and engineering are "not for the faint of heart," says one student. Engineering requires a B average in entry-level courses for acceptance into the major. The Scripps Institute of Oceanography is also excellent, due to the university's advantageous location. Computer science and chemistry also get strong recommendations, but you really can't go wrong in any of the hard sciences. Although the humanities and social sciences are not as solid in comparison, political science and psychology get strong backing from students. The math department, however, is less than adequate. In addition, the

> "The courses here are challenging and intellectually stimulating, but there are also a lot of fun classes too."

university lacks a full-fledged business program, and the administration states that UC–San Diego is not the place to go for practical or career-oriented courses. Imaginative interdisciplinary offerings include computer music, urban planning, ethnic studies, and a psychology/computer science program in artificial intelligence, as well as majors devised by students themselves.

Like most of the UC campuses, San Diego operates on the quarter system, which makes for a semester's worth of work crammed into ten weeks. Science students find the load intense. "The courses here are challenging and intellectually stimulating, but there are also a lot of fun classes too," says one senior. Students have a choice of six libraries, some good for research, others better for socializing. Despite the quality of research done by the faculty, half a dozen of whom are Nobel laureates, students find that the typical scenario of research over teaching seen at most large research universities is not as common at UC–San Diego. "Professors here are brilliant and conduct research throughout the year, but they also have a desire to share their knowledge with their students," says a communication major.

UC–San Diego's five undergraduate colleges, each of which (except the newest) has about three thousand students, have their own sets of general education requirements, their own personalities, and differing ideals upon which they are based. Prospective freshmen apply to UC–San Diego—the admissions requirements are identical for each college—but students must indicate their college preference. Revelle College, the oldest, is the most rigorous and mandates that students become equally

> "UCSD is still shaping its new admissions policy to maintain ethnic diversity on campus."

acquainted with a certain level of coursework in the humanities, sciences, and social sciences, as well as fulfill a language requirement. Muir allows more flexibility in the distribution requirements. "Generally, Muir students are considered dumb blondes, while Revelle students are considered nerdy," says a recent graduate. Thurgood Marshall College was founded to emphasize and encourage social awareness; like Revelle, it places equal weight on sciences, social sciences, and humanities. However, it stresses a liberal arts education based on "an examination of the human condition in a multicultural society." Warren has developed a highly organized internship program that gives its undergraduates more practical experience than the others do. The newest college, Eleanor Roosevelt College ("Fifth"), devotes its curriculum to international and cross-cultural studies.

A theater major notes that UCSD's academic intensity "does not mean that all the students here are nerdy. They enjoy athletics and extracurricular activities, but

(Continued)

Phi Beta Kappa: Yes
Applicants: 32,539
Accepted: 41%
Enrolled: 25%
Grad in 6 Years: 70%
Returning Freshmen: 93%
Academics: ✍ ✍ ✍ ✍ ✍
Social: ☎ ☎ ☎ ☎
Q of L: ★ ★ ★ ★
Admissions: (619) 534-4831
Email Address:
   admissionsinfo@ucsd.edu

Strongest Programs
   Biology
   Psychology
   Applied Mechanics and
      Engineering
   Economics
   Political Science
   Oceanography
   Communications

The five colleges have their own sets of general education requirements, their own personalities, and differing ideals upon which they are based.

academic excellence is their priority." A short walk to the beach, however, reveals the student body's wild and crazy half-surfers and their fans, who celebrate the "kick back." Students jumping curbs on skateboards are common on this campus. Yet these beach babies are no scholastic slouches. Virtually all of them placed in the top 10 percent of their high-school class, and they had an average GPA of 3.8. The average student pulls a 3.0 GPA while at UCSD. Many students here choose to take five years to graduate in order to gain a higher GPA, and many of the scientists continue their studies after graduation. UCSD also ranks high among public colleges and universities in the percentage of graduates who go on to earn a Ph.D., and in the percentage of students accepted to medical school. Most of the 3 percent from out of state are from the other Southwestern states. Minority representation is high, with 35 percent of the student body Asian-American, 10 percent Hispanic, and 2 percent African-American. Affirmative action programs have been abolished in the UC system, but "UCSD is still shaping its new admissions policy to maintain ethnic diversity on campus," notes the administration—perhaps a response to all the student protests against the passing of the anti–affirmative action initiative.

Each of the university's colleges has its own housing complex, with either dorms or apartments. Eighty percent of the freshmen live on campus and are guaranteed housing for their first two years. "The residence halls are very nice, with all the amenities, including Ethernet hookups in every room," says an animal physiology major. By junior year, students usually decide to take up residence in La Jolla proper or nearby Del Mar, often in beachside apartments; only 36 percent of all the students live on campus. But that can be costly: the price ends up being inversely proportional to proximity to the beach. If you are willing to relinquish the luxury of a five-minute walk to the beach, a short commute will bring you relatively affordable housing.

"Most students hang out at the dance clubs, jazz bars, and great restaurants in the Gaslamp Quarter."

The immediate surroundings of UCSD, however, are definitely not affordable. "La Jolla," says a student, "is a wealthy, ritzy beach community. In no way is it a college town." Cars are, of course, an inescapable part of Southern California life, and owning one—many people do—makes off-campus living even more pleasant. Unfortunately, trying to park on campus can be difficult, though at least one student says that "parking is not nearly as bad here as it is at other schools." Dorm residents are required to buy a meal card, which gets them into any of the four campus cafeterias as well as the campus deli and burger joints.

The university is dry, so most of the real socializing seems to take place off campus. "Most students hang out at the dance clubs, jazz bars, and great restaurants in the Gaslamp Quarter," says a senior. Annual festivals include the Open House, Renaissance Faire, UnOlympics, and the Reggae Festival. Another annual festival pays tribute to a hideously loud and colorful statue of the Sun God, which is the unofficial mascot for this sun-streaked student body. Ten percent of both the men and the women try to beat the blahs by joining a fraternity or sorority. Alcoholic parties are banned in the residence halls, though students say lax RAs and good fake IDs make for easy underage drinking. Although campus life is relatively tame, students rely heavily on the surrounding area—but not La Jolla—for their entertainment. Students go to nearby Pacific Beach, and downtown San Diego with the zoo, Sea World, and Balboa Park, is only twelve miles away. Torrey Pines Natural Reserves are great for outdoor enthusiasts. Mexico—and the $5 lobster—is a half-hour drive (even nearer than the desert, where many students go hiking), and the two-hour trip to Los Angeles makes for a nice weekend jaunt.

Although San Diego is the farthest thing imaginable from a rah-rah school, it is rapidly becoming a Division III powerhouse, most notably in women's sports.

students must take a third of their courses) is excellent. Students seriously interested in the humanities or social sciences are often frustrated by the limited course offerings. "Science is what Caltech is all about," says a freshman chemical engineering student. "Even if you are a literature major, you have to take quantum physics/mechanics to even graduate."

Most students can access the campus computer system from their dorm rooms, and one student boasts that Caltech has "the best computer/student ratio in the nation." Speaking of the best, among Caltech's facilities are the Beckman Institute, a center for fundamental research in biology and chemistry, and the Keck telescope, the largest optical telescope in the world. Recently added to the campus is the Moore Laboratory, with ninety thousand square feet filled with high-tech equipment for engineering and communications majors.

In spite of a few geniuses who are impossible to understand or impossibly demanding, the professors tend to be good teachers. They are described by students as "extremely smart," "approachable," and "top-notch." Of course, they are usually more interested in research than in classes, but then again, so are most of their students. For many, summertime is the time to go SURF-ing, as in Summer Undergraduate Research Fellowships, which are grants that give three hundred undergraduates a chance to get a head start on their own research under a faculty sponsor. Some 20 percent of them publish their work in scientific literature, the administration estimates. Research is so much in the air, in fact, that many students agree that "the focus definitely leans toward research and the graduate population," which is slightly larger than the undergraduate.

"Science is what Caltech is all about," says a freshman chemical engineering student. "Even if you are a literature major, you have to take quantum physics/mechanics to even graduate."

"There is a social life here, it just revolves around homework."

After four years in high school as the resident math/science genius, most freshmen show up at Caltech a little wet behind the ears. Bragging about being first in your high-school class will impress no one at Caltech; you're just joining the club. Techers say most students have a hard time successfully balancing a social life with academic demands. One slogan says students can pick sleep, social life, or work. "There is a social life here, it just revolves around homework," says one sophomore. "The workload really dampens the social life," laments a freshman. Thirty percent of the student body comes from California, but the rest are drawn from all over the nation. Asian-Americans account for more than a quarter of each class, with African-Americans and Hispanics at 8 percent combined. This seeming lack of diversity was recently highlighted by the fact that, among the nation's elite institutions, Caltech was the only one to admit no black freshmen in the 1999 academic year. But, the school is taking steps to increase programming for women and minorities and improve relations with them. The school guarantees to meet the full demonstrated financial need of every admit, and there are merit scholarships awarded to students at the beginning of sophomore year.

Bragging about being first in your high-school class will impress no one at Caltech; you're just joining the club.

Perhaps the most distinctive attribute of Techers is their commitment to one another, a supportiveness sustained by an honor system that a recent student poll rated as the best aspect of life at Caltech. Based on the principle that "no one shall take unfair advantage of any other member of the Caltech community," it is maintained through four years of grueling academic pressure that, though intense, is curiously enough not competitive. "Faculty and administration trust us and we don't abuse the trust," a freshman says. Faculty gives take-home exams, and if the instructions say the exam is three-hour closed book, then the students all follow these instructions to the letter. Students rule themselves, and if violations of the honor code are suspected, "students decide if a violation was indeed made," describes one student.

There are no fraternities or sororities, but the seven coed on-campus houses inspire a loyalty worthy of the Greeks. The four older houses, which have been renovated, offer mostly single rooms, while the three newer dorms have doubles that have also been refurbished. Freshmen select their house during Rotation Week, when they spend an evening of partying at each one, indicating at week's end the four they like the most. Resident upperclassmen take it from there in a professional-sports-type draft that places each freshman in one of his or her top choices. For those business-minded types, there's Avery House, a dorm whose residents embody the spirit of entrepreneurship. Each dorm's dining hall serves, on a mandatory basis, standard institutional food from a central kitchen (a new food service has improved quality a bit), but other than for meals, students loyally support their home bases. Ninety percent of the entire student body live in one form of university housing or another.

The houses are the emotional center of Caltech life. The site of Caltech parties, they are also the scene of innumerable practical jokes perpetrated on staff members and seniors. "Caltech is definitely known for its pranks," notes a junior. On Ditch Day, seniors barricade their dorm rooms using everything from steel bars to electronic codes, leave clues as to how to overcome the obstacles, and disappear from campus. Underclassmen spend the day figuring out how to break in and claim the awaiting reward, which can range from the edible to...well, anything is possible. Perhaps the most unforgettable student prank was orchestrated during the 1984

"Caltech is definitely known for its pranks."

Rose Bowl game. UCLA was playing Illinois, and a group of Caltech whiz kids were playing with the scoreboard in an attempt to get national exposure for Caltech. They spent months devising a radio-control device that would allow them to take control of the scoreboard in the second half and flash pictures of their school's mascot, the beaver, as well as a new version of the score that had Caltech leading MIT by a mile.

A Caltech student's idea of fun is likely to be a little offbeat and creative. For example, the annual Pumpkin Drop (on Halloween, of course) involves immersing a pumpkin in liquid nitrogen for several days and then dropping it from the library roof so it shatters into a zillion frozen pumpkin shards. During finals week, stereos blast "The Ride of the Valkyries" at seven o'clock each morning, just the thing to get you going after that all-nighter. Although Pasadena has become a hip, trendy place for up-and-coming yuppies to hang out, L.A. is the original all-night city for Caltechers with a car—and even rarer—a free evening. As one stressed-out Techer notes, "When I have free time, I go to sleep."

When it comes to athletics, physical education, and recreation, Caltech sponsors a well-balanced and broad-based program. The program consists of eighteen NCAA sports including men's and women's cross-country, men's soccer, women's volleyball, water polo, men's and women's basketball, men's and women's fencing, baseball, golf, men's and women's tennis, and men's and women's track and field. Caltech has a large and varied program of physical education classes and boasts an excellent program of both undergraduate and graduate student intramural sports, with an 80 percent participation rate.

Although studying at one of the world's most renowned schools for scientific research can be exhilarating, students can face enormous stress and a social scene that leaves much to be desired. One electrical engineering major reflects, "You can play a sport that you hadn't heard of a year ago, you can be an actor in the winter play, or write for the newspaper. You can do it all if you don't let your studies take over your life." At this high-powered and demanding college, that may be easier said than done.

Overlaps

MIT, Stanford, UC–Berkeley, UCLA, Harvard

Calvin College

3201 Burton, Grand Rapids, MI 49546

An evangelical Christian institution that ranks high on the private-college bargain list. More than half the students are members of the Christian Reformed Church. Archrival of Michigan neighbor Hope and Illinois cousin Wheaton. Best-known in the humanities.

Christian values are as much a feature of the Calvin College experience as academics. Students are asked to define their religious beliefs on the admissions application, and a spiritual mentorship program offers to link students with "wise Christian friends" such as professors and staff. Religion also permeates the classroom environment. Says one senior, "Students at Calvin are encouraged to learn how to live in the world according to a Christian standard, because they are encouraged to apply their beliefs and perspectives to their learning." Along with Wheaton College in Illinois, Calvin is regarded as one of the country's top two evangelical colleges.

The educational wing of the Christian Reformed Church in North America, Calvin was founded in 1876. After outgrowing its first home, the college bought a large tract of land on the city's edge and built the present campus of more than 370 beautifully landscaped acres that encompass three ponds, playing fields, and a nature preserve. The campus includes a one hundred-acre woodland and wetland nature preserve that is used for class work, research, and recreation. Campus facilities are less than thirty-five years old and were designed by a pupil of architect Frank Lloyd Wright. The school is building a new communication center and a new conference center. The college is located in suburban Grand Rapids, which one senior describes as a "great community for a college to be located in." Students often head into town to volunteer or intern, or for social happenings.

Calvin students describe the overall academic environment as challenging but supportive. "Calvin's education keeps students on their toes. The workload is demanding and students have to stay on top of their schedules," a senior says. Every subject, the school believes, can be approached from a Christian perspective, integrating faith and learning. For instance, first-year students take courses such as Christian Perspectives on Learning and Developing a Christian Mind. The Communication Arts and Sciences department is highly respected for its reformed Christian perspective on the mass media and popular culture.

The core curriculum mandates Core Gateway courses, Core Capstone courses, Core Studies courses such as Physical World and Biblical Foundation, and Core Competencies courses including foreign languages and Rhetoric in Culture. Strong high school preparation and advanced-placement tests can help reduce these requirements. Minors in Asian studies and gender studies are new, along with a concentration in digital communications.

Traditionally, the school's strongest programs have been English and history, and the departments of music, math, and the natural sciences are outstanding. Calvin graduates have few problems getting accepted to graduate schools of law,

> **"Calvin's education keeps students on their toes."**

Website: www.calvin.edu
Location: Suburban
Total Enrollment: 4,324
Undergraduates: 4,286
Male/Female: 42/58
SAT Ranges: V 520–640
  M 530–660
ACT Range: 22–28
Financial Aid: 57%
Expense: Pr $
Phi Beta Kappa: No
Applicants: 1,870
Accepted: 98%
Enrolled: 57%
Grad in 6 Years: 71%
Returning Freshmen: 87%
Academics: ✏ ✏ ✏
Social: ☎ ☎ ☎
Q of L: ★ ★ ★ ★
Admissions: (616) 957-6106
  or (800) 688-0122
Email Address:
  admissions@calvin.edu

Strongest Programs:
  Education
  Business
  Psychology
  English
  Biology

medicine, or business. Students also recommend the education, social work, and nursing programs, as well as the engineering and communication arts departments, but cite the languages as weak. Students in the general business program can opt for a wide range of specializations, including marketing, human resources management, operations management, finance, and economics. Internships and small-business consulting opportunities are also integral parts of a student's program—Calvin is a member of the Christian College Consortium*—and there's a five-year co-op plan. The bachelor's degree in accounting has resulted in students passing the CPA exam at rates of 15–20 percent above the national average. Education is the most popular major, and the school is focusing more on technology and international education.

Class size is small—many have fewer than twenty-five students—and faculty members, all of whom must be committed to Christian teachings, are especially helpful. "The teachers here have challenged me to think in a way I thought not possible and their availability is uncomparable to any school." There are no teaching assistants, and professors are expected to reserve about ten hours per week for advising outside of class. Most devote more time than that to their students. "Even though the profs expect a lot, they truly want to see you succeed as a student," says a business major. Students use the interim month of January to pursue a variety of creative, low-pressure alternatives on or off campus. For those who opt for travel, there are opportunities for studying art and theater in England, and languages in Germany, Canada, and the Dominican Republic. Students who stay on campus can take such courses as Shakespeare's Greatest Hits or the provocative Toward a Theology of Wealth and Possessions. There's also an award-winning lecture series that brings in nationally known speakers.

> "Even though the profs expect a lot, they truly want to see you succeed as a student."

The administration reports that more than half of Calvin students are members of the Christian Reformed Church, though that proportion is dwindling. The school has a strong Dutch heritage but is becoming more diverse. The population is 85 percent white, 1 percent African-American, 1 percent Hispanic, and 2 percent Asian-American. "There are a lot of different people at Calvin, but everyone seems to be real with who they are and what they believe," says a student. Fifty-five percent are students are from Michigan and 8 percent are foreign-born. The Entrada program brings high-school students from ethnic minorities to campus for a residential summer program. The school offers more than 1,600 merit scholarships and a tuition gift-certificate program that allows families to prepay tuition, but there are no athletic scholarships.

> "Calvin students push each other to learn more in school, about themselves, and their Christian faith."

Freshmen and sophomores under twenty-one who do not live at home with their parents must live on campus. "The dorms are my favorite thing about Calvin," says a senior. "It is a 'suite' setup, no pun intended." Each residence hall and two apartment buildings have computer rooms in their basements. The "MOSAIC Community" lets students live in a residence hall designed to be multicultural. "Project Neighborhood" places Calvin students and two adult mentors in a college-owned house located in a core neighborhood in Grand Rapids.

Calvin's social life includes on-campus concerts and Thursday open-mic nights at Cave Cafe. "Social life is usually incorporated in the residence halls," a senior says. There is no Greek scene, and many of the social activities revolve around the housing units. Road trips include the beaches of Lake Michigan (a one-hour drive) or Chicago and Detroit (three hours distant). A popular annual event is Chaos Day, when each dorm (both the male and female wings) competes in athletic games. The huge Airband lip-sync competition in February is also a favorite activity, as are athletic contests versus Hope College. Calvin maintains an officially dry campus, and "the alcohol policy is pretty much followed to a T," says one junior.

While the Knights don't field a football squad, students love almost all other sports competitions, with men's soccer and basketball and women's basketball and volleyball. The men's basketball team and cross-country team each took the national championship in the NCAA Division III in 2000, which the women's cross-country team did in 1998 and 1999. Calvinites come face to face with each other in intramural competition.

Calvin's sense of community and the opportunity to serve meshes well with the strong Christian faith of most students. They come here looking for an environment that would combine faith-based learning with academic rigor, and they find it. "Calvin students push each other to learn more in school, about themselves, and their Christian faith," a senior says.

> **Overlaps**
>
> **Hope, Wheaton (IL), Grand Valley State, University of Michigan–Ann Arbor, Trinity Christian**

If You Apply To >

Calvin: Rolling admissions. Financial aid: Feb. 15. Housing: May 1. Campus interviews: optional, informational. No alumni interviews. SATs or ACTs: required. ACTs preferred. SAT IIs: optional. Essay question: interest in Calvin, academic experiences, religious beliefs, personal statement.

Canadian Colleges and Universities

Horace Greeley told ambitious young men of his generation to "go West." Today his admonition to young men and women seeking a quality college education at a fraction of the usual cost would probably be to "go North"—to Canada. A growing number of American students are discovering the educational riches that lie just above their northern border in this huge land of thirty million people that is known for its rugged mountains, bicultural politics, spirited ice hockey, and cold ale. What's drawing them is easy to discern.

The top Canadian universities are the academic equals of most flagship public universities and many leading privates in the United States, but the expense of a bachelor's degree is far lower, even taking travel into account. Canadian campuses and the cities in which they are located are safe places, and, unless one opts for a French course of study, there are no language and few cultural barriers. Canadian schools are strong on international exchange programs, and their degrees carry weight with U.S. graduate schools.

Canada has ninety institutions of higher learning ranging from internationally recognized research universities to the small undergraduate teaching institutions in the country's more rural areas; the country ranks second after the U.S. in the percentage of citizens attending university. Most of the larger universities are located in highly urban centers, but some are situated in smaller towns where they dominate the life of the community. Most are almost literally next door to the United States, within one hundred miles of the Canada–U.S. border. In this guide, we feature four of Canada's strongest universities: the University of British Columbia, McGill University, Queen's University, and the University of Toronto.

Institutions of higher learning in Canada were established from the earliest days of French settlement in the mid seventeenth Century, making them some of the oldest in North America. The precursors to the public universities in Canada were the small, elite, denominational colleges that sprang up in Quebec, in the Maritimes, and later in Ontario. A few private denominational colleges and universities still exist in Canada, but most have been subsumed into affiliations or associations with the larger universities. Education in Canada, including university education, became the exclusive jurisdiction of provincial governments. As the Canadian West was developed the large Western provinces of British Columbia, Alberta, Manitoba, and Saskatchewan set up provincially chartered universities similar to land-grant colleges in the U.S.

One of the key differences between Canadian and U.S. universities is that Canadian universities (and this is what they are, not "colleges") are primarily funded from public monies. Despite steady tuition increases in the past five years, the average Canadian student still only pays on average about $2,500 in Canadian dollars, or U.S. $1,700. Although non-Canadians may be charged up to six times the domestic rate, most costs are still lower than out-of-state tuition in the U.S. Tuition at the four universities described below ranges from U.S. $5,500 to $9,200.

Canadians have come to expect easy and affordable access to a uniformly high quality of education whether they live in Halifax or Vancouver. After diminishing government funding in the past several years, a now booming economy, a large government surplus, new federal initiatives grants for innovations and scholarships, and the universities' own aggressive fund-raising campaigns bode well for the continued growth and quality of Canadian higher education in the immediate future.

Federal and provincial loans and grants that are readily available to Canadian students are generally not available to students from the U.S. and other countries. However, the majority of universities with competitive admissions, particularly those featured in *The Fiske Guide*, offer merit-based awards and scholarships to students of all nationalities. American students who attend leading Canadian schools can apply their U.S. student assistance funds, including Stafford Loans and Pell Grants as well as the recently implemented HOPE Scholarship and Lifetime Learning tax credits.

The requirements for obtaining a degree are set by each institution, as are the admission requirements and prerequisites. Unlike the U.S., Canada does not offer nor require its own students to take a Canadian college entrance test. Some Canadian universities admitting students from the United States will require the results of SAT or ACT scores along with high-school marks from academic subjects in the last two or three years of high school. In general, top universities are about as selective as their American counterparts.

Application fees vary by institution, as do deadlines. Canadian universities are aware of the May 1 deadline operative in the U.S., and try to accommodate. Applications to the University of Toronto and Queen's University in Ontario are handled centrally through the Ontario Universities' Application Service. McGill handles applications directly and accepts both Web-based and paper applications. British Columbia has its own application; it can be mailed, but encourages students to apply online. Canadian universities differ widely in the amount of credit and/or advanced standing they offer for Advanced Placement Examinations or International Baccalaureate Higher Level Examinations.

The following admission requirements apply to applicants from an American school system. The University of British Columbia bases admission decisions on the average on eight full-year academic courses over the last two years of high school, and there are also specific program requirements for students entering the science-based faculties. SAT test results are not required, but if students submit them, the results can be helpful in the evaluation process. McGill bases its assessment of American high-school graduates on the overall record of marks in academic subjects during the final three years of high school, class standing, and results obtained in SAT I and SAT II and/or ACT tests. Queen's wants applicants with a minimum score of 1200 on SAT I (with at least 580 in the verbal section and 520 in the mathematical one) and looks at class rank. There are also program-specific requirements for programs where mathematics and/or biology, chemistry, and physics are a requirement. Toronto's Arts and Science faculties want a high grade-point average and good scores on the SAT I and on three SAT II subject tests. ACT and CEEB Advanced Placement Examination scores are also considered.

It is hard to beat Canadian universities for the quality of student life. Although many students commute, most of the universities in Canada offer on-campus housing; some even guarantee campus housing for first-year students. Universities offer active intramural and intercollegiate sports programs for both men and women, and the usual student clubs, newspapers, and radio stations provide students with opportunities to get involved and to develop friendships. As in the United States, student-run organizations are active participants in university life, with leaders serving on university committees and lobbying on issues ranging from creating more bicycle paths to keeping tuitions low. Few Canadian campuses are troubled by issues of student safety or rowdiness. In the larger urban centers, Canadian campuses reflect the rich cultural diversity of Canada's cultural mosaic, and most encourage their students to gain international experience by spending a term or a full year abroad.

Americans wondering about the currency of a Canadian degree in the U.S. should be reassured that top American and multinational countries—the likes of Archer Daniels Midland, Chase Manhattan, IBM, Microsoft, Nortel Networks, and Solomon Smith Barney—actively recruit on Canadian campuses, as do American graduate schools. According to the Institute of International Education in New York, more than seven thousand Canadians are currently enrolled in graduate schools in the United States.

The one thing that is different for U.S. and other international students intending to study in Canada is that they will have to obtain a Student Authorization, equivalent to a visa, from Canadian immigration authorities. Getting a Student Authorization is fairly straightforward for American citizens, but this slight bureaucratic hurdle is a reminder that Canada, for all of its similarities in language and culture with the United States, is still another country. For many American students who have chosen to study in Canada, this is part of the draw—they get to enjoy all the excitement of studying abroad in a foreign country with few of the cultural and none of the linguistic barriers to overcome. One of the most pleasant differences American students soon discover is how far their American dollar goes in Canada with the favorable exchange rate.

The Association of Universities and Colleges of Canada has a website at www.aucc.ca. Another good source of scholastic information is the website of the Canadian Embassy in Washington D.C. at www.canadianembassy.org/studyincanada.

Canadian universities are currently playing host to about three thousand American students on their campuses, and as a result of funding cutbacks and internationalization policies in the early 1990s, they have become increasingly active in recruiting students from south of the border. This is but one more reason why it makes sense for more young Americans to check out the "Canadian option." Canada, eh?

University of British Columbia

Vancouver, British Columbia, Canada V6T 1Z1

Natural beauty is the first thing that draws Americans to Vancouver—and Canada's premier western university. A similar scale to places like University of Washington but with two major differences—no big-time sports to unite the campus and limited dorm life.

What do two prime ministers of Canada, three provincial premiers, an astronaut, a world-renowned opera singer, and a Nobel Prize winner have in common? Give up? They are all graduates of the University of British Columbia. Founded in 1908, UBC offers students solid programs in business and science, ready access to beaches and mountains, and a diploma with instant name recognition. Though the massive campus can sometimes feel isolating, students are nevertheless happy to be here. After all, not everyone can lay claim to such illustrious company.

Located just twent-five minutes from downtown Vancouver, UBC's striking Point Grey campus covers a peninsula that borders the Pacific Ocean and is bounded by an old-growth forest. Mountains—perfect for skiing—loom in the distance. Architectural styles are a mix of Gothic and modern, and students can enjoy a leisurely stroll through the university's botanical gardens. Recent campus additions include the Chan Centre for the Performing Arts, the Centre for Integrated Computer Systems Research, and the $50 million Forest Sciences Centre.

According to the UBC administration, the university's mission is to "offer students an intellectually challenging education...that prepares them to become citizens of...the twenty-first century through programs that are international in scope, interactive in process, and interdisciplinary in content and approach." Strong programs include microbiology, international relations, economics, and business administration. Asian studies is highly regarded, and theatre majors benefit from the new Chan

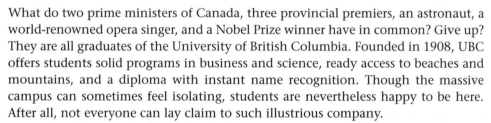
"Everyone can fit in because the student body is so diverse and large."

Centre for the Performing Arts. Other popular majors include psychology and computer science. The administration admits that some home economics and agricultural science courses could be strengthened, and one student grumbles about his 8:00 A.M. philosophy lecture: "Who can focus on the big questions at that time of the morning?"

Website:
  www.welcome.ubc.ca
Location: Suburban
Total Enrollment: 35,248
Undergraduates: 28,811
Male/Female: 43/57
SAT Ranges: N/A
ACT Range: N/A
Financial Aid: N/A
Expense: Pub $
Phi Beta Kappa: No
Applicants: 18,642
Accepted: 41%
Enrolled: 53%
Grad in 6 Years: 87%
Returning Freshmen: 88%
Academics: ✑ ✑ ✑ ✑ ½
Social: ☎ ☎
Q of L: ★ ★ ★
Admissions: (604) 822-8999
Email Address: international.
  reception@ubc.ca

Strongest Programs:
  Economics
  Microbiology

(Continued)
Business Administration
Computer Science
Computer Engineering
Asian Studies
International Relations

Freshmen benefit from a wide array of first-year programs, including Imagine UBC, a first-day orientation. Arts Foundation is a series of three courses that offers an enriched, integrated approach to broad interdisciplinary themes in arts and humanities. Qualified students can take advantage of Science One, featuring team-taught courses in biology, chemistry, math, and physics. Student exchange programs are available through 145 partner universities around the globe, and co-op programs in engineering, science, arts, commerce, and forestry give students an opportunity to earn while they learn. In addition, honors and double-honors programs are available to super-brains and budding geniuses.

The academic climate is exactly what you would expect from a university of UBC's stature. "It requires a lot of hard work to achieve an A at UBC," says a senior. Most classes have less than fifty students, though mammoth lectures are not uncommon for freshmen. Faculty receive mixed reviews, depending largely on the department. "Most profs are focused on their students and will help whenever possible," says a senior. A junior, however, grumbles that many professors "are either too old and need to be retired...or too young and without experience." Academic advising is a mixed bag, with some students complaining that finding a knowledgeable advisor can be time-consuming.

"We can do anything we want in Vancouver."

With nearly forty thousand students attending, it's no surprise that UBC's student population is a melting pot. "Everyone can fit in because the student body is so diverse and large," says a senior. The typical UBC student is bright, hardworking, and gregarious. Though government subsidies make UBC a relatively affordable institution, at least one student says "those with tons of money" will fit in best. A history major divides his classmates into two categories: commuters "who come in their fancy new cars with cell phones" and "those who live on campus and enjoy the community spirit." Minorities are well represented on campus (Asians make up the largest contingency), and the university encourages diversity through a series of special programs. Hot political issues include homosexual rights, abortion, and sexual harassment. UBC offers seventy-five merit scholarships to qualified students and athletic scholarships in seventeen varsity sports.

Qualified students can take advantage of Science One, featuring team-taught courses in biology, chemistry, math, and physics.

Only 5 percent of the students—mostly freshmen and sophomores—live in college housing, which is described as "quite nice and well maintained." The rest must fend for themselves against Vancouver's pricey rental market or commute from home. On-campus options include coed complexes (primarily for freshmen), university apartments, and family units for upperclassmen. Theme houses are another alternative, and offer like-minded students the opportunity to mingle. Dorm food encourages dieting, although "there are a couple of low-cost/good-food places that are always busy," reports a senior. Security is adequate, and features a walking escort service and nightly shuttle, though "most people just walk to where they want to go."

On-campus options include coed complexes (primarily for freshmen), university apartments, and family units for upperclassmen. Theme houses are another alternative and offer like-minded students the opportunity to mingle.

On such a large campus, isolation is a real threat. "You need to get in touch with other students quickly when you get here or you could feel lost on such a big campus," says a freshman. A senior adds, "To get the full value of UBC, you must willingly seek out clubs to join. Otherwise, you can feel lost and alone." Social life largely "depends on the crowd you hang with," according to one student. For partying types, there are the requisite beer bashes and toga parties, courtesy of UBC's small but active Greek scene—one of the few places where underage drinkers can sneak a sip of booze. Alcohol-free alternatives include university-sponsored events, such as movies and guest speakers. Popular campus events include Storm the Wall, long-boat racing, and the Arts County Fair.

Vancouver offers students countless opportunities for fun and contribution. "We can do anything we want in Vancouver," says a senior. "Most people go downtown for social events, bars, and shopping." Beautiful weather draws students outdoors and to nearby beaches and mountains for in-line skating, snowboarding, and swimming. Varsity and intramural competition are favorite pastimes; popular sports include soccer, basketball, hockey, volleyball, and skiing.

"If you're not confident and outgoing…you might be lost or lonely [at UBC]," admits a junior. Indeed, spending four years at this mammoth university can be isolating for the shy student. But for those willing to take control of their social lives, UBC offers an impressive academic milieu.

If You Apply To ➤

British Columbia: Early admission: Feb. 28 (domestic). Regular admissions: Mar. 31. Financial aid: Apr. 15. Housing: May 1 (for non-Canadians). Does not guarantee to meet demonstrated need. No campus or alumni interviews. SATs: recommended. SAT IIs: optional. No essay question.

McGill University

Montreal, Quebec, Canada H3Z 2E2

The Canadian university best-known south of the border. Though instruction is in English, McGill is located in French-speaking Montreal. Americans will not find the degree of extracurricular life available in the U.S. Only the self-motivated need apply.

Strong preprofessional programs and a diverse student body are just two of the drawing cards of McGill University. But beware: this is not a place for those in need of attention. "McGill is a very independent school," says a senior. "It is not a place for the student who needs lots of personal contact." Though Montreal's freezing weather and the university's impersonal atmosphere can leave some feeling cold, those who are willing to boldly go forward can expect to fit right in. With such notable alumni as singer Leonard Cohen, musician Burt Bacharach, astronaut Julie Payette, and actor William Shatner (*Star Trek's* Captain Kirk), it's easy to see why enterprising men and women from around the world flock to McGill University.

A junior describes McGill's eighty-eight-acre campus as "an oasis in the heart of the city." Located in downtown Montreal, amidst the hustle and bustle, the campus provides students with ample greenspace and a welcome respite from the decidedly urban atmosphere of the city. Campus buildings range from "Gothic-like" structures with vines growing up the sides to more modern (read: ugly) constructions ("You can ignore them if you try hard," says a senior). Trees and greenery dot the campus landscape, and mountain ranges rise into the sky to the north and south. The new Montreal Genomics and Proteomics Centre building and new Trottier Information Technology Building have recently been completed.

Though the most popular majors are psychology and English, there is no denying that the university's strengths lie in preprofessional programs such as medicine, law, and engineering. The management program is renowned, and students cite political science, religious studies, and philosophy as sure bets. The sciences receive uniform praise, and the school has recently opened its School of Environment, where environment-related courses are offered. For those who want to escape Montreal's brutal winter weather, there are internships, field studies in Barbados, exchange programs with more than five hundred partner universities around the world, and study-abroad options via the Canadian University Study Abroad Program (CUSAP).

Website: www.mcgill.ca
Location: City center
Total Enrollment: 28,552
Undergraduates: 21,757
Male/Female: 43/57
SAT Ranges: N/A
ACT Range: N/A
Financial Aid: 35%
Expense: Pub $
Phi Beta Kappa: No
Applicants: 16,952
Accepted: 55%
Enrolled: 47%
Grad in 6 Years: N/A
Returning Freshmen: N/A
Academics: ✍ ✍ ✍ ✍ ½
Social: ☎ ☎ ☎ ☎
Q of L: ★ ★ ★ ★
Admissions: (514) 398-3910
Email Address:
admissions@mcgill.ca

Strongest Programs:
Medicine
Law
Engineering

(Continued)
Management
Environmental Studies
Music

To fulfill the university's general education requirements, students must first choose which discipline (or faculty) to enter; popular choices include psychology, English, political science, mechanical engineering, and economics. A senior says, "It is important to consider the university on the basis of which faculty you would be interested in, because they vary greatly and operate almost as independent units." On average, students must earn 120 credits to graduate with a four-year degree. Freshmen must accumulate six to twelve credits in three of four disciplines, including languages, math and science, social sciences, and humanities, and declare a major before their sophomore year. Upon entering their major, students have a menu of course options that includes honors programs and double majors.

"The quality of teaching is tremendous." Regardless of the major, students can expect classes to be demanding. "McGill definitely keeps you on your toes," says a sophomore. Classes tend to be large—especially for freshmen—and students must be willing to seek out professors and advisors. "Students looking for small classes and personalized education...would not fit in at McGill," warns a political science major. "In many undergrad programs, classes are huge," agrees a psychology major. "However, classes are often accompanied by smaller tutorial sessions where students get more focused attention with professors or teaching assistants." Professors receive high marks for their knowledge and accessibility outside of class. "The quality of teaching is tremendous," says a student. "Our first two weeks of classes are the best because the institution is so big you can 'shop' for the best professors." Academic advising is a bureaucratic tangle—"My suggestion is to get to know a professor in your area and ask him or her your questions," says a student. McGill's 6.1 million library holdings are reportedly adequate, though "not outstanding."

Though the most popular majors are psychology and English, there is no denying that the university's strengths lie in preprofessional programs such as medicine, law, and engineering.

McGill students are a diverse lot—more than 150 countries are represented here—and the only common thread among students seems to be their fierce independence. "McGill students represent the world," says one student. "They are energetic, friendly, and cosmopolitan." Students report little racial hostility, and hot political issues include local politics and university funding. Qualified students are eligible for 1,807 scholarships of $2,000 to $15,000. There is also a work-study program for those in need of financial assistance. There are no athletic scholarships. "Once you have started at McGill, they will do everything they can to help you graduate," says a grad student.

The university's five traditional and fourteen alternative residence halls house 8 percent of the student population, primarily freshmen from out of town. Dorms run the gamut from "cement box room" to "gorgeous studio flat." Party animals will feel free to crank up the stereo in Molson or McConnell, while bookworms might be better suited

"McGill students represent the world." for Gardener. Douglas denizens enjoy their hall's quaint charm, and women who want to skip the coed scene can find a room in Royal Victoria College, an all-female dorm. "Almost every building has its own cafeteria and the food is generally good," says a senior. Off-campus apartments are a popular alternative for upperclassmen, who take advantage of Montreal's clean, affordable housing. Despite its urban location, the McGill campus is safe and security is considered more than adequate. "There are student organizations like 'Walksafe' and 'Drivesafe' that will walk or drive students home at night regardless of where they are or where they are going," reports one student.

Drinking is a popular pastime, but underage drinkers are few and far between since the legal age in Quebec is eighteen.

"There is a thriving social scene at McGill," says one student. Though there are "considerable on-campus social activities, with many clubs and associations," most students venture off campus and into the bars and clubs of Montreal for fun and adventure. "Montreal's rich musical, artistic, and young culture is intoxicating," says a sophomore. A senior adds, "The city of Montreal is absolutely essential to student life. Students live, work, and play there." Drinking is a popular pastime, but underage drinkers are few and far between since the legal age in Quebec is eighteen. "Alcohol is served on campus, but students are asked to show their IDs to prove their age," reports a modern languages major. Well-attended campus events include homecoming, a winter carnival, and Frosh Week activities. Popular roadtrips include New York City, Ottawa, and Toronto. Ski slopes are less than an hour away.

> **"The city of Montreal is absolutely essential to student life. Students live, work, and play there."**

Football, basketball, and ice hockey are the most popular varsity sports. According to one student, hated opponents include "our crosstown rivals at Concordia" and "our archenemies at Queen's University, in Kingston, Ontario. Both schools are very old and this is a long-standing traditional rivalry." Intramurals offer would-be jocks an opportunity to blow off steam after classes and on weekends. "As you walk through campus, you are sure to pass by a soccer, flag football, or rugby game on one of the numerous fields," says a student. New athletic facilities are a welcome addition for varsity athletes and "those of us who just like to work out," says a senior.

Overachievers and independent types do best here. "Slackers would be happier elsewhere," quips a senior. Large classes, brutal winters, and mountains of red tape are part of the McGill experience. Nevertheless, most seem happy to be here. "No one is here to hold your hand and make decisions for you," says a student. "But not to worry. You will have a great time—guaranteed!"

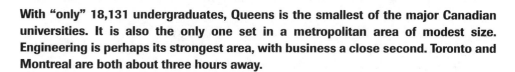

If You Apply To ➤ | **McGill:** Regular admissions: Jan. 15. Housing: Apr. 18 (American students). Does not guarantee to meet demonstrated need. No campus or alumni interviews. SATs or ACTs: required. SAT IIs: required (three, depending on program). Accepts electronic applications. No essay.

Queen's University

Kingston, Ontario, Canada K7L 3N6

With "only" 18,131 undergraduates, Queens is the smallest of the major Canadian universities. It is also the only one set in a metropolitan area of modest size. Engineering is perhaps its strongest area, with business a close second. Toronto and Montreal are both about three hours away.

Students at Queen's University approach work and play with equal zeal and enjoy a potent mix of school spirit and intellectual drive. Success requires energy and a willingness to get into the thick of things. "People who aren't interested in being a part of the school community are better off at a school that isn't such a big family," warns a sophomore. Solid academics, a pervasive school spirit, and longstanding traditions make life at this storied university unique—and demanding. "Getting into Queen's is just the first challenge," says a senior. "Succeeding at Queen's is another battle."

The 161-acre Queen's campus is located on the north shore of Lake Ontario, just minutes from the heart of Kingston, Ontario ("the limestone city") and directly between Montreal and Toronto. "Almost all buildings are constructed

Website: www.queensu.ca
Location: City center
Total Enrollment: 18,131
Undergraduates: 12,469
Male/Female: 44/56
SAT Ranges: N/A
ACT Range: N/A
Financial Aid: N/A
Expense: Pub $ $
Phi Beta Kappa: No

(Continued)

Applicants: 26,651
Accepted: 47%
Enrolled: 25%
Grad in 6 Years: 95%
Returning Freshmen: 96%
Academics: ✍ ✍ ✍ ✍ ½
Social: ☎ ☎ ☎ ☎
Q of L: ★ ★ ★ ★
Admissions: (613) 533-2218
Email Address:
  admissn@post.queensu.ca

Strongest Programs:
  Engineering
  Commerce
  Music

using limestone," explains a senior, "a Kingston tradition started by navy stone masons after the War of 1812." Historically significant buildings have been maintained and "there are some modern buildings with a lot of glass to provide a bright and welcoming atmosphere." Ample greenery and open spaces provide students a place to stretch out under the sky and hit the books. A new $57-million chemistry building features a 250-seat multimedia lecture theater and environmentally friendly labs that consume less electricity and produce less waste.

Established in 1841 by Royal Charter of Queen Victoria, Queen's offers undergraduate degrees in a variety of faculties, including arts, science, engineering, commerce, education, music, nursing science, and fine art. Academics are unilaterally solid, but the most demanding are engineering and commerce. The bachelor of commerce program was the first of its kind in Canada, and provides students with an internationally focused liberal business education, enhanced by new leadership modules and the

> **"The Queen's student seems to take on the leader role and is more likely to succeed."**

integration of technology. The newly restructured School of Computing offers Bachelor of Computer degrees in biomedical computing, cognitive science, and software design, as well as BA and BS degrees.

General education requirements vary by program, but all students can expect to complete a rigorous series of core and elective courses. Students participating in the Queen's International Study Centre are whisked away to the university's England campus, where they enjoy small classes and integrated field studies while residing in a fifteenth century castle. In addition, there are exchange programs with universities around the world.

The academic climate is challenging and competitive, which comes as no surprise to students. "Queen's is fairly competitive," says a junior, "but not bloodthirsty." The general consensus among struggling students is that As are hard to come by. "After working your butt off and reading stacks of textbooks, your grades pale in comparison to the marks of students at other universities," gripes a biology major. Classes tend to be large for freshmen and sophomores, but dwindle in size as one approaches graduation. The majority of classes are taught by full professors who receive praise for their accessibility and intelligence. "The teachers I have had have been thorough, challenging, and concerned about my success," says a junior. Office hours and special "wine and cheese" functions

> **"Extracurricular activities are a must, not an option!"**

give students ample opportunity to mingle with faculty. Students report that there is little trouble getting into desired classes, and "there is lots of counseling available for students who need it."

Queen's students are an industrious, intelligent group, and most are used to academic success. "The Queen's student seems to take on the leader role and is more likely to succeed," asserts one student. School spirit runs high and campus issues include rising tuition fees—and just who is responsible for the cost. Students come from every Canadian province and eighty countries, and a sociology major says that "Queen's is very PC and inclusive, regardless of gender, race, religion, or sexual orientation." A large percentage of the student body is active in extracurriculars, and school spirit is a must. Though there are no athletic scholarships, nearly eight hundred merit awards of $1,000 to $12,000 are handed out annually. "I have had great help through scholarships and financial aid," relates a senior. "There is quite a lot of money for you...you just have to go after it."

Twenty-five percent of the student body live in one of eleven residence halls, and all freshmen are guaranteed a place to hang their hat. "The residences are very comfortable and the custodial staff is in every day, becoming your parents away from home," says a junior. Coed and single-sex dorms are available. A mandatory

With forty-one varsity teams, Queen's athletic program is not only the largest in Canada, but also ties with Harvard University for the largest program in North America.

meal plan gives freshmen a wide variety of foods to choose from, including pasta, salad, pizza, and a soup-and-salad bar. The surrounding city also offers a plethora of dining options. "Kingston is known in our house as the 'city of restaurants,'" says a student. "They are everywhere." After freshman year, most students pack their bags and head off campus to the "student village," where comfortable apartments are available. In fact, 80 percent of Queen's students live within a fifteen-minute walk of campus. Though always a concern, safety is practically a nonissue on campus. Students report that they feel quite safe and that security is more than adequate.

Make no mistake about it, Queen's students know how to have a good time. "Social life is huge at Queen's," says a student. Adds another, "Campus pubs and city pubs have both found their niche." On Thursday nights, students flock to campus bars such as Afie's for a drink or two (or three), while Saturday nights are reserved for city bars and nightclubs. The legal drinking age is nineteen, and kiddies will have a tough time skirting the law. "The bouncers in Kingston actually have a couple of brain cells and can spot a fake ID from ninety kilometers away," says a senior. Nonalcoholic alternatives include school-sponsored movies and extracurricular clubs (there are more than 220!). "Extracurricular activities are a must, not an option!" says one student. Frosh Week is a favorite event with "cheers that even the most blasé of students will be shouting out with pride by the end of the week." The school is steeped in Scottish tradition, and it's normal to see kilt-wearing bandsmen at important campus events.

Once the capital of Canada, Kingston is described as the "very much a university town." There are several universities in the area (including the Royal Military College), and downtown provides students with places to shop. "Kingston itself has several clubs, three malls, a number of muse-

"Queen's has its own culture. Don't be afraid to engage it."

ums, numerous gyms, and three or four movie theaters," says a student. The city's relative isolation makes it the favored stomping ground for students without wheels. Town-gown relations are good, and students are very active in the community. Toronto and Montreal (less than three hours away) are popular roadtrips.

With forty-one varsity teams, Queen's athletic program is not only the largest in Canada, but also ties with Harvard University for the largest program in North America. Popular sports include men's and women's rugby, women's squash, rowing, golf, and women's lacrosse. The annual "kill McGill" football game against rival McGill University draws pigskin-crazed students from every corner of campus; homecoming is reputed to be a raucous affair featuring "alumni from the 1920s parading around the football field during halftime." Intramural competition is fierce, too, and nearly every student is involved on some level. A student says, "There is so much school spirit, sometimes it makes you sick."

Life at Queen's University is one of extremes. "Students who are able to balance work and pleasure fit in best here," says a junior. The pressure to succeed can be tough and expectations are high. But for those who pull it off, the rewards are well worth the effort. "Queen's has its own culture," says a student. "Don't be afraid to engage it."

Overlaps

University of Toronto, University of Western Ontario, McGill University, University of Waterloo, University of Ottawa

If You Apply To ➤ **Queens:** Regular admissions: Feb. 28. Financial aid: Mar. 15. Does not guarantee to meet demonstrated need. Campus interviews: optional, informational. No alumni interviews. SATs: required. SAT IIs: required (for engineering candidates only). No essay question.

University of Toronto

Toronto, Ontario, Canada M5S 1A3

U of T is the largest institution in the *Fiske Guide* and one of the biggest in the world. It is also, for most readers, in a foreign country. If ever there were a place where go-getterism is a necessity, this is it. In the absence of American-style school spirit, U of T students cut loose to find their fun in the city of Toronto.

Website: www.utoronto.ca

Location: City center

Total Enrollment: 56,112

Undergraduates: 43,278

Male/Female: 44/56

SAT Ranges: N/A

ACT Range: N/A

Financial Aid: 50%

Expense: Pub $ $

Phi Beta Kappa: Yes

Applicants: 44,074

Accepted: 61%

Enrolled: 37%

Grad in 6 Years: 72%

Returning Freshmen: 95%

Academics: ✑ ✑ ✑ ✑ ½

Social: ☎ ☎ ☎

Q of L: ★ ★ ★

Admissions: (416) 978-2190

Email Address:

ask@adm.utoronto.ca

Strongest Programs:

Arts

Science

Engineering

Medicine

Education

Students find plenty of reasons to love Toronto, their home away from home. "We are near museums, the art gallery, the bar and club district, and Lake Ontario," says one satisfied senior.

Students at the University of Toronto avoid getting lost in the shuffle by taking part in a unique residential college system that allows them to model their educational experience after their own personalities. Each college has a distinct character and appeal, yet blends seamlessly into the university's overall academic milieu. "Someone who wants to be involved in university life will have great opportunities here," says a student.

Toronto is so large that it spans three campuses. The St. George campus is situated in downtown Toronto and features Gothic architecture and historic buildings, though one students describes the setting as "very much similar to a nuclear power plant." Two suburban campuses—one in Mississauga and one in Scarborough—feature more modern structures. Newer facilities include the Joseph L. Rotman School of Management building and a new residence hall for graduate students.

Students apply directly to one of nine colleges, seven of which are on the St. George campus. Each college has its own set of admissions requirements, but international applicants can expect to submit SAT I and three SAT II scores. Advanced Placement testing is also considered. Strong programs include engineering, medicine, and education. First-Year Seminars are taught by the faculty's leading scholars and provide freshmen with cross-disciplinary discussions in intimate class settings. In addition, there are

"The quality of teaching is excellent."

study abroad programs around the world, internships, co-op programs, and specialized cross-disciplinary courses. Sophomores can choose from nearly one hundred research opportunities outside the classroom, where they work side by side with the university's most renowned professors. Newer programs include an architectural studies major and programs in forest conservation and health and disease.

"The academic climate is extremely competitive," says a junior. "This is encouraged by the university, which only allows a set percentage of students in a class to get an A." Students report that class size can be a problem and it's not uncommon to have more than one hundred classmates, even in upper-level courses. Still, most large classes break into smaller tutorials, and even freshmen are taught by full professors. "The quality of teaching is excellent," says one student. "Most professors really do care and take time to help out students and get to know them better." With so many students vying for classes, it can be difficult to get desired courses. "In special cases, instructors are usually willing to admit extra students who really need to get into the class," says a senior. Academic advising is described as "comprehensive" and "readily accessible to students." U of T's extensive library system holds 12.8 million volumes and "most are open seven days a week," according to one happy bibliophile.

"U of T is a very urban, active school and the students tend to be focused, chic, determined, and goal-oriented," says a junior. Though Toronto is becoming increasingly popular with outsiders, students from Ontario still make up 89 percent of the student body. International students comprise 5 percent, and students say that the university is "a very inclusive and accepting environment." Political correctness is "a given at this university, not an issue," says a freshman. Top students (and there are many!) vie for 2,400 admission scholarships and two thousand in-course awards. There are no athletic scholarships.

Top students (and there are many!) vie for 2,400 admission scholarships and two thousand in-course awards.

Eleven percent of the student body are residential students, and all are affiliated with one of the nine undergraduate colleges, which act as "local neighborhoods." "Even though fifty thousand people attend U of T, all undergraduate Arts and Sciences students choose a college to belong to," explains a junior. "This college has nothing to do with their academic studies, but allows them to meet people from various programs and take part in social events. It breaks the students into smaller communities." Each college has its own residences, which reflect the unique character of its students. St. Michael's College maintains a rich Roman Catholic tradition, while University

"U of T is a very urban, active school."

College has a predominantly Jewish student body. Students of New College enjoy air-conditioned dorm rooms, and Victoria College houses more than 750 students. The dorms are "clean, comfortable, and have a great social atmosphere," says a student. There are various dining options (mostly residence-specific), and all are well regarded. Campus security is adequate, according to most, and students say that they feel safe on campus.

Social life is quite active and takes place both in the city, where nightclubs beckon, and on campus. "There are pub nights and other social events held on campus," says a junior. "Hart House (which is the social and recreational center) has pool tables, an athletic wing, restaurants, and common rooms." The legal drinking age is nineteen, and students report that "alcohol abuse is not tolerated on campus." For those wishing to party without the aid of chemicals, there are university-sponsored events, including movies, guest speakers, and countless extracurricular clubs. Frosh Week gives students an excuse to get rowdy and enjoy themselves.

Students find plenty of reasons to love Toronto, their home away from home. "We are near museums, the art gallery, the bar and club district, and Lake Ontario," says one satisfied senior. "There are quite a few shops in the area and the Eaton Centre is just a subway ride away." Shopping is a favorite pastime,

"There is a lot to do here in terms of social activity."

as are movies and excursions to the shores of Lake Ontario. Students also support a wide array of volunteer programs. "There is a lot to do here in terms of social activity," says one senior.

Toronto fields numerous varsity sports teams; popular sports include hockey, basketball, and soccer. Still, "school spirit is a little low," says a junior. "I believe that this is because so many people commute and only come to school for classes." Rivals include Queen's University and Western Ontario. Intramural competition is popular, and many students can be found cheering the Toronto Raptors, the city's professional basketball team.

A junior acknowledges that those coming to U of T "must be prepared for a large campus with thousands of students," but goes on to say that "most people are friendly and so relationships are easy to form." Though the mammoth campus can seem daunting at first, those who are willing to take their academic lives by the reins will be rewarded with an exceptional educational experience and a wealth of friends. "People who enjoy academic activities should come here," asserts a sophomore. "We have everything!"

Overlaps

York University, Queen's University, McGill University, University of Western Ontario

If You Apply To ➤

University of Toronto: Early decision: Feb. 1. Regular admissions: Mar. 1. Guarantees to meet demonstrated need (for Canadian residents). No campus or alumni interviews. SATs or ACTs: required. SAT IIs: required. Accepts the Common Application. No essay question.

Carleton College

100 South College Street, Northfield, MN 55057

Less selective than Amherst, Williams, and Swarthmore because of its chilly Minnesota location. Yet Carleton retains its position as the premier liberal arts college in the upper Midwest. Predominately liberal, but not to the extremes of its more antiestablishment cousins.

Website: www.carleton.edu
Location: Small city
Total Enrollment: 1,936
Undergraduates: 1,936
Male/Female: 48/52
SAT Ranges: V 640–750
  M 640–720
ACT Range: 28–32
Financial Aid: 51%
Expense: Pr $ $ $
Phi Beta Kappa: Yes
Applicants: 4,061
Accepted: 37%
Enrolled: 34%
Grad in 6 Years: 89%
Returning Freshmen: 94%
Academics: 🖊 🖊 🖊 🖊 🖊
Social: ☎ ☎ ☎
Q of L: ★ ★ ★
Admissions: (800) 995-2275
Email Address: admissions@
  acs.carleton.edu

Strongest Programs:
  Mathematics
  Computer Science
  Chemistry
  Physics
  English
  History
  Economics
  Psychology

Minnesota is many things: the land of ten thousand lakes, home to the massive Mall of America, birthplace of lore from Hiawatha to Paul Bunyan, and proud parent of the Mississippi River. Beyond all that history-book stuff, tucked into a small town in the southeastern corner of the state, is Carleton College, arguably the best liberal arts school in the expansive Midwest. Classes are tiny, professors are enthusiastic, and students are itching to explore academia and the world beyond their doorstep. "I love this place!" says a freshman.

Surrounded by rolling farmland, Carleton's 955-acre campus is in the small town of Northfield, whose one-time status as the center of the Holstein cattle industry brought it the motto "The City of Cows, Colleges, and Contentment." Lakes, woods, and streams abound, and you can traverse them on twelve miles of hiking and cross-country skiing trails. The city boasts of its fragrant lilacs in spring, rich summer greens, red maples in the fall, and glistening blanket of white in winter. There's even an eight hundred-acre arboretum, put to good use by everyone from jogging jocks to bird-watching nature lovers. When it's -8 degrees, the new indoor recreation center provides a rock-climbing wall, gym, putting green, sports courts, track, and dance studio. Carleton's architectural style is somewhat eclectic—everything from Victorian to contemporary, but mostly redbrick.

> **"The courses require a lot of work," asserts a student, "but it's more of a cooperative atmosphere rather than competitive."**

Carleton's top-notch academic programs are no less varied: the sciences—biology, physics, astronomy, chemistry, geology, and computer science—are among the best anywhere, and scores of Carleton graduates go on to earn Ph.D.s in these areas. Of all the liberal arts schools in the country, Carleton's undergrads were recently awarded the highest number of National Science Foundation fellowships for graduate studies. English, history, economics, and biology get high marks, too. Engineers can opt for a 3–2 program with Columbia University or Washington University in St. Louis, and for geologists seeking fieldwork—and maybe wanting to thaw out after a long Minnesota winter—Carleton sponsors a program in Death Valley. Closer to home at the "arb," as the arboretum is affectionately known, environmental studies majors have their own wilderness field station, which includes a prairie-restoration site. At the opposite end of the academic spectrum, the arts also flourish. Music and studio art majors routinely get into top graduate programs, even though Carleton lacks a conservatory and doesn't emphasize performance, a music major says.

Distribution requirements ensure that a Carleton education exposes students not only to rigor and depth in their chosen field, but also to "a wide range of subjects and methods of studying them," administrators say. All students must show proficiency in English composition and a foreign language while fulfilling requirements in four broad areas: arts and literature, history, philosophy and religion, social sciences, and math and natural sciences. There's also a Recognition of Affirmation and Difference requirement, under which students must take at least one course dealing with a non-Western culture, and a senior comprehensive project is required in every

"Even the worst dorms aren't *that* bad."

major field. Carleton offers interdisciplinary programs in Asian, Jewish, urban, African and African-American, and women's studies. A new concentration in Cross-Cultural Studies brings in foreign students to discuss global issues and dynamics with their American counterparts. A biochemistry concentration has been added, while Social Thought has been dropped. Nearly 70 percent of students spend at least one term abroad, and many take advantage of programs available either through numerous organizations, including Carleton and the Associated Colleges of the Midwest.* The school's 799,000-volume library is bright, airy, and—much to the delight of caffeine-stoked night owls—open until 1:00 A.M. Students love the four-year-old center for mathematics and computing, which brought together all campus computing functions for the first time.

With highly motivated students and a heavy workload, Carleton isn't your typical mellow Midwestern liberal arts college. The trimester calendar means finals may be just three months apart, and almost everyone feels the pressure. The six-week Christmas vacation is Carleton's way of dealing with the cold winters. "The courses require a lot of work," asserts a student, "but it's more of a cooperative atmosphere rather than competitive." Nearly a third of all classes have ten students or fewer, so Carls are expected to participate actively. Carleton's faculty members are very committed to teaching. "They are very skilled in their areas, and they know how to challenge their students without talking over them," says a senior. "Freshman are always taught by full professors and immediately feel like a vital component of the Carleton environment."

"The best way to describe the people here would be two words," says a freshman: "Nerdy and weird." Seventy-seven percent of Carleton's students hail from outside Minnesota, half are from outside the Midwest, and most attended public schools. Both coasts are heavily represented, and more than fifteen foreign countries send at least one student. African-Americans and Hispanics account for 10 percent of the total student body, and Asian-Americans for another 8 percent. But most Carls have a few things in common, such as being intellectually curious yet laid-back, individualistic but into building a community feel on campus. Their earthy dress and attitude are very distinguishable from their more traditional crosstown cousins at rival St. Olaf College. The Carleton campus is rather left of center, concerned with issues including the environ-

"It's a great place to feel safe and sound."

ment, multiculturalism and affirmative action, gay rights, and sexism. Qualified students receive Carleton-sponsored National Merit and National Achievement scholarships every year, and students call financial-aid packages "definitely adequate." Carleton is need-blind for all but 5 to 10 percent of applicants, and guarantees to meet the full demonstrated need of all admits.

Campus accommodations range from comfortable old townhouses to modern hotel-like residence halls. "Even the worst dorms aren't *that* bad," says a student. Everyone is guaranteed a room for four years, although "it can be difficult to get the exact room you want," a wise senior explains. Best of all are the ten college-owned

With highly motivated students and a heavy workload, Carleton isn't your typical mellow Midwestern liberal arts college. The trimester calendar means finals may be just three months apart, and almost everyone feels the pressure.

off-campus "theme" houses, which focus on special interests such as foreign languages, the outdoors, or nuclear-power issues. With the exception of the Farm House, an environmental studies house sitting on the edge of the arb, all the theme houses (including Women's Awareness House) are situated in an attractive residential section of town close to campus. Dorms are coed by room, but there are two halls with single-sex floors. Davis is the recommended dorm, although Burton enjoys a "fun" reputation. Everyone who stays on campus must be on a meal plan, and dining-room fare is "getting better," a music major says.

Absent a Greek system, Carleton's social life tends to be relaxed and informal, and often centers on going out with friends. People go to parties on campus, or if they are of drinking age, bar hop around town. "There are very diverse happenings on any given weekend evening," says a senior. There are activities for those who pass on imbibing; a group called Co-op sponsors dances and Wednesday socials every two weeks, free movies, and special events like Comedy Night. Students agree that Carleton makes little more than token efforts to enforce the drinking age. "A few people are problem drinkers, a few never drink, most drink responsibly and socially," which goes for underage students, too. And a history major adds, "there is no pressure to participate in anything you don't want to do."

Northfield itself is a quaint, history filled town with a population of about seventeen thousand. There are old-style shops and a beautiful old hotel. "It's a great place to feel safe and sound," a senior sighs. "It's steeped in tradition and Minnesota friendliness." Students often frequent the St. Olaf College campus and a night spot known as the Reub'n'Stein. Minneapolis–St. Paul, thirty-five miles to the north, is a popular road-trip destination. Since students aren't allowed to have cars on campus, Carleton charters buses on weekends.

About a third of the students play on varsity teams, but about two-thirds play intramurals. The track, swimming, tennis, basketball, and baseball teams are competitive, as are the championship cross-country ski teams. Popular events include the Winter Carnival, the Spring Concert, and Mai-F'te, a gala celebrated on an island in one of the two lakes on campus. Traditions include the week-long freshman orientation program, where—during opening convocation—students bombard professors with bubbles as the faculty members process. There's also the annual spring softball game that begins at 5:30 A.M. and runs as many innings as there are years in Carleton's existence. The all-campus 10:00 P.M. scream on the eve of final exams keeps fatigued studiers awake. Notorious outlaw Jesse James failed to rob the Northfield Bank, lo those many years ago, and Northfield still celebrates with a Wild West bank raid reenactment every year. (The robbery was thwarted by brave townsfolk, and the gang broke up immediately afterward.)

It can be cold in Minnesota, in a face-stinging, bone-chilling kind of way. And the classes are far from easy. But Carleton is a warm campus, and the academics are challenging without being impossible. Carls toe the line between individuality and community, which makes for personal growth and lifelong friendships. "The people you debate with in the dining hall on Friday afternoon are the same people you party with on Friday night," a senior says. It seems Carleton provides all the ingredients for a promising college career.

Carnegie Mellon University

5000 Forbes Avenue, Pittsburgh, PA 15213-3890

CMU is the only premier technical university that also happens to be equally strong in the arts. Applications have more than doubled in the past ten years, so it must be doing something right. One of the few institutions that openly matches better financial-aid awards from competitor schools.

Students at Carnegie Mellon don't have to choose between soaking up the high drama of Shakespeare and experiencing the fast-paced dot-com world. The university is known for both its science offerings and strong drama and music programs. But scholars can't be too focused on their particular course of study—Carnegie Mellon continues to make every effort to offer both its technical and liberal arts students a well-rounded education that requires a lot of hard work but promises great results.

Carnegie Mellon was formed by the merger of Carnegie Tech and the Mellon Institute, resulting in a self-contained 103-acre campus attractively situated in Pittsburgh's affluent Oakland section. Next door is the city's largest park and its major museum, named after—you guessed it—Andrew Carnegie. Campus buildings range from early-1900s Beaux Arts style to contemporary eyesores. Construction was recently completed on the Purcell Center for the Arts, and work continues on an addition for the School of Computer Science and an addition to the Graduate School for Industrial Administration.

Carnegie Mellon is divided into six undergraduate colleges: Fine Arts, Humanities and Social Sciences, the Carnegie Institute of Technology, the Mellon College of Science, the School of Computer Science, and the School of Industrial Management. Each has its own distinct character and admission requirements, so applicants may want to contact the admissions office to find out about the varying policies. All the colleges, however, share the university's commitment to what it calls a "liberal-professional" education, which makes the liberal arts extremely relevant while stressing courses that develop technical skills and good job prospects. Humanities and social science types can major in applied history, professional writing, or public policy, for example, instead of traditional disciplinary concentrations.

> **"Carnegie Mellon is very intense, so lots of time is dedicated to class assignments and group projects."**

Under the University Choice Program, a select group of students is allowed to design an individualized freshman-year course of study directed toward their particular interest, and can defer the selection of a major until sophomore year. In addition, the Fifth-Year Scholars program provides full tuition for outstanding students who want to remain at CMU for an additional year to pursue a course of study that interests them.

Most departments at Carnegie Mellon are strong, but exceptional ones include chemical and electrical engineering. While some humanities courses are praised, most students agree that CMU is definitely more of a science-oriented school. Each college requires core work from freshmen; in the College of Humanities and Social Science, for example, students are introduced to computers in a required first-year philosophy course, using the machines to work on problems of logic. Two majors—logic and computation in the philosophy department, and cognitive science through the psychology department—combine computer-science technology with such fields as artificial intelligence and linguistics. The university created a Department of Modern Languages and a Bachelor of Science and Arts degree program was added recently along with a Science and Humanities Scholars Program.

Website: www.cmu.edu
Location: City outskirts
Total Enrollment: 8,514
Undergraduates: 5,106
Male/Female: 64/36
SAT Ranges: V 600–700
  M 680–760
ACT Range: 27–32
Financial Aid: 80%
Expense: Pr $ $ $
Phi Beta Kappa: Yes
Applicants: 14,621
Accepted: 36%
Enrolled: 25%
Grad in 6 Years: 77%
Returning Freshmen: 93%
Academics: ✍ ✍ ✍ ✍
Social: ☎ ☎ ☎
Q of L: ★ ★ ★
Admissions: (412) 268-2082
Email Address:
  undergraduate-admissions
  @andrew.cmu.edu

Strongest Programs:
  Computer Science
  Engineering
  Drama
  Music
  Industrial Management
  Business
  Architecture

As one student bluntly puts it, the courses at CMU are "extremely rigorous with many hours expected outside of the classroom. Expect to work hard if you come here." The College of Fine Arts' drama department, the first and still one of the best in the country, concentrates on performance, and its faculty is made up of highly regarded working professionals. While the program embraces the art of performance, freshman must take English and history as well as a basic computer course. After that it's drama all day, every day. Students at CMU work hard, no doubt about it. "Carnegie Mellon is very intense, so lots of time is dedicated to class assignments and group projects," a student says. However, nearly all the classes are small, with fewer than thirty students. Most students agree that the Carnegie Institute of Technology is by far the most difficult college. Professors rate high with most students, who praise their availability and willingness to help. "Most professors are very eager to help and make sure that material is understood," says a sophomore psychology major.

Carnegie Mellon's professional focus shows through in its internship program. A number of five-year, dual-degree options exist, including a joint BS/MS or a co-op program in metallurgical engineering and materials science that places students in the metals industry. Other engineers and scientists vie for a spot in the Junior Year in Switzerland Program. Humanities and social sciences students can spend a semester in England, and political science majors can go to Washington. One innovative program allows students to receive a bachelor's degree, teaching certificate, and master's degree within five years. But to counteract the tendency toward a narrow, preprofessional focus, the university-wide core curriculum requires courses such as Fundamentals of the Art of Communication, Fundamentals of Computing, and Foundations of Human Thought and Values. The idea is to give students with diverse interests a shared intellectual background. As Herbert Simon, the Nobel Prize-winning economist who helped design the core curriculum, puts it, "We want to provide some common topics of conversation besides sports, the weather, and sex."

"We are very diverse and therefore very culturally aware."

Nevertheless, Carnegie Mellon remains one of the most fragmented campuses in the nation. Students divide themselves between the actors, dancers, and other artsy types and the engineers, scientists, and architects. In any case, students are united in their quest for a good job after graduation. Still, many complain about the fact that students will give up sleep to study, and that this kind of academic orientation can often hinder social life. "Sometimes there just isn't very much social life, but many students prefer it that way," says one student.

Once a very regional institution, drawing mostly Pennsylvania residents, Carnegie Mellon now counts about 70 percent of its students from out of state. Nearly one-third are from minority groups, including 20 percent Asian-American, 3 percent African-American, and 5 percent Hispanic. "We are very diverse and therefore very culturally aware," a biology major says. Censorship of Internet newsgroups, because some provide access to "cyberporn," has garnered national headlines and stirred up student protests. Other students say a big issue is the nearly two-to-one male to female ratio. The university says it remains committed to need-blind admissions, but it provides larger proportions of outright grants in financial-aid packages to "academic superstars." CMU has also stopped guaranteeing to meet the financial need of all accepted students, but now offers an early evaluation of financial-aid eligibility for interested prospective students. The financial aid office encourages students who have received more generous packages from competing schools to let CMU know so they have an opportunity to match or better them.

Housing, which is guaranteed for all four years, offers old and newer buildings, the most popular being university-owned apartments. Upperclassmen get first pick, with freshman assignments coming from a lottery of the remainder. "The dorms are generally very comfortable and well maintained, with ample living space," says one student. The best dorms for freshmen are Donner, Resnik, and Morewood Gardens. Most halls are coed, but a few are men-only. Students can remain in campus housing as long as they wish, and nearly 70 percent do so each year. Meal plans are said to be restrictive and expensive.

With all the academic pressure at CMU, it's a good thing there are so many opportunities to unwind, especially with the entire city of Pittsburgh close at hand. The Greek system provides the most visible form of on-campus social life, and 22 percent of the students belong. For those who choose not to fraternize, coffeehouses, inexpensive films, dances, and concerts in nearby Oakland, plus downtown Pittsburgh itself (opera, ballet, symphony, concerts, and sporting events just twenty minutes away by bus) provide plenty of alternatives. Once every four years, the College of Fine Arts sponsors the Beaux Arts Ball, an

A number of five-year, dual-degree options exist, including a joint B.S./M.S. or a co-op program in metallurgical engineering and materials science.

> **"It's driven, but there's no better place to be interacting with people of so many disciplines who are so focused."**

absolutely amazing all-night masquerade party. The administration is desperately trying to curtail underage drinking, so far with only modest success. Some students say the penalties for being caught are harsh, but others maintain that the rules are "vaguely known."

One event that brings everyone together is the Spring Carnival, when the school shuts down for a day and a big top is constructed in a parking lot. Students set up booths with electronic games, and fraternities race in buggies made of lightweight alloys designed by engineering majors. Students put on original "Scotch and Soda" presentations, two of which—*Pippin* and *Godspell*—went on to become Broadway hits. But in a sports-crazed town like Pittsburgh, Carnegie Mellon's Division III varsity teams often have trouble getting attention. "I had to pass out flyers to try to get people to attend the football game Homecoming weekend!" laments a cheerleader. Both the men's and women's soccer teams recently won divisional championships.

CMU appeals to those yearning for the bright lights of Broadway or the glowing computer screens of the scientific and business worlds. And with a broad range of liberal arts and technical courses available and required, there's no doubt students leave CMU with a well-rounded education as well as an impressive diploma. "It's driven, but there's no better place to be interacting with people of so many disciplines who are so focused," says one senior.

Overlaps
MIT, Cornell University, Penn, Stanford, Northwestern

Case Western Reserve University

P.O. Box 128016, Cleveland, OH 44112-8016

The Cleveland Browns always lose to the Pittsburgh Steelers and CWRU is still trying to catch up with Carnegie Mellon. Students may sing its praises, but Cleveland isn't exactly Boston, or even Pittsburgh. On the plus side, students get an outstanding technical education at Case with solid offerings in other areas.

Website: www.cwru.edu

Location: Urban

Total Enrollment: 9,216

Undergraduates: 3,381

Male/Female: 61/39

SAT Ranges: V 600–710
  M 640–730

ACT Range: 27–31

Financial Aid: 49%

Expense: Pr $ $

Phi Beta Kappa: Yes

Applicants: 4,663

Accepted: 74%

Enrolled: 22%

Grad in 6 Years: 78%

Returning Freshmen: 90%

Academics: ✍ ✍ ✍ ✍

Social: ☎ ☎

Q of L: ★ ★ ★

Admissions: (216) 368-4450

Email Address:
  admission@po.cwru.edu

Strongest Programs:

Engineering

Accounting

Anthropology

Biology

Physics

Music

Psychology

Nursing

Forget Atari, typewriters, and cassette players—Case Western Reserve University offers students the chance to learn and live on a high-tech, computer-savvy campus. Cutting-edge equipment and strong arts and science programs create a comprehensive, intellectually stimulating environment. Though known for turning out brainy leaders in technology, CWRU is just as strong in the arts.

Case Western Reserve is located on the eastern edge of Cleveland at University Circle, an artistic 550-acre area of parks and gardens that is home to more than forty cultural, educational, medical, and research institutions. The buildings represent an eclectic mix of architectural styles, and several are listed on the National Register of Historic Places. The Veale Convocation, Recreation, and Athletic Center was recently renovated to include a new 3,100-square-foot exercise room and fifty new pieces of fitness equipment. Latest to be unveiled are a $33 million science building and a new building for the highly regarded Weatherhead School of Management.

The product of a marriage between Case Institute of Technology and Western Reserve University in 1967, the university is composed of the College of Arts and Sciences and the Case School of Engineering. Students take one of four core curricula to fulfill their general education requirements, depending on their major. Only after students declare their majors are they formally enrolled in one of the colleges. A pilot program called SAGES (Seminar Approach to General Education and Scholarship) allows 150 freshmen to learn through seminars, community service, internships, research projects, and some traditional classes, with an emphasis on communication, information technology, diversity, and ethics.

Among the strongest academic programs in the College of Arts and Sciences are anthropology, art history (conducted with the adjoining Cleveland Museum of Art), management, music (linked with the nearby Cleveland Institute of Music), and psychology. The Case School of Engineering boasts one of the world's first departments in biomedical engineering. Other leading programs include mechanical and aerospace engineering, macromolecular science, mathematics, and physics. As testimony to CWRU's outstanding programs in polymer science and in materials science and engineering, the university received a grant from NASA for the study of materials in space. There are majors in both computer engineering and computer science. Students cite English, philosophy, and the languages as being weak and "often overshadowed by engineering and science." A combined math/physics major was recently added, along with a minor in childhood studies. The College Scholars Program takes outstanding undergraduates in the arts, humanities, and sciences or engineering who want to take what they learned in the classroom into the real world. Some of the past emphases have been on medical ethics, Africa, dreams and fantasy, and urban design.

"Regardless of how intelligent a person is, everyone here must work hard to do well."

Classes tend to be smaller and professors more available at the College of Arts and Sciences than at the Case School of Engineering. The administration explains that engineering students find their professors more accessible as they move out of the introductory courses and focus on a specialty. The typical advanced class is limited to twenty students, and students often participate in research.

While it would seem that mixing engineering types with liberal arts majors would be chemically and intellectually impossible, all insist that the groups mix, especially when students load up with double (and even triple) majors. "Students here are very intelligent and they work very hard," a senior says. "Regardless of how intelligent a person is, everyone here must work hard to do well." Some even take six or seven courses in one semester. Academic competition exists, but does not rule the campus. "Students are grade focused, but at the same time help one another in any way possible," says one accounting major. "The competition is not cut-throat."

Most CWRU students have their eyes on the prize that comes after graduation, which makes preprofessional majors a big hit. The university offers integrated BA/MA, BS/MS, and BSE/MS degree programs, and the Senior Year in Absentia program lets enterprising students substitute their final undergrad year for their first year of professional school. The best bet of all may be the Preprofessional Scholars program, in which top freshmen who plan careers in law, medicine, or dentistry are given conditional acceptance into the CWRU professional schools in their fields.

Sixty-nine percent of the freshmen come from the top tenth of their high-school class, and 42 percent come from outside Ohio. Asian-Americans make up 13 percent of the student body, African-Americans make up 5 percent, and Hispanics make up 2 percent. The school stresses respect for diversity, and has developed a university-wide program called Share the Vision, designed to foster respect for different values, ideas, opinions, and ethnic, cultural, and racial differences. Although CWRU students are highly motivated toward their careers, it doesn't prevent them from donating their time to a worthy cause or two. Habitat for Humanity and activities organized through Alpha Phi Omega are popular options. Case Western Reserve offers students a wide variety of possibilities for meeting costs. The university distributes more than four hundred merit

"Campus security is fantastic."

scholarships per year, ranging from $500 to full tuition. No athletic scholarships are offered. A four-day orientation gets freshmen up to speed on Case Western Reserve life, and students desiring a longer introduction can attend an optional three-day camp just before the regular program.

All freshmen are now housed together on the campus's North side. Students seem generally satisfied with the housing situation at CWRU (73 percent live on campus), but some complain that dorms are old and rooms are small. Upperclassmen seeking more sophisticated living quarters enter a room draw for better choices. Housing is coed, save for one women's dorm and several off-campus men's fraternity houses. Apartments are available but expensive and often a long trek from campus, and financial aid awards are trimmed if students move off campus. Most students living on campus take their meals in one of three cafeterias, which do not exactly draw gastronomic raves. When the munchies hit, snacks are available at one of the twelve food operations on campus.

Forget all those things you heard in the past about Cleveland. It has made a smashing comeback and is a "great city for students" and a "cultural cornucopia" of art galleries, theaters, restaurants, bars and clubs, and many areas for shopping, says a senior. A car is pretty necessary for getting around Cleveland, but bus service has lately been beefed up and students can pay $25 a semester for unlimited rides. Cleveland is home to the Rock & Roll Hall of Fame, as well as to the Indians professional baseball team. On the downside, crime is a potential problem, but a veritable fleet of police officers, security guards, and campus escorts has the campus covered. "Campus security is fantastic," gushes a computer engineering student. The sandy beaches of a rejuvenated Lake Erie are just a few minutes away, and a university-owned farm is a great picnic place. Quaint Chagrin Falls, about a half-hour away, and Cleveland Heights' Coventry neighborhood, a manageable bus ride away, has shops and restaurants.

When CWRU students pledge their undying love and devotion, it can as easily be to their computers as to a hottie of the opposite sex. Rationalizes one student: "You may have trouble finding a date on most weekends, but if your computer crashes on a Friday night, it will be up and running by Saturday morning." Even after-class activities often have an academic flair. Engineering Week, for instance, features competitions such as the Mousetrap Car Race (all cars must run on a one-mousetrap engine) and the Egg Drop (a foolproof protective package for the tossed egg is key). The Film Society's weekend movies are popular, as are the frequent events sponsored by the University Program Board. Alcohol policies are relatively strict, and students say they have further worsened social life. "Most fraternities are dry, and there are no bars or pubs on campus," laments a senior. A Peer Helper Network trains student volunteers to be nonjudgmental listeners and sources of referral for students with problems ranging from alcohol abuse to sexual harassment. About one-third of the men and about 16 percent of women are Greek. "Social life is what you want to make it at CWRU," a senior says.

"Social life is what you want to make it at CWRU."

Sports are welcomed at CWRU, though they don't dominate campus. The track and field, women's softball, basketball, and swimming teams have done well recently, along with male swimmers and wrestlers. The dorm-centered intramural program is popular. And the twenty-six-mile Hudson Relays, held the last week of the spring semester, pits teams of runners from the four classes against one another. There's a spiffy racquetball and squash complex and a field house with an Olympic-size pool.

CWRU is always trying to better itself and enhance its already high-level academic programs. For the engineers and scientists, the university provides a stellar education to propel students to the tops of their fields, and the liberal arts program has only done good things to round out the student body. Down-to-earth and intelligent CWRU students are challenged by bright, dedicated faculty. "CWRU is home to amazing professors who care about their students," a senior says.

Overlaps

Northwestern, Ohio State, Carnegie Mellon, Washington University, Cornell University

If You Apply To >

CWRU: Early decision: Jan. 1. Regular admissions and financial aid: Feb. 1. Housing: May 1. Does not guarantee to meet demonstrated need. Campus interviews: recommended, informational. Alumni interviews: optional, informational. SATs or ACTs: required. SAT IIs: recommended. Accepts the Common Application and electronic applications. Essay question: writing sample. Audition required for artists and musicians.

The Catholic University of America

Washington, DC 20064

There are other Roman Catholic–affiliated universities, but this is *the* Catholic University. Catholics make up 80 percent of the student body here (versus roughly half at nearby Georgetown). If you can't be in Rome, there is no better place than D.C. to work and play. CU even has a Metro stop right on campus.

Website: www.cua.edu
Location: City outskirts
Total Enrollment: 5,493
Undergraduates: 2,609
Male/Female: 46/54
SAT Ranges: V 540–640
M 520–630
ACT Range: 22–29
Financial Aid: 58%
Expense: Pr $ $
Phi Beta Kappa: Yes

Founded in 1887 under a charter from Pope Leo XIII, The Catholic University of America was the brainchild of United States bishops who wanted to provide an American institution where the curriculum was guided by the tenets of Christian thought. Over time, the university has garnered a reputation as a research-oriented school that also provides a strong undergraduate, preprofessional education and an appreciation for the arts.

Catholic's campus comprises 145 tree-lined acres, an impressive layout for an urban university. Buildings range from ivy-covered brownstone and brick to ultra-modern, giving the place a true collegiate feel. Catholic is one of the few colleges in the country that began as a graduate institution, and grad students still outnumber their younger counterparts. Six of its ten schools (arts and sciences, engineering, architecture, nursing, music, and philosophy) now admit undergrads, while two others (social service and religious studies) provide undergraduate programs through arts and sciences.

Students have excellent options in almost any department at CUA. Apart from politics (which all agree sets the tone on campus), the history, English, drama, psychology, and physics departments are very strong. Philosophy and religious studies are highly regarded and have outstanding faculty members as well. The School of Nursing is one of the best in the nation, and engineering and architecture are also highly regarded. Architecture and physics have outstanding facilities, the latter enjoying a modern vitreous-state lab, a boon for both research and hands-on undergraduate instruction. Also, a high-speed fiber-optic network connects the entire campus to the Internet. For students interested in the arts, CUA's School of Music offers excellent vocal and instrumental training, and there's also a program in musical theater. Students cite communications and business as weaker than others. The library is modest for a school of this size.

Students at CUA need at least forty courses in order to graduate. In the School of Arts and Sciences, approximately twenty-five of these must be from a core curriculum spread across the humanities, social and behavioral sciences, philosophy, environmental studies, religion, math and natural sciences, and languages and literature. English composition also is required. The brightest students can enroll in a twelve-course interdisciplinary honors program that offers sequences in the humanities, philosophy, and social sciences. CUA's library offers approximately 1.49 million volumes.

Standard off-campus opportunities are augmented by internships at the British and Irish parliaments, NASA, the National Institutes of Health, the Pentagon, and the Library of Congress. The School of Architecture and Planning hosts summer classes for seniors and grad students to study in Italy and a host of European and Mediterranean countries. The Rome study-abroad program for design students incorporates design studio, field study, history, theory, and the Italian language. Finally, two students are chosen each year to spend a fall semester at the Fondazione Architetto Rancilio (FAAR) in Milan to study themes including architecture,

"The quality of teaching is excellent. Professors are usually very willing to help students."

urban studies, and technology. CUA also offers accelerated degree programs in which students can earn bachelor's and master's degrees in five years, or six years for a joint BA-JD. CUA is part of the eleven-university Consortium of Universities of the Washington Metropolitan Area and the Oak Ridge Associated Universities consortium. The latter is comprised of eighty-seven U.S. colleges and a contractor for the federal Energy Department. The program gives students access to federal research facilities.

Although Catholic University is research oriented, most classes have fewer than twenty-five students. That means special attention from faculty members. It also means that there's no place to hide. "The teachers push us to work hard but at the same time apply the subjects to everyday living," a history major reports. The faculty is given high marks by students. "The quality of teaching is excellent. Professors are usually very willing to help students," praises a veteran. Clergy are at the helm of certain graduate schools, but the School of Arts and Sciences has a primarily lay faculty, with priests occupying less than 16 percent of the teaching posts. Its chancellor is the archbishop of Washington, and Catholic churches across the country donate a fraction of their annual collections to the university. One downside of being the only Catholic school with a papal charter is that officials in Rome, who do not always warm up to American traditions of academic freedom, keep a sharp eye on the theology department.

Catholicism is clearly the tie that binds the student body. Sunday Masses are so well attended that extra services must be offered in the dorms. Says one administrator,

(Continued)
Applicants: 3,117
Accepted: 87%
Enrolled: 20%
Grad in 6 Years: 70%
Returning Freshmen: 84%
Academics: ✍ ✍ ✍ ✍
Social: ☎ ☎ ☎
Q of L: ★ ★ ★
Admissions: (202) 319-5305
Email Address: cua-admissions@cua.edu

Strongest Programs:
  Nursing
  Politics
  Drama
  Architecture
  Music
  Greek and Latin
  Physics
  Engineering

A fifteen-minute Metro ride brings students to the center of downtown D.C. and the Capitol. Georgetown, bustling with great shopping, bars, restaurants, and art galleries, is only a half-hour away.

"We like students to leave with Catholic values, but most of them come here with those values in the first place." Eighty percent of the students belong to the faith. Most are from the Northeast, and are primarily white. African-Americans and Hispanics comprise 7 and 4 percent of the student body, respectively. Another 4 percent are Asian-American, and foreign students account for 3 percent. Ninety percent are from out of state, and 54 percent of freshmen rank in the top quarter of their high-school class. Politically, students are fairly conservative, and the big issues on campus include abortion and gay/lesbian rights. "Everyone is basically the same at Catholic—white, upper-middle-class Catholics," says one student.

The university maintains a need-blind admissions policy. It does not guarantee to meet the full demonstrated need of all admitted, but 64 percent of aid recipients are offered full demonstrated need. Thirty-one lucky students—one from each archdiocese in the nation—receive a full-tuition merit scholarship. There are 450 additional merit scholarships available ranging from $1,000 to full tuition, along with various types of financial aid. There are no athletic scholarships.

Fifty-eight percent of the students live in the dorms, seven of which are coed by floor. The spacious and ultramodern Centennial Village (eight dorms and six hundred beds laid out in suites) is available to all students, many of whom flee CUA's strict visitation (no guests past 2:00 A.M.) and alcohol policies and move into apartments of their own. The best dorms for freshmen are Spellman and Flather (coed), and Conaty (women). Dorm food is fairly

> "We like students to leave with Catholic values, but most of them come here with those values in the first place."

tasty, and there's always the Rathskeller, or Rat, the campus bar and grill where students can get a late-night meal or brunch and dinner on weekends. Emergency phones, shuttle buses, and escort services are provided as part of campus security, and students agree that they always feel safe on campus as long as they are careful.

When students want to explore the city, they need only walk to the campus Metro stop and then enjoy the ride. Capitol Hill is fifteen minutes away; the stylish Georgetown area, with its chic restaurants and nightspots, is only a half hour away. CUA students do indulge in some serious partying. Some of their favorite locales include the Irish Times, Colonel Brook Tavern, the Tune Inn, and Kitty's. Its no wonder most students agree that the social scene is "off campus at various bars, clubs, and coffeehouses in D.C." Only 1 percent of the men and women join the Greek system. No one under twenty-one can drink on campus, and most students agree that this policy is effective in curbing underage drinking. Also, alcohol "abuse" has been added as an offense in addition to use, possession, and distribution. For those eager to repent the weekend's excesses, there are student ministry retreats. Annual festivals on the campus calendar include a week-long Homecoming celebration, Beaux Arts Ball, Christmas Holly Hop (held in New York City), and Spring Fling. A time-honored winter tradition is sledding down Flather Hill on cafeteria trays.

Sports on campus means varsity and intramural competition. CUA's athletic teams compete in Division III, and the men's basketball team won the 2001 championship. Other solid men's teams include baseball, swimming, and lacrosse. Volleyball, field hockey, softball, and swimming are the strongest women's teams. Intramural and varsity athletes alike enjoy the beautiful $10 million sports complex. Many students use their strength for community service, including the Christian-based Habitat for Humanity, in which they build houses for needy families.

When discussions first raised the idea of a Catholic university, the man who would become the university's first rector, Bishop John Joseph Keane, argued for an institution that would "exercise a dominant influence in the world's future" with a superior intellectual foundation. Now, more than one hundred years later, CUA offers students a wealth of preprofessional courses spanning the arts and sciences.

Overlaps

American, Villanova, Loyola (MD), Boston College, Georgetown

The founders' quest for "a higher synthesis of knowledge" is constantly being realized at CUA, a unique university and a capital destination.

If You Apply To ➤

Catholic: Early action: Nov. 15. Regular admissions: Feb. 15. Financial aid: Feb. 1. Housing: June 1. Does not guarantee to meet demonstrated need. SATs or ACTs: required. SAT IIs: required (writing and foreign language). Accepts the Common Application and electronic applications. Essay question: local, national, international issue of concern; historical figure to meet. Music applicants must audition.

Centre College

600 West Walnut, Danville, KY 40422

Centre is college the way it used to be—gentleman scholars, football games, and fraternity pranks (preferably done in the nude). There is also the unparalleled closeness between students and faculty that comes with a student body of 1,070. Compare to Sewanee, DePauw, and Kenyon.

Centre College is a small liberal arts school with plenty to brag about. It is the only private institution to have a Phi Beta Kappa chapter and has produced two-thirds of the state's Rhodes Scholars over the last forty years. Still, it's not all work and no play for the students. There are also more than one hundred different social groups, clubs, and societies to choose from.

Located in the heart of the beautiful Kentucky Bluegrass hills, Centre's campus is a mix of old Greek Revival and attractive modern buildings. Centre is the forty-eighth oldest college in the country, and takes great pride in its historic landmarks. More than fourteen buildings on campus are listed in the National Registry of Historic Places. Sinking Spring, an early Native American campsite and possible location of Thomas Harrod's cabin, is their oldest site of interest.

More than 95 percent of Centre's faculty hold a Ph.D. or equivalent degree. "I cannot emphasize enough the excellence of Centre College faculty," says a sophomore. The general education curriculum requires students to complete courses in expository writing, math, foreign language, and computing, as well as two courses in each context (aesthetic, the natural world, society and fundamental questions). In addition, freshmen must participate in a first-year seminar, which is offered in the January term. Some examples of the seminars include courses on cloning, American utopianism, and leadership. Professors are very highly regarded here.

Economics, biology, history, English, and government are generally considered Centre's best departments, and consequently are the most popular majors. Glassblowing enthusiasts will find one of the few fully equipped undergraduate facilities in the nation, which is part of a strong arts program. The computing facilities, including the Unix lab, are

"I cannot emphasize enough the excellence of Centre College faculty."

on a continuous growth spurt to keep up with a growing demand. Among the weaker departments are the foreign languages, such as German, but students say they're improving, citing the addition of Japanese as a language option. But perhaps the biggest academic drawback at Centre is the reality that, with fewer than 1,100 students enrolled, course offerings in many areas are limited.

Two-thirds of students take advantage of the school's study abroad programs, which includes programs in London, Strasbourg, and Mexico. And because of Centre's

Website: www.centre.edu
Location: Small town
Total Enrollment: 1,070
Undergraduates: 1,070
Male/Female: 44/56
SAT Ranges: V 570–700
  M 560–670
ACT Range: 25–29
Financial Aid: 62%
Expense: Pr $
Phi Beta Kappa: Yes
Applicants: 1,265
Accepted: 82%
Enrolled: 29%
Grad in 6 Years: 73%
Returning Freshmen: 89%
Academics: ✍ ✍ ✍ ½
Social: ☎ ☎ ☎
Q of L: ★ ★ ★
Admissions: (800) 423-6236
Email Address:
  admission@centre.edu

Strongest Programs:
  English
  History
  Biology
  Biochemistry
  Economics
  Art
  Drama

4–1–4 calendar, there are a number of three-week winter-term classes that involve group travel and opportunities to study abroad in such places as France, Vietnam, Africa, and the Bahamas. As a member of the Associated Colleges of the South,* Centre also offers its students programs in Central America. A 3–2 liberal arts and engineering program in collaboration with four major universities, including Columbia and Vanderbilt, is also available. The new January term, known as the "Centre Term," allows students to enroll in just one three week class.

Many students come from middle- to upper-middle-class Kentucky families, and are considered to be "preppy" and conservative. "Students are politically engaged on a wide range of issues," a sophomore government and economics major

"Students are politically engaged on a wide range of issues."

says. The student body is overwhelmingly white (93 percent), with African-Americans accounting for 3 percent, Asian-Americans 2 percent, and Hispanics less than 1 percent. Seventy-one percent of the students hail from Kentucky, and most attended public high school. Students typically head directly into the work force after graduating, rather than attend graduate or professional schools. Centre offers its students academic scholarships ranging from $4,500 to $24,000.

Virtually all of Centre's students live on campus. Freshmen occupy single-sex dorms, while upperclassmen have the option of living in halls that are coed by floor. Hillside is divided into separate six-person units, each with three bedrooms and a living room. "The dorms are all really nice compared to what I've seen at some other schools," a freshman says. An apartment was recently purchased and remodeled to provide additional housing, and ten new fraternity and sorority houses have created another favored living option for the 47 percent of men and 68 percent of women who belong to the Greek system. Everyone eats together in the main dining hall, Cowan Dining Commons. Though students have complained about the food in the past, improvements made to the facility have brought with them improvements in the cuisine. Meal plans range from ten meals to nineteen meals, and a flexible dollar spending-option is available as well. The surrounding community provides several decent restaurants when students really need a break.

Centre's social life is centered on campus, with students hanging out in dorms and frequenting Greek parties. "There are fraternity parties, contests, concerts, movies, etc," a senior says. Lexington, a thirty-minute drive away, is a popular draw on weekends for dates and films, as well as shopping. And road trips to the countryside are common, where there are plenty of places to go camping and fishing. Other quaint traditions include a serenade for the president by the senior women in their bath towels, and faculty Christmas caroling for the freshmen. Then there's

"There are fraternity parties, contests, concerts, movies, etc."

the long-held tradition of "Running the Flame," which has students running from the fraternity houses, around a sculpture and back—"naked, of course." Although the college is in a dry county and the nearest bar is twenty miles away, the campus has a unique alcohol policy, which students refer to as the "unoriginal container" policy. "If you have your drink in a cup and are acting responsibly, no one will ask you how old you are," reports one student. Another says, "If you are cited for public intoxication, then you must take a class on the dangers of alcohol."

Students may attend most events at the college's separately endowed Norton Center for the Arts, which brings phenomenal art, music, and drama to campus free of charge. "This is a great facility that attracts high-quality musicians and other performers," boasts one student. The Carnegie Club provides fine dining and offers special theme dinners on weekends and evenings before performances.

The women's basketball team was among the best in the nation in 2000-2001, and joins women's soccer and volleyball and men's football, soccer, and basketball as the most popular sports. Centre's football team has been around for one hundred years, but there's one moment in its history that outshines them all. In 1921, Centre beat then-powerhouse Harvard, 6–0, an event that has been called the greatest sports upset in the first half of the twentieth century. Although the football team has lost the national spotlight, it's still fairly competitive on the Division III level. Students love to brag most about Centre's expansive intramural program.

Centre College is a David in a world of academic Goliaths. What it lacks in size, it more than makes up for in quality. With a rich history spanning more than 180 years, Centre has put the bigger, more well-known schools on notice that they haven't heard the last from this small college.

Overlaps

University of Kentucky, Transylvania, Vanderbilt, Furman, Rhodes

If You Apply To ➤

Centre: Early action: Dec.1. Regular admissions and financial aid: Feb. 1. Does not guarantee to meet demonstrated need. Campus interviews: recommended, informational. Alumni interviews: optional, informational. SATs or ACTs: required. SAT IIs: optional. Accepts the Common Application and electronic applications. Essay question: personal statement.

College of Charleston

Charleston, SC 29424

C of C is a public university about half the size of University of South Carolina that offers business, education, and the liberal arts. It compares to William and Mary in both scale and historic surroundings but is far less rigorous academically. Must address its housing crunch to reach the next level.

Whether sampling the traditional Low Country cuisine or delving into a wide range of courses offered at this 232-year-old school, students at the College of Charleston know they are getting a quality education in a beautiful setting. Founded as Colonial South Carolina's first college, C of C has moved beyond its traditional roots to become a well-respected institution throughout the Southeast.

Located in Charleston's famous Historical District, the campus features many of the city's most historic and venerable buildings. More than eighty of its buildings are former private residences ranging from the typical Charleston "single" house to the Victorian. The campus has received countless regional, state, and local awards for its design, and has been designated a national arboretum. Students who complain that the current library is small are cheered by the fact that construction recently began on a state-of-the-art library. A sports facility and business center were recently completed, as was the Jewish Studies Center.

C of C has a core curriculum based strongly in the liberal arts and focused on the development of writing, computing, language acquisition, and thinking skills. Each student is required to complete six hours in English, history, mathematics or logic, and social science; 8 hours in natural sciences; and twelve hours in humanities and a modern or classical foreign language. Biology and chemistry are two of the strongest programs; many of the graduates end up at the Medical University of South Carolina a few blocks down the street. Marine biology is also strong, and students use the South

"The professors at C of C are not only knowledgeable and caring, they are inspirational."

Website: www.cofc.edu
Location: Urban
Total Enrollment: 11,617
Undergraduates: 9,934
Male/Female: 36/64
SAT Ranges: V 540–620
M 540–610
ACT Range: 22–26
Financial Aid: 76%
Expense: Pub $
Phi Beta Kappa: No
Applicants: 8,356
Accepted: 65%
Enrolled: 25%
Grad in 6 Years: 53%
Returning Freshmen: 81%
Academics: ✑ ✑ ✑
Social: ☎ ☎ ☎ ☎
Q of L: ★ ★ ★ ★
Admissions: (843) 953-5670

(Continued)
Email Address:
admissions@cofc.edu

Strongest Programs
Intermodal Transportation
Marine Biology
Business
Communications
Psychology
Education

Carolina marshes and beaches for a research laboratory. The most popular major is business, followed by education, communications, social science, and biology. Arts management, historic preservation, and international business are among the most recent additions to the curriculum. Many of the new performing arts majors take advantage of internship opportunities with Charleston's annual Spoleto Music Festival. Study-abroad options include the International Student Exchange Program and the Sea Semester.*

The academic climate at C of C is challenging but not cut-throat. The majority of classes at the college are limited to twenty-five students and students report the quality of teaching is excellent. "The professors at C of C are not only knowledgeable and caring, they are inspirational," boasts a Spanish major.

More than a third of the students hail from out of state, and one-quarter graduated in the top tenth of their high-school class. Asian-Americans and Hispanics combine to make up 2 percent of the student body, and African-Americans make up another 9 percent. Many students report that diversity is greatly valued, while others feel that racism is a concern on campus. In order to enhance diversity, C of C

"Charleston is amazing for all its variety."

has initiated several new programs and policies dealing with the issues of race, sexual harassment, and physical safety, along with many others that are already in place. The college offers hundreds of merit scholarships, as well as athletic scholarships in nine sports. A payment plan allows students to spread the cost of tuition over the course of the semester, a handy option some 20 percent of the students take advantage of.

Lack of dorm space is one of C of C's biggest problems—only 21 percent live on campus—and students say the rooms that do exist are horrible. "Most of the dorms are horrible, damp, small concrete cells and are not well maintained," a sophomore says. A new freshman dorm should help ease the crunch. In order to get a room, students advise applying early. Late applicants are doomed to scour Charleston for housing, which is usually expensive. Commuters also complain about the high cost of parking.

No matter where they live, students enjoy Charleston, with its festivals, plays, and scenic plantations and gardens. "Charleston is amazing for all its variety," an economics major says. Traditions of the Deep South provide a great backdrop for the more sophisticated side of Charleston, which includes a small but well-stocked

"City ordinances severely limit the nightlife."

art museum and some fabulous restaurants. There are social events such as movies and plays for students to enjoy on campus as well as all that the town of Charleston has to offer. Students party off campus in local clubs and apartments as well as on campus, where 14 percent of the men and 18 percent of the women belong to frats and sororities, respectively. Due to a well-enforced policy on drinking, students report that it is difficult to be served on campus if you are not twenty-one, but off campus is not a problem. Women far outnumber men, but females looking to beat the odds can always go to the Medical University of South Carolina or the Citadel Military College, which are both in Charleston.

A very old tourist town, Charleston has a "hostile attitude toward college kids," complains one student. "We are taken advantage of every day. City ordinances severely limit the nightlife and try to force kids out of the downtown area." Based on your tastes, however, you may find the historic quality charming and inspiring. On weekends, students head for "the Grand Strand," Myrtle Beach, which lies ninety miles north, or head south to Savannah and Hilton Head. Folly Beach, a great, small sandy strip, is only about twenty minutes away. Others enjoy taking a journey out of state to Georgia or North Carolina.

Many of the new performing arts majors take advantage of internship opportunities with Charleston's annual Spoleto Music Festival, while marine biology majors use the area's marshes and beaches as a research laboratory.

The absence of a football team is a common gripe among students, but other athletics are relatively popular. The men's basketball, soccer, and sailing teams are popular. On the female side, basketball, volleyball, and sailing draw a lot of participants.

The College of Charleston has set its sights on becoming the finest public liberal arts and sciences institution in South Carolina and it seems to be on its way. With a strong liberal arts foundation, an honors college, and opportunities to study abroad, students at C of C can take advantage of big opportunities at this small school.

If You Apply To ➤ | **College of Charleston:** Rolling admissions. Regular admissions: June 1. Guarantees to meet demonstrated need. No campus or alumni interviews. SATs or ACTs: required. SAT IIs: optional. Accepts the Common Application and electronic applications. Essay question: optional, personal statement.

University of Chicago

1116 East 59th Street, Chicago, IL 60637

Periodically, the news media reports that students at the University of Chicago are finally loosening up and having some fun. Don't believe it. This place is for true intellectuals who don't mind working hard for their degrees. Less selective than the top Ivies, but just as good. Social climbers apply elsewhere.

The University of Chicago attracts a very specific kind of student: one eager to eschew the superficial trappings of Ivy League prestige; one who is much more passionate about physics or Plato than about finding a great party. "This is a place that has always been very proud of its nerdiness," boasts a senior. To make the school more attractive to high-school seniors, U of C's administration has responded by launching a controversial campaign. The core curriculum has been reduced, and plans include increasing the undergraduate population, building new recreational facilities, and expanding student activities. "The administration has taken many steps to make the college a more fun place to go to school," says a sophomore.

Chicago's 190-acre tree-lined campus is located in the integrated neighborhood of Hyde Park, an eclectic community on the South Side of Chicago surrounded by low-income communities on three sides and Lake Michigan on the fourth. Town-gown relations are said to be calm, and crime is no more a problem than in any other urban setting, but African-American students complain that they are too often mistaken for trespassers by local police. The campus itself is self-contained and architecturally magnificent. The main quads are steel-gray Gothic—gargoyles and all—and the newer buildings are by Eero Saarinen, Mies van der Rohe, and Frank Lloyd Wright.

> "This is a place that has always been very proud of its nerdiness."

Historically, Chicago has been recognized for its graduate programs. But administrators and faculty members alike are beginning to realize that they must concentrate on the holistic experience the school offers undergraduates if Chicago has any hope of remaining competitive with schools like Stanford, Harvard, and Princeton. On the undergraduate level, though, Chicago remains unequivocally committed to the view that a solid foundation in the liberal arts is the best foundation for any walk of life, and that theory is better than practice. Thus, music students study

Website: www.uchicago.edu
Location: Urban
Total Enrollment: 12,327
Undergraduates: 3,917
Male/Female: 59/41
SAT Ranges: V 620–730
  M 630–730
ACT Range: 27–31
Financial Aid: 59%
Expense: Pr $ $ $ $
Phi Beta Kappa: Yes
Applicants: 5,361
Accepted: 33%
Enrolled: 57%
Grad in 6 Years: N/A
Returning Freshmen: 95%
Academics: ✑ ✑ ✑ ✑ ✑
Social: ☎ ☎
Q of L: ★ ★ ★
Admissions: (773) 702-8650
Email Address: college-admissions@uchicago.edu

Strongest Programs:
Economics

(Continued)
English
Sociology
Anthropology
Political Science
Geography
Geophysical Science
History
Linguistics
Mathematics

musicology but learn calculus along with everyone else. Indeed, half of a student's forty-two courses at Chicago, regardless of major, are taken as part of general education requirements called the common core. Dubbed by one student as the "hallmark of a Chicago education," the core curriculum has undergone a controversial reduction, down from twenty-one courses to fifteen or eighteen (depending on the foreign language requirement) and the replacement of long-standing Western civilization courses with others focusing on European civilization. What used to account for half of a student's total coursework now takes up only one-third. Requirements include courses in science and math, humanities and civilization, social sciences, and a foreign language. Sound intense? It is, students say, especially because courses are crammed into eleven-week quarters, rather than thirteen- or fourteen-week semesters. In addition to the core, seniors are encouraged to undertake final-year projects, which need not be in their area of concentration (although 99 percent of the time they are).

Chicago's brilliant and distinguished faculty is certainly its greatest asset. Although U of C was founded in the tradition of the German research universities, professors here take their teaching role quite seriously. "I have had renowned professors with years of study and experience in their fields," says a student. "In addition, lectures are informative and enjoyable." The university's dedicated professors get more time to teach and do research than they would elsewhere, since Chicago is one of the few schools in the country with full-time advisors to help students with academic and other matters. Most classes have about twenty-five students, and practically none are larger than fifty. A computerized enrollment system makes getting into sought-after classes a little less grueling. Although classes are small, students say graduating in four years is not a problem.

> **"The administration has taken many steps to make the college a more fun place to go to school."**

The economics department, a bastion of neo-liberal or New Right thinkers, is Chicago's main academic claim to fame and the most popular major. But biology, English, history, psychology, and political science also draw crowds. Chicago was father to both sociology and political science as scholarly disciplines, and these two programs remain among the best anywhere. The university also prides itself on outstanding interdisciplinary programs and area studies such as East Asian, South Asian, Middle Eastern, and Slavic. The New Collegiate Division of the university offers popular interdisciplinary programs such as Fundamentals: Issues and Texts, and newer majors include computer science and cinema and media studies. Students cite art and design, psychology, and foreign languages as weaker than most.

If Chicago gets too cold and snowy, students may study abroad on one of seventeen programs that reach most corners of the globe. A combined-degree program also allows the most motivated premeds to earn a B.A. and an M.D. in eight years, with acceptance to Chicago's medical school occurring after the second undergrad year. Other qualified undergrads are able to register for courses in all of the university's graduate and professional schools—law, divinity, social service, public policy, humanities, social sciences, biological and physical sciences, and business. "Those who are ready can accelerate as fast as the faculty and facilities permit," explains an administrator.

A combined-degree program also allows the most motivated premeds to earn a B.A. and an M.D. in eight years, with acceptance to Chicago's medical school occurring after the second undergrad year.

Since Chicago is committed to the quarter system it pioneered, the first term starts in late September and is over by Christmas. For practical purposes, this means virtually uninterrupted work straight through the school year, a long summer vacation, and three exam weeks a year. The one concession to the work ethic is a two-day reading period between the end of classes and the beginning of exams. All five of the university's libraries are excellent, containing one of the most extensive collections in the country; "much bigger than an undergrad would ever need."

Chicago has more graduate and professional students than undergraduates, and the climate on campus reflects the lopsided ratio. Some describe it as a high-pressure "grind," but it also translates into an enormous number of research projects and a better-than-even chance that an ambitious undergraduate can get a diploma having coauthored a journal article or two. "Chicago students care about their time here, which means that a lot of students are concerned about grades, curriculum, and the quality of their education," says one student.

With one hundred-plus extracurricular clubs and programs, everyone should be able to find something of interest on campus.

Only 21 percent of Chicago's student body come from Illinois; a high percentage hail from the East Coast, and many were raised in academic homes; 87 percent were in the top fifth of their high-school class. Fifty-nine percent go on to further study of some kind, which is why the university is known as "teacher of teachers." Asian-Americans account for a sizable 27 percent of Chicago's students, while blacks contribute 4 percent and Hispanics represent 5 percent. Both conservatives and liberals are "ably present and vocal," and interests run the gamut from government and politics to music. "Political correctness is pointedly ignored. Students simply treat each other fairly," says one junior. Most students dress in a come-as-you-are style. Freshman orientation, which the administration says was invented at U of C in 1924, is known as O Week, and it's a time when students make lasting friendships.

"We have incredible housing."

"We have incredible housing," boasts one student. And he's got a point, considering that one dorm, Shoreland, is a former luxury hotel located on the shore of Lake Michigan. There are twelve dorm complexes on campus, some new and sterile, others old and modeled after Cambridge or Heidelberg, and all coed by room or floor. Shoreland is the largest and most social, but it's also half a mile from campus, a definite hike when the wind is howling off the lake (from November to April). All rooms are connected to a campus-wide computer network, and some are equipped with kitchens. About two-thirds of the students live on campus, and housing is guaranteed for four years. Food is said to be "mediocre but plentiful," and while freshmen and residents of certain dorms are required to be on a full-meal contract, others can buy a meal plan or purchase individual meal coupons.

The nine fraternities and two sororities don't play a very large role in campus life, although frat parties are reasonably well attended. "Social life is very individualistic," says one student. There are two campus bars, both of which are fairly strict about not serving anyone underage, but the administration has never really cracked down on drinking, which "really isn't a social necessity here," says a student. Other weekend entertainment options on campus include low-cost flicks in the five hundred-seat movie theater, dorm

"Everybody was strange at the University of Chicago! It was paradise."

parties, and a plethora of cultural activities. Still, one student asks, "We're in Chicago, where else should we go?" He's referring, of course, to downtown, with its internationally acclaimed symphony, museums, and other cultural facilities. Though everything is accessible by public transportation, cars are a nice luxury if you can find a parking place. With 100-plus extracurricular clubs and programs, everyone should be able to find something of interest on campus.

Robert Maynard Hutchins, the famous president of Chicago from 1929 to 1951, once opined that "having fun is a form of intelligence." As evidence that such views are acceptable, the university belongs to the University Athletic Association, which includes other academically minded schools, such as Johns Hopkins and New York University. To everyone's surprise, the recently resurrected football team has already had a couple of winning seasons. Chicago fans often fill Stagg Field to its 1,500-seat capacity to support the school's teams, and the Scholarly Yell they shout out is one of the best cheers around: "Themistocles, Thucydides/The Peloponnesian

Wars/X-squared, Y-squared, H2SO4/Who for, what for/Who the hell are we cheering for?/Go Maroons!"

Athletes here are well respected, and—remember, this is the University of Chicago—have a higher overall GPA than the student body as a whole; the wrestling team and women's soccer squad sport all-Americans. Both Chicago's men's and women's soccer teams have been to the Division III Final Four, while the softball team has won the UAA championship in the past. The basketball team, which has been playing since 1896, posted a 22–12 record a couple of years ago, its greatest number of victories in a single season ever. Even weekend warriors get in on the action at Chicago; intramurals attract an enthusiastic three-quarters of the student body. Hans Brinker types flock to the Midway, site of the 1893 World's Fair, which is flooded every winter for skating. In addition, there's Kuviasungnerk (the Eskimo term for happiness), an esoteric winter carnival that features ice sculptures, hockey, poetry readings, and fireside lectures on Arctic food and the meteorology of cold fronts. Only at the University of Chicago!

U of C students take pride in both their individuality and their intellectual prowess. They come to college to flex their scholarly muscle, not raise their alcohol tolerance. They place a premium on academics, not extracurriculars, and at graduation they are rewarded for their efforts—as one says, "Once this is over, you'll be good enough to tackle anything." Film director Mike Nichols described his own years as an undergraduate here as "wide open," adding that "everybody was strange at the University of Chicago! It was paradise." Current students would likely agree.

Overlaps

Harvard, Cornell University, Stanford, Northwestern, Columbia

If You Apply To ⮞

Chicago: Early action: Nov. 15. Regular admissions: Jan. 1. Financial aid: Feb. 1. Guarantees to meet demonstrated need. Campus interviews: recommended, evaluative. Alumni interviews: optional, evaluative. SATs or ACTs: required. No SAT IIs. Essay question: something that reminds you of your past; why a newspaper story of importance interests you; improvise a story, play, or dialogue; a creative work that's a key to your worldview.

University of Cincinnati

P.O. Box 210091, Cincinnati, OH 45221-0091

In most states, UC would be the big enchilada. But with Ohio State two hours up the road and Miami U even closer, Cincinnati has to hustle to get its name out there. The inventor of co-op education, it offers quality programs in everything from engineering to art—and a top-ranked men's basketball team to boot.

Website: www.uc.edu
Location: City outskirts
Total Enrollment: 27,327
Undergraduates: 20,039
Male/Female: 51/49
SAT Ranges: V 460–590
  M 470–600
ACT Range: 19–25
Financial Aid: 48%
Expense: Pub $ $ $
Phi Beta Kappa: Yes

Many first-time visitors to Cincinnati are surprised to find an attractive and very livable city. As they traverse the city's hilly roads, they are in for another surprise—its university. Not only is the University of Cincinatti renowned for its extensive research programs, the school's co-op program is also one of the largest of any public college or university in the country.

The compact campus nudges up to the edge of the downtown area and is centered at the top of a hill. Ultramodern buildings rise up next to traditional ivy-covered Georgian halls. A $300 million construction project is underway to create a "Main Street" in the center of campus, which will consolidate all student activities. A new dorm under construction is one of several planned. A new medical research facility and performing arts complex recently joined the campus. Research is a UC specialty. Campus scientists have given the world antiknock gasoline, the electronic organ, antihistamines, and the U.S. Weather Bureau. UC is also the place where, in 1906, cooperative education was born, allowing students to earn while they learn. Across the Cincinnati curriculum, there is an abundance of co-op opportunities available. Nearly 4,000 students take advantage of them. In all, forty-two programs offer the popular five-year professional-practice option.

The colleges of engineering; business administration; and design, architecture, art, and planning (the schools with the most co-op students) are the best bets at UC. The university's music conservatory, one of the best state-run programs in the field, also offers broadcasting training. The schools of nursing and pharmacy are well-known and benefit from UC's health center and graduate medical school. The most popular major is marketing. In addition, education is a strong program. The Cincinnati Initiative for Teacher Education requires all education majors to complete a five-year program that ends in an entire year of internships in different education environments. Education students earn two bachelor's degrees: one in education and one in a liberal arts subject. The two-year University College is Cincinnati's open-admissions unit, which prepares less-qualified students to transfer into four-year programs and offers a variety of vocational degrees, including paralegal technology and robotics. A new Department of Biomedical Engineering was founded in 2001. Inventureworks is a new program for design and business students that allows them to brainstorm on new products for international companies.

The academic grind is determined largely by the major. Fields such as engineering, business, and nursing require a substantially larger academic commitment. "Most classes are laid-back until you are admitted to your degree program," says a sophomore. But another student notes "UC harbors a certain competitive spirit." Some courses end up being quite large (in popular design courses, two people to a desk is not unusual), and students say about 20 percent of their classes have up to one hundred students. One fine asset is the school's huge library, which has 1.9 million volumes and is completely computerized.

UC has taken steps to improve the quality of the undergraduate education by strengthening its general education requirements to focus on critical thinking and expression, and expanding its honors program. Additionally, UC has adopted its Pedagogy Initiative, which allows students to interact with professors and encourages them to develop

"Most classes are laid-back until you are admitted to your degree program."

questions in the classroom. Freshmen must take English and math as well as a contemporary issues class; other requirements vary by college. A third of the faculty members hold outside jobs, bringing fresh practical experience to the classroom.

All but 8 percent of the student body comes from within the state, but the student body is fairly diversified. "Students at UC are very diverse, and represent all different levels of academic ability, experience and interests," says one student. There are art types and business types, liberals and conservatives. African-Americans, Asian-Americans, and Hispanics comprise 15, 3, and 1 percent of the student body, respectively. Diversity, feminine issues, campus construction, and rising tuition are the hot topics on campus. The school offers over 1,500 merit scholarships ranging from $1,500 to full tuition, and 370 athletic scholarships for men and women. While students say they have noticed the budget squeeze in terms of services being cut and the hiring of new personnel curtailed, the school is growing. "Our school is constantly changing," says a triple major who notes a campus-wide joke is that UC stands for "Under Construction."

A mere 10 percent of UC students live on campus. Noncommuting freshmen and athletes are required to live in the six coed and single-sex dorms, which are described as adequate but crowded. Students say the lack of parking facilities is a much bigger deal than housing conditions. Many upperclassmen, especially the

(Continued)
Applicants: 10,745
Accepted: 82%
Enrolled: 41%
Grad in 6 Years: 45%
Returning Freshmen: 70%
Academics: ✍ ✍
Social: ☎ ☎ ☎
Q of L: ★ ★ ★
Admissions: (513) 556-1100
Email Address:
   admissions@uc.edu

Strongest Programs:
   Engineering
   Graphic Design
   Business
   Architecture
   Art
   Planning
   Education

More than 1,500 students receive more than $11 million in scholarships each year, but are required to participate in a service-learning program each year.

older and married students, consider off-campus living far better than dorm life, and inexpensive apartments can usually be found. Food in the two cafeterias located on opposite ends of the campus is "bland and unappetizing," and many students find stopping at the plastic village of fast-food joints surrounding the campus a tastier, cheaper, and more convenient option.

Merchants have turned the area surrounding UC, called Clifton, into a mini college town with plenty to do. A bus line running by the campus takes undergraduates into the heart of the "Queen City" of Cincinnati in minutes. There the students find museums, a ballet, professional sports teams, parks, rivers, hills, and as many large and small shops as anyone could want. Still, the students advise caution, especially at night, when maneuvering through the campus and the "somewhat run-down" urban neighborhood surrounding it. On-campus activities include everything from a mountaineering club to Internat (the international students association) to clubs in various majors. Fraternities and sororities are small but are still the most active places to party on campus, usually opening their functions to everyone. The university sponsors some events, such as the massive but still wacky Springfest, which spotlights local bands playing all day and lots of "crafts and food and beer." The most popular road trips are the city of Cleveland and white-water rafting in West Virginia.

In sports, men's basketball, track, and swimming teams have captured recent titles, along with the volleyball and women's swimming teams. Football, track, soccer, baseball, and women's crew are also popular. Everyone mentions the football rivalry with Miami (of Ohio) as a game you won't want to miss, and the same holds true when the men's basketball squad takes on Xavier University. Weekend athletes also take advantage of UC's first-rate sports center.

The University of Cincinnati and surrounding city offer students opportunities for a hands-on education and the full college experience. Students who attend UC not only get a good education at a reasonable price, they also get a chance to put what they've learned into practice outside of the halls of academia.

Overlaps

Ohio State, Miami University (OH), Ohio University, Bowling Green State, Toledo.

If You Apply To >

UC: Rolling admissions: Jan. 15. Does not guarantee to meet demonstrated need. Campus interviews: optional, informational. No alumni interviews. SATs or ACTs: required. SAT IIs: optional. Accepts the Common Application and electronic applications. No essay question. Apply to particular program.

Claremont Colleges

In 1887, James A. Blaisdell had the vision to create a group of colleges patterned after Oxford and Cambridge in England. More than a century later, the five schools that comprise the Claremont Colleges thrive as a consortium of separate and distinct undergraduate colleges with two adjoining graduate institutions, a theological seminary, and botanical gardens. As families can sometimes get, the colleges coexist, interact, and experience their share of both cooperation and tension. Ultimately, however, the Claremont College Consortium forms a mutually beneficial partnership that offers its students the vast resources and facilities one might only expect to find at a large university.

The colleges are located on 317 acres in the Los Angeles suburb of Claremont, a peaceful neighborhood replete with palm trees, Spanish architecture, and the nearby San Gabriel Mountains. The picture-perfect California weather can sometimes be marred by smog, courtesy of the neighbors in nearby L.A., but the administration claims the smog level has declined dramatically in the past few years.

None of the five undergraduate colleges that make up the Claremont Colleges Consortium—Claremont McKenna, Harvey Mudd, Pitzer, Pomona, and Scripps—is larger than a medium-size dorm at a state school. Each school retains its own institutional identity, with its own faculty, administration, admissions, and curriculum, although the boundaries of both academic work and extracurricular activities are somewhat flexible. Each of the schools also tends to specialize in a particular area that complements the offerings of all the others. Claremont McKenna, which caters mainly to students planning careers in economics, business, law, or government, has eight research institutes located on its campus, while Harvey Mudd is the choice for future scientists. Pitzer, the most liberal of the five, excels mainly in the behavioral sciences, and at the all-women Scripps, the best offerings are in art and foreign languages. The oldest of the five colleges, Pomona ranks as one of the top liberal arts colleges anywhere, and is the one Claremont school that is strong across the board, with the humanities especially superb.

Collectively, the colleges share many services and facilities, including art studios, a student newspaper, laboratories, an extensive biological field station, a health center, auditoriums, a 2,500-seat concert hall, a 350-seat theater, bookstores, a maintenance department, and a business office. The Claremont library system makes more than 1.9 million volumes available to all students, though each campus also has a library of its own. Faculties and administrations are free to arrange joint programs or classes between all or just some of the schools. Courses at any college are open to students from the others (approximately 1,200 courses in all), but each college sets limits on the number of classes that can be taken elsewhere. Perhaps the best example of academic cooperation is the team-taught interdisciplinary courses, which are organized by instructors from the different schools and appeal to a mix of different academic interests.

The Claremont Colleges draw large numbers of students from within California, although their national reputation is growing. These days, about half the students hail from other Western and non-Western states, with a sizable contingent from the East Coast. The tone at Claremont is decidedly intellectual—more so than at Stanford or any other place in the West—and graduate programs in the arts and sciences are more common goals than business or law school. Anyone who is bright and hardworking can find a niche at one of the five schools. Unfortunately, despite their excellence, the Claremonts are also among the most underrated colleges in the nation.

The local community of Claremont is geared more to senior citizens than college seniors. "Quiet town of rich white people—boring," yawns an English major. A sophomore says, "Most of the stores have strange granny knick-knacks or cosmic aura trinkets." Still, "the Village," a quaint cluster of specialty shops (including truly remarkable candy stores), is an easy skateboard ride from any campus, though the shades come down and the sidewalks roll up well before sunset. Students report that the endless list of social activities offered at the colleges make up for the ho-hum town of Claremont. For hot times, Hollywood's glamour and UCLA-dominated Westwood are within sniffing distance, and a convenient shuttle bus makes them even closer for Claremont students without cars. Nearby mountains and the fabled surfing beaches make this collegiate paradise's backyard complete. Mount Baldy ski lifts, for instance, are only fifteen miles away, and you'll reach Laguna Beach before both sides of your favorite tape are played out. For spring break, Mexico is cheap and a great change of pace.

On campus, extracurricular life maintains a balance between cooperation and independence. Claremont McKenna, Harvey Mudd, and Scripps field joint athletic teams, and the men's teams, especially, are Division III powers, due to the exploits of CMC athletes. Pomona and Pitzer also compete together. Each of the five colleges has its own dorms, and since off-campus housing is limited in Claremont proper, the social life of students revolves around their dorms. "Scripps itself is quiet but parties at Harvey Mudd and Claremont McKenna can get pretty wild," admits a Scripps student. There are no fraternities, except at Pomona, where joining one is far from de rigueur. All cafeterias are open to all students, and most big events—films, concerts, etc.—are advertised throughout the campus. Large five-school parties are regular Thursday, Friday, and Saturday night fare. Social interaction among students at different schools, be it for meals or dates, is not what it might be. Pomona is seen as elitist, and its admissions office has been known to try to distance itself from the other colleges. Occasional political squabbles break out between liberal faculty and students at Pitzer and their conservative counterparts at Claremont McKenna. For the most part, students benefit not only from the nurturing and support within their own schools, each of which has its own academic or extracurricular emphasis, but also from the abundant resources the Claremont College Consortium offers as a whole.

Following are profiles of each undergraduate Claremont College.

Claremont McKenna College

890 Columbia Avenue, Claremont, CA 91711

Make way, Pomona—this up-and-comer now has the lowest acceptance rate in the Claremont Colleges and is no longer content with being a social sciences specialty school. CMC is half the size of a typical liberal arts college and 50 percent smaller than Pomona. Still developing a national reputation.

Website: www.
claremontmckenna.edu
Location: Suburban
Total Enrollment: 1,044
Undergraduates: 1,044
Male/Female: 53/47
SAT Ranges: V 650–740
M 660–740
ACT Range: 28–32
Financial Aid: 71%
Expense: Pr $ $ $ $
Phi Beta Kappa: Yes
Applicants: 2,898
Accepted: 29%
Enrolled: 32%
Grad in 6 Years: 86%
Returning Freshmen: 94%
Academics: ✍ ✍ ✍ ✍ ½
Social: ☎ ☎ ☎
Q of L: ★ ★ ★
Admissions: (909) 621-8088
Email Address: admission@
claremontmckenna.edu

Strongest Programs:
Economics
Government
International Relations
Premed
Prelaw
Business
Accounting
Sciences

At Claremont McKenna College, the students not only have parties, they study them, too. Political parties, that is. As a member of the Claremont Colleges consortium, CMC boasts top programs in government, economics, business, and international relations. In addition, Claremont McKenna has eight research institutes located on campus, which offer its undergraduates ample opportunities to study everything from political demographics to the environment. The arts and humanities are also available, but Claremont McKenna is better suited to those with high ambitions in business leadership and public affairs.

The fifty-acre campus, located thirty-five miles east of Los Angeles, is mostly "California modern" architecture with lots of Spanish tile roofs and picture windows that look out on the San Gabriel Mountains. Described by one student as "more functional than aesthetic," the physical layout fits right in with the school's pragmatic attitude. Roberts Hall is a state-of-the-art academic center housing classrooms, seminar rooms, a computer laboratory, and faculty offices. Fans of William Tell can take advantage of the school's new archery range.

Claremont McKenna offers top programs in economics and government, but the international relations, prelaw, premed, and business programs are also considered strong. The biology, chemistry, and physics departments are greatly enhanced through the use of Keck Science Center, an outstanding facility providing students with hands-on access to a variety of equipment. In addition, the eighty-five-acre Bernard Biological Field Station is located just north of the CMC campus and is available to students for field work. The administration candidly admits that computer science and engineering are not as fully developed as most departments.

CMC's extensive general education requirements include two semesters in the humanities; three in the social sciences; two in the natural sciences; a semester each in mathematics, English composition and literary analysis, and Questions of Civilization; and a Senior Thesis. The college offers popular 3-2 programs in management engineering and a 4–1 MBA program in conjunction with the Claremont Graduate University. Nearly 40 percent of Claremont McKenna students take advantage of its study-abroad programs to countries including Australia, Brazil, Costa Rica, Japan, and numerous others. CMC also offers active campus exchange programs with Haverford, Colby, Spelman, Morehouse, and universities in Quebec, Canada, and Germany. Another popular program is the Washington Semester program, in which students can intern with E-Span, the State department, the White House, and lobbying groups.

> **"Everyone at the college seems to be driven by something."**

The academic climate is fairly strenuous at Claremont McKenna, but not overwhelming. "People can be very hard on themselves as far as academics are concerned," says a sophomore, "but it is not a very competitive campus." The students at CMC give most professors high marks with the exception of the occasional prof who "should have chosen the field over the classroom." Freshmen are always taught by full professors in classes that rarely exceed twenty-five students. "We don't do the whole 'TA' thing here," asserts a junior.

Freshmen are always
taught by full professors in
classes that rarely exceed
twenty-five students.

The CMC student body is 53 percent Californian, with most everyone else from west of the Mississippi. Many attended public high school and 81 percent graduated in the top tenth of their class. "Everyone at the college seems to be driven by something," says a student. "Overachievers abound." The student body is 67 percent white; Asian-Americans comprise the largest minority at 15 percent. Hispanics comprise 10 percent while African-Americans make up 4 percent. One student says that while the administration and student body traditionally have been conservative, the student body is becoming "more politically balanced." Adds a junior, "We have a very equal split between conservative and liberal students. So, while they are not always politically correct, they are politically active." All freshmen take part in a five-day orientation program that

"They dust and vacuum our rooms and clean our bathrooms!"

includes a beach trip and a reception with the president and department chairs. The school guarantees to meet the demonstrated need of accepted applicants and offers fifty merit scholarships of $1,000 to $5,000 a year. There are no athletic scholarships (no, not even for archers).

Almost all CMC students (96 percent) live on campus "because of the social life." The maid service probably doesn't hurt. "They dust and vacuum our rooms and clean our bathrooms! We do nothing (except study, of course)!" declares a happy resident. All the residence halls are coed; freshmen are guaranteed a room. Stark Hall, an eight-story residence hall, gives students more living options. A cluster of on-campus apartments equipped with kitchen facilities is a popular option for upperclassmen. Dorm food is said to be adequate, and students can eat in dining halls at any of the other four colleges, though the best bet may be CMC's Collins Dining Hall.

Most students agree that the social life at CMC is more than adequate, thanks to the five-college system. "Needless to say, our parties usually center on alcohol," admits one student. Another student adds, "You could easily lead a full and crazy social life without ever leaving campus." In addition to the usual forms of revelry, a calendar full of annual bashes includes Monte Carlo Night, Disco Inferno, Oktoberfest, Chez Hub, and the Christmas Madrigal Feast. Enthuses a junior, "Beer golf is also an interesting tradition. Golf clubs, tennis balls, and beer...need I say more?" "SYRs—Screw or Set Up Your Roommate dances—are also pretty popular," a government major says. Ponding, another unusual CMC tradition, involves being thrown into one of the two campus fountains on one's birthday. The

"Basketball games rock this campus."

college sponsors an outstanding lecture series at the Marion Minor Cook Athenaeum on Monday through Thursday nights each week. Before each lecture, students and faculty can enjoy a formal gourmet dinner together and engage in intellectual debates. Road trips to Joshua Tree, San Francisco, Las Vegas, and Mount Baldy are highly recommended by the students.

Athletics are an important part of life at Claremont McKenna. A third of the students play varsity sports, and CMC men tend to dominate the teams jointly fielded with Harvey Mudd and Scripps (for women). Recent conference championships have been won by women's basketball, cross-country, track and field, and tennis and men's track, soccer, and cross-country. Top rivalries include Pomona, both in athletics and academics, one student claims. "Basketball games rock this campus," another student says.

CMC may be a small college, but its mission is to produce great leaders. "Leadership pervades almost everything that goes on here," says a junior. "Claremont McKenna builds character, fosters a sense of ambition among its students, and drives them to set their sights high."

Overlaps
UC–Berkeley, Stanford, UCLA, Pomona, UC-San Diego

Harvey Mudd College

301 East 12th Street, Kingston Hall, Claremont, CA 91711

The finest institution than nobody outside of the techie world has ever heard of. Future Ph.D.s graduate from here in droves. Rivals Caltech for sheer brainpower and access to outstanding faculty. Offers more exposure to the liberal arts than most technically oriented schools.

Website: www.hmc.edu
Location: Suburban
Total Enrollment: 701
Undergraduates: 695
Male/Female: 75/25
SAT Ranges: V 670–740
   M 720–790
Financial Aid: 57%
Expense: Pr $ $ $ $
Phi Beta Kappa: No
Applicants: 1,517
Accepted: 42%
Enrolled: 31%
Grad in 6 Years: 78%
Returning Freshmen: 91%
Academics: ✑ ✑ ✑ ✑ ½
Social: ☎ ☎ ☎
Q of L: ★ ★ ★
Admissions: (909) 621-8011
Email Address:
   admission@hmc.edu

Strongest Programs
   Engineering
   Math
   Physics
   Chemistry

Students here take a third of their courses in the humanities, the most of any technical college.

A top-ranked technical institution, Harvey Mudd College strives to give its students a sense of balance. Although it's a leading provider of high-quality programs in science and engineering, it also emphasizes a well-rounded education with knowledge in the humanities. Harvey Mudd also encourages balance in work and play, and manages to maintain a community feeling in both realms. Although the academic climate is challenging here, the students go out of their way to assist each other, says one engineering major. This desire to help is fostered by the faculty's encouragement of cooperation and team projects.

HMC's mid-'50s vintage campus of cinder-block buildings even "looks like an engineering college; it's very symmetrical and there's no romance." In addition, the buildings have little splotches all over their surfaces that students have dubbed "warts"—not a very attractive picture. While most technical schools tend to have a narrow focus, HMC has come up with the novel idea that even scientists and engineers "need to know and appreciate poetry, philosophy, and non-Western thought," says an administrator.

Students here take a third of their courses in the humanities, the most of any engineering college in the nation. Up to half of them can be taken by walking over to another Claremont school. To ensure breadth in the sciences, students take another third of their work in math, physics, chemistry, biology, engineering design, and computer science. The last third of a student's courses must be in one of six major areas: biology, computer science, chemistry, physics, engineering, or math. And finally, to cap off their HMC experience, all students must complete a research project in their major, as well as a senior thesis in the humanities and social sciences.

"We're spoiled with small classes taught by Ph.D.s."

Of the six majors, engineering is considered not only the strongest but the most popular by students, with physics not far behind. In the past few years, the number of biology faculty has more than doubled, and with the completion of the Olin Science Center, HMC's program in science is a strong one. Students rave about the engineering clinic program, which plops real-life engineering tasks (sponsored by major corporations and government agencies to the tune of $34,000 per project) into the laps of students. There's also a Freshman Project that allows neophytes to tackle "some real-world engineering problems." The computer science major has been considered weak in the past but students say there have been improvements.

Whatever department students end up in, the workload at HMC is no cakewalk. One student says the academics are a bit like "drinking from a fire hose...this is one tough school." Still, an engineering major says that the intense academics foster a sense of camaraderie among students. "No matter how busy my classmates are with their own work, they always seem to be available to help me when I run into problems." The absence of graduate programs means that undergraduates get uncommon amounts of attention from even top faculty. Students love the small-college atmosphere. "We're spoiled with small classes taught by Ph.D.'s," says a student. "Their dedication is amazing and their knowledge immense." The campus-wide honor code is strongly supported by the student body. These budding technicians are also top achievers: 91 percent graduated in the top 10 percent of their high-school class.

"Prospective students should know that it can be temporarily damaging to their egos to come to a school with so many bright students," says a junior. Forty percent of the students are homegrown Californians. African-Americans and Hispanics combine for 6 percent of the student body, while Asian-Americans weigh in at over 26 percent. A staggering 42 percent of a recent freshman class was composed of National Merit Scholars. The administration advises that prospective applicants should be "passionate" about some aspect of math, science, or engineering. Political correctness is not an issue on campus, and "political awareness is pretty low," according to one senior.

Engineering is the most popular major, and students rave about the engineering clinic program, which plops real-life engineering tasks into the laps of students.

"Due to the dominant male population, social life can be rather strained."

Five older dorms and two newer, more modern ones are all coed and mix the classes. "They are definitely the engineering-school type–functional and efficient," notes a freshman. They range from Atwood ("study hard, party hard") to North ("way cool, so very"). The dorms are also ideal for computer whizzes: all are wired for online access to the HMC mainframe. Campus security is considered ample, especially with the school's recent installations of campus phones, additional lighting, and fences. Workshops in self-defense are also offered for those who are interested.

The college has no fraternities, and most social life takes place in and around the dorms where there are parties every weekend. "Social life is dorm life," says a computer science major. Despite their heavy workload, most HMC students find abundant social outlets, even if it's just joining the parade of unicycles that has overrun the campus. One student complains, "Due to the dominant male population, social life can be rather strained." Another student describes the town of Claremont as "a wonderful place if you're married or about to die." However, most students say there is always fun to be had at one of the five campuses. Down-and-dirty types often frequent the Mudd Hole, a pizza-pinball-Ping-Pong hangout. Underage drinking is "compliments of a peer over twenty-one," as one student puts it. For a school so young, Mudd is rife with tradition, including the annual "pumpkin caroling" trip at Halloween, in which students serenade professors' homes with doctored-up Christmas carols. Another night of screwball fun is the Women's Pizza Party, in which men don dresses and crash a meeting of the Society of Women Engineers. There is also an annual Five Class competition among the four classes and the handful of fifth-year students, complete with amoebae soccer and relay races that include unicycles (backward), peanut butter and jelly, and slide-rule problem solving.

Another night of screwball fun is the Women's Pizza Party, in which men don dresses and crash a meeting of the Society of Women Engineers.

Mudd fields varsity sports teams with Claremont McKenna and Scripps, and mainly because of all the CMC jocks, the teams do extremely well. The men's teams in soccer, track, cross-country, tennis, water polo, and swimming are nationally ranked in NCAA Division III. Women's teams in soccer, basketball, swimming, tennis, and track are perennial high achievers. Not long ago, some enterprising Mudders stole archrival Caltech's cannon, elevating the Mudd-Caltech rivalry to include a soccer game dubbed the Cannon Bowl. Intramurals, also in conjunction with Scripps and CMC, are even more popular. Traditional sporting events include the

HMC is right on the heels of Caltech as the best technical school in the West.

Black and Blue Bowl, an interdorm game of tackle football, and the Freshman-Sophomore Games, which climax in a massive tug-of-war across a pit of vile stuff.

"Harvey Mudd's problem right now," complains one senior engineering major, "is that it is not well known outside of the western United States." Nevertheless, HMC is right on the heels of Caltech as the best technical school in the West. Mudd doesn't promise you'll end up the owner of your own mining company—or president of anyone else's—within a decade of graduation, but it does offer a gem of a technical education perfectly blended with a dash of humanities and social sciences. HMC's intimate setting also offers something bigger schools can't: a sense of family.

Overlaps

UC–Berkeley, MIT, Caltech, Stanford, UCLA

If You Apply To ➤

Harvey Mudd: Early decision: Nov. 15. Regular admissions: Jan. 15. Financial aid: Feb. 1. Guarantees to meet demonstrated need. Campus interviews: recommended, informational. Alumni interviews: not available. SATs: required. SAT IIs: required (writing, math II, and one other). Accepts the Common Application. Essay question: compare and contrast relationship between art and science; meaningful moment; describe yourself.

Pitzer College

1050 North Mills Avenue, Claremont, CA 91711

Offers a haven for the otherwise-minded without the hard edge of nonconformity at places like Evergreen and Bard. Traditional strengths lie in the social and behavioral sciences. Still more than 60/40 female, but much more selective than it was ten years ago.

Website: www.pitzer.edu
Location: Suburban
Total Enrollment: 921
Undergraduates: 921
Male/Female: 38/62
SAT Ranges: V 560–670
M 550–640
ACT Range: 24–28
Financial Aid: 60%
Expense: Pr $ $ $ $
Phi Beta Kappa: No
Applicants: 2,282
Accepted: 54%
Enrolled: 10%
Grad in 6 Years: 66%
Returning Freshmen: 82%
Academics: ✍ ✍ ✍
Social: ☎ ☎ ☎
Q of L: ★ ★ ★
Admissions: (909) 621-8129
Email Address:
admission@pitzer.edu

As the most laid-back of the Claremont colleges, Pitzer College offers students a creative milieu, abundant opportunities for intellectual exploration, and a sense of fierce individualism. Founded in the '60s, this small school has changed with the times but continues its tradition of progressive thought and open social attitude.

Even the campus is, well, different. The classroom buildings are modernistic octagons, and the grass-covered "mounds" that distinguish the grounds "are perfect for sunbathing and Frisbee," says one student. In keeping with Pitzer's free-wheeling style, each student has the maximum freedom to choose which classes he or she would like to take. A lively freshman seminar program sharpens students' learning skills, especially writing. Students select from forty majors in sciences, humanities, and social sciences. Almost anything in the social and behavioral sciences is a sure bet, especially psychology (the most popular major), anthropology, sociology, political science, and organizational studies. A psych course, Sexual Deviance, wins the most-popular-class award

"The professors rock!" gushes a senior. "They are all dynamic, brilliant teachers."

hands down. The art department also garners praise, while most courses in Pitzer's weaker areas—math and the natural sciences—can be picked up at one of the other Claremont schools. New majors have been added in environmental science and biology/chemistry.

Interdisciplinary inquiry is encouraged and original research is common. Pitzer students take advantage of Claremont's abundant foreign-study options, including a program in international and intercultural studies combining language proficiency, cultural study, and an off-campus Challenge semester. Class size is generally small, promoting close interaction between students and faculty. "People work together with their professors to create a classroom climate that is supportive and engaging," says a psychology major. "The professors rock!" gushes a senior. "They are all dynamic, brilliant teachers." Academic advising gets the thumbs-up as well. A student says that advisors are "profs in our own majors, so they are knowledgeable."

Individualism is a prized characteristic among Pitzer students, more than half of whom are from California. Pitzer has a substantial minority community: African-Americans and Hispanics make up 21 percent of the student body, and Asian-Americans make up 10 percent. A senior describes his peers as leaders. "These kids design their own majors, coordinate student protests, devise community education programs, and ultimately tend to fight for what they believe in." Lest anyone get the idea that Pitzer students are too far out in left field, many of them eventually go on to graduate or professional school. Adequate financial aid is guaranteed to those students in need, and Pitzer offers scholarships to twenty outstanding students.

Seventy-five percent of students live on campus. One student describes the dorms as "livable but outdated." Boarders can choose from a variety of meal plans in the dining hall (which never fails to have a vegetarian plate), join a food co-op, or cook on their own. Campus security is ever-present; a student says, "Pitzer seems to be more safe than other campuses because campus security is so effective." One interesting campus curiosity is Grove House, a structure students saved from the wrecking ball nearly two decades ago and moved to campus. It houses a dining room, study areas, and art exhibits.

Pitzer has no Greek organizations, nor does it want any, and social life tends to be fairly low-key. Kohoutek is the big party: "A weeklong art-music fest celebrating the comet that never came," says a senior. Activities include bands, food, and a "whole week of hoopla." The college enforces the twenty-one-year-old drinking age, and all parties that serve alcohol must be registered. Dances, cocktail parties, and cultural events do much to occupy students' leisure time, but without a car things can get claustrophobic. According to one student, Pitzer "doesn't have enough athletic spirit," but the Pomona-Pitzer football team—"The Sage Hens"— has had winning seasons and the school fields a variety of teams within the Southern California Intercollegiate Athletic Conference. Students play a large role in Pitzer's community government and sit on all policy committees, including those on curriculum and faculty promotion.

Pitzer attracts open-minded students looking for the freedom to go their own way. Notes one student: "Pitzer is the only Claremont school that can claim to be genuinely different, in terms of race, religion, sexual orientation, and political belief. Pitzer is an amalgamation of every color of the spectrum."

Individualism is a prized characteristic among Pitzer students, more than half of whom are from California.

"Pitzer seems to be more safe than other campuses because campus security is so effective."

Pitzer has no Greek organizations, nor does it want any, and social life tends to be fairly low-key.

Overlaps

UC–San Diego, UC–Santa Barbara, UCLA, University of Southern California, UC–Berkeley

If You Apply To ➤ | **Pitzer:** Regular admissions: Jan. 15. Financial aid: Feb. 1. Guarantees to meet demonstrated need. Campus interviews: recommended, informational. No alumni interviews. SATs or ACTs: required. SAT IIs: recommended (English and two others). Accepts the Common Application and electronic applications. Essay question: significant social issue; how do you represent your generation; greatest life lesson.

Drive 5½ hrs - from SanFran.
45 min from L.b.

Pomona College

333 North College Way, Claremont, CA 91711

The great Eastern-style liberal arts college of the West. Offers twice the resources of stand-alone competitors with its access to the other Claremonts. Location an hour east of L.A. would be ideal except for the choking smog that hangs over the area during the warmer parts of the year.

Website: www.pomona.edu
Location: Suburban
Total Enrollment: 1,549
Undergraduates: 1,549
Male/Female: 51/49
SAT Ranges: V 670–760
   M 670–750
ACT Range: 29–32
Financial Aid: 53%
Expense: Pr $ $ $ $
Phi Beta Kappa: Yes
Applicants: 3,612
Accepted: 30%
Enrolled: 35%
Grad in 6 Years: 89%
Returning Freshmen: 99%
Academics: ✑ ✑ ✑ ✑ ✑
Social: ☎ ☎ ☎
Q of L: ★ ★ ★ ★
Admissions: (909) 621-8134
Email Address:
   admissions@pomona.edu

Strongest Programs
   English
   International Relations
   Economics
   Neuroscience
   Foreign Languages
   Media Studies

Pomona College, located just thirty-five miles east of the glitz and glamour of Hollywood, is the undisputed star of the Claremont College Consortium. This small, elite institution is the best liberal arts college in the West, and its media studies program (film and television) gets top billing. But the school's prestigious reputation doesn't get to the heads of Pomona's friendly students. "Students here are very open about different types of people—[Pomona] prides itself on its diverse community," chirps one Sage Hen (the school's mascot). With stellar liberal arts programs and a brilliant atmosphere, Pomona College wins for best supporting role.

The architecture is variously described as Spanish Mediterranean, pseudo-Italian, or, as a sophomore puts it, "a perfect mix of Northeastern Ivy and Southern California Modern." The administration building, Alexander Hall, is described as "postmodern with Mediterranean influences," and one notices more than one stucco building cloaked in ivy and topped with a red-tile roof on campus, as well as eucalyptus trees, canyon live oaks, and an occasional "secretive courtyard lined with flowers." By virtue of its location and beauty, Pomona's campus has served as the quintessential collegiate milieu in various Hollywood movies, including *Beaches* and, appropriately enough, *How I Got into College*. New facilities include the Andrew Building for Sciences and the Smith Campus Center.

Classes at Pomona are challenging. "Most courses are very rigorous," says a student. "Professors expect students to participate actively in class discussions." Another student asserts, "I'm surrounded by so many brilliant students, but students here are not consumed by their academics as they have an uncanny ability to balance the fine line between academics and social life." One undergrad estimates the average student spends twenty to thirty hours a week studying outside the classroom.

Economics, biology, English, psychology, neuroscience, and politics are the most popular majors at Pomona. Newer programs include media studies and cognitive science, and a reorganized self-study curriculum in the history department. One Pomona student reports that the history, chemistry, and politics departments are "rigorous and familial in that students are challenged to their limits by figures (professors) who are somewhat parental but very professional." As for weak spots, students say they tend to avoid a "small number of professors as opposed to entire departments or programs."

A required freshman seminar offers an introduction to critical inquiry through intensive writing on subjects such as Icons of America: The Madonna Factor, Deviance and the Devil, and What is Wrong with Killing People?: An Introduction to Ethics. Freshman seminars are designed to "teach students well and early how to use the classroom, foster discussion, step away from destructive competitive behaviors, and push to work collaboratively and supportively." Although no specific course or department is prescribed for graduation, students must take courses that meet the Perception, Analysis, and Communication requirement. Students must also enroll in at least two courses that are

"Students here are very open about different types of people."

writing-intensive, and one course designated speech-intensive, and must demonstrate proficiency in a foreign language. Educational opportunities abound at Pomona. Students can spend a semester at Colby or Swarthmore, pursue a 3–2 engineering plan with the California Institute of Technology, or spend a semester in Washington, D.C., working for a congressman. Nearly one-half of the students take advantage of study-abroad programs offered in twenty-two foreign countries, and many others participate in programs focusing on six cultures and languages at the Oldenborg Center. In addition, the Summer Undergraduate Research Program (SURP) provides students with the opportunity to conduct funded research with a faculty member in their area of study.

This small, elite institution is the best liberal arts college in the West, and its media studies program (film and television) gets top billing.

Classes are small at Pomona—the average is fourteen students—and the faculty makes a point of being accessible. It's not uncommon for professors to hold study sessions at their houses. "My professors have managed to combine their extensive experience and their research with continually inspired teaching and new ideas," a junior waxes. An ever-popular take-a-professor-to-lunch program gives students free meals when they arrive with a faculty member in tow, and there is even a prof who leads aerobics classes open to all interested parties. "For the most part, my professors are engaging and intelligent," a senior says. A classmate adds, "I know many of my professors on a personal level and feel that even after graduation, I can call them up for advice, good conversation, and possibly a free lunch!"

Pomona tends to attract "people who produce work of exceptionally high quality, but who also know how to relax and have fun," notes one student. Thirty-seven percent of the students are Californians, and a growing percentage venture from the East Coast. Pomona is proud of its diverse student body: 5 percent are African-American, 10 percent are Hispanic, and 18 percent are Asian-American. "We want to move beyond debates about statistics and make real integration happen among different ethnic groups," says a politics major. There is a healthy mix of liberals and conservatives on campus, though the leftists, especially the feminist wing, are much more vocal. "There is a high degree of political correctness on campus," claims one student, "though this does not preclude students from speaking their minds." One interesting way students voice their issues is by painting the Walker Wall. Anyone is allowed to paint any message they want on the wall, and four-letter words and descriptions of alternative sexual practices show up on a regular basis. The student government is active, and the administration is credited with respecting students' opinions. Pomona is need-blind in admissions and meets the full demonstrated need of all those who attend. Admissions officers are on the look-out for anyone with special talents and are more than willing to waive the usual grade-and-score standards for such finds. A five-day freshman orientation program divides the new arrivals into groups of six to twelve students headed by a sophomore. "We provide a great deal of support in acclimating students to a college environment," says a senior.

"We provide a great deal of support in acclimating students to a college environment."

The vast majority of Pomona students (96 percent) live on campus all four years. The dorms are coed, student-governed, and divided into two distinct groups. Those on South campus are family-like, fairly quiet, and offer spacious rooms and those on the North end have smaller rooms with a livelier social scene. Housing "kicks a** for freshmen," according to one blunt student, while "sophomores kind of get screwed." Freshmen must live on campus and are placed in a "sponsor group" with two guardian upperclassmen, creating a "quasi-family away from home." Upperclassmen generally get single rooms or spacious two-room doubles that sometimes include fireplaces. The open courtyards and gardens are popular study spots. A handful of students isolate themselves in Claremont proper, where apartments

A required freshman seminar offers an introduction to critical inquiry through intensive writing on subjects such as Icons of America: The Madonna Factor, Deviance and the Devil, and What is Wrong with Killing People?: An Introduction to Ethics.

are scarce and expensive. Boarders must buy at least partial meal plans. The food is good, with steak dinners on Saturday and ice cream for dessert every day. Students with common interests can occupy one of the large university houses; there is a vegetarian group and a kosher kitchen, both of which serve meals to other undergraduates. Pomona has a well-established language dorm with wings for speakers of French, German, Spanish, Russian, and Chinese, as well as language tables at lunch. Campus security is ever-present: "Officers are approachable and easy to find," says a student, "and they create a reassuring presence on campus." Another adds, "The biggest nuisances are occasional incidents of bike theft or theft from dorm rooms."

Students at Pomona often spend Friday afternoons relaxing with friends over a brew at the Greek Theater. Social life begins in the dorms, where barbecues, parties, and study breaks are organized. There are movies five nights a week, and students also enjoy just tossing a Frisbee on the lawn. One student wanted to be sure that incoming freshmen and transfers knew of the Coop's (student union) "best milkshakes west of the Mississippi" and its "game room, with pool, Ping-Pong, pinball, and assorted video games." "With the five-college system, there's always something going on somewhere," asserts another Pomona enthusiast. Five-college parties happen nearly every weekend. During midterms and finals, however, the campus is a "social ghost town." Of more concern is the poor air quality, described by a junior as "oppressive on hot days during the fall semester. Most students are willing to live with the smog, but at least one student complains, "I'd prefer to breathe clean air."

Pomona is unique among the Claremont Colleges in that it has six nonnational fraternities (four coed; there are no sororities), each with its own party rooms on campus. Seven percent of the men and 2 percent of the women join up. There is

"Once you take advantage of the five-college system, you realize how cool it is."

"no peer pressure to join frats," and no fraternity rivalry. As for booze, "Kegs are not allowed in dormitories, but there is an 'out of sight, out of mind' policy in which students can have as much alcohol in their rooms as they want," reports one student. Alcohol is not much of a problem, according to another student: "At Pomona no one feels pressured to drink or not drink. I've had a great time at parties completely sober, no one looks at me like I'm a nerd, and I respect others even if they drink." Harwood dorm throws the five-college costume party every Halloween, and interdorm Jell-O fights keep things lively. Freshman orientation gets interesting, too. "Every freshman participates in a traditional ceremony involving gates and bird noises," reports a student. "I can't say too much because the rest is a secret!"

Time was a time when Pomona was an athletic powerhouse; the football team even knocked off mighty USC on Thanksgiving Day back in 1899. Currently, women's basketball, tennis, soccer, and swimming, and men's football, baseball, soccer, track, and water polo are strong programs. Intense rivalry exists between the colleges in the Claremont consortium; basketball games between Pomona, Pitzer, and CMS are "particularly heated." Intramurals, including hotly contested innertube water-polo matches, attract many participants, and Pomona's $14 million athletic complex makes its facilities the best of the Claremonts.

"Pomona offers a unique and desirable juxtaposition of rigorous academics and comfortable social atmosphere," says a student. Another student says, "Once you take advantage of the five-college system, you realize how cool it is." The strongest link in an extremely attractive chain, Pomona continues to symbolize the rising status of the Claremont Colleges—and the West in general—in the world of higher education. There are few regrets about coming to Pomona. Says a senior, "We're in California. The sun is always shining. What's the problem?"

<table>
<tr><td>

If You Apply To ≫
</td><td>

Pomona: Early decision: Nov. 15. Regular admissions: Jan. 1. Financial aid: Feb. 1. Guarantees to meet demonstrated need. Campus or alumni interviews (students choose one): recommended, evaluative. SATs or ACTs: required. SAT IIs: required (writing and two others). Accepts the Common Application and electronic applications. Essay question: personal statement and choice of most important scientific development; influential character; or how diversity affects college experience.
</td></tr>
</table>

Scripps College

1030 Columbia Avenue, Claremont, CA 91711

Scripps is a tiny, close-knit women's college with coed institutions literally right next door. Only Barnard and Spelman offer the same combination of single-sex and coed. Innovative Core Curriculum takes an interdisciplinary approach to learning.

Scripps College offers a solid, well-rounded education with a distinctly female sense of community. Founded in 1926 by newspaper publisher Ellen Browning Scripps, the college continues to pursue the mission of its founder: "to educate women by developing their intellects and talents through active participation in a community of scholars." "Scrippsies," as they are sometimes called, are by and large a moderate to liberal group, with a sprinkling of radical feminists (who will kill you if you call them Scrippsies). All are interested in "proving their worth and combating sexism, stereotypes, and sexual assault."

Scripps's scenic thirty-acre campus, listed in the National Register of Historic Places, offers a tranquil, safe, and comfortable environment. The architecture is Spanish and Mediterranean, with Roman roof-tiled buildings and elegant landscaping. "We have more than twenty courtyards and a dozen fountains," says one student. A new student commons—including dining facilities and the Motley Coffeehouse—residence hall, and pool are the most recent campus additions.

At the heart of the Scripps academic offerings is the Core Curriculum, a closely integrated sequence of three interdisciplinary courses focusing on ideas about the world and the methods used to generate these ideas. All students are required to take one course in each of the four disciplines: fine arts, letters, natural sciences, and social sciences. In addition, there is a foreign language, mathematics, and multicultural requirement, and all students must complete a senior thesis or project in their chosen field. "Courses are generally quite rigorous," says one student, noting that "my grades are my own business, and I don't feel the need to compare them with my classmates or peers."

> **"We have more than twenty courtyards and a dozen fountains."**

Anything in the humanities is a good bet at Scripps. The languages (especially French and Spanish) are particularly strong; history and psychology are also good. The strong fine arts program gets an additional boost with the Millard Sheets Art Center, which includes a state-of-the-art studio and a freestanding museum-quality gallery. Psychology tops the list of most heavily enrolled majors, followed by studio art and English. Math is weaker than most departments, but students are quick to point out that the five-college system makes it easy to find solid offerings in every field. The Keck Science Center, a joint facility for students studying the sciences at Scripps, Claremont McKenna, and Pitzer, is a prime example of the camaraderie among Claremont schools. Hispanic studies is the newest Scripps major.

The Career Planning and Resources Office helps Scripps women integrate elements of their college experience in setting goals relevant to their lives at Scripps and beyond. Computers appear across the curriculum and are located in dorms for

Website: www.scrippscol.edu
Location: Suburban
Total Enrollment: 816
Undergraduates: 798
Male/Female: 0/100
SAT Ranges: V 600–700
  M 570–660
ACT Range: 25-30
Financial Aid: 47%
Expense: Pr $ $ $
Phi Beta Kappa: Yes
Applicants: 1,200
Accepted: 64%
Enrolled: 26%
Grad in 6 Years: 77%
Returning Freshmen: 77%
Academics: ✍ ✍ ✍ ½
Social: ☎ ☎ ☎
Q of L: ★ ★ ★ ★
Admissions: (909) 621-8149
Email Address:
  admission@scrippscol.edu

Strongest Programs:
  English
  Studio Art
  Biology
  Psychology
  Foreign Languages
  Music
  Politics/International
    Relations

convenience. Students usually have no problem getting the courses they want. Inside those courses, students are lavished with attention from professors. "They have chosen to teach at a women's college because they are serious about educating women," says a sophomore. Adds a first-year, "The teachers here are terrific and very knowledgeable and supportive of the students."

Forty-six percent of Scripps women are from California. African-Americans account for 3 percent of the student body, Hispanics 6 percent, and Asian-Americans make up another 16 percent. As for relations between various ethnic groups on campus, a sophomore notes that "most people seem to mingle without a fuss." Gay rights, race issues, and women's issues are always a hot topic and "liberalism is generally expected," says a student.

> **"I feel supported and encouraged to be outspoken and confident with myself as a student and a woman."**

The college holds several programs on cultural diversity and has adopted "Principles of Community." The college doles out twenty-six merit scholarships of half-tuition annually to outstanding students. Freshmen take part in a week long orientation, and all are assigned to a peer mentor for the whole year.

Ninety-two percent of the students live in one of the eight small, home-style dorms, which are well maintained, luxurious, and even have "character," according to one chemistry major. "The dorms are beautiful and well maintained," says a sophomore. Many of the dorms boast their own reflecting pools and inner court-yards; a number of the rooms have balconies and are furnished with antiques and beautiful rugs. Students praise the dining facilities, which serve vegetarian alternatives at every meal. Students agree that campus security is good. "Scripps is a very safe campus," says a student, "because campus security is good and because we take precautions."

Campus social life centers around the residence halls, which take turns throwing parties. Scripps is adamant about stopping underage drinking, and the school's alcohol policy is rather strict but it isn't foolproof. One student reports, "Underage students can still get alcohol through their older friends if they want it." Students hang out in the Motley, a coffeehouse, relax at $2 movies on Friday or Saturday nights, or attend the five-college parties that take place nearly every weekend. For male companionship, "Claremont McKenna is just across the street," cheers one sophomore. As far as traditions go, "at the end of orientation week there's Scripps Under the Stars, an exercise in shared humiliation for first-year women," reports a senior. "Everyone does skits or songs on the Wood Steps; it is followed by an ice cream social." Scripps fields joint athletic teams with CMC and Harvey Mudd, and conference championships have been won by the soccer, tennis, swimming, cross-country, and basketball teams.

Scripps has the appeal of being both a women's college with its supportive environment and part of the diverse academic and social university environment of Claremont. As a lit major sums up: "I feel supported and encouraged to be outspoken and confident with myself as a student and a woman. Scripps is dedicated not only to education but also to the empowerment and success of women."

Overlaps

UCLA, UC–Berkeley, Smith, University of Southern California, Wellesley

Clark University

950 Main Street, Worcester, MA 01610-1477

If Clark were located an hour to the east, it would be the hottest thing since Harvard. Worcester is not Boston, but Clarkies bring a sense of mission to their relationship with this old industrial town. Clark is liberal, tolerant, and world-renowned in psychology and geography.

For nearly a century, Clark has been in a class of its own—advancing curriculum and launching programs not seen anywhere else. The first all-graduate school in the country, it was also the only American university where Sigmund Freud lectured. Clark recently became the first school anywhere to offer a doctorate program in Holocaust history, and now it has made a compelling offer to students: study hard during your undergraduate years and get an extra year of education for free.

The compact fifty-acre urban campus has "enough ivy, tall maples, and collegiate brick buildings to make a traditionalist happy." Buildings range from remodeled Victorian-era residences, former homes of prosperous Worcester merchants, to the architecturally award-winning Robert Hutchings Goddard Library. Clark is always renovating one building or another, and careful restorations have brought a renewed sense of the history of the area. In the past decade, half of the fifty buildings on campus have been either completely renovated or newly built. Jonas Clark Hall, the oldest building on campus, was completely restored, maintaining its prominence as the main academic classroom facility in the center of campus. The recently added Lasry House is home to the Strassler Family Center for Holocaust and Genocide Studies, and the new Traina Center for the Arts just opened. A statue of famed psychoanalyst Sigmund Freud stands stoically in the center of the campus, marking the spot where he lectured.

> "It is a great environment because the professors want the students to learn and grow."

Though the majority of students are now undergrads, Clark was founded as the country's first all-graduate school. "Courses give students exposure to intensive assignments and a rigorous approach toward problem solving, analytical reasoning, and the like," says one senior. Some seminars are limited to fifteen students; 75 percent of classes have twenty-five or fewer. In first-year seminars, which never have more than fifteen students, students have isolated strands of DNA, explored the workings of the brain, discussed origins of modern sports, and interned at local elementary schools. The psychology and geography departments have national reputations, the latter having churned out more Ph.D.s than any other school in the nation. The American Psychological Association was founded on campus, and preeminent psychologist Carl Jung received an honorary degree at Clark. The departments of government and international relations, history, and chemistry are also strong, while the physics, music, and theater departments receive mixed reviews from students. The school has added two new concentrations: Urban Development and Social Change, and Environment and Society. In the USDC program, students have helped revitalize Clark's own neighborhood, called Main South, in Worcester. The Cultural Identities and Global Processes concentration was recently phased out.

In the first two years, broad academic exploration is the focus. Each student must complete a program of liberal studies, which includes two critical thinking courses in two categories—verbal expression and formal analysis—and six perspectives courses in the following areas: aesthetics, comparative analysis, history, science, language and culture, and values. International studies students take courses in

Website: www.clarku.edu
Location: Center city
Total Enrollment: 2,955
Undergraduates: 2,138
Male/Female: 40/60
SAT Ranges: V 530–640
 M 530–630
ACT Range: 22–28
Financial Aid: 55%
Expense: Pr $ $ $
Phi Beta Kappa: Yes
Applicants: 3,704
Accepted: 68%
Enrolled: 20%
Grad in 6 Years: 72%
Returning Freshmen: 85%
Academics: ✍ ✍ ✍ ✍
Social: ☎ ☎ ☎
Q of L: ♥♥♥
Admissions: (508) 793-7431
Email Address:
 admissions@clarku.edu

Strongest Programs:
 Psychology
 Geography
 Government and International
 Relations
 Environmental Studies
 Holocaust and Genocide
 Studies
 History

those areas with an international bent. Interdisciplinary programs are also popular—women's studies is especially good—and students may design their own majors.

Internships are encouraged in all academic areas and through the fourteen-college Worcester Consortium.* Special offerings include taking courses or attending international research conferences at the Clark University Center in Luxembourg. More than 20 percent of all Clark students spend at least one semester studying abroad at one of fourteen sites with which the school is affiliated. Clark also offers a special bonus with the Fifth Year Free Program, which allows students with a B-plus average or better to get a combination bachelor's/master's degree with, you guessed it, the last year at no cost. As for the academic climate, courses are "as rigorous as you want them to be," a history student says. Professors get high marks from students. "They challenge you to learn, and they help you along the way. It is a great environment because the professors want the students to learn and grow."

Forty percent of Clark's students are from Massachusetts; another large contingent hails from New York and other parts of New England. International students representing about ninety foreign countries make up 9 percent of the student body; 4 percent of students are African-American, 3 percent are Hispanic, and 4 percent are Asian-American. Students tend to support the diversity. "Clark is a place where students from so many different places come together to learn, hang, and party," a junior says. The university also has a collaborative educational program with historically African-American Howard University. Politically, Clark seems to have a reputation for being "extremely liberal," as one student points out, and also socially aware. "Clark is a place where issues can be brought to the front and talked about," says one government major. Another student says, "There is always a group willing to get involved with a hot issue." The Multicultural Center provides space for a wealth of groups and has a grant-funded director to host regular programs exploring race relations and diversity. Clark offers 302 merit-based scholarships that cover part of the tuition, and several special tuition-payment plans. Community-oriented students can score Making a Difference scholarships, each worth $44,000 plus $2,500 to support summer service projects.

"Clark is a place where issues can be brought to the front and talked about."

Housing options at Clark are highly regarded by most students. Three-quarters live in campus housing, which is described as comfortable and well maintained. There is free cleaning service, though freshman living space is described as "lacking in aesthetics." Students must play the "room roulette" lottery to get housing, and all dorms, except one, are coed by floor or wing. Freshmen and sophomores are required to live on campus, and many juniors and seniors live in cheap apartments close to campus. The on-campus dweller must subscribe to one of several meal plans, and there is a vegetarian option. All students can get a cash card encoded with their student ID number that will allow them to eat anywhere on campus including the Bistro, an international café.

"Almost everyone does something for the neighborhood."

Worcester boasts ten colleges but is hardly what you would call a college town. "It offers everything but a social atmosphere for those under twenty-one," a junior says. The offerings include numerous restaurants, dance clubs, concert halls, a resident symphony, theater companies, and good science and art museums. It's also home to the Centrum, a 13,000-seat arena that draws some of the top touring bands in the country. Students seem pretty happy to mix with townspeople and volunteer for community service, especially through the Big Brother-Big Sister program. "Worcester needs a lot of help, and Clark likes to help," a senior says. "Almost everyone does something for the neighborhood." When Clarkies need a change of pace they travel to Boston, Vermont, New Hampshire, Maine, or Providence.

There are no Greek organizations on campus, but over-twenty-one upperclassmen frequent a few local bars. The campus pub was recently converted into a place called Grind Central, a coffeehouse that offers gourmet coffee, pastries, live entertainment, and various games in a cozy atmosphere. As for booze, "Campus policies are strict in writing, but hard to enforce," says one senior. Be careful, though. No kegs are allowed on campus, and students say this rule is enforced. Other on-campus options include movies, plays, comedy clubs, concerts, and the popular Speakers Forum. One business major explains that Clark is "not a big 'party school.' It's more like a 'hang out with your friends' school." Another student adds, "Social life is a combination of planned events and random parties."

"Social life is a combination of planned events and random parties."

Coping with the cold New England winters includes quaffing cups of hot chocolate and dreaming about Spree Day—"what every Clarkie lives for," one student says. Spree Day comes as a complete surprise; students awake to canceled classes and a carnival and popular band waiting to entertain them. Completely different is Academic Spree Day, when all undergraduate research is celebrated. While Clark has never had a reputation as a jock school, it is respectable in several sports. The men's basketball team reached the Division III Elite Eight in 2001, and the women's basketball team reached the Sweet Sixteen in 2000. Other top women's teams include cross-country, which participated in the Worcester City Championships, and the field-hockey and crew teams. A 4,300-square-foot fitness center houses cardiovascular machines, strength-building machines, and free weights. Clark has opened a new field house, renovated the tennis courts, and renovated the baseball, soccer, and lacrosse fields.

The slogan "challenging convention, changing our world" sums up Clark's focus. The school strives to be a pioneer in the way it teaches, pursues new knowledge, and blends doing and thinking. Clark is willing to challenge old ideas and add to students' roles in the community and society. With an engaging staff, beautiful campus, and tight-knit community, Clark offers its students a world of opportunity.

Overlaps

Boston University, University of Massachusetts at Amherst, Brandeis, Wheaton (MA), Skidmore

If You Apply To ➣ **Clark:** Early decision: Nov. 15. Regular admissions, financial aid, housing: Feb. 1. Does not guarantee to meet demonstrated need. Campus and alumni interviews: recommended, evaluative. SATs or ACTs: required. SAT IIs: optional. Essay question: significant experience with meaning; issue of personal, local, national, or international concern; person of significance; fiction character, historical figure, or creative work and its influence on you; personal topic.

Clarkson University

Holcroft House, Box 5605, Potsdam, NY 13699

You know you're in the north country when the nearest major city is Montreal. Over the river and through the woods lies Clarkson, one of the few small, undergraduate-oriented technical universities in the nation. The atmosphere is informal and close-knit. Compare to Lehigh, Bucknell, and Union.

At Clarkson University, engineering and ice hockey reign supreme. More than half of the student body is enrolled in the engineering program, and the hockey team is a perennial contender for top honors. Students at this tiny school take advantage of a quality technical education and a small-town environment that offers plenty to do, especially during the sled dog days of winter.

Website: www.clarkson.edu
Location: Small town
Total Enrollment: 2,949
Undergraduates: 2,610

(Continued)

Male/Female: 75/25

SAT Ranges: V 520–620
   M 560–660

Financial Aid: 81%

Expense: Pr $ $ $

Phi Beta Kappa: No

Applicants: 2,584

Accepted: 81%

Enrolled: 32%

Grad in 6 Years: 70%

Returning Freshmen: 87%

Academics: ✍ ✍ ✍

Social: ☎ ☎

Q of L: ★ ★ ★

Admissions: (315) 268-6479

Email Address:
   admission@clarkson.edu

Strongest Programs:
   Engineering
   Chemistry
   Management
   Physics
   Biology
   Math
   Computer Science

The tiny town of Potsdam, New York, is cloistered away between the Adirondacks and the St. Lawrence River. The "hill campus," where most freshmen and sophomores live and take classes, relies mainly on modern architecture and lots of woods and wildlife. Personal computers are a must, and countless resources exist on the campus network, which can be accessed from dorm rooms. Opened in 2000, the Bertrand H. Snell building houses the School of Business and the School of Liberal Arts.

Engineering isn't the only thing at Clarkson, but it certainly gets top billing; 49 percent of the students are in the program. The combined programs in electrical/computer engineering and mechanical/aeronautical engineering earn the highest marks from students. Clarkson's School of Business has added majors in business and technology management, e-business, financial information analysis, and information systems and business processes. Project Arete allows students to earn a double major in management and a liberal arts discipline. The school also offers degree programs in computer and aeronautical engineering. Physics and chemistry are the strongest offerings in the sciences, and would-be doctors have the benefit of a joint program combining biology and—you guessed it—engineering. The liberal arts and humanities are cited by students as being weaker than other departments.

As part of their Foundation Curriculum requirements, all students at Clarkson are required to take six liberal arts courses; two in mathematics; two in science; and one each in computer programming, engineering, and management. Freshmen are required to take a two-semester Great Ideas course along with a personal wellness course. A convocation program for new students is designed to introduce them to distinguished speakers and performers whose appearances may broaden their educational horizons. About thirty freshmen are invited to participate in the honors program, which offers specially developed courses and research experiences.

Clarkson prides itself on intimacy and personalized instruction, and the fact that 80 percent of the Foundation courses are taught by full-fledged faculty members proves that it's no idle boast. "The professors here are very intelligent, readily available, and willing to help their students in any way they can," says an environmental science and policy major. Another student adds, "The professors are excited by the subjects they teach and it shows." Clarkson isn't the academic pressure cooker that many technical institutes are, but it really depends on whom you talk to. "The academic climate here is

"The professors are excited by the subjects they teach and it shows."

fairly rigorous but not to the point where it's overwhelming," says a business administration and social science double major. A senior adds, "Students mainly help each other out and have a laid-back demeanor." The bottom line of a Clarkson education is getting a job after graduation, and students uniformly praise the career counseling office and note with pride Clarkson's high placement rate. One junior says that the career center is "very good at getting students to think about their futures."

At Clarkson the students are friendly, serious-minded, and down-to-earth; radicals are notably absent. Seventy percent of the students graduated in the top quarter of their class. Seventy-two percent are New Yorkers, and 3 percent are from abroad. Clarkson has trouble luring minorities to its remote locale; the combined total of African-Americans, Hispanics, and Asian-Americans is 6 percent. "Our campus definitely needs more minority students," says a senior. All accepted applicants demonstrating financial need are offered some aid, but not necessarily enough to meet full need. Clarkson awards a handful of merit scholarships each year, ranging from $1,000 to $8,000. Athletic scholarships are offered for ice-hockey players only.

Students are required to reside on campus all four years, unless exempted to live in a Greek house. Most dorms are centrally located and are cleaned every day. "The dorms are comfortable and very well maintained," says a student. Four of the

Engineering isn't the only thing at Clarkson, but it certainly gets top billing; 49 percent of the students are in the program.

dorms are all-men and the rest are coed by floor. All freshman are housed with students in their major areas of study and in some instances in their department, giving them the chance to study and learn together. Many underclassmen are housed in conventional dorms, but university-owned townhouse apartments offer more gracious living. "The dorm situation is handled by the lottery, and housing improves based on your class year," a senior reports.

In keeping with Clarkson's "come as you are" atmosphere, the social scene is low key. "There are activities, such as comedians, picnics, and other types of entertainment on campus," says one senior. "However, a good deal of socializing also takes place off campus." Eleven percent of the men and 16 percent of the women join the Greek system. Fraternity beer blasts are the staple of weekend life, and those not into the Greek scene (and over twenty-one) can head to the handful of bars in downtown Potsdam. Nearby SUNY–Potsdam is also a source of social life, especially for men frustrated by Clarkson's three-to-one male/female ratio. Drinking is prohibited on campus, and residence-life staff are on the watch for violators; however, students report that it's still easy for the underaged to be served off campus. For those who crave the bustle of city nightlife, Ottawa and Montreal are each about an hour and a half away by car.

"A good deal of socializing also takes place off campus."

When it comes to sports, men's hockey is first and foremost in the hearts of Clarkson students—the only one in which the university competes in Division I. The team has been ECAC champ in recent years, and contends for the national championship with other blue-chip teams like archrivals Cornell and St. Lawrence. The ski teams, Nordic and Alpine, are among the best in the nation, and men's baseball and golf and women's soccer and basketball are also strong. For weekend athletes, an abundance of skiing and other outdoor and winter sports is within easy driving distance.

For those seeking a technical education without having to worry about big-school problems, Clarkson will be like a breath of mountain-fresh air. Come January, you'll feel like an Eskimo, but at least you'll have a high-tech igloo.

Overlaps

Rochester Institute of Technology, Rensselaer Polytechnic, University of Vermont, Cornell University

If You Apply To ➢

Clarkson: Early decision: Dec. 1, Jan. 15. Regular admissions: Mar. 15. Financial aid: Mar. 1. Does not guarantee to meet demonstrated need. Campus interviews: recommended, informational. Alumni interviews: optional, informational. SATs: required. Accepts the Common Application and electronic applications. Essay question: personal statement.

Clemson University

Sikes Hall, Box 345124, Clemson, SC 29634-5124

Clemson is a technically oriented university in the mold of Georgia Tech, Virginia Tech, and North Carolina State. Smaller than the latter two and more focused on undergraduates than Georgia Tech, Clemson serves up its education with ample helpings of school spirit and small-town hospitality.

Nestled in the foothills of the Blue Ridge Mountains, Clemson University is a place where Southern spirit continues to flourish. The campus occupies terrain that once was walked by John C. Calhoun, former Southern senator and a Civil War-era rabble-rouser of the first degree. Today Clemson features quality academics in technical

Website: www.clemson.edu
Location: Small town
Total Enrollment: 17,465

(Continued)

Undergraduates: 14,066
Male/Female: 54/46
SAT Ranges: V 525–620
  M 555–640
ACT Range: 23–27
Financial Aid: 11%
Expense: Pub $ $
Phi Beta Kappa: No
Applicants: 10,472
Accepted: 64%
Enrolled: 45%
Grad in 6 Years: 71%
Returning Freshmen: 84%
Academics: ✑ ✑ ✑
Social: 🌫 🌫 🌫 🌫
Q of L: ★ ★ ★ ★
Admissions: (864) 656-2287
Email Address:
  cuadmissions@clemson.edu

Strongest Programs:
  Engineering
  Architecture
  Biological Sciences
  Business

No haven for carpetbaggers or liberals, Clemson is best at serving those whose interests lie in technical fields.

areas such as engineering and biology, and big-time athletics supported by strong school spirit.

CU's 1,400-acre campus is situated on what was once Fort Hill Plantation, the homestead of Thomas Green Clemson. The campus is surrounded by seventeen thousand acres of university farms and woodlands and offers a spectacular view of the nearby lake and mountains. Architectural styles are an eclectic mix of modern and nineteenth-century collegiate. New additions to the campus include a student center.

Electrical engineering is the university's largest department, and computer engineering is among the nation's best in research on large-scale integrated computer circuitry and robotics. Chemists enjoy the impressive Hunter Laboratory. The College of Architecture, one of the school's most selective programs, offers intensive semesters at the Overseas Center for Building Research and Urban Study in Genoa, Italy. A fantastic resource for science enthusiasts and history buffs is the library's collection of first editions of the scientific work of Galileo and Newton. Because of the prevailing technical emphasis, most students interested in the liberal arts head

> **"It can be competitive to receive a room if you don't send your housing information on time."**

"down country" to the University of South Carolina. Undergraduate teaching has always been one of Clemson's strong points, and for students interested in pursuing a liberal arts curriculum, the school has degrees in fine arts, philosophy, and languages and enjoys a strong regional reputation for its history program. "My favorite academic department has been the political science department," says a senior marketing major. "The professors have challenged me and really helped me to learn while showing me they care." Highly motivated students should consider Calhoun College, Clemson's honors program—the oldest in South Carolina—open to freshmen who scored 1200 or above on their SATs and ranked in the top 10 percent of their high-school graduating class. Clemson also offers exchange programs in Mexico, Scotland, Ecuador, Spain, England, Australia, and Italy.

General education requirements include courses in communication and speaking, computer skills, mathematical sciences, physical or biological science, humanities, and social science. Each student is assigned a faculty advisor for help and guidance. "My academic advisors are perfect," says a health science major. Academically, the level of difficulty varies. "Most intro courses are not that difficult," one senior says. However, "the upper-level courses are rigorous." Students report some problems finishing a degree in four years, and class registration can be a hassle.

Clemson's student body has a definite Southern air, as 70 percent of the undergrads hail from South Carolina, with most of the rest from neighboring states. The average Clemson student is friendly and conservative, and though, as a public institution, the school isn't affiliated with any church, there is a strong Southern Baptist presence on campus. "We are creative, hard working, and love to be challenged," says an economics major. Thirty-seven percent were in the top tenth of the high-school graduating class. African-Americans make up 7 percent of the student body, and Hispanics and Asian-Americans account for less than 2 percent combined. The university offers three hundred academic scholarships and as many athletic scholarships as the NCAA allows. One students grumbles that "student athletes get to register for classes first and sometimes get priority treatment."

> **"Clemson is an awesome college town."**

Housing gets positive reviews, and 47 percent of the students live on campus, usually during their first two years. Most of the dorms are single-sex, though coed university-owned apartment complexes are also an option. "It can be competitive to receive a room if you don't send your housing information on time," warns a student. Clemson House and Calhoun Courts, the coed halls, are considered the best places to be. The food is typical dorm fare. Upperclassmen can cook for themselves, and each dorm has kitchen facilities.

After class, many students hop on their bikes and head to nearby Lake Hartwell. The beautiful Blue Ridge mountain range is also close by for hiking and camping, and beaches and ski slopes are both within driving distance. Atlanta and Charlotte are only two hours away by car, and Charleston is four hours away on the coast. Aside from the sports teams, fraternities and sororities provide most of the social life. Fifteen percent of Clemson men and 22 percent of women go Greek. Though Clemson empties out a bit on away-game weekends, there are still plenty of off-campus parties where the main activity is drinking beer. The town itself is pretty small, with a few bars and movie theaters, but some students love it. "Clemson is an awesome college town," a marketing major says.

Sports still help make the world go 'round at Clemson, and on weekends when the Tiger teams are playing there are pep rallies, cookouts, dances, and parties for the mobs of excited fans. The roads leading to campus are painted with large orange pawprints, an insignia that symbolizes great enthusiasm for Clemson sports. So, too, are half the fans at an athletic event, making the stands look like an orange grove. Football fever starts with the annual First Friday Parade, held before the first home game, and on every game day the campus dissolves into a sea of Tiger orange. Clemson has regained its former gridiron glory under the leadership of Coach Tommy Bowden. Hordes of Tiger fans cram "Death Valley" for every game and are especially rowdy when the eviled University of South Carolina Gamecocks are in town. Other very competitive athletic teams include basketball, baseball, and men's track.

No haven for carpetbaggers or liberals, Clemson is best at serving those whose interests lie in technical fields. School spirit is contagious, fueled by a love of big-time college sports, and becomes lifelong for many Clemson students. Everyone can become part of the Clemson family, from Southern belle to Northern Yankee, as long as they're friendly, easygoing, not aggressively intellectual, and enthusiastic about life in general and the Tigers in particular.

Calhoun College, Clemson's honors program—the oldest in South Carolina—is open to freshmen who scored 1200 or above on their SATs and ranked in the top 10 percent of their high-school graduating class.

Overlaps

University of South Carolina, College of Charleston, UNC–Chapel Hill, University of Georgia, North Carolina State

If You Apply To >

Clemson: Rolling admissions: May 1. Does not guarantee to meet demonstrated need. Campus interviews: optional, informational. No alumni interviews. SATs or ACTs: required. SAT IIs: required (math II for math placement). No essay question.

Colby College

Lunder House, Waterville, ME 04901

The northernmost outpost of higher education in the East. Colby's picturesque small-town setting is a short hop from the sea coast or the Maine wilderness. No frats since the college abolished them twenty years ago. A well-toned, outdoorsy student body in the mold of Middlebury, Williams, and Dartmouth.

Colby College emphasizes learning on both a global and local level. Its strong programs in international studies and environmental studies ensure that Colby students gain theoretical knowledge about the world around them, and its top study-abroad program provides them with practical experience in that world.

Website: www.colby.edu
Location: Small city
Total Enrollment: 1,814

(Continued)

Undergraduates: 1,814

Male/Female: 47/53

SAT Ranges: V 630–700
  M 620–690

ACT Range: 27–31

Financial Aid: 34%

Expense: Pr $ $ $ $

Phi Beta Kappa: Yes

Applicants: 3,907

Accepted: 36%

Enrolled: 33%

Grad in 6 Years: 88%

Returning Freshmen: 95%

Academics: ✍ ✍ ✍ ✍ ½

Social: ☎ ☎ ☎

Q of L: ★ ★ ★ ★

Admissions: (207) 872-3168

Email Address:
  admissions@colby.edu

Strongest Programs:
  Government
  Environmental Studies/Policy
  Economics
  Science
  English

The library tower is the most noted feature of the college's architecture, and the blue light atop it is viewed with much affection.

While Colby students relish their travels, they still cherish this small liberal arts college for its happy, friendly, and oh-so-wholesome qualities.

Secluded from the hustle and bustle of the rest of the world in the rustic setting of Waterville, Maine, Colby sits on a high hill with beautiful views of the surrounding countryside. Its 714 acres include a wildlife preserve, miles of cross-country trails, and a pond that is used in winter as an ice-skating rink. Colby's buildings are Georgian in architecture with a few more modern structures sprinkled in. The oldest buildings are red brick with white trim, ivy, and brass nameplates above their hunter-green doors. The more contemporary buildings blend a touch of modernity to the more classic style.

As a small college with a history of innovation and educational excellence, Colby boasts a faculty that is devoted to undergraduate teaching. "The quality of teaching is superb," a senior says. "The faculty and staff encourage and guide students to do their best work." Academic standards are high, especially in the most popular programs—biology, English, economics, government, and psychology. The foreign study and languages program also has an excellent reputation. Less traditional programs in creative writing, women's studies, and East Asian studies get rave reviews from students. Not quite up to par are administrative science, math, and American studies. New programs on the academic roster include minors in indigenous peoples of the Americas and Jewish studies.

Ninety-nine percent of the freshmen begin their Colby careers with the COOT program (Colby Outdoor Orientation Trips), four-day excursions by bicycle, canoe, or foot through Maine's wilderness. Once they are back to civilization, curling up with their books is a popular activity. "Libraries are packed after hours," one senior notes. The library tower is the most noted feature of the college's architecture, and the blue light atop it is viewed with much affection. Every year, students honor the light with a Blue Light Night party, and a key campus saying is "Keep the blue light burning." The library has a decent-sized collection—around 940,000 volumes—and boasts several online catalogs and CD-ROM computer reference sources. An electronic research classroom helps students and faculty mine information from the Internet.

The academic climate at Colby is challenging but not overwhelming, according to students. "Everyone seems to put in their hours at the library, but at the same time there is a very low sense of competition, if any at all," reports an American studies major. Each student gets a free computer account for unlimited hours of interactive bliss. Faculty advisors help a great deal and advise students on graduate schools and post-graduation jobs. Students also

"The quality of teaching is superb."

sing the praises of the career-services office, which helps students market themselves and brings a multitude of companies up from Boston and New York for interviews.

Colby was the first college to establish a special January program, and students must take three to graduate. During this short term, motivated undergraduates find an internship or study-abroad program or prepare an in-depth report. Other, less serious undergrads might head for the ski slopes or southern beaches and write a quick paper at the end of the month, though they must get a good enough grade to receive credit. Despite the beautiful surroundings, four years on the outskirts of Waterville (population 20,000) is more than many students can take. Incoming freshmen can pack off for Cuernavaca or Dijon to fulfill their language requirement, delaying enrollment until the second semester. There are also Jan-Plan trips to everywhere from Nicaragua to Vietnam, and juniors regularly seek out foreign- or college-exchange opportunities. Popular destinations are Bermuda (for biology), Connecticut's Mystic Seaport, Kyoto, and the great cities of Europe; even China is a possibility. With all of these options, it's no wonder that nearly 75 percent of Colby students spend some time abroad. Still, the administration likes to share the two "big secrets we Mainers like to keep" about Maine winters: the winters are beautiful, and they are a lot harsher and colder in the telling than in the living. For would-be engineers, there are joint 3–2 programs with Case Western Reserve, Dartmouth, and the University of Rochester, as well as exchange programs with Clark Atlanta and Howard. The Oak Institute organizes symposia on international human rights; most recently an anti-child labor crusader from Pakistan and a rural development advocate from the Congo have been institute fellows.

Social and political issues abound on the Colby campus. "PC is definitely an issue here, but not in a stifling way," says one student. Minorities make up 10 percent of the student body (5 percent Asian-American, 3 percent African-American, and 2 percent Hispanic). There are

"Students enjoy learning and the beauty that surrounds them."

several groups on campus that celebrate different cultures, and the college has implemented a program that pairs freshman students of color with upperclassmen mentors. Ninety-one percent of Colby freshmen placed in the top quarter of their high-school class, and a senior describes Colby students as "bright, vivacious, and happy." Students are admitted without regard to their financial need, and Colby remains committed to meeting the "full calculated eligibility" of all admitted applicants. There are no academic or athletic scholarships.

The campus is divided into three residence-hall groups, each with live-in faculty members. Students have a lot of autonomy over their living conditions, even to the point of setting dining-hall menus. Students can choose a "quiet" residence hall (never "dorm" at Colby), where there are posted hours for making noise, or a "chem-free" house for teetotalers. The dorms are "beautiful," but one student gripes that it's difficult to get rooms other than doubles. Thanks to the new senior apartments, only 4 percent of upperclassmen move off campus. On-campus dwellers use computerized meal cards for the four dining halls.

The well-entrenched fraternity and sorority system was abolished in 1984, when most Colby students were still learning their ABCs. While one might think that anger among students still lingers, many students say they chose Colby because of the absence of a Greek system. Despite the campus's remote setting, Colby students never seem to be at a loss for things to do—road trips to L.L. Bean and Freeport, Camden, skiing at Sugarloaf, Belgrade Lakes for swimming, Acadia National Park to camp—though drinking is high on many people's lists. It's still pretty easy for underage students to get alcohol on campus, even though the administration has poured a lot of resources into stemming the tide of student drinking. "Kegs can be delivered to dorms for lounge parties on Friday and Saturday nights," one student notes. All-campus parties are given by each of the residential commons, but private parties have become especially popular since they are less likely to attract the attention of the state liquor inspector. The town of Waterville is not exactly thriving: "It is an economically depressed mill town," a senior says.

An enthusiasm for outdoor sports is the major nonacademic credential needed to become a content Colby undergraduate, and the annual winter carnival and snow-sculpture contest are the pinnacle of winter celebration. Athletics have come a long way since the first intercollegiate croquet game here back in 1860, and Colby excels at men's cross-country, soccer, football, and basketball. Women have done very well in lacrosse, crew, outdoor and indoor track, and swimming. The overwhelming majority of students participate in some twenty-six intramural sports. Drama and music are popular extracurricular activities, and numerous productions and concerts are mounted each semester.

Students aiming for a well-rounded liberal arts education may find what they want at Colby. "Students enjoy learning and the beauty that surrounds them," a senior says. "They have a lot of school pride." Colby offers a progressive and challenging academic

Athletics have come a long way since the first intercollegiate croquet game here back in 1860, and Colby excels at men's cross-country, soccer, football, and basketball.

Overlaps

Middlebury, Bowdoin, Bates, Dartmouth, Williams

climate, outstanding professors, and opportunities abroad while promoting the fun and tradition that makes up so much of the college experience.

If You Apply To ➤

Colby: Early decision: Nov. 15. Regular admissions: Jan. 1. Guarantees to meet demonstrated need. Campus interviews: recommended, informational. Alumni interviews: optional, informational. SATs or ACTs: required. SAT IIs: optional. Accepts the Common Application and electronic applications. Essay questions (any one): hopes and fears of the future; describe hometown; global issue of importance; something you've read that has caused you to change your view of the world.

Colgate University

13 Oak Drive, Hamilton, NY 13346

At 2,773 students, Colgate is smaller than Bucknell and Dartmouth but bigger than Hamilton and Williams. Like the other four, it offers small-town living and close interaction between students and faculty. Greek organizations are still well-entrenched despite administrative efforts to neutralize them.

Website: www.colgate.edu
Location: Rural
Total Enrollment: 2,782
Undergraduates: 2,773
Male/Female: 48/52
SAT Ranges: V 620–670
  M 630–700
ACT Range: 26–30
Financial Aid: 43%
Expense: Pr $ $ $ $
Phi Beta Kappa: Yes
Applicants: 6,040
Accepted: 38%
Enrolled: 31%
Grad in 6 Years: 89%
Returning Freshmen: 95%
Academics: ✐ ✐ ✐ ✐ ½
Social: ☎ ☎ ☎
Q of L: ★★★
Admissions: (315) 228-7401
Email Address:
  admission@mail.colgate.edu

Strongest Programs:
  Biology
  Economics
  Foreign Language and
    Literature
  History
  Philosophy
  Political Science

One of the nation's elite liberal arts colleges, Colgate is also the most selective of the "almost-Ivy" group, competing for applicants with Cornell and Dartmouth. With its beautiful campus, fine faculty, zealous (sometimes overzealous) alumni, and spirited student body, the university, named for the man who founded the famed toothpaste empire, brings pride to the Colgate name. "Whenever I drive into Hamilton I get that excited feeling," says a proud student. "Colgate becomes your home."

Back in 1880, William Colgate gave $50,000 to the fledgling university—enough to get its name changed from Madison to Colgate. Though Colgate is called a "university," it is actually a small liberal arts college. Colgate's 515-acre campus is located on a hillside overlooking the village of Hamilton in rural New York. Its ivy-covered limestone buildings are all set amid tree-lined drives and lush green spaces, perfect for rugby, Frisbee, or a host of other outdoor diversions. Recent projects include a new university bookstore to allow the move of the current bookstore downtown. In 2001, Little Hall, a state-of-the-art building that houses the art and art history programs, provided needed extra work and teaching space for the growing department.

Colgate's interdisciplinary first-year seminar program gives freshmen a chance to meet top faculty and congregate in small groups. The faculty first established an interdisciplinary core program in 1928, and, while it has been adapted over the years, the core has been a foundation of the curriculum ever since. The latest revision examines the development of Western and non-Western cultures and gives students a personal view of science and technology. The school also requires proficiency in a foreign language. Add to that one of fifty majors (or design your own), four physical education classes, and a swim test, and you have the Colgate version of a liberal arts education.

Among the concentrations in the liberal arts curriculum, English/writing, economics, psychology, philosophy/religion, history, and political science stand out. The college offers four concentration programs in environmental studies: environmental biology, geography, geology, and economics. A major in Japanese has recently been added. All language instruction programs are linked to off-campus study groups led by Colgate professors, and the Lawrence Hall Language Labs and classrooms offer state-of-the-art language studies facilities. Colgate's curriculum has an international flavor, and more than half of all students take advantage of the school's off-campus study programs—which include three domestic programs, like the one in Bethesda, Maryland at the National Institutes of Health. In addition to the Maritime Studies Program* and the Sea Semester,* Colgate's international study options, many led by their own professors, include England, Japan, Nigeria, Russia, Poland, Central America, France, Germany, Switzerland, and Spain. One of the newest and most exciting off-campus study programs emphasizes the historical, environmental, and geographical diversity of Australia, and gives the students the opportunity to travel there. The Center for Ethics and World Studies brings nationally known authorities to campus to focus on different subjects each year.

Colgate works hard to keep its class sizes small; 99 percent of the courses have fewer than fifty students. Perhaps Colgate's greatest asset is a talented and dedicated faculty. "I have never been so challenged and richly rewarded in class," says one student. A classmate adds, "Professors make themselves available to students beyond their office hours." Undergraduate research is one of Colgate's greatest strengths, and its faculty receives accolades for involving students in research. Each summer, more than one hundred students assist professors in their work. Academic advising is administered through the First-Year Seminar instructor, giving all students a classroom relationship with their advisor. Career advisors receive praise, too. "They are organized and ready and willing to help you write a résumé, contact alumni and network, look for a job or internship, or prepare for an interview."

Incoming freshmen get the campus to themselves for orientation, and some go on a week-long camping trip before that to make friends and see the Adirondacks. For the 80 percent of Colgate grads who go directly to jobs rather than graduate school, the career counseling center is a blessing. Many students credit both the center and Colgate's strong and loyal alumni network with helping them land their first job.

"The student body is made up of driven, successful students who embody the philosophy of 'Work hard, play hard'," says a student. With a combined minority population of only 17 percent, many students lament Colgate's lack of diversity. "Our effort to create a more diverse student

"All the rooms are a good size, and the beds are comfortable."

body is one of the main issues facing Colgate today," explains one underclassman. Colgate has implemented an honor code that was developed, written, and passed recently by the students. Though there are no merit or athletic scholarships available, Colgate does meet the demonstrated financial need of all admitted students. "Financial aid is very competitive. Colgate will give you a great offer the first time around instead of making you squabble over the figures," says one freshman. "The aid is above and beyond any I received at other schools."

Colgate's housing options range from traditional buildings with fireplaces to new ones that seem more like hotels than dorms. "Residence life is more appropriate than housing because of the all-encompassing nature of the services," one student explains. Another student adds, "All the rooms are a good size, and the beds are comfortable." The university offers various special-interest housing, including a substance-free dorm. About 250 upperclassmen are allowed to live off campus each year, and the remaining 88 percent live in university housing.

Despite the renovation of some bars downtown and the addition of a Chinese take-out restaurant, Hamilton is essentially the same place it was two or three generations ago. The town of three thousand is not a social Mecca by any stretch of the imagination. "The town of Hamilton is not a college town at all," laments a junior. Another student adds, "It's more of a village than a town. Don't come here looking for NYC because you won't find it!" There's one very welcome addition to the town's main street, thanks to Colgate. The college recently opened the Barge Canal Coffee Company in a downtown storefront. The informal coffeehouse, open to

All language instruction programs are linked to off-campus study groups led by Colgate professors, and the Lawrence Hall Language Labs and classrooms offer state-of-the-art language studies facilities.

Colgate's curriculum has an international flavor, and more than half of all students take advantage of the school's off-campus study programs, which include three domestic programs, like the one in Bethesda, Maryland, at the National Institutes of Health.

faculty, students, and townspeople, has been very popular among Colgate students. "Besides serving up some mean Java, the atmosphere is terrific, cheap, and there are games, puzzles, magazines, and books to occupy your hours," gushes a sophomore art/theater major.

Thirty-nine percent of men and 33 percent of women belong to Greek houses, so these still provide many of the social options as well as considerable controversy over whether their values are conducive to a healthy campus environment. The university has increased its funding of student activities fourfold in the last decade, and has stepped up its efforts to offer alternatives to frat parties and alcohol. Such measures are the latest signs of a running battle between the faculty and alumni over the proper balance between academics and social life that has plagued Colgate for decades. The campus pub and Edge Café offer on-campus social options, and dance parties have recently attracted enthusiastic participation. Spring Party Weekend and Winterfest are popular annual traditions as is Octoberfest, which features pumpkin carving and a huge bonfire. Under the category of clean fun are the traditional rites of passage that punctuate the Colgate calendar. Among them are torchlight processions in the fall for first-years and the spring for seniors, and, of course, the Colgate versus Cornell hockey game.

Colgate students love athletics. Colgate's teams play in Division I and, despite being a David among many Goliaths, win more than their share of games. Hockey, football, and basketball are the top varsity spectator sports, and the teams are fierce competitors in the Eastern leagues. Men's and women's soccer also draw great crowds.

"Personal attention can be found wherever you look for it."

The men's football team has been league champ, and women's teams have also brought home trophies in field hockey, volleyball, and softball. Colgate also gives its students plenty of space to play and compete, including the Sanford Field House, the Lineberry natatorium, the nationally recognized Seven Oaks golf course, a trap range, a rock quarry for climbing, miles of trails for running and cycling, as well as sailing and crew facilities at scenic Lake Moraine, five minutes north of town.

Colgate is a cozy college with a much larger view of the world. "Personal attention can be found wherever you look for it," raves one student. "The administration is looking to a bright new future with students and faculty examining the university and making changes where necessary." Committed to undergraduate education, the college offers ample opportunities to have diverse and intense academic experiences either on campus or in a foreign land under the active guidance of dedicated faculty.

Overlaps

Dartmouth, Cornell University, Williams, Bucknell, Middlebury

If You Apply To ➤ **Colgate:** Early decision: Nov. 15, Jan. 15. Regular admissions: Jan 15. Financial aid: Feb. 1. Guarantees to meet demonstrated need. Campus and alumni interviews: optional, informational. SATs and SAT IIs (writing and two others) or ACTs required. Accepts the Common Application and electronic applications. Essay question: Common Application essays and supplemental essay on rotating topics.

Colorado College

14 East Cache La Poudre, Colorado Springs, CO 80903

The Block Plan is CC's calling card. It is great for in-depth study and field trips but less-suited to projects that take an extended period of time. The allure of the Rockies draw outdoor enthusiasts and East Coasters who want to ski. CC is the only leading liberal arts college between Iowa and the Pacific.

Imagine being able to focus on a single class at a time, instead of running from one class to another and juggling homework assignments all semester long. That's how it works at Colorado College. CC is the only college in the nation offering what is called the Block Plan, and this unusual approach has quickly earned this school a cool reputation among small liberal arts colleges.

Founded in 1874, Colorado College is located at the foot of Pikes Peak near downtown Colorado Springs in a neighborhood district recognized by the National Historic Register. Many campus buildings are also part of this register, including Cutler Hall (1879), the college's first building, and Palmer Hall, named after William J. Palmer, founder of Colorado Springs and a major force behind the establishment of the college. Prevailing architectural styles include Romanesque and English Gothic. The school is currently engaged in a ten-year master plan that will feature new buildings and facilities.

As at most schools, students take eight courses between early September and mid-May. For three-and-a-half-week periods, students concentrate exclusively on the subject at hand. At the end of each session is a four-and-a-half-day block break during which students relax, head for the hills, or take part in concerts, plays, or other offerings scheduled for such periods. This academic plan defines the school. "Because of our block program, courses can be very rigorous," a senior says. "To miss one day is like missing a week." Yet the advantages of the Block Plan are numerous. Students can immerse themselves in one subject and concentrate on it without having to spread themselves thin with a complicated schedule or let one course slide in order to get caught up in another. Students and teachers are flexible to odd scheduling needs by offering classes at unique times and in unique places—for instance, astronomy at midnight and anthropology work in Mexico. Class size is limited to twenty-five (average size is fifteen), and most students get into the classes they want. The method of securing seats is handled like an academic auction. At the beginning of each year students are given eighty points to "bid" on the classes they want. Those who bid the most for a particular class get a spot. If you're going to have one class at a time it helps to like the teacher, and CC students praise their professors. "The professors here are intelligent and caring," says a senior.

There are, of course, trade-offs to the block approach. Students say it is sometimes hard to integrate courses when you are taking them one at a time. There's also the danger of student and faculty burnout because of the amount of material crammed into such a short time and the intensity inherent in keeping a single subject in your mind without diversions.

The ability to take lab classes outside and a seventy thousand-square-foot science complex make Colorado College's science program a favorite among the students. Classes that focus on fieldwork are particularly popular. "There is something extremely satisfying about going onsite and actually seeing firsthand what you were reading about the night before," says an English major whose introductory geology class featured trips to the Garden of the Gods, a nearby geological wonderland. But

> **"Because of our block program, courses can be very rigorous."**

Website:
www.ColoradoCollege.edu
Location: Urban
Total Enrollment: 1,952
Undergraduates: 1,921
Male/Female: 45/55
SAT Ranges: V 580–690
M 610–680
ACT Range: 26–30
Financial Aid: 44%
Expense: Pr $ $ $ $
Phi Beta Kappa: Yes
Applicants: 3,402
Accepted: 69%
Enrolled: 20%
Grad in 6 Years: 79%
Returning Freshmen: 94%
Academics: ✑ ✑ ✑ ✑
Social: ☎ ☎ ☎ ☎
Q of L: ★ ★ ★ ★
Admissions: (719) 389-6344
Email Address: admission@
coloradocollege.edu

Strongest Programs:
Biology
Geology
English
Mathematics
Psychology
Neuroscience
Drama
Philosophy

not all field trips are so close: students fly to the Caribbean to study coral biology. Additionally, the school sponsors its own programs in Germany, France, and Mexico, and the college offers programs in such far-flung spots as Chicago, London, India, Japan, Russia, Tanzania, the Czech Republic, and Hong Kong, as well as several other study-abroad opportunities through the Associated Colleges of the Midwest.*

While some students complain that interdisciplinary study is difficult under the Block Plan, an Asian studies major and a women's studies major help to focus interdisciplinary agendas. "Weaker" offerings are in American Ethnic and Latin American studies. Some also believe that foreign languages are not at their best in the Block Plan. The college offers a popular program in Southwest studies, which includes spending time at the school's Baca campus, located 175 miles away in the historic San Luis Valley. For more variety, students can design their own majors or take advantage of the International Affairs Option or the American Ethnic Studies program.

As part of the general education program, all students are required to take two courses in the Western tradition; three courses in the natural sciences, including lab and field study; two additional courses in either non-Western or minority cultures; and some foreign language study. They may also choose what is called a thematic minor, five closely related courses that examine an issue or theme, a cultural group, an area of the world, or a time period. The library, with 440,000 volumes, is long on hours (open until 2:00 A.M.), but, students complain, sometimes short on books necessary for classwork. A First Year Experience program gets students into the groove of this unorthodox and intensive academic setup. FYE uses a theme which changes every two years, a recent one being on "Order and Chaos."

Students at Colorado College are a bright and independent lot. Sixty-nine percent are from outside Colorado, and 87 percent graduated in the top quarter of their high-school class. And while some claim that there has been an influx of conservatives, students agree that generally social attitudes are rather liberal. The college provides forums for many varied organizations, including the Bisexual, Gay, and Lesbian Alliance; the Feminist Collective; the College Republicans; the Jewish Chaverim; and the Black Student Union. But the political fervor is not overpowering. "All social and political issues are alive on campus, but not rampantly," a junior psychology major says. Minorities account for 12 percent of the student body—2 percent are African-American, 6 percent Hispanic, and 4 percent Asian-American—and the school is trying to attract more. The admissions office places great weight on the essay, and 10 percent of each year's freshmen begin their work at summer school, take off the fall, and then settle into the regular routine in January. The college guarantees to meet the demonstrated need of most students, and it offers merit scholarships in the natural sciences and mathematics. Thirty-seven athletic scholarships are awarded to male ice-hockey players and female soccer stars (the school's only Division I teams).

"There is something extremely satisfying about going onsite and actually seeing firsthand what you were reading about the night before."

Seventy-four percent of the students live on campus. Dormitories differ architecturally, from large brick halls to small wooden houses. They also differ by specialty: freshman, same-sex, language, or cultural theme, for example. The college recently spent $10 million to renovate the three primary residence halls. Students are required to live on campus for three years, but housing is guaranteed for all four years. On-campus students usually subscribe to at least ten meals a week in the dining halls, but one student, citing the food provided, concludes, "I guess we're expected to feed ourselves on thought instead."

The women's volleyball, men's soccer, women's lacrosse, and men's hockey teams have had major victories in Divisions I and III competitions. The sunny, dry

Colorado weather is excellent for off-campus outdoor sports. The Freshman Outdoor Orientation Trips (FOOT) help out-of-staters sort out the options: backpacking, skiing, mountain climbing, hiking, rafting, bicycling, and even windsurfing. Students frequently camp at a college-owned mountainside cabin. Campus nightlife includes dorm-sponsored and fraternity parties. Sixteen percent of the men and 18 percent of the women join fraternities and sororities. Despite rather stringent rules for on-campus parties and stricter enforcement of the twenty-one-year-old drinking age, most students agree with a junior who says, "As long as the doors are shut, the students get away with underage drinking." For those who don't want to drink alcohol, the campus center hangout, Benjamin's, serves great milkshakes. The college sponsors a wide variety of activities, and the hockey games entertain many students. The spring festival, Llamapalooza, brings about ten different bands to play outdoors.

"All social and political issues are alive on campus, but not rampantly."

The Block Plan is not for everyone, but it makes a lot of sense to its many fans. At any rate, the innovative plan makes or breaks Colorado College, and a decision to go to CC is a decision in favor of the college's academic agenda. Says one student succinctly, "It's why we're here."

Overlaps

University of Colorado, Middlebury, University of Denver, Colorado State, Whitman

---

If You Apply To ➤ **Colorado College:** Early action: Nov. 15. Regular admissions: Jan. 15. Financial aid: Feb. 15. Housing: June 20. Guarantees to meet demonstrated need. Campus interviews: optional, informational. No alumni interviews. SATs or ACTs: required. No SAT IIs. Accepts the Common Application and electronic applications. Essay questions: piece of art or literature that is meaningful; experience with a different culture; or important issue of local, national, or international concern. Also, explain educational objectives and why Colorado College.

University of Colorado at Boulder

BEST BUY

Campus Box 30, Boulder, CO 80309-0552

Boulder is a legendary place that draws everyone from East Coast ski bums to California refugees. The scenery is gorgeous and the science programs are first-rate. The University of Arizona is the only public university of similar stature in the Mountain West. Check out the residential academic programs.

Wild buffalo may be all but extinct on America's Great Plains, but they're in boisterous residence, proudly wearing gold and black, at Ski U—otherwise known as the University of Colorado at Boulder. The majestic Rocky Mountains provide a breathtaking backdrop and boundless playground for CU students seeking a respite from their books. The active social scene emphasizes nature, fitness, sports, and outdoor pursuits. There are "so many programs and different kinds of people on campus," says a fine arts major. "The environment is just friendly and beautiful."

Tree-shaded walkways, winding bike paths, open spaces, and an incredible view of the dramatic Flatirons rock formation makes CU's six hundred-acre Boulder campus a haven for students from both coasts and for Colorado residents eager to pursue knowledge in a snowy paradise. Campus buildings, in a rural Italian style, are Colorado sandstone with red-tile roofs. In fact, the campus tends to look and feel a bit Ivy League, which is not surprising when you know that CU's architect also worked for Yale and Princeton. The forty-five thousand-square-foot Discovery Learning Center opened in fall 2002, giving engineering students nine new labs in which to tackle society's challenges with videoconferencing and other high-tech

Website: www.colorado.edu
Location: Suburban
Total Enrollment: 29,609
Undergraduates: 23,998
Male/Female: 52/48
SAT Ranges: V 540–640
   M 530–620
ACT Range: 22–27
Financial Aid: 33%
Expense: Pub $ $
Phi Beta Kappa: Yes
Applicants: 18,487
Accepted: 79%
Enrolled: 34%
Grad in 6 Years: 65%

capabilities. The University Memorial Center has received a $27 million facelift and expansion, and the Williams Village residence-hall complex will add hundreds of on-campus apartments beginning in fall 2003.

The best of Colorado's public universities, CU–Boulder has worked hard to shed its persistent party-school image. Entering freshmen choose from five colleges: arts and sciences (the easiest), business and administration, architecture and planning, music, and engineering and applied science (the hardest, students say). Transfers may apply to two additional schools: journalism and education. Each has different entrance standards and requirements; music, for example, requires an audition. General education requirements for the 70 percent of students who enroll in arts and sciences are designed to provide a broad background in the liberal arts to complement their major specialization. The requirements cover four skills-acquisition areas—writing, quantitative reasoning and math, critical thinking, and foreign language—and seven content areas: historical context, culture and gender diversity, U.S. context, natural sciences, contemporary societies, literature and the arts, and ideals and values.

"The environment is just friendly and beautiful."

In a typical semester, CU may offer 2,500 courses in one hundred fields. Among the best choices are molecular and cellular biology, which take advantage of state-of-the-art electron microscopes. CU–Boulder also receives the second-most NASA funding of any university in the nation, leading to unparalleled opportunities for the design, construction, and flight of model spacecraft—and to fifteen CU alumni having worked as astronauts. CU distinguished professor Carl Weiman and adjunct professor Eric Cornell of the National Institute of Standards and Technology won the Nobel Peace Prize for Physics in 2001 for creating a new form of matter that occurs at a few hundred billionths of a degree above absolute zero. Business, history, engineering, and psychology are likewise strong, students say. "I've had some amazing teachers that really inspired me," says a junior business major. But a senior warns that in arts and sciences classes, "I've been taught by numerous TAs, amateurs, difficult-to-understand instructors, and mediocre professors."

Boulder has tried to make its mammoth campus smaller through "academic neighborhoods" focusing on topics such as leadership, diversity, natural or social sciences, international studies, engineering, music, and the American West.

"The dorms are well maintained, and it's a great place to meet new people."

Through these programs, students take one or two courses, limited to twenty-five students each, in their residence halls. For students having trouble choosing from the CU smorgasbord, the FallFEST program simplifies course selection. Up to 250 freshmen may participate in FallFEST, which lets them register in groups of twenty-five for a prepackaged set of core courses. The groups meet for weekly discussions with a faculty member and peer advisor. The Presidents Leadership Class is a four-year scholarship program that exposes the most promising students to political, business, and community leaders through seminars, work and study trips, and site visits. The new Undergraduate Academy offers special activities and advising for one hundred and fifty to two hundred of CU's most "intellectually committed" students, chosen for their excitement about learning and academic success.

Two-thirds of CU's student body comes from in-state, and by state regulation that fraction can be no lower than 45 percent, on average, over a three-year period. Hispanics and Asian-Americans each comprise 6 percent of the total, and African-Americans are a paltry 2 percent. Important issues include environmental awareness, efforts to make the campus more diverse, a lack of parking, and the ever-escalating cost of attending CU. "Figuring out how to discipline a handful of CU rioters while not affecting thousands (who aren't involved in protests) is

Boulder has tried to make its mammoth campus smaller through "academic neighborhoods" focusing on topics such as leadership, diversity, natural or social sciences, international studies, engineering, music, and the American West.

another challenge," quips a senior. "CU is a very liberal school that overlooks the many common issues on other campuses…yet has a couple of unusual ones."

First-year students are required to live on campus, where rooms are "comfortable, well kept, and secure," says a recent graduate. "The dorms are well maintained, and it's a great place to meet new people," agrees a junior. Due to a shortage of rooms, however, most upperclassmen move into nearby off-campus apartments. Those who want to stay on campus are advised to make early reservations for Farrand, Sewall, or Kittredge halls. All rooms come with microwaves, refrigerators, cable TV, and Internet hook-ups. Improved lighting, emergency call boxes, and safety programs like Night Walk/Night Ride, which provides volunteer escorts after dark, keep students feeling safe. An alternative to the dining hall is the student-run Alferd Packer Grill. The grill provides fast food under innocent auspices, but Boulder students and trivia buffs know that Packer was a controversial nineteenth-century folk figure known as the "Colorado Cannibal." Still hungry?

Eight percent of CU men and 12 percent of women go Greek, though fraternity and sorority parties have changed dramatically since CU's chapters became the first in the nation to voluntarily make their houses dry. On campus, the ban on alcohol is taken seriously, and dorms are officially "substance-free"—get caught with booze three times while underage, and you'll be booted from school housing. Off campus "the local bars in Boulder are very strict," says a senior. As at most schools, "it is not a problem for underage students to get alcohol" from upperclass friends, says a junior. Still, "there is something here for absolutely everyone and every interest," one student says. "I do not party often, yet feel CU's social life does not impose that lifestyle onto me," another echoes. "Students will find they can party like the best—or not."

On campus, CU offers movies, theater performances, speakers, dances, and barbecues. For the culturally minded, the university and the city of Boulder offer films and plays, the renowned Colorado Shakespeare Festival, and concerts by top rock bands. Boulder "is an awesome town," says a business major. "The campus is what makes the town. It is young, alive, and a great place for young people to be." Even

"Football games on campus are a great experience, with fellow students showing school spirit."

so, Denver is only thirty miles away, easy to reach with a free bus service that runs from there to Boulder, through campus, and back again. Day trips to ski resorts like Breckenridge, Vail, and Aspen largely replace weekend getaways here, but for those who've got to get out of the cold, Las Vegas isn't so far, says one student. For a quick night out, the Eldora ski area—with twelve lifts, fifty-three trails, runs up to two miles long, and a vertical drop of as much as 1,400 feet—is just a half hour from campus.

Aside from skiing, exercise is the leading extracurricular activity at CU. The school's Triathlon Club has won the USA Triathlon National Challenge for six years running, and CU–Boulder has also captured national titles in cycling and mountain biking for the past two years. Mountain-climbing enthusiasts have even interpreted CU as "Climb with Us." Just $68 a year gives students access to the sprawling recreation center, with swimming pools, squash and racquetball courts, three weight rooms, and an ice-skating rink. (Ninety percent of CU students use the facility regularly.) The football team, which competes in the Big 12, has had its share of success, too. A rowdy rivalry with Nebraska gets students riled up; they even took down the goalposts after their Buffaloes routed the Cornhuskers in 2001. "Football games on campus are a great experience with fellow students showing school spirit," a junior business major says. Ralphie, the live buffalo who acts as CU's mascot, doesn't miss a game.

For focused students who can deal with the ever-present distraction of the Rockies and who are willing to take the initiative required to become more than a

The Triathlon Club has won the USA Triathlon National Challenge for six years running, and CU–Boulder has also captured national titles in cycling and mountain biking for the past two years.

Overlaps

Colorado State, UCLA, University of Arizona, University of Illinois, University of Minnesota

number at a school this size, the welcoming environment of CU–Boulder just may be the place to kick off your boots and stay awhile. If you want to exercise your body as well as your mind, forget the ivy-covered bricks and gray city skies endemic to so many eastern institutions, and consider going west instead.

If You Apply To ➢

CU-Boulder: Rolling admissions. Regular admissions: Jan. 15 for freshmen, Apr. 1 for transfers. Financial aid: Apr. 1. Housing: May 1. Meets demonstrated need of 54%. Campus interviews: optional, informational. No alumni interviews. SATs or ACTs: required. Accepts electronic applications. Essay question: personal statement about educational aspirations, travel and work experience, creative talents, factors affecting your academic record.

Colorado School of Mines

1811 Elm Street, Golden, CO 80401-1842

The preeminent technical institute in the Mountain West. Twice as big as New Mexico Tech, one-tenth the size of Texas Tech. Best-known for mining-related fields but strong in most areas of engineering. Men outnumber women three to one, and Golden provides little other than a nice view of the mountains.

Website: www.mines.edu
Location: Small town
Total Enrollment: 3,350
Undergraduates: 2,556
Male/Female: 75/25
SAT Ranges: V 540–650
   M 620–680
ACT Range: 24–29
Financial Aid: 74%
Expense: Pub $ $
Phi Beta Kappa: Yes
Applicants: 2,703
Accepted: 67%
Enrolled: 33%
Grad in 6 Years: 64%
Returning Freshmen: 84%
Academics: ✍ ✍ ✍ ½
Social: ☎ ☎ ☎
Q of L: ★ ★
Admissions: (303) 273-3220
Email Address:
   admit@mines.edu

Strongest Programs:
   Mining Engineering
   Petroleum Engineering
   Metallurgical and Materials
      Engineering
   Geophysical Engineering

Golden, Colorado is home to two American institutions: Coors Brewing Co., which taps the Rockies for its legendary brews, and the Colorado School of Mines, where students learn to tap the Rockies for coal, oil, and other natural resources. This top technical institute has always had excellent programs in geological, chemical materials, and mining engineering. Now administrators are working to strengthen offerings in the humanities and social sciences, recognizing the need to offer "an interdisciplinary approach to traditional perspectives of technology." The school's small size and rugged location endear it to the mostly male students who shoulder heavy workloads to earn their degrees—and starting salaries after graduation can approach $60,000 a year.

CSM's 373-acre campus sits in the shadow of the spectacular Rocky Mountains. Architectural styles range from turn-of-the-century gold dome to present-day modern, and native trees and greenery punctuate the lush lawns. Campus beautification continues, and a $10 million research facility is now being built. Within the next two years, CSM will begin $24 million of new construction and renovation of dorms and sorority houses plus a $4 million all-weather track, Astroturf playing field, and other outdoor athletic facilities.

Academics at Mines are rigorous. All freshmen take the same first-year program, which includes chemistry, calculus, physical education, physics, design, environmental systems, quantitative chemical measurement, and the Freshman Success Seminar, an advising and mentoring course designed to increase retention. Because of CSM's narrow focus, the undergraduate majors—or "options," as they're called—are quite good. There's plenty of variety, as long as you like engineering; programs range from geophysical, geological, and petroleum to civil, electrical, and mechanical. Courses in a student's option start in the second semester of sophomore year, after yet more calculus and differential equations. Through the Liberal Arts and International Studies Department, CSM students are given another perspective on technology and its impact on culture and society. Courses such as Humankind and Values, Society and Decisions, and International Relations address human issues related to technological advances and expose students to an interdisciplinary-liberal arts discourse.

(Continued)
Geological Engineering
Chemical Engineering

Pass/fail grading is unheard of at Mines, but failing grades are not. "Most students come here with straight As and end up failing tests, passing classes with Cs and Ds," says a junior. "It is hard to adjust, but it happens at least once to everyone." The quality of teaching leaves something to be desired, says a chemical engineering major: "Some teachers make me fall asleep and are hard to pay attention to, others will teach well, and only a few capture my attention and keep it." Adjunct professors—those who work in the fields they teach—draw raves for bringing real-world application into the classroom. The required two-semester EPICS program—the acronym stands for Engineering Practices Introductory Course Sequence—helps develop communications, teamwork, and problem-solving skills with weekly presentations and written reports.

CSM supplements coursework with a required six-week summer field session, enabling students to gain hands-on experience. Each year, about 130 students are chosen for the Guy T. McBride Honors Program in the humanities, which includes seminars and off-campus activities—including a summer trip to Washington, D.C., centered around public affairs—that encourage students to think differently about the implications of technology. CSM also offers the opportunity to live and study at more than fifty universities worldwide in Europe, Australia, Latin America, Asia, and the Middle East. Each year, forty to sixty undergraduates participate in research.

CSM is a state school, and 76 percent of its students are from Colorado. Minority enrollment continues to increase: Hispanics comprise 6 percent of the student body, Asian-Americans 5 percent, and African-Americans 1 percent. Politics aren't prevalent on campus, probably because the workload is so consuming, and "there are not a lot of issues that people talk about," says a chemical engineering major. Perhaps they're too busy watching for the next oil or aerospace boom or bust.

Thirty percent of CSM students—mostly freshmen—live in the residence halls, which have been renovated to include air-conditioning and carpet. Most buildings are coed, though the preponderance of men results in a few single-sex dorms. The "old" dorms have conventional doubles, but the newer and more popular Weaver Towers house students in five-room suites. Most upperclassmen move to fraternity or sorority housing, college-owned apartments, or off-campus condos and houses. There are no concerns about crime, students say. "Mines police are on constant watch for speeders, stop-sign runners, and cars parked in 'No Parking' or 'Teacher Parking' zones," one student says.

Courses such as Humankind and Values, Society and Decisions, and International Relations address human issues related to technological advances and expose students to an interdisciplinary-liberal arts discourse.

"CSM is probably one of the last places where you will find true student athletes. "

There is life outside of the library here, though it is well hidden. Six fraternities and two sororities attract 20 percent of the men and the same fraction of women. Rush is dry, and, owing to the school's small size, those serving the alcohol almost always know the age of those trying to obtain it making it tough for the underage to imbibe. Social life includes house and frat parties, comedy shows, Homecoming, and Engineering Days—a three-day party with fireworks, a pig roast, tricycle races, taco-eating contests, and twenty-five-cent beers. The celebration includes the M-climb, which has freshmen hike up Mount Zion lugging white rocks then arrange them in a giant letter M at the top.

CSM's location at the base of the Rockies means gorgeous Colorado weather (make sure to bring sunscreen) and easy access to skiing, hiking, mountain climbing and biking. "We're right next to Denver, and Boulder is just up the road," says a math major. Aside from offering big-city museums, concerts, and sports teams, Denver is home to many government agencies and businesses involved in natural resources, computers, and technology as well as the regional offices of the U.S. Geological Survey and Bureau of Mines. Golden itself hosts the National Earthquake Center, the National Renewable Energy Laboratory, and, of course, the Coors Brewery. (The

CSM supplements coursework with a required, six-week summer field session, enabling students to gain hands-on experience.

three thousand-foot pipeline that runs from the Coors plant to campus is there to convert excess steam from the brewery into heat for the school—not to supply the frats with fresh brew.) The biggest complaints are too much homework and not enough girls, not exactly a recipe for weekend mayhem. Road trips to Las Vegas or Texas provide some respite.

Despite the abundance of wacky school traditions, CSM competes in Division II, so there aren't many true athletic rivalries. The tennis team recently won a conference championship, and the wrestling, track, and swimming teams qualified to compete for national titles. "CSM is probably one of the last places where you will find true student athletes," notes one student. "We play for fun." Still, three of the school's coaches have received Coach of the Year honors.

> **"We are all a little different than other college students because we are career-oriented, problem-solving engineers."**

"Mines is a school to be endured, not enjoyed," says another student. And yet as much as they complain about it, men and women here praise the institution's small size, emphasis on engineering, and the continuing relevance of its curriculums, even as the job market changes. "We are all a little different than other college students because we are career-oriented, problem-solving engineers," says a junior. While a CSM education may not stretch students' cultural horizons, it does enable them to support themselves in fine fashion after graduation—as they seek new and better ways to power our world, uncover natural resources, shelter us from the elements, and move people and information.

Overlaps

University of Colorado, Colorado State, MIT, Texas A&M, University of Texas

If You Apply To ➢

CSM: Rolling admissions: Jun. 1. Financial aid: Mar. 1. Housing: May 1. Guarantees to meet demonstrated need. Campus interviews: recommended, informational. Alumni interviews: optional, informational. SATs or ACTs: required. SAT IIs: optional. Accepts electronic applications. No essay question.

Columbia College

212 Hamilton Hall, New York, NY 10027

Columbia may soon leave Yale in the dust as the third-most selective university in the Ivy League. Applications have doubled in the past ten years for one simple reason: Manhattan trumps New Haven, Providence, Ithaca, and every other Ivy League city. But the heart of Columbia is still the Core.

Website: www.columbia.edu
Location: Urban
Total Enrollment: 21,547
Undergraduates: 7,593
Male/Female: 50/50
SAT Ranges: V 650–760
  M 650–740
ACT Range: 29–34
Financial Aid: 60%
Expense: Pr $ $ $ $

Though students entering Columbia College will, of course, expect the rigorous academic program they'll encounter at this Ivy League school, there's no room here in the heart of Manhattan for the bookish nerd. Students must be streetwise, urbane, and together enough to handle one of the most cosmopolitan cities in the world. "It's an Ivy League school with a campus in the leading cultural center of the United States," says a sophomore. CC lets its students experience life in the Big Apple, but serves as a refuge when it becomes necessary to escape from New York; ideally, Columbians can easily be part of the "real world" while simultaneously immersing themselves in the best academia has to offer.

Although Columbia is among the smallest colleges in the Ivy League, its atmosphere is far from intimate. With a total university-wide enrollment of 21,000 students, says one, "it's easy to feel lost." Still, the college is the jewel in the university's crown and the focus is "unquestionably oriented toward undergraduate education," reports a classics major. Columbia's campus has a large central quadrangle in front of Butler Library and at the foot of the steps leading past the statue of Alma Mater to Low Library, which is now the administration building. The red-brick, copper-roofed neoclassical buildings are "stunning," and the layout, says an undergrad, "is well thought out and manages to provide a beautiful setting with an economy of space."

Columbia is an intellectual school, not a preprofessional one, and even though 60 percent of the students aspire to law or medical school (they enjoy a 90 percent acceptance rate), "we are mostly content to be liberal artists for as long as possible," says an English major. Almost all departments that offer undergraduate majors are strong, notably English, history, political science, and psychology. Chemistry and biology are among the best of Columbia's high-quality science offerings. The geology department owns two hundred acres in Rockland County, home to many rocks and much seismographic equipment. There are thirty-five offerings in foreign

"It's an Ivy League school with a campus in the leading cultural center of the United States."

languages, ranging from Serbo-Croatian to Uzbek to Hausa. The fine arts are not fabulous but are improving thanks to departmental reorganization, new facilities, and joint offerings with schools such as the Juilliard School of Music. And while the administration admits that the economics and computer science departments are geared too much toward graduate students, at least the comp-sci undergrads benefit from an abundance of equipment. Columbia offers many challenging combined majors such as philosophy/economics and biology/psychology. The East Asian languages and cultures department is one of the best anywhere. New programs in Asian-American studies, Latino studies, and American studies have recently been added to the curriculum. There is also an African-American studies major and a women's studies major that delves into topics from the Asian woman's perspective to the lesbian experience in literature.

The kernel of the undergraduate experience is the college's renowned core curriculum. While these courses occupy most of the first two years and can become laborious, students generally praise them as worthwhile and enriching: "You learn how to read analytically, write sharply, and speak succinctly, and you are exposed to the greatest ideas in Western art, music, literature, and philosophy," exclaims an enlightened sociology major. A junior adds, "The core is the highlight of our education, providing the basis for all other classes and giving you an amazing familiarity with Western civilization...it's been one of the best parts of my experience." The value of the Western emphasis of the

"We are mostly content to be liberal artists for as long as possible."

core, however, is a subject of perennial debate. "Why should we study the Western tradition when it represents sexism, racism, imperialism, and exploitation?" asks one incensed student. "The canon is composed almost exclusively of dead European males." Yet, as it has since World War I, the college remains committed to the core while at the same time expanding the diversity of the canon and requiring core classes on non-Western cultures.

Two of the most demanding introductory courses in the Ivy League—Contemporary Civilization and Literature Humanities—form the basis of the core. Both are year-long and taught in small sections, generally by full profs. "Nearly everything I'd grown up believing was questioned in one way or another. They forced me to examine my life and to ponder how I fit into the big picture," states an art history major. LitHum (as it is affectionately called) covers about twenty-six masterpieces of literature from Homer to Dostoyevsky, usually with some Sappho, Jane Austen, and Virginia Woolf thrown in for alternative perspectives. CC examines political and

(Continued)
Phi Beta Kappa: Yes
Applicants: 14,135
Accepted: 12%
Enrolled: 63%
Grad in 6 Years: 90%
Returning Freshmen: 97%
Academics: ✍ ✍ ✍ ✍ ✍
Social: ☎ ☎ ☎
Q of L: ★ ★ ★
Admissions: (212) 854-2522
Email Address: ugrad-admiss@columbia.edu

Strongest Programs:
  English
  History
  Political Science
  Economics
  Dance
  Drama
  Chemistry
  Biology

To call Columbia diverse would be "a gross understatement. We make Noah's Ark look homogeneous," says a sophomore.

moral philosophy from Plato to Camus, though professors have some leeway in choosing twentieth-century selections. One semester each of art and humanities is required and, while not given the same reverence as their literary counterparts, are eye-opening all the same. Foreign language proficiency is required as are two semesters of science; two semesters of "extended core" classes dealing in cultures not covered in the other core requirements; two semesters of phys ed; and Logic and Rhetoric, a one-semester argumentative writing class that first-year students reportedly "either love or hate."

Columbia is hardly a cakewalk academically, and students always have something to read or write. Student-faculty interaction is largely dependent on student initiative. Additional interaction stems from professorial involvement in campus politics and forums and from the faculty-in-residence program, which houses professors and their families in spruced-up apartments in several of the residence halls.

"Columbia has always been known for its tradition of social and political activism."

First-year students are assigned a faculty advisor and receive a departmental advisor when they declare majors at the end of sophomore year. Columbia students can take classes at Barnard, which maintains its own faculty, reported to be "more caring and involved than Columbia's." As at Barnard, students can also take graduate-level courses in several departments, notably political science, gaining access to the resources of the School of International and Public Affairs and its multitude of regional institutes. For students wishing to spend time away from New York, there are summer, semester, and one-year programs at the Reid Hall campus in Paris; other programs include opportunities with Kyoto University in Japan, Howard University in Washington, D.C., Oxford or Cambridge in England, and The Free University of Berlin.

To call Columbia diverse would be "a gross understatement. We make Noah's Ark look homogeneous," says a sophomore. In fact, Columbia has the largest percentage of students of color in the Ivy League; 10 percent are African-American, 8 percent are Hispanic, and 19 percent are Asian-American. About 17 percent of the students come from New York City and another 15 percent from elsewhere in the state, especially Long Island. Socially, the campus is also diverse. In a city such as New York, "diversity is assumed," says one student. Another adds, "We have Euros, WASPs, jocks, grinds, sorority bunnies, Deadheads, fashion plates, a sizable Jewish population, and plenty of sideburn-sporting, cigarette-smoking, espresso-sipping, angst-ridden folks who own only black clothing."

Columbia remains one of the nation's most liberal campuses. "Columbia has always been known for its tradition of social and political activism," says a junior. "Students are not afraid to protest to get what they want." No one group dominates campus life. Although 6 percent of the men and 6 percent of the women go Greek, Columbia is hardly a Hellenocentric campus, namely because, as a junior argues, "the frats are chock-full of athletic recruits, the organizations—even the coed ones—are deemed elitist and politically incorrect, and there are too many better things to do in NYC on a Friday night than getting trashed in the basement of some random house." The advent of coed houses has raised interest in Greek life as has the arrival of sororities open to both Columbia and Barnard women.

"This is not a school that rallies together at football games."

With the New York housing market out of control, 95 percent of Columbia students live in university housing, which is guaranteed for four years. Security at the dorms is rated as excellent by students, and every person entering has to flash an ID to the guard on duty at the front door or be signed in by a resident of the building. One exciting aspect of Columbia housing is that many rooms are singles, and it is possible to go all four years without a roommate. Carman Hall is the exclusively first-year dorm and "the fact that you get to meet your classmates compensates for the noise and hideous cinder-block walls," says a music major. First-year students can also live in buildings with students of all years. "Living with upperclasspeople was great. They knew the ins and outs of the university and the neighborhood. It wasn't the blind leading the blind," offers a junior. First-year students are automatically placed on a nineteen-meal-a-week plan and take most of those meals at John Jay, an all-you-can-eat "binge-a-rama with salad bar, deli, grill, and huge dessert bar." Many soon-bloated students scale down their meal plans or convert to points, a buy-what-you-want arrangement with account information stored electronically on student ID cards. Several dorms have kitchens, allowing students to do much of their own cooking. Some students dine at the kosher dining hall at Barnard.

Social life on campus is best described as mellow. Rarely are there big all-inclusive bashes, the exceptions being fall's '60s throwback, Realityfest, and spring's Columbia-fest. "The social scene here is well balanced between school events, concerts and dances, and the variety of activities the city offers," says a senior.

Columbia athletics don't inspire the rabid loyalty of, say, a Florida State, because "Columbia students are individualists," according to one sophomore. "This is not a school that rallies together at football games." Still, the fencing teams are superlative, and men's soccer and basketball are also strong. As an urban school, Columbia lacks team field facilities on campus; however, merely one hundred blocks to the north there are the modern Baker Field, home of the football stadium, the soccer fields, an Olympic track, and the crew boathouse. On campus, the Dodge Gymnasium, an underground facility, houses four levels of basketball courts, swimming pools, weight rooms, and exercise equipment. The gym is often crowded and not all the stuff is wonderful. "It does the job, as well as providing for the best pickup basketball this side of Riverside Park," notes a sophomore. Intramural and club sports are popular, with men's and women's Ultimate Frisbee both national competitors.

Columbians are proud that they are going to college in New York City, and most would have it no other way. Explains an art history major: "Choosing to isolate oneself in the middle of nowhere for four years isn't what college is about. It's about taking one's place as an adult in an adult society. Columbia is the perfect place for that."

| **Overlaps** |
| Harvard, Yale, Brown, Penn, Cornell |

| **If You Apply To** ➢ | **Columbia:** Early decision: Nov. 1. Regular admissions: Jan. 1. Financial aid: Jan. 1. Housing: Jan. 1. Meets demonstrated need of 60%. Campus interviews: not available. Alumni interviews: optional, evaluative. SATs or ACTs: required. SAT IIs: required (writing and two others). Essay: personal statement. |

University of Connecticut

28 North Eagleville Road, Box Unit 3088, Storrs, CT 06269-3088

Squeezed in among the likes of Yale, Brown, Wesleyan, Trinity, and UMass—all within a two-hour drive—UConn could be forgiven for having an inferiority complex. But championship basketball teams, both men and women, have ignited Husky pride, and the university's mammoth rebuilding project is boosting its appeal.

Founded more than a century ago as an agricultural college—this is where America learned to get more eggs per chicken by leaving the lights on in the coops—the

| **Website:** www.uconn.edu |

(Continued)

Location: Rural

Total Enrollment: 21,427

Undergraduates: 14,716

Male/Female: 48/52

SAT Ranges: V 520–610

   M 530–630

Financial Aid: 79%

Expense: Pub $ $ $

Phi Beta Kappa: Yes

Applicants: 13,760

Accepted: 62%

Enrolled: 37%

Grad in 6 Years: 69%

Returning Freshmen: 88%

Academics: ✐ ✐ ✐ ✐

Social: ☎ ☎ ☎

Q of L: ★ ★ ★

Admissions: (860) 486-3137

Email Address:

   beahusky@uconn.edu

Strongest Programs:

   Biosciences

   Communication Sciences

   Business

   Education

   Engineering

   Pharmacy

   History

   Linguistics

University of Connecticut has emerged as a comprehensive university offering a vast selection of academic programs as well as opportunities to study abroad, participate in research, or join one of its 250 organizations or clubs. "The academic competition is strengthening at UConn," comments a senior. "No longer are we a 'safety school,' but rather, I think, one of the top choices in New England and across the country."

The four thousand-acre campus, about twenty-three miles northeast of Hartford, is an architectural potpourri consisting of a mix of collegiate Gothic and neo-classical architecture and half-century-old red-brick structures. The campus is graced with Swan Lake and Mirror Lake and is completely surrounded by dense woods. The school is undergoing a remarkable transformation thanks to UConn 2000, a $1-billion state-financed program to renew, rebuild, and enhance the university that would be the envy of the most heavily endowed private university. Campus construction and ongoing renovations are the norm, sparking jokes about "University of Construction," but the results are a slew of shiny new state-of-the-art facilities. Currently underway are a new School of Pharmacy, a forty thousand seat football stadium, and student-union renovations, and the Connecticut legislature has earmarked another $1.3 billion in improvements through 2015.

At UConn, preprofessional programs, such as the biosciences, are strong, as are business, education, engineering, pharmacy, history, linguistics, psychology, and, of course, agriculture. The basic sciences, especially biology, are solid, but the fine arts department is cited as weak. Engineering is very demanding, and, as at many schools, the department has a relatively high attrition rate, with many students switching to the less-rigorous Management Information Systems. UConn is the only public university in New England to offer majors in environmental engineering, computer science, computer engineering, and metallurgy and materials engineering. With new majors in engineering physics and biomedical engineering, it is also the only public school to offer undergraduate degrees in fourteen engineering specialties. There is a new special program in medicine and dentistry, which is also not offered at any other public university in New England. Students who meet the criteria set by the program are guaranteed admission to UConn's School of Medicine or School of Dental Medicine.

"The faculty at UConn are top-notch, especially outside the classroom."

Core requirements include study in eight areas: expository writing, mathematics, literature and the arts, culture and modern society and non-Western/Latin-American studies, philosophical and ethical analysis, social scientific and comparative analysis, science and technology, and two courses in foreign language (which can be waived if a student has studied three years of a single language in high school). All freshmen are now enrolled in seminar-style writing classes as well.

The university offers advising programs specifically designed for freshmen and sophomores. The First Year Experience program provides a series of special seminars and classes taught by senior faculty to help students with the transition into university life. The Academic Center for Exploratory Students provides advisors to students who are undecided about their majors during their first four semesters at UConn, though course selection advising receives mixed reviews from students. Faculty here are highly regarded. "The faculty at UConn are top-notch, especially outside the classroom," says a senior. Full professors teach most lectures, and labs and discussion groups are run by teaching assistants. Another student remarks that "the counseling program is wonderful."

The UConn Honors Program is an attractive option for talented scholars. Residence-hall floors are offered to freshman honors students, and a newly opened residence hall is specifically reserved for sophomore, junior, and senior level honors students. Approximately 15 percent of the undergraduate population are involved in hands-on research. Engineering, business, pharmacy, and honors students are required to participate in research projects, and each year two teams of finance majors operate the $1 million Student Managed Investment Fund. The university's Eurotech Program places engineering students with interests/studies in a particular language in jobs overseas, and several programs for disadvantaged or underprivileged students are available. In addition, 5 percent of undergraduates participate in the study-abroad program, which allows students to travel to more than thirty countries. UConn also has five regional campuses around the state that offer the first two years of the university's undergraduate program as well as selected four-year degree programs. Students who complete their work satisfactorily at these schools are automatically accepted at the Storrs campus for their last two years.

In addition to athletic scholarships, about 1,700 merit scholarships are offered for a wide range of skills and abilities, ranging from $1,500 to $12,500. Sixty-eight percent of freshman are from Connecticut. Nearly half of the entering students were in the top quarter of their high-school class, and a majority went to public high schools. Minority enrollment comprises 16 percent of the student body, including 6 percent Asian-American, 5 percent African-American, and 5 percent Hispanic. The university is continuing its efforts to attract minority students and has brought in many new faculty members who boast culturally and ethnically diverse backgrounds. Opportunities for multicultural studies abound, including an African-American Cultural Center, Asian-American Cultural Center, Latin American and Puerto Rican Cultural Center, and the new Rainbow Center, a gay, lesbian, bisexual, and transgender educational resource. "There isn't really a typical UConn student," says a junior. "We have a wide diversity on campus and we all celebrate that." Women's rights, residential living, and homophobia are hot campus political issues.

"We have a wide diversity on campus and we all celebrate that."

Sixty-five percent of the students live in university housing, which is available to everyone who wants it. Though a few dorms are single-sex, most are coed by floor. "The dorms are comfortable but small," claims a communications major. Most older dorms are being renovated and updated with Ethernet access. Students living on campus now have access to "HUSKYvision," a network of data, video, and voice communication services that includes everything from replays of lecture videos to course registration. There are several apartment complexes near campus, but most students say that living on campus is much more convenient. Several meal plans are available to dorm residents, but many students would just as soon go out to the snack bar for some ice cream, freshly made with some help from those cows that you can see as you drive out of campus.

The school does a pretty good job of enforcing the alcohol policy on campus. "If students are caught underage, they are subject to disciplinary hearings and can be asked to leave campus," explains one student. This doesn't stop everyone as one student recalls, "There are a lot of dorm parties, and the two major bars are fun but get crowded at times." There are three nearby bars: Ted's, Huskie's, and Civic Pub. Although fraternities do provide something of a party scene, only 7 percent of men and 6 percent of women go Greek.

"There are lots of events that are university sponsored on campus."

The town of Storrs is small and rural, and students complain about the "boring" surroundings. But, as one student notes, "UConn is a town within itself," with almost everything a student could need available on campus. To make up for the lack of on-campus entertainment, the Student Board of Governors provides a multitude of activities. "There are lots of events that are university sponsored on campus," says a marketing major. Popular legend (students always "know someone who did it") has it that there is one residential activity available at UConn that

Popular legend has it that there is one residential activity available at Uconn that most other colleges can't offer: cow tipping—that is, sneaking up on unsuspecting cows (who sleep standing up) and tipping them over.

Students who meet the criteria set by the program are guaranteed admission to UConn's School of Medicine or School of Dental Medicine.

most other colleges can't offer: cow tipping—that is, sneaking up on unsuspecting cows (who sleep standing up) and tipping them over. The administration contends that this is a myth. UConn's students are also very involved in community service, and the Center for Community Outreach provides many opportunities to volunteer. For most big-city needs, Hartford is only thirty minutes away, and Boston, New York City, Cape Cod, and the ski slopes of Vermont are within weekend road-trip range.

Basketball is by far the most popular sport at UConn; the Huskies are a perennial Big East powerhouse and in 1999 won the ultimate prize: the NCAA national championship. In a state that has no professional sports teams, UConn's women's basketball team is the pride of not only the campus but of the Nutmeg State. The Lady Huskies, NCAA Division I champions in 2000, 2002, and 2003 routinely sell out the Hartford Civic Center for their home games, and they are the only women's basketball team that operates in the black. Football isn't huge at UConn, but a decision to upgrade the football program from IAA to IA could change that. Annual campus events include Homecoming, Winter Weekend, and Midnight Madness—the first official day of basketball practice.

Students at UConn aren't "cowed" by the plethora of offerings, and those seeking greener pastures will be hard-pressed to find a more dynamic public institution. According to one student, "the best thing here is the mix of big school resources, small school community, and, of course, Husky Mania!"

Overlaps

University of Massachusetts, Boston University, Northeastern, University of Rhode Island, Boston College

If You Apply To >

UConn: Rolling admissions. Early action: Dec. 1. Regular admission: Feb 1. Campus interviews: optional, informational. No alumni interviews. SATs or ACTs: required. SAT IIs: optional. Accepts the Common Application and electronic applications. Essay question: what you can contribute to UConn.

Connecticut College

270 Mohegan Avenue, New London, CT 06320-4196

Like Vassar and Skidmore, Connecticut College made a successful transition from women's college to coed. The college is strong in the humanities and renowned for its study-abroad programs. It is also an SAT I-optional school. New London does not offer much but at least it is on the water.

Website: www. connecticutcollege.edu
Location: Suburban
Total Enrollment: 1,879
Undergraduates: 1,835
Male/Female: 41/59
SAT Ranges: V 626–701 M 608–682
ACT Range: 26-29
Financial Aid: 46%
Expense: Pr $ $ $
Phi Beta Kappa: Yes

Connecticut College is a small liberal arts school where students aren't "led around by the hand," a sophomore says proudly. "We are treated and respected like adults and expected to act as such." The school's professors here focus on teaching, helping students follow the example of Conn College's camel mascot: to drink up and store knowledge. Thanks to a student-run honor code, students also feel comfortable leaving their doors and bikes unlocked on campus. They're tested on what they've learned during unproctored final exams scheduled at their convenience within a ten-day window. "This is one of the kindest places you could ever come to," says an English major. "People genuinely care about each other."

Sitting majestically atop a hill, Conn College's lovely campus provides beautiful views of the Thames River (pronounced the way it looks, not like the "Temz" that Wordsworth so dearly loved) on one side, and Long Island Sound on the other. The campus is set on a 750-acre arboretum with a pond, wetlands, wooded areas, and hiking trails. The granite campus buildings are a mixture of modern and collegiate Gothic, neo-Gothic, and neo-Classical architecture. The school recently finished a regulation-size soccer field and new squash courts and renovated a section of the Shain Library into the Charles Chu Asian Art Reading Room.

Since its 1911 founding as a women's college, Conn has been dedicated to the liberal arts, broadly defined. The school's dance and drama departments are superb, and talented dance students often take a few semesters off to study with professional companies. Theater majors may work with the Eugene O'Neill Theater Institute, named for New London's best-known literary son. Chemistry majors may use high-tech gas chromatograms and mass spectrometers from their very first day; other schools typically reserve these gadgets for upperclassmen with more experience. The school's Ammerman Center for Arts and Technology lets students examine the links of theater, film, music, dance, writing, and other artistic pursuits to the world of math and computer science. Students also give high marks to the popular English, psychology, and government programs. And the Study Away/Teach Away initiative allows groups of Conn College students and faculty members to spend a semester living and working together at a university abroad in locations as far-flung as Vietnam, South Africa, and Egypt. Conn College also participates in the Twelve-College Exchange* and Venture Program consortiums.*

The school's general education requirements include one foundation course in each of seven broad areas: physical and biological sciences, mathematics and logic, social sciences, literature and the arts, creative arts, philosophical and religious studies, and historical studies. Students must also fulfill a foreign language requirement, take two writing-intensive or writing-enhanced courses, and participate in three general education tutorials. Each student is guaranteed $3,000 from the school for a summer internship sometime during his or her four years. "Because the school will pay, some students are able to get internships at places that would not normally hire interns," says a chemistry major.

An economics major says Conn College professors are impressive, though the school's financial woes have forced it to curtail some hiring and made classes on obscure topics less common. "You will be wowed by both the professor's teaching ability and his or her scholarship," says an English major. "And then that same professor will invite your class over for dinner." Professors are always willing to provide extra help, and it's not uncommon to see them having coffee with students at the Student Center. "I've been chal-

"We are treated and respected like adults and expected to act as such."

lenged to reach beyond accepted norms—to question myself and my society, to think critically and interdisciplinarily," says an anthropology major. "The people here are great, but the faculty makes it better," adds a psychology and sociology major. Students say they work hard and are motivated to achieve but compete with themselves, rather than each other. "Students don't go around interrogating one another about how they did on the last test," says a sophomore.

Despite strenuous effort, diversity has been slow in coming to Conn College. The student body remains 80 percent Caucasian, mostly from New England and the Mid-Atlantic States. African-Americans and Asian-Americans each comprise 3 percent, and Hispanics add 2 percent. Freshmen must attend a session on issues of race, class, and gender, run by a panel of peers representing different cultures, socioeconomic backgrounds, sexual orientations, and physical disabilities. Conn College's diversification efforts have been helped by the school's decision to emphasize high-school transcripts, rather than the SAT I, as a measure of achievement and potential in the admissions process.

Ninety-eight percent of Conn College students live on campus, where freshmen are assigned to doubles, triples, or quads. Dorms house students of all ages,

(Continued)
Applicants: 4,318
Accepted: 34%
Enrolled: 32%
Grad in 6 Years: 82%
Returning Freshmen: 93%
Academics: ✏ ✏ ✏ ✏
Social: ☎ ☎ ☎
Q of L: ★ ★ ★ ★
Admissions: (860) 439-2200
Email Address:
   admission@conncoll.edu

Strongest Programs:
   Psychology
   Sciences
   English
   International Studies
   Foreign Languages
   Dance

The school recently finished a regulation-size soccer field and new squash courts and renovated a section of the Shain Library into the Charles Chu Asian Art Reading Room.

and are run by seniors who apply to be "house fellows." Roommates tend to be well matched, because incoming students complete a three-page questionnaire about personal habits before coming to campus, says a sophomore. Most upperclassmen get single rooms, perhaps in the River Ridge Apartments, though that's no longer guaranteed because the student body has grown. Buildings range from older, more traditional structures to newer facilities known as the "plex" dorms, which "are all very clean and sterile, and remind many of a hospital," says a chemistry major. Among the seven specialty houses are Earth House (environmental awareness), the Abbey House co-op (where students cook their own meals), Unity House (fostering relationships across ethnic and racial boundaries), and houses dedicated to substance-free living, quiet lifestyles, and international languages.

Because Conn lacks a Greek system, most activities—including coed intramural sports—revolve around the dorms, which sponsor weekly keg and theme parties. Also keeping students busy are movie nights, comedy shows, student productions and dances—sometimes with out-of-town bands and DJs. The alcohol policy fits

"The school seems more concerned about student safety than anything."

under the honor code, so students under twenty-one can't imbibe at the campus bar. That said, "the school seems more concerned about student safety than anything," says an English major. "They don't slap every underage drinker on the wrist." Conn is helping redevelop New London, which is home to defense-contractor General Dynamics and drug-maker Pfizer. The town "has definitely improved since my freshman year," says a junior. Unfortunately, adds a sophomore, "most students do not know about the small coffee shops, bookstores, and restaurants located in the town, mainly because they do not venture off 'the Hill.'"

Students do get involved in the life of New London through volunteer work, with about 50 percent participating in some way each year. From soup kitchens to tutoring to Habitat for Humanity, students who want to give back will find no shortage of opportunities. A college van makes it easy to get to and from work sites. When students get the urge to roam, the beaches of Mystic and other shore towns are twenty minutes from campus. Farther away—yet still close enough for a weekend visit—are Providence, Rhode Island; New York City; Boston; and camping, hiking, and skiing in Vermont or upstate New York. Students eagerly anticipate two annual traditions: October's Camel Olympics, which pits dorms against each other in games ranging from *Scrabble* to Capture the Flag, and Floralia, an all-day music festival the weekend before spring finals, which the Dave Matthews Band recently headlined.

The Conn Camels compete in Division III of the NCAA. Among the most popular sports, for both men and women, are track and field, lacrosse, rowing, soccer, and cross-country. Men's ice-hockey games against rival Wesleyan draw crowds, and a T-shirt brags that Conn football has been undefeated since 1911 (the joke's on you if you believe that, since Conn—as a former women's college—has never had a team!). Between classes or at the end of the day, students of all skill levels can enjoy the natatorium's pool and fitness center and the field house's rowing tanks and climbing walls.

There are plenty of reasons to head to this little college on the hill—even if a great football team isn't one of them. On its friendly campus, Conn College fosters strong student-faculty bonds, and takes pride in its ability to challenge—and trust—students in the classroom.

Overlaps

Wesleyan, Tufts, Bates, Skidmore, Middlebury

If You Apply To ➤

Conn College: Early decision: Nov. 15. Regular admissions: Dec. 15 (supplement), Jan. 1 (Common Application and other materials). Financial aid: Jan.15. Guarantees to meet demonstrated need. Campus interviews: recommended, evaluative. Alumni interviews: optional, evaluative. SAT Is: optional. SAT IIs: required (any three or the ACT). Accepts the Common Application and electronic applications. Essay question: Common Application questions.

Cooper Union

30 Cooper Square, New York, NY 10003

BEST BUY

As college costs skyrocket, so does the popularity of Cooper Union's free education in art, architecture, and engineering. Expect Ivy-level competition for a place in the class here. Instead of a conventional campus, Cooper Union has the East Village—which is quite a deal.

Some say the best things in life are free. In most cases, they're probably wrong. But not in the case of the Cooper Union for the Advancement of Science and Art. If you manage to get accepted into this top technical institute, you get a full-tuition scholarship and some of the nation's finest academic offerings in architecture, engineering, and art. With cool and funky Greenwich Village in the background and rigorous studying in the forefront, college life at Cooper Union may seem to be faster than a New York minute. Whatever the pace, though, no one can deny that a CU education is one of the best bargains around—probably the best anywhere. The only problem is that its acceptance rate is lower than most of the Ivies.

The school was founded in 1859 by entrepreneur Peter Cooper, who believed that education should be "as free as water and air." With hefty contributions from J. P. Morgan, Frederick Vanderbilt, Andrew Carnegie, and various other assorted robber barons, the school was able to stay afloat in order to recruit poor students of "strong moral character." Today, students must pay a few hundred dollars for nonacademic expenses, but tuition is still free.

In place of a traditional collegiate setting are three academic buildings and one dorm plunked down in one of New York's most eclectic and exciting neighborhoods. The stately brick art and architecture building is a beautiful historic landmark. Built of brick and topped by a classic water tower, the dorm blends right in with the neighborhood. The Great Hall

"If you can't accept different kinds of people, you shouldn't come here."

was the site of Lincoln's "Right Makes Might" speech and the birthplace of the NAACP, the American Red Cross, and the national women's suffrage movement. Wedged between two busy avenues in the East Village, Cooper Union offers an environment for survivors. One mechanical engineering major describes the climate as "a tropical rain forest. Only the truly dedicated should come here."

The academic climate is intense, yet cooperation is critical, according to students. "We all feed off each other and strive for our best, but rivalry is low," says an architecture major. A junior adds, "You don't know the meaning of stress until you've been through Cooper." The curriculum is highly structured, and all students must take a sequence of required courses in the humanities and social sciences. The first year is devoted to language and literature and the second to the making of the modern world. In some special circumstances, students are allowed to take courses at nearby New York University and the New School for Social Research. The nationally renowned engineering school, under the tutelage of the nation's first female engineering dean, offers both bachelor's and master's degrees in chemical, electrical,

Website: www.cooper.edu
Location: Urban
Total Enrollment: 907
Undergraduates: 870
Male/Female: 65/35
SAT Ranges: V 510–760
    M 510–780
Financial Aid: 40%
Expense: Pr $
Phi Beta Kappa: No
Applicants: 2,216
Accepted: 13%
Enrolled: 69%
Grad in 6 Years: 80%
Returning Freshmen: 90%
Academics: ✍ ✍ ✍ ½
Social: ☎
Q of L: ★ ★ ★
Admissions: (212) 353-4120
Email Address: N/A

Strongest Programs:
    Architecture
    Electrical Engineering
    Art

mechanical, and civil engineering as well as a bachelor of science in general engineering. "Architecture and engineering are the most acclaimed, but then, these occupations are more mainstream, and graduates get big money and success," reflects an art major. "It's harder to measure success in the art school." The art school offers a broad-based generalist curriculum that includes graphic design, painting, sculpture, photography, and video but is considered weak by some students. The architecture school, in the words of one pleased participant, is "phenomenal—even unparalleled." Requirements for getting into each of these schools vary widely—each looks for different strengths and talents—hence the differences in test-score ranges.

The Cooper Union library is small (ninety thousand volumes), but contains more than one hundred thousand graphic materials. Classes are small and, with a little persistence, are not too difficult to get into. Professors are engaging and accessible. "One of the best aspects of this college is that everyone is taught by full professors," reports a junior. A professional counseling and referral service is available, as is academic counseling, but the school's small size and its rigorously structured academic programs set the classes the students take and eliminate a lot of confusion or decision making. Reactions on career counseling vary between "horrible" from an art major to "excellent" from an engineering major. Students "tend to talk to other students, recommending or insulting various classes and profs around registration time," notes a senior.

Strong moral character is no longer a prerequisite for admission, but an outstanding high-school academic average most certainly is. Prospective applicants should note, however, that art and architecture students are picked primarily on the basis of a faculty evaluation of their creative works. For engineering students, admission is based on a formula that gives roughly equal weight to the high-school record, SAT scores, and the SAT IIs in mathematics and physics or chemistry.

"The students here tend to be incredibly driven people," says one student, noting that some classmates have spent "literally twenty-four hours at the drafting desk." Sixty-one percent of the students are from New York State, and more than half of those grew up in the city. Most are from public schools, and many are the first in their family to attend college. Forty-four percent of the students are from minority groups, most of them Asian-Americans (27 percent); 6 percent are African-American, and 8 percent are Hispanic. One student attests that diversity is not an issue at CU: "We are a racially mixed student body that stays mixed. There's no overt hostility and rare self-segregation. One of the officers of the Chinese Student Association is a large black man from Trinidad. Need I say more?" The campus is home to ethnically-based student clubs, but, according to one student, membership is not exclusive: "In other words, you can be white and be a member of Onyx—a student group promoting black awareness." According to one senior, CU is a very liberal place: "If you can't accept different kinds of people, you shouldn't come here." For students who demonstrate financial need, help with living expenses is available.

"The East Village is great place to be young, with tons of bars and culture."

Students love the dorm, a fifteen-story residence hall that saves many students from commuting into the Village or cramming themselves into expensive apartments. It is noteworthy that housing here is guaranteed only to freshmen. The facility is composed of furnished apartments with kitchenettes and bathrooms complete with showers or tubs and is "in great condition and well maintained," states one resident. A less enraptured dweller notes, "Rooms are barely big enough to fit a bed, a table, and a clothes cabinet." Still, each apartment does have enough space for a stove, microwave, and refrigerator. So you can cook for yourself or eat at the unexciting but affordable school cafeteria or at one of the myriad nearby delis and coffee bars.

The combination of intense workload and CU's location means that campus social life is limited, though the administration hopes the dorm will promote more on-campus social activities. "Many students will say that Cooper social life is dead," notes a junior. "In many ways they are right." On the other hand, as one senior puts it, "The East Village is great place to be young, with tons of bars and culture." About 20 percent of the men and 10 percent of the women belong to professional societies. Drinking on campus is allowed during school-sponsored parties for adult students—otherwise, no alcohol on campus. But as one student puts it, "This is New York; one can be served anywhere." The intramural sports program is held in several different facilities in the city, and the games are popular. Students organize clubs and outings around interests such as soccer, basketball, skiing, fencing, Ping-Pong, classical music, religion, and drama. And of course, the colorful neighborhood is ideal for sketching and browsing. McSorley's bar is right around the corner, the Grassroots Tavern is just down the block, and nearby Chinatown and Little Italy are also popular destinations. The heart of the Village, with its abundance of theaters, art galleries, and cafés, is just a few blocks to the west. The Bowery and SoHo's galleries and restaurants are due south; all of midtown Manhattan spreads to the northern horizon.

Getting into Cooper Union is tough, and once admitted, students find that dealing with the onslaught of city and school is plenty tough as well. But most students like the challenge. "The workload, living alone in New York, and the administrative policies force you to act like an adult and take care of yourself," explains a senior. Surviving the school's academic rigors requires talent, self-sufficiency, and a clear sense of one's career objectives. Students who don't have it all can be sure that there are six or seven people in line ready to take their places. That's quite an incentive to succeed.

Art and architecture students are picked primarily on the basis of a faculty evaluation of their creative works.

Overlaps

NYU, Columbia, Cornell University, MIT, Carnegie-Mellon

If You Apply To ➤ **Cooper Union:** Rolling admissions (for art applicants, by invitation). Early decision (for art and engineering applicants): Dec. 1. Regular admissions: Jan. 1 (architecture), Jan. 10 (art), Feb. 1 (engineering). Financial aid and housing: May 1. All students receive full-tuition scholarships. No campus or alumni interviews. (Portfolio Day strongly recommended for art applicants.) SATs: required. SAT IIs: required for engineering (math and physics or chemistry). Apply to particular program. Essay question: varies by school.

Cornell College

600 First Street West, Mount Vernon, IA 52314-1098

One-course-at-a-time model is Cornell's calling card. Cornell's main challenge: trying to lure students to rural Iowa. With a student body of about one thousand, Cornell lavishes its students with personal attention. Though primarily a liberal arts institution, Cornell has small programs in business and education.

If you were ever torn between finishing your biology project or writing a paper for English (and both project's titles started to lean toward "Is cloning OK if it gets school work done?") you may want to consider Cornell College. They take a "One-Course-At-A-Time" (OCAAT) approach, which has students only taking one course during a three-and-a-half week term. The school, founded twelve years before that *other* Cornell in Ithaca, New York, divides its calendar into nine terms, each separated by a four-day break. Students take a single course during eight of the terms, and may use the extra term for a vacation or for a ninth course at no extra charge. All of the students seem to agree that the "One-Course-At-A-Time method, the close-knit community, and the available staff," add up to a great experience.

Website:
   www.cornellcollege.edu
Location: Rural
Total Enrollment: 986

(Continued)

Undergraduates: 986
Male/Female: 42/58
SAT Ranges: V 490–640
   M 510–620
ACT Range: 22–27
Financial Aid: 71%
Expense: Pr $ $
Phi Beta Kappa: Yes
Applicants: 1,182
Accepted: 70%
Enrolled: 37%
Grad in 6 Years: 63%
Returning Freshmen: 79%
Academics: ✍ ✍ ✍
Social: ☎ ☎ ☎
Q of L: ★ ★ ★
Admissions: (319) 895-4477
   or (800) 747-1112
Email Address: admissions@
   cornellcollege.edu

Strongest Programs:
   Art
   Biology
   Education
   Philosophy
   Politics

Cornell students can take off-campus courses in all parts of the world, such as Marine Science Research in the Bahamas, Advanced Spanish in Spain, or Greek Archaeology in Greece.

Cornell is one of only two colleges or universities in the nation with its entire campus listed on the National Register of Historic Places. The area is perched on a hilltop overlooking the Cedar River valley, and the view from the bell tower of majestic King Chapel is unequaled in the region. One of Cornell's academic buildings has been renovated into the Law Hall Technical Center, while the performing arts facility has a new 280-seat theatre.

Cornell, Colorado College, and Tusculum College are the only schools in the nation to employ the One-Course-At-A-Time schedule. As a result, the classes are "challenging and at a quick pace, but you can quickly adjust" says a senior. The schedule means that some students graduate in three and a half years while others take the full four years; nearly half graduate with a double major. If that sounds intimidating, it is. Administrators praise the program, claiming it improves the quality of liberal education and allows students to get accustomed to the pace of the business world, where "what needs to be

"The quality of teaching is excellent."

done needs to be done quickly and done well." A final advantage is academic advising. With a grade every four weeks, trouble can be spotted quickly. The downside of the approach is that it can be difficult to pursue cumulative subjects like math and the natural sciences and that a one- or two-day absence can knock you right out of a term. Still, students claim that while the "courses are challenging, they are not overwhelming and because classes are smaller, there is less competition and more interaction between the professors and students." If you have the temperament and attention span for a highly concentrated learning method, Cornell can be an enriching.

The school stays true to its liberal arts mission with noteworthy programs in English, psychology, and philosophy. Economics/business, biology, and education—primary and secondary—are also popular majors. Weaker areas include languages, religion, and computer science. If liberal arts is your mission, Cornell offers need-based financial aid and awards academic and service scholarships of up to $20,000. Also, under a work-study program, the college hires student tutors to provide free help to those in need.

To graduate, all students must complete thirty-two courses with at least twenty-one outside any single department and at least one in each of the following areas: English, fine arts, foreign language, humanities, math, science, and social science. Another route to graduation is the Bachelor of Special Studies (BSS) degree program, in which students and their advisors design a personalized major with no general requirements.

In addition to their core classes, Cornell students can take off-campus courses in all parts of the world, such as Marine Science Research in the Bahamas, Advanced Spanish in Spain, or Greek Archaeology in Greece. They can also spend a semester at sea or in any one of thirty-six countries

"RAs are pretty lenient unless the situation becomes unsafe."

through Associated Colleges of the Midwest* programs. Combined degrees and co-op programs are offered in several subjects, and the short breaks between courses include recreational and educational activities such as symposia, Music Mondays, carnivals, and athletic events.

Students praise Cornell's faculty, who make their home telephone numbers standard information on course syllabi. The school does not employ graduate assistants, and class size seldom exceeds twenty-five students. "The quality of teaching is excellent. Almost all the professors have a Ph.D. in their fields," says one junior. Freshmen are matched with academic advisors before orientation and meet with them before classes to plan a program of study. Students choose classes through a bidding system rather than first-come, first-serve registration, and seniors are assured of getting the classes they need.

Thirty percent of students at Cornell are Iowans; other Midwestern states are also well represented. African-Americans, Hispanics, and Asian-Americans make up 5 percent of the student body. Consciousness of the school's gay, lesbian, and bisexual community and the general diversity of the student body—or lack thereof—is improving. Students report that "women's rights, diversity issues, and gay and lesbian issues" are the biggest social and political issues talked about on campus.

Ninety-two percent of students live on campus, where renovations have improved and are continuing to improve the condition of some older housing stock. Two apartment buildings are available to upperclassmen; about half of the dorms are coed, and freshmen get their pick of rooms. Overall, the dorms are comfortable, but there are complaints that they are "not as well maintained as they could be." Everyone eats together in the Commons, where the food service draws jeers, although one junior feels complaints are due to the fact that "if you have the same type of food every day, anyone would be sick of it."

The nearby town of Mount Vernon "is very picturesque." Most students either love the town's idyllic pace—a few local bars and a lot of peace, quiet, and safety—or long for more excitement. Cedar Rapids and Iowa City, less than half an hour away, boast a more collegiate nightlife. Those who prefer the weekend road trip head for Chicago, which is less than four hours away. Parties in the dorms are pretty much a thing of the past, and some of the residence halls and floors are substance free. According to one junior, "Many students get of-age students to buy for them." Another student says, "RAs are pretty lenient unless the situation becomes unsafe." Off-campus rules seem to be fairly strict; most of the students agree that "it is increasingly difficult for underage people to be served in Mount Vernon's bars."

Cornell's athletic teams have competed in the Iowa Intercollegiate Athletic Conference since 1998 and have been to the NCAA men's basketball tournament five times, most recently in 1994. Recently, the tennis team won the Women's Tennis Conference Championship. In both men's and women's sports, the 113-year-old rivalry with Coe College continues unabated.

While the intensive One-Course-At-A-Time workload combined with the cold Iowa winters might appear daunting, there are few complaints. Instead, students praise the sense of community, high quality of teaching, and the flexibility of their schedules. For those with a "one-track mind," Cornell offers a top-notch education in a supportive community.

Students praise Cornell's faculty, who make their home telephone numbers standard information on course syllabi.

Overlaps

Coe, University of Iowa, Colorado College, Luther, Iowa State

If You Apply To ➤

Cornell College: Rolling admissions. Meets demonstrated need of 45%. Campus interviews: recommended, informational. No alumni interviews. SATs or ACTs: required. Accepts the Common Application and electronic applications. Essay question: how you have integrated classroom learning into nonacademic life; the fictional character you would spend a day as; the possession or trait that most reveals your character.

Cornell University

Ithaca, NY 14850

Cornell's reputation as a pressure cooker comes from its preprofessional attitude and "we try harder" mentality. Spans seven colleges—four private and three public. (Tuition varies accordingly.) Strong in engineering and architecture, world-famous in hotel administration. Easiest Ivy to get into.

Despite the intense academic atmosphere, Cornell social life beats most of the other Ivies hands down.

Cornell has a long tradition for being the lone wolf among the Ivy League universities. So it should come as no surprise that Cornell has taken another huge step away from its Ivy League counterparts by announcing its intention to become the finest research university for undergraduate education in the nation. Cornell's president recently unveiled a $400 million, ten-year plan to improve undergraduate education by combining education and research and having all freshmen live in the same residential area. With rain, drizzle, slush, and snow known as "the four seasons of Ithaca," just walking to class across the vast and hilly campus can be challenging. Cornell's highly talented student body and notoriously competitive academics probably make it, in the words of one student, "the only place where you walk up a forty-five-degree incline in twenty-degree weather to get 30 percent on a prelim."

Aside from the great strides in undergraduate education, Cornell also has its stunning campus to lure students to upstate New York. Perched atop a hill that commands a view of both Ithaca and Cayuga lakes, the campus is breathtakingly scenic; or, as the saying goes, "Ithaca is gorges." Ravines, waterfalls, and parks border all sides of the school's campus. The Cornell Plantation, more than three thousand acres of woodlands, natural trails, streams, and gorges, provides space for walking, picnicking, or contemplation. In addition to completing their north campus residential community, Cornell has also renovated both the Lincoln Hall and the Martha Van Renessaler Hall. Currently, they are working on improving the College of Industrial and Labor Relations and the College of Agriculture and Life Sciences.

"I am always impressed by the professors' real interest in helping students in addition to their research."

At the undergraduate level, Cornell has four privately endowed colleges: architecture, art, and planning; arts and sciences; engineering; and hotel administration. "Our school of hotel administration is among the best in the world," raves one junior. Cornell is also New York State's land-grant university. Therefore, three other colleges are operated by Cornell under contract with New York State: agriculture and life sciences, human ecology, and the school of industrial and labor relations (ILR). Thirty-seven percent of the students in these state-assisted colleges are New York State residents who pick up their Ivy League degrees at an almost-public price (tuition at these schools is slightly steeper than SUNY rates).

The College of Arts and Sciences boasts considerable strength in history, government, and just about all the natural and physical sciences. The English program has turned out a number of renowned writers, including Toni Morrison, Thomas Pynchon, and Richard Farina. Foreign languages, required for all A&S students, are also strong, and the performing arts, mathematics, and most social science departments are considered good. Among the state-assisted units, the agriculture college is one of the best in the nation and a good bet for anyone hoping to make it into a veterinary school (there's one at Cornell with state support). The School of Hotel Administration comes as close as anything at Cornell to being an undergraduate business school, and is, along with ILR, world renowned. Human ecology is among the best in the nation in home- and human-service-related disciplines. (It also offers a wine-tasting course that draws students from across the university.) In the Department of Applied Economics, the undergraduate business major is one of few taught by faculty separate from the graduate business school. This separation allows them to have a more focused undergraduate environment. The Johnson Museum, designed by I. M. Pei, has been rated as one of the ten best university museums in America. Students enjoy the $22 million theater arts center, designed specifically for undergraduates. Students say the math department needs improvement.

Student-faculty relations at Cornell are a mixed bag, but for the most part students do have a lot of respect for their professors. "I am always impressed by the professors' real interest in helping students in addition to their research," says an Operations Research and Industrial Engineering major. Lower-level courses are generally large lectures, though many are taught by "charismatic profs" who try to remain accessible. The largest course on campus, Psych 101, packs in more than one thousand, but students report that scintillating lectures make it a well-loved rite of passage. Some undergrads complain that it is difficult to get into popular courses unless you are a major. "There are times when students don't get into courses, but that's usually for classes with limited enrollment," explains one junior. The administration, however, is hoping that the decision to make undergraduates a priority will improve most of the problems in the lower-level courses. For now, first-year students do have access to senior faculty members, including such notables as novelists Alison Lurie and Dan McCall, through mandatory Freshman Seminars. In addition to their thematic focus, most of the seminars stress writing skills.

The Fund for Educational Initiatives gives professors money to implement innovative approaches to undergraduate education, which have included a visual learning laboratory and a course on electronic music. Cornell was early among universities to add women's studies to the curriculum and continues to be an innovator, with programs in Asian-American studies and by offering its students programs like its Sea Semester.*

Cornell academics are demanding and foster an intensity found on few campuses. "The easiest Ivy to get into; the toughest to get out of," quips one student. "Students spend four to five hours per night on coursework, and at least half the weekend is spent hitting the books." Another student adds, "The courses here are very difficult but can be mas-

> **"Program houses and co-ops are wonderful alternatives to dorm life."**

tered if the student puts in enough effort." University-wide, 95 percent of Cornell students ranked in the top quarter of their high-school class, so those who were the class genius in high school should be prepared for a struggle to rise to the top. To cope with the anxieties that the high-powered atmosphere creates, the university has one of the best psychological counseling networks in the nation, including an alcohol-awareness program, peer sex counselors, personal-growth workshops, and EARS (Empathy, Assistance, and Referral Service).

The library system is superb. Cornell students have access to more than 6.4 million volumes, 63,500 journals, and one thousand networked resources in the nineteen branches around campus. The resources on the Olin Graduate Library's first floor are available to anyone, and a pass from a professor gets you into the graduate stacks. Within the beautiful, underground Carl A. Kroch Library, students study in skylit atriums and reading rooms and move about the renowned Fiske Icelandic Collection and the Echols Collections, the finest Cambodian collection on display.

Academically, Cornell is a veritable plethora of opportunities offering more than four thousand courses in seven colleges and schools. Co-op programs are available to engineering and human ecology students, and Cornell-in-Washington, with its own dorm, is popular among public policy students. Students looking to study abroad can choose from more than two hundred programs and uni-

> **"The easiest Ivy to get into; the toughest to get out of."**

versities throughout the world, including those in Indonesia, Belgium, Ireland, and Nepal. Research opportunities are outstanding at Cornell, and students can take part in some of the most vital research happening in the nation. Recent research findings include solving the mystery of how Jupiter's rings are formed and discovering a new technology to make computer software less vulnerable to bugs.

Prospective students apply to one of the seven colleges or schools through the central admissions office, and admissions standards vary by school. The mixture of state and private, preprofessional, and liberal arts at one institution provides a

> *Cornell's highly talented student body and notoriously competitive academics probably make it, in the words of one student, "the only place where you walk up a forty-five-degree incline in twenty-degree weather to get 30 percent on a prelim."*

diversity of students rare among America's colleges. City slickers and country folk, engineers and those with an artsy flair all rub shoulders here. Just over half of Cornell's students are out-of-staters; another 7 percent are foreign. African-Americans and Hispanics account for 10 percent of the students, and Asian-Americans 16 percent more. "Cornell is open to all ideas as long as they do not harm another group or person," says one student. Cornell offers many workshops and discussion groups aimed at increasing tolerance. The state-assisted schools draw a large number of in-staters, as well as many students from New Jersey, Pennsylvania, and New England, while arts and sciences and engineering draw from the tristate metropolitan New York City area, Pennsylvania, Massachusetts, and California. Whatever their origin, students seem self-motivated and studious. Upon graduation, 55 percent of Cornell students take jobs, and 31 percent continue to graduate and professional schools.

Cornell is need blind in admissions and guarantees to meet the demonstrated need of all accepted applicants, but the proportion of outright grants—as opposed to loans that must be repaid—in the financial-aid package varies depending on how eager the university is to get students to enroll. The Cornell Installment Plan (CIP) allows students or their parents to pay a year's or semester's tuition in monthly interest-free installments. The university also takes pride in the alumni-developed Cornell Tradition, a unique program of fellowships for students on financial aid who are willing to work extra hours each week. In addition to their salaries, these students receive up to $2,500 to partly replace loans. Another scholarship, called the Cornell Research Scholars, provides paid research opportunities, need-based loan forgiveness, and one summer of funded research for the most academically gifted students who demonstrate an interest in research.

Many changes are in store for Cornell housing as a result of the new plan to transform undergraduate education. The university recently received a $100 million pledge from an anonymous donor to reach this goal. North Campus will receive two new residence halls and a dining room and will become the home of all freshmen. West Campus will be transformed into a post-freshman-year living and will have faculty leadership from all the undergraduate schools and colleges at Cornell. A few students are housed in two dorms on the edge of Collegetown, the blocks of apartments and houses within walking distance of the campus. There are dorms devoted to everything from ecology to music, and cultural houses include Chinese, Jewish, and American Indian (the only facility of its kind in the nation). "Program houses and co-ops are wonderful alternatives to dorm life," says one student. Also available

"Cornell is open to all ideas as long as they do not harm another group or person."

are a small number of highly coveted suites—six large double rooms with kitchens and a common living area. More than half of Cornell students—and most juniors and seniors—live off campus. Many try their luck in Collegetown, where demand keeps the housing market tight and rents high, while others live in fraternity and sorority houses. Cornell's food service is reputedly among the best in the nation. There are seven dining halls that function independently, so, one student enthuses, "there are at least 28 different entrées for each meal." Milk products and some meats come right from the agriculture school, and about twice a semester a cross-country gourmet team—the staff of a famous restaurant—prepares its specialties on campus.

Despite the intense academic atmosphere, Cornell social life beats most of the other Ivies hands down. Once the weekend arrives, local parties and ski slopes are filled with Cornell students who have managed to strike a balance between study and play. Collegetown bars offer good eats and drinks, but those under twenty-one are barred. However, there is plenty to do at Cornell aside from drinking, students report. "We go to movies, plays, concerts, or just go out to dinner with friends," says a senior. With 25 percent of men and 20 percent of women pledging, fraternities and sororities also play a significant role in the social scene. Big events include Fun in the Sun (a day of friendly athletic competition), Dragon Day (architecture students build a dragon and parade it through campus), and Springfest (a concert on Libe Slope).

Students celebrate the last day of classes—Slope Day—by hanging out at Libe Slope. There are also innumerable concerts and sporting events. In addition, there are more than four hundred extracurricular clubs ranging from a tanning society to a society of women engineers.

Hockey is unquestionably the dominant sport on campus (the chief goal being to defeat Harvard), and camping out for season tickets is an annual ritual. The Big Red football program has been somewhat revived after years in the Ivy League cellar. Cornell boasts the largest intramural program in the Ivy League; it includes more than 100 hockey teams organized around dorms, fraternities, and other organizations. The aforementioned "four seasons of Ithaca" can make walking to class across the vast and hilly campus challenging, but with the first snow of the winter, "traying" down Libe Slope becomes the sport of choice for hordes of fun-loving Cornellians. Ithaca boasts "wonderful outdoor enthusiast stores," says one student. It also hosts Greek Peak Mountain for nearby skiing, Cayuga Lake for boating and swimming, and lots of space for hiking and watching the clouds roll by.

Like most other Ivy League universities, Cornell is a premiere research institution with a distinguished faculty and outstanding academics. What sets it apart is the university's willingness to stray from the traditional Ivy League path as it did with the announcement of its plan to make undergraduates its highest priority. Cornell University is a pioneer in the world of education, and students unafraid to blaze their own trail will feel at home here. "There is no one way to characterize a Cornell student and I think that's what sets us apart," says one student. "Anyone is welcome here and anyone can find their niche."

<aside>

Overlaps

Penn, Columbia, Northwestern, Brown, Yale

</aside>

If You Apply To ➢ **Cornell:** Rolling notification (College of Agriculture and Life Sciences, School of Industrial and Labor Relations, and School of Hotel Administration only). Early decision: Nov. 10. Regular admissions: Dec 15. Financial aid: Feb. 15. Housing: Processed upon admission. Campus interviews: required for school of Hotel Admin. and College of Architecture, Art, and Planning, informative. Alumni interviews: recommended, informational (varies by program). SATs or ACTs: required. SAT IIs: required (varies by program). Essay question: applying classroom knowledge; influential person; or ask and answer your own question; and personal statement (optional). Apply to individual programs or schools.

University of Dallas

1845 East Northgate Drive, Irving, TX 75062

Bulwark of academic traditionalism in Big D. Despite being a "university," U of D has only 1,200 undergraduates. Except for the Business Leaders of Tomorrow program, the curriculum is exclusively liberal arts. The only outpost of Roman Catholic education between Loyola of New Orleans and University of San Diego.

While many universities around the nation have reexamined their Eurocentric core curriculums, the University of Dallas—the best Roman Catholic college south of Washington—remains proudly dedicated to fostering students in "the study of great deeds and works of Western civilization." "Imagine a party where someone makes a joke about Plato or Dante, and everybody cracks up. That's UD in a nutshell," says

<aside>

Website: www.udallas.edu
Location: Suburban
Total Enrollment: 3,542
Undergraduates: 1,200

</aside>

(Continued)

Male/Female: 42/58

SAT Ranges: V 550–670
  M 540–660

ACT Range: 23–28

Financial Aid: 27%

Expense: Pr $

Phi Beta Kappa: Yes

Applicants: 1,175

Accepted: 78%

Enrolled: 31%

Grad in 6 Years: 61%

Returning Freshmen: 83%

Academics: ✍ ✍ ✍

Social: ☎ ☎

Q of L: ★ ★ ★

Admissions: (972) 721-5266

Email Address: undadmis@
  acad.udallas.edu

Strongest Programs:
  Biology
  English
  Politics
  Psychology
  History

one student. And appropriately for a Roman Catholic school, much of the focus is on Rome, where most of the sophomore class treks every year. The unique and intense program focuses on the art and architecture of Rome, the philosophy of man and being, classical literature, Italian, and the development of Western civilization.

UD's 744-acre campus occupies a pastoral home in a Dallas suburb on top of "the closest thing this region has to a hill." Texas Stadium, home of the Dallas Cowboys, is right across the street. A major portion of the campus is situated around the Braniff Mall, a landscaped and lighted gathering place near the Braniff Memorial Tower, the school's landmark. The primary tone of the buildings is brown, and the architecture, as described by one student, is "post-1950s, done in brick, typical Catholic-institutional." While it may not be a picture-perfect school, it does have a beautiful chapel and a state-of-the-art science building. A new four-building Art Village is home to enlarged sculpture, painting, printmaking, and ceramics creations.

The curriculum can be daunting for those unaccustomed to the rigors of a more traditional liberal arts education. There's a heavy dose of classics (which leads to those late-night Roman jam sessions). English is the most popular major, followed by politics, economics, math, and history. Political philosophy is also a popular major, although students claim that most courses tend to be slanted toward the conservative side. One junior reports "philosophy and politics set the tone of the campus." Students say the math and education departments need improvement. The Business Leaders of Tomorrow program can be completed in addition to any undergraduate major. It includes introductory courses in business management, an internship, a mentor who is a business professional, and a choice of electives from the Graduate School of Management—all designed to prepare students to be future leaders. Premed students are well served by the biology and chemistry programs, and a majority of UD graduates go on to grad school.

The Rome semester is considered part of the UD Western Civilization core curriculum, which takes up close to half the requirements for a bachelor's degree. Included in the core are heavy doses of philosophy, history, literature, science, and math, as well as a serious foreign language requirement. Two theology courses (including Scripture and Western Theological Tradition) are also required of all students. Those inclined toward the sciences may take advantage of the John B. O'Hara Chemical Science Institute, which offers a hands-on nine-week summer program to prepare new students for independent research.

"Philosophy and politics set the tone of the campus."

Students report that the academic pressure and the workload can be intense. "The academic climate here is extremely rigorous," says a classics and drama double major. "You can either decide that the work is difficult and strive to accomplish, or get overwhelmed and crumble." A senior English major describes the school as "competitive and rigorous, based strongly on critical thinking, examination, writing, and discussion." The university uses no teaching assistants, and professors are easy to get to know. "We have outstanding faculty who are personally committed to students and to teaching them and not to advancing their own academic status," one student says. Getting into the small, personal classes is rarely a problem, and counseling receives high marks.

"UD is an ultraconservative university," says one senior. "Liberals are not exactly welcomed with open arms, although there are numerous forums for discussion."

About 70 percent of UD students are Catholic, and many of them choose this school because of its religious affiliation. Fifty-six percent are from Texas, and 13 percent of the student body are Hispanic. Seven percent are Asian-American and 1 percent is African-American. Students say that racial tension is not a problem on campus, although UDers tend to lean to the right politically. "UD is an ultraconservative university," says one senior. "Liberals are not exactly welcomed with open arms, although there are numerous forums for discussion." Tradition and religion govern rules on dorms and conduct.

UD offers various merit scholarships, ranging from $1,000 to full tuition, but no athletic scholarships. Everyone under twenty-one who doesn't reside at home with their parents must live on campus in single-sex or coed-by-floor dorms, "where visitation regulations are relatively strict," one student reports. As for the dorms, they're "not luxurious, but they are comfortable," one student reports. The most popular dorms are Jerome (all-female) and Madonna (all-male). At Gregory, the dorm reserved for those who like to party, the goings-on are less than saintly. In addition to a spacious and comfortable dining hall with a wonderful view of North Dallas, there is Rathskeller, which serves snacks and fast food (and great conversation). A car is a must for off-campus life since there is virtually no reliable public transportation in the Dallas/Fort Worth Metroplex.

The University of Dallas is unusual for a Texas school in that its entire population does not salivate at the sight of a football or basketball. Save for the Groundhogs, UD's rugby team, students rarely mention their Division III athletics. "Athletics will always be overshadowed by the academic commitments of the students," says one student. Intramural sports, on the other hand, are well organized and very popular, and chess is a favored activity. With no fraternities or sororities at UD, the student government sponsors most on-campus entertainment. Three free movies a week, dances, and visiting speakers are usually on the agenda. Church-related and religious activities provide fulfilling social outlets

> **"The academic climate here is extremely rigorous."**

for a goodly number of students. Annual events include Mallapalooza, a spring music festival, and Groundhog, a party on Groundhog's Day weekend. Then there's Charity Week in the fall, when the junior class plans a week's worth of fund-raising events. Each year students dread Sadie Hawkins Day and the annual Screw Your Roommate dance—dark nights of the soul, each. The university can be vigorous in enforcing restrictive drinking rules, and, as a result, it is difficult for a minor to drink at campus events.

Students describe Irving as "a suburb, just like any other," but the Metroplex offers almost unlimited possibilities, including a full agenda for bar-hopping on Lower Greenville Avenue, about ten minutes away. The West End and Deep Ellum offer a taste of shopping and Dallas's alternative music scene. And for the more adventurous, New Orleans isn't too far away.

UD is without a doubt the best Catholic-affiliated university south of Washington, D.C. Students pride themselves on being the "Philosopher Kings of the twenty-first century," but their roots go back to the Roman thinkers of an earlier era. The mix of religion and liberal arts can serve a certain breed of students well. In the words of one senior, "The best thing about the college is the amazing respect that professors have for their students, especially after Rome. It makes you feel like you can accomplish anything, and after four years at UD, you usually can."

> *UD is without a doubt the best Catholic-affiliated university south of Washington, D.C. Students pride themselves on being the "Philosopher Kings of the twenty-first century," but their roots go back to the Roman thinkers of an earlier era.*

Overlaps

University of Texas–Austin, Texas A&M, Notre Dame, Baylor, University of Texas–Arlington.

If You Apply To ➤

Dallas: Early action: Dec 1. Regular admissions, financial aid, and housing: Feb. 15. Does not guarantee to meet demonstrated need. Campus interviews: recommended, evaluative. Alumni interviews: optional, informational. SATs or ACTs: required. SAT IIs: optional. Accepts the Common Application. Essay question: describe a character in fiction, a historical figure, or a creative work (as in art, music, science, etc.) that has had an influence on you, and explain that influence.

Dartmouth College

6016 McNutt Hall, Hanover, NH 03755

The smallest Ivy and the one with the strongest emphasis on undergraduates. Traditionally the most conservative member of the Ivy League, it has been steered leftward in recent years. Ivy ties notwithstanding, Dartmouth has more in common with places like Colgate, Williams, and Middlebury. Great place for those who like the outdoors.

Website: www.dartmouth.edu
Location: Rural
Total Enrollment: 5,386
Undergraduates: 4,057
Male/Female: 52/48
SAT Ranges: V 660–760
  M 670–760
ACT Range: 29–33
Financial Aid: 47%
Expense: Pr $ $ $ $
Phi Beta Kappa: Yes
Applicants: 10,188
Accepted: 21%
Enrolled: 50%
Grad in 6 Years: 92%
Returning Freshmen: 96%
Academics: ✍ ✍ ✍ ✍ ✍
Social: 🍷 🍷 🍷 🍷 🍷
Q of L: ★ ★ ★
Admissions: (603) 646-2875
Email Address: admissions.
  office@dartmouth.edu

Strongest Programs:
  Biological Sciences
  Computer Science
  Engineering
  Economics
  Languages
  Psychological and Brain
    Sciences
  Studio Art
  Women's, Native American,
    and Environmental
    Studies

Dartmouth is truly a different species of Ivy. The Big Green has the highest graduation rate in the United States; it is one of the safest campuses in the United States; it is a college among universities; it has the smallest total enrollment in the Ancient Eight; and it is the most undergraduate-friendly. All of this has resulted in a mad rush of high-school students lining up for admission.

Dartmouth has turned out lots of businessmen but relatively few academicians, something the administration has been trying to change for some time now. When former president James Freedman was hired in the 1980s, he was charged with the task of "leading Dartmouth out of the sandbox" and making it a hospitable place with a more scholarly feeling. He said then that he wanted students "whose greatest pleasures may not come from the camaraderie of classmates but from the lonely acts of writing poetry, or mastering the cello, or solving mathematical riddles, or translating Catullus." (The reference to Catullus may have been the president's little esoteric joke. The Latin poet Catullus wrote erotic, sometimes obscene, verse on topics that included his passion for his mistress Lesbia, a boy named Juventius, and the sexual excesses of Julius Caesar.) Today's Dartmouth hardly resembles the Dartmouth of yesteryear, when liberal elements—mainly women and minorities—squared off against the self-proclaimed heirs of the Dartmouth tradition.

Set in the "small, Norman Rockwell town" of Hanover, New Hampshire, Dartmouth's picturesque campus is arrayed around a quaint New England green with Baker Library at one end and the college-owned Hanover Inn at the other. Although the campus architecture ranges from Romanesque to postmodern, the dominant theme is copper-topped Colonial frame. The nearest significant urban area (Boston) is two hours away, but major artists (including Itzhak Perlman) and groups visit the Hopkins Center for the Creative and Performing Arts, adding a touch of culture to the rural campus. Recent additions include the new $30 million Berry Library.

"Courses are generally very rigorous."

Much is questioned and considered at Dartmouth, and academic excellence is a given. "Courses are generally very rigorous," says a senior, citing "a semester's worth of material crammed into ten weeks." The Big Green also rates as one of the top in the country for undergraduate teaching. Three professional schools—business, engineering, and medicine—provide additional resources, but Dartmouth's passion still lies in undergraduate liberal arts. Most popular majors include government, history, English, biology, and economics. Students complain that teaching in the math department could improve. Dartmouth is perhaps best known for foreign languages, including Hebrew and Arabic, which are taught through the Intensive Language Model developed by John Rassias, a nationally renowned language professor. Computer science is also among the best in the nation, thanks in no small part to the late John Kemeny, the former Dartmouth president who coinvented time-sharing and the BASIC language. With the most extensive undergraduate facilities in the nation, computer literacy is a way of life at Dartmouth; indeed, the school has gone further than any other college in the nation in extending computing and word processing to every aspect of the curriculum, from physics to philosophy. Virtually every academic classroom and all residential dorms are networked. Dartmouth is also the first of the Ivies and one of the first in the nation to implement a wireless network so students can do research and check their email from the center of the Green.

Dartmouth also offers its students a wide variety of special programs, including the Presidential Scholars Program, which offers one-on-one research assistantships with faculty, and the Senior Fellowship Program, which empowers students to undertake interdisciplinary research projects. Another program, the Women in Science Project, encourages female students to pursue their interest in science, mathematics, and engineering, offering mentors, speakers, and even research apprenticeships for first-year students. Still another bonus is the Montgomery Fellowships, which bring well-known politicians, writers, and others to the campus for periods ranging from a few days to several months.

Students are generally enthusiastic about their professors. "I have amazing profs who are excellent teachers as well as excellent scholars," says a government major. Another student adds, "Professors often hold study sessions during the weekend before exams and

"I have amazing profs who are excellent teachers as well as excellent scholars."

invite you for dinner in their homes." Academic and career counseling resources are abundant but vary in quality. "The initial advising system for freshmen is minimal," says a senior, "and after the first year, students must take the initiative in developing advising relationships of their own."

Incoming students receive immediate instruction for the use of the written word at the college level: a composition course followed by a mandatory freshman seminar with an emphasis on writing. Students must also take ten courses distributed across the following areas: arts, literature, philosophy, religion or history, international studies, social analysis, technology or applied science, quantitative reasoning, and natural or physical science. Students are expected to become proficient in at least one foreign language and must take courses in U.S., Western, and non-Western studies. In addition, Dartmouth has a senior culminating activity—a thesis, public report, exhibition, seminar, production, or demonstration—which allows students to pull together the work of their major and add a creative and intellectual twist of their own.

The school's most notable eccentricity is the Dartmouth Plan, whereby the school operates year-round with four ten-week terms a year, including one during the summer. The D Plan allows students to take classes any of the four seasons they wish, with only the requirement that they be on campus during their entire freshman and senior years and the summer after their sophomore year. Students use their time off for jobs, internships, or travel. About 60 percent of the student body spend at least one term participating in one of Dartmouth's forty-four programs of foreign study, either for intensive language training or a departmental study (drama in London or environmental studies in Zimbabwe, for example). The college is also part of the Twelve College Exchange* and the Maritime Studies Program.*

Dartmouth was founded in 1769 to educate Native Americans, and since 1969 the college has made serious efforts to attract them. Dartmouth has the most outstanding Native American program in the country today, and 3 percent of the student body is made up of Native students. The formerly all-male school

"Students at Dartmouth are passionate and busy."

went coed in 1972, and nearly half of the current student body is female. African-Americans account for 5 percent of the student body, Hispanics for 6 percent, and Asian-Americans for 10 percent. "Students at Dartmouth are passionate and busy,"

The school's most notable eccentricity is the Dartmouth Plan, whereby the school operates year-round with four ten-week terms a year, including one during the summer.

Most first-year students begin their Dartmouth career with a camping trip led by an upperclass student or faculty member, and the Outing Club is the most popular student organization.

says a student. Another adds that students tend to be "incredible, interesting, and brilliant," and (perhaps missing the irony) "humble." Dartmouth is need-blind in admissions and guarantees to meet the demonstrated financial need of all accepted students. It was the first of a growing number of privately financed institutions to go into the business of selling tax-exempt bonds through a state authority to under-write loans to families at low interest rates. Within the last few years, Dartmouth has added roughly $4 million to its scholarship resources, mainly through reduced loan amounts for students. Additionally, Dartmouth is trying to lure more middle-class students to campus by offering bigger grants to students whose parents earn less than $60,000 per year. No merit scholarships are awarded, and athletic scholarships are prohibited at all Ivy League institutions.

On the housing front, the thirty-four dorms have been grouped into eleven clusters that organize activities and programs and provide a sense of community. There are also several academic affinity and special-interest housing options. Separate first-year housing will be provided as an alternative starting with the class of 2005. Rooms are large and homey—some of the older ones have working fire-places—and the maintenance service even cleans the bathrooms. "Dorms are generally

"In Hanover, it's odd when strangers don't smile at you as you pass them in town."

very comfortable, well maintained, and full of character," says an Italian and bio-chemistry major. Housing is guaranteed only for the first year, but some students say that getting a room can be a problem. "Recently some sophomores (the class with the worst priority) have had trouble getting housing on campus," one senior explains. And what about food? Students establish a declining balance account at the beginning of each term, the size of which is left up to the individual. First year students, however, must stick to a standardized plan for their first term. Eighty-seven percent of students live on campus. Students do live off campus, but gener-ally in larger, rented homes with several other students rather than in apartments.

Dartmouth's Greek system is nationally famous for, among other things, having inspired the movie *Animal House*, cowritten by a 1963 Dartmouth grad; fraternities and sororities claim 34 percent of the men and 27 percent of the women, respec-tively. The college's powerful and intensely loyal Greek alumni are the self-appointed keepers of the flame. This burgeoning family tree began to take root in the days before the interstate highway system, when Dartmouth males had nothing to do on Saturday nights but participate in male-bonding activities of the sort rarely seen these days outside beer commercials. Almost twenty years ago, the faculty rec-ommended abolishing the fraternities and, according to one junior, they continue to be a point of contention. After an outcry from the alumni, the school compro-mised by putting the most boisterous on probation. Under the two-year Student Life Initiative, a Greek-life steering committee has developed a set of more rigorous stan-dards for the system. The Initiative has made significant progress in creating more social and residential alternatives for students throughout campus. Recent additions include a new dance club in the student center, a joint kosher-halal dining facility, and free athletic tickets. The Big Green also has the most elaborately organized alumni associations in the country—testimony to the loyalty it inspires. It seems as if every other grad has a title like deputy assistant class secretary, and many return to Hanover when they retire, further cementing their bonds with the college (and driving local real-estate prices beyond the reach of most faculty members).

Greeks are no mean contributors to the college's longtime nickname of its sur-rounding city, "Hangover." In response to the excessive imbibing of some fraternity members, Dartmouth was one of the first to develop a counseling and educational program designed to combat the abuse of alcohol. The administration has set out on a long-range plan to curb fraternity drinking and provide alternative student

The administration has set out on a long-range plan to curb fraternity drinking and provide alternative student opportunities.

opportunities. There is, however, a bar on campus called the Lone Pine Tavern, which is described by one student as a place "where students play everything from Scrabble and chess to checkers and Jenga while listening to jazz and acoustic groups."

Of all Dartmouth's traditions, perhaps the best known is Winter Carnival, an annual festival that draws seekers from all over the Eastern seaboard. In one popular Homecoming ritual, freshmen build a bonfire sixty-four railroad tiers high and run around the flames the number of times of their year. During the spring, students celebrate Green Key weekend, which one student calls, "an excuse to drink under the guise of community service." Another unusual tradition, Tubestock, is a day when the entire sophomore class floats down the Connecticut River in rafts.

To the city dweller, Hanover is halfway to the North Pole, but to the outdoors lover it's nearly paradise. "In Hanover, it's odd when strangers don't smile at you as you pass them in town," admits a senior. Residents of Hanover flock to theater productions and women's basketball games alike. Dartmouth students serve as tutors, coaches, and role models for the children here. Dartmouth's own ski area is twenty minutes distant, the Connecticut River is even closer for canoeing and kayaking, and the great outdoors is literally steps away. More adventurous types take to the wilds of Dartmouth's twenty-seven thousand acre land grant in the northeast corner of the state, where cabins can be rented for $5 a night. Most first-year students begin their Dartmouth career with a camping trip led by an upperclass student or faculty member, and the Outing Club is the most popular student organization.

Love of the outdoor life extends to varsity athletics. Recent success stories include the coed sailing team, the men's cross-country, rowing, soccer, skiing, and basketball teams, and the women's basketball, ice hockey, lacrosse, and soccer teams. Few Dartmouth students miss the biannual excursion to the Dartmouth–Harvard football game, when thousands of Big Green devotees descend upon Cambridge. Dartmouth's sports center boasts, among other things, a 2,100-seat arena, a four thousand square-foot fitness center, and the only permanent three-glass-wall squash court in North America. Recent construction includes the $3 million Scully-Fahey Field, an artificial-athletic-turf facility.

Perhaps the best thing about Dartmouth is its combination of superior academics, a blossoming social life, and a small community atmosphere. Dartmouth enjoys a tremendous sense of community and tradition, which, while supporting an amazing diversity of talents, interests, and backgrounds, allows one to speak of a common Dartmouth experience. Students love the "work hard, play hard" ethic, and most cannot imagine themselves attending school anywhere else in the world.

> ## Overlaps
>
> **Harvard, Brown, Princeton, Cornell, Yale**

If You Apply To ➢

Dartmouth: Early decision: Nov. 1. Regular admissions: Jan. 1. Financial aid: Feb. 1. Housing: July 1. Guarantees to meet demonstrated need. Campus and alumni interviews: optional, evaluative. SATs or ACTs: required. SAT IIs: required (any three). Accepts the Common Application and electronic applications. Essay question: highlight of summer; which pursuits outside or inside school most important; highlight of academic experiences; and create an essay question and answer it.

Davidson College

P.O. Box 1737, Davidson, NC 28036

"The Dartmouth of the South" is how Davidson has always been styled. Goes head to head with Washington and Lee (VA) for honors as the most selective liberal arts college below the Mason–Dixon Line. At 1,673 students, it is slightly bigger than Rhodes and Sewanee and slightly smaller than W&L.

Website: www.davidson.edu
Location: Small town
Total Enrollment: 1,673
Undergraduates: 1,673
Male/Female: 49/51
SAT Ranges: V 620–710
  M 615–700
ACT Range: 26–31
Financial Aid: 30%
Expense: Pr $ $ $ $
Phi Beta Kappa: Yes
Applicants: 3,363
Accepted: 35%
Enrolled: 40%
Grad in 6 Years: 90%
Returning Freshmen: 96%
Academics: ✍ ✍ ✍ ✍ ½
Social: ☎ ☎ ☎
Q of L: ★ ★ ★ ★
Admissions: (800) 768-0380
Email Address:
  admission@davidson.edu

Strongest Programs:
  International Studies
  History
  English
  Biology
  Political Science
  Premed/Medical Humanities
  Psychology

Davidson College is a leader among the elite liberal arts schools of the South, and students from all over the country are taking note. Curiously overlooked by many because of its small size and Southern locale, Davidson could be described as an "Ivy wannabe." But the size, along with strong core requirements and a pervasive honor code, distinguish this school from many of its contemporaries and draw cheers from students. "The small size allows for lots of support, and it is very easy to find your place," says a senior.

Located in a beautiful stretch of North Carolina's Piedmont, Davidson's wooded campus features Georgian and Greek Revival architecture. The central campus is a designated arboretum that develops, maintains, and displays a collection of the woody plants that thrive in the area. It's used as an outdoor laboratory for students, and markers identify the varieties of trees and shrubs. Despite the building boom, Davidson retains its original quadrangle (circa 1837) and two dorms and literary society halls built in the 1850s. The new Alvarez College Union and Duke Family Performance Hall make up the Knoblach Campus Center, and the old campus center is being renovated into a music building.

Davidson operates under an honor code that allows students to take exams independently and to leave doors unlocked. "Everyone follows it in academics and life," says one junior. "It is not uncommon to see money taped to a bench or a pole saying it was found there." Every entering freshman agrees in writing to abide by the code, and all work handed in is signed with the word "pledged."

"The small size allows for lots of support, and it is very easy to find your place."

Core requirements are extensive, spanning fine art, literature, history, math, religion, philosophy, science, social science, physical education, composition, cultural diversity, and foreign languages. Many can be met through a two-year interdisciplinary humanities program.

The academic climate is said to be "strenuous" but not cut-throat. "The courses are demanding and challenging, but the atmosphere is not competitive," a senior says. The most popular majors are English, biology, political science, history, and psychology. Areas that do not receive high marks include economics and philosophy. The faculty is highly praised by students. "Professors are all focused on teaching and very helpful and accessible, as well as experts in their fields," says an economics major. A junior notes faculty-student interaction is not limited to the classroom: "I've been to professors' houses for desserts, chicken dinners, and movies."

Academic options are plentiful. "Davidson students truly want to learn and enjoy knowledge. It is common for academic discussions to occur just for fun," says a math major. The Center for Interdisciplinary Studies allows students to develop and design their own interdisciplinary majors. A 3–2 engineering program is available in conjunction with five other excellent universities. The college is committed to foreign studies—more than 60 percent of the students go abroad—and the Dean Rusk Program for International Studies beefs up offerings in this field. Armed with a Sloan Foundation grant, the college is attempting to integrate technological studies and the liberal arts through courses such as From Petroleum to Penicillin, and

Sex, Technology, and Morality. The School for Field Studies allows biology majors to spend a semester studying environmental issues in other countries. The college has added a concentration in education and also offers concentrations in applied math, gender studies, ethnic and international studies, medical humanities, neuroscience, computer science, and Southern studies. Back home, class size is restricted; you won't find a room other than the cafeteria with more than fifty students in it. More than 70 percent of all classes have fewer than twenty students.

Most Davidson students come from affluent and otherwise august Southern families and are the children of doctors, ministers, and businessmen. Many are Presbyterian, as the school has strong Presbyterian roots. There is an unusually strong national feel here; less than 20 percent of the student body hails from in state. Five percent of the student body is African-American, 3 percent Hispanic, and 3 percent Asian-American. An Andrew Mellon Foundation grant is helping the school welcome minorities by increasing diversity

> "Davidson students truly want to learn and enjoy knowledge."

programs in dorms, educating faculty on specific student populations, and hosting artist- or scholar-in-residence programs. Davidson lures top students with a number of annual merit scholarships, and athletic scholarships are available in twenty sports. Freshmen are guaranteed to have all demonstrated financial needs met, and the need is usually met for all four years. The five-day orientation program is elaborate and includes such activities as a regatta, scavenger hunt, and Freshman Cake Race. The financial-aid packages usually get good reviews. "When compared to all of the other schools I applied to, Davidson had the most generous aid package and also contained the least portion in loans," a senior biology major says.

Ninety-one percent of students live on campus in coed or single-sex dorms. A new performance hall and student union opened recently. Freshmen are housed together in two five-story halls and get to eat in Vail Commons, which gets high marks for food and socializing. Freshmen receive special attention from the Residence-Life Office staff, who devote considerable time to finding the best match for future roomies. Upperclassmen may live either in the dorms, off campus,

> "The dorms at Davidson are much, much nicer than most other college dorms."

or in college-owned cottages on the campus perimeter that hold about ten students each. Seniors get apartments with private bedrooms. "The dorms at Davidson are much, much nicer than most other college dorms," a senior says. Most upperclassmen dine in one of ten eating clubs—seven fraternities and three all-women houses—that maintain their own cooks and serve meals family-style.

The eating clubs are the center of social life on campus. All but one are situated in Patterson Court, where freshmen are not allowed for the first three weeks of school. The fees the houses charge go toward not only meals but also parties and other campus-wide events. The fraternities, which 41 percent of men join, are not much different from the eating clubs, and freshmen simply sign up for the group they want to join on Self-Selection Night with no "rushing" allowed. Davidson adds to the egalitarianism by requiring that most parties—"at least two per weekend" at the eating clubs—be open to the entire community. Still, a few students feel the need for social outlets other than Patterson Court. "Davidson is definitely not a suitcase school," a senior says. "In fact, some people would say that one of Davidson's flaws is that there is too much going on on campus and it's hard to choose which events to go to." Alcohol policies work to an extent, but it's always easy for underage students to be served.

Students hit coffee shops and cafés in Davidson and volunteer there, but not much else goes on in the small town for students. North Carolina's largest city, Charlotte, is twenty miles away, and students traverse there for clubs and other attractions.

Curiously overlooked by many because of its small size and Southern locale, Davidson could be described as an "Ivy wannabe."

The School for Field Studies allows biology majors to spend a semester studying environmental issues in other countries.

The neighboring town of Cornelius is only a ten-minute drive, so students can catch movies and a drink there. The school's small-town setting is quiet and quaint, and Davidson maintains facilities at nearby Lake Norman for sailing, swimming, and water-skiing. Myrtle Beach and skiing are several hours away, albeit in different directions. Intramural sports are popular, and there's a titanic athletic complex. Davidson's varsity athletic teams compete in the Southern Conference, and the men's basketball and women's volleyball teams brought home championships recently.

Davidson is strengthening its position as a top liberal arts school as more and more high-achieving students around the country hear of the opportunities and homey atmosphere at this little ol' Carolina school. "From enjoying a beer with a professor to the college president who holds a strawberries-and-champagne party for seniors to freshman hall mixers, people make Davidson," one satisfied senior says.

If You Apply To ➢ **Davidson:** Early decision: Nov. 15. Regular admission: Jan. 2. Financial aid: Feb. 15. Guarantees to meet demonstrated need. Campus and alumni interviews: optional, informational. SATs or ACTs: required. SAT IIs: recommended. Accepts the Common Application. Essay question: significant experience; important issue; influential person; influential character.

University of Dayton

300 College Park, Dayton, OH 45469-1300

Among a cohort of second-tier Roman Catholic institutions in the Midwest that includes Duquesne, Xavier (OH), U. of St. Louis, DePaul, and Loyola of Chicago. Drawing cards include business, engineering, education, and the sciences. The city of Dayton is not particularly enticing and UD's appeal is largely regional.

Anyone who thinks that this generation's crop of college students subscribes to postmodern cynicism ought to take a peek at Dayton, where optimism and Christian charity are alive and well. Dayton students work hard and play hard, and according to one senior English major, "We know when to study, but we know how to have a good time."

Founded by the Society of Mary (Marianists), Dayton continues to emphasize that order's devotion to service. More than one thousand students volunteer their time in twenty-five different public service areas. And like many religiously affiliated schools, Dayton prides itself on the closeness and sense of community among its students and faculty members. "I hate to use a cliché," says one education junior, "but UD is one big happy family."

UD's campus is on the southern boundary of the city, secluded from the traffic and bustle of downtown. The more historic buildings on the park-like campus make up the central core of the campus and blend architectural charm with modern technological conveniences. And the campus is full of wide-open space, recreational areas, and beautiful landscaping. The Jesse Philips Humanities Center features a state-of-the-art multimedia lab and recital hall with the latest sound and recording equipment. The Bombeck Family Learning Center (named for the late UD alumnus Erma Bombeck) has undergone a $3.8 million conversion.

UD students take full advantage of the strong offerings found in engineering, business, education, and the sciences. The most popular majors are communication, marketing, psychology, mechanical engineering, and biology. Weaker offerings include music, theater, and physical education. Most students agree that the academic climate can be either demanding or laid back, depending on the course and the major. "The academic climate is challenging," says a senior, "but the university provides as much tutorial and faculty support as needed." A classmate adds, "Many courses are very difficult, but students also try to help each other learn."

Dayton's general education requirements include courses in five "domains of knowledge": arts, history, philosophy and religion, physical and life sciences, and social sciences. Faculty members in the College of Arts and Science have developed a twelve-course core curriculum that satisfies the general education requirements through an interdisciplinary program that clumps mandatory classes into sequences pertinent to academic disciplines. Programs initiated recently include majors in operations management, economics, and business economics. Students with at least a 1300 combined SAT score or a 30 ACT score and who place in the top 10 percent of their graduating class or have a 3.7 GPA may join the University Honors Program. This involves taking special courses, including one that hosts a nationally renowned guest author. The administration notes that the majority of the participants who have applied to graduate school have won a full assistantship or fellowship.

The Interdepartmental Summer Study Abroad Program is a popular ticket to Europe's most exciting cities, while the Immersion Program in Third World countries is much praised by participants. Students in engineering, business administration, computer science, and biology can take advantage of the cooperative education opportunities, and everyone can benefit from the information science center, which houses computer classrooms and labs. All students purchase a computer upon entering UD in conjunction with the university's computer requirement.

Most classes are kept to minimum sizes, between twenty-five and fifty students, and students speak enthusiastically about contacts with professors outside of the classroom. "Students receive great personal attention from their teachers," says a sophomore. New students unsure of their majors can take advantage of First Year Experience, a structured program where students are required to meet with their advisors once a week. This enables freshmen to explore majors, set career goals, schedule for upcoming terms, as well as learn about the services, facilities, and opportunities UD has to offer.

Students, the majority of whom are Roman Catholics, tend to be "conservative, fun-loving...with a passion for the 'J. Crew' image," says one student. Two-thirds of Dayton's students are native Ohioans. Minorities make up only 6 percent of the student population. The Task Force on

"We know when to study, but we know how to have a good time."

Women's Issues, an Office for Diverse Student Populations, and an updated sexual-harassment policy demonstrate UD's growing sensitivity to campus issues. More than 24 percent of incoming students rank in the top tenth of their high-school class, an indication that UD is perhaps more selective than it is given credit for. Dayton's athletic scholarships go to all sports except football. There are also many scholarship and leadership awards that go to those with superior academic credentials.

Seventy-six percent of students are campus residents; those that live off campus generally live adjacent to it. First-year students can choose from three residence halls, one of which is smoke-free, and housing is generally available for all undergraduate students. Upperclassmen often enter the lottery for coveted university-owned apartments and houses located in an adjacent student neighborhood, that also contains privately owned homes. Students praise the clean and well-maintained rooms: "UD housing is awesome," exclaims one enthusiast. The best dorm for freshmen, according to many, is Marycrest, with "huge rooms and loads of storage space." Sophomores have an opportunity to live in Virginia Kettering, a residence hall whose amenities evoke luxurious apartments and is also known as "the Hilton on

(Continued)
Email Address:
admission@udayton.edu

Strongest Programs:
Communication
Engineering
Teacher Education
Business
Prephysical Therapy

Sophomores have an opportunity to live in Virginia Kettering, a residence hall whose amenities evoke luxurious apartments and is also known as "the Hilton on the Hill."

The L. William Crotty Center for Enterprise Leadership recently opened in 1999, allowing enterprising students to jumpstart their own business ventures.

the Hill." The food in the dining halls that dot the campus is generally well received; one dining hall is located in one of the first-year dorms, another in the sophomore complex, and the third is centrally located in the student union.

The student neighborhood (a.k.a. "the Ghetto") serves as a sort of continuous social center. A lit porchlight beckons party-seeking students to join the weekend festivities. Because the university owns most of the properties, a twenty-four-hour campus security patrol keeps watch over the area. Block parties are perennial warm-weather favorites, but most smaller affairs are also popular. Much of the social life takes place here or on campus. The more adventurous weekend excursions are trips to Ohio State University, Ohio University, and Cincinnati or Indianapolis. But the best road trip is the Dayton-to-Daytona trip after spring finals, a seventeen-hour trek that draws loads of students each year. Partying on campus is commonplace and controlled, but parties have sized down due to the university's enforcement of the twenty-one-year-old drinking age. Kegs are allowed only at parties where the legal drinking age of the partiers can be validated. Still, "There is a 'three strikes, you're out' policy regarding drinking, but students at UD, on average, enjoy drinking and have no problem being served at off-campus parties. Greek organizations draw 14 percent of UD men and 19 percent of the women, with all chapters playing an active role in the community service and social life.

"UD housing is awesome."

More important, though, are sports, particularly basketball. The football team, which is Division I-AA, plays in the Pioneer Conference and the soccer team won the 2000 Atlantic 10 regular-season championship. UD is in the Atlantic 10 for Division I athletics in all other sports. When students aren't cheering, they can participate in an extensive intramural program. Other activities in the city include a minor-league baseball team, art institute, aviation museum, symphony, and ballet, which are all just minutes away from campus by bus. A large shopping mall is also easily accessible. Those who hunger for a more cosmopolitan atmosphere can frequent Cincinnati and its restaurants, shops, and sports arenas.

The success of Dayton's attempts to provide its students with a high quality of life and a sense of cohesiveness is reflected in many of the students' comments about the terrific social life and family like atmosphere among both students and faculty. Dayton's Board of Trustees established a long-range plan called "Vision 2005," which builds upon Dayton's strengths as a Roman Catholic, Marianist, comprehensive university. As a mid-size university where the undergraduates come first, Dayton has managed to maintain an exciting balance of personal attention, academic challenge, and all-American fun.

Overlaps

Miami University (OH), Ohio University, Xavier, Ohio State, University of Cincinnati

If You Apply To ➤

Dayton: Rolling admissions: Jan. 1 (priority). Financial aid: Mar. 31. Campus interviews: recommended, informational. No alumni interviews. SATs or ACTs: required. No SAT IIs. Accepts electronic applications. Essay question: personal statement addressing your background.

Deep Springs College

Deep Springs, CA Mailing address: Dyer, NV 89010-9803

Picture twenty-five Ivy League–caliber men living and learning in a remote desert outpost—that's Deep Springs. DS occupies a handful of ranch-style buildings set on fifty thousand acres on the arid border of Nevada and California. Most students transfer to highly selective colleges after two years.

At Deep Springs College, all work and no play doesn't make Jack a dull boy; it makes him one of twenty-five or so male students at this two-year institution that doubles as a working ranch. Bonding is easy here, and students enjoy a demanding and individualized education based on ranch life. Both, it seems, demand the same things: hard work, commitment, and pride in a job well done. Deep Springs College students are also rewarded for their efforts in other ways: tuition is free and so is room and board. Students pay only for books, travel, and personal items; the average cost of one year at Deep Springs is $500.

Many of the men who work, study, and live at this college have shunned acceptance at Ivy League schools to embrace the rigors of a truly unique approach to learning. Deep Springs students tend to be of the academic Renaissance-man variety with wide-ranging interests in many fields. Almost all transfer to the Ivies or others of the most prestigious universities after their two-year program, and 70 percent eventually earn a doctorate.

California's White Mountains provide a stunning backdrop for the Deep Springs campus, set on a barren plain 5,200 feet above sea level near the only water supply for miles around. The campus is an oasis-like cluster of trees and a lawn with eight "somewhat ramshackle" ranch-style buildings that were built from scratch by the class of 1919. Deep Springs is twenty-eight miles from the nearest town, a thriving metropolis known as Big Pine, population 950. The focal point of campus is the Main Building, a venerable ranch house that includes dorm rooms, a computer room, and offices. Faculty houses and the dining facilities are grouped around the circular lawn a few yards away, and the trappings of farm life surround the tiny settlement. The college has 170 acres under cultivation, mostly with alfalfa, and an assortment of barnyard animals. Once threatened with extinction (thanks to meager financial resources), the college launched a capital campaign that generated $18 million in only six years. True to its practical spirit, the school used much of the money to enhance facilities and put itself back on track to a long future.

Founded in 1917 by an industrialist who made a fortune in the electric-power industry, Deep Springs today remains true to its charter "to combine taxing practical work, rigorous academics, and genuine self-government." Ideals of self-government, reflectiveness, frugality, and community activity have weathered more than seventy-five years of a grueling academic climate. "The work here is very rigorous," says one student. "If you don't want to work hard physically, mentally, and emotionally, this isn't the place for you." Explains a freshman, "Our classes are very small—my largest so far had eighteen students—so it's hard to hide the fact that you haven't done a reading." Academic learning is the primary activity here, but stu-

"If you don't want to work hard physically, mentally, and emotionally, this isn't the place for you."

dents are also required to perform twenty hours per week of labor, which can include everything from harvesting alfalfa to cooking dinner. When asked which are the best majors, one wit exclaims, "Dairy is the most popular, but many students swear by irrigation."

Website:
    www.deepsprings.edu
Location: Rural
Total Enrollment: 26
Undergraduates: 26
Male/Female: 100/0
SAT Ranges: V 660–800
    M 690–800
Financial Aid: N/A
Expense: Pr $
Phi Beta Kappa: No
Applicants: 150
Accepted: 8%
Enrolled: 95%
Grad in 6 Years: N/A
Returning Freshmen: 95%
Academics: ✑ ✑ ✑ ✑ ½
Social: ☎
Q of L: ★ ★ ★
Admissions: (760) 872-2000
Email Address:
    apcom@deepsprings.edu

Strongest Programs:
    Liberal Arts
    Environmental Studies
    Philosophy

The students' input carries a lot of weight at this school. They help choose the college's faculty and even elect one of their own to be a voting member on the board of trustees. They play a determining role in admissions and curricular decisions. And they abide by a spartan community code that bans all drugs, including alcohol, and forbids anyone from leaving Deep Springs Valley, the fifty square miles of desert surrounding the campus, while classes are in session, except for medical visits and college business. Lest these rules sound unnecessarily strict, keep in mind that these are all decided upon and enforced by the student body, not the administration.

Like almost everything else about it, Deep Springs has an unorthodox academic schedule: two summer terms of seven weeks each, and a fall and spring semester of fourteen weeks each. Between seven and ten classes are offered every term. The faculty consists of three "permanent" professors (they sign on for five years), plus an average of four others who are hired on a temporary basis to teach for a term or two. The quality of particular academic areas varies as professors

"We all enjoy a comfortable level of deep brotherhood."

come and go. Overall, however, the teaching quality is reported to be "superb." "Professors here eat with students daily," reports one student. "I've often continued discussions over lunch and dinner that started a few hours earlier in class." Although the curriculum is altered yearly, students predict that literary theory and philosophy will always remain superior. The students control the academic program and quickly replace courses—and faculty—that do not work out. Foreign language offerings are still sparse, and lack of high-tech lab equipment puts a damper on chemistry and physics courses. "In eighth grade at least I had a microscope," says a student. Currently, the only required courses are in public speaking and composition.

Deep Springers aren't much for the latest conveniences, but computers have taken the campus by storm; there's one in each student's room, plus several in a common area. With class sizes ranging from two to fourteen, there is ample opportunity for close student-faculty interaction. Close living arrangements have fostered a kind of kinship between faculty and students. Students routinely visit their mentors in their homes, sometimes to confer on academic matters and sometimes to play soccer with their children.

Deep Springers can truly boast of being hand-picked to attend; of the approximately two hundred applications received each year, only thirteen students are accepted. Most DS students are from upper-middle-class families and typically rank in the top 3 percent of their high-school class. Many Deep Springers are transplanted urbanites; the rest hail

"One cool thing about DS is that you can do anything you want to your room."

from points scattered across the nation or across the seas. Political leanings run the gamut, and there is diversity even among this small population: seventy-six percent of the student body are white; Asian-Americans make up 20 percent; and Hispanics account for 4 percent. "We all enjoy a comfortable level of deep brotherhood," says a student. The college's single-sex status is a source of much discussion, as well as "the extent to which we're justified in removing ourselves so thoroughly from mainstream culture," states a freshman.

Dorm selection and maintenance is entirely the responsibility of the students. "One cool thing about DS is that you can do anything you want to your room," says a student. "Our walls are painted mauve and there is a pink queen-sized bed hanging from the ceiling called the 'Love Loft.'" Students all pitch in preparing the meals, from butchering the meat to milking the cows to washing the dishes. Given the sequestered location of DS, crime is not an issue. Safety, however, is another matter. "Sometimes we get charged by bulls," admits one student.

Social life can be a challenge. "Socializing takes place on the front porch when people gather and smoke," reports one student. When the moon is full, students go out en masse in the middle of the night to frolic in the seven-hundred-foot-high Eureka Sand Dunes with Frisbees and skis. "We slide down the Eureka Valley sand dunes au naturel," says one student. As for "recent technological advancement," they used to have one telephone line for the whole school; now they have six. Perhaps the most popular social activity on campus is conversation over a cup of coffee in the dining hall, where the chatter is usually lively until the wee hours of the morning. Other common activities are road trips to nearby national parks, hikes in the nearby mountains, and horseback riding. The Turkey Bowl, the potato harvest, the two-on-two basketball tournament, and Sludgefest, an annual event involving cleaning out the reservoir, are only some of the time-honored Deep Springs traditions. Critics of Deep Springs charge that DS cultivates arrogance and social backwardness among students who were too intellectual to be in the social mainstream during high school. They argue that students who come here are doomed to be misfits for life, citing a survey that shows many Deep Springers never marry. While that charge is debatable, even supporters of Deep Springs confess to a love-hate relationship with the college.

Perhaps more than any other school in the nation, Deep Springs is a community where students and faculty interact day to day on an intensely personal level. Though the financial commitment is small, the school demands an intense level of personal commitment. All must quickly learn how to get along in a community where the actions of each person affect everyone. Urban cowboys who dream of riding into the sunset are in for a rude awakening. For a select few, however, the camaraderie and soul-searching fostered in this tight-knit community can be mighty tempting—just stay clear of those bulls.

University of Delaware

Newark, DE 19716

Plenty of students dream of someday becoming Nittany Lions or Cavaliers—even Terrapins—but not many aspire to be Blue Hens. The challenge for UD is how to win its share of students without the name recognition that comes from big-time sports. Less than half the students are in-staters.

Sure, Delaware is a small state, but its flagship university is growing in reputation every year. The mid-sized University of Delaware offers a plethora of academic offerings, from engineering to education, all bolstered by ample research and study-abroad opportunities. Students say classes are more challenging as the competition to attend UD becomes more acute. Add in a healthy helping of rowdy athletic traditions, a thriving social scene, and a welcoming town atmosphere, and UD begins to resemble that all-American college experience that so many students seek.

Delaware's spacious one thousand-acre campus is an attractive mix of Colonial and modern geometric buildings with a sufficient number of shady and tanning areas. The campus is set among one of the nation's oldest Dutch elm groves, and in

Website: www.udel.edu
Location: Small city
Total Enrollment: 18,673
Undergraduates: 15,731
Male/Female: 41/59
SAT Ranges: V 530–610
  M 550–630
ACT Range: 22-26
Financial Aid: 37%

(Continued)

Expense: Pub $
Phi Beta Kappa: Yes
Applicants: 18,209
Accepted: 53%
Enrolled: 35%
Grad in 6 Years: 72%
Returning Freshmen: 88%
Academics: ✍ ✍ ✍
Social: ☎ ☎ ☎ ☎
Q of L: ★ ★ ★
Admissions: (302) 831-8125
Email Address:
admissions@udel.edu

Strongest Programs:
Chemical Engineering
Business Administration
Biological Sciences
Psychology
Nursing
English
History
Political Science

the fall the trees on the mall "set the mood for academia," one student says. The hub of the campus is a grassy green mall flanked by a distinguished-looking group of classic Georgian buildings. DuPont Hall, the home of College of Engineering, has been completely renovated with sixty thousand square feet of space for offices and laboratories.

Delaware's academic menu includes more than 124 majors ranging from the usual liberal arts and science departments to vocational programs like fashion merchandising. Boasting one of the largest undergraduate research programs in the country—six hundred students take part each year—Delaware recently added majors in health behavior management, food business management and technology, and information systems. Other new concentrations include cell and molecular biology and genetics, ancient Greek and Roman studies, music management, biomedical engineering, and aerospace. Engineering, especially chemical engineering, is generally agreed to be UD's specialty, with business not far behind. Elementary education, biology, and psychology are popular majors, and the music department is upwardly mobile, with a number of faculty members who have impressive professional performance credits. Meanwhile, students report that the math department could stand improvement. For those seeking a change of scenery, more than sixty study-abroad programs are available in twenty-five countries.

Most students find that courses at UD are becoming more challenging and rigorous as the school trains its sights on incoming students with increasingly impressive transcripts. "Due to the fact that it is getting so competitive to get into UD, the classes are becoming more competitive," says a history education major. Students in all programs must take reading and writing courses and a course stressing multicultural, ethnic, or gender content. Grading standards and quality of instruction are high. The outstanding honors program enrolls about five hundred students a year, and the undergraduate research and humanities semester programs also attract many of the university's best and brightest.

Students report that they have little trouble getting into classes, and they can take a couple of classes during the winter session to reduce their courseload during the regular semester. Most faculty members are accessible and "great." "The professors here are highly regarded in their fields, and they are almost always willing to include students in their research projects," a student says. Academic advising receives mixed reviews. "If you make the effort to get in touch with them then they are definitely there for you," a sociology major says. Career counselors, however, receive high marks across the board. "They can help you get a part-time job, an internship, and help with résumé writing and finding a job after graduation," one senior reports.

Only 41 percent of the student body are from the First State; many of the rest are from the Northeast. Most students are from public schools and according to one senior include the "hardworking and active," as well as the "very apathetic." Some students bemoan the lack of cultural diversity on campus. "Walking around

"The classes are becoming more competitive."

campus, you see a lot of white folks," a sociology major says. African-Americans account for a mere 6 percent of the student population, and Hispanics and Asian-Americans combine for another 6 percent. But many students note that the administration is trying to promote multiculturalism with "'beefed-up' diversity awareness and education." More than a quarter of freshmen receive merit scholarships, ranging from $1,000 to a complete package, and scholarships are also available in several sports, art, and music. In order to get the academic scholarships into the hands of the most deserving, the university maintains a search program that matches eligible Delaware students with potential scholarships.

Except for those commuting from home, freshmen are required to live on campus. Housing placement is done through lottery, but at least it's guaranteed housing for all four years, provided application deadlines are met. UD provides a wide assortment of accommodations, including coed and single-sex dorms (some with visiting hours and some without), singles, apartments, and suites. "My bed is better than mine at home," raves one criminal justice major. The special-interest communities, such as French House, International House, and Martin Luther King Jr. House, are now all located in three residence halls. All told, half of the students live in some form of university housing, while the commuters engage in mortal combat for nearby parking spaces. But a large number of students also live in houses and apartments within walking distance to campus. Meal plans must be purchased by students living in traditional residence halls. Other on-campus students and commuters can use cash, points, or a nontraditional meal plan.

"Our school no longer has its party-school reputation," observes a senior. This is partly due to the administration-imposed ban on alcohol at campus parties and tighter ID-checking standards in downtown bars. The administration imposed a "three strikes and you're out" policy for the dorms: three alcohol violations and you're sent off campus. Off-campus houses and apartment parties offer more open action, and popular bars such as Stone Balloon draw huge crowds every weekend. There is a nonalcoholic bar on campus, and dry dances are held on Friday nights. Fraternities and sororities claim 15 percent of men and women.

Newark's Main Street is the center of campus and downtown, so it's where "the city and the campus really come together," says a sociology major. Among the other necessities of suburban life, Newark itself offers coffee shops that feature local bands. New York, Washington, Baltimore, and Philadelphia all lie within a few hours' drive. Depending on the season, Rehoboth Beach and ski slopes in Pennsylvania offer diversion. Spring Fling is an annual bacchanal held every spring, and Mallstock is a music festival and carnival on the campus's central green.

"Our school no longer has its party-school reputation."

The school's athletic bent emerges on fall Saturdays when Blue Hen football is the big attraction ("Go Hens!"), with tailgate picnics before the game and parties afterward. The football team, baseball team, and women's basketball team all claimed recent conference championships. The women's lacrosse team also attracts a loyal following, along with men's basketball and track and field. Intramural sports are popular, and arena events benefit from the six thousand-seat sports center.

Students at UD know when they've got a good thing: an ever improving public university, an extremely broad span of academic options, and a strong sense of school spirit. And all of it on a beautiful campus. While it might take less than an hour to drive through Delaware, those in search of a quality education might want to stop and give this institution a hard look.

Delaware's academic menu includes more than 124 majors ranging from the usual liberal arts and science departments to vocational programs like fashion merchandising. The school also boasts one of the largest undergraduate research programs in the country—six hundred students take part each year.

Overlaps
University of Maryland, Penn State, Rutgers, Villanova, Boston University

If You Apply To ➢

Delaware: Early decision: Nov. 15. Regular admissions: Feb. 15 (Jan. 15 for scholarships). Financial aid: Mar. 15. Housing: May 1. No campus or alumni interviews. SATs or ACTs: required. SAT IIs: optional (recommended for honors program). Accepts the Common Application and electronic applications. Essay question: what has shaped your values; ethnic/cultural heritage; the value of reality TV.

Denison University

Granville, OH 43023

Denison shut down its Frat Row in an effort to shift the spotlight from partying to academics. Not quite as selective as Kenyon, and draws more Easterners than competitors such as Wittenberg and Ohio Wesleyan. Denison has a middle-of-the-road to conservative student body and one of the most beautiful campuses anywhere.

Website: www.denison.edu
Location: Small town
Total Enrollment: 2,107
Undergraduates: 2,107
Male/Female: 43/57
SAT Ranges: V 550–650
   M 560–660
ACT Range: 25–29
Financial Aid: 43%
Expense: Pr $ $ $
Phi Beta Kappa: Yes
Applicants: 3,336
Accepted: 58%
Enrolled: 28%
Grad in 6 Years: 73%
Returning Freshmen: 87%
Academics: ✑ ✑ ✑ ½
Social: ☎ ☎ ☎ ☎ ☎
Q of L: ★ ★ ★
Admissions: (740) 587-6276
   or (800) DENISON
Email Address:
   admissions@denison.edu

Strongest Programs:
  Chemistry/Biochemistry
  English and Creative Writing
  Physics
  International Studies
  Computer Science
  Philosophy
  Geology
  Theater

Denison University is changing its image as a laid-back cousin of the Northeast's elite liberal arts colleges. The university has affirmed a renewed commitment to academics by closing the residential fraternity houses and making a concentrated effort to move academics from the backseat to the driver's seat. "Denison has changed from a Greek-dominated preppy school to a much more diverse and academically focused university," says a biology major. "Each entering class seems to have more impressive academic statistics than the one before," adds a senior.

Set in the rolling Welsh hills of central Ohio, Denison offers a panoramic view of the surrounding valley. With its huge maples and sloping walkways, the beautifully landscaped campus is reminiscent of a rustic New England hamlet, the town of Granville having, as described by a student, "a very charming, not quite of this earth appeal." The buildings, an ensemble of red bricks and white columns, include some of the most attractive Colonial architecture on any campus in the Midwest. Not everything here is reminiscent of the good old days, though. The new Samson Talbot Hall for Biological Sciences is equipped with the latest technology. A new Campus Common is to bring together several academic and administration offices along with an underground parking garage. Renovations were recently completed on residential halls.

For a small liberal arts college, Denison offers a substantial array of academic options. Denison also encourages internships and off-campus study through the programs of the Great Lakes Colleges Association* and the Associated Colleges of the Midwest,* and the May Term program offers students more than two hundred internships around the country in a broad range of careers. The top-notch geology and physics departments enjoy a state-of-the-art facility, complete with a planetarium and laser spectrometer, which was funded by the F. W. Olin Foundation. The college also places a premium on students doing both independent and collaborative research with faculty. Almost one-third of Denison students are in the honors program, which offers more than fifty courses each year and is known for its "Chowder

"Each entering class seems to have more impressive academic statistics than the one before."

Hour," where students and faculty gather for an informal presentation while dining on a faculty member's culinary specialty. Denison's "Arete" was chosen best honors-program newsletter by the National Collegiate Honors Council. Environmental studies is another of Denison's fastest-growing programs and has the benefit of a 350-acre biological reserve and a state-of-the-art research station. Biology, economics, and history are among the college's strongest departments. A boom in summer research opportunities over the past ten years now allows more than one hundred students, over half of them science majors, a stipend for close work on their own projects with professors. Physical education is a bit flabby, but the university is taking steps to whip it into shape. The university library is small, with only about 325,000 volumes, but the computer facilities are excellent, and an online network allows students access to collections at other Ohio colleges.

All students must take Words and Ideas, designed to develop reading and writing ability, and must also choose a second First-Year Seminar that focuses on one of a wide array of topics. Other inquiry courses await sophomores and upperclassmen, as do general education requirements that include life and physical sciences, foreign languages, and American Social Institutions. While this may sound intimidating, students say that some of the courses that count for general education credit are actually quite popular: World Cinema, Human Sexuality, Computer Science, and Creative Writing. Students have nothing but praise for their professors. "The professors and their teachings are what make Denison the academic powerhouse that it is," enthuses a senior history major. "Teachers are always available for their students and will make special times to meet with them."

Fifty-three percent of Denisonians are from out of state, mostly from the Midwest or East. The administration has made great strides in enhancing the status of intellectual achievement and tolerance on campus, yet the atmosphere continues to feel more conservative than at, say, Kenyon or Oberlin. Students here "must keep Abercrombie and J. Crew in business," says one. Another says a sizable number of people fit that preppy image, but

"The student body includes a wide variety of opinions and styles."

underneath it all, "The student body includes a wide variety of opinions and styles." Ironically, says a student, "One issue that remains pervasive is the lack of diversity, and it is this issue that often unites students." Statistics prove this out—African-Americans, Hispanics, and Asian-Americans combine for just 12 percent of the student body.

Community service is an important part of the Denison experience, and the college supports a number of service-learning courses that incorporate community involvement into their subject matter. One of the most popular service-oriented activities is the Licking River Roundup, where students canoe down the river and pick up all the trash they find.

Denison has been extremely aggressive in wooing students with more than eight hundred merit scholarships. Some of the awards, such as the Wells, Dunbar, and Faculty Achievement awards, are aggressively competitive and cover full tuition. Others (notably the $3,000 to $7,000 Alumni awards) are handed out to virtually anyone who can afford the balance of the bill. All the emphasis on merit scholarships has depleted Denison's reserves for need-based aid, but the university continues to meet at least 93 percent of need for two-thirds of the students who require assistance.

Denison is truly a residential college. Ninety-eight percent of its students live on campus, but Denison offers a wide variety of living situations. Crawford Hall, the freshman dorm, is specially geared to the needs of newcomers, with counseling, entertainment, and information. At Taylor House, academic leaders and scholars live in apartment-style units. The Homesteaders live in student-built solar-paneled cabins on a farm a mile away from campus and raise much of their own food. Some upperclassmen find the requirement to live on campus confining. "Students' biggest complaints revolve almost always around living at Denison," says a history major. Others applaud the requirement as yet another means of enhancing the sense of community. Dining hall food generally earns praise. Campus security is said to be good, and students pretty much feel safe in town.

People are enthusiastic about sports at Denison, and many teams, most notably men's and women's swimming and diving, contend for league and national championships. Denison has won the North Coast Athletic Conference All Sports Championship for five consecutive years. Other standouts include men's cross-country, lacrosse, and tennis, and women's indoor track and field, tennis, soccer, and softball. Enthusiasm reaches a fever pitch during Homecoming Weekend. Friday night

The university has affirmed a renewed commitment to academics by closing the residential fraternity houses and making a concentrated effort to move academics from the backseat to the driver's seat.

Almost one-third of Denison students are in the honors program, which offers more than fifty courses each year and is known for its "Chowder Hour," where students and faculty gather for an informal presentation while dining on a faculty member's culinary specialty.

features an all-campus gala highlighted by a chocolate volcano. Intramurals are very popular, and Denisonians get especially riled up for any competition against Kenyon and Ohio Wesleyan.

Greek life may not rule anymore, but neither has it been totally banished. Roughly a third of the men and 44 percent of the women still join, though the demise of "Fraternity Row" has forced many to search off campus for fun, especially if it involves alcohol. "Denison observes state and federal laws regarding underage drinking and campus security, and the residential-life staff do enforce the policies," says a history major. Still, most students consider on-campus drinking safe. Simply put, one student says, "Alcohol consumption is high." On campus, social outlets such as plays, concerts, and movies are sponsored by Denison and/or the Student Activities Council.

> "One finishes a Denison semester feeling closer to the school than when he/she started."

Tiny Granville is loved for its Main Street USA qualities, but "it's so quaint" is not synonymous with "it so rocks." "Granville is dullsville," says an environmental studies major. "The entire town rolls up by 10:00 P.M." The commercial and cultural facilities that Granville lacks can be found in Newark and Columbus, the state capital and home to Ohio State University, just forty-five minutes away by car or bus.

Denison University's warm sense of community always made the weekend party scene sizzle—and now it's firing up the classrooms, too. Small classes encourage students to be comfortable with each other and with the unique perspective each brings from his own particular background. Students still affectionately refer to their school as "Camp Denidoo," and these are indeed happy campers. A senior sums it up: "One finishes a Denison semester feeling closer to the school than when he/she started. It is a sense of growth and accomplishment that only helps further foster the community Denison wishes to establish: one of learning and knowledge."

Overlaps
Miami University (OH), Kenyon, College of Wooster, Ohio State, Bucknell

If You Apply To ➤

Denison: Early decision: Nov. 15, Jan. 15. Regular admissions: Feb. 1. Financial aid: Jan. 1 for scholarships. Meets demonstrated need of 51%. Campus and alumni interviews: recommended, evaluative. SATs or ACTs: required. SAT IIs: optional. Accepts the Common Application and electronic applications. Essay question: significant experience or achievement; issue of concern; influential person; most meaningful activity.

University of Denver

2199 South University Boulevard, Mary Reed Building, Denver, CO 80208

The only major middle-sized private university between Tulsa and the West Coast. DU's campus in residential Denver is pleasant but uninspiring. Brochures instead tout Rocky Mountain landscapes. DU remains a haven for ski bums and business majors.

Website: www.du.edu
Location: City outskirts
Total Enrollment: 9,188
Undergraduates: 3,751
Male/Female: 42/58
SAT Ranges: V 510–610
  M 500–610

The oldest private university in the Rocky Mountain region, the University of Denver provides plenty of options for students looking to hit the books or hit the slopes. A school with a rich heritage, DU boasts a strong business program, and the school's location offers ample opportunities for making job contacts and enjoying the beautiful Colorado landscape.

DU's 125-acre main campus is located in a comfortable residential neighborhood only eight miles from downtown Denver and an hour east of major ski areas. The north campus is home to the law school, the school of music, and several other programs, including the Women's College. Architectural styles vary, and include Collegiate Gothic, brick, limestone, Colorado sandstone, and copper. Special facilities on campus include centers for Judaic studies, Latin American studies, the environment institute, and fine arts. Nearby Mount Evans (14,264 feet) is home to the world's loftiest observatory, a DU facility available to both professors and students.

DU is known for its business school, especially the hotel, restaurant, and tourism management offerings, and for its innovative core curriculum. The school's preprofessional programs are feeders for graduate schools (almost 60 percent of DU's student body are grad students) and new businesses in the booming West. International studies is another strength, backed by lots of opportunities for study abroad, while chemistry, atmospheric physics, music, psychology, and computer science have solid reputations. Students praise the School of Communications for its numerous internships, television studios, and computer lab. Outstanding undergrads can get early admittance to DU's graduate schools of business, international studies, and social work, completing both undergraduate and graduate degrees in five years. Despite the inherent pressure of a quarter system, the academic climate is relatively relaxed. Students say that there is little competition with each other, though students at DU routinely push themselves to do their best. Professors receive high marks for their intelligence and passion. "Many of the professors are invested in the lives of students and are genuinely concerned for them and their education," says a senior. The Partners in Scholarship program pairs students and professors in research projects across the academic spectrum.

The DU core curriculum has received much praise from the National Endowment for the Humanities and is consistent with the national trend toward structured college curriculums. All undergraduates, poets and engineers alike, must take one year of English, arts and humanities, social sciences, and natural sciences; additional requirements include a quarter of oral communication and two quarters of mathematics. Each student must enroll in the University of Denver Campus Connection, a seminar in which first-year students are introduced to college life and are paired with faculty mentors for advising. The Student Orientation and Registration Program (SOAR) helps smooth the transition to freshman life, with programs in the summer as well as when classes begin.

"Many of the professors are invested in the lives of students and are genuinely concerned for them and their education."

University rules stipulate that all core courses must be taught by senior faculty. Course titles include The Making of the Modern Mind, Multiple Voices of America, and Understanding Human Conflict. "At first I thought, 'Who wants to take these science, art, and English classes?'" explains a business major. "But now that I've completed the core, I feel better about myself and my world knowledge. Now I can speak of Goya, Berlioz, and define my favorite artists with a knowledge of the period, styles, and works." The average undergraduate class size is twenty-one students, though introductory courses can be much larger. A rigorous honors program is available, as are numerous study-abroad options.

By and large, students come from fairly affluent families. One student jokes that "the stereotypical DU student drives a brand-new SUV, wears only Abercrombie and Gap clothing, and skis every weekend." Forty-four percent of the students are from Colorado; minorities account for 15 percent of the student body, and on the whole, race relations are considered good. Because it is one of the few private colleges in the West, DU is also among the most expensive in the region. There are a number of merit and athletic scholarships available to help those who qualify. The financial-aid office is notorious for including parent loans in the packages offered to students.

(Continued)
ACT Range: 21–27
Financial Aid: 43%
Expense: Pr $ $ $ $
Phi Beta Kappa: Yes
Applicants: 3,303
Accepted: 84%
Enrolled: N/A
Grad in 6 Years: 69%
Returning Freshmen: 84%
Academics: ✑ ✑ ✑
Social: ☎ ☎ ☎ ☎
Q of L: ★ ★ ★ ★
Admissions: (800) 525-9495
Email Address:
admission@du.edu

Strongest Programs:
Biological Sciences
Accountancy
Psychology
Hotel, Restaurant, and
    Tourism Management
English
Fine Arts
Business
Environmental Science

Each student must enroll in the University of Denver Campus Connection, a seminar in which first-year students are introduced to college life and are paired with faculty mentors for advising.

Every January, all thoughts of academics are put aside for the three-day Winter Carnival. Top administrators, professors, and students all pack off to Steamboat Springs, Crested Butte, or some other ski area to catch some fresh powder and see who can ski the fastest, skate the best, or build the most artistic ice sculptures.

Students are required to live their first two years on campus in the residence halls. "The dorms are comfortable enough," says a sophomore. "They have a beautiful view of the mountains, and at sunset or during lightning storms, students often crowd around lounge windows to watch." The Johnson-McFarlane hall ("J-Mac") is supposed to be the best place for freshmen, though another student says that the Towers are a much quieter on-campus option. Freshman and sophomore dorm residents must sign up for a fifteen- or nineteen-meal-a-week plan. Greeks can live and dine together in their houses. Since there are no restrictions concerning off-campus living for upperclassmen, many juniors and seniors opt for the decent quarters found within walking distance of campus.

With consistently beautiful sunny weather and great skiing, hiking, and camping less than an hour away in the Rockies, many DU students head for the hills on weekends. Besides various ski areas, one can explore Estes Park, Mount Evans, and Echo Lake. Additionally, DU is near Moab, Albuquerque, and Las Vegas, the Mecca of all American road trips. Since Denver is not primarily a college town, many students with cars head for Boulder (home of the University of Colorado), about thirty miles away. For those staying home, the transit system makes it easy to get to downtown Denver. Once there, the options are tremendous and include great local restaurants, bars, and stores, many of which cater to students. About 15 percent of the men and 8 percent of the women join fraternities or sororities.

Greeks tend to dominate the social life, and several students mention the Border Bar as a hot spot. Wednesday is pub night at the $10 million student center. Drinking policies abound, and although DU enforces the law, students say it's no harder for an underage student to imbibe at DU than any other school in the country.

When it comes to sports, peace-loving '60s types and partyers unite when the DU hockey team, a national powerhouse, skates out onto the ice, especially against archrival Colorado College. Women's gymnastics also competes successfully in Division I,

> "The dorms are comfortable enough. They have a beautiful view of the mountains."

while men's and women's soccer, basketball, tennis, skiing, and swimming, along with men's baseball and women's volleyball, have returned to Division I play. Intramural sports, for those with less ability but just as much competitive spirit, also are popular. Every January, all thoughts of academics are put aside for the three-day Winter Carnival. Top administrators, professors, and students all pack off to Steamboat Springs, Crested Butte, or some other ski area to catch some fresh powder and see who can ski the fastest, skate the best, or build the most artistic ice sculptures. In the spring, the whole campus turns out for the annual Chancellors Barbecue.

Students like DU for its modest size and friendly atmosphere. And while there remain some moneyed students with attitude problems, these types are balanced by more down-to-earth kids. As the school pushes for a more diverse student body, and emphasizes teaching and technology, the Denver University is becoming better known and looking to a day when it will be better known for its intellectual rigor than its gorgeous setting in the Rocky Mountains.

Overlaps

University of Colorado, Colorado State, Colorado College, University of Northern Colorado, Puget Sound

If You Apply To ➤

DU: Rolling admissions. Financial aid: Feb. 15. Does not guarantee to meet demonstrated need. Campus interviews: recommended, evaluative. Alumni interviews: optional, informational. ACTs or SATs: required. SAT IIs: optional. Accepts the Common Application and electronic applications. Essay question: What are you thinking, feeling, or laughing about and why?

DePaul University

One East Jackson Boulevard, Chicago, IL 60604

Gets the nod over Loyola as the best Roman Catholic university in Chicago. DePaul's Lincoln Park location is like New York's Greenwich Village without all the headaches. Especially strong in business and the performing arts. The student body is about half Catholic.

DePaul University boasts a "small-school feel with big-school opportunities," says a sophomore, even though its enrollment has doubled in the past fifteen years. The school's location in the heart of Chicago and a spate of campus construction has transformed DePaul from the "little school under the tracks" to Chicago's version of NYU. Moving beyond its Roman Catholic roots, DePaul values diversity and is largely a feeder to Chicago's business community. "Everyone has a place here," says a freshman. "Incoming students need to come with open minds."

DePaul has two campuses. The Lincoln Park campus, with its state-of-the-art library, is home to the College of Liberal Arts and Sciences, the School of Education, the Theater School, and the School of Music, as well as residence halls and academic and recreational facilities. Lincoln Park itself is a fashionable Chicago neighborhood with century-old brownstone homes, theaters, cafés, parks, and shops. The Loop, or "vertical," campus in downtown Chicago, houses the Law School, the School for New Learning, and the College of Commerce in four high-rise buildings—fifty-six stories in all. The DePaul Center, a $70-million teaching, learning, and research complex, is the cornerstone of this campus. The two sites are 20 minutes apart on the elevated train.

DePaul's name is closely associated with Midwestern business and law, and undergraduates can find internships with local legal and commercial institutions. The School of Accountancy draws many majors and is reported to be the most challenging department in the College of Commerce, which

"Everyone has a place here."

has added majors in e-business and management information systems. Programs in music and theater are renowned, while the School of Computer Science, Telecommunications and Information Systems has new majors in computer graphics and animation, e-commerce technology and network technology. The School of Education and several of the science departments (including biology, chemistry, and physics) have been rejuvenated, and the impressive prelaw program balances the strong liberal arts and business offerings. DePaul serves "the above-average to very good student who is career oriented," administrators say. According to students, professors in the English and math departments aren't as strong as their peers elsewhere.

At DePaul, courses are small, and professors teach at all levels. In fact, the administration appoints student representatives from each school and college to faculty promotion and tenure committees. Social activities bring undergraduates and faculty members together, and students receive a phone book with all the profs' home numbers. "All of my instructors have been friendly and very willing to help any student succeed," says a student in the College of Commerce. The faculty has many real-world practitioners who provide savvy academic and career advice, students say, helped in their guidance by results of basic-skills proficiency tests given at the Student Development Center. Students take a common core, with a first-year program of courses in composition and rhetoric, quantitative reasoning and exploring, and discovering Chicago; a sophomore seminar on multiculturalism in the U.S.; and a junior-year program in experiential learning, including foreign

Website: www.depaul.edu
Location: Urban
Total Enrollment: 20,548
Undergraduates: 12,436
Male/Female: 40/60
SAT Ranges: V 510–610
  M 500–610
ACT Range: 21–26
Financial Aid: 80%
Expense: Pr $ $
Phi Beta Kappa: No
Applicants: 8,117
Accepted: 73%
Enrolled: 34%
Grad in 6 Years: 59%
Returning Freshmen: 84%
Academics: ✍ ✍ ✍
Social: ☎ ☎
Q of L: ★ ★ ★
Admissions: (800) 4-DEPAUL
  or (312) 362-8300
Email Address: admitdpu@
  wppost.depaul.edu

Strongest Programs:
  Accounting
  Computer Science
  Finance
  Music
  Theater

DePaul's name is closely associated with Midwestern business and law, and undergraduates can find internships with local legal and commercial institutions.

study, service learning, or internships. Students also complete a series of "learning domains," consisting of arts and literature, philosophical inquiry, religious dimensions, scientific inquiry, social science, and history, and B.A. recipients are required to take three foreign language courses. The highly selective honors program includes interdisciplinary courses, a modern language requirement, and a senior thesis. Study-abroad options include programs in France, Hungary, Italy, England, Germany, China, Japan, South Africa, Greece, and Mexico.

Founded in 1898 by the Vincentian Fathers, DePaul is run by priests who also teach some courses, and (voluntary) Mass is still held every day. Seventy-nine percent of DePaul students hail from Illinois. "DePaul is mainly attended by kids with money," says a sophomore. "Noticing girls dressed up like they were going to a nightclub just to go to a 9:40 A.M. class threw me for a loop." Hispanics, African-Americans, and Asian-Americans are well represented in the student body—33 percent total—and DePaul wants to boost this figure by reaching out to disadvantaged inner-city students with academic potential. Human rights, gay rights, and the environment are big issues on campus. "DePaul is very liberal, and almost goes too far in its political correctness," says a computer science major. Vincentian Day, a day of service to the city held at the beginning of each year, is popular.

> **"All of my instructors have been friendly and very willing to help any student succeed."**

Traditionally, DePaul has been a commuter school; only 20 percent of the students live on campus, but those who do like their digs. Two "traditional" dorms lack air-conditioning, but the majority of the "spacious and clean" residence halls are "very well-maintained and comfortable," says a finance major—apply early to secure a bed! The university has seven modern coed dorms, and one includes parking, key in this densely populated neighborhood. Another provides apartment living with furniture and built-in kitchens and bathrooms. While Chicago may have a high-crime reputation, students say campus security is visible, with officers patrolling in cars and on foot and dorms requiring students to swipe ID cards at two or three places before allowing entrance. There are also about fifty emergency blue-light telephones, a freshman says.

Fraternities draw eight percent of DePaul students, and sororities four percent; not surprisingly, with the school's proximity to Chicago's clubs (especially on Rush Street), sporting events, and bars, most social life occurs off campus. In the warmer months, the beaches of Lake Michigan beckon downtown students, while the annual outdoor Fest concert—suspended in 2001—and the Gamble (the biggest frat party) attract large crowds from both campuses. "There are plays to see all over the city, concerts happening all the time, and a lot of great restaurants, too," says a computer science major. "A fake ID is almost necessary," says a marketing major. On campus, the alcohol policy forbids beer in the dorms except for those over twenty-one, behind closed doors.

On the sports scene, men's basketball is the headline story, beginning with the Midnight Madness of each fall's first practice in October. The game against Notre Dame always draws a capacity crowd, though Loyola is DePaul's oldest rival. The Lady Blue Demons softball team won an NCAA regional championship and a conference championship in 1999, and also reached the NCAA Final Four. Basketball also rules in the solid intramural program.

> **"There are plays to see all over the city, concerts happening all the time, and a lot of great restaurants, too."**

DePaul's student body is becoming more diverse as it increases in size, an admirable achievement. The administration credits the school's "increased academic reputation" for growth, but students say DePaul's popularity is due as much to the special bonds they feel with fellow Blue Demons. "The diversity of the student population makes this school a special place," says a freshman. "Each person brings his or her traditions and shares them with others."

If You Apply To ➤

DePaul: Rolling admissions. Early action: Nov. 15. Regular admissions: Feb. 1. Financial aid: April 1. Does not guarantee to meet demonstrated need. Campus interviews: optional, informational. No alumni interviews. SATs or ACTs: required. SAT IIs: optional. Apply to particular schools or programs; music and theater require auditions. Accepts electronic applications. Essay questions: who or what influenced your decision to apply to DePaul; proudest accomplishment.

DePauw University

313 South Locust Street, Greencastle, IN 46135

DePauw is a solid Midwestern liberal arts institution in the mold of Illinois Wesleyan, Ohio Wesleyan, Denison, and Dickinson. Its Greek system is among the strongest in the nation and full of students destined for Indiana's business and governmental elite.

DePauw is like a vintage New England liberal arts school plunked down in Middle America and given a flat Midwestern accent. The administration has focused on pumping up school spirit and on raising its academic standards. The results are apparent. "The university has become very academically oriented and more selective," says one freshman. Indeed, DePauw graduates populate the Indiana business and government elite. Other important changes have also occurred on campus, including a student judicial code, an enlarged student congress, and integration of technology into the curriculum.

DePauw is set amid the gently rolling hills of west-central Indiana. The lush green campus is dotted with a combination of older buildings and modern redbrick structures. At the center of it all is a well-kept park with fountains and a reflecting pool. Among DePauw's more notable facilities are the multimillion-dollar Science and Mathematics Center, with its science library and plenty of computer terminals, and the magnificent four-building Performing Arts Center, which holds a music library, practice rooms, theater, auditorium, and recital hall. Depauw also completed a residence hall renovation project, and the entire campus has recently been wired for data, phone, and video lines. New additions to the campus also include a tennis and track facility for indoor competition, as well as an art building with studios, classrooms, and gallery space.

> **"Students are challenged in their courses to define and stand for their own beliefs."**

The student body is as career-oriented as they come. The Center for Management and Entrepreneurship and the Center for Contemporary Media are both extremely popular. DePauw offers its students four prominent honors and fellows programs: Honors Scholars, Media Fellows, Management Fellows, and Science Research Fellows. An international business concentration revolves around three majors: political science, economics, or foreign language. Students major in one of these areas while taking selected courses in the other two and participate in an internship abroad. Summer research opportunities are around, especially in the sciences. Newly available are the Information Technology Associates Program and the Student Technology Assessment, Resources, and Training Program, which give students the chance to enhance their liberal arts education with these practical skills. Economics, communications, and computer science are considered to be the

Website: www.depauw.edu
Location: Small town
Total Enrollment: 2,219
Undergraduates: 2,219
Male/Female: 44/56
SAT Ranges: V 540–640
  M 560–650
ACT Range: 24–28
Financial Aid: 45%
Expense: Pr $ $
Phi Beta Kappa: Yes
Applicants: 3,004
Accepted: 53%
Enrolled: 39%
Grad in 6 Years: 79%
Returning Freshmen: 92%
Academics: 🖉 🖉 🖉 ½
Social: ☎ ☎ ☎
Q of L: ★ ★
Admissions: (765) 658-4006
Email Address:
  admission@depauw.edu

Strongest Programs:
  History
  Sociology
  Communications
  Biology
  English
  Economics
  Computer Science

Close to half the students study off campus through programs with the Great Lakes Colleges Association or in a variety of other study-abroad experiences.

strongest among students, while art and education receive a poor grade. DePauw has recently added majors in black studies, environmental geoscience, and biochemistry, and minors in film, jazz, Jewish, Japanese, Russian, and European studies.

For upperclassmen, the January winter term is an ideal time for independent study, exchanges with other schools, or mission trips to the Third World. All students can do semester-long internships. Close to half the students study off campus through programs with the Great Lakes Colleges Association* or in a variety of other study-abroad experiences. The administration makes sure that all students receive a healthy dose of liberal arts. Bachelor's degree requirements in the College of Liberal Arts call for courses from six areas: natural sciences and mathematics, social and behavioral sciences, literature and the arts, historical and philosophical understandings, foreign language, and self-expression. In addition, each student must demonstrate competence in writing, quantitative reasoning, and oral communication. First-year seminars are offered in several departments, and students are required to enroll in them.

The academic climate at DePauw seems to grow increasingly demanding. "Students are challenged in their courses to define and stand for their own beliefs," says one senior. The professors are highly praised. "Professors have high expectations," says an English major. "Each professor is an expert in his or her field."

DePauw students are "intellectually curious, philanthropically minded, and socially active," according to one student. In contrast to other liberal arts colleges, DePauw has succeeded in attracting a relatively strong minority population, in part because it has encouraged the formation of African-American fraternities and sororities. In addition, the growing presence of a new affinity group of dynamic multicultural students recruited by the Posse Foundation in New York City signifies strides toward a comfortably diverse campus. However, Caucasians still comprise 87 percent of the student body, with African-Americans accounting for 5 percent, Hispanics for 2 percent, and Asian-Americans for 2 percent. Academic scholarships are awarded, valued from $1,000 to $27,600; there are no athletic scholarships available. Three-quarters of DePauw students volunteer their time with area churches and social-service agencies, and there are scholarships for those involved with community service.

"The dorms are being renovated and are looking great!"

Ninety-five percent of DePauw students live in university housing, and students report that the buildings are well maintained but overcrowded. "The dorms are being renovated and are looking great! Each dorm has a computer lab, a commons area, and a TV lounge," says one junior. Many students recommend Humbert Hall to freshmen because of its hotel-like atmosphere. Men and women joining the Greek system must wait until sophomore year to move into the fraternity or sorority houses. Students report no trouble getting the type of room they desire, and all students are guaranteed some form of housing. Only a few students are allowed to move off campus, which is considered a "privilege" and is decided by lottery.

In addition, the growing presence of a new affinity group of dynamic multicultural students recruited by the Posse Foundation in New York City signifies strides toward a comfortably diverse campus.

While a whopping 77 percent of the men and 74 percent of the women go Greek; these organizations have been working hard to change the stereotypical view of Greek social life. They have devised a risk-management policy and instituted a community council to review conduct violations that come before the university for action. Rush is delayed until second semester so freshmen can at least unpack their bags before setting off in search of a house, and fraternities still maintain the old custom of having "house moms." Students say that it's very easy for underage drinkers to drink, especially at fraternity parties. Another student warns, however, "Fake IDs should not even be attempted here, because they get confiscated quicker than you can take them out." Many upperclassmen prefer smaller group gatherings and the quieter atmosphere of the bars in town.

Well-attended varsity athletic contests tend to turn into social events, especially the annual football game against archrival Wabash College. This rivalry is the oldest west of the Alleghenies and is played for possession of the much-cherished Monon Bell, hence the popular T-shirt that reads, "Beat the bell out of Wabash." Golf, basketball, cross-country, swimming, and soccer teams have all brought home SCA conference championship trophies. In a takeoff of Indiana University's famed Little 500 bike race, DePauw sponsors a Little 5 of its own, with Greeks and independents pitted against each other over a forty-mile course. The women's basketball team advanced to the Division III Final Four, and men's basketball made it to the Elite Eight in 2002.

> **"While education is very important here, so is the chance to grow socially and spiritually."**

Though rural Indiana is hardly a mecca of entertainment opportunities, Greencastle has the basic necessities—such as a movie theater, bowling alley, and several pizza places—and Indianapolis is only forty-five minutes away. "Greencastle lacks a college-town atmosphere," says a senior. "It is fine for sustaining day-to-day living but doesn't offer many alternatives to the university." Another student adds, "The town is cute but not terribly exciting." Several state parks and a lake for the sailing club are nearby. St. Louis, Chicago, and Cincinnati make for good road trips.

For a small school, DePauw offers a multitude of opportunities including strong academics, abundant extracurricular activities, and a variety of study-abroad options. "While education is very important here, so is the chance to grow socially and spiritually," says one student. "DePauw offers its students an excellent opportunity to sample every aspect of college life."

Overlaps

Indiana, Purdue, Denison, Notre Dame, Washington University

If You Apply To >

DePauw: Early decision: Nov. 1. Regular admissions: Feb. 1. Financial aid: Feb. 15 (in-state), Apr. 1. Does not guarantee to meet demonstrated need. Campus interviews: recommended, evaluative. Alumni interviews: optional, evaluative. SATs or ACTs: required. SAT IIs: optional. Accepts the Common Application and electronic applications. Essay question: teacher with greatest influence.

Dickinson College

P.O. Box 1773, Carlisle, PA 17013

Dickinson occupies a historic setting in the foothills of central Pennsylvania. Known foremost for study abroad and foreign languages, Dickinson's curriculum combines liberal arts with a business program that picks up the international theme. Competes head to head with nearby Gettysburg.

Dickinson College was chartered just six days after the Treaty of Paris recognized the United States as a sovereign nation—and tradition still holds a special place here. Each fall, freshmen bound up the stone staircase of the oldest building on campus, where they pass through glass doors to sign their names in the school's ledger. Afterward, the doors are locked until commencement, when graduates proceed through them into the world beyond Dickinson. While the ceremonies symbolize the separation between college and real life, by the time graduation rolls around, most students already knows what awaits them—65 percent have participated in one of the school's thirty-two study-abroad programs, which span twenty countries and six continents. "It's a place of opportunity," says a sophomore. "I've

Website: www.dickinson.edu
Location: Small town
Total Enrollment: 2,208
Undergraduates: 2,208
Male/Female: 42/58
SAT Ranges: V 580–670
   M 570–650
ACT Range: 25–29
Financial Aid: 59%

(Continued)

Expense: Pr $ $ $
Phi Beta Kappa: Yes
Applicants: 4,094
Accepted: 51%
Enrolled: 28%
Grad in 6 Years: 80%
Returning Freshmen: 89%
Academics: ✐ ✐ ✐ ✐
Social: ☎ ☎ ☎
Q of L: ★ ★ ★
Admissions: (717) 245-1231
Email Address:
    admit@dickinson.edu

Strongest Programs:
    Foreign Languages
    Political Science
    English
    Biology
    Psychology
    International Business and
        Management
    Teacher Certification

"Dickinson is like an endless buffet, where you can pick and choose anything you want to do," says a sophomore. *"Everyone's plate is different, but we all have something in common."*

been here two years, and I haven't heard the word 'no.' It is an amazing place to grow and learn more than just academics."

Almost all of Dickinson's Georgian buildings are carved from gray limestone from the college's own quarry, which gives the place a certain continuity. Even the three-foot stone wall that encloses much of the wooded sixty-eight-acre Dickinson yard is limestone. The campus is part of the historic district of Carlisle, an economically prosperous central-Pennsylvania county seat nestled in a fertile valley. The Stern Center for Global Education has been renovated to house the departments of international studies, business and management, and East Asian studies. The new Milton E. Asbell Center for Jewish Life will provide a central place for students to study, celebrate holidays, and meet with visiting rabbis.

Dickinson is best known for its workshop approach to science education, for its outstanding and comprehensive international education program, and for the depth of its foreign language program—twelve tongues are offered, including Chinese, Japanese, Hebrew, Portuguese, and Italian. A 3–3 program with the Dickinson School of Law (part of Penn State) allows students to accelerate their legal studies, and the international business and management major exposes aspiring executives to economics, history, financial and business analysis, internships, and overseas education. The biochemistry and molecular biology major requires coursework in four departments and completion of an independent research project, a boon for aspiring physicians. The teaching certification program may become more popular with Dickinson's Teachers for Tomorrow program, which gives a $10,000 cash award and $10,000 grant for career advancement to students who teach high school for four years after graduation.

To help students gain an appreciation for the liberal arts and the broader world, Dickinson requires two courses each in humanities, social sciences, natural and mathematical sciences, and crosscultural studies. One course must be writing-intensive. In addition, the required Freshman Seminar Program introduces new students to college-level study and reflection, with quirky courses such as "Images of the Suburbs," "Star Trek: Temporal Anomaly," and "The Role of Wine in American Society." Academics are rigorous, but not cut-throat. "Students are encouraged to pursue their goals as far as possible," says a French major. "Teachers challenge us to reach beyond our comfort

"It is an amazing place to grow and learn more than just academics."

zones." There are no graduate students at Dickinson, so professors teach all classes. "The teachers are so good that sometimes I feel like I'm being spoiled," says a sophomore. "Professors are consistent and organized," agrees a freshman.

Most Dickinson students are white, upper-middle-class, and from suburban areas of the Northeast. Forty-one percent hail from the Keystone State. They tend to be principled, competitive, relatively conservative, and highly motivated to find good-paying jobs. "Students are ambitious and open minded, mostly," says a freshman. They "are very involved and motivated in various areas of student life, from academics to athletics to the arts," adds a classmate. African-Americans, Hispanics, and Asian-Americans each account for 2 percent of the student body. Partnerships with New York's Posse Foundation in New York and the Philadelphia Futures Foundation promise to help boost these numbers.

Dickinson guarantees housing for four years, so 92 percent of students live on campus, though that number may decrease now that all seniors have the option of moving off campus. Freshmen have their own dorms, including one for women only. Upperclass dorms are coed by floor except for a complex of townhouses with eight-person suites. The college recently transformed an abandoned factory into a combination of art studios and loft-style apartments with 118 beds for juniors and seniors. "The buildings themselves are old and traditional, but the interiors are renovated and up-to-date," says a sophomore. A wide variety of special-interest housing, such as Spanish House, Arts House, Multicultural House, Equality House, and Tree House, is also available.

Most of Dickinson's social life occurs on campus, and most of that revolves around fraternities and sororities, which attract 25 percent of the men and 26 percent of the women. "However, there are always alternatives, such as movies, concerts, and plays," says a freshman, as well as stand-up comics, dances, and performances of *a cappella* and improvisational comedy troupes. When it comes to alcohol, Dickinson follows Pennsylvania state law: you must be twenty-one to drink. Monitors check IDs at parties, and only those who are old enough get wristbands entitling them to booze. That said, "underage students can easily find alcohol," says a biochemistry and molecular biology major. Students look forward to annual traditions like Freshman Olympics, the Fall Fest arts festival, and the Spring Fest carnival. "Put down the book and carry a blanket

"The teachers are so good that sometimes I feel like I'm being spoiled."

to Morgan Field to hear some live music," explains one senior. "Kick off the shoes, and enjoy the inflatable rides in the warm, spring sun just in time before finals."

Carlisle, "a small town in the middle of nowhere," isn't a typical "college town," but it is "bigger than you think," says a French major. "There's all kinds of things to do, restaurants to eat at, and foreign films to see." Big Brother–Big Sister programs, the Alpha Phi Omega community-service fraternity, and programs like Adopt-a-Grandparent help bring the school and community together. "Plus, it's really nice to go into one of the 'mom and pop' stores, and actually know 'mom and pop,'" says a sophomore. In the spring and early fall, Maryland and Delaware beaches beckon; they're just two- to three-hours' drive. Come winter, good skiing is a half-hour away. Budding politicians can intern in Harrisburg, the state capital, which is twenty miles from campus, and nature lovers will enjoy hiking the Appalachian Trail, just ten minutes away. For those who crave urban stimulation, the best road trips are to Philadelphia, New York, and Washington, D.C. They're accessible by bus or train—a good thing, since freshmen can't have cars.

Dickinson students get riled up for any match against top rival Franklin and Marshall, which it battles each year for the coveted Conestoga Wagon trophy. The women's cross-country team and indoor and outdoor track and field squads have won Centennial Conference championships in recent years. Dickinson also squares off each year with Gettysburg College for the Little Brown Bucket. Intramurals are a favorite of the fraternities, and dorms also organize teams. A nineteen-acre park provides teams with two soccer fields, two softball fields, and lighting for night games. Students may also assemble club teams to compete with other schools in sports where Dickinson doesn't field varsity squads, such as ice hockey.

If you're interested in the breadth of a liberal arts education, it could very well begin at Dickinson—and end someplace between West Africa, Eastern Europe, and South America. The college's nurturing, concerned community of students and faculty remains dedicated to mutual success and achievement. "Dickinson is like an endless buffet, where you can pick and choose anything you want to do," says a sophomore. "Everyone's plate is different, but we all have something in common."

The required Freshman Seminar Program introduces new students to college-level study and reflection with quirky courses such as "Images of the Suburbs," "Star Trek: Temporal Anomaly," and "The Role of Wine in American Society."

The college recently transformed an abandoned factory into a combination of art studios and loft-style apartments with 118 beds for juniors and seniors. Morgan Hall, the largest dorm on campus, has also been renovated.

Overlaps
Gettysburg, Franklin and Marshall, Bucknell, Lafayette, American

If You Apply To ➤

Dickinson: Early decision: Nov. 15, Jan. 15. Early action: Dec. 15. Regular admissions and financial aid: Feb. 1. Meets demonstrated need of 98%. Campus interviews: recommended, informational. Alumni interviews: optional, informational. SATs or ACTs: optional. SAT IIs: optional. Accepts the Common Application and electronic applications. Essay question: uses Common Application questions, plus additional essay on why student is a good match for Dickinson.

Madison, NJ 07940-4063

From Drew's wooded perch in suburban Jersey, Manhattan is only a thirty-minute train ride away. That means Wall Street and the UN, both frequent destinations for Drew interns. Drew is New Jersey's only prominent liberal arts college and one of the few in the greater New York City area.

Website: www.drew.edu
Location: Suburban
Total Enrollment: 2,412
Undergraduates: 1,537
Male/Female: 40/60
SAT Ranges: V 560–670
    M 550–650
Financial Aid: N/A
Expense: Pr $ $ $ $
Phi Beta Kappa: Yes
Applicants: 2,545
Accepted: 71%
Enrolled: 23%
Grad in 6 Years: 84%
Returning Freshmen: 86%
Academics: ✍ ✍ ✍
Social: ☎ ☎ ☎
Q of L: ★ ★ ★
Admissions: (973) 408-DREW
Email Address:
    cadm@drew.edu

Strongest Programs:
    Political Science
    English
    Biology
    Psychology
    Theater

Drew University's roots date back to 1867, when Wall Street wizard Daniel Drew founded it as a Methodist theological seminary. The school has since maintained a balance between reverence for the past and an exciting race toward the future. This tiny liberal arts university offers students intimate classes and a caring faculty, successfully upholding its original commitment to providing a broad liberal arts–based education. One senior describes Drew as a "supportive, yet challenging place to grow and learn."

The school occupies 186 acres of peaceful woodland in the upscale New York City suburb of Madison and is known as "The University in the Forest." Fifty-six campus buildings peek through splendid oak trees and boast classic and contemporary styles, a physical reflection of Drew's respect for both scholarly traditions and progressive education. The school is currently sprucing up the atmosphere through a reforestation project and construction of a $20 million arts center for the theater and studio arts departments.

> **"Drew has and is still striving for the best technology."**

Political science is Drew's strongest undergraduate department. Drew's president, former New Jersey governor Tom Kean, annually teaches a course titled Governing a State. Political science majors can also take advantage of off-campus opportunities in Washington, D.C., London, Brussels, and the United Nations in New York City. Other popular majors include psychology, English, biology, economics, and theater. The Dana Research Institute for Scientists Emeriti offers opportunities for students in biology, chemistry, physics, mathematics, and computer science to do research with distinguished retired industrial scientists. Even more impressive is a program whereby students can earn a B.A. and M.D. from Drew and the University of Medicine and Dentistry of New Jersey/New Jersey Medical School in seven years. Future financiers can follow in the footsteps of the school's founder and take advantage of Drew's Wall Street Semester, an on-site study of the national and international finance communities. Other new programs include minors in Holocaust studies, archeology, and linguistic studies.

Students give low grades to the music department, which is handicapped by a lack of adequate practice and performance facilities. "The building the department is housed in seems like it's ready to cave in!" a senior theater arts major says. Drew's commitment to liberal arts education includes a lofty goal: universal computer literacy. In fact, every full-time student is provided with a notebook computer and supporting software, which students take with them when they graduate. The school's campus-wide fiber-optic network links all academic buildings and many residence halls. "Drew has and is still striving for the best technology," a senior psychology major says.

> **"It's hard to get a nice room until junior year."**

General education requirements, which take up a third of each student's total program, involve coursework in natural and mathematical sciences, social sciences, humanities, and arts and literature. Students must also show competency in writing, and each first-year student enrolls in seminars limited to sixteen people, 80 percent of which are taught by senior faculty. The theater arts department works closely with the Playwrights Theater of New Jersey (founded by faculty member Buzz McLaughlin) to produce plays that are written, directed, and designed by students. Drew has long been a proponent of study-abroad programs, including the Drew International Seminar program, where students study another culture in depth on campus, then spend three to four weeks in that country.

Maintaining a rigorous study schedule is key, according to many upperclassmen. The industrious grind of hard work is fueled by a cast of highly praised, interactive faculty who generate enthusiasm and ambition. "Professors not only love questions during class but also encourage students to see them outside of class if they need help or to discuss the latest current issue relative to their class," a psychology major says. Some students complain that professors can be less than enthusiastic about teaching introductory classes. Drew's library complex, a cluster of three buildings, contains more than four hundred and fifty-thousand titles and offers ample study accommodations, though some students complain that some collections are outdated.

Fifty-six percent of Drew's students are from New Jersey, and 64 percent hail from public high school. "We are a diverse campus, a campus made of many different ethnicities, skin colors, religions, sexual orientations, hair colors, etc.," says a senior. Merit awards for incoming freshman range from $8,000 to full first-year tuition. Students can also win arts scholarships worth $10,000 each and minority scholarships ranging from $1,000 to $15,000.

Ninety percent of the students live in university housing, which includes both single-sex and coed dorms and six theme houses. Themes have included Earth House, Umoja House, Womyn's Concerns, Asia Tree House, and Spirituality Home. Some students lament their quality, but the school is renovating many dorms. Several housing options are available to upperclassmen, from dorm rooms of all sizes to suites and townhouses. A lottery gives housing preference to seniors and juniors, and most freshmen reside in dorms situated at the back of campus, which aren't the best. "It's hard to get a nice room until junior year," a senior says. Still, most students live on campus because housing prices in Madison are out of reach for collegians. Although the dorms have kitchenettes, everyone must buy the meal plan, which does not receive high ratings from students.

"One of the best things about Drew is that there is something always going on."

There is no Greek system, but social life mostly takes place on campus. Officially, nobody under twenty-one is allowed to drink, but alcohol is said to be easy to come by. Students say there is little pressure to drink. Two on-campus coffeehouses, The Other End and The Space, are very popular party alternatives. Free, on-campus social programming is extensive. "One of the best things about Drew is that there is something always going on," one junior reports. "Each semester there is something new as a way to represent the variety of interests about Drew students." New York City is a short train ride away, and Philadelphia, the Jersey Shore, and the Delaware River are close by.

The First Annual Picnic, held on the last day of classes and numbered like Super Bowls (FAP XVII), provides an opportunity to enjoy live music and food. On Multicultural Awareness Day, students are excused from one day of classes to celebrate cultural diversity by attending lectures, workshops, and social events. Drew also launched an initiative to give all students and staff opportunities to participate in diversity training.

The commuter town of Madison tends to get discouraging reviews as a college town by students who feel its wealthy residents don't take too kindly to Drewids, as

The First Annual Picnic, held on the last day of classes and numbered like Super Bowls (FAP XVII), provides an opportunity to enjoy live music and food.

Drew has long been a proponent of study-abroad programs, including the Drew International Seminar program, where students study another culture in depth on campus, then spend three to four weeks in that country.

they affectionately call themselves. "Madison is in denial that it's a college town," a senior says. "Stores close at 5 P.M., there is no nightlife and everything's expensive." However, Community Day—designed to bring students and residents together—has become an annual event, and approximately 50 percent of students volunteer in activities such as "Mentors at Drew" and "the Honduras Project," in which a group of Drew students traveled to Honduras to help an orphanage. Madison does provide several shops and restaurants within walking distance of campus. The New Jersey Shakespeare Festival is in residence part of every year, and offers both performances and internships.

Students used to seem more interested in intramural sports than in the school's Division III varsity teams, but interest has grown as the teams have become more successful. The $15 million athletic center is a 126,000-square-foot state-of-the-art facility that seats four thousand and is used by varsity sports teams and intramural programs.

Drew University always suffers by comparison to nearby Ivy League Princeton University, a fact many Drewids resent. But at a time when most colleges are gearing their courses more and more toward the job market, Drew remains dedicated to the well-rounded intellect.

Overlaps

Rutgers, NYU, College of New Jersey, Boston University, Muhlenberg

If You Apply To >

Drew: Early decision: Dec. 1, Jan. 15. Regular admissions and financial aid: Feb. 15. Does not guarantee to meet demonstrated need. Campus interviews: recommended, informational. Alumni interviews: optional, informational. SATs: required. Accepts the Common Application and electronic applications. Essay question: significant achievement, important issue, influential person, influential character.

Drexel University

3141 Chestnut Street, Philadelphia, PA 19104

Drexel is a streetwise, no-nonsense technical university in the heart of Philadelphia. Go to school, work an internship, go to school again, work again—that's the Drexel way. Like Lehigh, Drexel also offers programs in business and arts and sciences, and its most distinctive offering is a College of Media Arts and Design.

Website: www.drexel.edu
Location: City center
Total Enrollment: 13,128
Undergraduates: 10,582
Male/Female: 63/37
SAT Ranges: V 520–620
  M 540–640
Financial Aid: 78%
Expense: Pr $ $ $
Phi Beta Kappa: Yes
Applicants: 10,355
Accepted: 65%
Enrolled: 34%
Grad in 6 Years: 54%
Returning Freshmen: 87%

For career-minded students who want to bypass the soul-searching of their liberal arts counterparts, Drexel University offers both solid academics and an innovative co-op education that combines high-tech academics with paying job opportunities. "If you want a good job, you go to Drexel and you do co-op." It's easy to see why Drexel University is nicknamed "the Ultimate Internship."

"Drexel's campus is impressive for its downtown Philadelphia location, with gardens and greenery on every block," says a student, "but the campus is woven tightly into the fabric of the city." The buildings are simple and made of brick; most are modern and in good condition. Sitting just west of the city center and right across the street from the University of Pennsylvania, the campus is condensed into about a four-block radius. Students are encouraged to use a shuttle bus between the library and dorm at night, and access to dorms, the library, and the physical education center is restricted to students with ID, so most feel safe on campus.

Cooperative education is the hallmark of the curriculum, which alternates periods of full-time study and full-time employment for four or five years, providing students with six to eighteen months of money-making job experience before they graduate. And the co-op possibilities are unlimited: students can co-op virtually anywhere in this country, or in eleven foreign countries, and 98 percent of undergraduates choose this route. Freshman and senior years of the five-year programs are spent on campus, and the three intervening years (sophomore, prejunior, and junior) usually consist of six months of work and six months of school. A precooperative education course covers such topics as skills assessment, ethics in the workplace, résumé writing, interviewing skills, and stress management. Each co-oping student has the opportunity to earn from $7,000 to $30,000 while attending Drexel. And although some students complain that jobs can turn out to be six months of make-work,

> **"It starts out laid-back but after a while you begin to feel the competitiveness."**

most enjoy making important contacts in their potential fields and learning while earning. "It starts out laid-back but after a while you begin to feel the competitiveness," mentions one sophomore. "Keep in mind Drexel works on trimesters, so it keeps you on your toes."

To accommodate the co-op students, Drexel operates year-round. Flexibility in requirements varies by college, but in the first year everyone must take freshman seminar, English composition, mathematics, and Cooperative Education 101; engineering majors must also complete the Drexel Engineering Curriculum, which integrates math, physics, chemistry, and engineering to make sure that even techies enter the work force well-rounded and able to write as well as they can compute and design. Students enjoy the seven hundred thousand-volume library, which features a computerized card catalog, good hours, and lots of room for studying. Professors receive high praise from most, and are noted for their accessibility and warmth. Says one student, "They take a great interest in the students and are always willing to offer assistance or direction outside of class."

Drexel's greatest strength is its engineering college, which churns out more than 1 percent of all the nation's engineering graduates, B.S. through Ph.D. The electrical and architectural engineering programs are particular standouts. The College of Arts and Sciences is well recognized for theoretical and atmospheric physics; chemistry is also recommended. The futuristic Center for Automated Technology complements the strong computer science program. Students mention that the biology and chemistry departments are weak, primarily due to lack of organization and foreign teachers who are hard to comprehend. One film and video major says, "The dramatic writing major is lacking in popularity due to its placement under the College of Design rather than Arts and Sciences."

The performance-oriented student body is 64 percent Pennsylvanian, with another large chunk of students from adjacent New Jersey. The foreign student population is 13 percent, while Asian-Americans and African-Americans account for 20 percent of the student body. Twenty-three percent of Drexel undergrads grad-

> **"Our biggest rivalry is our feud with Delaware. We delight in sacrificing blue plastic chickens!"**

uated in the top tenth of their high-school class, and the student body tends to lean right politically. "This is a science and technology school full of conservative students who don't really have the time to worry about liberal issues," says a student. In addition to need-based financial aid, a wide range of athletic and merit scholarships (the latter in amounts up to $10,000 per year) is offered.

Freshmen live in one of six coed residence halls, including a luxurious high-rise, but many upperclassmen reside in nearby apartments or the fraternities, which are frequently cheaper and more private than university housing. Overall, 28 percent of the students live in the dorms; another third commute to campus from home. The cafeteria offers adequate food and plenty of hamburgers and hot dogs, but it's far away from the dorms. While on-campus freshmen are forced to sign up for a meal

(Continued)
Academics: ✍ ✍ ✍
Social: ☎ ☎
Q of L: ★ ★
Admissions: (215) 895-2400
Email Address:
   enroll@drexel.edu

Strongest Programs:
   Engineering
   Graphic Design
   Architecture
   Film and Video

It's easy to see why Drexel University is nicknamed "the Ultimate Internship."

To accommodate the co-op students, Drexel operates year-round.

Students take full advantage of their urban location by frequenting clubs, restaurants, cultural attractions, and shopping malls in Philadelphia, easily accessible by public transportation.

plan, most upperclassmen make their own meals; the dorms have cooking facilities on each floor. If all else fails, nomadic food trucks park around campus providing quick lunches.

With so many students living off campus and the city of Philadelphia at their disposal, Drexel tends to be a bit deserted on weekends. A student notes, "In a single weekend, I may play paintball in the Poconos, swim at the Jersey shore, see an opera in Philadelphia, and go mountain biking in nearby Wissahickon Park." Friday-night flicks are cheap and popular with those who stay around, and dorms sponsor floor parties. The dozen or so fraternities also contribute to the party scene, especially freshman year, but a handful of smaller sororities has little impact. Still, Greek Week is well attended by members of both sexes, as is the spring Block Party, which attracts four or five bands. The Greeks recruit 7 percent of the men and women. Drinking is "not a big deal to everyone," and campus policies are strict; dorms require those of age to sign-in alcohol, and limit the quantities they may bring in.

The co-op program often undermines any sense of class unity, and can strain personal relationships. Activities that depend on some continuity of enrollment for success—music, drama, student government, athletics—suffer most. "It's hard to get people involved because of the amount of schoolwork and co-ops," says one woman. There is no football team, but men's basketball and soccer are strong. "Our biggest rivalry is our feud with Delaware," admits one frenzied student. "We delight in sacrificing blue plastic chickens!" Men's and women's swimming and women's volleyball also generate interest. An extensive intramural program serves all students, and joggers can head for the steps of the Philadelphia Art Museum, just like Rocky did in the movies. Students take full advantage of their urban location by frequenting clubs, restaurants, cultural attractions, and shopping malls in Philadelphia, easily accessible by public transportation.

"When I graduate, I will be prepared and proud of it."

Aspiring poets, musicians, and historians may find Drexel a bit confusing. But for future computer scientists, engineers, and other technically oriented minds, the university's unique approach to learning inside and outside the classroom could give your career a fantastic jumpstart. As one satisfied customer explains, "The terms are intense, the activities unlimited, but Drexel graduates are surely among the most capable and motivated individuals I have ever met. When I graduate, I will be prepared and proud of it."

Overlaps

Penn State, Temple, Villanova, Rutgers, LaSalle

If You Apply To ➤

Drexel: Rolling admissions. Financial aid: May. 1. Does not guarantee to meet demonstrated need. Campus interviews: recommended, informational and evaluative. No alumni interviews. SATs: required. SAT IIs: optional. Accepts electronic applications. Apply to particular schools or programs.

Duke University

2138 Campus Drive, Durham, NC 27708

What fun to be a Dukie—face painted blue, rocking Cameron Indoor Stadium as the Blue Devils score again. Duke is the most selective private university in the South, though not as tough for out-of-staters to get in as public archrival UNC. Duke is strong in engineering and offers public policy rather than business.

Duke University is one of a few U.S. colleges where solid academics and championship-caliber sports teams manage to coexist. It might be south of the Mason-Dixon Line, and may seem a bit wet behind the ears compared to the nation's oldest and most prestigious northeastern schools, but Duke is competing with them and winning its fair share of serious students as well as athletes. The rising star in the South, Duke now competes on an even footing with the Ivies and Stanford.

Founded in 1838 as the Union Institute (later Trinity College), Duke University is young for a school of its stature. It came into being in 1924 thanks to a stack of tobacco-stained dollars called the Duke Endowment. Duke's campus, located in the lush North Carolina forest, is divided into two main sections, West and East, and also includes an adjacent 8,300-acre forest and enough open space to satisfy the most diehard outdoors enthusiast. West Campus, the hub of the university, is laid out in spacious quadrangles and dominated by the impressive Gothic chapel, a symbol of the university's Methodist tradition. Constructed in the 1930s, West includes residential and classroom quads, the administration building, Perkins Library (with 4.2 million volumes, nearly 8.9 million manuscripts, and two million public documents), and the student union. East Campus, built in the 1920s, consists primarily of Georgian red-brick buildings. Most of Duke's arts facilities are here, as are dorms renovated in 1995 to house all first-year students together, "for a sense of class unity, which works quite well," says a freshman. East and West are connected by shuttle buses, though many students enjoy the mile-or-so walk between them along wooded Campus Drive. New construction includes the Wilson Recreation Center, a Visitor's Center at the Sarah P. Duke Gardens, and a storage center for the library. Sopho-

> **"Students are given considerable freedom, and with it, responsibility."**

mores are now required to live on West Campus along with juniors, and a new residence hall is under construction to round out accommodations as part of this new plan. A new building is also in the works for the Center for Human Genetics.

Duke today includes two undergraduate schools: The Pratt School of Engineering and Trinity College; the latter resulted from a merger of the previously separate men's and women's liberal arts colleges. The school's engineering programs—particularly electrical and biomedical—are national standouts. The natural sciences, most notably ecology, biology, and neuroscience, are also first-rate. The proximity of the Medical Center enhances study in biochemistry and pharmacology. Duke's literature, English, and Romance studies programs have received heightened national attention and student interest. The English department has rebuilt after losing Stanley Fish and some of its other superstars. Duke is lately stressing inquiry-based learning in science classes and is also revamping the economics sequence.

Duke's Sanford Institute of Public Policy offers an interdisciplinary major—unusual at the undergraduate level—that trains aspiring public servants in the machinations of the media, nonprofit organizations, government agencies, and other bodies that govern our lives. Internships and apprenticeships are a big part of the program. Additionally, Duke offers more than one hundred interdisciplinary courses in areas such as genetics, statistics, and decision sciences and hemispheric studies, bolstered by the John Hope Franklin Center for International and Interdisciplinary Studies. More than 40 percent of Duke students study abroad, and for those who want a break from campus without leaving the country, Duke has arts and public policy programs in New York and a media arts and industries program in Los Angeles.

Trinity College's Curriculum 2000, part of the traditional undergraduate coursework known as Program I, requires courses in four general areas of knowledge: arts and literature, civilizations, social sciences, and natural sciences and mathematics. Students must achieve competency in foreign language, writing, and research, while

Website: www.duke.edu
Location: Small city
Total Enrollment: 11,926
Undergraduates: 6,203
Male/Female: 51/49
SAT Ranges: V 650–740
   M 670–760
ACT Range: 29–33
Financial Aid: 35%
Expense: Pr $ $ $ $
Phi Beta Kappa: Yes
Applicants: 13,976
Accepted: 26%
Enrolled: 44%
Grad in 6 Years: 94%
Returning Freshmen: 96%
Academics: ✍ ✍ ✍ ✍ ✍
Social: ☎ ☎ ☎ ☎
Q of L: ★ ★ ★ ★
Admissions: (919) 684-3214
Email Address: undergrad-admissions@duke.edu

Strongest Programs:
   Ecology
   Neuroscience
   Engineering
   Political Science
   Public Policy
   Languages
   Economics
   Literary Studies

When college counselors say Duke is hot, they don't mean because it is in the South. It's up there with the Ivies and the select few other colleges that compete with them for students.

also fulfilling requirements in areas called modes of inquiry and focused inquiries. Curriculum 2000 "makes the general distribution requirements harder to fulfill," complains a freshman. "It makes dozens of new requirements for graduation. Some of them seem a little silly." All students also must complete three Small Group Learning Experiences: one seminar course during the freshman year, and two more as upperclassmen. Students must finish thirty-four courses to graduate; those who wish to explore subjects outside and between usual majors and minors may choose Program II, to which they are admitted after proposing a topic, question, or theme, for which they plan a special, individualized curriculum with faculty advisors and deans. "Students are given considerable freedom, and with it, responsibility," says a student.

> **"People are always working and studying in pairs and larger groups, even in classes with heavy curves."**

When college counselors say Duke is hot, they don't mean because it is in the South. It's up there with the Ivies and the select few other colleges that compete with them for students. Courses here are rigorous, and the academic atmosphere has become more intense, particularly in the sciences. Still, "people are always working and studying in pairs and larger groups, even in classes with heavy curves," says a freshman. "A prime reason I chose Duke was that it seemed just like an Ivy League school, minus the 'kill the curve-setter' attitude." In recent years, the university has focused resources on undergraduate education, reducing the number of non-professors who teach incoming students and having senior professors teach more classes. The nationally recognized FOCUS program, groups of seminars clustered around a single, broad theme such as Evolution and Humankind or International Pop Culture, offer another way to get to know faculty members. Despite Duke's relatively large undergraduate population, 83 percent of courses here have twenty-five or fewer students.

Duke's Sanford Institute of Public Policy offers an interdisciplinary major—unusual at the undergraduate level—that trains aspiring public servants in the machinations of the media, nonprofit organizations, government agencies, and other bodies that govern our lives.

Only 15 percent of Duke students are from North Carolina, although a large fraction of the student body hails from the South, and the Northeastern corridor sends a fair-sized contingent, too. Ten percent of students are African-American, 6 percent are Hispanic, and 12 percent are Asian-American. Students of different ethnicities and races tend to "self-segregate," students say, producing little tension, but also little interaction. Overcoming these self-imposed barriers has been an ongoing quest for students and administrators, who conduct a diversity orientation program each year.

Duke's southern gentility is reflected in the look here, which is generally neatly pressed on guys and maybe a bit outfitty on women, in contrast to the thrown-together anti-status uniform of jeans and sweats that dominate on some other campuses. Duke is also a culturally active campus; theater groups thrive, and the Freewater Film Society shows classic movies each week. During the summer, Duke is home to the splendid American Dance Festival. Undergraduates use the school's cable-television system to make and broadcast parodies of game shows and other entertainment.

> **"There is always more than enough going on."**

Despite the imprimatur of wealth evident here, Duke admits students without regard to financial need, and guarantees to meet all accepted applicants' full demonstrated need. Dozens of merit scholarships are offered, ranging from $2,000 to a full ride, and some include six weeks of summer study at Oxford University, or simultaneously attend Duke and UNC. There are a number of scholarships earmarked for outstanding African-Americans. Unlike most other universities of its academic stature, Duke hands out hundreds of athletic scholarships annually.

Eighty-three percent of Duke undergrads live on campus, and each student is loosely affiliated with one of sixty "living groups," ranging in size from fourteen to

250 students, in a nod to the college- or house-based living units at some Ivy League schools. Student programmers and resident advisors plan lectures and social activities for these groups, and a total of more than 350 faculty members are affiliated with one group or another. The university also operates residential houses for fifty to 120 students, led by a faculty master and his or her family, under the expanding Faculty-in-Residence program. All freshmen dwell together on East Campus, a move aimed at insulating them from the wilder aspects of Duke's social scene and making it easier to introduce them to the life of the mind. Fraternities and sororities, which attract 29 percent of men and 42 percent of women, do not have their own houses, so members live in designated areas of the residence halls. The West Campus, home to frat men, boasts the liveliest nightlife. There are also special-interest dorms, focused on themes such as women's studies, the arts, languages, and community service. University-owned apartment buildings popular with upperclassmen are located on two nearby satellite campuses. Students use prepaid meal cards to order chow, either from the main dining hall, known as the Pits, or from a full-service restaurant or an on-campus pizza shop, which delivers. Unused "money" is refunded at the end of the semester, an unusual and much-appreciated policy.

The nationally recognized FOCUS program, groups of seminars clustered around a single, broad theme such as Evolution and Humankind or International Pop Culture, offers another way to get to know faculty members.

As a college town, Durham doesn't quite measure up to Ann Arbor, Michigan; Madison, Wisconsin; or Boulder, Colorado, but "there is always more than enough going on," says one student. Fraternity parties are open to everyone, and the free shuttle-bus service that connects the school's various dorm and apartment complexes runs until 4 A.M., making it easy to socialize in rooms or suites. "Alcohol, it seems, is quite easy to find," says a freshman. During the basketball season, games always sell out, and in the off-season, movies are an option for those tired of the frat-party scene. Off campus, many of Durham's year-round residents fall into the eighteen-to-thirty-five demographic, and the town boasts bars and clubs aplenty to feed and water them, as well as the beloved Durham Bulls, the local minor-league baseball team, which coined the term "bullpen." Popular road trips include nearby Chapel Hill, home of archrival

"By far, basketball season brings out the best of student support."

UNC, or Raleigh, the state capital and home of North Carolina State University. In warm weather, the broad beaches on North Carolina's outer banks are two to three hours away, while ski slopes are three to four hours distant in winter. The popular Oktoberfest and Springfest bring in live bands and vendors peddling local crafts and exotic foods each fall and spring.

"Duke–Durham relations do leave something to be desired," says a student dismayed by the contrast between the school's wealth and the economic depression afflicting Durham. However, students take part in plenty of community-service projects, including tutoring in local schools. And Durham is adjacent to the more affluent Research Triangle Park, the largest research center of its kind in the world, about fifteen minutes from campus. Duke, North Carolina State, and the University of North Carolina at Chapel Hill created the park for nonprofit, scientific, and sociological research. Many Silicon Valley technologies companies have East Coast outposts in the park, which has helped make the Raleigh/Durham area one of the most productive regions in the nation, with the highest percentage of Ph.D.s per capita in the U.S.

At the opposite end of the spectrum, Duke's official motto is Eruditio et Religio only to a few straight-laced administrators; everyone else knows it as "Eruditio et Basketballio," which translates more or less as "To hell with Carolina"—the University of North Carolina, Duke's archrival for supremacy in the Atlantic Coast Conference. At games, students get the best courtside seats, where they make life miserable for the visiting team. Their efforts paid off when the Blue Devils won the national Division I championship for the third time in a decade. "By far, basketball season brings out the best of student support," a senior says. Indeed, sports-crazed Blue Devils erect a temporary "tent city" to vie for the best seats. This is far from "roughing it"—students form groups to hold their places so that some fraction can go to class and keep their peers on track academically, while those who hold down the fort may check their email thanks to lampposts with Internet jacks. The women's basketball team has come on strong and made it to the NCAA Final Four twice in the last three years. Women's golf and men's lacrosse won 2002 championships. Women's and men's tennis and men's cross-country are also part of the unusually strong athletic program, while football is conspicuously weak. For part-time jocks, there are two intramural leagues, one for competitive types and one for strictly weekend athletes, which draw heavy participation from the Greeks.

Duke is new, and it's old. Take a walk around the up-to-date campus and see the latest technology, but listen for the whisper of the Old South through those big old trees. Duke is cool, in fact, it can sometimes seem as if the "coolest"—and smartest—students from schools all over the country got together and decided to make this their destination. And Duke is hot. No wonder, with all those success-oriented students who almost define the term "well-rounded."

If You Apply To ➤

Duke: Early decision: Nov. 1. Regular admissions: Jan. 2. Financial aid and housing: Feb. 1. Guarantees to meet demonstrated need. Campus interviews: optional, evaluative. Alumni interviews: recommended, evaluative. SATs or ACTs: required. SAT IIs: required (writing and two others, or writing, math and one other for engineering applicants). Accepts the Common Application. Essay question: a book that changed your understanding of the world, others or yourself; people you admire even though you disagree with them, most profound or surprising intellectual experience, or a matter of importance to you. Also requests a statement on whose feedback the essay writer solicited and how that person assisted and was or was not helpful.

Earlham College

Drawer 192, Richmond, IN 47374

Earlham is among the proud circle of liberal and nonconformist colleges in the Midwest that includes Oberlin, Grinnell, and Beloit, to name a few. Less than half the size of Oberlin and comparable to the other three, Earlham must hustle to attract students to the small, industrial city of Richmond.

Earlham is unusual among quality liberal arts institutions in that it prides itself on a strict faithfulness to the Quaker traditions of community and cooperation, both during and after college. The school supports its students and encourages them to work hard, dream big, and achieve much. "Earlham's Quaker traditions are what distinguishes it from other colleges," says a math and psychology double major. "The school attracts a wide variety of people, but most have the same values and principles of living."

The eight hundred-acre campus is seated in the small city of Richmond, yet is only a short distance from the major metropolitan areas of Cincinnati and Indianapolis. Georgian-style buildings dominate the campus, surrounded by mature trees and plantings. The most recent addition to campus is the Landrum Bolling Center for Interdisciplinary Studies and Social Sciences (try saying that three times fast!). The center houses lecture halls, seminar rooms, a computer lab, and technologically outfitted classrooms. The Japanese gardens on campus are a symbol of the college's long friendship and joint programs with Japan.

Students say the academic climate at Earlham is demanding. "The courses are challenging but a dedicated student can keep up," says a peace and global studies major. There are strict distribution requirements, including a two core humanities sequence, two courses in religion and philosophy, four natural sciences, one fine arts, and four courses in athletics, physical education, and wellness. All courses stress the development of library skills, and students praise the library staff and the facilities. Faculty and students have unrestricted access to major online databases from professors' desks.

Cooperative and group learning are vital parts of the academic approach, and class discussion rather than lecture is the predominant learning style. In fact, Earlham created a major called human development and social relations that mixes sociology, anthropology, and psychology and aims to help students understand and work with other people, countries, and institutions. Earlham faculty members are selected for their

"Earlham's Quaker traditions are what distinguishes it from other colleges."

excellence in teaching and their ability to cross various disciplinary lines. "My teachers push me and are my mentors," says a freshman. "I love my profs—they're incredible!" Another student adds, "Most professors are willing to spend time in and out of class going over difficult concepts or discussing interesting ones." The close-knit atmosphere of Earlham continues into the classroom, and students find this to be quite an advantage. Students rate academic advising highly, saying that they may discuss their plans with advisors over dinner. "My faculty advisor is outstanding," says a junior. "I meet with her often to go over classes, to check in, or just to socialize."

Top fields at Earlham are the sciences, especially biology and geology. A special stress is put on Japanese studies, a field in which Earlham is a national leader. (Notes one student: "Richmond, Indiana is on all the U.S. maps in Japan because the Earlham presence is so strong there.") Other solid departments are English and PAGS (Peace and Global Studies program). Biology is the most popular major, followed by human development and social relations, psychology, peace and global studies, and English. Eighteen percent of recent graduates go on to some sort of graduate study, although volunteer and service programs are popular postgraduation choices. In addition, both prelaw and premed students enjoy high acceptance rates at graduate schools

There are more than two dozen off-campus programs, including the semester in Japan, as well as programs in Mexico, Kenya, and the American and Canadian wilderness. About 70 percent of the students eventually take advantage of at least one of the off-campus study programs. The school is also affiliated with the Great Lakes Colleges Association.*

While not particularly diverse racially, Earlham casts a wide net geographically; less than a third of the students are Hoosiers. African-Americans make up 9 percent of the student population, and Asian-Americans account for 2 percent. "Earlham students are from a wide variety of social, cultural, and economic backgrounds," says a biology major. "You would think that this would cause frequent confrontations, but everyone seems to get along." "EC's Quaker background makes this a very politically

"Earlham students are from a wide variety of social, cultural, and economic backgrounds."

active and 'correct' community (though not to the extreme)," says a senior. Rights of all kinds—women's, gay, animal, environmental—are also a big deal at Earlham, and campus organizations exemplify Earlham's commitment to various causes. Groups range from Action against Rape to BLAC (Black Leadership Action Coalition).

At Earlham, students are strongly encouraged to live on campus, and 90 percent do. Single, double, and triple rooms are comfortable, good-sized, and fairly well

(Continued)
Grad in 6 Years: 69%
Returning Freshmen: 84%
Academics: ✍ ✍ ✍ ✍
Social: ☎ ☎ ☎
Q of L: ★ ★ ★ ★ ★
Admissions: (765) 983-1600
Email Address:
admission@earlham.edu

Strongest Programs:
Psychology
Foreign Languages
International Studies
Natural/Physical Sciences
Japanese Studies
English

"EC's Quaker background makes this a very politically active and 'correct' community (though not to the extreme)," says a senior.

maintained, students say. "You can't expect luxury, but many dorms offer personality in return," says one denizen. Examples? "Olvey-Andis is loud and friendly. Earlham Hall and Barrett aren't very spacious. Hoerner has horribly thin walls but is cozy," says one student. "Some college houses are bordering on decrepit, but in general, housing is varied, accessible, and easy to obtain," says a senior. Freshmen have reserved space in each dorm, and upperclassmen divide up the remaining rooms by lottery or petition to live together. Juniors and seniors may move from the dorms into one of twenty-four college-owned apartments and houses, including a working farm, although demand usually exceeds supply. Most people eat at the college dining hall on one of the three meal plans. A vegetarian main course and a salad and health-food bar are available in the large cafeteria.

Quaker beliefs and Indiana's liquor laws prohibit alcohol on campus, but students find the dry campus policy far from intolerable. "The policy creates an environment that doesn't focus on alcohol," one sophomore notes. "If you don't drink, it is very easy to find other options." There are no fraternities or sororities, so fun at Earlham includes movies, bands, hiking in the woods, and time at the Breadbox, a student-run coffeehouse that features student performers. Popular road trips include Cincinnati and Oxford, Ohio (home to Miami University), and Indianapolis. An International Festival highlights music and cultural exhibits; Sunsplash, an outdoor reggae festival in the fall,

> "You can't expect luxury, but many dorms offer personality in return."

and Umoja, an African-American celebration, are also popular. An air-guitar and lip-sync contest is a popular winter activity. Almost all students participate in music or theater activities.

Men's and women's varsity athletics (NCAA Division III) receive equal support at Earlham. The men's cross-country and basketball teams are strong, as are women's soccer and basketball. Nearly a third of the student body participate in seventeen sports.

Earlham functions rather independently of the small city of Richmond and vice versa. "Relations between the college and town haven't always been amazing," reports a sophomore, "but that's beginning to change due to the success of the Earlham Volunteer Exchange." City-oriented people may have to make an adjustment to the slower life, but Richmond, which is not a typical college town, does offer a symphony, theater, several parks, and a minor-league baseball team, and it is big enough to supply part-time jobs and volunteer activities for many students.

Life at Earlham is a collection of paradoxes: it's a liberal school stuck in a small, conservative city, and while its physical location is isolated, the school is known for its expertise in international studies. Despite the paradoxes, most graduate ready to take on the world, thanks to the school's cooperative, can-do spirit and caring student-faculty community. As one sophomore peace and global studies major puts it, "Earlham will take you around the world, but it'll make sure your feet are planted on the ground when you come home."

Overlaps

Grinnell, Oberlin, Kenyon, Macalester, Guilford

If You Apply To ➤ **Earlham:** Early decision: Dec. 1. Early action: Jan. 1. Regular admissions: Feb. 15. Financial aid: Mar. 1. Does not guarantee to meet demonstrated need. Campus interviews: recommended, evaluative. Alumni interviews: optional, evaluative. SATs: required. SAT IIs: optional. Accepts the Common Application and electronic applications. Essay question: choose one from five options: important issue, significant experience, or valued relationship; significant book, piece of writing, or research article; analysis of H. L. Mencken's critique of Christianity; the balance of freedom and responsibility; the importance of creativity.

Eckerd College

4200 54th Avenue South, St. Petersburg, FL 33711

There are worse places to go to school than the shores of Tampa Bay. Eckerd's only direct competitor in Florida is Rollins, which has a business school but is otherwise similar. Marine science, environmental studies, and international studies are Eckerd's biggest draws.

Attending Eckerd College demands willpower. Why? In the words of an international business major: "We are right on the water, and it is like going to college in a resort." With free canoes, kayaks, boats, coolers and tents always available for student use, it's a wonder anyone studies. But study they do, as a new president and student affairs staff have lured more capable students to Eckerd with small classes, skilled professors, renovated housing, and a reinvigorated social scene. "The standard of education and competition has improved dramatically," says a computer science major.

Founded in 1960 as Florida Presbyterian College and renamed a decade later after a generous benefactor (of drugstore fame), Eckerd considers itself nonsectarian. Still, the school maintains a formal "covenant" with the major Presbyterian denomination, from which it receives some funds. The lush, grassy campus is located on the tip of a peninsula bounded by the Gulf of Mexico and Tampa Bay, with plenty of flowering bushes, trees, and small ponds—and it's not unusual to spot dolphins frolicking in the adjacent waters. Campus buildings are modern, and none are taller than three stories. The Hough Campus Center and Triton Pub have been completely remodeled, and construction of a new library and technology center began recently.

Freshmen arrive three weeks early for orientation, where they take a one-credit seminar on the skills required for college-level work. First-years also take a year-long course called Western Heritage in a Global Context, which focuses on influential books, and they must meet composition, foreign language, information technology, oral communication, and quantitative skills requirements to graduate. Also required are one course in each of the four academic areas—arts, humanities, natural sciences, and social sciences—plus one course each in environmental and global perspectives. The capstone senior seminar, organized around the theme "Quest for Meaning," asks students to draw on what they've learned during college to find solutions to important issues. Popular departments include marine science, business management, biology, international business, and psychology. The Russian and German departments suffer because each has only one professor. Because the emphasis of Eckerd's music program is vocal and keyboard performance, instrumentalists get short shrift.

> **"We are right on the water, and it is like going to college in a resort."**

In addition to strong programs in watery subjects like marine science, Eckerd pioneered the 4–1–4 term schedule, in which students work on single project, for credit, each January. Concentrating on a single subject sparks strong student-faculty bonds, and every student has a faculty mentor—there are no graduate assistants at the blackboards. "The professors are very personable, down-to-earth, helpful, and exciting to listen to," says a psychology major. The academic climate is fairly competitive, "without making you feel miserable if you don't do well," says a marine science major. New majors include business administration, communications, and East Asian studies, and minors are now available in legal studies and leadership studies. A Freeman Foundation grant has funded significant new coursework in the Chinese and Japanese languages.

Website: www.eckerd.edu
Location: City outskirts
Total Enrollment: 1,582
Undergraduates: 1,582
Male/Female: 44/56
SAT Ranges: V 520–610
  M 520–610
ACT Range: 22–28
Financial Aid: 53%
Expense: Pr $ $
Phi Beta Kappa: No
Applicants: 1,930
Accepted: 78%
Enrolled: 28%
Grad in 6 Years: 67%
Returning Freshmen: 77%
Academics: ✑ ✑ ✑
Social: ☎ ☎ ☎
Q of L: ★ ★ ★ ★ ★
Admissions: (727) 864-8331
Email Address:
  admissions@eckerd.edu

Strongest Programs:
  Marine Science
  Environmental Studies
  International Relations
  International Business
  Biology
  Economics
  Creative Writing
  Psychology

In addition to strong programs in watery subjects like marine science, Eckerd pioneered the 4–1–4 term schedule, in which students work on single project, for credit, each January.

While St. Petersburg isn't a college town—a senior calls it "old people central"—a side benefit to the school's location is the Academy of Senior Professionals, a group of senior citizens who mentor undergrads. Academy members, who come from all walks of life, take classes with students, work with professors on curriculum development, help students with career choices, and lead workshops in their areas of expertise. About half of Eckerd's students study abroad, in countries from Austria and France to Bermuda and China. The school also has its own campus in London, England. Marine science programs include a Sea Semester* and the Eckerd College Search and Rescue, which performs more than three hundred marine rescues annually and inspires a popular campus T-shirt that tells students to "GET LOST! Support Eckerd Search and Rescue."

Eckerd students "are extremely hardworking, caring, and passionate," says a junior. "They attempt to find the right mix between academic, extracurricular, and social activities," a senior adds. Important campus issues include environmental and wildlife awareness, gay rights, and feminism, students say. Nearly two-thirds of the student body hails from out of state; 10 percent are foreign. Hispanics are the largest minority group, at 4 percent of the total, and African-Americans and Asian-Americans account for 2 percent each. The annual Festival of Cultures has "amazing food, awesome dancing, and cultural activities from around the world," says a sophomore.

Seventy-two percent of students live in one of eight housing quads, separated from the rest of campus by the imaginatively named Dorm Drive. Some residence halls are single sex, and others are coed by floor. Rooms are fairly large and air-conditioned, and waterfront views and beach access are in-your-face—and free. Two trendy townhouse- and apartment-style residence halls provide suite living above and beyond the standards of other dorms, and other dorms have been renovated to add computer labs and kitchens in lounges. Still, says a junior, "very few dorms are well maintained, and most are relics from the '60s and '70s. There isn't any trouble getting a room, because many students have moved off campus."

"The professors are very personable, down-to-earth, helpful, and exciting to listen to."

There are no Greek organizations at Eckerd, and a strict alcohol policy—no kegs on campus, no alcohol at university events—means wristbands at campus parties, even for those over twenty-one. The policy has been relaxed a bit to allow students of drinking age to imbibe at the campus bar, the Triton Pub, and to drink in public areas of the dorms. Students say those who are underage still manage to get booze and consume it in their rooms, away from prying eyes. Off campus, it's next to impossible for underage students to be served at bars and restaurants, students say—though they do enjoy the new Baywalk shopping complex, about fifteen minutes from campus, with a stadium-seating movie theater, bars, and restaurants.

New majors include business administration, communications, and East Asian studies, and minors are now available in legal studies and leadership studies. A Freeman Foundation grant has funded significant new coursework in the Chinese and Japanese languages.

Students who don't like the new, quieter atmosphere engendered by Eckerd's stricter alcohol policies eschew the concerts, lectures, shows, and games arranged by Palmetto, the student activity board, for the nightclubs and bars of Latin-flavored Ybor City, a section of Tampa about thirty minutes away. Tampa and St. Pete also offer a Salvador Dali museum and professional baseball, football, hockey, and soccer teams. Tempting road trips include Orlando's Walt Disney World and Islands of Adventure theme parks, Miami's South Beach, and that hub of debauchery on the delta, New Orleans.

Eckerd doesn't have a football team, but intramural athletics range from flag football to the assassin game, in which students try to shoot their peers with dart guns, pit dorms against each other in serious contests. Varsity teams compete in NCAA Division II, and in 2001, the men's basketball squad went to the southern regional playoffs, while the men's tennis team got to the Final Four. The sailing team has qualified to compete for national championships in three events:

women's, coed, and dinghy. Weekend warriors and varsity athletes alike benefit from a new athletic complex with baseball, soccer, and softball fields. Still, says a junior, athletic teams "are very poorly funded, and it shows on the field."

Eckerd continues "to strive to link experiential, service, and international learning to traditional classroom learning in the arts and sciences," administrators say. That the school has emphasized these new traditions of scholarship, service, and multiculturalism while maintaining its reputation for fun in the sun is all the more remarkable because Eckerd is not even fifty years old.

If You Apply To ➤

Eckerd: Rolling admissions: May 1. Financial aid: Apr. 15. Housing: May 1. Meets demonstrated need of 70%. Campus interviews: recommended, evaluative. Alumni interviews: optional, informational. SATs or ACTs: required. SAT IIs: recommended (writing and math I or math II). Accepts the Common Application and electronic applications. Essay questions: significant concern and how you'll address it in college; influential event or person; book, movie, play, or piece of music that's impacted you.

Emerson College

120 Boylston Street, Boston, MA 02116-4624

Emerson is strategically located in the heart of Boston's theater district and within walking distance of the city's major sites. Communication and the performing arts head the list of strong programs. With roughly 4,300 undergraduates, Emerson is a smaller alternative to neighboring giants Northeastern and Boston U.

Those who aspire to a career in Hollywood may want to make a four-year pit stop in Boston first. There they will find Emerson College, a small liberal arts school that offers strong programs in communications and the performing arts. Here, students take notes from professors who also happen to be working directors, producers, actors, and writers. It's an approach that put students in the spotlight and asks them, "Are you ready to be heard?"

Founded in 1880, Emerson is located on Boston Common in the heart of the city's theatre district and features a mix of nineteenth-century brownstones and modern high-rise buildings. Much of the surrounding city is accessible by foot, including the historic Freedom Trail and the Boston Public Garden. Current projects include the eleven-story Tufte Performance and Production Center that will house expanded performance and rehearsal space, a theatre design/technology center, a makeup lab, a costume shop, classrooms, and television studios. Future plans call for the development of a fourteen-story college center and residence hall.

Emerson was founded with an emphasis on oratory and performance, and the school still offers a plethora of strong programs in this vein. Undergraduates may choose from more than twenty majors, including acting, broadcast journalism, dance/theatre, film, media studies, and writing, literature, and publishing. General education requirements consist of a combination of

"Are you ready to be heard?"

interdisciplinary seminars and traditional courses. All students must take courses in four areas: a Communication Core, a Liberal Arts Distribution, Global and Multicultural Perspectives, and Ethics and Values. Interdisciplinary seminars of no more than twenty students stress the interrelationships between different communication fields; recent seminars include *Minds and Machines, Ways of Knowing: Philosophy and Literature,* and *Words, Imagination, Expression.*

Website: www.emerson.edu
Location: Urban
Total Enrollment: 4,339
Undergraduates: 3,412
Male/Female: 42/58
SAT Ranges: V 570–660
  M 540–630
ACT Range: 23–29
Financial Aid: 28%
Expense: Pr $ $ $
Phi Beta Kappa: Yes
Applicants: 4,071
Accepted: 47%
Enrolled: 33%
Grad in 6 Years: 63%
Returning Freshmen: 84%
Academics: ✍ ✍ ✍
Social: ☎ ☎
Q of L: ★ ★
Admissions: (617) 824-8600
Email Address:
  admission@emerson.edu

Strongest Programs:
  Film

(Continued)
Acting
Creative Writing
Communication Sciences
   and Disorders

The most popular major is film, followed closely by acting, creative writing, marketing communication, and journalism. The atmosphere can be intense, according to students. "The students themselves are highly competitive and expect the best," says a junior. "The teachers and courses tend to meet this standard." The college provides students with access to state-of-the-art equipment and facilities—including digital editing labs, Avid composers, recording studios, and fully-equipped television studios—and the campus is home to the oldest noncommercial radio station in Boston.

For those seeking a spotlight and stage elsewhere, Emerson offers a semester-abroad program at Kasteel Well (The Netherlands), where students are housed in a restored thirteenth-century castle complete with moats, gardens, a gate house, and peacocks. Film students may attend a summer program in Prague, and approximately two hundred students

> "The students themselves are highly competitive and expect the best."

vie annually for a semester-long internship at Emerson's Los Angeles Center. Back on campus, students may cross-register with nearby Suffolk University, Wheelock College, and the six-member Boston ProArts Consortium.

Nearly two-thirds of all classes have less than twenty-five students, and professors receive high marks for their knowledge and accessibility. "The quality of teaching is greatly enhanced by the small student-faculty ratio and the availability of profs outside of class," says a communications disorders major. Though adjunct professors teach a large portion of freshman classes, students seem to appreciate their real-world advice—especially considering the competitive nature of a career in the arts. The library holds 193,000 volumes, mostly related to communication and performing arts, and students may also take advantage of more than seven hundred thousand volumes in the collections of ten nearby academic and museum libraries.

Though adjunct professors teach a large portion of freshman classes, students seem to appreciate their real-world advice— especially considering the competitive nature of a career in the arts.

Emerson students are a "truly specific breed," according to a junior. "They tend to be driven in the communication and performing-arts worlds. They are the bright student who isn't looking for a typical liberal arts education; ones with strong, yet open minds." Nearly two-thirds hail from outside of Massachusetts, and 72 percent come from public high schools. "Emerson students are different because individuality doesn't create barriers," says a student, "but instead enhances creativity." Whites account for 85 percent of the student body, African-Americans 2 percent, Hispanics 3 percent, and Asian-Americans another 2 percent. Hot campus issues include gay/lesbian relations and a constant debate among students about "where the tuition

> "With two hundred thousand college students, there are always things happening."

money goes." Emerson offers 251 merit scholarships to qualified applicants, ranging from $4,000 to a half-ride. There are no athletic scholarships.

Forty-five percent of students live in one of four residence halls, some on special theme floors including the Writer's Block (cute, huh?), and the Wellness and Digital Culture floors. "Freshmen get priority," says a student, "so upperclassmen have a harder time getting housing." Residence halls are comfortable and well maintained, and "definitely the hub for campus activity," according to a communication disorders major. Campus dining options include the Little Building and Zero Marlborough, which offer traditional college fare as well as vegetarian, vegan, and kosher selections. Students feel safe on campus, "although there isn't a strong security presence," according to a senior.

Forty-five percent of students live in one of four residence halls, some on special theme floors including the Writer's Block (cute, huh?), and the Wellness and Digital Culture floors.

Campus life gets two thumbs up from students. "I loved on-campus life!" gushes a student. "I was actively involved and loved every minute of my time on campus." More than fifty student organizations and performance groups offer students ample opportunity for involvement, including two radio stations, six humor and literary journals, ten performance troupes, and six production organizations. For those seeking less-structured playtime, there are the usual campus parties and gatherings. The Greek scene attracts 4 percent of Emerson men and women, and its share of party animals. Underage drinking is against college rules, and students note that there is little pressure to drink here.

Of course, for those inclined to "party hard," there is Boston, arguably the best college town in the nation. "With two hundred thousand college students, there are always things happening," says a student. Another gushes, "Boston is amazing." There are plenty of diversions, including museums, the Franklin Park Zoo, Freedom Trail, the Boston Symphony Orchestra, and major league baseball at Fenway Park. Volunteer opportunities abound, and "some kids say they learn just as much out of the classroom," according to a fifth-year student. Back on campus, popular festivities include Hand Me Down Night (during which outgoing club officers "hand down" their positions to incoming officers), Greek Week, and the New Student Revue.

Emerson fields twelve Division III athletic teams, and the Lions compete as a member of the Eastern College Athletic Conference. The college is also a charter member of the Great Northeast Athletic Conference; recent GNAC champions include the women's cross-country team and the men's basketball and golf squads. Emersonians also enjoy a strong intramural program and take advantage of a ten-thousand-square-foot fitness center featuring state-of-the-art fitness equipment, classes, and wellness workshops.

Emerson College is a place where students' talents and passions take center stage. Innovative academics, caring professors, and a strong connection to real-world experiences foster within students "an eagerness to learn and express ourselves creatively," says a theatre arts major. For those seeking a rich academic environment dedicated exclusively to communications and arts, this small New England college may be just the place to make themselves heard.

Overlaps

Boston University, New York University, Syracuse, Ithaca College, University of Southern California

---

If You Apply To ➤

Emerson: Regular admissions: Feb. 1. Financial aid: Mar. 1. Housing: May 1. Does not guarantee to meet demonstrated need. Campus interviews: optional, informational. No alumni interviews. SATs or ACTs: required. SAT IIs: optional. Essay question: personal statement.

Emory University

Jones Center, Atlanta, GA 30322

Often compared to Duke and Vanderbilt, Emory may be most similar to Wash U. in St. Louis. Both have suburban locations in major cities and both tout business and premed as major draws. If the campus is uninspiring, the suburban Atlanta location is unbeatable.

Emory University benefits from great weather, substantial funding from neighbor Coca-Cola, and talented students who come from far and wide to take advantage of it all. "Not only do students obtain a world-class education, they can also have fun doing it," says a freshman. Yet despite the infusion of financial resources and gifted faculty, leaders of Emory are still struggling to articulate a vision that will help it realize its potential as another Vanderbilt or Duke in the South and as a major player on the national scene.

Set on 631 acres of woods and rolling hills, Emory's campus spreads out from an academic quad of marble-covered, red-roofed buildings. More contemporary

Website: www.emory.edu
Location: Suburban
Total Enrollment: 10,945
Undergraduates: 5,630
Male/Female: 44/56
SAT Ranges: V 640–720
  M 660–740
ACT Range: 29–33

The FAME program (Freshman Advising and Mentoring at Emory) helps students adjust to college life, grouping them into sections of sixteen to eighteen peers, with faculty, staff, and student mentors.

structures dot the periphery of the lush, green grounds. Recent additions include centers for the performing arts and the sciences, and a new facility for the nursing school. The nucleus of campus has also been closed to all car traffic except for Emory shuttles. "The administration eventually wants to have a pedestrian campus," says a sophomore.

Emory's rigorous and comprehensive distribution requirements take up more than a third of every student's total coursework; they're divided into six categories, including Tools of Learning, the Individual and Society, and Aesthetics and Values. Students must also take two seminars during their academic careers—one tailored to freshmen (fifty to sixty are available each term, limited to eighteen students each), and one at an upper level. The FAME program (Freshman Advising and Mentoring at Emory) helps students adjust to college life, grouping them into sections of sixteen to eighteen peers, with faculty, staff, and student mentors. Entering freshmen seeking an even smaller environment may want to consider starting at Emory's two-year Oxford College, where six hundred students earn their associate's degrees in a "small-town" atmosphere, transferring to the main campus to finish up. Emory is also a member of the Atlanta Regional Consortium for Higher Education,* allowing students to take courses at other area schools. Students who wish to really get away can tap into the Center for International Programs Abroad, which offers more than sixty study-abroad options in other nations. And the school's Journeys of Reconciliation help cultivate relationships of education, partnership, service, and friendship with communities around the world.

> "Not only do students obtain a world-class education, they can also have fun doing it."

As Emory has built and renovated academic buildings, the school has also spent lavishly to draw new faculty members, adding star quality and teaching and research competence to key departments. Over the past decade, for instance, the chemistry and biology departments have been beefed up; they also benefit from physical proximity to the federal Centers for Disease Control. Archbishop Desmond Tutu has joined the faculty of the school of theology, while political science benefits from professors with ties to the Carter Center (named for the former president), who are also regular guests on nearby CNN. Students say economics, math and computer science, psychology, and English are strong, as are the premed offerings (especially neuroscience and behavioral biology), and the undergraduate business program. A 4–2 program enables students to earn bachelor's degrees at Emory, and then pursue master of science degrees in engineering at Georgia Institute of Technology. Recent additions to the academic menu include Chinese studies (offering a major and minor in Chinese language and literature) and American studies.

> "There is an unlimited amount of things to do in Atlanta."

Thirty percent of Emory students are Georgians, and a little over half are from the Southeast. New York, New Jersey, California, and Florida are also well represented. "Emory is a very diverse institution with people from various backgrounds," says a finance major. "Though it is in the South, Emory is in no way a 'Southern' school. The only time I hear a Southern accent is when I leave campus." The statistics bear that out: African-Americans constitute 9 percent of the student body, Asian-Americans 15 percent, and Hispanics 3 percent. The recent revamp of rules and regulations for Greek life sparked campus debate, and gay rights and racial issues are also topics of conversation. "Emory frequently hosts well-known speakers, such as Julian Bond, Alan Keyes, and Spike Lee, to speak on such issues," says a sophomore. Merit scholarships range from two-thirds of tuition to a full ride; there are no athletic scholarships.

Sixty-five percent of Emory's students live on campus; 1,500 hang their hat in Clairmont Campus, a residential facility for undergraduates and grad students.

Campus housing is guaranteed for four years, and dorms "are well-kept, with air-conditioning, heating, high-speed Ethernet connections, telephone connections, and free cable," says a sophomore. Rooms also have sinks and carpeting. Newcomers are housed together during the freshman year, which a junior calls "one of the best experiences I've had here." Campus dwellers are required to buy a meal plan, which can be used in the spacious dining hall inside the student center, or at other school restaurants, including a kosher deli, snack bar, and an ice-cream and frozen-yogurt parlor.

Fraternities and sororities attract 28 percent of Emory's men and 31 percent of women, and most students say the Greeks dominate the social scene on campus. Off campus, it's a different story. "There is an unlimited amount of things to do in Atlanta: Watch a Braves game, see a play at Fox Theatre, go to an exhibit at the High Museum, shop at Underground Atlanta or the Lenox Mall (to which Emory provides a free shuttle every Saturday), and the list goes on," says a finance major. Clubs and restaurants in the Buckhead neighborhood are also popular. Alcohol isn't allowed in the dorms, and resident advisors strictly enforce that policy, but an economics major says that "If you are not stupid, you won't get caught." One quirky highlight of the social calendar is Dooley's Week, a spring festival in honor of Emory's enigmatic mascot, William M. Dooley, who reportedly escaped from the biology lab almost one hundred years ago. "He's a guy in a top hat, cane, and skeleton suit," one student explains. "If

"Emory is a first-class institution."

he walks into your class, the professor either has to let you go, or get soaked by water guns." There's also a costume ball on Dooley's birthday, and band festivals in the spring and fall have recently brought Run-DMC and Ludacris to campus. Road trips are also plentiful, ranging from New Orleans for Mardi Gras to Disney World and the beaches of Florida and Alabama to Memphis, Tennessee—home of Graceland, great barbecue, and the Delta blues.

Emory doesn't field a varsity football team, which students say dampens school spirit, though the university is perennially ranked among the nation's top twenty-five in Division III for all-around athletic excellence. Men's and women's soccer, track and field, and swimming and diving are strong, as are baseball and women's cross-country. There's also an extensive intramural program, which takes advantage of Emory's George W. Woodruff Physical Education Center. Men's basketball competes in the University Athletic Association against such academic powerhouses as the University of Chicago, Johns Hopkins, and Carnegie Mellon.

While many Southern schools suffer from regional provincialism, Emory has cultivated a national reputation. And don't think about asking for a Pepsi to slake your thirst here—the largesse of another nearby soda company has given Emory the nickname Coca-Cola U. Even with the cola money, though, Emory hasn't won the name recognition of some of its academic peers. Yet students aren't concerned. "Emory is a first-class institution," says an international studies and sociology major.

Overlaps

Duke, Washington University (MO), University of Pennsylvania, Vanderbilt, Georgetown

If You Apply To ➤

Emory: Early decision: Nov. 1, Jan. 1. Regular admissions: Jan. 15. Financial aid: Feb. 15. Housing: May 1. Meets demonstrated need of 98%. No campus or alumni interviews. SATs or ACTs: required. SAT IIs: optional. Accepts the Common Application and electronic applications. Essay question: half-page on both a meaningful activity or work experience, and why Emory is a good match; and one to three pages on any subject of genuine interest to you.

The Evergreen State College

Olympia, WA 98505

There's no mistaking Evergreen for a typical public college. Never mind the way-out garb favored by its students. Evergreen's interdisciplinary, team-taught curriculum is truly unique. To find anything remotely like Evergreen, you'll need to go private and travel east to places like Hampshire or Sarah Lawrence.

Website: www.evergreen.edu
Location: City outskirts
Total Enrollment: 4,227
Undergraduates: 4,001
Male/Female: 42/58
SAT Ranges: V 540–650
   M 480–600
ACT Range: 18-21
Financial Aid: 51%
Expense: Pub $ $
Phi Beta Kappa: No
Applicants: 1,237
Accepted: 82%
Enrolled: 38%
Grad in 6 Years: 56%
Returning Freshmen: 69%
Academics: ✑ ✑ ✑
Social: ☎ ☎ ☎
Q of L: ★ ★ ★ ★
Admissions: (360) 867-6170
Email Address:
   admissions@evergreen.edu

Strongest Programs:
   Environmental Studies
   Media Arts
   Physical and Biological
      Sciences
   Social Science
   Computer Science
   Humanities

When it comes to bucking the mainstream, few schools are so insistent—and successful—as Evergreen State College. The school's unofficial motto: *Omnia extares*, Latin for "Let it all hang out," demonstrates the school's laid-back atmosphere. Founded in 1967 as Washington State's experimental college, Evergreen lacks grades, majors, and even departments. Students have almost unlimited control over their academic destinies, which a senior calls "the double-edged sword of choice and responsibility." This system may sound strange, but it works: among Evergreen's alumni is Matt Groening, creator of *The Simpsons*, *Futurama*, and *Life in Hell*.

Evergreen lies in a fir forest at the edge of Puget Sound and is within walking distance of the Washington coast. The peaceful, one thousand-acre campus includes a twenty-four-acre organic plant and animal farm, as well as 3,300 feet of undeveloped beach. It's a "beautiful, wooded location," says a senior. "The students who attend TESC are independent thinkers," adds a classmate. "They are interested in synthesis rather than separation." That said, most of Evergreen's buildings are boxy, concrete-and-steel creations, though the Longhouse Education and Culture Center is designed in the Native American style typical of the Pacific Northwest. Evergreen's Tacoma campus, for juniors and seniors, now has a science lab dedicated to public health and other environmental science studies, as well as a multimedia lecture hall seating 250 people.

At first glance, Evergreen's wide-open curriculum looks like Easy Street: no required classes and few traditional exams to slog through at the end of each ten-week quarter. And instead of signing up for a set of unrelated courses to fulfill requirements, students enroll in a coordinated "program," which may last as long as a year. Each program is team-taught by multiple professors; one recent program, Problems Without Solutions, for example, looked at topics like AIDS and homelessness from the perspective of political science, philosophy, anthropology, economics, statistics, and writing, while Motion and Matter incorporated physics, calculus, and chemistry. The integrated approach draws raves, but also warnings to expect a sizable workload. "The courses are very rigorous, and I find myself spending at least forty–fifty hours a week doing homework," says a sophomore. Freshmen select an interdisciplinary core program, while upperclassmen concentrate in more specialized areas, often concluding with a thesis or Individual Learning Contract developed with a faculty sponsor.

Since Evergreen lacks traditional departments, it's tough to assess the quality of various programs. But even without rankings and ratings, students say definite winners include expressive arts and film and media studies. The superb environmental

"The students who attend TESC are independent thinkers."

science program invariably fills up fast, and offers classes in ornithology, marine biology, and wetlands studies. To supplement their coursework, students may explore Puget Sound on one of Evergreen's two forty-foot boats, or spend seven weeks at a bird sanctuary in Oregon. "The sciences boast undergrads doing grad-level work for professors," says a junior. The animation program is a big draw, too, with Hollywood studios like Disney quickly snapping up graduates. These programs, along with the general penchant for activism, set the tone on campus.

Because Evergreen attracts many nontraditional students, administrators take advising and career counseling seriously; they've also asked faculty members to do more to help students adjust to life on campus. "You get an amazing amount of support and advising from your actual professors," says a sophomore. "Academic advising has also been very helpful!" Students give professors high marks for teaching skill—and more. "Professors actually care about the success of their students," says one student. "I've had professors give their home phone number to the entire class!" Because there is no tenure at Evergreen, there's less pressure for professors to conduct research and publish their findings—and less to distract them from their undergraduates. Still, individual interest and motivation are the keys to getting the most from four years at Evergreen.

Not surprisingly, "Greeners" are an environmentally conscious, nonconformist lot, open-minded and liberal; many are community-college transfers. Ideologically, the school remains one of the best choices for students who think they were born thirty years too late. If the '60s was your decade, take heart: special admissions consideration is given to applicants twenty-five years of age and older, as well as Vietnam-era veterans and

"The sciences boast undergrads doing grad-level work for professors."

applicants whose parents have not graduated from college. Three-quarters of Evergreen's students are homegrown Washington residents, and 17 percent are minorities, with Native Americans accounting for 5 percent, and African-Americans, Asian-Americans, and Hispanics each accounting for 4 percent of the student body. Important campus issues include abortion, women's rights, environmental issues, and various other political concerns. "Evergreen is very liberal," explains a sophomore. There are forty-five merit scholarships of up to $3,000 each, and athletic awards are once again available, as Evergreen enters Division II of the NAIA.

Twenty-one percent of Evergreen students, mostly freshmen and sophomores, live happily on campus, many in apartment complexes with single bedrooms, shared bathrooms—with bathtubs, not just shower stalls—and full kitchens, says a junior. Because housing can be expensive, and because it can be tough to get a room, most students live off campus, especially after their first year. An efficient bus system brings non-residents back to campus, though it helps to

"This is a place where you can transform your life."

have a car, students say. The food service on campus, Bon Appetit, offers a wide variety of dishes including vegan options, all of which are organic. Some students complain, however, that "the food on campus is more expensive than it should be."

Nearby Olympia (the state capital) doesn't really qualify as a college town, but it's progressive and open-minded—"it is a very community oriented city and very welcoming to Evergreen students," says one student. Situated at the southernmost point of the Puget Sound, Olympia naturally offers a lot of water-related activities. The city also has "beautiful trees and mountains for hiking," kept lush and green by the (interminable) rain, which stops in time for summer break and begins again by October. Seattle (an hour away) and the rugged Oregon coast (three to four hours) provide changes of scenery for students with wheels. The college offers all types of outdoor equipment for rent, from backpacks and skis to kayaks and sailboats. Evergreen's large College Activities Building houses a radio station, the student newspaper, and space for student gatherings.

You may laugh at Evergreen's mascot, an eight-foot clam named "Gooeyduck," for the large geoduck clams found in Puget Sound, but the school is getting more serious about organized sports. When it switched to NAIA Division II, Evergreen expanded its athletic program, adding women's volleyball and cross-country to

Not surprisingly, "Greeners" are an environmentally conscious, nonconformist lot, openminded and liberal; many are community-college transfers.

To supplement their coursework, students may explore Puget Sound on one of Evergreen's two forty-foot boats, or spend seven weeks at a bird sanctuary in Oregon.

soccer, swimming, tennis, and basketball. While the college hasn't brought home championships yet, it has produced two All-American swimmers and one All-American men's basketball player. Many students also enjoy intramural Frisbee, volleyball, skiing, and sailing. As might be expected at this nonconformist Mecca, fraternities and sororities don't exist; social life revolves around movies and parties with friends. The biggest annual event is Super Saturday, a huge community fair the day after graduation, featuring bands, arts and crafts, and ethnic foods.

To succeed at Evergreen, students must take an active role in shaping their educational experience. For a select group, that's an opportunity, rather than a burden. "This is a place where you can transform your life," says a junior. "For the future, we must protect the freedom we've enjoyed the freedom we've enjoyed for thirty-plus years," adds a classmate. That may prove a challenge, as many long-time faculty retire and current administrators seek to boost enrollment by 40 percent over the next few years. "Growth is resisted by students here, but state funding demands it," sighs a junior.

If You Apply To ➤

Evergreen: Rolling admissions: Mar. 1. Financial aid: Mar. 15. Housing: May 1. Meets demonstrated need of 51%. No interviews. SATs or ACTs: required. Accepts electronic applications. Essay question (optional): academic goals.

Fairfield University

Fairfield, CT 06824

Fairfield is one of the up-and-coming schools in the Roman Catholic universe. Undergraduate enrollment has grown by more than one thousand in the past decade. Strategic location near New York City is a major attraction. Lack of big-time sports keeps Fairfield from the Boston College/Holy Cross echelon.

Fairfield University, a comprehensive Jesuit school, focuses on "preparing students for lives of leadership and service in a constantly changing world." To provide a well-rounded education, the school combines solid academics, real-world opportunities in and outside of the classroom, and an abundance of community-service projects. No doubt about it, Fairfield is moving into the same class as older, more revered East Coast Jesuit institutions.

The university's physical beauty, a scenic, tree-lined campus just ninety minutes from Manhattan, is a source of pride. The administration takes pains to preserve a lush atmosphere of sprawling lawns, ponds, and natural woodlands. Buildings are a mix of collegiate Gothic, Norman chateau, English manor, and modern. The library, Campus Center, and Science Center have all undergone recent expansion, and the business school recently relocated to a new building with state-of-the-art teaching facilities, seminar rooms, and group study areas. Scholars enjoy a twenty-four-hour computer lab, Geographic Information Systems lab, and a wireless 125-person computer lab in the School of Nursing. A new fifty-one thousand-square-foot Athletic Center offers improved locker facilities for varsity players and an aerobics and free-weight area for weekend warriors.

> **"The dorms vary in quality depending on which building you are in."**

Despite the beautiful facilities, students may find it difficult to squeeze a workout into their demanding class schedules. Everyone must complete the liberal arts core curriculum, with two to five courses from each of five areas: math and sciences, history and social science, philosophy and religious studies, English and fine arts, and modern and classical languages. The core constitutes almost half of a student's total courseload.

Fairfield's main academic strengths are business (accounting, finance, and economics), the social sciences (sociology and psychology), and the natural sciences (biology and physics). "Fairfield is mainly known by reputation and in the literature as a liberal arts school, but I believe their biology program is underrated," says one biology major. Upperclassmen can now design their own majors.

Fairfield's academic climate is not cut-throat, but challenging nevertheless. "The nice part has been that although it has gained respect academically, it still retains its reputation while not making students feel as though they were in a competitive or cut-throat environment," one senior explains. Recent additions to the curriculum include minors in information systems; operations management; legal studies; classical studies; Irish studies, which has strong ties to the University of Galway; and Italian studies, which maintains strong ties to the Lorenzo de'Medici Institute in Florence. Engineering students may enroll in joint five-year programs with the Rensselaer Polytechnic Institute, Columbia University, or the University of Connecticut. MBA candidates can now have a concentration in e-business. Approximately 150 students study abroad each year, through their choice of more than one hundred programs in fifty nations. In the past two years,

"It's not the destination, but the journey that counts."

ten Fairfield students have been awarded Fulbright Scholarships for studies abroad. About eight percent are part of the four-year honors program. Sophomores can join the new Ignatian Residential College, in which they live together and, literally, explore the meaning of life. A new computer engineering program is developing.

Fairfield's advanced fiber-optic network brings email, Internet, and video capabilities to classrooms, offices, and dorm rooms. There are no graduate teaching assistants, hence no teaching assistants, and 98 percent of the classes have fewer than forty students.

The vast majority of Fairfield's students come from Roman Catholic families, and approximately one-quarter from Connecticut. Minority enrollment is small, with African-Americans constituting 3 percent of the student body, Hispanics 5 percent, and Asian-Americans another 3 percent. Students are somewhat self-conscious about their conservative, preppy image, referring jokingly to themselves as "J. Crew U." Volunteerism abounds, and tensions with beach residents of Fairfield top the list of current issues at the college. A peer group helps Fairfield deal with race relations and sexual harassment. Minority recruiting efforts include programs in Latin American, Asian, Women's, Judaic, and Black studies, and there are many diversity celebrations.

To help students with Fairfield's steep price, the school offers 160 merit scholarships annually, ranging from $7,000 to $12,500, and 165 athletic scholarships. Freshmen are introduced to Fairfield with a thorough orientation program. Two days of academic orientation and a parents' program occur in June, and a two-day orientation occurs in September before classes begin. All first-semester freshmen must complete the non-credit, non-graded First Year Experience Program.

Fairfield's "comfortable and well-maintained" residence halls house more than three-fourths of the student body. One senior admits some dorms are better than others: "The dorms vary in quality depending on which building you are in." But the school recently built a new upperclassman apartment village, and four of the traditional halls have been renovated. In one of the more unusual housing arrangements in American higher education, upperclassmen can move off campus to

(Continued)
Admissions: (203) 254-4100
Email Address:
   admis@mail.fairfield.edu

Strongest Programs:
   Biology
   International Studies
   Art History
   Religious Studies
   Sociology
   Accounting and Finance
   Mechanical Engineering

The rapidly expanding curriculum now includes minors in information systems; operations management; legal studies; classical studies; Irish studies, which has strong ties to the University of Galway; and Italian studies, which maintains strong ties to the Lorenzo de'Medici Institute in Florence.

nearby beach houses, which they can rent at off-season rates. Meal plan options are available to all students.

Fairfield's proximity to the beaches of the Long Island Sound, a quick five-minute drive from campus, provides students with a scenic social space for everything from romantic retreats to rowdy parties. Still, students say much of the social life takes place on campus, where sponsored events range from dances to hanging out at the coffeehouse and on-campus pub to concerts with stars like Blues Traveler and Billy Joel. Harvest Weekend at the end of October and Dogwoods Weekend at the end of April provide relief from the stress of studying. Road trips to New York (only an hour by train) and Boston are popular. The college recently instituted a new program for alcohol misuse or abuse. Students who violate rules must attend educational programs focused on substance abuse to remedy their records. "Students still drink though, regardless of penalties," a senior says. Although Jesuits are very much in evidence, and often live in the dorms, students say they do not hinder the social scene. The Campus Ministry draws a large following, with daily Masses, retreats about three times a semester, and regular community-service work including two weeks of programs in the Caribbean and Latin America.

As for the surrounding area, one junior says Fairfield is not a college town and beach residents don't always approve of beach-apartment students and their activities. "Most Fairfield residents use FU facilities, but they treat the students like garbage," complains one student. Community-service work in the less advantaged community of nearby Bridgeport is a common pastime for Fairfield students.

Athletics have come of age at Fairfield, with a number of women's sports leading the way. Women's volleyball reached NCAA qualifiers during the 2000 and 2001 seasons, while women's basketball earned an at-large bid to the NCAA tournament in 2001. Men's soccer and women's lacrosse and field hockey have also brought home trophies. Men's and women's basketball both draw crowds, and the boisterous home-court fans, who come to games in full Fairfield regalia, have been dubbed the "Red Sea." The university recently eliminated varsity football and men's ice hockey as a budget-cutting move. Living up to the Jesuit motto of sound mind and sound body, many students play on intramural teams, whose exploits are copiously chronicled in the campus newspaper. The school also takes pride in its high graduation rate for athletes, regularly one of the highest rates in the country.

Like those graduation rates, Fairfield University is on the upswing. By working on preserving and updating facilities, expanding academic offerings and helping students find their roles in society, Fairfield is hoping to attract more students dedicated to its motto: "It's not the destination, but the journey that counts."

Overlaps

Villanova, Boston College, Providence, Loyola (MD), College of Holy Cross

If You Apply To ➢ **Fairfield:** Early decision: Nov. 15. Regular admissions: Feb. 1. Financial aid: Feb. 15. Does not guarantee to meet full demonstrated need. Campus and alumni interviews: optional and informational. SATs or ACTs: required. SAT IIs: optional. Accepts the Common Application and electronic applications. Essay question: from Common Application and a personal statement.

Gainesville, FL 32611

It should come as no surprise that UF is a world leader in citrus science. Throw in communications, engineering, and Latin American studies to the list of renowned programs. Among Deep South public universities, only the University of Georgia rivals UF in overall quality.

Set on two thousand acres of rolling, heavily forested terrain in north-central Florida, the University of Florida is an athletic powerhouse, an academic dynamo, and a bastion of diversity. The school is massive and is getting more so. But then bigger can be better, as the university continues to see a boost in applications, bolstering the school's selectivity and causing one student to report that the climate on campus is "becoming more academically oriented, but not too stuffy!"

The central campus, which is listed as a National Historic Area, has twenty-one buildings from the early twentieth century on the National Register of Historic Places. Buildings are designed in the collegiate Gothic architectural style, featuring red brick with white trim. More than a dozen new buildings or additions to existing ones have been finished in the past few years. More are to be completed by 2004, including a residence hall and a health professions complex. Newer facilities include a 233,000-square-foot physics building and a residential living complex. Size matters when it comes to being able to boast a list of superlatives, it seems, such as UF's having the world's largest citrus research center, a microkelvin laboratory capable of producing the coldest temperature in the universe, a world-class bell carillon, a federally funded world-class brain institute, and the Florida Museum of Natural History, which is said to be one of the nation's top ten.

Academically, UF is strongest in preprofessional areas, and is known for its programs in engineering, tax law, and pharmacy. Business administration is the most popular major, followed by finance and psychology. Other popular majors are accounting, electrical engineering, elementary education, and advertising. The schools of engineering, medicine, law, business, education, and journalism are winners, according to student critics. The well-known College

> **"Most professors have a tremendous amount of professional experience and are very enthusiastic."**

of Journalism and Communications was the first to offer students an electronic newsroom, and broadcasting students run their own radio and television stations. UF's honors program is reserved for students with 3.6 GPAs and SAT scores of at least 1280 overall. Students mention foreign languages and math as weaker areas (too many TAs), along with fine arts and music. The University Scholars Program offers $2,500 stipends for research working one on one with a faculty member. Regardless of a student's main interests, he or she has a good chance of finding a major program, since only two universities, Ohio State and Minnesota, offer more degree programs on one campus than UF.

To complement the preprofessional leanings of its students, UF has a general education program through which students must fulfill credits in composition, literature and arts, historical and philosophical studies, international studies and cultural diversity, social and behavioral sciences, mathematical sciences, and the physical and biological sciences, to be taken over the four-year B.A. program. There is also a six-credit International Diversity focus requirement. Internships abound, along with volunteer and leadership opportunities, and foreign study in such places as Brazil, Israel, Colombia, Japan, China, or more than a dozen cities in Eastern and

Website: www.ufl.edu
Location: Center city
Total Enrollment: 46,515
Undergraduates: 33,639
Male/Female: 52/48
SAT Ranges: V 550–650
 M 570–670
ACT Range: 24–28
Financial Aid: 64%
Expense: Pub $ $ $ $
Phi Beta Kappa: Yes
Applicants: 18,625
Accepted: 63%
Enrolled: 53%
Grad in 6 Years: 70%
Returning Freshmen: 92%
Academics: 🖉 🖉 🖉 🖉
Social: ☎ ☎ ☎ ☎
Q of L: ★ ★ ★ ★
Admissions: (352) 392-1365
Email Address:
 freshman@ufl.edu

Strongest Programs:
 Engineering
 Counselor Education
 Tax Law
 Latin American Studies
 Journalism/Communications
 Chemistry
 Anthropology
 Citrus Science
 Business

Western Europe. Recent program additions are degrees in Middle School Education and in Digital Arts and Sciences.

Like many supersized universities, UF suffers from an impersonal environment and a mountain of bureaucracy. Occasionally, lectures in the College of Business Administration have to be videotaped (and also offered through cable television) so everyone can see them. Although course registration has been frustrating for some in the past, all first-year students are now guaranteed seats through the university's telephone registration system. The professors are often praised. "The quality of teaching is very high," says one junior. "Most professors have a tremendous amount of professional experience and are very enthusiastic." Academic pressure varies with each major and each student. "Classes can be challenging," one student says. "The academic qualifications of our students are steadily increasing; thus, studying is of growing importance."

Faculty advisement is said to be fair, and is bolstered by the Academic Advising Center. Experiences differ among students, with one junior reporting that advising is "atrocious" and that advisors often lack a genuine interest in students' needs. To

"There's no hostility between ethnic groups, but not very much mixing."

improve academic counseling, students receive personalized letters as they reach thirty, forty-five, and sixty hours, telling them of specific grade and course requirements in their programs. A similar program is being developed to track freshmen and transfers in engineering and political science. An "incredible" career resource center has many students singing its praises: here students can seek advice, conduct research, and interview for jobs.

Florida has a largely homegrown student body: more than 95 percent of the young scholars on campus are Floridians, and 86 percent finished in the top fifth of their class in high school. Despite the geographical homogeneity, students claim they're a diverse bunch. A veteran says that diversity "is a highly emphasized subject" at UF. People Awareness Week, a multicultural celebration, has grown into a popular campus event, and UF recently established a Latino-Hispanic Cultural Center to serve the majority minority on campus. Many of the African-American student body belong to their own set of fraternities, and notes one student, "There's no hostility between ethnic groups, but not very much mixing." Hispanics make up 11 percent, Asian-Americans 7 percent, and African-Americans another 8 percent of the students. UF offers more than two hundred athletic scholarships, as well as 3,100 merit scholarships. National Merit Scholars automatically qualify if they list UF as their first choice.

Housing is iffy in terms of getting a room if you're not a first-year student. Selection is governed by a Social Security number lottery, and there are just not enough rooms for everybody. Freshmen are guaranteed space, but after that the

"The social life is awesome."

unlucky must fend for themselves in the off-campus housing market. Only 21 percent of the undergraduates get campus housing, available in doubles, triples, or suites. Most of the dorms are coed by floor. Fraternity and sorority houses provide another housing alternative. Students on campus eat on the university's meal plan, which is "pretty bad," or use the dorm kitchens. There are also several student pubs on campus.

Students love their home away from home—Gainesville—described by one agriculture economics student as "a great college town." A city of about 125,000 midway between the Atlantic Ocean and the Gulf of Mexico, Gainesville offers plenty of stores, restaurants, and bars as well as a sports arena. Campus security is excellent.

The university owns a nearby lake, which is "great for lazy Sundays" as well as more vigorous water sports, and there are more than enough parks, forests, rivers, and streams close by for backpacking, camping, and canoeing. "The social life is awesome," a student reports. Fifteen percent of the men and women join fraternities and sororities, making Florida's Greek system one of the nation's largest. The best road trips are to UF away football games and, of course, the beach.

Sports are a year-round obsession at Florida. The university has one of the top intercollegiate programs in the nation, with varsity competition for men and women in sixteen sports, including nationally ranked teams in football, baseball, track, golf, tennis, gymnastics, volleyball, and swimming and diving. In the fall, Gator football sets the campus on its ear with a flurry of "big weekend" social events, most notably the annual Homecoming extravaganza—"Gator Growl"—which boasts a half-million-dollar budget and attendance averaging seventy-eight thousand people each year. New head coach Ron Zook emerged from the shadow of legendary coach Steve Spurrier to lead the football squad to a post-season bowl game and a big win over the University of Georgia. Basketball is the biggest winter spectator sport, and both the men's and women's swimming teams are powerhouses. Women's sports are generously funded and also get a fair amount of fan support; a new women's softball stadium now highlights that program. After men's football and basketball, women's gymnastics and volleyball are the next most popular, and women's tennis has enjoyed national prominence, as has men's golf. Intramural sports are also big, and a sixty-thousand-square-foot fitness park offers aerobics, martial arts, basketball, racquetball, softball, squash, strength conditioning, tennis, and volleyball.

For some students, the sheer size of UF is overwhelming. For others, that's a drawing card. Whether standing in line at registration or for kickoff at the football stadium known as "the Swamp," loyal Gators certainly have spirit. And they aren't shy about saying so. As one student comments, at UF she has found "top-notch academics with unparalleled athletics: the best of both worlds!"

> **Overlaps**
>
> **Florida State, University of Central Florida, University of South Florida, University of Miami (FL), Duke**

> **If You Apply To ➤**
>
> **Florida:** Rolling admissions. Campus interviews: optional, evaluative. No alumni interviews. SATs or ACTs: required. SAT IIs: required for some programs. Essay question.

Florida Institute of Technology

150 West University Boulevard, Melbourne, FL 32901-6975

FIT is practically a branch of the nearby Kennedy Space Center, so it should come as no surprise that aeronautics and aviation are specialties. The Atlantic ocean is also close at hand, an ideal spot for marine biology. With a total enrollment of only 4,409, FIT is the smallest of the major technical institutions in the Southeast.

Students at the Florida Institute of Technology can explore the endless depths of the ocean and shoot for the stars. With the ocean around the corner and Cape Canaveral only forty minutes away, it's not surprising that some of the most cutting-edge work in water-related sciences and space happens here. The combination of academic excellence and a bustling Central Florida location—just an hour from the dizzying lights of Walt Disney World—has students flocking to this innovative school.

Founded in 1958 to meet the needs of engineers and scientists working at what is now Kennedy Space Center, Florida Tech's contemporary 130-acre campus features

> **Website:** www.fit.edu
> **Location:** Small city
> **Total Enrollment:** 4,409
> **Undergraduates:** 2,191
> **Male/Female:** 66/34
> **SAT Ranges:** V 510–620
>   M 550–650

(Continued)

ACT Range: 22–28

Financial Aid: 77%

Expense: Pr $ $

Phi Beta Kappa: Yes

Applicants: 2,157

Accepted: 82%

Enrolled: 31%

Grad in 6 Years: 56%

Returning Freshmen: 77%

Academics: ✏ ✏ ✏

Social: ☎ ☎ ☎

Q of L: ★ ★ ★

Admissions: (321) 674-8030

Email Address:
   admission@fit.edu

Strongest Programs:
   Aeronautics/Aviation
   Computer Engineering
   Electrical Engineering
   Mechanical Engineering
   Marine Biology

more than two hundred species of palm trees and botanical gardens in a tropical setting. Campus architecture ranges from modern to Georgian Gothic. Newer facilities include the state-of-the-art Olin Engineering Complex, Olin Life Sciences Building, and Clemente Center for Sports & Recreation.

If you're considering Florida Tech, make sure you have a strong background in math and science, especially chemistry and physics. Few students major in the less practical sciences. Though many students grouse that Florida Tech is too expensive for their tastes, students who plan their education well are able to get high-paying technical jobs immediately following graduation. Prospective aviation students can major in aviation management, aviation meteorology, aviation computer science, as well as aeronautics with or without flight option. The flight school has a modern fleet of thirty airplanes and three flight-training devices, and the precision-flying team regularly wins titles. Florida Tech, the only independent technological university in the Southeast, garners some of the best young minds in the country. The computer and mechanical engineering majors have gained popularity recently, although marine biology is still a popular major. New concentrations include aviation meteorology and business information systems. Weaker areas are the humanities, due to the institute's technical orientation.

"If you don't study, you don't pass."

The academic climate at FIT is challenging. "The courses are designed to challenge all the students in the class and the courses are very rigorous," says an ecology major. An aviation computer science major reports that "every class I go to people are comparing grades. If you don't study, you don't pass." Classes, especially labs, have strict ceilings, but it's usually possible to graduate in four years with the help of academic advisors who can open "closed" sections. Graduate teaching assistants are not overused. "The professors are passionate about the subjects they teach at Florida Tech," says one student. "They go out of their way to help their students understand the material."

All majors offer co-op programs and senior independent research at the Indian River Lagoon or on the RV Delphinus, a sixty-foot research boat the school owns. Recent marine research includes manatee preservation, beach erosion, and sea-turtle studies. Most students, however, are job-minded; 80 percent go to work after getting their degrees; 17 percent head to graduate school. Regardless of major, everyone must take courses in communication, physical or life science, math, humanities, and social sciences.

Thirty percent of Florida Tech students are out-of-staters, while nearly 30 percent arrive from out of the country. "One of our nicknames is 'Foreign Tech,'" says a sophomore. The student body is 56 percent white, yet political correctness and diversity-related issues seem to be taken in stride because of the preponderance of international students. Like any school, the students "vary from kooky to crazy and nerd to jock," says a political science major. A sophomore says FIT "is a great place to learn about different cultures." Florida Tech offers 129 merit scholarships, ranging from $5,000 to $12,500, and forty-five athletic scholarships in six sports. Incoming freshmen are welcomed with a week-long orientation program highlighted by trips to Disney World and the beach, just three miles away. On campus, freshmen may take part in the University Experience Program, which helps first-years adapt to college life.

"The rooms here are comfortable and convenient and much larger than in most college dorms."

Dorms at Florida Tech are modern, air-conditioned (whew!), and well-maintained. Forty-nine percent of students make their home on campus. "The rooms here are comfortable and convenient and much larger than in most college dorms," says a

The flight school has a modern fleet of thirty airplanes and three flight-training devices, and the precision flying team regularly wins titles.

marine biology major. Freshmen are required to live on campus in large double rooms. Four-student apartments are available to a small percentage of qualifying upperclassmen by lottery. Students who live off campus are drawn by cheap rent and not much else, because Melbourne "is not much of a college town," reports an aviation major senior. The meal plan is an open, unlimited arrangement, and students report that the food is survivable.

Most Florida Tech students who don't have cars choose bikes as their favorite mode of transportation. Diversions can be found in Orlando (with Epcot, MGM Studios, and Animal Kingdom abutting Disney World) or at the Kennedy Space Center. Students also hit the road for other Sunshine State cities, including Tampa, Key West, Miami, Daytona, and St. Augustine. Watching space shots from campus with a trained eye (and a cold brew) is a treasured pastime. The campus bar, the Rat, is a popular hangout. Otherwise, though, campus social life is predictably hampered by the low male/female ratio. "There's a greater influx of females to the school that will dramatically improve the social scene," says a molecular biology major. Another student adds, "The social life at Florida Tech is what you make of it, which means sometimes you have to create your own fun."

Fraternities and sororities are slowly becoming more popular at Florida Tech, claiming 17 percent of the men and 11 percent of the women. "The Greek organizations offer excellent extracurricular activities that help you both socially and academically," says a sophomore. And while the campus is officially dry, every frat party has beer that the underage eagerly guzzle, students say. Besides partying, students spend their off time surfing, fishing, hanging out at the beach, shopping, or going for a "Sunday drive" (in the sky) with a flight-school student. Every April, students brace for the invasion of other collegians on spring break. Techies also look forward to Greek Week and intramural sports competitions. With so much water around, it's not surprising that crew is awesome.

Whether it's surveying marine coral fifty feet down or the sky thirty thousand feet up, students at Florida Tech get hands-on experiences that serve to sharpen the school's already specialized, high-quality academics. The administration is focusing on capital improvements and keeping equipment on the cutting edge, so the school is always growing. And with beaches and amusements within manageable distances, students find themselves having some real fun in the sun while they prepare for high-flying careers.

Dorms at Florida Tech are modern, air-conditioned (whew!), and well-maintained. Forty-nine percent of students make their home on campus.

Overlaps

University of Florida, Florida State, Embry-Riddle, University of Central Florida, University of Miami (FL)

If You Apply To ➤

Florida Tech: Rolling admissions. Financial aid: Mar. 15. Campus and alumni interviews: recommended, informational. Alumni interviews: recommended, informational. SATs or ACTs: required. SAT IIs: optional. Accepts the Common Application. Essay question: personal profile of career goals, work or military experience; leadership, community involvement, and athletic activities.

Florida State University

A2500 University Center, Tallahassee, FL 32306-2400

With an assist from its football program, FSU's popularity has burgeoned in recent years. Not that there weren't some quality programs to begin with. The motion picture school is among the best around, and business and the arts are also strong. So long as the football team beats the hated Gators, all is well.

Florida State University has long been synonymous with football, but students at this Sunshine State university enjoy success off the gridiron, too. Here, you could have a Nobel laureate for a professor, study in one of the finest science facilities in the Southeast, or get your feet wet in state government through an internship at the state capitol. The choices are plentiful at FSU, and the pace of life makes it possible to taste a little of everything: a wide array of academic choices, Florida sunshine, and some rowdy football.

FSU is located in Tallahassee, a land described as the "Other Florida": the one with rolling hills, flowering dogwoods and azaleas, and a canopy of moss-draped oaks. Glistening Gulf of Mexico waters are only half an hour away. The main campus features collegiate Georgian structures surrounded by plenty of shade trees, with some modern facilities sprinkled in. Situated on 463 compact acres, the campus is the smallest in the state university system—it's just a ten-minute walk from the main gate on the east side to the science complex on the west side. The University Center, which wraps around the football stadium, offers centralized services, including counseling, financial-aid offices, undergraduate studies, and an active career center. Improvements to the campus include a new Student Life Building and the recently renovated Williams building. Bicycling and skating are popular forms of transportation, though the parking garage provides spaces for more than one thousand cars and a free shuttle bus circles campus for those without wheels.

FSU has outstanding programs in music, drama, art, and dance; it's moving up fast in the natural sciences with improved equipment and facilities in physics, chemistry, and biology. The College of Medicine, which focuses on serving the elderly and underserved communities, is the university's newest. FSU has twenty-five programs rated exemplary by the state university system, more than any of the other ten system schools. Communications, statistics, and business (especially accounting) have strong reputations in the Southeast. The most "wired" campus in the state, FSU has 1,700 computers available to undergraduates. The School of Motion Picture, TV, and Recording Arts has consistently won an impressive array of national and international awards. For gifted students, the honors program offers smaller classes and closer faculty contact, as well as forty special seminars each year. Certain students can even earn their degrees in three years. And Directed Individual Study courses offer undergraduates the chance to participate in independent research projects with faculty direction. Recent academic changes include a new College of Medicine and an increase in distance learning opportunities within the colleges. Internships and political jobs abound for tomorrow's politicians, since the state capitol and Supreme Court are nearby.

"The quality of teaching is excellent."

Students report the academic climate is somewhat laid back but that "the courses are rigorous." Recently, liberal studies requirements were reduced from forty-nine to thirty-six hours, common prerequisites were established, and the total hours for a bachelor's degree were dropped to 120 (with a few exceptions). The general education requirements—courses in math, English, history and social sciences, humanities and fine arts, and natural sciences—are reported to be among the easier classes at FSU. Within FSU's liberal studies program, students must also complete six hours of multicultural understanding coursework—three focusing on diversity within the Western experience and three focusing on cross-cultural studies. Freshmen must take math and English, and may find a TA at the helm in these courses. But overall, faculty members do teach. "The quality of teaching is excellent," a senior says. For those with wanderlust, FSU offers extensive study-abroad options. They include year-long placements in Italy, England, and Spain and summer programs in Greece, Vietnam, Switzerland, France, Costa Rica, Russia, the Czech Republic, and Barbados. The university is making strides in the world of distance

The School of Motion Picture, TV, and Recording Arts has consistently won an impressive array of national and international awards.

learning, allowing some students with an associate's degree to earn their bachelor's degree online. Five undergrad and five master's majors are online.

Perhaps not surprisingly, FSU's student body has a distinctly Floridian flavor: in-staters comprise 81 percent of the group. Nearly two-thirds of the student body are white; 13 percent are African-American, and 9 percent are Hispanic. There's little evidence of racial tension on the diverse campus. Seminoles are a mixture of friendly small-towners and city dwellers, and political tastes tend toward the conservative. While tuition is a hot topic of campus conversation, so are issues like voter registration, the environment, and student-government concerns.

Sixteen percent of FSU's students live in the university dorms, all of which are air-conditioned and wired for Internet access. Students may opt for typically spacious older halls or newer ones that tend to be more cramped. The dorms get mixed reviews, and the number of students who can live in them is limited; rooms are assigned on a first-come, first-served basis. Upperclassmen generally forsake the housing rat race and move into nearby apartments, houses, or trailers, where they take advantage of the city and campus bus systems (substantially cheaper and infinitely easier than driving and parking a car in FSU's infamously crowded lots) to get to school. The dorms are equipped with kitchens; meal plans that offer "good but expensive" food are also available.

> "The school has been known as the number-one party school, so the social life is fine."

When they're not studying, dorm parties, plays, concerts, and films keep FSU students busy. "The school has been known as the number-one party school, so the social life is fine," a freshman says. Those with a good ID can head for one of Tallahassee's bars or restaurants, which fall somewhere between "college hangout" and "real world." Generally, though, students give the area a thumbs-up. As for Greek life, 13 percent of the men and 13 percent of the women join fraternities and sororities, which constitute another important segment of the social scene.

In sports, the big-time Seminole football team won two national titles in the '90s and was runner-up in 2000. Going to games is an integral part of the FSU social scene, especially when games are against FSU's two most hated rivals: the University of Florida and the University of Miami. FSU's baseball team also draws an enthusiastic following, as do the Lady 'Noles volleyball and softball teams.

While Florida State has all the elements of a party school, the merrymaking here doesn't seem to reach the riotous excesses for which some universities are known. FSU students take pride in their school and what it has to offer. "It is a place I can consider almost like my home," says a business major.

For gifted students, the honors program offers smaller classes and closer faculty contact, as well as forty special seminars each year. Certain students can even earn their degree in three years.

The university is making strides in the world of distance learning, allowing some students with an associate's degree to earn their bachelor's degree online.

Overlaps

University of Florida, University of Central Florida, University of South Florida, University of Miami (FL), Florida International

If You Apply To ➤

Florida State: Regular admission: Mar. 1. Financial aid: Feb. 15. Does not guarantee to meet demonstrated need. No campus or alumni interviews. SATs or ACTs: required. SAT IIs: not used. Accepts the Common Application and electronic applications. Essay question: Important issue, significant life experience or achievement, influential person.

Fordham University

Rose Hill Campus: 441 East Fordham Road, Bronx, NY 10458
Lincoln Center Campus: 113 West 60th Street, New York, NY 10023

With the current euphoria for colleges in New York, Fordham has climbed a few notches on the selectivity scale. There is no better location than Lincoln Center, where the performing arts programs are housed. The Bronx campus is less appealing but better than the horror stories you may hear.

Website: www.fordham.edu
Location: Urban
Total Enrollment: 13,843
Undergraduates: 7,062
Male/Female: 39/61
SAT Ranges: V 540–630
  M 535–630
ACT Range: 22–28
Financial Aid: 70%
Expense: Pr $ $ $
Phi Beta Kappa: Yes
Applicants: 10,663
Accepted: 55%
Enrolled: 28%
Grad in 6 Years: 75%
Returning Freshmen: 89%
Academics: ✍ ✍ ✍
Social: ☎ ☎ ☎
Q of L: ★ ★ ★
Admissions:
  (800) FORDHAM
Email Address:
  enroll@fordham.edu

Strongest Programs:
  Business
  Theater and Drama
  Psychology
  English
  Philosophy
  Theology
  History

Any New Yorker could tell you that the Bronx and Manhattan simply do not have the same feel. So students must choose wisely when deciding between Fordham University's two distinct campuses. The Rose Hill campus in the Bronx is an oasis of trees, green grass, and Gothic architecture within the hectic and fast-paced Big Apple. But head to the university's Lincoln Center campus in Manhattan and feel the metropolitan, industrial setting of a fast-paced, no-nonsense city. The Jesuit philosophy and motto of Fordham University, "Wisdom and learning," is maintained by the emphasis on a liberal arts education spread over these two campuses in New York City. And this philosophy is further enhanced by the rich sense of diversity that Fordham offers its students.

Although the university is an independent institution, its Jesuit heritage rings loudly through its concern for liberal values on both campuses. For most students, the Roman Catholic influence is positive, and many students say that the Jesuit tradition is the

"I have had the best teachers of my life."

school's best feature. If nothing else, the Catholic influence and the politics of the '90s keep the campus lively. "Because of the amount of Catholics here, there are differences in opinions concerning religious beliefs," says a junior theater major. "Yet I find the student body very liberal and free-thinking."

The eighty-five-acre Rose Hill campus (a.k.a. the countryside in the city) is home to Fordham College as well as to the undergraduate schools of business administration and general studies. Fordham College at Rose Hill, the largest liberal arts school, is full-scale back to basics in the broadest sense. The imaginative core curriculum, which takes up almost half of a student's courseload, concentrates on developing a liberal arts foundation in three distinct but interlocking stages: the history of the Western world, study of the contemporary world, and an introduction to the various disciplines scholars choose in studying both the past and the present. The business program is especially strong in marketing, accounting, and finance, and it provides hundreds of internships in all areas of Manhattan's business community, many leading to jobs. Freshmen are required to take courses in literature, English composition (which students cite as weak), foreign languages, history, philosophy, and theology.

The Manhattan campus at Lincoln Center, the performing arts complex, has its own college as well as the law school and other graduate programs. Started as an alternative-style urban institution with no grades, it has become more traditional over the years and now shares the common core curriculum with Rose Hill. The university recently agreed to take over Marymount College, a small women's college in Tarrytown, New York, where Fordham has already leased space for graduate programs. Under the merger agreement, Fordham will continue to operate Marymount as a women's college while looking for ways to integrate the two institutions.

Both colleges have strong humanities departments: Rose Hill's strengths include history, philosophy, psychology, and economics, while Lincoln Center's forte is, appropriately enough, theater. A BFA in dance is offered in conjunction with Alvin Ailey; students must be accepted both by Fordham's admissions committee and Alvin Ailey's audition panel. Communications/media studies is praised at both schools, but some students cite the lack of an on-campus television studio as a major fault. Both colleges offer interdisciplinary majors, including black and Puerto Rican studies, and preprofessionals may enter 3–2 engineering programs at Columbia or Case Western Reserve. Rose Hill offers an innovative set of seminars, taught by the philosophy and theology departments, to help upperclassmen involved in community service analyze their experiences. Classes are assigned to freshmen during their fall semester, but they have the option to change their given schedule. Overall, students say faculty members are accessible and knowledgeable. "I have had the best teachers of my life," a junior gushes.

The college has been seeking to build its national appeal and residential character.

"Most Fordham students are liberal, open-minded, social, intelligent, and don't take themselves too seriously."

Faculty advising leaves something to be desired, but the career counseling center is said to have an abundance of material and information on jobs and internships.

Sixty-three percent of the students are from New York, and nearly two-thirds are from private or parochial high schools. Sixteen percent of Fordham's undergraduates are African-American or Hispanic, and the minority community is vocal. The atmosphere at both campuses is less intellectual than at nearby Columbia and New York universities, and Fordham students must motivate themselves. An American studies major says, "Most Fordham students are liberal, open-minded, social, intelligent, and don't take themselves too seriously." A large number of students receive financial aid. There are six hundred merit scholarships, with stipends ranging from $7,500 to $23,540. Athletic scholarships are available as well. Responding to a declining commuter population and an increasing housing crunch, the university offers a $4,000 tuition discount for entering freshmen who continue to live at home and commute to the college.

Responding to a declining commuter population and an increasing housing crunch, the university offers a $4,000 tuition discount for entering freshmen who continue to live at home and commute to the college.

The college has been seeking to build its national appeal and residential character. Seventy percent of the students now live on campus. Lincoln Center students gladly welcome the twenty-story, 850-bed dorm, so they don't have to deal with pricey rents in nearby apartments or in two specially priced hotels. Still, others live at home. One student says the dorms are "roomy and well-structured."

And what's there to say about the social life? "New York has so much to offer and it's right outside the gates," says a sophomore. The school sponsors some extracurricular activities, including an intramurals program in Central Park, but they pale against the city's vast cultural smorgasbord. Students say there's much happening on campus, too, including parties, movies, social events, bands, and plays, and there's a pub and coffeehouse. The university's cultural affairs program brings the Bronx campus students into the Big Apple for a little high life; Manhattan is, after all, just half

"Winning draws big crowds and gives the campus a new level of energy."

an hour away by train, subway, or college shuttle bus. Two of the most enjoyable events of the year are Spring Weekend and Homecoming. "The ten o'clock scream," a ritual every Thursday night in which everyone leans out their window and screams for one minute, is a favorite stress reliever.

Both Rose Hill and Lincoln Center students agree that theirs is not a typical college town. But the Bronx community does play a large role in the Rose Hill students' lives, including volunteering. The Rose Hill campus is backed up against the Bronx Zoo, the beautiful botanical gardens, and Belmont, the "Little Italy" of the Bronx. Of course, since we are talking about New York City, students must constantly be aware of their surroundings. But guards at each entrance to the campus and roving security give Rose Hill a safe feeling within the city.

The marvelous Lombardi Athletic Center (named for that famed alumnus) inspires an active program of club sports and intramurals, while "grandstand athletes" especially enjoy rooting for the varsity basketball team, not to mention the rapidly improving football and baseball teams. The basketball team is competitive nationally, and one student says it is a source of pride on campus. "Opponents named the Fordham Gym one of the most feared in the whole nation. They view our loyalty to our team and having to come to the Bronx and face a Fordham home crowd as intimidating," a former student says. Fordham is a member of the Atlantic 10 and has produced championship men's baseball and women's rowing teams. Says one sports-minded student, "Winning draws big crowds and gives the campus a new level of energy."

And it's that high level of energy that continues to propel Fordham University into the future. This school, like its home city, is built on the idea that diversity and a strong sense of community need not be mutually exclusive.

Overlaps

NYU, Columbia University, Boston College, Boston University, Villanova

If You Apply To ➤

Fordham: Early decision: Nov. 15. Regular admissions, financial aid, and housing: Feb. 1. Does not guarantee to meet demonstrated need. Campus and alumni interviews: optional, evaluative. SATs or ACTs: required. SAT IIs: optional. Apply to particular school or program. Accepts the Common Application and electronic applications. Essay question: significant life experience; personal identification with a literary character; important issue.

Franklin and Marshall College

637 College Avenue, Lancaster, PA 17604-3003

F&M is known for churning out hard-working preprofessional students. Faces tough competition from the likes of Bucknell, Gettysburg, Lafayette, and Dickinson for Pennsylvania-bound students. Known for business, the sciences, and internships on Capitol Hill.

Website: www.fandm.edu
Location: Small city
Total Enrollment: 1,854
Undergraduates: 1,854
Male/Female: 51/49
SAT Ranges: V 580–670
   M 590–680
Financial Aid: 49%
Expense: Pr $ $ $
Phi Beta Kappa: Yes
Applicants: 3,534
Accepted: 56%
Enrolled: 26%
Grad in 6 Years: 83%
Returning Freshmen: 91%
Academics: ✍ ✍ ✍ ✍
Social: ☎ ☎ ☎
Q of L: ★ ★ ★
Admissions: (717) 291-3951

At Franklin and Marshall College, set in the serene hills of Pennsylvania's Amish country, you have to be extra careful when driving. You never know when your Saturn may come nose to nose with a horse and buggy—and they don't have antilock brakes. While the city has modernized beautifully, parts of this historic town and many of its residents look much the same as they did when President James Buchanan insisted in 1853 that Marshall College merge with Franklin College in his hometown of Lancaster.

F&M's 125-acre campus is surrounded by a quiet residential neighborhood shaded by majestic maple and oak trees. The campus itself is an arboretum and boasts forty-seven buildings of Gothic and Colonial architecture. The College Square complex, which offers a Laundromat, printing service, two restaurants for student dining, and a bookstore, appeals to students seeking a study respite. Recent additions to the campus include a new art museum and a revamped center for the performing arts. A main-stage theatre is also under construction, reflecting the college's recent focus on the arts.

Although there are no required courses freshman year, four out of five students enroll in First-Year Residential Seminars. Participating students live together in groups of sixteen on coed freshman floors and study a major theme or concept within a discipline. Recently, the college curriculum was significantly revised. General education requirements include writing and language requirements, one course in three different "Foundation" areas, and one course each in the arts, humanities, social sciences, natural sciences, and non-Western cultures. Collaborations are optional opportunities to get course credit for an experience that includes working with others.

The chemistry, biology, geosciences, and government departments are highly praised, while foreign languages are weaker. Course offerings in modern languages have been expanded, with majors only in French, German, and Spanish and minors in Italian, Greek, and Russian. However, faculty members have been added in Russian, Hebrew, and Japanese. New majors in biochemistry and molecular biology have also been added, and the college recently created an international studies program. A program in biological foundations of behavior offers students an interdisciplinary major with a focus on either animal behavior or neuroscience. In addition, many students engage in independent study or research with faculty during the academic year, or have internships or independent studies on campus during the summer. A preprofessional college in line with Lafayette and Bucknell, F&M has an excellent reputation for preparing undergrads for medical school, law school, and other careers. Students praise career services for its innovative approach to placing students in jobs—staff send out emails to keep students apprised of opportunities.

Approximately fifty Marshall and seventy-five Presidential scholars are named each year. Marshalls receive a $12,500 tuition grant, a Macintosh computer, and the chance to apply for up to $3,000 in research travel funds. Presidential scholars receive a $7,500 tuition grant. F&M also offers two Rouse scholarships worth full tuition, books, and fees. The school also offers merit-based financial aid to outstanding students of ethnic backgrounds that have been traditionally underrepresented in higher education. There are no athletic scholarships.

Students uniformly describe the coursework as rigorous. The atmosphere at F&M can be competitive, and "the workload is always an issue," says a senior. Nonetheless, "what makes us different from other schools is that we somehow manage to combine a casual attitude with a pretty killer workload," says a history major. Students rate the quality of teaching as outstanding, and the relatively small student body and intimate class sizes help create a strong sense of community between students and professors.

"The faculty at F&M made my experience what it was—stimulating, intellectually maturing, open, insightful, and never redundant."

"The faculty at F&M made my experience what it was—stimulating, intellectually maturing, open, insightful, and never redundant," says a senior. F&M offers cross-registration with two other small Pennsylvania colleges—Dickinson and Gettysburg—and several domestic-exchange and cooperative-degree programs. In the summer, the college sends students to countries such as Japan and Russia, and nearly 25 percent study in locations around the world during the junior year. Others participate in the Sea Semester.*

Seventy-five percent of students rank in the top quarter of their graduating high-school class, and students hail from forty states and sixty-two countries. Merely one-third are from Pennsylvania. Asian-American students comprise 3 percent of the student body; African-Americans and Hispanics represent 3 percent each. Although the student body is fairly homogeneous, students say it has become more diverse in recent years. An occasional political debate may waft through the murmurs of light social exchanges during dinner, but according to one student, the big issue on campus is the lack of issues on campus. Fummers do, however, take an interest when it comes to extracurricular activities and social opportunities. The 115 clubs on campus attest to that, as does an unusually high level of participation in community-service activities.

(Continued)
Email Address:
admission@fandm.edu

Strongest Programs:
Biology
Chemistry
Geosciences
Physics
Business
Government
English

"What makes us different from other schools is that we somehow manage to combine a casual attitude with a pretty killer workload," says a history major.

An occasional political debate may waft through the murmurs of light social exchanges during dinner, but according to one student, the big issue on campus is the lack of issues on campus.

Student housing, all coed, ranges from campus dorms to theme houses, a co-op, and private apartments near the campus. Although dorm rooms can vary greatly in size, students say they are very well maintained. "The dorms here are clean and comfortable," says a sophomore. All dorms also have also heating, air-conditioning, carpet, hard wiring, and cable. Every student is guaranteed housing; freshmen and sophomores are required to live on campus, while many juniors and seniors live off campus in houses and apartments. Boarders eat most of their meals in the campus cafeteria under a flexible meal plan, but students are issued debit cards that they may use at a number of different food stops on campus. Food has been a common complaint in the past but seems to be improving.

Regarded by the college as independent social organizations, nine fraternities and three sororities are integral to much of the nightlife, although the residence halls and special-interest groups offer a range of alternatives, including concerts, comedians, and Ben's Underground, a popular student-run nightclub. Hildy's, a tiny local bar, is a favorite campus meeting place. In recent years, the student-run and college-funded College Entertainment Committee has brought the Gin Blossoms, Rusted Root, Live, Ben Folds Five, and Vertical Horizon to the campus.

Lancaster is a historical and well-to-do city of sixty thousand people located in a larger metro area of three hundred thousand. Although most students say they wouldn't describe it as a "typical college town," Lancaster offers about a dozen movie theaters, scores of shops, a farmer's market, brick-and-cobblestone streets (with hitching posts for the Amish horses and buggies), and a plethora of quaint restaurants and cafés.

"People who complain that there is nothing to do just aren't looking hard enough."

Students have a measured, realistic appreciation of its urban amenities and rural ambiance. The Amish culture draws the interest of some students, and many frequent the charming farmer's market to shop for handmade quilts. "People who complain that there is nothing to do just aren't looking hard enough," says one senior. Those with a hankering for contemporary action take road trips to Philly, Baltimore, Washington, D.C., and New York City. The biggest annual event is Spring Arts, which is held the weekend before the last week of classes and includes student air-band contests, live concerts, art exhibits, games, booths, and barbecues. Other highlights include the freshman Pajama Parade, the Sophomore Sensation, the Senior Surprise, International Day, Black Cultural Arts Weekend, and Flapjack Fest (when professors serve pancakes to students).

The college has a good selection of intramural sports, which include popular coed competitions. In addition to a being wrestling powerhouse, F&M boasts recent victories in men's basketball, swimming, and indoor track and women's tennis and volleyball. Varsity squads are called the Diplomats, a name that is irresistibly abbreviated to "the Dips." But after years of yelling "Go Dips," some F&M football fans have resorted to calling their team the Fighting Amish—a name that some members of the local community might not find too amusing. The annual football game against Dickinson for the Conestoga Wagon trophy is always a crowd-pleaser.

Franklin and Marshall's small size and peaceful location don't leave students feeling bored or isolated. In fact, many students say on-campus activities have improved lately, and they don't have to go far to find action. The atmosphere at F&M is warm and welcoming, and the campus is largely self-sufficient. While some students complain of being overworked or stressed, most tell tales revealing a college experience that blends rigorous academics with a healthy dose of fun.

Overlaps
Dickinson, Gettysburg, Lafayette, Bucknell, Lehigh

Furman University

3300 Poinsett Highway, Greenville, SC 29613

Furman's campus is beautiful, and the swans are definitely a nice touch. At 3,252 total enrollment, Furman is nearly twice the size of Davidson and half the size of Wake Forest. As befits its Baptist heritage, Furman is a conservative place and still a largely regional institution.

Some call it the "Country Club of the South." Others refer to it as the "Furman Bubble." And if you're in with the traditional in-crowd here, you love it. But beyond the lush lawns and tight-knit student body, Furman University has made a name for itself as a solid liberal arts institution. An emphasis on undergraduate research and a traditional curriculum brought up-to-date with lots of active participation by students give this school its distinct atmosphere.

The campus is so beautiful that townspeople treat it as a city park. On weekends, people wander Furman's 750 acres of lush countryside featuring a formal rose garden, an outdoor amphitheater, fountains, and flowering trees and shrubs; others picnic beside its man-made lake full of swans and ducks. The architectural style of the campus, designed specifically for Furman, features elements of Greek Revival and Colonial Williamsburg, with porches and pediments and distinctly Southern touches. One senior rhapsodizes, "On pretty days you can walk around the lake, feed the swans, [or] play golf or tennis on wonderful facilities." The most recent additions to the campus include student apartments, the Hartness Welcome Center, and the Bryan Center for Military Science. The James Duke Library is getting a new wing; Hipp Hall, a twenty-thousand-square-foot building for the departments of Education and Economics and Business Administration and an advanced technology center, is the latest addition to the campus.

> **"On pretty days you can walk around the lake, feed the swans, [or] play golf or tennis on wonderful facilities."**

Furman sees itself as a new type of liberal arts college, one that recognizes how fast the world is changing. The rather hefty general education requirements include freshman composition, five humanities courses, one to three courses in math, two courses each in natural sciences and social sciences, one course in fine arts, one course in health and exercise science, one course from the Asian-African program, one to three courses in a foreign language, and nine events a year from the Cultural Life Program. Freshmen must take a special course to fill the composition requirement. According to students, the political science department has some of the most desirable faculty and courses, along with numerous opportunities for internships and international study. Chemistry, political science, music, and psychology are the school's strongest departments, while communications is said to be somewhat underresourced. Recent additions to the curriculum include concentrations in environmental, women's, classical, and Latin American studies. Furman students take three courses during the fall and spring terms, and two courses during the shorter eight-week winter term.

Website: www.furman.edu
Location: City outskirts
Total Enrollment: 3,252
Undergraduates: 2,767
Male/Female: 45/55
SAT Ranges: V 590–690
   M 590–680
ACT Range: 26–30
Financial Aid: 39%
Expense: Pr $ $
Phi Beta Kappa: Yes
Applicants: 3,564
Accepted: 61%
Enrolled: 34%
Grad in 6 Years: 80%
Returning Freshmen: 92%
Academics: ✑ ✑ ✑ ½
Social: ☎ ☎ ☎
Q of L: ★ ★ ★
Admissions: (864) 294-2034
Email Address:
   admissions@furman.edu

Strongest Programs:
   Chemistry
   Psychology
   Political Science
   Music
   Biology
   History

Students say the academic climate at Furman is intense. "The coursework is very demanding and the professors expect you to focus all of your time on their particular course," says one political science major. The low student/faculty ratio results in small class size and excellent student-faculty relations. One student says, "The classes are very engaging, and the professors are good about helping students outside of class." The prized Furman Advantage and other special programs fund a legion of upperclassmen who hold research fellowships, internships, and teaching assistantships in their fields of study. Furman also traditionally sends one of the largest student delegations to the annual National Conference of Undergraduate Research. Study-abroad options include a special exchange program with Kansai-Gaidai University in Japan and study in the Middle East, England, France, Spain, Germany, Central and South America, and Africa. Furman is also a member of the Associated Colleges of the South* consortium.

Diversity, both cultural and religious, is a hot issue on campus. Most Furman undergrads are white Southerners from middle- to upper-class families with politically conservative backgrounds, and just under a third are actually from South Carolina. Although many denominations are represented at Furman, the Baptist influence has been the tradition on campus. In 1992, Furman broke its ties with the South Carolina Baptist Convention after a 166-year affiliation. African-Americans make up 6 percent of the student body, and Hispanics and Asian-Americans barely weigh in with 2 percent combined. More than 60 percent of Furman graduates go straight into the workforce after college; 31 percent go on to professional and graduate schools. Each year, Furman awards a variety of merit scholarships, which range from $500 to a full ride, as well as 251 athletic scholarships.

Furman is somewhat unusual among universities of its ilk in that it maintains a dry campus. One senior explains, "Freshman and sophomore dorms are fairly strict, with resident advisors in each hall, although plenty of drinking still occurs. North Village [a new university-owned apartment building] is much more relaxed. If there are no noise violations or outright violations, what goes on in your apartment is private." All dorms are equipped with telephone, cable TV, and Internet access. Dorms at Furman have created long-lasting friendships for many. "Resident life here is a blast!" says a senior. All students have a choice of several different meal plans. The PalaDen is organized into food courts, and options include a breakfast bar, salad bar, Chinese food, grilled items, Italian pastas, and a section for yogurt and baked goods. Students refer to the campus as the Furman Bubble because of the high level of safety and security that surrounds them. "My biggest worry is parking tickets, if that tells you anything," says one student.

"Resident life here is a blast!"

The Student Activities Board sponsors movies, dances, coffeehouses, and bowling and skating parties. According to students, most parties and Greek functions take place off campus. "Furman is a dry campus but the students here still know how to have fun, with or without alcohol" says a communications studies major. Greenville has also become a popular spot, with a wide variety of coffeeshops, bars, and clubs. And the Peace Center for the Performing Arts attracts many students to downtown Greenville, where they can attend Broadway shows and see first-rate performing artists. "Greenville is a great city with a revitalized downtown and a good population," says a senior. "There are fantastic restaurants to choose from, popular bars and clubs, and an impressive music scene." Atlanta is a two-and-a-half-hour drive away; skiers can hit the slopes after a two-hour drive; and for dedicated sojourners, the great South Carolina beaches are about four hours from campus.

Thirty percent of men and 35 percent of women belong to one of the eight fraternities and seven sororities on Furman's campus. And while fraternities and clubs are popular, there are several other organizations available. A large number of students also choose to devote spare time to the Collegiate Educational Service Corps, which organizes community social-service projects such as the annual May Day-Play Day carnival, which converts the Furman campus into a student-sponsored playground for underprivileged children. Football and basketball games are favorites on campus. During the past few years, football, cross-country, women's and men's tennis, women's golf, and men's and women's soccer have won the Southern Conference Championships. Almost 70 percent of the students compete for the coveted All Sports Trophy by participating in the well-organized intramural games, which range from flag football to horseshoes.

> **"Greenville is a great city with a revitalized downtown and a good population."**

While many universities are emphasizing diversity and inclusiveness of people from all walks of life, the Furman "Bubble" may indeed seem like "The Country Club of the South" to some. But they can't burst the bubble of the many faithful applicants who feel comfortable here and would love to spend four years in such a beautiful and challenging environment.

<table>
<tr><td>Overlaps
Wake Forest, Vanderbilt, UNC–Chapel Hill, University of Georgia, Emory.</td></tr>
</table>

<table>
<tr><td>If You Apply To ➤</td><td>Furman: Early decision: Nov. 15. Regular admissions and financial aid: Jan. 15. Meets demonstrated need of 84%. Campus and alumni interviews: optional, informational. SATs or ACTs: required. SAT IIs: optional, required for home-schooled students. Accepts the Common Application and electronic applications. Essay question: personal statement.</td></tr>
</table>

George Mason University

4400 University Drive, Fairfax, VA 22030-4444

Located in one of the richest suburbs in American, GMU is poised to become a major university. Though still mainly a commuter school, campus housing continues to grow. The presence of prominent conservatives such as Walter Williams have added cachet to economics and public policy.

Just forty minutes from the White House and the Smithsonian, smack in the middle of greater Washington, D.C.'s budding high-tech corridor, stands a fledgling university that is a leading center of conservative political and economic thought. George Mason University's urban campus and symbiotic relationship with the surrounding region contrast starkly with Virginia's two other major universities, which have held classes for a hundred years in the relative isolation of Charlottesville and Blacksburg. With just thirty years on its Fairfax campus—and only forty-five years of life experience—GMU is clearly the new kid on the block.

Founded as a sleepy outpost of the University of Virginia, GMU sits on a 583-acre, wooded campus in the Washington, D.C., suburb of Fairfax, Virginia. Campus architecture is modern and nondescript; most structures were erected after the mid-'70s. GMU's ten-thousand-seat arena, the Patriot Center, hosts both sporting and entertainment events. In addition, a new aquatic and fitness center, featuring two pools, a whirlpool, and coed saunas, was recently completed. And although GMU's campus doesn't have the Colonial ambiance or tradition of William and Mary or UVA, its namesake does have the same Old Virginia credentials. George Mason drafted Virginia's influential Declaration of Rights in 1776, and he later opposed ratification of the federal Constitution because there was no Bill of Rights attached.

<table>
<tr><td>Website: www.gmu.edu</td></tr>
<tr><td>Location: Suburban</td></tr>
<tr><td>Total Enrollment: 24,897</td></tr>
<tr><td>Undergraduates: 15,802</td></tr>
<tr><td>Male/Female: 44/56</td></tr>
<tr><td>SAT Ranges: V 480–580
M 490–590</td></tr>
<tr><td>ACT Range: 19–23</td></tr>
<tr><td>Financial Aid: 59%</td></tr>
<tr><td>Expense: Pub $</td></tr>
<tr><td>Phi Beta Kappa: No</td></tr>
<tr><td>Applicants: 8,106</td></tr>
<tr><td>Accepted: 68%</td></tr>
<tr><td>Enrolled: 39%</td></tr>
<tr><td>Grad in 6 Years: 48%</td></tr>
<tr><td>Returning Freshmen: 76%</td></tr>
<tr><td>Academics: ✍ ✍ ✍</td></tr>
</table>

(Continued)

Social: ☎ ☎
Q of L: ★ ★
Admissions: (703) 993-2400
Email Address:
  admissions@gmu.edu

Strongest Programs:
  Economics
  Engineering
  Public Policy
  Business Administration
  Government
  English
  Communications
  Information Technology

Mason's general education requirements stipulate that all students take the equivalent of two courses in English composition, humanities, social sciences, and math and sciences. Students who prefer to find their own way can design a major under the Bachelor of Individualized Study program. The academic climate is intense but manageable. "The courses here are not too rigorous," says a sophomore, "but professors expect excellence from students." If they do fall behind or need some guidance, academic counseling is likely to put them back on course. Advisors "have been so helpful and really supportive," says a marketing major.

Mason has grown by leaps and bounds for most of the past two decades; recent additions to the curriculum include degree programs in classical studies, international transactions, computational sciences, public policy, and urban systems engineering. Another option is the New Century College degree program, which teams small groups of faculty and undergraduates on projects that can be easily connected to the world outside GMU. However, though it is growing up fast, Mason's youth shows in a number of ways. First, programs taken for granted at more established universities are just hitting their stride here. Next, GMU's relatively small endowment means almost constant tuition increases. Last, some of the school's facilities are just plain inadequate for its more than twenty thousand students. The library, for example, has fewer than seven hundred thousand volumes, though it now subscribes to more than three hundred online databases and allows students to borrow books from all eight members of the Washington Research Library Consortium.

> **"The courses here are not too rigorous, but professors expect excellence from students."**

The lack of resources in the library may present less of a problem for GMU's career-focused students, who seem to like learning on the job: 70 percent enter the working world after graduation, and just 20 percent proceed to graduate and professional schools. Psychology tops the list of popular majors, and economics—which boasts its own Nobel laureate—is probably the strongest department. Other well-regarded majors include computer science, nursing, engineering, and English; not surprisingly, given the school's location, the public policy department also receives accolades. The drama department, once a weak sister, is now part of the Institute of the Arts, created to make arts an intrinsic part of every student's GMU experience. The institute includes a professional theater company, which hosts actors and playwrights in residence.

> **"The dorms are nice enough, but most students still prefer to live off campus."**

Eighty-six percent of GMU students are home-grown, and Mason's student body is fairly diverse, likely due to the diversity of the surrounding area. Minorities make up 28 percent of the student population—9 percent African-American, 6 percent Hispanic, and 13 percent Asian-American. Students are politically aware and tend to lean rightward. That said, racial tensions haven't been a problem, perhaps thanks to the four-year-old Stop, Look, and Learn program. The program attempts to increase campus discussion on prejudice, discrimination, and harassment. Athletic and merit scholarships are available to those who qualify.

George Mason has been a commuter school for much of its short existence, but there is on-campus housing, and 19 percent of undergrads choose this option. Another several thousand live around campus in university-sponsored housing. The administration admits that room and board costs are inflated because the university's entire housing stock dates from 1978 or later, which means the buildings are modern and air-conditioned—but still being paid for. And though the dorms are comfortable and well-maintained, there's still a lot of building to do. "The dorms are nice enough, but most students still prefer to live off campus," says a junior. Freshmen live together in Presidents Park, while other students get rooms on a first-come, first-served basis, based on class status. Those looking for an active social life

The lack of resources in the library may present less of a problem for GMU's career-focused students, who seem to like learning on the job.

should definitely consider a stint in the dorms, particularly in Presidents Park or the Freshman Center. But freshman dorms are dry, and you can get the boot if you're caught having a party with alcohol.

GMU's University Center, with its food court, movie theater, classrooms, computer labs, and study areas, has become the center of on-campus social life. The center is a convenience and a lure for students who commute to school and have gaps between classes. On the weekends, students find a predictable assortment of malls and shopping centers in Fairfax, just southwest of D.C., but off-campus parties and the sights and sounds of downtown Washington, Georgetown, and Old Town Alexandria beckon when the sun goes down. Best of all, these are only a short commute away via a free shuttle bus to the subway. Those searching for a more lively collegiate scene take road trips to other local schools, including James Madison and UVA.

With barely a generation of history under its belt, Mason is notably lacking in traditions and annual events: "Come here and invent one!" a student urges. Patriots Day and Mason Day are the two major bashes, in addition to Homecoming, Greek Week, and International Week. GMU competes in Division I, and basketball dominates the sports scene since there's no football team. Any game against James Madison University draws a big crowd. Other successful teams include women's soccer, men's and women's track, and women's volleyball. Intramurals are catching on, now that many games are held in the Patriot Center.

The name of George Mason may not have the cachet of George Washington, James Madison, or the other luminaries of Virginia history who have had universities named for them. But with improving academics, a growing and improving physical campus, and the rich cultural and economic resources of Washington, D.C., Mason's namesake looks like it's set to follow in those other schools' fine footsteps.

With barely a generation of history under its belt, Mason is notably lacking in traditions and annual events: "Come here and invent one!" a student urges.

Overlaps

Virginia Tech, James Madison, Mary Washington, University of Virginia, University of Maryland

If You Apply To ➤

Mason: Regular admissions: Feb. 1. Meets demonstrated need of 40%. Campus interviews: required, informational. Alumni interviews: optional, informational. SATs or ACTs: required. SAT IIs: optional. Accepts the Common Application. Essay question: personal statement.

George Washington University

2121 I Street NW, Washington, DC 20052

Ten years ago, GW was a backup school with an 80 percent acceptance rate that was maligned for its lack of identity. But the allure of Washington, D.C. has proved to be a strong drawing card, and GW now accepts less than half who apply. Still not much for school spirit, GW is the nation's leader in internships per capita.

Like Washington itself, George Washington University draws students from all over America—and around the world. Upon arrival, they find a bustling campus in the heart of D.C., with ready access to Smithsonian Institution museums, the Folger Shakespeare Library and the Library of Congress, and other national treasures, including top political officials as guest speakers and visiting professors. Since Congress chartered GW in 1821, perhaps it's not surprising that the school has learned well from nearby government agencies how to create red tape. "GW is more like a business with consumers than a university with students," a senior laments.

Website: www.gwu.edu
Location: Urban
Total Enrollment: 22,184
Undergraduates: 10,063
Male/Female: 44/56
SAT Ranges: V 570–660
M 580–670

(Continued)

ACT Range: 24–29
Financial Aid: 42%
Expense: Pr $ $ $ $
Phi Beta Kappa: Yes
Applicants: 15,960
Accepted: 48%
Enrolled: 33%
Grad in 6 Years: 74%
Returning Freshmen: 92%
Academics: ✑ ✑ ✑ ½
Social: ☎ ☎ ☎
Q of L: ★ ★ ★
Admissions: (202) 994-6040
Email Address:
    gwadm@gwu.edu

Strongest Programs:
    Political Communications
    History
    International Affairs
    Electronic Media
    International Business
    English
    Biology
    Computer Science

A new building for the Elliott School of International Affairs, with residence-hall space and five floors of classrooms, as well as more dorms and a new hospital, are under construction on the main campus.

"Bureaucracy is huge, office staff is rude, and money is everything. However, it has made some wonderful expansion possible, and put us where we are today."

Where the school is today includes two campuses—the main, older campus in the Foggy Bottom neighborhood, on Pennsylvania Avenue near the White House, and the new Mount Vernon campus, with five residence halls and some classroom buildings, a few miles away. The Foggy Bottom campus has a mix of renovated federal row houses and modern buildings, while the wooded Mount Vernon campus spans 26 acres near Georgetown, and also includes athletic fields, tennis courts, and an outdoor pool. Formerly a women's college, all GW students are now permitted to take classes and attend activities at Mount Vernon, though certain programs and academic initiatives are geared toward women. A new building for the Elliott School of International Affairs, with residence-hall space and five floors of classrooms, as well as more dorms and a new hospital, are under construction on the main campus. "We are always under construction, and therefore at war with Foggy Bottom residents," sighs a criminal justice major.

Aside from the Elliott School, freshmen may enroll in the School of the Engineering and Applied Science, the School of Business and Public Management, the School of Media and Public Affairs, and the Columbian College of Arts and Sciences, which is the largest undergraduate division. During the freshman year, all undergraduates take English composition. Other requirements vary by school. To graduate from the college, students fulfill requirements covering seven areas of knowledge: literacy, quantitative and logical reasoning, natural sciences, social and behavioral sciences, creative and performing arts, humanities, and foreign languages and cultures.

For highly motivated and capable undergraduates seeking a challenge, GW's honors program offers special seminars, independent study, and a University Symposium on both campuses. The intensive Enosinian Scholars Program culminates with a written thesis and oral examination. The School of Engineering also offers an honors program, in which students work with professors on research projects; a team recently collaborated with America Online to create a wireless-technology lab. GW added a women's studies major in 2000, and introduced majors in biomedical engineering, biological anthropology, and athletic training in 2002. The school also began offering a minor in film studies and joint-degree programs combining a bachelor's degree in political science or economics with a master's in public policy. GW's political communications major, which combines political science, journalism, and electronic media courses, is one of the few undergraduate programs of its kind, and benefits from its Washington location. Students say history, English, political science, and international affairs are also among the school's best departments. Geology and statistics— "None of the profs speak English," a senior complains—need work, they say.

"**GW is more like a business with consumers than a university with students.**"

GW's academic climate has become more rigorous because the school is raising standards with each entering class, says a criminal justice major. "The overall climate is one of healthy competition," a history major reasons. "The threat of not getting a good job after graduation is a bigger motivator than a love of academia." Two-thirds of the classes taken by freshmen have twenty-five students or less; professors handle lectures and seminars, and TAs facilitate discussion or labs. "So many of my teachers have taught in interesting ways," says a history and psychology major. "They make it exciting to go to class." Still, almost half of GW's faculty members divide their time between the halls of academia and the corridors of power, with many holding high-level government positions. "Avoid the 'super-profs,'" says a junior history major. "They tend to cancel classes more, for things like an appearance on CNN." Then again, those connections help GW students get summer internships and part-time jobs with Congress members and the K Street lobbying firms a few blocks away.

Given GW's location and its improving academic reputation, students "are smart, politically savvy, and ambitious," says a junior. "They are used to being leaders and achievers, not as much scholars." Six percent of the students are African-American, 5 percent are Hispanic, 10 percent are Asian-American, and nearly 5 percent come from foreign countries. "The diversity of the campus sets it apart," says a senior. As you might expect, political issues important on the national stage are also important here. "Every issue big in the news is big on campus," says a mechanical engineering major.

Sixty-two percent of GW students live in campus housing, where "everyone is guaranteed a room, but it might not be the one they want," says a freshman, since sophomores get first pick in the lottery. Dorms are "palatial, mostly renovated former hotels or apartments," with private bathrooms and fast Internet links, says a junior. "D.C. rents are so high and the dorms so nice that many people stay." Those who move off campus

> **"Our rivalries with schools like Georgetown are more social than athletic."**

typically find group houses in Foggy Bottom, or go to nearby neighborhoods like Dupont Circle and Georgetown, just a short walk from campus. Some also choose the Maryland or Virginia suburbs, where housing stock is newer and a little more affordable, since they're just a short subway ride away. Most freshmen are assigned to suites with up to four roommates in Thurston Hall, the biggest and rowdiest dorm on campus. They may also choose one of twenty-four Living and Learning Communities, groups of students who share similar interests. These groups have gone to the Kennedy Space Center for a rocket launch and to New York City to tour the United Nations.

Fourteen percent of GW men and 11 percent of the women go Greek, though "the Greeks don't have lots of public parties because most of them don't have houses," says a junior. "People tend to gather with friends, either at apartments or bars." That said, a D.C. Police crackdown on underage drinking has made it extremely difficult for those under twenty-one to be served at off-campus restaurants and pubs. Major annual events include the Fall Fest and Spring Fling carnivals, with free food and nationally known entertainment, such as The Roots and Busta Rhymes. Popular road trips include the beaches of Ocean City, Maryland, and Virginia Beach, Virginia. Philadelphia and New York City are easily accessible by bus or train, a boon since most GW students don't have cars.

GW doesn't field a football team, but its men's and women's basketball teams have won Atlantic 10 conference championships in recent years. During Family Weekend, Midnight Madness launches spirit week—and the beginning of basketball season. The gymnastics squad is also strong, and the men's and women's rowing teams compete on the Potomac River, right in GW's backyard. "Our rivalries with schools like Georgetown are more social than athletic," says a history major. The school's unofficial mascot is the hippopotamus.

A popular GW T-shirt proclaims: "Something Happens Here." Something certainly has happened on *both* of the school's campuses in the past five years, says a junior. "GW has gone up in status, scholarship, and quality of life, recruiting stellar students and becoming far more selective," the history major says. "We're expanding the physical campus while dramatically improving existing traditions of achievement and work." For students interested in urban living, in the heart of the nation's political establishment, GW may be a very good choice indeed.

GW added a women's studies major in 2000, and introduced majors in biomedical engineering, biological anthropology, and athletic training in 2002.

Overlaps

Boston University, Georgetown, NYU, American, University of Maryland

GW: Early decision: Nov. 1, Dec 1. Regular admissions: Jan. 15. Financial aid: Jan. 31. Housing: Jan. 15, March 1 (early decision); May 1 (regular admissions). Campus and alumni interviews: recommended, evaluative. SATs or ACTs: required. SAT II: recommended (math, writing, science). Accepts the Common Application and electronic applications. Essay question: why GW; how GW's strengths compare to your view of the "ideal" college experience, or a graded sample of creative or fiction writing. Media and Public Affairs applicants have an additional essay on political communication, electronic media, or journalism.

Georgetown University

Washington, DC 20057

For everyone who wants to be a master of the political universe, this is the place. Only a handful of Ivy League schools and Stanford are tougher to get into than Georgetown. In all the excitement over D.C., students can forget the Jesuit affiliation, which adds a conservative tinge to the campus.

Website:
www.georgetown.edu
Location: Center city
Total Enrollment: 12,688
Undergraduates: 6,422
Male/Female: 47/53
SAT Ranges: V 640–730
M 650–730
ACT Range: 28–32
Financial Aid: 55%
Expense: Pr $ $ $ $
Phi Beta Kappa: Yes
Applicants: 15,327
Accepted: 21%
Enrolled: 47%
Grad in 6 Years: 91%
Returning Freshmen: 98%
Academics: 🖉 🖉 🖉 🖉 ½
Social: ☎ ☎ ☎ ☎
Q of L: ★ ★ ★ ★
Admissions: (202) 687-3600
Email Address: N/A

Strongest Programs:
Government
Chemistry
Philosophy
Business
International Relations
Diplomatic History
International Economics

As the most selective of the nation's Roman Catholic schools, Georgetown University offers students an intellectual milieu that is among the nation's best. With unparalleled access to Washington, D.C.'s corridors of power, aspiring politicos benefit from the university's emphasis on public policy, international business, and foreign service. For avid sports fans, there is the powerful basketball team. The national spotlight shines brightly on this elite institution, drawing dynamic students and athletes from around the world.

From its imposing, hilly location blocks from the Potomac River, Georgetown affords its students an excellent vantage point from which to survey the world. The 104-acre campus reflects the history and growth of the nation's oldest Jesuit university. The Federal style of Old North, home of the school of business administration, which once housed guests such as George Washington and Lafayette, contrasts with the towers of the Flemish Romanesque-style Healy Hall, a post–Civil War landmark on the National Register of Historic Places.

Although Georgetown is a Roman Catholic university, founded in 1789 by the Society of Jesus, the religious atmosphere is by no means oppressive. Just over half of the undergraduates are Catholic, but all major faiths are respected and practiced on campus. That's partially due to the pronounced international influence here. International relations, diplomatic history, and international economics are among the hottest programs, as evidenced by former Secretary of State Madeline Albright's return to the School

"Departments usually select their best faculty to teach introductory courses."

of Foreign Service. Through its broad liberal arts curriculum, GU focuses on developing the intellectual prowess and moral rigor its students will need in future national and international leadership roles. The curriculum has a strong multidisciplinary and intercultural slant, and students can choose from several programs abroad to round out their classroom experiences.

Would-be Hoyas may apply to one of four undergraduate schools: Georgetown College, School of Nursing and Health Studies, McDonough School of Business, and the Walsh School of Foreign Service, which gives future diplomats, journalists, and others a strong grounding in the social sciences. Prospective freshmen must declare intended majors on their applications, and their secondary school records are judged accordingly. This means, among other things, intense competition within the college for the limited number of spaces in Georgetown's popular premed program.

Georgetown's liberal arts program is also very strong: American studies gets favorable reviews, as do history, government, English, and, of course, theology. The School of Foreign Service stands out for its international economics, regional and comparative studies, and diplomatic history offerings. SFS also offers several five-year undergraduate and graduate degree programs in conjunction with the Graduate School of Arts and Sciences. The business school balances liberal arts with professional training, which translates into strong offerings in international and intercultural business as well as an emphasis on ethical and public policy issues. A new major, operations and information management, prepares students to understand business processes and the information systems that support them. The School of Nursing and Health Studies runs an integrated program combining the liberal arts and humanities with professional nursing theory and practice, and offers a major in Health Studies. The Faculty of Languages and Linguistics, the only undergraduate program of its kind nationwide grants degrees in nine languages, as well as degrees in linguistics and comparative literature. The computer science department has been bolstered by the recruitment of a chair with a national reputation, but students continue to cite it and the anthropology department as weak.

Georgetown's general education requirements are of two types: applicable to all students (literature, philosophy, and theology), and specific to certain divisions (chemistry, biology, physiology, math, philosophy, and sociology for nursing students, for example). The library holds 2.2 million volumes and features quiet study areas, audiovisual equipment, and access to special collections. That GU views most subjects through an international lens as evidenced by the 38 percent of students who study abroad. University-sponsored study programs in eighty-five countries— in Asia, Latin America, Poland, Israel, France, Germany, and at the university's villas in Flo-rence, Italy, and Alanya, Turkey—attract the

"The campus feels very safe."

culturally curious. First-years read the same novel during the summer and the author visits campus during the first few weeks for a daylong seminar. There are no special academic requirements for the freshman year, but about thirty Georgetown College freshmen are accepted annually into the liberal arts colloquium.

Georgetown likes to boast about its faculty, and well it should. "Departments usually select their best faculty to teach introductory courses," says a junior. Professors "really love teaching and have a passion for their area of expertise," adds an international politics major. Academically, the environment is tough but manageable. Says a biochemistry major: "Most students are extremely motivated, but there is virtually no competition between students." A sophomore adds that GU students "pursue knowledge for the sake of knowledge."

The GU community includes students from all over the United States and abroad. Ninety-nine percent are from outside the District of Columbia, and 8 percent are foreign. African-Americans and Hispanics make up 11 percent of the undergraduate group, and Asian-Americans comprise 9 percent. A student committee works with the vice president for student affairs to improve race relations and develop strategies for improving inclusiveness and sensitivity to issues of multiculturalism.

Students take studying seriously; they also say that each faculty member likes to think you're majoring in his or her subject. Seventy-five percent of graduates move directly into the job market after graduation, helped by the more than 127 résumé-building clubs, organizations, and student government activities available at this incubator for aspiring public leaders. Georgetown offers no academic merit scholarships, but it does guarantee to meet the full demonstrated need of every admit, and some 160 athletic scholarships draw male and female athletes of all stripes.

University-owned dorms, townhouses, and apartments accommodate two-thirds of students, and the university guarantees housing for three out of four years.

Georgetown likes to boast about its faculty, and well it should. "Departments usually select their best faculty to teach introductory courses," says a junior.

The university's strict enforcement of the twenty-one-year-old drinking age has led to a somewhat decentralized social life, not necessarily a bad thing.

All dorms are coed, and some have more activities and community than others. "All have great amenities like Ethernet and landscaping," says one student. Two dining halls serve "passable" food, but the popular student-run coffeeshop offers more palatable options. Although D.C. has a high crime rate, GU students feel relatively safe on campus thanks to the school's ever-present Department of Public Safety and its walking and riding after-dark escort services. "The campus feels very safe. We are also in a self-contained community, so much of the D.C. crime stays out," an underclassman says.

Jesuits, who know all about secret societies, frown upon fraternities or sororities at their colleges, and so there are none at Georgetown. The university's strict enforcement of the twenty-one-year-old drinking age has led to a somewhat decentralized social life, not necessarily a bad thing. Alcohol is forbidden in undergrad dorms, and all parties

> "Georgetown's location and its student body are its greatest assets."

must be registered. The dozens of bars, nightclubs, and restaurants in Georgetown—Martin's Tavern and the Tombs are always popular—are a big draw for students who are legal, but they can get pricey. The Hoyas, a campus pub in the spectacular student activity center, is a more affordable alternative. Popular annual formals such as the Diplomatic and the Blue/Gray Ball force students to dress up and pair off.

Washington offers unsurpassed cultural resources, ranging from the museums of the Smithsonian to the Kennedy Center. "We have all the opportunities of Washington, D.C., without the city streets cutting through our campus," says a biochemistry major. "Georgetown's location and its student body are its greatest assets." And given the city's excellent public transit system and the absence of on-campus parking, a car is probably more trouble than it's worth.

And speaking of Hoya basketball, should you notice the hills begin to tremble with a deep, resounding, primitive chant—"Hoya...Saxa...Hoya...Saxa"—don't worry; it's just another Georgetown basketball game. Their mascot, the Hoya, is derived from the Greek and Latin phrase, "hoya saxa" which means, "what rocks!" Some say it originated in a cheer referring to the stones that comprised the school's outer walls. The Hoya team is always tough, especially when Syracuse, Villanova, or UConn come to town, and GU often figures prominently in the NCAA postseason tournament in March. The thrill of victory in intramural competition at the superb underground Yates Memorial Field House is not to be missed, either.

For anyone interested in discovering the world, Georgetown offers an outstanding menu of choices. Professors truly pay attention to their undergrads and the diverse students who are "hard-working, diligent, caring individuals," says one sophomore. "Georgetown is a place where students of all backgrounds, all traditions, and all faiths come together for a common purpose of educating each other and making an impact on the world."

Overlaps

Boston College, Harvard, University of Pennsylvania, NYU, Notre Dame

If You Apply To ➤

Georgetown: Early action: Nov. 1. Regular admissions: Jan. 10. Financial aid: Feb. 1. No campus interviews. Alumni interviews: required, evaluative. SATs or ACTs: required. SAT IIs: recommended. Apply to particular schools or programs. Essay question: personal statement plus one additional question for each school.

University of Georgia

212 Terrell Hall, Athens, GA 30602-1633

What a difference free tuition makes. Top in-state students now choose UGA over highly selective private universities. Business and journalism head the list of sought-after programs. The college town of Athens boasts great nightlife and is within easy reach of Atlanta.

The University of Georgia is arguably the fastest-rising public university in the country. As recently as a decade ago, it was known primarily for its dynamite football team—a sleepy party school that would readily accept virtually anyone with a high-school diploma and a pulse. But a big boost from Georgia's Hope Scholarship program, which pays tuition and fees for Georgia residents with at least a B average, has turned UGA into a highly selective flagship public university that is able to pick and choose from among the region's best high-school seniors. The average SAT score and grade point average for entering freshmen has soared, and the university has moved aggressively to provide programs to challenge its new and brainier breed of students. Enthusiasm for "them Dawgs" has never been greater.

Situated on 605 acres, Georgia's attractive campus is speckled with greenery and wooded walks. The older north campus, which houses the administrative offices and law school, features nineteenth-century architecture and landscaping while more modern buildings and residence halls are found on the southern end of campus. A striking feature is the university's lush botanical garden. Founded in 1785, Georgia is the nation's first chartered state university, and spent most of its first two centuries expanding. New facilities include a $43 million student learning center and the $28 million Center for Applied Genetics Technologies.

Despite great strides toward improving the quality of education and the campus, some UGA undergraduates still take a low-key approach to the life of the mind. Many of the toughest academic requirements are found in premedical, preveterinary, and other preprofessional concentrations, as well as in the highly regarded honors program. UGA's strongest programs include business (especially accounting and management), education, journalism, law, studio art, ecology, and genetics. A major in film studies, and minors in Arabic and TESOL are just a few of the newest additions to UGA's undergraduate program. The core curriculum requires students to complete a total of forty-two

> **"I have had very good teachers in my time here, many exceptional."**

semester hours in humanities and fine arts, English, science, mathematics, technology, social sciences, environmental literacy, and four to five hours of electives. Selected freshmen can participate in the BIG (Busily Involved at Georgia) Event, a three-day retreat the summer before enrollment designed to introduce students to UGA history and resources, improve leadership skills, and help them adapt to new academic and social challenges of college.

The faculty at the University of Georgia receives high marks from the students. "I have had very good teachers in my time here, many exceptional," says a history/political science major. Registration for classes, previously a formidable process at UGA, has been significantly simplified by a computerized registration system that allows students to enroll electronically. First pick for all courses usually goes to honors students and varsity athletes, and the rest follow by seniority. Gut courses can be found for those intent upon attending Camp Georgia, but serious students may partake of several special programs, such as a five-year business/engineering degree offered in conjunction with Georgia Tech. In addition, UGA offers study

Website: www.uga.edu
Location: Small city
Total Enrollment: 32,317
Undergraduates: 24,829
Male/Female: 44/56
SAT Ranges: V 550–650
 M 560–650
ACT Range: 23–28
Financial Aid: 47%
Expense: Pub $ $
Phi Beta Kappa: Yes
Applicants: 13,578
Accepted: 62%
Enrolled: 53%
Grad in 6 Years: 69%
Returning Freshmen: 91%
Academics: ✍ ✍ ✍
Social: 🍷 🍷 🍷 🍷 🍷
Q of L: ★ ★ ★
Admissions: (706) 542-2112
Email Address:
 undergrad@admissions.uga.edu

Strongest Programs:
 Business
 Education
 Law
 Journalism
 Studio Art
 Ecology
 Genetics

abroad programs in fourteen different countries. Summer courses, night classes, and free tutorial sessions are also available as well as high-quality services for the student with learning disabilities. The school also offers courses and additional resources as a member of the Atlanta Regional Consortium for Higher Education.*

The university's student body is overwhelmingly Georgian (90 percent) and 67 percent are public school graduates. Many belong to one of more than a dozen religious organizations on campus (the Wesley Foundation is the largest) or become members of one the other

> "Housing is OK, but it could be better as far as being newer or nicer."

five hundred-plus campus organizations. African-Americans account for 5 percent of the students, and Hispanics and Asian-Americans combine for 6 percent. Georgia makes its admissions decisions without regard to student financial need. The school does not guarantee to meet the demonstrated need of every admit, but 45 percent of enrolled students are offered complete financial aid packages. There are hundreds of merit scholarships and most in-state freshmen receive the Georgia Hope Scholarship, which covers full tuition. Up to one hundred of the top undergraduates participate in the Foundation Fellows program, which provides a full scholarship plus international travel and research.

Tales of miscreant air-conditioning and elevators in some regular dorms often lure freshmen to the high-rise variety, where they find the smallest rooms on campus. Most upperclassmen prefer the roomier low-rise dorms, if they haven't already moved off campus. The residence halls are described as "well-maintained and convenient." One student says, "Housing is OK, but it could be better as far as being newer or nicer." Students aren't required to buy one of the two meal plans (for five or seven days a week), but most do. There are three dining halls plus the student union's snack bar.

On-campus activities are numerous. "Social life abounds," says one senior. Downtown Athens—a well-known spot on the national rock map, having spawned such hit groups as R.E.M. and the B-52's—borders the university and provides bus service and an abundance of diversions. Students rate it a "10" as a college town. "Downtown Athens, with shops, clubs, restaurants, bars, and a great music scene, is the center of social activity," says one student. One nightclub enthusiast notes that many of the clubs in Athens cater to UGA students and admit those who are under

> "There is a place for students with any interest here at UGA."

twenty-one as long as they get a stamp saying they can't drink. It is difficult but not impossible to obtain alcohol on campus. "There is an alcohol culture here at UGA, especially downtown," says one student. "Some people say Athens is a drinking town with a football problem," says another.

Athens residents worship UGA's fierce football team, which won the Sugar Bowl in 2002. Other sports have been impressive lately as well, though the 2003 men's basketball season was cut short due to an ethics scandal. The men's tennis team won the 2001 national championship. UGA's women's gymnastics team is strong. Men's and women's golf teams, women's basketball, and swimming and diving teams regularly capture conference and national titles as well. The university has everything the weekend jock could want, including indoor and outdoor tennis and swimming; handball, racquetball, and tennis courts; and a jogging and exercise trail. Athletic rivalries with Auburn, Florida, and Georgia Tech make the hairs stand up on the Bulldogs' necks.

Georgia's twenty-eight fraternities and twenty-two sororities provide much of the social activity, though a campus policy banning open parties has put a damper on things. Only 16 percent of the men and 19 percent of the women go Greek, but almost everyone attends at least a couple of Greek bashes each year. Atlanta is only an hour away, and Savannah and Myrtle Beach are other popular getaways. Students descend on Florida en masse twice a year: first for the Florida football game and then for spring break.

Selected freshmen can participate in the BIG (Busily Involved at Georgia) Event, a three-day retreat the summer before enrollment designed to introduce students to UGA history and resources, improve leadership skills, and help them adapt to new academic and social challenges of college.

Overlaps

Georgia Tech, Georgia Southern, Florida State, Emory, University of North Carolina

With more than twenty-four thousand undergraduates, UGA is not a school where students are coddled. But outstanding educational opportunities—like scientific research and the honors program—await serious students, just as football games and live music await those who want to coast. Says one satisfied Dawg: "There is a place for students with any interest here at UGA."

<table>
<tr><td>If You Apply To ≻</td><td>Georgia: Rolling admissions. Financial aid: Aug. 1. Does not guarantee to meet demonstrated need. No campus or alumni interviews. SATs or ACTs: required. SAT IIs: recommended. Accepts electronic applications. Essay question: challenge faced and overcome; symbol that represents you.</td></tr>
</table>

Georgia Institute of Technology

Atlanta, GA 30332-0320

As the South's premier technically oriented university, Ma Tech does not coddle her young. That means surviving in downtown Atlanta and fighting through a wall of graduate students to talk with your professors. Architecture and big-time sports supplement the engineering focus.

If your college daydreams feature parties, bars, and dates rather than lecture halls, libraries, and exams, Georgia Institute of Technology may not be the school for you. On the other hand, if you see college as a stepping stone to a high-paying, prestigious career, a place to work hard for four or five years, have a great time on the weekends, and graduate with a solid professional direction, then you may want to think about "Tech." Georgia Tech students take their studies and future careers—mainly engineering—very seriously. But when the whistle blows, they let down their crew cuts, stash their pocket protectors, and become wild members of the "Rambling Wreck of Georgia Tech."

Located just off the interstate in Georgia's capital city, Georgia Tech's 330-acre campus consists mainly of modern buildings. In 1996, the physical plant was completely transformed by the construction of the Olympic Village on Tech's campus. Its glorious remnants include seven new residence halls, an aquatic center, a coliseum, a sports performance complex, and an amphitheater.

Tech academics are as rigorous as they come, but "that's why a degree from Georgia Tech means so much," claims a senior chemical engineering major. "The courses are challenging and the workload requires a great deal of self-discipline," says an electrical engineering major. Before your heart starts missing beats at the thought of this grind, take heed: "Tech students are not dull. We take school seriously but also make time for social activities,"

> "Tech students are not dull. We take school seriously but also make time for social activities."

says a senior. The institute is a national leader in most engineering fields, notably electrical, computer, civil, industrial and systems, as well as mechanical and aerospace. Materials, ceramic, chemical, and nuclear engineering programs are also part of the curriculum. Degree programs in international affairs and public policy combined with the institute's engineering and science offerings prepare students to make policy in the increasingly technological and global markets of the twenty-first century.

Website: www.gatech.edu
Location: City center
Total Enrollment: 14,805
Undergraduates: 11,043
Male/Female: 66/34
SAT Ranges: V 600–690
  M 650–730
Financial Aid: 24%
Expense: Pub $ $ $ $
Phi Beta Kappa: No
Applicants: 8,899
Accepted: 57%
Enrolled: 43%
Grad in 6 Years: 68%
Returning Freshmen: 90%
Academics: ✐ ✐ ✐ ✐ ✐
Social: ☎ ☎
Q of L: ★ ★
Admissions: (404) 894-4154
Email Address:
  admissions@success.gatech.edu

Strongest Programs:
  Engineering
  Architecture

The faculty at Georgia Tech is renowned for its research. They have turned out volumes of learned tracts over the years and have aided in the development of Star Wars defense technology and the space shuttle.

Aside from the technical fare, there is an increasingly popular management college, and a strong school of architecture, which is known for its work in historic preservation and energy conservation. The liberal arts are somewhat weaker, but the general education requirements ensure that all students receive some schooling in the humanities and social sciences. Also weak are the building construction and physics departments. Since most coursework requires computers, students are faced with long lines at the 375 computer labs. Newer additions to the curriculum include a biomedical engineering major and a film and new media concentration.

Five years of college is common at Georgia Tech because of the rigorous academic requirements for engineering students and the popularity of the co-op program. More than three thousand students finance their education and gain on-the-job experience by working half a school year and going to classes the other half through the school's co-op program. Special travel programs include a year in Paris for architects, a summer in London for chemical engineers, and a graduate-level degree from Metz, France. Other popular study abroad destinations include Oxford and Australia. By graduation day, 62 percent of the students have jobs and 20 percent have committed to graduate and professional schools. The school also offers courses and additional resources as a member of the Atlanta Regional Consortium for Higher Education.*

The faculty at Georgia Tech is renowned for its research. They have turned out volumes of learned tracts over the years and have aided in the development of Star Wars defense technology and the space shuttle. Some argue that undergraduate teaching has suffered in the process. "Most of our professors conduct impressive research and some are more interested in the research than in teaching their students," says an international affairs major. Still, Georgia Tech does have many stellar professors. "The professors here are knowledgeable and well-respected in their fields," says one student. Don't seek too many cozy seminars at Tech: many classes are large—often more than one hundred students. Stringent grading is the rule at Tech: "The biggest problem is trying not to get 'shafted' by professors who must have a certain percentage of their students get low grades in order to 'even out the class average,'" complains a sophomore computer science major.

"Many of the dorms have full kitchen facilities and individual bedrooms."

Nearly two-thirds of Georgia Tech's largely male student body come from Georgia—the vast majority went to public school, and 60 percent ranked in the top tenth of their high-school class. Political apathy is the norm; most students are too busy studying to pay attention to politics. A senior admits that a fair amount of Tech students "could be considered nerds by society as a whole" but is quick to point out that "there are thriving alternative, artsy, and gay/lesbian cultures here." One in four Tech students is a racial minority, with African-Americans accounting for 8 percent of the student body, Hispanics 3 percent, and Asian-Americans 14 percent. The Office of Minority Educational Development helps minority students adjust to life at Tech. To limit burgeoning enrollment, out-of-state applicants must meet slightly higher criteria than their Georgia counterparts. The university does not guarantee to meet the demonstrated financial need of every accepted applicant, but a variety of merit scholarships are awarded each year. In addition, 291 students receive athletic scholarships each year.

Don't seek too many cozy seminars at Tech: many classes are large—often more than 100 students.

In 1996, Georgia Tech was briefly transformed into the Olympic Village, and when the Olympiads departed, they left Tech with brand-spanking-new dormitories and "refurbished" old ones. "The housing at Tech is awesome," says a junior. "Many of the dorms have full kitchen facilities and individual bedrooms." More than half of Techies live in dorms, and freshmen are guaranteed a room. Most halls are single-sex, though visitation rules are lenient. Students who go Greek often live in their chapter houses; housing off campus is generally comfortable, but parts of the surrounding neighborhood are unsavory. While some students feel infallible despite the urban area, others are more cautious: "I don't go out by myself at night, but during the day the campus is fine. There are campus police and student escort services until 4:00 A.M.," says a senior. Tech has two large dining halls on campus, where the food is said to be "adequate and somewhat overpriced."

Tech's hometown is "Hot-Lanta," as the students refer to it, and it offers an endless supply of social and dining opportunities. As one student says, "Atlanta is one of the most exciting cities in the nation. The people are friendly, there are a lot of young adults, a great social atmosphere, good cultural activities, beautiful (and green) spaces, and a booming economy." Another student adds, "Atlanta has more to do than would be possible in a lifetime." Tech students can be found at restaurants or movies in midtown Atlanta, or at teeming bars in Atlanta's Buckhead district. The city also offers plenty of community service opportunities. More than a quarter of the students belong to one of the dozens of fraternities and sororities, which are responsible for a good deal of the on-campus social scene. Greek or not, however, students study much of the weekend (often in groups), although just about everyone takes time out for a sporting event or evening entertainment. "The basketball season at Georgia Tech is awesome and students generally camp out for tickets to the big games," says one student.

Tech's varsity sports have become as big-time as any in the South. During the past few years, Georgia Tech teams have taken home trophies in tennis and track, women's volleyball and track, and men's basketball, where the graduation rate for non-whites is zero. Techies look forward to Homecoming Week, which culminates in the Rambling Wreck Parade of student-owned cars. There's also a traditional "rivalry with the neighboring University of Georgia that escalates each Thanksgiving at the annual 'Georgia game,'" a

"We don't fit the mold, we make it."

student explains. Among its many other traditions are some that may seem odd to the uninitiated: "Stealing the T is the most famous prank." Students try to remove the huge yellow letter T from the tower on the administration building and then return it to the school by presenting it to a member of the faculty or administration. The recent addition of alarms, motion sensors, and heat sensors on the T has made the task more difficult but "certainly not impossible for a Georgia Tech engineer," says an electrical engineering major. Another is the Mini 500, a 15-lap tricycle race around a parking garage with three pit stops, a tire change, and a driver rotation.

Georgia Tech students like to say, "We don't fit the mold, we make it." They are proud of their self-direction and promising futures. As one senior says, "The students here are intelligent, independent, and driven by very high expectations for the future." Georgia Tech supports their drive by recruiting faculty who are leaders in their fields and by making the campus an enjoyable place to spend four to six years studying. Lively school traditions and the thriving city of Atlanta are waiting for Techies when they're finally ready to take a break.

Overlaps
University of Georgia, MIT, Georgia State, Emory, Georgia Southern

If You Apply To >

Georgia Tech: Regular admissions: Jan. 15. Financial aid: Mar. 1. Housing: May 1. Meets demonstrated need of 32%. No campus or alumni interviews. SATs or ACTs: required. SAT IIs: optional. No essay question. Looks for high math and science aptitude.

The college by the battlefield is strong in U.S. history—that's a given. The natural sciences and business are also popular, and political science majors enjoy good connections in D.C. and New York City. Students can also take courses down the road at Dickinson and Franklin and Marshall.

Website: www.gettysburg.edu
Location: Small town
Total Enrollment: 2,377
Undergraduates: 2,377
Male/Female: 50/50
SAT Ranges: V 580–650
   M 590–660
Financial Aid: 57%
Expense: Pr $ $ $
Phi Beta Kappa: Yes
Applicants: 4,364
Accepted: 53%
Enrolled: 29%
Grad in 6 Years: 76%
Returning Freshmen: 91%
Academics: ✑ ✑ ✑ ½
Social: ☎ ☎ ☎
Q of L: ★ ★ ★
Admissions: (717) 337-6100
   or (800) 431-0803
Email Address:
   admiss@gettysburg.edu

Strongest Programs:
   English
   History
   Psychology
   Natural Sciences
   Business
   Political Science

Mention the word "Gettysburg," and patriotic heart palpitations and echoes of the "Battle Hymn of the Republic" are likely to result. Whether the reference is to the Pennsylvania town steeped in Civil War history or the small, high-caliber college located in the famed battlefield's backyard, a certain pride and reverence become immediately evident. This feeling is not lost on students at Gettysburg College, who come to southeastern Pennsylvania to acquaint themselves with American history while gearing up for the future.

Situated in the midst of gently rolling hills, Gettysburg's two-hundred-acre campus is "a historical treasure," an eclectic assemblage of Georgian, Greek, Romanesque, Gothic Revival, and modern architecture, plus several styles not easily categorized. One campus building—Penn Hall—was actually used as a hospital during the Battle of Gettysburg. Rumor has it that ghostly soldiers can still be seen walking the grounds.

Indoors, the English department, home of the *Gettysburg Review*, is among the strongest at Gettysburg, as are the natural sciences, which are well endowed with state-of-the-art equipment. The fine psychology department offers opportunities for students to participate in faculty research. The management major is the most popular. Also popular, of course, is the excellent history department, which is bolstered by the school's nationally recognized and prestigious Civil War Institute. The library system boasts more than 345,000 volumes, a library/learning resource center, and an online computer catalog search. "I don't think there are any weak departments," says a student, "just some that are smaller." These include physics and classics.

"It's obvious that teachers spend a lot of time and effort on the material that they present to the class."

The small class sizes make for close student-faculty relationships. "It's obvious that teachers spend a lot of time and effort on the material that they present to the class," says a senior. Advising draws praise from students. "[My advisor] is always there for me, professionally, academically, and personally," says one happy undergrad. The academic honor code contributes to the atmosphere of community and mutual trust. The popular first-year seminars aim at strengthening reasoning, writing, and speaking skills. Another popular program is the Area Studies Symposium, which focuses each year on a different region of the world and offers lectures and films for the whole campus in addition to academic credit for participating students. There are disciplinary programs such as environmental studies, Latin American studies, and biochemistry and molecular biology.

Gettysburg sponsors a Washington semester with American University, a United Nations semester through Drew University in New Jersey, and cooperative dual degree programs in engineering and forestry. Most departments offer structured internships, and the chemistry department offers a summer cooperative research program between students and professors in which most majors participate and work on a joint publication. Through the Central Pennsylvania Consortium, students may take courses at two nearby colleges—Dickinson and Franklin and Marshall. Outstanding seniors may participate in the Senior Scholar's Seminar, with independent study on a major contemporary issue, but all students have a chance to do independent work and/or design their own majors. Study abroad programs are global and popular with 250 students taking part each year.

Conservative, white, and middle- to upper-middle-class describes 95 percent of Gettysburg's students. "As opposed to our rivals, I would say our students are more attractive and pretty ambitious," quips a senior. Though the administration is trying to lure more minorities with activities sponsored by the Intercultural Advancement Division, African-American, Asian-American, and Hispanic enrollment totals 7 percent. Students are so interested in public service that the school set up a Center for Public Service to direct their community activities. "Gettysburg has a continuous concern for the connection between the classroom and life off and beyond the campus," reports a

Situated in the midst of gently rolling hills, Gettysburg's two-hundred-acre campus is "a historical treasure."

"The residence life staff is excellent."

veteran. Three-quarters of the students come from public high school, and the majority were in the top quarter of their high-school class. No athletic scholarships are available, and the number of offerings based on academic merit varies by year.

"The residence life staff is excellent," enthuses one denizen. "Freshman year they match you up very well and are conscientious about making sure you are happy in your residence." Campus housing is guaranteed all four years, and students can choose from apartment-style residence halls, special interest halls, and the new Quarry Suites. The top scholars in each class get first crack at the best rooms. Student rooms have been added in renovated historical properties (some reputed to be haunted) on campus, and there are more options for interest housing and suite living. About a fifth of the men live in fraternity houses; the sororities are nonresidential. Off-campus apartments lure 10 percent of the upperclassmen, but freshmen are required to remain in the residence halls. There are a variety of dining options, including the ever popular Café 101, the campus snack bar and grill room where many students take their regular meals. Kitchens are also available in the residences for upperclassmen.

The top scholars in each class get first crack at the best rooms.

Social life at the 'Burg involves the Greek system and other activities. Forty-four percent of the men belong to the dozen fraternities; the seven sororities draw 26 percent of the women. Greek parties are open and attract crowds eager to dance the night away, although students insist that "they definitely aren't the only source of fun on campus." A Student Activities Committee provides alternative social events, including concerts, comedians, bus trips to Georgetown, movies, and campus coffeehouses. Favorable reviews have come in for the campus nightclub. Those who get the munchies can make the short walk to the Lincoln Diner or take a brief road trip to Stavros, a locally famous pizza parlor. Officially the campus is dry, but like many such campuses, drinking can be done, albeit carefully, students report. The orchards and rolling countryside surrounding the campus are peaceful and scenic, and there is a small ski slope nearby. Students also get free passes to the historic attractions in town. Many participate in the November 19 Fortenbaugh Lecture by noted historians commemorating the Gettysburg

"You want to make your own major? *Do it!* Want to form a new club? *Do it!*"

Address and in the yearly wreath-laying ceremony in front of the Eisenhower Admissions Office to commemorate the general's birthday. Geared toward the tourist trade because of its historical legacy, Gettysburg occupies a spot "in the middle of nowhere but not far from anywhere," within an hour and a half of Washington, D.C., and considerably closer to Baltimore, where students enjoy the scenic Inner Harbor area.

About a quarter of Gettysburg's students earn varsity letters, and the college boasts a strong athletic program. Women's field hockey and swimming are traditionally strong, while men's lacrosse is ranked nationally. Both the men's and women's soccer teams have competed in the Division III playoffs. The annual football game against Dickinson draws a good turnout, and the Little Brown Bucket, mahogany with silver handles, is passed to the team that wins. Both track and swimming frequently produce All-Americans.

At Gettysburg, "everyone is valued," according to one senior, and students' can-do spirit is supported by the college. "You want to make your own major? *Do it!* Want to form a new club? *Do it!*" For those seeking a small school with solid academics might consider getting their education with a Gettysburg address.

<table>
<tr><td>Overlaps</td></tr>
<tr><td>Bucknell, Dickinson, Franklin and Marshall, Lafayette, Richmond</td></tr>
</table>

If You Apply To ➤ **Gettysburg:** Early decision: Feb. 1. Regular admissions and financial aid: Feb. 15. Meets demonstrated need of 95%. Campus interviews: strongly recommended, evaluative. No alumni interviews. SATs or ACTs: required. SAT IIs: optional. Essay question: significant experience; important issue or person.

Gordon College

255 Grapevine Road, Wenham, MA 01984

Gordon is the most prominent evangelical Christian college in the New England and competes nationally with Wheaton (IL) and Calvin. Not quite in the Boston area, but close enough.

At Gordon College, ancient biblical dictates have a huge impact on campus life. They regulate the very boundaries of what's acceptable in speech and conduct, as the school seeks to nourish equally students' academic and spiritual sides. In a fast-changing world, the school's mission remains constant: "To graduate men and women distinguished by intellectual maturity and Christian character." Students praise the school because "it challenges academically while incorporating a strong Christian faith," says a junior. For a select group, Gordon's solid academics, traditional values, and caring faculty are indeed a blessing.

Gordon is located on Massachusetts' scenic North Shore, three miles from the Atlantic Coast and twenty-five miles from Boston. The campus sits on hundreds of forested acres with five lakes. Academic buildings and dorms are clustered in one small section, so it doesn't take more than two or three minutes to walk anywhere on campus. Most structures are Georgian influenced, traditional red brick, except for the old stone mansion that houses administration and faculty offices. A new parking structure, with space for more than two hundred cars, and a new residence hall were recently completed.

Because religious commitment is seen as an enhancement to, not a threat against, serious academic inquiry, Gordon's core curriculum includes forty-six hours of introduction to Christianity and the liberal arts. Courses are distributed among religion, the fine arts, humanities, social and behavioral sciences, natural sciences, math, and computer science. Freshmen also take a first-year seminar on faith, character, and social thought; the conservative John Templeton Foundation has recognized this program for its academic excellence and character-building ability. The most popular majors are communications, English, and biblical and theological studies, followed by psychology and sociology/social work. "Courses are rigorous,

> **"Courses are rigorous, and demand you work hard, but it's not too much to handle."**

Website: www.gordon.edu
Location: Suburban
Total Enrollment: 1,694
Undergraduates: 1,624
Male/Female: 35/65
SAT Ranges: V 560–650
  M 540–640
ACT Range: N/A
Financial Aid: 79%
Expense: Pr $
Phi Beta Kappa: No
Applicants: 1,244
Accepted: 77%
Enrolled: 54%
Grad in 6 Years: 68%
Returning Freshmen: 88%
Academics: ✍ ✍ ✍
Social: ☎ ☎
Q of L: ★ ★ ★ ★
Admissions: (978) 927-2300 x4817 or (800) 343-1379
Email Address: admissions@ hope.gordon.edu

Strongest Programs:
  Biblical Studies

(Continued)
Music
English
Social Work
Biology
Education

and demand you work hard, but it's not too much to handle," says a Bible and English major. Administrators say the physics department and some language programs are weak, and they recommend study abroad.

On campus, Gordon's faculty receives high marks; a history major calls the quality of teaching "impeccable," and another student notes that professors "are very interested in what students think." Off-campus opportunities include stints in Washington, D.C., for aspiring politicos, in Michigan for environmentalists, in Los Angeles for filmmakers, and trips abroad through the Council for Christian Colleges and Universities.* The college also has its own program in Orvieto, Italy, focused on the country's history, art, and language, and a tropical biology semester in the Philippines. Each year, about sixty-five students take cooperative-education jobs that offer work experience at high-tech firms, publishing houses, and service organizations in the area.

Hard-working Christians come to Gordon from all over the U.S. seeking "a supportive environment without the strict rules of some Christian colleges," says a biology and Chinese studies major. Still, the regional diversity doesn't translate into ethnic diversity. "Most of the students are white, middle-class, New Englanders," says a sophomore. "Overall, they are open and very friendly, willing to help and cooperate in academics and campus endeavors." African-Americans and Asian-Americans each constitute 1 percent of the student body, while Hispanics represent 2 percent. Gordon students face the same campus issues as their peers at most colleges—homosexuality and tolerance, for example—but are required to sign a Statement of Faith promising acceptance of racial and gender equality, and moderation in behavior. "Abortion is a huge issue," says a sophomore. "Most of the campus leans Republican."

Students are required to sign a Statement of Faith promising acceptance of racial and gender equality, and moderation in behavior.

Eighty-eight percent of Gordon students live in the "coed dorms," where men and women live in separate wings of the same buildings—separated by a lobby, a lounge, and a laundry room. Persons of the opposite sex may traverse these barriers only at specified times. The dorms are "nice, but crowded," says a senior. Because freshmen get priority in the housing lottery, "you may not get your first choice." The newest dorm, Fulton Hall, opened in 2001. Permission to move off campus is granted only after the dorms are filled.

Social life at Gordon is "nice and relaxing," says an economics major, though a business major complains it "needs more variety and participation." As drinking and smoking are forbidden on campus (and may result in suspension or expulsion), students focus on chapel services and Bible

"A good portion of the student body comes out to the games."

study outside of class. Those who are twenty-one or older may drink off campus, but are expected to do so responsibly. Other options include weekend excursions to Boston (twenty-five miles away), church-related functions, movies, and an occasional square dance. Everyone looks forward to Homecoming, the Winter Ball formal (held in a castle), and the Last Blast spring party. Each year, the most popular guys in each class face off in the "hilarious" Golden Goose talent show, where the winner is crowned "Mr. Gordon."

For outdoorsy types, Gordon's setting on rugged Cape Ann is ideal, though others might describe it as isolated. The campus has cross-country ski trails and ponds for swimming, canoeing, and skating. The ocean is a quick bike ride away, nice beaches are available on Cape Cod and in Maine, and students frequently ski New Hampshire's nearby White Mountains. Volunteering through prison ministry and in soup kitchens and local churches is popular, and missionary road trips take students to Tennessee, Florida, and Washington, D.C.

When it comes to sports, Gordon competes in NCAA Division III, and "a good portion of the student body comes out to the games" when the opponent is rival

Eighty-eight percent of Gordon students live in the "coed dorms," where men and women live in separate wings of the same buildings—separated by a lobby, a lounge, and a laundry room.

Endicott College, says a history major. The women's basketball and tennis teams brought home conference championships in 2001, and the women's volleyball and field hockey teams went on to the NCAA tournament, while the men's soccer team qualified for the East Coast Athletic Conference playoffs.

Gordon students appreciate the shared sense of purpose and spirit fostered when all members of the community adhere to the gospel of Christ. While most students cherish the close community here, the school's small size can lead to gossip, frustration, and a feeling of claustrophobia. "Gordon is nicknamed 'the Gordon Bubble' because it is not an accurate representation of the real world," says a junior. "However, students do have a choice, to accept this idea"—or not. Even if they don't, most go forth happily at graduation, equipped with lasting friendships (and sometimes spouses), and prepared to work as global servant-leaders.

If You Apply To ➤

Gordon: Early decision: Dec. 1. Rolling admissions: Mar. 1. Financial aid: Mar. 1. Meets demonstrated need of 17%. Campus interviews: required, evaluative. No alumni interviews. SATs: required. SAT IIs: optional. Accepts the Common Application (with supplemental forms) and electronic applications. Essay question: Do you consider yourself a Christian?; Why a college like Gordon?; your response to a meaningful educational experience or achievement, or a pressing issue in American life.

Goucher College

1021 Dulaney Valley Road, Towson, MD 21204

This is not your grandmother's Goucher. One a staid women's college, Goucher has added men and a more progressive ambience, similar to places like Skidmore and Sarah Lawrence. Strategically located near Baltimore and not far from D.C., Goucher offers an excellent internship program.

Website: www.goucher.edu
Location: Suburban
Total Enrollment: 1,996
Undergraduates: 1,221
Male/Female: 29/71
SAT Ranges: V 560–660
  M 540–630
ACT Range: 23–27
Financial Aid: 59%
Expense: Pr $
Phi Beta Kappa: Yes
Applicants: 2,146
Accepted: 73%
Enrolled: 22%
Grad in 6 Years: 65%
Returning Freshmen: 83%
Academics: ✑ ✑ ✑
Social: ☎ ☎ ☎
Q of L: ★ ★ ★
Admissions: (410) 337-6100

Goucher, a private, liberal arts and sciences college, has a strong reputation for quality academics—especially in the sciences—and for combining classroom study with extensive off-campus and international experiences. Once a women's college, Goucher is now committed to empowering men and women of all ages and backgrounds, educating and representing them equally in an intimate setting. "Students get to know each other very well and experience a great educational environment at the same time," one sophomore says.

Indeed, Goucher has a long-standing history of excellence. Phi Beta Kappa established a chapter on campus only twenty years after the college was founded, and the college ranks among the nation's top fifty liberal arts colleges in turning out students destined for Ph.D.s in the sciences. Set on 287 landscaped acres in the suburbs of Baltimore, Goucher's wooded campus features lush lawns, stately fieldstone buildings, and rare trees and shrubs from all corners of the globe. Yet despite the pastoral ambiance, the campus is only a short walk from the suburban community of Towson.

"Goucher has challenging academics without the competition."

A rigorous general education program forms the foundation of every Goucher student's education. The core curriculum requires a first-year colloquium (Frontiers), one course in each of the humanities, social sciences, and mathematics, a lecture/lab course in the natural sciences, computer proficiency, and four physical education courses (including first-semester Transitions). Of Goucher's offerings, the science department's are arguably the strongest, with a nuclear magnetic resonance spectrometer and scientific visualization lab available for student use. Other facilities include dedicated research space, a greenhouse, and an observatory with a six-inch refractor telescope. The dance and education departments are also strong. Physics, once cited as weak, has been strengthened and is now offered as a major.

An honors program offers special team-taught interdisciplinary seminars for participants from freshman through senior years. Interdisciplinary programs include international studies, peace studies, American studies, Judaic studies (in cooperation with Baltimore Hebrew University), and a program in theory, culture, and interpretation. There's also a German minor offered through Loyola College (MD), and a 4–1 program in international business ending with a Goucher B.A. and an M.A. with California's Monterey Institute of International Studies. Future engineers can take advantage of the 3–2 program offered in conjunction with the Whiting School of Engineering at Johns Hopkins University.

For those with wanderlust, Goucher sponsors working trips to numerous countries, including Israel, France, Spain, Ghana, and Germany, as well as an exchange program with a Ukrainian university. In addition, Goucher students may take courses at nearby Johns Hopkins and seven smaller area colleges. The campus library houses 280,000 volumes and draws complaints from some students, mainly because it closes at 6:00 P.M. on Saturdays. However, Goucher students have free access to the libraries at Hopkins and other nearby schools.

> "Many different views are represented at Goucher, and people are very accepting of others' opinions."

Faculty members here devote most of their time and energy to undergraduate teaching and have a good rapport with students. "The quality of teaching is excellent and provides the students with a relaxed environment for learning," says a sophomore computer science major. Each freshman has a faculty advisor to assist with the academic and overall adjustment to college life, which are made easier by Goucher's trademark small classes and individual instruction. A sophomore adds, "Even if I hated everything else here, I would stay for the close interaction with engaging teachers." The top students strive for better, and many hold leadership roles. Another student says, "Goucher has challenging academics without the competition." In addition to their academic work, all Goucher students are required to do a three-credit internship or

> "Most people have small gatherings in their rooms instead of raging parties."

off-campus experience related to their major. Popular choices include congressional offices, museums, law firms, and newspapers. Another option is the three-week-long Public Policy Seminar in Washington, D.C., where students meet informally with political luminaries.

Thirty-eight percent of Goucher's students are homegrown, and most of the rest hail from Pennsylvania, Virginia, New York, and New Jersey. African-Americans, Hispanics, and Asian-Americans together make up 12 percent of the student body. Diversity, one student says, "is discussed easily in the small Goucher community," and students agree that multiculturalism is an important campus issue. Students are described as open-minded and accepting. "Many different views are represented at Goucher, and people are very accepting of others' opinions," a freshman says. Goucher offers merit scholarships for those who are qualified, some providing full tuition, room, and board each year. And coeducation seems to be working well; applications for recent classes have increased substantially, and enrollment is up. However, women still make up nearly three-quarters of the student body.

Goucher has four coed dormitories, divided into thirteen residential units of about fifty students each. Seventy percent of students live on campus. Freshmen double up in spacious rooms, while upperclassmen select housing through lotteries; the available singles usually go to juniors and seniors, though a lucky sophomore may

(Continued)

Email Address:
admissions@goucher.edu

Strongest Programs:
Psychology
English
Communications
Management
Sciences

The science departments are arguably the strongest, with a nuclear magnetic resonance spectrometer and scientific visualization lab available for student use.

Interdisciplinary programs include international studies, peace studies, American studies, Judaic studies (in cooperation with Baltimore Hebrew University), and a program in theory, culture, and interpretation.

Future engineers can take advantage of the 3–2 program offered in conjunction with the Whiting School of Engineering at Johns Hopkins University.

occasionally get one. A sophomore says: "We have great cable and Internet/voicemail hookups." The administration has been offering incentives to upperclassmen, encouraging them to move off campus to avoid a housing crunch; women who want an apartment closer to male-dominated Johns Hopkins can usually get one.

And what about the social life? "There is very little social life on campus, and the college does a very poor job of organizing events," says one freshman. Another says, "Most people have small gatherings in their rooms instead of raging parties." Access to a car is a virtual necessity, for many students travel to nearby universities (Loyola and Towson State) or Baltimore's Inner Harbor for entertainment. Students who are of age frequent restaurants and bars in Towson, the small but bustling college town a five-minute walk away. Goucher has no sororities or fraternities, but the close-knit housing units hold periodic events, and the college hosts weekend movies, concerts, and lectures. Major annual social events include Rocktoberfest, Spring Fling, and the Blind Date Ball each fall ("It can be great, or your roommate can be dead at sunup," a sophomore quips). Biggest of all is GIG, Get-into-Goucher Day, when classes are unexpectedly canceled and the whole campus celebrates. Popular road trips include Ocean City, New York, Philadelphia, and Washington, D.C.

Since Goucher was a women's college until 1987, women's athletics are more highly developed than those at many coed schools. The women's lacrosse team is popular, along with men's basketball and lacrosse. The genteel sport of horseback riding is popular, thanks to the indoor equestrian ring, stables, and beautiful wooded campus trails. Goucher also has several tennis courts, a driving range, practice fields, a swimming pool, and saunas.

Nostalgic alumnae no doubt shed some tears at the passing of the old Goucher, but the switch to coeducation seems to be bettering the school. Its traditional Southern stance has slowly evolved into a more Northern-looking slant. And more recently, its bucolic location, large investment in technology, strong academic reputation, and "all those girls" have helped bring more guys to Goucher. Every year that the percentage of men at Goucher creeps toward 50, this quaint school comes closer to becoming truly coed—and to proving that the genders can succeed in tandem.

Overlaps

American, Skidmore, University of Maryland–College Park, Towson, George Washington

If You Apply To ➤ **Goucher:** Early Decision: Nov. 15. Early action: Dec. 1. Regular admissions: Feb. 1. Financial aid: Feb. 15. Guarantees to meet demonstrated need. Campus interviews: recommended, informational. Alumni interviews: optional, informational. SATs or ACTs: required. SAT IIs: optional. Accepts the Common Application. Essay questions: significant experience or achievement; personal, local, national or international issue and why it is important to you; significant person; topic of own choosing.

Grinnell College

Grinnell, IA 50112

Iowa cornfields provide a surreal backdrop for Grinnell's funky, progressive, and talented student body. At 1,338 students, Grinnell is half the size of Oberlin. That translates into tiny classes and tutorials of thirteen students or fewer. Grinnell's biggest challenge is simply getting prospective students to the campus.

Website: www.grinnell.edu
Location: Small town
Total Enrollment: 1,338

"Go West, young man, go West," said Horace Greeley to Josiah B. Grinnell in 1846. The result of Grinnell's wanderings into the rural cornfields, fifty-five miles from Des Moines and sixty miles from Iowa City, is the remarkable college that bears his name. Yet despite its physical isolation, Grinnell is a powerhouse on the national scene. Ever progressive, it was the first college west of the Mississippi to admit African-Americans and women, and the first in the country to establish an undergraduate department of political science. It was once a stop on the Underground Railroad, and its graduates include Harry Hopkins, architect of the New Deal, and Robert Noyce, inventor of the integrated circuit, two people who did as much as anyone to change the face of American society in the twentieth century. Grinnell is now second only to Carleton as best liberal arts college in the Midwest.

The school's 108-acre campus is an attractive blend of collegiate Gothic and modern Bauhaus academic buildings and Prairie-style houses. (Architecture buffs should take note of the dazzling Louis Sullivan bank facade just off campus.) The Noyce Science Center, a technological showpiece, recently underwent a $15.3 million renovation, and a seventy-five thousand-square-foot addition to the Fine Arts Center—including gallery, studio, performing, and rehearsal space—has been completed. New dorms, athletic fields, a physical education complex, and student center are in the works.

> **"All courses are rigorous—it's just on a scale of rigorous to more rigorous."**

True to its liberal arts focus, Grinnell mandates a first-semester writing tutorial, modeled after Oxford University's program, but doesn't require anything else. The more than thirty tutorials, limited to thirteen students each, help enhance critical thinking, research, writing, and discussion skills, and allow first-year students to work individually with professors. When it comes to declaring a major, students determine their own course of study with help from faculty. Strong departments include the natural sciences and foreign languages, including German and Russian, bolstered by an influx of research grants, including one from the National Science Foundation. Beware of language courses if you aren't planning to major in the field, though: "I took an intermediate class in Spanish first semester freshman year, and I spent three hours in class as well as about eight hours outside of class on homework, and two hours in Spanish lab," says a drained sophomore. The chemistry department (including a newer biological chemistry major) draws majors with independent research projects, and English, anthropology, sociology, and economics are popular, too.

Grinnell's standards are high, and 30 percent of alums move on to graduate and professional schools. Students who don't mind studying, even on weekends, will be happiest here. "All courses are rigorous—it's just on a scale of rigorous to more rigorous," says a senior. Adds a sophomore: "Even the art classes are demanding." During finals, perhaps to help ease the stress, costumed superheroes run around the library giving out candy, says a sociology major. Teaching is the top priority for Grinnell faculty members, since the college awards no graduate degrees, there are no teaching assistants. "The profs act as responsible guides to our

> **"Everything you need is accessible by foot and within ten minutes (excepting Wal-Mart)."**

explorations of the texts," says an English major. "My current profs describe the expectations as difficult to meet, in that students expect magic in the classroom," reports a philosophy major.

Academic advising is also well-regarded, as students are assisted by the professor who leads their first-year tutorial, and then choose another faculty member in their major discipline: "Faculty really do take a great interest in the success of students inside and outside of the classroom," says a psychology major. It's rare to find classes with more than fifty students, and 76 percent of classes taken by freshmen have fewer than twenty-five. When campus becomes too stressful, students may study abroad in more than one hundred locations, through the Associated Colleges of the Midwest* consortium and Grinnell-in-London. Fifty percent of students spend some time away from campus, and financial aid extends to study abroad,

(Continued)
Undergraduates: 1,338
Male/Female: 46/54
SAT Ranges: V 630–730
   M 620–710
ACT Range: 27–32
Financial Aid: 58%
Expense: Pr $ $
Phi Beta Kappa: Yes
Applicants: 1,980
Accepted: 65%
Enrolled: 28%
Grad in 6 Years: 84%
Returning Freshmen: 92%
Academics: ✐ ✐ ✐ ✐ ½
Social: ☎ ☎
Q of L: ★ ★ ★
Admissions: (641) 269-3600
Email Address:
   askgrin@grinnell.edu

Strongest Programs:
   Foreign Languages
   Biology
   Chemistry
   History
   English
   Political Science
   Religious Studies

Grinnell is now second only to Carleton as best liberal arts college in the Midwest.

administrators say. Co-ops in architecture, business, law, and medicine, and 3–2 engineering programs are also available.

Grinnell is a bit of Greenwich Village in corn country. Despite the rural environment, the college attracts an urban clientele, especially from the Chicago area. "Students at Grinnell are very multi-talented—athletes, musicians, actors, activists, writers, on and on," says a religious studies major. "I am amazed by the diversity of talent." That diversity doesn't extend to the student body, which is 5 percent Hispanic, 5 percent Asian-American, 3 percent African-American and 71 percent white, but it does influence the issues about which students get excited. Women's rights, gay rights, labor rights, human rights, globalization, the environment, and groups like PAFA (the Politically Active Feminist Alliance), GEAR (Grinnell Escalating AIDS Response) and Fearless (formed to combat gender-based violence) set the tone. Grinnell benefits from a hefty endowment, considering the school's size, thanks to portfolio managers who are among the best in the country.

The college guarantees four years of campus housing and 85 percent of students take advantage of the dorms, each of which has kitchen facilities, cable television, and a computer room. All but two dorms are coed, and after freshman year, students participate in a room draw, which can be stressful but usually works out. "Self-governance in the halls makes for tight communities," says a senior—as does some recent overcrowding, which has occasionally placed two students in a room designed for one. Students who move off campus, mostly seniors, live just across the street, and the smallness of campus means "you can't avoid embarrassing exes—ever," cautions a philosophy major. There are two dining halls, one on each side of campus, and meal plans range from full board to just dinner. Special family-style dinners are served every other Wednesday. Safety is a non-issue, quips a sophomore: "We live in a small town in the middle of Iowa!"

"This is a pretty controlled drinking scene."

That town, Grinnell (pop. 9,100), is "delightfully small," says a sophomore. "Everything you need is accessible by foot and within ten minutes (excepting Wal-Mart)." Still, a senior complains, "There's a McDonald's in town now, so we can't claim to be that far outside of civilization, though most would like to." Community service helps bridge the town–gown gap, with some students serving as tutors and student teachers at the local high school and others participating in mentoring programs and community meals, among other projects. Outdoor recreation is popular, and nearby Rock Creek State Park lends itself to biking, running, camping, kayaking, and cross-country skiing, as well as other pursuits sponsored by the Grinnell Outdoor Recreation Program, or GORP. There are a few bars and pizza joints downtown, but for those craving bright lights, Iowa City and Des Moines are within an hour's drive, and the college runs a shuttle service to reach them. Chicago and Minneapolis are each about four hours distant.

With no fraternities or sororities, intramurals and all-campus parties revolve mainly around the dorms. Each dorm periodically sponsors a party using wordplay from its name in the title. For instance, Mary B. James Hall puts on the Mary-Be-James party, for which everyone comes in drag. As for alcohol, a senior reports, "The policy is very relaxed." That said, there have been problems with excessive drinking and alcohol poisoning, leading to mandatory age identification and campus security supervision at all parties, explains a sophomore. "This is a pretty controlled drinking scene," adds a senior. "The policy is, don't have alcohol outside, don't drink underage, do take care of each other. As a self-governed institution, we pride ourselves on our community-oriented ways of addressing alcohol problems."

Nondrinkers need not fear, however. Grinnell's social groups and activities range from the Society for Creative Anachronism and the Black Cultural Center to improvisational workshops, poetry readings, symposia, concerts, and movies—

"you name it, it's all free to students," says a history and secondary education major. Highlights of the campus calendar include semiformal Winter and Spring Waltzes ("Yes, we really waltz"), where "most people wear formals and look very nice, not a common occurrence at a school where comfort is the usual standard and women rarely wear makeup," notes one student. At Disco, "everyone dresses up in clothes from the '70s and dances all night." Other noteworthy events include a band/tie-dyeing fest called Alice in Wonderland, Titular Head (a festival of five-minute student films), Pipe Cleaner Day ("May 5 generally brings upwards of twenty thousand of the sculptable wires to campus"), and the Zirkle Circle, described by a senior as "a spontaneous dance around a famous campus sculpture, usually after imbibing intoxicating liquids."

Grinnell competes in Division III, and the men's cross-country, basketball, and women's swimming teams won conference championships in the 2000–01 season. The football team finished the 1998–99 season with a championship. Athletics aren't the focus here, though a senior does say that the "honor G" letter on the uniforms of varsity athletes is "very cool."

Grinnell wouldn't put a grin on every prospective college student's face. "Most of us don't apologize for what at first turns people off about Grinnell," explains a senior. "We like being in the middle of Iowa, we like that you've probably never heard of us, we love that won't come here because you want a big name." There's no denying that Grinnell is a real gem of a school—a first-rate liberal arts college out in the cornfields.

Overlaps

Carleton, Macalester, Oberlin, Washington University (MO), Swarthmore

If You Apply To ➤ **Grinnell:** Early decision: Nov. 20. Regular admissions: Jan. 20. Financial aid: Feb. 1. Guarantees to meet demonstrated need. Campus interviews: recommended, evaluative. Alumni interviews: optional, informational. SATs or ACTs: required. SAT IIs: optional. Accepts the Common Application and electronic applications. Essay question: changed opinion; original essay on any subject (expository, fictional, or poetic, but descriptive of applicant's style and abilities); or why you favor a rural education.

Guilford College

5800 West Friendly Avenue, Greensboro, NC 27410

One of the few schools of Quaker heritage in the South. Emphasizes a collaborative approach and is among the most liberal institutions below the Mason-Dixon line. A kindred spirit to Earlham in Indiana. Guilford's signature program is justice and policy studies.

Founded in 1837 by the Religious Society of Friends (Quakers), Guilford College has remained true to the sect's teachings, emphasizing community, equality, and justice. Faculty members value students' opinions and have them over for dinner. "We sit in a circle in the classroom, and call our professors by their first names," says a senior. Hewing close to the Quakers' philosophy of inclusiveness, a Guilford education is informed and enriched by interdisciplinary courses and community service.

Located on 340 wooded acres in northwest Greensboro, Guilford's redbrick buildings are mainly in the Georgian style. The school is the only liberal arts college in the Southeast with Quaker roots, as well as the oldest coeducational institution in the South and the third oldest in the nation. During the Civil War, Guilford was one of a few Southern colleges that remained open—perhaps because it was also an embarkation point on the Underground Railroad. New additions include the Frank Family Science Center, with optical and radio telescopes, opened in 2000.

Website: www.guilford.edu
Location: City outskirts
Total Enrollment: 1,490
Undergraduates: 1,490
Male/Female: 47/53
SAT Ranges: V 520–650
  M 500–600
ACT Range: 22–29
Financial Aid: 51%
Expense: Pr $ $
Phi Beta Kappa: No
Applicants: 1,355

(Continued)

Accepted: 79%

Enrolled: 31%

Grad in 6 Years: 72%

Returning Freshmen: 77%

Academics: ✐ ✐ ✐

Social: ☎ ☎

Q of L: ★ ★ ★ ★

Admissions: (800) 992-7759

Email Address:
admission@guilford.edu

Strongest Programs:
Business Management
Education
English
Geology
Physics
Psychology

In the summer, students may participate in a five-week seminar that includes hiking, camping, and geological and biological research in the Grand Canyon, or in a seminar on the East African rift, which includes a three-week trip to Africa.

Wireless Internet connections are available in the Hege Library, where students may check out laptop computers from the circulation desk.

In addition to their majors, Guilford students fulfill general education requirements in three areas: Foundations, Explorations, and Capstone. All students must also demonstrate quantitative literacy. Foundations consists of four skills and perspectives courses. The college has five areas of study—arts, business and policy, humanities, natural sciences and math, and social science—and the first set of Explorations courses provide academic breadth outside the area covered by a student's major and concentration. The second set of Explorations courses consists of three critical perspectives classes, one each from the categories of intercultural, social justice and environmental responsibility, and U.S. diversity. During the senior year, students take an interdisciplinary studies course to meet the Capstone requirement.

Students say Guilford's best programs include physics, religious studies, peace and conflict studies (owing to the Quaker influence), and political science. New majors include computer information systems, computing and information technology, health sciences, and forensic biology. Some students avoid the highly regarded management program because they're "more interested in changing the world than doing business," says a political science major. The political science department is rebuilding after two of three full-time faculty members left, a major says: "One of the faculty has been replaced, but only by a temporary visiting professor who has not gotten marks for his teaching." When it comes to teaching, Guilford has high standards—instruction should be "thorough, meaningful, applicable to real life, and most of all, interesting!" says a psychology and health sciences major. Guilford's academic climate is "very laid-back, just like all other aspects of the school,"

"We sit in a circle in the classroom, and call our professors by their first names."

says a junior. "However, that doesn't mean that the academics aren't rigorous, because they are extremely challenging." Guilford believes that experiential learning adds immeasurably to classroom work, so the college offers study abroad from China and Japan to Mexico, Germany, and France. In the summer, students may participate in a five-week seminar that includes hiking, camping, and geological and biological research in the Grand Canyon, or in a seminar on the East African rift, which includes a three-week trip to Africa.

Despite its small size, Guilford gives students the tools needed for ground-breaking work. Physics majors get professional-grade optics and robotics equipment, and students working on complex geology and chemistry projects have access to the Scientific Computation and Visualization Facility, with more than twenty Unix workstations for information-based modeling. Perhaps not surprisingly, Guilford publishes both the *Journal of Undergraduate Mathematics* and the *Journal of Undergraduate Research in Physics*. Wireless Internet connections are available in the Hege Library, where students may check out laptop computers from the circulation desk.

Guilford students are quite literally a colorful bunch, says a justice and policy studies major. "We have people with pink and blue hair," he says. "We have our share of hippies, and many athletes as well. Throw in the mix a couple of Republicans and some run-of-the-mill college students, and the result is a diversity of thought and conflict that makes Guilford an exciting place to spend four years." Students come from forty states, twenty-five countries, and a range of socioeconomic backgrounds, although most are liberal. "We work to quell institutional racism, homophobia, and violence in the world," a political science major explains. African-Americans comprise 11 percent of the student body, Hispanics 2 percent, and Asian-Americans 1 percent.

Seventy-three percent of students live in Guilford's dorms, which got new furniture and carpeting, big-screen TVs, remodeled kitchens, and upgraded heating and air-conditioning systems in the fall of 2000. On-campus apartments, for juniors and seniors, are comparable in price to off-campus digs—a good thing, since getting permission to move off campus is tough. Bryan is the party dorm, and English (for men) and Shore (for women) are the single-sex quiet dorms. The female residents of Mary Hobbs, a co-op dorm built in 1907, do their own housekeeping in exchange for cheaper rent. Binford has a large freshman population, and a substance-free floor that spawned a circus club two years ago! Food in the college cafeteria is awful, but unfortunately, students say, it's nearly impossible to opt out of the meal plan.

Guilford's social life revolves around more than forty registered clubs and organizations, ranging from the Entrepreneur's Network and Strategic Games Society to Hillel and the African-American Cultural Society. No alcohol is allowed at college functions, but it remains pretty easy for underage students to drink—despite efforts to impose fines on those who are caught. Serendipity, a celebration of spring with games, mud wrestling, streakers, big-name musicians like the Violent Femmes, and "a sense of mass disorientation," is a cherished tradition. "If you love to drink and be loud, and throw chairs and trash cans off of balconies and buildings, then you will have a great time," says a senior. "If you are more mature, the social scene can be a little dry."

Getting off campus and back will be easier now that Guilford plans a free shuttle service, also stopping at some of the five other schools in the area, and running until 2 A.M. on weekends.

Beyond the campus gates, students find all of the essentials—Wal-Mart, some clubs in downtown Greensboro (only 10 minutes away), the ethnic restaurants of Tate Street, and the college's Quaker Village, which has a $1 movie theater, pool hall, and a Starbucks. Getting off campus and back will be easier now that Guilford plans a free shuttle service, also stopping at

"We have our share of hippies, and many athletes as well."

some of the five other schools in the area, and running until 2 A.M. on weekends. Popular road trips include UNC-Chapel Hill (one hour), Asheville and the mountains (three-and-a-half hours), and the Outer Banks beaches (four hours).

Guilford's athletic teams compete as the "Fighting Quakers," and students love the oxymoron, as in their cheer: "Fight, fight, inner light! Kill, Quakers, kill!" Students root for the football team in the annual Soup Bowl against Greensboro College, while the men's golf team brought home the NCAA Division III national championship in 2002. The women's basketball team won conference championships in 2001 and 2002, and the women's rugby team plays in prom dresses once a year. Because of Guilford's emphasis on developing the whole person, physically, mentally, and spiritually, students are encouraged to participate in school-sponsored outdoor adventures, such as a ropes course, sailing, and white-water rafting.

While Guilford has evolved from its humble beginnings as a lone Southern outpost of liberalism, it remains devoted to the traditional Quaker goal of "educating individuals not only to live, but to live well." Unfortunately, a cash crunch has led the school to raise tuition and downsize some departments. "The student body has gotten richer, and has less compassion for things that really matter," says a senior. Adds a junior: "I'm really scared that in another few years, Guilford will be just another small Southern school"—which would be a shame.

Overlaps
Elon, Oberlin, Goucher, Earlham, UNC–Chapel Hill

If You Apply To ➤

Guilford: Early decision: Nov. 15. Early action: Jan. 15. Regular admissions: Feb. 15. Financial aid: Mar. 1. Does not guarantee to meet demonstrated need. Campus interviews: recommended, evaluative. Alumni interviews: optional, evaluative. SATs or ACTs: required; personal portfolio or presentation may be substituted. SAT IIs: optional. Accepts the Common Application and electronic applications. Essay question: compare your experiences to those of others; relate the work of an admired or disliked artist, public figure, scientist, or writer to your own experiences; compare Palmer's concepts of "community" and "lifestyle enclave" to personal experience. Graded writing sample also required.

800 West College Avenue, St. Peter, MN 56082

A touch of Scandinavia in southern Minnesota, GA is a guardian of the tried and true in Lutheran education. With Minnesotans comprising nearly 80 percent of the students, GA is less national than cross-state rival St. Olaf. Extensive distribution requirements include exploring values and moral reasoning.

Website: www.gac.edu
Location: Small city
Total Enrollment: 2,545
Undergraduates: 2,545
Male/Female: 43/57
SAT Ranges: V 550–670
  M 550–670
ACT Range: 23–28
Financial Aid: 68%
Expense: Pr $
Phi Beta Kappa: Yes
Applicants: 2,163
Accepted: 76%
Enrolled: 41%
Grad in 6 Years: 80%
Returning Freshmen: 89%
Academics: ✏️ ✏️ ✏️
Social: ☎ ☎ ☎
Q of L: ★ ★ ★
Admissions: (507) 933-7676
Email Address:
  admission@gustavus.edu

Strongest Programs:
  Physics
  Psychology
  Classics
  Spanish
  Chemistry
  Communications Studies

The sidewalk running through the middle of the spacious Gustavus Adolphus College campus is nicknamed the "Hello Walk," because it's a tradition for students venturing down the path to greet one another—whether they've met or not. "You can smile at anyone on the sidewalk, and they, most likely, will smile back," says a sophomore. "It's really a supportive place." GA is named for Sweden's King Gustav II Adolph (1594–1632), who is credited with making Sweden a major European power and defending Lutheranism against the Catholics. While the king's battle victories earned him the title "Lion of the North," he was also an advocate of education and culture. Save for the women now attending classes, King Gustav would probably feel at home at the college that bears his name, where a not-so-subtle Swedish influence pervades everything from the buildings to the curriculum.

The 330-acre GA campus is perched on a hill overlooking the Minnesota River valley, about sixty-five miles southwest of the Twin Cities. The campus architectural theme is, not surprisingly, Scandinavian, dominated by subdued, semi-modern to modern brown brick buildings. Highlights include the 113-year-old Victorian Old Main Building and the centrally located Christ Chapel, with spires and shafts resembling a crown. Thirty bronze works by sculptor-in-residence Paul Granlund are strategically placed, and the 130-acre Linnaeus Arboretum and Interpretive Center offers plant study and retreats. The campus boasts one thousand new trees and many new windows, carpets, computers, and roofs—all grim reminders of the March 1998 tornado that caused more than $60 million in damage. Students have clamored for more of the two apartment-style dorms that had to be built because the storm destroyed the college's oldest residence hall.

In the classroom, students will find an academic smorgasbord, as GA aims to offer an education both "interdisciplinary and international in perspective." Among more innovative programs, students may choose majors in Scandinavian studies, environmental studies, women's studies, or materials science—or they may design their own. GA's strongest programs include physics, chemistry, biology, classics, and communication studies. The accounting major is weaker, administrators say. Outside the classroom, learning opportunities come from several internationally renowned meetings held on campus each year, including the Nobel Conference, a two-day meeting of scientific experts from all over the world; the May Day peace conference, held the first Wednesday in May; and the International Festival, incorporating a diversity-focused conference called Building Bridges.

"You can smile at anyone on the sidewalk, and they, most likely, will smile back."

To fulfill core requirements, Gustavus students have two options. Curriculum I includes twelve courses from seven areas of knowledge, plus a first-term seminar covering liberal arts skills such as critical thinking, writing, speaking, and recognizing and exploring values. Curriculum II is an integrated twelve-course sequence focused on related classic works from various disciplines. The sixty students who select this option—on a first-come, first-served basis—start with the first four courses in the liberal arts core: Historical Perspective I and II, The Biblical Tradition, and The Individual and Morality. In addition to the core courses, students must satisfy a "writing across the curriculum" requirement, with three courses that have a substantial amount of writing, and the first-term Values in Writing seminar, which explores questions of value while emphasizing critical thinking, writing, and speaking.

Overall, academics at Gustavus are rigorous, but study groups are common. "Faculty will challenge you, and you will be pushed, but everyone's there for you at the same time," says a biology and history major. Undergraduate research is a hallmark—despite the library's paltry 250,000 volumes—and Gustavus Adolphus students recently presented forty-two papers at the National Conference on Undergraduate Research, the third-highest total in the nation. That's not as surprising when you consider that each year, thirty-five freshmen are selected for the Partners in Scholarship program, which matches undergraduates with faculty research mentors and gives them annual grants of $7,500. For the professionally minded, Gustavus offers 3–2 engineering programs with the University of Minnesota and Minnesota State University Mankato.

When winter winds force almost everyone indoors during the January term, Gustavus students (known as Gusties) may take concentrated study on campus, or enjoy travel and co-op opportunities. Gustavus sponsors study-abroad programs at five colleges and universities in Sweden, as well as in Japan, India, Malaysia, Australia, Russia, the Netherlands, and Scotland. Back on campus, students find professors knowledgeable and friendly. "They always have their doors open for additional help," says a classics major.

"The dorms are clean and have nice furniture."

For all its good points, though, this liberal arts college is hardly a model of diversity. In fact, the population is more reminiscent of Garrison Keillor's Lake Wobegon: 94 percent of students are white, 76 percent are Minnesotan, and about 55 percent are Lutheran. "Gustavus is pretty much the epitome of 'Minnesota nice,'" says a sophomore. Some students lament the lack of diversity, and the school has responded by expanding minority recruitment efforts. The Greek system, the use of wind power, and U.S. politics are among the myriad issues and causes that occupy students' minds. "People are whiny about various things, but most of it is minor," says a biology and history major. "The biggest complaint would probably be about being 'too busy.' As overachievers, Gustavus students tend to get very involved, and then realize that you can only do so much."

Eighty percent of Gusties live in the dorms, where housing is guaranteed for four years, and most underclass rooms are doubles. "The dorms are clean and have nice furniture," plus twenty-four-hour computer labs, says a biology major. Substance-free floors are available, and smoking is prohibited in all residences. Norelius is exclusively for freshmen and sophomores, which helps them form friendships and encourages group activities. Two dorms with single rooms and apartment-style suites, and some college-owned houses, are exclusively for upperclassmen, who get priority at room draw. Juniors and seniors, and

"Gustavus has a great feeling of community and opportunity."

all students over twenty-one, may also request permission to live off campus. Twenty-seven percent of the men and 22 percent of the women go Greek, but GA's social life is not centered around fraternities and sororities.

Instead, students look forward to college-sponsored events, such as outdoor movies, concerts (Five for Fighting played last spring), variety shows, and the annual Earth Jam outdoor concert. Extracurricular involvement in music is very strong, says a freshman: "There are two orchestras, two bands, seven choir groups, and numerous other smaller ensembles." They all perform together at the Christmas in Christ Chapel concert, for which more than five thousand tickets are usually sold. The Dive is a popular on-campus dry bar, and the college offers periodic trips to Mankato—ten miles away—and to the Twin Cities, for shopping at the Mall of America or a Minnesota Twins baseball game. "It gets to the point where there is almost too much to choose from," says an overwhelmed senior. Because students twenty-one and older may drink in their rooms, with the door closed, underage students may easily get alcohol if they want it, but students say drinking isn't a popular pastime. The town of St. Peter "could be characterized as cute, quaint, and somewhat rural," says a sophomore, but it has "a great coffee shop, a thrift store, and the nicest people you'll find anywhere." There are also many opportunities to give back, through tutoring or mentoring younger kids, or working at the local nursing home.

The GA football team has a loyal following, particularly in annual match-ups against St. Olaf, and that rivalry extends to men's swimming, which brought home a conference championship last year. Numerous GA teams participated in NCAA Division III national championship competition, with women's ice hockey and men's tennis placing third, and women's tennis and men's golf coming in fifth.

King Gustav would no doubt be pleased with the achievements of students at his namesake college, whether in the classroom and the lab, or on the ski slopes and athletic fields. "Gustavus has a great feeling of community and opportunity," says a senior. For the future, the school is emphasizing "diversity and vocational reflection, or finding your place inside a larger community," says a freshman. Doing so shouldn't be too hard for students here, who leave with a solid arts-and-sciences foundation after four years in this close-knit haven.

If You Apply To > **Gustavus Adolphus:** Early decision: Nov. 15. Early action: Jan. 15. Rolling admissions and financial aid: Apr. 1. Housing: June 1. Does not guarantee to meet demonstrated need. Campus interviews: recommended, informational. No alumni interviews. SATs or ACTs: required. SAT IIs: optional. Accepts the Common Application and electronic applications. Essay question: significant experience; what you hope to gain from college; personal goals; or submit a writing sample from one of your classes.

Hamilton College

198 College Hill Road, Clinton, NY 13323

Hamilton is among network of elite, rural, northeastern liberal arts colleges that extends from Colby in Maine through Middlebury and Williams to Colgate, about half-an-hour's drive to Hamilton's south. Hamilton is on the small side of this group and emphasizes close contact with faculty and a senior project requirement.

Website: www.hamilton.edu
Location: Rural
Total Enrollment: 1,755
Undergraduates: 1,755
Male/Female: 49/51
SAT Ranges: V 600–690
   M 600–680
Financial Aid: 60%
Expense: Pr $ $ $ $
Phi Beta Kappa: Yes

Back in 1978, Hamilton was a traditional men's college that seemed to have everything: money, prestige, and academic excellence. But after 166 years of bachelorhood, Hamilton decided to walk down the aisle with Kirkland College, the artsy women's college next door that was founded under Hamilton's auspices a decade before. The marriage was rocky at first, but the gender wars eventually gave way to cooperation. Today, Hamilton is much the richer for its diverse heritage, combining old school traditionalism with a touch of right-brain flair. Women may be from Venus and men from Mars, but at Hamilton both sexes have found common ground.

Set on a picturesque hilltop overlooking the tiny town of Clinton and crafted of rich, warm brownstone, the old Hamilton campus features a glorious array of collegiate Victorian architecture whose beauty is punctuated only by the eyesore that houses the library. By contrast, the adjacent Kirkland campus consists of boxy concrete structures of a 1960s "brutalist" vintage. Straddling the ravine that divides the two campuses, and joining them literally and figuratively, is a Student Activities Building that features a diner, lounges, and areas where students and faculty can relax. In all, Hamilton owns more than 1,200 acres of woodlands, open fields, and glens with many lovely trails for hiking or cross-country skiing within the grounds. Construction was recently completed on residence halls for sixty students.

In the classroom, Hamilton is pure liberal arts. English, economics, and government top the list of most popular majors, the latter enjoying a national reputation in public policy. In fact, the Arthur Levitt Public Affairs Center is emerging as a model public policy think tank where students can actively engage in research for local, regional, and state social service organizations and government agencies. The natural sciences are also strong, with up-to-date equipment and small labs. Under a grant from the National Science Foundation, the geology department sends students to Antarctica for research each year, and Hamilton's rocky terrain provides fertile research territory for those who remain. The economics and psychology departments are unusually productive in terms of research and publication, often giving undergrads a piece of the action. The nationally recognized physics department has been nominated for prestigious awards. The administration admits that the rhetoric and communication department needs to be strengthened.

A major curriculum reform went into effect for the class of 2005 and features a series of proseminars—classes of no more than sixteen that require intensive interaction—that emphasize writing, speaking, and discussion. There will also be a required sophomore program that stresses interdisciplinary learning and culminates in an integrative project with public presentation. Hamilton is among the few colleges that requires all seniors to produce an independent project in their area of concentration. Up to seven outstanding seniors—designated as Senior Fellows—replace their normal courseload with a fellowship project that culminates in a written thesis and a public lecture to the college community. Another interesting development is the administration's decision to allow students to choose what standardized tests they submit for admissions. Beginning with the class matriculated in the fall of 2002, candidates to Hamilton may submit results from the SAT-1, the ACT, three SAT-2 tests, three Advanced Placement (AP) tests, three International Baccalaureate or higher level tests, or three scores in different areas of study from any mix of the above to include an English test, a quantitative test, and a test of the student's choice. Hamilton offers year-long or semester-long programs in France, Spain, and China and terms in Washington, D.C. About two-thirds of graduates have an off-campus study experience. Students can earn a B.A. in liberal arts from Hamilton and B.S. in engineering with Columbia University, Rensselaer Polytechnic Institute, and Washington University of St. Louis in a 3–2 program. Other similar 4–2 programs are also available.

Hamilton students take pride in their school's dedication to quality instruction. "I am constantly reminded of how lucky I am to be taught by such intelligent and caring people," boasts a psychology major. "They have vast knowledge about their subjects and are very motivated to make sure their students are truly learning." Students report that the courses here are challenging, but that classmates are supportive, not competitive with each other. "Expectations are high, but students have access to any help they might need," says a mathematics major. Small classes add to the experience; many have ten students or fewer. Faculty members make sure they are available outside of class, and often give out their home phone numbers and invite students to lunch or their homes. "They will take you out for a cup of Joe and

> "I am constantly reminded of how lucky I am to be taught by such intelligent and caring people."

(Continued)

Applicants: 4,601
Accepted: 35%
Enrolled: 29%
Grad in 6 Years: 85%
Returning Freshmen: 92%
Academics: ✍ ✍ ✍ ✍ ½
Social: 🕾 🕾 🕾 🕾
Q of L: ★ ★ ★
Admissions: (315) 859-4421
Email Address:
  admission@hamilton.edu

Strongest Programs:
  Sciences
  Social Science
  Asian Studies

The Arthur Levitt Public Affairs Center is emerging as a model public policy think tank where students can actively engage in research for local, regional, and state social service organizations and government agencies.

Under a grant from the National Science Foundation, the geology department sends students to Antarctica for research each year, and Hamilton's rocky terrain provides fertile research territory for those who remain.

a muffin at Café Opus," explains one junior. "You have access to everyone in the school. Even President Tobin holds 'office hours' on the porch where you can go and talk to him."

The student body is composed of 39 percent New York residents (most from downstate), and 63 percent public high-school graduates. The majority of students are social, outdoorsy, and fans of J. Crew. "Sometimes the people here can be rather cliqueish," notes a freshman. "Overall, I find the people very down-to-earth and well-rounded." Minority enrollment makes up 12 percent, with African-Americans comprising 4 percent. Big issues on campus involve race relations, gay and lesbian rights, and alcohol policies. Hamilton offers a handful of merit scholarships ranging from $5,000 to $10,000 each, but no athletic scholarships.

Housing at Hamilton is varied, including old fraternity houses that were renovated and turned into dorms and three- or four-person apartments. "The only complaint that I have ever heard about housing is the housing lottery," says one junior. "If you are smart, you will just become an RA and live in a nice single and not go through the lottery." The Hamilton side of campus is reputed to be the place for party animals, while the Kirkland dorms have a more mellow, individualistic reputation.

"Overall, I find the people very down-to-earth and well-rounded."

On the Hamilton side, students have likened Dunham to a "dungeon," but note that its problems are outweighed by its social draw for freshmen. Both sexes and all four classes are mixed together in most of the halls, a number of which have been renovated to create small-group living units. Rooms are assigned to first-year students; upperclassmen rely on a lottery system. At the top of the list are several stately mansions that offer posh amenities. Students have the option of living in a coed cooperative house, and several substance-free, smoke-free, and quiet houses. All told, 96 percent of Hamilton students reside on campus. A student food co-op offers opportunities for experimental cooking, which can make up for the rather unpopular food services.

Another interesting development is the administration's decision to allow students to choose what standardized tests they submit for admissions.

Twenty-three percent of the men and 17 percent of the women join fraternities and sororities, despite housing rules that ban frat houses from campus. Most students stay on campus to socialize. Some say options are limited, but others find more than enough to keep them occupied. An old barn was recently reopened as a campus pub, and the campus activities board sponsors comedians, a casino night, and concerts with some popular college acts like the Goo Goo Dolls, Blues Traveler, Indigo Girls, and Barenaked Ladies.

For those interested in other forms of leisure, Clinton has good cross-country skiing, and there's plenty of room for walking or jogging on campus. Students describe the town as "storybook" but also not very exciting. "There are bars and the pizza is rather good if you put enough blue cheese on it," says a junior. The nearest small city, Utica, is only ten minutes away by car and offers a few more attractions. Culture-seekers with time on their hands can hop a bus or drive to Boston, New York, Toronto, or Montreal, all about five hours away. Students always anticipate the last day of

"We love our snow at Hamilton College."

class in the spring for Class and Charter Day, a campus-wide picnic with games and bands and other related activities.

In athletics, Hamilton finished in the top twenty-five of nearly four hundred colleges eligible for the Sears Cup, which recognizes overall athletic excellence. Men's soccer scored the UCAA championship and advanced to the NCAA Division III tournament, while men's basketball capped an undefeated season by winning the UCAA championship. In their third straight trip to NCAA competition, the women's cross-country team placed ninth in Division III championships in 2001. The school recently started a varsity crew team, which has been extremely popular.

Students' school spirit, which often seems dormant, is on display at the annual Citrus Bowl, where Hamilton students pelt the opposing goalie with oranges after the first goal of the first home hockey game is scored. In football, a major event is the annual Rocking Chair Classic against Middlebury (the winner keeps the chair). Intramurals also are popular.

Hamilton students are, by necessity, hearty. "We love our snow at Hamilton College," says a government and theater major. Feb Fest is a chance to do just that—the school has concerts and games all centered on snow. "It's a chance to enjoy our perpetually cold weather and have some fun with it," says one senior. Perhaps to counter the cold, Hamilton has shown a knack for community building, evident not only in its thriving marriage with former neighbor Kirkland and its warm relationship with the town of Clinton, but also in its successful use of cozy seminars, labs, and co-ops in the education and socialization of its small student body.

If You Apply To ➤ | **Hamilton:** Early decision: Nov. 15. Regular admissions: Jan. 15. Guarantees to meet demonstrated need. Campus interviews: recommended, evaluative. Alumni interviews: optional, evaluative. SATs or ACTs: required. SAT IIs: recommended. Accepts the Common Application and electronic applications. Essay question.

Hampden-Sydney College

P.O. Box 667, Hampden-Sydney, VA 23943

The last bastion of the Southern gentleman and one of two all-male colleges (without a coordinate women's college) in the nation. H-SC is a feeder school to the Virginia business economic establishment in Richmond. Picturesque rural setting evokes the old South.

At Hampden-Sydney College, where "men are men and women are guests," awkward Southern boys have become cultured and refined adults for more than two centuries. Tradition is treasured at this small, all-male liberal arts college nestled in south-central Virginia's rolling hills. With the school's century-old Code of Honor, students keep their doors open, leave their bicycles unlocked, and take exams without proctors, all without fear of mischief. "The community environment is great," a senior says. "We speak to everyone on the sidewalk, even if we don't know them."

Hampden-Sydney's 660-acre campus, surrounded by farmland and woods, features mainly redbrick buildings in the Federal style. The nearby town of Farmville, population 6,600 and home to Longwood College, offers restaurants, stores, and a movie theater; it's just five miles from H-SC, but one

> **"During the week, students work exceedingly hard."**

student describes the town as "a black hole inside a time warp." Despite its lack of bright lights, the town does provide numerous community service and outreach opportunities. A campus volunteer group called Good Men, Good Citizens spearheads projects such as tutoring, highway clean-up, and Habitat for Humanity home-building.

Hampden-Sydney's most popular major is economics, which may help explain why more than half of the school's alumni have pursued business careers. The department offers concentrations, including managerial and mathematical concepts; instruction is "intensive," a junior says. History, English, and religion are also

Website: www.hsc.edu
Location: Rural
Total Enrollment: 1,026
Undergraduates: 1,026
Male/Female: 100/0
SAT Ranges: V 500–620
   M 510–610
ACT Range: 20–25
Financial Aid: 48%
Expense: Pr $ $
Phi Beta Kappa: Yes
Applicants: 925
Accepted: 77%
Enrolled: 46%
Grad in 6 Years: 60%
Returning Freshmen: 79%
Academics: ✍ ✍ ✍
Social: ☎ ☎ ☎ ☎
Q of L: ★ ★ ★ ★
Admissions: (800) 755-0733

(Continued)

Email Address:
hsapp@hsc.edu

Strongest Programs:
Economics
Biology
Chemistry
Physics
English
Rhetoric
Classics

A campus volunteer group called Good Men, Good Citizens spearheads projects such as tutoring, highway clean-up, and Habitat for Humanity home-building.

Men seeking members of the opposite sex can find them at four all-female schools nearby—Sweet Briar, Hollins, Mary Baldwin, and Randolph-Macon Women's College.

popular, and the rhetoric program has earned international recognition, administrators say. The Wilson Center for Leadership in the Public Interest puts a public-service focus on the study of political science, preparing students for government work and garnering high marks in return. The school's small size offers many opportunities to work closely with professors, but has some academic drawbacks, including few computer courses and less than thirty majors total. The fine arts program, with concentrations in music, theater, and visual arts, has begun emphasizing performance rather than the study of these disciplines, but it suffers from a lack of facilities and student interest.

Students at Hampden-Sydney strive to maintain a balance between work and play. "During the week, students work exceedingly hard," says a junior economics major. "By the time the weekend rolls around, it is the exact opposite." Agrees a senior: "Classes are tough, but not insurmountable." To graduate, students must demonstrate proficiency in rhetoric and a foreign language, along with completing seven humanities courses, three in the social sciences, and four in the natural sciences and mathematics. Classes are small; more than three-quarters have twenty-five or fewer students, and the rest have fifty or less. "Most courses require strict attendance," a history major says—after all, with a class of twelve or fourteen students, your presence or absence will certainly be felt. "It is not a cake walk," says a managerial economics major. "When you come here, teachers challenge students to think deeper." Most H-SC professors live on campus, and encourage students to drop by their offices often. Some even make house calls to find out why a student missed class. Because of the emphasis on small sections, underclassmen may not get their first-choice courses or instructors. The school is seeking two additional economics instructors to help alleviate the crunch, one student says.

H-SC students are conservative, opinionated, and goal-oriented, not surprising given the college's reputation as a finishing school for Virginia's political and economic establishment. Sixty-three percent of students are state residents, and 94 percent are white. African-Americans make up 4 percent of the student body, and Hispanics and Asian-Americans account for 1 percent each. The college has added a Director of Intercultural Affairs to help increase tolerance for diversity. As a Division III school, Hampden-Sydney offers no athletic scholarships. There are 168 merit awards, ranging from $3,000 to $18,000 a year.

"There can be some trouble getting the room that a student wants, because everyone wants basically the same rooms."

Ninety-seven percent of students live on campus, as housing is guaranteed for four years, and H-SC is renovating older residence halls with mostly single rooms to offer more apartment-style living. "The rooms—not all, however—are spacious and bright," says a psychology and music major. "There can be some trouble getting the room that a student wants, because everyone wants basically the same rooms." All rooms have Internet connections, cable television, and private phone lines. Cushing Hall, built in 1824, is the dorm of choice for first-year students, with "big rooms, excellent parties, and at least three ghosts."

Students praise the close-knit atmosphere fostered by Hampden-Sydney's all-male status. "Brotherhood amongst your peers" is what makes the place special, says a senior. Men seeking members of the opposite sex can find them at four all-female schools nearby—Sweet Briar, Hollins, Mary Baldwin, and Randolph-Macon Women's College. Those who make a love connection will be glad to know that H-SC's dorms have twenty-four-hour visitation. When rural Virginia gets too insular, H-SC students can be found on road trips to the University of Virginia and James Madison University, Virginia's beaches, or Washington, D.C. The ski slopes of Wintergreen are also within three hours' drive.

Hampden-Sydney's social nexus is the Circle, the site of eleven of the school's twelve fraternities, which claim 33 percent of the students. Virginia law says students under twenty-one can't drink, but that doesn't seem to be a problem here. "Most bars will not serve underage very easily, but at frats and on campus, we drink beer like water from freshman year until we graduate," says a senior. The annual spring Greek Week brings out the *Animal House* aspect of Hampden-Sydney's budding gentlemen. Homecoming and various music festivals are also eagerly anticipated.

Perhaps because of all that testosterone on campus, Hampden-Sydney men are competitive, and that spells excellence in athletics. Football is big; students attend games in coat and tie, and H-SC's football rivalry with Randolph-Macon (not the famed women's college!) is the oldest in the South. At the annual pre-game bonfire, the college rallies to sing songs and hear student and faculty leaders vilify the enemy and extol "the garnet and gray." While football has the most players, basketball draws the most spectators. The school's basketball, lacrosse, and soccer teams have recently won conference championships, and for weekend warriors, intramurals are available in seven sports.

Hampden-Sydney may seem like the school that time forgot, with its anachronistic emphasis on courtesy, manners, and integrity. But for students seeking a sense of community, close interaction with faculty, long-lasting friendships, and some good old-fashioned Southern hospitality, H-SC is worth a look. As a campus T-shirt attests: "We say grace, we say Ma'am—if you ain't into that, we don't give a damn!"

> ## Overlaps
> **Virginia Tech, Randolph-Macon, James Madison, Bridgewater, University of Virginia**

If You Apply To ➤ **Hampden-Sydney:** Early decision: Nov. 15. Early action: Jan. 15. Regular admissions: Mar. 1. Financial aid: May 1. Meets demonstrated need of 20%. Campus interviews: recommended, informational. No alumni interviews. SATs or ACTs: required. SAT IIs: recommended. Accepts the Common Application and electronic applications. Essay question: A prominent person you would interview; significant experience or achievement; why you have saved a personal object or item; experience with those of different race, background, or culture.

Hampshire College

P.O. Box 5001, Amherst, MA 01002-5001

Part of a posse of nonconformist colleges that includes Bard, Bennington, New School University, and Sarah Lawrence. Instead of conventional majors, students complete self-designed interdisciplinary concentrations and independent projects. Gains breadth and resources from the Five College Consortium.

If the Five Colleges—Hampshire, the University of Massachusetts at Amherst, Smith, Mount Holyoke, and Amherst College—were each represented by one of the five members of the hapless Scooby Doo cartoon crew, then Hampshire College would be freewheeling Shaggy, who always seemed to have the most fun (and usually ended up solving the case in an unconventional way). Hampshire is one of the most freewheeling—and intellectually rigorous—colleges in the country, with no tests, no grades—and no traditional majors. Students develop their own programs of study and projects on which to be evaluated. "It's a real luxury to be this much in control of what and how you learn," says a senior. "It really makes you appreciate your own abilities."

Located in the Pioneer Valley of western Massachusetts, Hampshire's eight hundred–acre campus sits amid former orchards, farmland, and forest. Buildings

Website: www.hampshire.edu
Location: City outskirts
Total Enrollment: 1,175
Undergraduates: 1,175
Male/Female: 44/56
SAT Ranges: V 600–700
M 550–650
ACT Range: 21–29
Financial Aid: 54%
Expense: Pr $
Phi Beta Kappa: No

(Continued)
Applicants: 1,785
Accepted: 62%
Enrolled: 27%
Grad in 6 Years: 56%
Returning Freshmen: 83%
Academics: ✍ ✍ ✍ ✍
Social: ☎ ☎ ☎
Q of L: ★ ★ ★
Admissions: (413) 559-5471
Email Address:
  admissions@hampshire.edu

Strongest Programs:
  Film and Television
  Photography
  Environmental Studies
  Communication
  Cognitive Science
  Creative Writing

are eclectic and contemporary, and the school is most proud of its bio-shelter, arts village, and multisports and multimedia centers.

Instead of grades, Hampshire professors hand out "meaningful assessments," which consist of written evaluations and critiques. Degrees are obtained by passing a series of examinations and independent studies. The first hurdle, known as Division I, consists of courses or projects in each of five multidisciplinary schools: Natural Science; Social Science; Cognitive Science; Interdisciplinary Studies; or Humanities, Arts, and Cultural Studies. A typical test in Division I is a single project or paper, two courses, or an experiment presented to one or two professors.

The second hurdle, Division II, is each student's "concentration"—the rough equivalent of a major elsewhere. The concentration consists of individually designed courses, independent work, and often fieldwork or internships. Division III, or "advanced study," begins in the fourth year. Students are asked to complete a sizable independent study project centered on a specific topic, question, or idea, much like a senior thesis. Because of the division system, there are as many curriculums at Hampshire as there are students; each individual must devise a viable, coherent program, specific to himself or herself. Not surprisingly, competition is virtually nonexistent, and the academic climate is "challenging, empowering, liberating, in the sense that it allows students to study what they love," says a philosophy major. The common denominator is a heavy workload, an emphasis on self-initiated study, close contact with faculty advisors, and the assumption that students will eventually function as do graduate students at other institutions. (One popular campus T-shirt says Hampshire is "The Undergraduate Graduate School.")

Given the emphasis on close working relationships with faculty and those "meaningful assessments" in place of grades, the importance of qualified, attentive faculty is not to be underestimated. Students at Hampshire heap praise on their professors. "The professors are the best," says a junior. "They get genuinely excited

> **"The professors are the best. They get genuinely excited about their courses because they get to choose what they teach."**

about their courses because they get to choose what they teach." The Hampshire academic year has fall and spring semesters, each four months long, and an optional January term, and internships and other real-world experience are encouraged during all three. Despite Hampshire's somewhat unstructured nature, a large percentage of grads do go on to graduate school, and many Hampshire students begin their own businesses in fields such as computer programming, construction, or film production.

Hampshire's flexibility is ideal for artists, and the departments of film and photography are dazzling, which is also the reason they are overcrowded. Hampshire is strong in the social and natural sciences, "but limited in scope," says a dance and critical theory major. Communications, creative writing, and environmental studies are also good bets, and Hampshire was the first U.S. college to offer an undergraduate program in cognitive science. A popular program called Invention, Innovation, and Creativity exposes students to the independent reasoning and thinking essential to the process of inventing.

For courses in modern and classical languages, students must travel to another school in the Five College Consortium,* as Hampshire doesn't offer foreign language instruction. Although the school's library is a quiet and pleasant place to study, it has only 114,000 volumes. Still, if you count the library resources at all five institutions, students have ready access to more than eight million volumes. There is no extra cost to use the other schools' facilities or the buses that link them.

Hampshire draws students from across the country who tend to be "free-loving, innovative-thinking scholars who challenge institutions and bureaucracy," says an English major. But a senior grumbles that "because of the way Hampshire has been

Instead of grades, professors hand out "meaningful assessments," which consist of written evaluations and critiques. Degrees are obtained not by accumulating course credits, but by passing a series of examinations and independent studies.

advertised, the people who come here are more mainstream kids whose parents can afford to pay full tuition." The minority community is relatively small—4 percent of students are African-American, 3 percent Hispanic, and 4 percent Asian-American—and most students would like to see these numbers rise. "Hampshire is very progressive, with many self-declared anarchists, Marxists, Greens and (a few) Libertarians among the ranks of staff, faculty and students," says an education major. "Hampshire conservatives usually vote Democratic."

First-year students live in coed dorms, about one-third in double rooms. Many single rooms are available for older students, who may move to one of more than one hundred "mods"—apartments in which groups of four to ten students share the responsibility for cleaning, cooking, and maintaining their space. "The dorms and apartments were quickly and cheaply built, and have problems," warns a senior. Adds a junior: "Although the quality of housing is not horrible, people often have problems finding compatible people to live with, and in an area where they want to live." Special quarters are available for nonsmokers, vegetarians, and others with special preferences; it's not easy to move off campus.

"There is a large effort by some factions of the students, staff, and faculty to make Hampshire live up to not only its stated ideals, but also its immense possibilities."

On weekends, many students head for Boston, New York, Hartford, or, in season, the ski trails of Vermont and New Hampshire. But there are plenty of cultural resources within the Five College area, and the free buses to Amherst (the ultimate college town), Northampton, and South Hadley (all about twenty minutes away) are always crowded. The annual Spring Jam brings live bands to campus, and throughout the year there's almost always a party going on, including the drag ball and the much-anticipated Halloween bash, an intense, all-campus blowout complete with fireworks. A tradition called "Div Free Bell" celebrates the completion of Division III requirements—and graduation—with soon-to-be alumni ringing a bell outside the library, surrounded by friends.

Hampshire is no place for competitive jocks, since many sports are coed and primarily for entertainment (there never was a football team here). The school offers paid instructors in a handful of sports, but most students organize their own clubs (men's and women's soccer and basketball are the biggies, and there's also the competitive Red Scare Ultimate Frisbee Team) and intramural teams. The outdoors program offers mountain-biking, cross-country skiing, and kayaking; equipment may be borrowed free. The school also has its own climbing wall and cave, a gym with solar-heated pool, and a coed sauna.

Hampshire's drive for academic freedom and experimentation gives students the chance to explore their own interests under the guidance of well-qualified professors. At the same time, they are ultimately accountable for what they accomplish—and they hold their school to the same high standards. Says a junior: "There is a large effort by some factions of the students, staff, and faculty to make Hampshire live up to not only its stated ideals, but also its immense possibilities—to be a progressive and self-critical alternative educational institution that really asserts itself as a leader in the fight for social justice."

There's a heavy workload, an emphasis on self-initiated study, close contact with faculty advisors, and the assumption that students will eventually function as do graduate students at other institutions.

Overlaps

Bard, Sarah Lawrence, Oberlin, NYU, Brown

Hampshire: Early decision: Nov. 15. Early action: Jan. 1. Regular admissions and financial aid: Feb. 1. Housing: June 1. Does not guarantee to meet demonstrated need. Campus and alumni interviews: recommended, evaluative. SATs or ACTs: optional. SAT IIs: optional. Accepts the Common Application and electronic applications. Essay questions: personal statement, and sample of academic work or persuasive critical essay on a complex issue.

Hartwick College

Oneonta, NY 13820

Hartwick is known for its cozy atmosphere and ability to take good care of students. Combines arts and sciences with a nursing program. The campus is beautiful but small-town upstate New York has proven to be a hard sell in recent years.

Website: www.hartwick.edu
Location: Small city
Total Enrollment: 1,446
Undergraduates: 1,446
Male/Female: 44/56
SAT Ranges: V 500–610
  M 510–610
Financial Aid: 78%
Expense: Pr $ $ $
Phi Beta Kappa: No
Applicants: 1,970
Accepted: 89%
Enrolled: 25%
Grad in 6 Years: 57%
Returning Freshmen: 74%
Academics: ✍ ✍ ✍
Social: ☎ ☎ ☎ ☎
Q of L: ★ ★ ★
Admissions: 888-HARTWICK
Email Address:
  admissions@hartwick.edu

Strongest Programs:
  Anthropology
  Biology
  Geological and
    Environmental Sciences
  English
  Management
  Sociology
  Chemistry

Hartwick has been working to change its reputation from party school to a quality liberal arts and sciences college. Judging from the innovations of the last few years, it is making strides, especially in its science offerings. Upon entering, each student receives a notebook computer to keep through college and beyond, to use in class, at the library, or in the room to surf the Internet. Hartwick's dedication to forging a new path through technology has set it apart from other liberal arts colleges less quick to jump on the bandwagon.

Hartwick's campus has a New England feel with its ivy-covered, redbrick buildings and white cupolas, gables, and trim. The campus setting on the Oyaron Hill, overlooking the city and the Susquehanna Valley beyond, provides a breathtaking view, though the steepness of the campus may have some wishing for the legs of a mountain goat. A new $12-million science center offers a lab-rich environment including centers for biotechnology, ecology, environmental sciences and policy, and science communications. The science facility has been renovated and expanded to include new classrooms and labs, a tissue culture lab, electron microscopes, a greenhouse, an herbarium, a cold room, a biotechnology "clean lab," and a graphics imaging lab.

Hartwick's liberal arts and sciences framework ensures that its students are exposed to what one administrator terms "a broad swath of human knowledge." The most popular major is management, followed by psychology and English. Students are enthusiastic about political science and English, as well as life sciences, which one student accurately terms an "up-and-coming" program. Art and music also are praised, while modern and classical language and philosophy are works in progress.

Hartwick's general education program is divided into five areas: continuity (Western tradition), interdependence, science and technology, critical thinking and effective communication, and choices. Among the voluminous requirements are two Great Books courses, a course in Western and non-Western culture, foreign language, two decision-making seminars, a course in the creative or performing arts, and a senior research thesis. Another example of Hartwick's academic enrichment is the honors program that provides students with the opportunity to design and carry out a coherent program of study characterized by challenges exceeding those offered in typical course work required for graduation. The course offerings are necessarily limited by Hartwick's small size, but the Individual Student Program (ISP) enables students to create their own major dealing with a particular interest, and students may take courses at the nearby State University College at Oneonta (SUCO).

"The college is competitive and rewarding at the same time for students who work hard."

"The college is competitive and rewarding at the same time for students who work hard," says one senior. Hartwick offers other unconventional learning options, many of them in off-campus locations. Students have traveled to all parts of the world while pursuing their Hartwick education. In addition to offering trips to Chiang Mai, Thailand, for first-year students, there is a field station used by the biology department on an island in the Bahamas, and Hartwick owns a closer, lakeside environmental campus. The Awakening Challenge, completed by freshmen as part of orientation, is also an option for management majors who want to test their leadership skills. The four-week January term is also a favorite time to explore the world beyond Oneonta.

The faculty wins universal praise from the students. "The professors demand a lot of their students, but they also show appreciation for hard work," says a psychology major. Private tutoring and help sessions are offered, along with an innovative freshman Early Warning program that identifies struggling students early and offers counseling. Academic advising is said to be helpful, and "the career center goes above and beyond what is expected" to aid students, according to a senior.

Hartwick has traditionally attracted a somewhat less academically oriented student body than most of the colleges with which it competes, but has been working to alter this image. Twenty-one percent of students come from the top tenth of their class. Sixty-four percent are from New York State, especially upstate, and most of the rest come from New England or the Mid-Atlantic states. The student body is 85 percent white; 5 percent are African-American, 3 percent Hispanic, and 1 percent Asian-American. Students at the Wick are generally from "fairly well-to-do" families and tend to be socially active and politically sedate. Hartwick college awards merit scholarships that range from $4,000 to $18,000, and there are thirty athletic scholarships for Division I men's soccer and women's water polo.

In general, the dorms receive mixed reviews, but the administration is hoping for more positive reactions since all residence halls have been renovated and improved recently. Upperclassmen covet a place in one of the four townhouses described by one as "the yuppie version of on-campus living." Freshmen, sophomores, and juniors are required to live on campus, though the latter may move

"The professors demand a lot of their students, but they also show appreciation for hard work."

into one of the fraternity or special-interest houses. Each dorm has designated quiet hours, though they may not always be observed. Hartwick's environmental campus, Pine Lake, has cabins that are heated by pellet stoves and a lodge where environmentally inclined students can live in rustic style. One student says that it is "very selective, but well worth the application process." On-campus students eat at a single dining commons, where the food has been dubbed "not so bad." Some wish that campus security would make its presence known a bit more than they do.

From campus, it's only a short walk, bike ride, or bus ride downhill into the small city of Oneonta, with its tantalizing profusion of bars. But the underage Hartwick students usually don't get past the front doors of these taverns, and the administration is tough about enforcement on campus. No alcohol is allowed in dorm rooms. Tamer entertainment includes Saturday movies as well as occasional lecturers and comedians, and just hanging out at the student union. The Greek system attracts 15 percent of the men and 17 percent of the women. Popular campus-wide bashes include a Last Day of Classes party, the Holiday Ball, and Winter and Spring Weekends, the latter of which features the notorious "Wick Wars," a school-wide sports competition. Walking to class each day provides great hill workouts for your ski legs, and skiing is popular throughout the region. Another nice diversion is Pine Lake, which offers cross-country trails, swimming, boating, and fishing. Nearby Cooperstown offers entertainment for baseball and history buffs.

In addition to offering trips to Chiang Mai, Thailand, for first-year students, there is a field station used by the biology department on an island in the Bahamas, and Hartwick owns a closer, lakeside environmental campus.

Colorful autumns pave the way for long, cold winters, and it helps to have a bit of mountain goat in your gene pool.

Though traditionally a soccer school, Hartwick has fielded a football team for nearly a decade. The Mayor's Cup Soccer Tournament weekend is a big event. Hartwick is nationally ranked at the Division I level in soccer; the remainder of the teams compete in Division III. The women's water polo team has been a real success story, having been Eastern Collegiate Conference Tournament champions in 2002. The women's field hockey team reached the NCAA semifinals, and conference championships have been won by men's basketball, swimming, and baseball, and by the women's basketball, soccer, and lacrosse teams. Intramurals are popular as well.

Hartwick is developing into an academically competitive liberal arts and sciences college and shedding its image as a place to party. The T-shirts sold on campus that read "Smartwick" broadcast the students' attitudes about their education and Hartwick's growing reputation. "Over the past five years, Hartwick has adjusted with the times and undergone some major changes," says a student. The changes have allowed Hartwick to forge a path into the new millennium.

Overlaps

Ithaca, SUNY-Oneonta, Hobart and William Smith, St. Lawrence, SUNY-Cortland

---

If You Apply To ➤

Hartwick: Early decision: Jan. 15. Regular admissions: Feb. 15. Financial aid: Feb. 1. Campus interviews: recommended, informational. Alumni interviews: optional, informational. SATs or ACTs: SATs preferred. SAT IIs: optional. Accepts the Common Application and electronic applications. Essay question: significant experience, personal statement, influential person, character in fiction or history, topic of your choice.

Harvard University

Byerly Hall, 8 Garden Street, Cambridge, MA 02138

An acceptance here is the gold standard of American education. Gets periodic slings and arrows for not paying enough attention to undergraduates, some of which is carping from people who didn't get in. It takes moxie to keep your self-image in the midst of all those geniuses, but most Harvard admits can handle it.

Website: www.fas.harvard.edu
Location: City outskirts
Total Enrollment: 18,036
Undergraduates: 6,684
Male/Female: 54/46
SAT Ranges: V 700–800
M 700–790
ACT Range: 30–34
Financial Aid: 70%
Expense: Pr $ $ $ $
Phi Beta Kappa: Yes
Applicants: 18,161
Accepted: 11%
Enrolled: 79%
Grad in 6 Years: 97%
Returning Freshmen: 96%
Academics: ✍ ✍ ✍ ✍ ✍
Social: ☎ ☎ ☎
Q of L: ★ ★ ★ ★

Over the past 350-plus years, the name Harvard has become synonymous with excellence, prestige, and achievement. At this point, Harvard University is the benchmark against which all other colleges are compared. It attracts the best students, the most academically accomplished faculty, and the most lavish donors of any institution of higher education nationwide. Sure, some academic departments at Hah-vahd are smaller than others, but all have faculty members who have made a name for themselves, many of whom have written the standard texts in their fields. Olympic athletes, concert pianists, and Rhodes Scholars blend in nicely here, ready to embrace the challenges and rewards only Harvard's quintessential Ivy League milieu can offer.

Spiritually as well as geographically, the campus centers on the famed Harvard Yard, a classic quadrangle of Georgian brick buildings whose walls seem to echo with the voices of William James, Henry Adams, and other intellectual greats who trod its shaded paths in centuries past. Beyond the yard's wrought-iron gates, the campus is an architectural mix, ranging from the modern ziggurat of the science center to the white towers of college-owned houses along the Charles River. Loker Commons, a student center beneath the new Annenberg freshman dining hall, provides a place for students to meet and philosophize over gourmet coffee or burritos of epic proportions. The Barker Center for humanities has emerged from the shell of the Union, the old freshman dining hall, and the Maxwell Dworkin building, which houses the computer science and engineering departments, has also been completed.

Harvard's state-of-the-art physical facilities are surpassed only by the unparalleled brilliance of its faculty. Under its "star" system, Harvard grants tenure only to scholars who have already made it—usually someplace else—and then gives them free rein for research. It seems like every time you turn around, a Harvard professor is winning a Nobel Prize or being interviewed on CNN; every four years, half the government and econ departments move to Washington to hash out national policy. But one of Harvard's finest qualities is also one of its biggest problems. "You can have unlimited contact with professors, but it must be on your initiative," notes a biology major. "But, this is not a small liberal arts college where people will reach out to

> **"You can have unlimited contact with professors, but it must be on your initiative."**

you." That's not to say profs are completely uncaring. Most teach at least one undergraduate course per semester, and even the luminaries occasionally conduct small undergraduate seminars (including those reserved for freshmen, which can be taken pass/fail). Harvard also sponsors a faculty dining program, encouraging professors to eat at the various residential houses and chew over ideas as well as lamb chops.

Harvard's best-known departments tend to be its largest; economics, government, biology, English, and biochemistry account for a large chunk of majors. But many smaller departments are gems as well: East Asian studies is easily tops in the nation. And under the leadership of Henry Louis Gates, the African-American Studies department has assembled the most high-powered group of black intellectuals in American higher education. Smaller, interdisciplinary honors majors, to which students apply for admission, boast solid instruction and happy undergraduates, too. These programs—social studies, history and science, history and literature, and folklore and mythology—are the only majors that require a senior thesis, although many students elect to do one in other departments.

Harvard's visual and environmental studies major serves filmmakers, studio artists, and urban planners, and concentrations in women's studies and environmental sciences have been well received. Students can also petition for individualized majors, typically during the sophomore year. All students must choose some sort of major at the end of their freshman year, a year earlier than most schools. The field of concentration can be changed later, but Harvard expects its students to hit the ground running. Regardless of the department, students uniformly complain about the overuse of teaching fellows

> **"The courses at Harvard are very demanding. If you choose to be competitive, you'll find the competition can be cut-throat."**

(graduate students) for introductory courses in mathematics and the languages. TFs aren't all bad, though, says a junior: "They can give good advice, having just been in our position." Besides, it's easier to ask "dumb questions" of mere mortals than of the demigod-like professors.

Back in the mid-1970s, Harvard helped launch the current curriculum reform movement. The core curriculum that emerged ranks as perhaps the most exciting collection of academic offerings in all of American higher education. The best and brightest freshmen can apply for advanced standing if they have enough Advanced Placement credits. And should you not find a class you are looking for, admittedly highly unlikely, Harvard offers cross-registration with several of its graduate schools and the Massachusetts Institute of Technology.

In formal terms, the core requires students to select eight courses, or a quarter of their program, from a list of offerings in six different "modes of inquiry": foreign cultures, historical studies, literature and arts, moral reasoning, sciences, and social analysis. For the three or four most popular courses, enrollment is limited by the number of seats in the various large auditoriums on campus; sometimes places in these lectures are determined by lottery. Freshmen also face quantitative reasoning

(Continued)
Admissions: (617) 495-1551
Email Address:
college@fas.harvard.edu

Strongest Programs:
Economics
Biology
Social Studies
Government
English
African-American Studies
East Asian Studies
Anthropology
Music
History of Science

Students can also petition for individualized majors, typically during the sophomore year.

and foreign language requirements, as well as a semester of Expository Writing (Expos), taught mainly by preceptors.

For many students, the most rewarding form of instruction is the sophomore and junior tutorial, a small-group–directed study in a student's field of concentration that is required in most departments within the humanities and social sciences. Teaching of the tutorials is split between professors and graduate students, and the weight of each party's responsibility varies with the subject and the professor. Juniors and seniors seek out professors with whom they want to work.

The oft-made claim that "the hardest thing about Harvard is getting in" is right on target. Failing out takes real effort. Once on campus, the possibilities are endless for those who are motivated. Then again, Harvard can feel uncaring and antisocial. While it offers unparalleled resources—including fellow students—brilliant overachievers who desire the occasional ego-stroke might be better off at a small liberal arts college. Although most students feel little competition, the academic climate is still intense. "The courses at Harvard are very demanding," says a social studies major. "If you choose to be competitive, you'll find the competition can be cutthroat." Sooner or later, all roads lead to Widener Library, where incredible facilities lie in wait (and where snow-covered steps make prime sledding runs in the winter).

Harvard does have one thing its $19 billion endowment can't buy: a diverse, high-powered, ambitious, and exciting student body. You will meet smooth-talking government majors who appear to have begun their senatorial campaigns in kindergarten. You will meet flamboyant fine arts majors who have cultivated an affected accent all their own. You will sample the intensity of Harvard's extracurricular scene,

"Despite what you may think, Harvard people have parties and Harvard people date!"

where more than 6,600 of the world's sharpest undergrads compete for leadership positions in a luminous galaxy of extracurricular opportunities. "Most of the social life takes place on campus, and there are a million things to do," says a history/government double major. "Yes, despite what you may think, Harvard people have parties and Harvard people date!" Stressed-out students can count on help from a variety of quarters, including the various deans' offices, the Bureau of Study Counsel, the Office of Career Services ("dedicated to working with Harvard students and alums for the rest of their lives," claims a senior), and counselors associated with each residential house. All students participate in week-long orientation, and the First-Year Urban and Outdoor Programs help students acquaint themselves with one another and the Boston area.

No one can tell you exactly what it takes to gain admission to Harvard (and if anyone tries, apply a large grain of salt), but here's a hint: 90 percent of the current student body ranked in the top tenth of their high-school class and two-thirds went to public high school. Though there are a few old-money types who probably spit up their baby food on a Harvard sweatshirt, their numbers are smaller than one might imagine on this liberal campus. (Many enter as sophomores when no one is looking.) Undergrads come from all fifty states and scores of foreign countries, although the student body is weighted toward the Northeast. Minority groups account for nearly a third of the enrollment. There are no merit or athletic scholarships to ease the pain of Harvard's hefty tuition, but a generous financial aid policy recently added $2,000 annually to every student aid package.

In the past, women students benefited from "dual citizenship" in both Harvard and Radcliffe colleges, receiving degrees ratified by the presidents of both colleges. However, Radcliffe has been phased out as a separate institution; everyone is now considered a Harvard student, though students can still take advantage of Radcliffe's network of professional women, researchers, and alumnae.

Every first-year class lives and eats as a single unit in Harvard Yard, a privilege made more enticing by recent renovation of all the freshman dorms. Freshmen now eat in Annenberg Hall, the new name for beautifully renovated Memorial Hall. For their last three years, students live in one of twelve residential houses, built around their own courtyards with their own dining halls and libraries. All the houses are coed, and each holds between three hundred and five hundred students. Designed as learning communities, the upperclass houses come equipped with a complement of resident tutors, affiliated faculty members, and special facilities, from art studios to squash courts. Each house has a student council, which plans programs and parties and arranges the fielding of intramural teams. Students are now randomly assigned (with up to fifteen friends) to one of the houses, but some houses still retain a personality from the days of old when each stood for a particular ideology, interest, or economic class. "Harvard housing is beautiful," says a history of science major. "Freshmen have amazing rooms and upperclass houses are great."

The nine houses along the Charles River feature suites of rooms, while the three houses at the Radcliffe Quad, a half-mile away, offer a mixture of suites and single rooms. Some students value the greater privacy of the Quad houses' singles; others consider it equivalent to a Siberian exile, especially during harsh Cambridge winters. The older dorms provide spacious wood-paneled rooms, working fireplaces, and the gentle reminders of Harvard's rich traditions. Most rooms are also wired for direct Internet access. With all these features and amenities, it's no wonder few students move off campus.

Nowhere but Harvard does the identity of a school— its history, its presence, its pretense—intrude so much into the details of undergraduate life.

What socializing there is at Harvard tends to occur on campus and in small groups. "It's certainly normal to spend Friday and Saturday nights studying," says a philosophy major. With the exception of the annual all-school Freshman Mixer and the annual theme festivals each house throws, parties tend to be private affairs in individual dorm rooms. Though Harvard does enforce the drinking age at university events, in individual houses, it's up to the resident tutors. For some, the key to happiness in Harvard's high-powered environment is finding a niche, a comfortable academic or extracurricular circle around which to build your life. Outside activities include about eighty plays performed annually, two newspapers and several journals, and plenty of community service projects.

The possibilities of Harvard's social life are increased tenfold by Cambridge and Boston, where there are many places to have fun. Harvard Square itself is a legendary gathering place for tourists, shoppers, bearded intellectuals, and coffeehouse denizens. The American Repertory Theater by Robert Brustein, transplanted from Yale in the mid-1980s, offers a season of professional productions and nearly as professional student shows. Cambridge also enjoys an exceptional selection of **"Cambridge/Boston is the ultimate college town. Everything is geared toward the students."** new and used bookstores, including the Starr Bookshop (behind the Lampoon building), McIntyre & Moore, Grolier Books, and, of course, the Harvard Bookstore and the mammoth Harvard Co-op, known universally as "the Coop." Boston itself features Faneuil Hall, the Red Sox, the Celtics, and fifty-two other colleges. "Cambridge/Boston is the ultimate college town," says an English major. "Everything is geared toward the students."

Harvard's athletic facilities are across the river from the campus, and their incredible offerings often go unnoticed by students buried in the books. Both the men's and women's squash and crew teams are perennial national powers, and the men's ice hockey team draws a crowd of few, but dedicated, fans. The women's lacrosse team is strong, as are tennis, swimming, and sailing. As for football, the team has been doing better in recent years, but the season always boils down to the Yale game, memorable as much for the antics of the spectators and marching band as for the fumbles of the players. Intramural sports teams are divided up by house, and each fall, league champs play teams from Yale the weekend of the Game.

Another fall highlight is the annual Head of the Charles crew race, the largest event of its kind in the world, where as many as two hundred thousand people gather to watch the racing shells glide by.

Nowhere but Harvard does the identity of a school—its history, its presence, its pretense—intrude so much into the details of undergraduate life. Admission here opens the door to a world of intellectual wonder, academic challenges, and faculty minds unmatched in the United States—but then drops students on the threshold. "I have quickly gained exposure to major theories in literature, psychology, anthropology, social sciences, and evolutionary biology," says a junior. "I gauge myself by how many allusions in *The New Yorker* I understand." That's the way Harvard is; what other kind of place could produce statesmen John Quincy Adams and John F. Kennedy, pioneers W.E.B. DuBois and Helen Keller, and artists T.S. Eliot and Leonard Bernstein? But beware: it is only the most motivated and dedicated student who can take full advantage of the Harvard experience. Others who attempt to drink from the school's perennially overflowing cup of knowledge may find themselves drowning in its depths.

If You Apply To ➤ **Harvard:** Early action: Nov. 1. Regular admissions: Jan. 1. Financial aid: Feb. 1. Housing: May 1. Guarantees to meet demonstrated need. Campus interviews: optional, informational. Alumni interviews: optional, evaluative. SATs or ACTs: required. SAT IIs: required (any three). Accepts the Common Application. Essay question: uses Common Application questions.

Haverford College

Haverford, PA 19041-1392

Quietly prestigious college of Quaker heritage. With an enrollment of 1,138, Haverford is half the size of some competitors but benefits from its relationship with nearby Bryn Mawr. Close cousin to nearby Swarthmore but not quite as far left politically. Exceptionally strong sense of community.

Website: www.haverford.edu
Location: Suburban
Total Enrollment: 1,138
Undergraduates: 1,138
Male/Female: 48/52
SAT Ranges: V 640–730
　M 640–720
Financial Aid: 44%
Expense: Pr $ $ $ $
Phi Beta Kappa: Yes
Applicants: 2,574
Accepted: 33%
Enrolled: 35%
Grad in 6 Years: 92%
Returning Freshmen: 96%
Academics: ✐ ✐ ✐ ✐ ✐
Social: ☎ ☎ ☎

Life at Haverford College is defined by the school's honor code, which lets students schedule their own final exams, take unproctored tests, and police underage drinking on their own, among other responsibilities. "The honor code creates a community with academic integrity, where people trust, respect, and are concerned for each other," says a junior. "It is written, ratified, and maintained by students; we really feel ownership for our college and community." While Haverford is smaller and less well known than some of its peers, it remains one of the finest liberal arts colleges in the country, especially for students who want to work hard and play hard (65 percent of Fordians were varsity athletes in high school). In response to the oft-heard dig "I've never heard of Haverford," one student says he and his friends have adopted a slogan from humor columnist (and Haverford alum) Dave Barry: "We haven't heard of you either!"

Founded under Quaker auspices in 1833, Haverford functions much like a family. The campus consists of 204 acres just off Philadelphia's Main Line railroad, and resembles a peaceful, well-ordered summer camp. The densely wooded campus has an arboretum, duck pond, nature trails, and more than four hundred species of shrubs and trees. Architectural styles range from nineteenth- and early twentieth-century stone buildings to a sprinkling of modern structures here and there. The combination enhances the sense of a balanced community, bringing together two traditional Quaker philosophies: development of the intellect and appreciation of nature. The 140,000-square-foot, $50 million Koshland Center for Integrated Natural Sciences (for the departments of astronomy, biology, chemistry, physics, math, and more) was recently completed.

Haverford's curriculum reflects commitment to the liberal arts. Biology, English, history, political science, and philosophy are well regarded and popular, and sixteen new minors were recently introduced. Unusual offerings include a philosophy seminar called From Zen Buddhism to Contemporary Public Black Intellectuals and a course on Happiness, Virtue, and the Good Life. Haverford's general education requirements call for three courses in each of three divisions: social sciences, natural sciences, and humanities. One of these nine courses must fulfill a quantitative reasoning requirement, and students also must demonstrate foreign language proficiency and complete a semester each of coursework in freshman writing and social justice.

The bicollege system that includes Bryn Mawr allows Haverford students to major in subjects such as art history, growth and structure of cities, and environmental studies. Also, by combining resources with Bryn Mawr and nearby Swarthmore, Haverford offers students an extensive language program: Japanese, Chinese, Italian, and Russian, in addition to the traditional languages. The

> **"Professors are really there because they like to teach."**

unique relationship between Bryn Mawr and Haverford dates to the days when Haverford was all-male, over two decades ago. However, students at each institution can still take courses, use the facilities, eat, and even live in the dormitories of the other. Haverford and Bryn Mawr students cooperate on a weekly newspaper, radio station, orchestra, and other clubs and sports, and a free shuttle bus connects the campuses. Cross-registration is also available at Swarthmore and the University of Pennsylvania. Students can transfer to Penn after their junior year to complete an engineering major after two more years. Haverford also allows students to take time off; some work, while others travel or enroll at other schools, such as Spelman, Claremont McKenna, Pitzer, or Fisk, for a semester or two. Study abroad in one of thirty-three countries attracts 35 to 40 percent of juniors.

Since there are no graduate students at Haverford, undergraduates often help professors with research, and several publish papers each year. In fact, Haverford's biggest strength may be its faculty members, 64 percent of whom live on campus. "Professors are really there because they like to teach," one senior says. "Those that have been excellent have really changed the way I look at things." Perhaps because of the intense classroom interaction, the workload is sizable, although students say they don't worry about each others' grades and try to squeeze in non-scholarly pursuits, too. "Everyone I know is involved in the community," says a philosophy major. "I spend a lot of time in the library, but I feel like my life is really balanced." Advising is ever-present: freshmen are matched with

> **"Everyone I know is involved in the community. I spend a lot of time in the library, but I feel like my life is really balanced."**

professors who work with them from their arrival until they declare majors two years later, while upperclass "Customspeople" are resources and mentors for living groups of nine to sixteen first-year students.

One of Haverford's most distinctive features is the honor code that governs all aspects of campus life. The code, administered by students and debated and re-ratified each year at a meeting called Plenary, helps instill the values of "integrity, honesty, and concern for others." While the social honor code encourages students to "voice virtually any opinion so long as it is expressed rationally," that can mean self-censorship, says a philosophy major. "Sometimes you feel like you are walking

(Continued)

Q of L: ★ ★ ★ ★ ★
Admissions: (610) 896-1350
Email Address:
  admitme@haverford.edu

Strongest Programs:
  Biological and Physical
    Sciences
  English
  History
  Political Science
  Economics

The second phase of the 140,000-square-foot, $50 million Koshland Center for Integrated Natural Sciences (for the departments of astronomy, biology, chemistry, physics, math, and more) was recently completed.

on eggshells to avoid offending anyone," the student says. In good Quaker tradition, the faculty makes decisions by consensus rather than formal voting, and students also play a large role in college policy, through the Honor Council, Students' Council, and membership on college committees.

Only 19 percent of the Haverford's students hail from Pennsylvania, but a large percentage are East Coasters nonetheless. Approximately 13 percent of students are Asian-American, 5 percent are Hispanic, and 6 percent are African-American. "Diversity is a huge issue: race, religion, geography, class, sexuality, world views," says a freshman. Though the college is nonsectarian, the Quaker influence lives on in the form of an optional meeting each week. And politics lean toward the liberal: "People say that is it easier to come out as a gay male on campus than a Republican male," quips a junior.

Haverford's residence halls are spacious and well maintained, and 64 percent of available rooms are singles—even for freshmen—so it's not surprising that 98 percent of all students live on campus. That said, a junior cautions that "the singles may be the size of closets," and a classmate describes the cinder-block residence halls as "riot-proof"—a vestige of '60s architecture—with "mazelike hallways and winding staircases." All dorms are coed, but students may request single-sex floors. Freshmen are guaranteed housing, and even sophomores, who draw last in the lottery, can usually get decent rooms. The extremely popular, school-owned Haverford College Apartments sit on the edge of campus. These include one- and two-bedroom units, each with a living room, kitchen, and bathroom. Upperclassmen in the apartments

"People say that is it easier to come out as a gay male on campus than a Republican male."

may cook for themselves, but all others living on campus (and all freshmen regardless of where they live) must buy the meal plan, which includes weekend board. Crime is virtually nonexistent, owing to the school's location in the ritzy Philadelphia suburbs, "surrounded by luxury-car dealerships and expensive stores." Muses a philosophy major: "I've even seen people leave their laptops in the library and go to dinner."

While the community spirit at Haverford works well for academics and personal development, it doesn't always carry over to the social scene. Without fraternities and sororities, Haverford and Bryn Mawr hold joint campus parties. These alcohol-soaked affairs can get tiresome after freshman and sophomore years, which is why students tend to spend at least part of their junior years abroad. The alcohol policy respects the law of the commonwealth of Pennsylvania—no drinking if you're under twenty-one—and is connected, as well, to the honor code. "Students drink underage on every college campus, and our policy creates a realistic and safe space that keeps students from getting hurt and entrusts them with their own responsibility," explains a political science major. For non-drinkers, there are frequently free movies, concerts, and other activities on campus. Other traditional events include the weekend-long Haverfest—Haverford's approximation for Woodstock—as well as the winter Snowball dance and Taste the Rainbow drag ball.

Life in the close-knit, introspective environment that is Haverford can get stifling, but there are easy escapes: downtown Philadelphia is twenty minutes away by train, offering bargain orchestra tickets, museums, concerts, and Flyers, Eagles, and Phillies games, along with great restaurants and the New Orleans-like rowdiness of South Street. New York City, Washington, the New Jersey beaches, Pocono ski areas, and Atlantic City are only a couple hours away by car. Many students participate in the Eighth Dimension, which coordinates volunteer opportunities.

The football team at the Ford has been undefeated since 1972, when the administration eliminated it, so soccer, a sport in which Haverford played in the first intercollegiate game more than eighty years ago, has become most popular. Track and cross-country are also strong, with the men's and women's teams winning regional championships in the last few years. Every year, Haverford and archrival Swarthmore vie for the Hood Trophy, awarded to the school that wins the most varsity contests between the two. Haverford also boasts the number-one varsity college cricket team in the country because, well, it's the only school with one! Intramural sports are popular, especially because participation counts toward the six quarters of athletic credit Haverford requires during the freshman and sophomore years. In spite of all the rivalries, these Quakers have struggled to justify their peace-loving heritage with the desire to bash opponents' brains out on the court or the field. For now, students root for the Black Squirrels, and cheer with this gem: "Fight, fight, inner light—kill, Quakers, kill!''

Haverford's small size is both the reason many students choose this often-overlooked school—and the source of their frustration after a couple of terms here. With just over 1,100 students, "other people will tell you who you hooked up with while drunk at a party before you can remember it," sighs a junior. "You can never be anonymous." Even so, Haverford students have no regrets. Says a freshman: "Kids here are overly friendly, chill, dynamic, intelligent people who are easy to get along with and great to be around.''

> **Overlaps**
>
> **Swarthmore, Brown, Amherst, Wesleyan, Penn**

If You Apply To ➤ **Haverford:** Early decision: Nov. 15. Regular admissions: Jan. 15. Financial aid: Jan. 31. Guarantees to meet demonstrated need. Campus interviews: recommended (required for those living within 150 miles of campus), informational. Alumni interviews: recommended, informational. SATs or ACTs: required. SAT IIs: required (writing and two others). Accepts the Common Application and electronic applications. Essay question: personal statement that reveals something other application materials have not covered and how the honor code would change you or help you grow.

University of Hawaii at Manoa

2530 Dole Street, Room C200, Honolulu, HI 96822

Who wouldn't want to go to Hawaii for college? To make it work, aim for one of UH's specialties, such as Asian studies, marine science, and travel-industry management. Bear in mind the measly 55 percent graduation rate. Too many luaus and not enough studying can be a bad combination.

One of the goals of the University of Hawaii at Manoa is to "serve as a bridge between East and West." This multiculturalism is evident in everything from course offerings to the student body. And while you may be thinking about surfing as much as studying, don't be fooled: it will take more than a great tan to earn your degree here.

The UH campus occupies three hundred acres in the Manoa Valley, a residential Honolulu neighborhood. The architecture is regionally eclectic, mirroring historical and modern Asian Pacific motifs, and is enhanced by extensive subtropical landscaping. "There are many plants and trees that make our campus more environmentally friendly," says a sophomore. UH offers bachelor's degrees in eighty-eight fields. Among the best are astronomy, Asian and Pacific area studies, languages and the arts, ethnomusicology, and tropical agriculture. It should come as no surprise that marine and ocean-related programs are also first-rate. The university also takes pride in its programs in engineering, geology and geophysics, international business, political science, and travel industry management. Both medical and law schools are gaining

Website: www.hawaii.edu
Location: Center city
Total Enrollment: 17,004
Undergraduates: 11,785
Male/Female: 46/54
SAT Ranges: V 480–580
  M 510–630
Financial Aid: 30%
Expense: Pub $ $
Phi Beta Kappa: Yes
Applicants: 8,714
Accepted: 76%
Enrolled: 44%
Grad in 6 Years: 55%

(Continued)
Returning Freshmen: 82%
Academics: ✍ ✍
Social: ☎ ☎
Q of L: ★ ★ ★
Admissions: (808) 956–8975
Email Address: ar-info@
   hawaii.edu

Strongest Programs:
   Astronomy
   Asian and Pacific Area
      Studies
   Languages
   Travel Industry Management
   English as a Second
      Language
   Ethnomusicology
   Tropical Agriculture
   Geosciences

reputations for excellence. UH has also recently added a B.A. degree in information and computer science. Beyond these few specialties, programs are adequate but hardly worth four years of trans-Pacific flights for students from the mainland. The math department is cited by several students as the school's biggest problem. Students describe the academic climate as "fairly competitive" and somewhat laid-back.

Despite the relaxed atmosphere, core requirements are extensive. All students must take a semester in expository writing and math, two courses in world civilization, two years of a foreign language or Hawaiian, and three courses each in the humanities, social sciences, and natural sciences. There are freshman seminar classes that offer small-group learning in a variety of subjects. Desirable classes and times are said to be difficult to get into for freshmen and sophomores. You may need to talk to profs, one student advises. Another problem seems to be that certain classes are only offered one semester a year. The academic advising is described as "good" if you know the professor and know what you want to study. Nonacademic counseling rates "an 8 out of 10," for one student. "They will help you with everything from career planning to a marital dispute."

> "On the whole, UH seems to be an academically focused campus, meaning that school is for on campus and socializing is for off campus."

Hawaii stands out among major American universities in that 78 percent of the students are of Asian descent. Caucasians account for 20 percent, and African-Americans and Hispanics, 1 percent each. The different groups seem to get along well, according to students. Mainland Americans account for about 7 percent of the students, and another 3 percent are foreign. "Hawaii is a unique place where diversity is recognized and accepted. There are many mixed-race students and many interracial couples," a senior says. Hot campus issues include gay rights, campus parking, and Hawaiian sovereignty. Especially promising students can compete for more than 108 merit scholarships, and a total of 310 athletes get grants-in-aid.

Hawaii stands out among major American universities in that 78 percent of the students are of Asian descent.

Only 21 percent of the student body live in campus housing, which is parceled out by a priority system that gives preference to those who are from across the sea. Students recommend the four towers, Ilima, Lehua, Lokelani, and Mokihana; the rooms are small, and the hallways are happening. "Students never know what to expect," one student explains. If you're thinking about off-campus housing, take note: the administration warns that housing in Honolulu is scarce and expensive. Once you are accepted into housing, continuous residency is not that difficult to obtain. Cafeterias are located throughout the campus and serve "edible" fare.

Because of all the commuters, UH is pretty sedate after dark. "On the whole, UH seems to be an academically focused campus, meaning that school is for on campus and socializing is for off campus," a psychology major says. Many students hit nearby dance clubs or movies, or else head for home. Four percent of the men and two percent of the women join the tiny Greek system. Drinking is not allowed in the dorms. A couple of local

> "Many do not recognize the high quality of education possible through choosing challenging courses and instructors who urge achievement and high-quality work."

hangouts provide an escape, and the campus pub, Manoa Garden, is also an option. Lest anyone forget, some of the world's most beautiful resorts—Diamond Head and all the rest—are less than a twenty-minute drive away. Waikiki Beach? Within two miles' reach. And round-trip airfare to the neighboring islands—including Maui, Kauai, and the Big Island—is not unreasonable.

Because of all the commuters, UH is pretty sedate after dark.

About the only thing that generates excitement on campus are the athletic teams, the Rainbow Warriors, with football, volleyball, basketball, baseball, and swimming among the top draws. The Rainbow women's teams are also well supported, especially the championship volleyball team. The Homecoming Dance is one of the most popular events of the year. But what students really look forward to is Kanikapila, a festival of Hawaiian music, dance, and culture. Don Ho, eat your heart out.

Students seeking warm weather and great surfing won't be disappointed at UH, but mainlanders should think twice about it unless they are set on one of the university's specialized programs. It's up to you, one student says, to get the best out of UH. "Many do not recognize the high quality of education possible through choosing challenging courses and instructors who urge achievement and high-quality work." And if you can catch a few waves in the process, so much the better.

If You Apply To ➤ | **UH:** Rolling admissions: May 1. Financial aid: Mar. 1. Housing: May 1. Guarantees to meet demonstrated need. Campus interviews: optional, informational. No alumni interviews. SATs or ACTs: required. Achievement tests: optional. No essay question.

Hendrix College

1600 Washington Avenue, Conway, AR 72032

Along with Millsaps and Rhodes, Hendrix is the class of mid-South liberal arts colleges. Hendrix is the smallest and most progressive of the three and has a strong emphasis on international awareness. Small-town Arkansas is a tough sell, and the college accepts the vast majority of students who apply.

Hendrix College sits in the heart of the Bible Belt, but it is surprisingly liberal. Academics are demanding but students are laid back—even radical—in their political and social views. Ironically, healthy dialogue about tough issues such as gay rights, the environment, and capital punishment draws students together. Graduating students leave Hendrix with more than a degree; they also come away with good friends and well-tested beliefs. "Hendrix students are also very intelligent, and it's not unusual to hear a group having an intellectual discussion while eating in the cafeteria," says one junior.

Hendrix's compact and comfortable campus stretches for 160 acres between the Ouachita and the Ozark mountains. College land boasts more than eighty varieties of trees and shrubs, and more than ten thousand budding flowers each spring. The main campus—with its own lily pool, fountain, and gazebo—occupies about one-fourth of the total acreage. The red brick buildings are a mix of old and new, and a pedestrian overpass connects the main campus to the college's athletic facilities and a wooded fitness trail. The campus is undergoing a building boom. An art facility is being built with $3 million from an anonymous donor, and a new home for the Hendrix-Murphy Foundation Programs in Language and Literature recently opened. Other new additions include new and renovated facilities for science and social science.

Hendrix is strong in many areas, but natural and social sciences are definitely the school's forte—35 percent of students major in biology or psychology. Students also give high marks to English, history, religion, philosophy, and politics. "I have never been so challenged before," raves one sophomore. Less inspiring are the college's education and physical education programs. Doing well at Hendrix means keeping

Website: www.hendrix.edu
Location: Small town
Total Enrollment: 1,085
Undergraduates: 1,079
Male/Female: 46/54
SAT Ranges: V 570–690
  M 550–650
ACT Range: 25–31
Financial Aid: 45%
Expense: Pr $
Phi Beta Kappa: Yes
Applicants: 1,056
Accepted: 82%
Enrolled: 26%
Grad in 6 Years: 62%
Returning Freshmen: 84%
Academics: ✍ ✍ ✍
Social: 🐦 🐦 🐦 🐦
Q of L: ★ ★ ★ ★
Admissions: (501) 450-1362
  or (800) 277-9017
Email Address:
  adm@hendrix.edu

Strongest Programs:
Chemistry
Mathematics
History
Religion
Psychology
Economics and Business

up with the workload. "The courses and classwork are rigorous. Professors expect a lot out of you," says a junior. This means plenty of time in the $10-million library, but students say the intensity fosters collaboration rather than competition.

At Hendrix, undergraduate research takes priority, and students get the chance to present original papers at regional and national symposia. Hendrix offers exchange programs in Austria and England, sends aspiring ecologists to Costa Rica and budding archaeologists to Israel, and allows other students to get course credit for internships at U.S. embassies and organizations such as the National Institutes of Health and Agency for International Development. About 40 percent of Hendrix students participate in study abroad. The school is also a member of the Associated Colleges of the South* consortium, and offers five-year programs with Columbia, Vanderbilt, and Washington University in St. Louis for aspiring engineers.

> "Hendrix students are also very intelligent, and it's not unusual to hear a group having an intellectual discussion while eating in the cafeteria."

Hendrix freshmen participate in a ten-day orientation program, which includes a two-day, off-campus trip emphasizing outdoor experiences, urban exposure, or volunteer service. The school implemented a new curriculum recently, including a common Foundations of World Cultures course for freshmen. Professors from many departments teach the course, which considers the lasting importance and global influence of Western and non-Western traditions. Students are also required to complete one course from a category called Challenges of the Contemporary World, and to complete courses in seven learning domains—scientific inquiry, historical perspectives, social and behavioral analysis, literary studies, expressive arts and values, beliefs, and ethics. The new curriculum also includes writing, foreign language, physical education, and quantitative analysis requirements. Additionally, the school changed from a three-term system to a semester calendar.

The two Fs that dominate social life at most Southern schools—football and fraternities—can't be found at Hendrix.

Sixty-nine percent of Hendrix students are from Arkansas, and 75 percent are white, but students say diversity isn't a big issue on campus. Instead, students celebrate diversity unrelated to skin color, with events such as the Miss Hendrix drag show and pageant, where proceeds are given to charity. "Hendrix students are highly concerned with the environment, globaliza-

> "Hendrix students are highly concerned with the environment, globalization, and corporation reforms."

tion, and corporation reforms," says a junior. "A liberal/progressive stance is the norm on campus." A sophomore describes students as "smart, friendly, tolerant, interested in current affairs, and politically liberal." The college offers merit scholarships to academically qualified students, but there are no athletic scholarships.

All but one of Hendrix's dorms are single-sex, and freshmen are required to live on campus, which students say adds to the sense of community. Each residence hall has a personality all its own: Galloway (women's) is most beautiful; Raney is a perpetual summer camp; Veasey and Martin are party dorms; and Couch houses 90 percent of the school's vegetarians. Eighty percent of students live on campus, but some seniors get permission to move into nearby college-owned apartments. "The hardest thing at Hendrix is getting off-campus permission, not getting an on-campus room," says a junior. Each dorm has a kitchen for general use, and there's now a "port for every pillow," providing students with direct connection to the Internet. Upperclassmen have access to "brand-new, beautiful, suite-style houses," says a biology major.

About 40 percent of Hendrix students participate in study abroad, in locales such as Austria, England, and Costa Rica.

The two Fs that dominate social life at most Southern schools—football and fraternities—can't be found at Hendrix. Students are proud of their independence; the annual Hendrix Olympics allows them to celebrate the absence of Alphas, Betas, and Gammas from campus. Other major affairs include the Toga Party, Oktoberfest, and Beach Bash, as well as the annual Toad Suck Daze, a rollicking carnival that features bluegrass music. Last but not least is the Shirttail Serenade, in which first-year men from each dorm croon out a song-and-dance routine in their shirts, ties, shoes, socks—and underwear—for freshman women. The latter rate each performance on the basis of singing, creativity, legs, and so on, and respond two days later with their own Long Shirts/Short Skirts Serenade.

Conway offers shops and restaurants, but it is not seen as a college town and gets mixed reviews from students. Most social life takes place on campus, or on the campuses of two other nearby colleges. "We are working to improve relationships between Conway and Hendrix. One way happens to be through volunteering," says a sophomore. Faulkner County, where the school is located, is officially "dry," so students must travel thirty miles to Little Rock for booze—or find older peers to help out. "Underage students find little difficulty in getting alcohol if they choose to," says a sophomore. Other popular road trips are Memphis (two hours by car) and Dallas and Oklahoma City (each five hours' drive), for concerts and the like. For those who stay in town, the Volunteer Activities Center coordinates participation in projects on Service Saturdays.

There's no football team to cheer for, but basketball, soccer, baseball, and softball are hot sports on campus. Rhodes College is the chief rival. For outdoor buffs, the college sponsors trips around Arkansas for canoeing, biking, rock climbing, and spelunking.

Musician Jimi Hendrix—whose mug inevitably adorns a new campus T-shirt each year—once asked listeners "Are you experienced?" After four years at Hendrix College, with small classes, an emphasis on research, and a laid-back atmosphere in which to test their beliefs and boundaries, students here can likely answer "Yes!"

Overlaps

University of Arkansas, University of Central Arkansas, Rhodes, Vanderbilt, Southwestern

If You Apply To ➤

Hendrix: Rolling admissions. Financial aid: Feb. 15. Housing: May 1. Does not guarantee to meet demonstrated need. Campus interviews: recommended, evaluative. Alumni interviews: optional, informational. SATs or ACTs: required. SAT IIs: optional. Accepts the Common Application and electronic applications. Essay question: meaningful experience or achievement; issue of personal, local, national, or international concern; influential literary or artistic work; how influential individual has changed your life; or why Hendrix is a good match for you.

Hiram College

P.O. Box 96, Hiram, OH 44234

At only 1,190 students, Hiram is the smallest of the prominent Ohio liberal arts colleges. Less nationally known than Wooster or Denison, Hiram attracts the vast majority of its students from in-state. Many classes are taught in seminar format, and an extensive core curriculum ensures a broad education.

Hiram College's secluded campus breeds a strong sense of community among its students. "Hiram has a unique character," extols one junior. "Because of its small size...students get noticed, not lost in the shuffle." But for all their emphasis on closeness, Hiram students are hardly homebodies—more than 50 percent study abroad in locales ranging from Europe to Australia to Costa Rica. The school's flexible schedule makes it even easier to split campus for a while. Clearly, these Hiram Dawgs are loyal to their school but always willing to learn new tricks.

Set on a charming hilltop campus that occupies the second-highest spot in Ohio, Hiram is blessed with an abundance of flowers and trees as well as a nice view

Website: www.hiram.edu
Location: Rural
Enrollment: 1,190
Undergraduates: 1,190
Male/Female: 43/57
SAT Ranges: V 520–640
   M 500–620
ACT Range: 20–27

(Continued)

Financial Aid: 86%

Expense: Pr $ $

Phi Beta Kappa: Yes

Applicants: 1,022

Accepted: 79%

Enrolled: 32%

Grad in 6 Years: 66%

Returning Freshmen: 77%

Academics: ✍ ✍ ✍

Social: ☎ ☎ ☎

Q of L: ★ ★ ★

Admissions: (800) 362-5280

Email Address:
    admission@hiram.edu

Strongest Programs:
   Biology
   Chemistry
   English
   History
   Psychobiology
   Environmental studies
   Communications
   English/Creative writing

Hiram is a bit isolated, and there are few distractions in town, so students must make their own fun.

of the valley below. The prevailing architectural motif is New England brick, and many Hiram buildings are restored nineteenth-century homes. The college recently renovated Bowler Hall, the oldest standing structure on campus, investing $1.5 million to transform it into a modern, air-conditioned dorm while retaining its eleven-foot ceilings and Victorian charm. A new $6.2 million science facility provides ample space for students studying biology, one of the most popular majors, along with education, premed, psychology, and management.

Future tycoons don't get the same fieldwork opportunities as budding doctors and researchers, though. Hiram's bio majors work at a 260-acre, college-owned ecology field study station a mile away, with a specialized lab, a seventy-acre beech and maple forest, artificial river, and numerous plant and animal species. Other sciences, especially chemistry, are also strong at Hiram. Weaker areas are music, physics, and French. Recent additions to the curriculum include a major in biochemistry, biomedical humanities, and a minor in international studies.

> **"Hiram has a unique character. Because of its small size...students get noticed, not lost in the shuffle."**

Hiram offers several unusual summer opportunities, most notably the Northwoods Station up in the wilds of northern Michigan, where students choose courses ranging from photography to botany and geology to writing. And Hiram is the only affiliate college of the Shoals Marine Lab, run by Cornell University and the University of New Hampshire, which offers summer study in marine science, ecology, coastal and oceanic law, and underwater archeology.

Hiram's core curriculum is extensive. All students must complete two courses from each of the college's four divisions (fine arts, humanities, natural sciences, and social sciences), plus the Freshman Colloquium, a writing and speaking skills seminar, and an upper-division interdisciplinary requirement. First year students are also enrolled in a seminar with a focus on western intellectual traditions and an emphasis on writing.

The Hiram Plan allows students to cover a breadth of material in three courses during each semester's longer twelve-week session, and to focus on a seminar-style class during the additional three-week term. Even nonseminars are small, though; 75 percent of Hiram's courses have twenty-five or fewer students, allowing for an impressive degree of faculty accessibility. "At Hiram, students have every professor's home phone number, and they encourage us to call their office or home whenever we have any questions," says a junior.

Hiram goes to great lengths to offer outstanding travel abroad programs. Professor-led trips make it to all corners of the globe, and all participating students get academic credit. Students can also study at Hiram's Rome affiliate, John Cabot International University, and transfer their credits. Hiram's unique academic calendar allows ample opportunity for off-campus endeavors of all types, including the Washington Semester* at American University, which Hiram helped found.

> **"We always have tons of things happening on campus."**

Eighty percent of Hiram students are in-staters, and many of the rest hail from New York and Pennsylvania, though the administration is working to broaden the college's geographic base. Minority students are present, too, with African-Americans constituting 8 percent and Asian-Americans and Hispanics together comprising another 2 percent. International students, minorities, and gays are said to feel welcome, as "We are known for our diversity," says a history major. Hiram heads off race-related conflict with a dorm program called Dialogue in Black and White that encourages open discussion on multicultural issues. There's also a one-credit course that has as its final project the creation of a plan of action on campus race relations. In addition to need-based financial aid, Hiram awards merit scholarships ranging from $3,000 to $15,000. Hiram lures good students with irresistible financial aid. "My financial aid package at Hiram is unbelievable," says a junior. "After applying to larger, cheaper public universities, I came to realize it would actually cost me less to attend Hiram."

Almost all Hiram students—93 percent—live on campus, and everyone who wants a room gets one. "Ours are much better than some I have seen at other schools," says a junior. Community lounges in each hall boast big-screen TVs and computer labs. Most halls are coed, and students choose between twenty-four-hour quiet, twenty-four-hour noise, and a happy medium. Upperclassmen who like their location can stay in the same room year after year. Most students live in two-person suites; the popular (and larger) triples and quads are scarcer and thus harder to get. Dorm dwellers are required to buy the meal plan, which does not always receive five-star reviews, but two gourmet dinners each term liven up the menu.

When the weekend rolls around, don't expect to find all Hiram students gathered around a keg. There are dorms designated as totally dry, and the college has cracked down on underage drinking. Still, students admit that it's easy for underage students to get alcohol if they really want to drink.

Hiram is a bit isolated, and there are few distractions in town, so students must make their own fun. Typically, that means hanging out in each other's rooms, or if they're twenty-one, at CJ's Down Under, an on-campus pub that serves pizza (and features karaoke on Tuesdays). The Student Programming Board plans concerts, comedians, speakers, movies, and both formal and informal dances. "We always have tons of things happening on campus," says one student, noting the college also sponsors trips to events. Cleveland's Jacobs Field is a short road trip away. Cleveland's Rock and Roll Hall of Fame can get students rockin' all year round, and Cedar Point amusement parks get them rollin' in good weather, along with Geauga Lake and Sea World. Sometimes the college offers free tickets to concerts, plays, and ballets in town. Every semester also brings a surprise Campus Day, when classes are cancelled and a slew of activities planned. Other diversions include an excellent golf course three miles away, a college-owned cross-country ski trail, and good downhill slopes about an hour distant.

> "After applying to larger, cheaper public universities, I came to realize it would actually cost me less to attend Hiram."

Hiram is hardly a mecca for budding athletic superstars, but it does have a decent Division III sports program. Football, baseball, and soccer are among the most popular men's teams, while soccer, volleyball, and softball attract women. A fitness center is open to all.

Without being extreme, Hiram has a distinct personality. Those looking for a school where anonymity will be ensured need not apply. People here are so close that they share an equivalent of the secret handshake. "Everyone smiles at you as you pass—faculty, staff, a senior football player, a freshman chemistry major, the lady that vacuums in the morning, the gardener," says a junior. Indeed, those seeking a friendly, all-American institution with a touch of internationalism might want to give Hiram a serious look.

Hiram goes to great lengths to offer outstanding travel abroad programs. Professor-led trips make it to all corners of the globe, and all participating students get academic credit.

Overlaps

Wooster, John Carroll, Mount Union, Miami University (OH), Wittenberg

If You Apply To ➤   **Hiram:** Rolling admissions. Early decision: Dec. 1. Regular admissions: Feb. 1. Financial aid: Mar. 1. Does not guarantee to meet demonstrated need. Campus interviews: recommended (required for scholarship consideration), evaluative. Alumni interviews: optional, informational. SATs or ACTs: required. SAT IIs: optional. Accepts the Common Application and electronic applications. Essay question: last book you read; government spending; space exploration a good thing or not; most significant invention ever; your choice.

Hobart and William Smith Colleges

Geneva, NY 14456

Coordinate single-sex colleges overlooking one of New York's Finger Lakes. Because of the two-college system, relations between the sexes are a little more traditional. Greek life and the men's lacrosse team set the pace of the social scene. Geneva is an old industrial town.

Website: www.hws.edu
Location: Small city
Total Enrollment: 1,892
Undergraduates: 1,892
Male/Female: 45/55
SAT Ranges: V 540–620
  M 540–620
Financial Aid: 65%
Expense: Pr $ $ $ $
Phi Beta Kappa: Yes
Applicants: 2,928
Accepted: 69%
Enrolled: 27%
Grad in 6 Years: 80%
Returning Freshmen: 85%
Academics: ✍ ✍ ✍
Social: ☎ ☎ ☎
Q of L: ★ ★ ★
Admissions: (315) 781-3472
Email Address:
  admissions@hws.edu

Strongest Programs:
  Creative Writing
  Environmental Studies
  Architectural Studies
  Biology
  Political Science
  History
  Economics
  Teacher Certification

Students at Hobart College for men and William Smith College for women have the best of both worlds—each school has its own dean, admissions office, and student government, but their "coordinate system" means students eat together, study together, and even live together in co-ed residence halls. "It's like being at an all-girls' school, with men around all the time!" says a senior. There's an easy-going sense of community here on the shores of upstate New York's Seneca Lake. "The best thing about H-WS is the family-like atmosphere between the faculty and students."

The H-WS campus stretches for two hundred tree-lined acres, with a "beautiful forest and farmlands and a wildlife preserve," says a studio art major. Architectural styles range from Colonial to postmodern, with stately Greek Revival mansions and ivy-clad brick residences and classrooms. The Rosenberg Hall of Science and facilities for William Smith athletics were added after

> "A big social issue on campus is apathy. We have tons to do, but not enough students are getting involved."

fund-raising efforts finished more than $30 million ahead of their $75 million goal. Ground has been broken on a new academic building for the social sciences, which should be finished by late 2003.

The colleges' innovative curriculum begins with an interdisciplinary first-year seminar capped at sixteen students, which emphasizes writing and critical thinking. Instead of traditional distribution requirements, students complete a major and minor, or a double major, one from a traditional department and one from an interdisciplinary program. Some of the newest majors include international relations, European Studies, and media and society. "Courses are intense and rigorous, but the atmosphere is very cooperative," says an economics major. "Students work with each other and the faculty to get ahead." Professors expect a lot, and apply these high standards equally to students in their introductory and advanced courses, a biology and public policy major says. Perhaps that's because small classes are the norm; two-thirds have twenty-five or fewer students.

The colleges take pride in their creative writing, environmental studies, and architectural studies programs, the latter especially unusual for a small school. Biology is enhanced by a cooperative arrangement with the New York State Agricultural Experiment Station, also located in Geneva. Programs in teacher certification include four semesters of student teaching, helping to prepare those who will motivate the next generation. Hobart and William Smith also encourage students to take a term away from campus, with programs in twenty-eight cities, ranging from Copenhagen, Rome and Edinburgh to Sao Paolo, Taipei, and even New York and Los Angeles. Qualified students may also participate in the honors program, the Venture Program,* and independent research.

New Yorkers make up half of H-WS's student body; a third are graduates of private schools. Though hardly diverse—African-Americans constitute 6 percent, Hispanics 4 percent, and Asian-Americans 3 percent—the campus abounds in good intentions. Departments of women's, African-American, and third world cultural studies are small but flourishing, less surprising when you know that H-WS President Mark

Gearan directed the Peace Corps before arriving on campus. Major campus issues include world hunger and trade, environmentalism, and gender equity ("all fresh-men are first-years"), students say. "A big social issue on campus is apathy," adds a sophomore. "We have tons to do, but not enough students are getting involved." Students also get riled up about the lack of a student union building and the administration's ban on fraternity parties. H-WSers are "very independent, very reactionary," explains a senior. "They take matters into their own hands."

Ninety percent of H-WS students live on campus, where first-years may opt for single-sex or coed dorms, and usually get their first choice. Favorites include Geneva (Hobart) and Hirshon (William Smith), while Durfee, Bartlett, and Hale halls, known as "Miniquad" and formerly the most avoided living spaces on campus, are again popular among Hobart men. Sophomores, who may find themselves on the short end of the stick in the housing draw, typically live in a large coed complex known as J-P-R (for Jackson, Potter, and Rees halls). Juniors and seniors may choose from suites, twenty-one on-campus houses, or the "Village at Odell's Pond," where townhouses have four to five bedrooms and two bathrooms each. Housing is guaranteed for four years, so only sixty-five or seventy-five seniors typically live off campus, says an arts and education major.

Six Hobart fraternities claim 20 percent of the college's men, who aren't permitted to pledge until sophomore year, and there are no sororities at William Smith (so much for the Socratic mean), so Greek life is an option, not an imperative. For men who'd rather not join in, Bampton House (the men's honors house) and McDaniel's House are good bets. Women may choose smaller residence halls, like Blackwell and Miller houses, which contribute to a feeling of community without rigid structure. William Smith has also retained a number of traditions typical of women's colleges, most notably Moving Up Day, in which seniors symbolically hand over their leadership role to juniors. (Hobart, not to be left out, has a similar event called Charter Day.)

Geneva is the embodiment of "small-town America," a junior says. Forget bright lights; the best you'll do here are a few coffee shops, a pool hall, a video-rental store, and a upscale grocery within walking distance of campus—and even those don't stay open late. The annual Celebrate Service, Celebrate Geneva Day brings more than five hundred students and faculty members together for community service projects, ranging from tutoring to working in soup kitchens to home-building with Habitat for Humanity. Students also look forward to the two-day Folk Fest, a music-, food-, and craft-filled party now held in the fall. There's a "zero tolerance" policy for underage drinking, and those who aren't twenty-one will find it tough to buy alcohol on campus, but "it's relatively easy" for anyone to get a beer at off-campus pubs, says a senior. On weekends, "the outdoor recreation program hosts a variety of activities in the Adirondacks and surrounding areas,"

"It has become more academic and less party-oriented in the four years I've been here. The administration is seeking to make this a top-tier institution."

says a biology and environmental science major. "Rochester, Ithaca, and Syracuse are all about forty-five minutes away, providing easy weekend travel." Some intrepid souls really looking to escape trek as far as New York City, Washington, D.C., and Toronto, Canada.

Sports are the most popular diversion from studying here. Each spring, the campus comes alive with mania for men's lacrosse, which has a long-standing rivalry with Syracuse. The team won sixteen straight NCAA Division III championships before joining Division I in 1995, and made it to the NCAA playoffs in 1998, 2000, and 2002. The William Smith field hockey team won national titles in 1997 and 2000, and the lacrosse and soccer teams reach their Final Fours nearly every year.

Departments of women's, African-American, and third world cultural studies are small but flourishing, less surprising when you know that H-WS President Mark Gearan directed the Peace Corps before arriving on campus.

The William Smith field hockey team won national titles in 1997 and 2000, and the lacrosse and soccer teams reach their Final Fours nearly every year.

Overlaps
Skidmore, Union, Hamilton, St. Lawrence, Ithaca

Hobart and William Smith Colleges may not be as well known as some other northeastern schools—a popular campus T-shirt explains, "Not Williams...Not Smith...William Smith!"—but that may be changing, students say. "It has become more academic and less party-oriented in the four years I've been here," says a senior. "The administration is seeking to make this a top-tier institution."

Hollins University

(formerly Hollins College)
Roanoke, VA 24020

Hollins is among a trio of western Virginia women's colleges—along with Sweet Briar and Randolph-Macon. Hollins is in the biggest city of the three, Roanoke, and has long been noted for its program in creative writing. Social life often depends on road trips to Washington and Lee and Virginia Tech.

Website: www.hollins.edu
Location: City outskirts
Total Enrollment: 1,091
Undergraduates: 818
Male/Female: 0/100
SAT Ranges: V 510–660
 M 490–600
ACT Range: 22–27
Financial Aid: 61%
Expense: Pr $ $
Phi Beta Kappa: Yes
Applicants: 560
Accepted: 81%
Enrolled: 34%
Grad in 6 Years: 65%
Returning Freshmen: 81%
Academics: ✑ ✑ ✑
Social: ☎ ☎ ☎
Q of L: ★ ★ ★ ★
Admissions: (540) 362-6401
Email Address:
 huadm@hollins.edu

Strongest Programs:
 English/Creative Writing
 Psychology
 Visual Arts/Film

Don't tell the students at this small liberal arts university that the time for single-sex education has passed, or you may find yourself being shown the door. When president Jane Rasmussen forecast financial disaster and suggested that the university consider going coed, she was unanimously ousted by the school's trustees. Make no mistake, the students here are fiercely loyal to the original mission of this small university and will fight to keep it intact.

Described by *The New York Times* as "achingly picturesque," the neoclassical red brick buildings at Hollins date back to the mid-nineteenth century. Modernization is occurring, though, with the Wyndham Robertson Library—Virginia's first national literary landmark—completed in 1999. The facility holds 250,000 titles, a two-story periodicals reading room, multimedia production equipment, and a screening room. The cafeteria was also renovated, and the old library will be turned into a center for art history, studio art, film, and photography. A visual arts center is in the works as well.

Whether it's the award-winning writing program, the highly prized honor system, or the student-administered Independent Exam System, which allows students to take exams when they choose (within limits) and without faculty supervision, Hollins has much to offer. The academic program is rigorous but not brutally so. "Hollins's academic climate seems to be a mix of students who are serious about their work and tend to be competitive, while those who are more laid back can find classes

"Hollins's academic climate seems to be a mix of students who are serious about their work and tend to be competitive, while those who are more laid back can find classes where they have a minimal amount of work."

where they have a minimal amount of work," says a communications and French double major. The history, political science, English—particularly creative writing—and psychology departments are the strongest on campus, students say. Art is also a popular choice; a link to Christie's in London offers a yearlong opportunity to learn about galleries and auction houses, with strong emphasis on writing and research. Natural sciences and the new programs in business and computer science suffer because the emphasis here is on liberal arts, according to students.

(Continued)
Dance
Biology
Communications Studies

Hollins changed its general education requirements in the fall of 2001 to emphasize the integration of areas of knowledge and the acquisition of specific skills. Students must now take at least eight credits in humanities, social sciences, fine arts, and natural and mathematical sciences and must demonstrate competence in written and oral communications, quantitative reasoning, and information technology. Two terms of physical education are also mandatory. Self-motivated students are encouraged to design individualized majors. Hollins does offer a combined-degree program in engineering and architecture, and, as a member of the Seven-College Exchange* consortium, allows students to cross-register at other participating institutions.

"Hollins women are distinguished by their passion for life, self-confidence, and determination."

Those with wanderlust may spend semesters at Hollins's extended campuses in England, France, Mexico, Spain, or Japan. They may also study in Ireland, Austria, Greece, or Italy; a service-learning program takes altruistic (or sun-seeking) students to Jamaica every year. The January term offers a break for on-campus projects, travel, or internships; alumnae help arrange housing in Washington and other cities. Classes here are small; more than three-quarters have twenty-five or fewer students, and none have more than fifty. "Simply put, the professors are incredible," says a freshman.

Self-motivated students are encouraged to design individualized majors.

Back when Hollins was seen as a finishing school, its women were once disparaged as "Hollie Collies." Now they are seen as a mix of types, though not so much of ethnicities. The student body is 89 percent Caucasian. Asian-Americans and Hispanics each comprise 2 percent, and African-Americans comprise another 5 percent. But not everyone is typical, and just about every type is welcomed on campus now as well. Forty-five percent of students are Virginians, and 24 percent graduated in the top tenth of their high-school class. "Hollins women are a unique blend of independence, creativity, spontaneity, and intelligence," says one sophomore. "Hollins isn't for everyone—Hollins women are distinguished by their passion for life, self-confidence, and determination. If

"The social atmosphere is comfortable, warm, and accepting."

there's an issue of concern, on or off campus, Hollins students are the first to recognize and initiate change." Students are friendly, and upperclass women are supportive of their younger peers, says an art history major. "The social atmosphere is comfortable, warm, and accepting," she says.

Dorms at Hollins range from the modern Tinker and Randolph to century-old houses on the Front Quad called East, West, and Main. The latter have wide front porches and halls, high ceilings, and hardwood floors in some of the "large, spacious, airy" rooms, says an economics major. Some rooms also include brass doorknobs, walk-in closets, and even fireplaces. "Singles are easily obtainable for students who feel strongly about not having a roommate," says a freshman. Eighty-nine percent of students live on campus, where security is described as "on the ball."

After class, the Hollins Outdoor Program offers hiking or spelunking in the beautiful Shenandoah Valley and Blue Ridge Mountains. The on-campus stable complements the school's equestrian program, which brought home a 2002 Intercollegiate Horse Show Association championship. Women's tennis won the Old Dominion Athletic Conference in 2002, and the swim team has won national Division III championships. In addition to the lacrosse, field hockey, golf, soccer, basketball, and tennis teams, Hollins offers fencing.

Those with wanderlust may spend semesters at Hollins's extended campuses in England, France, Mexico, Spain, or Japan. They may also study in Ireland, Austria, Greece, or Italy; a service-learning program takes altruistic (or sun-seeking) students to Jamaica every year.

The city of Roanoke has a small museum, ethnic restaurants, a farmers' market, and artsy stores, says a junior. Students give back through a group called SHARE, which organizes volunteer work through the Society for the Prevention of Cruelty to Animals, Habitat for Humanity, and organizations serving local children and the elderly. "There are no clubs for us to dance at, and the bar scene is disappointing," says a student, although the college does offer discounted cab vouchers so that students who imbibe don't drink and drive.

Hollins shuns sororities, but sporadic student efforts to bring them to campus draws lively debate. The school organizes school-wide mixers and maintains several traditions, such as the annual Tinker Day sometime after the first frost. Classes are canceled, everyone eats Krispy Kreme Donuts in her PJs, and the whole school dresses up in "wacky costumes" and hikes to the top of Tinker Mountain for songs, performances, and a lunch of fried chicken and cake. On Ring Night, juniors receive their class rings from seniors, and on Hundredth Night seniors put on skits to celebrate the Hundredth night before graduation. Drinks are available in the on-campus snack bar, but it's almost impossible for underage students to be served at college events because everyone knows everyone, and two forms of ID are required anyway. Road-tripping remains the preferred social option, and favored destinations are Hampden-Sydney College, Virginia Tech, the University of Virginia, and Washington and Lee.

Loyal students continue to cry "Better dead than coed!" Hollins University has known all along what many private and public school educators and parents are rediscovering—that single sex education is terrific for the right kind of student. Hollins has made a specialty of educating women for a long time and not only turns out independent women with a grounding in the liberal arts but provides a cozy, enjoyable atmosphere in which to learn.

Some rooms also include brass doorknobs, walk-in closets, and even fireplaces.

Overlaps

Randolph-Macon, Mary Baldwin, Sweet Briar, Mary Washington, Virginia Tech

If You Apply To ➢

Hollins: Rolling admissions: Feb. 15 for priority. Early decision: Dec. 1. Financial aid: Feb. 1. Does not guarantee to meet demonstrated need. Campus interviews: recommended, informational. Alumni interviews: optional, informational. SAT or ACT: required. SAT IIs: recommended (writing and two others). Accepts the Common Application and electronic applications. Essay question: choose one: personal or career goal; volunteer service you have performed; how you express your creativity or have used it to solve problems; a woman you admire outside your family.

College of the Holy Cross

Worcester, MA 01610

A tight-knit Roman Catholic community steeped in church and tradition. Many students are the second or third generation to attend. Set high on a hill above gritty Worcester, an hour from Boston. Sports teams compete with (and occasionally beat) schools ten times HC's size.

Website: www.holycross.edu
Location: City outskirts
Total Enrollment: 2,811
Undergraduates: 2,811
Male/Female: 48/52
SAT Ranges: V 560–660
  M 580–660

Students at Holy Cross, a Roman Catholic college in the heart of New England, are devoted to the Jesuit tradition of becoming "men and women for others." They're a "happy, driven" bunch, says a senior. Peers and professors alike offer support and spiritual guidance, and bonds forged in the lab or on the field are strengthened through activities like SPUD (Student Programs for Urban Development), which provides community service opportunities. The classroom focus is critical thinking and writing, but the school's proximity to nine other colleges in the Boston area mean Crusaders focus on their social lives, too. "One might think that HC, being a conservative school, would be clique-ish," says a junior. "However, that is not the case—everyone is friendly."

Located on one of the seven hills overlooking the industrial city of Worcester, the 174-acre Holy Cross campus is a registered arboretum. The school's landscaping has won a half-dozen national awards, including two first-place prizes, as the best-designed and planted campus in the nation. Architectural styles range from classical to modern, including Smith Hall, a fifty-six thousand-square-foot building for the departments of philosophy and religious studies, that was just completed. The facility also houses centers for interdisciplinary and special studies—such as deaf studies and gerontology—and for religion, ethics, and culture. The biology department's O'Neill Hall has been renovated and expanded. A 244-bed, apartment-style dorm will be completed this year.

Other Holy Cross award winners are its small classes—69 percent of those taken by freshmen have twenty-five or fewer students, the rest have fifty or less—which help faculty members keep in touch with undergraduates. "We don't have any TAs or grad students teaching," says a sophomore. "Students are expected to put in two to three hours of studying for every hour spent in class," adds a senior. Crusaders come from a variety of backgrounds and hometowns, though most are Irish Catholics from the northeast who want "to learn and excel," says a political science major. "Cooperation is encouraged to improve the learning experience."

Students give high marks to HC's premed, English, history, and economics and accounting programs. As might be expected, philosophy and religious studies are strong, and concentrations in Latin American studies and peace and conflict studies are popular, as these are the disciplines central to Jesuit missionary work. Holy Cross recently added community-based learning courses, which include two to two-and-a-half hours of weekly service with local volunteer, education, or health organizations, in addition to time in the classroom. Students say they tend to avoid the extremely difficult chemistry and physics

> "One might think that HC, being a conservative school, would be clique-ish. However, that is not the case—everyone is friendly."

departments and note that music, theater, and fine arts suffer because of their small size. However, as the student-faculty ratio in these departments is about two-to-one and tutorials are encouraged, carefully chosen seminars can be excellent.

For a decade, nearly a quarter of Holy Cross's first-year students have enrolled in the First Year Program, which attempts to answer a question adapted from Tolstoy, "How then shall we live?" The FYP includes seminars, each limited to fifteen students; shared readings; co-curricular events; and a common dorm. Aside from the FYP, Holy Cross's general education requirements comprise twelve courses in seven areas: arts and literature, religious and philosophical studies, natural and mathematical sciences, social sciences, language studies, historical studies, and cross-cultural studies. Ideas and thinking are the focus rather than preparation for a specific vocation.

Holy Cross is part of the Worcester Consortium,* which offers registration privileges at the region's most prestigious colleges and universities. Aspiring teachers will find education courses and student-teaching opportunities at local primary and secondary schools and a teacher certification program accredited by the Massachusetts Department of Education. Would-be engineers can choose Holy Cross's 3–2 dual-degree programs with Columbia or Dartmouth; a partnership with nearby Clark offers a B.A. and M.B.A., or a B.A. and master's in finance, in five years. Off-campus opportunities include academic internships in the community and the Washington Semester.* HC's honors program enables a small number of juniors and seniors to enroll in exclusive courses and thesis-writing seminars, while the Fenwick Scholars program helps students design and carry out independent projects.

(Continued)

Financial Aid: 50%
Expense: Pr $ $ $ $
Phi Beta Kappa: Yes
Applicants: 4,753
Accepted: 43%
Enrolled: 34%
Grad in 6 Years: 90%
Returning Freshmen: 95%
Academics: ✍ ✍ ✍ ✍
Social: ☎ ☎ ☎ ☎
Q of L: ★ ★ ★ ★
Admissions: (508) 793-2443
Email Address:
   admissions@holycross.edu

Strongest Programs:
   Biology/Premed
   History
   Economics
   English
   Psychology
   Political Science
   Philosophy/Religious Studies

Holy Cross recently added community-based learning courses, which include two to two-and-a-half hours of weekly service with local volunteer, education, or health organizations, in addition to time in the classroom.

Through the Venture Program* and partnerships with foreign universities, students may spend their junior year on one of eighteen programs in twelve European, Asian, and African nations. About one-fifth do so.

The religious influence at Holy Cross is somewhat greater than at other Jesuit schools—most students are Roman Catholic, one-third are in-staters, and only 46 percent attended public high school—but daily Mass is not required. The chaplain's office does offer an optional five-day silent retreat four times a year, in which student volunteers follow the spiritual exercises of Jesuit founder St. Ignatius Loyola. African-Americans make up 3 percent of the student body, Asian-Americans comprise 4 percent, and Hispanics account for 5 percent. "The college is concerned with increasing diversity, and has developed a task force for that purpose," says a biology major. "The college is also working on controlling underage drinking." There are no sororities or fraternities.

Seventy-eight percent of Holy Cross students live in the residence halls, where freshmen and sophomores have double rooms, and juniors and seniors may opt for two- and three-bedroom suites—with living rooms and bathrooms, but no kitchens. Floors are single-sex; buildings are coed. Most first-years live on "Easy Street," the row of five dorms (Healy, Leahy, Hanselman, Clark, and Mulledy) on the college's central hill next to the Hogan Campus Center. Wheeler, Loyola, Alumni and Carlin house mostly upperclassmen. Each dorm has its own T-shirt, and they compete against each other for prizes in athletic and other contests, says a philosophy major. Doors have combination locks, which means no worries about forgetting your keys when you walk to the shower. Students say they feel safe on campus. "Public safety officers make rounds often," says a junior. "Holy Cross is pretty well enclosed into itself" despite its location in Worcester, a gritty industrial center and New England's second-largest city.

"Cooperation is encouraged to improve the learning experi-

While Worcester isn't Boston, the town doesn't deserve its lousy reputation, students say. An hour from Beantown, Cape Cod's beaches, and the ski slopes of the White Mountains, Worcester "has everything you need—movies, clubs, restaurants, groceries, bars," says a junior. A school shuttle service takes students to the orchestra, the Worcester Centrum for athletic events and rock concerts, and the town's museum. Nightlife is good, especially with so many other schools nearby. HC abides by Massachusetts liquor law: Students under twenty-one can't drink at the campus pub. If they're caught with alcohol, they're put on probation and parents are notified. Still, as with most schools, students who seek to imbibe can find booze, regardless of their ages. Since students are discouraged from having cars, most take advantage of concerts, hypnotists, comedians, and other events organized by the Campus Activities Board. The college also organizes trips to New York City and Providence, Rhode Island.

Tradition is big at Holy Cross, from Alumni Weekend to HC by the Sea, a week in Cape Cod at the end of the year. Midnight breakfasts provide sustenance as students cram for finals, while the 100 Days weekend begins the senior class countdown to graduation. Spring Weekend has brought headliners like Run DMC and the Pat McGee Band to campus. Would-be matchmakers can set up their roommates on dates at the "Opportunity Knocks" dance. And of course, given the high percentage of Irish Catholic students, St. Patrick's Day is an occasion for celebration. Students cheer with religious zeal when the Crusaders battle Boston College at HC's football stadium, which holds 23,500 screaming fans. Men's basketball and women's field hockey, soccer, and basketball teams have recently won Patriot League Championships.

Holy Cross is keeping the faith—its emphasis on Catholicism and the Jesuit tradition, that is—even as administrators place a renewed emphasis on academics. Four new tenure-track faculty, designated Edward Bennett Williams Fellows, are charged with teaching and pursuing research in English, religious studies, sociology, and philosophy that bears directly on the college's mission as a Jesuit institution focused on the liberal arts. Still, students here haven't forgotten how to have fun, as a campus T-shirt proclaims: "Purple Reign all the way!"

Hood College

401 Rosemont Avenue, Frederick, MD 21701

The newly coed Hood will face a challenging task in building a coed environment. A major asset: Hood's strategic location one hour from Baltimore and D.C. Hood's distinctive core curriculum stresses thematic study, and a Freshman Colloquium program ensures that all students have a common touchstone.

Some might label small, private women's colleges as out-of-touch or sequestered from the real world. They haven't been to Hood College. This liberal arts school an hour north of the nation's capital is focused on moving its students out into the world and preparing them for a wide spectrum of careers. The school has remained true to its deep roots and traditions while maintaining a confident, forward-looking vision, reflected in the administration's decision to allow men into its residential program. You won't find many shrinking violets here. "Hood students are independent and great leaders," says a biochemistry major while a junior adds that "students feel welcome the moment they step on campus."

Hood was founded in 1893. Its strikingly beautiful fifty-acre campus features redbrick buildings and lush, tree-shaded lawns in the historic Civil War town of Frederick. Hood is within an hour and a half of nearly thirty colleges, within minutes of a major National Cancer Institute research complex, plus high-tech firms, small and large businesses, and both Washington, D.C., and Baltimore. On campus, technology programs, already important, will get a further boost with the completion of a new science and technology center, which will house all of the natural and quantitative sciences.

Students see their school's biggest strength as its people: students, staff, and faculty. "There are so many cultures and ethnicities and traditions to be shared," says one junior. "I love living here. I'm having the time of my life." All incoming students participate in the Freshman Colloquium, a series of intellectual, social, and cultural events that focus on a different topic each

> **"Hood students are independent and great leaders."**

year. Sophomore Experience helps students pick a major and plan a career. The honor system also is an important part of a Hood education. The academic honor code permits unproctored exams and self-scheduled finals; the social code allows for self-governed residence halls where students call the shots in place of resident assistants.

Hood's required core curriculum is divided into three parts. Foundation courses include English, foreign language, computation, physical education, and fitness.

Website: www.hood.edu
Location: Small city
Total Enrollment: 1,607
Undergraduates: 784
Male/Female: 12/88
SAT Ranges: V 520-630
  M 520-620
ACT Range: 22-25
Financial Aid: 58%
Expense: Pr $ $
Phi Beta Kappa: No
Applicants: 502
Accepted: 74%
Enrolled: 30%
Grad in 6 Years: 62%
Returning Freshmen: 79%
Academics: ✏ ✏ ✏
Social: ☎ ☎ ☎
Q of L: ★ ★ ★
Admissions: (301) 696-3400
Email Address:
  admissions@hood.edu

Strongest Programs:
  Biology
  Management
  Psychology
  Education

Methods of Inquiry offers courses that acquaint students with scientific thought, historical and social/behavioral analysis, and philosophy. The Civilization section requires coursework in modern technology and Western and non-Western civilization at the junior-senior level. Even with these comprehensive requirements, there is still a great deal of flexibility; creative interdepartmental majors are often approved.

Hood's major strength lies in the sciences, especially the biology department, with its special focus on molecular biology, marine biology, and environmental science and policy. A new semester-long coastal study takes students along the East Coast on a biological educational mission. Education, especially early childhood, is a program of note, as is management. The graduate school, of mostly commuting students, is as large as the undergraduate programs. Newly-approved programs include an M.A. in humanities, thanatology, regulatory compliance, and education leadership.

Students recognize early on that the school demands they be committed to their studies. Students say the learning environment is more rigorous than competitive. "The professors expect only exceptional work, and they do all they can to assist every student," says a biochemistry major. In general, Hood students are "interested in their education and are serious and hardworking," says a sophomore. Hood students praise the competence and accessibility of the faculty. "The teachers want their students to succeed and are very accessible when students need help," says a math major. No one is taught by graduate assistants, and the average student-teacher ratio is nine to one. A computer network links every dorm room and academic building to the campus-wide information system, and students have twenty-four-hour Internet access.

> "If you don't like to stay on campus, there are restaurants, bars, clubs, malls, and coffee houses within ten minutes of the college."

If you really want to stimulate the brain cells, the four-year honors program features team-taught courses and a sophomore-year seminar on the ethics of social and individual responsibility with student involvement in a community-service project. One-third of students complete internships that include overseas jobs for language and business majors and legislative and cultural positions in Washington, D.C. With the outstanding resources of the Catherine Filene Shouse Career Center (including a national electronic listing for résumés), students have a leg up on their next step in life—60 percent of graduates go straight into jobs after graduation; 31 percent enroll in graduate or professional schools. A three-week May term offers a study tour to countries like France and Mexico.

The Hood student body is 61 percent Caucasian, and one student says that characterizing her classmates is difficult because "we all come from such different financial, cultural, ethnic, and personal backgrounds. The only thing I can say for sure is that we come here to learn." Eleven percent of the student body are African-American, while Hispanics and Asian-Americans each make up 2 percent. Twenty-three percent of Hood students are from out of state, with a large contingent from the Northeast. Students say major issues on campus include diversity, sexuality, and alcohol. Hood provides numerous merit scholarships, which can range from $1,000 to $18,795.

Hood's dorms are well liked, though "they need a face-lift," gripes one student. But a happier camper notes that "the rooms are a good size, all are air-conditioned, and each dorm has a cleaning staff that is here every day." The lottery system is based on seniority, and about half the students live on campus. Freshmen can expect to be assigned to doubles (seniors and juniors can compete for singles), and three small language dorms house students who choose to speak French, Spanish, or German exclusively.

Traditions abound at Hood. Annual events include the Class Ring dinner and formal, a performance of Handel's Messiah, and Spring Parties, a weekend of carnival activities and dances.

All incoming students participate in the Freshman Colloquium, a series of intellectual, social, and cultural events that focus on a different topic each year.

Social life among the students is centered around the dorms, as each has its own personality as well as its own house council, rules, and social activities. Students report that there are parties every weekend, along with movies, dances, or other forms of entertainment. The Whitaker Campus Center, with its pool tables, snack bar, bookstore, and meeting rooms, offers a great gathering place for residents and commuters twenty-four hours a day. "If you don't like to stay on campus, there are restaurants, bars, clubs, malls, and coffeehouses within ten minutes of the college (by car)," explains an English major. About an hour in the car brings students to the multiple diversions in Baltimore and Washington. Campus alcohol policies follow state law and the honor code, but in general drinking is not a big deal at Hood. "At parties students are carded and given a wristband before receiving alcohol," says a chemistry major. "Drinking in rooms among friends is harder to regulate." Students also frequent scenic Frederick, which is described as small, safe, and beautiful but without too much in the way of entertainment.

With a one hundred-year history, Hood is rife with traditions. Some of the most important ones include Class Ring dinner and formal, a performance of Handel's Messiah, and Spring Parties, a weekend of carnival activities and dances. In sports, tennis, field hockey, basketball, and volleyball are tops.

Students looking for the friendliness and security of a small campus along with the chance to prepare for high-flying careers find satisfaction at Hood. Traditions bring the campus close together, while the administration encourages students to explore the world. In the midst of all that, Hood students remember how to have fun. As one informal school motto goes: "We don't go to a girls' school without men, we go to a women's college without boys."

> **Overlaps**
>
> **Washington College, Western Maryland, Mount Holyoke, Goucher, Towson State**

If You Apply To ➤

Hood: Early action: Dec. 1. Regular admissions and financial aid: Feb. 15. Does not guarantee to meet demonstrated need. Campus interviews: recommended, evaluative. No alumni interviews. SATs or ACTs: required. SAT IIs: recommended. Accepts the Common Application and electronic applications. Essay question: leadership; major national event; Hood's motto *Corde et Mente et Manu*, Heart and Mind and Hand; significant experience or accomplishment.

Hope College

P.O. Box 9000, Holland, MI 49422

Hope has an in-between size—bigger than most small colleges but smaller than most universities. Evangelical in orientation, but less than a fourth of the students are members of the Reformed Church in America. In addition to the liberal arts, Hope offers education, engineering, and nursing.

Each fall since 1897, Hope College freshmen have spent three grueling hours engaged in "the Pull," an epic tug-of-war against the sophomores, who stand assembled on the opposite end of a 650-pound rope across the fifteen-foot-wide Black River. This annual tradition evokes the daily struggle Hope students face: to maintain their faith in a world eager to challenge it at every turn. The heritage of Hope's Dutch founders remains strong and visible on campus, but you don't have to be a member of the Reformed Church in America to appreciate the charms of this conservative Christian college.

The college, founded in 1866, is situated on six blocks near downtown Holland, the tulip capital of the nation (population 60,000) and a short bike ride from the shores

Website: www.hope.edu
Location: Small city
Total Enrollment: 2,999
Undergraduates: 2,999
Male/Female: 40/60
SAT Ranges: V 530–660
   M 540–670
ACT Range: 22–28
Financial Aid: 55%

(Continued)

Expense: Pr $
Phi Beta Kappa: Yes
Applicants: 2,110
Accepted: 88%
Enrolled: 39%
Grad in 6 Years: 71%
Returning Freshmen: 87%
Academics: ✍ ✍ ✍
Social: ☎ ☎ ☎
Q of L: ★ ★ ★
Admissions: (616) 395-7850
Email Address:
 admissions@hope.edu

Strongest Programs:
 Biology
 Chemistry
 Dance
 Education
 English
 Music
 Political Science
 Psychology
 Religion

The bachelor's-level
nursing program, offered
with Calvin College since
1982, became an
independent Hope-only
degree beginning with the
class of 2004.

of Lake Michigan. There's a lush pine grove in the center of campus, which features an eclectic array of buildings in architectural styles ranging from nineteenth-century Flemish to modern. A new $36 million Science Center is under construction and scheduled to be completed by 2005. Planning is underway for a second academic building for several departments and a new intercollegiate field house.

Among Hope's academic offerings, the sciences (especially biology, physics, and chemistry) stand out, with excellent laboratory facilities and faculty who are eager to involve students in their funded research. During the school year, undergraduates often conduct advanced experiments and even publish papers; come summer, more than seventy-five biology, chemistry, mathematics, computer science, and physics and engineering majors participate in research full-time. Not surprisingly, many science majors go on to medical and engineering schools and Ph.D. programs. For those otherwise inclined, Hope's offerings in political science, psychology, music, dance, and education are solid, too. Hope's Department of Communication is one of the Speech Communication Association's two nationwide Programs of Excellence. And Hope is one of only fourteen colleges and universities in the U.S. with accredited programs in art, dance, music, and theater. The First-Year seminar and GEMS (General Education in Math and Science) courses are two new fully implemented courses. Offerings in anthropology and journalism continue to be limited, administrators say. The bachelor's-level nursing program, offered with Calvin College since 1982, became an independent Hope-only degree beginning with the class of 2004.

Most Hope students select a major from one of the college's thirty-nine fields, although the truly adventurous may design their own composite major. Hope's general education program, designed around the themes "knowing how" and "knowing about," includes a first-year seminar, which provides "an intellectual transition into Hope." Courses in expository writing, health dynamics, math and natural science, foreign language, religious studies, social sciences, the arts, and cultural heritage are also required; some must have a focus on cultural diversity. Students also complete a senior seminar. "Hope college is very competitive in the academic area," says a business major. Professors get high marks, too. "I'm bowled away by the energy, creativity, and compassion that my professors pour into their teaching," says an English major.

Hope offers off-campus programs through the Great Lakes Colleges Association,* including semesters at other U.S. colleges and options combining classes and internships. Students may also study abroad in Austria, England, Greece, Japan, or Israel. The modern and classical language departments offer students proficient in a second language the chance to use their skills in volunteer work and research with faculty members, while the Visiting Writers Series gives students an opportunity to interact with noteworthy authors.

> **"Hope students are sincerely religious and often speak openly about their faith."**

Less than a fourth of Hope's students belong to the Reformed Church in America, but the student body is overwhelmingly Christian, white, conservative—and female. Thrice-weekly chapel is voluntary, but administrators say it's typically filled to capacity. "Hope students are sincerely religious and often speak openly about their faith," says one student. Seventy-six percent of students hail from Michigan; African-Americans, Hispanics, and Asian-Americans make up just under 5 percent of the student body. "The biggest social issue is that we aren't very diverse," says an accounting major, while another student feels "the biggest debate at Hope is over the Christian nature of the college." Homosexuality is another sensitive issue on campus. "Homosexual students often struggle to find a place in a student body that does not readily accept them," says one junior. Despite all of these issues students still feel that "one word that describes the campus community is friendly."

Hope's housing options include on-campus apartments, small houses called cottages, and traditional dorms, arranged in freshman clusters or coed by suite. First-year students are assigned dorms and roommates; upperclassmen get first pick in the annual lottery. Only seniors and married students may live off-campus, one reason why dorms are "very crowded," says a senior. "Housing is great except you are supposed to have seventy-five credits before you can live off campus," says a senior. "I believe after your sophomore year you should be able to be off campus." On-campus students eat in one of two large dining halls, where the fare—especially homemade bread and desserts—is tasty.

Most of Hope's social life takes place on campus. The Social Activities Committee brings in comedians, bands, and hypnotists, shows movies in campus auditoriums, and plans the Spring Festival carnival, Winter Fantasia dance, and May Day celebration. Seven fraternities and six sororities, all local organizations, claim 26 percent of the men and 28 percent of the women, but Hope's campus is officially dry. While there are no echoes of *Animal House* on campus, "it's easy to find alcohol at off-campus parties, especially fraternity parties," admits one student. Students caught drinking must perform community service, although plenty of students do that anyway, through activities like charity walks in Holland, a "very touristy town" with "great downtown shopping" and a "simple, slow-paced lifestyle." Holland is also the site of spring's Tulip Time, one of the largest U.S. flower festivals.

Perhaps not surprisingly, social preferences here lean more toward sports, games, and coffeehouses than to keg parties. But when Hope's cozy campus and the quaint town of Holland get too close for comfort, students find relief at the beaches of Lake Michigan or drive thirty minutes to Grand Rapids, which offers some large-city amenities and good weekend rental deals at the ski slopes. Chicago and Detroit are other typical destinations for those trying to hit the road.

On the field and on the court, Hope's Flying Dutchmen are fearless and talented Division III competitors. The men's football team won conference championships in three of the last four years, while the men's swim team recently finished fourth nationwide. Last year, Hope athletes and teams qualified for 11 NCAA championship tournaments. The college also won the Commissioner's Cup of the Michigan Intercollegiate Athletic Association for the sixth time in the past eight years; the trophy recognizes the school with the conference's best cumulative sports program for men and women. Especially important are any competition against Calvin (a century-old rivalry) and football versus Albion and Kalamazoo.

Hope continues to be considered one of the nation's leading liberal arts colleges. Without losing sight of its Christian roots, the campus is expanding, political issues are becoming more openly discussed, and students are getting involved in the community. "Hope students really like each other," brags an English major. "It's a close-knit community." Hope's challenge will be to retain this close-knit community and devotion to religion that are its hallmarks, while growing, changing, and improving to meet new students' needs and realities.

Hope offers off-campus programs through the Great Lakes Colleges Association,* including semesters at other U.S. colleges and options combining classes and internships.

Overlaps

Michigan State, Western Michigan, University of Michigan, Grand Valley State, Calvin

If You Apply To >

Hope: Rolling admissions. Meets demonstrated need of 85%. Campus interviews: optional, informational. No alumni interviews. SATs or ACTs: required. SAT IIs: optional. Accepts the Common Application and electronic applications. Essay question: what you have gained from and contributed to activities or employment; something important to you; and thoughts on careers and career preparation.

Houghton College

Houghton, NY 14744

The mid-Atlantic's premier evangelical Christian college. Women outnumber men by nearly two to one and enjoy perks such as a 386-acre horseback-riding facility. All students are required to take a Biblical literature class, and most go to chapel three times per week.

Website: www.houghton.edu
Location: Rural
Total Enrollment: 1,356
Undergraduates: 1,356
Male/Female: 36/64
SAT Ranges: V 520–650
   M 520–640
ACT Range: 21–28
Financial Aid: 76%
Expense: Pr $
Phi Beta Kappa: No
Applicants: 1,025
Accepted: 91%
Enrolled: 38%
Grad in 6 Years: 68%
Returning Freshmen: 88%
Academics: ✑ ✑ ✑
Social: ☎ ☎ ☎
Q of L: ★ ★ ★ ★
Admissions: (800) 777-2556
Email Address:
   admission@houghton.edu

Strongest Programs:
  Music
  Biology
  Bible
  English
  Education
  Psychology

Houghton College, located in the bucolic New York town that shares its name, "has a unique Christian atmosphere, combining academics, athletics, and service," says an English major. This liberal arts institution, run by the Wesleyan Church of America, celebrates its Christian heritage and tries to ensure that students do the same. Applicants must explain in their essays why they want to go to a Christian college, and thrice-weekly chapel attendance is a must. These strict mandates help create true community on campus. "Faculty and students have close relationships, and there is a Christ-centered attitude in every aspect of college life," says a psychology major.

> **"Houghton College has a unique Christian atmosphere, combining academics, athletics, and service."**

Houghton's scenic hilltop campus covers 1,300 acres of rural beauty, surrounded by vast expanses of western New York countryside. The academic buildings are a mix of area fieldstone and brick with ivy-covered walls. An art gallery displays student work and traveling exhibits. Students can go online with the laptops they get at matriculation; through Houghton's Educational Technology Initiative, the computer's price is included in the tuition bill.

Students say Houghton's academic climate is rigorous. "The level of competition is really up to the individual student, and courses are difficult, without being impossible," says a political science major. The school's most popular programs are education and biology, but psychology and music also draw crowds. The educational ministries, accounting, and computer science departments are weak. Unusual minors such as equestrian studies—which takes advantage of Houghton's 386-acre riding facility—and linguistics have been joined by newer programs such as intercultural studies. Across departments, faculty gets high marks for teaching and accessibility. "My professors have done a wonderful job making class stimulating," says a sophomore.

Once they've enrolled, Houghton students must complete general education requirements known as Integrative Studies, designed to provide a context and framework for the entire educational program. IS includes courses in writing, literature, communications, a foreign language, social science, history, physical education, math, natural science, religion, philosophy, and fine arts. A research requirement cuts across the curriculum. Freshmen must also take Biblical Literature, Principles of Writing, and a course titled

> **"Faculty and students have a close relationship, and there is a Christ-centered attitude in every aspect of college life."**

FYI (First-Year Introduction), aimed at easing the transition to college. The First-Year Honors Program allows about thirty students to spend the spring semester of their freshman year in London studying under two Houghton professors.

In recent years, Houghton has begun to emphasize off-campus study, with programs in Paris, Tanzania, Honduras, Australia, and many cities and countries in between. Students who want to get away within the U.S. can spend a semester at any Christian College Consortium* member school or participate in the American

Studies program in Washington, D.C., sponsored by the Council for Christian Colleges and Universities.* The Oregon Extension program lets thirty Houghton students spend the fall studying in the Cascade Mountains while Houghton's extension campus in Buffalo offers internships and provides living quarters for students completing student teaching assignments. A 3–2 engineering program with Clarkson University (NY) is available, too.

Fifty-seven percent of those who enroll at Houghton are from New York. The minority community is tiny, accounting for only 4 percent of the student body. Hot-button issues include "whether or not to have nudes in the art classes," a chemistry major says. Students are also concerned about campus expansion, town–gown relations, and the number of women in Houghton's faculty and administration, says an English major. The increasing use of technology sparked a campus debate when the school's board blocked access to some Internet sites with sexually explicit materials or references. "There were students on both sides of the censorship issue, and eventually some of the restrictions were loosened," says a junior.

Houghton's single-sex dorms and sixteen townhouses are "well cleaned and carefully maintained," with kitchens on each floor and free laundry. Students are required to live in the residence halls as freshmen and sophomores. There, in-room visitation is only allowed at weekly "open houses," but dorm lounges are open daily to members of the opposite sex. After their first two years, some students move off campus—80 percent of the total were dorm-

> "The level of competition is really up to the individual student, and courses are difficult, without being impossible."

dwellers at last count—but many opt for college-approved townhouses where regulations are self-imposed. This isn't exactly surprising, considering the other rules students voluntarily obey here, including abstention from tobacco, alcohol, drugs, and swearing, and optional Sunday church and Tuesday prayer meetings.

Houghton's boondocks village is truly small, lacking even a traffic light, says a junior. "It's us, a gas station, a coffee shop, and a pizza place," the student says. "Students are very involved in service projects," such as Big Brothers/Big Sisters and nursing home visitation, because the area surrounding the college is one of the poorest in New York State. Social life consists of on-campus movies, coffeehouses, concerts, and picnics. Because the student body is two-thirds female, dating can be a challenge. "You make your own fun at Houghton, or you go off-campus—usually Buffalo, Rochester, Olean, or Latchworth State Park," says a political science major. The college even has its own ski trails. The town of Houghton is "dry," and because college policy forbids alcohol, consumption is virtually nonexistent, says a freshman. "The student body does not put an emphasis on or find enjoyment in drinking," she notes. Students eagerly anticipate annual celebrations for Homecoming, Christian Life Emphasis Week, and the Christmastime Madrigal Banquets.

The First-Year Honors Program allows about thirty students to spend the spring semester of their freshman year in London.

Soccer is the spectator sport of choice at Houghton, especially since there is no football team. The women's squad won the Region IX Championship in 2001 to advance to the NAIA National Tournament for the third time in four years. The women's basketball and volleyball teams also advanced to their respective national tournaments recently. The school's sports facilities have undergone extensive renovation and now include new tennis courts, an all-weather track, and lighted soccer and field hockey fields. Intramurals, including pool and Ultimate Frisbee, provide fun competition for athletes of all levels.

Students don't come to Houghton for the surrounding town, which is thirty minutes by car from the nearest mall, or for the weather, which can be brutal once winter sets in. But they do come, and for good reason, says a sophomore: there's little to distract them from their studies, their campus's natural beauty, and their connection to God. "Students at Houghton are the best part—both as individuals and

Overlaps

Messiah, Roberts Wesleyan, Gordon, Grove City, Cedarville

as a community," the student says. "The close relationships with students and professors alike are the backbone of Houghton's specialness."

If You Apply To ➤

Houghton: Rolling admissions. Financial aid: Mar. 1, Nov. 15. Housing: Nov. 15. Does not guarantee to meet demonstrated need. Campus interviews: recommended, evaluative. No alumni interviews. SATs or ACTs: required. SAT IIs: optional. Music majors apply directly to music program. Accepts electronic applications. Essay question: when and how Christ became personal; how you are cultivating spiritual growth; why Houghton; opinion of the college's policies on drugs, alcohol and tobacco; how a liberal arts college will contribute to your goals.

Howard University

2400 Sixth Street NW, Washington, DC 20059

The flagship university of black America and the first to integrate the black experience into all areas of study. Strategically located in D.C., Howard depends on Congress for most of its funding. Preprofessional programs such as nursing, business, and architecture are among the most popular.

Website: www.howard.edu
Location: Center city
Total Enrollment: 10,211
Undergraduates: 6,541
Male/Female: 42/58
SAT Ranges: V 430–640
  M 410–680
ACT Range: 16–27
Financial Aid: 74%
Expense: Pr $
Phi Beta Kappa: Yes
Applicants: 5,964
Accepted: 53%
Enrolled: 42%
Grad in 6 Years: N/A
Returning Freshmen: 85%
Academics: 🖉 🖉
Social: ☎ ☎ ☎
Q of L: ★ ★ ★
Admissions: (202) 806-2700
Email Address:
  admission@howard.edu

Strongest Programs:
  African Studies
  Music
  Art
  Architecture
  Business
  Psychology

Perhaps it's no surprise that Howard University is located in the nation's capital, near the monuments and memorials erected to honor this country's history and heritage. This historically black university strives to educate its students about the great achievements of African-Americans and to honor the African-American perspective in the context of a traditional curriculum. Buoyed by the arrival of president (and alumnus) H. Patrick Swygert, Howard has strengthened its financial position and has begun implementation of a new strategic plan structured around "Leadership for America." The four-part plan focuses on strengthening academic programs and services, promoting excellence in teaching and research, increasing private support, and enhancing national and community service.

Founded in 1866 by Gen. Oliver Howard primarily to educate freed slaves, the university now operates four campuses and serves about ten thousand students. The eighty-nine-acre main campus houses most classrooms, dorms, and administrative offices, as well as the university center, the Founders Library, and the undergraduate library. The Howard Law Center is located on the west campus near Rock Creek Park; the Divinity School is located on a twenty-two-acre site in northeast Washington; and there's also a 108-acre campus in suburban Beltsville, Maryland.

"Come to Howard ready to study." Architecturally, the main campus is a blend of old and new, with numerous sculptures and murals created by Jacob Lawrence, Richard Hunt, Elizabeth Catlett, and the late Romare Bearden. The campus is an easy bus ride from the attractions of the nation's capital, all the more visible now thanks to a campus-wide window-replacement initiative. Auditoriums, office spaces, classrooms, galleries, and computer labs across campus have undergone large-scale renovation in recent years; the physics, chemistry, and fine arts facilities have also been completely redone.

Contrary to the advice of early black leaders such as Booker T. Washington, who argued in favor of technical training, Howard since its inception has promoted the liberal arts. This focus has served the school well; Howard's law school counts former Supreme Court Justice Thurgood Marshall among its alumni, and Nobel Prize-winning author Toni Morrison went here, too. The school also has excellent

(Continued)
Electrical Engineering

programs in African studies, music, art, and theater arts. Other intriguing academic options are accelerated programs for a B.S. on the way to a medical or dental degree, coursework in the institute of jazz studies, programs in zoology and engineering (especially electrical engineering), and programs in communication science and disorders. And despite Howard's historical focus on the liberal arts, preprofessional programs are among the most heavily enrolled here. The most popular major is nursing, followed by radio/TV/film and accounting. Programs in ancient Mediterranean and international studies are being developed. Weaker departments include classics and physics.

All students must complete general education requirements, which vary by school or college but uniformly encompass eighteen credits in social sciences and humanities and one Afro-American studies course. Freshman seminars and various other special programs for first-year students are available in the schools of communication, engineering, and arts and sciences. And seniors in arts and sciences must weather a comprehensive exam to graduate. In general, students say that the workload at Howard is demanding. "You must treat homework as a very important part of your life," admonishes a junior. "If you do not, it will be hard to get by in a majority of classes." Another student adds, "Come to Howard ready to study." Most students agree that professors are ready and willing to help when asked, though academic advising is not Howard's strength. "Sometimes, you may get professors who do not know how to break down anything," explains a psychology major. "Then, it is your job to talk up and ask questions. You must ask questions because a closed mouth does not get fed!" Students who need a break from the academic scene seek out internships in town or across the country. Many also study abroad at one of the more than two hundred institutions in thirty-six countries where Howard grants credit.

"Sometimes, you may get professors who do not know how to break down anything."

Eighty-three percent of Howard students are African-American, and 12 percent hail from foreign countries. Most come from decidedly middle-class backgrounds. Although Howard seems to be a very cohesive community, career-minded and highly motivated men and women fit in best, students say, and most are politically liberal. Hot issues include women's empowerment, student government, and fraternities, and sororities. Fraternities and sororities do not have their own housing or dining facilities, and only 2 percent of the men and women go Greek. Howard awards a wide variety of athletic scholarships, and merit scholarships are also available to students who maintain a 3.5 GPA. A deferred-payment plan also allows families to pay each semester's tuition in three installments. But even with financial aid, costs are steep; President Swygert hopes that will change as he encourages more alumni to give back to their alma mater.

Howard's law school counts former Supreme Court Justice Thurgood Marshall among its alumni, and Nobel Prize-winning author Toni Morrison went here, too.

Interestingly, Howard is one of a handful of universities in the nation supported partly by federal subsidies; these days, the school gets about 55 percent of its budget from Congress. Bethune Hall, a $14 million housing complex, has helped ease the space crunch, but only about half of Howard's students can be accommodated on campus. "Housing at Howard is average in regards to availability, maintenance, and comfort," says one student. Freshmen get room assignments, while upperclassmen take their chances in a lottery. The halls are coed, and the eleven residential computer labs have more than two hundred state-of-the-art machines for student use. But many students live off campus purely to avoid the mandatory meal plan. Still, the administration is doing its best to bring students back, and Drew, Meridian Hill, Baldwin, Carver, Truth, and Crandall halls have recently gotten facelifts.

Among America's historically black colleges and universities, Howard stands out as the standard-bearer, a longtime center of excellence and leadership.

Weekends bring an assortment of social happenings to campus, many of which take place in the student center. On-campus parties and sports events are always big draws, but the bars of Georgetown and Adams Morgan, the restaurants and clubs in the "New U" Street corridor, and the MCI Center arena (home to the NBA's Wizards and NHL's Capitals)—most accessible by public transit—also beckon. Though small in numbers, the Greeks are "an integral part of the university." Athletics are also an important presence on campus, particularly varsity basketball, soccer, football, and track, and the highlight of the season is always the grudge match with Hampton University to decide which school is the "true HU." Students list Howard's Homecoming as one of the best annual events, along with various Greekfests, concerts, and talent shows that alumni, current students, and members of the community enjoy together.

Among America's historically black colleges and universities, Howard stands out as the standard-bearer, a longtime center of excellence and leadership. Its scholarship and collections of artworks, rare books, manuscripts, and photographs are a repository of the African-American experience. The current generation of students is writing a new chapter of that very experience. The same might be said about those who receive their education at Howard.

Overlaps

Hampton, Clark Atlanta, Spelman, Morgan State, Florida A&M

If You Apply To ➤

Howard: Early action: Nov. 30. Regular admissions and financial aid: Apr. 1. Meets demonstrated need of 39%. Campus and alumni interviews: not available. SATs or ACTs: required. SAT IIs: required (writing only). Audition tape or portfolio required for fine arts applicants. No essay question unless applying for scholarship consideration by Early Action deadline.

University of Illinois at Urbana-Champaign

901 West Illinois, Urbana, IL 61801

Half a step behind Michigan and neck-in-neck with Wisconsin among top Midwestern public universities. U of I's strengths include business, communications, engineering, architecture, and the natural sciences. More than 90 percent of the student body hails from in-state.

Website: www.uiuc.edu
Location: Small city
Total Enrollment: 39,291
Undergraduates: 28,746
Male/Female: 56/44
SAT Ranges: V 550–670
   M 600–720
ACT Range: 25–30
Financial Aid: 35%
Expense: Pub $ $
Phi Beta Kappa: Yes
Applicants: 19,930
Accepted: 62%
Enrolled: 50%
Grad in 6 Years: 76%
Returning Freshmen: 93%
Academics: ✐ ✐ ✐ ✐ ✐

Homecoming weekend was invented at the University of Illinois, and whether cheering for the Illini, pledging one of seventy-five Greek houses, or celebrating Moms', Dads', or Siblings' Weekends, students here stir up a vibrant mix of school spirit and good times. This may look and feel like a laid-back Midwestern campus, but students work hard for the degrees they receive, especially in prestigious departments such as engineering and business administration.

The oldest land-grant institution, the Illinois campus was built in farm country between the twin cities of Champaign and Urbana. The park-like campus was designed along a mile-long axis where trees and walkways separate stately white-columned Georgian structures made of brick. Physically challenged students tend to appreciate the campus because it is flat and well-equipped with ramps and widened doorways. Students will soon take advantage of a new computer science center, which is nearing completion.

> **"Engineering and Business tend to be highly competitive, while Liberal Arts and Sciences and Applied Life Studies are more relaxed."**

Illinois has eight undergraduate colleges and more than 150 undergraduate programs; if nothing strikes your fancy, you may design your own. Requirements include six to nine hours of composition, three hours of quantitative reasoning, proficiency in a foreign language, and six hours each of cultural studies, natural sciences and technology, humanities and arts, and social and behavioral sciences. Engineering, architecture, business, education, and the sciences—especially agriculture and veterinary medicine—get high marks from students and lots of resources from administrators. The academic climate "varies by college," says a senior. "Engineering and Business tend to be highly competitive, while Liberal Arts and Sciences and Applied Life Studies are more relaxed."

Partially because of its size, Illinois can afford to support excellent programs across the university, including the expansion of undergraduate minors campuswide. For a huge university, registration can be relatively painless, thanks to an online system allowing course selection from one's own computer. Nevertheless, freshmen and sophomores, who register last, may have trouble getting into certain general education classes, like foreign languages. Professors and academic advisors can usually help if classes you need are full, but "if you don't get into the College of Education by your sophomore year, you won't graduate in four years," says a sociology major. "Accounting is a five-year major, and engineering is hard to do in four."

> "If you don't get into the College of Education by your sophomore year, you won't graduate in four years. Accounting is a five-year major, and engineering is hard to do in four."

The impressive Illinois library system, the largest public university facility of its kind worldwide, makes it easier to keep up with class work. Aside from engineering and business, other notable programs at Illinois include the Beckman Institute for Advanced Science and Technology, an interdisciplinary center designed to bring biological and physical sciences together to pursue new insights in human and artificial intelligence. The National Center for Supercomputing Applications at Illinois developed Mosaic, the predecessor to Netscape's Navigator World Wide Web browser. The undergraduate honors program includes faculty mentoring, intensive seminars, advanced sections of regular courses, and access to special resources. More than 1,400 undergraduates travel and study abroad each year, roaming one hundred countries around the globe, while the Ronald E. McNair Scholars Program helps fund independent, original research by minority, low-income, and first-generation college students who are completing bachelor's degrees. In a new class called LINC, students derive the satisfaction of community work while receiving academic credit for this real-world experience.

Illinois has its share of stellar faculty, including National Medal of Science winners and two dozen members of the National Academy of Sciences. "I have experienced professors with a passion in their areas as well as a sincere concern for the well-being of their students," says a sophomore. Even freshmen stuck in large lectures (think two thousand seats) will find some personal attention in the associated discussion sections, led by graduate teaching assistants. Freshmen Discovery Courses, seminars limited to twenty students, enable first-year students to interact closely with full professors. First semester freshmen can ease into the rigors of college level work in one of the "Learning Communities." In this program, groups of eighteen to twenty-one students go to two classes together and attend weekly discussions led by upperclassmen.

Ninety-three percent of Illinois undergrads are homegrown. But since Illinois stretches from the wealthy north suburbs of sophisticated Chicago to the unspoiled rural hills bordering Kentucky and encompasses classic farm towns as well as gritty working class cities, students do come from multiple backgrounds and fit less into the stereotypical "Midwest" mold than one might think. African-Americans and Hispanics combine for 12 percent of the student body, and there's an equal number

(Continued)
Social: ☎ ☎ ☎
Q of L: ★ ★ ★
Admissions: (217) 333-0302
Email Address:
admissions@oar.uiuc.edu

Strongest Programs:
Accounting
Agricultural Economics
Architecture
Engineering
Business Administration
Insurance/Risk Management
Psychology

Illinois attracts many socially oriented students who love parties and intramural sports, which may be why the Greek influence is particularly strong. Independents don't have to suffer boredom, though, as there are also more than 850 registered student clubs and organizations ranging from the rugby team to ethnic advocacy groups.

of Asian-Americans, due in large part to the administration's effort to attract high-achieving students through the President's Award of financial support for state residents. But even this moderate amount of diversity in the student body hasn't dampened what students admit is a "heated controversy" over the mascot, Chief Illiniwek, which is seen by many as an insensitive symbol. There are those on the other side who see it as honoring Native Americans. However, one junior says, "Most people prefer to stay out of political issues" at Illinois.

Thirty percent of students live in the U of I's twenty-two coed and single-sex residence halls, which range in size from fifty-one to 660 beds and are arranged in quadrangle-like groups. However, some dorms are quite a hike from classrooms, veterans warn. Daniel's Residence has been renovated. All bedrooms have fast Internet connections, and many residence halls house living/learning programs, such as WIMSE (Women in Math, Science, and Engineering) and Unit One (academic support and educationally focused programming). Each quad is a mini-neighborhood, with dining halls, darkrooms, libraries, music practice rooms, computers, and lounges creating a sense of community. "For some halls, the rooms are a little small," says a sophomore. "After your freshman year, there really is no trouble getting a room." The dorms have unique personalities, another student says, so it's important to choose the right one: "Champaign dorms are loud, party places, while Urbana is more focused on school. ISR has engineers, Allen is alternative, LAR is quiet, PAR is relaxed and fun, and FAR has air-conditioning in the rooms." Many sophomores live in fraternity or sorority houses; Illinois claims to have the largest Greek system anywhere, with more than seventy-five chapters drawing 22 percent of men and women as pledges. Many juniors and seniors move to off-campus apartments.

> "People used to say that Champaign was a drinking town with a football problem."

Illinois attracts many socially oriented students who love parties and intramural sports, which may be why the Greek influence is particularly strong. Independents don't have to suffer boredom, though, as there are also more than 850 registered student clubs and organizations ranging from the rugby team to ethnic advocacy groups. On most weekends, the Illini Union showcases bands, comedians, and hypnotists. The impressive Krannert Center for the Performing Arts, with four theaters and more than 350 annual performances, serves as the area's cultural center, while Assembly Hall hosts national touring acts, including popular rock bands. Students get a discount at both facilities. Chicago and the shores of Lake Michigan beckon when the weather warms up, and Mardi Gras makes for a good road trip in the dead of winter.

> "Urbana-Champaign is very alive and there are many student organizations that go out and have contact with the community."

Though drinking is prohibited in the dorms, nineteen-year-olds can get into bars—and can also get alcohol fairly easily. "People used to say that Champaign was a drinking town with a football problem," reports a student. For those who itch for the stimulation of a big city, the campus is just about equidistant from Chicago, Indianapolis, and St. Louis.

The Illini compete in the Big Ten and count as their biggest rivals Northwestern (football), Michigan (football), Indiana (basketball), and Iowa (both sports). The baseball and men's basketball teams won Big 10 championships in 2000 and 2001, respectively, and the football team made it to a post-season bowl game. The intramural program is extensive mainly because of the university's excellent sports facilities: sixteen full-length basketball courts, five pools, nineteen handball/racquetball courts, a skating rink, a baseball stadium, and the $5.1 million Atkins Tennis Center, with 6 indoor and 8 outdoor courts. Not surprisingly, the men's tennis team has brought home Big Ten championships in recent years.

Freshmen Discovery Courses, seminars limited to twenty students, enable first-year students to interact closely with full professors.

Overlaps

Northwestern, University of Michigan, University of Wisconsin, Notre Dame, Washington University (MO)

Don't be scared off by the enormity of the University of Illinois. Its size is probably its greatest asset, offering a multitude of opportunities to those who seek them out. "People see it as a campus in the middle of the cornfields," says a student, but actually, "Urbana-Champaign is very alive and there are many student organizations that go out and have contact with the community." Though state budget cuts have pushed tuition up and made freshman classes larger, students still leave with a great education and memories of good times outside the classroom.

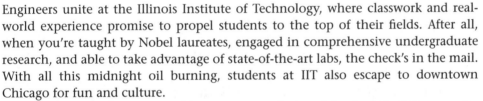

If You Apply To ➢ **Illinois:** Regular admissions: Jan. 1. Financial aid: Mar. 15. Does not guarantee to meet demonstrated need. No campus or alumni interviews. SATs or ACTs: required. Apply to particular schools or programs; music, dance, and theater applicants must audition. Essay question: personal statement.

Illinois Institute of Technology

10 West 33rd Street, Chicago, IL 60616

Forget about cheerleaders, homecoming games, and the other trappings of college life. IIT is about learning technology, getting a degree, and getting a job after graduation. IIT is all engineering with a little bit of architecture thrown in for good measure. If your goal is a technical job in the Chicago area, this is the place.

Engineers unite at the Illinois Institute of Technology, where classwork and real-world experience promise to propel students to the top of their fields. After all, when you're taught by Nobel laureates, engaged in comprehensive undergraduate research, and able to take advantage of state-of-the-art labs, the check's in the mail. With all this midnight oil burning, students at IIT also escape to downtown Chicago for fun and culture.

IIT's home is an urban, 120-acre campus designed by Ludwig Mies van der Rohe, the influential twentieth-century architect who directed the architecture school for twenty years. Founded in 1890, the school is just three miles south of Chicago's Loop, one mile west of Lake Michigan. Miesian-style buildings are adorned by trees and grassy open parks. Comiskey Park, home of the White Sox, is located directly across from the campus. The S.R. Crown Hall, home of IIT's College of Architecture, is considered a landmark, and fund-raising for the restoration of the building is underway. In fact, a major campus renewal is currently in progress including completion of a campus center and plenty of landscaping. A new biomedical research center is also planned for the main campus.

Engineering sets the tone at IIT. All engineering departments are outstanding. Computer engineering is the most popular major, followed by architecture, computer science, chemical engineering, and aerospace engineering. The sciences, physics in particular, are first-rate; high-energy physicist and Nobel laureate Leon Lederman teaches freshman—yes, freshman—physics. Computer literacy is demanded of all students. In addition, all freshmen take an introduction to the professions seminar, which includes discussion of innovation, ethics, teamwork, communication, and leadership. Multidisciplinary, group-based learning is big at IIT. Every student must complete two semester-long inter-profession projects that sharpen real-world skills. New academic options include a major in applied mathematics, biomedical engineering, engineering management, Internet communications, and professional and

Website: www.iit.edu
Location: Urban
Total Enrollment: 6,050
Undergraduates: 1,893
Male/Female: 75/25
SAT Ranges: V 590–690
  M 640–740
ACT Range: 25–30
Financial Aid: 54%
Expense: Pr $
Phi Beta Kappa: No
Applicants: 2,562
Accepted: 62%
Enrolled: 19%
Grad in 6 Years: 54%
Returning Freshmen: 88%
Academics: ✍ ✍ ✍ ½
Social: ☎ ☎
Q of L: ★ ★
Admissions: (312) 567-3025
Email Address:
  admission@iit.edu

Strongest Programs:
  Electrical
  Chemical

(Continued)
Mechanical
Aerospace Engineering
Architecture

technical communications. Weaker offerings include the social sciences and, not surprisingly, the humanities.

The architecture curriculum emphasizes a team approach that mixes third- through fifth-year students under the supervision of a master professor. Guided by an academic reorganization, the physical sciences have been bolstered, grouped together with career-oriented fields like psychology, political science, and computer information systems.

Along with humanities and social science courses, students must fulfill general education requirements that include mathematics, computer science, natural science, and engineering; writing is emphasized across the curriculum. IIT's academic climate is pretty unforgiving, students say. Both the workload and the competition are fierce. "You always have a lot of work to do, especially with homework and labs," says an electrical engineering major. Adds another student: "The courses usually require three hours of time outside class for every lecture hour." Professors always teach their own classes at IIT, while TAs are available for labs and extra help. Most students praise the faculty for their knowledge and tendency to offer as much help as is needed. About three-quarters of all classes have less than twenty-five students.

"Students at IIT study a lot."

In addition to meeting outside of class to go over problem sets or for career direction, IIT students and professors often work side-by-side on research projects. Engineering students have the use of sophisticated labs, and independent research labs in Chicago are also available. The five-year co-op program, another possibility for hands-on experience, helps lead IIT grads into high-paying jobs after graduation. Combined B.S./M.S. degrees in engineering, food safety and technology, and business administration and public administration are available, as is a B.S./J.D. program in law, in addition to a variety of newly designed master's tracks. To round out the combined program offerings, a B.S./M.S. in medical physics and an honors program for students seeking a B.S. in engineering along with an M.D. are offered in conjunction with the Chicago Medical School. There are study-abroad programs that include France, Spain, Scotland, and Germany.

"Students at IIT study a lot," reports a psychology major. A majority of IIT students graduated from public high school in the top fifth of their class. Out-of-state students account for 43 percent of the undergraduate population. Eighteen percent are from foreign countries. African-Americans and Hispanics constitute 15 percent of the student body, and Asian-American students constitute another 15 percent. Students say International Fest is one of the year's most popular events, and IIT offers a multitude of cultural awareness workshops to help avert potential problems. Politics and political correctness don't really stir up campus because "we are so conservative and diverse," says an aerospace engineering major. Perhaps it's not surprising that most IIT students spend much of their time thinking about classwork and future jobs, without much energy or enthusiasm for late-night debates. IIT offers 605 merit scholarships, ranging from $1,000 to a full ride, and seventy-seven athletic scholarships. IIT's ROTC program has grown and matured into one of the finest in the nation and even hosts a popular annual formal ball.

The university provides free shuttle bus service to downtown on weekends. Students take in some culture or hit the town's hip bars and restaurants.

As befits the school's urban location, a chunk of students commute. The 79 percent of students who live in residence halls report that rooms are "kind of small" but comfortable. Six of the seven dorms are coed, with one hall for women only. The McCormick Student Village is popular, and South and North are said to be the nicest dorms. Fowler has the biggest rooms, but no air-conditioning; the rest of the dorms have A/C. Some students live in apartments in the area or on Chicago's North Side; others inhabit one of the eight fraternities, which claim 21 percent of the men. Sororities nab only 3 percent of the women, but many students say the social aspect of

Greek life is a welcome addition to campus. The dining hall has several meal plans and a special vegetarian menu. Breakfast and lunch can also be eaten in the cafeteria at the student union, while the campus pub serves lunch and dinner. Engineers and architects—notorious late-night studiers—have to hit the library early, since it closes at 10:00 P.M. Though students tend to feel safe on campus, the surrounding area is a different story. "It is difficult to get to a doctor, pharmacy, or grocery store and feel safe unless you have a car," says a student.

IIT's six-block campus is contiguous to Chicago's "Gap" community, where historic but rundown homes are being rehabilitated to form one of the city's hottest new urban residential areas. Most students love exploring Chicago; the city skyline is beautiful and is a veritable museum, with buildings designed by the likes of Frank Lloyd Wright, Louis Sullivan, and, of course, van der Rohe. "Chicago is awesome—there is always something to do," a sophomore says, but adds that it can be a bit pricey. Thus, the university provides free shuttle bus service to downtown on weekends. Students take in some culture or hit the town's hip bars and restaurants. Lake Michigan is within jogging distance, and Chinatown is a walk away for lunch or dinner.

"Chicago is awesome—there is always something to do."

For students who stick around on weekends, "you have to create your own social life," a sophomore says. The Union Board offers movies, concerts, and comedians, and the Bog brings in bands on Thursdays and Saturdays. Students can also plan events like a formal on the Odyssey, a sightseeing boat, or an outing to the Chicago Symphony. The eight-day Winter Festival and the Spring Formal are other popular annual events. As for alcohol, the school follows the 21-year-old age law and students say it generally works. In sports-crazy Chicago, IIT athletic teams are not much of a draw. Students praise the men's baseball and swimming teams along with women's volleyball, which compete in the NAIA. The intramural program is strong, but students hate the fact that the facilities close at 5:00 P.M. on weekends. The Olympics occur every year at IIT when Greek Week and Sports Fest kick off, featuring Olympic-type competition for all students.

Shipping off to Chi-town to stare down the mammoth workload at IIT means a lot of work and a fair share of all-nighters. But the payoff is undeniable. Students who take advantage of this small school's ever-improving engineering departments will likely have their pick of careers after graduation. And with the innumerable diversions offered in the Windy City, students at IIT revel in the best of two worlds: a challenging academic climate and a great city to let off all that steam.

Overlaps

University of Illinois–Chicago, MIT, University of Illinois–Urbana-Champaign, Virginia Tech, Depaul

If You Apply To ➤ | **IIT:** Rolling admissions: Mar. 15. Early Action: Jan. 15. Housing: Jul. 1. Does not guarantee to meet demonstrated need. Campus interviews: optional, informational. No alumni interviews. SATs or ACTs: required. SAT IIs: optional. Accepts the Common Application and electronic applications. No essay question.

Illinois Wesleyan University

210 East University, Bloomington, IL 61702-2900

IWU is an up-and-coming small college with a low-key Methodist affiliation. The curriculum is basic liberal arts with additional divisions devoted to fine arts and nursing. Offers an optional three-week term in May that allows students to travel or explore an interest.

Website: www.iwu.edu
Location: Small town
Total Enrollment: 2,064
Undergraduates: 2,064
Male/Female: 44/56
SAT Ranges: V 580–680
M 580–680
ACT Range: 26–30
Financial Aid: 56%
Expense: Pr $ $
Phi Beta Kappa: Yes
Applicants: 2,795
Accepted: 57%
Enrolled: 37%
Grad in 6 Years: 80%
Returning Freshmen: 90%
Academics: ✏️ ✏️ ✏️ ½
Social: ☎ ☎ ☎
Q of L: ★ ★ ★ ★
Admissions: (309) 556-3031
Email Address:
iwuadmit@titan.iwu.edu

Strongest Programs:
Biology/Premed
History/Prelaw
English
Psychology
Mathematics
Music

Illinois Wesleyan University has its sights set on a special breed of student—the kind that isn't afraid to be many things at once. One recent student government leader, who appeared in a talent show juggling basketballs, tennis balls, and a racquet, performed some academic juggling as well with a double major in business administration and economics, tossing in a Spanish minor. Students here are very much encouraged to pursue multiple interests. In fact, 14 percent of the student body has two or more majors while also finding time for sports, music lessons, and other activities.

Founded in 1850, IWU occupies a seventy-two-acre campus site in a northside residential district of Bloomington. The heart of the campus is the central quadrangle, and tree-lined walkways connect buildings that range in style from gray stone Gothic to ultramodern steel and glass. A $23 million library recently opened along with a renovated gym and football stadium. The Hansen Student Center, built in the early 1920s, dazzles with a multi-million dollar makeover, complete with new mechanical equipment.

IWU is a mecca for students who have preprofessional interests, especially those with unusual interest pairings like management and music. The College of Fine Arts houses the three separate schools of music, art, and drama; music is the standout, having turned out opera star Dawn Upshaw. Among the top-notch programs in the College of Liberal Arts are biology, English, chemistry—where faculty members have received a National Science Foundation grant to develop a new curriculum that will merge organic and inorganic topics—and math. Students say the foreign language departments need improvement.

In addition to the usual fall and spring semesters, IWU has an optional, three-week May term. The courses during this term must have one of five features—curricular experimentation, nontraditional approaches to traditional subject matter, student-faculty collaboration, crossing of disciplinary boundaries, or experimental learning through travel, service, or internships. About half the students take a May term class, and about one-fourth take off-campus travel courses. The university's study abroad program offers students the opportunity to travel to countries such as England, Denmark, and Japan. The business administration department offers a Portfolio Management Course, in which students buy and sell orders overseen by a Client Board composed of University Trustees. IWU hosts an annual student research conference that attracts people from all disciplines.

> **"The community around the college is conservative, but the administration is very PC."**

The school's general education requirements emphasize critical thinking, imagination, intellectual independence, social awareness, and sensitivity to others. All first-year students must take a Gateway Colloquium, a topic-based, seminar-style class of fifteen that stresses critical reading, writing, discussion, and analytical skills and introduces students to the intellectual life of the university. Methodism founder John Wesley would no doubt be surprised to hear some of the topics, which include The Social and Political Implications of Motown, Barbie Meets the

Terminator, and Who Wants to Be a Millionaire? Students do jockey for high grades especially since the institution of a plus/minus grading system. The advantages of a focus on undergraduates are summed up by a biology/business major: "The administration emphasizes teaching quality in evaluating faculty, not research dollars and publications." Career counseling is excellent, says a student, adding that in planning your college career, "Academic advisors will give you as much or as little help as you want."

Students at IWU are mostly the homegrown variety, with 86 percent hailing from Illinois. Although IWU began admitting African-American students in 1867, the campus is still predominantly Caucasian. African-Americans account for only 3 percent of the student body, Hispanics 2 percent, and Asian-Americans 3 percent. "Most of the 'hot button' issues have a voice on campus (gays and lesbians, abortion, Christian groups, etc.), but I would not say we are a Madison or Berkeley of the 1960s here. The community around the college is conservative, but the administration is very PC," says an observant student. Active participation in groups like Circle K, the Alpha Phi Omega service fraternity, and Habitat for Humanity provides evidence for the social consciousness of the IWU campus.

Housing is guaranteed for four years, and 84 percent of the students live in the dorms, which receive stellar marks from residents. "The dorms are very comfortable and nice as dorms go. All have been recently renovated and their locations are almost all convenient—no class more than a five-minute walk," says a student. "Better living conditions than I'll have after graduation," quips an English lit

> "IWU continues to emphasize the pursuing of a variety of passions and talents to their fullest within an intellectually and socially nourishing environment."

major. The school recently eliminated single-sex dorms, and students must be twenty-one to live off campus. Campus security is described as "pretty good," and most students acknowledge that they feel safe on campus though common sense is a must.

Thirty-one percent of the men and women go Greek because fraternities and sororities are the focus of IWU's social life. Non-Greeks also use the system for social life, which translates into "lots of parties," according to one senior. A new alcohol policy allows of-age students to have beer and wine in their dorms; underage drinkers must trek off campus in search of a place to score booze. Each fall during Homecoming the fraternities and residence halls compete in the Titan Games to get appropriately psyched. Other annual festivities include the Far Left Carnival, the Gospel Festival, and Earthapalooza (on Earth Day). The Student Senate also sponsors guest speakers; Spike Lee, Bonnie Blair, and Maya Angelou have addressed the students in recent years.

Thanks to the proximity of Illinois State University in nearby Normal, IWU offers more than the typical small-college-town atmosphere. The total area school population of about twenty-five thousand helps to offer students at tiny IWU "the best of both worlds," says a senior. A sophomore says: "There are more restaurants per capita than anywhere else in the country." The best road trips are to Peoria or Urbana-Champaign (home of the University of Illinois), both forty-five minutes away, or to Chicago or St. Louis, each two-and-a-half hours away.

In the IWU arena, baseball and football are well and good, but basketball really gets students going; the men's team placed third in Division III in 2001. Although you wouldn't think of IWU as a jock factory, it was the launching pad for many-a-professional athlete, including longtime basketball star Jack Sikma and Doug Rader, former manager of the California Angels. In 2002, the football team shared the CCIW championship for the second straight year. The men's golf team captured league titles in 2001 and 2002. Women's volleyball and softball also rouse the fans

Although you wouldn't think of IWU as a jock factory, it was the launching pad for many-a-professional athlete, including longtime basketball star Jack Sikma and Doug Rader, former manager of the California Angels.

IWU is a mecca for students with preprofessional interests, especially those with unusual interest pairings like management and music.

Overlaps

University of Illinois, Northwestern, University of Chicago, Washington University (MO), Notre Dame

as does women's basketball. The Fort Natatorium houses a whopping fourteen-lane swimming pool, and the swim team had its share of stars along with the track team. Intramural sports include volleyball, badminton, and coed inner-tube water polo.

One of the better-kept secrets, Wesleyan is at once cozy and diverse, loaded with opportunities for ambitious students. This is a place that, according to one double major, "continues to emphasize the pursuing of a variety of passions and talents to their fullest within an intellectually and socially nourishing environment."

Indiana University

300 North Jordan Avenue, Bloomington, IN 47405

Though men's basketball is IU's most famous program, it may not be its best. That distinction could easily go to the world-renowned music school or to the distinguished foreign language program. IU enrolls three times as many out-of-staters as University of Illinois.

Website: www.indiana.edu
Location: Small city
Total Enrollment: 37,076
Undergraduates: 29,383
Male/Female: 47/53
SAT Ranges: V 480–600
  M 490–620
ACT Range: 21–27
Financial Aid: 62%
Expense: Pub $ $ $
Phi Beta Kappa: Yes
Applicants: 19,896
Accepted: 82%
Enrolled: 42%
Grad in 6 Years: 65%
Returning Freshmen: 88%
Academics: ✍ ✍ ✍ ✍
Social: 🍺 🍺 🍺 🍺
Q of L: ★ ★ ★ ★
Admissions: (812) 855-0661
Email Address:
  iuadmit@indiana.edu

Strongest Programs:
  Accounting
  Business

With more than thirty-five thousand students on its enormous campus, Indiana University is the prototype of the large Midwestern school. Indeed, President Myles Brand has boldly pledged that the school will become "America's New Public University." With strong academics, a thriving social scene, and some of the best sports teams around, this top-notch public institution is a testament to Hoosier determination.

Located in southern Indiana's gently rolling hills, the 1,800-acre campus boasts architecture from Italianate brick to collegiate Gothic limestone to the distinctive style of world-famous architect I.M. Pei. Other unique campus features include fountains, gargoyles, an arboretum of more than 450 trees and shrubs surrounding two reflecting pools, a limestone gazebo, and the Jordan River, a pretty creek that runs alongside a shaded path. The most recent campus addition is the 117,000-square-foot Theatre/Neal-Marshall Education Center. The new facility will house the African-American Cultural Center as well as new research studios, classrooms, and offices for the Department of Theatre and the Neal-Marshall Education Center.

IU's ten schools offer many majors and minors, cross-disciplinary study, an individually designed curriculum, intense honors and research programs, and yearlong study in twenty-seven countries (and sixteen languages). The highly touted business school, with its respected international studies component, is second only to arts and sciences in popularity. The internationally known Kinsey Institute for the Study of Human Sexual Behavior is housed on IU's campus, and the music school is tops in its field, setting the tone for much of the campus. Many of the communications programs have been merged into the new communications and culture department, and the university has also added a gender studies program, a new degree program in Environmental Science, and several new minors in international studies, telecommunications, sociology, criminal justice, chemistry, Russian and East European studies. IU has also introduced a new two-year online MBA program known as "Kelley Direct." Students don't complain about many departmental weaknesses but note that large introductory lectures, especially in the sciences, are a hazard of IU's size. The GradPact program guarantees that Indiana will pay all fees if a qualifying student has to stay on campus for more than four years. "IU is a four-year institution," says one economics major. "If a student takes longer than that, they probably have three majors, changed their majors, or are bad planners." Despite its size, Indiana prides itself on its liberal arts education—freshmen are admitted not to preprofessional schools but to the "university division." Majors are declared after one or two years, and the university discourages premature specialization. IU's communications and culture department advances the study of communication as a cultural practice, while the Environmental Science Joint Program is an undergraduate degree program that specifically considers the environment as a scientific entity.

(Continued)
Chemistry
Journalism/Communications
Languages
Music
Optometry
Fine Arts

General education requirements vary from school to school but usually include math, science, arts and humanities, social and behavioral sciences, English and writing, culture, and a foreign language. Students describe the academic climate as rigorous but not cut-throat. "With four thousand different courses per semester, a variety of intensity levels exist," says a marketing major. "There is a balance with room for both competitive overachievers and laid-back, carefree individuals." Students say they regularly share ideas with each other, and group projects are commonplace. Faculty members bring their research results directly to students, and some profs bring undergrads into their labs to assist with ongoing projects. Students say the quality of teaching is excellent. "The professors here are remarkable,"

"There is a balance with room for both competitive overachievers and laid-back, carefree individuals."

says an art history/telecommunications major. "They not only care about their field of study, they care about their students." As for advising, many students seem surprised by the personal attention they receive at such a large university, but they soon learn that many available resources are helpful to those students who seek them out. Some students complain of confusing bureaucracies and problems parking.

Seventy percent of IU students are from in-state, while the remainder hail from every state and more than one hundred foreign countries. Out-of-staters face much more rigorous minimum admissions standards, including rank in the top quarter of their high-school class and SAT scores in the 1050 to 1100 range. African-Americans comprise 4 percent of the student body, Hispanics 2 percent, and Asian-Americans 3 percent. By and large, students do not seem particularity concerned with social and political issues.

The school's rolling admissions system enables students to know their fate only a month after their application is filed. And while IU does not guarantee to meet the full demonstrated need of every admit, it admits on a need-blind basis and offers the Early Approximate Student Eligibility (EASE) program to help prospective freshmen gauge how much financial aid they will get. Merit scholarships are awarded to qualified students; applicants must be in the top 10 percent of their graduating class and have a minimum combined SAT score of 1200. There is also an "NCAA maximum" program of roughly 236 full athletic scholarships encompassing ten men's sports and nine women's.

Housing ranges from Gothic quads (coed by building) to thirteen-floor high-rises (coed by floor or unit, except for one all-women dorm), and halls are considered "clean and comfortable." One student explains the housing situation this way: "All dorms have laundry facilities, cafeterias, computer clusters, and undergraduate advisors, and some even have special amenities like language-speaking floors." A junior adds, "There is no trouble getting a room, but preference of dorm may be harder." Academic floors (requiring a GPA of 3.1 or better) are popular with more serious students who are not interested in the intense nightlife in the high-rises. Housing is guaranteed to all incoming freshmen, and those who stay in the university

The GradPact program guarantees that Indiana will pay all fees if a qualifying student has to stay on campus for more than four years.

housing system won't ever face rent increases. Based on results from a student survey, some dining halls have been modernized to resemble mall food courts with outlets offering international and healthful menus sprinkled among the fast-food options. Alcohol is prohibited in the dorms, which may explain why 61 percent of the student body lives off campus. Most off-campus residents choose apartments or small wooden houses with big front porches within walking distance of the campus or of the IU bus system.

Although campus organizations host numerous events, the most active on-campus groups, in terms of social life, seem to be the Greeks. About 16 percent of IU men and 16 percent of IU women are in the Greek system, and membership is a status symbol. Some complain of a polarized atmosphere. "There is a large separation between the Greek community and the rest of the social body," says a senior. Every fall there is a thirty-six-hour Dance Marathon to raise money for Riley's Children's Hospital in Indianapolis. The Little 500 bike race, which was modeled after the Indianapolis 500, is one of the most highly attended events of the year at Indiana. With concerts, ballets, recitals, and festivals right on campus, students are not lacking for things to keep them busy. The IU student union is the largest in the nation, and the range of extracurricular organizations is also impressive. The Office of Diversity Programs, Committee on Multicultural Understanding, and Students Organized Against Racism are a few more ways students can make a difference on campus. "Bloomington is a great, small college town," says one senior. "There are opportunities to get

"Bloomington is a great, small college town."

involved in the community if you seek them out." There are many excellent bars, shops, and restaurants, including one of the few Tibetan restaurants in the country. Locally, the area offers some impressive rock quarries (often used as illegal but refreshing swimming pools), miles of public forests, and three nearby lakes. Spelunkers will find heaven underground in the many nearby caves. Chicago, Cincinnati, Indianapolis, St. Louis, and even New Orleans are popular road trips.

Intramurals pale in comparison with varsity athletics here; basketball is an established religion in the state of Indiana. The Hoosiers basketball program is entering a new era now that the combative and controversial coach Bobby Knight has finally been fired. Although students and faculty are all eligible for tickets, they've got to get requests in early—and even those lucky enough to get tickets don't count on going to more than a quarter of home games. In 1998 and 1999, Indiana Hoosiers soccer team won back-to-back NCAA championships. In recent years, women's golf and women's tennis have both claimed at least a share of the Big Ten championship, and even the football team is beginning to draw red and white crowds. Recently, women's water polo has attained varsity status. Purdue is IU's traditional athletic rival, and teams play for the Old Oaken Bucket, found on a farm in southern Indiana in 1925 and alleged to have been used during the Civil War.

Most students feel the education they get at IU is worth every penny. They come away from Bloomington with knowledge, lifelong friends, and a new world view. "Indiana University offers so much more than just academics," says an accounting major. "You really can do it all here."

If You Apply To ➤

Indiana: Admissions deadlines: Feb. 1, fall; Nov. 1, spring. Campus interviews: recommended, informational. No alumni interviews. SATs or ACTs: required. SAT IIs: optional. No essay question.

University of Iowa

107 Calvin Hall, Iowa City, IA 52242-1396

A bargain compared to other Big Ten schools such as Michigan, Wisconsin, and Illinois. Iowa is world-famous for its creative writing program and Writers' Workshop. Other areas of strength include health sciences, business, and the arts. Future scientists should check out the Research Scholars Program.

At first glance, Iowa might seem to be a standard-issue Midwestern school. But beneath the bland exterior of fields and corn lies one of the most dynamic schools in the country—and one of the best buys to boot. Iowa has long been a major player in the creative worlds, particularly writing, and its small-town atmosphere is just one of many reasons students nationwide flock to this "budget Ivy League."

The 1,880-acre campus, located in the rolling hills of the Iowa River valley, is bisected by the Iowa River and merges with downtown Iowa City. Among the ninety primary buildings is Old Capitol, the first capitol of Iowa, a national historic landmark, and the symbol of the university. The primary architectural style of the campus buildings is Greek Revival and Modern. The newly renovated Seamens Center for the Engineering Arts and Sciences opened in the summer of 2000 along with a dining facility with nine meal stations. The campus is changing face with many new buildings, including a $47 million medical research facility and $37 million recreation complex.

Iowa has a long tradition in creative arts. It was one of the first universities to award graduate degrees for creative work and is also the home of the first Writers' Workshop. The school also prides itself on its International Writing Program, which brings a wide array of prominent authors to the campus. "The English department is stellar," raves one English major. "It's possibly the best in the country—at least for creative writing." Iowa's on-campus hospital is one of the largest teaching hospitals in the United States. The Health Sciences Center, affiliated with the hospital, encompasses five colleges: medicine, dentistry, pharmacy, nursing, and public health. Undergraduates benefit from the strong health center

> **"The English department is stellar. It's possibly the best in the country—at least for creative writing."**

course offerings in related health professions, such as physician's assistant or medical technician. Combined degree programs, which permit students to earn degrees across colleges, exist between liberal arts and a choice of the following: business administration, engineering, nursing, and the College of Medicine.

The University Honors Program provides special academic, cultural, and social opportunities to outstanding students in the Colleges of Business Administration, Education, Engineering, Liberal Arts and Sciences, Nursing, and Pharmacy. Honor students may also participate in the Research Scholars Program, which allows them to collaborate with faculty members on research projects. Iowa's study-abroad program gives students a chance to travel to forty-five different countries. Speech pathology, psychology, and fine arts programs are popular, while students report that the foreign language department is weak due to limited majors and low enrollment. Agriculture, veterinary medicine, forestry, architecture, and animal science are not offered at Iowa but are taught at its sister institution, Iowa State.

Each of the undergraduate colleges has its own general education requirements. Liberal arts students must take courses in rhetoric, natural science, social sciences, foreign language, interpretation of literature, historical perspectives, humanities, and quantitative or formal reasoning. Distributed general education, including

Website: www.uiowa.edu
Location: Small city
Total Enrollment: 28,768
Undergraduates: 19,603
Male/Female: 45/55
SAT Ranges: V 530–650
   M 540–670
ACT Range: 22–27
Financial Aid: 40%
Expense: Pub $ $
Phi Beta Kappa: Yes
Applicants: 11,836
Accepted: 85%
Enrolled: 40%
Grad in 6 Years: 65%
Returning Freshmen: 82%
Academics: ✍ ✍ ✍ ✍
Social: ☎ ☎ ☎
Q of L: ★ ★ ★
Admissions: (319) 335-3847
Email Address:
   admissions@uiowa.edu

Strongest Programs:
   Creative Writing
   Theater Arts
   Dance
   Music
   Health Sciences and
      Health Care
   Business
   Physics
   Psychology

courses in cultural diversity, foreign civilization and culture, and physical education, are also required. Iowa's academic climate is described by the students as moderately competitive and differing by major. "There is always a pack of students gunning for the number one spot in the class," says one chemistry major. "The only way to get on top and stay on top is to do your work and not slack off." Most classes have less than fifty students, although some introductory courses have more. Registration is done by computer, so the process is fairly easy. The University of Iowa's Four-Year Graduation Plan guarantees that students who fulfill certain requirements will not have their graduation

"Full professors have taught nearly every course I have taken, from freshman year up."

delayed by unavailability of a needed course. Students give their professors high marks. "Overall, the quality of the teaching has been terrific," says one biology major. "Full professors have taught nearly every course I have taken, from freshman year up." There are often smaller sessions led by graduate students as a way to make the classroom experience more accessible. Academic advising gets some hot and cold remarks, but according to one senior, "the career development program is great."

Sixty-eight percent of the undergraduates hail from Iowa with most of the rest coming from contiguous states, especially Illinois. African-Americans, Hispanics, and Asian-Americans account for about 7 percent of the student body; but, as the administration points out, the state of Iowa has only 4 percent minority population. Yet students say the campus is extremely tolerant and that almost anyone can find their niche at Iowa. Besides the athletic scholarships available in all sports, there are 880 other scholarships available with stipends ranging from $200 to $7,000. The Roy J. Carver Scholarships are awarded to eighty-two students who have overcome social or psychological barriers; it is one of the first awards that was bestowed on a former homeless man. Some students say they have been able to fund their entire education through scholarships. However, the school does not guarantee to meet the demonstrated financial need of every admit.

Students say that campus residence halls are clean but very sociable and therefore not very quiet. All are coed by floor or wing. Some students say that "campus housing is great, and very popular," while others think the dorms are "as satisfactory as dorms can be." A few students get sloughed off to temporary housing, so it

"Downtown Iowa city, which is practically in the center of campus, is bursting with nightlife even during the week."

is important to apply early. There are many praises for the custodial staff that keeps the buildings clean. Don't get too excited, though; your own room is up to you! Only 29 percent of the students live in university housing, and more than half live in apartments or houses that are adjacent to the campus. "Off-campus housing is popular but the high rents are often an issue," says one student. Each dorm has its own dining hall, and the food is described as "predictable and uninspired." The student union, improved by a $10 million renovation, includes a pastry and coffee shop, two cafeterias, and the State Room Restaurant.

Eleven percent of the men and 12 percent of women belong to fraternities and sororities, and these groups tend to play less of a role in the social life than they do elsewhere. "Social life at the University of Iowa is a very big part of the draw for many students," says one theatre arts major. "Downtown Iowa City, which is practically in the center of campus, is bursting with nightlife even during the week." There are two university theaters right on campus and many affordable cultural events take place at Hancher Auditorium. "The social life revolves around bars and movie theaters in town," says a sophomore. The Union Bar and Grill, Mickey's, Sports Column, and George's are all popular hangouts with students. The school

The school prides itself on its International Writing Program, which brings a wide array of prominent authors to the campus.

Although Iowa City is located in a semirural area, it still has a vast array of bars, dance clubs, restaurants, and other social activities.

officially follows the state policy regarding alcohol; the legal drinking age is twenty-one. But one senior says underage drinking is prevalent.

Although Iowa City is located in a semirural area, it still has a vast array of bars, dance clubs, restaurants, and other social activities. Yet for those who tire of the local scene, Chicago, Kansas City, or St. Louis are all within six hours by car, a short road trip by Midwestern standards. Skiing is another hour away in Minnesota. Riverfest, held at the Iowa Memorial Union and on the banks of the Iowa River, is a weeklong, all-campus event celebrating the long-awaited spring. Another annual event the students look forward to is the Iowa City Jazz Festival.

As for sports, there's that big football stadium, which now has the team it deserves. Iowa has become a national power and is a regular on New Year's Day bowl games. Hawkeye fans are serious about their team. But if you want a real power-house, look no further than the Hawkeye wrestling team, a perennial national champion. Both basketball teams and the softball teams have also claimed recent titles.

The University of Iowa not only boasts a beautiful campus with many improvements on the way, it offers students a seemingly endless range of academic programs, an abundance of social activities, and a friendly, welcoming climate. With its combination of quality academics, mammoth resources, renowned specialty programs, and extensive research opportunities, this Midwest school is anything but faceless.

If You Apply To ➢

Iowa: Rolling admissions. Does not guarantee to meet demonstrated need. No campus or alumni interviews. SATs or ACTs: required. SAT IIs: optional. Accepts electronic applications. No essay question. Apply to particular schools or programs.

Iowa State University

100 Alumni Hall, Ames, IA 50011

Visit ISU and you'll see why they call it Silo Tech. Agriculture and engineering are the twin pillars of the curriculum, and the university is a magnet for prevets. Ames is a small city and ISU must still endure barbs from certain snobby people in Iowa City.

Love for Iowa State University runs as deep as its Midwestern roots. Strong programs in engineering, business, and agriculture attract students from around the globe. The close-knit, small-town atmosphere fostered at this school of nearly twenty-eight thousand keeps them here.

The university has lavished attention on its park-like campus, located on a 1,984-acre tract in the middle of Ames, population 50,000. The campus, which boasts a combination of dignified old buildings and award-winning new ones, is a landmark of landscape design with numerous shady quadrangles with floral plantings and artwork that create a garden-like quality. History and tradition prevail, from the campanile, which serenades the campus with its carillon bells, to the huge public art collection including sculptures by Danish artist Christian Petersen. Howe Hall, the new home to aerospace engineering, boasts a virtual reality application center and a six-sided virtual reality cave. On-campus apartments and suites, the Palmer Development School, and an honors building are other recent additions to the campus. Much of the campus is closed to cars, largely for the benefit of walking,

Website: www.iastate.edu
Location: Small city
Total Enrollment: 27,823
Undergraduates: 23,060
Male/Female: 55/45
SAT Ranges: V 510–660
  M 540–690
ACT Range: 22–27
Financial Aid: 66%
Expense: Pub $ $
Phi Beta Kappa: Yes
Applicants: 10,658
Accepted: 90%
Enrolled: 44%

(Continued)

Grad in 6 Years: 64%
Returning Freshmen: 84%
Academics: ✎ ✎ ✎
Social: ☎ ☎ ☎
Q of L: ★ ★ ★
Admissions: (515) 294-5838
Email Address:
admissions@iastate.edu

Strongest Programs:
Engineering
Agriculture
Design
Veterinary Medicine

There's a plethora of new programs, ranging from technical communications to communication studies to sustainable agriculture.

Much of the campus is closed to cars, largely for the benefit of walking, bicycling, and in-line skating students as well as the swans (named Sir Lancelot and Lady Elaine) and the ducks who reside on Lake LaVerne.

bicycling, and in-line skating students as well as the swans (named Sir Lancelot and Lady Elaine) and the ducks who reside on Lake LaVerne.

When Iowa State opened in 1869 as a land-grant university, agriculture and engineering ruled the academic roost. These days, though, the liberal arts are at least as popular, and the College of Liberal Arts and Sciences is the largest of ISU's nine colleges. Among the university's one hundred-plus majors, the College of Agriculture still fields outstanding programs in animal science, agriculture technology, agribusiness, and agronomy. Other colleges include business, design, education, veterinary medicine, family and consumer sciences (formerly home economics), and the graduate college. There's a plethora of new programs, ranging from technical communications to communication studies to sustainable agriculture. Students find the academic climate competitive, but that can vary by program.

All undergraduates must take two semesters of English composition freshman year and demonstrate proficiency in English prior to graduation. Other general education requirements vary by college and focus on gaining breadth in the natural and social sciences, but everyone takes a half-credit course on the use of the library and a one-credit course on skills such as time management and test-taking. A modem network allows students to link their personal computers with the university system, and hundreds of Iowa State pages now inhabit the World Wide Web.

Students can also use the AccessPlus system of electronic kiosks sprinkled around campus to check the status of their university bill or financial aid package, print an unofficial transcript, or get their current schedules. An honors program enrolls nearly three hundred outstanding freshmen each year, many of whom live in honors housing. A summer language program in France, Germany, and Spain is one of fifty programs that students can choose from for work or study in thirty-five countries worldwide.

"We have some world class profs here who are doing important research."

Despite the university's size, professors teach most classes with the exception of some freshman English options. Students learn from faculty stars like Pulitzer Prize-winning author Jane Smiley. "We have some world class profs here who are doing important research," one senior says. A Spanish student adds the teaching is "undoubtedly excellent." Academic and career counseling draw praise, too, and advisors are "always readily available" to help students.

Seventy-seven percent of ISU's students are Iowans, though all fifty states and 118 countries are represented in the student body. Foreign students comprise another 5 percent of the student body. Iowa State was the first coed land-grant institution, but attracting minorities has proven more difficult: minority students account for just 12 percent of the student body. "We have a lot of farmers and small-town Iowans," says a senior. "This is a pretty white campus." To help remedy this situation, ISU launched a $25 million campaign aimed at increasing the number of scholarships available for minority students, student athletes, and student leaders. Freshman orientation has come to include the topics of race relations and cultural diversity, and entering frosh participate in learning teams through which groups of students with similar interests and career goals take courses together and live in the same dorms during their first year. In addition to need-based financial aid and a variety of athletic scholarships, many merit awards are available, ranging from $250 to $20,000.

Thirty-six percent of undergrads live in on-campus residence halls and apartments. Single-sex and coed dorms are available, and rooms are said to be comfortable and well maintained. One student indicates that the janitors throw a picnic every spring. "There is a great community. Each hall is divided into houses and they do activities and stuff together," says one senior. Special floors are available for international students, teetotalers, and particularly studious undergraduates; separate housing is available for married students. But "if students apply late and turn in their housing info late, they may have to live in the den of a dorm floor for a few days until housing is found for them." Each year, the food service sponsors a Favorites from Home contest, in which recipes entered by students are selected and adapted to feed thousands. Many upperclassmen live off campus, and Greek life claims 12 percent of men and 11 percent of women.

Iowa State is not simply located in Ames—in many respects it is Ames. "Ames has lots of entertainment and affordable options for students," says a junior. Des Moines, the state capital, is about 30 minutes away, and Iowa City, Minneapolis, and Chicago are other easy and enjoyable road trips. Socializing tends to stay on campus, with big-name bands playing at Hilton Coliseum and parties always rocking. The campus is supposedly dry, but according to one sophomore most older students will buy alcohol for minors. The big event every spring is a two-day campus festival called VEISHEA (an acronym for ISU's original five colleges), which features parades, exhibitions, food, and a fun-run. Another tradition is campaniling, where students must kiss under the campanile at the stroke of midnight to be considered "true" coeds. And students have learned not to walk over the Zodiac sign in the Memorial Union—it brings bad luck.

> **"Ames has a lot of entertainment and affordable options for students."**

In sports, basketball is king; the men's and women's teams are usual invitees to the NCAA tournament; both won Big XII championships in 2000 and 2001. The football team earned a post-season bowl bid, playing Boise State in the Humanitarian Bowl. The women's gymnastic team won the conference championship in 2000. An astounding 80 percent of the students participate in one of the largest intramural sports programs in the nation.

Students agree Iowa State has something for just about everyone, from farmers to globetrotters. Cows and computers seem to coexist happily at Iowa State, an institute founded to train future farmers that now churns out top-notch engineers experienced in the latest virtual reality and online technologies.

> *Each year, the food service sponsors a Favorites from Home contest, in which recipes entered by students are selected and adapted to feed thousands.*

Overlaps

University of Iowa, University of Northern Iowa, University of Illinois, University of Nebraska, University of Minnesota

---

If You Apply To ➤

Iowa State: Rolling admissions. Admissions: Aug. 1. Financial aid: March 1. Guarantees to meet demonstrated need. SATs or ACTs: required. No SAT IIs. Accepts electronic application. No essay question.

Ithaca College

953 Danby Road, Ithaca, NY 14850-7020

Students looking at Ithaca also apply to BU, Syracuse, and NYU. The common thread? Outstanding programs in the arts and media. Students also clamor to get into physical therapy. (Watch the November 1 deadline.) Cross-town neighbor Cornell adds curricular and social opportunities.

Just over the hill, in upstate New York, sits Ithaca: a small college with much to boast about. Known for its strong programs in the arts—including drama, television and film, and music—Ithaca emphasizes quality over quantity. This drive to innovate results partly from its desire to shine beyond the shadow of its much larger Ivy League neighbor, Cornell University. Its offerings mirror that of a large university,

Website: www.ithaca.edu
Location: Small town
Total Enrollment: 6,483
Undergraduates: 6,209

Male/Female: 45/55
SAT Ranges: V 540–630
  M 540–630
Financial Aid: 64%
Expense: Pr $ $
Phi Beta Kappa: No
Applicants: 10,505
Accepted: 66%
Enrolled: 25%
Grad in 6 Years: 72%
Returning Freshmen: 85%
Academics: 🖉 🖉 🖉
Social: 🏆 🏆 🏆 🏆 🏆
Q of L: ★ ★ ★
Admissions: (607) 274-3124
Email Address:
  admission@ithaca.edu

Strongest Programs:
  Music
  Physical Therapy
  Theater
  Communications
  Natural Sciences
  Psychology

The majority of Ithaca's classes are small—nearly three-quarters have twenty-five or fewer students.

but the school maintains small classes and "hands-on" learning more commonly found at small colleges.

Ithaca College is located in the center of the Finger Lakes region, on a six hundred-acre plot with spectacular views overlooking the city of Ithaca. None of the streamlined, modern campus buildings are more than a few decades old, since the college moved to its present location in the 1960s. Many believe the campus is one of the country's most beautiful, including author Tom Wolfe, who dubbed the school "the emerald eminence at the fingertip of Lake Cayuga." Newest campus additions include the Center for Health Sciences, a seven thousand-square-foot fitness center, and the Clinton B. Ford Observatory.

Through its five schools—music, communications, business, health sciences and human performance, and humanities and sciences—Ithaca offers more than one hundred majors and more than fifty minors. The newest include majors in writing, gerontology, health policies, and health sciences. With its prominent faculty and many opportunities for student performance, the college's reputation for music education and performance are almost unparalleled. The Park School of Communications has its own elaborate $12 million facility. The school has grown up alongside the broadcast industry and is known for programs in radio and TV production (the most popular major) and cinema and photography. The business school has grown rapidly over the past decade; all students now matriculate into the business administration major and declare one of eight concentrations after the first or second year.

In the School of Health Sciences and Human Performance, the physical therapy program is a national drawing card and boasts nearly a 100 percent placement rate; five-year B.S./M.S. programs in physical and occupational therapy are available in conjunction with the University of Rochester. Ithaca also offers a dual teacher certification program in health and physical education and majors in therapeutic recreation and environmental studies. In addition, Ithaca boasts one of the nation's most complete sports studies programs, with majors including exercise science, rehabilitation, athletic training, sports management, and sports communication.

Though not the most well known, with more than 2,200 students, Humanities and Sciences is the largest school on Ithaca's campus. The school has refocused its general education program around human communities, and students now explore how communities form, function, and express meaning. The program emphasizes global and historical perspectives through courses in self and society; science, mathematics, and formal reasoning; and human expression. Among the strongest of nineteen humanities and sciences departments are the natural sciences, which offer research and even publishing opportunities for undergraduates. The $23 million science building boasts state-of-the-art teaching and research facilities for biology, chemistry, and physics. To enhance student-faculty interaction, Ithaca redesigned Williams Hall, adding new computers and lab facilities for the departments of mathematics, computer science, and psychology. Theater arts offers solid acting and technical production programs, but the English and foreign language programs need work, students say. Health services administration, religious studies, audiology, and speech communications programs are no longer accepting new students.

> **"Professors always teach their own classes and are there for students if we need help."**

All Humanities and Sciences students are required to take writing and statistical analysis courses; H&S also offers an optional freshman seminar combining rigorous study of a selected subject with transition-to-college topics such as personal, social, and academic responsibility. Topics include Mathematical Art with Computers and Who Are We? What Do We Think? Applied psychology and telecommunications management are popular majors that cross disciplinary lines. Ithaca students can go to Cornell to take courses not offered on their campus, and vice versa. Other off-campus opportunities include internships and foreign-study programs in more than fifty countries in all corners of the world, including the Ithaca College London Center and internships in Washington, D.C., and Los Angeles.

The majority of Ithaca's classes are small—nearly three-quarters have twenty-five or fewer students—and praise for professors abounds. Students appear especially impressed by the fact that all classes (even labs) are taught by full professors, not TAs. "Professors always teach their own classes and are there for students if we need help," says a sophomore.

A senior describes the student body as "laid back and friendly." Students generally hail from the Northeast with nearly half from New York and most from middle- to upper-middle-class backgrounds. The school has a large, well-organized Jewish community, but the African-American, Hispanic, and Asian-American populations are small, combining for less than 10 percent of the student body. Students say the campus is becoming more diverse, and the administration's focus of late has been unity, with Unity Relays and Unity Day bringing together students and faculty from all walks of campus life. The new Center for the Study of Culture, Race, and Ethnicity offers academic courses and extracurricular activities. And the self-motivated thrive here. Nearly 1,600 merit scholarships are awarded each year, ranging from $3,000 to a full ride. There are currently no athletic scholarships offered.

> **"People truly seem to enjoy their four years here because of all the people you meet, outdoor activities, clubs, and organizations available to us."**

While there may be a figurative place for everyone at Ithaca, only 70 percent find a place to hang their hat on campus. Students cite the housing situation as a major campus issue. Though they are guaranteed space in the residence halls, arriving freshmen can find themselves squeezed into triples that used to be doubles or packed into a common-room lounge. But don't despair: many lounges have TVs, fireplaces, and terraces, and overcrowding is usually remedied by Thanksgiving, students report. Dorm rooms are comfortable and well maintained. By junior year, many students move off campus.

Since "Ithaca is gorges," there are plenty of opportunities to get out of those dorm rooms for hiking, biking, sledding, and skiing. Officially, Ithaca is a dry campus. On weekends, Ithaca students take advantage of an array of college-oriented activities on campus, in the town of Ithaca, and at next-door neighbor Cornell. "With Cornell on the other hill, it allows the students a ton of access to social life, educational experiences, and cultural development," a senior says. Students frequent restaurants, movies, clubs, and festivals downtown, or may road-trip to Cortland, Syracuse, and Binghamton, New York (each an hour away, with plenty of malls), or Philadelphia, Washington, D.C., New York City, or Canada, less than six hours' drive. Ithaca's Greek scene is low key, with three professional music frats and one social service sorority; only about 2 percent of men and women each join the organizations. Homecoming is an occasion for revelry as is the not-too-esoteric tradition of Terrace mudslides. All Ithacans also look forward to the annual Rocktoberfest, which features games, dunking booths, and revelry.

On the sports scene, the men's wrestling team is competitive nationally and football and baseball are competitive. Students really get into Ithaca's football rivalry against Cortland State, known as the "Cortaca Jug" match (or the Division III Super Bowl). Women's softball won the 2002 National Division III Championship. Sailing is a favorite warm-weather activity, and horseback riding is also available.

Ithaca College students are segregated by academic interest from day one due to the existence of five separate schools, but their diverse qualities and involvement on campus makes them unique. Overall, students at Ithaca seem to be a satisfied

Ithaca boasts one of the nation's most complete sports studies programs, with majors including exercise science, rehabilitation, athletic training, sports management, and sports communication.

Overlaps

Syracuse, NYU, Boston University, University of Massachusetts, Northeastern bunch, almost smug about their school's smallness and setting. "People truly seem to enjoy their four years here because of all the people you meet, outdoor activities, clubs, and organizations available to us," brags a junior.

James Madison University

Harrisonburg, VA 22807

JMU has carved a comfortable niche among Virginia's superb public universities. With more undergraduates than UVA and more than double the number at William and Mary, Madison is strong in preprofessional fields such as business, health professions, and education.

Website: www.jmu.edu
Location: Small town
Total Enrollment: 15,562
Undergraduates: 14,590
Male/Female: 42/58
SAT Ranges: V 540–620
   M 540–630
Financial Aid: 32%
Expense: Pub $ $
Phi Beta Kappa: No
Applicants: 14,114
Accepted: 64%
Enrolled: 36%
Grad in 6 Years: 80%
Returning Freshmen: 90%
Academics: ✑ ✑ ✑
Social: 🐾 🐾 🐾 🐾
Q of L: ★ ★ ★ ★
Admissions: (540) 568-5681
Email Address:
   gotojmu@jmu.edu

Strongest Programs:
   Science
   Integrated Science and
      Technology
   Health Professions
   Education
   Business

James Madison University means business. Business programs continue to garner national attention and attract top-notch students from coast to coast. The university is growing at a phenomenal rate, causing some to feel growing pains, but students at this laid-back Southern university have much to cheer about, including an emphasis on undergraduate teaching and close student-faculty interaction. Indeed, at JMU it's not simply "business as usual."

JMU is in the heart of the Shenandoah Valley, two hours from Washington, D.C., and Richmond, Virginia. Three distinct types of architecture make up the campus. The buildings on Front campus have red-tile roofs and are constructed of a distinctive limestone block known as bluestone. Newer buildings on the back campus are more modern and made of red brick. The third type features modern, beige buildings at the recently constructed College of Integrated Science and Technology campus. The university straddles Interstate 81, an outlet to several major East Coast cities. Recent construction includes a health and human services building, and numerous facilities are getting upgrades. A $170 million bond issued from the state will bring a new physics and chemistry building, library, and arts center to campus, along with renovations to historical buildings.

> "I think that the teachers here are excellent."

James Madison University is recognized nationally for programs within the business major; social sciences and education are also strong. The most popular majors at JMU are marketing, psychology, and integrated science and technology. The sciences are also strong bets at JMU, and undergraduates in the biology department have even employed recombinant DNA technology to help develop organisms that produce biodegradable plastics. Also worth noting is the geology and geography departments' summer geology field camp for undergraduates. Although the math department is cited as weak, its development of a mathematical modeling laboratory is used by select undergrads to solve real-world applied math problems. "The academic climate is rather competitive. The courses are very rigorous and challenging," a senior warns. Programs in the health professions, business, information technology, integrated science and technology, and science have all been expanded, and the school has placed a new focus on teacher education, especially science teacher education.

The General Education Program requires each student to take courses in several clusters, including Skills for the 21st Century, Arts and Humanities, the Natural World, Social and Cultural Processes, and Individuals in the Human Community. The idea is to offer students a basis for life-long learning by challenging them to become active in their own education and to explore the foundations of knowledge. Freshmen are offered a variety of programs to help smooth their transition into the university. Freshmen Adventures, held before and after the beginning of the freshman year, gives students an opportunity to meet while hiking, navigating, and looking forward to the coming term.

As Madison's enrollment has now exceeded fifteen thousand, the school is suffering some growing pains, and parking—or rather the lack of space for parking—is a constant complaint, although a new five hundred-vehicle parking deck has eased the situation. With undergraduates far outnumbering grad students, JMU's main mission is undergraduate teaching. "I think that the teachers here are excellent," says one student. "They are very cooperative and are willing to work with you." Students say that faculty advising can be hit or miss. But if you are willing to find the time, some students say that even weekly meetings with these gurus are possible. Those looking for a more intense intellectual experience can check out the honors program, which offers small classes and opportunities for independent study. Many upper-level programs encourage undergraduate participation with faculty research, another plus of this school. If JMU gets a little confining, students may opt for a semester in London, Paris, Florence, Salamanca, and Martinique.

The sciences are strong bets at JMU, and undergraduates in the biology department have even employed recombinant DNA technology to help develop organisms that produce biodegradable plastics.

"I loved living on campus my first two years, and I miss it now."

Don't look for a lot of diversity among fellow students at JMU. Ninety-five percent attended public high school, and 71 percent are from Virginia. In fact, there's a general effort to keep out-of-state enrollment under thirty percent at JMU. African-Americans account for just 4 percent of the student body, and Hispanics and Asian-Americans combine for another 6 percent. A public administration major says the school is "not a diverse campus compared to rival universities." JMU offers 174 merit scholarships ranging from $400 to $2,000 and 365 athletic scholarships for men and women in a variety of sports.

Forty-one percent of the students live in the dorms, which run the gamut from the old high-ceiling variety to newer, air-conditioned models that come complete with carpet and a fitness center in the building. "I loved living on campus my first two years, and I miss it now," says a junior. While most upperclassmen opt to move off campus to nearby apartments or houses, they still feel like part of the campus community. And "anyone with twelve or more credit hours is guaranteed housing," one student notes. Students rave about the meal plan, which has a growing number of options to choose from including a salad bar and low-calorie meals.

Programs in the health professions, business, information technology, integrated science and technology, and science have all been expanded, and the school has placed a new focus on teacher education, especially science teacher education.

And what do students do for a good time? "Life at JMU is always exciting. When students have free time, there is always a play, concert, sporting event, or party to attend," says a student. A classmate agrees: "Many Greeks hold parties on JMU's Greek row, but you do not have to be Greek to have fun!" Much of the social life is off campus, including in nearby apartment complexes. Although the school does not allow underage drinking on campus, "minors can find ways to drink" and have no problem getting served off campus. The Greek system attracts 11 percent of the men and 13 percent of the women, though most agree that going Greek is by no means mandatory. Greeks and independents alike participate in JMU's many annual rites, including Homecoming and Christmas on the Quad. As for road trips, the favorite destination seems to be the University of Virginia, almost an hour's

"When students have free time, there is always a play, concert, sporting event, or party to attend"

drive to the south. Equally enticing, however, are the many natural delights of the Shenandoah Valley, including hiking, camping, and even skiing, all nearby. Most students find local Harrisonburg a friendly Southern town, though it doesn't necessarily embrace the college. Says one senior media arts and design major, "Harrisonburg is a small town, but has an incredible array of restaurants and shopping spots."

The fans here are known as the Electric Zoo and are enthusiastic about their sports teams. Conference, state, and regional championships have been won in recent years by the men's archery, soccer, and swimming and diving teams, while the women have captured crowns in swimming and diving, cross country, lacrosse, and volleyball. The football team made the national quarterfinals twice in the '90s, and the program has sent many players to the NFL. Intramural sports are very popular and bring out the weekend warrior in participating students.

Though JMU still has a ways to go before establishing itself as a front-rank national university, it is making considerable progress. The school is growing, but not outgrowing its Southern charm. "Everyone is so nice and polite! The people are wonderful and the area in general—the Shenandoah Valley—is a beautiful location to live in," says one happy junior.

> ## Overlaps
>
> **Virginia Tech, University of Virginia, College of William and Mary, George Mason, Mary Washington**

> ## If You Apply To ➤
>
> **JMU:** Early action: Nov. 1. Regular admissions: Jan. 1. Financial aid: March 1. Housing: May 1. No campus or alumni interviews. SATs or ACTs: required. SAT IIs: English required for course placement. Accepts electronic applications. Essay question: one-page personal statement.

The Johns Hopkins University

3400 North Charles Street, Baltimore, MD 21218

The Hop's reputation as a premed factory can be misleading. It's apt, but Hopkins also has fine programs in international relations (with D.C. close at hand) and a variety of liberal arts fields. In the absence of a football team, the national powerhouse lacrosse team is a major rallying point.

Website: www.jhu.edu
Location: Urban
Total Enrollment: 5,358
Undergraduates: 3,961
Male/Female: 59/41
SAT Ranges: V 640–730
M 680–760
ACT Range: 28–32
Financial Aid: 55%
Expense: Pr $ $ $ $
Phi Beta Kappa: Yes
Applicants: 9,127
Accepted: 34%
Enrolled: 32%
Grad in 6 Years: 87%
Returning Freshmen: 96%

The pursuit of academic excellence and the need to achieve are what fuel the typical student at the Johns Hopkins University. This Baltimore school has garnered widespread acclaim for its top-notch professors, incredible resources, and unparalleled research opportunities. Students who attend this elite university know they are at the top of the game, and they burn the midnight oil to stay there. "When you put this many great minds together, people are going to push each other to do well," says one public health major. "But after Hopkins, you are prepared for anything the real world throws at you."

The arts and sciences and engineering schools are located on the picturesque 140-acre Homewood campus, located just three miles north of Baltimore's revitalized Inner Harbor. Tree-lined quadrangles, open lawns, and playing fields make for an idyllic setting on the edge of a major urban center. The architecture on this woody urban campus is mainly Georgian red brick, with several recently built, more modern structures scattered throughout. A new chemistry building will house several research programs. The Mattin Student Arts Center houses clubs, fine arts, and other student amenities, and a new recreation center offers indoor tennis, racquetball, and other fitness activities. Students say both facilities have enlivened the campus.

As much as some try to deny it, premeds dominate the campus. Nearly 30 percent of entering freshmen say they are premed, and biomedical engineering tops the list of most popular majors (followed by international studies, computer science, biology, and economics). The university's hospital provides excellent research opportunities, and the Bloomberg School of Public Health offers a popular undergraduate major. Medicine at JHU plays such a major role in campus life that students sometimes fear it "overshadows the vibrant undergrad life that exists at Homewood." Biomedical engineers also enjoy a strong department—many say it's the hardest department at the school thanks to its intense workload. But that doesn't deter a Hopkins student. The only departments that really receive any criticism from students are math and classics. Hopkins now offers B.S. degrees in molecular and cellular biology, physics and astronomy, and a special B.S./M.S. in biology and biophysics. The school is developing a new major in environmental engineering, and there is a new minor in computer integrated surgical systems. Whether it's science or the humanities, undergraduates say their professors are "easy to reach and eager to help." One sophomore complained that grade inflation is nonexistent at Hopkins.

> "When you put this many great minds together, people are going to push each other to do well."

(Continued)

Academics: ✑ ✑ ✑ ✑ ½
Social: ☎ ☎ ☎
Q of L: ★ ★ ★
Admissions: (410) 516-8171
Email Address:
gotojhu@jhu.edu

Strongest Programs:
English/Writing
History
International Studies
Biomedical Engineering
Art History
Biology
French

Although Johns Hopkins is a firm supporter of traditional scholarship, there are no university-wide requirements other than a four-course writing component. Each major has its own distribution requirements, and there are several creative seminar offerings for freshmen. Students can receive a B.A. in creative writing through the Writing Seminars program, where they study with authors and playwrights such as John Barth. But students warn that these writing courses are quite popular, and getting into them can be difficult. The Humanities Center espouses a casual, interdisciplinary approach, and with maximum curriculum flexibility allowed them, undergraduates are free to range as broadly or focus as specifically as they want. Students can get a dual degree in music performance with the Peabody Conservatory. There also are broad "area majors," such as social sciences and behavioral sciences, humanistic studies, or natural sciences, and students can choose from a cluster of related disciplines to design their own program. Even the strictly structured engineering course plan stresses the importance of interdisciplinary and interdepartmental exposure.

Students also benefit from the well-developed graduate side of Johns Hopkins. The International Studies Program, for example, is enriched by its offerings at the university's Bologna Center in Italy, Nanjing Center in China, and at its Nitze School of Advanced International Studies in nearby Washington, D.C. Undergraduate research is also a hallmark of a Hopkins experience, with 70 percent of students having at least one research experience. The provost awards 60 grants of up to $2,500 each for undergraduates to do summer research.

Overall, students find the academic climate competitive but not overwhelming. "Most of this university's students graduated at the top of their high-school class, and are used to working hard," says a Spanish major. "JHU is a place where their growth and development—both academic and social—is fostered." Hopkins is one of the toughest schools in the country, and the workload reflects that. "There are very few slackers here," one student says. There is a premajor faculty advisor for freshmen, and Arts & Sciences students are encouraged to wait until at least their sophomore year to declare a major. Johns Hopkins also generously allows freshmen to take an entire semester on a pass/fail basis to ease them into the academic rigor of the place. After this "honeymoon" period, students buckle down to a Herculean workload. Some relief is offered, however—the optional January intersession—during which students can take courses or pursue independent study for one or two credits.

About 70 percent of students have at least one research experience, and the school also awards sixty grants of up to $2,500 each for undergrads to do summer research.

Hopkins students are remarkably talented and proactive, with 73 percent from the top tenth of their high-school class. Politically, Johns Hopkins is usually considered rather conservative, but that might be changing. "We're hip on diversity," says one junior. "Southern Society lives peacefully with the Black Student Union, the Jewish Students Association and the Muslim Students Association cosponsor events, frat guys tolerate the Gay, Bisexual, Lesbian, and Transgender Alliance and vice versa." Some students have rallied to support a living wage for workers, while other issues on campus include the Middle East conflict. But be careful: "It is very important to be politically correct on this campus," one senior says. Sixty-six percent of the school is Caucasian, 19 percent Asian-American, 4 percent African-American, and 2 percent Hispanic. Geographically, most students come from the Mid-Atlantic states and New England—only 12 percent come from Maryland.

Hopkins's endowment is among the top twenty in the country at nearly $1.8 billion, and it strives to meet the full demonstrated financial need of virtually every admit. Hopkins generously rewards the extraordinarily talented with eighteen hefty Hodson Trust scholarships worth $20,000 annually, regardless of need, and renewable annually for those who keep a 3.0 GPA. The Hodson Success Scholarship, based on need, replaces the loans in the aid packages of selected students from underrepresented minority groups. Twenty-four athletic scholarships are also awarded in women's and men's lacrosse, where Hopkins is a perennial national powerhouse. Word is that non-premeds are looked on with particular favor by the financial-aid office.

Freshmen and sophomores are required to live on campus in either single-sex or coed-by-floor dormitories. Twenty-five percent of the upperclassmen, once left to fend for themselves, are now guaranteed housing in one of six residence halls or university-owned "luxury" apartments. Juniors and seniors, however, often choose to scope out the row houses and apartment buildings that surround JHU. "The dorms are well maintained and fairly comfortable," says one student. "But they are very expensive for the room you get." All in all, 54 percent of Hopkins undergrads live in university housing.

According to students, the social scene at Hopkins is improving. "Social life has been on a continual rise since the early '90s," says one senior. "Events continue happening off campus, and are slowly re-centering on the campus itself." With one-third of the students dispersed among the city's apartment buildings, rowdy dorm parties and all-campus events are few and far between. But fraternity parties can be found on the weekends, though only 18 percent of the men and 19 percent of the women belong. The twenty-

"There are very few slackers here."

one age drinking limit is officially enforced, with violators facing disciplinary action. "Students can get alcohol at frat parties, but sometimes it's more difficult at local bars," one senior says. With more than two hundred student groups on campus, somebody is always hosting some event. The student-run Milton S. Eisenhower symposium brings internally acclaimed speakers to campus.

But the biggest and most popular undergraduate social event of the year is the annual student-organized Spring Fair, which draws crowds from the surrounding communities as well. Downtown Baltimore and the famed Inner Harbor are not too distant, and some of the city's best attractions, such as the art museum, aquarium, and Wyman Park, are right near campus. Trendy Baltimore hotspots—like Canton, Fells Point, and Little Italy—draw big crowds. Students also head to downtown for plays, the symphony, films, clubs, restaurants, the zoo and major league sports; Camden Yards, home of baseball's Orioles, is the most commodious park in the country. "Baltimore has the appeal of a city with the closeness of a town," says a political science major. Of course, that urban reality means parking can be hard on campus, some students say. When things become tiresome, Annapolis and Washington, D.C., are less than an hour by car, and Philadelphia and New York are just a train ride away. In the warmer months, a trek out to the Delaware and Maryland beaches takes the mind off studying.

When the stellar lacrosse team takes the road against opponents, students often take advantage of the opportunity to road-trip with them. Undergrads come together—even leaving the library at times—to cheer on their nationally acclaimed Blue Jays and release some study tension. Women's and men's basketball **"Everyone here has an interesting life story."** and men's soccer have each brought home conference trophies recently. Always a welcome alternative to the books, Hopkins's intramural sports program provides some playing time for other students.

With one of the world's premier medical and scientific programs as well as first-rate programs in areas as diverse as writing, international studies, and art history, Johns Hopkins University is clearly among the best schools in the country. "Everyone here has an interesting life story," says one upperclassman. "It is at this university that we are able to join together and grow and learn from each other while achieving academic excellence." For those seeking top-notch professors, incredible resources, and unparalleled research opportunities, Johns Hopkins is hard to beat. Student truly take pride in the fact that they belong to the cream of the academic crop—even if they're not premed.

Overlaps

Harvard, Penn, Cornell University, Yale, Princeton

If You Apply To ➢

Johns Hopkins: Early decision: Nov. 15. Regular admissions: Jan. 1. Financial aid: Feb. 1. Does not guarantee to meet demonstrated need. Campus and alumni interviews: optional, informational. SATs or ACTs: required. SAT IIs: required (writing and two others or ACT). Accepts the Common Application and electronic applications. Essay question: how do you hope your peers remember you, and how would professors recommend you in a letter of reference; personal statement.

Kalamazoo College

1200 Academy Street, Kalamazoo, MI 49006-3295

The "K" Plan should appeal to both the nontraditional student and the practical-minded. Those with wanderlust get to travel the world while enjoying hands-on learning experiences. Those looking for a leg up on the job market get it through K-zoo's extensive internship program.

Kalamazoo College is a small school in a small city in America's heartland. But college subsidies enable 85 percent of students to study abroad during their years here, making the school a launching pad to the world. In addition to international education, the school's "K" Plan emphasizes teaching, internships (80 percent of students have at least one), and independent research (as seniors, all students complete a year-long project, with one-on-one faculty supervision). Despite snowy winters, the environment is warm and supportive, thanks to the school's "beautiful campus, friendly people, and open minds," says a theatre major.

Life on Kalamazoo's wooded, sixty-acre campus centers on the Quad, a green lawn where students ponder their destinies and play Ultimate Frisbee with equal ease. With its rolling hills, Georgian architecture, and cobblestone streets, the campus has the quaint look more typical of historic New England than of nearby Kalamazoo, which, with surrounding communities, has 225,000 residents. Recent

Website: www.kzoo.edu
Location: City outskirts
Total Enrollment: 1,322
Undergraduates: 1,322
Male/Female: 43/57
SAT Ranges: V 590–700
  M 600–690
ACT Range: 26–30
Financial Aid: 43%
Expense: Pr $ $
Phi Beta Kappa: Yes
Applicants: 1,422

(Continued)

Accepted: 70%

Enrolled: 32%

Grad in 6 Years: 69%

Returning Freshmen: 91%

Academics: ✎ ✎ ✎

Social: ☎ ☎ ☎

Q of L: ★ ★ ★ ★

Admissions: (616) 337-7166

Email Address:
admission@kzoo.edu

Strongest Programs:
Biology/Health Science
Psychology
English
Economics

campus construction includes a renovated fine arts building opened in the fall of 2001.

Kalamazoo operates on the quarter system, and students must spend their entire first year on campus. Still, many freshmen begin the year with a "land-sea adventure," three weeks of rappelling and backpacking in the mountains of Canada, followed by sailing a brigantine ship down Lake Huron to Windsor, Ontario. By the end, they're convinced they can survive anything, including the rigors of a Kalamazoo education (and the long Michigan winters). Once safely ashore on campus, they begin to fulfill distribution requirements, including three courses each in language, cultures, social sciences, and literature and fine arts, and two courses each in philosophy or religion and in math, natural sciences, or computer science. Also required are a first-year writing seminar and a quantitative reasoning course, as well as a senior individualized project—an internship, artistic work, directed research, student teaching, or a traditional thesis, basically anything that caps off each student's education in some meaningful way.

After their freshman year, most of K-zoo's undergrads meet life's challenges with suitcase in hand, studying wherever their heart takes them, for the regular tuition price. A variety of off-campus programs are available, including those offered by the Great Lakes College Association.* Kalamazoo's new Center for Experiential Education is another resource for information on careers, internships, and study abroad.

Many freshmen begin the year with a "land-sea adventure," three weeks of rappelling and backpacking in the mountains of Canada.

"There is a great sense of trying to complete work as well as have fun."

"All students have a faculty advisor whom they choose, so they can pick the type of person they want guidance from," says a junior. "Professors serve as advisors, and since they know the faculty and classes available better than anyone, they do a great job!" adds a senior.

Kalamazoo aims to prepare students for real life by helping them synthesize the liberal arts education they receive on campus with their experiences abroad. This has filled the school with overachievers, says a religion major. "The academic climate is rigorous, but the students are supportive of each other," adds a classical studies major. "The only competition is for yourself, to do better each time." Still, students do seek balance, says a theatre major: "There is a great sense of trying to complete work as well as have fun." The natural sciences are exceptionally good and students heap praise on the psychology and languages departments, although economics draws the most majors. Asian studies, music, and education are candidly cited as weaker by administrators. Professors give students lots of individual attention and are rewarded with some of Michigan's highest faculty salaries. "Our professors really care," says a junior. "They are passionate, and for the most part, classes are superb."

Founded in 1833 and formerly associated with the American Baptist Churches, Kalamazoo is the oldest college in Michigan. Twenty-four percent of students come from out of state, and minorities comprise 10 percent of the student body—3 percent

"We have many groups whose ideas are opposing, yet are very respectful of each other's beliefs and activities."

African-Americans, 2 percent Hispanic, and 5 percent Asian-American. Many K-zoo students crave more diversity on campus. "It's been diversified somewhat, but not enough," says a religion major. "That's the ongoing goal." Other hot topics are women's rights and homosexuality, students say, although debate is far from rancorous. "We have many groups whose ideas are opposing, yet are very respectful of each other's beliefs and activities," a junior explains.

Seventy-five percent of students live on campus, but with two to three hundred students away each quarter because of the K Plan, a certain instability pervades all activities, from athletics to student government to living groups in the coed residence halls, where suites hold one to six students. "Students are always coming and going," one laments. "This makes it hard for relationships and sometimes you don't see your friends for six to nine months." Dorms aren't divided by class standing, but Trowbridge is a good choice for freshmen. Those who return from abroad with bags of dirty laundry will be glad to know that dorm washers and dryers are free. While there are no Greek organizations at K-zoo, theme houses offer a more community-oriented atmosphere, including family-style dinners. The central dining hall's food is no match for its decor: six "motif" rooms each reflect a single nationality, such as the English pub, with wood panels and stained-glass windows. Although dorms require key cards for entry, "security is a big joke," says a senior. "Granted, we live in a safe area, but if something ever did happen, security is pretty useless."

The city of Kalamazoo "thrives on college life," says one student. The city, the college, and Western Michigan University, across the street, "are intertwined, and students love to work outside through organizations like Habitat for Humanity," as well as in local churches and schools. On campus, students look forward to a casino night called Monte Carlo, Homecoming, Spring Fling, and the Day of Gracious Living, a spring day where, without prior warning, classes are canceled and students relax by taking day trips or helping beautify the campus. (One popular T-shirt: "The end of learning is gracious living.") Off campus, Kalamazoo offers the typical collection of restaurants, theaters, and bars; K-zoo students also benefit from the physical proximity of colleges such as Western Michigan, where they may use the library or attend cultural events, as the college lacks a central place for students to hang out. Students also appreciate the city's proximity to Lake Michigan's beaches and Chicago's urban playground.

> "Students are always coming and going."

For those who equate college with big-time athletics, Kalamazoo has something to offer—even if it's not nationally televised games or tens of thousands of screaming fans. The Kalamazoo Hornets have a long-standing rivalry with Hope College, culminating in the football teams' annual competition for the "infamous wooden shoes," where the Hornets are cheered on by fans known as "the stingers." Kalamazoo also has an outstanding men's tennis team, which has won conference titles for the past sixty-three consecutive years. However, an economics and business major reports that "Frisbee golf is the thing to play, and K's golf course is used by Kalamazoo students, some faculty, and some townies."

"Study hard, party hard" is not the official motto of Kalamazoo College, but it might as well be. At this increasingly selective school, graduates leave with solid liberal arts preparation, made more thoughtful by required senior-year individualized projects and by near-ubiquitous study abroad. Well-traveled, well-grounded, and well-prepared for real life, students here can proudly say "whoop-dee-doo for Kalamazoo."

The central dining hall's food is no match for its decor: six "motif" rooms each reflect a single nationality, such as the English pub, with wood panels and stained-glass windows.

Overlaps

University of Michigan, Michigan State, Northwestern, Western Michigan, Chicago

If You Apply To ➤

Kalamazoo: Early action: Nov. 15. Early decision: Dec. 1, Jan. 15. Regular admissions and financial aid: Feb. 15. Housing: May 1. Meets demonstrated need of 38%. Campus interviews: recommended, evaluative. No alumni interviews. SATs or ACTs: required. Accepts the Common Application and electronic applications. Essay question: significance of multicultural education; situation where you've made a difference; someone or something that had a lasting impact; or how Kalamazoo will help you achieve personal and educational goals.

University of Kansas

1502 Iowa Street, Lawrence, KS 66045

Memo to out-of-staters: Lawrence is not flat as a pancake and does not resemble Dorothy's home in "The Wizard of Oz." University of Kansas has a gorgeous campus and is one of the premier college bargains in the United States. Strong programs in a full slate of professional schools.

Website: www.ku.edu
Location: Small city
Total Enrollment: 28,849
Undergraduates: 20,610
Male/Female: 47/53
ACT Range: 22–28
Financial Aid: 34%
Expense: Pub $ $
Phi Beta Kappa: Yes
Applicants: 9,005
Accepted: 68%
Enrolled: 66%
Grad in 6 Years: 56%
Returning Freshmen: 81%
Academics: ✍ ✍ ✍ ✍
Social: ☎ ☎ ☎ ☎
Q of L: ★ ★ ★ ★
Admissions: (785) 864-3911
Email Address: adm@ku.edu

Strongest Programs:
Architecture and Urban
Design
Education
Environmental Studies
Journalism
Nursing/Pharmacy
Social Welfare
Business
Engineering

With solid academics, outstanding extracurricular programs, winning athletics, and a stellar social life, the University of Kansas is one of higher education's best buys. It might be in the center of the conservative Midwest, but KU itself is an oasis of tolerance and open-mindedness. Recently, KU has taken steps to become more selective and the results are evident: the university admitted its highest-achieving class on record in 2001. And those students who are extremely dedicated can plunge into a great honors program the school provides to court them in its efforts to raise its academic profile

The one thousand-acre campus is set atop Mount Oread ridge—once a lookout point for pioneer wagon trains—and spread out on rolling green hills overlooking valleys. Let's face it—Kansas isn't the first place that comes to many people's minds when asked to think of the most beautiful scenery anywhere. Never mind the wooded and hilly Lawrence campus is one of the most gorgeous in the United States. Many of the buildings are made of indigenous Kansas limestone. But the real beauty of the campus lies in its landscape, particularly the breathtaking foliage that appears each autumn. There are nearly as many trees on campus—nineteen thousand at last count—as there are undergrads. Recent construction includes renovations to the football stadium and a new parking garage. Murphy Hall, part of the School of Fine Arts, has been renovated to include rehearsal rooms, recording studios, a computing technology lab, and a comprehensive music and dance library. The Kansas Memorial Student Union just underwent a pricey renovation to expand the bookstore, food service areas, and space for student organizations. Work on an engineering building, a recreation center, and housing improvements are kicking off as well.

"We embrace differences."

KU applicants apply to the individual school of their choice. Those not admitted to one of the professional schools will automatically be considered for admission to the College of Liberal Arts and Sciences, where 70 percent of the undergraduate population is enrolled. Students in most of the professional schools, with the exception of engineering, architecture, and fine arts, spend their first two years completing the liberal arts requirements. The general education curriculum is intended to expose students to the foundations of the humanities, sciences, and social sciences. It also includes math, English, and oral communication, and requires courses in both Western and non-Western civilization. Foreign language and laboratory science courses are required as well for all B.A. candidates.

Of the fourteen graduate and professional schools, those most noted for undergraduate programs are architecture and urban design, allied health, fine arts, social welfare, pharmacy, nursing, education, business, and engineering. The journalism, architecture, and business programs receive rave reviews from students. The lower-rated programs include math, Western civilization, and the oft-maligned physical education. Those in the top 20 percent of their high-school class and with high SAT (last year, more than 1240) or equivalent ACT scores should definitely look into the Mount Oread Scholars program, which offers a dorm, networking, and small classes with top professors. The Indigenous Nations Studies Program—a graduate program that focuses on indigenous people's issues—offer an undergraduate class to introduce students to this new area of study. The biological sciences, formerly six separate departments, have been reorganized into one unit, and the international studies program now offers students an opportunity to receive a co-major.

Students describe the academic atmosphere as fairly competitive. Professors earn high marks for their teaching ability and dedication, while some students complain about the number of graduate students teaching courses. There is a great range in class size; introductory chemistry takes the prize as the largest, with more than eight hundred students, but most classes range from twenty to fifty students. Aside from the usual coursework, options include independent study or the more than 75 study-abroad programs in fifty-two countries, including Brazil, France, Germany, and Ghana. Kansas provides several area study programs supported by language instruction in more than twenty languages. The top-ranked Latin American, Spanish, and Portuguese studies programs, which benefit from an exchange with the University of Costa Rica, are three good examples. Perhaps the downside to having a great department like that, along with a two-year requirement, is the foreign language phobia that some students here have developed. "They think it will be either hard or boring," says a senior. Undergraduates at KU may receive research awards to work with faculty members in publishing papers and poetry. And students are pleased with their library system, which includes a 3.5 million-volume main library, a research library, and science and engineering libraries.

The basketball team is legendary and James Naismith, who invented basketball, was KU's first coach—and the only one with a losing record.

Sixty-eight percent of the students are from Kansas, and most of the rest are fellow Midwesterners (with lots from Chicago). The most vocal groups on campus are African-Americans, gays, and lesbians. Vocal yes, highly represented, no: African-Americans, Hispanics, and Asian-Americans combined account for only 10 percent of the students. Gay rights, diversity, alcohol policies, and the Middle East conflict are hot topics. KU, with its famous steep hill and more affluent profile, is called "Snob Hill" by students at other Kansas schools who come from humbler origins. However, students think they're a pretty friendly lot. "I have been to both the East and West Coasts, and nowhere did I find kinder, more open-minded students as we have here," asserts a biology major. "We embrace differences," says a senior. Out-of-staters must have a 2.5 high-school GPA or a 24 on the ACT to get in. KU gives out about five thousand academic merit awards and 353 more benefit from a wide variety of athletic scholarships. Freshman orientation

"I visited nine campuses, and this town had me from hello."

begins with a series of one- or two-day summer sessions. And the seven days before classes are officially called Hawk Week, but are more commonly known as Country Club Week because of all the partying that goes on—though it's been less in recent years due to tougher liquor laws.

Only 18 percent of the students live in university housing, and both coed and single-sex dorms are available. Students have described some of the housing as "ugly" and in great need of repair, though renovations have cleaned up many problem areas. "It is quite easy to find on-campus living quarters in all shapes and sizes—most of which are comfortable and affordable," says an English major. Students with 2.5 GPAs can live in one of the ten scholarship halls where fifty men or women live in a cooperative-type arrangement. A vast majority of KU students live off campus in Lawrence apartments, which are considered expensive only by Kansas standards. A dining complex called Mrs. E's provides extended-hour access to food court-style meals for 2,500 residence-hall occupants.

The university's bus system is run entirely by students and is much appreciated by tenderfeet, especially because that great big hill seems to double in size during the cold, windy winters. Lawrence, with its myriad boutiques, restaurants, and bars, receives rave reviews from students. "I visited nine campuses, and this town had me from hello," says a psychology and business major. Students describe the town as "kind of artsy, kind of alternative," and volunteerism in the community among students seems to be on the rise. City slickers can trek off to Topeka, the state capital, or to Kansas City, each less than an hour's drive. The KC airport makes for easy long-distance transportation, and the area is also served by Amtrak.

The Greek system, which attracts 17 percent of the men and 18 percent of the women, tends to be a major force in the on-campus social life, though tension does exist between Greeks and independents. Sorority rush is completely dry, but rumor has it that the frats are a little more lenient when it comes to alcohol. Overall, the social scene is very much alive and well. More than four hundred organized groups keep things lively; other extracurricular activities include movies, poetry readings, and concerts. Scholarship halls, dorms, and other student groups sponsor large campus parties and events, but most of the social life takes place off campus.

KU varsity teams—the only ones in the nation that carry the name Jayhawks—compete in the tough Big 12 Conference. The basketball team, which won the Big 12 Championship for the third consecutive year in 1999, is legendary, and James Naismith, who invented basketball, was KU's first coach—and the only one with a losing record.

The school year kicks off with Hawk Week, the official welcome for new students. The traditional "Rock Chalk Jayhawk" KU cheer is enough to bring a pang of nostalgia to the heart of even the most grizzled Kansas alum. To demonstrate their loyalty to the Jayhawks, thousands of students show up for the first basketball practice of the season at 12:01 A.M. on October

"We love to be challenged, and to challenge the status quo."

15. This nocturnal tradition is lovingly labeled "Midnight Madness." KU's most-hated rival is Missouri, and the winner of the annual football game takes possession of an "alumni spirit drum." Favorite road trips are determined by where the basketball team is playing. The women's basketball team is also worth watching, as are the men's and women's tennis teams and the women's swimming and diving team.

With KU's huge number of high-ranking academic programs, its national reputation (the nonbasketball one) has certainly improved. "We love to be challenged, and to challenge the status quo," writes a senior. And that's just what the university is doing, pushing up in the rankings and making Kansas one heck of a deal.

Overlaps

Kansas State, University of Missouri, Washington University (MO), University of Nebraska, University of Illinois

If You Apply To ➤ | **Kansas:** Rolling admissions. Financial aid: Mar. 1. Housing: Feb. 15. No campus or alumni interviews. SATs or ACTs: required. SAT IIs: optional. Apply to particular school or program. Accepts electronic applications. Essay question: personal statement (only for scholarship consideration).

University of Kentucky

100 Funkhouser Building, Lexington, KY 40506-0032

The State of Kentucky is better known for horses and hoops than higher education, but University of Kentucky is working to change that. The basketball team is still a championship contender, but so too are programs in business, engineering, and health fields.

You probably know that the University of Kentucky Wildcats are perennial attendees at the NCAA postseason basketball tournament. What you may not know is that the University of Kentucky's excellence stretches beyond its winning athletic teams—into outstanding medical and premedical programs, scientific research involving both professors and students, and a social calendar packed so full of Southern tradition that it would make even the most composed debutante's head spin.

The University of Kentucky campus, home to a major public research university as well as a community college, contains a mixture of old and new, modern and traditional buildings that date back to the late 1890s. The campus buildings indicate a transition beginning with the original redbrick structures to designs using contemporary glass and concrete as one moves south following the path of development. Most visitors would agree that the grounds are well-maintained, organized around the comfortable park-like spaces influenced by Frederick Law Olmsted's design. The campus contains a vast amount of mature trees and lawns set in a natural arrangement of open spaces, typical of the great land-grant universities. Of course, UK's location in the heart of one of the finest horse-breeding areas in the world makes it a natural place for the Gluck Equine Research Center, a headquarters for research into horse diseases. The new William T. Young Library is ranked thirtieth among public research libraries by the Association of Research Libraries.

Students sing the praises of many departments at UK, but several unique programs stand out. The Lexington campus is home to the Gaines Center of the Humanities, which is unusual in its study of public higher education. Lexington also hosts the Patterson School of International Diplomacy, one of the smallest yet most respected schools of its type in the country. The chemistry department turned out three National Science Foundation fellowship winners in 1998–99, a feat matched only by Harvard, Cornell, Rice, Princeton, and the Massachusetts Institute of Technology. Weaker areas include lower-level "monster" science classes, which one student describes as "extremely large and not at all personalized." All but 10 percent of classes at UK have fifty or fewer students, unusual for a state university, but undergraduates still complain about trouble getting into courses they need, especially entry-level offerings. According to a marketing major, students "have difficulty if they are freshmen, because most of them have to take the same classes, and sometimes they don't get the right times—or the classes at all." It's hard to complete the engineering, health, business, and architecture programs in four years, students say. Term-time internships, known as co-ops, also complicate, but enliven, the picture.

> "My professors have always shown a genuine concern for my grades."

Students praise UK's professors. "My professors have always shown a genuine concern for my grades," says a sophomore. TAs and full professors teach about the same number of freshman classes. The Central Advising Service, or CAS, is helping to improve the quality of academic guidance, though one student notes, "I do wish I had more assistance from my advisors on which classes to take."

To graduate, all students must take mathematics and a foreign language, as well as written and oral communication classes and a statistics, calculus, or logic course. The core program, called University Studies, also requires exposure to natural and social sciences, humanities, an introduction to cross-disciplinary education, and experience with non-Western ways of thinking. Additionally, all freshmen are encouraged to take an academic orientation class called UK101, designed to help them adjust to college life. The academic climate is laid-back, but students shouldn't expect easy As. "When it comes to study time and classwork, the students are always competing with themselves to earn the best grades they can," explains a junior.

For upperclassmen, UK offers a number of joint programs with other colleges and universities, including Transylvania, Centre, and Georgetown (in Kentucky).

Website: www.uky.edu
Location: Center city
Total Enrollment: 23,060
Undergraduates: 16,841
Male/Female: 48/52
ACT Range: 22–27
Financial Aid: N/A
Expense: Pub $
Phi Beta Kappa: Yes
Applicants: 8,320
Accepted: 73%
Enrolled: 32%
Grad in 6 Years: 53%
Returning Freshmen: 79%
Academics: ✍ ✍ ✍
Social: ☎ ☎ ☎ ☎
Q of L: ★ ★ ★
Admissions: (859) 257-2000
Email Address:
admissio@pop.uky.edu

Strongest Programs:
Business
Premed
Predentistry
Nursing
Engineering
Chemistry

UK is a member of the Academic Common Market, which provides students in fifteen states the opportunity to pay in-state tuition at any of these states' schools if they want to enroll in a program not offered in their home state.

There's also a cooperative program with the Army and Air Force ROTC. Students studying prevet at UK will find coveted slots reserved for them at Auburn and Tuskegee in the advanced veterinary medicine program, at in-state tuition rates. UK is a member of the Academic Common Market, which provides students in fifteen states the opportunity to pay in-state tuition at any of these states' schools if they want to enroll in a program not offered in their home state.

"UK students are typically self-assured, slightly competitive, and outgoing," says a psychology major (perhaps practicing analysis for her future career). The UK student body hails from all fifty counties in Kentucky, with 13 percent from out of state and 4 percent from foreign countries. The student body is predominantly white; African-Americans account for 6 percent of students, and Hispanics and Asian-Americans combine for a little more than 3 percent. Despite these small numbers, students say diversity is valued. "Respectfulness is an issue," says one student. "But Southern hospitality abounds." The university aims to be an "inclusive learning community," achieving academic excellence by working toward "social responsibility and community building, with particular focus on equity, fairness, and safety for each person," among other initiatives. Merit scholarships, ranging from $500 to a full ride, are offered to qualified students.

> "UK students are typically self-assured, slightly competitive, and outgoing."

Kentucky's dorms are clean and convenient, as well as a great way to meet people, students say, though there's quite a range of what amenities you may get. Dorms are located on three parts of the campus—north, central, and south. North campus housing is old, but the halls are small, so they afford a chance to form close relationships. They're also within a short walking distance of classrooms, the student center, and the bookstore. South campus offers newer dorms with small rooms and air-conditioning, while Central campus offers the biggest rooms. Recommended for freshmen: Kirwan-Blanding Complex, since "everything seems to happen there." Getting a room is not a problem as long as you apply by the deadline. Also, since students are not required to live on campus, only 25 percent do.

Students say that while Lexington is a great place to go to school, it's not a typical college town. "Lexington is almost 250,000 people strong," an upperclassman explains. "It's small enough to drive across town easily, but large enough not to see everyone you know when you go to Wal-Mart." Despite the lack of diversity on campus, Lexington abounds with a multitude of ethnic eateries, as well as theaters, shopping malls, and nightspots. On campus, students enjoy movies, presentations, seminars, and athletic events, the most popular being basketball games at the legendary Rupp Arena. Other campus activities include the Little Kentucky Derby, a week-long student-run festival that features a balloon race and concerts. Among the highlights of any student's career at UK are two one-month periods—one in the fall, one in the spring—when students spend afternoons at Keeneland Race Track enjoying the tradition of Kentucky horse racing.

> "Respectfulness is an issue, but Southern hospitality abounds."

About 15 percent of the men and 17 percent of the women go Greek, but fraternities and sororities offer the great majority of on-campus activities, as well as opportunities for volunteer work in the community. The university has a strict no-alcohol-on-campus policy that is enforced, but it doesn't tend to impact students with fake IDs. When it's time for a road trip, UK students head to Cincinnati and Louisville (one hour away), or to Atlanta and Chicago (six hours)—that is, if they're not taking leisurely Sunday drives through nearby Blue Grass country. And the best road-trip destinations are anywhere there's a steamy, noisy gym and a basketball team ready to play UK's always-strong Wildcats. Home games at Lexington's Rupp Arena—what one student calls "a magical experience"—are consistently packed.

"In Kentucky, basketball is like a second religion," agrees another true-Blue Wildcat fan. Although screaming yourself hoarse for five guys hitting the hardwood may not be as genteel as cheering while sipping a mint julep at the track, for many students, the mix of collegiate craziness and old-world Southern hospitality found in Lexington is just what they want.

Kenyon College

Ransom Hall, Gambier, OH 43022-9623   740·427·5776 -admissions office

Kenyon is a pure liberal arts college plunked down in the middle of the Ohio countryside. More mainstream than Oberlin, more serious than Denison, and more selective than Wooster, Kenyon is best-known for English and a small but distinguished drama program.

Kenyon College maintains a pure liberal arts and sciences emphasis that's less and less common in the world of higher education. Students here are proud of what sets Kenyon apart from other liberal arts colleges. "The small student body and the friendliness of the students makes for a genuine community feeling," explains one student. "At Kenyon, you really feel like you are sharing a great college experience with great people."

The oldest private college in Ohio, Kenyon's eight hundred-acre campus sits on a hillside overlooking a scenic view of river, woods, and fields. The college's oldest building, Old Kenyon, dates from 1826, and is said to be the first collegiate Gothic building in America. The Brown Family Environmental Center includes a butterfly garden and extensive perennial gardens planted with community donations. A new education building opened at the BFEC in 2001. In addition to new science facilities and a new greenhouse, which opened during the 2000–01 academic year, renovations have been completed on the building housing the psychology department. The athletics and physical education department have added a new softball field and new tennis facilities. There are plans for a new fitness, athletic, and recreation complex slated to be completed in the fall of 2005.

Kenyon's focus on the liberal arts makes for a challenging, but largely noncompetitive, learning environment. "Kenyon students are typically concerned with wanting to perform well, but are not very competitive with each other and not interested in doing well at the expense of peers doing worse," says a student. In fact, at Kenyon, it's hard to find a weak department. "Smaller departments such as Classics and Math draw fewer students, but still offer great courses," says one student.

English, a nationally renowned subject at Kenyon since the 1930s, is the most popular major, and it, along with the drama department, set the tone of campus life. This is, after all, home to *The Kenyon Review*, a prestigious literary quarterly, and a school about which alum E. L. Doctorow has said, "Poetry is what we did at Kenyon, the way at Ohio State they played football." Political science is said to be solid, drawing undecided majors with its introductory class, "Quest for Justice," because it

Website: www.kenyon.edu
Location: Rural
Total Enrollment: 1,558
Undergraduates: 1,558
Male/Female: 45/55
SAT Ranges: V 600–700
  M 580–680
ACT Range: 27–31
Financial Aid: 44%
Expense: Pr $ $ $
Phi Beta Kappa: Yes
Applicants: 2,063
Accepted: 66%
Enrolled: 33%
Grad in 6 Years: 84%
Returning Freshmen: 92%
Academics: ✍ ✍ ✍ ✍
Social: ☎ ☎ ☎
Q of L: ★ ★ ★
Admissions: (800) 848-2468
Email Address:
  admissions@kenyon.edu

Strongest Programs:
  English
  Art
  Biology
  Dance

(Continued)
Drama
History
Economics
International Studies
Political Science

"introduces the material in such a way that you're left hungry for a greater understanding of it!" says one devotee. The Integrated Program in Humane Studies, which incorporates English, history, political science, and art history, is also popular.

The hallmark of Kenyon's academic philosophy is an almost fanatical devotion to the liberal arts and sciences. "Academic life at Kenyon is rooted in three strong tenets," an administrator explains. "That students thrive when they can work closely with their professors; that they can best explore their own potential when they have enough flexibility to experiment; and that they learn most productively in an atmosphere of cooperation." Pre-professional opportunities include 3–2 engineering programs with several universities, and with high acceptance rates to graduate programs in law, business, and medicine, Kenyon's emphasis on arts and sciences is clearly yielding positive results. In fact, three out of four recent Kenyon grads took jobs when they finished, rather than continuing on to graduate or professional schools. The Career Development Center helps sort out grad schools and employment opportunities, both summer and post-graduation. Kenyon awards approximately sixty merit scholarships a year ranging from $13,000 to $26,000.

While there is no core curriculum at Kenyon, all students must complete at least one unit of credit in the college's four divisions: humanities, fine arts, social sciences, and natural sciences. Students must also complete requirements in quantitative reasoning and foreign language study. Change is constant at Kenyon, including changes in curriculum. American studies, which used to be a concentration, has now been designated

"Kenyon students are typically concerned with wanting to perform well."

as a major. A bevy of academic counselors, including upperclassmen and professors, help ensure that freshmen stay on the right track. About 20 percent of juniors are invited by their departments to read for honors, and about 15 percent graduate with departmental honors. The culmination of each student's coursework at Kenyon is the senior exercise, which may take the form of a comprehensive examination, an integrative paper, a research project, or some combination of these.

Classes are small at Kenyon—the majority have twenty-five or fewer students—and even the larger introductory courses use a two-part format in which students meet for lectures one week and split up for discussion sections with the professor the next. "Kenyon professors are passionate about what they teach and are great at communicating their knowledge and inspiring students to learn," asserts a junior. "Not only can you get extra help or discuss course material further, but you also get to know them and they get to know you on a more personal level," adds a senior.

Twenty-five percent of Kenyon students are Ohioans, and together, African-Americans, Hispanics, and Asian-Americans make up just 10 percent of the student body. "Although ethnic diversity is something Kenyon needs to work on at the moment, there really isn't a 'model' Kenyon student," says a junior. The anti-sweatshop and Free Tibet movements that have been sweeping the nation's campuses have found their homes at Kenyon as well; on-campus political issues include the formulation of a new sexual harassment policy and underage drinking. "Large-scale movements such as those against sweatshops or in favor of eliminating the death penalty find support in groups like Amnesty International and Activists United, and environmentally conscious students have recently formed a group called REEL (Resource and Energy Efficient Living) that is making big changes on campus," says a student.

English, a nationally renowned subject at Kenyon since the 1930s, is the most popular major, and it, along with the drama department, set the tone of campus life.

All Kenyon students live on campus, with housing guaranteed for four years. Freshmen start in five dorms at the north end of campus, and most move south to recently remodeled housing the next year. Although renovations and expansions are always in the works, they are currently having some trouble keeping up with demand. Rooms are selected via a harrowing housing lottery, and typically upperclassmen "opt for one of the historic dorms—Old Kenyon, Hannah or Leonard, or one of the campus-owned apartments—the Aclands, Bexleys, or New Apartments." Most dorms are coed. Rather than their own houses, fraternities occupy sections of the south-campus dorms, making that area the center of the party scene. "In general, the school could improve its housing options, but it is nice that by the time you are a junior, you are basically guaranteed an apartment," says one student. Everyone, including those in the apartments with kitchens, must eat college chow; dining halls operate on each end of the campus, though only one is open on weekends.

The school's Greek system draws 36 percent of the men but only 10 percent of the women, and the frats throw lively parties that are open to all. Like most campuses, Kenyon is slowly moving away from the animal-house paradigm of social life. "Most of the social life is student-initiated and takes place on campus," says one senior. "There is always something going on from the opportunity to participate in game shows to try and win a trip to the Bahamas, listening to student bands or bands that come from nearby schools, karaoke contests, or watching the movie that the Kenyon Film Society shows." Gambier is a small town, with a couple of bars and no movie theaters, but there

"Most of the social life is student-initiated and takes place on campus."

are a few more options fifteen minutes away in Mount Vernon, to which the college runs a daytime shuttle bus. On-campus events and college-sponsored activities are growing more popular to help keep boredom at bay. With its deli, market, inn, restaurant, bank, and post office, Gambier is at least quaint. Students enjoy buying real maple syrup, fresh bread, and cheese from Amish farmers with stands on its main street on Saturdays.

Kenyon remains defined by its traditions, the most hallowed of which is renewed each year as incoming freshmen sing college songs to the rest of the community from the steps of Rosse Hall. Departing seniors sing the same songs at graduation. On Matriculation Day each October, after a formal ceremony, freshmen sign a book that contains the signatures of virtually every Kenyon student since the early 1800s. Other major events include Homecoming and the Summer Send-Off. To break February's icy cold, the school holds a formal ball called Philander's Phling, remembering founder Philander Chase; an alum donates money for the dance. There are two small ski areas near campus, but for those seeking adventure further from home, Columbus and Ohio State University are a forty-five-minute drive south. The adventurous sometimes road-trip to Cleveland (home of the Rock and Roll Hall of Fame), Cincinnati, Chicago, or even Canada.

The hallmark of Kenyon's academic philosophy is an almost fanatical devotion to the liberal arts and sciences.

In addition to its emphasis on academics, Kenyon was instrumental in establishing the North Coast Athletic Conference, which includes a number of academically strong Midwestern schools, including longtime rival Denison. A junior cites the annual hockey game versus Denison, when "both teams have to drive to Newark and a surprising number of fans

"The community atmosphere of Kenyon makes it a special place."

from both colleges attend." The women's tennis and basketball teams are reigning conference champs, while Kenyon's swimming and diving teams dominate Division III competition. The school leads the nation with forty-two NCAA Division III postgraduate scholarships. Soccer games against Ohio Wesleyan draw large crowds. Clubs sponsor everything from Frisbee to water polo.

Kenyon introduces the upper crust of the Eastern seaboard to rural Ohio, and often makes it hard for them to tear themselves away. For the many young artists, writers, and budding intellectuals here, it's hard to face the end of their four years. "The community atmosphere of Kenyon makes it a special place," says a senior. "At Kenyon, you are around a group of people who love being where they are."

Overlaps

Denison, Oberlin, Bates, Carleton, Hamilton

Kenyon: Early decision: Dec. 1, Jan. 15. Regular admissions, financial aid, housing: Jan. 15. Meets demonstrated need of 44%. Campus interviews: recommended, evaluative. Alumni interviews: optional, evaluative. SATs or ACTs: required. SAT IIs: optional. Accepts the Common Application and electronic applications. Essay question: special interests, experience, or achievement.

Knox College

2 East South Street, Galesburg, IL 61401

This friendly and progressive Illinois college was among the first in the nation to admit African-Americans and women. Offers close interaction with faculty and pure liberal arts. More mainstream than Beloit and Grinnell and just more than half as big as Illinois Wesleyan.

Website: www.knox.edu
Location: Small city
Total Enrollment: 1,143
Undergraduates: 1,143
Male/Female: 44/56
SAT Ranges: V 540–690
    M 560–660
ACT Range: 24–29
Financial Aid: 73%
Expense: Pr $ $
Phi Beta Kappa: Yes
Applicants: 1,428
Accepted: 72%
Enrolled: 19%
Grad in 6 Years: 71%
Returning Freshmen: 88%
Academics: ✍ ✍ ✍
Social: ☎ ☎ ☎
Q of L: ★ ★ ★
Admissions: (309) 341-7100
Email Address:
    admission@knox.edu

Strongest Programs:
    Biology
  ' Creative Writing
  · Music
    Math
    Political Science
  ' Psychology

Knox College, with the unconventional Prairie Fire as its mascot, has long made a name for itself by breaking away from the conventions of the day. Founded in 1837 as the Knox Manual Labor College in Galesburg, Illinois, this liberal arts college was the first in the state to graduate an African-American student and among the first in the nation to admit women. And through a warm and supportive academic community, the college continues to foster a strong sense of individualism.

Located in the heart of the Midwest—almost midway between Chicago and St. Louis—the eighty-two-acre campus has spacious, tree-lined lawns and a dynamic mixture of architecture that reflects the 145-year span of construction dates of existing buildings. Old Main, constructed in 1857, is a National Historic Landmark and the only building remaining from the 1858 Lincoln-Douglas debates.

Students say the academic relationships at Knox are infused with a spirit of cooperation and equality. Beyond the classroom, students, faculty, and administrators make decisions on boards together, each with identical voting power. First-year students confront the core issues of liberal education in Preceptorial, a one-term seminar examining questions of ethics and truth through multidisciplinary reading and critical writing. But while many schools have small, intense classes for first-year students, Knox takes things a bit farther by mandating an advanced preceptorial for seniors. This class connects their expertise in their major to a broad topic. Other graduation requirements require all students to demonstrate proficiency in math and a foreign language, and take two classes in each of the following: math, humanities, and social science. Interdisciplinary courses are also required, and revisions to the general education guidelines will

"The beauty of Knox is the openness and accessibility of professors!"

likely bring curriculum changes. Knox also boasts the Ford Foundation Research Fellowship Program, which was created in the mid-1980s to encourage students to consider careers in college teaching and research. Ford Fellows work with selected faculty mentors to design and carry out a research project in an area of interest. Through this permanently endowed foundation, Knox is able to offer stipends for summer research to a full one-fifth of the junior class. Moves like these have helped Knox earned a national reputation for its independent undergraduate research. More than 70 percent of students do some type of independent study.

Strong departments include creative writing, math, psychology, political science, and the natural sciences, with biology attracting lots of research grant money. The school's literary journal, *Catch*, has won national awards. Students can take part in the Chicago Semester in the Arts, and dramatists also benefit from several theaters, including one with a revolving stage. Students cite the modern languages and philosophy as weak. Study abroad options include programs in more than twenty countries, and the college is a member of the Associated Colleges of the Midwest consortium.*

Knox operates on an honor system that allows students to take tests in any public area unproctored, but few students would even think of cheating. "Courses are extremely rigorous. They are filled with in-depth discussion, large amounts of reading and multiple writing projects," says a junior. Where faculty is concerned, students offer uniformly glowing reviews for their performance in the classroom and availability outside of it. "The quality of teaching is top-notch. The beauty of Knox is the openness and accessibility

"Political correctness is huge. We're pretty conscious of the words we choose."

of professors!" raves an English literature major. Nearly 80 percent of students have fewer than twenty-five students. Knox's trimester system packs a great deal of studying into a short period, but students are only required to take three courses per term.

Knox's student advising system is praised by students. "On one of your first days on campus as a first year, your Faculty Advisor takes his or her advisees out to dinner," says one sophomore. "Academic advising has been excellent for me, and advisors are always available to discuss anything ranging from future plans to personal problems," adds a junior. An early identification of premed freshmen guarantees ten students admission to Rush Medical College in Chicago if they maintain a four-year B average. Knox also offers 3–2 or 3–4 programs in engineering, nursing, medical technology, law, and architecture.

More than 70 percent of students do some type of independent study and Knox has earned a national reputation for its independent undergraduate research.

The bulk of students (48 percent) are from Illinois, and 10 percent of students come from foreign countries. American minorities make up 12 percent of the student body (4 percent African-American, 4 percent Asian-American, and 4 percent Hispanic), and maintain an active profile on campus. "There is no typical student at Knox. Students come here with vastly different backgrounds, political leanings, interests, and goals," says a junior. While Knox does not seem to be a terribly politically active school, there appears to be a commitment to diversity across campus. One of the most popular forms of activism is "chalking," where students write messages in chalk on campus walkways. "Political correctness is huge. We're pretty conscious of the words we choose," says a sophomore. A senior points out freshmen are always called "first-years." Most students went to public high school, and 67 percent graduated in the top quarter of their class. Merit scholarships, from $5,000 to full tuition, are available, but athletic scholarships are not.

Housing is not a problem on the Knox campus; renovations have improved housing for most students, though some students complain that most rooms are not air-conditioned. "Our suite system is particularly nice because people have common living space," says one junior. Coed living arrangements are available, although most

"Our suite system is particularly nice because people have common living space."

freshmen live in single-sex suites with one or two upperclassmen as residential advisors. Students suggest freshman women would be happiest in Post Hall, while men should try to live anywhere in Old Quad. Older students may band together with friends or form a special-interest or theme suite. The five fraternities are residential; the two sororities are not. It takes a minor miracle for students to obtain permission to move off campus, which has become a common complaint among juniors and seniors. Food service, as at many colleges, gets a thumbs-down, with some students lamenting that it is difficult to get off the board plan. Security is "very visible on campus, driving around in their 'chariots of justice,' or golf carts," says a student.

Galesburg is a small Midwestern railroad town, and some students say they had trouble adjusting to the sounds of locomotives. At one time this city of about

Knox operates on an honor system that allows students to take tests in any public area unproctored, but few students would even think of cheating.

thirty-five thousand was a center of abolitionism, and the honorary degree that the college bestowed on then presidential candidate Abraham Lincoln was his first formal title. Relations between the town and school haven't been the greatest, but students say that is changing. Nearby Lake Storey offers boating, water slides, and nature trails, and students looking for more excitement can travel to Peoria, about forty miles away. Slightly farther away, Chicago is about 140 miles to the northeast. Weekends are filled with dances, campus activities, and fraternity parties. A third of the men and 13 percent of women go Greek, but you don't have to join to find fun. The alcohol policy is liberal, and as one sophomore notes, "Personal responsibility is valued above all." One of the best all-time traditions is Flunk Day. At 5:30 on a spring morning, Old Main's bell rings and classes are canceled to make way for dunk tanks and Jell-O pits. One sophomore proudly notes "the newest tradition on campus is to steal a cafeteria tray during the first snow of the year and go sledding down the Knox Bowl."

Athletics generate a reasonable degree of enthusiasm. Both the men's and women's golf teams won conference championships in 2001. Every fall, the football team endures lots of hard Knox against archrival Monmouth to bring home the highly prized Bronze Turkey Award, a throwback to the time when the game was played on Thanksgiving Day.

Knox may not be a well-known school, but students here have little else to complain about. Academics are the priority and students are encouraged to be individuals, but the close-knit atmosphere helps them form strong connections with different types of students and down-to-earth professors.

Overlaps

Beloit, Illinois Wesleyan, University of Illinois, Grinnell, Augustana

If You Apply To ➤

Knox: Early action: Nov. 15. Regular admissions: Feb. 1. Financial aid: Mar. 1. Meets demonstrated need of 93%. Campus interview: recommended, evaluative. Alumni interviews: optional, informational. SATs or ACTs: required. SAT IIs: optional. Accepts the Common Application. Essay question: significant experience; issue of concern; discuss work of art, drama, literature, or music.

Lafayette College

118 Markle Hall, Easton, PA 18042

Geographically close to Lehigh, but closer kin to Colgate and Hamilton. Does offer engineering, as do Swarthmore, Trinity (CT), and Union. Attracts relatively conservative, athletic students who work hard and play hard. A recent spate of building shows Lafayette's financial health.

Website: www.lafayette.edu
Location: City outskirts
Total Enrollment: 2,330
Undergraduates: 2,330
Male/Female: 51/49
SAT Ranges: V 560–650
  M 600–680
ACT Range: 25–29
Financial Aid: 60%
Expense: Pr $ $ $

With the number of applicants going up each year, and its acceptance rate steadily dropping, Lafayette College is taking its pick from among the nation's brightest students. With less than two dozen students in most classes, this small liberal arts college boasts an intimate academic milieu that draws praise from students. One of the few liberal arts schools of its size to offer engineering, Lafayette has also won respect for its technical and scientific programs.

Lafayette is situated on a stately hill in Easton, Pennsylvania, just one and one-half hours west of New York City and even closer to Philadelphia. The campus has an eclectic blend of architectural styles and more than 125 species of trees. The main library holds 490,000 volumes, with a twenty-four-hour study area and online access to the card catalog from the comfort of dorm rooms. A $20 million expansion of the library will add thirty thousand square feet of open learning space—a common theme in many Lafayette buildings. The new $10 million Oeschsle Center for Psychology and Neuroscience features three remote observation labs that allow students to watch their subjects—be they fish or human—without the subjects knowing it. And the renovation of three engineering buildings will create the new ninety thousand-square-foot Acopian Engineering Center, slated to open in the fall of 2003. The center will be open 24/7 and feature lots of open work spaces and glass walls to build a sense of shared purpose—and allow for extra mingling.

Lafayette's engineering, economics, and government and law programs are among the most popular majors, followed by English and psychology. Physics and chemistry are among the toughest courses of study, and students shun them as a result. One junior says the biology department seems to "focus on the needs of upperclassmen only," while a senior notes that the campus's music facilities aren't great "for someone really serious about music." The standard course load is four classes a semester, and all first-year students take an interdisciplinary seminar designed to engage them as

> "The school has recently added many more lights and security cameras."

thinkers, speakers, and writers. In the second semester of sophomore year, students take a second seminar, to promote scientific and technological literacy. All students must take an intensive writing course, as well as four units in both math and natural sciences and humanities and social sciences. Students working for a B.A. must meet a foreign culture requirement through foreign language studies or study abroad—Lafayette ranks eleventh nationally in the number of students who study abroad—or complete a group of courses providing intensive exposure to a specific foreign culture. The EXCEL program pays students who take research positions with faculty. "Not only did I get paid and get a great mentor, but we have two publications and two more hopefully on the way!" gushes a psychology major. "How's that for an undergraduate institution?"

Engineering students, too, may explore a foreign culture through an unusual arrangement with the Free University of Brussels, which allows them to study abroad while maintaining normal progress toward their degrees. Students agree that profs at Lafayette don't "dish out As, you really have to work for them." While the campus isn't "bookwormish," courses are challenging and the professors are demanding yet accessible, according to an English major. Still, in case Lafayette gets claustrophobic, cross-registration is available with other schools in the Lehigh Valley Association of Independent Colleges.*

While only 29 percent of Lafayette students are Pennsylvanians, and 63 percent attended public high school, it sometimes doesn't seem that way. "Most students are white, wear khakis and sweatshirts, and are from middle- and upper-class backgrounds," says a physics major. Lafayette may be somewhat apathetic and generally conservative as a result, one student says. "Once I saw a group of students protesting the quality of the food," recalls the math major, "but within an hour or two, they were hungry enough to stop for lunch." But students notice that the administration is working hard to attract international students to beef up the campus' small minority population. The Greek system, which attracts 26 percent of men and 43 percent of women, is also a concern. Administrators are trying to de-emphasize fraternities and sororities, and not all students approve.

Ninety-seven percent of students live on campus, and housing is guaranteed for all four years. Possibilities include Greek houses as well as independent dormitories and college-owned apartments with a variety of living and eating arrangements. The school is busily renovating and modernizing some of the older dorms, but still, one student says the range of housing goes from dingy to "Taj Mahal." Keefe Hall, a new dorm, is "more like a hotel," says a senior, while South College Hall, recently

(Continued)

Phi Beta Kappa: Yes
Applicants: 5,195
Accepted: 39%
Enrolled: 29%
Grad in 6 Years: 85%
Returning Freshmen: 96%
Academics: ✐ ✐ ✐ ✐
Social: ☎ ☎ ☎ ☎ ☎
Q of L: ★ ★ ★
Admissions: (610) 330-5100
Email Address:
  admissions@lafayette.edu

Strongest Programs:
  Engineering
  Economics/Business
  Chemistry
  Art
  Biology
  Psychology/Neuroscience
  English
  Government/Law

Engineering students, too, may explore a foreign culture through an unusual arrangement with the Free University of Brussels, which allows them to study abroad while maintaining normal progress toward their degrees.

renovated, has more washers and dryers and "nicer and newer facilities," says a classmate. A sixty-person residence hall has special-interest floors organized around themes such as science and technology. There's a lottery system that determines which dorm a student will live in, but most get into the dorm of their choice. Ruef and South College are more social, while Watson Hall and Kirby House are quieter, students say. Most upperclassmen, including women and non-Greek males, join meal plans at fraternities or the social dorms. And this is hardly a "suitcase school": everyone stays around for the weekends, a senior says. Students feel safe on campus, though like many schools, there have been a few assaults. "The school has recently added many more lights and security cameras, per students' requests," says a government major.

Most social life now takes place off-campus, because Greek houses are becoming less powerful, says a geology major. For students with cars, or those willing to hop a bus or train, the bright lights of Philadelphia, New York, and Atlantic City beckon on weekends, as do hiking the Appalachian Trail or touring the nearby Binney & Smith factory where Crayola crayons are made—a big "draw," if you know what we mean. The Lafayette Activities Forum plans plays, movies, concerts, and coffeehouses for those who wish to stay on campus. Parties are BYOB, and all sororities and some fraternities are dry; fraternities that host parties where alcohol is served must have third-party security, says a psychology and history major. But even though the college has taken to stricter enforcement of its alcohol policies, "it is there if you want it." The arts program brings a range of performers to campus,

"I have met professors who truly desire that their students learn and experience success."

and blue-collar Easton has a rich history as one of three cities where the Declaration of Independence was publicly read. The town has become more "college-friendly," and now has more stores and restaurants that cater to the college crowd. From College Hill and Downtown to the South Side, the city offers plenty of opportunity for volunteer work in schools, prisons, rehabilitation center, hospitals and environmental sites, under the auspices of Lafayette's Community Outreach Center.

The Lafayette Leopards women's lacrosse teams brought home Patriot League championships in 2001 and 2002, while the annual football game against nearby Lehigh is intense—students claim it's the oldest rivalry in the U.S., and when the two teams play, extra bleachers must be installed to accommodate the crowd. Women's field hockey, basketball, and indoor track and field are also strong, as are football, men's track, and soccer. All Leopard varsity teams compete in Division I except for football, which is I-AA. For those not up to varsity level, there is an extensive intramural program, buoyed by a state-of-the-art, $35 million Kirby Sports Center. The most important nonathletic campus event of the year is All-College Day, a spring festival with beach balls, bathing suits, bands, and the like.

On this small, leafy campus something great is happening, says an international studies major. "I have met professors who truly desire that their students learn and experience success," the senior says. "I have met students who gladly give of their time to help their peers. And I have met staff who serve students cheerfully and selflessly." Lafayette students know they're "at the center" of the college, getting more attention than they'd receive at a larger school. But that doesn't mean Lafayette "spoon-feeds" its students, a senior says. "If you want help you need to seek it out," the psychology major says. "Once you do, though, it's all over the place!"

Lake Forest College

555 Sheridan Road, Lake Forest, IL 60045

The only small, selective private college in the Chicago area. The college generally attracts middle-of-the-road and conservative students. In the exclusive town of Lake Forest, students can baby-sit for corporate CEOs at night and get internships at their corporations during the day.

Lake Forest, lovingly referred to as the "Enchanted Forest" by many of its students, is a laid-back liberal arts college. The school's true bounty is most apparent in its improving academics, fueled by small classes and dedicated professors, and a familiar, laid-back atmosphere among the student body. "Classes are challenging and competitive, but the small class size allows students to form close bonds with professors, which makes for a more open atmosphere," a junior English and psychology major says.

With its mixture of century-old Gothic and modern glass structures, Lake Forest's 107-acre campus is storybook beautiful. Located on Chicago's North Shore, about an hour from the heart of downtown, the campus has three parts: North, Middle, and South. Each has a mix of residence halls and academic facilities. The college recently opened the Cleveland-Young International Student Center, to provide seminar and library space in addition to living quarters for all incoming foreign students. In addition, a new varsity locker room has opened in Halas

> "The professors are open-minded and incorporate a wide range of ideas as well as their own."

Hall, formerly the home of the Chicago Bears, which the college shares with the Chicago Fire professional soccer team. Other newly renovated facilities include Nollen Hall and Deerpath Hall with such noteworthy enhancements as central air-conditioning and a fitness center. The wealth and seclusion of Lake Forest make the college a real dreamland—but also feed the insularity that many students come with or begin to feel once on campus. Nature lovers can explore the wooded ravines on the many undeveloped acres leading to Lake Michigan.

Students are expected to fulfill a variety of course requirements at this small liberal arts school. A general education curriculum requires two credits of natural and mathematical sciences, two credits of humanities, two credits of social sciences, and two classes in cultural diversity. In addition, freshmen must take a seminar-style Freshman Studies course and seniors must complete a senior seminar or senior thesis. Students say that academic intensity depends largely on the individual student. "The campus is separated into students who care about their education and those who don't," says a junior. "The general atmosphere of the college is laid-back, and though about half of the students opt to take challenging classes and pursue internships in the cite, Lake Forest is not a stressful environment." Students who seek more academic autonomy value the Independent Scholar program, which allows undergrads to create their own majors across traditional disciplines. There's also the Richter Apprentice Scholars program, which encourages freshmen to join faculty

Website: www.lakeforest.edu
Location: Suburban
Total Enrollment: 1,277
Undergraduates: 1,260
Male/Female: 42/58
SAT Ranges: V 510–620
  M 510–630
ACT Range: 23–28
Financial Aid: 70%
Expense: Pr $ $
Phi Beta Kappa: Yes
Applicants: 1,607
Accepted: 69%
Enrolled: 30%
Grad in 6 Years: 65%
Returning Freshmen: 79%
Academics: ✍ ✍ ✍
Social: ☎ ☎ ☎ ☎
Q of L: ★ ★ ★
Admissions: (847) 735-5000
Email Address:
  admissions@lakeforest.edu

Strongest Programs:
  Business
  Economics
  Psychology
  Politics
  Biology

members in conducting scholarly research—and then to consider careers in research and teaching.

Students say LFC's best departments are business, economics, English, and the sciences. The $4 million Student/Faculty Science Research Center provides plenty of lab and office space for students and faculty alike. The theater and music departments are said to be weaker, owing to limited faculty and facilities. The "Information Revolution" has inspired LFC to create a new program in Communications, and students can benefit from the new Latin American studies major as well. Comparative literature has been dropped. Students who don't like what's offered at Lake Forest can create their own classes, provided they find professors to teach them.

Lake Forest believes deeply in the value of study abroad, and many students participate in programs such as the Greece and Turkey Program, where archeological sites and museums provide cultural classrooms, or the marine biology program, which includes work at a tropical field station. Unlike part-time internships at other schools, Lake Forest interns work full-time in business, education, social and political activities, and at nonprofit agencies. The International Internship program has placed students in organizations including the Paris Cultural Affairs Department, UNESCO, UNICEF, and Eurospace. Lake Forest students also can be found in secondary schools and multinational corporations in both Paris and Santiago, Chile. The school is a member of the Associated Colleges of the Midwest* too, which offers programs in Russia, Zimbabwe, Japan, India, and central Europe, among other locales.

While Foresters like the small class sizes, flexible academic guidelines, and large doses of individual attention, nothing seems to compare to the quality of the faculty. Professors "are very knowledgeable in their departments and are very good at engaging students in interesting learning activities," raves an English and psychology major. Adds another English major: "The professors are open-minded and incorporate a wide range of ideas as well as their own." Students praise the Career Development Center for its symposia, workshops, and résumé clinics. One satisfied students says, "The CDC is available to students at any time and are very able to find jobs and internships for students."

"North campus is nice, but no parties. Half of the students live on South campus, which is the party place."

When it comes to recruiting, Lake Forest prides itself on its interstate appeal. Fifty-seven percent of students come from outside the Land of Lincoln, with many from either New England or the Mid-Atlantic states. Another 43 percent of Foresters come from Illinois, and international students account for 13 percent. African-Americans comprise 5 percent of the student body, Hispanics 3 percent, and Asian-Americans 4 percent, though this doesn't seem to bother anyone much. "The majority of students are not very politically active or 'PC' for that matter," one student says. For the most part, students do not get involved in any major social or political issues on campus. One thousand merit scholarships are available to qualified students.

Few students have the megabucks to live off campus in affluent Lake Forest, so 85 percent live in the dorms, where housing is coed by floor or quad unit except for one single-sex dorm. "North campus is nice, but no parties," says an in-the-know senior. Middle campus dorms are seen as more "academic" while the South campus is the older, wilder area. "Half of the students live on South campus, which is the party place," claims one student. In response to student requests, the school recently made Nollen Hall and McClure Hall completely substance-free. Each residence hall has a computer room and a television lounge; some rooms even have fireplaces. Freshmen are assigned rooms by the dean of students, while upperclassmen fend for themselves through a lottery based on seniority. Deerpath, an all-freshmen dorm, is by all accounts the top spot, and a recently completed $7 million renovation added air-conditioning, an aerobics and fitness center, and a state-of-the-art computer network. An honors dorm is home to the brainy crowd. Students have complained about not having cable TV, and that is now on its way. Everybody eats in a pleasant central dining hall, the social beehive of the campus, where unlimited helpings are served except on Thursday, which is steak and shrimp night.

The party scene on LFC's campus has picked up with the arrival of fraternities and sororities, which attract 18 percent of men and 22 percent of women, though parties are open to all. Students report they can drink behind closed doors, and it's a breeze for underage students to get alcohol. Says a junior: "many students are 'written up' for open alcohol, however, seldom are seriously punished for drinking underage." For students not interested in the frat scene, LFC offers movies, speakers, and coffeehouses with musical and comedy acts. Major events on the campus social calendar include the Festival of Ra, the Egyptian god of the sun, held every spring with a week of games, parties, talent shows, pie-throwing contests, and Jell-O wrestling.

> "Lake Forest is a very upscale town with many beautiful big homes and buildings."

Other festivities celebrate ethnic and cultural diversity, such as Semana Latina (Hispanic culture) and CelebrAsian. Since the movie *Class* was filmed at Lake Forest, each entering freshman class gets an encore presentation. The Big Chill in February is something akin to a winter carnival, and for diehard traditionalists, there's always Homecoming weekend in the fall.

Though Chicago is only an hour away by train, it helps to have a car for maximum freedom to get downtown and to other suburbs. "Lake Forest is a very upscale town with many beautiful big homes and buildings," says a junior. "There are mostly expensive stores and restaurants in town and the people of Lake Forest aren't very involved with the college." Neighboring communities like Highwood have bars—most notably Rainbows and the Wooden Nickel—frequented by students. The recent construction of a coffeehouse now provides Foresters with a setting for informal, nonalcoholic mixing. Aside from pure socializing, a few students take part in volunteer programs with low-income students in Chicago-area high schools. Another program sends students to the Appalachian Mountains in Virginia and Tennessee every spring break to help local townspeople repair substandard housing.

Lake Forest isn't exactly what you'd call a football factory, but the school does field a number of competitive athletic teams. Hockey is undoubtedly the biggest sport on campus, but men's handball is a perennial international collegiate champion. The volleyball, handball, swimming and diving, and women's basketball have excelled recently. More than 65 percent of LFC students participate in athletics at some level, from club to varsity sports.

While Lake Forest still has a substantial contingent of spoiled rich kids who are there just to drink their college years away, the college is also working hard to attract sharp minds who are searching for a safe, cloistered environment and professors who know all of their students by name. "The small class size, close relationships with professors, small and unique town, and easy access to Chicago," are a few of the things that make Lake Forest special, according to one senior.

Overlaps

Northwestern, Boston University, NYU, American University, Denison

If You Apply To ➤

Lake Forest: Early decision: Jan. 1. Early action: Dec. 1. Regular admissions: Mar. 1. Campus interviews: recommended, evaluative. Alumni interviews: optional, informational. SATs or ACTs: required. SAT IIs: optional. Accepts the Common Application and electronic applications. Essay question: personal statement.

Lawrence University

706 East College Avenue, Appleton, WI 54912

One of two small colleges in the nation that combines the liberal arts with a first-rate music conservatory. (Oberlin is the other.) Occupying a secluded spot in southern Wisconsin, Lawrence is comparable to Beloit in size but not quite as nonconformist.

Website: www.lawrence.edu
Location: Center city
Total Enrollment: 1,323
Undergraduates: 1,323
Male/Female: 46/54
SAT Ranges: V 560–700
  M 580–700
ACT Range: 25–30
Financial Aid: 71%
Expense: Pr $ $ $
Phi Beta Kappa: Yes
Applicants: 1,629
Accepted: 68%
Enrolled: 20%
Grad in 6 Years: 67%
Returning Freshmen: 87%
Academics: ✍ ✍ ✍ ✍
Social: ☎ ☎ ☎
Q of L: ★ ★ ★
Admissions: (800) 227-0982
Email Address:
  excel@lawrence.edu

Strongest Programs:
  Music
  Drama
  Biology
  Physics
  Psychology
  English

Lawrence University is an unpretentious school that can appeal to both the left and right side of students' brains. For those with an analytical bent, there is Lawrence's uncommon laser physics program. More creative types can take advantage of the school's renowned Conservatory of Music, one of only two at a small liberal arts college (the other is at Oberlin).

Lawrence's campus is on a wooded bluff above the Fox River, perfect for long walks, jogging, or simply meditating underneath the trees. It was chosen in 1847 by one of Appleton, Wisconsin's, earliest settlers. The pristine eighty-four-acre campus reflects several architectural styles of the past 150 years, including classical revival, 1920s Georgian-inspired, and 1950s and 1960s institutional, unified by their limestone color. The award-winning Wriston Art Center and the Conservatory's Ruth Harwood Shattuck Hall of Music (both designed by Lawrence graduates) bring contemporary architectural touches to the campus. Youngchild Hall, which also houses science programs, recently received $11 million in upgrades, and a new $15.3 million dorm is being built.

The second coeducational college established in the nation, Lawrence was founded to educate German immigrants and Native Americans. While coeducation was shocking, innovators at Lawrence didn't stop there. More than fifty years ago, administrators introduced the Freshman Studies program, a required two-term course focusing primarily on the great works of art, music, and literature of primarily the Western tradition. These days, general education requirements at Lawrence include Freshman Studies, distribution requirements and diversity, foreign language, and writing-intensive courses. Most departments now offer minors, and newly added programs include Japanese and an ethnic studies minor.

At the school's Conservatory of Music, first-year music students are offered courses including theory and analysis, keyboard skills, sight-reading, ear training, and applied study in music. The Conservatory's instrument collection includes an 1815 Broadwood piano identical to Beethoven's Broadwood, and a Guarneri violin. There is also a first-rate jazz group along with classical and world music programs; it offers a bachelor's degree in music within its liberal arts environment, plus a unique five-year bachelor's and master's program that receives regular national acclaim. "Music is the unifying theme at Lawrence," says one student. "Almost everybody plays it or studies it or likes to listen to it and talk about it." A five-year program allows students to earn two degrees—one in music and one in another subject.

Overall, however, the most popular major is biology, followed by music performance and history. Students say that they tend to avoid the anthropology department because it is "really small and understaffed." Students are encouraged to spend at least one of the year's three terms off campus. Lawrence is known for its London Study Center, which allows students to take classes "across the pond" while taking advantage of the city's many cultural activities. Other off-campus programs involve the Kurgan Technical Pedagogical Institute in Russia, Waseda University in Japan, and the Ecoles des Beaux Arts in France. Programs in marine biology research are held in the Cayman Islands. In all, forty off-campus programs are available.

Back on campus, Lawrence students appreciate their professors' expertise and experience. They say faculty members are accessible and highly encouraging of intellectual curiosity while still showing compassion for all of students' needs. "Their dedication to students is unsurpassed, and it is rare when students do not meet with their professors outside of class," a senior physics major says. Because of the three-term calendar, the academic climate is intimate and intense. "The courses are tough, and nobody has an easy time getting As," confides a senior. Students choose their own faculty advisors and meet with them at least once a term. The system gets top-notch reviews from students.

Most of Lawrence's students hail from Wisconsin or the Midwest. Most attended public high school, and 76 percent graduated in the top quarter of their class. The student body is described as a diverse group of individuals. "It's not unusual to find a classical violinist who majors in physics or a chemistry major who also minors in studio art," notes one junior. Minority enrollment is only about 10 percent, with Asian-Americans the largest group at less than 3 percent. International students account for 9 percent of the student body, representing more than forty countries. The political climate on campus is somewhat liberal—there's a leftist newspaper—but "sometimes outside politics can have a hard time penetrating the campus," a sophomore says.

The dorms at Lawrence are well populated; all but 3 percent of students live on campus. That's because you have to get permission to move off, which is no easy feat. A full 30 percent of men and 22 percent of women go Greek at Lawrence, and that gives the men the opportunity to live in their houses. Sororities can claim a house through a new group-housing program. Two dorms are reserved for upperclassmen, and six small university-owned houses handle overflow. All halls are coed, by room or by floor, and all have laundry facilities, kitchens, televisions, Internet links, and lounges. Students praise the variety of housing choices. They report the older halls are more elegant, but the newer ones are more practical, with extra storage space and other amenities. "The dorms all have their own special reputations, but they are all clean, comfortable, well maintained, and close to everything," raves one sophomore. On-campus students have a choice of meal plans and eat in one of the two dining halls, where meals are reportedly monotonous.

Social life at Lawrence stays almost entirely on campus, although some say it's beginning to move off campus because of stricter alcohol policies. It's almost impossible for underage students to be served at the on-campus bar, but the story is different at private parties and dorm rooms. A sophomore notes that "the university does not support or enable underage drinking, of course, but no one is here to baby-sit you either." Fraternity parties, room parties, conservatory concerts, film series, coffeehouses, and art openings keep students busy. "There is usually enough going on on campus to keep everyone busy enough," says a junior. Those over twenty-one frequent Pat's Tap and the Wooden Nickel in town. The school radio station also broadcasts a fifty-hour trivia contest in January, in which each hall has its own team, and students stay up for the entire weekend answering offbeat questions. Once spring finally arrives, students look forward to a popular arts festival aptly called Celebrate! Octoberfest is also a big event, held in conjunction with the city of Appleton.

And what would a Midwest fall Saturday be without football? The Lawrence team draws good crowds almost every weekend. Women's cross-country and soccer have brought home recent Midwest Conference championships. Men's basketball is notable, too. The sparkling recreation center helps students fend off midwinter blues, sometimes in very strange ways: five years ago, 187 "Larries" set a Guinness world record by traveling 220 feet on a 120-foot toboggan in Appleton's Memorial Park. Participating in a rousing game of intramural broomball, which is ice hockey

Lawrence is diversifying its curriculum, recently adding Japanese language instruction within the Asian studies program, as well as a minor in ethnic studies.

Student-housing opportunities will grow when the school opens a new $15.3 million, 79,500-square-foot dorm, which will house 179 students.

The sparkling recreation center helps students fend off midwinter blues, sometimes in very strange ways: five years ago, 187 "Larries" set a Guinness world record by traveling 220 feet on a 120-foot toboggan in Appleton's Memorial Park.

played on shoes with brooms as sticks and kickballs as pucks, is a must for students, even if all you do is watch.

Students rarely venture into Appleton for fun; although the campus can seem suffocatingly small, there's not much to do in the town. "Students do almost nothing in town," complains a senior who notes there are not enough cultural opportunities. The nearest grocery store is a five-minute drive away, as is the nearest theater, and many students see a car as a necessity. A music student says that most students don't go off campus often to do things, though administrators insist that townspeople frequently visit for theater, concerts, art exhibits, and lectures. Volunteerism is popular, however, and students regularly take part in activities such as tutoring at local schools. The best road trips are Milwaukee (two hours), Green Bay (half an hour), and Chicago (four hours). There are also weekend seminars at Bjorklunden, the college's 425-acre estate on the shores of Lake Michigan.

With its outstanding liberal arts curriculum, knowledgeable and caring faculty, an administration that treats students like adults, and a charming country setting, Lawrence University is easily one of the best little-known schools in the country. And for students with a musical ear, Lawrence's symphony of offerings sounds especially pleasant.

Overlaps

University of Wisconsin at Madison, Macalester, Oberlin, Northwestern, Grinnell

If You Apply To ➤

Lawrence: Early decision: Nov. 15. Early action: Dec. 1. Regular admissions: Jan. 15. Financial aid: Mar. 1. Guarantees to meet demonstrated need. Campus interviews: recommended, informational. Alumni interviews: optional, informational. SATs or ACTs: required. SAT IIs: Optional. Music applicants must audition. Accepts the Common Application and electronic applications. Essay question: movie, play, book or piece of music that has challenged your thinking; significant experience, achievement, or risk; or what you would do with a year of funding.

Lehigh University

27 Memorial Drive West, Bethlehem, PA 18015

Lehigh is built on the powerful combination of business and engineering. Lehigh occupies a middle ground between the techie havens, such as Rennselaer and Drexel, and the liberal arts/engineering institutions such as Bucknell and Union. By graduation, students are primed for the job market.

Website: www.lehigh.edu
Location: City
Total Enrollment: 6,479
Undergraduates: 4,650
Male/Female: 59/41
SAT Ranges: V 593–660
  M 620–710
Financial Aid: 45%
Expense: Pr $ $ $
Phi Beta Kappa: Yes
Applicants: 8,088
Accepted: 47%
Enrolled: 29%
Grad in 6 Years: 83%

Lehigh University's reputation as a factory producing skilled engineers has traveled far and wide. But the P.C. Rossin College of Engineering and Applied Science is only one of four undergraduate divisions at this multifaceted school. From the College of Arts and Sciences (the school with the highest enrollment) to the College of Education and the College of Business and Economics, Lehigh combines the academic resources of a large research university with the collegial atmosphere of a much smaller institution. Students choose from a vast selection of courses; classroom work is challenging, but not overwhelming. "Lehigh perfectly combines competitive academics with a great social life," says a junior.

Grand old oaks shade the buildings on Lehigh's 1,600-acre campus, which is tucked into the side of an eastern Pennsylvania mountain. Architectural styles range from ivy-covered collegiate Gothic to modern glass and steel. The Goodman Athletic Campus provides first-class practice and playing facilities for Lehigh's sports teams, including a sixteen thousand-seat stadium and fields for the lacrosse and field hockey squads.

Because so much of Lehigh's reputation rests on its consistently strong engineering program, the school is investing $75 million over the next few years to enhance critical academic programs such as optoelectronics, bioscience, and biotechnology. New majors, including business economics and supply-chain management, augment already-notable programs in the College of Business and Economics, such as accounting, finance, management, and marketing. The College of Arts and Sciences boasts strong psychology, political science, architecture, and biology departments, although students say the math and journalism/communications programs suffer because of their small size. Despite its emphasis on science and engineering, Lehigh also has active theater and music programs; non-majors may join student ensembles, which have toured Europe, Asia, and the U.S.

Requirements vary by college, and engineers face the most. Regardless of major, all freshmen must take two semesters of English (the second is said to be better than the first). Special degree options include seven-year programs, offered with two Pennsylvania medical schools, that lead to bachelor's and medical or dental degrees, and a five-year arts and engineering program, leading to B.A. and B.S. degrees. Co-ops allow certain engineering students to spend eight months working for a major-related company—and getting paid to do so—while still graduating in four years. Lehigh is big on connecting disparate disciplines, with a four-year integrated business and engineering curriculum, five-year programs leading to a B.A. or B.S. and a master's in education, plus teacher certification, and the combined education-MBA program, geared to future school administrators. IP3—the acronym stands for integrated product, process, and project—brings engineering, business, and arts students together to design and make products for sponsoring companies.

Lehigh also offers more than fifty study-abroad options in thirty countries, some through the Lehigh Valley Association of Independent Colleges.* And every summer, the Martindale Scholars Program sends a dozen select juniors to another country, where they interview business and political leaders and write reports on the country's economy for a journal.

The workload at Lehigh is heavy, especially in engineering and business; students are ambitious, and many pursue double majors. "Each class is expected to be the student's top priority," says a psychology major. "It seems that you are always racing against the curve," agrees a materials science and engineering major. Except for first-year English classes, professors teach all courses, with teaching assistants handling weekly recitation sections. Eighty-three percent of courses have fifty or fewer students, and "Lehigh is very good at making it so that you can take all the courses you need,

"Lehigh perfectly combines competitive academics with a great social life."

and most of those you want, in four years," says one student. (Those who can't, or don't want to, but manage to maintain a 3.75 GPA are eligible for a fifth year of study tuition-free.) For academic or career planning, professors "are more than delighted to help, but you need to approach them," a senior says.

Lehigh's two main libraries include a card catalog accessible from most computers on campus, including those in students' rooms; virtually all rooms in campus buildings, including dorms, have high-speed Internet access. Also noteworthy is the International Multimedia Resource Center, which gets news broadcasts from more than twenty-five countries via satellite. Even those not yet on campus quickly learn how wired Lehigh is: through the Lehigh Clipper Project, students accepted for early admission may take Web-based freshman courses without charge, getting a jump on graduation requirements.

Only 28 percent of Lehigh's students come from Pennsylvania, three-quarters are white, and the majority graduated from public high schools. Diversity is improving— African-Americans and Hispanics now constitute 6 percent of the student body, and

(Continued)
Returning Freshmen: 94%
Academics: ✍ ✍ ✍ ✍
Social: ☎ ☎ ☎ ☎
Q of L: ★ ★
Admissions: (610) 758-3100
Email Address:
  admissions@lehigh.edu

Strongest Programs:
  Engineering
  Accounting
  Finance
  Sciences
  Architecture

Asian-Americans add 6 percent—but still could be greater. "Students are very driven to succeed," says one. "They tend to come from money, and have a strong desire to do the same." Things are changing, albeit slowly, thanks to a decrease in drinking and a new emphasis on the arts and humanities, students say. "Our campus used to be very Republican and conservative, but now I think it's liberal," says a senior.

Two-thirds of Lehigh students live on campus; freshmen and sophomores are guaranteed housing, and freshmen must live in Sayre Park Village or Campus Square. "There are two types of freshman dorms: Lower Cents, small halls that are more close-knit at the end of a year, and the Freshman Quad buildings, which are large and introduce a lot of people in one year," one student says. "Most of the rooms are spacious, with a lot of storage," adds another. Sophomores and juniors generally live in Greek houses—38 percent of men join fraternities and 43 percent of women pledge sororities—or in apartment-style dorms, while seniors move off campus, where some apartments are closer to their classes than their old dorm rooms. Other options include special-interest housing, such as Umoja House for interested African-Americans and Hispanics, and residential colleges, in which faculty masters, resident assistants (known as "gryphons"), and students from all classes live together. Lehigh's dining service has been honored with the Ivy Award, given by the restaurant industry to first-class restaurants such as Spago in Los Angeles, as well as to educational institutions including Harvard and Notre Dame.

Social life at Lehigh revolves around "the Hill," where most fraternities and a new sorority are located. Students look forward to the craziness of Greek Week carnivals each semester, with toga races, pie-eating contests, and reasonably continuous partying, ending in a huge, free picnic and live concert. Like many universities, Lehigh is struggling with an entrenched drinking culture; it's one of ten schools nationwide to get a grant from the Robert Wood Johnson Foundation to help curb alcohol abuse. New policies aim to make the campus a "healthier, safer living and learning environment" by changing Lehigh's culture—placing stricter rules on parties and tailgating, and expanding alcohol-free programming. Administrators point to a 50 percent drop in campus crime as proof of progress. "The social life is very party-oriented, but they are trying to move away from that," agrees a materials science and engineering major.

> **"Our campus used to be very Republican and conservative, but now I think it's liberal."**

The bustling campus stands in contrast to the worn condition of Bethlehem, a once-great steel town. However, the town has drawn a number of emerging information-technology companies, many with ties to Lehigh professors and the university's mountaintop research park. Lehigh has also joined a $400 million redevelopment effort that will include a Smithsonian Institute Museum of Industry, a multiplex theater, and a large new hotel and conference center. While the university's immediate neighborhood, South Bethlehem, "has a pretty bad reputation," says a senior, "I love it, and feel very safe." By contrast, the student says, "North Bethlehem is beautiful and historic," with an active downtown and cultural district.

For non-Greeks, or those who don't want to end the evening soaked in beer, various clubs and organizations sponsor concerts, comedians, performances, and other diversions, often at the striking Zoellner Arts Center or the 6,000-seat Stabler Arena. Center-city Bethlehem is five minutes from campus, and one in four students volunteers in the community, often at the Boys and Girls Club or through America Reads. In late August, just before classes begin, the town hosts Musikfest, a celebration with oompah bands, "chicken dancing" (that's a polka), international foods, arts and crafts, and free concerts. Shortly thereafter, CelticFest is underway. For those with wheels, Philadelphia is an hour's drive, and New York City is barely two; students may buy

> **"The average Lehigh student not only has intelligence, but can communicate it as well."**

tickets to Broadway shows for $15 through the university. Skiers will appreciate the close proximity of the Poconos in the winter, while sun worshippers can enjoy the nearby Jersey shore in the early fall and late spring.

While Lehigh's varsity wrestling team has been strong for years, the biggest deal is still the annual sell-out football game against Lafayette. Lehigh is a Division I-AA powerhouse, winning titles in 2000 and 2001, and its rivalry with Lafayette is one of the oldest on the east coast. "I hate football," says one Mountain Hawk (the Lehigh mascot), "but I go to this game." Women's swimming is also strong, bringing home two championships recently. Even weekend warriors will find something to cheer about in the Taylor Fitness Center's weight room, two pools, and racquetball and squash courts.

Lehigh students proudly juggle rigorous classes and a packed extracurricular calendar. They give college life more than the old college try—and expect to succeed. "Students at Lehigh University set the perfect example of combining academic vigor and social interaction," a journalism major says. "The average Lehigh student not only has intelligence, but can communicate it as well."

> ## Overlaps
> **Bucknell, Boston College, Penn State, Cornell, University of Pennsylvania**

If You Apply To ➤ **Lehigh:** Early decision: Nov. 15. Regular admissions: Jan. 1. Financial aid: Mar. 1. Meets demonstrated need of 42%. Campus interviews: recommended, informational. No alumni interviews. ACTs or SATs: required. SAT IIs: required (all three may not be math-related). Apply to particular colleges. Accepts the Common Application and electronic applications. Essay question: why Lehigh is a good match for you; greatest high-school accomplishment; what can you contribute to Lehigh.

Lewis & Clark College

0615 Southwest Palatine Hill Road, Portland, OR 97219-7899

The West Coast's leader in international and study-abroad programs. Politically liberal, but not so far out as cross-town neighbor Reed. Portfolio Path to admission allows students to finesse standardized tests. With Mount Hood visible in the distance, there is a wealth of outdoor possibilities.

The nineteenth-century explorers Lewis and Clark struck out from middle America to find where the trail ended, and their travels took them to Portland, a lush, green paradise by the Willamette River that's often—and unfortunately—overshadowed by its seemingly hipper neighbor to the north, Seattle. The college that bears the explorers' names gained notoriety for graduating a former White House intern named Monica Lewinsky. But it's the school's international focus—more than 7,500 Lewis & Clark students have explored the world since 1962—and its setting in a quiet, residential neighborhood not far from Portland's brewpubs, coffeehouses, and hiking trails, that continue to draw high achievers.

Lest students become too enchanted overseas, Lewis & Clark lures them back with a gorgeous campus perched atop fir-covered bluffs overlooking the river. The campus is an old estate, complete with elaborate gardens, fountains, and pools, where cement is almost nonexistent and the roads are instead paved with cobblestones. Newer structures, added among the traditional Tudor buildings, reflect the heritage of Native American tribes of the Northwest. New residence halls and an expansion of the Law School were recently completed.

Lewis & Clark requires that all students achieve competency in a foreign language and international study; more than half of the students fulfill these

Website: www.lclark.edu
Location: Suburban
Total Enrollment: 2,947
Undergraduates: 1,682
Male/Female: 40/60
SAT Ranges: V 590–670
M 570–660
ACT Range: 25–29
Financial Aid: 53%
Expense: Pr $ $
Phi Beta Kappa: Yes
Applicants: 2,859
Accepted: 68%
Enrolled: 22%
Grad in 6 Years: 63%
Returning Freshmen: 80%
Academics: ✍ ✍ ✍

requirements by studying overseas for a semester or more. Students may travel to countries including Australia, China, Colombia, Ecuador, Japan, Kenya, Germany, France, and Scotland, and may also study in a number of American cities—some study in two or three countries. Freshmen also take a class called Inventing America, where they analyze the formation of the United States. In addition to the international requirement, students must complete courses in scientific and quantitative reasoning, creative arts, foreign languages, and physical education.

Not surprisingly, the most popular major at Lewis & Clark is international affairs, followed closely by psychology and English. The business major has been dropped, and the economics program now offers concentrations in international, management, public policy, or theory. "History is heavily underrated; it is a fantastic program," says a religious studies major. "Political science is very strong. Computer science has a good history of job placement." Music and art are well regarded, but students report difficulty getting into certain courses—even for majors—because these departments are small. Honors programs are available in all majors, and 3–2 programs in engineering are also offered.

> **"Courses are thorough, but not excessive."**

Lewis & Clark offers a Portfolio Path to admission, where students present a package representing their talents and interests and don't have to submit SAT or ACT scores as a reward. In addition to essays and other items required of students who send in test scores, PP students supply three teacher recommendations and graded samples of high-school work, such as essays, lab reports, or samples of art or music. Some students who use this approach feel standardized tests don't do them justice, while others have "incredible test scores." The key to a good portfolio is a "well-rounded approach," administrators say. "The more creative, the better, but be sure it's not solely artwork or writing samples."

Given this open attitude, it's not surprising that L&C students are not cutthroat. The atmosphere is "challenging and motivational, but not oppressive," explains a student majoring in psychology and sociology/anthropology. "Courses are thorough, but not excessive." Freshmen and graduating seniors get priority in the registration process, helping ensure graduation in four years for those who declare majors early and plan a way to fit in all of the requirements. Grad students don't teach classes, and professors get high marks. "They are experienced, approachable, personal, insightful, helpful, and enthusiastic," says a sophomore. "The professors are my favorite thing about this school," adds a junior. Every year, students and faculty members organize three major symposia—one on international affairs, one on environmental affairs, and the other on gender studies.

> **"Students are liberal, conservative, hippie-ish, and also just run-of-the-mill, average people."**

Lewis & Clark tends to attract West Coasters seeking an emphasis on the liberal arts; it's also a haven for easterners who see L&C's open and outdoorsy feel as the antithesis of the typical prep school or fancy suburban high-school scene. "Students are liberal, conservative, hippie-ish, and also just run-of-the-mill, average people," says a freshman. Those who succeed are very independent, adds a junior: "So many students study abroad that often it is hard to make strong connections and keep them. People have to be flexible. Students are friendly, but do not tend to be highly sociable." The campus is only 65 percent white, but administrators have still made boosting diversity a priority. "L&C students are very liberal," says a philosophy major. "They like to pour their energy into social causes and community service. They also tend to want to take their academics and relate them to social change." The center for service draws students to volunteer projects that aim to combat AIDS and homelessness, among other causes.

Lewis & Clark offers a Portfolio Path to admission, where students present a package representing their talents and interests and don't have to submit SAT or ACT scores as a reward.

A residency requirement keeps students on campus their first two years, and most move off campus after that. Owing to the college's hilltop location, lucky dorm residents have views of Mount St. Helens, Mount Hood, or the Portland skyline. There are six coed residence halls and one that's all women, as well as theme floors for students involved in performing arts, foreign languages, outdoor pursuits, and other programs. Dorms are comfortable and spacious: "Not five-star, but livable," says a sophomore. Despite L&C's location in a residential section of Portland, safety is a priority—residence halls have card-swipe entry systems and door alarms, and campus security has officers on duty twenty-four hours. Aside from the Fields Dining Room (a.k.a. the Airplane Hangar because of its high ceilings and width), students may eat at two student-run restaurants that also host study breaks, movie nights, and musical performances.

Lewis & Clark requires that all students achieve competency in a foreign language and international study; more than half of the students fulfill these requirements by studying overseas for a semester or more.

Fun-seekers at Lewis & Clark rely primarily on SOFA (Students Organized for Activities) for on-campus movies, contests, dances, and talent shows, although "there aren't many campus-wide social events," says a junior, perhaps because there's no Greek system. On the weekends, College Outdoors sponsors trips to Mount Hood (great skiing, about an hour distant) or the coastal beaches (an hour and a half). Seattle and Vancouver, B.C., three- and six-hours' drive, are favorite road trips, as are San Francisco and Las Vegas when there's more time. Despite the famous rains of the Pacific Northwest, the campus is officially dry; per Oregon law, no one under twenty-one may drink, except perhaps in a room with a closed door and a few friends. The neighborhood immediately surrounding the college is pleasant, affluent suburbia, which means few stores, restaurants, or bars. The activity of downtown Portland—mostly on Hawthorne Boulevard in the southeast section, and in the Pearl District or on 23rd Street in the northwest quadrant—is fifteen minutes away on the city's public transit system or the campus shuttle service, the Pioneer Express. "Portland is very serious about underage drinking," says a sophomore. "A convincing fake ID is required for participation in the bar scene."

"Portland is very serious about underage drinking."

As might be expected at a school in the outdoorsy northwest, Lewis & Clark has excellent athletic facilities and a well-organized intramural program. The men's basketball team won the Northwest Conference in 1999–2000 and 2000–01, and individual athletes from the cross-country and track and field teams have participated in NCAA championships. Women's basketball, softball, tennis, and volleyball are also popular.

Lewis & Clark College draws students who are "outdoor enthusiasts, athletically involved, academically curious," says a sophomore. "Students tend not to be career-oriented, and are instead rather laid back," adds a junior. That's not to say they are lazy; in fact, it's just the opposite. Like the school's mascot, students are knowledge-seeking pioneers—ones who would have made Lewis and Clark, the explorers, proud.

Overlaps
University of Oregon, University of Puget Sound, Willamette, UC—Santa Cruz, Colorado College

If You Apply To ➤

Lewis and Clark: Early action: Dec. 1. Regular admissions: Feb. 1. Financial aid: Mar. 1. Meets demonstrated need of 55%. Campus interviews: recommended, informational. Alumni interviews: optional, informational. SATs or ACTs: required (except Portfolio Path). SAT IIs: optional. Accepts the Common Application and electronic applications. Essay question: significant person or experience; issue of local, national, or international concern; situation or experience that changed your values or opinion; character in a book to whom you can best relate.

Louisiana State University

110 Thomas Boyd Hall, Baton Rouge, LA 70803

In the state that invented Mardi Gras, students come to LSU for both a good time and a good education. The latter can be had in business, engineering, and life science fields. Administrators are trying to make LSU a more serious place with rising admission standards and curbs on underage drinking.

Website: www.lsu.edu
Location: Urban
Total Enrollment: 31,392
Undergraduates: 26,518
Male/Female: 47/53
ACT Range: 21–26
Financial Aid: 28%
Expense: Pub $ $
Phi Beta Kappa: Yes
Applicants: 10,536
Accepted: 79%
Enrolled: 64%
Grad in 6 Years: 58%
Returning Freshmen: 83%
Academics: ✍ ✍
Social: 🐯 🐯 🐯 🐯 🐯
Q of L: ★ ★ ★
Admissions: (225) 578-1175
Email Address:
    admissions@lsu.edu

Strongest Programs:
    Accounting
    Engineering
    Economics
    Political Science
    Physics
    English
    Animal Science
    Plant Biology

Whether it's the abundance of azaleas and Japanese magnolias, the smell of Cajun cuisine, the sororities' antebellum mansions, or the diehard football rivalry with Ole Miss, few schools evoke the spirit of the South like Louisiana State University. Students here enjoy tailgate parties, road trips to New Orleans, and festivals such as Groovin' on the Grounds—and somehow squeeze in classes, too.

LSU's campus includes more than 250 principal buildings on the main 650-acre plateau—most in the Italian Renaissance style, with tan stucco walls and red-tile roofs. They sit along the banks of the Mississippi River on the grounds of a former plantation. Lakes and huge oak trees diffuse the strong sun and help temper Louisiana's legendary humidity. "LSU is a special place because of its beauty and tradition. The large oaks and arches make this campus so unique," says a sophomore. The life science building was recently expanded and an addition to Nicholson Hall, the physics building, is underway.

The historic acceptance at LSU of New Orleans' theme "Laissez les bons temps roulez!" (Let the good times roll!) is shifting as administrators work overtime to make the school competitive. Formerly an open-admissions university for state residents, LSU has been tightening its standards, requiring all freshmen to have successfully completed 17.5 high-school units in designated academic areas, including computer studies and a foreign language. For out-of-state applicants, grades and test scores are weighed equally. Students encounter a rigorous core curriculum, including thirty-nine semester hours in six areas: English composition, analytical reasoning, arts, humanities, and the natural and social sciences.

Students give high marks to LSU's French, design, theater, agriculture, history, and geology departments, and note that while the sciences are solid, they're tough. Engineering and accounting are also highly regarded. And, as one of the nation's twenty-five sea-grant colleges (as well as a land-grant college), LSU's offerings in coastal studies and coastal ecology are notable as well. Across the board, students praise the faculty, and say graduate students mainly teach lab sections in the sciences. "Teachers have office hours available and really care about their students," says a sophomore kinesiology student.

Although some faculty members' preoccupation with research can be annoying, most are accessible to undergraduates. Indeed, contact with professors here is said to be better than average, and freshmen are often taught by full professors. The academic and career counseling programs generally get good reviews. But taking initiative seems good advice at this thirty thousand student hub of activity, where a junior reports that "general advisors are not readily available, but department advisors are very accessible and willing to help."

"LSU is a special place because of its beauty and tradition."

Nine out of ten LSU Tigers are Louisiana residents, but don't try to paint them with the stereotypical Southern conservative brush. "The students here are very diverse. Everyone can find a group they can fit in with," says a dietetics major. Still, just a few years ago, students were proudly calling LSU "the deepest of the Deep South universities." Whites comprise 79 percent of the student body, African-Americans

10 percent, Hispanics 3 percent, and Asian-Americans 4 percent. Nearly 2,500 merit scholarships are available to qualified students and standout athletes can vie for 460 athletic awards in eighteen sports.

Housing is available to all students who apply, and 23 percent of students live in campus residences. Upperclassmen tend to prefer off-campus housing. The dorms get mixed reviews, and students say the process of getting a room can be frustrating. The best dorms for freshman women are said to be Herget or Miller, and for men it's Kirby Smith. All dorms are single-sex with visiting hours, and students report that rooms fill up quickly, so it's important to apply early. The meal plans that come with dorm dwelling are reportedly inexpensive. Campus security is "good and improving," says one student. "I feel very safe. There are emergency boxes everywhere," adds another. The school has a nighttime transit system so students don't have to walk alone.

A co-op program lets students combine coursework with paid on-the-job training in business, industry, or government agencies. It's mainly used by engineering, basic sciences, business administration, and agriculture students.

> **"The students here are very diverse. Everyone can find a group they can fit in with."**

Though the administration is working hard to improve academic standards, make no mistake about it: LSU offers one of the wildest party atmospheres around. One way to ensure a nonstop campus social life is to join one of the Greek organizations that draw 12 percent of the men and 16 percent of the women. The campus is theoretically dry, and a junior says, "LSU has cracked down heavily on underage drinking." Still, students admit that a determined underclassman can find booze, and drinking off campus is easy. The student union offers a wide variety of events, including movies, plays, concerts, fashion shows, lectures, and banquets. "There are also rodeos, live bands, and other activities that make LSU unique," a sophomore says. Homecoming is one of the year's biggest events, and Mardi Gras is always a popular draw. Road trips to Elvis Presley's Memphis birthplace and Florida beaches are popular.

No one is forced to spend their years at LSU shuttling between keg parties and the stadium, but few can resist the temptations of the Big Easy.

While Tiger football is king in Baton Rouge, LSU athletes have also earned their laurels (and national-championship trophies) in men's baseball and men's and women's track and field. When the Tigers are on the road, the campus tends to empty out as students follow the team or find their fun else-

> **"I love it so much, I plan to stay here after graduation!"**

where, often to Oxford, Mississippi (home of Ole Miss), or South Bend, Indiana (Notre Dame). Students are pleased with life in Baton Rouge, and one junior says, "I love it so much, I plan to stay here after graduation!" As the state capital, the city offers numerous chances to get involved in politics or volunteer programs.

LSU offers a range of academic opportunities in a setting with a traditional Southern feel. No one is forced to spend their years at LSU shuttling between keg parties and the stadium, but few can resist the temptations of the Big Easy. However, the school is looking ahead—raising admissions standards and striving for smaller classes and more funding. The trees and traditions date back more than a hundred years, but the focus is on the future.

Overlaps

University of Southwestern Louisiana, Tulane, Loyola (LA), Southeastern Louisiana, Louisiana Tech

If You Apply To ➢

LSU: Rolling admissions. Financial aid: Dec. 15 (for full scholarship). Does not guarantee to meet demonstrated need. Campus interviews: optional, informational. No alumni interviews. SATs or ACTs: required. No SAT IIs. Accepts electronic applications. No essay question.

Loyola University–New Orleans

6363 St. Charles Avenue, Box 89, New Orleans, LA 70118

There are at least four Loyolas in the nation but only one where you can go to Mardi Gras and still get back in time for class. New Orleans is an ideal setting for this Roman Catholic university with strengths in business and the arts. More progressive than any other Deep South location.

Website: www.loyno.edu
Location: Urban
Total Enrollment: 5,509
Undergraduates: 3,792
Male/Female: 37/63
SAT Ranges: V 540–640
   M 520–620
ACT Range: 23–28
Financial Aid: 54%
Expense: Pr $ $ $
Phi Beta Kappa: No
Applicants: 3,416
Accepted: 70%
Enrolled: 36%
Grad in 6 Years: 56%
Returning Freshmen: 81%
Academics: ✍ ✍ ✍
Social: ☎ ☎ ☎
Q of L: ★ ★ ★
Admissions: (800) 4-LOYOLA
Email Address:
   admit@loyno.edu

Strongest Programs:
   Music Therapy
   Music Business
   Voice/Opera
   Finance
   International Business
   Economics
   Communications
   Premed

Loyola University students lay claim to the best that New Orleans has to offer while basking in the attention of this community-focused liberal arts school. Its "peaceful, beautiful campus" provides a respite from the wild side of the Big Easy—while keeping the clubs and bars of the French Quarter just a historic streetcar ride away. The South's largest Roman Catholic university, Loyola's strongest programs draw a wide range of students, each "looking to receive a great education and have fun while we're here," says one junior.

The school's attractive and well-kept twenty-acre main campus, in the University section of Uptown New Orleans, mixes Tudor, Gothic, and modern structures. It overlooks acres of Audubon Park and, beyond, the mighty Mississippi River. Two blocks up St. Charles Avenue, Loyola's Broadway campus has an additional four acres, home to the Loyola School of Law, the Twomey Center for Peace through Justice, the visual arts department, and a residence hall. The J. Edgar and Louise S. Monroe Library houses five-hundred-thousand volumes, a center for community literacy, an art gallery, two multimedia classrooms, and Internet connections for laptop computers every 7.5 feet.

"We are sitting in the birthplace of jazz, and it shows."

Loyola offers comprehensive undergraduate degree programs in the College of Arts and Sciences. The communications major wins points with students; Loyola once owned the only TV and radio stations in New Orleans. "Every year, the communications department has winning advertising and public relations teams, and the newspaper constantly wins awards," according to one student. Also in demand is the international business program in the College of Business Administration and virtually any major in the College of Music. "We are sitting in the birthplace of jazz, and it shows," says a junior. Students are advised to "be quick about" registering for needed classes. There are no teaching assistants, and students love that most of their professors have doctorates. "The quality of the professors is extraordinary," a sophomore says. "They want to see their students succeed." Students take twenty-four credits of introductory courses and twenty-four more of advanced courses in English, history, math, philosophy, religious studies, social sciences, natural science, and humanities/arts.

Loyola is not a land of library addicts. "A student can make Loyola as competitive as he or she wants it to be," a student says. "There are those who are definitely overachievers, and then those just trying to get by." First-year students participate in a three-day orientation and can take advantage of more than twenty-two learning communities designed around various majors. Loyolans also benefit from the New Orleans Consortium, with cross-registration and library access at Tulane, Xavier, the University of New Orleans, and other schools in the area. Study-abroad programs take students to Belgium, Ireland, Mexico, France, Spain, and China. There's a 3–2 liberal arts/engineering arrangement with Tulane for those who'd rather stay here.

"Campus is one of the safest spots in New Orleans."

Fifty-one percent of Loyola students are Louisiana natives, and many of the remaining students are from the Southeast. Religion—specifically Roman Catholicism—has a significant influence on campus. "At Loyola, a student can experience the Jesuit concept of the Magis...and what the locals call 'Lagniappe,' a little something extra," says a junior. Daily mass is voluntary, but many students attend. Hispanics constitute 13 percent of the student body, African-Americans 9 percent, and Asian-Americans 5 percent. Recent hot-button issues at Loyola have included abortion rights, gay rights, and that perennial student gripe, campus parking. Loyola awards more than 1,900 scholarships each year, ranging from $1,000 to $24,000 annually, but there are no athletic scholarships.

Most Loyola students commute from home or off-campus apartments; 75 percent of first-years and 39 percent of the total undergrad population live on campus. The school has renovated two residence halls. The rooms are "comfy," but it can be hard for sophomores to find space on campus, some students say. As for safety, always an issue in a big city, one public relations major says "campus is

Loyola is not a land of library addicts. "A student can make Loyola as competitive as he or she wants it to be," a student says. "There are those who are definitely overachievers, and then those just trying to get by."

"The school is small enough that you always see a familiar face, but large enough to meet new people."

one of the safest spots in New Orleans. Campus security officers patrol on foot, by bike, and in golf carts, SUVs, and mini-vans." "No matter where you are on campus, you can see a blue light" on a call box that summons guards, explains a junior.

Loyola fields baseball and basketball teams in the Gulf Coast Athletic Conference, NAIA Division II. Basketball, men's flag football (no real pigskins at Loyola), and women's volleyball are popular pastimes. An athletic complex features racquetball and basketball courts, an Olympic-size pool, and steam and sauna rooms.

Aside from sweating on the field, students volunteer their sweat equity with the Loyola University Community Action Program, a coalition of eleven organizations that provides community-service opportunities. Fraternities and sororities are rarities at Jesuit schools, but are popular at Loyola, with 16 percent of the men and 17 percent of women choosing to belong. Major campus-wide social events include the annual Riverboat Dance, Swamp Stomp, Loyolapalooza, and Loup Garou, a concert featuring big-name bands. February brings Mardi Gras, of course—the school shuts down that week. As for underage drinking, Louisiana law requires that you be at least twenty-one to buy alcohol, but only eighteen to consume it in a private residence. While Loyola maintains that dorms are private residences, the school has also established a Coalition to Reduce Underage Drinking. But as one student says: "We live in New Orleans. They can't be too strict."

It can't be New Orleans without a mention of Mardi Gras—the school shuts down that week in February when the city says "Laissez les bons temps roulez," French for "Let the good times roll."

Students at Loyola know how to "Laissez les bons temps roulez," French for "Let the good times roll." Whether they're working closely with caring professors or relaxing with friends amid Bourbon Street's boundless energy, students are satisfied with their choice. "The school is small enough that you always see a familiar face, but large enough to meet new people," says one junior. "I couldn't imagine getting the same experience anywhere else."

Overlaps

Tulane, Louisiana State, NYU, Boston College, University of Miami (FL)

Loyola: Rolling admissions. Financial aid: Mar. 1. Housing: May 1. Does not guarantee to meet demonstrated need. Campus interviews: recommended, informational. Alumni interviews: optional, informational. Audition required for admission to the College of Music and the Department of Drama and Speech. Portfolio required for admission to the Visual Arts Program. SATs or ACTs: required. SAT IIs: optional (writing is for placement only). Accepts the Common Application and electronic applications. Essay question: discuss an "assumed truth" that you now question; what obstacles face your generation; topic of your choice.

Macalester College

1600 Grand Avenue, St. Paul, MN 55105

UN Secretary General Kofi Annan, '61, typifies one of Mac's hallmarks: an internationalist view of the world. Carleton has a slightly bigger national reputation, but Mac has St. Paul, a progressive capital city. Mac is the only leading Midwestern liberal arts college in an urban setting.

Website: www.macalester.edu
Location: City outskirts
Total Enrollment: 1,822
Undergraduates: 1,822
Male/Female: 42/58
SAT Ranges: V 640–730
  M 610–710
ACT Range: 28–31
Financial Aid: 68%
Expense: Pr $ $
Phi Beta Kappa: Yes
Applicants: 3,480
Accepted: 50%
Enrolled: 29%
Grad in 6 Years: 83%
Returning Freshmen: 91%
Academics: ✐ ✐ ✐ ✐ ½
Social: ☎ ☎ ☎
Q of L: ★ ★ ★ ★
Admissions: (651) 696-6357
Email Address:
  admissions@macalester.edu

Strongest Programs:
  Economics
  Religious Studies
  Chemistry
  Math
  Biology

The school has an "activist culture" when it comes to issues of local, national, or international import— sweatshops, fair trade, bombing Iraq, and gay rights, among others.

Macalester College, in the midst of the Twin Cities' hustle and bustle, might have been plucked from San Francisco's Haight-Ashbury district and set down in the Great Plains. The school has an "activist culture" when it comes to issues of local, national, or international import—sweatshops, fair trade, bombing Iraq, and gay rights, among others. However, students reserve their loudest shouts of protest for Mac's top brass, who refuse to give them "input and control over administrative decisions, like tenure," says a junior. With its Scottish roots and international focus,

"Everyone has a place at Mac—everyone."

Mac is worth a look if you can brave the bitter winters. "For every story Mac students have about their inadequate high-school experience, they have one about a trip abroad, a secret talent, or how they became commencement speaker," one student confirms. "Everyone has a place at Mac—everyone."

Macalester is located in a friendly, family oriented neighborhood near the Mississippi River, midway between Minneapolis and St. Paul, Minnesota, and one block from a tree-lined avenue with some of the state's most beautiful historic homes. The self-contained, fifty-three-acre campus hosts a mix of architectural styles, with buildings arranged around the 115-year-old Old Main, a splendid Victorian structure listed on the National Register of Historic Places. The unifying theme is red brick, the better to set off the octagonal Weyerhauser Chapel, constructed of black glass. The $18 million Campus Center opened in 2001, with seventy thousand square feet of space for students to meet, work, and socialize, plus dining facilities with cuisine from around the world. The 41,500-square-foot Kagin Commons, built at a cost of $7.7 million, opened in 2002.

Mac's extensive general requirements include eight semester hours each of social sciences and natural sciences (or math); twelve hours of humanities and fine arts (at least four in the fine arts); eight hours of diversity (four domestic, four international); and proficiency in a foreign language (equivalent to four hours of study). Everyone begins with one of more than thirty first-year courses, each capped at sixteen students and taught by a professor who becomes their advisor. About half of the classes include an added benefit: living on the same floor of a residence hall. Seniors must also complete a capstone experience involving original work, a seminar, or a performance. Mac's academic strengths include economics, religious studies, math, chemistry, and biology; the school's impressive science facilities include an observatory, an animal operant chamber, and labs for electronic instrumentation and laser spectroscopy. New options include majors in Japan studies and East Asian studies. Administrators say weaker programs include Russian, music, linguistics, and sociology.

There's an emphasis on collaboration and working together at Mac, to handle the challenging workload, and students say most pressure to do well comes from within. "We are always pushed to the maximum of our abilities, yet the environment is laid back and encouraging," says a Japan studies major. "It is impossible to go here and not be intellectually fulfilled," agrees a political science major. "The courses are always turning out to be tougher than I think they are going to be."

Teaching is paramount, with professors often having students over for dinner or taking their classes for drinks at a local watering hole. "Few students regularly skip class," one student says. "You virtually never have to take a class with an adjunct professor, though I've found them to be especially sprightly." More than one hundred students do stipend-supported research with Mac professors each summer, and since a number of faculty members play intramurals, students may find professors dishing off passes on the basketball court.

Macalester students come from every state and eighty-eight other nations; 23 percent are Minnesota natives. In addition, nearly half of the school's students participate in study abroad, through approved independent programs or the Associated Colleges of the Midwest.* Mac undergraduates may also cross-register at five other Twin Cities colleges or enroll in cooperative-degree programs in engineering, nursing, and architecture with larger Mid-western schools. Despite Mac's small size, the student body is 4 percent African-American, 3 percent Hispanic, and 5 percent Asian-American. According to the president, Macalester welcomes students who "want an academic challenge, to encounter new ideas and cultures, and to make an impact in their communities." Political debate is lively, and "race, gender, and Earth consciousness are always hot-button issues," says a political science major. "Mac students are all left-leaning—even the Republicans."

> "It is impossible to go here and not be intellectually fulfilled."

While Mac students may harbor radical political and social viewpoints, they live in traditional residences, with double rooms for the first two years, when they're required to live on campus, and suites for upperclassmen. Single-sex floors are guaranteed to those who want them; many students have single rooms, and some live in language houses. Residents of the kosher house prepare their own meals, and elsewhere on campus, chow has vastly improved with the opening of the new campus center. Seventy-two percent of students remain in college-owned digs, and more would probably stay if there were room—"juniors cannot get housing," laments a Japan studies major. Still, "off-campus living is one of the best reasons to come here," says a junior. "The surrounding neighborhoods are friendly, and many Mac students live there."

Without Greek organizations and given the proximity of a major metropolitan area ("only a $1 bus ride away"), Mac's on-campus social life "is wanting," one student says. "Many students cling to their first-year friends until they graduate." Thank goodness, then, for the close proximity of Minneapolis and St. Paul, with their bookstores, coffeeshops, restaurants, bars, and movie theaters, plus dance and jazz clubs and professional sports teams. The Mall of America is also nearby, though Mac students tend to tire of it quickly, and at

> "Mac students are all left-leaning—even the Republicans."

least one warns that "it is impossible to get anywhere without a car—the public transportation in the Twin Cities is deficient." For those with wheels, the best road trips include Chicago; Madison, Wisconsin; and Duluth and Bemidji, Minnesota, "to see Babe the Blue Ox," reports a senior.

During the first weekend in May, Macalester hosts the annual Scottish Country Fair. More than one hundred bagpipers descend on Mac's main lawn in something like "a scene from *Braveheart*," blaring away from 8 A.M. until 6 P.M. Other popular events include Spring Fest and the annual Brain Bowl football game against in-state rival Carleton, "the only school we can't chant 'We are smarter than you!' to," says a communications studies major. Although men's and women's soccer recently joined the debate team as champions, the math and computer programming teams are the ones that often compete internationally. "The days of ruthless rivalry are over and done with," quips another student. "Mac athletics are all about lazy fun in the sun."

During the first weekend in May, Macalester hosts the annual Scottish Country Fair. More than one hundred bagpipers descend on Mac's main lawn in something like "a scene from Braveheart," blaring away from 8 A.M. until 6 P.M.

Seventy-two percent of students remain in college-owned digs, and more would probably stay if there were room—"juniors cannot get housing," laments a Japan studies major.

Overlaps

Carleton, Wesleyan, Oberlin, Washington University (MO), Brown

Macalester students are an open-minded, friendly bunch who are more politically and socially progressive than their peers at similar institutions, says a Japan studies major. As the school keeps "rushing toward Ivy League–ness, the intellectual caliber of professors and students continues to rise," adds a junior. Still, the student says, one thing hasn't changed: "Students at Mac are brightly skeptical about everything in the world—this is their distinguishing trait."

University of Maine–Orono

Orono, ME 04469

A sleeper choice for out-of-staters amid better-known public universities such as UMass, UNH, and UVM. Not coincidentally, Maine is the least expensive of the four. A popular marine sciences program flourishes here, as do forestry and a range of preprofessional programs.

Website: www.umaine.edu
Location: Rural
Total Enrollment: 10,282
Undergraduates: 8,229
Male/Female: 48/52
SAT Ranges: V 480–590
  M 490–600
ACT Range: 20–25
Financial Aid: 69%
Expense: Pub $ $ $ $
Phi Beta Kappa: Yes
Applicants: 4,783
Accepted: 81%
Enrolled: 43%
Grad in 6 Years: 57%
Returning Freshmen: 77%
Academics: ✍ ✍
Social: ☎ ☎ ☎ ☎
Q of L: ★ ★ ★
Admissions: (877) 486-2364
Email Address: um-admit@
  umaine.edu

Strongest Programs:
  Forestry and Agriculture
  Engineering
  Marine Sciences

Maine is known for its hardy residents, whose insistence on braving harsh winters and the state's rugged wilderness has helped create community in hamlets like Freeport and Bar Harbor. Students find much of the same close-knit feeling at UMaine–Orono, where more than 8,000 undergraduates help themselves to a range of strong academic programs at a reasonable cost. They believe in their roles as custodians of the state's breathtaking natural resources, even taking a break from classes to keep the place pristine on Maine Day. "When I came here, I thought I was settling for a state school," says a nursing student. "But I have really enjoyed my first year." Things should only improve, with renovations to the student union nearly done and construction of a new dorm planned.

Situated on an island between the Stillwater and Penobscot rivers, UMaine's 660-acre campus centers on a large, tree-shaded grass mall. Architectural themes at this flagship of the state university system range from English academic to contemporary. A new extension to the science lab is underway, and a recreation center is in the works. The school also recently received a $25 million grant for a new marine research facility.

UMaine's seven undergraduate colleges have been restructured into five schools with greater interdisciplinary emphasis: education and human development; business, public policy, and health; engineering; liberal arts and sciences; and natural sciences, forestry, and agriculture. The Honors Program, one of the oldest in the nation, admits about two hundred students with SAT scores of 1200 or higher; it will become a free-standing college soon. Specific requirements vary from college to college, though all students must demonstrate writing proficiency and take two physical or biological science courses, eighteen credits in human value and social context, six credits in math (including statistics and computer science), and at least one ethics course. A capstone experience in the major is also mandatory.

The engineering programs are widely viewed as the most demanding on campus. Other best bets include forestry and agriculture, Canadian studies, and marine science. The forest engineering program has been restructured and renamed forest operations science, and a new media major has been added. The interdisciplinary Institute for Quaternary Studies collaborates with other research centers around the world in focusing on the Quaternary period, a time of glacial and interglacial cycles leading up to the present.

(Continued)
Business Administration
Biology
Education
Music

The university library, one of the state's finest, is the regional depository for American and Canadian government documents, and houses some of alumnus Stephen King's papers. Former U.S. Senator William S. Cohen, a UMaine faculty member before he became defense secretary in the Clinton administration, donated his personal papers to the university as well. The papers, which chronicle Cohen's twenty-four-year congressional career, will be used to develop a nonpartisan center on international policy and commerce focused on teaching, research, and public service, and named in Cohen's honor. They are also available to scholars interested in Cohen's career.

"We have a program where people can actually sign contracts with the university to graduate in four years, or the rest of their education is free."

Students don't expect long lines at registration, which can be done over the phone, online, or with their departments, and report that graduating in four years is virtually certain, unless you pursue a double major or choose the engineering or music programs. "We have a program where people can actually sign contracts with the university to graduate in four years, or the rest of their education is free," reports a junior. The Academic and Career Exploration program lets students work with professionals in different areas before declaring their degree choices. "Classes are tough and competitive," says an anthropology major. "Students have adopted a mellow attitude and take it in stride." Every department "has its one easy professor," adds a social work major. "I still learned a lot."

The engineering programs are widely viewed as the most demanding on campus. Other best bets include forestry and agriculture, Canadian studies, and marine science.

Outside the classroom, internships and co-ops are available in most fields, and there's a Semester-by-the-Sea and a Lobster Institute for nautical types. Juniors who want a reprieve from Maine's often brutal winters can head for Brazil, while the heartier types choose Canada, Scandinavia, and Ireland. Most students, however, are immune to the weather, since 83 percent are from Maine and many of the rest hail from other parts of New England. In fact, the student body is 93 percent white—and perhaps because of that, is relatively oblivious to social and political controversy. "Lots of people are environmentally conscious, but political correctness is absolutely not an issue," says an international affairs major. "You can be whoever you are." Merit scholarships offer $1,000 to $7,700 a year for qualified students, and there are another 150 athletic awards.

The Honors Program, one of the oldest in the nation, admits about two hundred students with SAT scores of 1200 or higher; it will become a free-standing college soon.

Fifty-five percent of UMaine students live off campus, in Orono, nearby Bangor, or the sparsely populated area in between. Dorms are coed or single-sex; some have gyms, computer labs, or apartment-style suites, with "plenty of space for two students" in a room, according to a senior. Still, not everyone is happy:

"Lots of people are environmentally conscious, but political correctness is absolutely not an issue."

"Sometimes the furniture doesn't match," one junior complains. Some housing or wings are set aside for specific majors. Dining-hall food is average, while Greeks may eat in their chapter houses.

Despite UMaine's relatively isolated location, the campus pulses with social life; more than 150 student organizations plan plays, carnival nights, concerts, and comedy hours. Partiers find their niche off campus, at bars, clubs, and house parties. Big winter events are the "bed sled" race, in which students race beds down a campus hill, and the annual carnival, featuring a school-wide snow-sculpting competition. Come spring, students go all out for April's Bumstock Weekend, a three-day event featuring bands playing outdoors from dawn 'til dusk.

The Academic and Career Exploration program lets students work with professionals in different areas before declaring their degree choices.

The mid-sized town of Orono offers a few bars, a dollar theater, and some other hangouts. Buses to Bangor, a fair-sized city ten minutes away, run every fifteen to twenty minutes. A car is helpful, although there are gripes about parking. UMaine students tend to be outdoor enthusiasts, and popular road trips include Acadia National Park, skiing at Sugarloaf USA, L.L. Bean's twenty-four-hour store in Freeport, and the real-life Mt. Katahdin, which appears on Bean's logo. More urban types enjoy Bar Harbor, Boston, or Montreal, just four hours away (and with a lower drinking age and cheaper drinks). Hockey reigns here, especially when played against New Hampshire, Boston University, or Boston College, and the Black Bears are perennial champions. Intramurals cover a range of sports from swimming and wrestling to hoopball (golf with a basketball) and broomball (ice hockey with a dodgeball and a broom, played with shoes instead of skates).

UMaine is a big school that "feels small," says a theater major. Combine the state's natural beauty with an increased emphasis on top-quality facilities and increased student-faculty interaction, and it's no surprise that this campus draws more die-hard "Maine-iacs" each year.

Overlaps

University of Southern Maine, University of New Hampshire, University of Maine–Farmington, University of Vermont, University of Massachusetts—Amherst

If You Apply To ➤

Maine: Rolling admissions. Financial aid: Mar. 1. Does not guarantee to meet demonstrated need. Campus interviews: optional, informational. No alumni interviews. SATs or ACTs: required. Accepts Common Application and electronic applications. Essay question: personal statement on academic goals and objectives or essay of student's choice.

Manhattanville College

2900 Purchase Street, Purchase, NY 10577

Though coed for more than thirty years, Manhattanville is still almost 70 percent female. Strong programs include art, education, and psychology. Among the few small colleges in the NYC area, Manhattanville is a quick train ride from the city. Portfolio system emphasizes competency rather than rote learning.

Website: www.mville.edu
Location: Suburban
Total Enrollment: 2,443
Undergraduates: 1,400
Male/Female: 31/69
SAT Ranges: V 530–780
  M 530–720
ACT Range: 20–24
Financial Aid: 70%
Expense: Pr $
Phi Beta Kappa: No
Applicants: 2,105
Accepted: 61%
Enrolled: 32%
Grad in 6 Years: 53%
Returning Freshmen: 78%
Academics: ✏️ ✏️ ✏️

Manhattanville sees its mission as "educating students to become ethically and socially responsible leaders for the global community." The Portfolio System, Manhattanville's distinct approach to undergraduate education, requires students to create a body of work reflecting their entire college career. Students must craft a freshman assessment essay, a study plan and program evaluation, specific examples of work in writing and research, and a résumé. The Portfolio Program, however, is only one way Manhattanville encourages individuality and personal growth. Personal attention is another. "You can go in and have a Diet Pepsi with the president," says one senior. "You're not just a number."

Manhattanville College, which began as a Roman Catholic academy for girls on Houston Street in New York City, pulled up stakes in the 1950s for a 125-acre estate in Purchase, New York. Today, the campus is located in wealthy Westchester County, near the town of White Plains—home to several major corporations but just twenty-eight miles from the excitement of the Big Apple. The focal point of the campus, which was designed by Central Park architect Frederick Law Olmsted, is Reid Hall, a nineteenth-century replica of a Norman castle.

Manhattanville's distribution requirements include courses in five areas: humanities, social sciences, fine arts, mathematics and sciences, and languages. Students must demonstrate English writing competency as well. Freshmen complete the Preceptorial, a two-semester introduction to college-level work, as well as a library and information studies course. Manhattanville's strongest offerings include art and design (enhanced by the proximity of New York City's many museums and galleries), music, and education, while economics and psychology are also popular. M-ville's School of Education, which offers two five-year masters programs, boasts a near-perfect passage rate for the New York State Teaching Exam. The languages—French, Spanish, Asian studies, and classics—attract the fewest majors. Students, who used to avoid math and science because of the difficulty of the classes and the age of some labs, can now enjoy facilities that are independently ranked among the top one hundred wired colleges in the country. Students may also opt to design their own major. Career Services, which offers internship opportunities at over 350 locations in the New York metro area and beyond, is "phenomenal," securing placements at places such as MTV, Metropolitan Museum of Art, Fox News, U.S. Senate offices, MasterCard, Dedicated Records, PepsiCo, and the Westchester County Board of Legislators. The school has recently reestablished the physics program and established new minors in communication and social justice.

(Continued)
Social: ☎ ☎ ☎
Q of L: ★ ★ ★
Admissions: (800) 328-4553
Email Address:
admissions@mville.edu

Strongest Programs:
Management
Art
Psychology
Education

The academic climate at Manhattanville is fairly laid back, "yet not to the point where no one is really serious about classes," says a sophomore. The low student-faculty ratio and the quality of teaching get high marks. More than 90 percent of freshmen classes have twenty-five or fewer students. Perhaps that's why "everyone knows your name," according to an English/history major. The Board of Trustee's scholarships offer qualified students an Honors Preceptorial. An Honors Seminar and honors programs within majors are also available. The college also offers dual degree programs with New York Medical College (MS in physical therapy or MS in speech language pathology) and Polytechnic University (MS in computer science or MS in information technology). The college has exchange programs with Mills College and with American University's World Capitals Program, plus study-abroad options in England, France, Germany, Ireland, Italy, Japan, Mexico, and Spain.

"Everyone knows your name."

Forty-seven countries and thirty-two states are represented by Manhattanville's student body. Females outnumber males by a ratio of two to one. Twenty-nine percent of undergraduates come from outside of New York, while 13 percent come from overseas. Hispanics comprise the largest minority group at 15 percent, followed by African-Americans at 6 percent and Asian-Americans at 3 percent. The college does not guarantee to meet the need of every admit, but there are nearly one thousand merit scholarships available, ranging from $2,000 to $10,000.

"You can go in and have a Diet Pepsi with the president," says one senior. "You're not just a number."

Sixty-eight percent of Manhattanville's students live on campus in one of four dorms, which have lounges, communal kitchens, laundry rooms, cable TV, and Internet access. Freshmen are assigned rooms which are "quite comfortable" according to a first-year art major, while upperclassmen enter a lottery—and complain they never get what they want. Campus dwellers can choose fifteen- or nineteen-meal-a-week plans, and can also use their meal cards at Café de Ville (a deli-type eatery), the convenience store, and vending machines. Students can also order "room service" three times a semester. The dining hall has been renovated and offers fresh-baked goods and a well-stocked salad bar.

"Purchase is not a college town at all, but we are close to NYC."

Manhattanville's hometown, Purchase, "is not a college town at all, but we are close to NYC," says a senior. With increasing numbers of male students enrolling, things seem to be picking up, and with no fraternities or sororities, off-campus parties are usually open to all. The student programming board is working to improve the social life, with weekend events such as dinners, formals in the castle, parties, comedy and talent shows, plays, and concerts. The student center has a movie theater.

Thirty student-run organizations help to fulfill the cultural, intellectual, and social interests of the student body, but off-campus bars still draw many students—whether of age or not. "It's really boring because so many kids leave on weekends," one student says. "There's hardly any parties, so if you want to study, go here." On campus alcohol policies are said to be strict. "We don't really serve alcohol often on campus," says a political science major. "But of course, kids still drink." Road trips include Rye Beach in the warmer months and upstate New York or Vermont for skiing in the winter. The college offers a free van service that runs into NYC, and a new bus service takes students to nearby outlets with movies, theaters, videos, bowling, billiards, restaurants, clubs, and shopping. Every spring, students look forward to Quad Jam, "an all-day, all-night concert and carnival and party." There's a Fall Jam and midnight brunches during finals served by faculty and staff.

Manhattanville athletics has seen tremendous growth and success, and now offers eighteen NCAA Division III sports. In just their second year, the women's ice hockey team was ranked fifth in the nation. Women's tennis, volleyball, and softball are solid, and men's soccer, ice hockey, lacrosse, golf, basketball, and baseball are also successful. In 2000, the men's tennis team won the Skyline Conference championship. Intramurals sometimes draw flak because of organizational problems, but overall, students enjoy them. Weekend warriors and letter-winners alike applaud the college's gym, fitness center, swimming pool, tennis courts, and athletic fields.

Manhattanville's size can be both an asset and an annoyance, say students. The familial atmosphere can get claustrophobic at times, but for those wishing to be part of a close but growing community, Manhattanville may be worth a look.

Overlaps
Fordham, NYU, Manhattan, Iona, Hofstra

If You Apply To ➤

Manhattanville: Early decision: Dec. 1. Rolling admissions, financial aid: Mar. 1. Housing: July 1. Meets demonstrated need of 39%. Campus interviews: recommended, informational. Alumni interviews: optional, informational. SATs or ACTs: required. SAT IIs: optional. Accepts the Common Application and electronic application. No essay question.

Marlboro College

Marlboro, VT 05344

Marlboro is a hilltop home to several hundred nonconformist souls. Each develops a plan of concentration that culminates in a senior project. One of the few colleges in the country that is governed in town-meeting style where student votes carry equal weight with those of the faculty.

Website: www.marlboro.edu
Location: Rural
Total Enrollment: 380
Undergraduates: 290
Male/Female: 41/59
SAT Ranges: V 580–680
M 500–620

Marlboro College is only one half-century old, but already the college is known far and wide as an innovator in liberal arts education. It was founded on the principles of independent and in-depth study just after World War II, when returning GIs renovated an old barn as the college's first building while living in Quonset huts. And today's Marlboro students are just as trail-blazing; they prepare for the next century by digging into self-developed Plans of Concentration, including one-on-one tutorials and a thesis or project judged by visiting outside examiners from "the best Eastern colleges and universities." With three hundred students and thirty-eight faculty members, Marlboro is its own little world, where students enter as novices and leave as pros.

Positioned atop a small mountain, surrounded by maples and pines, and with a gorgeous view of southern Vermont, Marlboro's physical beauty is striking. Buildings are adapted from barns, sheds, and houses that stood on three old farms that today make up the 350-acre campus. Among the renovated structures, many with passive solar heating, are nine dormitories, a library, a science building, art studios and music practice rooms, a 350-seat theater, and a campus center. Above the athletic field is the college's astronomical observatory. The school recently completed a new art gallery and studio, photography lab, and sculpture studio, and it is working with a professor of architecture from Yale to develop a campus planning model.

While some schools see growth as a sign of their success, Marlboro intends to remain one of the nation's smallest liberal arts institutions. Administrators believe that the size stimulates dynamic relationships between students and faculty, making learning happen both inside and outside the classroom. This isn't a place where students can fade into the background: the institution relies on everyone to share their talents and skills. The same philosophy will apply to the college's new Graduate Center; its first programs—a master of arts in teaching with Internet technologies and a master of science in Internet strategy management—are as innovative as the college's heritage.

The cornerstone of an undergraduate Marlboro education is the Plan of Concentration, which each student develops independently. Juniors and seniors "on plan" take most coursework in one-on-one tutorials with the faculty sponsors. Seniors present their thesis or project to their sponsors, who are backed up by outside examiners, experts in the student's field unaffiliated with the college. The administration boasts that by bringing in these outsiders for two- to three-hour oral examinations of its seniors, Marlboro has created its own accountability system, ensuring that neither students nor faculty at this isolated institution are cut off from the most current academic thinking. Faculty

"Everything at Marlboro screams 'interactive learning.'"

members often find the exams as stressful as the students, as it means their teaching is being judged by outsiders. The only other requirement is the Clear Writing course, usually completed freshman year. Marlboro's flexibility should not be confused with academic flabbiness, though. Grades are an integral part of the evaluation process, professors are stingy with As, and most students work hard.

Marlboro offers solid instruction in literature, writing, environmental science, sociology, psychology, and theater. Administrators and students alike praise the World Studies program, which provides an eight-month professional internship and/or study experience abroad. Music and math are said to be weaker, and since one professor can constitute an entire discipline at Marlboro because of the college's small size, a personality conflict may mean problems with a whole department. Even that can be remedied, though; in most years, students can choose among 250 courses and more than six hundred tutorials. Only six had more than twenty students. Students give most profs high marks and appreciate the low student/teacher ratio: "Everything at Marlboro screams 'interactive learning,'" says one student.

In the old independent Yankee spirit, Marlboro's library operates on the honor system, where students sign out their own books twenty-four hours a day. It is the same for the computer center, science, and humanities buildings. The school has only one security guard. "I feel really safe here," says one freshman. "Everyone is out at night and nobody's worried about assault—except maybe by bears." Indeed, the college operates on a New England town-meeting style of government involving students, faculty, staff, and their spouses in every aspect of policymaking. Students can

(Continued)
Financial Aid: 95%
Expense: Pr $ $
Phi Beta Kappa: No
Applicants: 308
Accepted: 80%
Enrolled: 40%
Grad in 6 Years: 40%
Returning Freshmen: 78%
Academics: ✍ ✍ ✍
Social: ☎ ☎ ☎
Q of L: ★ ★ ★ ★
Admissions: (800) 343-0049
Email Address:
admissions@marlboro.edu

Strongest Programs:
World Studies
Writing and Literature
Environmental
Studies/Biology
Sociology
History

Marlboro is its own little world, where students enter as novices and leave as pros.

veto the faculty members on hiring and retention decisions, and it takes a two-thirds vote of the faculty to override them.

Clearly, 1960s-era liberalism is still the dominant political tone on this campus. A big issue these days is parking: "Should students be able to park on campus, or are cars too hideously ugly to be seen at Marlboro?" asks a psychology major. Minority enrollment continues to be low (4 percent), in spite of the administration's program to recruit and support poor rural Vermonters. The college offers fifty merit scholarships of up to $5,000 every year, but no athletic scholarships for the single reason that there are no varsity sports.

The dorms are mostly coed, and students say they have a "rustic" appeal. "The rooms are huge, something I took for granted until I visited friends at other schools," says one dorm-dweller. Housing is based on credits, so freshmen have triples, sophomores have doubles, and upperclassmen have singles. Twenty-two percent of students live off campus in Brattleboro, twenty minutes away, and shuttle to and from campus in a school van.

Students agree that the town of Marlboro, highlighted by a post office and general store, isn't much to write home about. Most head to Brattleboro for its restaurants, bookstores, and coffeeshops. As might be expected, Marlboro has no Greek organizations; a new staff member was recently hired to coordinate the planning of student activities like poetry readings, trips to Boston and New York City, vans to local movie theaters, and pumpkin-carving contests. Snowball fights by the library are a big draw in winter. On Community Work Day, students and faculty skip class and work together to improve the campus through various manual labor projects. The annual Cabaret and Halloween parties are unofficial costume contests showcasing student creativity.

> **"The rooms are huge, something I took for granted until I visited friends at other schools."**

The school mascot, the Fighting Dead Trees, is emblazoned on the shirts of the ever popular co-ed soccer team, and broomball, a variation of ice hockey played on shoes with brooms instead of sticks and a kickball instead of a puck, is also always popular for athletes and spectators. The "incredibly dynamic" outing club ensures plenty of opportunities to enjoy the local wilderness, including hiking and cross-country skiing on runs that radiate from the center of campus. Excellent downhill skiing is only a few minutes' drive away.

This iconoclastic school continues to push the academic envelope and remains proud of doing and being the unexpected. And that suits students here just fine. Says a student, "Basically, we're a bunch of crazy, dedicated, love-struck, joyful, cynical, conscious freaks who go blasting around campus in a frenzy of creative and destructive energy."

Overlaps

Hampshire, Bennington, Bard, Earlham, Evergreen State

If You Apply To ➤ **Marlboro:** Early decision: Nov. 15. Early action: Jan. 15. Regular admissions: Mar. 1. Financial aid: Mar. 1. Housing: May 1. Guarantees to meet demonstrated need. Campus interviews: required, evaluative. Alumni interviews: optional, evaluative. SATs or ACTs: required. SAT IIs: recommended. Accepts the Common Application and electronic applications. Essay question: academic paper of student's choice (research paper, book report, expository essay) and autobiographical statement. Encourages "nontraditional" students.

Marquette University

Milwaukee, WI 53201-1881

Marquette is an old-line Roman Catholic university along the lines of St. Louis University and Loyola of Chicago. Milwaukee is not a selling point, and the university's clientele is mainly from the southern Wisconsin/northern Illinois corridor. About 80 percent of the students are Catholic.

At Marquette University, students practice what they preach. Rooted in traditional Jesuit doctrines, the educational experience at this university has not left its Roman Catholic origins behind, and includes emphasis on civic responsibility, community service, and personal growth. Innovative programs combine classroom theory with volunteer opportunities in Milwaukee and beyond.

Eighty acres of "concrete with interludes of grass and trees," Marquette University is located just a few blocks away from the heart of downtown Milwaukee. While offering the advantages of an urban setting, its campus does have plenty of open spaces suitable for everything from throwing a Frisbee to throwing a barbecue. Although most of the buildings are relatively modern, the campus is the site of the oldest building in the Western Hemisphere, the St. Joan of Arc Chapel, which was built in France in 1400 and later transported to Wisconsin. The new $30 million dental school building is completed; current construction includes the John P. Raynor S. J. Library and the Al McGuire Center athletic facility. A campus beautification project is also underway.

Marquette has added several new majors, including biological sciences, physics, statistics, physician's assistant studies, physiological sciences, management information systems, and social welfare and justice. Students are no longer being admitted into the social work and dental hygiene majors, and some students complain that the university is notorious for dropping majors without warning. "The physical therapy and physician assistant programs are very competitive and have a great reputation," remarks a junior. "Also the business and engineering schools are well known throughout the country." Through an affiliation with the Milwaukee Institute of Art and Design, two art minors, studio art and art history, are available. Marquette has its own art museum and an active theater program.

> **"We do a lot of community service and work a lot with the city of Milwaukee."**

Recently, a new general education core curriculum was put into effect. The program is comprised of nine subject areas: diverse cultures, human nature and ethics, histories of cultures and societies, individual and social behavior, theology, literature/performing arts, mathematical reasoning, rhetoric, and science and nature. In addition to myriad study-abroad programs, the university is the proud owner of the Les Aspin Center for Government located in Washington, D.C., which allows students to take courses in philosophy, political science, and theology, while simultaneously participating in an internship with a federal government agency.

Many classes are limited to fifty students, but students usually manage to get into the ones they want. The administration encourages students to "put our beliefs into practice" through volunteer activity, which serves the elderly, the sick, and the poor in the Milwaukee area and elsewhere. "We do a lot of community service and work a lot with the city of Milwaukee," one student says. Student religious organizations are active, and weekly Masses are held in the dorms by the resident priest. Roman Catholics understandably predominate in the student body, but religious practice is left to the individual. The academic climate is described as challenging

Website: www.marquette.edu
Location: Urban
Total Enrollment: 10,832
Undergraduates: 7,499
Male/Female: 45/55
SAT Ranges: V 520–630
 M 520–640
ACT Range: 23–28
Financial Aid: 58%
Expense: Pr $ $
Phi Beta Kappa: Yes
Applicants: 6,743
Accepted: 84%
Enrolled: 29%
Grad in 6 Years: 74%
Returning Freshmen: 87%
Academics: ✍ ✍ ✍
Social: ☎ ☎ ☎
Q of L: ★ ★ ★
Admissions: (414) 288-7302
 or (800) 222-6544
Email Address:
 admissions@marquette.edu

Strongest Programs:
 Dentistry
 Physical Therapy
 Law
 Biomedical Engineering
 Biology
 Nursing
 Philosophy

Physical therapy wins much praise from students, and the College of Arts and Sciences is applauded for its political science, biology, and psychology programs.

The university is the proud owner of the Les Aspin Center for Government located in Washington, D.C., which allows students to take courses in philosophy, political science, and theology while participating in an internship with a federal agency.

While offering the advantages of an urban setting, its campus does have plenty of open spaces suitable for everything from throwing a Frisbee to throwing a barbecue.

rather than cut-throat. A senior says, "I would categorize the academic climate to be competitive." Students give the counseling and academic advising mixed reviews.

An honors program with small classes is available for about seventy highly motivated students in each year, while the Freshman Frontier program offers admission and intensive assistance to students "who did not reach full academic potential in high school."

Although the university actively recruits in thirty-five or so states and several U.S. territories, most of the student body is from the Midwest, 48 percent from Wisconsin itself. In general, Marquette boasts a friendly collection of middle-class students, most of whom did well enough to graduate in the top quarter of their high-school class. Like their curriculum, Marquette students are vocationally oriented; 96 percent of graduates go into the job market or on to the military, volunteer service, or advanced study. African-Americans and Hispanics combine to make up 9 percent of the student body, while Asian-Americans make up another 4 percent. "Lack of diversity," is one of the students' biggest complaints according to a senior. Marquette offers a very successful Educational Opportunity Program, which enables low-income, disadvantaged students, most of whom are minorities, to have the advantage of a college education. There are a variety of merit scholarships, ranging from $4,000 to full tuition. In fact, nearly 50 percent of the student body receive merit-based aid of one form or another.

"The people are amazing—laid back, friendly, and involved."

As for on-campus life, all but two residence halls are coed, and the campus offers several apartment options. Residency is required for freshmen and sophomores, but by junior year an overwhelming majority of students choose to move off campus, though housing is guaranteed for all undergraduate students through a lottery. A student's ID card validated for food service ensures entrance into any of the halls' cafeterias. The university works hard to keep the campus safe, though some say it's difficult in the neighborhood. In addition to residence-hall guards, the school has blue-light emergency phones throughout the campus and operates a safety patrol escort program (to provide safe travel between the campus and surrounding residential areas) and an intracampus shuttle service complete with vans known as "limos."

Students are less than enthusiastic about the city beyond the campus, characterizing Milwaukee as "not exactly 'college town USA.'" Even so, students say they have plenty of opportunities for community service. "Marquette has a great service learning program that allows the students to take part," says one student. An old advertising slogan once claimed that "Milwaukee Means Beer," and few Marquette students would disagree. The city has more bars on a single block than are found in some entire cities. Marquette is stricter than most universities in enforcing the drinking age, but getting served off campus is not as difficult, and most students happily declare alcohol is there for the getting. Another well-loved tradition is the Miracle on Central Mall, the annual lighting of the campus Christmas tree and accompanying Mass. There are fraternities and sororities, and they attract about 8 percent of the men and women.

Sports fans will be impressed with Milwaukee's Bradley Center, close to campus and home to Marquette basketball and the NBA's Milwaukee Bucks. Nature lovers can head to Lake Michigan, a forty-minute walk from campus, or to Kettle Moraine, a glaciated region ideal for hiking and cross-country skiing. Chicago is only ninety-five miles away. As the school grows, varsity sports are gaining a higher profile, and men's and women's track, men's soccer, and women's tennis are strong, while the women's cross-country and soccer teams won conference championships in 2000.

Still, no matter how dynamic the basketball team or how impressive the facilities, it's the family atmosphere that make Marquette what it is. One student says the best thing about the school is that "the people are amazing—laid back, friendly, and involved." The classes challenge and the instructors lead the way.

University of Maryland–College Park

College Park, MD 20742

The name says Maryland, but the location says Washington, D.C. Students in College Park can jump on the Metro just the same as they do at Georgetown or American. Maryland is nothing if not big, and savvy students will look to programs such as the College Park Scholars for some personal attention.

For good luck on exams, University of Maryland students rub the nose of Testudo, the school's terrapin mascot. But even without touching the revered statue, most students here feel lucky to be at a school with so many courses, such a diverse student body, and state-of-the-art research programs and institutes. "The student body is diverse and active in many extracurriculars. Students do not just attend classes but become part of the school," gushes one happy camper.

Maryland's Georgian brick buildings are arranged in graceful quadrangles around the grassy 1,200-acre campus. New facilities include an arena, a research greenhouse complex, the Chemistry Teaching Building, South Campus Commons Apartments, and a parking garage. Students select a major from one of the twelve schools and colleges; Maryland has earned a strong reputation for its engineering, physics, and computer science departments, as well as the Robert H. Smith School of Business and Philip Merrill College of Journalism.

As might be expected at such a large school, bureaucracy is ever-present, starting with the general education requirements that comprise a third of every undergrad's total course load. These include classes in writing, math and the sciences, humanities and the arts, social sciences and history, as well as two upper-level classes outside the major, and one course focusing on cultural diversity. For students at the extremes of the academic spectrum, there's a "very impressive" honors program and an intensive educational development and tutoring program. Students participating in individual studies combine established majors and create their own programs; other options for those feeling fenced-in on campus include internships in nearby Washington, D.C., and Baltimore and study abroad in locations such as Costa Rica, Israel, and Sweden. Mary-

> "The student body is diverse and active in many extracurriculars."

land isn't so big that it can't get bigger. Several new offerings include a science journalism specialization, a meteorology-physics concentration, and a certificate program in Lesbian, Gay, Bisexual, Transgender Studies. Some new centers have been established, including one for Undergraduate Research, and the Maryland Institute for Minority Achievement and Urban Education was recently instituted.

Maryland's curriculum "is rigorous, but not overwhelming," says a cell biology major. Lower-level courses tend to be large and impersonal ("easy to hide in, even easier to skip"), but the corresponding weekly discussion sections led by teaching assistants offer personal attention. The situation improves by junior year, when classes of twenty to forty students become the norm. "The teachers expect a lot of students, but they also give a lot back," says an elementary education major.

Website: www.umd.edu
Location: Suburban
Total Enrollment: 34,160
Undergraduates: 25,099
Male/Female: 51/49
SAT Ranges: V 560–660
  M 590–690
Financial Aid: 42%
Expense: Pub $ $ $
Phi Beta Kappa: Yes
Applicants: 19,647
Accepted: 55%
Enrolled: 41%
Grad in 6 Years: 64%
Returning Freshmen: 91%
Academics: ✍ ✍ ✍
Social: ☎ ☎ ☎
Q of L: ★ ★ ★
Admissions: (301) 314-8385
Email Address: um-admit@ uga.umd.edu

Strongest Programs:
  Business
  Management Information
    Systems
  Engineering
  Journalism
  Computer Science
  Government and Politics
  Physics

"Courses do require a lot of reading." Faculty members are "knowledgeable and enthusiastic," but as might be expected given Maryland's size, students must seek them out for extra help, feedback, or assistance. The career center is "very helpful," according to a computer science major. He adds, "Academic counseling is always available. I had no problem planning my own program and getting it approved."

Only 30 percent of Maryland's freshmen may come from out of state; overall, 73 percent of students are Bay State natives, and New York and New Jersey are also well represented. Middle-class backgrounds predominate, and "the people are generally nicer and more open than at other schools," says a senior. Diversity is more than just a buzzword: 13 percent of students are African-American, 5 percent are Hispanic, and another 14 percent are Asian-American. Important campus issues include the equitable distribution of student-activity fees between various clubs and organizations, local and national politics (given College Park's proximity to the capital), and the environment, students say.

Thirty-nine percent of Maryland students live on campus in single-sex or coed dorms; freshmen are guaranteed housing, and while many juniors and seniors seek off-campus accommodations, those who stay on campus all four years will find their digs improve as they gain seniority. (Upperclassmen also have the option of on-campus apartments and suites.) "There is a huge demand for campus housing," says a senior, adding, however, "There are lots of housing options around the university." Decisions on financial aid and housing are affected by acceptance date, so the earlier you apply, the better off you'll be. Freshmen generally live in high-rises or low-rises; South Campus features air-conditioning, carpeting, and new furniture. Safety features include triple locks on dorm-room doors, blue-light emergency phones, and walking and riding escort services to transport students after dark. "Security is good. We have a very defined campus, and we keep unauthorized visitors to a minimum," says a student.

"There is a huge demand for campus housing."

Social life at Maryland revolves around nonalcoholic events such as concerts, movies, and speakers, as well as around the traditional fraternity parties and football and basketball games. The university's reputation as a haven for those who prefer partying to studying is changing as students with better credentials apply, but it's still true that in the dorms, at local pubs, and in nearby Baltimore and Washington, D.C., there's always something happening. On campus, only students over twenty-one may drink, in accordance with state law; the policy works "50 percent of the time," says one student. "RAs monitor dorms," warns one student. Nine percent of the men and women go Greek, but they don't dominate the tone of campus life. At a school this big, extracurricular activities and participants come in every shape and size.

"Talk to professors, join clubs, attend campus meetings, and people will know you."

Despite College Park's highly social atmosphere, Maryland's suburban campus can feel too small. A few bucks and a few minutes on the Metro (Washington's subway system) brings Terps into downtown D.C. at a hare's pace. Back on campus, favorite annual events include Art Attack, in which local artists share their crafts and national touring artists perform an evening concert, and Homecoming.

Terrapin basketball fans are unsinkable and not always civilized, turning out en masse to cheer against Duke. The football program continued its impressive run last season by racking up ten regular season wins and a post-season bowl game victory. The men's lacrosse and baseball teams also draw crowds, as do women's lacrosse (national champions from 1995 through 2000) and field hockey.

The University of Maryland's overwhelming size is a both a blessing and a curse for the increasingly capable undergraduates here. On one hand, they may choose from an ever-growing variety of courses, and they live and study among a diverse group of peers. On the other, largeness can translate into crowded dorms, long lines at registration, big classes, parking problems, and hassles everywhere. Still, a junior insists, getting lost in the shuffle "is totally avoidable. Talk to professors, join clubs, attend campus meetings, and people will know you."

Mary Washington College

1301 College Avenue, Fredericksburg, VA 22401

Mary Washington could easily be mistaken for one of Virginia's elite private colleges. MWC offers just as much history and tradition—but at a much lower price. Once a women's college, it is still over two-thirds female. On the selectivity chart, MWC ranks behind only UVA and William and Mary among Virginia public universities.

Strolling among Mary Washington College's elegant buildings of red brick and white columns has led more than one pleased parent to declare, "Now this is what a college should look like." Indeed, for an aura of history and tradition, few schools stack up to this small college in Fredericksburg, a site of Civil War action and the boyhood town of George Washington. If the campus architecture puts some people in mind of the University of Virginia, it's no accident: MWC was the all-female branch of that august institution before going coed and cutting its ties in 1970. Of course Mary Washington is not just beautiful, but smart, too. Easily mistaken for one of Virginia's elite private colleges, Mary Washington has gained a reputation as one of the premium public liberal arts colleges and continues to attract bright students from around the globe.

Located in historic Fredericksburg, this is the college-campus prototype, featuring classical Jeffersonian buildings, sweeping lawns, brick walkways, and breathtaking foliage. Of course, beauty these days requires that you also be in shape, so a brand new fitness and recreation center is in the works. Other newer buildings include a $13.5 million science center.

Mary Washington's core curriculum emphasizes its strong liberal bent. Students select courses to meet specific goals in the arts, literature, natural and social sciences, and mathematics. English composition, five writing-intensive courses, and foreign language competency are also required. Students also must complete across-the-curriculum general education requirements in five areas: written communication, oral communication, race and gender, global awareness, and the environment. For majors, business and English are popular programs, and two of the best. Political science and international affairs are very strong, as is a unique program in historic preservation. Among the sciences, biology is the clear favorite. The administration concedes that the dance and Russian departments are weaker because declining enrollments forced cutbacks.

> **"Now this is what a college should look like."**

Students are encouraged to take on research projects of their own design, and several departments offer grants for work abroad or in the U.S. Many students study

Website: www.mwc.edu
Location: Small city
Total Enrollment: 4,483
Undergraduates: 4,132
Male/Female: 35/65
SAT Ranges: V 570–660
 M 560–650
ACT Ranges: 25-29
Financial Aid: 65%
Expense: Pub $
Phi Beta Kappa: Yes
Applicants: 4,320
Accepted: 55%
Enrolled: 36%
Grad in 6 Years: 69%
Returning Freshmen: 88%
Academics: ✍ ✍ ✍ ½
Social: ☎ ☎ ☎
Q of L: ★ ★ ★ ★
Admissions: (800) 468-5614
Email Address:
 admit@mwc.edu

Strongest Programs:
 Historic Preservation
 Psychology
 English
 Biology
 International Affairs

(Continued)

History

Political Science

abroad during their junior year. The college's location, roughly an hour from both Washington, D.C., and the state capital, Richmond, is a handy asset for approximately 350 budding politicos who seek internships every year. Because of the rise in Mary Washington's popularity, some students are concerned about potential overcrowding. "There aren't huge difficulties getting into courses that students want or are required to take," says an economics major. "Often, you are unable to get the exact days or time that you would like, but the college makes an effort to provide enough sections of each course when it is in high demand." Most profs will

"Each building is a community, not simply a place to live."

use the force-add system to let people into full classes; but this doesn't always work, especially in the psychology department, which is notoriously strict. A senior says, "It is hard to finish the teaching program in four years. But on the whole, graduating on time is definitely possible."

The close ties between students and faculty are a great source of pride at Mary Washington, where classes usually have fewer than twenty-five students and rarely more than fifty. "The quality of teaching I have received has been phenomenal," says one historic preservation major.

Indeed, for an aura of history and tradition, few schools stack up to this small college in Fredericksburg, a site of Civil War action and the boyhood town of George Washington.

In general, Mary Washington students are a "friendly and unpretentious" bunch. "They respect each other based on the MWC Honor Code. Students are hard working and ambitious in their pursuit of academic excellence and job opportunities," says a junior. Students tend to be conservative and not socially active, although Middle Eastern politics have drawn some debate and prompted demonstrations. Mary Washington may act and look like a private school, but her state school status is showing just a bit. "As a public institution, the college has been affected by Virginia politics and many student organizations suffer from budget cuts." African-Americans make up 3 percent of the student population, Hispanics 3 percent, and Asian-Americans 5 percent. Sixty-five percent of the student body is from Virginia, and a large majority continues on to jobs after graduation, rather than graduate school. The college offers five hundred merit scholarships ranging from $500 to $10,000, but no athletic scholarships.

Students have great affection for MWC housing, and the vast majority resides on campus. "Each building is a community, not simply a place to live," reports a junior. "The rooms are a good size—comparable to a room at home." The seventeen residence halls offer many different living arrangements, including foreign language floors, service-learning options, and special theme units. Each room includes

"There is always something to do, but it won't come looking for you."

access to the college's advanced fiber-optic network, cable TV, and telephone service. Once they find a room that suits

Once they find a room that suits them, students can "homestead," or retain that room for their remaining years.

them, students can "homestead," or retain that room for their remaining years. In addition to standard cafeteria service, students can use their meal cards to eat at a campus snack bar with full restaurant service until 1 A.M.

Small and friendly, nearby Fredericksburg is a "quaint, historic town." While it lacks some of the nightlife of a larger community, it has plenty of museums offering Civil War exhibits. For dance clubs and bars, it's not far to Richmond or D.C. Likewise, women frustrated by the disadvantageous gender ratio can reach UVA in an hour and a half, and Georgetown in even less. Both the scenery of the Chesapeake Bay and hiking in the Blue Ridge Mountains are roughly an hour away, due east and west, respectively. On campus, plenty of events are held by various student organizations. Although there are parties both on and off campus on any given weekend, alcohol does not dominate the social scene, and there are no fraternities or sororities. A band plays the campus snack bar most Thursday nights, and the student council often sponsors dances. "There is always something to do, but it won't come looking for you," says one history major.

Even though Mary Washington doesn't have a football team, other sports are alive and well. Since the inception of the Capital Athletic Conference, MWC has won more conference championships than all other conference members combined. Men's and women's cross-country and tennis and men's soccer have all been championship winners in recent years. The women's lacrosse team reached the NCAA Final Four during the 2001 season. Non-varsity types also use the seventy-six-acre sports and field complex, complete with an Olympic-size pool, for a variety of intramural and club sports, including men's and women's rugby and crew.

Mary Washington students take an uncommon interest in college traditions. Several annual outdoor parties, including Grill on the Hill and Weststock, never fail to attract a large crowd. All third-year students brace themselves for Junior Ring Week, during which they are the victims of practical jokes prior to receiving their rings from the school's president. Another tradition is Devil-Goat Day, an all-day competition pitting odd- and even-yeared classes against each other in events such as sumo wrestling, jousting, and the Velcro wall. Homecoming is observed with the usual round of sporting events (particularly soccer), dances, and dinners. The multicultural festival is also popular.

With a first-rate liberal arts education in an intimate environment and at a public school price, Mary Washington College is a smart choice for anyone seeking the most bang for their buck. It offers a pleasing blend of beautiful architecture, first rate faculty, and serious, down-to-earth students who appreciate it all.

> **Overlaps**
> University of Virginia, College of William and Mary, James Madison, University of Richmond, Virginia Tech

If You Apply To ➤
Mary Washington: Early decision: Nov. 1. Regular admissions: Feb. 1. Financial aid: Mar. 1. Does not guarantee to meet demonstrated need. No campus or alumni interviews. SATs or ACTs: required. SAT IIs: recommended. Accepts the Common Application and electronic applications. Essay question: personal statement and your sense of honor.

University of Massachusetts–Amherst

Amherst, MA 01003

A liberal Mecca in cosmopolitan and scenic western Massachusetts. UMass boasts strong study-abroad programs and an international flavor. Science and engineering are also strong. Ready access to privates Amherst, Hampshire, Mount Holyoke, and Smith via the Five College Consortium.

The University of Massachusetts at Amherst, a leading land-grant university with more than a century of tradition, offers students a dizzying array of majors and extracurricular options. Students can live in one of the nation's top college towns, take advantage of an extensive research program and strong honors program, and enjoy an endless supply of social opportunities—without emptying their wallets. "The school is special because it combines a city environment with a rural one," says one happy senior. "We are surrounded by a diverse student population and talented faculty."

UMass's sprawling 1,463-acre campus is centered on a pond full of ducks and swans, while architectural styles range from Colonial to modern. The school is located on the outskirts of Amherst, a city that combines the energy of a bustling cosmopolitan center with the quaintness of an old New England town. Students agree that Amherst caters to college life. New additions on campus include the Animal Care

Website: www.umass.edu
Location: Small town
Total Enrollment: 24,678
Undergraduates: 19,368
Male/Female: 48/52
SAT Ranges: V 500–610
  M 510–620
Financial Aid: 46%
Expense: Pub $ $
Phi Beta Kappa: Yes
Applicants: 18,625
Accepted: 73%

(Continued)

Enrolled: 31%
Grad in 6 Years: 59%
Returning Freshmen: 84%
Academics: ✍ ✍ ✍ ½
Social: ☎ ☎ ☎ ☎
Q of L: ★ ★ ★
Admissions: (413) 545-0222
Email Address: mail@
admissions.umass.edu

Strongest Programs:
Chemical Engineering
Computer Science
Electrical and Computer
Engineering
English/Creative Writing
Linguistics
Philosophy
Psychology

Facility; the first phase of the Engineering and Computer Science Complex, with a second phase on the way; and an addition to the School of Management building.

Of UMass's nine undergraduate colleges and schools, offerings in management and engineering are top-ranked. Polymer science is notable, as is the English department, which features such names as Pulitzer Prize–winning poet James Tate, and John Edgar Wideman, a two-time PEN/Faulkner Award winner and MacArthur "Genius Grant" Award recipient. Political science, creative writing, and international studies also draw praise. New to the menu are bachelor of arts programs in Earth systems and linguistics, while biology, math, computer science, and the natural sciences are regarded as especially tough. Students report little difficulty getting into courses they want or are required to take. Engineering students may face a bit of a challenge in finishing in four years; they are required to take 130 credit hours while most programs require 120 credit hours.

> **"The school is special because it combines a city environment with a rural one."**

All undergraduates must complete two courses in writing; six Social World courses, including literature, arts/liberal arts, historical studies, social and behavioral sciences, and an interdisciplinary elective; three courses in biological and physical science; one basic math skills course; and a course in analytic reasoning. Freshmen must also complete the College Writing Program, taught in sections of twenty-four or fewer. The school's honors program, Commonwealth College, offers qualified students special courses and sponsors interdisciplinary seminars, student gatherings, service projects, a newsletter, and a housing option. Students seeking to stand out from the "Masses" might consider the interdisciplinary major in Social Thought and Political Economy or the bachelor's degree in the Individual Concentration program, a design-it-yourself major. The study abroad program offers options in thirty different countries, including Japan, the Netherlands, and Australia. The Center for Student Business offers one of the most unique programs at UMass, allowing students to staff and manage nine campus businesses, and learn how to work with others and resolve conflicts professionally.

UMass's intellectual and political climate is extraordinarily fertile for a state university, perhaps in part because of its membership in the Five College Consortium.* This special alliance allows students to attend UMass and take courses at the other four consortium schools: Amherst College, Smith, Hampshire, and Mount Holyoke. Students say that generally, the quality of teaching at UMass is excellent. Full professors teach most courses, and some of the larger ones are broken down into smaller sections with graduate-level teaching assistants. Academic and career counseling receive mixed reviews, and it is usually up to students to pursue career help.

> **"There are always rallies about better programs and aid for minorities."**

The majority of UMass students are white public-school graduates from Massachusetts who make a beeline for the job market after graduation, especially since out-of-state enrollment is capped at 25 percent of students. African-Americans and Hispanics make up 9 percent of the student body, while Asian-Americans constitute 8 percent. The university has established cultural centers on campus providing activities and support for students from different backgrounds, but affirmative action is still an issue, students report. "There are always rallies about better programs and aid for minorities," says a senior. Students from other New England states are treated as Massachusetts residents for admission purposes if their own state schools don't offer the programs they want. Students have also cried out against state budget cuts, which have cost the school programs.

UMass has the sixth-largest residence-hall system in the country. Forty-two dorms, organized in five residential areas, house 59 percent of students. Freshmen

Commonwealth College offers honors students special courses and sponsors interdisciplinary seminars, student gatherings, service projects, a newsletter, and a housing option.

can choose single-sex or coed living and also submit a list of their preferred living areas, and they're required to live on campus through sophomore year. About half of the freshmen end up in the Southwest Area, a "huge, citylike complex" with five high-rise towers and eleven low-rise residence halls. The university is expanding its Residential Academic Programs, which allow first-year students with similar interests to live and study together in specialized interdisciplinary courses to ease their transition into campus life. Approximately 35 percent of freshmen participate. Upperclassmen tend to move off-campus. "Our dorms are well maintained and very comfortable compared to other private as well as state universities," says one satisfied resident.

UMass offers an abundant social life, marked by "noisy dorms, overflowing fraternities, and off-campus parties," says a freshman. "Social life is better than any place on Earth," raves a junior. Both on campus and off, alcohol policies are strict and well enforced. First-time underage offenders are sent to alcohol-education programs. The school is losing its reputation as "ZooMass." Nearly two dozen fraternities and sororities occupy 6 percent of the men and 5 percent of the women, but they are somewhat out of the mainstream. A free public-transportation system allows maximum mobility not only among the Five Colleges but also to nearby towns, which are graced with a number of exceptional bookshops. The annual Spring Concert around the pond is a daylong event where musicians such as U2, Bob Dylan, and the Beastie Boys perform.

Settled in the Pioneer Valley and surrounded by the Berkshire foothills, Amherst is close to good skiing, hiking, and canoeing areas. It's also ninety miles west of Boston, 150 miles north of New York City, and twenty-five miles south of Vermont and New Hampshire, making a car very useful (and very expensive if you get too many tickets from overzealous campus cops, students say). Varsity sports are popular, and UMass has been a model for achieving gender equity in athletics. "Midnight Madness," the first men's basketball practice of the season, held annually at midnight with everyone invited, is a hot campus ticket. The football team recently won a conference championship, as have men's baseball and swimming and women's basketball, crew, cross-country, field hockey, softball, soccer, tennis, lacrosse, and track. Two on-campus gyms offer facilities for the recreational athlete, and two Olympic-size skating rinks mark the recent reintroduction of intercollegiate hockey to the university.

"Social life is better than any place on Earth."

UMass is big enough to offer a vast number of academic and extracurricular opportunities, but also big enough to feel impersonal and overwhelming. While a senior likes the size and says, "I've met tons of people here who have positively affected my life," a freshman grumps, "It is such a typical university rat race!" UMass might be best for students who are sure where they are going—and not shy about demanding what they need to get there.

If You Apply To ➢ **UMass:** Regular admissions: Feb. 1. Financial aid: Mar. 1. Housing: Jul. 19. Rolling admissions. Meets demonstrated need of 90%. Campus and alumni interviews: optional, informational. SATs or ACTs: required. SAT IIs: optional. Accepts the Common Application and electronic applications. Essay question: personal circumstances or academic experiences.

Massachusetts Institute of Technology

Room 3-108, 77 Massachusetts Avenue, Cambridge, MA 02139

If you're a science genius, come to MIT to find out how little you really know. No other school makes such a massive assault on the ego (with little in the way of support to help you pick up the pieces). Technology is a given, but MIT also prides itself on leading programs in economics, political science, and management.

Website: http://web.mit.edu
Location: Urban
Total Enrollment: 10,090
Undergraduates: 4,258
Male/Female: 58/42
SAT Ranges: V 670–760
   M 740–800
ACT Range: 30–34
Financial Aid: 59%
Expense: Pr $ $ $ $
Phi Beta Kappa: Yes
Applicants: 10,671
Accepted: 16%
Enrolled: 56%
Grad in 6 Years: 92%
Returning Freshmen: 97%
Academics: 🖉 🖉 🖉 🖉 🖉
Social: ☎ ☎ ☎
Q of L: ★ ★ ★
Admissions: (617) 253-4791
Email Address:
   admissions@mit.edu

Strongest Programs:
   Engineering
   Science
   Architecture
   Economics
   Management

MIT is, in a word, excellence. With a student body that averaged near-perfect scores on the math portion of their SATs, and verbal scores not far behind, this is a place that restores faith in the American educational system. Engineering, science, and math are MIT's specialties, but students come here to learn about everything—and learn they certainly do.

MIT is located on 154 acres that extend more than a mile along the Cambridge side of the Charles River basin facing historic Beacon Hill and the central sections of Boston. The main campus of neoclassical architecture carved from limestone was designed by Welles Bosworth and constructed between 1913 and 1920. Since then, more modern designs in brick and glass have been added. The buildings give off a utilitarian aura; most are even known by number instead of by name. Athletic playing fields, recreational buildings, dorms, and dining halls are closely arranged on the campus and provide a sense of unity. Sculptures and murals, including the works of Alexander Calder, Henry Moore, and Louise Nevelson, are found throughout the campus.

Originally called Boston Tech and now frequently referred to as "the Tute," MIT stresses science and engineering studies with a "concern for human values and social goals." Every science and engineering department is superb. The biology department is a leader in medical technology and the search for designer genes. Nevertheless, pure sciences tend to play second fiddle to the engineering fields that, along with computer science, draw the bulk of the majors. Electrical engineering and computer science are almost universally credited as tops in the nation. Students in these two areas may now pursue a five-year-degree option, where they can obtain a professional master's degree upon completion of their studies. Biomedical, chemical, and mechanical engineering; physics; and the tiny aeronautics department are also highly praised programs. The most popular majors include biology, mechanical engineering, chemical engineering, and management. The humanities are strong here as well, though not on par with more technical programs.

MIT has always attracted top nontechnical professors, including such luminaries as linguist Noam Chomsky. Economics, political science, management, urban studies, linguistics, graphics for modern art, and holography—plus anything that can be linked to a computer—are strong, and the tiny minority who major in these subjects receive enough personal attention to make any college student envious. "Some professors really know how to engage the interest of the student," says a senior.

MIT is tops in technology, but also strong in the social sciences. The administration worries that engineers of the future will need to possess not only first-rate technical skills but also a better understanding of the social system in which they

> **"Some professors really know how to engage the interest of the student."**

will be operating. As one dean put it, "Too many MIT graduates end up working for too many Princeton and Harvard graduates." The general education program does require undergraduates to take at least eight courses that stress such fundamental academic themes as literary traditions and the origins of political institutions. Perhaps to ensure that they will be able to make their future discoveries known, students must also complete a two-phase writing requirement. Technical types are also able to choose a minor in a nontechnical field, in subjects ranging from philosophy to women in society. There's also a four-class physical education requirement as well as a mandatory swimming test to be passed by the end of freshman year.

One of MIT's most successful innovations is the Undergraduate Research Opportunities Program (UROP), a year-round program that facilitates student-faculty research projects. Considered one of the best programs of its kind in the nation, it allows students to earn course credit or stipends for doing research. The Experimental Study Group allows freshmen and sophomores to set a self-paced course of study as they learn through tutorials instead of in the traditional lecture format. Many students have access to even the world-renowned professors and the Nobel Prize winners, who carry lighter teaching loads to allow them time for students and research. Faculty advising is "pretty good for freshmen," one student says, but after that, "it's as good as you make it." The library system, which includes a recently expanded architecture facility, is vast and contains more than two million volumes, including some one-of-a-kind manuscripts on the history of science and technology. One library is even open twenty-four hours a day, and "some students spend the majority of their time (awake or asleep) there," one student reports.

A mandatory pass/fail grading system helps freshmen adjust to "MIT brain-stretching": freshmen receive grades of P, D, or F in all subjects they take. P means C-or-better performance; Ds or Fs do not receive credit or appear on the permanent record. Grades or not, most MIT students set themselves a breathtaking pace. "MIT is intense and will take you for quite a ride," a biology/premed student says. "The courses demand your full attention and a lot of extra work," another says. Some relief from "tooling" (that is, studying) is found through the optional January period of independent activities offering noncredit seminars, workshops, and activities in fields outside the regular curriculum as well as for-credit subjects. Participation in the engineering co-op program, junior year abroad, or cross-registration at all-female Wellesley College are other helpful ways to get young noses away from the grindstone. Academic and psychological counseling are well thought of by students. A student-run hotline provides all-night peer counseling. Many upperclassmen return to school at least two weeks before classes start, "to help integrate the freshmen."

While MIT somewhat justly earned an image as a "conservative, rich white boys' school" in the past, there is certainly enough racial if not gender variety to beat the rap today. African-Americans account for 6 percent of the student body, Hispanics 11 percent, and Asian-Americans a hefty 27 percent. If anything, women may feel "a different tone, as the campus is three-fifths male." Almost 100 percent of students come from the top tenth of their high-school class, and average SAT and ACT scores are simply mind-boggling. "The average MIT student can be characterized as having a passion and singular drive for what they really want in life," offers a chemical engineering major. MIT helps financially needy students pay the super-hefty tuition bill, and it also guarantees to meet demonstrated need. It does not give purely merit or athletic scholarships, but it has its own parent-loan fund with favorable interest rates to augment the federal-loan programs.

All freshmen are now required to live in dorms, eliminating the harried housing gauntlet. Cat lovers will be glad to learn that the MIT administration, which once cracked down on surreptitiously harbored kitties in dorm rooms, has backed off its no-pets-except-fish policy and permitted students to bring their beloved cats with them. Cats, however, face one admissions requirement not yet extended to

Though students often wonder what life at a so-called typical college would have been like, chances of survival and even satisfaction at MIT are excellent.

"The average MIT student can be characterized as having a passion and singular drive for what they really want in life."

Almost 100 percent of students come from the top tenth of their high-school class, and average SAT and ACT scores are simply mind-boggling.

undergraduates: they must be spayed or neutered. Guaranteed housing is either single-sex or coed; the dorms are in the middle of campus, and most of the fraternities and living groups are a mile or less away across the Charles. Ninety-five percent of the undergraduates live on campus, and mandatory meal plans exist, depending on the living group. Some dorms have kitchens, and the meal plan is optional. Dorms without kitchens have a required meal plan. Frat-types feast on spreads prepared by their full-time cooks, and the Kosher Kitchen, run by Hillel, provides some refuge for others.

MIT's social scene is varied. There's Greek life, to which 45 percent of the men and 25 percent of the women belong. Then there are campus movies and lectures. There's the ubiquitous workload, worming its way into the uneasy consciousness of a techie's every waking hour. And there's the great city of Boston, with its many restaurants, clubs, parks, shopping opportunities, and more than fifty other colleges. On-campus dances, parties, and dorm activities keep other students busy. Most on-campus drinking for over-twenty-one students is relaxed and accepted, "as long as the alcohol does not result in unlawful behavior or cause any problems," a student explains. For those with the urge to roam, the multifaceted greater Boston metropolis lies only a few subway stops away.

When the MIT megabrains take a break, practical jokes, or "hacks" (described by one student as "practical jokes with technical merit"), are sure to follow. In past years, popular hacks have included disguising the dome of the main academic building as a giant breast, unscrewing and reversing all the chairs in a five hundred-seat lecture hall, and, of course, welding shut Harvard's gates. Hacking can also involve late-night explorations by students in the tunnels and shafts that run through restricted parts of the campus, a practice that's definitely frowned upon by the school.

When not studying or hacking, these engineering jocks often turn into real jocks: MIT fields the second-highest number of intercollegiate varsity sports in the country with thirty-nine (Harvard has forty-two). Athletic accomplishments in the past three years include Constitution Athletic Conference championships in men's

"MIT is intense and will take you for quite a ride."

cross-country; the New England Women's 8 title in crew; and national championships for the air pistol and women's sports pistol teams. Hockey is popular, and even more popular is the extensive, well-organized intramural program, with sports ranging from Ping-Pong, billiards, and bowling to the more traditional basketball and volleyball. Everyone has access to MIT's extensive athletic facilities. Supposedly, there are more clubs and organizations at MIT than at any other school in the country, and a sampling of the offerings explains why. The Rocket Society, the Guild of Bell Ringers, a singing group called the Corollaries, and the Exotic Fish Society are only a few of the diverse interests on this campus.

Though students often wonder what life at a so-called typical college would have been like, chances of survival and even satisfaction at MIT are excellent. Students are able to comprehend the incredible experience of attending one of the nation's leading academic powerhouses. A biology major puts it bluntly: "It will take you right up to what you think your limits are, and then MIT will shatter them and make you realize how great your potential is."

If You Apply To ➤

MIT: Early action: Nov. 1. Regular admissions: Jan. 1. Financial aid: Jan. 11. Guarantees to meet demonstrated need. Campus interviews: optional, informational. Alumni interviews: required, evaluative. SATs or ACTs: required. SAT IIs: required (writing, history, or science and math). Essay question: create your own question; or explain an opinion you had to defend. Looks for aptitude in math and science.

University of Miami

P.O. Box 248025, Coral Gables, FL 33124-4616

Football is the main reason UM is on the map, but it isn't the only reason. Renowned programs in marine science and music are big draws; business is also strong. Housing takes the form of a distinctive residential college system that offers living/learning opportunities.

Year-round sunshine and the colorful Miami culture could make even the most dedicated students forget why they are at college. But at the University of Miami, students can have their fun and get a solid education at the same time. Trash-talking has been replaced by a renewed focus on academics, though the 'Canes have lost none of their South Florida swagger.

Twenty minutes from Key Biscayne and Miami's beaches, and ten minutes from downtown Miami, the university's 260-acre campus is located in tranquil suburbia. With its own lake in the middle of the campus (and on the cover of most brochures), the campus is architecturally varied, from postwar, international-style structures to modern buildings, most with open-air breezeways to let in the warm, salty winds. The state-of-the-art Francis L. Wolfson School of Communications building recently opened.

Miami has one of the nation's top programs in marine biology, and was the first university to offer a degree in music engineering. Miami's main strengths are in the preprofessional and professional areas. The school also boasts an unusual program in jazz, and students recommend any of the strong premed offerings. Chemistry majors have access to a nuclear magnetic resonance spectrometer, an essential tool for modern chemistry. The school's six-year medical program for outstanding students, and dual degree (grad/undergrad) programs in law, marine science, business, physical therapy, biomedical engineering, and medicine receive high marks. Women's studies and philosophy are said to be weaker. Business management is the most popular major, followed by visual and performing arts, biology, health professions, and engineering.

Students report that most classes can be rigorous or laid back, and give professors high marks for knowledge and accessibility. Full professors teach most courses. "The quality of teaching I have received is second to none," a sophomore says. "I have received that personal attention I wanted from my classes and professors." Though many have a preprofessional bent, students at Miami receive a broad liberal arts education. Distribution requirements vary from school to school, but general education requirements include proficiency in English composition, mathematics, and writing across the curriculum (courses that involve a substantial amount of writing). In addition, a certain number of credits must be earned in each of three areas of knowledge: natural sciences, social sciences, and arts and humanities. Students looking for a change

> **"We have students from all fifty states and more than 110 foreign countries."**

of pace can take advantage of Miami's summer-semester program in the Caribbean. In addition, the study abroad program offers more than forty study-abroad options in countries such as Australia, Israel, France, Japan, the Netherlands, and Argentina.

Highly motivated students in any field can apply to the school's comprehensive honors program, which enrolls students who were in the top tenth of their high-school class and have a combined SAT score of at least 1360. About 15 percent of each freshmen class enrolls. UM still attracts its share—though it's declining—of beach bums who drop by for a couple of classes in the morning, spend the rest of

Website: www.miami.edu
Location: Suburban
Total Enrollment: 13,963
Undergraduates: 8,955
Male/Female: 45/55
SAT Ranges: V 530–630
  M 540–650
ACT Range: 22–28
Financial Aid: 54%
Expense: Pr $ $ $
Phi Beta Kappa: Yes
Applicants: 13,088
Accepted: 53%
Enrolled: 15%
Grad in 6 Years: 62%
Returning Freshmen: 82%
Academics: ✍ ✍ ✍
Social: ☎ ☎ ☎ ☎
Q of L: ★ ★ ★
Admissions: (305) 284-4323
Email Address:
  admission@miami.edu

Strongest Programs:
  Marine Science
  Music
  Business
  Political Science
  Biology/Premed

the day at the shore, and almost never see the inside of the library. That's a shame, though; the facility is one of the best in the region, with more than two million bound volumes and another three-million-plus on microform.

Thirty-eight percent of UM's students come from out of state, mostly from the Northeast, Ohio, and the Chicago area. UM is unique among universities of its caliber in the incredible diversity of its student body; Hispanics account for a substantial 31 percent of the total, African-Americans 11 percent, and Asian-Americans 6 percent. Nine percent are foreign-born. Students say that diversity is one of UM's best assets. "We have students from all fifty states and more than 110 foreign countries," says an English/political science major. "When I lived on campus at U of M, I think the most wonderful experience was hearing three different languages spoken by groups of students on my way from the dorm to the classroom." The school's large number of Hispanics is traceable to the influx of Cuban and other Caribbean refugees into southern Florida, and at times it seems that Spanish is the mother tongue on campus. The Latin influence mixes colorfully with that of the wealthier New Yorkers, many of whom view their time at "Sunshine U" as an extended vacation. The one characteristic everyone seems to share is the hope of getting high-paying jobs after graduation. Nearly two thousand merit scholarships and athletic awards in several sports ease the school's hefty price tag for qualified students.

"The majority of students at Miami fit into the trendy, clubbing profile."

Miami offers a distinctive system of five coed residential colleges, modeled after those at Yale University. Each college is directed by a Master, a senior faculty member who organizes seminars, concerts, lectures, social events, and the monthly community dinner. Faculty members often host study breaks in their homes and provide guest speakers from all walks of life to discuss current issues. Generally, students give the dorms average marks; less than 40 percent of students live on campus, and others bunk in off-campus apartments or Greek houses. Still, all dorm housing at Miami is coed, and students can choose apartment-style housing when they tire of the residential colleges' closeness. Scrounging up grub on campus is easy; the residential colleges have their own cafeterias with a variety of plans, from five to twenty meals, and there is a kosher alternative.

On the weekends, Miami students frequent nearby bars or the Campus Rat, home also to the popular Fifth Quarter post-football-game parties. On-campus alcohol policies are relatively strict for underage students, sometimes including parental notification for offenses. Fraternities still manage to thrive, accounting for 12 percent of the men and providing a space for most of the underage drinking at UM (although not during rush, which is dry). The sororities, with no housing of their own, attract 13 percent of the women. Many of the fraternities and sororities are small (averaging about thirty members), but they often join forces in throwing parties.

If keg parties aren't your scene, though, UM offers a plethora of other social opportunities. Those who shun sand between their toes bike down to the boutiques in Coconut Grove, Bayside, or South Beach, or attend on-campus events, such as International Week, Sportsfest, and the Cardboard Boat Races. "The majority of students at Miami fit into the trendy, clubbing profile," explains a psychology major.

"It is the whole college experience at U of M."

"They like trendy up-to-date clothes, and going to clubs in order to see and be seen." Public transportation runs in front of the residential colleges, but most students recommend a car in order to get "the full Florida effect." Parking can be a problem, though, says a senior: "If you want a parking space, you need to get to school by 8:00 A.M., and parking decals are way too expensive." The best road trips are Key West, Key Largo, and, of course, UM football games, especially those against Florida State.

Though hurricane season hits most of the Southeast coast in late summer, in Miami, 'Cane season lasts straight through New Year's. Under the tutelage of new head coach Larry Coker, the 'Canes capped off an impressive 2001–2002 season with a national championship win in the Rose Bowl. Although football is undisputed king of the hill on campus, men's baseball, basketball, and tennis and women's track and field have also captured recent championships. A $14 million rec center, with juice bar and spa, and the annual intramural Sportsfest, also draw crowds.

It's hard to imagine a school in the Sunshine State without a generous allotment of fun, and UM is no exception. Life really is a beach for students at the University of Miami, although its days as a beach-bum hideout are long over. These days, UM students are just as likely to search long and hard for the perfect instrumental phrase or mathematical proof as they are to scope out the perfect wave. "It is the whole college experience at U of M," says one sophomore. "It is so fulfilling and rewarding."

If You Apply To ➤   **Miami:** Early decision and early action: Nov. 15. Regular admissions: Feb. 15. Financial aid: Mar. 1. Does not guarantee to meet demonstrated need. No alumni or campus interviews. SATs or ACTs: required. SAT IIs: optional. Apply to particular schools or programs. Accepts the Common Application and electronic applications. Essay question: experience or achievement that is special to you; personal, local, or national concern important to you; person who has had significant influence on you; role of academic integrity.

Miami University (OH)

301 S. Campus Avenue, Oxford, OH 45056

Rather than disappear into the black hole of Ohio State, top students in the Buckeye state come here to feel as if they are going to an elite private university. MU has a niche like William and Mary's in Virginia—though MU is twice as big. Miami's top draw is business, and its tenor is conservative.

This Miami is about one thousand miles from South Beach, but that doesn't mean it's without sizzle. The academic kind, of course. Miami University is actually tucked into a corner of Ohio and is gaining national recognition as an excellent state university. Students rave about the picture-perfect campus, high-caliber student body, and access to a wide variety of academic challenges—and at a low sticker price.

The university is staked out on two thousand wooded acres in the center of an urban triangle of approximately three million people, encompassing Cincinnati and Dayton, Ohio, and Richmond, Indiana. The campus is dressed in the modified Georgian style of the Colonial American period and it remains as impeccably groomed as its students, who give the school one of its nicknames, "J. Crew U." New additions to campus include an academic center, a training facility for athletes, a child-care facility for faculty and students, and a baseball field.

Miami University was founded in 1809 to provide a classical liberal education, and has never strayed from its central commitment to liberal arts. Still, many of the university's strongest offerings are in the School of Business Administration. Other popular programs include accounting, architecture, international studies, education, and zoology. For those with an inclination toward forestry or the paper industry, the university's unique pulp and paper science technology degree is in a league of its own. Students say the theater and history departments could use improvement.

University requirements, or foundation courses, provide for a broad education, and all undergraduates must complete foundation courses in English composition,

Website: www.muohio.edu
Location: Rural
Total Enrollment: 16,946
Undergraduates: 15,153
Male/Female: 45/55
SAT Ranges: V 550–640
  M 580–660
ACT Range: 24–28
Financial Aid: 16%
Expense: Pub $ $ $ $
Phi Beta Kappa: Yes
Applicants: 12,500
Accepted: 74%
Enrolled: 37%
Grad in 6 Years: 80%
Returning Freshmen: 90%
Academics: ✍ ✍ ✍ ✍ ½
Social: ☎ ☎ ☎
Q of L: ★ ★ ★
Admissions: (513) 529-2531

(Continued)
Email Address:
  admission@muohio.edu

Strongest Programs:
  Accountancy
  Business Economics
  Music
  Chemistry
  Botany
  International Studies
  Architecture
  Computer Science

fine arts, humanities, social sciences and world cultures, biological and physical sciences, and mathematics, formal reasoning, or technology. Additional requirements include twelve credits of advanced liberal education focus consisting of nine credits of thematic and sequential study in-depth outside of the student's major, and three credits of the Senior Capstone Experience, which ties in liberal education with the specialized knowledge of their major.

The academic atmosphere at Miami is competitive but not cut-throat. "The classes are challenging, and a great majority of students put academic performance first, making peer interaction a big plus," says one English major. Most students are conscientious about their grades, says a senior who has "never taken a class here lightly." The professors at Miami are described as "exceptional." "Teaching is Miami's biggest strength," raves one senior. Fifty percent of classes have less than twenty-five students, and most are taught by full professors, though graduate students do pop up. Many students complain that it's very hard to get required classes, especially foundation courses. "I've had to force-add classes or wait to take them in the summer," gripes a speech communications major.

Approximately 40 percent of students take advantage of a wide array of study-abroad opportunities. The Dolibois European Center in Luxembourg offers a semester or year-long program in the liberal arts, and an opportunity to live with a foreign family. Exchange programs with universities in Denmark, Japan, Brazil, Mexico, Austria, and England are available as well as summer programs in France, Italy, Germany, Russia, the Caribbean, Asia, and Scotland. There is a new major in mechanical engineering. Undergraduate research gets a lot of attention at Miami— the competitive Undergraduate Research Scholars program gives one hundred students a stipend, free tuition, and an expense account to complete a ten-week academic project. More than one thousand undergrads participate in research activities each year, and there also are several leadership programs.

"Miami is made up of a lot of preps who are well-dressed and have money to spend," says one student. Another adds that "a lot come from upper-middle class families where Mom and Dad pay for everything." Eighty-nine percent of the student body are white, 4 percent African-American, and 2 percent each Hispanic and Asian-American. Seventy-three percent of students are from Ohio, and the campus has a reputation for conservatism. In recent years, Miami has begun an effort to attract more students of color with programs such as the Minority Professional Leadership Program.

> **"The classes are challenging, and a great majority of students put academic performance first, making peer interaction a big plus."**

Forty-five percent of the student body call the campus home, and dorm rooms are reported to be very nice and well kept, thanks to friendly cleaning staff. A few of the dorms remain single-sex and are accompanied by visitation rules. Most upperclassmen find good, cheap off-campus housing by their senior year, but remain very involved on campus. Campus security is said to be good, and students report that they feel safe.

Miami has a lively on- and off-campus social life, although students complain that social restrictions on campus are on the rise. "Many get busted for underage drinking. If you get caught, you have to take a substance-abuse class and do one hundred hours of community service," explains one student, but it's still "relatively easy" to get served. A lot of socializing takes place in the restaurants, bars, and clubs of Oxford. Twenty-four percent of the men and 27 percent of the women involved in fraternities or sororities. In fact, Miami is known as the "mother of fraternities" because several began here.

Ice hockey, which is one of the top ten programs in the country, is extremely popular, and the women's precision ice skating team is the only one at collegiate level in the nation.

The town of Oxford "is as good as it gets." One students explains: "The students comprise two-thirds of its population, and most of its shops cater to the students. It is a wonderful and distinct 'college town.'" Cincinnati is about thirty-five miles away. The well-organized intramural program provides teams for just about every sport (including the ever-popular korfball and broomball), and the Student Recreational Sports Facility is well used.

After nearly seventy years, Miami University has changed the name of its sports teams from the Redskins to the Redhawks, out of respect for Native Americans. The university will, however, keep using the portrait of an Indian chief as its logo since the Miami Tribe urged them to do so. Swimming, tennis, and volleyball are among Miami's best varsity sports, but football and men's basketball reign as the most popular spectator sports. For women, soccer and swimming teams do well. Ice hockey, which is one of the top ten programs in the country, is also extremely popular, and the women's precision ice skating team is the only one at collegiate level in the nation. For cycling enthusiasts, the annual 20/20 Bike Race is one of the largest collegiate events of its kind in the U.S. Other annual events include Green Beer Day in March, Make a Difference Day in cooperation with Oxford, Homecoming, and continued rivalries with Ohio University.

"Miami is made up of a lot of preps who are well-dressed and have money to spend."

Miami University of Ohio has broken out of its regional reputation and is now looked upon as a rising star in the nation's state-university network. With plenty of opportunities for research, travel, and leadership experiences, it's not hard to see why. The school effectively combines a wide range of academic programs with the personal attention ordinarily found only at much smaller institutions. As one senior says, the students "are working towards a future."

Overlaps
Ohio University, Ohio State, Indiana University, University of Dayton, Notre Dame

If You Apply To ➤ **Miami:** Early decision: Nov. 1. Regular admissions: Jan. 31. Financial aid: Feb. 15. Housing: May 1. Does not guarantee to meet demonstrated need. Campus interviews: optional, informational. No alumni interviews. SATs or ACTs: required. SAT IIs: optional. Accepts the Common Application and electronic applications. Essay question: impact of a class from high school; a teacher you admire.

University of Michigan

1220 Student Activities Building, Ann Arbor, MI 48109-1316

The most interesting mass of humanity east of UC–Berkeley. UM is among the nation's best in most subjects, but undergraduates must elbow their way to the front to get the full benefit. Superb honors and living/learning programs are the best bet for highly motivated students.

One of the nation's elite public universities, Michigan offers an excellent faculty, dynamite athletics, an endless number of special programs to the most interesting collection of students east of Berkeley. "Michigan is a special place because it has a deep history and reputation," says a senior. "It is an excellent school and no matter what degree you have, it is respected."

Situated on 3,129 acres, Michigan's campus is so extensive that newcomers may want to come equipped with maps and a compass to find their way to class. The university is divided into two main campuses. Central Campus, the heart of the university, houses most of Michigan's 19 schools and colleges. North Campus, which is two miles northeast of Central, is home to the College of Engineering,

Website: www.umich.edu
Location: Suburban
Total Enrollment: 38,103
Undergraduates: 24,412
Male/Female: 50/50
SAT Ranges: V 570–670
  M 610–710
ACT Range: 26–30
Financial Aid: 54%

(Continued)

Expense: Pub $ $ $ $
Phi Beta Kappa: Yes
Applicants: 24,109
Accepted: 52%
Enrolled: 43%
Grad in 6 Years: 83%
Returning Freshmen: 95%
Academics: ✍ ✍ ✍ ✍ ✍
Social: ☎ ☎ ☎
Q of L: ★ ★ ★
Admissions: (734) 764-7433
Email Address:
  ugadmiss@umich.edu

Strongest Programs:
  Premed
  Engineering
  Art and Design
  Architecture
  Music
  Film and Television
  Journalism/Communications
  Business

School of Music, School of Art and Design, College of Architecture and Urban Planning, and the new Media Union. Other campus areas include the Medical Center complex containing seven hospitals and fifteen outpatient facilities, and South Campus, featuring state-of-the art athletic facilities. Architecturally, the main drag of campus features a wide range of styles, from the classical Angell Hall to the Gothic Law Quad. Recent renovations include a new parking deck, stadium expansion, and refurbished residence halls. More projects are on the way.

Academically, students describe the courses as challenging and rigorous but not cut-throat competitive. "Although some students are overly ambitious, most are willing to share their notes and study together," says a senior. The university ranks among the best in the nation in many fields of study, mainly because it attracts some of the biggest names in academia to teach and research in Ann Arbor. The College of Literature, Science, and the Arts is the largest school at Michigan. The College of Engineering and School of Business are well-respected, and the university's programs in health-related fields are also top-notch. Students report that professors are "knowledgeable." One student says, "The professors here are intelligent and seem to enjoy teaching." Students claim excellent academic and career advising is available, but only for those who seek it. The administration, however, notes the

> "Michigan is a special place because it has a deep history and reputation. It is an excellent school and no matter what degree you have, it is respected."

advising office, which registers nearly 12,000 clients each year, offers individually tailored services and workshops. The Career Planning and Placement Office processes about 120,000 transactions each year, provides individual and group career counseling/planning and individual job placement, and works with 950 companies annually in recruiting UM graduating students.

One of Michigan's most distinct characteristics is its special academic programs, which seek to offer the best of both worlds—personalized attention and a large university setting. Approximately 627 active degree programs, including about 226 undergraduate majors as well as individualized concentrations are offered, mainly through the College of Literature, Science, and the Arts. Some of these special programs include double majors, accelerated programs, independent study, field study, and internships. In addition, students can choose from several small interdisciplinary programs. The instructors live and teach in the residential hall in the Residential College and the Lloyd Hall Scholars Program. The Comprehensive Studies Program allows students to become part of a community of scholars to work in programs designed to best realize an individual student's potential.

The University of Michigan's Honors Program, considered to be one of the best in the nation, offers qualified students special honors courses, opportunities to participate in individual research or collaborative research, seminars, and special academic advisors. A preferred admissions program guarantees 150 top high-school students admission to Michigan's professional programs in dentistry, biomedical engineering, social work, architecture, or pharmacy, provided they make sat-

> "Although some students are overly ambitious, most are willing to share their notes and study together."

isfactory progress during their first years. The Undergraduate Research Opportunities Program enables students to work outside the classroom with a small group of students and a faculty member of their choice. The most popular majors at University of Michigan are business administration, mechanical engineering, psychology, English, and political science, but students say the statistics department needs improvement. Michigan also offers a number of foreign language majors not found many other places, including Arabic, Armenian, Persian, Turkish, and Islamic studies. The newest addition to the undergraduate program is the organizational studies major.

No courses are required of all freshmen at Michigan, but all students are required to complete some coursework in English (including composition), foreign languages, natural sciences, social sciences, and humanities. Students in the College of Literature, Science, and the Arts must also take courses in quantitative reasoning and race or ethnicity. In addition, the university offers a series of seminars designed specifically for freshmen and sophomores, which are taught by tenured and tenure-track faculty.

Off-campus opportunities abound at the UM. Students have the chance to visit and study abroad in more than thirty different countries, including Australia, China, Costa Rica, Finland, France, Greece, India, Ireland, Japan, Russia, Sweden, and Turkey. Some specific programs include a year abroad in a French or German university, a business program in Paris, summer internships in selected majors, and special trips organized by individual departments.

The University of Michigan's admissions office sifts through some of the best students in the country, with 69 percent of the students in the top tenth of their high-school class. Two-thirds of the undergraduates are from Michigan. The student body is remarkably diverse for a state university. In fact, Michigan's Program on Intergroup Relations, Conflict, and Community was recognized by former President Clinton's Initiative on Race as one of fourteen "promising practices" that successfully bridge racial divides in communities across America. Minorities now comprise one-fourth of UM's total enrollment, an all-time high. African-Americans and Hispanics combined make up 13 percent of the student body, and Asian-Americans make up another 12 percent. There is a large and well-organized Jewish community at Michigan, and gays and lesbians are also organized and prominent. While the student body is more conservative today than it was a decade ago, it is still "most noticeably liberal," says a history major, and political issues flare up from time to time on campus.

Michigan really socks it to out-of-staters with a $13,000-plus surcharge. However, the university guarantees to meet the demonstrated financial need of all admitted Michigan residents. Students can also vie for merit scholarships of up to $25,000 as well as 408 athletic scholarships for men and women. Dormitories at the University of Michigan traditionally have

"We are ranked high enough to be known for our academic success, but we still have a reputation for having a good time."

well-defined personalities. Sixties-inspired types and "eccentrics" find the East Quad the "most open-minded dorms" (the residential college is here). The Hill dorms are "more sedate." For those seeking alternative housing arrangements, a plethora of special-interest housing is available, including substance-free residence halls. On-campus housing is comfortable and well-maintained. "The dorms are a tad small but livable with a little bit of work," says a history major. Overcrowding is a thing of the past thanks to a major renewal and improvement project; residence halls were actually under capacity last fall. Housing is guaranteed for all incoming freshmen, leaving many upperclassmen to play the lottery. For the student who wants to live off campus, the UM housing office provides information, listings, and advice for finding suitable accommodations. Other alternatives include fraternity and sorority houses, and a large number of college- and privately owned co-ops.

Detroit is a little less than an hour away, but most students become quite fond of the picturesque town of Ann Arbor. "It's a great city with something for everyone," says a political science major. "There are coffeehouses, bars, sporting events, movie theaters, and a lot more." A surprising variety of visual and performing arts are offered in town and on campus. Underage drinking is not allowed, and a senior has a stern warning for any potential schemers: "Your fake ID will be taken. Plan on it. Do not be surprised, no matter how good it is." An annual art fair held in Ann

Arbor draws craftspeople from throughout the nation and Canada. Many lakes and swimming holes lie only a short drive away and seem to keep the large summer-term population happy. As one junior says, "we are ranked high enough to be known for our academic success, but we still have a reputation for having a good time." Michigan winters, though, are known for being cold and brutal. Seventeen

"Ann Arbor is a great city with something for everyone." percent of the undergraduates go Greek, though these groups are the bane of campus liberals. Many students also volunteer in the community. One senior explains, "Most students get involved, especially if it has something to do with helping kids."

Football overshadows nearly everything each fall as students gather to cheer, "Go Blue." In 1999, the Wolverine football team won the Big Ten Conference championship, as did the baseball, men's cross-country, men's and women's gymnastics, women's indoor track, and the women's softball teams. Attending football games is an integral part of the UM experience, students say, and "you shouldn't be allowed to graduate if you haven't gone to a hockey game," quips a sophomore. Intramurals, which were invented at the University of Michigan, provide students with a more casual form of athletics.

The University of Michigan strives to offer its students a delicate balance between academics, athletics, and social activities. On one hand, this is American college as it's characterized in movies like *Animal House*—football and fraternities. But it's also a college with a fine faculty and top-rated programs, intent upon making America competitive in the 21st century. For assertive students who crave spirit and action as well as outstanding academics, Michigan is an excellent choice.

If You Apply To ➤ **Michigan:** Rolling admissions. Regular admissions: Feb. 1. Financial aid: Mar. 15. Guarantees to meet demonstrated need of in-state students. Campus and alumni interviews: optional, informational. SATs or ACTs: required. SAT IIs: optional. Essay question: personal statement. Apply to particular school or program. Policies and deadlines vary by school.

Michigan State University

250 Administration Building, East Lansing, MI 48824

Most people don't realize that Michigan State is significantly bigger than University of Michigan. (Classes via videotape don't help the situation.) Students can find a niche in strong preprofessional programs such as hotel and restaurant management, prevet, business, and engineering.

Michigan state began as an agricultural school, and like most seeds planted in well-tended fields, the school's "cash crop"—a solid education in a friendly and fun-loving atmosphere—grows stronger each year. It offers all the positive aspects of a large city and the safety of a town. The school's focus has broadened to include would-be engineers, entrepreneurs, hoteliers, and doctors of the veterinary, traditional, and osteopathic persuasions, in addition to future farmers. But the more than forty thousand students who populate East Lansing have one thing in common: "Everyone has a smile for you here," says a communications major. "I noticed it from the first day."

MSU's parklike campus is a unique blend of the traditional and the innovative. The older heart of the campus, north of the Red Cedar River, boasts ivy-covered brick buildings, some built before the Civil War and listed on the National Register of Historic Places. This area houses five colleges and includes the MSU Union and ten residence halls. Across the Red Cedar is the medical complex, the modern residence hall complexes, and not one but two eighteen-hole golf courses. On the southernmost part of campus are University Farms, where researchers keep up MSU's reputation as a premier land-grant university through work in agricultural and animal production. New additions and renovations on campus include a six-story biomedical and physical science building and the National Superconducting Cyclotron Laboratory.

The academic climate at MSU can be as daunting as its size. "The academic climate at MSU is fairly competitive," says a sophomore. "A lot of the competition comes from whether or not students challenge themselves by taking rigorous courses." The computerized enrollment system has done away with long registration lines, and advisors can help with overrides for classes that

> "The academic climate at MSU is fairly competitive. A lot of the competition comes from whether or not students challenge themselves by taking rigorous courses."

are technically full. Most lectures are given by professors, who students describe as caring and "very approachable." Reports a child development for elementary education major, "I believe I have received a high quality of teaching." Labs and smaller recitation sections are led by less-skilled TAs, students say. Also controversial among students is the technique of teaching some classes via cassettes or videotapes, followed by twenty-minute discussion sessions with graduate assistants and one writing session per week. But in general, students praise the teaching, especially in smaller, upper-level courses, which garner more personal attention from the top professors. Academic advising also gets high marks: "The advisors are very helpful, you just have to take the initiative to seek out their help," says a sophomore.

As a land-grant university, MSU traditionally has been strong in agriculture and preveterinary science. However, psychology, accounting, finance, engineering, education, and criminal justice are also among the school's top drawing cards. Math is cited as weaker than most. Recent curricular additions include environmental biology and zoo and aquarium science. MSU boasts the nation's first school of packaging, and student trainees from the Hotel, Restaurant, and Institutional Management program staff the university hotel. General education requirements include math, tier I and II writing courses, a 2000 and 3000 level social sciences course, two courses in arts/humanities, and one physical and biological science course with a lab. There is a strong international component, too. With eighty study abroad programs located

> "The advisors are very helpful, you just have to take the initiative to seek out their help."

in over forty countries around the world, it's not surprising that MSU sent more than thirteen hundred students to terms away last year, more than any other U.S. research university.

Despite MSU's farm-school heritage, most students are urban types from the state of Michigan. They're not all the same, though. Indeed, African-Americans and Hispanics account for 12 percent of students, and Asian-Americans make up 5 percent. Relationships across ethnic and racial lines are calm, and a communications major says, "Sharing of views—and respect for others' views—is encouraged." Each year hundreds of students receive scholarships for outstanding academic performance that range from $200 to $21,060. Athletic scholarships lure devotees of many different sports.

With a capacity of nearly eighteen thousand, MSU's residence system is the largest of any university in the nation. Almost half of all undergrads live on campus. MSU has divided its massive college into two smaller residential colleges, James

(Continued)
Expense: Pub $ $
Phi Beta Kappa: Yes
Applicants: 24,246
Accepted: 65%
Enrolled: 43%
Grad in 6 Years: 69%
Returning Freshmen: 89%
Academics: ✍ ✍ ✍
Social: ☎ ☎ ☎ ☎
Q of L: ★ ★ ★
Admissions: (517) 355-8332
Email Address:
  admis@msu.edu

Strongest Programs:
  Education
  Accounting
  Finance
  Hospitality Business
  Communications
  Psychology
  Criminal Justice
  Packaging

With eighty study abroad programs located in over forty countries around the world, it's not surprising that MSU sent more than thirteen hundred students to terms away last year, more than any other U.S. research university.

Madison (organized around the social sciences) and Lyman Briggs (emphasizing the natural sciences and math). Each houses fewer than one thousand students and aims to create the feeling of a small undergraduate institution. Three much bigger living-learning complexes, each with about four residence halls, are also available, giving residents access to libraries, faculty offices, classrooms, counseling, cafeterias, and recreation areas. "The dorms are very nice, but very different depending on the side of campus you live on." An honors college brings the brightest freshmen together, houses them separately if they wish, and assigns them a special advisor. Other living-learning programs, known by their catchy acronyms, include RISE (focus on the environment), ROIAL (arts and letters), ROSES (science and engineering), and STAR (Support-Teamwork-Achievement-Resources).

Freshmen and sophomores usually live in "clean and well-maintained" residence halls with populations from 250 to more than twelve hundred. The halls offer various living options, including single-sex or coed, high-rise or low-rise, smoking or nonsmoking, and extra quiet or alcohol free. Room and board includes various meal plans at any of the cafeterias sprinkled throughout the residence halls, all of which receive good reviews. For juniors and seniors, apartment living often becomes the thing, in college-owned facilities or in East Lansing. But parking places are in chronically short supply. Fraternity and sorority members mostly live in their own off-campus houses. And despite its bucolic surroundings, campus safety is as much of an issue here as anywhere: State has its own police force, green light emergency phone system, and riding and walking escort services for those who need to travel at night.

"The university and the city work hard on relations and many students are active in the community."

With so many people concentrated in one spot, it's no wonder the residence halls and active Greek system (18 percent of the student population) sponsor popular MSU social events. As at most schools, the rule on alcohol is "no one under twenty-one is served," but a zero-tolerance policy—meaning that police can Breathalyze any student suspected of being under the influence—gives the rule teeth here. Other popular leisure-time fare includes picnics, pizza-eating contests, hall Olympics, hayrides, and ice-skating outings. The annual Michigan Festival brings big-name performers such as R.E.M., Elton John, and the Red Hot Chili Peppers to campus. The town of East Lansing, where the Land Shark and Rick's are popular hangouts, is a short walk from campus and many students do volunteer work in the community. "The university and the city work hard on relations and many students are active in the community," says a junior.

Weekends are dominated by Big Ten athletic competitions, with the Michigan-MSU rivalry especially fierce. A sophomore proudly describes the pregame ritual: "During the week before the U of M-MSU football game, students guard our mascot Sparty, the largest free-standing ceramic statue in the world, and protect him from sneaky Wolverines." More than a few times, the Spartans have upset their archrivals in football and basketball; they even won the 2000 NCAA championship. The marching band is also a national award winner.

"During the week before the U of M-MSU football game, students guard our mascot Sparty, the largest free-standing ceramic statue in the world, and protect him from sneaky Wolverines."

With so many outstanding programs in such a pretty, friendly place, it's easy to see why students here are so content. Once they recover from the initial shock caused by State's large size, most thrive on the opportunities offered at such a large school. "The beautiful campus, diverse student body, and ability to speak your mind freely," are what make this school special, according to one student.

Overlaps

Middlebury College

Middlebury, VT 05753

One of the few small liberal arts colleges where applications have surged significantly in the past ten years. Students are drawn to the beauty of Midd's Green Mountain location and strong programs in hot areas like international studies and environmental science. Known worldwide for its summer foreign language programs.

The nickname of Middlebury College—"Club Midd"—may bring to mind a tropical resort, but this school's rigorous academics are far from a four-year vacation. The campus, with its picturesque sunsets, excellent skiing, and rural Vermont charm is a paradise for those interested in environmental studies, second and third languages, and a tight-knit community where highly motivated and intelligent students and faculty truly care about each other. "Even in the coldest and snowiest months, Middlebury is still a warm and welcoming place," says a senior.

The college's 350-acre main campus overlooks the village of Middlebury, Vermont, which a religion major describes as "full of character." The eighteen hundred-acre mountain campus, site of the Bread Loaf School of English, the Bread Loaf Writers' Conference, and the college's

> **"The plans for even more unbelievable and impressive facilities put our brand-new, $60 million science building to shame."**

Snow Bowl, is nearby. Old Stone Row cuts across the campus, where buildings with simple lines and rectangular shapes evoke the mills of early New England. (Middlebury was founded in 1800.) Academic halls and dormitories of marble and limestone sit in quadrangles with views of the Adirondacks and Green Mountains. "I wish I could still be here in two years!" exclaims a junior. "The plans for even more unbelievable and impressive facilities put our brand-new, $60 million science building to shame."

Even with the recent building boom, Middlebury's priorities remain inside the classroom: one-fourth of the faculty teaches languages and literature. Between June and August, Middlebury banishes English from its campus and teaches hundreds of "linguiphiles" other tongues through "immersion"—students live, learn, and, hopefully, think only in their chosen language. The language departments continue their excellent instruction during the school year; especially notable are German, Chinese, and Japanese. Although there is no foreign language require-

> **"Everyone talks about Middlebury having the highest study hours per week, and if that is true, I wouldn't be surprised."**

ment, just about everyone studies another dialect, if only to take advantage of Middlebury's campuses in France, Germany, Italy, Spain, and Russia. About two-thirds of students study abroad; the school is also a member of the Maritime Studies Program.*

Other highly touted Middlebury departments include English (the most popular major, bolstered by its connections to Bread Loaf), psychology, and economics. "Courses are demanding, and students work hard to do well," says a sophomore.

Website: www.middlebury.edu
Location: Small town
Total Enrollment: 2,307
Undergraduates: 2,307
Male/Female: 48/52
SAT Ranges: V 670–740
  M 670–730
ACT Range: 29–32
Financial Aid: 35%
Expense: Pr $ $ $ $
Phi Beta Kappa: Yes
Applicants: 5,411
Accepted: 23%
Enrolled: 42%
Grad in 6 Years: 87%
Returning Freshmen: 97%
Academics: ✍ ✍ ✍ ✍ ½
Social: ☎ ☎ ☎
Q of L: ★ ★ ★
Admissions: (802) 443-3000
Email Address: admissions@
  middlebury.edu

Strongest Programs:
  Political Science
  Language Study
  Environmental Studies
  Biology
  Economics
  English/Literary Studies
  International Studies
  Dance and Theater

Adds a political science major, "Everyone talks about Middlebury having the highest study hours per week, and if that is true, I wouldn't be surprised." Still, a literary studies major notes that, "Professors really encourage cooperative learning." While administrators claim there's no "objective" way to measure which departments are weak, some students feel studio art is too small to accommodate all those interested, and computer science and math "don't attract large numbers," says a junior. New programs include a neuroscience major and a course in Portuguese that will eventually be developed into a major.

Middlebury students must take a discussion-based, writing-intensive First-Year Seminar with only fifteen people; the instructor serves as advisor to those enrolled until they declare a major. By the end of sophomore year, students must complete a second writing-intensive course. In addition to a ten- to sixteen-credit major, students must also satisfy distribution requirements in seven of eight academic areas:

> **"In most cases, the professors know the name of every student in a class by the end of the second week."**

literature, the arts, philosophical and religious studies, history, physical and life sciences, deductive reasoning and analytical processes, social analysis, and foreign language. Students also take four cultures and civilizations classes, and two non-credit courses in physical education. With all of these requirements, it's no wonder students and faculty become close. "In most cases, the professors know the name of every student in a class by the end of the second week," says a senior.

Seventy-two percent of Middlebury's students graduated in the top tenth of their high-school class, and students of color constitute 14 percent of the student body. The school's partnership with New York City's Posse Foundation brings ten inner-city students to the school each year. Lack of parking is a perennial complaint, and students are concerned about issues of race, gender, and sexual orientation—there's a gender studies academic house that has its own social functions and may become residential in the future, and a substance-free social house now offers living space. One student says that because of the emphasis on tolerance and not stirring up bad feelings, "nothing ever happens." Middlebury's small, close-knit community can also make the place claustrophobic, says a literary studies major: "Sometimes you just want to be anonymous, and it's absolutely impossible."

Few Middlebury students live off campus (5 percent), since tuition includes guaranteed housing for four years. A variety of "palatial" coed dorms offer suites, augmented by college-owned group houses, the Environmental House (where residents

> **"Housing is almost as intense and competitive as academics —but you can't really lose."**

cook all of their own food), academic interest houses, and more "standard" situations. Rooms for upperclassmen are distributed by lottery, based on seniority, which a junior says is "almost as intense and competitive as academics—but you can't really lose." It's easy to get a single room, even as a sophomore, students report. The meal plan is served at five dining halls, which set high marks for both their décor and their victuals.

Students at Middlebury play as hard on the weekends as they work during the week. Most stay on campus for school-sponsored movies, discussions, or parties at the Greek-like coed social houses. Kegs are outlawed in the dorms, but permitted at parties, which must be registered and also offer non-alcoholic drinks and snacks. "Underage students do not need to be served—they serve themselves," says a senior. The college's Grille provides an alternative, with performers throughout the week and weekend.

Off campus, Middlebury is a "rural Vermont farming town" that is "oriented almost exclusively to the college." It has necessities such as fast food, a grocery store, drug store, hardware store, and clothing shops, but the administration regularly airlifts or buses in culture and entertainment. February can be grim because the snow here comes early and stays late, so road trips are popular. The progressive city of Burlington is forty-five minutes away, while Montreal is barely three hours' drive, Boston four, and New York City five. Middlebury's own Snow Bowl ($100 for the season) and proximity to most Vermont ski slopes make this a paradise for ski fanatics, a breed Middlebury attracts in predictably large numbers.

Middlebury athletics draw rabid fans, especially when on cheering the powerful ski and ice hockey teams—men's and women's—that compete in Division III against archrival Williams. Men's swimming and men's and women's lacrosse are also strong, having brought home conference championships recently. The administration shows its support, too,

> **"Volunteer work is very important. Altruism is alive at Middlebury!"**

by favoring student-athletes in admissions. Perhaps the biggest outdoor activity of all is the three-day Winter Carnival, an annual extravaganza including parties, cultural events, an all-school formal, sporting competitions, snow sculpture, and ice-skating at an outdoor rink. Townspeople support the school's hockey games, and students give back through volunteer work with children, women, the elderly, and local schools. "Volunteer work is very important," says a political science major. "Altruism is alive at Middlebury!"

Students have noticed physical changes at Middlebury over the past few years, with more in the works, including a library due for occupancy in 2004. But some things have remained the same—namely, the combination of "excellent academics with endless extracurricular opportunities," says a sophomore. "My friends sing in a cappella groups, climb mountains, and direct films," says a senior. Despite Middlebury's location in rural Vermont, who said anything about isolation?

Overlaps

Dartmouth, Williams, Bowdoin, Amherst, Brown

If You Apply To ➤

Middlebury: Early decision: Nov. 15 (preapplication and Common Application); Dec. 15 (preapplication) and Jan. 1 (application). Regular admissions: Dec. 15 (preapplication) and Jan. 1 (application). Financial aid: Nov. 15, Jan. 1. Guarantees to meet demonstrated need. Campus and alumni interviews: optional, evaluative. The ACT or any three SAT IIs, AP exams or IB exams as long as those submitted include a writing test, a quantitative test, and one of the student's choice. Accepts the Common Application and electronic applications. Essay question: one Common Application essay; and describe an experience in which your values were tested.

Millsaps College

1701 North State Street, Jackson, MS 39210

Millsaps is the best liberal arts college in the deep, deep South. Its largely pre-professional student body typically has sights set on business, law or medicine. Typically compared to Hendrix, Rhodes, and Sewanee, though less selective than the last two.

Millsaps College, long a finishing school for well-bred Southern belles and gentlemen, is also one of the best liberal arts institutions in the deep South. It boasts an urban location in Mississippi's capital city, and a quality premed curriculum. Its Heritage Program, an interdisciplinary approach to Western culture, is nationally recognized, though hard-partying Greeks dominate the social scene. "We're half spoiled little rich kids who sleep through classes and half academically minded students who are here on scholarships," explains a sophomore. That said, "mostly, everyone really gets along," says a freshman. "Since the school is so small, a great sense of community is established—and that includes all faculty, up to the president!"

Website: www.millsaps.edu
Location: Center city
Total Enrollment: 1,330
Undergraduates: 1,221
Male/Female: 46/54
SAT Ranges: V 540–650
   M 550–650
ACT Range: 23–29

(Continued)

Financial Aid: 60%

Expense: Pr $

Phi Beta Kappa: Yes

Applicants: 952

Accepted: 86%

Enrolled: 40%

Grad in 6 Years: 70%

Returning Freshmen: 83%

Academics: ✍ ✍ ✍

Social: ☎ ☎ ☎

Q of L: ★ ★ ★

Admissions: (601) 974-1050

Email Address:
admissions@millsaps.edu

Strongest Programs:
Accounting
Business Administration
Economics
Biology/Premed
Classics
Education
English
History

Millsaps is situated in the center of Jackson, but owing to the city's small size, it offers the ivory-tower serenity of a less urban environment. The Bowl—according to legend, the crater of an extinct volcano—marks the center of campus, surrounded by an eight-foot wrought iron fence. Dotting the rest of campus is a mix of modern and traditional buildings, dominated by the 122-foot, copper-sheathed Millsaps Tower at the east entrance. The $17.3 million Campus Life Complex opened in January 2000, with offices for student organizations, a coffee house and cafeteria, fitness facilities, and a stage for outdoor events.

Millsaps requires students to complete 128 semester hours to earn a degree, all but eight of which must be taken for a letter grade. All students must also complete ten multidisciplinary courses designed to develop their skills in reasoning, communications, quantitative thinking, valuing, and decision-making—including four in the humanities and four in the sciences and math. Students begin the humanities sequence with either Heritage or Topics of the Ancient World. All freshmen also take a one-hour Perspectives class, led by an academic advisor, to aid in adjusting to college life, and all new students take the Introduction to Liberal Studies seminar, which emphasizes critical thinking and writing. Mandatory freshman and senior seminars provide perspective on the work in between.

> **"We're half spoiled little rich kids who sleep through classes and half academically minded students who are here on scholarships."**

Among the best programs at Millsaps are English—"We have the leading Eudora Welty scholar," says a freshman—and education, where students get involved with the Jackson Public Schools from introductory-level classes. The Else School of Management, Millsaps' business school, offers strong programs in accounting, business administration (the most popular major), and economics. Premedical courses, including those in biology and chemistry, are also well-regarded. There's a new German major, and concentrations in American studies, environmental studies, human services, and international studies have been added. Physics and political science suffer somewhat because each has only two faculty members, administrators say.

No course at Millsaps has more than fifty students, and three-quarters have twenty-five or less. "I've had maybe one or two professors thus far that I'm not impressed with," says a sophomore. "Overall, our quality of teaching is high." A freshman agrees, calling faculty members, "so intelligent, so active, so accessible." Off campus, students may do research for credit at Tennessee's Oak Ridge National Laboratory or at the Gulf Coast Research Laboratory, or they may intern for credit with local businesses or in

> **"Since the school is so small, a great sense of community is established—and that includes all faculty, up to the president!"**

government offices. Each year, about twelve upperclassmen are accepted into the Ford Teaching Fellows Program, letting them work closely with a faculty member to learn about teaching—and paying them for their time in the classroom. Students eager to see how government works may participate in the Washington Semester,* while those seeking passport stamps may spend summers in London, Paris, Munich, Florence, Nice, the Yucatan, or Costa Rica. Cooperative programs are also available through the Associated Colleges of the South* consortium, of which Millsaps is a founding member.

Millsaps has broadened its recruiting efforts, and 42 percent of students now come from out of state. They're also getting smarter: 46 percent of a recent freshman class graduated in the top tenth of their high-school class. While Millsaps was the first college in Mississippi to voluntarily adopt open admission for minority students, it's still far from diverse. African-Americans now account for 11 percent of the student body, Asian-Americans 2 percent, and Hispanics 1 percent. "Millsaps

Among the best programs at Millsaps are English—"We have the leading Eudora Welty scholar," says a freshman—and education, where students get involved with the Jackson Public Schools from introductory-level classes.

emphasizes diversity—an honorable goal, to be sure, but one that is odd considering we're over 80 percent white," says an English major. "There's been a lot of conversation lately about reconciling academic freedom with being a church-affiliated school. The election that considered removing the Confederate battle flag from the Mississippi state flag was also a hot topic."

Most Mississippians view Millsaps as a hotbed of liberalism—noting that the school's coed dorms confirm their worst fears. Freshmen, however, are still required to live in single-sex halls. Seventy-six percent of students stay in campus housing— mostly, grouses a sophomore, because they lose a third of their scholarship money if they leave. "It has been difficult for underclassmen to get rooms," the student reports. "Dorms are—in general—nice, but not luxurious." Junior and senior men may live in one of four fraternity houses; there is no sorority housing, even though the Greek system claims 45 percent of men and 48 percent of women.

> "Millsaps emphasizes diversity —an honorable goal, to be sure, but one that is odd considering we're over 80 percent white."

Each year, about twelve upperclassmen are accepted into the Ford Teaching Fellows Program, letting them work closely with a faculty member to learn about teaching—and paying them for their time in the classroom.

The social scene at Millsaps revolves around the fraternity houses, which are usually open and rocking from Wednesday through Saturday nights. Greek rush is now held after fall midterms instead of during the first hectic week of school, but that hasn't dampened the party spirit. The school's alcohol policy says only students of age may drink, and then only in their rooms—but students say the rule is only loosely enforced. "For the non-drinker, there are people who are active with clubs and projects," says a freshman. Easy road trips include New Orleans and Memphis; closer to campus, ten miles to the north, is a huge reservoir, popular for weekend water sports. Major Madness is a favorite annual event, offering a week of open mic nights, hypnotists, and comedians, and culminating in a weekend-long festival in the Bowl, with food, games, and live music.

Millsaps competes in NCAA Division III, as a member of the Southern Collegiate Athletic Conference (SCAC), so it isn't nearly as sports-crazy as most Southern campuses. For the men, football, basketball, baseball, and soccer draw the largest crowds; basketball, soccer, softball, and volleyball are the most popular among women's teams. "We have a rivalry with Mississippi College that lots of Millsaps folks are hard-core about, and lots of MC folks couldn't care less about," quips a sophomore. "Or, as a friend of mine says, 'A one-sided rivalry—isn't that called hatred?'"

> "We have a rivalry with Mississippi College that lots of Millsaps folks are hard-core about, and lots of MC folks couldn't care less about."

In a state renowned for its legendary blues and warm deltas, Millsaps College remains a well-kept secret. Small classes ensure plenty of time to get to know fellow students and faculty members. Emphasizing "scholarly inquiry and intellectual growth," in the words of the Honor Code, Millsaps is built around "a spirit of personal honesty and mutual trust." And that's one tradition that never gets old.

Overlaps
University of Mississippi, Mississippi State, Rhodes, Mississippi College, University of the South

If You Apply To ➤

Millsaps: Early action: Dec. 1. Rolling admissions: Jun. 1. Financial aid: Mar. 1. Housing: May 1. Guarantees to meet demonstrated need. Campus interviews: optional, informational. No alumni interviews. SATs or ACTs: required. SAT IIs: optional. Accepts the Common Application and electronic applications. Essay question: community, state, national, or world issue in which you've gotten involved; what fictional character would you be and why; the most memorable or significant hour of your life.

5000 MacArthur Boulevard, Oakland, CA 94613

One of two major women's colleges on the West Coast. Mills has the Oakland area to fall back on, including UC-Berkeley, where students can take classes. Mills is strongest in the arts, though it does offer small programs in preprofessional areas such as communications and business economics.

Website: www.mills.edu

Location: City outskirts

Total Enrollment: 1,162

Undergraduates: 728

Male/Female: 0/100

SAT Ranges: V 520–660
M 490-610

ACT Range: N/A

Financial Aid: 73%

Expense: Pr $ $ $

Phi Beta Kappa: Yes

Applicants: 431

Accepted: 85%

Enrolled: 31%

Grad in 6 Years: 63%

Returning Freshmen: 80%

Academics: ✍ ✍ ✍

Social: ☎ ☎ ☎

Q of L: ★ ★ ★

Admissions: (800) 87-MILLS

Email Address:
admission@mills.edu

Strongest Programs:
English
Computer Science
Creative Writing
Dance
Psychology
Music
Studio Art
Political, Legal, and
Economic Analysis

Only a short drive from the majestic Golden Gate Bridge is another kind of unique passageway: Mills College, a preeminent women's college where diverse academic pursuits, from studio art to computer science, blend to create a challenging learning environment. The students here are no shrinking violets. Having gone on strike to keep men out despite budget troubles, the women of Mills are confident, well-rounded, and vocal. After four years at this small school, a departing senior asks: "Where else can you find such tremendous women making the world more positive and rich?"

The school's fascinating history started in 1852, when it began as a young ladies' seminary serving the children of California gold rush adventurers who were determined to see their daughters raised in an atmosphere of gentility. Now, the combination of student diversity and educational opportunity guarantees that no one can graduate without having her horizons well expanded. It is a place where issues are debated and analyzed, and many students are politically active in such groups as NOW, Young Women's Political Caucus, and League of Women Voters. Make no mistake—"It's very key to be P.C." on a campus where sexuality, class, and race can dominate heated debates.

> **"Where else can you find such tremendous women making the world more positive and rich?"**

The park-like 135-acre campus boasts both historic and modern architecture set among rolling meadows, woods, and a meandering creek. Residence halls and classrooms are located within easy walking distance of one another. New additions include an aquatic center, education complex with a lab school, and a new plaza for outdoor gatherings. In an effort to make itself more attractive to prospective students, the college developed a series of interdisciplinary lower-division seminars including Science and Pseudoscience, Music and the Written Word, and Tribal Cultures in Fact and Fiction. At least half of each student's work must be taken outside of her major field, and students must take two courses in each of the following areas: natural sciences and math, social sciences, fine arts, and humanities. In addition, every Mills student must take at least two writing and interdisciplinary classes, such as Cuisine History, as well as a course in multiculturalism, like Voices in Hispanic Poetry.

Classes range from small to smaller; 90 percent of the classes taken by freshmen have fewer than twenty-five students. "There are high academic standards and a serious environment, but a cooperative feeling," says an art major. A junior reports that test grades are not posted. Instead, "There is an emphasis on wanting the students to thrive without grade-comparing." The professors are highly regarded, friendly, and accessible. With a remarkable 60 percent of them women, there's no shortage of excellent female role models. Faculty also play a large role in helping advise students on course and career choices, though the general quality of formal advising "varies a lot," says a molecular biology major.

> **"There are high academic standards and a serious environment, but a cooperative feeling."**

English, history, psychology, art, and dance are all praised by Mills students. But most agree the natural sciences are the most improved; premed students enjoy a 75 percent acceptance rate at med schools. Popular among prelaw students is the interdisciplinary program in administration and legal studies. The fine arts department is Mills's traditional stronghold, and electronic and computer music specializations within the music program are worthy of note, as is the fact that Mills was the first women's college to offer a major in computer science. Students and the administration consider that pioneering move to have been a good investment in what is now among the best mathematics and computer science programs around. Newer majors include public policy, environmental science, and a joint bachelors/masters program in economics. Foreign languages are somewhat limited—only French, German, and Spanish are offered, though others can be taken through cross-registration at Berkeley.

Mills students are encouraged to explore beyond the Oakland campus, and many take advantage of the excellent programs abroad and exchanges with other American schools. A year at a women's or coed college in the East is especially popular. Mills has concurrent cross-registration agreements with UC–Berkeley and most Bay Area universities, with five-year engineering programs with several of the same schools.

The college developed a series of interdisciplinary lower-division seminars including Science and Pseudoscience, Music and the Written Word, and Tribal Cultures in Fact and Fiction.

"Most halls are very charming and have their own unique style."

Opportunities for internships abound. Students take advantage of the fully automated $6-million F.W. Olin Library, with access to the huge facilities at Berkeley.

Three-quarters of Mills women are from California, and most attended public school. Asian-Americans, Hispanics and African-Americans make up 10 percent each of the student body. A full 70 percent ranked in the top quarter of their graduating class. An influential subgroup of the student body is "resumers," women returning to college after a break of several years.

Four Mediterranean-style old dorms and three California-modern hill dorms offer a plethora of spacious single rooms. "Most halls are very charming and have their own unique style," a junior says. Only 55 percent of the students live on campus, so there's not much of a housing crunch. Students can freely take advantage of cooperative housing, college-owned apartments, and French- and Spanish-language wings. Older dorms are more homey, with high ceilings and long windows. Each of the older dorms has its own dining room, in which traditions are very important.

Each Wednesday night a sit-down candlelight dinner is served, and each year students feast on a Christmas dinner of Cornish game hens and flaming plum pudding.

Each Wednesday night a sit-down candlelight dinner is served, and each year students feast on a Christmas dinner of Cornish game hens and flaming plum pudding. Another old-dorm dining tradition is the Candle Passing ceremony: a candle is passed around the table until the honored woman blows it out. Students living in the three newer dorms eat together at the commons. And there isn't a place on campus where the food is not excellent.

Fears about a stunted social life on this tiny campus quietly linger throughout. "It's not as nurturing as you might think," a senior says. Building an active social life requires an "open and adventurous spirit." While many students agree that the social options on campus are lacking, others enjoy activities such as going to a movie or dance on campus, having a party in their rooms, or going into Berkeley or San Francisco. "The greater Bay Area is teeming with life," a

"Students are very proactive and socially aware."

social change major says. Frat hops are popular around Berkeley, and many a man is let into Mills functions. Of course, friendships and romances among women are understandably strong.

With a bus stop on campus, it is easy to get around Oakland and into San Francisco to take advantage of the dining, dancing, and cultural resources of both cities. Farther away, there's the college ski lodge in the Sierra Nevadas and gambling in scenic Reno. The NCAA Division III varsity teams in tennis, cross-country and soccer have been successful—two of the soccer players were named to the 2001 all-conference team. Participation in student government and other campus organizations is strong. Other activities include Amnesty International and environmental activism. "Students are very proactive and socially aware," a junior confirms.

Mills College may not bustle, but its students make up for the relative serenity by tackling tough social issues, diverse course offerings, and ideas from their independent-minded peers. The size makes one-on-one attention a given while its Bay Area setting offers social and cultural options in one of the most vibrant parts of the country.

If You Apply To ➤

Mills: Regular admissions: Feb. 1. Early action: Nov. 15. Financial aid: Feb. 15. Meets demonstrated need of 73%. Campus and alumnae interviews: recommended, informational. SATs or ACTs: required. SAT IIs: recommended. Accepts the Common Application and electronic applications. Essay question: submit sample of graded analytical paper or essay from the past year.

University of Minnesota–Morris

600 East 4th Street, Morris, MN 56267-2199

The plains of western Minnesota is an unlikely place to find a liberal arts college—and a public one at that. Minnesota–Morris is cut from the same cloth as UNC–Asheville, St. Mary's of Maryland, and Mary Washington. The draw: private-college education at a public-university price.

Website: www.mrs.umn.edu
Location: Small town
Total Enrollment: 1,870
Undergraduates: 1,870
Male/Female: 41/59
SAT Ranges: V 500–630
  M 540–630
ACT Range: 22–28
Financial Aid: 90%
Expense: Pub $ $ $ $
Phi Beta Kappa: No
Applicants: 1,254
Accepted: 80%
Enrolled: 55%
Grad in 6 Years: 60%
Returning Freshmen: 83%
Academics: ✑ ✑ ✑ ½
Social: ☎ ☎
Q of L: ★ ★ ★
Admissions: (800) 992-8863
Email Address: N/A

Strongest Programs:
  Premed

The University of Minnesota–Morris is far more comprehensive than its small size might indicate. Founded by a Roman Catholic nun as a school for Native Americans, Morris has since grown into a full-fledged university with solid academics, a dedicated faculty, opportunities for collaborative research, and options for study abroad. One of the four University of Minnesota campuses, Morris has become a quality public liberal arts college where personal attention is commonplace.

The school lies on 130 acres in west-central Minnesota, which for some students means "mootown." The campus is composed of twenty-six traditional brick-and-mortar buildings loosely arranged around a central mall. A $28-million addition to the science building has doubled the size of the science and math facility, and a new $5 million fitness center serves the entire community.

In the classroom, Morris students must complete at least ninety credits of general education coursework outside their major, in subjects ranging from writing, foreign language, mathematical and symbolic reasoning, and artistic performance to historical perspectives, human behavior, communication, fine arts, physical and biological sciences, and the global village. Freshmen are also required to take a diversity seminar. Among major fields, the sciences and math are highly regarded, as is Morris's psychology department, which is known for breakthrough studies of daydreams. Preprofessional programs for wanna-be doctors, lawyers, veterinarians, pharmacists, and physical therapists are recognized, too.

"The small size allows you to get more help from professors."

One of the college's innovations is Morris Academic Partners, in which select students receive a stipend to conduct their own research with a faculty member. The merit-based Undergraduate Research Opportunities Program offers financial rewards to students for research, scholarly, or creative projects undertaken in collaboration

(Continued)
Predentistry
Preveterinary
Engineering
Natural Sciences
Math

with a faculty member. Students in the English Language Teaching Assistant Program travel to schools in foreign countries to assist English teachers. The study abroad program at Morris allows students to live and learn in Africa, the Middle East, Asia, the South Pacific, and Europe. Newly christened majors include statistics and anthropology.

Class sizes at Morris are generally small by public university standards: 90 percent have fifty or fewer students. The quality of teaching is "outstanding," says a management major. "Professors are always more than willing to sit down with you and discuss things," adds a freshman. Faculty also receive high marks from students for their individualized approach and willingness to get to know students as people, not just numbers on a class list. Every freshman is assigned an academic advisor who must approve his or her schedule. "I can always get the help I need from academic or career counseling," says a sophomore.

Morris draws 81 percent of its students from Minnesota, and 60 percent of last year's freshmen graduated in the top quarter of their high-school class. They are an active bunch, and proud of their academic standing, as illustrated by a popular jeer at archrival Duluth: "It's better to fail at Morris than graduate from Duluth!" Minorities comprise 16 percent of the student body at UMM, including a large contingency

One of the college's innovations is Morris Academic Partners, in which select students receive a stipend to conduct their own research with a faculty member.

> **"Professors are always more than willing to sit down with you and discuss things."**

of Native Americans. The school is partnered with the Anti-Defamation League's World of Difference Institute, dedicated to decreasing prejudice and increasing intergroup understanding and communication. UMM offers a wide variety of merit and athletic scholarships. And in keeping with its heritage, Morris automatically grants free tuition to Native Americans.

Fifty-four percent of Morris freshmen live on campus in one of five residence halls. Upperclassmen either move off campus or enter a lottery for space in a campus apartment complex. The dorms feature a twenty-four-hour visitation policy with kitchenettes on every floor and a TV lounge on the ground level. "I found living in the freshman dorms to be a pleasurable experience," says student. "It was a quick and easy way to meet people." Students find campus safe, and say even the dining halls aren't a danger zone: "There are salad bars for lunch and dinner, and food service is more than willing to fix a special lunch," says a math major.

The phrase "Make your own fun" might well have been invented here, since students are left to their own devices when it's time to relax. "There are always activities taking place on campus," says one student. "Activities occurring off campus usually involve close friends getting together." That's because the drinking age is strictly enforced on campus and in local bars. Some students use weekends to participate in community service. Others head for home with laundry bags in tow.

Once each quarter, Morris sponsors a Diversity Jam in which all ethnic groups are celebrated.

For those who stick around campus, more than ninety clubs and student organizations are available, focusing on everything from juggling to geology. Morris sponsors several outstanding music groups, including a jazz ensemble that was selected to play at the 1994 Jazz Festival in Amsterdam.

> **"I found living in the freshman dorms to be a pleasurable experience. It was a quick and easy way to meet people."**

Intramural sports are also a big hit, especially basketball, volleyball, wrestling, and football. Morris competes in Division II, and crowds gather to cheer on the basketball, football, baseball, and women's wrestling teams, among others.

A home on the range at UMM isn't for everyone; some might chafe at the school's low-key social life and relative isolation. But for those looking to test their academic stamina for four years, Morris offers a way to leave distractions behind. "The small size allows you to get more help from professors," says one happy student. And the affordable price tag sure doesn't hurt.

Overlaps

Gustavus Adolphus, University of Minnesota–Twin Cities, St. John's University/College of St. Benedict, Concordia–Moorehead, St. Thomas

Morris: Early action: Dec. 1, Feb. 1. Regular admissions: Mar. 15. Guarantees to meet demonstrated need. Campus and alumni interviews: recommended, informational. SATs or ACTs: required. SAT IIs: optional. Accepts electronic applications. Essay question: how UMM will contribute to your intellectual development and overall growth.

University of Minnesota–Twin Cities

240 Williamson, 231 Pillsbury Drive SE, Minneapolis, MN 55455

Not quite as highly rated as U. of Wisconsin or U. of Michigan, but not quite as expensive, either. In a university the size of Minnesota, the best bet is to find a niche, such as the honors program in the liberal arts college. Strong programs include engineering, management, and health fields.

Website: www.umn.edu/tc/
perspective
Location: Urban
Total Enrollment: 46,597
Undergraduates: 27,699
Male/Female: 48/52
SAT Ranges: V 530–650
   M 550–680
ACT Range: 22–28
Financial Aid: 47%
Expense: Pub $ $
Phi Beta Kappa: Yes
Applicants: 15,436
Accepted: 76%
Enrolled: 46%
Grad in 6 Years: 51%
Returning Freshmen: 84%
Academics: ✑ ✑ ✑ ✑
Social: ☎ ☎ ☎
Q of L: ★ ★ ★
Admissions: (612) 625-2008
Email Address:
   admissions@tc.umn.edu

Strongest Programs:
   Chemical Engineering
   Psychology
   Journalism
   Management
   Biology
   Theater
   Dance

The University of Minnesota, like the nearby Mall of America, can be overwhelming, with its seemingly limitless variety of offerings and gargantuan size. With more than 150 majors, UM offers an abundance of academic choices. "The size allows for what seems like endless opportunities and experiences," says a child psychology major. "The location allows for job experience and lots of social activities."

The vast Twin Cities campus actually consists of two campuses with three main sections, and within each the architecture is highly diverse. The St. Paul campus encompasses the colleges of agriculture, food, and environmental sciences, natural resources, human ecology, veterinary medicine, and biological sciences. The Minneapolis campus is divided by the Mississippi River into an East Bank and a West Bank that are home to the other colleges and most of the dormitories, as well as most of the fraternities and sororities. Both campuses offer a blend of traditional and modern architecture, with columned buildings seated next to sleek geometric structures.

> **"The size allows for what seems like endless opportunities and experiences. The location allows for job experience and lots of social activities."**

The two campuses are five miles apart and linked by a free bus service. Academic facilities are excellent, beginning with the five-million-volume library system, which is the fourteenth largest in North America. Every one of the colleges has its own library, many of which are good places to study. A 695-acre arboretum is used for research and teaching. New additions include a tennis/hockey arena, architecture building, molecular/cellular biology building, and remodeled student union.

Minnesota offers more than 150 undergraduate majors in twenty-eight separate schools. The Institute of Technology is notable for the options it offers for tutorials and internships; its electrical and mechanical engineering programs are particularly strong and well-subscribed. Psychology, the most popular major on campus, has a good reputation, as do political science, management, economics, law, and journalism. Undergraduates also have access to more esoteric fields, from aging studies and biometry to therapeutic recreation and mortuary science. Anthropology, foreign languages, and math could be better, students say.

While efforts to limit class size have been stepped up and the school is focusing more on undergraduates, classes still top out at three hundred-plus, with introductory classes typically the largest. While Minnesota is a large school, the thoughtful student can find ways of rising out of the sea of anonymity. "You have to work hard and be willing to compete if you want to make yourself known at such a large school," says one junior. The place is crawling with potentially helpful teaching assistants, and the excellent honors program in the liberal arts college allows close contact with faculty members as well as leeway to enroll in certain graduate courses and seminars. Students say the academic climate varies by school. "Classes are quite competitive and leave the student with a sense of true accomplishment. The workload is intense, but manageable," says one student.

While undergraduates have had a difficult time enrolling in courses, the use of computer registration has made life a lot easier. One junior reveals, "If a class is closed and somebody really needs it, they can usually get a magic number from the department to be able to register for it." The administration attributes the school's low six-year graduation rate to the fact that students are likely to center their lives in spheres outside the university—in work and off-campus homes. However, the four-year plan guarantees graduation in four years provided students follow program requirements, including frequent academic counseling and specific coursework.

Professors receive high marks from most students as being approachable and knowledgeable. "They are all experts in the fields they teach, many with national recognition for teaching, research, or publications," says a sophomore business student. Students find plenty of internship opportunities at the many corporations and government agen-

> **"Classes are quite competitive and leave the student with a sense of true accomplishment. The workload is intense, but manageable."**

cies in the Twin Cities area. The university is on a semester system, and almost all classes have a pass/fail option (limited to no more than a quarter of a student's courses).

Sixty-three percent of students at the university come from the top quarter of their high-school class, and 72 percent are from Minnesota. Minorities constitute 20 percent of the students, with 4 percent African-American, 2 percent Hispanic, and 8 percent Asian-American. Students hail the diversity. "There is a lot more diversity on our campus than most Big Ten schools because we are located in a metropolitan area," says a sophomore. Tuition hikes are a main gripe of students. But there is need-based financial aid, over seven hundred merit scholarships—worth up to $48,000—each year and athletic awards in all major sports.

Dorm life at Minnesota follows the big school, wait-in-line theme. Twenty-four percent of all undergraduates and three-quarters of freshmen live in residence halls, as there are now eight traditional halls and one new apartment-style facility, with at least one more on the way. Dorm rooms are hard to obtain, and parking spaces for all those commuters are almost as scarce. Students who have rooms get the chance to keep them for the next year. The administration ensures that new freshmen who apply for housing by May 1 have a room. "Residence halls are great places for freshmen and sophomores. These living areas are designed with programs to fit lower-division students," a sophomore says. Once you're

> **"There is a lot more diversity on our campus than most Big Ten schools because we are located in a metropolitan area."**

there, you're required to join a meal plan. Campus security is adequate, although bike thefts are common. "Have common sense and you'll be safe," a freshman psychology major says.

Since so many students live off campus, on-campus social life is described as low-key but not the only diversion available. Underage drinking is banned, and students say the policy usually works. The downtown areas of the Twin Cities are easy to get to by bus, and there are scores of good bars, restaurants, nightspots, and movie theaters. "Downtown and uptown also provide plenty of entertainment, but it is not necessary to go off campus to find something to do," a freshman says.

This is an athletically inclined bunch of students, as both intramural and varsity sports are popular. The men's basketball team went to the 1997 NCAA Final Four and won the 1998 National Invitational Tournament championship, but the pennants in the gym have been taken down due to an academic fraud scandal prompted by the revelations that, among other things, staff members had completed tests and papers for basketball players. Wrestling, baseball, and hockey have brought home trophies more recently. Students always hope the current season will be one in which the gridiron Gophers take home the roses in a bowl victory, but short of that,

"Downtown and uptown also provide plenty of entertainment, but it is not necessary to go off campus to find something to do."

a victory over Michigan for custody of the Little Brown Jug is cause for celebration. The extent of the University of Minnesota's rivalry with the University of Wisconsin is considerable, especially since U of M has a large Wisconsin population. Intramural competition can go on well past midnight.

Minnesota can get brutally cold in the winter, but for those who enjoy skiing or skating, that's no hardship. For students who want to avoid the winter winds, many of the campus buildings are linked by underground tunnels. In the spring and summer, Minnesota's famed ten thousand lakes offer swimming, boating, and fishing. More than four hundred extracurricular organizations offer respite from the books. The Carnival Weekend put on by the Greeks each April to raise funds for charity is the biggest such event on campus. Spring Jam, which features regional and local bands and is described by one student as "Homecoming in Spring but better," and Campus Kick-off Days in the beginning of the fall quarter are much-anticipated activities.

Anonymity is almost a given at a university of this size. But for those who don't mind working among the masses, there are a plethora of campus resources to take advantage of. Says one junior: "A lot of students are attracted to the university because of its top programs, its reputation, and its size."

If You Apply To ➤ | **Twin Cities:** Rolling admissions: Dec. 15 (priority). Housing: May 1. Campus and alumni interviews: optional, informational. SATs or ACTs: required. Accepts electronic applications. No essay question.

University of Missouri at Columbia

130 Jesse Hall, Columbia, MO 65211

Mizzou is renowned for one of the top journalism schools in the nation, but engineering, business, and education are also standouts. Enrolls only about half the number of out-of-state students as archrival University of Kansas. Columbia is a quintessential college town.

The University of Missouri pays tribute to the past while continuing to evolve into a top-notch academic and research institution. The school constantly wins awards for its innovative programming, while capital improvements on campus get thumbs-up from students. Students say Mizzou covers all the bases. "It not only gives me the tools for my career," says a journalism major, "it has also challenged me and helped shape my character."

The oldest public university west of the Mississippi, Mizzou's spacious, tree-filled campus is flanked by mansion-like fraternity and sorority houses. The Francis

Quadrangle Historical District, with nineteen National Historic Landmark buildings, is the core of the Red Campus (so named for the predominant color of brick). Central to this area are the sixty-foot granite columns of the original Academic Hall—the building was destroyed by fire in 1892. To the east of the columns is the original tombstone of Thomas Jefferson. The White Campus consists of vine-covered limestone buildings, symbolized by the Memorial Union Tower. New additions include the $28 million Cornell Hall for the College of Business, the four-court Green Tennis Center, and a renovation of lab space in Stephens Hall. Construction continues on the $58 million Life Sciences Center.

With more than 250 degree programs and twenty schools and colleges, Mizzou offers a comprehensive set of choices for basic and advanced study. Young writers can get intensive training at the Center for the Literary Arts, and then hands-on experience with the Columbia Missourian, the six thousand-circulation local daily paper edited by J-school faculty members. KBIA, MU's National Public Radio station, is popular among students and has the second-highest number of listeners of any public radio station in the nation. Not surprisingly, newspapers like *The New York Times* and *The Washington Post* send recruiters to campus. Agriculture is also nationally ranked, especially in the areas of agricultural economics and applied research for farm communities. The College of Engineering maintains several notable undergraduate segments, including biological and civil engineering. The College of Business is highly competitive and features a five-year bachelor's/master's accounting program, while the College of Education has added a degree in middle school education and made recent strides to integrate more technological experiences into its courses. There is a new bachelor's degree in environmental geology, and several departments have sharpened their Internet-based offerings.

Committed preprofessionals will be glad to know that MU offers highly able and directed freshmen guaranteed admission to its graduate-level programs in medicine, law, veterinary medicine, nursing, and health-related professions. Mizzou is also one of the leading public research institutions in the country

"While the class work can be difficult, the professors and faculty are committed to the students' success."

for the number and range of lab and scholarly opportunities it offers undergraduates. Undergraduate research projects range from breast cancer research to plant genomics. The school has received millions of dollars over recent years from the National Science Foundation and others to continue expanding research opportunities. MU is also committed to making study abroad opportunities affordable for all students.

MU's general education program has been revamped to facilitate a strong "distribution of knowledge" requirement, in addition to two writing-intensive courses, math/reasoning and computer proficiency, and a capstone experience. In addition, students must take eighteen hours of courses in areas outside their major. Full professors teach the lecture courses at Mizzou, supplemented by a weekly discussion session led by a teaching assistant to go over material presented in class. A freshman reports that professors are "there to help students succeed and hold plenty of time outside of class for students' questions or concerns."

Students say the courses at Mizzou are challenging but not impossible if you are willing to work hard. "While the class work can be difficult, the professors and faculty are committed to the students' success," says a senior. Owing to MU's size, classes can fill up quickly, but professors do give overrides for students who must take certain credits at specific times. Missouri guarantees the availability of coursework to complete a degree in four years. The study-conscious will find plenty of room and resources in the MU library system. Mizzou's libraries have more than three million books, five million microfilms, and sixteen thousand periodicals. (Thank goodness there's a course on how to use it all.)

(Continued)
Expense: Pub $ $
Phi Beta Kappa: Yes
Applicants: 9,678
Accepted: 89%
Enrolled: 48%
Grad in 6 Years: 65%
Returning Freshmen: 85%
Academics: ✏️✏️✏️
Social: ☎ ☎ ☎ ☎
Q of L: ★ ★ ★
Admissions: (573) 882-7786
Email Address:
    mu4u@missouri.edu

Strongest Programs:
    Journalism/Communications
    Biology
    Psychology
    English
    History
    Engineering
    Agriculture
    Geology

Mizzou was the first university in the nation to create a mascot-conservation program. The Mizzou Tigers for Tigers works to ensure that there will be wild tigers for as long as there are Mizzou Tigers.

The Mizzou campus is home mostly to Missourians (86 percent), though every state in the union and more than one hundred foreign countries are represented. African-Americans account for 6 percent of the student body, while Asian-Americans and Hispanics combine for 4 percent. To boost its minority population, MU has established several scholarship programs designed especially for them. It's also opened a state-of-the-art, $2.4 million Black Culture Center and an Asian Affairs Center. More than one thousand merit scholarships are available to academically gifted students; 370 athletic scholarships are available in a plethora of sports.

Forty-two percent of MU students live on campus, and freshman under age twenty are required to do so. Residence halls have double rooms and are often crowded and noisy—and thus are incredibly fun places to be, though single-sex halls, a few single rooms, and round-the-clock quiet floors are also available. Dorm choice is first come, first serve and half of the halls offer coed living by floor or wing. Students can also choose to live in one of twenty-eight "learning communities," where residents share a common interest, such as engineering, arts, or nursing. About 75 percent of students choose a Freshman Interest Group—there are more than eighty to choose from—where fifteen to twenty students with shared academic interests live in the same residence hall and enroll in three classes together. The programs are "very conducive to learning," says a senior. Dorm dwellers are required to purchase meal plans, but credits can be used at all-you-can-eat dining halls, coffee bars, and take-out stands, among many options. Most upperclass students move into one of Columbia's many apartment complexes, primarily in search of single rooms. The fraternity and sorority houses are livable (the frat houses less so), although not all members can fit; 23 percent of Mizzou men and 27 percent of women go Greek.

"Columbia is the ideal college town. It's safe, it's not too big, it has many things to do for people of all ages, and it's easy to get around in."

Mizzou, a champion of tough alcohol policies, works hard to maintain a dry campus and has won national awards for its alcohol prevention program. "Of course, not everyone abides by the policy; sometimes successfully, frequently not," a junior says. Students say MU's social life is packed with options, including movies, shopping, eating out, the usual Greek parties, and great parks and hiking areas on the outskirts of town. "Columbia is the ideal college town," says one student. "It's safe, it's not too big, it has many things to do for people of all ages, and it's easy to get around in."

Columbia offers the benefits of a large city—a versatile bar scene, lots of pizza joints, coffee shops, and expensive boutiques—and the friendly atmosphere of a small town. Students support the town by engaging in community service and the community caters to them in return; their concern even goes beyond the borders of campus to the plight of the wild tiger and the preservation of its habitat. At Mizzou, service goes hand-in-hand with learning; in partnership with the Office of Service Learning, the university offers more than seventy-five courses designated as service-learning. Road trips to St. Louis, Kansas City, and Lake of the Ozarks offer a change of scenery.

Mizzou's Tigers compete in the Big 12, and basketball and football games draw big crowds. In fact, the entire town turns out in black and gold for any football game. The heated rivalry with Kansas dates back to 1891 in football, but can be traced back to the Civil War, when Kansas abolitionists sparred violently with pro-slavery Missouri farmers. An indoor practice facility for football, baseball, softball, and soccer and a track/soccer complex offers seating for two thousand fans. MU's popular intramural program has nearly two dozen sports and two skill divisions, so bloodthirsty competitors and weekend warriors alike can get what they want.

Overlaps

University of Kansas, University of Illinois, Indiana University, University of Missouri at Rolla, Kansas State

The University of Missouri knows that sticking with its long-standing goals of academic growth and abiding by its old traditions, such as Homecoming, encourages students to be well-grounded but constantly growing. Quality teaching, ample research opportunities, and a dynamic college town make Mizzou an increasingly popular choice in higher education.

If You Apply To ➤	**Mizzou:** Rolling admissions. Financial aid: Mar. 1. Campus and alumni interviews: not available. SATs or ACTs required; ACTs preferred. No SAT IIs. Accepts electronic applications. No essay question.

Montana Tech of the University of Montana

1300 West Park Street, Butte, MT 59701-8997

If you go to Montana for college, you're probably interested in either rocks or trees. Montana Tech covers the former, with strong programs related to mining and petroleum engineering. Montana Tech is a third bigger than New Mexico Tech and about the same size as Colorado School of Mines.

Students at Montana Tech like to dig into their work and aren't afraid to get their hands dirty. Plunked down in the midst of western mining country, Montana Tech, as you might expect, shines in land-related engineering fields like petroleum, mining, and geophysics. Students get a hands-on education geared toward "things metallic" (as the school's motto loosely translates). In fact, the school's mascot is Charlie Oredigger, and students are affectionately dubbed "diggers."

Situated on a shoulder of "the richest hill on earth" (some of the greatest copper, molybdenum, zinc, and manganese deposits in the world), Montana Tech's 50-acre campus is composed of 16 buildings of Classical college brick architecture. This is exemplified by Main Hall, constructed in 1900, and the Engineering, Laboratory, and Classroom building (the ELC), built in 1987 and modernized to the tune of $850,000. Other unique features on campus include the Museum Building, which houses one of the country's largest mineral collections; an Earthquake Studies Office, which records tremors throughout southwestern Montana; and the Montana Bureau of Mines and Geology, a research arm of the college that produces geological and mineralogical maps and publications. Recent campus additions include a residence hall and renovations to the student union and a chemistry/biology building with all new labs.

> **"The academic climate is competitive and we do have rigorous courses."**

Tech's degree programs emphasize the study of minerals, energy, and the environment, but students graduate with a well-rounded education. Strong degree programs include environmental engineering, business information and technology, and general engineering (formerly engineering science). Efforts have been made in recent years to strengthen the basic sciences underlying the engineering programs, and faculty is constantly upgrading classes technologically to prepare better job and graduate school candidates. The school also works to place upperclassmen in summer jobs in their fields. Everyone faces general education requirements including communications, humanities, social sciences, mathematical sciences, and life sciences, although students say the nonscience offerings are weak. For those who

Website: www.mtech.edu
Location: City outskirts
Total Enrollment: 2,067
Undergraduates: 1,978
Male/Female: 55/45
SAT Ranges: V 490–590
  M 480–620
ACT Range: 19–25
Financial Aid: 70%
Expense: Pub $
Phi Beta Kappa: No
Applicants: 585
Accepted: 97%
Enrolled: 70%
Grad in 6 Years: 44%
Returning Freshmen: 70%
Academics: ✍ ✍ ✍
Social: ☎ ☎
Q of L: ★ ★ ★
Admissions: (406) 496-4178
Email Address:
  admissions@mtech.edu

Strongest Programs:
  Engineering
  Information Technology

want more than just a straight-science experience, Tech has a major in science and technology that attempts to relate liberal arts to today's increasingly technological society. Newer additions to the curriculum include a BS in general science and general engineering. Montana Tech also continues to add degree programs in software engineering, nursing, and biological sciences.

Academic work at Tech is rigorous, with gym the only subject that can be taken pass/fail. "The academic climate is competitive and we do have rigorous courses," says a sophomore. "But with the small student-teacher ratio, free tutoring, and numerous computers on campus, help is always available." Faculty members have a genuine interest in teaching and work hard to accommodate students. In addition, the typical professor holds a terminal degree. "It is very rare for anybody but professors with Ph.D.s to teach," says a child psychology major. Freshmen are taught mostly by full professors and never by graduate students. Students must sit down with their academic advisors each term to discuss their schedules. "Tech prides itself on helping their students and they do a good job," says one senior.

"Everyone really supports the teams, especially if they are playing a rival of ours."

Eighty-five percent of Tech's students are from Montana, and the majority were the "brains or the nerds from high school," according to a sophomore. Residents and nonresidents alike must be in the top half of their high-school class or graduate with a 2.5 GPA and score at least 22 on ACT composite or 1030 on the combined SAT to gain admission. Student diversity stems from the 3 percent foreign enrollment. Minorities account for a mere 2 percent of the student population. The student body is conservative and "nerdy," a junior business major says. Students vie for merit scholarships, ranging from $250 to $20,000. There are 48 athletic scholarships distributed among football, basketball, volleyball, and golf. Registration and incidental fees are waived for some Montana state residents, including war orphans and those of at least one-fourth Native American blood.

Twelve percent of the students live in Prospector Hall, which is "comfortable and spacious," but those who can't fit are often forced to live in married student housing. Prospector includes modern baths, carpeting, exercise rooms, and kitchens, and it is "in the middle of everything." Each room is wired with a microcomputer connected to the campus mainframe. The school likes freshmen to live on campus, but the vast majority of upperclassmen live either in the many nearby apartments or in houses with reasonable rents. The campus is said to be safe, without much crime. "I've never heard of any problems," says a senior. "We live in Montana, remember." For students without cars, there's a bus service that runs into town.

Butte (population 40,000) gets a fair enough rating as a college town, although it is suffering from a collapse of the mining industry. One native, a mechanical engineering major, says the community takes a lot of pride in the school. Social activities—many of which are sponsored by clubs—take place both on and off campus. Underage drinkers have a difficult time getting served in town, but, like any school, can find alcohol if they want it, students say. The ratio of men to women is evening out: 55 percent male to 45 percent female. On weekends, students who don't go home attend music or comedy shows on campus, see movies, go to a game, or frequent the bars in town. Butte's setting—nestled in the slopes of the Continental Divide—is magnificent for skiing, fishing, hiking, and camping. Yellowstone Park is a favored road trip.

The student union features a dining area, game room, bookstore, student-owned FM radio station, and a television where students are known to tune in to cartoons in the afternoon. St. Patrick's Day is widely celebrated on and off campus, and on M-Day, part of a three-day festival before spring finals, students whitewash the large stone "M" on a hill above campus and host the largest bonfire in the state.

Athletics at Tech, which competes in the NAIA, are up-and-coming, and jocks are generally considered "cool." The most popular varsity sports are football and women's basketball; one T-shirt reads, "Tech football: a miner miracle." But other varsity teams, including men's and women's cross-country teams and women's volleyball, are also strong. Tech students take advantage of the excellent intramural program and the facilities of the modern physical education complex. Tech's biggest rival is Western Montana College, and freshman football players from WMC face off with those from Tech in an annual boxing match known as the "Smoker." "Athletics is big here," says a liberal studies major. "Everyone really supports the teams, especially if they are playing a rival of ours."

Montana Tech's students know why they've chosen their school: they want a solid grounding in earth-related engineering disciplines at a reasonable cost. Though state budget cuts have reduced the number of credits required to graduate, the school still boasts an impressive 95 percent job placement rate for graduates. Tech doesn't offer your typical college experience, but for would-be miners and geophysicists, its programs offer mountains of opportunity.

<aside>
Overlaps

Montana State, University of Montana, Carroll College, Colorado School of Mines, Gonzaga
</aside>

<aside>
If You Apply To ➤

Montana Tech: Rolling admissions. Campus and Alumni interviews: optional, informational. SATs or ACTs: required; ACTs preferred. Accepts common and electronic applications. No essay question.
</aside>

Mount Holyoke College

50 College Street, South Hadley, MA 01075-1488

One of two women's colleges, with Smith, that are members of the Five College Consortium in western Massachusetts. Less nonconformist than Smith and Bryn Mawr. MHC is strongest in the natural and social sciences, and one among the few colleges to have a program devoted to leadership.

The women of Mount Holyoke will be the first to tell you that the nation's first all-female college is not a girls' school without men, but a women's college without boys. The women who choose MHC value tradition, leadership, and achievement, and eagerly support one another as each strives to meet her goals. Students rave about the quality of teaching and the small classes, and while they complain about the heavy workload, most bring that challenge upon themselves as they seek intellectual fulfillment. "I'm encouraged to explore and be adventurous, to learn about myself and the world," says a junior. "Also, no one fits into one specific category. Athletes are also involved in student government and other organizations—it's a total mix."

Mount Holyoke is located in the heart of New England, on 800 acres of rolling hills, dotted with lakes and waterfalls. Modern glass-and-stone buildings stand alongside more traditional ivy-covered sandstone structures. Highlights include the Japanese Meditation Garden and Teahouse, an art building with studios and a bronze-casting foundry, an 18-hole championship golf course, and an equestrian center. The school's $33 million Unified Science Complex will be finished in 2004. It includes a new, multistory building with 40,000 square feet of lab and classroom space, as well as renovations to Carr Laboratories and Shattuck Hall, built in 1955

<aside>
Website: www.mtholyoke.edu
Location: Small town
Total Enrollment: 2,038
Undergraduates: 2,037
Male/Female: 0/100
SAT Ranges: V 600–690
   M 570–660
ACT Range: 25–30
Financial Aid: 68%
Expense: Pr $ $ $ $
Phi Beta Kappa: Yes
Applicants: 2,881
Accepted: 49%
Enrolled: 36%
Graduate in 6 Years: 79%
Returning Freshmen: 90%
Academics: 🖋🖋🖋🖋
</aside>

(Continued)

Social: ☎ ☎ ☎

Q of L: ★ ★ ★ ★

Admissions: (413) 538-2023

Email Address:
admission@mtholyoke.edu

Strongest Programs:
English
Biology
Psychology
Politics
International Relations
Mathematics
Chemistry

and 1932, respectively. The Blanchard Campus Center is being renovated to make room for a cyber café, coffee bar, art gallery, game room, and performance space.

Despite the physical modernization everywhere on campus, curriculum at this 163-year-old institution remains decidedly traditional. Students complete three humanities courses, two courses from two different science and mathematics disciplines (with at least one lab), two social science courses, and one course in multicultural perspectives. They must also take six units of physical education, and either two elementary foreign-language courses, or one intermediate or literature course in another language. A total of 128 credits are needed to graduate; 32 must be in the major, and 16 credits are also required in a minor field. A small number of exceptional students are invited into the First-Year Honors Tutorial Program, where two or three students are paired with a professor to delve deeply into a given topic. The college also offers more than 25 first-year seminars each fall, and more than a dozen in the spring, covering topics and disciplines from biology to women's studies. These courses, which are writing- or speaking-intensive, are aimed at developing skills in analysis and critical inquiry. Some also include field trips to museums or events in Boston and New York.

Mount Holyoke has a long tradition of strength in the sciences and mathematics, and a quarter to a third of each graduating class majors in these disciplines. The school has top-of-the-line chemistry labs, along with a solar greenhouse, a scanning electron microscope, several nuclear magnetic resonance spectrometers, and a linear accelerator. Also well-equipped are the students who emerge from these labs: Mount Holyoke produces more female Ph.D.s in chemistry and biology than any other liberal arts college. Five-year dual-degree programs enable students to combine A.B. degrees from MHC with B.S. degrees in engineering from the University of Massachusetts, Dartmouth, or Caltech, or with master's degrees in public health from UMass. Other popular programs include English and psychology; every year, the college hosts the oldest forum for presenting undergraduate psychology papers. "Students are passionate about academics, and this passion is contagious," says an English major. "It is easy to excel because the climate is conducive to hard work, passionate inquiry, and dedication." Astronomy, classics, and medieval studies attract the fewest majors.

"It is easy to excel because the climate is conducive to hard work, passionate inquiry, and dedication."

Although some of Mount Holyoke's intro courses have fifty or more students, most have twenty-five or fewer. Still, students report few problems getting into required courses or graduating on time. "The only class I couldn't get into was fencing, my freshman year," a politics major says. The emphasis on learning through reading and discussion means that students develop close relationships with professors, who "are absolutely accessible, love what they do, and make students their main priority," says a senior. "Many of my professors have even invited an entire class to their houses for dinner," says a history major. The school's honor code makes possible self-scheduled, self-proctored final exams. After those tests is the optional January winter term, where many students opt for a two-credit, nontraditional course, or an off-campus internship in New York or Washington, D.C. About 25 percent of MHC students seeking a complete change of scenery spend all or part of junior year in another country. The Twelve-College Exchange Program* offers opportunities in more than twenty-five locales, while Mount Holyoke also has its own study-abroad programs. Those interested in the sea may be interested in the Maritime Studies Program.*

Mount Holyoke produces more female Ph.D.s in chemistry and biology than any other liberal arts college.

While Mount Holyoke attracts students from all over the nation and the world, 20 percent are Massachusetts natives. African-Americans make up nearly 5 percent of the student body, Asian-Americans almost 10 percent, and Hispanics 4 percent.

"MHC is very politically correct and very liberal," a biology major reports. "Gay rights, diversity, and equality for all are some of the big issues." Fair labor rights have also been a focus, an English major says. The Student Coalition for Action is a very large and popular campus group, dedicated to social change. Merit scholarships are available, ranging from $5,000 to $20,000.

Eighty-nine percent of Mount Holyoke's students live in the 19 residence halls, each of which has its own dining facility. "The smallest rooms here are average on other campuses, and they only get bigger from there!" gushes a politics major. "My room has hardwood floors and a walk-in closet." Most dorms are also very homey, with living rooms, TV lounges, and baby grand pianos; all serve milk and cookies (as well as healthier fare, like hummus and vegetables) every night at 9:30 P.M. Students from all four classes live together, in groups of 65 to 130 students each. After the first year, they take their chances in a lottery, for both dorms and rooms. Juniors and seniors usually get singles, while freshmen and sophomores have double rooms. Some residence halls also offer apartment-style living.

Students find the Five College Consortium* one of Mount Holyoke's greatest assets. A free bus service runs every 20 minutes between MHC and UMass, Amherst, Smith, and Hampshire, multiplying a Holyoke woman's access to academic, social, and cultural opportunities. "If you want to party every weekend, you can, but if you want to relax, you can," a senior says. "The college and various cultural organizations host events on campus every weekend," adds a classmate. Some of the best road trips include Boston, Montreal, and New York City. Closer to campus, the South Hadley Center has eateries, a pub, shops, and

> "Gay rights, diversity, and equality for all are some of the big issues."

apartments, though students say that Amherst and Northampton provide more shopping options. Alcohol policies ban open containers, kegs in the dorms, and any drinking by women under 21. Students say they're not excessively enforced.

Perhaps more than their counterparts at Smith and Wellesley, Mount Holyoke women have made a virtue out of the school's most visible "vice": the lack of men. Women fill all leadership positions, thanks to a strong and supportive community spirit, and boys are just down the road at Amherst or UMass. Like most happy families, Mount Holyoke students take pride in tradition. Upon arrival, each first-year student is assigned a secret elf (a sophomore), a big sister (a junior), and a disorientation leader (a senior). Each class also has a color and a mascot, and class spirit is huge, especially for the annual Junior Show. Every fall on Mountain Day, students wake up to ringing bells, classes are canceled (even the library is closed), and everyone treks up Mount Holyoke to picnic and see the foliage.

Mount Holyoke competes in Division III, and its equestrian team is legendary (most recently adding the 2002 Tournament of Champions prize to its already-overflowing trophy case). At the varsity level, field hockey, swimming, and indoor track are also strong, though the college encourages athletic participation at all levels with a demanding 18-hole golf course, jogging trails, and two lakes. The 20-acre equestrian center includes a fifty-seven-stall barn, two riding areas, a training and show area, and seating for 300. Crew regattas and rugby take the place of football games, and students come out in force when the opponent is another of the Seven Sisters.

MHC has the best of both worlds—far enough from civilization to provide plenty of open green space, while just close enough to New York and Boston to permit easy access. An atmosphere of tolerance prevails, with opinions (mostly liberal) widely expressed and celebrated. The rich fabric of tradition underscores the college's proud history and makes for wonderful memories. "The sense of community created by our small college setting brings together the diverse student body," says a junior.

The college offers more than 25 first-year seminars each fall, and more than a dozen in the spring, covering topics and disciplines from biology to women's studies. Some also include field trips to museums or events in Boston and New York.

Five-year dual-degree programs enable students to combine A.B. degrees from MHC with B.S. degrees in engineering from the University of Massachusetts, Dartmouth, or Caltech, or with master's degrees in public health from UMass.

Overlaps

Smith, Wellesley, Bryn Mawr, Vassar, Tufts

Mount Holyoke: Early decision: Nov. 15. Regular admissions and financial aid: Jan. 15. Guarantees to meet demonstrated need. Campus and alumnae interviews: recommended, evaluative. ACTs or SATs: optional. SAT IIs: optional. Accepts the Common Application and electronic applications. Essay question: why Mount Holyoke is a good match for you; most meaningful activity; and one of the following: an institution, charity or cause you would support, and why; the wisest advice you've received, and how you've used it; influence of other cultures on sense of self; important person, experience or achievement. Also requires a two- to five-page paper written in the 11th or 12th grade, with a teacher's comments.

Muhlenberg College

2400 Chew Street, Allentown, PA 18104-5586

There is a definite Muhlenberg type: serious, ambitious, and buttoned-down. Muhlenberg is the only eastern Pennsylvania/New Jersey liberal arts college with a serious religious affiliation—Lutheran. Strong in premed, prelaw, preanything.

Website:
www.muhlenberg.edu
Location: City outskirts
Total Enrollment: 2,100
Undergraduates: 2,100
Male/Female: 44/56
SAT Ranges: V 550–640
M 560–650
Financial Aid: N/A
Expense: Pr $ $
Phi Beta Kappa: Yes
Applicants: 3,822
Accepted: 35%
Enrolled: 41%
Grad in 6 Years: 84%
Returning Freshmen: 93%
Academics: ✍ ✍ ✍
Social: ☎ ☎ ☎
Q of L: ★ ★ ★ ★
Admissions: (484) 664-3200
Email Address: admissions@
muhlenberg.edu

Strongest Programs:
Premed/Biology
Prelaw
English/Writing
Theatre Arts and Dance
Business
Psychology

When a popular school pseudonym is "The Caring College" rather than some crack referring to booze or babes, you know you're in for a different experience. That's the case with Muhlenberg College, a small liberal arts school that nurtures its students. Muhlenberg holds its students to rigorous academic standards, and they know it. From its solid Lutheran roots to its current standing as a top premed school, Muhlenberg shows students it really does care. "Academic excellence is, by far, the top priority," says a junior, "but the people are warm, friendly, compassionate, and truly care about making Muhlenberg the best possible place for everyone." Guess that slogan does fit after all.

Set on 75 park-like acres, the Berg campus is a combination of older Gothic stone structures and newer buildings in a variety of architectural styles. Prominent facilities include a lovely chapel, the high-tech Trexler Library, a forty-acre biological field station and wildlife sanctuary, and a forty-eight-acre arboretum with more than 300 species of wildflowers, broadleaf evergreens, and conifer trees. The campus also boasts a football stadium and all-weather track, and the 50,000 square-foot Trexler Pavilion for the Performing Arts that has a dramatic forty-five-foot glass outer shell and houses a variety of performing spaces. Two new dorms, Robertston and South, recently opened overlooking Lake Muhlenberg, and the communications building recently reopened with new radio and television studios.

Muhlenberg's regional reputation rests on its premedical program, which continues to attract large numbers of students. An agreement with Philadelphia's Hahnemann University Medical School guarantees seats for up to six Muhlenberg students each year. The college's theater arts program is also a national draw, and a few alumni have even gone on to star on Broadway. Science lab equipment at Muhlenberg is cutting-edge, and a comprehensive natural science major allows for a sampling of it all. The Living Writers course is offered every other year and has brought a number of noted authors to campus, including Robert Pinsky, Jay Wright, and Alice Fulton. Muhlenberg sends study groups to Washington, D.C., and students may spend semesters abroad in countries from England, France, Spain, and Germany to Argentina, the Czech Republic, Japan, Australia, and Scotland. Any program sponsored by the International Student Exchange is also available, and Muhlenberg is member of the Lehigh Valley Association of Independent Colleges* consortium.

The college offers three honors programs, the Muhlenberg Scholars Program, the Dana Associates Program, and the new RJ Fellows Program, which focuses on the ramifications of change. Each is limited to 15 students per entering class. They carry an annual $3,000 stipend and culminate in an in-depth mentored senior research project. Psychology is Muhlenberg's most popular major, followed by business, biology, theatre arts, and communications. Sociology is making a comeback with energetic new faculty, while the Russian studies and preseminary programs are not as strong. General education requirements are organized into two major groups: Skills (writing, oral expression, reasoning, and foreign language) and Perspectives (literature and the arts, meaning and values, human behavior and social institutions, historical studies, physical and life sciences, and other cultures.) Each freshman

"Content is difficult but made manageable by the way professors teach the material."

is assigned a First-Year Advising Team, usually consisting of four students (a student mentor, a student advisor, and two academic advisors) and a faculty member. One Spanish/premed double major says her science advisor helped pick classes to prepare her for medical school, while her Spanish advisor explained how language skills would serve her well as a doctor.

The fun-filled, three-day freshman orientation program carries one requirement: learning the alma mater and then hightailing it to the president's house to serenade him. All freshmen also take a writing-intensive, discussion-intensive First-Year Seminar, with enrollment capped at 15. About two-thirds of freshman courses have fewer than 25 students, and since there are no graduate students, there are no teaching assistants. "Content is difficult but made manageable by the way professors teach the material," says a psychology major. "They also make themselves available for help outside of class."

Muhlenberg draws 30 percent of its students from Pennsylvania, and many from adjacent New Jersey. The campus is 91 percent white, but "we have a diverse pool of interests, which creates a lively campus in terms of politics and social awareness," says a biology major. Cultural appreciation is emphasized as Muhlenberg strives for a more ethnically and religiously varied campus. Students stay involved in the community by volunteering as tutors and with groups such as Habitat for Humanity and Planned Parenthood. A political science professor has started a student-run polling institute, which is raising campus awareness and activism.

Muhlenberg encourages on-campus living and guarantees housing to all undergraduates except transfers, so 88 percent of students live in campus residences. All dorms have computer labs, study lounges, and vending machines. Prosser's coed wing makes it a good choice for freshmen, while upperclassmen praise the Muhlenberg Independent Living Experience, or MILE, townhouses. Two new dorms, Robertson and South, house 140 students in single, air-conditioned rooms overlooking Lake Muhlenberg. Other popular choices include New West and Benfer, where students live in eight-person suites that have their own bathrooms. Freshmen choose from a seven- or five-day meal

Muhlenberg's regional reputation rests on its premedical program, which continues to attract large numbers of students.

"The environment that engulfs the campus with friendliness and warmth makes Muhlenberg feel truly like home."

plan, where options include a salad bar, pasta station, soup-and-bread line, brown-bag lunches, "wellness" entrées, and the ever-popular ice cream machine. For some a measure of having "arrived," Starbucks has a coffee bar in the student union.

Most social life at Muhlenberg takes place on campus. The Muhlenberg Activities Council (MAC) provides comedians every Thursday evening—recent visitors have included Jimmy Fallon and Dave Chappell—current movies in the Red Door Café, live band concerts (Counting Crows headlined a recent show), and new movies on the lawn. City buses stop five minutes from campus for trips to Allentown proper and area malls. There also are daily bus runs to New York City (for clubbing and theater), Philadelphia (for nightlife and cheese steaks), and Baltimore and Washington, D.C. Outdoorsy students can pick up the Appalachian Trail for a little hiking.

Twenty-six percent of men and women each pledge their undergraduate years to fraternities and sororities, but Greek life does not dominate the social scene—and it's becoming less important now that rush doesn't occur until sophomore year. Alcohol is forbidden if you're underage, per Pennsylvania law and the school's "no tolerance" policy, but is "available for those who make the effort to find it," a senior says. Big social events include East Fest, Homecoming, Deck Party, the Scotty Wood basketball tournament, the Mr. Muhlenberg awards—which parody the Miss America pageant—and the Henry Awards, the college's version of the Oscars. There's also a candlelight ceremony where freshmen write down their college goals, reexamining them the day before graduation.

For the athletically inclined, intramural sports arouse a great deal of passion. Football, men's and women's golf, women's softball, and women's soccer are strong, winning Centennial Conference championships and NCAA tournament bids. Muhlenberg's Life Sports Center offers a pool, basketball court and other all-purpose courts, and a jogging track. Also popular is Frisbee golf; there's an 18-hole course on campus, where play goes on during all seasons and all hours of the day and night. Any contest against Johns Hopkins draws crowds, students say.

Though it's a former steel town once scorned in a Billy Joel song, Allentown is also home to this regionally respected liberal arts school that is constantly improving its arts and hard science programs. Muhlenberg has produced Fulbright Fellows and Udall Scholars, but it also ensures that every student excels at his or her own pace. "The environment that engulfs the campus with friendliness and warmth," a senior says, "makes Muhlenberg feel truly like home." Now that's a caring college.

Overlaps

Lafayette, Gettysburg, Rutgers, Dickinson, Skidmore

If You Apply To ➤ **Muhlenberg:** Early decision: Jan. 15. Regular admissions and financial aid: Feb. 15. Housing: May 1. Meets demonstrated need of 90%. Campus interviews: recommended, evaluative (required, along with a graded paper, if students choose not to submit SAT scores). Alumni interviews: optional, informational. SATs or ACTs: optional. SAT IIs: optional. Accepts the Common Application and electronic applications. Essay question: significant experience or achievement; issue of personal, local, national, or international concern; influential person; influential fictional character, historical figure, or creative work; topic of your choice.

University of Nebraska at Lincoln

12 Administration Building, Lincoln, NE 68588-0415

Everybody knows Nebraska football, but in other areas UNL has a lower profile. Fewer out-of-staters attend Nebraska than, say, University of Kansas or Iowa. Agriculture is still the biggest drawing card, and the music program is also strong. Because of the state's demographic makeup, diversity is limited.

Website: www.unl.edu
Location: Center city
Total Enrollment: 22,764
Undergraduates: 17,985
Male/Female: 52/48
SAT Ranges: V 500-640-630
  M 520-650
ACT Range: 21-27

Right downtown in the capital of the Cornhusker State is the University of Nebraska at Lincoln, a school that is making 21st century additions to its campus and its curriculum. More than twenty thousand students call UNL home, and their school pride is contagious. On crisp fall weekends, when spirits are high and the Big Red football arcs through the air, Huskers cheer and paint the town of Lincoln red and white in a show of appreciation for their alma mater. In fact, on home-game Saturdays, the stadium is the third largest "city" in the state, holding 5 percent of the population. Away from the stadium, in the classrooms, UNL has more reason to cheer with top programs ranging from music to agriculture to journalism.

UNL spreads across two campuses. The East Campus is home to the colleges of agricultural sciences and natural resources, human resources and family sciences, law, and dentistry. Most entering students end up on the larger City Campus, where the architectural style ranges from the modern Sheldon Art Gallery designed by Philip Johnson to the architecture building, which is on the National Register of Historic Places. There are also several malls, an arboretum, and a sculpture garden. This is the home of six of the eight undergraduate colleges: architecture, arts and sciences, journalism and mass communications, business administration, fine and performing arts, engineering and technology, and the teachers college. In the past two years, the UNL has completed a major addition to and renovation of the student union, added more university-owned apartments, and constructed a much-needed six hundred-car parking garage. More than $93 million of new construction and renovations are underway across the campus.

> **"It's possible to pursue only honors classes and research, but there are also those who just 'get by.'"**

Nebraska's College of Agricultural Sciences and Natural Resources, known for its outstanding programs in food science and technology, agribusiness, and animal science, is housed in a $19 million complex. The school of music's opera program has received national attention, and the performing arts programs benefit from the $18 million Lied Center for the Performing Arts, which seats 2,300. Education, business administration, and psychology are some of the most popular majors. New programs include majors in engineering, film studies, architectural engineering, natural resources, rangeland ecosystems, and even grazing livestock systems. UNL can be academically challenging—by choice. "It's possible to pursue only honors classes and research, but there are also those who just 'get by'," says one premed student.

Nebraska's Comprehensive Education Program provides students with a common set of educational experiences across the majors and colleges. It has four components: Information Discovery and Retrieval (1 course), Essential Studies (9 courses), Integrative Studies (10 courses), and Co-Curricular Experience. To help freshmen get oriented, a one-semester University Foundations class covers the inner and outer workings of the campus, organized around academic subjects. The classes may provide a real foundation for success at the school, but that doesn't always make them exciting. "We have a library course that is required for all freshmen that students hate, but it's required," grumps one student. Big Red Welcome combines entertainment and food in a carnival setting to welcome new students, and the SIPS program (Summer Institute for Promising Scholars) is a six-week preorientation session for incoming minority students. The J.D. Edwards Honors Program gives computer science and management students internships to complement their coursework. The Undergraduate Creative Activity and Research Experience Program provides a stipend for students after freshman year who want to participate in research with a professor.

> **"There are not many minority students on campus, [which] creates tension."**

Getting into courses in the most popular areas, especially education, business, and engineering, can be a problem, students say; preregistration is a must. Though many top profs teach introductory courses, freshmen and sophomores should expect to spend much of their time with graduate teaching assistants. But one junior had a different experience. "I've been fortunate to have had great professors. Many have been recognized by students or the university for their incredible dedication to students and their fields." Students also can study abroad in places such as Costa Rica, Germany, Mexico, and Japan.

The UNL student body is mostly conservative and from the Cornhusker State. Asian-Americans make up 3 percent of the student body, with African-Americans

(Continued)

Financial Aid: 65%
Expense: Pub $
Phi Beta Kappa: Yes
Applicants: 7,266
Accepted: 79%
Enrolled: 62%
Grad in 6 Years: 53%
Returning Freshmen: 80%
Academics: ✍ ✍ ✍
Social: ☎ ☎ ☎ ☎
Q of L: ★ ★ ★
Admissions: (800) 742-8800
Email Address:
   nuhusker@unl.edu

Strongest Programs:
   Agribusiness and Agronomy
   Animal Science
   Architecture
   Audiology and Speech
      Pathology
   Music
   Textiles, Clothing and Design
   Food Sciences
   Journalism

Most entering students end up on the larger City Campus, where the architectural style ranges from the modern Sheldon Art Gallery designed by Philip Johnson to the architecture building, which is on the National Register of Historic Places.

and Hispanics 4 percent combined. A senior says, "There are not many minority students on campus, [which] creates tension." Other hot-button issues include underage drinking, homosexuality, and abortion.

Still, UNL is big and there's a group or activity for everyone; fraternity and house parties, roller skating, the movies, eating out, visiting coffee shops and bars (for those of age), and road trips to Omaha or Kansas City are just some of the activities that keep students busy. For many, the fall semester revolves around football weekends and postseason bowl games. "Football games are like religious celebrations," says a sophomore. "It's so hard to understand until you've been in the atmosphere."

Twenty-five percent of students live in the university's single-sex or coed dorms, and there's usually no trouble getting a room. Dorm lotteries favor those wanting to stay in the same room or on the same floor. Students say the dorms are clean and well-maintained, though the freshman dwellings can be a bit cramped. Each room also is wired for the Internet. Freshmen, who must live on campus, are welcomed to the residence halls through the FINK program, which is friendlier than it sounds (the acronym stands for Freshman Indoctrination of New Kids). New furniture is being moved into dorms this year.

Fraternities draw 11 percent of UNL men and sororities attract 12 percent of the women. They offer both social events and a chance to get involved in the Lincoln community. Homecoming, Greek Week, and Ivy Day are among the most-anticipated campus events, as is The End, new alcohol-free

> "Football games are like religious celebrations. It's so hard to understand until you've been in the atmosphere."

programming at the end of each semester during "dead week" and finals week. For those who want to indulge, plenty of bars are within walking distance of UNL, providing relief to students dissatisfied with the dry campus. So committed is the administration to keeping a distance between students and alcohol that it has obtained a grant to combat high-risk drinking among students. It's difficult to be served on campus, and one student says the ban on alcohol has made some on-campus parties as exciting as bingo night. Some say Lincoln itself is a great college town, with shopping, theaters, restaurants, and movies. One psychology major begs to differ. "Lincoln is a very 'homey' place, but truth be told, it doesn't have much to offer in terms of cultural events." That said, Omaha is only 45 minutes away. Pachyderm enthusiasts will be delighted by the Nebraska Museum of Natural History's outstanding collection of prehistoric elephant skeletons. Beyond the sidewalks are miles of flat road and plains ideal for biking, cross-country skiing, and snowmobiling.

In addition to football, UNL is a men's gymnastic powerhouse, and is gaining a reputation in women's volleyball and basketball and men's baseball. In all, Husker teams finished in the top 10 nationally in more than 10 sports in the past two years, and has won nine Big 12 championships since 2000. The football team played for the 2001–02 national championship (and lost to an undefeated Miami Hurricanes squad). The biggest football rivalries are with Colorado and Oklahoma. Husker fans proclaim that if forced to choose between going to Oklahoma and going to hell after death—well, it would be a tough choice.

At Nebraska, future agriculture experts mingle with techno-whizzes, while teachers-in-training brush elbows with architecture mavens. "Nebraska as a state is known for being very welcoming and friendly," says a sophomore. "Our students definitely reflect those qualities as well." Whether studying overseas, immersing themselves in an internship, or going wild on Saturday afternoon, students here know how to make the most of their time as Cornhuskers.

Overlaps

Wayne State, Creighton, Chadron State, Nebraska Wesleyan, Iowa State

If You Apply To >

Nebraska: Rolling admissions: June 30. Campus and alumni interviews: optional, informational. SATs or ACTs: required. SAT IIs: optional. Accepts electronic applications. No essay question.

New College of Florida

(Formerly New College of the University of South Florida)
5700 North Tamiami Trail, Sarasota, FL 34243-2197

New College is the South's most liberal institution of higher learning—apologies to Guilford. With an enrollment of 634, New College is about one-third the size of a typical liberal arts college. The kicker: New College is a public institution and one of the nation's best buys.

The New College of Florida blossoms with a madhatter's world of unique students, edge-of-the-envelope traditions, and the ability to create an academic future entirely of your design. This 35-year-old school has done away with grades and GPAs, so students compete with themselves, not with their classmates. Students are encouraged to "know that they are part of something completely different, out of the norm, definitely unique, irreproducible, and in many ways amazing," extols one sophomore. The mere existence of the place is proof that it's possible to find success through individualism.

New College began in 1960 as a private college for academically talented students, but when inflation threatened its existence in the mid-1970s, it offered its campus to the University of South Florida. Today, NCF serves as Florida's independent honors college, but is an academically independent entity. Clearly, the school still has a mind of its own, as do its students, who thrive on "self-motivation and academic dedication," says a biology major, as well as the occasional purple mohawk, distaste for wearing shoes, and ability to proclaim themselves as "weird."

New College's campus is adjacent to Sarasota Bay and consists of historic mansions from the former estate of circus magnate Charles Ringling, abutting modern dorms designed by I.M. Pei. The central quad is filled with palm trees, and sunsets over the bay are spectacular. New College shares its campus with the Sarasota branch of USF, which offers upper-level courses in business, education, and engineering. New facilities include two 70-bed apartment-style residence halls, a building with library, office, and classroom space for the natural sciences, and a marine biology research center.

> **Students are encouraged to "know that they are part of something completely different, out of the norm, definitely unique, irreproducible, and in many ways amazing."**

The administration once had absolutely no required core curriculum, but now has added a liberal arts and math and computer literacy requirement to provide "each student with the depth and breadth of knowledge characteristic of a good liberal arts education." The new rules go like this: each student must pass eight courses in three broad areas (humanities, natural sciences, and social sciences), plus one math class and proof of general competence in computer literacy. The school calendar, however, is still unique: the two fourteen-week semesters are separated by a month-long January Interterm, during which students devise and carry out their own research or conduct group projects. Students work out a "contract" with their

Website: www.ncf.edu
Location: Suburban
Total Enrollment: 634
Undergraduates: 634
Male/Female: 35/65
SAT Ranges: V 660–750
  M 590–680
ACT Range: 27–30
Financial Aid: 73%
Expense: Pub $
Phi Beta Kappa: No
Applicants: 490
Accepted: 61%
Enrolled: 50%
Grad in 6 Years: 60%
Returning Freshmen: 81%
Academics: ✍ ✍ ✍ ✍
Social: 🐿 🐿 🐿
Q of L: ★ ★ ★
Admissions: (941) 359-4269
Email Address:
  admissions@ncf.edu

Strongest Programs:
  Biology
  Psychology
  Literature
  Anthropology

advisor each semester and receive written evaluations instead of grades. Seven semester-long contracts and three independent study projects lead to an area of concentration, capped by a senior thesis and an oral baccalaureate examination. Due to the highly individualized nature of the curriculum, getting into some classes can be a challenge, especially for science majors looking to fulfill requirements for grad school admission, says one student. The workload can be intense, and the shape of any student's program depends heavily on the outlook of his or her faculty sponsor, and students say advising—both academic and career-oriented—is readily available.

New College doesn't offer the specialized courses of a large university, but there's still plenty to choose from, especially for students interested in the social sciences, the humanities, and the physical sciences, where a 1,100-gallon sea water system is available for lab experiments in animal behavior and physiology. Anthropology wins raves, and many students gravitate toward biology, psychology, literature, and sociology. The computer science concentration was dropped, and a partial concentration in theatre was added. Fine arts suffers from a lack of core faculty, and it remains to be seen whether the interdisciplinary international studies program will really pull professors together from various departments, administrators say. Regardless of discipline, the Jane Bancroft Cook Library makes up for its small—less than 300,000 volumes—size with a language lab, videotape viewing area, an interlibrary loan program with the entire state university system of Florida, and a classroom equipped for teleconferences.

Students praise the personalized attention they receive from New College professors, since graduate students and teaching assistants don't lead classes here. During a typical semester, about half of the students are engaged in one-on-one tutorials, and most other classes are seminars. All disciplines provide the opportunity for original research and students

"You can even create a class if there is not already one in existence."

also may conduct field research around the globe, including the study of coral reefs in Honduras, Buddhism in India, and history in Europe. "You can even create a class if there is not already one in existence," says a gender studies major. The academic climate at New College is rigorous, though without grades, competition is "more about motivation and responsibility."

In keeping with the revolution theme, students on this relatively cosmopolitan campus tend to be creative liberal types with '60s nuances. Seventy percent of students hail from Florida, perhaps because New College has yet to make a national name for itself. Minorities account for 12 percent of the student body. Social and political issues run the gamut from animal rights and Tibetan independence to vegan issues and helping Mexican migrant workers. In general, "political awareness is more important than political correctness," says one senior. A new Diversity and Gender Center explores race and gender relations and reconciliation through lectures, movies, and weekly discussions.

Seventy-two percent of students live in campus housing. Rooms in the Pei dorms "are gigantic and have their own bathrooms," says a senior. The Dart dorms, two apartment-style halls, accommodate 140 students in two-bedroom, two-bath suites with a kitchen, living area, and—of course—air-conditioning (as essential as food and water in the Sunshine State). Rooms are chosen by lottery; though in the past older students were encouraged to move off campus to make room for new students, the new dorms are drawing them back, students report. "There is fierce competition for favored rooms," an upperclassman says. As for security, the campus is "shockingly safe," says a sociology major.

On campus, social life is T-shirts-and-shorts relaxed. "Walls," free-form parties every Friday and Saturday night, can last until 4 or 5 AM. the following morning. Loudspeakers line Palm Court and students sign up to reserve a night and play whatever music they want. The PCPs (Palm Court Parties) are "blown-out-of-proportion Walls" that occur during Halloween, Valentine's Day, and Graduation. It's not hard for underage students to drink. While some students call Sarasota "old-timers ville," it does offer plenty of cultural enrichment (and beautiful beaches). The Ringling Museum of Art and the Asolo State Theater adjoin the campus, and many New College instrumentalists perform with the Florida West Coast Symphony, Sarasota's professionally led symphony orchestra. In the past, students have raised their own fees to fund plays, films, and programs like AIDS awareness. The open road to Tampa, Gainesville, Key West, New Orleans, Atlanta, and even Washington, D.C. ("to protest stuff"), beckons when Sarasota becomes too quiet.

New College is definitely not a haven for jocks, since it fields no varsity teams, somewhat of an oddity in football-crazy Florida. The yearly faculty-student softball game is popular, and anyone can play. Students also look forward to the Crucial Barbecue in January with music and mud wrestling, the Male Chauvinist Pig Roast, the SemiNormal, a semiformal event on the bay, and the Bowling Ball, a formal-dress occasion at a bowling alley. While the school has a 25-meter swimming pool, students complain than it closes at 10 P.M. The nearby ocean (which does not close) is a bigger draw.

The classes at NCF are seminar-like, the atmosphere is hippie beach, and the students are one-of-a-kind. All together, nobody at New College could ever complain of being bored. The school's reputation for eccentricity doesn't impede students' academic motivation or their love for learning—whether they're learning belly dancing, biology, origami, or psychology. A sophomore sums up the New College experience this way: "One sunny afternoon at the New College, complete with fierce hugs, shared snacks, passionate debate, and unconditional kindness…restores your faith in humanity."

Forget the pep rallies and tailgate parties. Popular New College events include the Male Chauvinist Pig Roast, the SemiNormal, a semiformal event on the Sarasota Bay, and the Bowling Ball, and the Cardboard Boat Regatta.

Overlaps

University of Florida, Florida State, Eckerd, Hampshire College, Rollins

---

If You Apply To ➤

New College: Rolling admissions: May 1. Campus interviews: optional, evaluative. No alumni interviews. SATs or ACTs: required. SAT IIs: optional. Accepts the Common Application and electronic applications. Essay question: why New College; views on an important issue.

University of New Hampshire

Grant House, 4 Garrison Avenue, Durham, NH 03824-3510

UNH looks and feels like a private college, and its tuition hits the pocketbook with similar force. Expensive though it may be, UNH draws more than half of its students from out of state. Strong in the life sciences, especially marine biology, and in business and engineering.

Students at the University of New Hampshire know how to get their hands dirty, and this solid public institution provides them with countless opportunities to do so. Whether studying marine life in the nearby Atlantic waters or human life on another continent, UNH students enjoy the myriad of research options available to them.

The university's wide-open grassy campus hosts a blend of modern facilities and ivy-covered brick buildings. The sprawling lawns are surrounded by three thousand acres of farms, fields, and woods. During the past few years, UNH has invested in

Website: www.unh.edu
Location: Small town
Total Enrollment: 13,650
Undergraduates: 11,040
Male/Female: 42/58
SAT Ranges: V 500–600
  M 510–610

(Continued)

Financial Aid: 50%

Expense: Pub $ $ $ $

Phi Beta Kappa: Yes

Applicants: 10,093

Accepted: 76%

Enrolled: 33%

Grad in 6 Years: 71%

Returning Freshmen: 85%

Academics: ✐ ✐ ✐

Social: 🍷 🍷 🍷 🍷 🍷

Q of L: ★ ★ ★ ★

Admissions: (603) 862-1360

Email Address:
admissions@unh.edu

Strongest Programs:
Business Administration
Biological Sciences
Environmental Studies
History
English
Hospitality Management
Kinesiology

large-scale construction and renovation projects, including a recent $19 million expansion and renovation of Diamond Library. The project resulted in a 207,000-square-foot building with three grand reading rooms and state-of-the-art technology. The Donald M. Murray Journalism Laboratory, featuring more than $100,000 of computer and projection equipment, was also completed recently. The new $8.5 million environmental technology building is a multi-disciplinary science and engineering facility. Pettee Hall, built in the 1930s, was renovated and now houses high-tech teaching facilities for the School of Health and Human Services.

UNH's emphasis on traditional academic programs is enhanced by interdisciplinary programs and the many research opportunities offered by its seven undergraduate schools. Business and engineering are the most respected programs, and the English department has a fine creative writing program. The Whittemore School of Business and Economics now includes options in entrepreneurial venture creations, information systems, international business and economics, management, marketing, and accounting; students can also design their own track. Marine biology is also considered stellar, due to UNH's proximity to the water. Environmental studies, chemistry, kinesiology, and nursing all are strong as well. UNH's programs in Classics, French, German, Italian, Japanese, Russian, and Spanish recently merged into a new Department of Languages, Literatures, and Cultures. Qualifying students can begin an honors program featuring small classes in freshman year. Philosophy is mentioned as a weak department.

The university's general education requirements apply across the board and mandate completion of 10 courses from eight categories: writing skills; quantitative reasoning; biological, physical, and technological sciences; historical perspectives; foreign cultures; fine arts; social science; and works of philosophy, literature, and ideas. Freshman composition is mandatory as part of a four-course writing intensive requirement. Classes are relatively small, almost always 50 students or fewer, and TAs only facilitate discussion sections or labs. The academic climate, says a freshman, "is in the middle. It is as competitive as you make it." "Classes for my major are competitive because students are constantly under the gun to improve," says an economics/political science major. Recent additions include majors in environmental engineering and European cultural studies and minors in youth drama and musical theater.

UNH prides itself on producing undergraduates with research experience. The Undergraduate Research Opportunities Program provides about 100 research awards each year for undergraduates to work closely with faculty on original projects. A recent undergraduate research conference drew 200 participants. Budding scientists and sociologists have opportunities to work at research centers for space science and family violence; other students can take advantage of the Institute for Policy and Social Science Research, the Center for Humanities, the Institute for the Study of Earth, Oceans, and Space and the Center to Advance Molecular Interaction Sciences.

"It is as competitive as you make it." The Interoperability Lab enables students to work with professors and businesses on cutting-edge problems of computing equipment compatibility. The Isle of Shoals Marine Laboratory, which operates several research projects with Cornell University, is just seven miles off the coast. And then there's UNH's Technology, Society, and Values Program, designed to address the ethical implications of the computer age. UNH's study abroad program offers exchange programs with more than 170 U.S. colleges via the Center for International Education. Students can even earn a dual major by combining foreign study and classes in international affairs with those of any other program.

While UNH is New Hampshire's major public institution, it has long been popular with out-of-staters, who make up 39 percent of its students. The school is working on becoming more diverse; only 4 percent of the student body are minorities, which students mention as an area of concern. A special task force at the University is working on keeping the minority students in school until graduation and in helping them network. Social issues at UNH include alcohol awareness and—as might be expected in a place with such lush natural beauty—the environment. The school offers more than 2,300 merit scholarships ranging from $500 to $7,500; awards are also available for athletic prowess.

UNH's emphasis on traditional academic programs is enhanced by interdisciplinary programs and the many research opportunities offered by its seven undergraduate schools.

Fifty percent of UNHers live in the school's thirty-one single-sex and coed dorms. "The dorms are great," says a junior who enjoys having cable channels and a cable line for Internet access. The dorms offer special-interest groupings, lounges, fireplaces, TV lounges, study rooms, and kitchenettes. A 360-students suite-style dorm and new dining hall are being built, and Murkland Hall, which dates back to 1926, is being renovated. "Housing is pretty reasonable," says a freshman. "Of course, there is the problem of having more kids than rooms." Freshmen and sophomores are guaranteed dorm rooms; most upperclassmen live off campus or in Gables and Woodside, on-campus apartment complexes,

"The majority of campus is very outdoorsy and active."

though one senior recommends staying on campus as long as possible to avoid "missing too much fun." Students also gripe that parking is difficult on campus. "Campus security is great," says one student. "Most everyone feels safe."

Less than a five-minute walk from campus is the beautiful little town of Durham, which caters to the student clientele. Along Main Street, Durham has many restaurants, coffeehouses, a grocery store, an ice cream parlor, and a few bars, which have been divided into separate sections (for legal consumers of alcohol and everyone else). Greek groups claim 5 percent of UNH men and women. The Greeks also throw parties, which are subject to the university's no-tolerance alcohol policy that evicts from on-campus housing underage students caught with alcohol more than once. One science major reports that violations also entail "protective custody for the night and a letter sent to your parents." For nondrinkers, the university offers weekend social events including concerts, dances, movies, and coffeehouses. Popular road trips include Boston and the White Mountains, or apple picking at a nearby farm. Late nights at L.L. Bean have also become commonplace, and Homecoming, Greek Week, Winter Carnival, Casino Night, and Spring Fling draw crowds every year. And every four years, New Hampshire takes the spotlight when the state holds the nation's earliest presidential primaries.

The dorms offer special-interest groupings, lounges, fireplaces, TV lounges, study rooms and kitchenettes.

UNH teams that regularly enjoy national rankings and generate strong spectator interest include men's and women's ice hockey, which recently won the NCAA Championship, and students celebrate the first UNH goal of each game by inexplicably throwing a large fish onto the ice. Women's gymnastics, men's and women's basketball, and football are also impressive. The university has a strong intramural sports program, involving thousands of students.

When there's no game to watch or postgame revelry to indulge in, nature provides UNH students with more than enough to do—if they can find time off. (The school's nickname is the University of No Holidays, since an exceptionally generous winter break limits the number of days off during other seasons.) Skiing, camping, fishing, and hiking in nearby forests are favorite seasonal pastimes, and the Outing Club is among the most popular student activities. "The majority of campus is very outdoorsy and active," a senior says.

New Hampshire's only public university offers a huge variety of programs. That's one reason it attracts so many students from out of state. Another is that it's a place where students feel comfortable—academically, socially, physically, mentally.

Overlaps

University of Massachusetts at Amherst, University of Vermont, University of Connecticut, Northeastern, Providence

New Hampshire: Early action: Dec. 1. Regular admissions: Feb. 1. Financial aid: Mar. 1. Housing: Feb 1. Campus interviews: optional, informational. No alumni interviews. SATs or ACTs: required. SAT IIs: optional. Does not guarantee to meet demonstrated need. Accepts the common and electronic application. Apply to particular school or program. Essay question: risk you have taken, meaningful photograph, topic of your choice, recent activities if previous applicant or have been away from school.

The College of New Jersey

(formerly Trenton State College)
P.O. Box 7718, Ewing, NJ 08628-0718

TCNJ is a public liberal arts institution in the mold of William and Mary or UNC–Asheville. Also offers business and education. More than nine-tenths of the students are homegrown Garden Staters. A smaller, more personal alternative to Rutgers.

Website: www.tcnj.edu
Location: Suburban
Total Enrollment: 6,848
Undergraduates: 5,973
Male/Female: 41/59
SAT Ranges: V 560–650
M 580–680
Financial Aid: 33%
Expense: Pub $ $
Phi Beta Kappa: No
Applicants: 5,988
Accepted: 51%
Enrolled: 41%
Grad in 6 Years: 80%
Returning Freshmen: 96%
Academics: ✍ ✍ ✍ ✍
Social: ☎ ☎ ☎
Q of L: ★ ★ ★
Admissions: (609) 771-2131
Email Address:
admiss@vm.tcnj.edu

Strongest Programs:
Biology
Chemistry
History
Elementary Education
Music
Psychology
Business
Computer science

The College of New Jersey is a public institution with an emphasis on undergraduates more commonly found at a private school. TCNJ offers professors focused on teaching and a campus physically similar to one found down the road at Princeton University—without the Ivy League price tag. Formerly a teachers' college, TCNJ strives to provide students opportunities in a host of other fields. The small size makes for closeness among students and faculty.

TCNJ is set on 289 wooded and landscaped acres in suburban Ewing Township, six miles from Trenton. The picturesque Georgian Colonial architecture centers on Quimby's Prairie, surrounded by the original academic buildings of the 1930s. A flock of Canada geese makes its home in one of the two campus lakes.

To graduate, students must earn 120 credits for all BS programs in the School of Business, BA programs except for teacher preparation, and the Bachelor of Science in Nursing. In addition, the list of majors and study abroad opportunities continues to grow. The First Year Experience program is a required two-semester sequence consisting of From Athens to New York and Society, Ethics, and Technology. It is designed to ease students into the demanding reality of college life with an approach that integrates academics, individual development, and social understanding. Ten hours of community service is part of the requirement. Says an alum who's returned to work in admissions: "Every student is expected to get involved and leave the college a better place for having been here." Also required of incoming freshmen: Expectations, a one-day program to help students and parents understand what they can expect from the college and what the college expects of them; the ten-week College Seminar, to smooth the transition to college; Welcome Week, which gives freshmen a chance to meet their classmates and become acquainted with the campus; and Summer Readings, which exposes students to the kind of scholarship and dialogue they can expect at The College of New Jersey. Recent choices include *Race Matters* by Cornel West and Ralph Ellison's *Invisible Man*. Other requirements include two semesters each of rhetoric and mathematics, twenty-six credits of "perspectives on the world," and three semesters of foreign language (arts and sciences students only).

> **"Every student is expected to get involved and leave the college a better place for having been there."**

Consistent with the school's origins as a teachers' college, elementary education is popular, and the business school is strong, as are the natural sciences. Sociology and health and physical education are considered weak. Academically, TCNJ is competitive and getting more so. Not everyone sees the school's rising star as a benefit. "Becoming an Ivy League–type school," one student complains, means that they are "getting rid of the fun on campus." The college offers a combined, four-and-one-half-year BS/MA in law and justice, taught jointly by TCNJ and Rutgers; a seven-year BS/MD degree program with the University of Medicine and Dentistry of New Jersey; and a seven-year BS/OD degree with SUNY College of Optometry. TCNJ also offers foreign study in eleven countries and is a member of the International Student Exchange Program, giving students access to 131 colleges and universities across the U.S., including Alaska, the Virgin Islands, Puerto Rico, and Guam. The college has no teaching assistants, and faculty members get high marks. Getting into their courses, though, can be frustrating, and students can find their hopes of graduating in five years disappearing as fast as spots in classes during registration.

The school has no cap on out-of-state admissions, but only 5 percent of TCNJ's students are non-Jerseyans; 63 percent of the freshmen graduated in the top tenth of their high-school class, and 65 percent attended public high school. The college has aggressively pursued minority students, and today, African-American, Hispanic, and Asian-American students account for 17 percent of the student body. "If you don't leave this school very well educated in polit-

"If you don't leave this school very well educated in political correctness, then you were obviously unconscious."

ical correctness, then you were obviously unconscious," says a marketing major who praises the school for its diversity. The school has begun ongoing symposia on the Middle East and Afghanistan in the wake of September 11. Merit scholarships range from $500 to $12,000. "TCNJ brings in many of the best New Jersey students who are accepted to Ivy League schools but cannot afford them," says a senior.

Dorm housing, which is described as "very good" and "well-maintained," is only guaranteed for freshmen and sophomores, though 60 percent of all students (and 95 percent of first-years) live on campus. Freshmen hang their hats in either Travers-Wolfe, a two-building, 10-story hall, or Lakeside, a four-building complex. After that, students can enter the lottery for about 2,100 upperclass spaces in the apartment-style townhouses, Community Commons, the recently built residence hall, or try one of several local apartment complexes. Although suburban Ewing doesn't really cater to students, funky New Hope, PA, and preppy Princeton, NJ, are just up the road; restaurants, bars, movie theaters—and this being New Jersey, many malls—are within a short drive. State alcohol policies are strictly enforced, and the underage shouldn't hope to imbibe at the campus bar, the Rathskeller. Six percent of men and 8 percent of women belong to fraternities and sororities, which provide many of the off-campus parties. Cam-

"TCNJ brings in many of the best New Jersey students who are accepted to Ivy League schools bu can't afford them."

pus programming includes dances, concerts (Billy Joel, Fiona Apple), and movies. Road trips to Philadelphia and New York, each about an hour away and accessible by train, are also highly recommended.

The College of New Jersey's twenty-one varsity teams are big fish in the small pond of NCAA Division III; since 1979, they've won dozens of Division III crowns and runner-up titles. In the 2001-02 school year, thirty-four athletes won fifty-three All-American awards. Students rally around the football and basketball squads, especially when archrival Rowan comes to town, and the women's field hockey, lacrosse, and soccer teams have a faithful following. TCNJers also look forward to several annual events, including Homecoming, a Family Fest Day, and—the spring-time favorite—Senior Week.

The College of New Jersey is one of the nation's "budget Ivies," with reasonable tuition and a location that offers media types, artists, and budding scientists a relaxed suburban haven within shouting distance of the editors, producers, directors, curators, and pharmaceutical companies of New Jersey, Pennsylvania, and New York.

Overlaps
Rutgers, Villanova, University of Delaware

New Jersey Institute of Technology

University Heights, Newark, NJ 07102

NJIT is one of the few public technical institutes in the Northeast. It occupies a middle ground between the behemoth Rutgers and smallish Stevens Institute. Offers engineering, architecture, and management. At nearly four to one, NJIT's gender ratio is particularly skewed.

Website: www.njit.edu
Location: Urban
Total Enrollment: 8,862
Undergraduates: 5,698
Male/Female: 78/22
SAT Ranges: V 490–590
   M 530–630
Financial Aid: 60%
Expense: Pub $ $ $
Phi Beta Kappa: No
Applicants: 2,227
Accepted: 65%
Enrolled: 26%
Grad in 6 Years: 46%
Returning Freshmen: 80%
Academics: ✑ ✑ ✑
Social: ☎
Q of L: ★ ★
Admissions: (800) 925-NJIT
Email Address:
   admissions@njit.edu

Strongest Programs:
   Architecture
   Computer Science
   Engineering
   Environmental Science

The New Jersey Institute of Technology provides a no-frills technological education that prepares students for a future in an ever-changing global workplace. NJIT's challenging programs emphasize education, research, service, and—not surprisingly—economic development. It's an enticing combination for students seeking a high-tech, low-cost education.

NJIT's urban forty-five-acre campus is dotted with twenty-four buildings of diverse architectural styles, ranging from Elizabethan Gothic to contemporary design. Some of New Jersey's greatest cultural institutions are just blocks away, including the Newark Museum, Symphony Hall, and the New Jersey Center for the Performing Arts. Construction is nearly constant on campus, the latest encompassing a student services mall, renovation of labs, a dorm, and a new Building Sciences Complex.

NJIT is composed of the Newark College of Engineering, the School of Architecture (the only state-supported one in New Jersey), the School of Management, the College of Science and Liberal Arts, and the Albert Dorman Honors College. More than one hundred entering freshmen made up the Dorman class in 1998, and enrollment in the college is almost five hundred students. Top applicants are offered a spot in Dorman as NJIT freshmen, and they can stay as long as they keep their grades up. Perks of Dorman membership include guaranteed dorm rooms, research opportunities, and accep-

> "The academic climate is extremely competitive. It requires hours of study just to keep up. I often meet with members of my class or go to the learning center to stay on top of things."

tance into the B.S./M.S. program after completion of five courses for the undergraduate major. Engineering, architecture, and computer science garner the most student praise, while mechanical and electrical engineering are especially challenging. Perhaps not surprisingly, students say humanities are weak. Every incoming student gets a personal computer, which can be purchased after graduation at a reduced rate. Computers are integrated into almost every subject. To graduate, students must fulfill general education requirements in areas ranging from English to management. All freshmen take calculus I and II, English composition, computer science, physical education, and Freshman Seminar, a course that introduces students to university life.

Programs in Internet engineering and pharmaceutical engineering have been added to the curriculum, as well as an MS program in power engineering and a

Ph.D. in biomedical informatics. NJIT has also worked with Rutgers to create a number of joint-degree programs, from biology to history.

Most NJIT courses have fifty students or fewer. While some say the atmosphere can be low-pressure in certain fields, an electrical engineering student relates his experience this way: "The academic climate is extremely competitive. It requires hours of study just to keep up." An actuarial science major says he finds it challenging as well. "I often meet with members of my class or go to the learning center to stay on top of things." The administration assists students in other ways if they are having a difficult time, arranging for leaves of absence or extra semesters with a lighter courseload. "Graduating in four years would be miraculous at NJIT," especially for some engineering students, says one. Some have problems getting into classes with enrollment caps that are offered only once a year. But one student confides that if a freshman has all of the prerequisite courses, he has a good chance of graduating on time.

Students give teaching quality average to high marks. Since most profs have worked in industry, they can offer job information along with academic assistance. However, some grumble that understanding the coursework is easier than understanding the professors. "Many professors have strong accents, which makes it very hard for students to understand the lecture," says a future civil engineer. Academic advising is spotty, students say, but career counseling is helpful in preparing students for the job hunt. NJIT's most-favored academic option is the co-op program, which enables juniors to get paid for two six-month periods of work at technical companies.

As New Jersey's comprehensive technological university, NJIT attracts a wide range of students with different interests. But, one sophomore laments, "We need women." African-Americans comprise 11 percent of the student body, while Hispanics represent 10 percent. Asian-Americans account for 23 percent, and 12 percent hail from out of state or from foreign lands. World Week—with cultural performances and ethnic foods—is a popular spring event. Tolerance is not a problem here as it is on some other campuses. But students say it's a shame that ethnic groups tend to stick together and not mingle. As at many other campuses, social issues have become even more complex. "After 9/11, the political issues began to swell because of the diversity among students," says one student.

"Many professors have strong accents, which makes it very hard for students to understand the lecture."

NJIT has a chapter of Tau Beta Pi, the national engineering honor society. The university does not guarantee to meet the financial aid of all admits, but offers about 1,200 merit scholarships, ranging from $500 to tuition and room and board. The college works with local businesses to recruit qualified minority scholars, offering them scholarships and summer jobs.

NJIT is still primarily a commuter school, with students living at home to cut costs, so getting a room is no problem. NJIT's four residence halls can accommodate one-third of the students. Freshmen and students living farthest away get first crack at the rooms, and those who get in are guaranteed space the next year. Consensus has it that the best freshman dorms are Redwood Hall and Cypress. Upperclassmen move into fraternity houses or nearby off-campus apartments. The dorms and frats both have kitchen facilities. Because of its urban location, safety is always a consideration at NJIT. However, students praise the security efforts the school has undertaken. "Public safety officers are always around," says an electrical engineering major.

All that commuting (and the four-to-one male/female student ratio) definitely puts a crimp in the social life. Plus, many students tend to not be big partiers. There are some outlets, though, for those who are. About 7 percent of the men and 5 percent of the women join the Greek system. One of the best annual campus events is

Every incoming student gets a personal computer, which can be purchased after graduation at a reduced rate.

Students give teaching quality average to high marks. Since most profs have worked in industry, they can offer job information along with academic assistance.

Spring Week, which includes bands, novelties, and a semiformal. Diwali, the Indian festival of lights, and Chinese New Year also give undergrads pause to party. Another option is the beach, an hour away, with windsurfing and sailing equipment courtesy of NJIT. Most students agree that the administration's strict alcohol policies work, but it doesn't seem to be much of an issue in the first place. A junior simply states, "Alcohol is not a problem here."

NJIT students take pride in their athletic prowess. Men's and women's volleyball are the most popular sports on campus, followed by basketball, swimming, and

> **"After 9/11, the political issues began to swell because of the diversity among students."**

tennis. The outstanding athletic facilities are open to all, and include an indoor running track, fitness center, racquetball and squash courts, a six-lane pool, and areas for weight training, archery, or aerobics. Outdoor facilities include lighted tennis courts, a sand volleyball court, and a multiuse soccer stadium seating one thousand. A proud (and sweaty) tradition is the Hi-Tech Soccer Classic, which pits NJIT athletes against rivals from MIT, RPI, and Stevens Institute of Technology.

NJIT students are motivated and goal-directed; they've chosen their school because they want a top-notch technical education without the topflight price tag. Academics are the priority here, and if the social life is less than electrifying, students deal with it. After all, they know highly skilled jobs will beckon after graduation. Getting through is a challenge, but there's ample compensation available for NJIT alums in the technologically dependent workplaces of today—and tomorrow.

Overlaps

Stevens Institute of Technology, Rensselaer, Georgia Tech., Rutgers

If You Apply To ➤ | **NJIT:** Rolling admissions. Does not guarantee to meet full demonstrated need. Campus interviews: recommended, evaluative. No alumni interviews. SATs: required. SAT IIs: required (math I or II). Essay question: Why NJIT? Architecture applicants must submit portfolio of work

University of New Mexico

P.O. Box 4895, Albuquerque, NM 87196-4895

UNM is shaped by the encounter between Hispanic, Native American, and white culture. Studies related to Hispanic and Native cultures are strong, and in a land of picture-perfect sunsets, photography is a major deal. Technical programs are fueled by government labs in Albuquerque and Los Alamos.

Website: www.unm.edu
Location: Urban
Total Enrollment: 24,705
Undergraduates: 16,806
Male/Female: 43/57
SAT Ranges: V 480–610
 M 470–600
ACT Range: 19–25
Financial Aid: N/A
Expense: Pub $
Phi Beta Kappa: Yes

UNM's heritage goes back to 1889, when New Mexico wasn't even a state, and the university's strengths are still rooted in the rich history of the American Southwest. New Mexico excels in areas such as Latin American affairs and Southwest Hispanic studies. Lest you think it is a typical state school, consider that many students are commuters or of nontraditional age. UNM also boasts New Mexico's only law, medical, and architecture and urban planning schools, as well as its only doctor of pharmacy program.

Seated at the foot of the gorgeous Sandia Mountains, in the lap of Albuquerque, the beautifully landscaped campus sports both Spanish and Pueblo Indian architectural influences, with lots of patios and balconies. The duck pond is a favorite spot for sunbathing, and the mountains, which rise majestically to the east, are visible from virtually any point on campus. A new student residence center opened in 2001, and a childcare center is being built.

UNM offers more than four thousand courses in eleven colleges and two independent divisions, running the gamut from arts and sciences, education, and engineering to management, fine arts, and the allied health fields. Academic and general education requirements vary, but the core curriculum mandates three English courses focused on writing and speaking, two courses in each of the humanities, social and behavioral sciences, and physical and natural sciences, and one course in each of the fine arts, a second language, and math. Those reluctant to specialize can spend a few semesters in the broad University College, which also offers the most popular degree, a bachelor of university studies. Freshmen are encouraged to participate in the Freshman Forum and Core Legacy Courses. Engineering and fine arts freshmen can join interest groups, who share suites in a new dorm. The Tamarind Institute, a nationally recognized center housed at UNM's School of Fine Arts, offers training, study, and research in fine-art lithography. Anthropologists may root around one of New Mexico's many archeological sites, and engineers

> **"UNM is a very diverse university and political correctness is practiced by most students."**

may join in major solar-energy projects. Other popular majors include biology, education, psychology, and nursing and business management. Despite the school's large size, a computerized registration system keeps track of course requests, notifying students who register early when additional sections of courses they need are created.

By virtue of its location, UNM enjoys a diverse mix of cultures, even though 86 percent of students are state residents. A large minority student enrollment—29 percent Hispanic, 2 percent African-American, and 4 percent Asian-American—reflects this cultural diversity. A cultural awareness task force and student diversity council work to keep race relations from becoming rancorous, while the new student orientation program includes a cultural awareness component, and a full-time human awareness coordinator develops diversity-related programs for the residence halls. UNM also hosts the Arts of the Americas, a broad cross-cultural program that involves U.S. and Latin American artists in festivals, classes, and exhibits. "UNM is a very diverse university and political correctness is practiced by most students," a junior says. Many classes, and several complete degree programs, are offered in late afternoon and evening sessions, and about half of the student body takes advantage of these after-hours options.

Many UNM students commute, and students say finding parking spots continues to be difficult as a result. With only 10 percent of students living on campus, the dorms are "mostly a stopover before finding off-campus housing." One fairly new apartment complex offers students a reprieve from the older "shoddy and high-rent" units across the street from

> **"Most students feel safe, including the female population."**

the campus. An escort service, emergency phones, good lighting, and police who patrol around the clock help students feel safer. "Most students feel safe, including the female population," one student says. And although students say campus food is not worth the wait in line, more edible fare is available from campus delis and on nearby "junk-food row."

Albuquerque is New Mexico's largest city, and it offers a variety of cultural attractions, including the nation's largest hot-air balloon fiesta, a growing artists' colony, and concert tours to charm the ears. Santa Fe is an hour away. Those with cars or pickup trucks take advantage of the state's natural attractions: superb skiing in Taos, the Carlsbad Caverns, the Sandias, as well as excellent hiking and camping opportunities. For the historically inclined, numerous Spanish and Indian ruins are within an easy drive. And for those who yearn for more exotic locales, study abroad programs beckon from Mexico, Brazil, Venezuela, Costa Rica, and Scotland.

(Continued)

Applicants: 4,914
Accepted: 90%
Enrolled: 57%
Grad in 6 Years: 40%
Returning Freshmen: 71%
Academics: ✏️ ✏️ ✏️
Social: ☎ ☎ ☎
Q of L: ★ ★ ★
Admissions: (505) 277-2446
Email Address:
apply@unm.edu

Strongest Programs:
Southwest Hispanic Studies
Photography
Lithography
Geology
Environmental Studies
Laser Optics
Latin American Affairs

UNM's campus is more diverse than most, with Hispanics making up one-third of the student body and whites making up just over half.

Alcohol, though banned on campus, is readily available, according to most students. Though only 3 percent of the men and 2 percent of the women go Greek, fraternity and sorority parties keep the campus police busy on weekend nights. Most students enjoy partying at home or at nearby campsites, "watching the sunset, starting at about 9:00 P.M., with a cooler of beer stocked to last the day." Annual social events include Welcome Back Days in the fall and Nizhoni Days, a celebration of Native American culture. Each spring the whole campus turns out for a four-day fiesta with food and live music.

The men's basketball and football squads and the women's softball, soccer, and volleyball teams usually draw crowds. Each year, UNM parcels more than 250 athletic scholarships for male and female athletes, in sports ranging from skiing and swimming to soccer and wrestling.

UNM's campus and educational emphases keep in mind the Indian pueblos that surround the school. For those not concerned about having a "complete" college experience, and for students balancing college with a part-time job, UNM offers a sun-drenched location that satisfies—precisely because its academic climate is as relaxed as the rolling desert dunes.

If You Apply To ➤
UNM: Regular admissions: July 1. Financial aid: Mar. 1 (priority). Does not guarantee to meet demonstrated need. No campus interviews. Alumni interviews: optional, informational. ACTs or SATs: required, ACTs preferred. SAT IIs: optional.

New Mexico Institute of Mining and Technology

Campus Station, Socorro, NM 87801

New Mexico Institute of Mining and Technology has evolved so much since its founding that it's outgrown its name. Founded as the New Mexico School of Mines, the college now emphasizes computer science, chemical and electrical engineering, and information technology. New Mexico Tech continues to expand and change with the times, as evidenced by its growing reputation in anti-terrorism training and research.

Website: www.nmt.edu
Location: Rural
Total Enrollment: 1,588
Undergraduates: 1,256
Male/Female: 62/38
ACT Range: 23–29
Financial Aid: 55%
Expense: Pub $
Phi Beta Kappa: No
Applicants: 343
Accepted: 84%
Enrolled: 75%
Grad in 6 Years: 38%
Returning Freshmen: 74%
Academics: ✍ ✍ ✍

Tech's tree-lined campus, seventy-six miles south of Albuquerque, is dotted with picturesque, white adobe and red-tiled buildings and plenty of grassy open spaces that "capture the spirit of the Southwest." The new Jones Hall Annex houses classrooms, labs, and offices. New student apartments consist of suites with private bedrooms. NMT owns 20,000 acres adjacent to the town of Socorro (population 9,000), including Socorro Peak, which provides a mother lode of research and testing facilities. A thunderstorm lab sits on another mountaintop twenty miles away. Not surprisingly, mountain bikers, runners, astronomers, hikers, campers, rock climbers, geologists, rock hounds, and scenery enthusiasts feel right at home here.

NMT offers a number of excellent programs in three main areas: science, engineering, and natural resources. The departments of earth and environmental science, petroleum, and environmental engineering are among Tech's best, as is the program in hydrology, but administrators admit that the mineral engineering department could be bolstered. Freshmen can participate in the First Year Experience Program, in which they are grouped by major under a peer facilitator. New programs have been added in information technology and engineering mechanics. The arts are not what

NMT is about, so don't look for an excess of stellar offerings. The closest thing to a well-regarded program in the soft sciences is technical communication.

The student body is said to contain its share of nerds—75 percent, calculates one senior. "However, they tend to be extremely smart," he adds. As might be expected, then, students are drawn to Tech's spacious library, which holds 255,000 books. Computer facilities are, naturally, quite good. And teaching gets high marks, though because of Tech's relatively small size, most courses in the technical fields are offered sequentially, and students who don't take a cluster all the way through may wait several semesters before the necessary course is offered again. To graduate, students must take courses in calculus, physics, chemistry, English, technical writing, humanities, social sciences, and foreign language. Students say it's tough to finish all requirements in four years. A chemical engineering major says students get frustrated because, "They never have enough time to finish projects and homework."

Tech's student/faculty ratio is quite low for a technical school, and though professors are research-oriented, they do take teaching seriously. Class sizes vary, though 93 percent have fifty or fewer students. Jobs with mineral industries, research laboratories, and government agencies are available through the five-year cooperative work-study program. Undergraduates can also work part-time at research divisions on campus,

> "Some advisors really care about their students and try to help, while others sign your forms and can't wait to get back to their research."

including the New Mexico Bureau of Mines and Mineral Resources, the Petroleum Research and Recovery Center, the Energetic Materials Research and Testing Center, and the National Radio Astronomy Observatory's VLA and VLBA facilities. The terrorism training and research comes through NM Tech's association with the Energetic Materials Research and Testing Center. As 99 percent of the faculty does research and most hire undergraduates, opportunities for scientific investigation and independent study are plentiful. Quality advising, on the other hand, is not: "Some advisors really care about their students and try to help, while others sign your forms and can't wait to get back to their research," gripes a biology major.

Only 17 percent of Tech's undergraduates are from out of state, and 2 percent are foreign nationals. Hispanics account for 20 percent of the student body, African-Americans 1 percent, and Asian-Americans 3 percent. Thirty-eight percent of students are female—high for a technical school. "The issues mostly are about how someone got a better grade than so and so," says a chemical engineering student. Tech's housing facilities have improved and expanded since the days when women resided in the school's trailer park. Students can now live in suites with private bedrooms, a kitchen, and a living room. Forty percent of students live on campus, which one resident

> "The issues mostly are about how someone got a better grade than so and so."

describes as "comfortable but a little crowded." A bit of legwork can turn up decent and "incredibly cheap" housing off-campus. Plus, dorm-dwellers are required to buy the meal plan, and the food is said to be less than appealing. Luckily, and not surprisingly, the Mexican food available makes the town taco heaven.

Otherwise, the town, Socorro, is far from being a student paradise. A mining-turned-farming area in one of the most sparsely populated areas in the Southwest, it can only be described as tiny. Boredom may be a problem here, especially if you are under twenty-one, says a senior, though he admits that in its own way, Socorro "grows on a person." The good news is the spectacular weather, where something called rain is in danger of becoming a distant memory, and the nearby desert and spectacular mountains provide a wealth of outdoor opportunities. According to one Techie, "This is a small Western town with a deep Hispanic and Indian culture—it's very relaxed." Still, even those who enjoy the scenery and their classmates' company

(Continued)

Social: ☎ ☎
Q of L: ★ ★
Admissions: (505) 835-5424
Email Address:
admission@admin.nmt.edu

Strongest Programs:
Earth Science
Electrical Engineering
Physics

Tech's student/faculty ratio is quite low for a technical school, and though professors are research-oriented, they do take teaching seriously.

Not surprisingly, mountain bikers, runners, astronomers, hikers, bikers, campers, rock climbers, geologists and rock hounds, and scenery enthusiasts will be at home here.

see a direct correlation between sanity and access to a car, which can take them to Albuquerque and El Paso, or the Taos ski slopes.

With no Greek system and little excitement in Socorro, it's no wonder students at Tech have always had to work to make their own fun. The alcohol policy—"in your room only, over twenty-one only"—works in residence halls with active resident advisors. But a senior says, "It is very easy for minors to find alcohol." There are no varsity sports at Tech, but the men's and women's rugby and soccer teams do travel to challenge other schools. Many students also enjoy an extensive intramural pro-

> **"This is a small Western town with a deep Hispanic and Indian culture—it's very relaxed."**

gram and the school's eighteen-hole golf course. And in the absence of teams to cheer for, Tech's most popular annual events are 49ers Weekend, a Homecoming tribute to the miners of yore with gunfighters and a bordello/casino, and Spring Fling, a mini-Homecoming. Fall Fest, a new event, welcomes new and old students back to campus.

With just over 1,200 undergraduates, New Mexico Tech boasts one of the most intimate and up-to-date technical educations—and certainly some of the best weather—in the nation. NMT is an island of intensity in the otherwise calm New Mexico desert, but those who make it through four years leave with a top-notch technical education at a rock-bottom price.

Overlaps

New Mexico State, University of New Mexico, Colorado School of Mines

---

If You Apply To ➤

New Mexico Tech: Rolling admissions: Aug. 1. Financial aid: Mar. 1. Meets demonstrated need of 90%. Campus interviews: recommended, informational. No alumni interviews. SATs or ACTs: required. SAT IIs: optional. Accepts electronic applications. No essay question.

New School University–Eugene Lang College

(formerly New School for Social Research)
65 West 11th Street, New York, NY 10011

Eugene Lang College is home to about four hundred street-savvy, free-thinking students. New York City is the campus, and Lang offers little sense of community. In keeping with the New School's traditional ties to Europe, an internationalist perspective predominates. Strong in the arts and humanities.

Website: www.newschool.edu
Location: Urban
Total Enrollment: 408
Undergraduates: 408
Male/Female: 32/68
SAT Ranges: V 570–673 M 470–633
Financial Aid: N/A
Expense: Pr $ $ $
Phi Beta Kappa: No
Applicants: 403
Accepted: 80%
Enrolled: 32%

Students seeking a typical college experience—large classes, rowdy football games, and rigid academic requirements—need not apply to Eugene Lang College. That's because Lang College has no majors, no departments, and not a single varsity sport. Instead, this small, urban liberal arts college offers individualized academic programs, small classes, and a campus that reflects the quirky and kinetic atmosphere of Greenwich Village. Students control their destiny at this school. Says a student, "Our unique tradition of innovative intellectualism is what makes the New School so special to students and valuable to the public as an institution."

Lang fits right in amid the brownstones and trendy boutiques of one of New York's most vibrant neighborhoods. The majority of Lang's classrooms and facilities are located in a single five-story building between Fifth Avenue and Avenue of the Americas on West 11th Street, although New School University occupies fifteen buildings in the Village. NYU and the excitement of Greenwich Village and Washington Square Park are only a few blocks away.

The New School was founded in 1919 by a band of progressive scholars that included John Dewey, Charles Beard, and Thorstein Veblen. A decade and a half later, it became a haven for European intellectuals fleeing Nazi persecution, and over the years it has been the teaching home of many notable thinkers, including Buckminster Fuller and Hannah Arendt. Created in 1978, the undergraduate college was renamed in the late '80s for Eugene Lang, a philanthropist who (surprise, surprise!) made a significant donation to the school.

The two most distinctive features of Lang College are the small classes—fewer than sixteen students—and the practice of having undergraduates design their own program of study with no required majors or distribution of courses. As freshmen, students choose from a broad-based menu of seminars, and as sophomores they select from five overarching areas of concentration: writing, literature, and the arts; social and historical inquiry; mind, nature, and values; cultural studies; and urban studies. In their final year at Lang, students take on advanced "senior work" through a seminar or independent project in order to return to a broad plane of thought for a new perspective on the more specialized work of their middle years. The standard courseload is at least four seminars a semester, with topics such as From Standup to Shakespeare and the History of Jazz. All first-year students must take one year of writing and a series of workshops focusing on nonacademic concerns and library research skills. Because each student pursues an individualized educational program, cooperation, not competition, is the norm. "Teachers and students have a lot of freedom to shape the nature, pace, and expectations of courses," says a student. "The general atmosphere is more communal than competitive."

> "Teachers and students have a lot of freedom to shape the nature, pace, and expectations of courses."

Lang's top offerings include political and social theory, anthropology, history, literature, and literary theory. Its city location lends strength to the urban studies and education programs. Writing is highly praised, especially poetry, and theater is strong. The natural sciences and math are weak areas, though courses are offered through an arrangement with nearby Cooper Union. While introductory language courses are plentiful, upper-level language offerings are limited. And the college has beefed up its offerings on the history and literature of Third World and minority peoples, which were already better than those at most colleges. The professors at Lang are well versed and engaging, according to many students. "We get an exceptional degree of personal attention from highly trained and involved professors who are prominent and respected in their fields."

The main academic complaint is that the range of seminars is somewhat limited by the small size of the school, but outside programs offer more variety. After their first year, students may enroll in courses outside Lang from a limited number of approved classes in other divisions of New School University. A joint B.A./B.F.A. with Parsons School of Design has proven very popular. There's also a B.A./B.F.A. program in jazz and a B.A./M.A. in media studies with the New School's communications department. A newer addition is the exchange program with Sarah Lawrence College, established to provide motivated students with additional academic opportunities. Advanced students also have the option of taking courses in the Milano Graduate School of Management and Urban Professions and the graduate faculty offerings in the social sciences. The New School's library is small, but students have access to the massive Bobst Library at nearby New York University.

> "Whatever is desired can be found somewhere in New York City."

Lang College attracts a disparate group of undergraduates, but most of them can be described as idealistic and independent. "The students at Eugene Lang are mostly neo-hippies or activists," says one student. Some are slightly older than conventional

(Continued)
Grad in 6 Years: 85%
Returning Freshmen: 85%
Academics: ✍ ✍ ✍
Social: ☎
Q of L: ★ ★ ★
Admissions: (212) 229-5665
Email Address:
  lang@newschool.edu

Strongest Programs:
  Writing
  Fine Arts
  Education Studies
  Cultural Studies

The New School was founded in 1919 by a band of progressive scholars that included John Dewey, Charles Beard, and Thorstein Veblen. A decade and a half later, it became a haven for European intellectuals fleeing Nazi persecution.

Because each student pursues an individualized educational program, cooperation, not competition, is the norm.

college age (sometimes they are transfers from other schools) and are used to looking after themselves. Twenty-one percent of the students are African-American or Hispanic, another 3 percent are Asian-American, and 4 percent are foreign. A junior says that most of his classmates "want the freedom of an interdisciplinary education at a small school in a big city." Forty-two percent of Lang's students are from New York City and many cite the school's location as one of its best features. "Whatever is desired can be found somewhere in New York City," says a junior. "It's a nice place to be if you want to party or be a stone-cold intellectual." Lang College admits students regardless of their finances, and strives to meet the demonstrated need of those enrolled. However, the school does not guarantee to meet the demonstrated financial need of all admits. A deferred-payment plan allows students to pay tuition in ten installments, and there are various loan programs available. There are no academic-merit or athletic scholarships.

Dorm life at Lang engages only about half of the student body, though the rooms are in good shape. One student offers this assessment: "Union Square is comfortable and fun to live in. Loeb Hall is the newest and is mostly for freshman. Marlton Hall is in sort of a drab location...and is just old and generally uncomfortable." Off-campus dwellers live in apartments, in the Village if they can afford it, or in Brooklyn or elsewhere in the New York City area. Eighty percent of freshmen live on campus. A meal plan is available, but most students opt for the hundreds of delis, coffee shops, and restaurants that line the Avenue of the Americas.

"Since we generally live off campus, our lives are off campus as well."

The social network at Lang is quite small, and like many things, is left up to the student. "Since we generally live off campus, our lives are off campus as well," says one student. The social activities found on campus generally involve intellectual pursuits such as poetry readings and open-mic nights, as well as typical college activities like the student newspaper and the literary magazine. A popular annual festival allows students to write, cast, design, direct, rehearse, and perform plays—all in one twenty-four-hour period. Occasionally, students organize dances and parties, like the Spring Prom, a catered affair with live music that is "a satirical offshoot of the high-school tradition." Students generally avoid drinking on campus, and when they do imbibe, alcohol is "far from the central focus of activity," asserts a junior.

Students relish the freedom they are given at Eugene Lang College. For a student who yearns for four years of "traditional" college experiences, Lang would be a disappointment. But for those desiring an intimate, seminar-style education in America's cultural center, with an emphasis on reading, analytical writing, and critical discussion, Lang offers all of the stimulation of the city it calls home.

Overlaps

Sarah Lawrence, NYU, Bard, Hampshire, Fordham

If You Apply To ➤ **Eugene Lang:** Early decision: Nov. 15. Regular admissions: Feb.1. Meets demonstrated need of 80%. Campus interviews (or by telephone): required, evaluative. No alumni interviews. SATs or ACTs: required. SAT IIs: optional. Essay question: explain how your community has affected your thinking; or discuss a social, economic, or political issue of personal importance; and personal statement. Seeks "independent" students.

Don't count on getting into NYU just because Big Sis' did. From backup school to the hottest place in higher education, NYU's rise has been breathtaking. The siren song of Greenwich Village has lured applicants by the thousands. Major draws include the arts, media, and business.

New York University used to be the darling of high-school academic counselors because it was a respectable alternative for students snubbed by the Ivies. No more! NYU is still no Columbia, but a growing number of top students are opting for its diet of quality academics and a rich cultural life in the ultimate urban setting: Manhattan's Greenwich Village. NYU students have attitude without being stuck up. They're hip and sophisticated while still socially committed. In short, students at NYU feed their minds while taking a succulent bite out of the Big Apple.

NYU has campuses and centers throughout New York, but is centered at Washington Square. Trendy shops, galleries, clubs, bars, and eateries crowd neighboring blocks; SoHo, Little Italy, and Chinatown are just blocks away. Modern and historic NYU academic buildings mix with nineteenth-century brick townhouses surrounding Washington Square Park (the closest thing NYU has to a quad), where parades of rappers, punks,

> **"Like all things at NYU, the academic climate is diverse and varied."**

Deadheads, junkies, and dealers surround a replica of the Arc d'Triomphe in Paris. A student center with a one-thousand-seat theater is under construction.

The city scene is a defining part of the NYU experience. So, too, is the wide range of academic programs. The Tisch School of the Arts trained directors including Martin Scorcese, Spike Lee, and Oliver Stone, and current undergrads continue to win many national-student filmmaker awards. Tisch also boasts excellent drama, dance, photography, and television departments, and it's not uncommon to see students who haven't yet finished B.F.A. degrees performing in Broadway shows.

Future bulls and the bears of Wall Street find a home at the Stern School of Business, where they benefit from a center for Japanese and American business and economic studies. Another favorite department among students (and New York corporations who recruit them after graduation) is accounting, known for its high job-placement rate. The arts and sciences are strong, with English, journalism, history, political science, and applied math winning highest marks. There's an increased emphasis on foreign exchange and study abroad, with new campuses in London and Buenos Aires; programs in Paris, Madrid, Florence, and Prague; and exchanges with universities in Chile, Mexico, Sweden, Denmark, and Germany. The Gallatin Division provides flexible schedules

> **"Security on campus is taken very seriously. Overall, students feel safe."**

and freedom from requirements for those wishing to engage in independent study or develop their own programs. NYU no longer offers concentrations in occupational therapy, physical therapy, and K–12 art education, but there are new programs in Hellenic studies, communications technologies, Chinese or Japanese education, international relations, and in social sciences, and anthropology. The "Speaking Freely" program encourages undergraduates to learn languages in their residence halls.

"Like all things at NYU, the academic climate is diverse and varied," says a sophomore. "Most students put a lot of effort into their studies, but the way they work varies from student to student." Premed, prelaw, and prebusiness students may encounter packed schedules and competitive classes, while Gallatin and Tisch

Website: www.nyu.edu	
Location: Urban	
Total Enrollment: 37,134	
Undergraduates: 19,028	
Male/Female: 40/60	
SAT Ranges: V 630–710	
M 600–710	
ACT Range: 27-31	
Financial Aid: N/A	
Expense: Pr $ $ $ $	
Phi Beta Kappa: Yes	
Applicants: 30,533	
Accepted: 29%	
Enrolled: 36%	
Grad in 6 Years: 75%	
Returning Freshmen: 91%	
Academics: ✍ ✍ ✍ ✍ ½	
Social: ☎ ☎ ☎	
Q of L: ★ ★ ★	
Admissions: (212) 998-4500	
Email Address: N/A	

Strongest Programs:
Drama / Theater Arts
Dance
Business
Art and Design
Film and Television
Music

students may have lots of spare time, students say. "It's hard to avoid the pressure," says a student majoring in drama and political science, with nine hours of acting class a day, and writing-intensive academic courses, too. At least the NYU library is accommodating—it's one of the largest open-stack facilities in the country, with more than three million volumes.

Under the Morse Academic Plan, freshmen and sophomores take courses including foreign language, expository writing, foundations of contemporary culture, and foundations of scientific inquiry. Like other large universities, NYU inflicts "gargantuan" introductory courses on freshmen, and graduate students lead foreign language sections, writing workshops, and the recitations that accompany lectures. Still, students say teaching is top-notch. Professors "are all accomplished writers and lecturers and are well-known, kind, personable, and hard workers," a sophomore says. Those qualifying for freshmen honors seminars study in small classes under top faculty and eminent visiting professors.

The variety of degree options here may tempt students to hang around the Village for more than four years. There's a five-year program offering a B.A. and a master's in science, and a seven-year dental program. NYU also has a five-year joint engineering program with New Jersey's Stevens Institute of Technology, and a B.A./M.D. program in which a student is admitted to NYU Medical School at the time of college acceptance. Freshmen selected as University Scholars travel abroad each year; the university sends more students to study abroad than any private university in the nation. Because of the school's location, internships ranging from jobs on Wall Street to assignments with film

"Social life is so eclectic and active all over campus and the city."

industry giants are easy to come by. The career center has thousands of listings for on-campus jobs, full-time jobs, and internships. "Career counseling is very comprehensive and dedicated to getting students into their fields," says a sophomore.

Thanks in part to the university's investment of new dorms, a majority of students (54 percent) now come from outside New York State and NYU enrolls the second-highest number of foreign students (behind the University of Southern California) among private institutions. Forty-six percent of NYU students are from New York State, primarily the city and nearby suburbs. African-Americans make up 6 percent of the student body, Asian-Americans 14 percent, and Hispanics 7 percent. Gender issues, social justice, the Israeli-Palestinian issue, and rights of all kinds—gay, lesbian, transgender, animal, human, and workers'—are most important now, students say.

An unusual psychological counseling program run by students, Peers Ears, tries to ensure that amid all the hubbub and the pressure of city living, students don't go off the deep end. New students are urged to attend an all-campus freshman orientation program, a program specifically designed for their school, or both. Students also meet with academic advisors—usually professors in their major department—at least once a semester. Advisors review course selections and give students permission to register, while also helping them stay on track toward graduation.

For concerned parents and students, the Office of Student Life, Protection, and Residence Halls hosts a series of workshops on keeping safe at NYU, and programs like the NYU Trolley and Escort Van Service provide door-to-door service for students until 3:00 A.M. "Security on campus is taken very seriously," says a student. "Overall, students feel safe." All residence halls have two people on duty at their entrances twenty-four hours a day, and visitors, including parents, must sign in and leave proper identification.

While NYU students once had to fend for themselves in New York's outrageous housing market, the university now guarantees four years of housing to all freshmen (and most transfers) who seek it. About a dozen dorms, ranging from old hotels to a converted monastery, provide a wide range of accommodations. Most rooms have private baths and are larger, cleaner, newer, and better equipped than many city apartments, enticing 55 percent of students to stay on campus. There are no "freshman halls," and rooms are assigned by lottery each spring. Amenities include central air-conditioning, computer centers, musical practice rooms, kitchens, and even, in some buildings, small theaters. The university provides free shuttle buses to dorms that are farther uptown than the Union Square area. And while three dorms have cafeterias, most students soon learn the real New Yorkers' secret—save the Uptown tourist places for special occasions and explore Downtown's array of ethnic restaurants that offer amazing food at cheap prices.

Students can't say enough good things about NYU's social life. "It's New York, come on," says a senior majoring in playwriting. On campus, there are concerts, movies, fraternity and sorority events (4 percent of the men and 2 percent of the women go Greek), and more than 250 clubs. The springtime Strawberry Festival includes free berries, cotton candy, outdoor concerts, and carnival amusements like a jumping bubble. Many students march in the city's Halloween Parade, which literally takes over Greenwich Village, while most spring and fall weekends find a city-sponsored street fair somewhere nearby. The Violet Ball, a dinner/dance held each fall in the atrium of Bobst Library, is an excuse to get dressed up. As for alcohol, underage students caught with it in public areas of dorms may lose their housing. The rest take their chances with the notoriously strict bouncers at bars and clubs around Manhattan.

While sports have not historically been NYU's strength, the women's basketball and men's fencing teams brought home the 2001 University Athletic Association Championship. Other Division III powers include women's fencing, men's volleyball, and men's and women's soccer. More than seven thousand students participate in intramural sports, with the usual standbys as well as hockey played on in-line skates, and arm wrestling. The Coles Sports Center has aerobics studios, bikes, rowing machines and a rooftop running track; students get in by showing their IDs. Road trips to Philadelphia, Boston or Washington are few and far between. "Why road trip when you are in NYC?" asks an educational theater major. "Social life is so eclectic and active all over campus and the city."

Like Boston University and George Washington University, NYU's identity is inextricably tied to the city whose name it shares. World-class arts offerings, plus nose-to-the-grindstone business classes, help push NYU grads to the tops of their fields, regardless of how disparate those fields are.

> *Like Boston University and George Washington University, NYU's identity is inextricably tied to the city whose name it shares.*

Overlaps

Columbia, University of Pennsylvania, University of California at Berkeley, Cornell, Boston

If You Apply To ➤ **NYU:** Early decision: Nov. 15. Regular admissions: Jan. 15. Financial aid: Feb. 15. Does not guarantee to meet demonstrated need. No campus or alumni interviews. SATs or ACTs: required. SAT IIs: recommended (writing and two others); required for applicants to the B.A./M.D. program. Accepts the Common Application (with NYU supplement) and electronic applications. Apply to particular schools or programs. Essay question: important person, place, or event in your life; describe the future; a value or ideal that is important to you; influential creative work.

University of North Carolina at Asheville

I University Heights, Asheville, NC 28804-8503

The "other" UNC happens to be one of the best educational bargains in the country. At just over three thousand students, UNCA is about half the size of fellow public liberal arts college William and Mary and one thousand students smaller than Mary Washington. Picturesque mountain location in a resort city.

Website: www.unca.edu
Location: Small city
Total Enrollment: 3,247
Undergraduates: 3,211
Male/Female: 42/58
SAT Ranges: V 530–640
  M 520–620
ACT Range: 21–27
Financial Aid: 39%
Expense: Pub $
Phi Beta Kappa: No
Applicants: 2,020
Accepted: 59%
Enrolled: 38%
Grad in 6 Years: 53%
Returning Freshmen: 80%
Academics: 🖉 🖉 🖉 🖉
Social: ☎ ☎ ☎
Q of L: ★ ★ ★ ★
Admissions: (828) 251-6481
Email Address:
  admissions@unca.edu

Strongest Programs:
  Psychology
  Management
  Environmental Studies
  Literature
  Biology

Whether it's the lush environment or the money you're saving, the University of North Carolina at Asheville will have you seeing green. This public liberal arts university offers all of the perks that are generally associated with pricier private institutions: rigorous academics, small classes, and a beautiful setting. And it does it for a fraction of the cost. Natural sciences are strong here, and students praise the close interaction between themselves and faculty. Any way you look at it, UNCA is a bargain that may have your friends turning green with envy.

Located in the heart of North Carolina's gorgeous Blue Ridge Mountains, the 265-acre campus lies in the middle of one million acres of federal and state forest near the tallest mountain in the East and the most heavily visited national park in the country. The campus was built in the 1960s, and much of the brick architecture reflects the style of that decade, although half of the buildings were added within the past few years. The Botanical Gardens at Asheville, adjacent to the main campus, features thousands of labeled plants and trees, and serves as a wildlife refuge and study center for botany students. The recently opened Glasshouse at Ramsey Library provides an interior greenspace that can be used as additional seating for the adjacent café and special events.

The university is dedicated to providing a liberal arts education that "teaches students to become their own best and lifelong teachers." The demanding core curriculum, among the nation's oldest, discourages channeling into disciplines too soon and focuses on uncovering diverse worldviews and cultural values. Each student takes a nationally recognized, four-course humanities sequence: the first three are historical surveys and the fourth a senior-level class that addresses modern society in light of its traditions. It may be tough, but it's also popular. There are also smaller requirements in English composition, math, social science, natural science, arts and ideas, and a foreign language.

> "Classes are rigorous, but with the small class sizes and amount of personal attention you receive, you are well prepared to succeed."

The academic climate is demanding and students admit that it can be competitive at times. "Classes are rigorous," says a senior, "but with the small class sizes and amount of personal attention you receive, you are well prepared to succeed." Political science, humanities, and literature receive near-unanimous praise, and one student says the once-struggling math department "is undoubtedly the strongest on campus." The most popular majors are psychology, management, environmental studies, sociology, and literature. Students cite chemistry and physics as being weaker than other offerings.

Asheville also offers 2–2 programs with NC State in engineering, forestry, and textile chemistry; study abroad is already an option in Europe, Asia, and South America. The UNCA Honors program offers special courses—as well as cultural and social opportunities—to motivated students who can make the grade. There are also ample opportunities for undergraduate research; in fact, nearly half of all students will have had an undergraduate research experience by graduation. A new interdisciplinary studies major allows students to develop an individual degree program that transcends the scope of a singe academic major. Professors are given high marks and noted for their passion and experience. "I don't think I can voice how awesome the teaching has been during my four years here," says a senior. "They make class interesting and are always helping students outside of class."

The head count at Asheville has risen dramatically over the past decade, but only 11 percent of the student body come from out of state. (The school limits its out-of-state admits to 18 percent.) A student says, "The school is located in the Bible Belt, but all political attitudes thrive here." Environmental causes, gay and lesbian issues, campus issues such as parking, and multiculturalism are a few of the buzzwords on campus. "The big subject right now is diversity in the student population," says a student. Currently, the college is 3 percent African-American, 1 percent Hispanic, and 1 percent Asian-American, but Asheville is making special efforts to bring more students who are "underrepresented" to the campus. Asheville offers 132 athletic scholarships in a variety of sports, as well as 390 merit scholarships ranging from $50 to $12,500.

The majority of the students commute from nearby communities, while 35 percent reside on campus. Students can choose from air-conditioned suites in Mills Hall, double occupancy in the Founders Residence Hall, or singles in the wooded Governors Village complex. There is no lottery, and freshmen are mixed in with upperclassmen. "There is plenty of room to live and relax in all dorms," notes a senior. "The newer dorms go first in reservations." For meals, students may eat dining-hall fare or grab a bite at any of the campus snack bars. Vegetarian entrées are available at most meals, in addition to a salad and sandwich bar. Crime is nearly nonexistent on campus, thanks to the school's rural location.

> There are ample opportunities for undergraduate research; in fact, nearly half of all students will have had an undergraduate research experience by graduation.

"I don't think I can voice how awesome the teaching has been during my four years here. They make class interesting and are always helping students outside of class."

After class, there's lots to do, especially for the many Asheville students with a hankering for the great outdoors. The college is surrounded by the Blue Ridge Mountains and the Smokies, where students can hike and rock climb; water buffs can go rafting on the nearby French Broad River. For students with cars, the Blue Ridge Parkway is a short drive away, while Spartanburg and Charlotte are one and two hours away, respectively. Real big-city action takes extra effort, though, since Atlanta is a four-hour trek. Asheville offers a tame but inviting nightlife, with popular hangouts like Boston Pizza and MacGuffy's. Most parties take place off campus, especially since RAs stalk underage drinkers in the dorms. "There is no tolerance for unsafe, underage, or unwise drinking," says a student. Four percent of the men and 3 percent of the women belong to fraternities and sororities, but their presence is not influential. There are more than seventy campus organizations, including a student newspaper, *The Banner*.

> The college is surrounded by the Blue Ridge Mountains and the Smokies, where students can hike and rock climb; water buffs can go rafting on the nearby French Broad River.

Involvement is no problem for the athletic teams. The Bulldogs boast Big South conference-championship teams in volleyball and men's basketball. Women's tennis has captured the league crown three times, and the soccer team has imported recruits from Germany and England. Most recently, women's cross-country has brought home conference trophies. Intramurals are at least as popular as the varsity sports. The Justice Center Sports Complex houses a pool, weight room, and dance studio.

Apart from athletics, several campus-wide events bring the school together each year, including Founders Day in October, Homecoming, a spring fling, and a mock casino night with an auction. Greenfest, a semester-based environment and beautification project, is also very popular. "There are lots of annual events, but the one I feel makes our campus unique is the annual Greenfest," says a student. "All groups on campus—faculty, staff, and students—come together for two or three days to help make a designated section of campus more beautiful."

"The school is located in the Bible Belt but all political attitudes thrive here."

All the ingredients for a superior college experience lie in wait at Asheville: strong academics, dedicated professors, and an administration that continues to push for excellence. "The people make Asheville special," notes a senior. "From the chancellor to the custodians, Asheville's people are committed every day to making this college a warm and inviting place." It's a place to get the kind of liberal arts education usually associated with private colleges—but for a lot fewer greenbacks!

Overlaps
Appalachian State, UNC–Chapel Hill, North Carolina State, UNC-Wilmington, UNC–Greensboro

<table>
<tr><td>

**If You
Apply
To ≻**

</td><td>

UNC–Asheville: Early action: Oct. 15. Regular admissions: Mar.15. Financial aid: Mar. 1. Does not guarantee to meet demonstrated need. Campus interviews: optional, evaluative. No alumni interviews. SATs or ACTs: required. SAT IIs: optional. Accepts electronic applications. No essay question.

</td></tr>
</table>

University of North Carolina at Chapel Hill

CB 2200, Jackson Hall, Chapel Hill, NC 27599-2200

Close on the heels of UVA as the South's most prestigious public university. With more than 80 percent of the spots in each class reserved for in-staters, admission is next to impossible for out-of-staters who aren't 6'9" with a forty-three-inch vertical jump. Chapel Hill is a quintessential college town.

Website: www.unc.edu
Location: Suburban
Total Enrollment: 24,892
Undergraduates: 15,608
Male/Female: 40/60
SAT Ranges: V 560–670
   M 570–670
ACT Range: 23–29
Financial Aid: 33%
Expense: Pub $
Phi Beta Kappa: Yes
Applicants: 16,569
Accepted: 37%
Enrolled: 56%
Grad in 6 Years: 82%
Returning Freshmen: 95%
Academics: ✍ ✍ ✍ ✍ ✍
Social: 🍷 🍷 🍷 🍷
Q of L: ★ ★ ★ ★
Admissions: (919) 966-3621
Email Address:
   uadm@email.unc.edu

Strongest Programs:
   Journalism
   Information and Library
      Science
   Philosophy
   Business
   Sociology
   Political Science
   Classics
   Drama

Welcome to "the Southern part of heaven," a place where the sky is Carolina Blue and the academics are red-hot. As the flagship campus of the state university system and the oldest public university in the United States, UNC–Chapel Hill has earned its place among the South's most prestigious universities. The atmosphere here is uniquely Southern, a rowdy mixture of hard work, sports fanaticism, and tradition that seems to attract bright, fun-loving students from everywhere.

UNC's campus occupies 730 acres dotted with trees, lawns, and thirty miles of brick-paved walkways. The architecture ranges from Palladian, Federal, and Georgian to postmodern, but red brick is the prevailing motif. The original administration building is a replica of the central section of Princeton's gorgeous Nassau Hall.

Chapel Hill offers eighty-six undergraduate degree programs. Strong programs include sociology, philosophy, chemistry, business, political science, journalism and mass communications, classics, and biology. One of the most popular on-campus offerings is the small honors seminars open to all undergraduates. UNC's honors program is nationally recognized as being one of the best in the country. A sophomore feels that the Carolina Leadership Development Office deserves recognition. "It administers programs, including the North Carolina Fellows Program (a highly selective four-year leadership development program), the Emerging Leaders Program, and the Womentoring Program, which matches female students with female faculty members who serve as mentors." The drama department runs a repertory company with professional actors, as well as sponsoring ten or more student productions a season. On the flip side, the administration admits that the geology department is not rock-solid.

"I have always felt challenged and enriched by classes."

General education requirements, which must be completed in the first two years, include multiple semesters of English composition, foreign languages, physical education, natural and social sciences, aesthetics, and history as well as single courses in mathematical science, philosophy, and cultural diversity. The low-pressure, low-tension academic atmosphere, unusual at a school of UNC's caliber, lets students set their own scholarly pace. "I've always felt challenged and enriched by classes," says one student. Another adds, "I find there are stimulating academic opportunities both inside and outside the classroom if students are looking to be challenged." Academic and social life are governed by a student-run honor system.

Registration is by web or telephone, and students register according to seniority. For those tired of the classroom rush, Research Triangle Park, a nearby research and corporate community, and home of the National Humanities Center, employs many students as research assistants. Foreign study is available in France, England, Germany, Italy, Spain, Latin America, Australia, and Japan during the academic year, and in more exotic places over the summer.

The Carolina faculty is, for the most part, top-notch. Professors keep regular office hours and welcome those students who seek them out. "I believe I have received an incredible education with some of the best professors in the nation," says one satisfied senior. Academic counseling, once less than stellar, has been revamped to the delight of students.

Under state guidelines, 82 percent of UNC's freshman class must be state residents, and the admissions office has no problem filling this quota with the cream of the North Carolinian crop. Thus, unless you're an athlete, out-of-state admission is extremely tough. Some Carolinians spend their childhoods talking about "when I get to Chapel Hill." A good number of them can't afford or don't want to pay for an Ivy League or private-school education. Big social and political issues on campus include multiculturalism, gender roles, local and national elections, and religious issues. African-Americans account for 11 percent of the student body, Asian-Americans 5 percent, and Hispanics 1 percent. This sports-minded school awards athletic scholarships in all of the major sports. Students also can vie for ninety-nine merit scholarships, ranging from $2,500 to $12,500. The university also offers a need-based loan program with low interest and repayment periods running as long as ten years after a student leaves school—quite a deal when you consider that UNC's tuition is already a bargain. The student government runs a part-time employment service that provides about five hundred student jobs.

> **"I believe I have received an incredible education with some of the best professors in the nation."**

Spring at Carolina brings a glorious flowering of azaleas and dogwoods, and, to the delight of returning students, no more housing lottery, which once made them scramble for rooms. Freshmen and returning students are guaranteed university housing, and returning students may reserve their rooms for the upcoming academic year. Housing on the north side of campus offers old but comfortable dorms; the south side offers high-rise cell blocks of cramped four-room suites, which are a good hike from classroom buildings (not to worry—there's a free campus shuttle). "Living in a dorm is one of the best experiences of college!" says one excited junior biology major. Students may opt to be part of a living/learning community; house themes include foreign languages, substance-free, wellness, and women's issues. Campus security is said to be good, and students feel relatively safe at UNC. "As a female, I try not to walk alone at night," says a senior, "but the university provides countless services to ensure that I generally don't have to ever walk alone." These services include free bus and shuttle rides, emergency call boxes, and a fully accredited campus police department.

"'College town' in the dictionary should show a picture of Chapel Hill," boasts one senior. Franklin Street, the main drag in town that runs across the northern boundary of campus, offers Mexican and Chinese restaurants, ice cream parlors, coffee houses, a Greek restaurant, vegetarian eateries, bakeries, a disco, and a generous supply of bars. Anyone wanting a secure handle on a social life should head straight for the fraternities or sororities, some of which date to the 1880s. The Greeks exert an influence far beyond their numbers (18 percent of undergraduates). Alcohol is readily available to those with a decent fake ID, though campus penalties for underage drinking are harsh. Students look forward to several annual festivals: Apple Chill, Festifall, and the North Carolina Literary Festival, which recently featured performances by numerous authors including bestseller John Grisham. Students are

> **"'College town' in the dictionary should show a picture of Chapel Hill."**

UNC's honors program is nationally recognized as being one of the best in the country.

Under state guidelines, 82 percent of UNC's freshman class must be state residents, and the admissions office has no problem filling this quota with the cream of the North Carolinian crop.

involved in the community, many through a unique service learning program for which they receive academic credit.

The Tar Heel varsity teams are extremely popular, especially football and, well, basketball, which is virtually always in the top twenty. A game with NC State makes any Carolina fan's heart beat faster, but Duke takes the prize as the most hated rival of all. "Everyone follows these games," says a student. "People go insane!" The slam-dunking Tar Heels play in the 21,750-seat Smith Center, named for retired coach Dean Smith, who just happens to be the winningest college basketball coach of all time. The school has taken more than 175 ACC championships since the league was founded in 1953. The baseball, tennis, and lacrosse teams are also strong, but the team with one of the best records (besides men's basketball of course) is the women's soccer team, which has claimed seventeen of the twenty NCAA championships awarded in their sport. Women also sport national championships in field hockey and basketball and conference championships in volleyball and track. A strong intramural program draws heavy participation. Those not quite so competition-minded can enjoy the $4.9 million student recreation center, which includes a weight-training facility, a place for aerobic dance, and the student wellness center. Those who crave fresh air can take advantage of the Outdoor Education Center, which offers mountain bike trails, an eighteen-hole Frisbee golf course, rope courses, and the longest zipline in the U.S.

Often touted as one of the best college buys in the country, the University of North Carolina at Chapel Hill gives students everything they want, both academically and socially. The two hundred-year history of this school creates an atmosphere of extreme pride, monumental school spirit, and a love for tradition. A student says, "I came to the University of North Carolina in hopes of finding a strong academic environment, outside-of-class opportunities, and a university peopled with students from diverse socioeconomic backgrounds who come together to educate one another, and I have not been disappointed."

Overlaps

North Carolina State, Duke, University of Virginia, East Carolina, Wake Forest

If You Apply To >

UNC–Chapel Hill: Early action: Nov. 15. (Early decision has been dropped.) Regular admissions: Jan. 15. Financial aid: Mar. 1. Guarantees to meet full demonstrated need. Campus interviews: optional, informational. No alumni interviews. SATs or ACTs: required. SAT IIs: required (math II). Accepts electronic applications. Optional essay question.

University of North Carolina at Greensboro

1000 Spring Garden Street, Greensboro, NC 27412

UNCG is a medium-sized alternative in the UNC system—half the size of Chapel Hill and three times bigger than Asheville. UNCG began its life as a women's college and remains about two-thirds female. Residential College program offers a first-rate living/learning option.

Website: www.uncg.edu
Location: Center city
Total Enrollment: 13,343
Undergraduates: 10,376
Male/Female: 32/68

At the University of North Carolina at Greensboro, an aggressive campaign is underway to make the school more "student-centered." Living Learning Communities have been developed to help meet the needs of freshmen and make the matriculation experience less daunting. The administration is also taking steps to make all students feel at home. "Being a student at UNCG is so much more than going to class, studying, and getting a degree," says a senior. "There's so much opportunity to get involved here and many ways to make your total college experience valuable and lots of fun."

Set on two hundred acres sprinkled with magnolia and dogwood trees, Greensboro's well-landscaped campus features a mix of Colonial, Georgian, brick, and modern architecture. Still standing is the original university building, the Victorian-style Julius Foust Building; built in 1892 and now on the National Register of Historic Places, it is located on a knoll in the center of the campus's original ten acres. The Elliot University Student Center has been expanded and renovated, and a $39 million science building will open its door soon, to the delight of budding campus scientists.

Within the College of Arts and Sciences, psychology, fine arts, and literature are strong. The university's program in human environmental sciences is also highly regarded, and business and nursing are the most popular majors. The School of Music has three ensembles, a symphony orchestra, three choral groups, and has won the National Opera Association's production competition three of the past four years. There are some unusual interdisciplinary programs, such as therapy training, which combines classes from the dance, education, fine arts, and theater departments. Greensboro's program in human environmental sciences is North Carolina's largest. New majors include special education and hospitality management, which prepares students for careers in hotel management, restaurant management, and other tourism fields. The general education requirements allow students to complete core requirements in as few as thirty-six semester hours, provided they have met requirements in global perspectives, writing across the curriculum, and speaking across the curriculum.

> "Being a student at UNCG is so much more than going to class, studying, and getting a degree."

The academic climate is rigorous and "very competitive," says a sophomore. Students take their education seriously, and so do the professors. "The teachers push you as well as support you," says a junior. Enrollments in introductory courses sometimes swell to more than one hundred, but preregistration is done through an online computer system. Those who make it into the residential college program enjoy the atmosphere of an intimate "academic community" with class sizes usually ranging from fifteen to twenty students. The school's residential college is among the nation's oldest living/learning programs. The honors program allows talented students the opportunity to tackle a broad interdisciplinary program through small seminars, while undergraduate research assistantships allow

> "The teachers push you as well as support you."

sixty-five students to work with faculty in all fields. To emphasize the importance of writing both as an essential skill and as a tool for learning, majors in the College of Arts and Sciences must take writing-intensive courses.

A summer orientation program allows freshmen to get their feet wet before classes begin. Each academic year starts off with the Fall Kickoff, when campus organizations line College Avenue with the trappings of their activities, creating a festival atmosphere. UNCG has more than 140 student organizations, including club sports, religious groups, service organizations, media groups, national societies, and professional organizations.

Ten percent of freshmen come from outside North Carolina, mostly from the South. African-Americans account for 20 percent of the student body, and the Neo-Black Society is very active on campus. Hispanics and Asian-Americans combine to make up 5 percent of the student body. According to a senior, "Diverse religions, ethnic makeups, sexual preferences, and educational backgrounds all converge on one campus—from extreme faddish clothing, tattoos, body-piercing, and hair-dyeing to the ultraconservative." Outstanding students can vie for hundreds of merit

(Continued)

SAT Ranges: V 460–570
    M 460–570
Financial Aid: 35%
Expense: Pub $
Phi Beta Kappa: Yes
Applicants: 6,619
Accepted: 75%
Enrolled: 11%
Grad in 6 Years: 46%
Returning Freshmen: 75%
Academics: ✍ ✍
Social: ☎ ☎
Q of L: ★ ★ ★
Admissions: (336) 334-5243
Email Address: undergrad_admissions@uncg.edu

Strongest Programs:
    Literature
    Biology
    Psychology
    Biology
    Environmental Studies
    Art and Design

To emphasize the importance of writing both as an essential skill and as a tool for learning, majors in the College of Arts and Sciences must take writing-intensive courses.

scholarships, which range from $1,000 to $12,000; 180 athletic scholarships are also offered.

Thirty-six percent of the undergraduates live in Greensboro's twenty-three residence halls, but students note that getting a room can be a challenge. "The past few years have been cramped and we have been experiencing a housing shortage," says a student. "But the rooms are OK." The Tower Village Apartments provide suite-style living on campus for three hundred lucky students who get private bedrooms. Rooms in the older buildings are spacious, those in the quad are more attractive, and the most modern, high-rise dorms offer cramped quarters. One-third of the dorms are single-sex, and at the beginning of the year, each residence hall votes on guidelines establishing the visitation policy for members of the opposite sex. For those who still want to avoid institutionalized living, off-campus housing is plentiful and cheap. Students who live on campus choose from a variety of meal-plan options in the university dining hall or in specialty shops.

> "Diverse religions, ethnic makeups, sexual preferences, and educational backgrounds all converge on one campus—from extreme faddish clothing, tattoos, body-piercing, and hair-dyeing to the ultraconservative."

Eight fraternities and eight sororities are a relatively recent addition to campus life, attracting 8 percent of the men and 6 percent of the women. For others, dances, coffee houses, concerts, movies, and other social activities pick up some of the social slack. "Greensboro is a wonderful, old Southern town," reports one student. Bars, restaurants, and stores are within walking distance, and the twenty-three thousand-seat Greensboro Coliseum, a scant two miles away,

> "Greensboro is a wonderful, old Southern town."

regularly plays host to rock bands and athletic events. Weekend trips are to the beach (three hours) or the mountains (two hours).

UNCG teams compete in Division I, and the university offers a comprehensive athletic program as part of the Southern Conference. Men's basketball and tennis and women's soccer have all brought home conference championships and continue to field solid squads. Intramurals are also popular.

Some students complain that Greensboro, living in the shadow of its big sister at Chapel Hill, lacks the reputation it deserves for providing a first-rate education in such diverse fields as liberal arts, nursing, and education. Others say it is becoming somewhat of a commuter school, but it may be too early to tell. With its strong academic offerings, a tight-knit community, and low cost, Greensboro is easily one of North Carolina's best values in higher education.

Overlaps

UNC–Chapel Hill, North Carolina State, Appalachian State, UNC–Charlotte, East Carolina

If You Apply To ➢

UNC–Greensboro: Rolling admissions. Financial aid: Mar. 1. Does not guarantee to meet demonstrated need. Campus interviews: optional, informational. No alumni interviews. SATs or ACTs: required. SAT IIs: optional. No essay question.

North Carolina State University

Box 7103, Raleigh, NC 27695-7103

It is hard for NC State not to have an inferiority complex next to high falutin' neighbors like Duke and UNC. But having them in the neighborhood is also a blessing—just ask the thousands of graduates who have gotten jobs in the Research Triangle. Engineering and business are the most popular programs.

Whether you're looking for a stellar education in engineering and textiles or a top-rated basketball program, North Carolina State is one of the bright leaves of the Tobacco Belt. NCSU offers students the benefits of a large school—reputable professors, a diverse student body, and plenty to do on weekends—while making sure that no one feels left out. Says one junior, "No matter how weird or crazy you are, there is someone just like you on campus."

The 107-year-old, 1,900-acre campus consists of redbrick buildings, brick-lined walks, and cozy courtyards dotted with pine trees. There is no dominant style, but more of an architectural stream-of-consciousness that reveals a campus that grew and changed with time. New facilities include a dining hall and toxicology building.

NCSU excels in the professional areas of engineering, pulp and paper science, statistics, design, agriculture, and forestry, which are the largest and the most demanding divisions. Not surprisingly, given its location in the heart of textile country, the school also boasts a first-rate textile school, the largest and one of the best such programs in the country. Business tops the list of most popular majors, followed by engineering and accounting. Even the most technical of majors requires students to take a broad range of liberal arts courses, although the humanities are far from the biggest game on campus. English and sociology get poor marks from students. University-wide general education requirements include two semesters each of English composition, math, and science, as well as foreign language proficiency and electives in the humanities and social sciences. Freshmen are required to take English and math, and there are numerous seminars and orientation courses in each area of academic interest.

> **"No matter how weird or crazy you are, there is someone just like you on campus."**

An important feature of NC State's approach to education is the cooperative-education program, through which students in all schools can alternate semesters of on-site work with traditional classroom time. There are also domestic and international exchanges with more than ninety-seven countries and a Residential Scholars program in which academic standouts live together and participate in weekly activities such as guest lectures. A First Year College program provides guidance and counseling for incoming students to introduce them to all possible majors. Many classes at State are large, but the faculty gets high grades for being accessible, interested in teaching, and friendly. Says a junior, "On a scale of one to ten, I would rate the quality of teaching here as an eight. I was taught by full professors as a freshman." Aside from regular hassles that come with attending a large school, the academic atmosphere is relatively relaxed. Free tutoring in most subjects is made possible by grants from state industries. The library contains six million volumes and is considered a good place to do research, but it's also a hot social spot.

The university benefits greatly from its relationships with Duke, the University of North Carolina at Chapel Hill, and private industry through the state's high-tech Research Triangle Park. The students at NC State are largely hard-working, bright North Carolinians. Some 91 percent are in-state students. "Students at NC State are

Website: www.ncsu.edu
Location: City suburbs
Total Enrollment: 29,286
Undergraduates: 19,839
Male/Female: 59/41
SAT Ranges: V 520–620
 M 550–660
ACT Range: 23–28
Financial Aid: 32%
Expense: Pub $
Phi Beta Kappa: Yes
Applicants: 11,835
Accepted: 66%
Enrolled: 49%
Grad in 6 Years: 62%
Returning Freshmen: 89%
Academics: ✍ ✍ ✍
Social: ☎ ☎ ☎
Q of L: ★ ★ ★
Admissions: (919) 515-2434
Email Address: undergrad_ admissions@ncsu.edu

Strongest Programs:
 Design
 Statistics
 Engineering
 Pulp and Paper Science
 Agriculture
 Forestry
 Textiles

very friendly, open, and down-to-earth," says a student. Seventy-four percent graduated in the top quarter of their high-school class, and 89 percent attended public high school. Ten percent of the student body is African-American, while Hispanics and Asian-Americans make up another 7 percent. Amid the public-school diversity, conservatism abounds, and the largest political organization is the College Republicans. Jocks and sports fans are visible, and the university offers 412 scholarships for men and women in twenty-two sports. Those with outstanding academic qualifications can compete for one of 108 merit scholarships that range from $1,000 to $23,000 per year. To be considered for merit awards, students must file a separate application in the early fall of their senior year in high school.

As for housing, 33 percent choose to stay on campus in one of twenty dorms. All students are guaranteed rooms for all four years. Sullivan and Lee are recommended for freshmen because they provide a mixture of academic and social activities. Most of the older dorms lack air-conditioning, and are described as "well maintained" though students admit that

"On a scale of one to ten, I would rate the quality of teaching here as an eight. I was taught by full professors as a freshman."

some of the dorms are ancient and need major reconstruction. Rooms range in size from spacious to cramped. Students report that dorm dwelling is actually more expensive than several off-campus units. Two big issues, students report, are parking and financial aid. One students says, "The financial-aid packets have caused me nothing but stress." About 35 percent of the students commute. If you don't mind such minor annoyances, off-campus housing and social activities are plentiful. A small percentage of students are housed in fraternities and sororities, and the international house is also an option. The dining hall feeds all freshmen and anyone else who cares to join the meal plan. It's an all-you-can-eat deal, and students can use their meal cards at numerous campus snack bars and sandwich shops.

As with many other schools, alcohol policies are not strictly enforced. The twenty-one fraternities and five sororities attract about 7 percent of the men and 11 percent of the women. The Greek scene provides much of the entertainment, but dorm and suite parties are also popular, and public transportation affords easy access to downtown, with its shops, restaurants, theaters, and night spots. The university is well integrated into Raleigh, and its proximity to three all-women's colleges helps alleviate the imbalance of the three-to-two male/female ratio. Annual events include Wolfstock, a band party, and an All-Nighter in the student center. Many students also like to head to the beach, which is less than two hours away, or to the ski mountains, which are about a three-and-a-half-hour trip.

With home close by for so many students, the campus does tend to thin out on weekends. Those who stay can cheer on the home teams, which do well in men's tennis, swimming, soccer, football, and men's and women's cross-country and track and field. But needless to say, basketball reigns supreme. The Wolfpack plays in the high-powered Atlantic Coast Conference. "We have an ongoing rivalry with the University of North Carolina," says a junior.

"The financial-aid packets have caused me nothing but stress."

Some crazy NC State fans have stormed nearby Hillsborough Street following game-day victories. The annual State versus Carolina football game usually packs the stadium, and the never-ending fight to "Beat Carolina!" permeates the campus year-round. Intramurals also thrive, and a particularly popular event is Big Four Day, when NC State's intramural teams compete against their neighbors at Duke, Wake Forest, and UNC–Chapel Hill.

North Carolina State seems to have overcome many of the obstacles associated with large land-grant universities. It has attracted a dedicated and friendly student body independent enough to deal with the inevitable anonymity of a state school, but spirited enough to cheer the Wolfpack to victory. NC State works well for both those who can shoot hoops and those who can calculate the trajectory of the same three-point shot.

Northeastern University

360 Huntington Avenue, 150 Richards Hall, Boston, MA 02115

Northeastern is synonymous with preprofessional education and hands-on experience. By interspersing a co-op job with academic study, students can rake in thousands while getting a leg up on the job market. With Boston beckoning, campus life is minimal.

At Northeastern University, students get the benefit of classroom schooling, workplace experience, and real-life exposure to Boston's hustle and bustle. A bonus is the opportunity to mingle with people from different lifestyles in an accepting environment. "Diversity is the word for NU. Every type of person from every walk of life goes here," says a chemical engineering major. It's a contrast to some of the nearby colleges with more homogenous student bodies.

Northeastern's sixty-six-acre campus is an urban oasis located in the heart of Boston, just minutes away from Fenway Park, shopping centers, nightclubs, cafés, Symphony Hall, and the Museum of Fine Arts. The campus's green spaces are interspersed with brick walkways, outdoor art, and a sculpture garden. Older buildings sport utilitarian gray-brick architecture while newer structures are of modern glass and brick design. During inclement weather, students can be found traversing the underground tunnel system that connects many campus buildings. A health sciences building and two residence halls are the latest campus additions.

> "Diversity is the word for NU. Every type of person from every walk of life goes here."

In order to enhance students' academic and co-op experiences, Northeastern University has switched from its academic quarter system to a semester calendar. The calendar will consist of fifteen-week semesters in the fall and spring and two 7½-week sessions in the summer. Full-time undergraduates will typically take classes for eight semesters and complete a total of three six-month co-ops during their five years at Northeastern. For students in the College of Arts and Sciences, there are many alternatives to the co-op, such as internships, study abroad, and undergraduate research opportunities. Each of the six colleges presents its own core curriculum, but all freshmen must complete English and diversity requirements. Freshmen are also required to attend the summer orientation program. New programs include an M.S. in physician assistant studies and B.S. degrees in architecture, information sciences, and computer engineering. An honors program is open to top students in all departments.

For six months' worth of work, students average nearly $12,000, which is generally used to defray college-related costs. Most of the jobs are in the Boston area and related to the student's major, and about half of Northeastern's grads, especially those in the more technical fields, end up taking jobs with one of their co-op

Website: www.neu.edu
Location: Urban
Total Enrollment: 18,180
Undergraduates: 13,963
Male/Female: 51/49
SAT Ranges: V 520-620
   M 540-640
ACT Range: 22–27
Financial Aid: 62%
Expense: Pr $ $ $
Phi Beta Kappa: No
Applicants: 16,173
Accepted: 63%
Enrolled: 29%
Grad in 6 Years: 50%
Returning Freshmen: 84%
Academics: ✐ ✐
Social: ☎ ☎
Q of L: ★ ★
Admissions: (617) 373-2200
Email Address:
   admissions@neu.edu

Strongest Programs:
   Business
   Health Professions
   Engineering
   Art
   Architecture
   Psychology
   Computer Science

(Continued)
Criminology

employers. Students warn, however, against becoming overly reliant on co-op advisors for good jobs or good advice. Plus, some students say that when the economy is on a downswing, co-op jobs are tougher to come by. Besides the money they can earn in co-op programs, outstanding students can compete for 1,462 merit scholarships that range from $2,500 to $32,000. And there are 279 athletic scholarships for a wide range of sports.

Undergrads say that most of their teachers are concerned with their needs, and most of Northeastern's classes have thirty-five or fewer students. A senior says, "Most professors avoid straight lecturing and use more interactive teaching methods." Scheduling can be difficult, as students sometimes find that courses they want are offered only when they're scheduled to be away on a job.

Northeastern, which was founded as a YMCA educational program, has traditionally served many local students from diverse socioeconomic backgrounds. Forty percent of the students are from Massachusetts, and most of the rest are from nearby states. African-Americans comprise 6 percent of the population. Hispanics makeup 4 percent of the student body, and Asian-Americans 8 percent. NU students find

Freshmen spend their first year, and seniors their last term, on campus. In between, students alternate eight quarters of study with either seven or eight on the job.

> **"Most professors avoid straight lecturing and use more interactive teaching methods."**

there is more than lip-service to diversity. "Pretty liberal thinkers," says a finance and political science student. But because so many participate in the co-op program, many "don't have a good connection to the university," says a senior. Northeastern has partnered with SquashBusters, a program in which urban middle- and high-school students receive tutoring and mentoring. They erected a new building, the SquashBusters Clubhouse, which is open to NU students for their own games.

Although 91 percent of freshmen live on campus, upperclassmen have a much harder time finding a place to sleep on campus. Some of the dorms have been showing their age, but NU recently completed several new residence halls, including the West Village complex, a thirteen-story apartment megaplex that houses up to six hundred students. "They're building dorms like crazy!" says one student. Off-campus options include privately owned apartments or suites located adjacent to the residence halls. Students speak highly of NU Public Safety.

The co-op program puts a strain on campus social life.

The co-op program puts a strain on campus social life. There are many clubs and activities, but the continuous flow of students on and off the campus tends to be disruptive. "I may see a friend one quarter in class and then not again for six months. It's hard to stay connected," a student explains. Fraternities and sororities attract 8 percent of the students. Those who are not in the Greek system find Boston with all its attractions to be a fully acceptable substitute.

In the winter, students head to the ski slopes of Vermont, and in balmier weather they're off to the beaches of Cape Cod and the North Shore. Not surprisingly in the city the Celtics made famous, the basketball team attracts adoring fans, especially after having produced the late Celtic star Reggie Lewis. But the biggest sports series of the year is the Beanpot Hockey Tournament, which pits

> **"I may see a friend one quarter in a class and then not again for six months. It's hard to stay connected."**

Northeastern against rival teams from Harvard, Boston College, and Boston University. Northeastern's female pucksters have frequently prevailed as champs. And the fleet-footed men's and women's track and cross-country teams, who work out in the newly renovated Bernard Solomon Indoor Track Facility, regularly leave their opponents blinking in the dust. The competitive nature of the sports teams, especially toward those also in the Boston area, is epitomized by one T-shirt that reads, "No—we don't want to B.U."

Northeastern is not the place for students seeking the traditional collegiate experience. But it is a school where people can easily fit in and be accepted, as long as they

Overlaps

Boston University, University of Massachusetts at Amherst, Boston College, University of Connecticut, University of New Hampshire have a good idea of what they want to do in life, or at least a strong desire to find out. If their co-op experience does not turn into a permanent job, it certainly gives them a jump on the job market over graduates who receive a traditional education.

Northwestern University

1801 Hinman Avenue, P.O. Box 3060, Evanston, IL 60204-3060

The most selective university in the Midwest. The Big Ten is not the Ivy League, and NU has more school spirit than its Eastern counterparts. Much more preprofessional than its nearby rival University of Chicago and than all of the Ivies but Penn. World renowned in journalism.

Northwestern University may have finally proved to the rest of the world what its students and faculty have known all along: NU is a school of winners. The university was briefly thrust into the national spotlight in 1995, when the long-suffering football team placed first in the Big Ten conference and went to the Rose Bowl. The hard work, pride, and dedication that were evident on the football field are also present in the academic halls of this challenging university. Northwestern has become a "hot" school seen on a par with the Ivies even though it lacks the strong liberal arts core of the great Eastern schools. Sleek new buildings with the latest technology are giving even more luster to prestigious programs.

Northwestern is situated on 231 acres about a dozen miles north of the Chicago Loop. Evanston is "gorgeous," students say, its leafy shores looking out on the sailboat-filled Lake Michigan in warm weather, and "lake effect" snow combining with the real thing to make it a Currier & Ives painting in winter. The newer buildings are located adjacent to a fourteen-acre lagoon, part of an eighty-five-acre lakefill addition built in the '60s.

> "The quarter system makes the academic climate at NU intense. It feels like people are constantly studying for midterms or finals."

This area provides students with a prime location for picnicking, fishing, running, cycling, rollerblading, or just daydreaming. Among the new additions to the campus are a 184-bed apartment-style dorm and a $125 million renovation to the Technological Institute.

As for the academic climate, Northwestern offers a choice of some widely known programs; among the six undergraduate schools, the School of Speech, the Medill School of Journalism, the School of Music, and the McCormick School of Engineering and Applied Science have national reputations. The School of Speech has excellent departments across the board, from theater and radio/TV/film to communicative disorders. The School of Journalism offers invaluable experience and the opportunity to make important job contacts through ten-week internships at fifty-two newspapers, forty-one magazines, and nineteen television stations across the nation. There's also a four-year accelerated B.S.J./M.S.J. program. A dazzling electronic studio centralizes Medill's state-of-the-art broadcast newsroom

Website:
   www.northwestern.edu
Location: Suburban
Total Enrollment: 15,649
Undergraduates: 7,816
Male/Female: 47/53
SAT Ranges: V 640–730
   M 660–750
ACT Range: 28–32
Financial Aid: 50%
Expense: Pr $ $ $ $
Phi Beta Kappa: Yes
Applicants: 13,988
Accepted: 34%
Enrolled: 41%
Grad in 5 Years: 92%
Returning Freshmen: 96%
Academics: 🖉 🖉 🖉 🖉 🖉
Social: ☎ ☎ ☎
Q of L: ★ ★ ★
Admissions: (847) 491-7271
Email Address: ug-admission
   @northwestern.edu

Strongest Programs:
   Engineering
   Economics
   Journalism
   Communications Studies
   Psychology

(Continued)
Theater
Music performance

and the speech school's radio/TV/film department. The McCormick School of Engineering and Applied Science is particularly strong in all aspects of engineering, and five-year co-op options are available. The physical and social sciences are the strongest of the liberal arts. The Asian studies program is newest on the academic roster.

Fine arts programs in the music school, particularly in the brass and wind departments, enhance the university's offerings, and a new major in dance has already drawn attention from students. There are many accelerated and combined-degree programs. Special academics programs like the Center for the Writing Arts, which sponsors one or more professional writers of national prominence to teach undergraduate courses, conduct seminars and present readings and discussions of their own work, are highly praised. Interdisciplinary programs, ranging from American culture, integrated arts, mathematical methods in the social sciences, and integrated sciences, are offered in eighteen fields. The Weinberg College of Arts and Sciences has a Junior Tutorial Program, in which small groups of under-grads in a variety of fields work with senior faculty members on advanced topics.

"The quality of teaching is out of this world."

Each of the undergraduate schools determines its own general education requirements, but the distribution requirements are similar. Each school requires a graduate to have coursework in "the major domains of knowledge"—science, mathematics and technology, individual and social behavior, historical studies, values, the humanities, and the fine arts. Unlike most schools on a ten-week quarter system, Northwesterners take four (not three) courses each quarter, except in engineering, where five are permitted. A senior says, "The quarter system makes the academic climate at NU intense. It feels like people are constantly studying for midterms or finals." The Primal Scream before each finals period (at the appointed time, everyone opens their window and screams) does help to relieve a small bit of the tension. Students can also take a break from the campus through any of twenty field-study programs and programs abroad in twenty-eight countries. Perhaps one reason students study so hard is the motivation provided by their professors. Most seem in awe of NU faculty members. "The quality of teaching is out of this world," says one senior. "I

"Most people have definite goals and work hard toward achieving them."

am friends now with so many of my teachers because they cared about my work and my ideas and my growth." Virtually all undergraduate courses, including required freshman seminars (of ten to fifteen students) in arts and sciences, are taught by regular faculty members. Introductory courses are larger than most, but the average 100-level class size is about thirty students. In response to student complaints, the university has expanded the advisory system.

All buildings are connected to the campus's fiberoptic system, so students can access the library and Internet from their rooms. They are supported by student consultants who live in each residence hall and are on call 24/7 to provide computer support. The library contains 4.15 million volumes. Its resources online include the catalog, more than seven hundred journals, and more than two hundred databases and indexes.

The abundance of preprofessionals has added to Northwestern's image as "young corporate America," and the acceptance rate for medical-school applicants is 63 percent while that of graduates at schools of business and law hovers around 90 percent.

Seventy-eight percent of the student body come from outside Illinois borders, and 82 percent graduated in the top tenth of their high-school class. Minorities represent 34 percent of the student body, with Asian-Americans accounting for 17 percent, African-Americans 6 percent, and Hispanics 5 percent. Some call the political atmosphere on campus "apathetic" or "conservative and passive"; others call it being driven toward achievement. "Most people have definite goals and work hard toward achieving them," says a senior. The abundance of preprofessionals has added to Northwestern's image as "young corporate America," and the acceptance rate for medical-school applicants is 63 percent while that of graduates at schools of business and law hovers around 90 percent. There are no academic merit scholarships, but NU does guarantee to meet the full demonstrated need of every admit, and it provides more than three hundred scholarships for its athletes. Loans for middle-income families are available through the university.

In response to student complaints, the university has expanded the advisory system.

With the addition of two residence halls in the past few years, there is now ample on-campus housing. "Rooms are spacious compared to other schools," says a junior. "My friends are always in awe of how big they are." However, housing is guaranteed only to freshmen. Dorms range from small single-sex houses to large coed buildings, the most popular of which are organized in suites of eight students around a common living room. Students may join thematic or nonthematic residential colleges, which bring students and faculty members together during faculty "firesides" or simply over meals. Themes for the residential colleges include communications, international studies, humanities, commerce and industry, performing arts, public affairs, and engineering. Fraternities and sororities also have their own houses. Students can choose to eat at the coffee house or any one of the many dining halls on campus. A variety of meal plans are available, including one that provides Sunday brunch and one offering Kosher food. Evanston offers some comfortable apartments to the 32 percent who live off campus, but rents are high and zoning laws prohibit occupancy of a house or apartment by more than three unrelated people. As for security, one student says, "Even though the campus is located so close to Chicago, I feel extremely safe."

"Our administration and the city government are always fighting."

Students agree that Evanston is not a great college town, and in fact there has traditionally been hostility between townspeople and students. "Our administration and the city government are always fighting," says one student. Another student feels the tension is lessening, and says, "One mayoral candidate ran on an 'anti-NU' platform and was soundly defeated." The town has built a new complex with a cineplex, hotel, and shopping mall.

For a night out, of course, there is that "toddlin' town," Chicago, right across the border. For those who don't think Chicago is their kind of town, Evanston will do nicely with its many excellent restaurants and trendy bars. Much of the social life on campus is centered around the Greek system, and 30 percent of the men and 39 percent of the women go Greek. For non-Greeks, on-campus entertainment opportunities are numerous, including theater productions, concerts, and movies. The school's alcohol policy is tough, but not always effective. "They don't really want us to have it, but students get it anyway," says one senior. The student government and Activities and Organizations Board sponsor an array of campus-wide events, such as the very popular thirty-hour Dance Marathon and Dillo Day, an end-of-the-year party with numerous bands and other activities. Another tradition is upheld when representatives of student organizations slip out in the dead of night to paint their colors and slogans on a centrally located rock. As a bonus to the social atmosphere as well as to educational hands-on experience, the campus has its own radio station, television studio, and award-winning newspaper, and, says one administrator, "Certainly any student who wishes to act, produce, direct, conduct, build scenery, or play in a musical ensemble has ample opportunity to do so."

The student government and Activities and Organizations Board sponsor an array of campuswide events, such as the very popular thirty-hour Dance Marathon and Dillo Day, an end-of-the-year party with numerous bands and other activities.

Football and tailgate parties are a traditional way of bringing alumni back and rousing the students to support the only non-state school in the Big Ten. The men's golf team brought home consecutive Big Ten championships in 1999, 2000, and 2001. The women's tennis team did that, and won again in 2002. Other competitive women's teams include volleyball, softball, field hockey, swimming, and NU's newest varsity sport: women's lacrosse. As far as facilities, NU is on par with many schools its size and larger, with the beautiful Norris Aquatics Center/Henry Crown

Sports Pavilion and the Nicolet Football and Conference Center, used for conditioning of varsity athletes. Then there is the Gleacher Golf Center, which the college boasts is "the finest indoor learning center in the collegiate world." The student-sponsored intramural program provides vigorous competition among teams from dorms and rival fraternities.

Adding to the luster of Northwestern's rising star are many more sleek new facilities and technological updates. One senior sums it up, saying, "The campus is gorgeous, it's right near Chicago, and the people are involved and interesting and diverse. It has the rigor and reputation of an elite university with a nice dose of Midwestern practicality and friendliness."

University of Notre Dame

220 Main Bldg., Notre Dame, IN 46556

The Holy Grail of higher education for many Roman Catholics. ND's heartland location and 85 percent Catholic enrollment make it a bastion of traditional values. Offers business and engineering in addition to the liberal arts. ND's personality is much closer to Boston College than Georgetown.

Website: www.nd.edu
Location: City outskirts
Total Enrollment: 11,054
Undergraduates: 8,208
Male/Female: 54/46
SAT Ranges: V 620–720
　M 640–730
ACT Range: 30–32
Financial Aid: 43%
Expense: Pr $ $ $ $
Phi Beta Kappa: Yes
Applicants: 9,385
Accepted: 36%
Enrolled: 61%
Grad in 6 Years: 94%
Returning Freshmen: 97%
Academics: ✎ ✎ ✎ ✎
Social: ☎ ☎ ☎
Q of L: ★ ★ ★
Admissions: (574) 631-7505
Email Address:
　admissio.1@nd.edu

Founded 159 years ago by the French priest Edward Sorin, the University of Notre Dame has come a long way from its fledgling days in a rustic log cabin. While it describes itself as "a Catholic academic community of higher learning," students need not be affiliated with the Roman Catholic church. According to the administration, "What the university asks of all its scholars is not a particular creedal affiliation, but a respect for the objectives of Notre Dame and a willingness to enter into the conversation that gives it life and character." An interest in football doesn't hurt, either.

With a total of 1,250 acres of rolling hills, twin lakes, and woods, the university offers a peaceful setting for studying. The lofty Golden Dome that rises above the ivy-covered Gothic and modern buildings and the old brick stadium, where in the 1920s Knute Rockne made the Fighting Irish almost synonymous with college football, are national symbols.

Liberal education is more than just a catchphrase at Notre Dame. No matter what their major, students must take the First Year of Studies, one of the most extensive academic and counseling programs of any university in the nation. The core of the program is a one-semester university seminar that is limited to twenty students per section and is writing-intensive. The remainder of each freshman's schedule is reserved for the first of a comprehensive list of general education requirements: one semester each in writing and mathematics and two semesters in natural science, as well as one semester chosen from theology, philosophy, history, social science, and fine arts. The First Year of Studies program also includes a strong counseling component in which peer advisors are assigned to each student, as are academic advisors and tutors if necessary. Administrators are quick to point out that, due in part to the success of the first-year support program, a whopping 97 percent of the freshmen make it through and return for sophomore year—the highest retention rate in the nation.

In the College of Arts and Letters, highly regarded departments include English, theology, and philosophy, while physics and chemistry are tops in the College of Science. Within the engineering school, chemical engineering rules. The College of Business Administration's accountancy program is ranked among the nation's best, and the chemistry labs in the Nieuwland Science Hall have first-rate equipment. While weak departments are hard to come by at Notre Dame, some students complain about the creative arts programs. The academic climate at Notre Dame is said

to be fairly rigorous. "The workload is very demanding," says a senior. "It requires the student to have very good time-management skills." And while the atmosphere is competitive, students agree that it is not cut-throat by any measure. Faculty members are praised for being dynamic, personable, knowledgeable, and accessible. "The professors here care a great deal about their students and it shows," says a biology major. Students report that it is sometimes hard to get all the classes you want during a particular semester, but that it's not difficult to graduate in four years.

Notre Dame offers a variety of special academic programs and options. One of the most popular is the Program of Liberal Studies (PLS), in which students study art, philosophy, literature, and the history of Western thought within their Great Books seminars. The Kaneb Center for Teaching and Learning, the university's most recent commitment to teaching, is based in DeBartolo Hall, an eighty-four-classroom complex with state-of-the-art computer and audiovisual equipment. The Arts and Letters Program for Administrators combines a second business major with liberal learning, and the College of Science also allows students the option of pursuing majors in two departments. In addition, Notre Dame offers programs in military and naval science, aerospace studies, and an international study program that allows students to travel to numerous countries around the world.

With a predominantly lay board of trustees and faculty, Notre Dame remains committed to "the preservation of a distinctly Catholic community." The president and several other top administrators are priests of the Congregation of the Holy Cross, and each dorm has its own chapel with daily Masses. Nearly 85 percent of the students are Catholic, leaving some skepticism about the comfort level of those who are not. Students feel Notre Dame nurtures their faith as well as their minds. The main social issues discussed on campus include abortion, gender and racial issues, homosexuality, and faith. Diversity is also a concern, and some students feel that it is a big problem. Minority enrollment is growing. African-Americans and Hispanics make up 10 percent of the student body, and Asian-Americans another 4 percent. Despite its relative cultural homogeneity, Notre Dame

A whopping 97 percent of the freshmen make it through and return for sophomore year—the highest retention rate in the nation.

"The workload is very demanding. It requires the students to have very good time-management skills."

recruits from all over the country; 88 percent of the students are from outside Indiana. The university offers competitive academic scholarships to students with outstanding high-school records and financial need, and 392 athletic scholarships are available.

Dorm life at Notre Dame appeals to 76 percent of the students. "Notre Dame dorm life is extraordinary," says a junior. "The dorm rooms are all very well-kept and very comfortable." Once assigned to a dorm during their freshman year, students are encouraged to stay in the same one until graduation. Fraternities are banned, and freshmen are spread out among all campus dorms. The single-sex dorms really become surrogate fraternities and sororities that breed a similar spirit of community and family. Parietal rules (midnight on weekdays, 2 A.M. on weekends) are strictly enforced. Boarders eat in either the North Quad or South Quad cafeterias, and must buy a nineteen-meal plan. For those who tire of institutional cuisine, the Huddle offers plenty of fast-food options as well as a pay-as-you-go snack bar. Students can also reserve the kitchen to cook their own meals.

Notre Dame has been open to female applicants since 1972, and with a fifty-five to forty-five breakdown in the freshman class, the ratio is now comparable to many other formerly all-male schools. ND's social life isn't as rambunctious as it once was, thanks to the policy that forbids alcohol at campus social events. The rules relating to alcohol in the dorms are a bit more relaxed, though kegs and drinking in the hallways are prohibited. For those who choose not to indulge, there are several groups dedicated to good times without alcohol. Most activities take place on campus

"Notre Dame dorm life is extraordinary."

and include parties, concerts, and movies. Each dorm holds theme dances about twice a month, and there's always the annual Screw Your Roommate weekend, where students are paired with the blind dates selected by their roomies. Another popular event is the An Tostal Festival, which comes the week before spring finals and guarantees to temporarily relieve academic anxiety with its "childish" games such as pie-eating contests and Jell-O wrestling. The annual Sophomore Literary Festival is entirely student-run and draws prominent writers and poets from across the country. Students are involved in the community through volunteer work. "Notre Dame students are very active in the community through a variety of service organizations," says a junior. The best outlet for culture is nearby Chicago, about ninety minutes away.

The talk of the fall semester at ND typically is football. With its proud gridiron heritage, there's nothing like the Fighting Irish spirit. From Knute Rockne and the Gipper right on down to modern-day greats like Joe Montana, the spirit of Notre Dame football reigns supreme. With new coach Tyrone Willingham in charge, the football squad racked up an impressive winning record and convinced many that the program is returning to its former glory. It wasn't intentional—at least that's what they say—but the giant mosaic of Jesus Christ on the library lifts his hands toward the heavens as if to signal yet another Irish touchdown. Tailgate parties are also celebrated events, occurring before and after the game.

Aside from football, Notre Dame offers one of the strongest all-around athletic programs in the country with nationally ranked teams in women's soccer, volleyball, basketball, tennis, softball, and fencing, and men's tennis, lacrosse, fencing, baseball, and cross-country.

"Notre Dame students are very active in the community through a variety of service organizations."

Diehard jocks who can't make the varsity will find plenty of company in ND's very competitive intramural leagues. The Bookstore Basketball Tournament, which is the largest five-on-five, single-elimination hoops tournament in the world with more than seven hundred teams competing, lasts for a month.

Everyone at the university, from administrators to students, is considered part of the "Notre Dame family." Traditions are held in high esteem. For those looking for high-quality academics, a friendly, caring environment, and an excellent athletics program, ND could be just the place.

Oberlin College

101 North Professor Street, Carnegie Building, Oberlin, OH 44074-1075

The college that invented nonconformity. From the Underground Railroad to the modern peace movement, Obies have been front and center. As at Reed and Grinnell, Oberlin's curriculum is less radical than its students. Oberlin is especially strong in the sciences, and its music conservatory is among the nation's best.

New and contrasting ideas are nothing new at Oberlin College, a liberal arts school tucked away in a small Ohio town. After all, it was the first American college to accept women and minorities. That pioneering spirit has not faded. With diverse academic challenges ranging from cinema studies to neuroscience, Obies thrive on higher thinking and exploring their myriad talents. The students here are "interesting, and more importantly, interested," one student says.

Oberlin's attractive campus features a mix of Italian Renaissance buildings (four designed by Cass Gilbert), late nineteenth- and early-twentieth century organic stone structures, and some less interesting 1950s barracks-type dorms. The buildings rise over flatlands typical of the Midwest, which do little to stop brutal winter winds. The Allen Art Museum, sometimes mentioned in the same breath as Harvard's and Yale's, is one of the loveliest buildings on campus, with a brick-paved, flower-laden courtyard and a fountain. An environmental studies building was dedicated in 2000, and another science center is under construction.

Oberlin has been a leader among liberal arts colleges seeking to promote their science offerings; biology and chemistry are two of the college's strongest departments, and undergraduates may major in interdisciplinary programs like neuroscience and biopsychology. Students rave about the religion department, where profs are "at the top of their game." Oberlin's conservatory of music holds a well-deserved spot among the nation's most prominent performance schools; the voice, violin, and TIMARA (Technology in Music and Related Arts) programs are especially praised. English is also lauded, and—not surprisingly at such a liberal school—interdisciplinary and self-created majors, such as black, Latin American, Russian, Third World, and women's studies, are popular. East Asian studies have long been outstanding at Oberlin as well; a

> **"We don't hide books from each other or erase term papers or steal research."**

study-abroad program at China's Yunnan University is available, and the two-year Shansi fellowship in an Asian country is a popular and sought-after post-graduate goal. The college has added a cinema/film studies major.

Oberlin's students are as serious about their schoolwork as they are about politics, justice, and other social causes. Courses are rigorous; heavy workloads and the occasional Saturday-morning class are the norm. Still, this is no smackdown school. "We don't hide books from each other or erase term papers or steal research," a religion major says. "It is an open atmosphere, very supportive and communal." Oberlin kids ask a lot of questions, which is how their professors like it. "We want an education more than a GPA," one student says. The pressure is somewhat minimized by the

Website: www.oberlin.edu
Location: Small town
Total Enrollment: 2,863
Undergraduates: 2,840
Male/Female: 43/57
SAT Ranges: V 630–730
  M 610–700
ACT Range: 26–31
Financial Aid: 55%
Expense: Pr $ $ $ $
Phi Beta Kappa: Yes
Applicants: 5,548
Accepted: 36%
Enrolled: 36%
Grad in 6 Years: 77%
Returning Freshmen: 90%
Academics: ✐ ✐ ✐ ✐ ½
Social: ☎ ☎ ☎ ☎
Q of L: ★ ★ ★ ★
Admissions: (440) 775-8411
Email Address: college.
  admissions@oberlin.edu

Strongest Programs:
  Neuroscience
  Biology
  Physics
  Creative Writing
  Environmental Studies
  Politics
  East Asian Studies
  Religion
  Music Performance

credit/no-entry policy, which allows students to take an unlimited number of grade-free courses (if they can get in). Plus, anything below a C is scratched from a student's transcript. Generally, however, students at Oberlin are gifted and want to challenge themselves. Recognizing that, most departments offer group and individual independent study opportunities and invite selected students to pursue demanding honors programs, especially during their senior year. Professors are "as excited about teaching as students are about learning," says a biology and dance major.

There are no requirements for freshmen at Oberlin, but general education requirements include proficiency in writing and math and nine credit hours in each of the three divisions—arts and humanities, math/natural sciences, and social sciences—plus another nine credit hours in cultural diversity courses, which include a foreign language. Students are also required to take one-quarter of the semester hours needed to graduate outside their major's division, and to participate in three January terms, during which they pursue month-long projects, traditional or unique, on or off campus. About twenty-five different freshman/sophomore colloquia are available, with enrollment limited to fifteen students each, and though the majority of other classes are limited to twenty-five students, the computerized registration system makes it easy to get in.

One of Oberlin's more unusual offerings is EXCO, an experimental college that offers students and interested townsfolk the chance to teach one another. "EXCO classes range from beer-making to sexual information to martial arts to the Beatles discography," notes one student. "Oberlin is a place that values almost any form of knowledge." Many learning opportunities are available beyond the town of Oberlin as well, with about 40 percent of students taking advantage of semesters at the Oberlin Center of European Studies in Strasbourg, France, or programs in China, London, France, Germany, and Dublin through the Great Lakes Colleges Association.* Sea lovers can travel to Mystic Seaport.* Back on campus, the Mudd Library has more than 1.5 million volumes and is a superb facility for research and studying or socializing; the famous A-level is the place to be on weeknights. Even more special is the music conservatory, with its 153 practice rooms, substantial music library, and more Steinway pianos under one roof (175 grands, twenty-one uprights) than anywhere else in the world. Qualified students can earn both a B.M. and a B.A. in a five-year dual degree program.

> "EXCO classes range from beer-making to sexual information to martial arts to the Beatles discography."

Obies are "sharp, honest, self-motivated, and self-questioning," says one student. Two-thirds come from public school and 74 percent are white. Still, 82 percent of students are from out of state, hailing primarily from the Mid-Atlantic states. African-Americans account for 8 percent of the student body, Asian-Americans 6 percent, and Hispanics 4 percent. Initiatives to increase diversity at Oberlin include advisors from various ethnic and racial backgrounds and a multicultural resource center with a full-time director. The campus is politically active, with issues of sexuality, race, and gender coming to the fore. One theater major says, "The campus is far left." A popular annual event is the Drag Ball, sponsored by the Lesbian Gay Bisexual Union, in which half the student body shows up in full drag. The event includes a runway competition and a disco string orchestra, and brought MTV's cameras to campus a few years ago. "Safer Sex Night is also quite an event,' says a sophomore. The annual Folk Fest attracts artists like Dar Williams, and students can drive to the majestic Severance Hall in Cleveland for some more serious tunes.

Seventy percent of Oberlin's students live on campus. They choose from among twenty-five dorms, ranging in size from fifteen to 235 people, several of which focus on foreign languages. "They're diverse architecturally and socially," notes one student. Some are stupendous: "We're talking closets so big they have windows." Students are guaranteed housing, but your choices get better as you gain upperclass standing. Only one dorm is single-sex; all dorms are four-class except Barrows, which is reserved for freshmen. The best dorms are said to be the program houses, including French House, African Heritage House, Russian House, and Third World House. Seniors and lucky juniors can land the preferred singles (thanks to their standing or good lottery numbers), but many move into cheaper off-campus apartments, although only a fraction are allowed off the college's meal plan. Oberlin's dining-hall system includes six dining rooms in four buildings, chosen through another lottery. An appetizing alternative to institutional fare can be found at one of the six co-ops that comprise the Oberlin Student Cooperative Association (OSCA), a $1 million-a-year corporation run entirely by students. Co-opers plan and prepare their own meals, and though only 12 percent of the student body actually live in these houses, almost 25 percent take their meals there, enjoying everything from homemade bread to whatever's left in the pantry before the next food shipment arrives.

Six dining co-ops comprise the Oberlin Student Cooperative Association (OSCA), a $1 million-a-year corporation run entirely by students.

Social life, like so much of the Oberlin experience, is what you make of it, students report. One student describes it as "tremendous" saying, "We're in the middle of farmland, yet I'm rarely bored." Another agrees, "It becomes a question of what can be fit into one's schedule." House parties, plays, movies, and conservatory performances are planned every other night. And

"We're in the middle of farmland, yet I'm rarely bored."

since there's no Greek system, nothing is exclusive. As for drinking, underage students can finagle booze, and of-age students are allowed to imbibe in their rooms.

The "tiny but complete" town of Oberlin offers the essentials, students say, including "a small-town movie theater, two bookstores, pizza places, banks, grocery stores, and a bakery with great doughnuts." Town-gown relations are symbiotic; "There's a lot of give and take on many levels," a philosophy major opines. Hospitals and a mentoring program for college-bound kids attract many Obies. If all else fails, Cleveland—including the Rock and Roll Hall of Fame and major league baseball—is ninety minutes away. "Trips to Cleveland for a nice dinner or a performance or protest are common," says a student. Other good road trips are Chicago (six hours) and Washington, D.C. (six-and-a-half hours).

Oberlin competes in the Division III athletics, but the varsity sports have lukewarm followings. That may be because Oberlin is a charter member of the North Coast Athletic Conference, which emphasizes scholarship and considers women's sports on par with men's. Women's lacrosse and tennis have both captured the NCAC championship in recent years; other decent teams include men's swimming, men's and women's soccer and track and field, and women's basketball. Participation in club sports, particularly rugby and Ultimate Frisbee, is on the rise, and there is now a golf team.

Oberlin might be small in size, but its emphasis on global learning, undergraduate research, and a vibrant liberal arts education helps it bust those statistical seams. Students are more likely to discuss local poverty than the quality of cereal choices in the dining halls, and can be found playing a Steinway or plugging away at astronomy. No matter what you find Obies doing, they'll be doing it their way. Like a popular Oberlin T-shirt says: "Think one person can change the world? We do."

Overlaps

Wesleyan, Brown, Vassar, Carleton, Swarthmore

If You Apply To ➤

Oberlin: Early decision: Nov. 15, Jan. 2. Regular admissions: Jan. 15. Financial aid: Feb. 15. Housing: June 1. Guarantees to meet demonstrated need. Campus and alumni interviews: recommended, evaluative. SATs or ACTs: required. SAT IIs: recommended. Accepts the Common Application and electronic applications. Essay question: Why Oberlin?

Occidental College

1600 Campus Road, Los Angeles, CA 90041

Oxy is a diverse, urban, streetwise cousin to the more upscale and suburban Claremont Colleges. Plentiful internships and study abroad give Oxy students real-world perspectives. Oxy's innovative diplomacy and world affairs program features internships in Washington and at the UN.

Website: www.oxy.edu
Location: Urban
Total Enrollment: 1,726
Undergraduates: 1,697
Male/Female: 41/59
SAT Ranges: V 540–660
  M 550–650
Financial Aid: 82%
Expense: Pr $ $ $ $
Phi Beta Kappa: Yes
Applicants: 3,276
Accepted: 57%
Enrolled: 25%
Grad in 6 Years: 75%
Returning Freshmen: 91%
Academics: ✑ ✑ ✑ ✑
Social: ☎ ☎ ☎
Q of L: ★ ★ ★ ★
Admissions: (323) 259-2700
Email Address:
  admission@oxy.edu

Strongest Programs:
  English
  Biology
  Theater
  Politics
  Economics
  Psychology
  Diplomacy and World Affairs

Occidental College is one of a handful of small colleges located in a big city. While some might feel stifled at a school with only 1,700 students, remember that Oxy is spitting distance from the glitz of Beverly Hills and the goofiness of Disneyland. Most students seem to appreciate the close-knit atmosphere fostered here and wouldn't have it any other way. "It's so friendly," says one student. "It truly feels like a family."

Set against the backdrop of the San Gabriel Mountains, Occidental's self-contained Mediterranean-style campus is a secluded enclave of flowers and trees between Pasadena and Glendale, minutes from downtown Los Angeles. Inside this urban oasis resides a thriving community of high achievers who don't for a moment believe that the liberal arts are dead, or even wounded. Required first-year cultural studies seminars include topics in human history and culture, emphasizing learning skills, critical thought, and a wide range of human activities, including art, philosophy, politics, and literature. Students must also complete one year each of English writing, foreign language, and science (with lab), one semester each of fine arts, math, and pre-industrial-era coursework, and three semesters of world cultures courses. Most students consider the core program, with its small classes and intimate labs, worthwhile. Upper-level classes often enroll fewer than a dozen students, and if students can't graduate in four years because classes were closed or were not offered, Oxy will pay for any necessary extra semesters. All this makes for lots of hard work. A sophomore says, "Students are competitive, but generally with themselves and not with other students." One student wryly says, "Transfer students make me nervous. Jeez, take a chill pill. It's only college."

"It's so friendly. It truly feels like a family."

As rigorous as its requirements are, Occidental encourages diverse learning experiences through internships, independent study, and study abroad. Students also can propose an Independent Pattern of Study to avoid a fixed distribution of courses. Independent study on special projects is possible under an honors program for outstanding students, and all departments offer honors courses. For aspiring techies, there is a computer science "emphasis," but no major. There is, however, a cognitive science major that combines math, philosophy, computers, and psychology. As for quality, many of Occidental's academic departments are excellent, with biology, psychology, politics, and an innovative diplomacy and world affairs program among the strongest, and economics the most popular. The college even has its own marine biology research vessel, the Vantuna. Perhaps because of Oxy's small size, the American studies, classics, and women's studies departments have less prowess, and there are no communications or foreign language majors. However, owing to Oxy's location, the television and film program is said to be strong.

Faculty members are readily available in and out of the classroom, and teaching is one of Occidental's strong points. "The quality of teaching at this institution is magnificent," says a sophomore. Emphasis is on ideas and their application, not memorization of meaningless facts. The great majority of classes have twenty-five or fewer students, and the university will not cancel classes because of small enrollment. And, since academic advisors are responsible for about four students per class (sixteen total), personal relationships develop quickly. "Professors are not only brilliant researchers but truly committed educators," says a kinesiology major. "They seem to really care about students' best interests." For those going stir-crazy on campus, Oxy has study-abroad programs in Western Europe, Japan, China, Mexico, Nepal, Zimbabwe, Hungary, Costa Rica, and Russia. For politicos, there's Oxy-in-Washington and Oxy-at-the-U.N. There are also 3–2 engineering programs with Cal Tech and Columbia University, exchange programs with Spelman and Morehouse colleges in Atlanta, and cross-registration privileges with Cal Tech and Pasadena's Art Center College of Design. Students may also take advantage of a new 4–2 biotechnology program with Keck Graduate Institute (of the Claremont Colleges).

A car—your own or someone else's—is practically a necessity, though the college runs a weekend shuttle service to Old Town Pasadena.

Occidental students represent forty-four states and twenty-six foreign countries. Whites comprise only slightly more than half of the student population; African-Americans make up 7 percent, Hispanics 14 percent, and Asian-Americans 15 percent. Perhaps not surprisingly, students tend to be liberal. Says one junior, "Oxy students are liberal and outgoing, effervescent, studious, trendy, diverse, and eager to learn." Since 1989, students here have won three

"Oxy students are liberal and outgoing, effervescent, studious, trendy, diverse, and eager to learn."

Rhodes scholarships, three Marshall scholarships, five Truman scholarships, three Fullbright fellowships, and a handful of other significant awards—proving that these students are no Oxy-morons. Administrators say "excellence and equity in education" is Oxy's top priority, though admission is not need-blind. Still, the college does offer a varying number of merit scholarships each year, ranging from $10,000 to $17,500. There are no athletic scholarships.

Students rave about Oxy's friendly and supportive environment but also complain that the school's smallness can lead to gossip and cliques. Upperclassmen on the "O-team" plan freshman orientation, the week before school starts. Housing is guaranteed; freshmen are required to live on campus and eat in the dining hall, though there are plenty of hole-in-the-wall eateries nearby, including Burger Continental (BC's), Auntie Em's, and the Big O. The eleven residence halls are small—fewer than one hundred students each—and coed by floor or room. One student raves, "It's everything a high-school senior hopes college dorm life to be!" Seventy-three percent of students live on campus in dorms ranging from "'five-star hotel' to 'this isn't too bad.'" What you get depends on your luck in the housing lottery, but everything is at least clean and well maintained. In fact, university housekeeping will clean your room for you three times a week. Students from all four classes live together, many in special-interest houses like the Multicultural Hall, the Environmental Quad, the Women's Center, or the Substance-Free Quad. A few students live off campus, although students characterize the surrounding neighborhood of Eagle Rock as "unsafe and declining economically and socially." Student escorts, shuttles, and a twenty-four-hour campus security system contribute to the feeling of safety.

Here's a tip: keep your birthday a secret, or on that unhappy day a roaring pack of your more sadistic classmates will carry you out to the middle of campus and mercilessly toss you in the Gilman Fountain. It's a tradition, after all.

While the bright lights of L.A. often beckon on weekends, on-campus social life can still be satisfying, students say, with Greek and other parties always an option and free tickets to the theater usually available. Fraternities and sororities, though declining on the Oxy social ladder, attract 10 percent of men and 9 percent of the women, but they are neither selective nor exclusive; students choose which to join, rather than being chosen, and

"It's everything a high–school senior hopes college dorm life to be!"

the frats must invite everyone to their functions. Alcohol policies are "pretty lax," says a film studies major. The annual Founders Day dinner-dance brings the campus together, and the Senior Smack offers graduates-to-be the chance to smooch whomever they've wanted to during the past four years. Other big events include parties such as Sex on the Beach and Da Getaway, a Roaring Twenties bash where students gamble with fake money and Charleston 'til they drop. Here's a tip: keep your birthday a secret, or on that unhappy day a roaring pack of your more sadistic classmates will carry you out to the middle of campus and mercilessly toss you in the Gilman Fountain. It's a tradition, after all.

When students become weary of the incestuous social life in the "Oxy fishbowl," they head for the bars, restaurants, museums, and theaters of downtown Los Angeles, where, one student notes, "you can find almost anything except snow." What! No snow? Never fear, the ski slopes of the San Gabriel Mountains are not far away. Neither is Hollywood nor the beautiful beaches of Southern California. When they tire of California, students try their luck in Las Vegas—or trek south of the border, into Tijuana. A car—your own or someone else's—is practically a necessity, though the college runs a weekend shuttle service to Old Town Pasadena. The weather is warm and sunny, but the air (cough! cough!) is often thick with that infamous L.A. smog.

Oxy's sports teams compete in Division III and draw a modest following. Football is the most popular, followed by men's basketball and soccer. Men's track and field is strong, and any match against rivals Pomona, Pitzer, Claremont McKenna, Scripps, and Harvey Mudd draws a crowd. The most popular intercollegiate sport of all, according to one student, is studying, but beach volleyball has fans, too. And don't forget that L.A. is home to the NBA's Lakers, the NHL's Kings, and baseball's Dodgers.

Occidental's creative, motivated—and diverse—students are not here for the bright lights and beautiful people of Los Angeles; those are just fringe benefits. Instead, students are drawn to this intimate oasis of learning by professors who hate to see anyone waste one whit of intellectual potential.

Overlaps

Pomona, Claremont McKenna, University of Southern California, UCLA, Stanford

If You Apply To ➤

Oxy: Early decision: Nov. 15. Regular admissions: Jan. 15. Financial aid: Feb. 1. Housing: May 1. Guarantees to meet demonstrated need. Campus interviews: recommended, evaluative. Alumni interviews: optional, evaluative. SATs or ACTs: required. SAT IIs: recommended. Accepts the Common Application and electronic applications. Essay question: significance of a personal picture or photo, or an in-depth conversation with someone of your choice.

Oglethorpe University

4484 Peachtree Road NE, Atlanta, GA 30319

Small wonder that brochures for Oglethorpe trumpet Atlanta as the college's biggest asset. In a region where most liberal arts colleges are in sleepy towns, Oglethorpe has the South's most exciting city at its fingertips. With only 1,112 undergraduates, Oglethorpe puts heavy emphasis on community.

Website: www.oglethorpe.edu
Location: City outskirts
Total Enrollment: 1,195
Undergraduates: 1,112
Male/Female: 35/65
SAT Ranges: V 560–680
   M 540–650
ACT Range: 23-29

Each Christmas, students at Oglethorpe University take part in a unique tradition. The Boar's Head Ceremony celebrates a student who years ago halted a stampeding wild boar by ramming his copy of Aristotle down the animal's throat. Though some may find it boorish, students at this small Southern school claim that it fosters a sense of family.

Founded in 1835, the school is named for the idealistic founder of the state of Georgia. Its 118-acre campus is located near suburban Buckhead, a ritzy area about ten miles north of downtown Atlanta. The heavily wooded, slightly rolling terrain is perfect territory for walks or long runs, and the beautiful campus has served as the backdrop for several movies and TV shows. Oglethorpe's academic buildings and some residence halls are in the English Gothic style; every year the campus plays host to the Georgia Shakespeare Festival.

Oglethorpe's strengths are business administration, English, biology, accounting, and psychology. Weaker bets are the fine arts and foreign language departments, though the latter does offer courses in Japanese, German, French, and Spanish. And whatever isn't offered at Oglethorpe can usually be taken through cross-registration at other schools in the Atlanta area.

Aspiring engineers may take advantage of 3–2 dual-degree programs with Georgia Tech, the University of Southern California, Auburn, and the University of Florida. The school also offers courses and additional resources as a member of the Atlanta Regional Consortium for Higher Education.* Oglethorpe also offers a wide variety of study-abroad programs, including a semester at Seigakuin University in Japan and sister-school exchanges in Argentina, the Netherlands, Germany, France, Russia, and Monaco. According to administrators, Oglethorpe "emphasizes the preparation of the humane generalist" and "rejects rigid specialization." That doesn't mean the curriculum's a cakewalk, though. "Classes are always challenging," says an English major. "I have never breezed through a class."

The university's guiding principle is the "Oglethorpe Idea," which says students should develop academically and as citizens. This philosophy is based on the conviction that education should help students make both a life and a living. All students take the sequenced, interdisciplinary Core Curriculum program at the same point in their college careers, providing them with a model for integrating information and gaining knowledge. In addition to the ability to reason, read, and speak effectively, the core asks students to reflect upon and discuss matters fundamental to understanding who they are and what they ought to be. The core requires Narratives of the Self (freshmen), Human Nature and the Social Order (sophomores), Historical Perspectives on the Social Order (juniors), and Science and Human Nature (seniors), plus a fine arts core course in music and culture or art and culture, and coursework in modern mathematics or advanced foreign language.

Oglethorpe's faculty may be demanding, but they're also friendly and helpful. "I would rate the teaching quality as an A. Freshmen are always taught by professors," a senior says. Another student adds, "The personal contact with each professor is what helped me learn more than anything I could have found in any book." Classes are generally small, and most

"Classes are always challenging. I have never breezed through a class."

students notice few problems at registration. Advising services are said to be helpful. The library's holdings are minuscule, though—just over 131,000 volumes.

What's an Oglethorpian like? The vast majority are smart, semiconservative offspring of middle- and upper-middle-class Southern families. Three-quarters ranked in the top quarter of their high-school class; most come from public schools, and more than half are native Georgians. "Piercings, BMWs, poor, rich, jocks, and nerds—we harbor them all," says a senior. Oglethorpe prides itself on being one of the first Georgia colleges to admit African-American students, and today 26 percent of the students are members of minority groups: roughly 17 percent are African-American, 3 percent are Asian-American, 3 percent are Hispanic, and 3 percent hail from abroad. There's a level of comfort with racial differences, students report. "I have never noticed any tension between different groups. People seem to be, as a whole, very accepting and open to all sorts of people," one student reports. Some students complain that their peers can be rather cliquish, but say that all in all, everyone gets along well.

Sixty-six percent of Oglethorpe's students choose to live on campus—and love it. "The dorms rock!" gushes an English major. Most rooms are suites with private

(Continued)

Financial Aid: 57%
Expense: Pr $ $
Phi Beta Kappa: No
Applicants: 574
Accepted: 86%
Enrolled: 37%
Grad in 6 Years: 70%
Returning Freshmen: 78%
Academics: ✍ ✍ ✍
Social: ☎ ☎ ☎
Q of L: ★ ★ ★ ★
Admissions: (404) 364-8307
or (800) 428-4484
Email Address:
admission@oglethorpe.edu

Strongest Programs:
Biology
Accounting
Business Administration
English
Psychology

Oglethorpe prides itself on being one of the first Georgia colleges to admit African-American students, and today 26 percent of the students are members of minority groups.

"The dorms rock!" gushes an English major. Most rooms are suites with private bathrooms, and some singles are available.

bathrooms, and some singles are available. Some students commute to campus; a quarter live in Atlanta—not a college town, but where the wild life is. "The social life on campus is secondary to most things at OU," one student explains. Fraternities and sororities, which claim 33 percent of the men and 22 percent of the women, throw parties that draw big numbers. Officially, the campus is dry, but underage students can find alcohol if they try, students agree. One sums up the policy by saying, "'Put it in a cup' is the usual thing." It's rumored that Oglethorpe barflies do more hopping than Georgia bullfrogs, and bars, clubs, and cafés abound within 10 minutes of campus.

Those who tire of the Oglethorpe scene can find excitement on the campuses of the dozen or so other colleges in the area ("Georgia Tech boys can be spotted from a mile away with their skinny, pale legs and baseball caps," says a student) or in downtown Atlanta, which at least one student considers "a great place to come to college." Atlanta proper offers everything you can imagine—arts, professional sports (including basketball's Hawks, football's Falcons, and baseball's Braves), and entertainment (ride the Great American Scream Machine at Six Flags). Facilities built for the 1996 Olympics also provide a diversion. Oglethorpe always has a big contingent going to Savannah for St. Patrick's Day and to New Orleans for Mardi Gras. The campus celebrates its origins once a year during Oglethorpe Day.

"The social life on campus is secondary to most things at OU."

Intramurals are important at Oglethorpe, sometimes more so than varsity sports. Perhaps Atlanta's diversions or the relatively small number of students on campus cause varsity sports to be a weak draw. Still, the Stormy Petrels men's golf team has brought home a Southern Collegiate Athletic Conference title, and basketball games against cross-city rival Emory are popular. The Georgia landscape makes possible a plethora of outdoor activities, including hiking at nearby Stone Mountain and boating or swimming in Lake Lanier (named for Georgia poet Sidney Lanier—Oglethorpe class of 1860).

Though Oglethorpe may lack widespread name recognition, its students get all the attention they need from a caring faculty on a close-knit campus. And being in a large city like Atlanta provides anything else that might be lacking ranging from great nightlife to internships and postgraduate employment with big-name corporations. In a sea of large Southern state schools, Oglethorpe stands out as a place where students come first.

Overlaps

University of Georgia, Emory, Georgia State, Georgia Tech, Mercer

If You Apply To ➤

Oglethorpe: Rolling admissions. Early action: Dec. 15. Financial aid: Mar. 1. Does not guarantee to meet demonstrated need. Campus interviews: recommended, evaluative. Alumni interviews: optional, informational. SATs or ACTs: required. SAT IIs: optional. Accepts the Common Application. Essay question: more about you.

Ohio State University

3rd floor, Lincoln Tower, 1800 Cannon Drive, Columbus, OH 43210

Ohio State may be the biggest university in the Big Ten, but it is far from the best. OSU has never achieved the reputation of a Michigan or a Wisconsin—partly because it has three major in-state rivals (Miami, Cincinnati, and Ohio U.) that siphon off many top students.

Think big. Think very big. Think very, very big. Envision a school with almost 50,000 students and too many opportunities to count. What might come to mind is Ohio State University, located in the heart of the state's capital, offering nineteen colleges and more than 10,444 courses in 175 undergraduate majors. If those numbers aren't staggering enough, consider the fact that OSU has thirty-four varsity teams, forty-four intramural sports, and fifty-one sports clubs. While students cite the school's size as both a blessing and a curse, all seem to agree that at OSU, the sky is the limit for those with a desire to sample its academic and other resources.

This mega-university stands on 3,200 wooded acres rubbing the edge of downtown Columbus on one side. On the other side, across the Olentangy River, is farmland associated with the College of Agriculture. OSU's architectural style is anything but consistent, yet it's all tied together in one huge redbrick package. "One part of the campus maintains a nostalgic air while another is relatively modern," observes a student. The grounds are nicely landscaped, and a centrally located lake provides a peaceful setting for contemplation.

Business, education, geography, industrial design, and engineering are among the school's most celebrated departments. OSU bills itself as the place to go for computer graphics and has a supercomputer center to back up its claim. It also boasts the largest and most comprehensive African-American studies program anywhere and turns out more African-American Ph.D.s than any other university in the nation. Furthermore, the university has the nation's only programs in welding engineering and geodetic science, and the state's only program in medical communications. Although immensely popular, students report that the English program needs improvement.

> "One part of the campus maintains a nostalgic air, while another is relatively modern."

The university's fundamental commitment to liberal arts learning means all undergrads must satisfy rigorous general education requirements that include at least one course in math, two each in writing and a foreign language, three in social science, four in natural science, and five in arts and humanities. To top it all off, students must complete a capstone requirement that includes a course on Issues of the Contemporary World. A quarterly selective admissions program has replaced OSU's old open-door policy, but a conditional-unconditional admissions policy allows some poorly prepared students to play catch-up in designated areas. Some 10,500 students receive merit-based scholarships while 560 athletes receive scholarships in seventeen sports.

Freshmen, who are grouped together in the University College before entering one of the degree-granting programs, find most introductory lectures huge. Teaching assistants, not professors, hold smaller recitation sections and deal on a personal level with students. "If you decide to attend OSU, come prepared to take responsibility for your education," says an animal science major. "The classes are large and the professors are very busy, so you will not be pampered." Students find that class sizes are whittled down as they continue in their fields of study. OSU's honors program allows 2,500 students to take classes that are taught by top professors and limited to twenty-five students each. Internships are required in some programs and optional in others, and possibilities for study abroad include Japan and the People's Republic of China. A personalized study program enables students to create their own majors.

Inside OSU's ivy-covered halls and modern additions are some of the best in up-to-date equipment and facilities, including a "phenomenal" library system with two dozen branches and nearly four million volumes—all coordinated by computer. Complaints about long registration lines have been answered by BRUTUS, Ohio State's Touch-Tone telephone registration system, which saves on time but does little to ease class overcrowding. It's becoming increasingly difficult to graduate within four years according to many students.

Website: www.osu.edu
Location: Center city
Total Enrollment: 48,477
Undergraduates: 36,049
Male/Female: 52/48
SAT Ranges: V 520–630
  M 590–660
ACT Range: 23–28
Financial Aid: 40%
Expense: Pub $
Phi Beta Kappa: Yes
Applicants: 19,968
Accepted: 73%
Enrolled: 41%
Grad in 6 Years: 56%
Returning Freshmen: 86%
Academics: ✐ ✐ ✐
Social: ☎ ☎ ☎ ☎
Q of L: ★ ★ ★
Admissions: (614) 292-OHIO
Email Address:
  askabuckeye@osu.edu

Strongest Programs:
  Business
  Premed
  Engineering
  Education
  Geography
  Industrial Design
  Linguistics
  Psychology

OSU has the nation's only programs in welding engineering and geodetic science, and the state's only program in medical communications.

Eighty-five percent of Ohio State's students come from Ohio, and the balance come largely from adjacent states. Every type of background is represented, most in huge numbers. Paradoxically, this school with its nationally recognized African-American studies program has a student body that is 8 percent African-American; Hispanics and Asian-Americans make up another 7 percent. One student bemoans the lack of integration between the African-American and Caucasian social groups. A psychology major, however, disagrees: "Ohio State has such a diverse population that it's easy for anyone to fit in." Several programs are aimed specifically at "enhancing" efforts to attract and retain minority students, including a statewide Young Scholars Program that yearly guarantees admission and financial aid to seventh graders following high school.

The residence halls that house 24 percent of the Ohio State masses are located in three areas: North, South, and Olentangy (that is, those closest to the Olentangy River). Freshmen—required to live either at home or in the dorms—are scattered among each of OSU's twenty-seven residence halls. Upperclassmen, when they don't head for off-campus life in Columbus, find the South campus section among the most desirable (it's

"Ohio State has such a diverse population that it's easy for anyone to fit in."

more sociable, louder, and full of single rooms). The Towers in the Olentangy section have gained more popularity since their conversion to eight-person suites. All in all, students have a choice of single-sex, coed (by floor or by room), or married-couples apartments if they want to live in campus housing. Computer labs are located in each residence area. A system of variable room rates based on frills (i.e., air conditioning, private bath, number of room-mates, etc.), as well as a choice of four meal-plan options, give students flexibility in determining their housing costs. Dormitory students have a choice of five dining halls, but others cook for themselves or eat in fraternity houses.

Such a large student market has, of course, produced a strip of bars, fast-food joints, convenience stores, bookstores, vegetarian restaurants, and you-name-it along the edge of the campus on High Street, and downtown Columbus is just a few minutes away. The fine public transportation system carries students not only throughout this capital city but also around the sprawling campus. In addition to the usual shopping centers, restaurants, golf courses, and movie theaters, Columbus boasts a symphony orchestra and ballet, and its central location in the state makes it easily accessible to Cleveland and Cincinnati. Outdoor enthusiasts can ski in nearby Mansfield, canoe and sail on the Olentangy and Scioto rivers, hike around adjacent quarries, or camp in the nearby woods.

Ohio State is a bustling place on weekends. "Student involvement is overwhelming," says one student. Various social events are planned by on-campus housing groups—floors, dorms, or sections of the campus. The Michigan-Ohio State football game inspires the best partying of the year, and other annual events include a Renaissance Festival and River Rat Day. Two student unions run eateries as well as movies on Friday and Saturday nights, and High Street's zillion bars, saloons, restaurants, and discos come to life. Campus policies prohibit underage drinking in dorms, but one partier discloses, "I can get served in almost any bar on campus." Just 5 percent of men and 6 percent of women on this vast campus belong to one of the 61 fraternities and sororities. By one account, these students make the Greek system "a way of life and isolate themselves from the rest of the student population."

Ohio State operates the largest and most expensive college sports program in the country—a $79 million a year operation led by the only athletic director in the country with his own Bobblehead doll for sale. The Buckeyes field teams in thirty-seven sports, from women's rifle to men's football. Non-recruited students should not expect to make any varsity team as walk-ons. But despair not, your chances of eventually graduating with a degree are much better than the varsity athletes (for male basketball players the odds are one in four), and you can take advantage of an ambitious intramural program that boasts a dozen basketball courts and twenty-six courts for handball, squash, and racquetball. "It rained one day and two hundred softball games were rained out," one student reports. For diehard basketball fans, the first official day of practice, Midnight Basketball, is a favored ritual.

OSU's sheer size is sometimes overwhelming to be sure, but students say they "thrive on the challenge and excitement of a big university." They enjoy "the freedom to pick and choose courses, programs, activities, and friends to fit their needs." For those who really want to be a Buckeye, jump in with both feet and heed the old campus saying: "Welcome to the Nut House."

<table>
<tr>
<td>

If You Apply To ➤

</td>
<td>

OSU: Rolling admissions. Meets demonstrated need of 12 percent. Campus interviews: recommended, informational. No alumni interviews. SATs or ACTs: required. SAT IIs: optional. Accepts the Common Application and electronic applications. Essay question.

</td>
</tr>
</table>

Ohio University

Chubb Hall 120, Athens, OH 45701-2979

OU is half the size of Ohio State and plays up its homey feel compared to the cast of thousands in Columbus. The Honors Tutorial College is a sure bet for top students who want close contact with faculty. Communications and journalism top the list of prominent programs.

Once known as the prototypical party school, Ohio University is shedding the image for that of a competitive public institution with a classical touch. Students and faculty members are still forced to chide well-meaning outsiders who confuse the school with its neighbor to the north, Ohio State. Students here will be quick to tell you that the schools have very different personalities, OU being much smaller and more liberal.

Established in 1804 as the first institution of higher learning in the old Northwest Territory, Ohio University is located in Athens, about seventy-five miles from Columbus, the state capital. Encircled by winding hills, the campus features neo-Georgian architecture, tree-lined redbrick walkways, and white-columned buildings all clustered on "greens," which are like small neighborhoods. Long walks are especially nice during the fall foliage season. Current campus beautification projects include a $25 million renovation of Grover Center, an athletic mall, and two new research facilities. In 2002, the university restored an art deco movie theater, "The Athena."

One of the focal points of an Ohio University education and something that sets the school apart from run-of-the-mill state institutions is the Honors Tutorial College. This unique program is modeled on the tutorial method used in British universities, notably Oxford and Cambridge. Students in the honors program take an individualized curriculum in a major field, including weekly tutorials with profs on a one-on-one basis. Most participants finish their degrees in three years and then go on to attend leading graduate programs with close to a 100 percent acceptance rate. Students are eligible for such special privileges as paid research apprenticeships, priority class registration, special library policies, and exemption from most university general education requirements. Other top areas are the College of Communication and its three offspring: the schools of telecommunications, visual communication, and journalism, which feature the latest graphics and computer equipment. One of the newest additions to the curriculum is the Global Learning Community Certificate, an

Website: www.ohiou.edu
Location: Rural
Total Enrollment: 20,163
Undergraduates: 17,178
Male/Female: 45/55
SAT Ranges: V 500–590
  M 500–600
ACT Range: 21–26
Financial Aid: 38%
Expense: Pub $ $ $
Phi Beta Kappa: Yes
Applicants: 12,433
Accepted: 78%
Enrolled: 39%
Grad in 6 Years: 70%
Returning Freshmen: 85%
Academics: ✍ ✍ ✍
Social: 🐦 🐦 🐦 🐦
Q of L: ★ ★ ★
Admissions: (740) 593-4100
Email Address: admissions.
  freshmen@ohiou.edu

Strongest Programs:
  Engineering
  Journalism

(Continued)
Business
Communications
Dance

innovative program that prepares students for leadership opportunities in a rapidly changing world. There is a new thirty-two-credit East Asian Studies Certificate and a twenty-four-credit Italian Studies Certificate open to students in any major.

General education requirements involve a minimum of one course in math or quantitative skills, two courses in English composition, one senior-level interdisciplinary course, plus 30 quarter hours in applied sciences and technology, social sciences, natural sciences, humanities, and cross-cultural perspectives. To lighten the load, you can take electives such as Humor Writing or the Language of Rock Music (so you can communicate better with Mom and Dad?). Study abroad offers worldwide destinations for anywhere from two weeks to one year though only 2 percent of students study abroad. Co-op programs are available for engineering students, and nearly anyone can earn credit for an internship.

> "Students at our college are laid-back people who like to have fun."

Regarding their profs, students are generally pleased with what they've found. "The professors at OU are qualified, approachable, and willing to help their students in any way possible," says a business administration major. Freshmen usually are taught by full professors with TAs handling study sessions. Classes of one hundred-plus students do exist, but the average class size for freshmen is about twenty-five. Getting into classes is difficult. "Even graduating seniors don't get the schedule they want," laments one student. Faculty advising is generally hit or miss. The academic climate at OU is debatable, depending on the classes and major you choose.

You'll find many classmates from the Buckeye State; 89 percent are Ohioans. "Students at our college are laid-back people who like to have fun," writes a sophomore. "They don't gel their hair too much." Almost everyone attended public high school and 18 percent graduated in the top tenth of their class. The student body is overwhelmingly Caucasian. Three percent are African-American; Hispanics and Asian-Americans combine for 2 percent. The university has established an Office of Multicultural Programs. However, a senior writes, "Most people are very open minded. OU differs from rival institutions because the quaint atmosphere makes it friendly and open." Ohio offers numerous merit scholarships and 381 athletic scholarships.

One of the newest additions to the curriculum is the Global Learning Community Certificate, an innovative program that prepares students for leadership opportunities in a rapidly changing world.

Campus housing is plentiful (forty dorms) and well liked. Almost everyone lives on campus for two years then moves into neighboring dwellings. Freshmen and sophomores live in one of three residential neighborhoods, or greens. Campus housing comes with a variety of options: coed, single-sex, quiet study, academic interest, and even an international dorm. At the "mods," six men and six women occupy separate wings but share a living room and study room. Upperclassmen usually move to fraternity or sorority houses, nearby apartments, or rental houses. Four different meal plans are available at four cafeterias and include fast-food counters next to regular dorm-food fare. "Freshmen and sophomores are required to purchase a meal plan," says a senior. "It is a major complaint along with the lack of parking."

> "Freshman and sophomores are required to purchase a meal plan. It is a major complaint along with the lack of parking."

The social life is vibrant. "Students here keep busy by going to parties and bars and attending the many social events available on campus," says a senior. Uptown features bars and clubs, campus and community activities such as plays, and guest speakers and performers. Some students also choose to participate in Greek life. Twelve percent of men and 14 percent of women join their ranks. The administration and some students have tried to downplay OU's party-school image by strictly enforcing the alcohol policy. But despite their efforts, students say that drinking is a problem and that binge drinking is not uncommon. Athens's fabled Halloween celebration, "a huge block party" with people from all over the Midwest wouldn't be missed by many students. The International Street Fair features food and music from the different cultures on campus. "Athens is the complete college town," says a communications major. "Most OU students feel a very strong affiliation with Athens and are very active members of the community." Volunteer opportunities, such as Habitat for Humanity and a local homeless shelter, are available through the Center for Community Service. Students also love to hike and camp at the nearby state parks or trek to Columbus.

Sports are a big draw at Ohio. Any competition pitting the Bobcats against hated Miami of Ohio draws a rowdy crowd. In 2001, the women's field hockey, swimming and diving, and soccer teams won NCAA Division I championships, as did the men's wrestling team. The Athens Criterium bicycle race draws competitors from throughout the nation.

There is something for nearly everyone at OU, from those interested in the classics to those with a practical bent. "The beauty of the school and its surroundings with lots of state parks extremely close makes it special," says a prelaw student. There is plenty of interaction with professors, especially in the honors program. Add to that a jumping social life, and Ohio University proves to be a quality institution with a reasonable price tag.

To lighten the load, you can take electives such as Humor Writing or the Language of Rock Music (so you can communicate better with Mom and Dad?).

Overlaps

Ohio State, Miami University (OH), Bowling Green, Kent State, University of Cincinnati

If You Apply To ➤

OU: Regular admissions: Feb. 1. Housing: May 1. Does not guarantee to meet demonstrated need. Campus and alumni interviews: optional, informational. SATs or ACTs: required. SAT IIs: optional. Essay question: optional personal essay.

Ohio Wesleyan University

South Sandusky Street, Delaware, OH 43015

OWU serves up the liberal arts with a popular side helping of business-related programs. In a region of beautiful campuses, Ohio Wesleyan's is nondescript. Like Denison, OWU is working hard to make its fraternities behave. Attracts middle-of-the-road to conservative students with preprofessional aspirations.

Ohio Wesleyan University is a small school with a big commitment to providing its students with a well-rounded education. Hallmarks at OWU are strong preparation for graduate and professional school, a solid grounding in the liberal arts, and an emphasis on having fun outside the classroom. Once known for its raucous students, this small university has overcome its hard-partying past and now offers its students a rewarding college experience.

Situated smack in the center of the state, OWU's spacious two hundred–acre campus is peaceful and quaint, with eleven buildings on the National Register of Historic Places. The architecture ranges from Greek Revival to Colonial to modern, with ivy-covered brick academic buildings on one side of a busy thoroughfare and dormitories and fraternities on the other side of the highway. Stately Stuyvesant Hall, with its majestic bell tower, is the main campus landmark. The R.W. Corns Center, which houses the economics department, information systems, and the writing center, has recently been renovated, and the science center is undergoing additional construction and improvements.

Website: www.owu.edu
Location: Small town
Total Enrollment: 1,886
Undergraduates: 1,886
Male/Female: 48/52
SAT Ranges: V 550–660
  M 550-660
ACT Range: 23-29
Financial Aid: 58%
Expense: Pr $
Phi Beta Kappa: Yes
Applicants: 2,257
Accepted: 78%
Enrolled: 33%

(Continued)

Grad in 6 Years: 58%

Returning Freshmen: 79%

Academics: ✑ ✑ ✑ ½

Social: ☎ ☎ ☎ ☎ ☎

Q of L: ★ ★ ★

Admissions: (740) 368-3020

Email Address:
owuadmit@cc.owu.edu

Strongest Programs:
Psychology
Zoology
Economics and Management
Sociology/Anthropology
English
History
Politics and Government
Biology

Preprofessional education has always been OWU's forte, and in 1998, the school placed all of its prehealth graduates in medical, dental, or veterinary schools. New additions to the curriculum include majors in neuroscience and East Asian studies, and the highly popular zoology and microbiology departments are interesting alternatives to the traditional premed route. The Woltemade Center for Economics, Business, and Entrepreneurship caters to budding entrepreneurs, and the music and fine arts programs offer both professional and liberal arts degrees. Students say the French department lacks "pizzazz."

A member of the Great Lakes College Association* consortium, Ohio Wesleyan offers numerous innovative curricular programs. The most prominent is the National Colloquium, a year-long series of lectures on a timely issue. Recent speakers have included David Wetherell, president and CEO of CMGI, and novelist Gloria Naylor. The Honors Program offers qualified students one-on-one tutorials and a chance to conduct research with faculty

> **"The quality of education and teaching on campus is excellent."**

members in areas of mutual interest. The Special Languages program offers the opportunity for self-directed study and tutoring by native speakers in languages such as Arabic, Chinese, Japanese, and modern Greek. Students can travel to Mexico for a community-service experience during spring break, while fine arts, theater, and music majors can spend a semester in New York City to study with professionals.

To graduate, OWU students must take a year of foreign language; three courses in each of the social sciences, natural sciences, and humanities; one course in the arts; and one course in cultural diversity. Students must also pass three mandatory writing classes to sharpen their written communication skills, but these aren't burdensome. Students universally laud OWU's faculty for ability and accessibility. "The quality of education and teaching on campus is excellent." The school highly values opportunities for students to interact closely with its thoughtful and dedicated faculty. "Professors are able to provide a lot of personal attention to students, making the quality of teaching very good," says an economics major.

Forty-seven percent of students come from Ohio; another big contingent consists of students from Mid-Atlantic and New England states, while recruits from Chicago and California are increasing. Students agree that diversity is valued on campus, but African-Americans make up only 5 percent of the student body, Hispanics 2 percent, and Asian-Americans 2 percent. Fifty-eight percent of students receive some type of financial aid, and merit scholarships recognizing academic or artistic ability ranging from $5,000 to $24,000 plus room and board are available.

All but one of the dorms are coed, and rooms are mostly apartment-style, four-person suites or doubles. Fraternities, unlike sororities, offer a residential option. Special-interest houses, such as Creative Arts House, House of Black Culture, House of Spirituality, and Women's House,

> **"I think that the housing is good but overbooking new students creates problems with the returnees getting the rooms they want."**

are available, as is Welch Hall, which is for students with GPAs over 3.2. "I think that the housing is good but overbooking new students creates problems with the returnees getting the rooms they want," says a sophomore. Seniors are now permitted to live off campus, a policy change that has received praise. Each meal eaten on the college plan subtracts a certain number of points (far too many in the opinion of most students) from students' accounts, but there are numerous culinary choices, from all-you-can-eat in the three dining halls to pizza and snacks from the college grocery store.

Does the buttoned-down seriousness of recent years mean that OWU has forsaken its heritage of raucous partying? Administrators certainly hope so. Trying to stamp out drunken binges, OWU slaps fines of up to $150 on all underage students

Romantics will enjoy the President's Ball the weekend before finals in the winter, and the famous Little Brown Jug harness race provides offbeat fun.

caught drinking and puts them on probation after the fourth offense. Nevertheless, one student says, "Most of the time when students drink and get loud, they get caught. That might not be the case if you drink quietly in your room." Part of OWU's commitment to mend its partying ways includes dry rush for all fraternities and an armband policy at parties. Greek membership, however, still attracts 44 percent of men and 34 percent of women. Among OWU's best-loved traditions are Fallfest and Monnett Weekend in the spring—campus-wide bashes for students, parents, and alumni that include bonfires, a Fun Run, and open houses for the Greeks. Romantics will enjoy the President's Ball the weekend before finals in the winter, and the famous Little Brown Jug harness race provides offbeat fun.

The Woltemade Center for Economics, Business, and Entrepreneurship caters to budding entrepreneurs, and the music and fine arts programs offer both professional and liberal arts degrees.

Delaware, a town of twenty-five thousand, is "very peaceful and friendly," reports one junior. Another student notes, "There is some involvement of the students in the community." Approximately 85 percent of the students volunteer in the community for Habitat for Humanity and other charitable organizations. Ohio's capital and largest city, Columbus, is only thirty minutes away by car and offers many job and internship opportunities. Lakes, farms, and even ski slopes are within a few hours' drive.

"Most of the time when students drink and get loud, they get caught. That might not be the case if you drink quietly in you room."

OWU sports rank seventh in the nation, according to the Sears Director's Cup Standings, which rates top all-around programs. The women's Battling Bishops basketball team has proven successful, and men's indoor and outdoor track have won NCAC championships. Sports fever carries over into single-sex and coed intramurals, and a massive annual game of Capture the Flag begins at eleven one night and lasts until the wee hours.

It's clear that Ohio Wesleyan University has much to offer its students, including close student-faculty interaction, quality academics, and a social atmosphere that fosters a sense of community. "Ohio Wesleyan is a place where the education goes well beyond the classroom," explains one student. "The family atmosphere and the opportunities that the college provides you in a diverse environment enrich the entire college experience."

Overlaps

College of Wooster, Denison, Wittenberg, Miami University (OH), Ohio State

If You Apply To ➤ | **Ohio Wesleyan:** Early decision: Dec. 1. Early action: Dec. 15. Regular admissions: Mar. 1. Financial aid: Mar. 15. Housing: May 1. Does not guarantee to meet demonstrated need. Campus interviews: recommended, evaluative. Alumni interviews: optional, informational. SATs or ACTs: required. SAT IIs: recommended. Accepts the Common Application and electronic applications. Essay question: significant experience, influential person, or value of community service to society. Places less reliance on standardized test scores than do similar colleges.

University of Oklahoma

1000 Asp Avenue, Room 127, Norman, OK 73019

Football aside, OU has historically been outclassed by neighbors like the University of Texas at Austin and the University of Kansas. But the signs of the improvement are there. Check out the Honors College, which boasts a living-learning option. OU is strong in engineering and geology-related fields.

Thanks to an aggressive self-improvement kick and a recent national football championship, Sooner Pride is at an all-time high. Indeed, there's much to cheer

Website: www.ou.edu

(Continued)

Location: Suburban
Total Enrollment: 25,498
Undergraduates: 19,230
Male/Female: 50/50
ACT Range: 22–27
Financial Aid: 90%
Expense: Pub $
Phi Beta Kappa: Yes
Applicants: 6,943
Accepted: 93%
Enrolled: 59%
Grad in 6 Years: 51%
Returning Freshmen: 83%
Academics: ✍ ✍ ✍
Social: ☎ ☎ ☎
Q of L: ★ ★ ★
Admissions: (800) 234-6868
Email Address: admrec@
   ouwww.ucs.ou.edu

Strongest Programs:
   Meteorology
   Finance and Accounting
   History of Science
   Chemistry and Biochemistry
   Petroleum and Geological
      Engineering
   Music
   English
   History

OU offers optional "Gateway to Learning" classes for freshmen, which provide a survey of the university's academic opportunities, services, and resources.

about at OU, including twelve additional endowed faculty positions, forty-eight presidential professorships, an Adopt-a-Prof program to encourage faculty mentoring, and roundtables, lectures, and dinner discussions at the president's house, open to all. "Our college is a new place in the last five years," says a senior English education major. "The administration's goal is for OU to be just as prestigious and stimulating as any Ivy League or private institution." A bit presumptuous, perhaps, but not bad for a school of whom a former president once said, "We want a university the football team can be proud of."

Located about eighteen miles south of Oklahoma City, OU's two thousand–acre Norman campus features tree-lined streets and predominantly redbrick buildings. Many are historic buildings in the Cherokee or Prairie Gothic style. The campus houses twelve colleges; six medical and health-related colleges are located on the OU Health Sciences Center campuses in Oklahoma City and Tulsa. Newer facilities on the Norman campus include the $15 million renovation of the Norman campus student union, a new addition for the Honors College in the Honors Residence Hall, and the physics and astronomy building at Nielsen Hall. The Sam Noble Museum of Natural History, which opened in mid-2000, is the largest university-based museum of natural history in the nation, with more than five million artifacts. OU recently completed a new intercollegiate wrestling facility, women's soccer complex, and the Barry Switzer Center.

All Oklahoma freshmen start out in the university college before choosing among several degree-granting institutions, including the colleges of architecture, arts and sciences, education, business administration, and fine arts. The engineering school offers specializations in geological, aerospace, petroleum, and environmental engineering; the petroleum program ranks among the best in the nation and is home to numerous recent national Black Engineers of the Year. OU has the state's only comprehensive fine arts college, with one of the nation's oldest collegiate ballet programs. In the College of Arts and Sciences, the natural sciences, notably chemistry, are strong. The state-of-the-art $50 million Energy Center houses some of the brightest energy-related programs under the sun. The College of Geosciences brings together Oklahoma's strong programs in meteorology, geology and geophysics, and geography.

OU offers majors in interesting fields such as Native American studies, African-American studies, energy management, Chinese, and public administration. Interestingly, the OU Native American studies program teaches more American Indian languages than any other institution in the United States. Future forecasters can stay on to get their master's degrees in professional meteorology, while the College

"Our college is a new place in the last five years."

of Education's rigorous, nationally accredited five-year teacher-certification program, Teacher Education Plus (TE-PLUS), incorporates field experience, mentoring, and instruction from thirty full-time professors. Students cite women's studies and film studies as among OU's weaker offerings. OU has recently added majors in environmental design, information studies, religious studies, and studio arts, among others.

A university-wide education curriculum, comprised of five core areas, has been approved by the Oklahoma State Regents for Higher Education. The general education requirements consist of three to five courses in symbolic and oral communication, including English composition, two courses in natural science, two courses in social science, four humanities courses, an upper-division General Education course outside the major, and a one-course Senior Capstone Experience. OU also offers optional "Gateway to Learning" classes for freshmen, which provide a survey of the university's academic opportunities, services, and resources. One participant comments, "Any incoming freshman wondering how to survive the first year should seriously consider taking Gateway as a ticket to ensured success at the University of Oklahoma." Another rich opportunity is the Presidential Travel and Study Abroad Scholarships, which provide $75,000 for students and faculty to study and conduct research around the globe.

For the academically ambitious, the Honors College offers small classes with outstanding faculty members, independent reading and research for credit, and interdisciplinary studies. It also has its own dorm, which houses two hundred of the program's twelve hundred students. Along with the Honors College, top students can apply for admission to the Scholarship-Leadership Enrichment Program, through which well-known lecturers from outside the university give seminars for academic credit. With all of these opportunities for

Students can check out wireless laptops from the library if they don't yet have their own.

"Any incoming freshman wondering how to survive the first year should seriously consider taking Gateway as a ticket to ensured success at the University of Oklahoma."

the bright and highly motivated, plus its reasonable price tag, it's no wonder OU attracts one of the highest concentrations of National Merit Scholars of any school in the nation. At the other end of the scale, however, special guidance counseling and a concerned tutorial staff are available for students who need remedial help.

Though OU is one of the smaller Big 12 schools, it can still overwhelm. A freshman orientation program, involving both students and faculty, tries to ease the transition to college, and when it's time to hit the books, students can check out wireless laptops from the library if they don't yet have their own. Class size is not generally a problem; advisors and professors can usually get students into most courses, even if they're officially closed, and with a little upfront planning and dedication to the coursework required for your major, students report little trouble graduating in four years. Students also give the faculty high marks and note that even freshmen encounter full profs, though 20 percent of undergraduate courses are led by graduate students. An English education major notes that students should utilize both faculty and departmental advisors; the former can offer perspective on their academic field, while the latter know OU's bureaucracy and logistics. Each college also offers advisors and support organizations, such as Project Threshold and the Minority Engineering Program.

OU's student body is primarily homegrown, with only 18 percent from outside the Sooner state. Minorities account for 28 percent of the student body; African-Americans and Native Americans make up 7 percent each, Asian-Americans 5 percent, and Hispanics 4 percent. Foreign students comprise almost 5 percent. The Center for Student Life has hosted programs such as "A Day of Dialogue on Race," but polit-

"All dorms are well maintained; some rooms are more comfortable than others."

ical correctness, acceptance of alternative lifestyles, and the power of the Greek system appear to be more pressing issues these days. OU awards 13,611 merit scholarships, ranging from $100 to $5,300, and 360 athletic scholarships in a variety of sports.

The university's residence halls provide a happy, if unremarkable, home to only 21 percent of the undergraduate students. Says one English major, "All dorms are well maintained; some rooms are more comfortable than others." Most halls have been renovated; some feature air-conditioned buildings with color-TV lounges and recreation rooms. (Of course, there are also basic box accommodations with no frills attached.) Most halls are coed by floor, and many of the lounge areas on the halls have been refurbished. "They are fantastic and fun," says a senior. Off-campus housing is affordable (most students choose this option); though fraternities draw 18 percent of the men and sororities 24 percent of the women, only 10 percent of students live in Greek housing.

The Thomas M. Cooley Guide recently selected the OU College of Law as one of the fifteen best law schools in the United States.

Students love the town of Norman, Oklahoma's third-largest city, which provides restaurants and shops plus numerous volunteer opportunities. "Around campus it is absolutely a college town," notes one student. Frat parties are the highlight of weekends at OU, as are annual events such as the road trip to Dallas for the OU–Texas game, the first-of-the-football-season Big Red Rally, the Medieval Festival, and the University Sing, a talent show.

OU sports big-time athletics as part of the Big 12 conference. The football team went undefeated in 2000–01 and brought home a national championship under second-year coach Bob Stoops. Other strong teams include men's gymnastics, men's basketball, men's wrestling, and women's softball and basketball.

There's a dedication and spirit of family evident in Norman, Oklahoma, these days, and not just among fans of Sooner football, says a senior. "A remarkable faculty, staff, and president are working to make OU a top-notch university, and help students do the same," she explains. OU students have a favorite saying: "Sooner born and Sooner bred, when I die, I'll be Sooner dead!"

Overlaps

Oklahoma State, University of Texas, Texas A&M, Texas Tech, Baylor

If You Apply To ➤

OU: Early action: rolling. Early decision: rolling. Regular admissions: June 1. Financial aid: June 1. Housing: rolling. Meets demonstrated financial need of 90%. Campus interviews: optional, informational. No alumni interviews. SATs or ACTs: required. No SAT IIs. No essay question.

University of Oregon

Box 1226, Eugene, OR 97403-1226

UO may be the best deal in public higher education on the West Coast. Less expensive than the UC system and less selective than the University of Washington, UO is a university of manageable size in a great location. The liberal arts are more than just a slogan, and programs in business and communication are strong.

Website: www.uoregon.edu
Location: Small city
Total Enrollment: 19,091
Undergraduates: 15,196
Male/Female: 47/53
SAT Ranges: V 493–615 M 495–607
Financial Aid: 45%
Expense: Pub $
Phi Beta Kappa: Yes
Applicants: 11,182
Accepted: 88%
Enrolled: 40%
Grad in 6 Years: 59%
Returning Freshmen: 82%
Academics: ✑ ✑ ✑ ½
Social: ☎ ☎ ☎
Q of L: ★ ★ ★ ★

Students at the University of Oregon say their school boasts "the world's coolest website." But they're not referring to the university's virtual presence on the Internet: they mean Autzen Stadium, home of their football team, the (mighty) Ducks. Sure, the joke's a little hokey, but its offbeat humor is typical of the laid-back, slightly eccentric attitude that prevails here in Eugene, where bicycles are the main form of transportation, recycling is a requirement, and littering is déclassé.

UO's buildings date from as early as 1876 to as late as 1999; they're surrounded by the university's lush 295-acre arboretum-like campus, which boasts two thousand varieties of dew-kissed trees. Most academic buildings were built before World War II and represent a blend of classical styles, including Georgian, Second Empire, Jacobin, and Lombardic. Residential facilities range from nineteenth-century Colonials to modern high-rises. Renovations of the Autzen football stadium have increased its seating capacity to fifty-four thousand. Other recent renovations include the Museum of Art and the Lundquist College of Business.

While a liberal arts emphasis underlies Oregon's entire curriculum, general education requirements are not highly structured. The calendar is composed of quarters, and students must take two terms of English composition, two years of foreign language (for a B.A.), one year of math (for a B.S.), and one term of a race- or gender-sensitive course, plus six courses in each of three areas: arts and letters, social sciences, and natural sciences. The academic climate is "laid-back, however, the courses that you choose to take can either be rigorous or not so hard," a senior economics major reports. Freshman seminars introduce students to top professors in small-group settings, and profs have to apply to teach them, a process students applaud. Freshman Interest Groups help new students acclimate to campus life through informal meetings and activities with upperclassmen.

Oregon's professional schools—journalism, architecture and allied arts, education, law, business, and music—are highly regarded, with journalism and business drawing the most student praise. Of the more than thirty-five departments in the College of Arts and Sciences, students give high marks (and high enrollments) to psychology and biology, and the science departments within this particular college offer many opportunities for research. Newer majors include an environmental science, studies, and policy major, and a biology major with an emphasis in marine biology.

"Our career center and university advisors are both excellent."

Highly motivated undergraduates may join the Honors College, a small liberal arts college with its own courses, and outstanding liberal arts majors may spend five years on campus to earn their master's degree in the Graduate School of Management. The student-run ESCAPE (Every Student Caring About Personalized Education) program provides credit for community volunteer work, while on-campus internships allow students to earn credit for work with university organizations and academic departments.

A telephone and Web registration program has improved the registration process so that it is no longer "like battling in an arena." One student notes that Advanced Placement credits help new students register earlier than their peers, since students get priority for the classes they request based on accumulated credits. The UO library system remains the best in the state, and students say the career center is "first-rate." "Our career center and university advisors are both excellent," says a senior. "We have not only departmental advisors, but also peer advisors as well as general academic advisors."

Blend two vegetarians, one track star, a frat brother, two tree huggers, three hikers, and one conservative. What have you got? Ten UO students. Some students say UO is one of the last collegiate strongholds for people who "are open minded and liberal politically." A student adds, "Students are very inclined to vote and arrange protests." In general, every part of the white Anglo-Saxon spectrum is well represented, with an especially heavy dose of the athletically inclined.

"Students are inclined to vote and arrange protests."

There is a noticeable contingent of international students, who account for 6 percent of the student body. Asian-Americans account for another 6 percent, African-Americans 2 percent, and Hispanics 3 percent. The 19 percent of students who come from out of state are mostly from California. Numerous merit scholarships of up to $5,000 and 283 athletic scholarships are awarded to qualified students.

Since there are no residence requirements and few dorms, 79 percent of the students live off campus in nearby apartments (although 64 percent of freshmen choose to live on campus). There are a number of thematic living arrangements—a crosscultural dorm, an academic-pursuit residence hall, a music dorm; students recommend Walton, Carson, and University Inn. Rooms in the residence halls tend to be small but clean and comfortable, and they have Internet connections. Any student can sign up for the meal plan in the two main dining halls; restaurants in the student union and off-campus fast food round out the menu.

Eugene, the second-largest city in Oregon, is "very supportive and involved—full of school spirit," a sophomore says. "But its not totally a 'college town' because there is a community separate from the UO," says a journalism and art major. Popular

(Continued)
Admissions: (541) 346-3201
or (800) BE A DUCK
Email Address: uoadmit@
oregon.uoregon.edu

Strongest Programs:
Architecture
Music
Creative Writing
Business
Chemistry
Journalism and
Communication
Psychology
Education

The UO library system remains the best in the state, and students say the career center is "first-rate."

hangouts include Old Taylor's and Rennies, and community- and public-service projects also draw crowds. The one drawback to all this fun is Oregon's weather: it rains and rains. "Eugene gets some sunny days in early fall, late spring, and summer," reports a veteran. "The winter rain is occasionally depressing, but it keeps the city green." Still, the moist climate rarely dampens enthusiasm for the many expeditions available through the university's well-coordinated outdoor program, from rock climbing to skiing. An hour to the west, the rain turns to mist on the Pacific Coast; an hour to the east it turns to snow in the Cascade Mountains. Students can also escape the weather year-round in the new recreation center, complete with rock-climbing wall and juice bar.

Ten percent of UO men and women join Greek organizations, which provide living space and interesting social diversions. Oregon's twenty-one-year-old drinking age means that alcohol is banned from college-owned dorms, but students claim this rule can be broken. "Most of the underage drinking takes place in secret because the UO has fairly strict policies, which are typically enforced," says a senior. Major events include the Eugene Celebration, the Oregon Country Fair, the Martin Luther King, Jr. Festival, and weekly street fairs attended by local vendors. University Day, which happens twice a year, offers students an opportunity to clean up their campus. The Willamette Valley Wine Festival is a fun road trip.

"Most of the underage drinking takes place in secret because the UO had fairly strict policies, which are typically enforced."

Second only to parties, athletic activities head the list of favorite free-time activities. The Ducks' biggest athletic rival is the Oregon State Beavers, and each year the Civil War game in football is huge. When students aren't on the tracks and fields themselves, they're trooping down to the stadium to join the Quacker Backers in cheering on the successful basketball and football teams. Track is also prominent; Nike is headquartered in nearby Beaverton.

A recent University of Oregon Orientation Week T-shirt sported a picture of a duck and the simple exhortation "Let your future take flight." UO offers ample opportunities for those with lofty ambitions to succeed. Indeed, UO's caring faculty, excellent academics, and abundance of social activities reveal that UO is all it's quacked up to be.

Overlaps

University of Washington, University of Colorado, Oregon State, UC–Davis, UC–Santa Barbara

If You Apply To ➤ **UO:** Rolling admissions. Financial aid and housing: Mar 1 (priority). Meets demonstrated need of those who meet eligibility and priority deadline of Mar. 1. Campus interviews: optional, informational. No alumni interviews. SATs or ACTs: required. SAT IIs: required if home schooled or graduate of nonstandard high school (English, math, one of choice). Accepts the Common Application and electronic applications. Essay question (required for students with GPA below 3.0): What motivates you to succeed?

Oregon State University

Corvallis, OR 97331-2106

The biggest dilemma facing the typical eighteen-year-old Oregonian is whether to be a Beaver or a Duck. Choose Beavers and get small-town life with professional programs in business, engineering, and life sciences. Choose Duck and hang with the ex-hippies in cosmopolitan Eugene.

Website: www.osu.orst.edu

With a wide range of academic programs, Oregon State University could very well be the setting of its own movie, titled *Planes, Trains, and Submarines*. You see, Oregon

State is one of just a handful of universities in the country with land-, sea-, and space-grant designations. Though the school might be happy to forget its many years of being called Moo U, that doesn't mean its agriculture department should go unnoticed. In fact, many of the contributions made by Oregon State researchers center on the field of agriculture. Still, there's more to OSU than fruits and vegetables. The school is strong in many departments, including biotechnology, forestry, and engineering.

Located in the pristine but rainy Willamette Valley, OSU's campus is a mix of older, ivy-covered buildings and more modern structures. In addition to the five hundred–acre main campus, OSU owns thirteen thousand acres of forestland near campus and numerous agricultural tracts throughout Oregon. Thousands of azalea and rhododendron bushes welcome springtime on campus with their colorful blooms, and summers are unfailingly sunny. (All that rain during the rest of the year has to be good for something, right?) Recent additions to the campus map include a forest resource lab, a residence hall, and a baseball field.

"The academic climate here fosters learning."

OSU's College of Liberal Arts ranks with Business and Engineering as the largest on campus, but there are many more preprofessionals than poets. With the exception of history and English, the liberal arts—including such standard fare as sociology, psychology, economics, and philosophy—play second fiddle to more practical, technical fields. The departments of engineering (with their up-to-date electrical and computer engineering building) and forestry are major drawing cards, and even though agriculture doesn't lure as many students as it used to, those who do come find excellent programs. Business administration is the most popular major, followed by exercise and sport science, liberal studies, general science, and psychology. The business school offers some of the finest business-related programs in the state, while the health and human performance program—a euphemism for home economics—has expanded its offerings recently. Newer degree programs include ethnic studies and environmental engineering.

OSU's extensive Baccalaureate Core requires courses in a variety of areas, including skills; perspectives; and difference, power, and discrimination. One writing-intensive course is required as well. Perhaps the core's most innovative facet is its "synthesis" requirement, in which upperclassmen take two interdisciplinary courses on global issues in the modern world. The campus's global awareness is also evident in the new International Degree, which can be coupled with any other course of study. Thus, students can earn a B.S. in forestry and a B.A. in international studies in forestry simultaneously. The

"The college has its intelligentsia, its social butterflies, its determined athletes, and any combination of those."

level of academic pressure varies by major, but even those in the various honors programs say they don't feel overworked. "The academic climate here fosters learning," says a business major. "The courses are challenging but manageable." Another adds, "I transferred here from a small, private school on the East Coast and I have never been so challenged." Students have good access to professors, but classes tend to be crowded, and one student notes that "many business and engineering people are bumped from their courses." (In fairness, that might be because of the major's immense popularity.)

Of particular note is OSU's Experimental College, where undergraduates spice up their semesters with noncredit courses in a range of imaginative subjects—everything from wine tasting to the art of bashing, a medieval war technique. Those who can afford a semester abroad may study at universities in England, France, Australia, Mexico, New Zealand, China, and Japan—or participate in individual exchange programs in still more countries. (Oregon State returns the favor, playing host to

(Continued)

Location: Small city
Total Enrollment: 18,034
Undergraduates: 14,877
Male/Female: 52/48
SAT Ranges: V 470–590
   M 480–610
ACT Range: 20–26
Financial Aid: N/A
Expense: Pub $ $ $
Phi Beta Kappa: No
Applicants: 9,588
Accepted: 88%
Enrolled: 36%
Grad in 6 Years: 58%
Returning Freshmen: 80%
Academics: ✐ ✐ ✐
Social: ☎ ☎ ☎
Q of L: ★ ★ ★
Admissions: (541) 737-4411
Email Address:
   osuadmit@orst.edu

Strongest Programs:
   Agriculture
   Biotechnology
   Forestry
   Engineering
   Business

Perhaps the core's most innovative facet is its "synthesis" requirement, in which upperclassmen take two interdisciplinary courses on global issues in the modern world.

about 1,500 foreign students from more than ninety nations each year.) The university's small-town location (population 45,000) makes it difficult to find much career-oriented part-time employment, and term-time internships are hard to come by. (OSU operates on a quarter system.) Students in almost all majors, however, can participate in the cooperative-education program, which allows them to alternate terms of study with several months of work in a relevant job.

Statistically, Oregon State certainly doesn't offer the most diverse student body. Nineteen percent graduated in the top ten percent of their high-school class. Seventy-nine percent of the students are from Oregon, and the 12 percent minority population is mostly Asian-American. Foreign students account for another 3 percent of the total. Communication between different racial and ethnic groups is poor, students report, despite a new ethnic studies program. Other big issues are underage drinking and tuition increases. Most Oregon Staters are conservative and "very all-American—not cowboys and not city slickers, but very middle-of-the-road in all respects," a business major observes. Says an engineering major, "The college has its intelligentsia, its social butterflies, its determined athletes, and any combination of those."

Freshmen are expected to live in college housing, though fraternity pledges have the option of living in their houses. Coed and single-sex options are available in the comfortable and well-maintained dorms, which house about a third of the students. "The residence halls are comfortable and well maintained, for the most part," says a forestry major. "They also offer many opportunities to get involved and meet new people." In addition to standard rooming situations, a new "wellness" hall offers an exercise room and low-calorie meals. Students can also choose life in one of eight cooperatives or the plentiful off-campus apartments. Foraging for food on your own generally beats so-so dorm grub; the better chow at frat and sorority houses is one motivation for students to go Greek, which about 15 percent of the men and 11 percent of the women do. Alcohol still flows freely at Greek affairs, but recent crackdowns by the administration and local police have begun to curb the most wanton debauchery.

> **"Civil War games between OSU and U of Oregon are a big part of every season."**

Cheering for the Beavers' nationally ranked wrestling team, which has had four top ten national finishes in the last five years, demands a lot of students' time and energy here, as does participation in the well-rounded intramural program. Benny Beaver, the school's former (and somewhat benign) mascot has been replaced by a more aggressive beaver that students have dubbed the "angry beaver". Other talented varsity squads include women's gymnastics, basketball, and volleyball, and men's football and baseball; the basketball team has the eighth-winningest program of all time among NCAA Division I schools. As for rivalries, one student says, "Civil War games between OSU and U of Oregon are a big part of every season."

Another popular student activity is complaining about the Willamette Valley weather: "People in the valley don't tan, they rust," warns one native. One reward for this sogginess, however, is the abundance of flowers that bloom in every color and shape each May. Many students consider Corvallis a good-size town; a number of bars and cheap theaters cater to their entertainment needs. Beautifully rugged beaches are less than an hour away, and some of the best skiing in the country can be found in the Cascade Mountains, two hours east. Hiking and rafting are nearby, too, and trips to powwows in the area and camping on the coast provide other good times. Popular campus traditions include the Greeklife Sing (featuring musical numbers staged by fraternity and sorority members) and the annual Fall Festival.

Oregon State University continues to build on its solid reputation as an agricultural institution, marching into the millennium as an old and faithful part of the state's university system. OSU doesn't scream for attention. Instead, it's content to be a "nice" college, in "a safe and pleasant little town," where professors are

The academic program at Penn is well supplemented by its huge and busy library, which houses more than three million volumes.

Despite all the preprofessional programs, Penn never lets its undergraduates stray too far from the liberal arts. All Penn students fulfill distribution requirements, which vary by school. All Wharton undergraduate students take a core curriculum that consists of courses in social structures, language, arts and culture, and science and analysis. Engineering requires students to take seven humanities courses, and the College of Arts and Sciences requires ten courses from seven sectors. There also is a writing requirement, and all freshmen are encouraged to take at least one course in the Freshman Seminar Program, designed to give students an opportunity to work closely with a faculty member. Strict academic policies and demanding professors exacerbate the academic pressure. But while students find the school competitive, not all are complaining. "Personally, I have found it to be a good competition," says one sophomore. "It keeps me on my toes." But unlike some other schools, Penn strikes a good balance between academics and social life. A senior adds, "Penn students seem to find a way to balance out the competitive atmosphere. We definitely strive to do well, and this involves a serious commitment to coursework. But we don't let this inhibit our Penn experience by keeping us in the library nonstop." Each year students evaluate every class themselves and publish their findings in a guide. Thousands of faculty and students give expression to Benjamin Franklin's adage that service to humanity is "the great aim and end of all learning." They work with local public-school students as part of academic coursework in disciplines as diverse as history, anthropology, and mathematics. There are tons of opportunities to volunteer—from tutoring to Big Brother/Big Sister to the Ronald McDonald House. Back in the classroom, one classics professor uses modern Philadelphia and fifth-century Athens to explore the interrelationships among community, neighborhood, and family.

Penn is a diverse campus; 20 percent of the population is Asian-American, and African-Americans and Hispanics combine for 10 percent. But students are not diverse in their brainpower—they're all smart. Ninety percent of the students rank in the top tenth of their high-school class. Nearly 60 percent come from public high school. Penn's Diversity

Thousands of faculty and students give expression to Benjamin Franklin's adage that service to humanity is "the great aim and end of all learning." They work with local public-school students as part of academic coursework in disciplines as diverse as history, anthropology, and mathematics.

"I have found the teachers to be very accessible and willing to help."

Awareness Program for freshmen helps students from various backgrounds blend more harmoniously. Freshman orientation includes skits that depict students in various situations of possible conflict and include discussions about each situation.

Penn admits students regardless of need but does not offer any merit scholarships, athletic or academic. Through its innovative Penn Plan, the university strives to ensure that virtually every family with a college-bound son or daughter, no matter what its income, can benefit from financial assistance. For some this means subsidized loans and other traditional forms of aid. Other possibilities under the Penn Plan, however, include prepayment and borrowing options designed with the rate of inflation in mind and aimed at families in the higher-income brackets. In all, Penn students have six payment-plan options.

Nearly all freshmen and 55 percent of all undergraduates live on campus and enjoy a wide range of living options. Dorms are coed. The Quad seems to be the hot spot, described as "beautiful, self-enclosed, and social" and "the greatest place in the world for freshmen." Upperclassmen reluctantly move to the high-rises across campus that look like "prefabricated twenty-four-story monsters" but do offer more space as well as kitchens. Students may also apply for a number of small College Houses, which provide a greater community experience. There are living-learning programs for those who are interested in the arts, Asian studies, etc., and want to be surrounded by others with the same interests. Rather than compete in the lottery

Undergraduates may work hard during the week, but in contrast to most Ivy League achievers, they leave it behind them on weekends.

Penn is more sports-
minded than most Ivy
schools, and football is the
biggie. The team has grown
accustomed to sitting on
the top of the Ivy League
and has sparked a
widespread revival of
school spirit.

for rooms, many juniors and seniors simply head off campus—"for the freedom, plus it's a lot cheaper," a junior says. Some end up in nearby renovated three-story houses in the neighborhood. "Off-campus living is just an extension of student neighborhoods, as we tend to stay in large groups," explains a senior. Like housing, the meal plans are optional (though strongly recommended in the freshman year as an important source of social life), and the food isn't all that bad for institutional fare, though there is no food served on weekends.

Undergraduates may work hard during the week, but in contrast to most Ivy League achievers, they leave it behind them on weekends. "Penn has a vibrant social scene," a junior says. "A lot of the social life takes place on campus because of the Greek system and the many student-run clubs, such as a capella singing groups and comedy and theater groups," says a sophomore. After an underage student suffered from alcohol poisoning, the university stiffened its alcohol policy, but with only limited effectiveness, say students. More than two dozen fraternities attract 30 percent of the men and provide "your basic meat-market scene." Similarly, sororities claim 30 percent of the women. The frats' exclusive claim to the houses along Locust Walk, the main artery on campus, has been undone: after some controversy, it was determined that non-Greeks, too, must be able to live at the social nexus of the campus.

Two big annual events at Penn are Spring Fling, a three-day weekend "nothing short of absolutely incredible fun," and Hey Day, when juniors, donning Styrofoam hats and bearing the president of the university on their shoulders, march down Locust Walk to officially become seniors, taking chomps out of each other's hats as they go. A less formal tradition is the Quad Streak, when uninhibited undergraduates run through the crowd naked. Road trips include New York City, Washington, D.C., Atlantic City, and even Maine and Florida. Downtown Philadelphia, only a few minutes away by foot, cab, or public transportation, offers enough social and cultural activities to make up for the less-attractive aspects of city living. "Students constantly take advantage of all the social and academic opportunities the city has to offer," a senior says. "I don't know if I would call it a college town, because there is so much else going on here, but there is plenty for students to do!" Students frequent sporting events, malls, South Street ("a miniature Greenwich Village"), and, of course, myriad bars and dancing joints.

Despite all the
preprofessional programs,
Penn never lets its
undergraduates stray too
far from the liberal arts.

Penn is more sports-minded than most Ivy schools, and football is the biggie. The team has grown accustomed to sitting on the top of the Ivy League and has sparked a widespread revival of school spirit. Tickets are free for those with a student ID. The Penn-Princeton rivalry is always a crowd pleaser. At the end of the

"Penn students seem to find a way to balance out the competitive atmosphere. We definitely strive to do well, and this involves a serious commitment to coursework. But we don't let this inhibit our Penn experience by keeping us in the library nonstop."

third quarter of each home game, everyone in the stands begins belting out the lyrics of the Penn fight song, and when they get to "Here's a toast to dear old Penn," the students shower

the field with burnt toast, "a moment that makes all Penn students proud," gushes a senior. Aside from football, recent Ivy championship teams include men's basketball and wrestling, and women's field hockey, basketball, and fencing. Nearly two dozen intramural sports bring thousands of less-seasoned athletes out to play each year, and all types of athletes benefit from the swanky track and weight-lifting facilities. Each spring, Penn hosts the prestigious Penn Relays, a track-and-field extravaganza that attracts the nation's best track athletes.

While its students work hard, Penn lacks the intellectual intensity of some of the top Ivies, and you can even detect some undercurrents of anti-intellectualism. Some undergraduates still carry a chip on their shoulder about not getting into Harvard or

Overlaps

Harvard, Princeton,
Yale, Cornell, Brown

Yale, and many more are quick to note that Penn is a member of the Ivy League. But most accept it for what it is: a first-rate university where you can live a relatively normal life. Penn is one Ivy League university where no one apologizes for having fun!

Pennsylvania State University

201 Old Main, University Park, PA 16802

Aside from UVA and UNC, there are precious few public universities more select ve than Penn State. With a student body the size of a small city, the university is stro g in everything from meteorology to film and television. The University Schola Program is one of the nation's elite honors programs.

Living it up with more than thirty-four thousand classmates in Happy Valley is the perfect college experience for some, though it might not fit everyone's idea of a good time. Those who can muster the energy to take advantage of Pennsylvania State University's fabled school spirit and immense academic offerings may find a home here. "It is an amazing university founded on excellence" says one senior. "You feel the strongest internal pride and love for Penn State. A very personal bond is forged forever."

Sporting an eclectic architectural mix, including white-columned brick, stone, and some modern apartments, this land-grant university continues to experience growth as major renovation and expansion projects continue. Newer facilities at the University Park campus include the Earth and Engineering Sciences building, the Hintz Family Alumni Center, the Pasquerilla Spiritual Center, and a renovation of the White building. "There is an ongoing plan to make Penn State bigger, better, and even more prestigious," says one elementary education major.

Penn State maintains strong programs in the scientific and technical fields such as earth sciences, engineering, agricultural sciences, and life sciences, as well as nutrition and family studies. The meteorology program boasts alumni worldwide, including the founder of AccuWeather, an internationally renowned private forecasting firm that is headquartered here. The newer School of Information Sciences and Technology is designed to prepare students for the digital age in the business world. On the other end of the spectrum, the Agriculture College has extensive facilities that include huge livestock barns. Dairy products from the school's cows are sold at an on-campus store, and courses are offered in the production of its famous ice cream. Students can choose from 225 baccalaureate programs, 155 graduate fields, and the Dickinson School of Law, located near the state capital. At a school of Penn State's size, there are bound to be some weaknesses. Students say cultural and ethnic studies—courses that focus on Asian and Latin American history—need help, while the administration continues to concentrate on improving the humanities in

> **"It is an amazing university founded on excellence. You feel the strongest internal pride and love for Penn State. A very personal bond is forged forever."**

Website: www.psu.edu
Location: Small city
Total Enrollment: 40,571
Undergraduates: 34,539
Male/Female: 53/47
SAT Ranges: V 530–630
M 60–660
Financial Aid: 77%
Expense: Pub $ $ $
Phi Beta Kappa: Yes
Applicants: 28,100
Accepted: %
Enrolled: 38%
Grad in 6 Years: 81%
Returning Freshmen: 93%
Academics: ⚖ ⚖ ⚖ ⚖ ½
Social: ☎ ☎ ☎ ☎
Q of L: ★ ★ ★
Admissions: (81 -5471
Email Address:
admissions@psu

Strongest Program
Agricultural Scien
Business logistics
Engineering
Human Development
Family Studies
Astronomy
Chemistry

(Continued)
Film and Television
Architecture

general. Increased funds are being allocated for program requests in the arts and liberal arts, but chronic underfunding by the state is an unwieldy obstacle.

General education requirements consist of forty-five credits that include several communications and quantification courses as well as humanities, arts, natural sciences, social and behavioral sciences, and health and physical education courses. The incorporation of critical thinking skills has been a priority in redesigning the general curriculum; Penn State's Schreyer Institute for Innovation in Learning is playing a central role in developing an academic culture of active and collaborative learning that helps graduates become critical problem solvers and lifelong learners. In addition, undergrads must enroll in "diversity-focused" courses that encourage awareness of minority concerns. One helpful program offered to freshmen is L.E.A.P (Learning Edge Academic Program), which gives new students the benefit of a big university while making it seem small. Students in L.E.A.P take a team approach by taking classes together and living together. But all this education can be put to good use with the "outstanding" career counselors, one senior says. A public relations major raved that the academic counselors "guide you in the right direction, but don't force discussions upon you." About 1,800 of the university's best and brightest are invited to participate in the University Scholars Program, which offers opportunities for independent study and graduate work as well as honors options in regular courses.

Those binoculars you use when sitting in the bleachers may come in handy in some of Penn State's intro-level lecture courses, which sometimes draw up to four hundred students. Though such enormous classes can feel impersonal, students rate the quality of teaching very high, one student gives faculty an A-. For cramming outside of class, the Penn State library contains approximately 4.6 million volumes, and a branch library is open twenty-four hours every day for the afterhours crowd. Not every major is a pressure-cooker, though science and engineering are generally tough. "Professors expect students to do their best," a junior says. Another upperclassman added that the classes are "very entertaining and intensive." A large number of students study abroad, and combined undergraduate/graduate degree options are available, as are co-op programs in engineering, distance learning, and student-designed majors.

> "There is an ongoing plan to make Penn State bigger, better, and even more prestigious."

Most undergraduates are residents of Pennsylvania, with 21 percent hailing from out of state and a 2 percent sprinkling of foreign students. Eighty percent ranked in the top quarter of their high-school class. Many students note that race and diversity issues are becoming more pronounced on a campus that is still pretty homogenous: Asian-Americans make up 5 percent of the undergrad population, and blacks and Hispanics combine for another 7 percent. "For the most part, people get along and respect each other," says a public relations major. A whopping 527 athletic scholarships are available, covering all NCAA-approved sports, as are a number of merit awards. Freshmen must live in the dorms, which students say are clean and comfortable, but crowded. More than 60 percent of students live off campus, often in downtown apartments. The meal plan operates on a point system where you pay for what you eat. More than half of Penn State's undergraduates spend their first two years at one of the university's seventeen campuses across the state, or at Penn State's Behrend College in Erie, which offers four-year programs, too.

Penn State's students take advantage of the picturesque and peaceful locale by engaging in outdoorsy activities, including skiing at a nearby slope, and sailing, canoeing, hiking, and renting cabins in Stone Valley. The university is "at the heart of State College," one student says. "The town comes alive while semesters are in session." State College offers some cultural events, such as symphonies, theatrical

About 1,800 of the university's best and brightest are invited to participate in the University Scholars Program, which offers opportunities for independent study and graduate work as well as honors options in regular courses.

shows, and ballets, while the Bryce Jordan Convocation Center hosts top-notch performers, including Linkin Park, Dave Matthews Band, Nelly, Ricky Martin, and Faith Hill. "The town itself is small, but gives a sense of community," a junior says.

Partying at Penn State is almost as legendary as the football team, which registered two national championships in the '80s. "There is something to do socially all the time!" raves a biology major. Students mostly go to bars and parties off campus in State College, where bouncers are "strict about ID-ing students." While the administration strives to keep booze out of underage hands, "it's still fairly easy to get ahold of," says a junior. The HUB, the campus union building, is open twenty-four hours, so students seeking nonalcoholic entertainment are encouraged to attend. The Greeks—which include 14 percent of Penn State men and 11 percent of women—have BYOB parties.

They don't call State College a "drinking town with a football problem" for nothing. When thousands of "insanely loyal" alumni converge on State College to cheer on their Nittany Lions in blue and white, the festivities include tailgate parties replete with marshmallow throwing, pregame parties, and postgame revelry. As a member of the Big Ten, Penn State's foes include Michigan and Ohio State, both of which make great road trips in addition to Philadelphia, Pittsburgh, and New York. Other popular events include the mid-July art festival, the Dance Marathon (which in 2002 raised $3.6 million for children with cancer), and, of course, Homecoming.

"Professors expect students to do their best."

While the football team captures its share of Big Ten titles, it's just one of twenty-nine varsity teams in town. In fact, Penn State teams have won nearly sixty national titles in a wide variety of sports, including men's and women's volleyball, women's soccer, field hockey, and fencing. There are three large gyms, a competitive-size pool, an indoor ice rink, and an extensive intramural program for the recreational athlete.

Penn State offers its students a host of academic challenges and plenty of fodder for stories about intense pride, community spirit, and football frenzy. Nobody said PSU students are necessarily modest about their love for their school. Just try to answer one of the school's favorite questions: "If God isn't a Penn State fan, why did he paint the sky blue and white?"

Those binoculars you use when sitting in the bleachers may come in handy in some of Penn State's intro-level lecture courses, which sometimes draw up to four hundred students.

Overlaps
University of Pittsburgh, Temple, University of Maryland, Indiana University of Pennsylvania, University of Delaware

---

If You Apply To ➢

PSU: Rolling admissions: priority consideration given if sent by Nov. 30. Financial aid: Feb. 15. Housing: Jan. 14. Meets demonstrated need of 5%. No campus or alumni interviews. SATs or ACTs: required. SAT IIs: optional. Accepts electronic applications. Essay question optional. Apply to particular school or program.

Pepperdine University

24255 Pacific Coast Highway, Malibu, CA 90263-4392

With apologies to Wellesley and Furman, Pepperdine has the most beautiful campus in America. Small wonder that its acceptance rate hovers at about one in three. Students must come to Pepperdine ready to embrace an evangelical Christian emphasis much stronger than, say, the Roman Catholicism of U. of San Francisco.

With picturesque surroundings, it's easy to confuse Pepperdine University with its nicknames—Pepperdine Resort and Club Med. Surrounded by the beautiful Southern

Website: www.pepperdine.edu

(Continued)

Location: Suburban
Total Enrollment: 7,476
Undergraduates: 3,068
Male/Female: 42/58
SAT Ranges: V 570–670
  M 580–680
ACT Range: 25–29
Financial Aid: 54%
Expense: Pr $ $ $ $
Phi Beta Kappa: No
Applicants: 5,393
Accepted: 36%
Enrolled: 35%
Grad in 6 Years: 68%
Returning Freshmen: 89%
Academics: ✍ ✍ ✍
Social: ☎ ☎
Q of L: ★ ★ ★ ★
Admissions: (310) 506-4392
Email Address: admission-
  seaver@pepperdine.edu

Strongest Programs:
  Business
  Accounting
  Communications
  Natural Science

California seashore, Pepperdine University might seem paradise found for students seeking sunshine rather than studies at this conservative, Christian-affiliated university, though students take their work and their worship seriously. "The philosophy of the school is that God and the academic experience must be married," says a senior telecommunications major. "This creates an intimate learning environment that prides itself on moral integrity and a high academic standard." Business and communications are the blessed programs, though other departments deserve recognition, too. Undergrads praise their educational opportunities, the strength of their school's spiritual community, and God's good grace in creating cute little bikinis for the vast sandy beaches beckoning below their hilltop campus.

There's no denying that Pepperdine's location—high in the Santa Monica Mountains, about twenty-five miles northwest of Los Angeles—is a strong selling point. The 830-acre Malibu campus, to which the school moved in 1972, overlooks the Pacific Ocean and features fountains, hillside gardens, mountain trails, and a twenty-minute-walk to the beach. Cream-colored, Mediterranean-style buildings topped with red terra-cotta roofs dot the landscape. A 125-foot-tall white stucco cross stands near the center of campus, reminding students and faculty of the school's affiliation with the Churches of Christ.

Pepperdine was founded in 1937 by George Pepperdine, a devout Christian who had amassed a fortune through his mail-order auto-parts supply company. The church's continued influence on the school pervades many aspects of campus life, from the prohibition of overnight dorm-room visits by members of the opposite sex to the requirement that students attend convocation—similar to chapel—fourteen times each semester. Students at Seaver College, Pepp's undergraduate school, must also take three religion courses. While drinking is officially prohibited on campus, the administration has lifted the ban on dancing, and now allows students to choose their own seats at convocation. Though restrictions like this would drive the average kid up a wall, most at Pepperdine like the "highly moral" atmosphere. Says one student: "In comparison to other schools, Pepperdine students generally have a more religious foundation and thus have high standards of moral integrity."

> **"The philosophy of the school is that God and the academic experience must be married."**

Seaver's academic programs aim to provide students "with a liberal arts education in a Christian environment and relate it to the dynamic qualities of life in the twentieth century." Individual classes are demanding, as is the required General Studies program, which includes a freshman seminar, a physical education course, three courses in Western heritage, two courses each in American heritage and English composition, and one class each in a foreign language and non-Western culture. However, faculty members are said to be accessible and responsive—not surprising when the average class has seventeen students. "The quality of teaching is very personal and exceptional," says an art major. Another student adds: "Because it is a small school, professors don't accept excuses or laziness. They demand a lot from their students and expect a high standard and quality of work."

The Business Administration Department is unequivocally the strongest and most popular department at Pepperdine, and it tends to set the tone on campus. The Communications Department, with majors including advertising, public relations, and journalism, is also highly touted, especially now that it boasts radio and television broadcasting studios. Biology and computer science are said to be strong, and sports medicine, rare at the undergraduate level, is both popular and well respected. Although music studios and a $10 million humanities and visual arts center have been built to enhance the Fine Arts Division, students still say art and music are relatively weak. Recent additions to the academic menu include minors in African-American studies, women's studies, and multimedia design. Juniors

Pepperdine's location—high in the Santa Monica Mountains, about twenty-five miles northwest of Los Angeles—is a strong selling point.

interested in European culture may spend a year at Pepperdine's own facilities near Heidelberg Castle, or in London or Florence. Other study-abroad programs are available in Japan and Australia; locations for summer study include France, Spain, Israel, Asia, and Russia.

Back on campus, students trying to complete term papers can use one of the 292 public computer terminals and the collections of Pepp's eight-facility library system, which boast more than 515,000 volumes and 375,000 titles on microfilm. The well-organized campus Career Center allows students sign up for job fairs, interviews, and individual and group career-counseling sessions.

One might expect students at this religiously oriented school to be conservative, and politically, they most definitely are. Many come from well-to-do Republican, California families; there is also a relatively high percentage of wealthy international students. Students joke that there's never a shortage of Porsches and BMWs on campus, but there is a shortage of places to park them. Hispanics account for 10 percent of the students, Asian-Americans 7

> **"Pepperdine tends to shy away from political activism."**

percent, and African-Americans 7 percent. The Republican influence is felt far and wide. Pepperdine has received millions of dollars from conservative Pittsburgh financier Richard Mellon Scaife. One student sums up the political climate gently: "Pepperdine tends to shy away from political activism."

Some say flashy student vehicles fit into the small, very wealthy community of Malibu better than the students themselves; the city sees the university as a catalyst for development, and that hurts town-gown relations. Because the social scene in Malibu is pretty slack, with a 10:00 P.M. noise curfew and high price tags for everything, students typically head to L.A., Hollywood, Westwood, and Santa Monica for fun. "For a large proportion of students, academics and their social lives take priority over religious matters," says a public relations major. "Parties on weekends are well attended, and probably draw a larger portion of students than church on Sunday." Twenty-four percent of men and 29 percent of women join one of six national fraternities or eight national sororities, which are playing a larger role in social life. Along with student government, they sponsor dances, movies, and other typical college activities, including the occasional illicit drink. "Pepperdine enforces a 'dry' campus, but 'damp' would be a better way of describing the residential community," says one student. "I think most of us would like to see Pepperdine get out of the dark ages in these matters."

Except for commuters, students are required to live on campus if they are single and under twenty-one. That's a good thing, says one senior, who declares that Pepperdine's dorms are "comfortable, convenient, and really quite nice." The single-sex dorms and apartments are connected to the campus computer network. Rooms are assigned on a first-come, first-served basis, and the housing stock consists of twenty-two dorms with twenty-six rooms each, a 135-room tower, and a seventy-five-unit apartment complex for juniors and seniors. Freshmen are typically assigned to suites with bathrooms, living rooms, and four double bedrooms. Some consider these arrangements crowded, but a junior says they "connect freshmen instantly to seven suitemates and friends." Despite the above-average

> **"Pepperdine enforces a 'dry' campus, but 'damp' would be a better way of describing the residential community."**

cost of living in the Malibu area, many upperclassmen choose to live off campus. The relatively new student union serves as the main campus social center, and annual events including Songfest, Family Weekend, and Midnight Madness draw crowds.

Sports receive a lot of attention at Pepperdine, with athletic scholarships offered in multiple sports, and a tennis pavilion and recreation center drawing varsity jocks and weekend warriors alike. The men's golf team and men's water polo team have

Faculty members are said to be accessible and responsive—not surprising when the average class has seventeen students.

Students joke that there's never a shortage of Porsches and BMWs on campus, but there is a shortage of places to park them.

recently won NCAA championships. Men's volleyball is always a contender for the national championship, and a Pepperdine men's tennis singles player has won the national title. Eleven club and intramural sports, including lacrosse, rugby, cycling, surfing, and soccer, keep students busy, as does the physical education department, with classes in everything from surfing to horseback riding.

Students here love to tease their well-manicured university with T-shirts proclaiming, "Pepperdine. 8 month party. 20K cover charge." But most seem to think the solid, values-oriented education they receive is worth the stiff price tag. Pepperdine faces a unique challenge in trying to marry the Christian focus of a Bible college with the academic rigor of a secular university—all in a location not known for the strength of its moral fiber.

Overlaps

University of Southern California, UCLA, UC–San Diego, UC-Santa Barbara, Stanford

If You Apply To ➤

Pepperdine: Early action: Nov. 15. Regular admissions: Jan. 15. Financial aid: Feb. 15. Housing: May 1. Does not guarantee to meet demonstrated need. Campus interviews: recommended, evaluative. No alumni interviews. SATs or ACTs: required. SAT IIs: optional. Accepts the Common Application and electronic applications. Essay question: current topics; ethical dilemma; or most embarrassing moment.

University of Pittsburgh

Bruce Hall, 2nd floor, Pittsburgh, PA 15260

With the city of Pittsburgh's rise in stature, Pitt has become a hot commodity. A state university in the mold of University of Cincinnati—not the state flagship, but strong in a host of mainly preprofessional programs. Unexpectedly, Pitt is among the nation's best in philosophy.

Website: www.pitt.edu
Location: City
Total Enrollment: 26,329
Undergraduates: 17,424
Male/Female: 47/53
SAT Ranges: V 530–630
  M 530–640
ACT Range: 22–29
Financial Aid: 70%
Expense: Pub $ $ $
Phi Beta Kappa: Yes
Applicants: 13,565
Accepted: 62%
Enrolled: 35%
Grad in 6 Years: 60%
Returning Freshmen: 85%
Academics: ✍ ✍ ✍
Social: ☎ ☎
Q of L: ★ ★
Admissions: (412) 624-PITT
Email Address:
  oafa+@pitt.edu

Pittsburgh has shaken off its idled steel-factory stigma and joined the ranks of the most livable cities in the U.S. The University of Pittsburgh has matured, too, becoming a formidable research institution. The school offers numerous opportunities for students pursuing technical, medical, and engineering careers, but leaves a great deal of room for exploration in the liberal arts. Students are encouraged to be individuals and carve out their own academic niche, either with multiple majors or certificate programs. Combine this with a satisfying social life, and Pitt has discovered one formula for a rewarding college experience.

Pitt began as a tiny educational academy in the Allegheny Mountains in 1787. Oh how times have changed. The university is now part of the landscape of shops, parks, museums, galleries, and apartment complexes that make up Oakland, the heart of Pittsburgh's cultural center. Spacious, light-filled, contemporary buildings and generic, modern office buildings make up the Pitt campus, but the architectural delight is a forty-two-story, neo-Gothic academic building, appropriately called the Cathedral of Learning, a national historic landmark. The stately and towering cathedral, with its unique Nationality Rooms, attracts one hundred thousand visitors annually. And contrary to images you may hold of inner-city Pittsburgh, the campus borders a 456-acre city park. The state has granted Pitt nearly $140 million for renovations and new construction. In the works are garden-style residence halls, practice fields, a 12,500-seat basketball arena, and many buildings at satellite campuses.

With ten undergraduate schools and more than 280 degree programs, Pitt rightfully claims to accommodate students with diverse needs. The academically motivated can take advantage of the excellent University Honors College, which an one sophomore gushes is "the best thing at Pitt. It can do so much for any students taking a serious interest in their education." It offers "small, intensive classes so students can work with professors and do independent research." Honors students publish the *Pittsburgh Undergraduate Review*, which receives submissions from students nationwide. Pitt's extensive research programs are its finest asset. The University of Pittsburgh is one of the top twenty institutions in the nation in terms of the federal research dollars that it attracts, and for good reason. Pitt astronomers discovered what appear to be two new planets orbiting a nearby star, and its physicians were the first to utilize gene therapy on a person with rheumatoid arthritis. The schools of engineering and nursing are excellent and attract high-caliber students. Premed students can even watch transplants at the famed University of Pittsburgh Medical Center, which is one of the world's leading organ-transplant centers. On the arts side, faculty and students in the music department consistently rake in more awards and fellowships than their counterparts at other U.S. universities.

Pitt now offers guaranteed admission into graduate programs in communication science, public and international affairs, dental medicine, law, medical school, and physical therapy, for outstanding freshman applicants. In two national studies, Pitt had four programs—philosophy, information science, history and philosophy of science, and nursing—ranked in the top six of their fields, and several others rated very high on the list. The College of Arts and Sciences (CAS) has academic requirements that include skill requirements in writing, quantitative and formal reasoning, foreign languages, and distribution requirements in the humanities, social and natural sciences, and foreign cultures. Psychology ranks among the

"I have never met a professor who is not willing to help a student outside of the classroom."

most popular majors, and a heavily subscribed option permits students to combine a business major with a CAS degree. The university has a new Center for International Studies and has added a B.S. in scientific computing. Qualified freshmen may enter the School of Engineering, the College of Business Administration, or the School of Nursing, as well as the College of Arts and Sciences.

For undergraduates who want to travel, the university cosponsors the Semester at Sea Program,* where students visit ports around the world and take classes at the same time. Closer to home, Pitt is a partner in the Pittsburgh Supercomputer Center, one of five such centers nationwide established by the National Science Foundation. The center houses the fastest computer in the world, performing one trillion calculations per second. There is also the Engineering Co-op, a program in which students alternate terms of study with work experience. Students in the co-op may take more than four years to graduate.

Pitt students take advantage of the school's flexible scheduling, which includes a strong evening program and summer sessions, and take on double and even triple majors, ensuring themselves of plenty of education and a degree that's well worth the money.

First-year students undergo an extensive orientation that includes three days in the summer focused on academics, another three days before the term starts, and a one-credit orientation seminar. Class sizes are not out of control. Out of 1,917 courses, 61 percent have fewer than twenty-nine students enrolled, and only 6 percent have one hundred or more. Most students agree that professors are very approachable. "I have never met a professor who is not willing to help a student outside of the classroom," says a biology major.

Eighty-six percent of all undergraduates are from Pennsylvania, including a substantial number from the Pittsburgh area. African-American students account for 9 percent of the student body, Asian-Americans 4 percent, and Hispanics 1 percent. Incoming freshmen discuss diversity during orientation, and a cultural diversity fair

The University Honors College offers "small, intensive classes so students can work with professors and do independent research."

is held at the beginning of the school year. To top that off, every student must take a pledge to promote civility on campus. The university admits students without reference to financial need, and 70 percent of undergraduates receive need-based financial aid. Pitt also offers six hundred merit awards of one thousand dollars to a full scholarship to qualified students. Athletic scholarships are also offered in nineteen varsity sports.

While student housing may have been scarce in the past, Pitt is working to increase the amount of on-campus living space. Thirty-five percent of full-time undergraduates live in on-campus university housing, which features eleven coed and single-sex dorms with liberal visitation hours and all kinds of rooming situations, from singles to seven-person suites. The new Bouquet Gardens apartments have been expanded, and more student housing will open as part of the new north campus. Sutherland Hall boasts a view of Oakland and the rest of the city, and offers its own computing lab. Suites in McCormick and Brackenridge halls have two-story windows in the living rooms. Lothrop Hall tends to attract the quieter students, and features attractive singles. Many students opt to live off campus "because it can be less expensive and students can have more freedom," says a biology major.

Pitt's urban location provides a wide variety of social activities. Within minutes of campus are shops, parks, museums, and sporting events. "I would say Pittsburgh is a great college town in which students can always find something to do," a sophomore says. Though only 10 percent of the men and 6 percent of the women belong to the Greek system, the fraternities and sororities play a vital role on campus. Many students say alcohol policies on campus are pretty tough for underage students. "Students somehow find a way to bring alcohol to campus," one student

> **"I would say Pittsburgh is a great college town in which students can always find something to do."**

confides. "However, the penalties are severe when students get caught." A senior notes that under-twenty-one students caught drinking are referred to the Pittsburgh police department. Students feel safe on campus, considering the extensive network of campus lighting, emergency phones, the shuttle bus route, and on-demand van system. In addition, Pitt students can ride the city PAT bus system for free to nearby neighborhoods to shop and go to coffee houses, bookstores, or movie theaters. Adjacent Schenley Park offers ice-skating, golfing, a pool, jogging trails, and tennis courts. Ski slopes and mountain trails are not far away, and road trips to Penn State and Philadelphia, Boston, and New York City are popular. Although the Pitt Panther football team has endured some unhappy (read: losing) seasons of late, the university is striving to change that by bringing in new coaches. Men's basketball is also popular, and competition is heated in Big East hoops.

Pitt boasts innumerable resources and opportunities for its students in the sciences and the arts, and is improving not only in its academics, but in the caliber of its student body. Pitt is raising its sights, and in many cases, breaking records. The university is molding its offerings to fit in with the new fields, such as bioengineering, that are dominating headlines.

Overlaps
Penn State, Duquesne, University of Maryland, Carnegie Mellon, University of Delaware

If You Apply To ➤

Pitt: Rolling admissions. Financial aid: Mar. 1. Housing: May. 1. Does not guarantee to meet demonstrated need. Campus interviews: recommended, informational. Alumni interviews: optional, informational. SATs or ACTs: required. SAT IIs: optional. Accepts the Common Application and electronic applications. Essay question: optional.

Presbyterian College

503 Broad Street, Clinton, SC 29325

A South Carolina liberal arts college that competes head to head with Wofford for students who want their education served up with plenty of personal attention. Programs in business and engineering complement those in the liberal arts. Lacks the urban allure of Oglethorpe or Furman.

Presbyterian College was founded in 1880 by William Plumer Jacobs, who wanted "education at a higher level" for students at a local orphanage. Today, its students continue to reach higher by embodying the school's creed: "While we live, we serve." This small liberal arts school is taking steps to keep up with the times, but staying focused on its mission of community service and helping the less fortunate.

PC is located on 234 acres in the South Carolina Piedmont, and its campus is a blend of oak trees, red bricks, and columns. All the buildings share a common Georgian architecture, and several are listed in the National Register of Historic Places. The campus is designed to resemble Jefferson's University of Virginia, with structures grouped around a series of three plazas that are great for reading, studying, or throwing a football. The library holds only 156,000 volumes but it is reportedly adequate and houses the Online Computer Library. New additions to the campus include a dorm for seniors, a football stadium, the Patrick Center for Admissions and Alumni, the Carol International House, and a new soccer field.

The school's mission to "develop students' mental, physical, moral, and spiritual capacities" has not changed during its 120 years. Approximately 50 percent of PC students volunteer each year for some type of community service. "We are a very service-oriented campus and are very involved in many areas of the community," says a junior early childhood and elementary education major. "Students are always out raising money for various philanthropies or playing with the kids," adds a senior business major. All students must

> **"We are a very service-oriented campus."**

complete a core curriculum that includes studies in English, the natural sciences, mathematics, foreign languages, religion, history, the social sciences, fine arts, and physical education. In addition, students must attend ten Cultural Enrichment Programs a year, which range from drama, film, and musical performances to lectures and panel discussions. These "CEPs" are very popular among students and are always well attended.

During the month of May or "Maymester," the biology department takes trips with its students. Some of the most recent trips have been to the Galapagos and Hawaiian Islands. The four-year honors program, open to any sophomore, junior, or senior with sufficient grades, includes special meetings with deans and dignitaries, a series of honors seminar classes in great issues, thinkers, and literary works, and opportunities for independent research. PC also offers several other opportunities for students such as the Oxford Program, Hansard Program, and Russell Program. The Oxford Program, which began in 1992, provides students with an opportunity to study in England at Corpus Christi College. Some students feel that the foreign languages, visual arts, and sciences are weaker departments, due to few resources and little interest.

Presbyterian College's academic climate is competitive, students say. "The courses require many hours of preparation and study," says a freshman. Students agree professors are the most valuable asset at PC. "I have found them to be passionate about their field and investing into the lives of students," a junior says.

Website: www.presby.edu

Location: Small town

Total Enrollment: 1,185

Undergraduates: 1,185

Male/Female: 44/56

SAT Ranges: V 520–600
M 520–600

ACT Range: 23–27

Financial Aid: 59%

Expense: Pr $

Phi Beta Kappa: No

Applicants: 951

Accepted: 78%

Enrolled: 43%

Grad in 6 Years: 78%

Returning Freshmen: 86%

Academics: ✍ ✍ ✍

Social: ☎ ☎ ☎

Q of L: ★ ★ ★ ★

Admissions: (800) 960-7583

Email Address:
admissions@presby.edu

Strongest Programs:
Business
Political Science
Education

"They invite students to dinner, attend school functions, and are there to teach and not do personal research projects." Assistants are nonexistent, and the classes are small. The career counseling and academic advising programs both receive good marks. "Faculty advisors are outstanding and very helpful," one senior says. The Winter Conference, held in January of each year, is a retreat for faculty, students, and staff, and provides them an opportunity to interact with the Thomas F. Staley Distinguished Christian Scholar.

Presbyterian follows a need-blind admissions policy. Each year the school offers academic scholarships, ranging from $1,500 to full tuition. Also, gifted athletes qualify for scholarships in nine sports.

Sixty percent of the PC student body hails from South Carolina herself. The great majority of incoming students attended public high school, and 29 percent graduated in the top tenth of their high-school class. Being Presbyterian is not a requirement to attend PC, though roughly one third of the students have this affiliation. Ninety-two percent of the student body are white. The administration admits the lack of cultural diversity on campus is a weakness and recently created the Southeastern Intercultural Studies Center to promote diversity and global citizenship. The biggest campus issues are underage drinking and the Greek system. "I think honestly that PC is in a bubble and that students do not seem to concern themselves with big social and political issues," a junior says. Most students describe their school as a genuinely friendly environment, and many attribute it to the caring faculty. "It is a place where you feel at home. Professors are interested in students' lives—inviting students to dinner is quite common—and the students are friendly and active." The student body is bound by an eighty-year-old honor code, which is taken quite seriously.

"People from other schools come to visit and are instantly jealous of our palaces."

With 89 percent of the students living on campus, there's a "nice community feel" to dorm life. "The dorms are extra nice," says a senior. "People from other schools come to visit and are instantly jealous of our palaces." Only seniors are allowed to live off campus. In an effort to improve the food at PC, they now use Sodexo Dining Service.

Clinton is a town of ten thousand inhabitants, and while it doesn't offer much for entertainment, students report many volunteer opportunities and a warm relationship between the college and townspeople. "Although there aren't many options or places to go hang out, the small-town atmosphere is one of my favorite things about PC," a senior says. PC students volunteer through the Student Volunteer Services program, the largest organization on campus. Most social life involves activities on campus, at fraternity court, or in the dorms. More and more students have been adopting the Greek life—which now encompasses 48 percent of the men and 46 percent of the women. PC has taken a firm stand against underage drinking, but a junior says, "Drinking goes on at all schools, and PC is no exception." Still, "there is no pressure to drink." Some of the campus traditions include the Blue Sox Festival at Homecoming, a candlelight Christmas service, and a beautiful graduation ceremony under the oaks with bagpipes and trumpets heralding students and faculty in full academic regalia.

"The Blue Hose show school spirit by showing off very unsightly legs."

The ten varsity sports teams compete in Division II of the NCAA and call themselves the Blue Hose, a reference to the stockings of their Scottish ancestors. In fact, some of the students wear kilts during athletic events. "The Blue Hose show school spirit by showing off some very unsightly legs," jokes a junior. The men's golf and soccer teams and the women's tennis teams have claimed recent conference championships. Men's football and basketball, and women's soccer, basketball, softball, and volleyball are also popular. The thirty-one-acre recreational facility, with lighted softball, football, and soccer fields, volleyball and horseshoe pits, a driving range, a basketball court, a track, and an amphitheater, keeps everyone active.

PC students are proud of their school's history, which includes its own tartan and a bagpipe processional at opening convocation and graduation that "bring chills if not tears every time." "It is probably one of the only schools in the country where every student can and will sing the fight song at the drop of a hat," one student says. Students say they feel fortunate to be a part of an up-and-coming college that encourages not only academic excellence but spiritual growth as well. "People and the tremendous involvement of students make PC a special place," says one satisfied student.

If You Apply To ➤

Presbyterian: Rolling admissions. Early action: Dec. 5. Regular admissions, financial aid, and housing: May 1. Does not guarantee to meet demonstrated need. Campus interviews: recommended, informational. No alumni interviews. SAT or ACT: required. Accepts the Common Application and electronic applications. Essay question: what would people be surprised to learn about you; Presbyterian College's motto; ethics of lying, cheating, and stealing.

Prescott College

220 Grove Avenue, Prescott, AZ 86301

Not a place where students fresh out of high school typically go. Those who succeed here love the outdoors and are looking for an alternative college experience. College of the Atlantic is the only other college in the _Fiske Guide_ remotely comparable. If you loved Outward Bound, consider Prescott.

Future _Survivor_ contestants take note: this tiny outpost in the wilderness of central Arizona is a perfect spot for the nature lover who seeks adventure, wants to learn survival skills, and likes studying outdoors. Where else but Prescott College could you major in adventure education or take courses like mountain search and rescue, ecopsychology, and wilderness rites of passage? Before any Prescott student sets foot in a classroom, the college sends him or her to the outback for three weeks of hiking and camping. Wilderness Orientation is an introduction to everything Prescott stands for: hands-on experience, personal responsibility, cooperative living, and stewardship of the environment.

Founded in 1966, Prescott retains the air of a 1960s commune. The student body has an abundance of shaggy mountain men and beaded daughters of the Earth, three-quarters of whom transferred from traditional four-year colleges. "Most Prescott students (like myself) have had negative experiences with large universities," says a senior environmental science/creative writing major. "We come here because we want to learn, not to have a fancy piece of paper hanging in our office." Another student describes her peers this way: "They have a clear vision and are committed to making a difference on the planet. They are each unique and talented in their own way and they have come to PC because they know it is the only college where they can study their particular passion."

Surrounded by national forest, the college's "campus" consists of a two-block-long handful of buildings in the small town of Prescott. The largest of the college's buildings was once a convent; its chapel is now used for meetings, art shows, and performances. Behind the chapel, a student center houses the Organic Alley and

Website: www.prescott.edu
Location: Small city center
Total Enrollment: 1,000
Undergraduates: 500
Male/Female: 50/50
SAT Ranges: N/A
ACT Range: 18–32
Financial Aid: 64%
Expense: Pr $ $
Phi Beta Kappa: No
Applicants: 334
Accepted: 84%
Enrolled: 54%
Grad in 6 Years: 54%
Returning Freshmen: 83%
Academics: ✍ ✍ ✍
Social: ☎ ☎
Q of L: ★ ★ ★ ★
Admissions: (800) 628-6364
Email Address:
   admissions@prescott.edu

(Continued)

Strongest Programs:
Adventure Education
Environmental Studies
Writing and Literature
Photography

community garden, which was once a volleyball court. The architectural style of the campus ranges from the historic 220 Grove to the Sam Hill Warehouse, a multi-purpose classroom, rehearsal, and performance space, and the small cottages of the admissions and advancement offices. A new student computer lab is three times the size of the lab it replaced. A recent library expansion doubled the space available for book storage and study; though the facility holds twenty-eight thousand volumes, students praise the helpful staff, and electronic systems offer online access to seventeen nearby municipal libraries. Other new additions include labs for students in the biology, geology, agroecology, and GIS (geographical information science) programs.

Prescott bills itself as a college "for the liberal arts and the environment," and most students envision themselves becoming teachers, researchers, park rangers, or wilderness guides. Adventure education, a major including everything from alpine mountaineering to sea kayaking, is a specialty. Also popular is environmental studies, which provides offerings of impressive breadth and depth for such a small school. The major in social and human development, a hodgepodge of sociology, psychology, and New Age mysticism including unorthodox courses such as Dreamwork Intensive, has been reconceptualized into integrative studies. IS is a "home" for core humanities and liberal arts areas such as religion, philosophy, and social sciences, as well as an "incubator" for new programs such as peace studies. Among the college's few concessions to practicality is the Teacher Education Program, which offers students teaching credentials in elementary, secondary, special, and bilingual education, and English as a second language. Prescott does not offer a comprehensive program in advanced math, chemistry, physics, and foreign languages other than Spanish. The school also lacks a developed sociology curriculum, which, given the state of sociology on most campuses, is not a major problem.

"There are no formal tests at Prescott."

Prescott's requirements for graduation are characteristically unorthodox. "There are no formal tests at Prescott College, with the exception of classes that award first-aid certification," explains one student. Instead of grades, faculty members give narrative evaluations. And rather than accruing credits, students design individualized "degree plans" that outline the competence (major) and breadth (minor) areas they will pursue, and the Senior Project (thesis) they will complete to demonstrate competence (graduate). Students must also obtain two levels of writing certification (college level and thesis level), and math certification, showing knowledge of college-level algebra.

"Ecological correctness is more of an issue than political correctness."

Prescott's calendar is divided into three periods, each with one ten-week quarter and one four-week block. During the quarters, students follow a traditional schedule, studying liberal arts and spending time doing fieldwork and student teaching. During the blocks, students pursue intense immersion in one course, most likely in the field, perhaps the backcountry of Baja, California, the alpine meadows of Wyoming, or even a local service clinic. Students can even take a one-month rafting trip down the Colorado River for credit! Summers may be spent studying field methods in agroecology at Prescott's thirty-acre Wolfberry Farm. Though Prescott does not offer a traditional study-abroad program, it encourages students to take courses at the Kino Bay Center for Cultural and Ecological Studies in Mexico.

While Prescott carefully studies the global problems of the environment, it does so in an intimate localized setting. Each class is limited to twelve to fourteen students, so "it is difficult to teach in this sort of environment if you are not dedicated," a senior says. There's no tenure track at Prescott, so publishing and research take a backseat to teaching. "The nature of PC courses (often in the field) help them

Prescott retains the air of a 1960s commune. The student body has an abundance of shaggy mountain men and beaded daughters of the Earth, three-quarters of whom transferred from traditional four-year colleges.

create intimate relations with their students," says a senior holistic health and spirituality major. "Teachers become lifelong friends."

"Students who go to Prescott College are earth lovers, animal lovers, activists, artists, musicians, outdoor adventurers, compassionate, thrill seekers, and dreamers," waxes one junior. Liberal politics predominate, though one student declares that "ecological correctness is more of an issue than political correctness." Prescott's unconventional approach entices many well beyond Arizona. Indeed, 35 percent of students come from the Northeast; only 6 percent are in-staters. The minority population is small, with African-Americans, Hispanics, and Asian-Americans making up only 4 percent of the total. Part of the problem is the college's meager supply of financial aid. Since the school's endowment is just one million dollars, needy students rely on government loans and grants.

> **"Housing is a hassle, but it always works out."**

Because the college has no housing, students fend for themselves in the town of Prescott, a rapidly growing community of approximately thirty-five thousand where almost everything is accessible by bicycle. The college assists with the apartment hunt by providing lists of available properties and by cosigning leases when necessary. "Housing is a hassle, but it always works out," one senior says. As for the townsfolk, students describe them as retirees who are extremely conservative. Prescott recently set up a meal plan, though many students still eat at home or in town.

Prescott social life is informal and spontaneous. Aside from environmental activities, Prescott offers a nationally recognized literary magazine, *Alligator Juniper*, and a chapter of Amnesty International. Those looking for nightlife can hit Whiskey Row, the town bar scene, or drive to Flagstaff (ninety minutes) or Phoenix (two hours). Though the college offers no athletics, students often participate in city sports leagues. Prescott's personal touch extends to graduation, a unique experience where each student is spoken about personally by a faculty member and then speaks on their own behalf.

Though Prescott lacks the financial resources and academic breadth of more established schools, it more than compensates with small classes, innovative programs taking full advantage of the nearby Southwestern wilderness, and a student body with '90s-style ambition and '60s-style social consciousness. If Grizzly Adams had gone to college, he probably would have chosen Prescott, where a popular T-shirt attests that "Education is a journey, not a destination."

> ### Overlaps
> **Evergreen State, Hampshire, Marlboro, Warren Wilson, Antioch**

If You Apply To ➤ **Prescott:** Regular admissions: Feb. 1, Sep. 1. Financial aid: Apr. 15. Does not guarantee to meet demonstrated need. Campus interviews: optional, evaluative. No alumni interviews. SATs or ACTs: optional. SAT IIs: optional. Apply to particular school or program. Essay question: autobiography, past academic experiences, and reasons for attending Prescott.

Princeton University

110 West College, Princeton, NJ 08540

More conservative than Yale and a third the size of Harvard, Princeton is the smallest of the Ivy League's Big Three. That means more attention from faculty and plenty of opportunity for rigorous independent work. Offers engineering but no business. The affluent suburban location contrasts with New Haven and Cambridge.

Website: www.princeton.edu

Location: Small town

Total Enrollment: 6,324

Undergraduates: 4,556

Male/Female: 53/47

SAT Ranges: V 680–770
  M 680–770

Financial Aid: 40%

Expense: Pr $ $ $ $

Phi Beta Kappa: Yes

Applicants: 14,875

Accepted: 11%

Enrolled: 68%

Grad in 6 Years: 96%

Returning Freshmen: 99%

Academics: ✑ ✑ ✑ ✑ ✑

Social: ☎ ☎ ☎

Q of L: ★ ★ ★

Admissions: (609) 258-3060

Email Address: N/A

Strongest Programs:
  Physics
  Molecular Biology
  Public Policy
  Economics
  Philosophy
  Romance Languages
  Computer Science
  Math

At Princeton, exclusivity is endemic. Admissions officers brush off countless valedictorians, athletes, and legacies with the contents of one thin envelope—sans mercy. A mere 11 percent of applicants are accepted, and those who get in find other entrances barred. Only graduating seniors may pass through a northern campus gate, such a sacred tradition that no uniformed sentries are needed to enforce it—no upstart undergraduates would dare step through it. But the wait is well worth it. Undergraduates at Princeton are surrounded by intellect and intensity and 250 years of finely honed educational tradition, delivered today by some of the nation's most brilliant, scholarly stars. And now that Princeton has decided to replace all loans in its financial-aid packages with grants, a lot more of those stars will be able to afford the place.

Cloistered in the secluded but upscale New Jersey town, Princeton's architectural trademark is Gothic, from the cavernous and ornate university chapel to the four-pronged Cleveland Tower rising majestically above the treetops. Interspersed among the Gothic are examples of Colonial architecture, most notably historic Nassau Hall, which served as the temporary home of the Continental Congress in 1783 and has defined elegance in academic architecture ever since. A host of modern structures, some by leading American architects Robert Venturi and I. M. Pei, add variety and distinction to the campus, but the ambiance is still quintessential Ivy League at its best. Among the newest additions are an athletic stadium and new student housing.

Princeton is unique in its scale (among the Ivies, only Dartmouth has a lower total enrollment) and its emphasis on undergraduates. For a major research institution, the university offers its students unparalleled faculty contact. With fewer graduate students to siphon off resources or consume faculty time than at large research universities, undergraduates get the lion's share of both; at last count, 70 percent of Princeton's department heads taught introductory undergraduate courses. Freshmen explore various texts and ideas that have shaped Western culture in interdisciplinary seminars taught by senior faculty members. Lovers of literature can study with Joyce Carol Oates or Toni Morrison, and nearly every other department has a few stars of its own. At least one or two of the small discussion groups that accompany each lecture course are led by senior professors, and the seminar program for freshmen based in the residential colleges further enhances student-faculty interaction. Every liberal arts student must fill distribution requirements in epistemology and cognition, ethical thought and moral values, historical analysis, literature and the arts, quantitative reasoning, social analysis, and science and technology. Students must also take writing courses. During their junior year, liberal arts students work closely with a faculty member of his or her choice in completing two junior papers—about thirty pages of independent work each semester in addition to the normal courseload. Princeton is also one of the few colleges in the country to require every graduate to complete a senior thesis—an enterprise that serves as a culmination of their work in their field of concentration.

> "The underclassmen spend too much time pining for the day when they, too, can join the closest thing Princeton has to cliques."

As one might expect, Princeton's small size means the number of courses offered is smaller than at other Ivies, but lack of quantity does not beget lack of quality. Princeton's math and philosophy departments are among the best in the nation, and English, physics, economics, molecular biology, public policy, and romance languages are right on their heels. Princeton is one of the few top liberal arts universities with equally strong engineering programs, most notably chemical, mechanical, electrical, and aerospace engineering, and computer sciences (which has its own facilities). In fact, the Department of Civil Engineering and Operations Research has split into two departments: Civil and Environmental Engineering and Operations

Research and Financial Engineering. One of Princeton's best-known programs is the prestigious Woodrow Wilson School of Public and International Affairs ("Woody Woo" to the students), which admits undergraduates on a selective basis. The university has undertaken a major effort to become a national center in the field of molecular biology, with a laboratory for teaching and research staffed by twenty-eight faculty members, including one who shared the Nobel Prize in medicine in 1995.

Princeton's semester system gives students a two-week reading period before exams in which to catch up, with first-term exams postponed until after New Year's, much to the dismay of many ski buffs and tropical sun worshipers. The university honor code, unique among the Ivies, allows for unproctored exams. The outstanding library facilities embrace five million volumes and provide five hundred private study carrels for seniors working on their theses; there are another seven hundred enclosed carrels in other parts of the campus.

About 10 percent of the student body take advantage of the opportunity to study abroad. Except for students with sufficient advanced standing to complete their degree requirements in three and a half years, leaves of absence must be taken by the year, not the semester, an impediment to "stopping out." The university does offer an intriguing five-year program that includes intense language in an Asian country and a joint bachelor's of law degree program. A limited number of courses can be taken on the pass/fail option and the University Scholars program provides especially qualified students with what the administration calls "maximum freedom in planning programs of study to fulfill individual needs and interests." Although the faculty gets high ratings for its academic advising, students are rather cool on the university's nonacademic counseling programs.

"There are no factories, toxic-waste dumps, or smokestacks, contrary to popular belief."

The majority of Princeton undergraduates are "highly organized, highly competitive, goal-oriented" students, both in terms of academics—high-school valedictorians make up 30 percent of each class—and extracurricular activities. African-American and Hispanic enrollment combined now stands at 13 percent, with Asian-American at 12 percent. While diversity is present, mixing is often not. "As an African-American, I can say that even the African-Americans are subdivided based on economics, place of origin, and whether you went to public or private school," explains one senior. And the campus remains socially conservative, with tweed and penny loafers adorning many students. Artists aren't a dominant social force on campus, but the administration hopes that renovations of the arts facilities, coupled with a $5.9 million expansion of the art gallery, will make the university more appealing to future Picassos and Baryshnikovs. As the southernmost of the Big Three, Princeton has traditionally attracted a sizable Southern contingent. This contributes to the atmosphere of social conservatism and strong sense of tradition that pervade the campus. African-Americans and women tend to feel less comfortable here than at comparable institutions.

Princeton undergraduates are admitted to the university without regard to their financial need, and those who qualify for aid get an appropriate package of benefits. There are no merit or athletic scholarships, but Princeton's financial-aid package is generous to middle-class families. Each student's Princeton experience begins with a week of orientation; five hundred each year participate in Outdoor Action, a few days of wilderness activities immediately preceding orientation.

In an attempt to improve the quality of life for freshmen and sophomores, Princeton has grouped many of its dorms into residential colleges, each with its own dining hall, faculty residents, and an active social calendar. Under this system, nearly all the freshmen and sophomores live and dine with their residential college unit, alleviating the formerly fragmented social situation. However, by providing a

Princeton is one of the few top liberal arts universities with equally strong engineering programs, most notably chemical, mechanical, electrical, and aerospace engineering, and computer sciences (which has its own facilities).

separate social sphere for these students, the system "creates a gulf between underclassmen and upperclassmen." And all too often the upper-level eating clubs steal the thunder from the college's social events. As a result, "the underclassmen spend too much time pining for the day when they, too, can join the closest thing Princeton has to cliques," says one student.

The university's turn-of-the-century Gothic dorms may look like crosses between cathedrals and castles, but conditions on the inside are often less glamorous. Some halls have amenities, including living rooms and bay windows. Several new dorms have helped ease the space crunch somewhat, and more dorms are planned as part of the school's 250th anniversary fund-raising campaign. Only 3 percent of the students live off campus. The modern and roomy Spelman dorms, which come complete with kitchens, are the best on campus and fill up quickly every year with seniors who do not belong to eating clubs.

Ah, yes, the eating clubs: Princeton's most firmly entrenched bastions of tradition. Run by students and unaffiliated with the school, they line Prospect Avenue, and have, for over a century, assumed the dual role of weekend fraternity and weekday dining hall. Of the twelve, seven admit members through an open lottery, but the other five still use a controversial selective admissions process called bicker (because of the wrangling over whom to admit), to the embarrassment of the administration and most of the students. While many of the clubs opened their doors to women back when Princeton went coed, two of the oldest and most exclusive—the Ivy Club and the Tiger Inn—remained all-male until 1991, when a court decision compelled them to admit women. Now all clubs are coed.

Catering exclusively to upperclassmen, the clubs provide a secure sense of community for their members. More than half of all sophomores join one of the clubs at the end of the year, becoming full-fledged members by the fall of their junior year. Annual dues vary; the most expensive is the Ivy Club, which charges its members almost five thousand a year. Unfortunately, the social options for those who choose not to join are limited. Some opt for life in independent dormitories or join the handful of Greek fraternities and sororities (not sanctioned by the administration) that have sprung up on campus over the past few years.

Princeton's campus is self-contained, but those who venture outside its walls will find the surroundings quite pleasing. "There are no factories, toxic-waste dumps, or smokestacks, contrary to popular belief," states one student. One side of the campus abuts quaint Nassau Street, which is dominated by chic (and pricey) boutiques and restaurants, most out of the range of student budgets, although coffee shops and affordable restaurants are becoming more prevalent. The other side of campus ends with a huge man-made lake that was financed by Andrew Carnegie so that Princetonians would not have to forgo crew. Students rarely venture much farther than New York or Philadelphia, each one hour away (in opposite directions) on the train. Few students complain about boredom, and many praise the affluent town of Princeton for the parks, woods, bike trails, and, most important, the quiet and safety it offers students. McCarter Theatre, adjacent to campus, is the nation's seventh-busiest performing arts center and houses Princeton's Triangle Club, which counted Jimmy Stewart and Brooke Shields as members. The roundup of annual campus events includes Communiversity Day, an international festival, and the P Party in the spring, which features a big-name band. Each year about two thousand students engage in volunteer activities such as tutoring, working in soup kitchens, or helping the elderly.

Princeton has the oldest licensed college radio station in the nation, plenty of journalistic opportunities, a prestigious debating and politics society (Whig-Clio) whose ranks included James Madison and Aaron Burr, and a plethora of arts offerings. The sports program includes several national championship teams, including men's lacrosse, men's heavyweight crew, and men's lightweight crew. The women's rugby club is also outstanding, having won its second straight national title as part of a fifty-nine-match winning streak. The men's basketball team is a phenomenal success, and has appeared in numerous NCAA championship tournaments. Well-attended events are found on the intramural fields, where teams from the eating clubs and residential colleges compete. Every fall, the freshman and sophomore classes square off in Cane Spree, an intramural Olympics that has been a tradition since 1869.

It's easy to be humbled at Princeton. Even the most jaded students must be awed and inspired when they think of those who've traversed the campus paths before them: former U.S. presidents James Madison and Woodrow Wilson attended the university, as did writer F. Scott Fitzgerald, to name just a few luminaries. While some may find the ambiance too insular, not many turn down membership in this very exclusive—and rewarding—club.

> **Overlaps**
> **Harvard, Yale, Stanford, MIT**

> **If You Apply To >**
>
> **Princeton:** Early decision: Nov. 1. Regular admissions: Jan. 1. Financial aid: Feb. 1. Guarantees to meet demonstrated need. Campus interviews: recommended, evaluative. Alumni interviews: optional, informational. SATs: required. SAT IIs: recommended (engineering applicants required to take either physics or chemistry and math I or II). Essay question: changes every year.

Principia College

Elsah, IL 62028

Prin is a tiny college in a tiny town about an hour from St. Louis. All students have ties to Christian Science. Prin is mainly liberal arts though it offers popular programs in mass communications and history. About 65 percent of the students travel abroad.

Students at Principia College eschew drugs, tobacco, and alcohol for the high that comes from spirituality, community, and the sense that they will one day help bless the world. Founded on the tenets of Christian Science and just an hour from St. Louis, this small liberal arts school is a haven for students who thrive on a climate that emphasizes the development of the whole person through academics, athletics, social interaction, moral standards, and a focus on character education. "The place empowers each student to be better than the best concept they've ever had of themselves," a junior says. "It makes people shine."

Principia students have always enjoyed the natural beauty of their 2,600-acre campus located on limestone bluffs above the mighty Mississippi River. The English village-style campus received National Historic Landmark designation in 1993. Many of the buildings, including most dormitories, were designed by California architect Bernard Maybeck, a contemporary of Frank Lloyd Wright. Maybeck urged Principia trustees to locate the college to its current spot when it was relocated from St. Louis, Missouri, in 1935. The campus draws on Colonial American, Tudor, medieval, and American vernacular stone building traditions. The College Chapel, whose bells ring out hymns every evening, is the symbolic center of campus. Newest additions to the campus include a one-thousand-square-foot art studio and new computer graphics labs.

As for academics, the school is particularly strong in education, studio art, history, biology/natural resources, and business administration. Mass communication

Website: www.prin.edu
Location: Rural
Total Enrollment: 554
Undergraduates: 554
Male/Female: 44/56
SAT Ranges: V 510–650
    M 510–620
ACT Range: 22–28
Financial Aid: 75%
Expense: Pr $
Phi Beta Kappa: No
Applicants: 252
Accepted: 89%
Enrolled: 50%
Grad in 6 Years: 98%
Returning Freshmen: 86%
Academics: ✍ ✍ ✍
Social: ☎ ☎ ☎
Q of L: ★ ★ ★ ★
Admissions: (800) 277-4648

(Continued)

Email Address:
collegeadmissions
@prin.edu

Strongest Programs:
Education
Studio Art
History
Biology/Natural Resources
Business Administration

majors have the added advantage of a television studio, FM radio station, and editing rooms at their disposal. Prin's science center provides students with an aviary, greenhouse, thirteen laboratories, and a computer weather center. Students complain that the theater department seems "on shaky legs at times," and foreign languages and sports management are considered weaker departments.

Although the academic climate is fairly competitive, the students say the emphasis is more on learning than on grade averages. With only ten weeks for each class in the quarter system, courses are "strenuous," says an art history major. "Each day is maximized by students and professors alike." Prin's professors generally receive high marks, save for the usual variance. "The professors do not just pump you full of information," says a religion major. "They want you to learn, and most teachers here will go the distance with the student willing to ask." The small class size provides intimate forums for discussing ideas and receiving individualized attention. General education requirements include proficiency in at least one foreign language as well as

"Each day is maximized by students and professors alike."

courses in the Bible, literature, history, the arts, religion or philosophy, social science, math, and lab science. Students must also fulfill requirements in moral reasoning, writing proficiency, and physical education as well as a survival swim test. Freshman also participate in an intensive writing seminar.

Approximately 72 percent of Prin's students take advantage of the excellent Prin Abroad as well as the Mini-Abroad programs. Students are also able to connect with administrators and entrepreneurs in the San Francisco Field Program, as well as other organizations and businesses in independent internships. Another interdisciplinary program, Diakonia, allows students to integrate academic study with off-campus community-service activity. Undergraduate research is popular—the student-led solar-car competition team created a sun-powered vehicle that placed seventh in the 2,400-mile American Solar Car Challenge 2001.

The student-led solar-car competition team created a sun-powered vehicle that placed seventh in the 2,400-mile American Solar Car Challenge 2001.

Despite their common faith, Principia students are geographically quite diverse. Most are from either the East or West coasts, and 81 percent are from out of state. Minorities constitute 4 percent of the student body. The school awards merit scholarships each year, ranging from $2,500 to $17,400. About 15 percent of each year's new students have transferred from other colleges, and there is a small but growing contingent of "nontrads," or students over the age of twenty-three returning to school or beginning college.

Everyone lives on campus and seems to love it. One student describes the dorms as "beautiful houses that feel like castles." After their first year, most students elect to become "house" members and stay in the same building—similar to a sorority or

"Principia prepares its students to bless the world."

a fraternity—for the duration of their stay at Prin. But as part of Prin's character education goal, students change rooms and roommates every quarter. Students pick up their meals in the "scramble room" and then eat together in the plush dining hall.

Settled in the 1800s, Elsah, Illinois, is small and quaint, and "hardly a town at all," says a global perspectives major, though there is a good frozen-custard shop. The social committee provides activities on the incredibly safe campus, but "for social butterflies, campus life is a bit of a bore," a junior says. Those with cars make friends fast. Nearby St. Louis is a quick one-hour getaway for your museums, zoos, and nightspots, and there are big-box stores within a half-hour from campus. Religious services are run by the Christian Science Organization (a.k.a. "the Org"). "Principia students interact on a more real level," a senior explains, "without the opportunistic and hazy influence of alcohol and drugs."

One of the most popular festivals is the springtime Whole World Festival, where international students have food, clothing, and display booths representing their home countries.

Principia's athletic teams score well in NCAA Division III competition. Cross-country, tennis, and soccer are strong for men and women. Principia's athletic facilities include a four-court indoor tennis center and Hay Field House, with its large gym and pool, as well as outdoor courts and running trails. Intramurals are popular, with competition usually organized by the houses. One of the most popular festivals is the springtime Whole World Festival, where international students have food, clothing, and display booths representing their home countries. Principia holds the oldest student-run public-affairs conference in the nation that draws internationally renowned speakers.

Prin's students are not shy about their adherence to Christian Science principles or the conservative nature of the campus. Indeed, they revel in the opportunity to fulfill their spiritual needs while benefiting from intense academic challenges. The campus attracts all kinds of students, but encourages them to develop their character. In the end, Principia's goal is to "allow me to be the best I," says a religion major. One freshman explains the bottom line: "Principia prepares its students to bless the world."

<table>
<tr><td>

Overlaps

Purdue, Indiana, Ball State, UCLA, UC–Berkeley

</td></tr>
</table>

<table>
<tr><td>

If You Apply To ➤

</td><td>

Principia: Regular admissions: March 1. Financial aid: June 1. Does not guarantee to meet demonstrated need. Campus interviews: recommended, informational. No alumni interviews. SATs: required. SAT IIs: required (foreign language for placement purposes). Essay question: significant book or creative endeavor; defend personal or political issue; or choose your own creative topic. Only college in the world that admits only Christian Scientists.

</td></tr>
</table>

University of Puget Sound

1500 North Warner, Tacoma, WA 98416

Ask anyone in Tacoma about UPS—the university, not the parcel service—and they'll tell you that Puget Sound delivers solid liberal arts programs with a touch of business. With easy reach of the Sound, the university specializes in all things Asia. Compare to Willamette and Whitman.

The University of Puget Sound has clarified its mission and significantly improved its focus on creating a high-quality undergraduate liberal arts experience for its students. Academic offerings—as well as the campus—have undergone dramatic changes, resulting in an increasingly selective admissions process and a renewed emphasis on learning. "Students are self-motivated, and an emphasis is placed on class discussion and critical thinking," says a freshman.

Founded in 1888, the university is cradled between the Cascade Range and the rugged Olympics, with easy access to the city life of Seattle and the natural beauty of Mount Rainier. Puget Sound's ninety-seven-acre campus boasts beautifully maintained lawns, native fir trees, and tons of other plants, trees, and greenery, thanks to the omnipresent rain. Most of the school's buildings, with their distinctive arches and porticos, were built in the 1950s and 1960s, but the university has experienced a building boom over the past few years. Recently, the Wheelock Student Center was renovated, resulting in expanded seating capacity and additional meal options in the main dining facility, and a new espresso bar was opened. Collins Library underwent seven million dollars in renovations and remodeling, resulting in twenty thousand square feet of additional study and bookshelf space. The administration building, Jones Hall, was renovated in the summer of 2001. Wyatt Hall, a new state-of-the-art academic building, was opened in September 2002. Trimble Hall, a new residence hall, was completed in the summer of 2002, as well as renovations to Payton Field.

<table>
<tr><td>

Website: www.ups.edu
Location: Suburban
Total Enrollment: 2,848
Undergraduates: 2,604
Male/Female: 39/61
SAT Ranges: V 580–680
  M 580–660
ACT Range: 24–29
Financial Aid: 54%
Expense: Pr $ $ $
Phi Beta Kappa: Yes
Applicants: 4,377
Accepted: 67%
Enrolled: 24%
Grad in 6 Years: 73%
Returning Freshmen: 84%
Academics: ✍ ✍ ✍ ½
Social: ☎ ☎ ☎
Q of L: ★ ★ ★ ★

</td></tr>
</table>

(Continued)

Admissions: (253) 879-3211

Email Address:
admission@ups.edu

Strongest Programs:
Asian Studies
Biology
Chemistry
History
International Political
     Economy
English
Mathematics
Computer Science

Students must complete an eight-course core curriculum, which includes two freshman seminars in writing and rhetoric and scholarly and creative inquiry. Other courses include mathematical approaches, humanistic approaches, natural scientific approaches, fine arts approaches, and connections. Students must take a Science in Context course where they defend answers to complex questions on scientific and public policy grounds. They also satisfy additional writing requirements within their major field and enroll in a freshman advising course during their first year. Additionally, first-years may participate in writing seminars, a highly selective classics-based honors program, or the Business Leadership Program. A $250,000 grant enabled Puget Sound to create a set of interdisciplinary business-related majors grounded in liberal arts.

After navigating through the requirements, students find a wealth of majors to choose from in Puget Sound's two undergraduate schools. The most popular majors are business, psychology and biology, English, and international political economy. The university has also developed a reputation as a jumping-off point—both literally and figuratively—to Asia. Its curriculum stresses two of the fastest-growing fields in the region: Asian studies and Pacific Rim economics. Nearly one-third of Puget Sounders take at least one Asian studies course, and thirty-five lucky students spend nine months traveling through Japan, Thailand, Korea, India, and Nepal, studying native art, architecture, politics, population, and philosophy. Puget Sound recently added minors in African-American studies, Latin-American studies, and environmental studies, and the physical education major is now exercise science, reflecting a program more grounded in liberal arts and sciences. The School of Occupational and Physical Therapy now offers a graduate degree as well.

"Freshmen are taught by full professors."

Regardless of the department or program, positive interaction with professors is a big selling point at Puget Sound. "Freshman are taught by full professors," a junior comments, "however, I think teaching ultimately is derived from the personality and character of the person and not status." The president holds monthly Fireside Dinners at her home, with a standing invitation to all. Classes generally have less than thirty students. For students interested in traveling abroad, Puget Sound offers a Pacific Rim/Asia studies program every three years.

Less than one-third of Puget Sound's students hail from Washington. The majority attended public high schools, and 75 percent were in the top quarter of their class. African-Americans and Hispanics combine for 5 percent of the student body. Asian-Americans, who constitute 11 percent, appear to be more integrated, and an active Hawaiian student organization sponsors a number of events, including a massive luau. Other student organizations exist for various minorities and special-interest groups. A senior biology major observes: "UPS is a very liberal campus. Political correctness and openness is encouraged." Puget Sound offers 1,646 merit scholarships, ranging from $1,000 to $9,000, for achievement and promise in general academics and specific talent areas, such as music, art, and debate.

"Dorms are fairly spacious and well maintained."

At Puget Sound, freshmen are guaranteed on-campus housing, and 57 percent of the student body reside in nine dorms. "Dorms are fairly spacious and well maintained," says one student. Spaces are reserved for freshmen in all dorms; Phibbs Hall and Todd Hall are the best choices, according to students. All rooms are connected to Ethernet and have voicemail. After their first year, students may move to one of many university-owned houses, possibly creating their own theme houses along the lines of the current "women in science," "outhaus" (outdoor adventure), and "multicultural" houses. Other options include four foreign-language houses, which

First-years may participate in writing seminars, a highly selective classics-based honors program, or the Business Leadership Program.

offer immersion in other cultures. Meals can be taken in the Wheelock Student Center, which has a dining area, game room, television lounge, and the student-run Pizza Cellar and Diversions Café.

"Social life depends on the person and their relationships with others on campus," says a senior. Twenty-three percent of men join fraternities, and 30 percent of women belong to sororities, providing ready opportunities to mix and mingle. But off-campus independent parties and school-sponsored activities such as the Mistletoast Winter Formal and Casino Night are also popular. Foolish Pleasures, a festival of short student-produced films, is another favorite. With the mountains and beaches so close by—Seattle is thirty minutes away by car, Portland is two hours south, and Vancouver, British Columbia, is three hours north—road trips are *de rigueur*. That's especially true during ski season, because the university rents out all the equipment necessary for a variety of weekend outings. Seventy-five percent of the undergraduates participate in community volunteer programs. While Tacoma is a nice place to live and offers plenty of opportunities for volunteer work, Seattle is where it's at. Back on campus, the alcohol policy states that if you live in the dorms and are under twenty-one, you can't drink. The Greek houses have banned kegs.

> "Social life depends on the person and their relationship with others on campus."

Among Puget Sound's varsity teams, the Loggers, women's cross-country, swimming, and volleyball, and men's swimming have won national championships. Men's cross-country is also strong. The annual football game with local rival Pacific Lutheran University unfailingly draws a crowd. As part of its move to Division III athletics, Puget Sound stopped offering athletic scholarships.

The University of Puget Sound stands ready to welcome students who appreciate the natural beauty of the outdoors, the unique challenge presented by the liberal arts, and the special bond that can be forged with professors in small classes. It's especially appealing for students who want to participate in the growing Asian economy. A junior says, "You get a quality education, make good friends, and virtually every opportunity is there if you go looking for it."

> ## Overlaps
> University of Washington, Lewis and Clark, Whitman, Willamette, Colorado College

---

If You Apply To ➤   **Puget Sound:** Early decision: Nov. 15, Dec. 15. Regular admissions and financial aid: Feb. 1. Housing: May 1. Meets demonstrated need of 48%. Campus interviews: recommended, evaluative. Alumni interviews: optional, informational. SATs or ACTs: required. SAT IIs: optional. Accepts the Common Application and electronic applications. Essay question: topic of your choice or one of the following: hometown's impact on your life, original work's effect on your thinking, experiences with diversity, time when humor has helped diffuse a difficult situation, responsibilities of an educated person, plan for accomplishing lifetime goal.

Purdue University

1080 Schleman Hall, West Lafayette, IN 47907-1080

Purdue is Indiana's state university for science and technology—with side helpings of business, health professions, and liberal arts. Purdue is nearly twenty times the size of Indiana's other technically oriented university, Rose-Hulman. Compare to Kansas State and Big Ten rivals Michigan State.

Most successful colleges in Indiana have three characteristics: a strong agricultural program, a powerhouse basketball team, and a conservative student body. Purdue University has all of these in abundance. Befitting its students' practicality, preprofessionalism

> **Website:** www.purdue.edu
> **Location:** Small city

(Continued)

Total Enrollment: 38,208
Undergraduates: 30,987
Male/Female: 57/43
SAT Ranges: V 500–600
  M 520–650
ACT Range: 23–28
Financial Aid: 71%
Expense: Pub $ $
Phi Beta Kappa: Yes
Applicants: 21,760
Accepted: 77%
Enrolled: 39%
Grad in 6 Years: 64%
Returning Freshmen: 89%
Academics: ✑ ✑ ✑ ½
Social: ☎ ☎ ☎
Q of L: ★ ★ ★
Admissions: (765) 494-1776
Email Address:
  admissions@purdue.edu

Strongest Programs:
  Engineering
  Technology
  Science
  Agriculture

rules, with top-notch engineering, aeronautics, agriculture, and management programs being especially good—and liberal arts being all but nonexistent.

Purdue is the main attraction in the small industrial town of West Lafayette. The campus architecture is traditional: a combination of redbrick and limestone buildings and lush shaded courtyards. The food sciences building, complete with extensive research labs, is the most recent addition. Among Purdue's most famous graduates are astronauts Neil Armstrong and Gus Grissom; Amelia Earhart was once a career counselor here.

The Purdue mission freely states that the school "does not offer comprehensive programs in some of the liberal and fine arts and some of the social sciences." That said, what it does, it does well. In fact, the university has awarded more bachelor's degrees in engineering than any other institution. And students flock to the five-year engineering co-op program, one of the most competitive on campus because it marries classroom study with real-world work. Purdue also offers a strong undergraduate program in flight technology, which includes hands-on training at the university's own airport. Generally, according to students, the pharmacy and management departments are likewise excellent, and the restaurant, hotel, institutional, and tourism management program has gained a following. Not surprisingly, the creative arts do not exist, save the required writing requirements. A physical education major was recently dropped.

"Most profs are very concerned with how well you do."

Each of the university's ten schools establishes its own, usually extensive, set of curriculum requirements, but all require English, math, and science at various levels, and some require a foreign language. All but 16 percent of courses have fifty or fewer students, and graduation requirements can be fulfilled in four years unless students change their major or elect a co-op. Faculty research projects can take away from their time with students. About half of freshman classes are taught by graduate students and academic advisors, who are available to answer questions and provide career advice. "Most profs are very concerned with how well you do, but there are some that are concerned with research," an industrial engineering major says.

Although Purdue offers rolling admissions, prospective students should apply early in their senior year of high school to beat the cutoff date for certain programs. The student body is fairly homogeneous, with more than two-thirds from Indiana and only 9 percent minorities: 3 percent African-American, 4 percent Asian-American, and 2 percent Hispanic. Still, the university has more foreign students than any other public university in the country. Although some complain that the campus looks like the world's biggest Abercrombie & Fitch catalog, Boilermaker pride is said to stretch across boundaries of race, gender, and background. Most, but not all, students are conservative. "It's usually the school of liberal arts hippies versus everyone else," reveals a junior. Merit scholarships of up to $20,000 are available to qualified students, and sporty types can vie for more than three hundred athletic scholarships.

Thirty-nine percent of students live in Purdue's dorms, where attendants enforce visitation hours between men and women; the notion of a "coed dorm"

"Students can easily find somewhere to fit in."

here means that both sexes share a dining hall and a lobby. Almost all freshmen live on campus, though they aren't required to, and Harrison Hall wins the Best Freshman Dorm Award. Dorms are clean and well maintained, and "offer amenities and services like recreational activities, laundry facilities, clubs, and cafeterias," says a hotel/restaurant management major. But, students say, as the student body has grown, it has become harder to get a room. Most upperclassmen hunt down inexpensive and accessible off-campus housing options. With more than forty officers on patrol, walking and riding escorts, and emergency call boxes, students feel safe.

The annual Grand Prix, where a week of fun and parties leads up to Saturday's go-cart races, takes place each spring.

Officially, Purdue is as dry as Death Valley, but according to a senior, "It is very easy for underage students to get alcohol." Forget the local bars, but fraternity and off-campus house parties are accessible to those underage. "There is too much drinking at Purdue," complains a junior. Greek life, though declining in popularity, is still described as "huge" by more than a few students. It now draws 17 percent of men and 14 percent of women. Most students stay close to campus to party, where the residence halls plan bowling, movies, and day trips, and where Purdue's more than 621 campus organizations provide a plethora of diversions. "With student organizations ranging from the BBQ society to professional development clubs, students can easily find somewhere to fit in," says an industrial management major. Community service, with organizations like Habitat for Humanity and Big Brothers/Big Sisters, is also a popular pastime. The annual Grand Prix, where a week of fun and parties leads up to Saturday's go-cart races, takes place each spring. Students also look forward to the Slater Slammer, a free Labor Day weekend concert. And while the drive to Indianapolis or Chicago is

"Hoosier by birth, Boilermaker by the grace of God."

not unbearable, most students use the weekends for forgetting the books, sleeping in, catching a flick, or frequenting Harry's Chocolate Shop—a longtime bar, not a candy store.

This is a big sports school with an extensive, all-purpose athletic facility, and the mammoth intramural program fosters animosity almost as intense as that felt for the Indiana Hoosiers on the varsity level. Boilermaker pride manifests itself at varsity games of all types, especially when the opposing team is "that school down south," in the annual struggle for possession of the Old Oaken Bucket. Every year, the winner adds a link to a chain on the bucket, with each in the shape of either an "I" or "P." The men's football team is strong, as is the women's basketball squad. Women's volleyball and softball are also popular, as are men's basketball and baseball.

Whether screaming themselves hoarse for their beloved Boilermakers or hitting the books, Purdue students get a healthy dose of academics and athletics, in a relaxed, almost rural environment. Like the saying goes, "Hoosier by birth, Boilermaker by the grace of God." For those planning to stay true to their Midwestern roots, shoot for the stars, or even go to the moon, Purdue might be the right place to spend four years.

Boilermaker pride manifests itself at varsity games of all types, especially when the opposing team is "that school down south," in the annual struggle for possession of the Old Oaken Bucket.

Overlaps

Indiana, Ball State, Indiana State, University of Illinois, University of Michigan

If You Apply To ➢

Purdue: Rolling admissions. Financial aid and housing: Mar. 1. Does not guarantee to meet demonstrated need. Campus and alumni interviews: optional, informational. SATs or ACTs: required. SAT IIs: optional (English composition, math, and lab science for home-schooled students). Accepts electronic applications. No essay question.

Randolph–Macon Woman's College

2500 Rivermont Avenue, Lynchburg, VA 24503

In its glory days, Randolph-Macon was one of the premier women's colleges in the nation. The coming of coeducation to places like Washington and Lee has cut into R-MWC's market, but it still manages to field fine programs in the liberal and fine arts. Unlike pastoral Sweet Briar, R-MWC has a suburban location.

Forget the absence of male students for a moment and consider the strengths of Randolph-Macon Woman's College: from its ever-expanding academic opportunities

Website: www.rmwc.edu

(Continued)

Location: Residential
Total Enrollment: 721
Undergraduates: 721
Male/Female: 0/100
SAT Ranges: V 540–670
  M 510–620
ACT Range: 23–29
Financial Aid: 56%
Expense: Pr $ $
Phi Beta Kappa: Yes
Applicants: 718
Accepted: 87%
Enrolled: 30%
Grad in 6 Years: 63%
Returning Freshmen: 77%
Academics: ✍ ✍ ✍
Social: ☎ ☎
Q of L: ★ ★ ★ ★
Admissions: (800) 745-7692
Email Address:
  admissions@rmwc.edu

Strongest Programs
  Psychology
  Biology
  English Literature
  International Studies
  Fine Arts
  Classics

Worldliness is part of life at R-MWC. The new Global Studies Initiative has sponsored immersion programs in South Africa and Zimbabwe, a peace study in Nagasaki and Hiroshima, and a theatre seminar in London and Stratford.

and world travel to its small classes and lovely dorms, this Southern school clearly has mastered progress while maintaining beloved traditions and a deep sense of sisterhood. Each student encounters an integrated series of classes, extra-curricular activities, internships, and career planning customized to meet their goals. One student finds the academic challenge, well, bracing. "I came from a very academically competitive high school, and I still look like an underachiever here!" she exclaims.

The college's one hundred–acre campus is located in a gracious residential area of Lynchburg, a city of almost eighty thousand on the James River at the foot of the Blue Ridge Mountains. The old and majestic buildings, arrayed in a semicircle, are strewn with purple wisteria vines and surrounded by grand trees that burst into bloom in the spring and melt into colors in the fall. Glass corridors called trolleys link nearly all campus buildings. Main Hall, built in 1893, houses student rooms, classrooms, and faculty and administrative offices. The college features well-equipped computer labs hooked up to the campus network and set off with scanners, printers, and Internet access—enough to grant it a slot among the most-wired campuses in the nation. The college's Maier Museum of Art houses one of the country's most extensive collections of nineteenth- and twentieth-century American art, and its one hundred–acre equestrian center is in the nearby Blue Ridge foothills.

At Randolph-Macon, adherence to the honor code inspires trust among students and faculty. While each student develops a tailor-made program designed with a faculty advisor, there are general education requirements in three areas: skills (composition, math, and a foreign language), distribution (courses in literature, artistic expression, history, philosophy or religion, and the social sciences), and dimensions (a women's studies course and three cultural diversity courses). Freshmen have to take either the College's Symposium or Greek Play, thematic reading courses that alternate annually. In addition to the traditional majors, students can also create their own course of study or take on interdisciplinary majors. New offerings include American Studies and Environmental Studies. There's also a major for students wanting to teach elementary school, and another for students in the nursing program with Johns Hopkins University. Worldliness is part of life at R-MWC. The new Global Studies Initiative has sponsored immersion programs in South Africa and Zimbabwe, a peace study in Nagasaki and Hiroshima, and a theater seminar in London and Stratford.

> **"I came from a very academically competitive high school, and I still look like an underachiever here!"**

Psychology is the most popular major, followed by biology, English, political science, and sociology. English, biology, and psychology are the strongest programs, students say. Smaller departments, such as music and physics, are cited as weaker, primarily due to their size. No matter which classes students choose, they will be small and taught by a devoted professor. The instructors are "as enthusiastic inside the classroom as they are during office hours," one sophomore says. Competitively selected student-faculty research projects are also popular.

R-WMC's library collection of nearly 197,000 volumes also provides more than six hundred magazine and journal titles, extensive audiovisual holdings, and domestic and foreign newspapers. Randolph-Macon participates in the Seven-College Exchange* and gives women opportunities to experience other campuses, including a year or semester abroad at the University of Reading in England, the Universidad de las Americas in Mexico, or the University of Economics in Prague. And the college participates in American University's Washington Semester program and the Tri-College Exchange. About 65 percent of R-MWC students intern in Lynchburg and places ranging from the Chicago Lyric Opera to Philip Morris USA to London's Imperial College.

On campus, students find small classes and attentive professors. "On a scale of one to ten, Macon's teaching is a twelve!" gushes one communications major.

Reed College

3203 S.E. Woodstock Boulevard, Portland, OR 97202

Reed is like a West Coast version of Oberlin or Grinnell, mixing nonconformist students with a traditional (and rigorous) curriculum. Only two-thirds of first-year students graduate in six years, a sign of Reed's demands and the fact that its students often live close to the edge.

Reed College, one of the most intellectual colleges in the country, has been home to thirty-one Rhodes Scholars, forty-eight Fulbright Scholars, two MacArthur Fellows, and two Pulitzer Prize winners, and is one of a handful of colleges that requires all students to write a senior thesis to graduate. On the thesis due date, seniors march from the library steps to the registrar's office in a Thesis Parade, inscribe their names on a giant thermometer known as the Thesis Meter, and then throw the Renn Fayre, an affair described by one student as "an all-blowout party lasting three days." Reed is home to, as one student puts it, "the eccentric, brilliant, and work-obsessed."

Located just five miles from downtown Portland, Reed's one hundred–acre campus consists of rolling lawns, winding lanes, canyon creek, and protected wetlands. Recent efforts to provide safe migration of native fish have included the installation of fish ladders, and non-native plants are also being removed from the area in order to protect the natural habitat. In addition to the canyon, the campus is also widely known for its 125 different species of trees. These two thousand majestic arbors are a mix of original Tudor Gothic brick, slate, and limestone; old Northwest Timber-style; and newer more modern facilities. Recent improvements include the new Kaul Auditorium, more residence halls, and renovations to the psychology building and theater annex. Underway are renovations and expansions of the Eric V. Hauser Library and the ETC (educational technology center).

The school offers unsurpassed intellectual opportunities in the liberal arts and sciences for its size. The Gray Fund helps to make this possible by bringing the Reed community together outside the classroom for field trips as well as sponsoring other cultural and social programs. All dormitory rooms are connected to a network providing twenty-four-hour access to hundreds of computers distributed throughout the campus. The school also provides a loan program that allows students to buy personal computers through small monthly payments to the school. The Triga Research Nuclear Reactor is run by students and staff who have passed an eight-hour Atomic Energy Commission examination.

> **"Reed's courses are extremely rigorous. The professors expect you to be intellectual equals who are seeking the experience that will bring you on a level with them."**

Although the college works within a structure of personal freedom, the curriculum is—contrary to what one might expect—highly traditional. All undergraduates must complete a full-year course or the equivalent in semester courses in each of the following divisions: literature, philosophy, and the arts; history and the social sciences; natural sciences; mathematics, logic, linguistics, or foreign languages. First-year students are required to pass a year-long humanities course taught by prestigious faculty. Juniors must pass a qualifying examination. Interdisciplinary programs and opportunities to design an individual major abound, and several 3–2 engineering, forestry and environmental science, visual arts, and computer science programs are also offered at Reed. Many students participate in Reed's study-abroad programs, available in nineteen overseas countries, including Germany, Russia,

Website: www.reed.edu
Location: City outskirts
Total Enrollment: 1,420
Undergraduates: 1,396
Male/Female: 46/54
SAT Ranges: V 640–740
  M 600–680
ACT Range: 27–31
Financial Aid: 50%
Expense: Pr $ $ $
Phi Beta Kappa: Yes
Applicants: 1,731
Accepted: 71%
Enrolled: 29%
Grad in 6 Years: 70%
Returning Freshmen: 83%
Academics: ✑ ✑ ✑ ✑ ½
Social: ☎ ☎ ☎
Q of L: ★ ★ ★ ★
Admissions: (503) 777-7511
Email Address:
  admission@reed.edu

Strongest Programs
  Biology
  Chemistry
  Psychology
  English
  Philosophy
  History
  Physics

China, France, and Costa Rica. Most students spend all four years at Reed in classes with twenty-five people or less.

Studying is a way of life at Reed, and some students say they have neither time nor inclination to do much else. Most take full advantage of the library's late hours. "Reed's courses are extremely rigorous," says one senior. "The professors expect you to be intellectual equals who are seeking the experience that will bring you on a level with them." A new employer relations program has improved relations with alumni, local employers, and parents and has boosted the effectiveness of the career-services office. The professors are willing to put as much energy into teaching as they demand from their students in class. Students rarely attend class unprepared for what is sure to be lively intellectual banter between inquiring and active minds. Faculty members must regularly write evaluations of students' work, and are known for their brutal honesty. Most courses are run as seminars or "conferences" with enrollments of twenty or fewer. Over the years, a quarter of Reed's grads have gone on for Ph.D.s, the highest percentage of any liberal arts college in the country.

Reed has been around for more than eighty years, and its offerings currently attract students from all over the nation. Only 14 percent of students come from Oregon, and most come from upper-middle-class backgrounds. "Freshpeople"—orientation Reed-style—includes a three-day backpacking trip, organized forays into Portland, and community-service projects. Despite the conservatism found on many of the nation's campuses, Reed seems committed to remaining an island of intellectual independence, diversity, and free thinking. "I feel that Reedies are unique in that we consciously cultivate and even glorify our oddity," one student explains. "[Students] run the gamut from pot-smoking hippies to radical vegan lesbian activists to outdoorsy athletic types to total nerds." Despite its wide-open attitude, minorities are poorly represented on campus; less than 1 percent are African-American, 3 percent are Hispanic, and Asian-Americans account for 5 percent, a situation many students lament. "Political correctness is another issue, but social/political responsibility and local government is definitely strong," says a biology major. Reed meets the full financial need of half its students, but no merit or athletic scholarships are available.

Sixty-five percent of the students live on campus in small, homey coed or single-sex dorms that usually house fewer than thirty people, and some of the rooms feature such niceties as fireplaces or balconies. "The dorms are great and each has its own set of quirks to deal with so no one is really better than another, although Old Dorm Block and Anna Mann are by far the most popular," claims one student. First-year students are guaranteed housing, while the rest must endure the lottery. "There can be problems after freshman year getting a room but it generally works out," states a senior. Singles usually go to on-campus seniors, but there is sufficient privacy for all; even most doubles have two rooms. Many upperclassmen prefer to live off campus, and houses to share are cheap and plentiful. On-campus students must join the meal plan and eat in the Commons, which includes ample vegetarian and vegan options. A salad bar adds some alimentary diversity, but students are most appreciative of the student-run coffee shops.

Just about everyone goes to the campus socials, which feature a wide variety of Pacific Northwest alternative bands. Movies, coffeehouses, intramural and club sports, and dinner out take up the rest of weekend time. The on-campus scene, though, could use some improvement. "The social life at Reed, like many other aspects of Reed life, is what you make of it," one student explains. The Halloween social is noted for its "utter zaniness" and "uninhibited bodily movements," and the end of every academic year brings the Renn Fayre, "a big party complete with live chess, a naked Slip 'n Slide, and any number of bizarre activities," says a student. One

Although the college works within a structure of personal freedom, the curriculum is—contrary to what one might expect—highly traditional.

"[Students] run the gamut from pot-smoking hippies to radical vegan lesbian activists to outdoorsy athletic types to total nerds."

The school maintains its own ski cabin on nearby Mount Hood with sleeping space for thirty.

way Reedies avoid the January blahs is to divide into teams that use recycled home-building materials to build catapults on the campus lawn and see whose contraption can propel an object the farthest. The only rule is that students have to fire something that won't put holes in buildings, the lawn or, of course, people. Paideia, ten days between semesters when students take "fun" classes, including Southern cooking and Shiatsu, is also a popular tradition among the usually stressed-out students.

Where there are college students, there is also alcohol. Students, however, say that drinking is not a high priority here. Drinking underage is forbidden per the Reed Honor Principle and college policy, however, "the administration realizes that an overzealous crackdown on drinking only leads to less safe drinking," a freshman explains. Quieter escapes include the beautiful Oregon coast, an hour away. Plus, Portland has lots to offer. "Portland is not a college town, but there are plenty of ways to get involved with the community," comments a history major. The school maintains its own ski cabin on nearby Mount Hood with sleeping space for thirty. There are no varsity athletics, although some clubs, such as basketball, soccer, and rugby, compete with clubs from other colleges in the area. One student reports that the lack of NCAA sports is the school's best quality. The closest thing Reed has to an official school mascot is the Doyle Owl, a three hundred–pound concrete structure that is regularly stolen from one dorm to the next. There is wide interest in sports on a casual basis, and the newly renovated sports center offers beautiful squash and paddleball courts, a swimming pool, a state-of-the-art weight room, and other facilities.

One thing is for sure—Reedies are an entirely different breed of student. "There are hundreds of details that make Reed the amazing place it is, and more are being created every day," says a history major. When asked whether or not his school had a slogan, one student gave us this unofficial motto found on some college T-shirts: "Atheism, Communism, and Free Love."

Overlaps

Oberlin, UC–Berkley, Brown, Stanford, Harvard

Rensselaer Polytechnic Institute

Troy, NY 12180-3590

If you can spell Rensselaer, you've already got a leg up on many applicants. RPI is one of the nation's great technical universities, along with Caltech, MIT, Worcester Polytech, and Harvey Mudd. The beauty of RPI is the chance for hands-on learning and synergy between technology and management.

Rensselaer is one of the first research universities to figure out what millions of students have known for decades: hands-on control of the learning process helps students retain much more than passive listeners do. The application to Rensselaer Polytechnic Institute asks, "Why not change the world?" The school has for years aided students in doing that by combining the newest possibilities of the Information Age with the tried-and-true values of hard work, experiential learning, and a firm grounding in "the application of science to the common purposes of life." Many courses are small seminars, allowing students to explore, experiment,

Website: www.rpi.edu
Location: City outskirts
Total Enrollment: 8,106
Undergraduates: 5,272
Male/Female: 76/24
SAT Ranges: V 580–680
M 650–720

(Continued)

ACT Range: 24–28

Financial Aid: 90%

Expense: Pr $ $ $ $

Phi Beta Kappa: No

Applicants: 5,542

Accepted: 67%

Enrolled: 20%

Grad in 6 Years: 77%

Returning Freshmen: 91%

Academics: ✐ ✐ ✐ ✐

Social: ☎ ☎ ☎

Q of L: ★ ★ ★

Admissions: (518) 276-6216

Email Address:
admissions@rpi.edu

Strongest Programs
Architecture
Engineering
Humanities and Social
    Sciences
Information Technology
Management and Technology
Science

create, simulate, and synthesize new ideas by exploiting technology and their own imagination.

Set high on a bluff overlooking Troy, New York, Rensselaer's 260-acre campus mixes modern research facilities and classical, ivy-covered brick buildings dating to the turn of the century. Recently, the school completed a $9.3 million renovation of the Student Union, concealing in its atrium a state-of-the-art wireless computing network that serves two hundred students on the building's two upper floors. Construction on two new major facilities—one for research in biotechnology and interdisciplinary studies, the other a center for electronic media and performing arts—began in 2002. A $7 million computer center contains one of the largest computer graphics laboratories in the nation; RPI is a national leader in the study and application of electronic media, and recently introduced a B.S. program in electronic arts.

> **"Sometimes professors may be hard to understand, but they are always willing to help students when they are confused with the subject material."**

It would be an exaggeration to say that technology is "God" at RPI, though the school's conversion of a Gothic chapel into a computer lab does hint in that direction. Even if it's not deified, technology remains omnipresent at this school, which pioneered the teaching of calculus via computer in the early '90s, and has been named one of Yahoo!'s most-wired campuses. Not surprisingly, all students are required to have their own laptop computer. Studio courses foster small-group interaction between students and professors, after which students return to their workstations for collaborative problem solving. RPI, which made its reputation as one of the nation's premier engineering schools, continues to excel in traditional favorites such as chemical and electrical engineering, as well as newer specialties like environmental and computer systems engineering. Computer science is the most popular major, followed by mechanical engineering and management. The nuclear engineering department has its own linear accelerator, while graduate and undergraduate students participate in research at the Center for Industrial Innovation.

RPI's Lally School of Management and Technology combines elements of a business school with the latest technical applications. Entrepreneurship is one of its specialties; budding entrepreneurs may participate in the Lally "Business Incubator," a support system for start-up companies run by Rensselaer students and alumni. Last fall, RPI began requiring all students to take courses in entrepreneurship or have an "entrepreneurial experience" before graduation. The BS program in information technology continues to attract top students, who often combine it with coursework in e-commerce or the arts. Majors in the humanities and social sciences are limited, and their quality is directly related to their applicability to technical fields. Still, all students must complete at least twenty-four credits in these areas, as well as at least twenty-four credits in physical, life, and engineering sciences, a minimum of thirty credits in their majors and a writing or writing-intensive course.

> **"Most students here are either geeky or frat boys. It's either 'Party! Party!' or 'Program my computer.'"**

About two-thirds of Rensselaer students are undergraduates, a high percentage for a top engineering school; because of this, RPI has worked hard to ensure that classes are smaller and more attention is paid to individual needs. Eighty-four percent have fewer than fifty students. Professors are extremely knowledgeable, and the quality of teaching is excellent. "Sometimes professors may be hard to understand, but they are always willing to help students when they are confused with the subject material," says a freshman. Juniors and seniors enjoy self-paced courses and occasionally paid positions helping with faculty research. Career counseling is helpful, and academic advisors get mixed reviews. All of the effort pays off: 70 percent of a recent RPI senior class went on to jobs after graduation, and 15 percent entered graduate or professional school.

For students who can't wait to start working, popular co-op programs in more than a dozen fields help them earn both money and credit. Those who already know what field they'll pursue may enter a seven-year dual degree program in medicine, a six-year program in law, and four- and five-year master's programs in biology, geology, and mathematical science. Although most engineering schools discourage studying abroad, Rensselaer offers exchange programs in several European countries, most notably at Switzerland's renowned Federal Institute of Technology.

More than half of RPI students are New Yorkers, and 90 percent ranked in the top quarter of their high-school class. RPI is fairly diverse, with Asian-Americans comprising 12 of the student body, African-Americans 4 percent, and Hispanics 5 percent. A slogan warns male students to import their girlfriends, since males outnumber females more than three to one. Students tend to be bright, studious, and technically savvy. "Most students here are either geeky or frat boys. It's either 'Party! Party!' or 'Program my computer.'" RPI is far from a center of political activism; one student says the biggest campus issue is choosing the Grand Marshal, who oversees a boisterous week-long carnival celebrating campus elections, during which professors are forbidden from giving tests.

Fifty-five percent of students live in university residence halls; freshmen are required to live on campus and, for the fall term, must buy the meal plan. The residence halls are well maintained and clean. "The dorms are definitely not the best part of campus life, but they aren't horrible," a sophomore says. All bedrooms have fast Internet links for every resident. In newly constructed Barton Hall, even the laundry room is wired for fast access to the Internet and RPI's campus network. Upperclassmen may keep their current room, enter the lottery to get something better, or live in college-owned apartments off campus, widely considered the nicest option. About half of RPI upperclassmen live in fraternity and sorority houses, where meals are served family-style; 30 percent of men and 20 percent of women go Greek.

"Hockey at RPI equals insanity."

Social life "is very good for the people who want it," one student says, but the male-female ratio is a major hassle, forcing lovelorn men to haunt Russell Sage (next door) or Skidmore (forty minutes away) in hopes of finding a mate. Other than Greek parties, weekend options at RPI include sporting events, live entertainment, concerts, movies, and a half-dozen local pubs—some of which students find easily accept fake IDs. Those under twenty-one can't have alcohol in the dorms, and fraternities aren't allowed to have "containers of mass distribution" (i.e., kegs) at parties; students are split as to whether those not of age are easily served. Extracurricular clubs, organized around such interests as chess, dance, judo, and skiing, are chartered and funded by a student-managed body that doles out more than $8 million annually.

Free shuttle buses run regularly from campus to downtown Troy, a former industrial revolution town, but there aren't many good reasons to make the trip. "Troy is a run-down city that is broke," says a mechanical engineering major. Students and Greek groups do get involved with community-service projects, though, and the town offers opportunities for internships. A six-screen movie theater is within easy reach, and for a taste of bigger-city nightlife, Albany is a half-hour's drive. For scenic excursions, the Berkshires, Catskills, Adirondacks, Lake George, Lake Placid, the Saranac Lakes, Montreal, and Boston are popular destinations.

The athletic scene at Rensselaer revolves around hockey, hockey, hockey, the school's only team playing in Division I. One of the biggest weekends of the year is Big Red Freakout, when all festivities center around cheering on the beloved Big

It would be an exaggeration to say that technology is "God" at RPI, though the school's conversion of a Gothic chapel into a computer lab does hint in that direction.

RPI requires all students to take courses in entrepreneurship or have an "entrepreneurial experience" before graduation.

Red. "Hockey at RPI equals insanity," one student says. "If you go to one hockey game all season, go to the men's hockey season opener. The place is packed with rowdy RPI students who scream and chant in unison." "Hockey has huge events and draw a big crowd all the time," adds another. RPI offers eighteen full scholarships to hockey players each year. Other varsity teams play in Division III, and the football, baseball, men's and women's basketball, and women's ice hockey and field hockey teams are most popular. Each year, Rensselaer's football players vie with rival Union College for the coveted Dutchman's Shoes, while a new fitness center helps even non-varsity players sculpt six-pack abs.

Students at RPI learn cutting-edge technology in an atmosphere based on teamwork and collaboration. They delight in the school's close-knit, down-to-earth feel, enhanced by a common interest in computers, gadgets, and other accoutrements of geekdom. While the gender imbalance generates grumbles from the outnumbered male students, after four years of immersion in some of the best educational technology in the nation, students leave RPI poised to influence the technical destiny anywhere.

Overlaps

Cornell, MIT, Carnegie Mellon, Rochester Institute of Technology, Worcester Polytechnic Institute

If You Apply To ➢

Rensselaer: Regular admissions: Jan. 1. Meets demonstrated need of 65%. Campus and alumni interviews: optional, informational. SATs or ACTs: required. SAT IIs: optional (writing, math, and chemistry or physics required for applicants to accelerated dentistry, law, physician-scientist, and podiatric programs). Accepts the Common Application and electronic applications. Apply to particular programs. Essay question: significant experience or achievement; influential person; or how your work will impact the twenty-first century; others depend on program.

University of Rhode Island

Kingston, RI 02881

URI is a smallish alternative to UMass and UConn. With Boston, Providence, and vacation hot-spot Newport within easy reach, there is plenty to do. Strong programs include engineering, marine science, and pharmacy. More than half of URI's students are out-of-staters.

Website: www.uri.edu
Location: Small town
Total Enrollment: 14,362
Undergraduates: 10,647
Male/Female: 44/56
SAT Ranges: V 490–590
M 490–600
ACT Range: NA
Financial Aid: 62%
Expense: Pub $ $ $
Phi Beta Kappa: Yes
Applicants: 9,758
Accepted: 75%
Enrolled: 23%
Grad in 6 Years: 57%
Returning Freshmen: 78%

Once known as a great party school, the University of Rhode Island is building a new reputation for challenging academics and friendly associations. In the years since President Robert Carothers cracked down on the wild drinking scene, the school has become more focused on Monday morning than Saturday night. "Over the years, URI has become more academically competitive," says one senior. "Many students are concerned about their academic performance."

URI's 1,200-acre campus is located in the small town of Kingston. Surrounded by farmland and only six miles from the coast, it is also within driving distance of cities such as Providence, Boston, and New York. The main academic buildings, a mixture of modern and "old New England granite," surround a central quad on Kingston Hill. At the foot of Kingston Hill lies the athletic buildings and agricultural fields. Work on a new $54 million eight thousand–seat convocation center—the largest building project ever at the University of Rhode Island—is nearing completion. The university is also putting $10.6 million into an addition and renovation to Ballentine Hall, home to the College of Business Administration. The men's and women's hockey teams will soon be able to enjoy a new $12 million, 2,500-seat ice arena, one of only two ice rinks in Rhode Island to operate year-round.

New students here are first enrolled in the University College, which offers courses in communication skills, fine arts and literature, natural and social sciences, letters, mathematics, foreign language, and culture requirements, while providing academic and career guidance. All new students take URI 101, a one-credit course intended to acquaint students with support services, co-curricular activities, and academic majors and career options. After a year or two in University College, students choose more specialized colleges, such as the well-regarded College of Pharmacy. The university also offers a marine and environment program, landscape architecture, and African and African-American Studies. Some majors require students to stay for five or six years, but most students graduate in four years. Freshmen often have full professors; more than 75 percent of professors have their doctorate. "I like knowing I have earned a grade as opposed to having it handed to me," says communications major. The university offers exchange programs with universities in Austria, England, France, Germany, Japan, Korea, Mexico, Spain, Venezuela, Quebec, and Nova Scotia. Students can also participate in the international engineering program, spend a year of the five-year program abroad, and major in both engineering and Spanish, German, or French. A Writing Center provides free tutorial assistance to anyone who wants feedback on any kind of college or extracurricular writing.

> **"Many students are concerned about their academic performance."**

Students mostly hail from the Northeast, and URI gives preference to in-state students who meet requirements. About 45 percent of entering freshmen are from Rhode Island. Although students say the campus is becoming more diverse, at least 75 percent of undergraduates are white. "Students at URI come from very diverse backgrounds, lifestyles, and interests," insists a psychology major. "The students are fairly open minded as a whole." Ninety percent of freshmen come from public schools. Ten percent of men and 12 percent of women join the active Greek community.

Though most freshmen live on campus, 63 percent of all undergraduates do not. Because of ongoing renovations, on-campus housing is tight. "They are renovating all the dorms, which is forcing many people off campus," says one senior. "The students who live on campus are forced to share a small room with three people," reports another. The good news is that students live in a sizable off-campus community near the beach. Students complain about a chronic shortage of parking but say that even freshmen are allowed to have cars. There is ample public transit. The university now has a strict alcohol policy, and students note that underage drinkers have a hard time finding an adult beverage on campus. "The policies are strict. They do work," says a communications major. "Alcohol is only permitted if you are twenty-one. You may have *one* six-pack in your room." URI has ten meal plans available to commuters and dorm residents. While the hearty New England winters are invigorating for some, many students wind up catching colds, earning URI the unflattering nickname Upper Respiratory Infection.

> **"I like knowing I have earned a grade as opposed to having it handed to me."**

Kingston is a sleepy New England college town. "The only thing of interest to students in Kingston is campus," says a senior. "There are many opportunities to get involved. Some attend the town council meetings while others organize beach cleanups," says a psychology major. URI is also within striking distance of both Rhode Island's famous beaches and the major New England ski slopes. Newport, with its heady social scene, is just twenty minutes away, and those feeling lucky can get to the Foxwoods Resort and Casino in forty-five minutes. Other fun road trips include Providence (thirty minutes), Boston (ninety minutes), and New York City (four hours). Many natives find going home on weekends a pleasant diversion, but on campus there are always movies and guest speakers, plus the usual Greek parties.

(Continued)
Academics: ✍ ✍
Social: ☎ ☎ ☎ ☎
Q of L: ★ ★ ★
Admissions: (401) 874-7000
Email Address:
uriadmit@uri.edu

Strongest Programs
Pharmacy
Engineering
Marine and Environmental
  Sciences
Communicative Disorders

All new students take URI 101, a one-credit course intended to acquaint students with support services, co-curricular activities, and academic majors and career options.

A Writing Center provides free tutorial assistance to anyone who wants feedback on any kind of college or extracurricular writing.

The campus coffeehouse hosts open mic nights, and movie theaters, clubs, and malls beckon just off campus. The student newspaper that covers it all has one of the most original names anywhere: *The Good 5¢ Cigar* (as in, "what this country needs").

Sports are big at Rhode Island, and basketball games are especially exciting. Midnight Madness (the team's first sanctioned practice of the year) is always well attended, and URI fans love it when the team defeats archrival Providence College. Another student favorite is Oozeball, an April volleyball tournament played in about two feet of mud. As befits the school's locale, sailing draws much interest, and the team regularly produces All-Americans. Students can find unique opportunities running businesses like a flower shop, a sound and lighting group, and a coffee house in the Memorial Union under full-time supervision but with a lot of independence.

Centrally located in dense New England, URI students are close to the beaches and ski slopes, and within easy reach of some major cities. The administration works hard and the students feel at home. "It is so big and has so much to offer that most people will find what they are looking for," says a senior.

> "Students at URI come from very diverse backgrounds, lifestyles, and interests."

If You Apply To ➤

URI: Early action: Dec. 14. Rolling admissions and financial aid: Mar. 1. Meets demonstrated need of 71%. Campus interviews: recommended, evaluative. Alumni interviews: optional, evaluative. SATs or ACTs: required. Essay question: personal statement (optional).

Rhode Island School of Design

2 College Street, Providence, RI 02903

The nation's best-known arts specialty school, RISD sits on a hillside adjacent to Brown. The campus offers easy access to downtown Providence, but it can't match the location of rival Parsons in New York's Greenwich Village. Offers an artsy architecture major in addition to programs in the visual arts.

Website: www.risd.edu
Location: City center
Total Enrollment: 2,119
Undergraduates: 1,849
Male/Female: 40/60
SAT Ranges: V 540-660
   M 540-650
Financial Aid: 39%
Expense: Pr $ $ $
Phi Beta Kappa: No
Applicants: 2,404
Accepted: 33%
Enrolled: 55%
Grad in 6 Years: 93%
Returning Freshmen: 95%
Academics: ✍ ✍ ✍ ✍

Founded in the late nineteenth century to address the country's need for more artisans and craftsmen, the Rhode Island School of Design has grown into a premier arts incubator. It's a place where today's artists and designers gather to share ideas and create tomorrow's masterpieces and architectural icons. RISD grants degrees in virtually every design-related topic, and like the varied curriculum, the students and their creations are as diverse as the colors on an artist's palette. "Attending RISD is literally eating, thinking, wearing, dreaming, and speaking art. You become it," says a junior graphic design major.

Though you might expect an art school like RISD to occupy funky, futuristic buildings, the predominant look here is Colonial New England. Set on the upgrade of College Hill, RISD sits at the edge of Providence's beautifully preserved historic district across the street from Brown University. Many campus buildings date from the 1700s and early 1800s; the mostly redbrick-and-white-trim group includes converted homes, a bank, and even an old church with the campus pub in what used to be its attic. The six-story Industrial Design building, designed by faculty member Jim Barnes, occupies the old Roitman furniture company warehouse. Its fifty thousand square feet are designed for wood- and metal-working and prototype making.

About the only thing RISD's campus doesn't offer is a lot of open space. Those wanting to toss a football or a Frisbee would be well advised to take up a sport better suited to the streets of Providence, like hopscotch or people-watching.

While RISD looks traditionally New England on the outside, behind its historic walls lies something else entirely. Students give the architecture, graphic design, and industrial design programs top marks, while liberal arts are considered more of a "joke." As a graphic design major explains, "Liberal arts is pretty limited, and it is hard to relate courses back to our majors." Another says, "The English department is not very likable or strong." That said, bachelor's and master's liberal arts concentrations in art history are available, complementing offerings in furniture design and architecture and interior architecture (for grad students). Landscape architecture is no longer available to undergraduates. RISD also offers cross-registration at adjacent Brown University for students seeking more diverse courses. The institute's highly specialized library contains 662,000 non-book items (prints, etc.) and 106,000 volumes, and students are likely to be found at their personally assigned studio carrels. Perhaps RISD's most prized facility is its one hundred thousand–piece art museum, a superlative collection that includes everything from Roman and Egyptian art to works by Monet, Matisse, and Picasso. A new wing has allowed more of these wonderful works to be viewed.

To graduate, students must be in residence for at least two years, and must complete a final-year project. They must also finish 126 credit hours—fifty-four in their major, eighteen in the Foundation Studies program (an integrated year of "functional and conceptual experiences" that leads to "an understanding of visual language"), forty-two in the liberal arts (art and architectural history, English, history/philosophy/social sciences,

> **"Liberal arts is pretty limited, and it is hard to relate courses back to our majors."**

some electives), and twelve in nonmajor electives. Hands-on studio courses abound, and most classes have fewer than twenty students. Still, a junior says, "Getting into required courses isn't usually a problem. Getting a teacher for a specific required course (known for teaching it well) can be." During RISD's winter session, six weeks between the first and second semesters, students are encouraged to take courses outside their major. And each year about thirty juniors and seniors venture to Rome for the European Honors Program, which offers independent study, projects with critics, and immersion in Italian culture.

While students at RISD don't "hit the books" in the traditional sense, the in-studio workload is tremendous. "Our Freshman Foundation program is nicknamed the RISD bootcamp," says a senior industrial design student. But "liberal arts classes are almost the opposite, very lax," notes a classmate. Students praise faculty members' knowledge and accessibility. "The quality of teaching at RISD surpassed all my expectations after the first month. Every teacher is a practicing designer or artist in their field," a junior says. A senior rates the teaching quality as excellent, saying "We are taught how to find our own solutions, not to plug in a given solution." Career and academic counseling both get high marks.

RISD students (referred to as "RISDoids" or "Rizdees") come to Providence to form a largely urban mix of styles and personalities. In a word, the school is diverse, and that can create tension. "Students here are open minded and very affirming. Any problems may have to do with economic class issues, foreign clashes, and limited racial diversity," a sophomore says. Indeed, only 6 percent of students are native Rhode Islanders, not surprising given the state's small size. Many of the rest are from the vicinity of other East Coast cities, notably New York and Boston. Though highly selective—67 percent of freshmen were on the top quarter of their high-school class—RISD will often take a chance on students who did not perform well in high school by the usual academic criteria, but make up for

(Continued)
Social: ☎ ☎
Q of L: ★ ★ ★ ★
Admissions: (401) 454-6300
Email Address:
admissions@risd.edu

Strongest Programs
Architecture
Illustration
Graphic Design
Industrial Design

While students at RISD don't "hit the books" in the traditional sense, the in-studio workload is tremendous.

that with special artistic talent. The racial makeup of the campus is fairly mixed, with Asian-Americans making up 11 percent of the student body, African-Americans 2 percent, and Hispanics 4 percent. Issues of ethnicity and sexuality top the campus agenda, though a senior says "generally, students are too wrapped up in their own little worlds to get organized and fight for anything." Tuition and fees here are steep, with the annual tab nearing $32,000. Though RISD offers some merit scholarships, athletic scholarships are nonexistent, and the school does not guarantee to meet financial need.

All noncommuting freshmen are required to live in coed dorms that one student says "can be a little beaten up by the artists who've lived there." The dorms are comfortable and feature common studio areas and connections to the campus computer network, but a graphic design major says "it is hard to get repairs done." The vast majority of upperclassmen move off campus to nearby apartments, many of which occupy floors

> **"Getting into required courses isn't usually a problem. Getting a teacher for a specific required course (known for teaching it well) can be.**

of restored homes; RISD also owns an apartment building and some renovated Colonial and Victorian houses. "Housing is good but there are too many students and not enough housing," a sophomore says. "Lotteries are vicious and many are left to find apartments on their own." All boarders buy the meal plan, which students say has improved as of late.

Despite a student body that looks like it could have been plucked from the streets of New York's Greenwich Village, RISD is not the place to come for wild and funky nightlife. "Social life?" asks a senior. With three eight-hour studios each week, plus two other classes (and that's just freshman year), "typical social activity is running out for a cup of coffee. If you're desperate, there's always Brown University." Providence also provides some social outlets. The Taproom shown on the campus map went dry years ago, and each year, those twenty-one and over vote on whether to allow drinking in their residences. But underage students can swill "as long as they're responsible and don't draw attention to themselves," an illustration major says. Though RISD isn't much for traditions, one big annual event is the Artist's Ball, a November formal where dress is "formal or festive, which has been interpreted as everything from chain mail to buck naked," says a senior. "The only other event we're known for is graduation, which can be a real circus." When claustrophobia sets in, students can flee to the RISD farm, a thirty-three-acre recreation area on the shores of nearby Narragansett Bay. Boston and New York are one and four hours away by train, respectively.

Though jocks are an endangered species at RISD, recreation opportunities abound. There is no intercollegiate sports program in the ordinary sense, though there is a hockey team, called the Nads (which, of course, leads to RISDoids hollering "Go Nads!"). Students do get involved in intramural sports, ranging from football and baseball to sailing and cycling. There's also a weight room for those who thrive on pumping iron.

Students come to RISD committed to their crafts, and most march to the beat of their own drummer as they rush from studio courses to gallery openings to exhibitions. But this professional preoccupation is not a problem. Students are confident the endless studio hours are starting them on the path to success. "Starting the first day of classes and enduring a lifetime, Foundation students learn what it means to push ideas, establish a productive work ethic, and cross the boundaries set by others," a graphic design student says.

Overlaps

Pratt Institute, Maryland Institute College of Art, Art Institute of Chicago, Syracuse, Parsons School of Design

RISD: Early action: Dec. 15. Regular admissions: Feb. 15. Does not guarantee to meet demonstrated need. No campus or alumni interviews. SATs or ACTs: required. SAT IIs: optional. No essay question.

Rhodes College

2000 North Parkway, Memphis, TN 38112-1690

BEST BUY

Goes head to head with Sewanee for the top spot in the pecking order of mid-South liberal arts colleges. While Sewanee has a gorgeous rural campus, Rhodes has Memphis. Economics and international studies head the list of strong programs. Like Davidson, Rhodes has historic ties to the Presbyterian Church.

Located in the city that gave us Elvis, W. C. Handy ("Father of the Blues"), Beale Street, and barbeque, Rhodes College emphasizes a strict honor code that builds trust and challenging academics that build confidence. Professors leave the classroom during exams, and there are no meal cards to prove who's on the meal plan. "We have a really strong community built upon trust and responsibility," one sophomore says. The combination creates a college experience that students say is gratifying and complete.

Rhodes was founded as a Presbyterian school in 1848 in Clarksville, Tennessee, and moved to Memphis in 1925. The one hundred–acre campus is located in a residential section of midtown Memphis, across the street from a 175-acre park housing the city's largest art museum, a golf course, and the Memphis Zoo. The original Gothic structures of brownish orange stone, leaded-glass windows, and slate roofs have served as models for all forthcoming buildings. With the exception of its underground science center, Rhodes's elegant, old-fashioned tonality remains intact. Thirteen of the original buildings are on the National Register of Historic Places. One new addition to the campus is the $22.5 million Bryan Campus Life Center, which provides extensive facilities for sports and fitness (squash and racquetball courts, a suspended indoor track, and a sports arena) and extracurricular activities.

> **"We have a really strong community built upon trust and responsibility."**

Rhodes offers a wide array of traditional and interdisciplinary programs. The natural sciences are Rhodes's forte (biology is the second most popular major), and labs are equipped with state-of-the-art equipment. Strong programs also exist in business administration—the top major—economics, and English (Renaissance literature is especially strong). "The economic and business departments have about 90 percent to 100 percent job placement," says a sophomore. The political science department has produced four national championship teams at the National Intercollegiate Mock Trial Tournament. A new partnership with St. Jude Children's Research Hospital lets students spend twelve weeks in the summer working with researchers, and continue their research the following year. The respected international studies program offers summer internships abroad in exciting locales such as Madrid, Hong Kong, and Johannesburg through the Buckman International Fellows program. And the burgeoning Greek and Roman Studies program offers a travel-study option that includes a twenty-four-day excursion to Greece and sizable scholarships. Rhodes is also a member of the Associated Colleges of the South consortium.*

Website: www.rhodes.edu
Location: City residential
Total Enrollment: 1,551
Undergraduates: 1,535
Male/Female: 43/57
SAT Ranges: V 600–700
  M 600–680
ACT Range: 26–30
Financial Aid: 36%
Expense: Pr $
Phi Beta Kappa: Yes
Applicants: 2,426
Accepted: 64%
Enrolled: 27%
Grad in 6 Years: 72%
Returning Freshmen: 89%
Academics: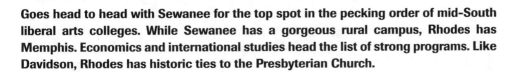
Social: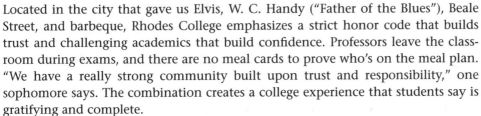
Q of L: ★ ★ ★ ★
Admissions: (901) 843-3700
Email Address:
  adminfo@rhodes.edu

Strongest Programs
  Biology
  Chemistry
  Physics
  International Studies
  English
  Economics
  Political Science
  Business Administration

In addition to standard distribution requirements and a foreign language mandate, all students must fulfill a humanities requirement that includes taking a four-course sequence from the following: Search for Values in the Light of Western History and Religion (SEARCH for short) or Life: Then and Now. The SEARCH course (previously called MAN) has been a staple of the school's curriculum for almost fifty years. It takes students through the whole history and culture of Western civilization, with a special emphasis on the Bible. Rhodes requires students to take two years of religion classes. But these aren't "Sunday School" courses: some of the profs are Buddhist, atheist, or feminist. With lectures, seminars, honors programs, one-on-one tutorials, studies at Oxford, supervised internships, bridge (multiple) majors, and independent Directed Inquiry, there are dozens of ways to get an education at Rhodes. In addition, Rhodes now has exchange programs in countries including France, Japan, Scotland, and Belgium. Also popular is the Dual Degree Program with Washington University, which has defined tracks for engineering students.

> "The economic and business departments have about 90 percent to 100 percent job placement."

The workload and academic environment is "competitive, though definitely not cut-throat," says a political science major, who calls the courses "manageable." More than 80 percent of classes have fewer than twenty-five students, which means professors are real people, not talking heads. "Most of the professors have been extremely knowledgeable and stimulating, and have really taken an interest in me as a person," a sophomore says. "The student-professor interaction is one of Rhodes's greatest advantages." Some students say they've had few problems at registration. "We have a high-tech computer program that successfully matches students with their courses based on the student's need or demand for a course," explains a political science major. Both academic and career counseling programs receive high marks. "My academic advisor is very on top of things and is involved in my life," says a biochemistry major.

Professors leave the classroom during exams, and there are no meal cards to prove who's on the meal plan.

Diversity has been a sticking point for Rhodes over the past few years. Most students are white, and 55 percent are from the top tenth of their high-school class. The flavor of Rhodes's student body is definitely Southern, and about a third of the undergraduates come from both rural and urban areas of Tennessee. The student body is 3 percent Asian-American, 4 percent African-American, and 2 percent Hispanic. "Changing close-minded and prejudiced mind-sets of some students is an issue at Rhodes," says an English major. The Black Student Association has been forthright in bringing concerns to the administration, which is receptive to ideas. The college has a healthy endowment, and while financial aid has been cut recently, the school still offers nearly three hundred merit-based scholarships.

All dorms are single-sex, air-conditioned, and clean; some attract students with a special "academic interest." Freshmen occupy their own single-sex residence halls (the best are said to be Glassell for men and Williford for women) while upperclassmen fend for the rooms they want in the yearly lottery. Housing has been tight, but the college recently opened a $15 million apartment complex that can house two hundred students. Twenty-five percent of the students live off campus, where room and board can be cheaper, but few recommend the move. "The quality of the dorms and proximity to classrooms" often means students "choose to stay on campus for all four years." Regarding meals, more than one student admits the food is "pretty bad." The cafeteria is affectionately called "The Rat," and the workers there are "Rat Ladies." Campus security is tight: an ironwork fence encircles the whole one hundred acres and residence halls remain locked at all times. Rhodes also has a twenty-four-hour escort policy and sixty emergency phones across campus.

> "The student-professor interaction is one of Rhodes's greatest advantages."

Much of social life takes place on campus. Activities include bands, movies, and amphitheater parties such as the Rites of Spring (three days of nonstop music, picnics, and a mud-slinging contest). The Greek scene draws quite a few Rhodents: 55 percent of the men join fraternities, 58 percent of the women pledge sororities. Since Greeks do not live in their houses, the tension between "Greeks and Freaks" is kept within reasonable bounds. But one history major quickly lost interest in the ubiquitous frat parties: "Once you've been to one, you've been to all!" The school's alcohol policy allows on-campus parties where those twenty-one or older wearing wrist bracelets can drink in the presence of underage students. For those not of age, getting booze is "fairly easy," a sophomore says. Memphis itself offers a wealth of activities, from live music to professional sports teams. Many students volunteer in the city, working with programs helping elderly, homeless, and hungry Tennesseans. Both the men's and women's cross-country teams have claimed recent titles, along with women's golf.

The Rhodents of Rhodes College say they adore the solid academics, atmosphere of trust and rich traditions of the South that make the college unique. "Rhodes's small size, student-professor interaction, Honor Code, and commitment to community make this a special place," says a political science major. As they like to say at Rhodes: "Our ivy is in a league of its own."

Overlaps

Vanderbilt, University of the South, Tulane, Wake Forest, Emory

If You Apply To ➤ **To Rhodes:** Early decision: Jan. 1. Regular admissions: Feb. 1. Financial aid: Mar. 1. Housing: May 1. Does not guarantee to meet demonstrated need. Campus interviews: recommended, evaluative. No alumni interviews. SATs or ACTs: required. SAT IIs: optional, required for homeschoolers. Accepts the Common Application and electronic applications. Essay question: significant person or experience; risk you have taken; ethical dilemma you have faced.

Rice University

6100 Main Street MS-17, Houston, TX 77005-1892

One of the few elite private colleges that makes the list of best buys. Rice is outstanding in engineering, architecture, and music. With less than three thousand undergraduates, Rice is smaller than many applicants realize. In lieu of frats, Rice has a residential college system like Yale and the University of Miami.

With top-notch programs in the liberal arts and sciences, a huge endowment, and a below-average tuition, Rice University is one of the best buys around. It is the dominant university in the Southwest, and second only to Duke in the entire South. Add to that a strong football team, a spirited student body, and an impressive success rate for graduates, and you've got yourself an incredible deal.

Created under the will of legendary Texas cotton mogul William Marsh Rice nearly one hundred years ago, Rice was modeled after such disparate institutions as progressive, tuition-free Cooper Union and the more traditional Princeton University. Despite its resemblance to other institutions, Rice maintains distinctive characteristics of its own. The predominant architectural theme of the campus, situated three miles from downtown Houston, is Spanish Mediterranean, and it's surrounded by a row of hedges—the singular buffer between the quiet campus and the sounds of the city. Two recent campus additions are the Baker Institute for Public Policy and a center for nanoscale science and technology.

The students tend to put a lot of pressure on themselves to succeed. "Most classes are graded on a curve," reports a managerial studies student. "So students are

Website: www.rice.edu
Location: Urban
Total Enrollment: 4,285
Undergraduates: 2,714
Male/Female: 56/44
SAT Ranges: V 650–760
    M 680–770
ACT Ranges: 30–34
Financial Aid: 85%
Expense: Pr $
Phi Beta Kappa: Yes
Applicants: 6,375
Accepted: 27%
Enrolled: 40%
Grad in 6 Years: 86%

Rice is the dominant university in the Southwest, and second only to Duke in the entire South.

not just competing to get an A, but also competing with each other to define what an A is."

And no matter how much coursework is assigned, "you can always be assured that someone else will have more." Science and engineering are the strongest programs here; competition in the engineering and premed programs is especially intense, and each year a good number of students who start in these fields retreat to the humani-

"Most classes are graded on a curve, so students are not just competing to get an A, but also competing with each other to define what an A is."

ties, which in general are less demanding. In fact, Rice has a long tradition of encouraging double, and even triple, majors in such seemingly opposite fields as electrical engineering and art history. Engineering is the most popular major, followed by English, managerial studies, biology, and economics.

Architecture is one of the finest undergraduate programs in the nation, and the space physics program works closely with NASA. The university excels in the sciences and engineering, and the SEs (as these students are called) still dominate the student body. Rice has a fairly new department of biochemistry and cell biology, housed in the up-to-date bioscience/bioengineering building. Under the Mellon Fellow program, selected humanities and social sciences majors may work with a faculty mentor on an academic project that offers a summer research stipend. Some students give less than favorable reviews to social and computer science offerings; foreign languages (especially German) aren't recommended either.

Under the area-major program, students can draw up proposals for independent interdisciplinary majors. An additional option is the "coherent minor" program, which can replace distribution requirements. Distribution requirements mean that science and engineering majors must take courses in humanities; social science and humanities majors must take them in science; and music and architecture students must take them all. Class size rarely presents a problem: "One of my classes has four students, and another one has about one hundred," reports a student, "and all the others are somewhere in between." Faculty members for the most part are friendly and accessible, sometimes providing upperclassmen with research opportunities. "The professors eat with students, attend parties, and

"One of my classes has four students, and another one has about one hundred, and all the others are somewhere in between."

even coach intramural teams," one student reports. Under an extensive advising system, incoming students are assigned two or three student counselors and two professors during the first two years. Everyone operates under the honor system, and most exams go unsupervised.

Those who want to take their education on the road can visit Swarthmore, and there are internships for engineering and architecture students. The library is stocked with most needed materials and, thanks to a renovation, has become more inviting. The career counseling program is a disappointment to many. "They essentially cater to engineering majors and pretty much forget about seniors in the humanities and social sciences," says one biology/anthropology major. But the administration reorganized the Career Services Center and now notes "limited data" as the only drawback.

Rice was founded to serve "residents of Houston and the state of Texas," but Texans no longer dominate the student body. Today, 51 percent of Rice students come from out of state, with high percentages transplanted from California, Florida, the Northeast, and other Southern states. Sixteen percent of the student body are Asian-American, 10 percent are Hispanic, and 7 percent are African-American. Many students claim that, by Texas standards anyway, they are liberal. Others report an intense amount of political apathy. Because much of the university's $3.2 billion endowment is dedicated to keeping tuition low, Rice costs thousands of dollars less than most other selective, private universities. Still, for all its riches, Rice is fairly provincial Texas. Rice guarantees to meet the full demonstrated need of every admit, and there are a variety of merit scholarships available every year, ranging from $1,000 to full tuition. There are also a number of athletic scholarships awarded to both men and women.

Fraternities and sororities are forbidden on campus—Rice's founder did not approve of elitist organizations—but their functions are largely assumed by the eight residential colleges, Rice's version of dorms. Each college houses about 225 students, who remain affiliated with it for all four years and develop a strong sense of community, even for those who later move off campus. Freshmen are randomly assigned to one of the eight coed dorms. Many freshmen enjoy rooms as spacious as their older colleagues, and a dormer contends that "no college is better than another, they're just different." Air-conditioning is a standard weapon against Houston's muggy climate. Everyone is guaranteed a room for at least three of the four years, though students sit through a lottery system. About 25 percent of the students go packing, many seeking quieter surroundings and cheaper rents. Students can eat at any of the college dining halls, and cafeteria-hopping can be a "great way to meet people." Though the food receives average marks for college cafeteria food, students report that it's getting better with each year. Apparently the salad bar and frozen-yogurt machines have won converts.

> **"No college is better than another, they're just different."**

Houston has plenty of nightlife, but to enjoy it bring a car; mass transit is virtually nonexistent. Luckily, parking on campus is easy. Galveston's beaches on the Gulf of Mexico are only forty-five minutes away, and heading for New Orleans, especially in February, can make a great weekend trip.

Ardent football fans abound at Rice; tearing down the goalposts after home victories remains a happy tradition. A familiar chant echoes, "Two, four, six, eight, our players graduate." Other strong programs include baseball, women's cross-country, men's indoor track, and both men's and women's tennis. Rice students go really wild for intramurals—the most popular pits the colleges against each other in a Beer-Bike Race in which coed teams of twenty chug cans of beer and speed around a bicycle track—which gives them a chance to let off academic steam.

Students don't have time to plan anything more formal on weekends than the traditional TGIF lawn parties on Friday afternoons, but campus-wide parties sponsored by one of the residential colleges spring up from time to time. Night of Decadence is Rice's Halloween party, where it is reported that the students appear in "lingerie or less." Drinking age or no, students are expected to unwind on the weekends. "People who study constantly are considered dullards, and people who are negligent about academics aren't taken seriously," a history and English major explains. If nothing else, there's always the campus movie.

Rice has a reputation for doing better in academics than in athletics. But the students don't mind too much. Instead they yell, "That's all right, that's OK, you're gonna work for us someday." In fact, 53 percent of them head straight to jobs after graduation, wasting no time in climbing those corporate ladders or hitching themselves to a dot-com. But most don't like to leave. They've had a terrific academic experience and a decent social life for four years, and their wallets are still thick thanks to a pint-sized tuition.

Fraternities and sororities are forbidden on campus— Rice's founder did not approve of elitist organizations—but their functions are largely assumed by the eight residential colleges, Rice's version of dorms.

Overlaps
Stanford, Harvard, MIT, Princeton, Duke

Rice: Early decision: Nov. 1. Early action: Dec. 1. Regular admissions: Jan. 1. Housing: Jan. 1, May 1. Guarantees to meet demonstrated need. Campus or alumni interviews: recommended, evaluative. SATs or ACTs required. SAT IIs: required (varies by program). Essay question: important experience, achievement, or interest; issue of concern; or influential person or event.

University of Richmond

28 Westhampton Way, Richmond, VA 23173

The former capital of the Confederacy is now crawling with Yankees—at least at the University of Richmond. Students come from points north to partake of warmer weather and Richmond's business-oriented curriculum. One of the few institutions with an entire school devoted to leadership.

Website: www.richmond.edu
Location: Suburban
Total Enrollment: 3,695
Undergraduates: 2,989
Male/Female: 50/50
SAT Ranges: V 590–680
  M 610–690
ACT Range: 27–30
Financial Aid: 33%
Expense: Pr $ $
Phi Beta Kappa: Yes
Applicants: 5,622
Accepted: 44%
Enrolled: 33%
Grad in 6 Years: 84%
Returning Freshmen: 90%
Academics: ✑ ✑ ✑
Social: ☎ ☎ ☎
Q of L: ★ ★ ★
Admissions: (800) 700-1662
Email Address:
  admissions@richmond.edu

Strongest Programs
  Business
  Biology
  Political Science
  International Studies
  English
  Leadership Studies

The University of Richmond may be located below the Mason-Dixon line, but you can forget about finding the South's laid-back feel here. Students are busy conquering tough classes, serving the community, and completing research and internships—all while trying to maintain an active social life. Small classes and terrific faculty interaction are just a few of the perks of being a Richmond Spider—and they even make up for having an arachnid for a school mascot. "The academic climate is very rigorous. Most students are very serious about academics—although they still allow time for fun, too," one sophomore says.

The school's 350-acre campus is situated amid rolling hills, stately pines, and a ten-acre lake. Located about fifteen minutes from the center of Richmond, the university's academic buildings, residence halls, and athletic and student-life facilities are designed in traditional collegiate Gothic architecture. Currently, the university is building Weinstein Hall, a 35,000-square-foot social science center. Renovations are underway on the Robins Sports Center, and there are plans to renovate the Boatwright Library.

Richmond offers students a unique gender-based coordinate college system. In addition to being a member of an academic division, undergraduates take part in one of the coordinate colleges—Richmond College for men, and Westhampton College for women. Each college has its own student government, traditions, and special programs. Business is the most popular major, followed by biology, social sciences, international studies, and English, all of which are considered strong programs. The business school enrolls students who have completed two years in the School of Arts and Sciences, and it's exceptionally popular among eager, financially ambitious students. Richmond has an excellent feel for international studies, and the E. Claiborne School of Business has an International Business Major. The

"The professors stretch students' minds and seek to know their students at a personal level."

Jepson School of Leadership Studies is, according to the administration, the nation's first school of its type and is dedicated to leadership in service to society. Majors in this school must complete an internship in a social-service organization. "The leadership school in its interdisciplinary nature gives students the best overall liberal arts experience," a senior leadership studies student says.

Students rave about the faculty, describing them as involved, accessible, and caring: "The professors stretch students' minds and seek to know their students at a personal level." One-third of students study abroad, three-quarters have at least one internship, and undergraduates are encouraged to do research—they can even get university funding for it. Richmond's general education requirements include courses in expository writing, foreign language to the intermediate level, and "fields-of-study" courses in areas such as social analysis and symbolic reasoning. A two-semester Core Course for all freshmen includes intensive reading and small, focused discussions, and is linked to campus activities such as musical performances. Many students note the academic rigors do not translate into an overly competitive environment. "The only person you compete against is yourself," one junior says. "In the Jepson school, there's so much group work you have to be laid-back and work together." In the new Richmond Quest, the campus spends a year discussing a question posed by a student in class and through activities. Freshmen who are invited into the Honors Law Program and maintain a 3.4 GPA while at Richmond are guaranteed admission into the university's law school without taking the LSAT.

Vigorous recruiting efforts have brought more students from out of state: only 15 percent are from Virginia. Although increasing diversity is a main mission of the school, the campus remains overwhelmingly white. Eighty-four percent of students are white, 5 percent are African-American, 3 percent are Asian-American, and 2 percent are Hispanic. International students make up 6 percent of the student body. Students from nearby colleges often refer to the school as the University of Rich Kids, but some Richmond students contend the campus is becoming more diverse. Richmond offers fifty-five merit scholarships, ranging from half to full tuition, including benefits, and 168 athletic scholarships for eleven sports.

> **"The only person you compete against is yourself."**

Campus housing, where 92 percent of students live, is given high marks. "The dorms are very well maintained and quite comfortable," a sophomore says. Most residence halls and student apartments are newly built or recently remodeled, and blend in tastefully with the older, more typically collegiate Gothic buildings. Several more are being renovated. Campus housing also includes townhouses—University Forest Apartments—but these options are open only to upperclassmen. One of students' biggest gripes has been that the men's and women's residence halls are separated by the campus lake. In response to these concerns, the administration has opened men's and women's halls throughout the Richmond campus. The individual halls, however, will remain single gender. Students report feeling safe on campus, thanks to a campus police force, shuttle bus, and emergency phones.

Programs such as WILL (Women Involved in Living and Learning) and Spinning Your Web, an orientation program for first-year men, are two approaches the university has tried to educate students on gender. On Proclamation Night, women write letters to themselves on their goals for college during a candlelight service, which they will read when they are seniors. During the Ring Dance, junior women don white gowns and are presented with their class rings. Freshman males have Investiture Night, when they officially are inducted into the university. Race relations are addressed through diversity workshops for all new students, and the administration reports student unions for multiculturalism, international students, and students of color are active.

Students report the weekend begins on Thursday. The Greek scene is popular–32 percent of men and half of the Richmond women go Greek. But those who want to steer clear of Fraternity Row have plenty of other opportunities. There are frequently comedians, movies, and

> **"The dorms are very well maintained and quite comfortable."**

bands on campus, and students can visit Tyler's Grill, a coffeehouse alternative established in the wake of an outcry over sexism in fraternity rush, or the Cellar, a student restaurant/bar. An end-of-year, campus-wide Pig Roast is well attended.

Vigorous recruiting efforts have brought more students from out of state: only 15 percent are from Virginia.

Many students note the academic rigors do not translate into an overly competitive environment.

Many students spend time volunteering in on-campus activities or with local community groups. Restaurants, bars, and clubs in downtown Richmond are popular spots. While most Richmond students prefer to stick around on weekends, those with wanderlust can head to Virginia Beach, Washington, D.C., and the Blue Ridge Mountains.

Richmond competes in Division I athletics and recently moved to the Atlantic 10. The men's baseball and basketball teams have brought home Colonial Athletic Association titles in the past. Men's football and soccer are also popular, along with women's soccer, basketball, swimming, and tennis. Games against rivals like William and Mary draw big crowds, and tailgating is regarded as a key social event. Intramural sports are popular, and the recently renovated Spider Sports Center includes Nautilus machines, cardiovascular free weights, and a wellness area.

Richmond is a good choice for students looking for beautiful surroundings and plentiful academic opportunities—especially in business, leadership, or liberal arts—but those who are also willing to devote time to helping others and to the social scene. "Class size, professor-student relations, and ease of getting around make the school wonderful," a senior says. Though classes are important, "volunteerism is a huge part of the UR culture."

Overlaps

University of Virginia, College of William and Mary, Wake Forest, Boston College, Georgetown

If You Apply To ➤

Richmond: Early decision: Nov. 15, Jan. 15. Regular admissions: Jan. 15. Financial aid: Feb. 25. Does not guarantee to meet demonstrated need. No campus or alumni interviews. ACTs or SATs: required. SAT IIs: required (Writing and Math Ic or IIc). Accepts the Common Application and electronic applications. Essay question: personal statement on yourself, a potential independent study, influential public figure, a pressing change in the world.

Ripon College

300 Seward Street, P.O. Box 248, Ripon, WI 54971

Everything about Ripon is small—the town, the college, and just about all the classes. Ripon is more conservative than Beloit and Lawrence and is more similar in atmosphere to places like DePauw and Knox. With fewer than one thousand students, Ripon is the smallest of the five.

Website: www.ripon.edu
Location: Small town
Total Enrollment: 903
Undergraduates: 903
Male/Female: 46/54
SAT Ranges: V 560–600
    M 580–610
ACT Range: 21-26
Financial Aid: 75%
Expense: Pr $
Phi Beta Kappa: Yes
Applicants: 847
Accepted: 84%
Enrolled: 28%
Grad in 6 Years: 59%

Ripon College is affectionately nicknamed the "The Cookie College," because it sits near a cookie factory. That sweetness pours over into the campus of the small college. "Ripon College is a special place because of the close relationships and friendliness of the students, staff, and faculty," says one delighted Red Hawk. It's a good thing Ripon students like each other so much, because the school enrolls just over nine hundred of them. And when it gets cold, students depend on each other and residents of their small town for just about everything.

Set on a hill in a tiny east-central Wisconsin town, just a block from Main Street, Ripon's 250-acre campus features tree-lined walks, wetlands, prairie, and woods, and a mixture of nineteenth- and twentieth-century architecture that gives the campus a "majestic" atmosphere. Founded as a coed school in 1851, Ripon is a place where the curriculum is rooted in tradition, and there is little room for dabbling in trendy educational fashions. Academic work does take a high priority among Ripon students, and while the quiet, rural setting has both cultural and down-home Midwestern activities for those who seek them out, there isn't much danger of twinkling neon lights distracting anyone from his or her studies. The courses are rigorous but not unusually so, and just as anywhere else, there are competitive people. "Because classes are so small, one feels the need to be always on top of studies," says a senior.

The chemistry and biology (especially premed) programs at Ripon are particularly strong and well known, and their students enjoy the benefits of the science center. Other departments that get high marks include English, history, politics and government, and psychology. The most popular majors are business, physical education, chemistry, history, and English. Communications, leadership studies, and Latin could use some improvement, students say. Recently, majors were added in early childhood education and physical sciences. An accelerated-degree program is available to students eager to finish college in three years.

> "Ripon College is a special place because of the close relationships and friendliness of the students, staff, and faculty."

Distribution requirements cover natural sciences and mathematics, foreign language, writing skills, behavioral and social sciences, fine arts, humanities, global studies, and physical education. In addition, freshmen are required to take First-Year Studies. Ripon students delight in their small classes; two-thirds of classes have twenty-five or fewer students. If the student/faculty ratio wasn't the reason they applied here, it's one reason they stay. "The professors are great, very knowledgeable, and focused on teaching, not research," says a junior. Students and professors are regularly on a first-name basis, and critiques of the academic advising range from superb to just plain excellent. Students report no problems getting the classes they need. For temporary changes of scenery, study abroad is available through the college's own programs in Chicago and overseas (German majors may study in Bonn), in addition to programs sponsored by the Associated Colleges of the Midwest.* The Fisk Exchange program with Fisk University has improved diversity and race relations by fostering a relationship between Ripon and the predominately African-American Southern university.

Sixty-four percent of the Ripon student body hails from Wisconsin, and others come from several states and foreign counties. The vast majority are white, upper-middle-class conservatives, with Asian-Americans, African-Americans, and Hispanics accounting for just 6 percent of the population. Twenty-one percent come from the top tenth of their high-school graduating class. With enrollment down, officials are hoping to get the school recognized and grow the student body to one thousand students. The college offers numerous renewable merit awards ranging from $1,000 to full tuition. No athletic scholarships are available.

> "The professors are great, very knowledgeable, and focused on teaching, not research."

Freshmen are housed together and are given a choice between coed and single-sex halls, as are the upperclassmen. Ninety-two percent of the students live on campus. For most dorms, those students who want singles will have to pay a premium each term. Some students say the maintenance of them could be better, but students are generally happy with dorm life. "The dorms are just an extension of the great Ripon community. By senior year, everyone has their own room," a senior says. All students eat in one large dining hall, and food is described as good and plentiful. Campus security measures include regular foot patrols and key cards for access to residence halls.

The small Midwestern town of Ripon (about 7,500 residents) is well known to history buffs as the birthplace of the Republican Party—which was founded at a meeting on the college campus on February 28, 1854, to be exact. One student says "the community is very willing to help us with anything." Where else do you find a community that holds a welcome-back picnic for students at the beginning of the

(Continued)
Returning Freshmen: 88%
Academics: ✍ ✍ ✍
Social: ☎ ☎ ☎
Q of L: ★ ★ ★
Admissions: (920) 748-8337
Email Address:
   adminfo@ripon.edu

Strongest Programs
   Education
   Business
   Social Sciences
   History
   English

Ripon is a place where the curriculum is rooted in tradition, and there is little room for dabbling in trendy educational fashions.

Frozen lakes and a blanket of snow are a natural part of the winter landscape, and students can cross-country and downhill ski, toboggan, skate, and attend dogsled and iceboat races.

year? Students return the favor in the form of volunteer work. For students who want to get away on weekends, Chicago is a three-hour drive; Milwaukee is just eighty miles away.

For those staying in town, local bars offer a break from boredom for those twenty-one and older. The school's new BYOB policy allows of-age students to imbibe on campus, while those under twenty-one must skirt school rules to drink. "But there is never pressure to drink and something else is always going on," a senior says. Other social activities include an array of concerts, plays, and cultural activities, including free Wednesday-night movies. A weekend of dancing and music in the spring attracts alumni back to the campus enclave. "There is plenty of things to do every weekend. We have comedians, jugglers, hypnotists, and one time, the Milwaukee Symphony Orchestra visited on campus," notes one satisfied freshman. Fifty-five percent of the men join fraternities and 21 percent of the women join sororities, and with all Greeks living in dorms and eating in the dining hall, there is little tension between them and nonmembers. Fraternity parties are the main form of campus social life, and Ripon is so darned friendly that independents are included in just about all Greek events.

> **"There is plenty of things to do every weekend. We have comedians, jugglers, hypnotists, and one time, the Milwaukee Symphony Orchestra visited on campus."**

Ripon is located in the wonderful North Woods territory, a spot in the state where the scattered trees begin to grow thicker and then give way to rugged pine forests. Frozen lakes and a blanket of snow are a natural part of the winter landscape, and students can cross-country and downhill ski, toboggan, skate, and attend dogsled and iceboat races. Nearby Green Lake boasts facilities for skiing and, when it's not winter ("for one month during the year," warns one student), facilities for water sports. Athletic matches against the rival team from Lawrence University usually draw excited crowds. Men's teams have been successful in recent years, snatching up conference championships in baseball (four times), football, soccer (twice), and tennis (twice). Men's basketball is also popular, along with women's basketball, volleyball, and softball. Athletes enjoy a women's softball field, intramurals field, baseball field, and six tennis courts—all fairly new.

The homey atmosphere is just one benefit of this small liberal arts college. Students appreciate the intimacy of their classes and the attention they get from their professors, and don't seem to mind that they can't just blend into the scenery or get lost in the back of the class. "People here care about your health and safety as well as the quality of your education," a freshman says.

Overlaps

University of Wisconsin at Madison, St. Norbert, Carroll, University of Wisconsin at LaCrosse, Marquette

If You Apply To ➤

Ripon: Rolling admissions. Regular admissions and financial aid: Apr. 1 (priority). Guarantees to meet demonstrated need. Campus interviews: recommended, evaluative. No alumni interviews. SATs or ACTs: required. SAT IIs: optional. Accepts the Common Application and electronic applications. Essay question (strongly recommended): discuss reasons for pursuing an education at Ripon.

Rochester, NY 14627

The name may conjure up a nondescript public university, but Rochester is a top-notch private university in the orbit of Carnegie Mellon, Case Western Reserve, Johns Hopkins, and Washington U (MO). The university has a scientific bent and is known as a haven for premeds.

The University of Rochester is not afraid of change. In 1996, this distinguished private university implemented its unique Rochester Renaissance Plan, and it has never looked back. The five-year plan, which includes a 20 percent reduction in the size of the freshman class, more merit scholarships, a refocusing of the curriculum, and new investments in library and computer/networking resources and campus facilities, has been the major catalyst in a new, improved, user-friendly University of Rochester.

Cold weather and snow are a given at the University of Rochester, but anyone who visits will find a flourishing community thriving on a clandestinely snug little ninety-acre campus, which nestles up to a bend in the Genesee River. One student acknowledges that the university has "perpetually gray [read: winter] skies," but finds comfort that "it's great for winter sports or studying or even sleeping late on a snowy Saturday." Another student adds, "The nippy winter days are perfect for sitting inside and hitting the books." Although a few buildings are modern—the Wilson Commons student center designed by I. M. Pei, for example—most of the older structures come in Greek Revival and Georgian Colonial styles. There is an aesthetically pleasing contrast between old and new, and the Eastman Quadrangle, with the library and original academic buildings, adds to Rochester's stately look. Recent construction projects include a 240,000-square foot building to house the Institute of Biomedical Sciences.

> **"The nippy winter days are perfect for sitting inside and hitting the books."**

Degree requirements vary slightly from college to college, but all are designed to ensure that students are exposed to the full range of liberal arts. The curriculum—appropriately but unimaginatively known as the Rochester Curriculum—focuses on three classic divisions of learning: humanities and arts; social science; and natural science, mathematics, and engineering. Students choose a major from one of these areas and also complete a cluster of three courses in each of the remaining two divisions. These clusters give students the opportunity for integrated study in diverse fields and the chance to participate in three very different types of learning. Freshmen have the option of taking seminar-style Quest courses, which teach them how to learn and how to make learning a lifetime habit. Quest courses can involve extensive work with original materials, existing and experimental data, and primary texts. Orientation Rochester-style includes a week-long fall festival called Yellow Jacket Days, designed to help new students "become fully integrated in the university community."

> **"I can say that Rochester students are a hard-working, fun-loving, positive group that puts a high value on academics."**

The university's 175 degree programs span the standard fields of study, but Rochester takes special pride in its famed Eastman School of Music. It also excels in the engineering and scientific fields—competition is keen to "beat the mean" among science majors. A cognitive science program—a cooperative venture among faculty in computer science, psychology, and philosophy—is innovative and popular. The Institute of Optics, the nation's first center devoted exclusively to optics, is

Website: www.rochester.edu
Location: Small city
Total Enrollment: 7,681
Undergraduates: 4,452
Male/Female: 51/49
SAT Ranges: V 590–690
   M 620–710
ACT Range: 26–30
Financial Aid: 70%
Expense: Pr $ $ $
Phi Beta Kappa: Yes
Applicants: 8,880
Accepted: 62%
Enrolled: 17%
Grad in 6 Years: 77%
Returning Freshmen: 95%
Academics: ✏ ✏ ✏ ✏
Social: ☎ ☎ ☎
Q of L: ★ ★ ★
Admissions: (716) 275-3221
Email Address: admit@
   admissions.rochester.edu

Strongest Programs
   Premedicine
   Engineering
   Music
   Optics
   Biology
   Psychology
   Economics
   Political Science

An unofficial Rochester tradition calls for each student to eat a "garbage plate" at the infamous dive called Nick's before graduating.

a leader in basic optical research and theory. The most popular majors include psychology, political science, economics, and biology. Students cite math and anthropology as being weak.

The academic climate at Rochester is challenging, owing much of that to its energetic professors, who are described as "extremely knowledgeable" and "enthusiastic about teaching undergraduates." No matter what their field of interest, students who are sufficiently advanced may combine undergraduate with graduate study. The Rochester Early Medical Scholars program offers highly qualified first-year students guaranteed admission to the medical school after four years. In addition, Rochester offers a tuition-free fifth year that allows students to explore interests outside their major. The Center for Work and Career Development receives praise for its vigorous preparation of seniors for the job market. Students may also study abroad, and the university sponsors programs in a variety of places ranging from Russia to Singapore, not to mention what one student calls a "chance of a lifetime" British Parliament internship program. A work-study program called Reach for Rochester provides students with on- or off-campus jobs, summer employment options, and individually tailored "experienceships."

Fifty-one percent of the students hail from New York State. Many also come from New England, and there's been a large jump in the numbers from Florida, the Midwest, California, and overseas. Asian-Americans make up 11 percent of the student body, while African-Americans account for 6 percent, and Hispanics another 5 percent. "I can say that Rochester students are a hard-working, fun-loving, positive group that puts a high value on academics," says a student. Campus issues include political correctness and anti-sweatshop campaigns, though one student notes political involvement is "lower than might be expected" due to a "lack of free time." In an effort to attract scholars, the university offers in-state applicants and children of alumni a $5,000 annual grant. Its strongest applicants are awarded a Rush Rhees Scholarship, which ranges from $5,000 to $10,000 per year.

> "Dorms are comfortable, modern, high-tech, very generously sized, well maintained."

As far as housing is concerned, there's virtually nothing but praise from the 78 percent of students who live on campus. "Dorms are comfortable, modern, high-tech, very generously sized, well maintained," a senior says. Some of the housing units offer such benefits as computer terminals, telephones with voicemail features, oak floors, and marble trim. All housing offers Internet access. New students are assigned to rooms—usually doubles—and upperclass students can usually get singles or suites through the lottery. Susan B. Anthony comes highly recommended. Single-sex, coed-by-floor, and coed-by-room dormitories are available. Though few students choose to live off campus, a new shuttle bus runs to and from the major off-campus living areas. Dormitory students may eat meals in the cafeteria, where a credit system ensures they pay per meal instead of in one lump sum. The fare served in the dining halls receives high ratings from students, especially the á la carte options such as tacos and burritos and the deli bar. Other meal options available include a kosher deli, the Common Ground Coffee House, and a submarine sandwich shop.

Twenty percent of the men and 14 percent of the women go Greek. "The Greek scene plays a large factor in social life here, but it is by no means the only social outlet," says one student. Yet, fraternities still contribute heavily to the social life of Greeks and independents alike by sponsoring parties and concerts. UR does have its own set of movie theaters that charge $3 or less per ticket, and campus concerts always draw a crowd. Despite the university's best efforts to enforce a stricter alcohol policy, underage drinking still occurs. "This school's policy in no way curtails underage drinking unless students take it upon themselves to obey," one student says. Many students take the free campus shuttle into "Rochchacha," where they may

The Institute of Optics, the nation's first center devoted exclusively to optics, is a leader in basic optical research and theory.

entertain themselves on the beaches of Lake Ontario, in the International Photography Museum at the George Eastman House, or at the Rochester Philharmonic Orchestra. Favored out-of-town ventures are Niagara Falls, about seventy miles westward, and, for the more venturesome, Toronto, 125 miles farther westward. Other popular activities include cappuccino at the student union, frequent ski trips, Yellow Jacket Days, and a spring fling known as Dandelion Day. The Viennese Ball and the Boar's Head Dinner are also popular events, as is the unforgettable Screw Your Roommate Dance. An unofficial Rochester tradition calls for each student to eat a "garbage plate" at the infamous dive called Nick's before graduating. Students are involved in the community through projects on and off campus, and Rochester was recently recognized nationally for its high percentage of student volunteers.

> "The Greek scene plays a large factor in social life here, but it is by no means the only social outlet."

The varsity sports teams are coming of age at Rochester, which competes in the University Athletic Association. For those who want something to cheer about, the golf team, the basketball teams, men's and women's soccer, tennis, and cross-country are all quite successful. Intramurals are a popular outlet for "ex-jocks from high school who miss their glory days gone by." Even if intramurals aren't your bag, Rochester has an $8 million sports complex, complete with basketball, tennis, squash, and volleyball courts; lighted rooftop tennis courts; a Nautilus fitness center; the Speegle-Wilbraham Aquatic Center with an eight-lane pool; and an indoor track.

In the past, students bemoaned the fact that the school didn't have a wider academic reputation, but that's changing due, in part, to the Rochester Renaissance Plan. Improvements have been made in the curriculum, the facilities, and just about anywhere you look on campus. "Prospective students who are unsure where their academic careers will take them will have no problem finding what excites them intellectually," says a junior. "But more importantly, they will build relationships with others that will last their entire lives." Rochester seems to be winning its battle for a spot among the nation's leading private universities. Now if they could only do something about all that snow.

Overlaps
Cornell University, Brown, SUNY–Binghamton, Northwestern, Washington University

---

If You Apply To ➤ | **Rochester:** Early decision: Nov. 1. Regular admissions: Jan. 15. Financial aid: Feb. 1. Housing: June 1. Guarantees to meet demonstrated need. No campus interviews. Alumni interviews: optional, informational. SATs or ACTs: required. SAT IIs: recommended. Musicians apply directly to the Eastman School of Music. Essay question: life in a different era; personal diversity. Looks closely at recommendations, activities, and "indications of intellectual curiosity and a zest for college life."

Rochester Institute of Technology

60 Lomb Memorial Drive, Rochester, NY 14623-5604

RIT is the largest of New York's three major technical universities—about double the size of Rensselaer. The school is strong in anything related to computers, business, and engineering, and in the city built by Eastman Kodak, photography is among the tops in the nation.

The first undergraduate school to offer programs in software engineering, imaging science, and microelectronics, the Rochester Institute of Technology is as career-oriented as they come. Students looking for challenging, up-to-date technological training will be at home at RIT, and those who are geared up and ready to go

Website: www.rit.edu
Location: Suburban
Total Enrollment: 14,430

(Continued)

Undergraduates: 12,029
Male/Female: 68/32
SAT Ranges: V 540–650
   M 580–680
ACT Range: 25–28
Financial Aid: 70%
Expense: Pr $ $
Phi Beta Kappa: No
Applicants: 8,493
Accepted: 69%
Enrolled: 38%
Grad in 6 Years: 61%
Returning Freshmen: 87%
Academics: ✍ ✍ ✍
Social: ☎ ☎ ☎
Q of L: ★ ★ ★
Admissions: (585) 475-6631
Email Address:
   admissions@rit.edu

Strongest Programs
   Photography
   Computer Science
   Engineering
   Business

RIT has the largest number of on-campus apartments in the country.

professional will be happy to know that the school places 2,700 juniors and seniors in full-time paid positions through its co-op program. At RIT, the focus is on career-oriented and technology-based academics. Be warned: if you're still trying to figure out how to set the clock on your VCR, or you only use computers to play solitaire, then the Rochester Institute of Technology is probably not the place for you.

The main campus is located on 1,300 suburban acres, six miles from downtown Rochester. RIT shares the city with six nearby colleges, making Rochester "quite a college town." The campus was built in 1968, when the institute moved from its original location downtown. The redbrick buildings have sharp, contemporary lines. Construction is a given these days, and current focus is on a new 125,000-square-foot Computing and Information Sciences Building.

RIT specializes in carving out niches for itself with unusual programs, and majors are offered in more than two hundred fields, from basic electrical and mechanical engineering to packaging science and new media design. Fortunately, applicants narrow the range of choices to a manageable size by applying to one of eight undergraduate colleges: applied science and technology, business, computing and information sciences, engineering, imaging arts and sciences, liberal arts, science, and the National Technical Institute for the Deaf (NTID). Created for the hearing-impaired, NTID offers students technical and professional training in more than thirty programs, including business, science and engineering, and visual communications. NTID students and faculty use a combination of communication methods including sign language, finger spelling, and visual aids, and the college boasts a placement rate of 95 percent. New programs include the nation's first undergraduate program in New Media. This program combines graphic design, printing, publishing, and information technology courses to help students prepare for jobs in digital-based media such as the World Wide Web.

> "The coursework is very, very tough, but not impossible.

Predictably, engineering is the most popular major, but one might be surprised to know that the third-most popular major is art and design. Information technology, business, and photography (Rochester is home to Eastman Kodak) also grace the top of the list. Academic programs include aerospace engineering, environmental management, hotel and tourism management, engineering technology, and a physician assistant program. The RIT School for American Crafts offers excellent programs in ceramics, woodworking, glass, metalcraft, and jewelry making, and students have the run of Bevier Gallery, where visiting artists provide firsthand instruction. The small College of Liberal Arts, which offers only six degree programs, is cited as weaker than the other colleges.

All students take liberal arts requirements, which total a third of their undergraduate work and include a senior seminar and project. These requirements are offered through the College of Liberal Arts and include courses in humanities, social science, and English composition. Students also must take three physical education courses, but the emphasis is more on health and wellness than competitive sports. Unlike many universities, RIT allows freshmen to schedule significant coursework in their major early on, and spreads out liberal arts requirements over a more extended period. RIT's academic pressure is fairly high, although it is not a competitive pressure. "The coursework is very, very tough, but not impossible," says a mechanical engineering major. "I feel that it is pretty competitive. The courses are challenging but well worth the work required," states another student. Many faculty members lead a double life with some kind of commitment to the professional world. "The professors have all been in the 'real world,' and can relate the theoretical to the applied," says one student. Career

> "I feel that it is pretty competitive. The courses are challenging but well worth the work required."

counseling is a "great system" according to students, but it is up to each individual to utilize the resources.

Fifty percent of entering freshmen come from outside New York State, and many of those are from New Jersey, Pennsylvania, and Connecticut. Minorities make up 15 percent of the student body: 5 percent are African-American, 3 percent are Hispanic, and 7 percent are Asian-American. Preprofessionalism is a common bond, but beyond that interests vary. The unique mix of art, engineering, business, and science students, along with the large number of deaf students, creates a diverse atmosphere on campus. "It seems like everyone has a different attitude toward school, and looks at it differently," explains one junior. RIT admits without regard to student financial need, and it meets the demonstrated need of 90 percent of the students for as long as the funds allow. RIT offers more than 1,800 renewable merit scholarships to each freshman class, ranging from $500 to $19,600, made without reference to need. Most of the time students are oblivious to the issues going on in the outside world because "we are too busy with our own work," a student says.

Seventy percent of full-time students live in college dorms and apartments, and students report that getting a room is not that difficult. Freshmen are required to live in the dorms, while upperclassmen can vie for campus apartments through a lottery. But that shouldn't be too tough since, according to the administration, RIT has the largest number of on-campus apartments in the country. Recently seven hundred new campus apartment units were added. Dorms are well maintained and offer a variety of living styles: single-sex, coed by room, or coed by floor. Special-interest floors range from nonsmoking to "mainstream" (with hearing-impaired students). Campus residents choose among several meal plans, all of which provide good food from the campus-run food ser-vice. Those who choose to live off campus take advantage of areas serviced by the school shuttle bus. Then there are the 7

"It seems like everyone has a different attitude toward school, and looks at it differently."

percent of men and 5 percent of women who choose to go Greek and live and eat in RIT's 17 fraternity and 7 sorority houses. Campus safety is largely a nonissue; most students feel secure.

Though the competition among peers at RIT probably won't drive students to drink, many indulge anyway. "It is for the most part a wet campus," says one observer. "There is no alcohol allowed on the dorm side of campus, and it is allowed in the apartments," explains a junior. The only facilities within walking distance of this sedate suburban campus are a variety of shopping plazas, including one of the largest between New York and Cleveland. Students take road trips to Buffalo, Syracuse, Rochester, and Canada. For those without transportation, there's always something to do on campus. Drama and other creative arts are less common than parties and movies, but a fine jazz ensemble and a chorus perform regularly. RIT also livens things up with several major weekend bashes throughout the year. Brick City Bash is held each spring, and is a favorite among some students. Intramurals attract the more active students, as do the twenty-three varsity sports. Men's hockey is the overwhelming favorite, a real winter crowd pleaser that draws even the campus commuters and local residents to the rink. Other sports such as men's basketball and lacrosse, and women's volleyball and softball, are strong but not followed.

For those seeking a competitive, high-tech education, RIT may be just the ticket. For all its other amenities, one of the best things about the school, says one student, "is that you get a good job when you graduate."

Created for the hearing-impaired, the National Technical Institute for the Deaf offers students technical and professional training in more than thirty programs, including business, science and engineering, and visual communications.

Overlaps
Rensselaer Polytechnic, University at Buffalo, Clarkson, Syracuse, Cornell University

Rollins College

1000 Holt Avenue, Box 2720, Winter Park, FL 32789-4499

Rollins is the marriage of a liberal arts college and a business school. A haven for Easterners who want to their ticket punched to Florida, Rollins attracts conservative and affluent students and world-class water-skiers. Rivals include Eckerd in St. Petersburg and the University of Miami.

Website: www.rollins.edu
Location: Suburban
Total Enrollment: 2,320
Undergraduates: 1,598
Male/Female: 53/47
SAT Ranges: V 540–630
  M 540–630
ACT Range: 24–28
Financial Aid: 40%
Expense: Pr $ $ $ $
Phi Beta Kappa: No
Applicants: 1,906
Accepted: 68%
Enrolled: 33%
Grad in 6 Years: 65%
Returning Freshmen: 83%
Academics: ✿ ✿ ✿
Social: ☎ ☎ ☎ ☎
Q of L: ★ ★ ★
Admissions: (407) 646-2161
Email Address:
  admission@rollins.edu

Strongest Programs
  English
  Theater/Drama
  Latin American Studies
  Chemistry
  Psychology
  Politics
  Philosophy
  Biology
  Economics

Central Florida is home to many of the world's greatest attractions. There's Walt Disney World, Sea World, and Universal Studios, to name a few. And for those seeking a quality education, the area offers an attraction of another sort: Rollins College. Here you can dig your toes in the sand while studying theater or biology, and enjoy making waves while making grades.

Although founded in 1885, Rollins's commitment to Spanish Mediterranean–style architecture was established in the 1930s. Capitalizing on its location on beautiful Lake Virginia, campus planners have succeeded in combining the natural beauty of the lakeside with consistent architecture. Recent additions include the Cornell Campus Center, with meeting rooms and dining facilities, the new bookstore complete with a coffee bar, an electronic research and information center, and the $10.1 million Alfond Sports Center.

The path to a bachelor's degree at Rollins leads all students through three areas of general education requirements: skills (writing, foreign language, public speaking, mathematical methods, decision-making); cognitive (Western and non-Western culture, natural world); and affective (expressive arts and literature). For freshmen acclimating to college, the fall-semester Rollins Conference eases the transition by placing them into groups of seventeen or fewer to discuss themes such as imaginary voyages, contemporary ethical issues, and the environment. Each group has a professor-advisor and two upperclass peer mentors. Students also have the opportunity to pursue independent research, and during a recent summer, seventeen chemistry majors did just that.

> **"You can't come here and expect to party and not study. To get decent grades, you have to work for them."**

Students give the philosophy department their highest marks, and also praise history, English, theater, psychology, environmental studies, international studies, and economics. The chemistry department turned out the winner of the 1987 Nobel Prize. Some students say they avoid the sciences, but only because instructors are so tough and science majors are so competitive. The Annie Russell Theatre hosts productions staged by the active theater department, which takes pride in having set the stage for such stellar actors as alumni Buddy Ebsen and Tony Perkins. A major in International Business was added recently, and future *Fortune 500* types can take an eight-course minor in business studies combined with a major selected from the liberal arts offerings, including the new biochemistry major. An Accelerated Management Program allows qualified freshmen to gain guaranteed admission to the Roy E. Crummer Graduate School of Business when they enter Rollins, leading to B.A. and M.B.A. degrees in five rather than six years.

While the workload at Rollins varies by major, academics are important. "You can't come here and expect to party and not study," says an international relations major. "To get decent grades, you have to work for them." That's made easier by the fact that there aren't any TAs here; teaching is the responsibility of professors. "It's probably the best part of Rollins, the individual attention of extraordinary professors," raves a sophomore. Many students take advantage of Rollins' study-abroad program, which offers programs in Sydney, Australia, and Merida, Mexico, for regular tuition costs, as well as internships in London.

Rollins draws 60 percent of its students from outside Florida and has more than its share of rich kids. Adequate financial aid, however, is available for BMW-deprived students, with merit scholarships for qualified students and athletic scholarships given to male and female standouts in eight sports. Twenty-six percent of the students are international students or members of minority groups, and each fall there's a week of programming aimed at celebrating diversity. Still, the school's homogeneity is a concern for some. "For the most part, the minority population at Rollins feels isolated," says one student.

Eighty-nine percent of the college's students live on campus in comfortable coed dorms. "The dorms are better than most hotel rooms," says a sophomore, though a senior warns "it's getting harder to get a room because of increasing enrollment." Freshmen who want to study should choose Ward, students say, while McKean is the social center. Some students live in special-interest houses or move off-campus. Dining facilities are located in the campus center and food is charged on a credit-card system, so students eat when they want and pay only when they eat.

The high-powered Greek scene claims 27 percent of the women and men at Rollins, so there's almost always a party somewhere. Still, "with downtown Orlando fifteen minutes away, everybody has something to do," says a sophomore. Also, the administration has clamped down on the social scene, with party monitors checking IDs and a student activity director attending each on-campus party. No open containers of alcohol may be carried on the campus grounds, and if you're caught with one, campus safety "will make you pour it out," says a history major. "The college tries hard to catch us, but sometimes we slip through." With beaches close by, students add sailing, sunbathing, and windsurfing to their daily activities, and the Florida Keys are a popular road-trip destination.

> "It's probably the best part of Rollins, the individual attention of extraordinary professors."

Fox Day is "a sacred tradition"—the president cancels classes for the day by placing a fox statue on the front lawn. Students look forward to the tradition every spring and, though they never know exactly which day the president will choose, almost everyone heads for the beach once the day arrives. Many students volunteer with programs such as Habitat for Humanity and tutoring at local schools. Orlando's offerings include entertainment complexes like Church Street Station and the Cheyenne Saloon, and amusement parks like Disney World, Epcot Center, and Universal Studios, complete with giant mechanical sharks.

Sports are also important and Rollins rules in water-skiing. Recent teams have struggled because Rollins is more academically competitive than many Division II opponents. However, the women's tennis team recently placed fourth in the NCAA national championships; the women's golf team captured second place in their own sport.

Students at Rollins may not realize how lucky they are. They have gorgeous new facilities to complement the natural beauty of Florida's sun and surf, plus a lake in their own backyard. Their biggest gripes are a lack of on-campus parking and a campus safety force too eager to hand out citations for expired meters or underage drinking. It's true that high tuition costs and a lack of diversity have some students

Fox Day is "a sacred tradition"—the president cancels classes for the day by placing a fox statue on the front lawn.

Overlaps
University of Florida, Stetson, University of Miami (FL), Tulane, Emory

concerned. But for those who want to put off entry into the "real world" just a bit longer, Rollins could be an ideal oasis in which to spend the next four years.

Rose–Hulman Institute of Technology

5500 Wabash Avenue, Terre Haute, IN 47803

Coed since 1995, Rose-Hulman offers the rare combination of technical education and personal attention. Only Caltech, Clarkson, and Harvey Mudd offer comparable intimacy in a technical environment. Nearby Indiana State and St. Mary's of the Woods help mitigate the skewed gender ratio.

Website:
www.rose-hulman.edu
Location: City outskirts
Total Enrollment: 1,749
Undergraduates: 1,573
Male/Female: 82/18
SAT Ranges: V 560-660
 M 630-720
ACT Range: 26-31
Financial Aid: 70%
Expense: Pr $ $ $
Phi Beta Kappa: No
Applicants: 3,034
Accepted: 67%
Enrolled: 20%
Grad in 6 Years: 77%
Returning Freshmen: 91%
Academics: ✍ ✍ ✍
Social: ☎
Q of L: ★ ★
Admissions: (812) 877-8213
Email Address:
admis.ofc@rose-hulman.edu

Strongest Programs
Optical Engineering
Chemical Engineering
Mechanical Engineering
Electrical Engineering

Understand one thing: the Rose-Hulman Institute of Technology is a haven for young engineers, but the school is hardly a refuge for the pasty nation. Though some Hulman students gleefully describe themselves as "big dorks," this small tech school fosters a sense of unity and takes pride in giving back to its community. "The students at Rose are the best of the best," says one mechanical engineering major. "They have a strong work ethic, desire to learn, and want for hands-on experience. There are few slackers here." With fewer than 1,600 undergraduates and only eleven majors, the Rose-Hulman Institute of Technology doesn't have much room for weakness.

Established in 1874, Rose-Hulman is the oldest private engineering school west of the Allegheny Mountains. It gets its name from Chauncey Rose, an entrepreneur who brought the railroad to Indiana, and the Hulman family, owners of the Indianapolis Speedway, who gave their fortune to the institution in 1970. Its two hundred–acre campus boasts an idyllic setting of trees and two small lakes. Newest to the campus is the Oakley Observatory, which houses eight telescopes and has a retractable roof, as well as the Hatfield Hall Performing Arts Center.

There's nothing like commiserating over a ton of coursework to forge tight bonds among Rose students. "We have an attitude that we are all in this together and it is easier to work together to survive," explains a chemical engineering major. "Classes are tough, but not impossible...although sometimes it does seem that way." The work requires much effort out of class in both groups and independent studies, but with full professors teaching every class, students get "lots of one-on-one attention." In addition to gems such as a major in optical engineering—the only undergraduate program of its kind in the country—Rose-Hulman also offers students double majors and humanities minors. Programs such as Fast Track Calculus enable students to accelerate in areas where they demonstrate special aptitude. Students in every program except math must work in a team and complete a project for an outside company, and all are required to take "College and Life Skills," which covers study skills, time management, and resume writing. Rose-Hulman Ventures gives students the chance to form companies after graduation. And given the technical focus of the school, the campus is awash with high-tech

"The students at Rose are the best of the best."

gadgets such as a 60 MHz nuclear magnetic resonance spectrometer, neutron how-itzers and generators, electron accelerators, and holography tables.

Rose-Hulman offers degree programs in engineering, chemistry, computer science, biology, math, and physics. It was the first private college to offer a bachelor's degree in chemical engineering, and this department remains among its strongest. Electrical and mechanical engineering are also popular with students, but for every student, a fifth of their academic program will consist of classes in the humanities and social sciences. A bachelor's program in Applied Biology was recently added. Chemistry students have to deal with outdated equipment. Rose-Hulman's library system is excellent in technical fields, but for anything else, students must trek to nearby Indiana State University, where they have free access. For the most part, though, students seem happy with the school's tech-oriented outlook. The humanities are named as some of the "most avoided" departments. As one sophomore puts it: "Many engineering minds find liberal arts very difficult."

Nearly all the students at Rose are white (94 percent) and used to academic success (96 percent were in the top quarter of their high-school class). Racial tension is said to be nonexistent, but many students are quick to point out that this is directly related to the school's extreme lack of diversity. One major change in the makeup of the student body has been the addition of women. Rose became coed in 1995, and already has a significant enough female population to warrant the existence of sororities and several women's sports teams. Rose-Hulman also offers nearly one thousand merit scholarships each year, worth $3,000 to $16,000. None of these scholarships cover the tuition, but "if you are accepted, they will find a way for you to attend."

> "Classes are tough, but not impossible...although sometimes it does seem that way."

While the work is hard, students say the dorms are "wonderful" and the rooms are "big, many are air-conditioned, and a maid service comes once a week to clean," says a mechanical engineering major. "They even make our beds!" exclaims one student. Freshmen are required to live on campus, and about half of the upper-classmen choose to live off campus. Greek life is big at Rose—45 percent of the men and women are in fraternities and sororities. Even though it's a dry campus, alcohol does flow. Resident assistants "are not pounding on doors for random searches because they treat students at adults." Concerts, outdoor movies, comedians, and musicians often swing by.

The town of Terre Haute gets about the same review from students as the cafeteria food. It is home to three colleges (St. Mary's of the Woods and Indiana State are close by), which means lots of co-eds and plenty of malls and eateries in the area. Terre Haute has "the basics": mall, stores, restaurants, theatres, and a museum. Students also get involved in volunteer activities, from the Lighthouse Mission to Bikes for Tykes. The most popular road trips are to Indianapolis, Chicago, and St. Louis. While students at some schools say their college town stinks, Rose-Hulman students are in the rare and unfortunate situation of contending with truly odious odors. "Terre Haute is a great town, but it's smelly because of the paper mill."

Feelings about Terre Haute aside, Rose students live a happy, active life. Lest anyone envision Rose-Hulman students as pale lab dwellers, be aware that athletics are very popular. More than 90 percent of the students are involved in intramurals, and even faculty members get into the act. Varsity teams play in Division III of the NCAA with football, basketball, baseball, and track and

> "Many engineering minds find liberal arts very difficult."

field among the strongest teams. The men's basketball team and women's softball teams took home the 2002 SCAC cochampionships. The Indianapolis Colts even use the facilities for their month-long summer camps. Homecoming brings a major class

The campus is awash with high-tech gadgets such as a 60 MHz nuclear magnetic resonance spectrometer, neutron howitzers and generators, electron accelerators, and holography tables.

Students in every program except math must work in a team and complete a project for an outside company, and all are required to take "College and Life Skills," which covers study skills, time management, and résumé writing.

Overlaps

Purdue, University of Illinois, University of Michigan, Georgia Tech, Northwestern

conflict: the freshmen build a bonfire and the sophomores do their best to destroy it. The bonfire is said to be so large, a senior reports, that the "Indianapolis airport reroutes airplanes around the area."

Rose provides an incredible technical education that ranks among the best in the country. Though the workload can be stressful, when classes are over and studying is put aside, "there is a family atmosphere here unlike anywhere I have seen," says a sophomore. Another student sums up by noting that "there are many familiar faces everywhere you go. Professors know your name, everyone works together, and everyone has their share of fun."

If You Apply To ➤   **Rose-Hulman:** Rolling admissions and financial aid: Mar. 1. Housing: Jun. 1. Meets demonstrated need of 24%. Campus interviews: recommended, informational. Alumni interviews: not available. SATs or ACTs: required. Accepts the Common Application and electronic applications. No essay question.

Rutgers–The State University of New Jersey

65 Davidson Road, Piscataway, NJ 08854-8097

Rutgers is a huge institution spread over three regional campuses and twenty-nine colleges or schools. Rutgers College on the New Brunswick campus is the most prominent. Literally everything is available: engineering, business, pharmacy, the arts, and the nation's largest women's college (Douglass College in New Brunswick).

Website: www.rutgers.edu
Location: Small city
Total Enrollment: 49,465
Undergraduates: 37,112
Male/Female: 45/55
SAT Ranges: V 510–620
  M 520–650
Financial Aid: 55%
Expense: Pub $ $ $
Phi Beta Kappa: Yes
Applicants: 26,593
Accepted: 67%
Enrolled: 36%
Grad in 6 Years: 69%
Returning Freshmen: 88%
Academics: ✍ ✍ ✍ ✍
Social: ☎ ☎ ☎
Q of L: ★ ★ ★
Admissions: (732) 445-3777
Email Address: admissions@
  asb-ugadm.rutgers.edu

Strongest Programs
  Accounting

Life at Rutgers University is all about choice. Choices between the more than one hundred undergraduate majors and four thousand courses offered between its campuses in New Brunswick, Newark, and Camden. Choices about which of the more than four hundred student organizations to join. Even choices about which library to visit since there are eighteen branches with holdings of more than three million volumes university-wide. "Rutgers's best quality is its wide variety of majors, classes, and social activities," says one junior.

Rutgers University has three regional campuses in Camden, Newark, and New Brunswick. Rutgers–New Brunswick, which has the largest concentration of students, is composed of five smaller campuses located along the Raritan River. The campuses are connected by a free university bus system and students travel among campuses to take classes. Rutgers–Newark is in a downtown section of Newark, giving the campus neighborhood a collegiate feel. The smallest campus in the Rutgers system is in Camden, located one stop away from the shopping and cultural offerings of downtown Philadelphia. The RUNet 2000 project, a $100-million infrastructure initiative in progress, promises to transform student-faculty interaction through access to voice, video, and data from just about any location on campus.

> **"Rutgers's best quality is its wide variety of majors, classes, and social activities."**

Among the nearly one hundred majors, the three most popular are psychology, biological sciences, and accounting. Especially strong academic programs include accounting, history, political science, and chemistry. The workload is steady for most students; science majors and pharmacy students can expect the heaviest load. "The courses here require a great deal of thought and outside preparation if you want to be successful," says a political science major. Recently added majors include cell biology and neuroscience; genetics and microbiology; biomedical engineering; evolutionary anthropology; and allied health technology. As at any big state university, registration can sometimes be a headache. But Rutgers now has telephone registration at its New Brunswick campus, and students say the situation has improved.

In an effort to reverse the traditional exodus of New Jersey high-school superstars from the state, Rutgers offers a variety of honors programs, including special seminars, internships, independent projects, and research opportunities with the faculty. Rutgers also provides its undergraduates with a chance to study abroad in Britain, Costa Rica, France, Germany, India, Ireland, Israel, Italy, Mexico, Switzerland, and Spain. Biology students have the run of the 370-acre Rutgers Ecological Preserve and Natural Teaching Area. In addition, Rutgers is also home to more than one hundred specialized research centers and institutes dedicated to the study of topics ranging from ancient Roman art to mountain gorillas. Professors generally get high marks. "I completely revere most of my professors," coos a junior. "They are intelligent, well respected in their fields, and present dynamic lectures."

Though the administration has been trying to increase the number of out-of-staters, in recent years more than 90 percent of Rutgers students have been from New Jersey. Nevertheless, the student population is as diverse as that of the state, with a good proportion of students from cities, suburbs, farms, and seaside communities. Minorities account for 37 percent of the students: 11 percent are African-American, 9 percent are Hispanic, and 17 percent are Asian-American. "I feel I've grown so much here and learned so much about being a member of a rich and diverse community," explains one senior. The school's administration

> "The courses here require a great deal of thought and outside preparation if you want to be successful."

takes pride in their Committee to Advance Our Common Purpose, for students who want to reduce prejudice and promote diversity on campus. In the past, the committee developed a World Wide Web page for multicultural resources and submitted a proposal for the creation of an Intercultural Relations Study Group.

The university has eight liberal arts schools spread out among its campuses, for those seeking a broad-based education. Seven colleges cater to the needs of students wanting a preprofessional school (business, nursing, life and environmental studies, fine and performing arts, engineering, and pharmacy). The school does not guarantee to meet the full demonstrated need of every admit, but 24 percent of the applicants are offered full demonstrated need. About four hundred students receive athletic scholarships in a wide range of sports, and more than 6,500 receive merit awards. Students say they have noticed budget cuts in terms of tuition increases, fewer course offerings, shorter hours at buildings around campus, and fewer administrators.

On-campus housing in New Brunswick accommodates 47 percent of full-time students. "There has been a big push recently to renovate the dorms, so most of them are really nice," says a history major. Another student says, "With the exception of a few mediocre dorms for freshmen, most are extremely large and have air-conditioning; some have free cable TV; and a good number are directly hard-wired with fiber-optic cables into the Internet." Current on-campus housing options include conventional dorms, special-interest areas, and apartment complexes with kitchens and living rooms. The university also offers a special dormitory for students who are trying to overcome addictions to drugs and alcohol.

The city of New Brunswick is an attractive place to go for a drink or dinner on the town. Just don't stray too far from the campus. True, Rutgers has its own police department that possesses the same training and powers as the New Jersey state police. "I personally don't feel safe in New Brunswick, so I restrict my outings to on-campus locations," one student admits. For those who want to hit the road for fun,

(Continued)
History
Pharmacy
Biological Sciences
Political Science
Psychology
Engineering

The city of New Brunswick is an attractive place to go for a drink or dinner on the town. Just don't stray too far from the campus.

New York City and Philadelphia are each only about an hour distant, and students flood the Jersey shore in springtime. The Rutgers College Program Council offers trips ranging from white-water rafting to mountain climbing to skiing. "The variety of activities at Rutgers provides you with the opportunity to have fun any way you desire," says one student. "There are lots of on-campus social activities," a senior explains. "Movies, coffeehouses, local and bigger bands, lectures, parties. Off-campus activity includes frat parties and bars." In the past five years, students enrolled in the Citizenship and Service Education Program at Rutgers contributed more than ninety thousand hours of service to communities across New Jersey. "Students definitely get involved in the surrounding community and do a lot of volunteer work," says a senior.

The Greek system, which attracts 2 percent of the men and women, is entirely off campus. While the school neither owns nor administers any of the Greek organizations, it does have a university office for Greek affairs, which oversees the welfare of those belonging to fraternities and sororities. Students say a lot of the nightlife for the New Brunswick campuses takes place at the Greek houses. Reportedly, it is "difficult to drink in dorms," but underage students drink if they really

"With the exception of a few mediocre dorms for freshmen, most are extremely large and have air-conditioning; some have free cable TV; and a good number are directly hard-wired with fiber-optic cables into the Internet."

want to. Each college has its own student center with pinball machines, pool tables, bowling alleys, and a snack bar. Major social events include Reggae Day at Livingston, Agricultural Field Day at Cook, and Oktoberfest for the campus as a whole. Pioneer Pride Night is Camden's big party. During Homecoming, tailgate parties are held in the stadium parking lot, featuring tons of food—including roast pigs and whole sides of beef—continuous music, and thousands of revelers.

Varsity, intramural, and club sports fill whatever gap is left by the social scene. In fact, the university fields the highest number of athletes—more than one thousand—of any university in the nation. The Rutgers baseball team is competitive, as are many other sports, including football, basketball, tennis, lacrosse, soccer, cross-country, and track. Women's basketball, fencing, soccer, softball, field hockey, tennis, and track teams are also strong. A member of the Big East in football, Rutgers faces a tough schedule that includes Boston College, Miami, Syracuse, and West Virginia. Big East Conference competition makes up for not getting to play Princeton, which in 1980 bowed out of what was then the oldest football rivalry in the nation.

Rutgers has a plethora of people and programs characteristic of large state universities. It also has a lot more, including loyal support from the state's legislature and private sector, and tuition at an affordable price. Says one satisfied student: "From the diversity of its majors and courses to the hundreds of student organizations on campus, Rutgers gives me a chance to explore a world of options."

Overlaps

College of New Jersey, Montclair State, NYU, Penn State, Rowan University

If You Apply To ➤

Rutgers: Rolling admissions: Dec. 15. Financial aid: Mar. 15. Housing: June 15. Meets demonstrated need of 24%. No campus or alumni interviews. SATs or ACTs: required. No SAT IIs. No essay. Apply to particular school.

Annapolis campus: P.O. Box 2800, Annapolis, MD 21404-2800
Santa Fe campus: 1160 Camino Cruz Blanca, Santa Fe, NM 87501-4599

Books, books, and more books is what you'll get at St. John's—from Thucydides to Tolstoy, Euclid to Einstein. St. John's attracts smart, intellectual, and nonconformist students who like to talk (and argue) about books. Easy to get in, not so easy to graduate.

Although they're separated by more than one thousand miles, the two campuses of St. John's College share one key characteristic—an all-consuming quest for knowledge in the classical tradition. There are no lectures and no traditional professors on either campus. Instead, classes are led by tutors, who guide students as they seek knowledge from one another and from the great philosophers and thinkers of our time and generations past. St. John's may be the most intellectual college in the country, making even erudite Chicago look like a party school. Although fully one-third go on to professional schools, students don't come here because they're racing on the fast track toward career goals. "All of us love to learn," says a senior on the Annapolis campus. "We believe in the value of education for its own sake."

Physically, the two St. John's campuses are more than just three time zones from one another. The Colonial brick structures of the small urban campus in Annapolis, with its historic 1742 central classroom building, are squeezed into of the city's historic district. With the Maryland state capitol and the U.S. Naval Academy in the neighborhood, St. John's exudes an old-world ambiance. The other campus occupies 250 acres on the outskirts of sun-drenched

"We believe in the value of education for its own sake."

Santa Fe. The adobe-style buildings, which stand silhouetted against the Sangre de Cristo Mountains, offer beautiful views of the city below. Though it's not near public transportation, students at St. John's in Santa Fe can get back to nature in a nearby national forest. Students may attend both campuses during their academic careers, and about a quarter do so.

St. John's has no professors in the usual sense because the Great Books—about 150 of the most influential works of Western civilization—are the teachers. Both campuses follow a curriculum that would have delighted poet and educator Matthew Arnold, who argued that the goal of education is "to know the best which has been thought and said in the world." The St. John's curriculum, known as the Program, has every student read the Great Books in roughly chronological order. Students discuss the books in seminars, write papers about them, and ponder, debate, and philosophize about the riddles of human existence they propose.

At St. John's there are no registration or scheduling hassles: the daily course of study for all four years is mapped out before a student sets foot on campus. It includes four years of mathematics, two years of ancient Greek and French, three years of laboratory science, a year of music, and, of course, four years of Great Books seminars. Freshmen study the Greeks and Romans, sophomores advance to the Renaissance, juniors cover the seventeenth and eighteenth centuries, and seniors do the nineteenth and twentieth centuries. Readings are from primary sources only: math from Euclid and Ptolemy, physics from Einstein, psychology from Freud, and so on for all fields. For about seven weeks in the junior and senior years, seminars are suspended, and students select a book or topic to study in depth with a tutor. The assumption is that the Great Books can stand on their own, representing the highest achievements of human intellect. Overall, students say the junior

Annapolis Website:
www.sjca.edu
Location: Center city
Total Enrollment: 538
Undergraduates: 472
Male/Female: 53/47
SAT Ranges: V 650–740
M 580–670
Financial Aid: 62%
Expense: Pr $ $
Phi Beta Kappa: No
Applicants: 464
Accepted: 78%
Enrolled: 31%
Grad in 6 Years: 71%
Returning Freshmen: 82%
Academics: ✍ ✍ ✍ ✍ ½
Social: ☎ ☎ ☎
Q of L: ★ ★ ★ ★
Admissions: (800) 727-9238
or (410) 626-2522
Email Address:
admissions@sjca.edu

Santa Fe Website:
www.sjcsf.edu
Location: City outskirts
Total Enrollment: 528
Undergraduates: 445
Male/Female: 56/44
SAT Ranges: V 630–680
M 570–620
ACT Range: 26–30
Financial Aid: 67%
Expense: Pr $ $
Phi Beta Kappa: No
Applicants: 360
Accepted: 83%
Enrolled: 63%
Grad in 6 Years: 54%
Returning Freshmen: 82%

(Continued)

Academics: ✐ ✐ ✐ ✐ ½

Social: ☎ ☎ ☎

Q of L: ★ ★ ★ ★

Admissions: (800) 331-5232
 (505) 984-6060

Email Address:
 admissions@mail.sjcsf.edu

Strongest Programs
 The Great Books Program

St. John's may be the most intellectual college in the country, making even erudite Chicago look like a party school.

year, with its advanced curriculum in math and the natural sciences, is the most challenging. "No one is taught at St. John's College; everyone simply learns," says a sophomore. Forget about multiple-choice tests and cramming, but don't expect to slide by simply because the curriculum doesn't include formal exams. "It's all rigorous," says a sophomore. "Some of it—studying calculus in the raw by reading Newton and Leibniz—is downright Olympic. Academically, we each do what we can, and roll with the punches. Having no written tests removes a lot of the anxiety, but none of the difficulty." Math, languages, and lab sciences are very strong, "but the music class sophomore year could use a bit more structure," says a classmate.

Though the curriculum is far more structured and classical than any other college's, the method of presentation is as radical as that of any alternative school. Tutors would be professors at any other institution; at St. John's they are considered only the most advanced students in class. Like true Renaissance men, tutors must be able to teach any subject in the curriculum, and in a few years' time, they do. Many never publish at all, and they put teaching above all else. Tutors "do not see St. John's as a springboard to a better career," a senior says. "They are here because they, too, believe this is the best education possible." Instruction is entirely by small discussion groups, where the tutor's responsibility is to lead and guide rather than lecture. Not surprisingly, student-faculty relations are excellent. "Students get disappointed when classes are cancelled, and complain that tutors do not assign enough papers," says a sophomore. Another sophomore muses that although the absence of lecturing professors works very well, it can also be a weakness of the system. "The rigor of the class depends on your tutors," says the student. "The education hasn't changed," says a senior, but, "We have a tutor committee on instruction that is always giving the program a little tweak."

Many St. John's students find they need a year off between sophomore and junior years; some switch from Annapolis to Santa Fe or vice versa, not only for a change of scenery, but also for a change of climate, as the Santa Fe campus, founded in 1964 to increase the size of St. John's without sacrificing the virtues of a small campus, is more relaxed than the comparatively uptight Annapolis campus. As

"No one is taught at St. John's College; everyone simply learns."

dutiful as the cadets at the Naval Academy across the street, Annapolis Johnnies come as close as students can to learning every waking hour of the day. "Some of us are disappointed by the fact that the college issues grades," says one. "What we do here is so unique it cannot be quantified and itemized by a letter."

The St. John's curriculum, known as the Program, has every student read the Great Books in roughly chronological order.

Though the reasons students choose St. John's are never simple, the common thread is a fierce love of learning. "In my room right now, there's me, a pretty clean-cut, East Coast kind of guy; my roommate, a sort of down-to-earth mountain man from West Virginia; and the green-haired guy from New York City from across the hall who likes Offspring," says a sophomore. Most students are bright, opinionated, and have no use for the status quo. "There aren't really any social or political issues that affect us on campus," says a senior. "We spend time on questions that have been asked for millennia." While tolerance is a given, "Political correctness is scoffed at," says another. Admission of qualified students is first-come, first-served. After all spaces fill up (the school keeps a strict cap on enrollment), admissions begin for the following semester. A fifth of the students are transfers from more conventional colleges—an act of devotion, since St. John's requires all students to begin as freshmen. Minorities represent 8 percent of the student body, and racial tension is virtually nonexistent, though intellectual snobbery is not unheard of.

Sixty-one percent of students, including most freshmen, live on campus. "Not all dorms at St. John's are created equal," says one student. "Some are almost luxurious (large rooms with individual thermostats and great views of campus) and some feel like upscale refugee accommodations (exposed pipes, bugs, squeaky beds)." Dorms in Annapolis are coed, and some buildings date to the mid-nineteenth century; their age shows in the showers, where "the water often changes temperature," says one shivering student. Dining-hall food on both campuses gets no stars in the reviews of many students. Upperclassmen typically live in off-campus apartments and houses, while those who stay in the dorms usually get single rooms. The Santa Fe campus has a collection of small two-story dorms housing twenty students each. Rooms are spacious and offer more scenic views than most luxury hotels, thanks to their seven thousand feet above sea level, on the edge of mountains that turn blood red at sunset.

> **"Some of it—studying calculus in the raw by reading Newton and Leibniz—is downright Olympic. Academically, we each do what we can, and roll with the punches. Having no written tests removes a lot of the anxiety, but none of the difficulty."**

Santa Fe undergraduates plunge into the outdoorsy activities made possible by their mountaintop location, while Annapolis students limit their adventures to well-organized intramural teams with names like the Druids and the Furies. The annual croquet tournament against the U.S. Naval Academy, across the street from the Annapolis campus, attracts five thousand spectators, who come dressed in their spring finery. Mass quantities of wine and cheese are consumed at this event. "Most of the time, we win," says one Johnnie. Road trips to Washington, D.C., Baltimore, New York, and Assateague State Park are options for students with cars; the annual spring-break trip to the Santa Fe campus is known as Wagons West. Some students venture south of the border on weekends. Blues and jazz clubs are popular diversions, as are coffee shops, movies, and malls.

Drinking is a favored release for Johnnies, who have of course read Plato's Symposium and are familiar with the likes of Rabelais. Although no one under twenty-one may be served at college-sponsored events, which are patrolled to prevent underage drinking, underage undergrads tip their share of the brew at smaller gatherings and in their rooms. "If you have a friend over twenty-one who buys you beer, the RAs will not generally disturb you unless you get out of hand—that is, if they catch you at all," says one student. Only students who are extremely rowdy or disruptive are reported to the dean's office, to face penalties including expulsion. The Santa Fe administration adds cigarette smoking to alcohol consumption as a frustrating problem. Popular annual events on the Annapolis campus include Lola's, a casino night sponsored by the junior class to raise money for Reality, a three-day festival of food, games, and general debauchery thrown for the seniors the weekend before commencement. "A big part of Reality is the Spartan Mad-Ball game, which pits the freshmen and seniors against the sophomores and juniors in a free-for-all," says a sophomore. "The only rule is no one can use motorized devices or excessively sharp objects." There are waltz and swing dances, the annual

> **"Some of us are disappointed by the fact that the college issues grades. What we do here is so unique it cannot be quantified and itemized by a letter."**

Seducers and Corrupters party for incoming freshmen, and Senior Prank, a day-long surprise party for the whole college community. While intramurals are popular, fencing is the only intercollegiate sport at Santa Fe, and there are none at Annapolis. Probably not a shock to anyone is the fact that there are no fraternities or sororities.

Students grumble that there are more "good-grade rich kids" now than the motley crew of environmentalists, Goths, and ultra-conservatives that had happily coexisted here; this is, after all, a school where seniors wear formal academic gowns to their oral examinations, which are open to the public. As they march by, midshipmen

Santa Fe undergraduates plunge into the outdoorsy activities made possible by their mountaintop location, while Annapolis students limit their adventures to well-organized intramural teams with names like the Druids and the Furies.

Overlaps

Annapolis: Kenyon, Chicago, Reed, Oberlin, Smith

Santa Fe: Reed, UC-Berkeley, UT–Austin, NYU, St. Johns of Maryland

from the nearby Naval Academy taunt St. John's students by chanting, "I don't want a real degree, that's why I go to SJC." Johnnies take it all in stride. "We think it's pretty funny," says one. "At least we can dress ourselves."

While many colleges and universities are trying desperately to grow and change, St. John's College remains a throwback to simpler times. Enrollment is strictly limited, and devotion to the Great Books Program is still cult-like. "We don't like having other people tell us what the truth is," says a student. "We want to find it for ourselves."

If You Apply To ➤

St. Johns: Rolling admissions: Mar. 1. Financial aid: Feb. 15. Campus interviews: recommended, evaluative. Alumni interviews: recommended, informational (Annapolis) or optional, evaluative (Santa Fe). SATs and ACTs: optional. SAT IIs: optional. Accepts Common Application with supplemental essays. Essay questions: evaluate strengths and weaknesses of your formal education and explain why you wish to attend St. John's; describe reading habits and experience with books, and discuss one aspect of a book that's shaped your thoughts, or submit an already-written paper on a topic of significance; and describe and explain important experience. Special attention given to essays.

St. John's University and College of St. Benedict

St. John's campus: P.O. Box 7155, Collegeville, MN 56321-7155
St. Benedict campus: 37 South College Avenue, St. Joseph, MN 56374-2099

St. John's is a throwback to the way college was fifty years ago: men and women on separate campuses and copious amounts of school spirit. Catholics comprise about 80 percent of the students and monastery brothers make up 20 percent of the faculty.

Website: www.csbsju.edu
Total Enrollment: 4,139
Undergraduates: 3,988
Male/Female: 47/53
SAT Ranges: V 520–650
   M 540–660
ACT Range: 23–28
Financial Aid: 62%
Expense: Pr $
Phi Beta Kappa: No
Applicants: 2,546
Accepted: 83%
Enrolled: 50%
Grad in 6 Years: 75%
Returning Freshmen: 90%
Academics: ✍ ✍ ✍
Social: ☎ ☎ ☎
Q of L: ★ ★ ★
Admissions: (800) 245-6467 (St. John's) or (800) 544-1489 (St. Benedict)
Email Address: admissions@csbsju.edu

St. John's University and the College of St. Benedict are two single-sex campuses, three miles apart, with a common heritage and mission: providing an educational and spiritual atmosphere where professors and students work in concert to tackle the issues of the day. There's a true closeness here, a feeling that encourages neighbors to look out for one another—and for those they don't yet know. The students are "laid-back, friendly, outgoing, intelligent, and all together fun," a nursing major says. "If someone doesn't hold a door open for you, you can suspect they aren't a student at SJU."

Owned and operated by the largest Benedictine monastery in the world, St. John's occupies 2,400 pristine acres in rural Minnesota, an area replete with forests, lakes, and wide-open spaces that are perfect for outdoorsy types. Alongside an ancient quadrangle erected by monks

"If someone doesn't hold a door open for you, you can suspect they aren't a student at SJU."

is a strikingly modern church designed by Marcel Breuer, with a towering bell banner and three-story stained-glass window. The campus itself is one of the main reasons many choose this school. St. Benedict, down the road in St. Joseph, is connected to St. John's by free shuttle service. That campus is an impressive combination of contemporary and carefully restored and maintained turn-of-the-century buildings. St. John's has invested nearly $20 million in facilities in recent years, including a football stadium overhaul, new outdoor and indoor tracks, renovation of Warner Palaestra, construction of an all-purpose field house, and the building of a 48,000-square-foot science center. New residences have been built on both campuses.

The most popular major is management, followed by biology, communication, nursing, and elementary education. Students say chemistry and physics are tough, and the strong medieval studies program benefits from the Hill Monastic Manuscript Library, one of the foremost microfilm collections of handwritten manuscripts. The forests on and around the campus are a boon to the field biology offerings. An innovative management program places majors in control of computer-simulated corporations and lets them try their hand at free-market enterprise.

St. Benedict shares extensive cross-registration programs and joint departments with St. John's, so students mix easily and comfortably. Owing to the schools' small size, every class has fewer than fifty students, and classes can fill up fast. Still, only education majors typically spend more than four years getting their degrees, because of student-teaching requirements. It can be hard for freshmen to snag popular elective courses, but in general, "the school makes sure you take what you need," says a St. John's communication major. The small classes also encourage strong student-faculty ties. "You come out of each class learning how to think critically," says a history and peace studies major. "I am often amazed by my professors," exclaims a St. John's senior. The schools help keep instruction quality high by asking students to evaluate their courses at the end of each semester. Monastery brothers make up 20 percent of the St. John's faculty, and sisters make up a contingent of the St. Benedict professors. "The profs really want students to succeed and are always available to help," says a French major.

The schools' core four-year curriculum reflects the tradition of the Benedictine focus on understanding the wisdom of the humanities, sciences, and fine arts. It starts with a first-year symposium and ends with a senior seminar. Students also take courses that examine issues from a gender or global perspective, and courses that emphasize discussion, quantitative reasoning, and writing. The schools have eliminated the optional January term, much to

"You come out of each class learning how to think critically."

students' dismay. On a brighter note, the Liemandt Family Service Learning program encourages students to engage in the community and complete projects, essays, and journals—with guidance from faculty—based on their experiences. About half the students study abroad to countries including Austria, Australia, China, England, France, Greece, Italy, Ireland, South Africa, or Spain; each is limited to about thirty participants. SJU sends more students to study abroad than any other small liberal arts college. Closer to home, there's also an honors program for exceptional freshmen, and sophomores can apply, too.

Though 80 percent of students are Roman Catholic, few resemble priests in training. In fact, almost three-fourths climb the corporate ladder after graduation. Eighty-three percent are from Minnesota, and most are white, public-school alumni from middle-class backgrounds. While the administration is trying to increase minority enrollment, minorities only make up 3 percent of the student body. "Diversity, or our lack of it," is now a big complaint among students, a senior says. The campus is not preoccupied with political correctness, students say, though human rights and international relations are important issues here.

Eighty-two percent of students here live on campus, and a committed residence staff, including the monks at St. John's and sisters at St. Benedict, oversees homey dormitory life. Lest you think a nun is watching your every move, "students have enough freedom in dorm rooms to make them comfortable," says a philosophy major. Incoming students are assigned to doubles on freshman floors in one of the six dorms, and a cleaning services attends to each room every day. Other options include small houses off campus for half a dozen students each, an experimental Christian community housing project of five units for 110 students, and college-owned apartments, including an earth-sheltered complex on the shore of a lake.

Religion may be the most dominant program on campus, but football is a close second. The team is a perennial Division III powerhouse, cheered on by a team of guys called "the Rat Pack" instead of a traditional pom-pom squad.

Upperclassmen who live off campus in a nearby town commute by car or college bus. "We have the big city nearby, and we live in the country," says a sophomore. "It has the perfect atmosphere."

Since there are no social fraternities or sororities, the social scene tends toward private or college-sponsored parties, as well as bar-hopping in St. Joseph and nearby St. Cloud, a city of fifty thousand that is fifteen minutes away by car. These towns also offer restaurants and coffee shops that are popular with students. For more refined tastes, the Stephen B. Humphrey Fine Arts Theater at SJU and the Benedicta Arts Center on the CSB campus host a wide variety of cultural events. For those seeking typical college fun, student groups host movies, sports events, dances, and parties, says a Spanish major. As you might imagine, it's pretty tough to drink while you're underage on these campuses. The best road trips are to Duluth, St. Paul, and Minneapolis, and many students take advantage of outdoor adventures in central Minnesota. Among the most popular annual happenings are the fall Watab Island party, Christmas tree lighting, formal dances each semester, the year-end spring Pinestock Folk Festival (named for the school's Pine Curtain setting), and the St. John's–St. Thomas football game, otherwise known as the Tommy-Johnnie.

"This team riles up the crowd like nothing you've seen."

Religion may be the most dominant program on campus, but football is a close second. The team is a perennial Division III powerhouse, and its fanatical following rivals the likes of Notre Dame with their devotion. Curiously enough, a team of guys functions as a cheerleading squad: "Instead of cheerleaders we have 'The Rat Pack' who cheer for our football team," says a junior. "This team riles up the crowd like nothing you've seen." SJU football, golf, and basketball have brought home conference championships in the past two years. The St. Benedict basketball team reached the NCAA finals. Non-varsity students can participate in intramural program.

Students at these two Catholic schools are "ultra-involved and well-rounded," traits one might not expect at a school featuring two monasteries. But those who attend St. John's and St. Benedict's revel in their small-town setting and the beauty of rural Minnesota while exploring Catholic ideals. With small classes, opportunities for research and study abroad, and a strong sense of community, these students are generally a contented lot. "It's an environment where saying 'hello' and 'good morning' to complete strangers is the norm," says a biology major. While they're holding the door for you, of course.

Overlaps

University of St. Thomas, St. Cloud State, Gustavus Adolphus, University of Minnesota, St. Olaf

If You Apply To ➤ **St. Johns and St. Benedict:** Rolling admissions. Financial aid: Mar. 1. Housing: May 15. Meets demonstrated need of 85%. Campus interviews: recommended, informational. No alumni interviews. SATs or ACTs: required. SAT IIs: optional. Accepts the Common Application and electronic applications. Essay question: personal statement.

St. Lawrence University

Canton, NY 13617

St. Lawrence is perched far back in the north country, closer to Ottawa and Montreal than Syracuse. Isolation breeds camaraderie, and SLU students have a special bond similar to that at places like Dartmouth and Whitman. Environmental studies is the crown jewel.

St. Lawrence University beckons those seeking an education that exercises both body and mind. Located deep in upstate New York, this school's excellent liberal arts curriculum is complemented by a close-knit community—and one of the best environmental studies programs in the nation. Students take full advantage of their pristine and rugged surroundings, and many prefer to find their thrills on the ski slopes and hiking trails rather than the dance floor or concert hall.

The St. Lawrence campus—which has undergone $80 million in construction and renovation over the past few years—is just ninety minutes from Ottawa, the Canadian capital. Hiking trails, a river, and a golf course surround thirty buildings, which sit centered on one thousand acres. Many buildings date from the late nineteenth century, and though their exteriors have been preserved, their interiors are fully modernized and up-to-date. Winter temperatures average between twenty and thirty degrees, but the good news is it's only a ten-minute walk between the two most distant buildings. A whole new world of athletic facilities has sprung up: a fitness center, field house with a track, tennis courts and climbing wall, soccer and football stadiums, and baseball and softball fields. After all that exercise, students can go chow down in their new dining hall.

> "The academic climate is mixed, split between those who are excited by their academics and those who don't care."

The building boom doesn't stop there—a 120-unit senior townhouse-style residence opened in 2003, and a new student center is to appear in 2004.

St. Lawrence offers a classical liberal arts education, emphasizing quality over quantity. Enrollment has been reduced to improve the student/faculty ratio, keep classes small, and allow for more team teaching. New majors include computer science, neuroscience, biochemistry, and global studies. St. Lawrence is well known for its environmental studies. Among the unique offerings are outdoor education courses in music and writing, and a student-run, self-sustainable residence. General education requirements can be satisfied through one of two tracks. The "standard track" requires one course in the natural sciences, one in social sciences, one in humanities, and one in any non-Western topic, plus two courses in "classical liberal arts" (math or symbolic logic, arts, and language). The "alternative track" is based on St. Lawrence's Cultural Encounters program, which includes core courses, foreign language study, science and mathematics, one semester of study abroad, and a senior seminar.

The university's First-Year Program—small, interdisciplinary, two-semester courses taught by professors from all departments, who then become academic advisors—is "a good stepping stone to get you into the college environment," says a junior. Biology is the most popular major, followed by psychology, economics, government, and English, but many students prefer less conventional programs, such as

> "There has been a steady improvement in the state of the dorms over the last four years."

Renaissance music. Administrators say the music department is small but growing steadily with the recent addition of an instrumental music faculty position.

Striving "to make the world our classroom," St. Lawrence augments its on-campus offerings with numerous study-abroad programs. More than half of the students head overseas to such places as Kenya, Japan, Russia, or India, or stay right nearby for the new "Adirondack semester" at Saranac Lake. Students may also take advantage of group-sponsored exchange programs in Denmark, Canada, Costa Rica, or Washington, D.C. Frequent trips to Ottawa for cultural and political events are part of the academic and extracurricular agendas. There are also five-year programs with other universities in engineering, nursing, and management. Some lucky students will have the opportunity of participating in the St. Lawrence University Fellows Program, which supports faculty-student research done in the summer before the student's senior year.

Website: www.stlawu.edu
Location: Village
Total Enrollment: 2,099
Undergraduates: 1,970
Male/Female: 48/52
SAT Ranges: V 520–620
  M 520–620
ACT Range: 22-28
Financial Aid: 70%
Expense: Pr $ $ $
Phi Beta Kappa: Yes
Applicants: 2,745
Accepted: 61%
Enrolled: 30%
Grad in 6 Years: 72%
Returning Freshmen: 85%
Academics: ✍ ✍ ✍
Social: ☎ ☎ ☎
Q of L: ★ ★ ★
Admissions: (315) 229-5261
Email Address:
  admiss@stlawu.edu

Strongest Programs
  Psychology
  Sociology
  Environmental Studies
  Math
  Speech and Theater
  English

The social life at SLU centers on campus, since—thanks to the school's small size—most students know each other.

St. Lawrence students speak highly of their professors, and say administrators have worked hard to increase the school's academic rigor over the past few years. That results in some disconnects: "The academic climate is mixed, split between those who are excited by their academics and those who don't care," says a senior. "But the coursework is pretty demanding." Small classes make for a lot of attention and assistance from professors. "I have had the opportunity to study with exceptional instructors who motivate me, interest me, and care about my future," an English and government major reports.

"Most of the social life revolves around Greek houses."

Still, most "Larries" agree that there is no cut-throat competition here. The emphasis on shared learning is furthered by the school's "residential college system," through which students living in the same dorm take a common interdisciplinary course team-taught by professors from multiple disciplines. To complement their year-long common course, first-year students live together in one of twelve residential "communities" with forty to fifty students each.

St. Lawrence students are a conventional bunch with a streak of outdoorsy non-conformity. The student body is predominantly white, with African-Americans, Hispanics, and Asian students constituting 5 percent of the student body. Qualified students vie for merit scholarships worth up to $15,000, and talented puck-pushers may take advantage of athletic scholarships in hockey.

Dorm life at St. Lawrence is your standard bed, dresser, chest of drawers, and desk-with-a-light. "There has been a steady improvement in the state of the dorms over the last four years," says a senior majoring in economics. Most rooms are well maintained, though students complain it sometimes takes a while for repair requests to be addressed. Most dorms also have coed wings, and students generally live in doubles. Freshmen are placed in their residential colleges, while everyone else gets rooms by lottery with priority given to upperclassmen (they get all the singles). Seniors occasionally gain permission to live off campus; 95 percent of the student body live on campus. Campus living also has its rewards: the food served in the dining hall frequently features student recipes. Twenty-five percent of the women and 14 percent of the men live and eat in sorority and fraternity houses. Other options for grub include the campus pub in the Student Center, a café in the physical education building, and a convenience store.

In varsity sports, men's hockey is the top draw—especially when played against archrival Clarkson.

The social life at SLU centers on campus, since—thanks to the school's small size—most students know each other. The university provides activities, such as a nonalcoholic campus nightclub, a new pool hall, four different current movies each week, and the campus coffeehouse—a great place to hear a band, acoustic guitarist, or comedian. Still, students say, "most of the social life revolves around Greek houses," where independent students are welcome, too. No hard liquor or kegs are allowed on campus, and the school has clamped down on underage drinking. However, at St. Lawrence, to "make a run for the border" doesn't mean heading for Mexican fast food; the purchasing age for liquor in Ontario is a mere nineteen years old.

Canton is a charming town of restored Victorian buildings and storefronts offering everything from bagels to handmade jewelry to bars and restaurants. As a college town, however, it rates "nonexistent," says a sociology major. Potsdam, ten minutes away, has more to offer.

On campus, the university's Winterfest is an annual two-week celebration of the season. On "Peak Weekend," the SLU Outing Club tries to "put St. Lawrence students on every peak in the Adirondacks." Most St. Lawrence students enjoy sports; the school's fine athletic facilities, including an indoor field house, eight squash courts, indoor tennis, a pool, and ropes course, cater to varsity athletes and weekend warriors alike.

St. Lawrence's on-campus golf course doubles as a running route and a cross-country skiing trail during the winter. Hiking and rock climbing are other outdoor exercise options, as is canoeing the St. Lawrence River. In varsity sports, men's hockey is the top draw, especially when played against archrival Clarkson. Championship teams include women's soccer, basketball, and track; men's soccer, basketball, track, and Lacrosse; and softball. Intramurals are the thing to do for almost everyone, with competition ranging from softball to hockey to volleyball.

With administrators raising the academic bar and a lengthy round of renovation and construction about to conclude, St. Lawrence is a school on the rise. It could be the ideal school for those seeking a small, caring environment—and wanting to get back to nature.

St. Mary's College of Maryland

St. Mary's City, MD 20686

A public liberal arts institution of the same breed as Mary Washington, UNC–Asheville, and William and Mary. St. Mary's historic but sleepy environs are ninety minutes from D.C. and Baltimore. With the Chesapeake Bay close at hand, St. Mary's is a haven for sailors.

St. Mary's is one of the best deals on the East Coast. Despite its religious-sounding name, the school is a public institution that has been designated the state's "honors college." Fifteen years ago, St. Mary's was just another complacent public college with a dazzling waterfront. But now, with rising test scores, increased state support, and growing numbers of applications, suffice it to say that St. Mary's is out to make waves. It also has the advantage of being one of the East Coast's prettiest schools, with its own beautiful marina located right on the St. Mary's River and plenty of opportunities to stroll along the shore and watch gorgeous sunsets.

St. Mary's got its start in 1840 as a women's seminary intended as a monument to the colonial birthplace of the state. The campus, built on a peninsula in southern Maryland where the Potomac River meets the Chesapeake Bay, is a mix of Colonial and modern architecture clustered directly on the waterfront. The college has taken advantage of its setting by establishing an outstanding center for marine research along the river. It's also part of an 1,100-acre

> **"Students can balance the more difficult courses with the easier ones so at no point is any one semester too difficult."**

national historic landmark commemorating Maryland's first colonial settlement; archeological digs dot the campus and provide opportunities for research. Crescent-shaped townhouses add a distinctly historic flavor to the campus. New tennis courts and a new baseball field are recent campus additions, as is the much-appreciated student center.

Students may sail through the bay, but not the academics; the curriculum is continuously improved and the courseload is getting tougher. "The academic climate is fairly rigorous," reports one student, though "students can balance the more difficult courses with the easier ones so at no point is any one semester too difficult." Students

(Continued)
Economics
Political Science
Psychology

have excellent departments to choose from, especially biology, which places many of its grads into top graduate schools and research positions. It is also the most popular major, followed by economics, psychology, political science, and English. The strong music department includes prize-winning pianist Brian Ganz as head of the piano faculty. St. Mary's has also created an independent student-designed major for more free-thinking types. A state-of-the-art science center, with fifty-five thousand square feet of classrooms, labs, and research space, benefits the already strong science departments.

All entering freshmen must take a course in English composition in addition to a math course, a foreign language, and Legacy, a history survey course. The ambitious general studies curriculum emphasizes Western heritage, writing, and math, but also includes art history, literature, science, and a philosophy course for juniors and seniors. The school offers study-abroad programs, including Oxford's Center for Medieval and Renaissance Studies; exchange programs in Germany, China, and France; and participates in the National Student Exchange. Closer to home, biology students can cruise the bay on the college's research boat. The Nitze Scholars Program, both highly respected and very selective, has further boosted St. Mary's academic standards. "Overall, the quality of teaching I have received has been excellent," an enthusiastic junior reports.

The strong music department includes prize-winning pianist Brian Ganz as head of the piano faculty.

> **"Overall, the quality of teaching I have received has been excellent."**

"My teachers have all been very knowledgeable of the subjects and were enthusiastic in attempting to spark my interests," a fellow classmate adds. All classes are taught by faculty, and most have twenty-five people or fewer.

St. Mary's students are "probably the most well-rounded and culturally aware population I have ever met," says a student. Eighty-eight percent of the student body hail from Maryland, and 77 percent are from public schools. More minority students are also finding their way to the peninsula; 7 percent of the school are African-American, 2 percent Hispanic, and 4 percent Asian-American. The big social issue on campus, according to students, is the environment. The political atmosphere on campus is described as fairly liberal and laid back. St. Mary's offers 218 scholarships for academic merit that range from $1,000 to $7,000, but there are no athletic scholarships.

Best of all are the eighty-one two-story townhouses that allow upperclassmen with sufficient credits to do their own cooking.

Students tend to enjoy living on campus, as 82 percent reside there at any given time. Options include five residence halls, three of which are coed, and a newly constructed complex of coed residential suites. Best of all are the eighty-one two-story townhouses that allow upperclassmen with sufficient credits to do their own cooking. "Everyone looks forward to having enough credits to get into a townhouse," remarks an anxious sophomore. Older students get preference if they decide to retain a room or want one nearby, and students select rooms based on the number of academic credits they have acquired. Those who do live off campus have enticing options, including old farmhouses and riverside cottages available for rent. Students who tire of cafeteria food can join the vegetarian co-op or just go catch their own fish and crabs.

> **"My teachers have all been very knowledgeable of the subjects and were enthusiastic in attempting to spark my interests."**

St. Mary's secluded location—about an hour and a half from either Washington, D.C., or Baltimore—means there's little nightlife off campus. The seclusion gets mixed responses from students: "St. Mary's is a pretty close community. Weekend social life is usually centered around a few parties that everyone attends," one student comments. Given the isolation of the campus, St. Mary's is a "make your own fun" kind of place. When students become tired of relaxing in the upperclassman townhouses and dorm rooms, they take it upon themselves to create their own activities. Campus organizations, including a film society, sponsor several events a week. In nice weather, students spend time enjoying the waterfront or nearby bike trails.

The main source of fun, of course, is the surrounding water and its sporty offerings.

The main source of fun, of course, is the surrounding water and its sporty offerings. "It's virtually impossible to graduate without knowing how to sail," says one student. The waterfront also becomes the focus of campus-wide activities, including World Carnival, an Earth Day celebration, and the cardboard boat race held each fall. More than 70 percent of students become involved in community service.

Although certainly not known for its athletics, Division III St. Mary's has recently taken off. The coed and women's sailing teams, coached by a former member of the U.S Sailing Team, have won several national championships, and the women won the Sloop National Championship several years back. Women's sailing and men's lacrosse are also strong. The Ultimate Frisbee golf club team has a heated rivalry with Navy, and even attracts considerable alumni interest. A popular T-shirt reads, "St. Mary's college football—undefeated," but of course, there is no football team.

St. Mary's is bent on establishing itself as one of the country's premier public liberal arts colleges. Though its small size and isolation can be stifling at times, most students appreciate the close bonds that are created at this school. With its unique blend of learning and life on the waterfront, says one student, "It's like your parents are paying for you to live at a vacation resort for eight months of the year."

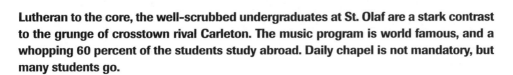

If You Apply To ➤

St. Mary's: Early decision: Dec. 1. Regular admissions: Jan. 15. Financial aid: Mar. 1. Does not guarantee to meet demonstrated need. Campus interviews: recommended, informational. Alumni interviews: optional, informational. SATs or ACTs: required. SAT IIs: optional. Accepts electronic applications. Essay question: title of autobiography; what you wanted to be when you grew up; most significant invention.

St. Olaf College

1520 St. Olaf Avenue, Northfield, MN 55057-1098

Lutheran to the core, the well-scrubbed undergraduates at St. Olaf are a stark contrast to the grunge of crosstown rival Carleton. The music program is world famous, and a whopping 60 percent of the students study abroad. Daily chapel is not mandatory, but many students go.

Northfield, Minnesota, which bills itself the city of "Cows, Colleges, and Contentment," is home to St. Olaf College—and the blondest student body this side of Oslo. This small Midwest school was founded by Norwegian Lutheran immigrants, was named for the country's patron saint, and aims to be "an excellent liberal arts college of the church." One student describes her peers at St. Olaf as "Minnesota nice," adding, "You can't go anywhere without saying 'hi' to people. Even if you don't know a person, there is still a feeling of belonging to the same community. We are friendly, outgoing, hardworking, and we love to have fun."

St. Olaf's meticulously landscaped 350-acre campus, featured in several architectural journals, is located on Manitou Heights, overlooking the Cannon River valley and the city of Northfield. More than ten thousand trees, native prairie, and a wetlands wildlife area surround the thirty-four native limestone buildings that form the campus. The student union, the Buntrock Commons, offers dining and food services, a bookstore, post office, conference and banquet facilities, movie theater, and game room. The three-level, eighty-four thousand–square foot Dittman Center, housing the art and dance departments, opened in 2001. Under construction is the even larger Tostrud Center, which will be home to recreational and exercise facilities.

Website: www.stolaf.edu
Location: Small town
Total Enrollment: 3,011
Undergraduates: 3,011
Male/Female: 42/58
SAT Ranges: V 580–680
  M 570–680
ACT Range: 25–29
Financial Aid: 61%
Expense: Pr $ $
Phi Beta Kappa: Yes
Applicants: 2,463
Accepted: 76%
Enrolled: 40%
Grad in 6 Years: 80%
Returning Freshmen: 93%

All students at St. Olaf complete a general education requirement that covers three areas: foundation studies, core studies, and integrative study. A first-year seminar emphasizing writing, a foreign language, math, oral communication, and physical education fulfill the first area. Two courses in each of six disciplines—Western culture, multicultural studies, art, literary studies, biblical studies, and theological studies—with two courses in natural sciences and two in social sciences, complete the second requirement. A course in ethical issues and perspectives fulfills the third area. Typically, fourteen to sixteen courses satisfy the general education requirements; some courses may fulfill requirements in more than one area.

Students give the nod to biology and chemistry, and the college also boasts a solid premed program; economics, psychology, English, and math are also popular majors. The music department draws high praise; it offers many performance opportunities with five school choirs, a band, and an orchestra. The choirs are often featured at church services and other religious events, and can regularly be heard singing with the Minnesota Orchestra. Weaker academic departments include family resources and sociology. In the last quarter-century, the college has cultivated an international agenda for its students and faculty, and has created the largest international studies

> **"You can't go anywhere without saying 'hi' to people. Even if you don't know a person, there is still a feeling of belonging to the same community."**

program in the country among liberal arts colleges. Programs are available in forty-eight countries. The Finstad Center conveys knowledge about the challenges, risks, rewards, opportunities, and responsibilities of being an entrepreneur. Research is available in the sciences and psychology, and the Center for Integrative Studies allows students to form their own majors. All students get faculty advisors, and the vast majority of students graduate in four years. Students who participate in the intensive, nontraditional program—the two-year Great Conversation course in classic works—live together in one dorm to facilitate late-night study sessions. Additionally, since the program in international studies is an important part of the school's curriculum, more than 60 percent of students take advantage of study-abroad opportunities, including those offered through membership in the Associated Colleges of the Midwest* consortium.

Faculty members at St. Olaf are highly praised by students. "All my professors have known my name and have had much interaction with students," a sophomore chemistry major says. Instructors participate in and out of the classroom, reportedly having as many as ten hours of open office time a week. Still, just because professors want to see them succeed doesn't mean students can coast. "The academic climate is fairly competitive and the expectations of professors are pretty high and they push you to do your best," one student says. There's also an annual study break where professors serve their stressed-out pupils ice cream.

Diversity is by far the hottest topic at St. Olaf. The student body is extremely homogeneous: 88 percent are white—a situation the administration says it is working to change through workshops and other awareness programs. Students also recognize that while there is no overt hostility among white and minority students, there is a degree of separatism. "They come from wealthy families and have not had exposure to diversity

> *"Unfortunately, there is a typical or stereotypical Ole. They are typically blond, well-off, and very attractive. At the same time, two people who may look like they are similar may have very different views," a sophomore says.*

> **"All my professors have known my name and have had much interaction with students."**

(of culture, religion, opinions) in their lives," opines a freshman. Most students are high achievers from Midwestern public schools, drawn in part by hundreds of merit scholarships ranging from $500 to $9,000 per year. Despite their similar backgrounds, students say they have their differences. "Unfortunately, there is a typical or stereotypical Ole. They are typically blond, well-off, and very attractive. At the same time, two people who may look like they are similar may have very different views," a sophomore says.

Ninety-six percent of students live in on-campus housing, with college-owned houses available off campus, and freshmen are assigned double rooms in twenty-student "corridors," each with two junior counselors. Dorms are coed by floor, and each has its own personality. Rooms are selected by lottery, which students consider very fair. Students eat in a large modern cafeteria, where the food is considered above average for college fare. Every December, the dining hall serves a special meal of traditional Norwegian cuisine, including lutefisk, which "tastes awful," according to one junior philosophy major.

Opinions diverge on St. Olaf's social life. Some students blame peer apathy for the lack of things to do, noting "it's what you make of it." Others grouse about the dry campus or students' efforts to circumvent it, yet "most students seem to make very satisfying friendships that extend beyond the drinking scene," according to one student. "If you're looking for adventure and excitement, this is not the place to be," advises a freshman. Most weekend activities are on campus, including a nightclub called Lion's Pause and a coffeehouse, the Alley. The fine arts department provides many music, theater, and dance performances. And because there are no fraternities or sororities at St. Olaf, any large-scale weekend partying usually occurs off campus—at the few bars in town, or even better, at crosstown rival Carleton College. The Student Activities Committee sponsors occasional dances, speakers, and cultural events, covered by student fees and at-the-door ticket sales. Daily chapel services, though not mandatory, are heavily attended, and studying is always another weekend option

In the city of Northfield, there is little of social interest for St. Olaf students aside from Carleton, Olaf's liberal neighbor and chief rival. The most talked-about annual event, running more than seventy-five years, is the four-day Christmas Festival during which choirs, orchestras, and bands combine in televised concerts celebrating the birth of Jesus. Many students volunteer in Northfield and report a friendly rapport with the community. "They work in town, volunteer at the food shelf and at the schools, and

"If you're looking for adventure and excitement, this is not the place to be."

have other programs to help out with the town," reports a senior. Nonetheless, for those with wanderlust, buses leave regularly for the twin cities of Minneapolis and St. Paul, which are less than an hour's drive, where one can experience a shopper's paradise at the huge Mall of America. Chicago is also a popular road trip.

St. Olaf has outstanding athletic programs. Women's cross-country and volleyball and men's swimming and baseball secured recent conference titles. The men's ski team is the reigning national champion, while the women's team ranked second in nationals. There is also an extensive intramural program, and broomball—ice hockey played with brooms instead of sticks, and shoes rather than skates—is the sport of choice in the winter. The St. Olaf football team competes against Carleton for the honor of having the statue in the town's square face the winning campus. The chorus of the school's fight song is "Um Ya Ya," which has become a popular chant on campus.

For those yearning for a school where spirituality and scholarship exist on the same exalted plane, St. Olaf is a good bet. It's a place where students work hard, are encouraged by good teachers, toughened by Minnesota winters, and nourished by strong moral values, in addition to hearty Scandinavian food.

In the last quarter-century, the college has cultivated an international agenda for its students and faculty, and has created the largest international studies program in the country among liberal arts colleges.

Overlaps

Gustavus Adolphus, Carleton, Luther, University of Wisconsin at Madison, University of Minnesota.

If You Apply To ➤

St. Olaf: Rolling admissions. Early decision: Nov. 15. Early action: Dec. 15. Financial aid: Feb. 15 (priority). Guarantees to meet full demonstrated need. Campus interviews: recommended, informational. No alumni interviews. SATs or ACTs: required. SAT IIs: optional. Accepts the Common Application and electronic applications. Essay question: define an ideal community; meaning of diversity; what you would like to research.

Saint Louis University

221 North Grand Boulevard, St. Louis, MO 63103-2097

This is not your father's SLU. The campus and surrounding neighborhood have been spiffed up in the past two decades, and SLU's campus is a pleasant oasis from the bustle of mid-town St. Louis. In addition to strengths in premed and communication, SLU has an unusual specialty in aviation.

Website:
  www.imagine.slu.edu
Location: Urban
Total Enrollment: 11,145
Undergraduates: 7,228
Male/Female: 45/55
SAT Ranges: V 540–650
  M 550–660
ACT Range: 24–29
Financial Aid: 63%
Expense: Pr $ $
Phi Beta Kappa: Yes
Applicants: 5,902
Accepted: 69%
Enrolled: 35%
Grad in 6 Years: 69%
Returning Freshmen: 86%
Academics: ✐ ✐ ✐
Social: ☎ ☎
Q of L: ★ ★ ★
Admissions: (314) 977-2500
Email Address:
  admitme@slu.edu

Strongest Programs
  Premed
  Prelaw
  Biology
  Aerospace Engineering
  Biomedical Engineering
  Communications
  Psychology

Within sight of Saint Louis's famed Gateway Arch, the historical gateway to the American West, sits Saint Louis University, the first university established west of the Mississippi River. SLU offers students a "slew" of programs, from aviation and engineering to public service, social work, and meteorology. The school's academic atmosphere is shaped by its Roman Catholic, Jesuit tradition; administrators ensure that each student receives personal care and attention, and expect graduates to contribute to society and lead efforts for social change.

The SLU campus has undergone an $870 million renovation and features pedestrian walkways, lush greenery, fountains, and sculptures, as well as the signature Saint Louis University gates at all entrances. Cupples House, a beautiful old mansion in the middle of campus, houses nineteenth-century furniture and an art gallery—and is just steps from the futuristic glass structure of the law school. Numerous renovations and campus additions have been completed over the last two years, including the opening of the John and Lucy Cook Hall; the Verhaegen Hall, which now houses the Paul C. Reinert, S. J., Center for Teaching Excellence; the Manresa Center, which was formally the Franciscan Friary; the Grand Forest apartments; the former Compton Heights Hospital reopened as Salus Center, which now includes the School of Public Health; the renovated Childgarden Building, which is now the Academic Resources Center; and the Saint Louis University Museum of Art. Plans are currently underway to renovate and expand the Busch Memorial Center as well.

> **"Students do not seem to avoid any particular department or program."**

In keeping with its strong Jesuit commitment to education in the broader sense, all SLU undergrads must complete distribution requirements in international cultures, fine arts, English, literature, science, social/behavioral science, mathematics, and history. Additionally, students must take philosophy and theology courses, such as SLUVision, which integrates community service with the philosophy and theology component. The most popular majors are physical therapy and psychology, while premed also gets high marks from students. As might be expected, philosophy and theology are outstanding. Weaker spots are hard to find; a junior insists that, "students do not seem to avoid any particular department or program." SLU attracts scholars from around the globe with one of the world's most complete microfilm collections of Vatican documents. Parks College, America's first certified college of aviation, offers degree programs in Aviation Science where students can become professional pilots. The College of Arts and Science's meteorology program provides students with an opportunity to study with specialists in satellite, radar, and mesoscale meteorology. The College of Public Service offers majors in communication disorders, educational studies, and urban affairs, which encourage students to put research into action.

Nearly two-thirds of SLU freshman class came from the top quarter of their high-school class, and a psychology major reports, "The courses are tough, but that's what brings people together." "I've had teachers set up study sessions, hold extra office hours, and give me home phone numbers," says a senior. "I feel a personal

SCU: Regular admissions: Jan. 15. Early Financial aid: Feb. 1. Housing: May 4. Does not guarantee to meet need. Campus interviews: optional, informational. No alumni interviews. SATs or ACTs: required. Accepts the Common Application and electronic applications. Essay question: time when anticipation outweighed experience; time when offered compassion.

Sarah Lawrence College

1 Mead Way, Bronxville, NY 10708-5999

The free-spirited sister of East Coast alternative institutions. Though SLC is coed, women outnumber men nearly three to one. Strong in the humanities and fine arts with a specialty in creative writing. Full of quirky, head-strong intellectuals who hop the train to New York City every chance they get.

It seems the only rule at Sarah Lawrence College is that rules are made to be broken. This elite liberal arts school prides itself on individualism and self-expression. "At SLC the climate is open to make it what you will," says one junior. Freedom and exploration are valued more highly than any tradition, and it's this commitment to the individual and the mind that makes Sarah Lawrence College a creative place to learn. "The students here are left-winged, right-brained people," says one student.

Founded in 1926, the college sits on a quaint, forty-acre campus. English Tudor buildings and mansions of converted estates intermingle with more modern structures. The landscape is hilly and green, with more than one hundred types of trees and abundant rock outcroppings. The school's founders believed that there should be as little physical separation as possible between life and work, so classrooms, dormitory suites, and faculty offices are all housed in the same ivy-covered buildings. The studio theater, recently renamed the Suzanne Werner Wright Theatre, has been completely renovated by an award-winning designer who also happens to be a faculty member.

> **"At SLC, the climate is open to make it what you will."**

It's tough to find two Sarah Lawrence students studying the same thing, because every student has an individually designed program of study, and almost no subject is out of bounds. Instead, you'll find uniquely combined concentrations, such as American history and cultural anthropology or sculpture and literature. Grades are recorded for transcript purposes only; more emphasis is placed on written faculty evaluations. Some students become overwhelmed here, but those who stay find that the combination of close faculty supervision and an endless slate of choices provide an experience unavailable elsewhere. "There are no mandatory classes, so each class is chosen by the student," says a freshman studying international relations.

Students will become intimately acquainted with the written word at Sarah Lawrence—one of the few things that everyone does here. Writing begins in the first year and continues relentlessly "across the curriculum" for the next three years. All first-year students take a First-Year Studies Seminar in one of more than thirty subjects. Each student meets with a professor individually each week to discuss his or her independent projects, academic plans, and transition to college. Undergraduate students must complete 120 credit hours in at least three of four academic areas. Other than that, undergraduates write their own academic ticket, with the help of their first-year seminar leader, who serves as an academic guru (called a "don" from the Latin for "gift"). "I absolutely love the don system," boasts a music, law, and French triple major.

Website:
www.sarahlawrence.edu
Location: Suburban
Total Enrollment: 1,553
Undergraduates: 1,214
Male/Female: 27/73
SAT Ranges: V 610–710
M 540–640
ACT Range: 25–30
Financial Aid: 57%
Expense: Pr $ $ $ $
Phi Beta Kappa: No
Applicants: 2,782
Accepted: 37%
Enrolled: 32%
Grad in 6 Years: 66%
Returning Freshmen: 94%
Academics: ✐ ✐ ✐ ✐
Social: ☎ ☎
Q of L: ★ ★ ★
Admissions: (914) 395-2510
Email Address: slcadmit@
sarahlawrence.edu

Strongest Programs
History
Literature
Psychology
Social Science
Writing
Visual and Performing Arts

At Sarah Lawrence, students take three courses each semester. Courses can last a semester or the full year, depending on the nature of the course. Students also work on independent projects with faculty members in individual, one-on-one conferences every two weeks for each of these classes. Perhaps because of the close personal contact with professors, the registration process is rigorous: students interview their prospective teachers to determine whether the course fits their academic plan, and to make sure the instructor is someone they respect and want to study with. Students get very involved with the individual projects that result from the seminar/conference system, which is modeled after Oxford University's and said to be intense. "At SLC, the climate is open to make it what you will," a junior says. Seminar enrollment is strictly limited, and even the largest lecture courses have only around sixty students. Getting into popular classes can be a problem, but the administration guarantees students at least two of their first three course choices each semester.

> "I absolutely love the don system."

The Sarah Lawrence writing program is one of the strongest in the country. Other highly rated fields include literature, visual arts, and psychology. The psychology department offers fieldwork at the college's Early Childhood Center. The premed program, more structured than other offerings, places nearly all of its eligible graduates into medical schools while science students have the opportunity to use the state-of-the-art Science Center, with 22,500 square feet of classrooms, labs, and computer workspaces. The film department has been upgraded with expanded offerings in filmmaking and film history, and environmental studies and computer science have expanded offerings as well. Students report that math and science are weak.

All first-year students take a First-Year Studies Seminar in one of more than thirty subjects. Each student meets with the professor individually each week to discuss his or her independent projects, academic plans, and transition to college.

Since individual attention is the cornerstone of the Sarah Lawrence educational philosophy, even grading is done personally. Teachers give students written evaluations twice a year, though conventional grades also go on record. The library, though small (224,000 volumes and more than one thousand periodicals), is a delight, with an area for eating and a pillow room for cozy studying and occasional dozing. For the travelers, there are academic years in Cuba, Oxford, Paris, Florence, and a London theater program for study at the British American Drama Academy.

Sarah Lawrence students are not your run-of-the-mill young American men and women; a campus T-shirt says "Sarah Lawrence, where even the squirrels wear black." While one student describes Sarah Lawrence as "a predominantly female-oriented school" (it used to be an all-women's school and women still outnumber men three to one), there appears to be very little tension between the sexes. And what about campus issues? Again, nothing is out of bounds here. "Political correctness does tend to be an issue here, but it is more socially enforced, and is not a manner of policy," a junior says.

> "Political correctness does tend to be an issue here, but it is more socially enforced, and is not a manner of policy."

Sixteen percent of SLC's students come from New York State—the bulk from nearby New York City—and most of the rest are from somewhere along either the East or West Coast. African-Americans make up 5 percent of the student body, Asian-Americans 4 percent, Hispanics 4 percent, and foreign students 6 percent. The school is working to increase diversity among students as well as faculty.

Sarah Lawrence students are not your run-of-the-mill young American men and women; a campus T-shirt says that "Sarah Lawrence, where even the squirrels wear black."

Eighty-seven percent of Sarah Lawrence students live on campus, where freshmen usually get doubles in the newer dorms and upperclassmen are guaranteed singles in the prettier, older dorms or college-owned houses. One popular dorm contains four townhouses, each with seven single rooms. In fact, accommodations are so good that there's been a bit of a housing crunch lately. "We are so spoiled by housing here, it's ridiculous," says one sophomore. And since Bronxville is a staid, super-rich suburb, off-campus students often commute from Westchester County's lower-rent districts or from New York City. The cafeteria cooking is good, and the health-food bar and student center's greasy spoon fill in the gaps. Most dorms also have their own kitchens.

Weekend life often revolves around New York City (half an hour away by train after a ten-minute walk to the station), where SLC's large theatrical contingent takes advantage of the art and culture of the Big Apple. For those who stick around over the weekend, there are free dances and movies, plays, poetry readings, guest lectures, and several tea and coffeehouses. There's also the end-of-the-year mega party, Bacchanalia,

> "I think it's fair warning to tell anyone considering applying here that you will never find a big-university-type party at Sarah Lawrence."

and the oldest college AIDS benefit in the country, the Deb Ball. Other traditions include Coming Out Week and May Fair, which brings community children to campus for games and food. "I think it's fair warning to tell anyone considering applying here that you will never find a big university type party at Sarah Lawrence," a junior says. Drinkers, largely ignored in the past, are now subject to tough rules regarding on-campus consumption. And although the relationship between the school and surrounding community is improving, Bronxville is still described as "too expensive," and one student notes SLC students are merely tolerated.

Sports are not a high priority among Sarah Lawrence's bookish undergrads. "There's virtually no athletics here," one student ventures. While the school does field several intercollegiate clubs (the Sarah Lawrence riders do well in equestrian competitions, and the tennis teams are strong), nary a "Go get 'em" is heard from these students.

The Sarah Lawrence community is an intimate one, and students say this is both a challenge and a blessing. The social life can be extremely stifling, a freshman says, but Sarah Lawrence students will gladly exchange a little excitement for extra time with their professors. For students willing to give up the idea of partying their way through college and get buried in their books, Sarah Lawrence offers a nearly extinct kind of liberal arts education. "There is no school like this one," boasts a junior. "From an administrative level to a faculty level to the student body—everyone is similar in their view of education and communication."

Overlaps
NYU, Oberlin, Bard, Smith, Vassar

If You Apply To ➢ **Sarah Lawrence:** Early decision: Nov. 15 and Jan 1. Regular admissions: Jan. 15. Financial aid: Feb. 1. Meets full demonstrated need of all admitted students who file on time. Campus interviews: recommended, evaluative. Alumni interviews: optional, evaluative. SATs or ACTs: required. SAT IIs: optional. (Three SAT IIs may be substituted for SAT) Accepts the Common Application and electronic applications. Essay question: a significant social, economic, or political issue; recent scientific advance; or a passage from art or literature and why it is important to you.

Skidmore College

815 North Broadway, Saratoga Springs, NY 12866

Like Vassar, Connecticut College, and Wheaton (MA), Skidmore is a successful convert to coeducation. Strong in the performing arts with an unexpected emphasis on business, Skidmore is top-notch when it comes to internships, study abroad, and student research. Instead of green lawns, Skidmore has the woods.

Website: www.skidmore.edu

Location: City outskirts

Total Enrollment: 2,544

Undergraduates: 2,488

Male/Female: 41/59

SAT Ranges: V 570–660
  M 580–660

ACT Range: 24–28

Financial Aid: 43%

Expense: Pr $ $ $ $

Phi Beta Kappa: Yes

Applicants: 5,633

Accepted: 42%

Enrolled: 25%

Grad in 6 Years: 77%

Returning Freshmen: 93%

Academics: ✍ ✍ ✍ ✍

Social: ☎ ☎ ☎

Q of L: ★ ★ ★

Admissions: (800) 867-6007
  or (518) 580-5570

Email Address:
  admissions@skidmore.edu

Strongest Programs
  Drama
  Studio Art
  English
  Biology
  Government
  Psychology
  Business
  Music

Students start with Foundation classes in expository writing and quantitative reasoning, followed by Interdisciplinary courses entitled Liberal Studies 1 and Liberal Studies 2.

Founded in 1903 as the Young Women's Industrial Club of Saratoga, Skidmore College still excels in the fine and performing arts that were then deemed proper for ladies—but little else remains the same. In 1961, as enrollment surpassed 1,300 and many of the college's turn-of-the-century Victorian buildings grew obsolete, a board member's gift enabled Skidmore to trade its Victorian campus in the heart of Saratoga Springs for 650 acres on the northwest edge of town. Since then, the campus has grown to forty-nine buildings on 850 acres, and the student body has doubled in size (and welcomed men). What hasn't changed? "The people, the education, and the massive amount of beautiful girls!" says a senior government major.

While contemporary in style, the buildings on Skidmore's Jonsson campus—as the tract is known, in honor of the donor who made it possible—are human in scale. They reflect the Victorian heritage of Skidmore's original Scribner campus in their aesthetic details. The campus was carefully planned to preserve natural beauty, with a feeling of freedom and wide horizon. From the covered walkways that unite residential, academic, and social centers on campus, the prevailing views are of the surrounding mountains, woods, and fields, and into the central campus "green." Teachers and students often meet informally, and academic resources are easily accessible.

Skidmore's mandatory core groups require courses under broad themes. Students start with Foundation classes in expository writing and quantitative reasoning, followed by Interdisciplinary courses titled Liberal Studies 1 and Liberal Studies 2. LS1, "The Human Experience," is team-taught by professors from many departments, and combines lectures, performances, readings, and discussions to examine the issues and dilemmas of human life. Students have many options for LS2, which must be completed by the end of

> **"Professors expect a lot. The course load is more than I expected."**

sophomore year, and which connects back to LS1. Also required are four Breadth courses—one each in arts, humanities, natural sciences, and social sciences—and two Culture-Centered Inquiry courses. One must be a foreign language, and the other may focus on either non-Western culture or cultural diversity.

Skidmore's programs in business and art are among its best, and those are the most and third-most popular majors, respectively. English, psychology, and biology are also well enrolled, perhaps because of their applicability to graduate study in medicine. Biology majors also may conduct fieldwork in the marsh at the northern end of campus. Through the Hudson-Mohawk Association of Colleges and Universities, students may take courses at Rensselaer Polytechnic Institute, Union College, and SUNY–Albany. There's also a cooperative program in engineering with Dartmouth College, a Washington semester with American University, a semester at the Marine Biological Laboratory in Woods Hole, Massachusetts, an ecosystems seminar at Arizona's Biosphere 2, a master of arts in teaching with Union, and M.B.A. programs with Clarkson University and Rensselaer.

Skidmore augments liberal arts offerings with preprofessional training. Studio art and art history majors frequently enroll in business classes, where they work in groups with business majors, and make presentations for actual executives. Another much-praised option is junior year abroad, especially when spent in a Skidmore-run program in France, England, Spain, or India. Students who just can't get enough time on campus may compete for summer grants—to fund collaborative research with professors, or attend one of the school's incredible summer programs. In addition, the University Without Walls offers older students a flexible and inexpensive route to a bachelor's degree through remote coursework, tutorials, and internships.

The academic climate at Skidmore is fairly laid back, though courses in all disciplines can be rigorous—"from the sciences to the physical education courses," says a senior. "Professors expect a lot," a sophomore agrees. "The courseload is more than I expected." Two-thirds of the courses have less than twenty students, so "participation and attendance are almost mandatory," says a business major. That said, it may be hard to get into the courses you want, says a geology major. "Every year, some of the most appealing courses close early, and the school has courses that aren't given every year or every semester," a social work major agrees.

Given Skidmore's hefty price tag—"tuition is more than Harvard," a senior gripes—it's not surprising that the students are typically well-off and from the Eastern seaboard, especially New York, New Jersey, and New England. "There is a broad range of students, from jocks to artsy ones, but most come from wealthier backgrounds and most are Caucasian," says a women's studies major. "There needs to be more school spirit, unity, and close-knit community," a classics major sniffs. Hispanics constitute 5 percent of the

> "There is a broad range of students, from jocks to artsy ones, but most come from wealthier backgrounds and most are Caucasian."

student body, Asian-Americans 4 percent, and African-Americans 2 percent. More than two decades of effort to recruit men has also paid off, and the gender ratio is slowly approaching 50/50.

Seventy-seven percent of Skidmore students live in the dorms, where they are guaranteed rooms for four years, though "it's always a struggle to get the room you want," says a senior. Most buildings have carpet, air-conditioning, and cozy window seats, though "some are not maintained well at all," says a sophomore. "The rugs are old and dirty, and the bathrooms are always having problems." A senior agrees: "The dorms need to be updated, but they are comfortable and safe." Dorms are integrated by class and are coed by floor or suite, with kitchenettes and lounges on every floor. The double rooms in South Quad tend to be livelier than those in North Quad. Sophomores aren't permitted to live off campus, but they "always dread room selection" because space limitations force them away from the main part of campus. Juniors and seniors typically get single rooms in the centrally located dorms, or move to apartments—on campus in Scribner Village, or off campus in Saratoga.

With no fraternities or sororities, Skidmore students flock to dorm parties, especially if there's live music. They're also eager participants in road trips to Albany, New York City, Boston, and Montreal. A campus event card is distributed to students over twenty-one who plan to drink on school grounds, though a business major notes that there are more than thirty bars within two blocks of campus. "Students here have big issues with alcohol and drug use—anyone could get alcohol at any time," a social work major agrees. "I believe students do this because there isn't much else to do." Skidmore's more traditional activities, which have lingered even after a quarter-century of coeducation, include Junior Ring Week, when juniors receive their class rings and a dance is held in honor of their initiation. Every year, there are also two or three formal dances at the Hall of Springs, which a senior calls "basically the fanciest reception hall ever." Students also look forward to

> "The community and the comfort level here are so high. Sometimes, it's like being in a bubble."

the Diva Night party, where a group devoted to sexuality awareness "creates a safe environment for all people, and promotes the 'diva' in everyone to come out," a geology major says.

The nearby Adirondacks make Skidmore a haven for backpackers and skiers, while the old resort town of Saratoga, with its healing springs and antique shops, offers plenty of culture, including the Saratoga Performing Arts Center and the country's oldest thoroughbred racetrack. Saratoga is also the summer home of the New York City Ballet, the New York City Opera, and the Philadelphia Orchestra. Students reach out to the community through Benefaction, a volunteer group connected to

Students look forward to the Diva Night party, where a group devoted to sexuality awareness "creates a safe environment for all people, and promotes the 'diva' in everyone to come out," says a geology major.

several local agencies and schools. Still, a senior quips, "students basically volunteer to keep all the local bars in business."

Skidmore's Thoroughbreds compete in Division III; men's and women's tennis and the equestrian team have claimed several conference championships in recent years. "There are no athletic rivalries, because sports are not real big here," says a government major. Students who do compete play mostly in the intramural sports program, which has more than twenty teams, a student commissioner, and 250 acres of new playing fields. Varsity athletes and intramural jocks alike enjoy the four hundred–meter, all-weather track and the athletic center, which includes a gym, fitness center, and locker rooms.

Skidmore continues to win the hearts of liberal, motivated students with its flexibility, openness, and receptivity to change and growth. Its small size means they have the opportunity to really get to know each other, says a business student. "The community and the comfort level here are so high," a women's studies major adds. "Sometimes, it's like being in a bubble."

> ### Overlaps
> Vassar, Connecticut College, Wesleyan, Tufts, Hamilton

> **If You Apply To** ➤
>
> **Skidmore:** Early decision: Dec. 1, Jan. 15. Regular admissions and financial aid: Jan. 15. Meets demonstrated need of 85%. Campus interviews: recommended, evaluative. Alumni interviews: optional, evaluative. SATs or ACTs: required. SAT IIs: recommended. Accepts the Common Application. Essay question: significant experience; important issue of personal, local, or national concern; important person; or significant fictional or historical character.

Smith College

College Lane, Northampton, MA 01063

The most left-wing of the nation's leading women's colleges. Liberal Northhampton provides big-city social life, and the Five College Consortium adds depth and breadth all around. With a total enrollment of more than three thousand, Smith is the biggest of the leading women's colleges.

Website: www.smith.edu
Location: Small city
Total Enrollment: 3,113
Undergraduates: 2,630
Male/Female: 0/100
SAT Ranges: V 590–700
 M 570–670
ACT Range: 25–30
Financial Aid: 59%
Expense: Pr $ $ $
Phi Beta Kappa: Yes
Applicants: 2,869
Accepted: 54%
Enrolled: 42%
Grad in 6 Years: 81%
Returning Freshmen: 91%
Academics: ✍ ✍ ✍ ✍ ½
Social: ☎ ☎ ☎

Heaven only knows what Sophia Smith would think of the women's college she founded in 1871 with the hope it would be "pervaded by the Spirit of Evangelical Christian Religion." There are still evangelicals at Smith, but today they join the rest of their schoolmates in crusading against societal injustices such as racism, classism, sexism, and heterosexism. Though the all-female school remains strongly committed to its liberal arts mission, it is also focused on placing women at the forefront of science and technology. Students here have an opportunity to become leaders in the male-dominated field of engineering, or study interdisciplinary fields, such as the newly added landscape studies.

Founded in 1871, Smith is located in the small city of Northampton, an artsy oasis in the foothills of the Berkshire Mountains. The 125-acre campus resembles a medieval fortress from the front gate, but inside it sparkles with many gardens, Paradise Pond, and a plant house. Buildings cover a range of styles from late eighteenth-century to modern, and the college has successfully retained its historic atmosphere while keeping facilities up to date. A new temporary engineering building, with exercise facilities for yoga, fencing, and rock-climbing, and a parking garage recently opened. A major renovation and expansion to the Fine Arts Center is underway, as is construction of a new campus center. Plans for a new science center, including permanent engineering facilities, are also in the works.

a six-lane swimming pool, and a riding ring. Interhouse competitions include everything from kickball to inner-tube water polo. Service Organizations of Smith (SOS) arranges for students to volunteer in about six hundred placements in Northampton, the surrounding communities, and on campus.

The strict evangelism is gone, and today's Smith women are far from Sophia Smith wannabes. But her namesake and spirit lives on at this eclectic, open-minded institution where women don lab coats, power suits, combat boots, and even white dresses at graduation. "You can be yourself, develop yourself, change yourself, and have a support group and acceptance from the community," says one happy junior. This unique institution readies women to be and do just about anything.

If You Apply To ➢

Smith: Early decision: Nov. 15 and Jan. 2. Regular admissions, financial aid and housing: Jan. 15. Guarantees to meet demonstrated need. Campus interviews: recommended, evaluative. Alumnae interviews: optional, evaluative. SATs or ACTs: required. SAT IIs: recommended (writing and two others). Accepts the Common Application and electronic applications. Essay question: significant academic or intellectual experience; significant person; a situation in which your beliefs were challenged; place you would like to have a summer internship.

University of the South (Sewanee)

735 University Avenue, Sewanee, TN 37383-1000

Sewanee is like a little bit of Britain's Oxford plunked down in the highlands of Tennessee. More conservative than Rhodes and Davidson, Sewanee is a guardian of the tried and true. Affiliated with the Episcopal Church, Sewanee still draws heavily from old-line Southern families.

Tradition is the word at University of the South, known simply as Sewanee after the city in which it is located. Episcopal bishop Leonidas Polk founded the university in 1857 and envisioned it as a distinguished center of learning in the South. Through the years, a host of customs have emerged: students wear gowns to class, dress up for football games, and adhere to an honor code. With proceeds from Tennessee Williams's estate, the university holds a prestigious annual conference to promote the art of writing and seats a theater complex bearing his name.

Sewanee is located atop Tennessee's Cumberland Plateau between Chattanooga and Nashville. The university's stately English collegiate Gothic buildings of native-mountain, beige-and-pink sandstone are home to both a college of arts and sciences and a seminary. Be prepared to do a good amount of walking around the campus, whose buildings are often widely spaced on the ten thousand acres fondly known as "the Domain." Noteworthy structures include the St. Luke's and All Saints Chapel, and Convocation Hall, built in 1886. Owned by twenty-eight dioceses of the Episcopal Church, the university calls its semesters Advent and Easter. The student body is overwhelmingly Christian, and students report that religion is often a big part of their lives. A new dining hall with a 450-seat formal eating room, a 250-seat informal room, and a 150-seat outdoor dining area was completed in 2001, and the university has broken ground for a new residence hall.

Sewanee's undergraduate curriculum is broad in the classical sense. All students must complete thirty-two full courses, including twenty-one courses outside the major field, and must attain an overall grade point average of at least 2.0 on all academic work. Students also must spend at least four semesters in residence, including

Website: www.sewanee.edu
Location: Village
Total Enrollment: 1,442
Undergraduates: 1,329
Male/Female: 48/52
SAT Ranges: V 570–670
  M 560–650
ACT Range: 24–28
Financial Aid: 39%
Expense: Pr $ $
Phi Beta Kappa: Yes
Applicants: 1,696
Accepted: 70%
Enrolled: 30%
Grad in 6 Years: 76%
Returning Freshmen: 91%
Academics: ✍ ✍ ✍ ✍
Social: ☎ ☎ ☎
Q of L: ★ ★ ★ ★
Admissions: (800) 522-2234
Email Address:
  admiss@sewanee.edu

(Continued)
Strongest Programs
  English
  History
  Mathematics
  Chemistry
  Geology

their final year. Core curriculum requirements include English and one other course in literature or English and a writing-intensive course, foreign language at the third-year level, math, a lab science, history, religion or philosophy, fine arts, and physical education. In keeping with the European tradition, Sewanee seniors take comprehensive exams in their majors as part of their graduation requirements. While students take the test, their friends decorate their cars and prepare for parties when they are finished.

The English department is unquestionably the top program on campus. The university publishes *Sewanee Review*, the nation's oldest continuously published literary quarterly, and sponsors the Sewanee Writers' Conference through the gift of (you guessed it) Tennessee Williams's estate. Big-name literary writers such as Russell Banks and Diane Johnson have conducted seminars in recent years for the hundreds of aspiring writers who add a touch of arty elan to

> "Most of the teachers are very good and/or very hard."

the otherwise traditional look of the campus. History and mathematics are also strong. Several of the science programs are top-notch, including chemistry and geology. Eighty-nine percent of pre-med, dentistry, and veterinary students go on to professional schools. Weaker departments include Italian and Japanese, primarily due to their small size. Of the study-abroad opportunities, the summer British studies program at Oxford is especially popular. A cooperative master's degree program in environmental science with Duke and Yale is offered. Unusual for a liberal arts schools is an offering for students in forestry and geology, which takes advantage of the mountains and forests on which the campus is perched.

Sewanee maintains many old customs and standards that add a quaint veneer—some might say stuffiness—to campus life. A voluntary dress code calls for women to wear dresses or skirts and men to wear jackets and ties to class. Professors as well as the numerous honors students (members of the Order of Gownsmen) wear black academic gowns to class. An honor code is strictly observed, and lying, cheating, or stealing usually results in expulsion. Students take the code so seriously that "professors are not present when we take exams," says a student.

Sewanee faculty members receive high praise from students. "Most of the teachers are very good and/or very hard," says a psychology major. Indeed, upper-level courses may contain as few as six people. Most Sewanee students understand what is expected of them academically. "In true Southern style, no one would admit to being competitive, but we are," says a junior anthropology major.

Tradition carries over into other aspects of life at Sewanee. Many students hail from Southern families, while "some proud Yankees" represent New York, New Jersey, Pennsylvania, and New England. The student population is 91 percent white,

> "It is beautiful and quaint and I would not change it, but the closest Wal-Mart is thirty minutes away."

with African-Americans the largest minority group at 4 percent. "Alternative lifestyles or minority students really stand out on campus compared to the general population," a junior warns. Sewanee offers several minority scholarships, including the Tutu Scholars program for students from South Africa. Sewanee awards 114 merit scholarships, but there are no athletic scholarships. A financing plan enables families to pay tuition in ten monthly installments. Students who maintain a 3.0 cumulative GPA may have the loan portion of their award replaced by a grant.

The town of Sewanee has a population of only about 3,500, not including students. "The university is the town, period," a junior says. "It is beautiful and quaint and I would not change it, but the closest Wal-Mart is thirty minutes away." Students are very involved in the community and often run into their professors in town. A whopping 95 percent of students live on campus. Most of the dorms are

The English department is unquestionably the top program on campus. The university publishes Sewanee Review, the nation's oldest continuously published literary quarterly, and sponsors the Sewanee Writers' Conference through the gift of (you guessed it) Tennessee Williams's estate.

single-sex, but renovated halls are now coed, and there are three coed language houses. "Dorms are either better than hotels or worse than Motel 6," a student quips. The few seniors who move off campus must live in university-approved housing. Many students complain about the quality of the food.

Although Sewanee is not known for student activism, the school's one concession to populist thinking is its policy that virtually no one gets cut from varsity sports squads. The most popular sport on campus is probably football—not so much because of the sport, but because games are social events where everyone shows up in coats and ties and dresses. There is also some serious competition going on; conference championships have been won by the men's soccer team, men's and women's tennis sent players to the national competitions, and the softball team won its division in 2002. The university recently made equestrian competition a varsity sport. Their facilities include a dressage area, jumps, more than thirty acres of pasture, individual paddocks, and miles of trails. The cheer here is: "Sewanee, Sewanee, leave 'em in a lurch. Down with the heathens and up with the Church. Yea, Sewanee's right."

> "The social life is incredible, the parties are outrageous. Parties on campus must end at 1 A.M., so everybody usually lingers off campus at another party until the wee hours."

The social life occurs, of course, on campus. Greeks provide an important social outlet, and 62 percent of the men and 65 percent of the women join up. Drinking is a fact of life here. "The social life is incredible, the parties are outrageous," says a sophomore. "Parties on campus must end at 1 A.M., so everybody usually lingers off campus at another party until the wee hours." Annual Fall and Spring Party Weekends, Homecoming weekend, the Shakespeare Festival, and a blues fest are popular campus happenings. For students who want to get out of town, the beautiful rural setting, complete with lakes, waterfalls, and even caves and caverns, makes outdoor activities popular. Students who occasionally feel a need for the "real world" can go to nearby Chattanooga, Memphis, or Nashville. A favorite trip is to the Jack Daniel's Distillery in Lynchburg.

For the most part, though, students are in no rush to get away. They seem content with their school's way of life, its rich past, beautiful location, and caring people. As one student puts it, "You're not a number here, you're a person. Teachers talk to you if you bump into them. They remember your name."

Overlaps

Vanderbilt, Rhodes, Furman, Washington and Lee, Davidson

If You Apply To ➤

Sewanee: Early decision: Nov. 15. Regular admissions: Feb. 1. Campus interviews: optional, informational. No alumni interviews. SATs or ACTs: required. SAT IIs: optional. Accepts the Common Application and electronic applications. Essay question: An issue of great concern and importance; or personal statement.

University of South Carolina

Columbia, SC 29208

In the state that started the Civil War, USC is still trying to fight off the image of being one step behind UNC–Chapel Hill. The university has paid big money to attract star professors and boasts one of the top international business programs in the nation. Criminal justice is also a specialty.

Website: www.sc.edu
Location: Center city
Total Enrollment: 23,000
Undergraduates: 15,506
Male/Female: 46/54
SAT Ranges: V 490–600
  M 500–610
ACT Range: 21–26
Financial Aid: 45%
Expense: Pub $
Phi Beta Kappa: Yes
Applicants: 11,176
Accepted: 70%
Enrolled: 42%
Grad in 6 Years: 58%
Returning Freshmen: 81%
Academics: ✍ ✍ ✍
Social: ☎ ☎ ☎
Q of L: ★ ★ ★
Admissions: (803) 777-7700
Email Address: admissions-
  ugrad@sc.edu

Strongest Programs
  Biology
  English
  International Business
  Psychology
  Criminal Justice
  Nursing
  Business

Whether it's football or international business, the students at the University of South Carolina are game—they're the Gamecocks and they've got plenty of fighting spirit. Sure, South Carolina's a somewhat crowded state university, but these Gamecocks rarely feel cooped up. The bevy of courses offered and plenty of interesting academic programs to explore make for a campus that seems to have a lot more space than it actually does. Which is not to say that South Carolina's an impersonal school—this is the South, after all. Gamecocks may lay claim to their school, but old-fashioned Southern charm still rules the roost.

Carolina's large modern campus is located right in the heart of Columbia, a city of more than 450,000 that is the capital of the state. Government buildings and downtown businesses are all within walking distance of the campus and serve as fertile hunting grounds for internship opportunities. Mild winters are typical. Snow—even a few flurries—is a traffic-stopping event. The old section of the campus, which dates back to the school's founding in 1801, includes the glorious oak-lined Horseshoe, composed of numerous nineteenth-century buildings, ten of which are now listed in the National Register of Historic Places.

The University of South Carolina offers seventy-nine professional, liberal, and technical bachelor's degrees to its undergrads. Biology is the most popular major, but the school is also known for its psychology, nursing, English, and criminal justice programs.

Students in the huge marine science program enjoy a splendid seventeen thousand–acre facility located about three hours from the main campus. The university is also the beneficiary of an excellent film library. Much of the economy of South Carolina is tied to foreign trade, and, fittingly, the university has developed a top-notch international business program. Art students have access to the latest cameras, editing stations, and computers, as well as kilns and other equipment necessary for their studies.

Among the liberal arts, English is one of the best departments in the region, and the natural sciences are strong. The four-level, one thousand–square-foot music building features studios, classrooms, a music and performance library, chamber and music rooms, recording studios, and a 250-seat lecture hall. A unique minor called medical humanities is designed for future medical students; it provides an understanding of the ethical, sociocultural, legal, economic, and political factors that affect medical practice.

Many classes are predictably large, and freshmen should not be surprised to find themselves taught by graduate students in "microphone classes" where they are known only by their Social Security numbers. In the past, registration has been a hassle, but students now have the option of using the Internet to register, making the task less troublesome. Required courses vary by college, but degree-seeking students must take a comprehensive two-year core curriculum, which generally forces freshmen to take

The USC–Clemson rivalry is one of the oldest and most colorful in college sports. The festivities begin weeks in advance and include a blood drive where the two schools compete for the most blood, the annual Tigerburn parade and bonfire, and lengthy all-night tailgating parties.

> **"I have had excellent advisors and they are very interested in my academic career."**

English, numerical and analytical reasoning (math or philosophy), humanities and social sciences (history and fine arts), natural sciences (lab science), and a foreign language. Also required for freshmen is University 101, a three-hour seminar designed to help freshmen adjust to the university. The University has a top-notch library, with numerous special collections, including the world's most comprehensive collection of F. Scott Fitzgerald research materials, and a recent acquisition of Ernest Hemingway materials. While responsibility for faculty contact rests squarely on the students, the student-teacher relationship seems good here. "I have had excellent advisors and they are very interested in my academic career," says a student.

The student body is 81 percent South Carolinian, and most come from public school. A full quarter are from the top tenth of their high-school class. Seventeen

Review, one of the four oldest continuously published literary quarterlies in the nation. SMU's history program has been enhanced by a $10 million endowment that began funding a Ph.D. program and the interdisciplinary Center for Southwest Studies; the center's programs are available to undergraduates as well.

The Cox School offers SMU's most popular major, business administration. The Business Associates Program pairs students with corporate mentors in Dallas for term-time internships and postgraduation jobs. Similarly, engineers have access to an extensive co-op program, thanks to Dallas's proximity to more than eight hundred high-tech companies. The John Goodwin Tower Center for Political Studies, named for the former U.S. senator, focuses on international relations and comparative politics.

> **"I have been in classes with engaging, brilliant faculty."**

Outstanding students can qualify for an accelerated three-year program at SMU, and the honors program has been revamped to emphasize internationalism and intellectual community. Additionally, thirteen study-abroad programs are available in places ranging from Austria to Australia; about four hundred students participate each year. SMU also operates a second campus near Taos, New Mexico, at historic Fort Burgwin, a mid-nineteenth century army outpost.

SMU prides itself on small classes; most courses have fifty or fewer students. Students find professors at the lectern, as teaching assistants conduct labs only. "I would give the quality of teaching I have received a one hundred," says a junior. "I have been in classes with engaging, brilliant faculty," one student says. The career center benefits from SMU's strong alumni network, but business and engineering students generally find more help here than liberal and fine arts majors do, students say.

The many conservative students here have welcomed speakers such as President George Bush and other Republicans as warmly as some other campuses might applaud speakers from more liberal camps. As one student describes, "the stereotypical SMU student is white, upper-class/upper-middle-class who could not get into Emory, Vanderbilt, Rice, etc." Another student counsels, "Don't be surprised to see Chanel book bags, khakis instead of jeans, BMWs, and Rolexes." But, insists a music, art, and history major, "The snobby stereotype of the school is not true."

More than 90 percent of students have received some sort of financial aid in recent years, and SMU is proud of its student-loan program, designed for middle-income families that do not meet federal guidelines for need-based loans. "Financial aid is given abundantly to high-quality students who normally cannot afford SMU." SMU also provides merit scholarships, ranging from $1,000 to $14,000, as well as 291 athletic scholarships.

Texans make up 57 percent of the SMU student body, which includes students from all fifty states and more than ninety foreign countries. Hispanics account for 8 percent, African-Americans 6 percent, and Asian-Americans about another 6 percent of the student body. While campus diversity has increased over the

> **"The stereotypical SMU student is white, upper-class/upper-middle-class who could not get into Emory, Vanderbilt, Rice, etc."**

past few years, ethnic groups tend to band together. Some attribute this division to the Greek system. But the administration is working to increase understanding among races, with activities such as Intercultural Student Orientation. And SMU students have begun to emerge from the "bubble" of their posh Park Cities location: administrators say community involvement is at an all-time high, with about one thousand students volunteering regularly for service projects.

About 48 percent of the students live on campus, and freshmen are required to do so; most upperclassmen find off-campus apartments or dwell in Greek houses (38 percent of the women and 37 percent of the men go Greek). All thirteen residence

Outstanding students can qualify for an accelerated three-year program at SMU, and the honors program has been revamped to emphasize internationalism and intellectual community.

Although it was founded by what is now the United Methodist Church, SMU is nondenominational and welcomes students of all faiths. The associate chaplain is a female rabbi.

halls are coed by floor, and a variety of options, such as an honors floor and an "expressive living" floor, are available. "The dorms are absolutely wonderful," says one student, who calls them "Hiltons" of the dorm world. Adds a classmate: "All the first-years live in the South Quad together. One thousand students living, eating, sleeping, and playing together cannot help but bond."

The extracurricular life at SMU is quite active, boasting 152 student organizations. "Most of the campus's social life revolves around the Greek life," says a self-identified sorority girl. "We hold most of the formals and theme parties. However, plenty of partying is done by non-Greeks." And Dallas, sophisticated and swinging, is always there. Since SMU is a dry campus, the city's bars and clubs hold even greater allure for those old enough to get in, or clever enough to sneak in with a fake ID. "It

> **"All the first-years live in the South Quad together. One thousand students living, eating, sleeping, and playing together cannot help but bond."**

is a fun college town although it is difficult to navigate without a car," remarks a student. The downside of having a car: the parking situation is ridiculous, and some students can practically wallpaper their roomy dorm walls with parking tickets. Road trips include South Padre Island (for sunning on the Gulf Coast), New Orleans (for Mardi Gras), Shreveport (for gambling), and Austin (for playing along Sixth Street).

SMU also offers outstanding cultural options. Each year, for example, the Meadows School sponsors more then four hundred theatrical performances, concerts, and exhibits. The on-campus Tate Forums provide informal question-and-answer sessions with national and international figures. Highlights of the campus calendar include Peruna's Birthday, a day honoring the mustang mascot, and the Celebration of Lights, when students gather to admire Christmas lights at Dallas Hall.

Students don't walk around hiding their heads just because sports have taken a backseat at SMU ever since a late-1980s football scandal and resulting NCAA sanctions. The team still gets fired up to play archrivals Texas and Texas Christian. And if they are losing, says one junior, students chant, "That's all right. That's okay. You're going to work for us some day." SMU competes in the Western Athletic Conference, and women's and men's swimming and diving, soccer (the soccer field was upgraded as a World Cup practice site), and track are among programs garnering national recognition.

SMU students will tell you that they are friendly as well as success-oriented. And many don't apologize for the nickname "Southern Millionaire's University," and will unabashedly describe themselves as "classy" and "cultural." If y'all are looking for a fine faculty that cares about undergraduates, and a school that serves up education with a healthy dose of Southern hospitality and athletic boosterism, then Southern Methodist is worth a look.

Overlaps

Texas, Texas Christian, Vanderbilt, Texas A&M, Tulane

If You Apply To ➤

SMU: Rolling admissions: Jan. 15 (priority). Early action: Nov. 1. Financial aid: Feb. 1. Housing: May 1. Does not guarantee to meet demonstrated need. Campus and alumni interviews: optional, informational. SATs or ACTs: required. SAT IIs: required for some. Accepts the Common Application. Essay question: create a family, community, or school tradition; what sets you apart; or a topic of your choosing.

Southwestern University

1001 E. University Avenue, Georgetown, TX 78626

Camouflaged beneath a nondescript name, Southwestern is a private-college alternative to Austin and Trinity (TX). Southwestern is about half the size of the latter and prides itself on individual attention and down-to-earth friendliness. Strong programs include communications and international studies.

Smack in the heart of the Lone Star State sits Southwestern University, a small liberal arts school with strong academics and top-notch professors. The focus here is not only on classroom studies, but students' total development as contributors in the post-grad world.

Southwestern is situated on seven hundred acres at the edge of the rolling Texas Hill Country. The oldest college in Texas, Southwestern maintains its affiliation with the United Methodist Church. The campus boasts turn-of-the-century Texas limestone buildings in a Romanesque architectural style. There are plenty of wide-open spaces, including a nine-hole golf course and outdoor tennis courts. Construction of new apartment-style residence halls was recently completed, as was a renovation of the fine-arts performance theater.

Rigorous classes mean hard work is the norm at Southwestern. But competition isn't the bottom line. "The courses really push the students to learn and to question," says a communications major. "You aren't in competition with others, just yourself." Biology, psychology, and business are considered the school's strongest programs and are quite popular with students. Weaker departments include computer science and dance. Non-Western language studies are getting a boost through the Language Learning Center. The Brown Symposium, held each spring, is an annual series of discussions and seminars organized around a single topic such as genetic engineering, computers in everyday life, or the achievements of a single scholar or artist.

> "The faculty are top-notch and really care about their material. You can really feel their passion."

Graduation requirements include eight hours of Foundation courses, thirty hours of Perspectives on Knowledge courses, and English Composition. There's also a stipulation that students take a foreign language through sophomore year and two hours of a fitness or recreational activity. The study-abroad program is very strong, and about half the students here take advantage of opportunities in London, Jamaica, Mexico, Hungary, Honduras, and Germany. Several student-exchange programs are offered as well. Internships are available, including those to study politics, foreign policy, journalism, and architecture in Washington, D.C. The New York Arts program offers students the chance to work with professional artists, designers, actors, and filmmakers in the Big Apple. Undergraduate research is encouraged in all majors. The biology department offers a summer research program to students interested in working with a faculty member, which also provides a $3,000 student stipend. In addition, Southwestern has been a member of the Associated Colleges of the South* consortium for more than a decade. A dual-degree program in engineering also is possible.

Nearly all classes have fewer than twenty-five students, so one-on-one attention and connections between professors and students abound. "The faculty are top-notch and really care about their material," a junior reports. "You can really feel their passion." Professors even occasionally invite students to their homes. "I love the personal attention I can get from faculty members," says a senior. "It lets me know that they care about me as a student and as a person." Perhaps because of

Website:
www.southwestern.edu
Location: Suburban
Total Enrollment: 1,320
Undergraduates: 1,320
Male/Female: 44/56
SAT Ranges: V 570–660
   M 570–670
ACT Range: 24–29
Financial Aid: 54%
Expense: Pr $
Phi Beta Kappa: Yes
Applicants: 1,561
Accepted: 59%
Enrolled: 35%
Grad in 6 Years: 70%
Returning Freshmen: 88%
Academics: 🐛🐛🐛
Social: ☎ ☎ ☎
Q of L: ★★★
Admissions: (512) 863-1200
Email Address: admission@
southwestern.edu

Strongest Programs
Art
Biology/Premed
Psychology
Education
Business
Communications
Political Science

their respect for their profs, Southwesterners take their academics seriously, and staying in to study is a legitimate excuse for not going out.

The student body is 81 percent Caucasian, 12 percent Hispanic, 2 percent Asian-American, and 3 percent African-American. Ninety-two percent of the students are Texans, with large numbers from the metropolitan areas of Houston, Dallas, and San Antonio. Most students are from middle-class families, which leads to a certain kind of homogeneity on campus. "The need for diversity is high," one student reports, adding that "opinions are not withheld and students know where they stand on an issue." SU's tuition is markedly less than at institutions of similar quality in other parts of the nation, and the university has several special tuition payment plans, including a new loan program for all families. The school also offers merit scholarships to each class, ranging from $1,000 to a full ride. There are no athletic scholarships.

> "The need for diversity is high."

> Perhaps because of their respect for their profs, Southwesterners take their academics seriously, and staying in to study is a legitimate excuse for not going out.

Over the past few years, Southwestern has changed a number of programs to keep up with the times. It developed a sexual-harassment policy involving students, faculty, and staff as advisors, and created a Gender Awareness Resource Center on campus to offer programs on gender communication and acquaintance rape. An alcohol coalition deals with alcohol issues on campus. All new students go through an afternoon diversity workshop called Facing Differences, which focuses on relating in spite of racial, ethnic, cultural, and other differences. The Bridge Builders helps students to examine their own views on issues such as racism and sexism with their Tunnel of Oppression program. Political correctness does not rule the day at Southwestern because "students question everything here," a junior says. As for student complaints, they wish the administration would listen to them a bit more. "P.C. is not so much the issue as respect," says a political science major.

Since Georgetown is on the small side (pop. 26,000), there is not an overabundance of off-campus housing. Eighty-three percent of the students live in university housing, which students say is "excellent" and "gorgeous." Most rooms of the coed and single-sex European-style residence halls are suite-like, and on-campus apartments also are available. Housekeepers clean up several times per week. One student says the new McCombs apartments are "spacious and very comfortable." Different meal plans are available, and students can also eat in the student union snack bar.

> "The Blue Hole is a beautiful swimming hole with a small waterfall where we spend our afternoons when it gets warm."

> All new students go through an afternoon diversity workshop called Facing Differences, which focuses on relating in spite of racial, ethnic, cultural, and other differences.

Most social life on campus is centered around the Greek system, to which 30 percent of the men and 36 percent of the women belong. The frats host house parties open to everyone most weekends, though one student says there is a rift between the "more conservative, pro-Greek students and the liberal, non-Greek students." For the latter, the fine arts department sponsors concerts and plays, and there are campus-wide picnics with carnival-style entertainment. During Homecoming, students look forward to Sing!, an event where students produce short musical skits about Southwestern.

Georgetown, once a stop on the famed Chisholm Trail, also has some of its own treasures. "The Blue Hole is a beautiful swimming hole with a small waterfall where we spend our afternoons when it gets warm," says a history major. For the real action, many students travel thirty minutes south to Austin's great restaurants, concerts, and live music shows on Sixth Street. Another popular campus activity is "rolling," where students pack as many people in a car as they can and drive very slowly on the back roads with blaring music. MallBalls begin and end the year with food, frivolity, music, and games on the Academic Mall. The official school policy prohibits underage drinking, but it's "extremely easy" for them to get booze, a senior says.

Rockefeller became governor in 1960 and made the building up of the university his major priority did SUNY begin its dramatic growth.

SUNY has now ripened into a network of four research-oriented "university centers," thirteen arts and sciences colleges, six agricultural and technical colleges, five "statutory" colleges, four specialized colleges, thirty locally sponsored community colleges, and four health science centers. The fruits of the labor, though practiced in as high-cost a state as there is, have become legitimately advertised as among the best bargains in the nation, particularly at the undergraduate level. Annual costs at institutions like SUNY–Albany are still barely more than half of what it costs to attend such hoary and prestigious publicly supported flagship campuses as California at Berkeley and the University of Michigan. Nevertheless, the SUNY system faces continuing budget cuts, and New York State's investment per capita in higher education as a whole is forty-seventh in the country.

Prospective students apply directly to the SUNY unit they seek to attend. Forty-six of the colleges, though, use a "common form" application that enables a prospective student to apply to as many as four SUNY campuses at the same time. The central administration runs a SUNY Admissions Assistance Service that helps rejected students find places at other campuses. Students who earn associate degrees at community or other two-year colleges are guaranteed the chance to continue their education at a four-year institution, though not necessarily at their first choice. The level of selectivity varies widely. Most community colleges guarantee admission to any local high-school student, but the university centers, as well as some specialized colleges, are among the most competitive public institutions in the nation. As part of a recent "standards revolution," SUNY trustees voted to adopt a new budgeting model designed to financially reward campuses that increase enrollment. Undergraduates at all liberal arts colleges and university centers pay the same tuition, but the rates at community colleges vary (and are lower). Out-of-state students, who make up only 4 percent of SUNY students, pay about double the amount of in-state tuition.

Mainly for political reasons, the State University of New York chose not to follow the model of other states and build a single flagship campus the likes of an Ann Arbor, Madison, or Chapel Hill. Instead, it created the four university centers with undergraduate, graduate, and professional schools and research facilities in each corner of the state. When they were created in the 1960s, each one hoped to become fully comprehensive, but there has been a certain degree of specialization from the beginning. They also decided not to establish a Division I football program, something that has lowered their visibility to out-of-state students.

Albany is strongest in education and public policy, Binghamton is best known for undergraduate arts and sciences, and Stony Brook is noted for its hard sciences. Buffalo, formerly a private university, maintains a strong reputation in the life sciences and geography but comes the closest of any of the four to being a fully comprehensive university. Critics of the system say that the decision to forgo a flagship campus guarantees a lack of national prominence, and the lack of big-time football or other sports programs has affected SUNY's reputation as well. Still, many insist that somewhere in the labs and libraries of these four university centers are lurking the Nobel Prize winners of this century. To these supporters, it's only a matter of time before SUNY achieves excellence in depth as well as breadth.

The thirteen colleges of arts and sciences likewise vary widely in size and character. They range from the twenty-six thousand–student College at Buffalo, whose 125-acre campus reflects the urban flavor of the state's second-largest city, to the rural and highly selective College at Geneseo, where half as many students nearly outnumber the year-round residents of the small local village. Still others are suburban campuses, such as Purchase, which specializes in the performing arts, and Old Westbury, which was started as an experimental institution to serve minority students, older women, and others who have been "bypassed" by more traditional institutions.

With the exception of Purchase and Old Westbury, which were started from scratch, the four-year colleges are all former teachers' colleges that have, for the most part, successfully made the transition into liberal arts colleges on the small, private New England model. Now they face a new problem: the growing desire of students to study business, computer science, and other more technically oriented subjects. Some have adjusted to these demands well; others are trying to resist the trend.

SUNY's technical and specialized colleges, while not enjoying the prominence of the colleges of arts and sciences, serve the demand for vocational training in a variety of two- and four-year programs. Five of the six agricultural and technical colleges—Alfred, Canton, Cobleskill, Delhi, and Morrisville—are concerned primarily with agriculture, but also have programs in engineering, nursing, medical technology, data processing, and business administration. The sixth, Farmingdale, offers the widest range of programs, from ornamental horticulture to aerospace technology. A new upper-division technical campus at Utica-Rome now provides graduates of these two-year institutions with an opportunity to finish their education in SUNY instead of having to head for Penn State University, Ohio State, the University of Massachusetts, or destinations in other directions.

Four of the five statutory schools are at Cornell University—agriculture and life sciences, human ecology, industrial and labor relations, and veterinary medicine—while the internationally known College of Ceramics is housed at Alfred University, another private university. In addition to Utica-Rome, the specialized colleges consist of the College of Environmental Sciences and Forestry at Syracuse, the Maritime College at Fort Schuyler in the Bronx, the College of Optometry in New York City, and the Fashion Institute of Technology, whose graduates are gobbled up as fast as they emerge by employers in the Manhattan Garment District.

The twenty-nine community colleges have traditionally been the stepchildren of the system, but the combination of rampant vocationalism and the rising cost of education elsewhere is rapidly turning them into the most robust members of the family. Students once looked to the community colleges for terminal degrees that could be readily applied in the marketplace. Now, with the cost of college soaring, a growing number of students who otherwise would have been packed off to a four-year college are saving money by staying home for the first two years and then transferring to a four-year college—or even a university center—to get their bachelor's degree.

Following are full-length descriptions of SUNY–Purchase, which is the liberal arts institution best known beyond New York's borders, SUNY–Geneseo, and the four university centers.

SUNY–Albany

1400 Washington Avenue, Albany, NY 12222

SUNY–Albany won't win any awards for campus beauty, but it does have some attractive programs. Albany is strong in anything related to politics, public policy, and criminal justice. Study-abroad programs in Europe and Asia are also a strength. Less than 5 percent of the students are out-of-staters.

Website: www.albany.edu
Location: Suburban
Total Enrollment: 17,204
Undergraduates: 11,884
Male/Female: 50/50
SAT Ranges: V 500–600
  M 520–610
Financial Aid: 48%
Expense: Pub $ $
Phi Beta Kappa: Yes
Applicants: 17,019
Accepted: 58%
Enrolled: 22%
Grad in 6 Years: 62%
Returning Freshmen: 85%
Academics: ✍ ✍ ✍ ✍
Social: ☎ ☎ ☎
Q of L: ★ ★ ★
Admissions: (518) 442-5435
Email Address:
  ugadmissions@albany.edu

Strongest Programs
  Criminal Justice
  Atmospheric Science
  Physics

Founded in 1844 to train teachers, SUNY–Albany is set up primarily for graduate research, but the school's outstanding education and public policy programs attract undergrads from around the nation who are eager to take advantage of vast resources.

Designed by Edward Durrell Stone, who also designed the Kennedy Center and Lincoln Center, SUNY–Albany's campus is modern and suburban. Almost all the academic buildings are clustered in the center of the campus, while students are housed in five symmetrically situated quads so similar in appearance that it usually takes a semester to figure out which one is yours. (Hint: the quads are named for periods in New York history—Indian, Dutch, Colonial, State, and Freedom—and progress clockwise around the campus.) A twenty thousand–square-foot sculpture studio opened recently, and construction has begun on a $78 million Life Sciences Building.

Most of the preprofessional programs are among the best of any SUNY branch. Students in the public administration and social welfare programs may take advantage of their proximity to the state government to participate in internships. Biology, physics, sociology, and psychology are other notable majors, and undergrads are clamoring for admittance to the university's business administration program, which is especially strong in accounting. The New York State Writers' Institute is the newest and least traditional of Albany's offerings, and with William Kennedy as head of the institute, the university's dream of becoming distinguished for its creative writing has nearly come true. The School of Nanosciences and Materials is another recent campus addition and the first of its kind in the nation.

"Alumni [Quad] has much more attractive rooms and ambiance overall."

All undergraduates must fulfill Albany's thirty-credit general education program, which includes courses in disciplinary prospectives, national and international perspectives, mathematics and statistics, pluralism and diversity, communication and reasoning competencies, and foreign language. If this liberal arts exposure whets your appetite for interdisciplinary study, try your hand at human biology, information science, or urban studies. The more career-minded can sign up for one of forty B.A./M.A. programs or opt for a law degree with the bachelor's in only six years. Many students take advantage of SUNY–Albany's superior offerings in foreign study. Don't be surprised if you find yourself sitting in class next to someone named Ivan; the university was one of the first in the nation to develop exchange programs with Russia (and China, for that matter).

(Continued)
Accounting
Business
Political Science
Social Welfare
Computer Science

Undergraduates may also study in several European countries as well as in Brazil, Costa Rica, Israel, Japan, and Singapore. Project Renaissance brings together groups of one hundred freshmen with a team of senior faculty, librarians, computer specialists, and assistants in a shared academic and living community. Participants engage in a year-long, unified course of study covering twelve hours of the university's general education requirements, and have access to special perks including housing and faculty mentors.

One undergraduate describes his peers as "intelligent, assertive, hardworking, urban—generally pretty fast company." Albany students tend to spend a lot of time thinking about their future. But, lest you get the wrong impression, "They're also highly motivated to party at every available moment," another adds. The student body comprises "bits and pieces of every Long Island high school and a dash of upstate, topped off with a Big Apple or two." All but 6 percent of the students are native New Yorkers, about one-third from Long Island and more than half from upstate New York. African-American and Hispanic enrollment now stands at 16 percent combined, while Asian-Americans make up another 7 percent. Racial issues are hot, but a senior says, "No problems, just a lot of diversity." SUNY–Albany is one of the more selective public universities in the nation, and 48 percent of the students are from the top quarter of their high-school class. SUNY–Albany makes available five hundred merit scholarships of $1,000 to $6,000 each.

> "The transportation system to and from campus is convenient and the cost of apartments is as cheap (or cheaper) than living on campus."

Fifty-eight percent of students live in university housing, which is described as "average." Freshmen and sophomores are required to live in dorms, and the Empire Commons housing facility, with apartment-styled space for 1,200 upperclassmen, eases the housing crunch. The coed quads are exceptionally friendly, surprisingly quiet, and comfortable. "They are compact and force unity and friendship," says one undergrad. Each floor of these dorms is divided into four- to six-person suites. But the word from most students is that the best dorms are in the Alumni Quad on the downtown campus. "Alumni has much more attractive rooms and ambiance overall," says a business major. Many students move off campus because "the transportation system to and from campus is convenient and the cost of apartments is as cheap (or cheaper) than living on campus," says a junior. Students on the main campus take their meals at any of the four dorms or at the campus center that includes a popular food court and bookstore, while downtowners haunt the cheap local eateries as well as their own cafeterias.

> "You can find an outlet here for even the most obscure interest, but this is not a school that will educate you when you're not looking."

While most people are serious about their work, a SUNY–Albany weekend starts on Thursday night for many. Students go to parties or go bar-hopping about town. Students warn that alcohol policies forbidding underage drinking are strict and well enforced. "It is easy for underage residents to drink on campus, but if you're caught there are severe penalties," says a student. The Greek life is experiencing something of a renaissance at Albany. Fraternities and sororities now attract 7 percent of the male and female students, and have become the main party-throwers on campus.

The Greek life is experiencing something of a renaissance at Albany. Fraternities and sororities now attract 7 percent of the male and female students, and have become the main party-throwers on campus.

SUNY–Albany is one of the more selective public universities in the nation.

Albany students tend to be traditional, but rites-of-spring festivals, mandatory after enduring the miserable upstate winters, have produced Guinness records for the largest games of Simon Says, Twister, and Musical Chairs. Fountain Day brings thousands of students together for the spring turn-on of the infamous podium fountain. Mayfest is a huge all-school concert party that brings in well-known as well as up-and-coming bands.

The natural resources of the upstate region keep students busy skiing and hiking. Treks to Montreal and Saratoga are popular. Plus, the student association owns and operates Dippikill, a private camp in the Adirondacks. Men's basketball, tennis, wrestling, and football and women's softball, volleyball, and basketball advanced to the NCAA Division II in 1995, and the school has made a recent move to Division I. Meanwhile, intramurals engender a great deal of student enthusiasm, and participation numbers in the thousands. Athletic scholarships are offered in a dozen different sports such as soccer, tennis, and golf, to name a few.

SUNY–Albany is not the concrete, sterile diploma mill it may appear to be. It's a place of opportunity for those willing to put in the hours and hard work. As one veteran warns, "You can find an outlet here for even the most obscure interest, but this is not a school that will educate you when you're not looking."

Overlaps

SUNY–Binghamton University, NYU, Boston University, Syracuse, Cornell University

If You Apply To ➢

SUNY–Albany: Early action: Dec. 1. Regular admissions: Mar. 1. Financial aid: Mar. 15. Does not guarantee to meet demonstrated need. Campus interviews: recommended, informational. No alumni interviews. SATs: required. No SAT IIs. Accepts electronic applications. Optional essay question: personal statement.

SUNY–Binghamton University

P.O. Box 6001, Binghamton, NY 13902-6000

If one hundred thousand screaming fans on a Saturday afternoon tickles your fancy, head two hundred miles southwest to Penn State. Binghamton has become the premier public university in the northeast because of its outstanding academic programs, such the Binghamton Scholars and Discovery Initiative, and its commitment to undergraduates.

Website:
  www.binghamton.edu
Location: Suburban
Total Enrollment: 12,820
Undergraduates: 10,167
Male/Female: 46/54
SAT Ranges: V 540–640
  M 580–670
ACT Range: 24-28
Financial Aid: 69%
Expense: Pub $ $
Phi Beta Kappa: Yes
Applicants: 17,391
Accepted: 45%

Binghamton is the smallest of the university centers and is the best public university in the country that never gets any respect—except from students. "I find the university is large enough to get super professors and to have cutting-edge resources, but small enough that I have had the opportunity to get to know some professors very well," says a junior. "Academic advising is always available," says another student.

Binghamton University is situated on more than eight hundred acres of open grassy areas that include a large nature preserve, trails, fountains, and a pond. "The surrounding countryside is breathtaking," one woman notes. The campus itself isn't bad either, if you like modern, "functional" buildings (all structures have been built since 1958). Some students say that from an aerial view the circular campus bears a striking resemblance to the human brain—a total coincidence and not a secret plan of the architects, the administration asserts. Recent construction includes two new housing units: Rockland/Saratoga and College in the Woods. The Field House and more residential buildings are also on the way.

The first thing that greets students who do gain admission is the general education program. This comprehensive curriculum requires new students to take courses in five areas: language and communication, creating a global vision, sciences and mathematics, aesthetics and humanities, and wellness. Engineering receives high marks from students, as do the Decker School of Nursing, which offers an accelerated bachelor's degree program for students with degrees in other fields, and the school of management, which offers a five-year B.S./M.B.A. program. In addition, qualified students enrolled in any undergraduate program may pursue the baccalaureate/M.B.A. in a five-year program. Biological science, chemistry, and English win rave reviews in Harpur College. Interdisciplinary fields of study include women's studies, medieval studies, Africana studies, Judaic studies, and Latin American and Caribbean area studies. If these don't satisfy a student's intellectual cravings, the Innovational Projects Board will oversee and help students design not only their own majors but courses as well.

Internship possibilities exist, as do numerous study-abroad programs. Undergraduate students are also encouraged to participate in faculty research projects. The Binghamton Scholars Program offers students of exceptional merit a chance to participate in a special four-year program that includes experiential and capstone courses. The new Discovery initiative, boasted as the only one of its kind in the country, offers students opportunities for self-assessment, skill-development, academic advising, tutorial assistance, career preparation, and collaborative learning. The Global Studies Integrated Curriculum (GSIC) offers students from any school or major a chance to explore global issues from a broad range of perspectives, to develop skills and knowledge relative to a particular world culture, and to pursue collaborative research related issues.

> "I find the university is large enough to get super professors and to have cutting-edge resources, but small enough that I have had the opportunity to get to know some professors very well."

Although there are complaints that research sometimes receives higher priority than teaching, professors generally receive good marks from students, and the university has benefited from the hiring of new professors thanks to increased state funds. "Professors are known in their fields but have not lost touch with how to teach," says a sophomore. Graduate teaching assistants (mainly those in the natural sciences) hold smaller group meetings to supplement large lecture courses that sometimes seat close to five hundred students. According to students, getting into needed courses can sometimes be difficult. Binghamton's strong academic reputation has been

> "Professors are known in their fields but have not lost touch with how to teach."

enhanced by a tough grading policy in which students are given an F rather than no credit, and pluses and minuses as well as straight letter grades. "You're not spoon-fed," says a student, "yet it's not rocket science." Students agree that the courses are challenging, yet competition among students is not heated. "I feel a good mix of competitiveness between students and professors," says a student. "Despite the number of really smart people here, the academic climate is surprisingly laid-back," remarks a senior.

Although Binghamton ranks as one of the best public arts and sciences schools in the nation, word of this is slow to cross state lines. The university attracts large numbers of New Yorkers (94 percent) who come seeking a lower-cost alternative to good private liberal arts colleges. The traditional upstate-downstate divisions of New York State politics are reflected in the student body, with upstaters complaining about provincial peers who think that "New York City is the only city in the world." African-Americans make up 7 percent of the student body, Hispanics 6 percent, and Asian-Americans 21 percent. The school does guarantee to meet full

(Continued)

Enrolled: 29%
Grad in 6 Years: 80%
Returning Freshmen: 91%
Academics: ✐ ✐ ✐ ✐ ½
Social: ☎ ☎ ☎
Q of L: ★ ★
Admissions: (607) 777-2171
Email Address:
    admit@binghamton.edu

Strongest Programs
    Anthropology
    Human Development
    Chemistry
    Engineering
    English
    History
    Management
    Nursing

Some students say that from an aerial view the circular campus bears a striking resemblance to the human brain—a total coincidence and not a secret plan of the architects, the administration asserts.

demonstrated financial need, and there's tough competition for the 757 merit scholarships of $250 to $10,000 doled out every year. More than 170 athletic awards are given in a variety of sports.

To help make the university seem a little smaller, residence halls are grouped into five residential areas. Dickinson is the oldest and most stately, but each area has its own personality and reputation. Fifty-six percent of the students live on campus. It pays to get your housing application in early; a student says, "Students who are mindful of the deadlines are guaranteed housing." The majority of juniors and seniors move off campus, where housing is plentiful and "moderately priced." Those who stay on campus say that the residence halls are "good-sized and comfortable."

Binghamton enforces the state's twenty-one-and-over drinking law. "No alcohol is allowed on campus," says a student. "But people drink in their rooms all the time." This has not damaged the social life for nondrinkers, however, as there is plenty of fun to be had at neighborhood bars, movies, concerts, quiet dinners off campus, and

"Spring Fling is a cool campus carnival. They always bring in a good band."

occasional campus-wide parties in the residence areas. In an effort to decrease drinking, the school is participating in the "Just the Facts" program, which offers students alternatives to drinking that include free movies, games, a coffee bar, and musical groups. Annual events among the dorms include the Passing of the Vegetables to bring in the winter season, Stepping on the Coat to usher in spring, and dorm wars. Another senior notes, "Spring Fling is a cool campus carnival. They always bring in a good band."

Binghamton the town gets mixed reviews from the students, but students agree that townies are friendly and there is a growing trend of community service and volunteer work. "It's not a typical 'college town,' but there is the strip of shops and bars and clubs," says a junior. There is a fraternity and sorority presence on campus—a total of thirty-three—with about 12 percent of the men and 15 percent of the women as members. Few students take major road trips on the weekends, but for those who need an escape, Syracuse, Ithaca, Cortland, and Oneonta are about an hour by car. The toughest part about road trips may be finding a parking space when you get back—permits currently outnumber spaces by about three to one.

Several Binghamton teams have brought home conference championships in recent years, and varsity sports have made the move to the NCAA Division I. On the wish list of many students is big-time football. For now, students must make do with co-rec football, where teams of three men and three women (always a female quarterback) stir up intense rivalries, and "traying" (downhill snow sledding on trays).

Binghamton is proud of its growing reputation as a public alternative to the Ivy League, and the school's reputation for value and excellence attracts an overwhelming number of highly qualified students. One says, "I've had some really good classes, but more than anything else I've connected with some of the greatest people I've ever met." Though some may argue that college is not the "real world," few can dispute the fact that Binghamton grads have a real education that will serve them well.

Overlaps

NYU, SUNY–Albany, SUNY–Stony Brook, Cornell University, SUNY–Buffalo

If You Apply To ➤ **Binghamton University:** Early action: Nov. 15. Regular admissions: Feb. 15. Financial aid: Mar. 1. Guarantees to meet full demonstrated need. No campus or alumni interviews. SATs or ACTs: required. No SAT IIs: optional. Accepts electronic applications. Essay question: thoughts about violence; or benefits of higher education.

Glamorous it is not, but SUNY–Buffalo offers solid programs in everything from business and engineering to geography and English. The majority of students come from western New York and a high percentage commute from home. The largest of the SUNY campuses.

In the world of higher learning, SUNY–Buffalo is a big fish in the big pond. As part of the mammoth State University of New York system, UB's resources are large enough to warrant two campuses—North and South. "Big university with a small-college atmosphere," comments one student. This former private university maintains a strong reputation in the life sciences and geography and is the most comprehensive of the SUNY schools. The resources are vast and the size is staggering; UB students must take care not to get eaten alive.

The North campus of SUNY–Buffalo, less than twenty years old and home to most undergraduate programs, stretches across 1,200 acres in the suburbs just outside the city line and boasts buildings designed by world-renowned architects such as I. M. Pei. Meanwhile, the South campus, along Main Street, favors collegiate ivy-covered buildings and the schools of architecture and health sciences, including the highly rated programs in medicine and dentistry. New facilities include much-needed on-campus housing.

On the academic front, the engineering and business management schools are nationally prominent, and architecture is strong. Occupational and physical therapy programs are also quite good. The English department is very strong, and notable for its emphasis on poetry. Poets visit the campus frequently, and students not only compose and read poetry, but study the art of performing it as well. French, physiology, geography, and music are highly regarded, but other humanities vary in quality. Math and German are also on the weak side, and physics is the least impressive among the sciences. Complaints occasionally surface about the lack of major programs in journalism and broadcasting, although courses in both disciplines are offered.

UB has a multitude of special programs, joint degrees (such as a five-year B.S./M.B.A.), and interdisciplinary majors as well as opportunities for self-designed majors and study abroad. Students accepted into the honors program enjoy smaller classes, priority in class registration, individual faculty mentors, and special scholarships regardless of need. Freshmen must also take

> "Most upper-level courses are challenging, and the general education courses require a lot of time."

University Experience 101, which orients students to UB's academic life, general social experience, and resources. General education requirements are standardized and include courses such as writing skills, math sciences, natural sciences, foreign language, world civilizations, and American pluralism. The university's newest programs include majors in dance, music theatre, computational physics, pharmacy, environmental engineering, biotechnology, and geological science.

"Most upper-level courses are challenging, and the general education courses require a lot of time," says a senior. Class size can be a problem, especially for freshmen. Scheduling conflicts are not unusual, and required courses are often the most difficult to get into. Students seem to accept that some degree of faculty unavailability is the necessary trade-off for having professors who are experts in their fields at a school where graduate education and research get lots of the attention. The

Website: www.buffalo.edu
Location: Suburban
Total Enrollment: 25,838
Undergraduates: 17,290
Male/Female: 54/46
SAT Ranges: V 500–600
  M 520–630
ACT Range: 22–27
Financial Aid: 70%
Expense: Pub $ $
Phi Beta Kappa: Yes
Applicants: 16,016
Accepted: 63%
Enrolled: 30%
Grad in 6 Years: 56%
Returning Freshmen: 85%
Academics: ✐ ✐ ✐ ✐
Social: ☎ ☎
Q of L: ★ ★
Admissions: (716) 645-6900
Email Address: ub-admissions@admissions.buffalo.edu

Strongest Programs
  Biological Sciences
  Business Administration
  Computer Engineering
  English
  Engineering
  Geography
  Occupational Therapy

academically oriented student body spends plenty of time in UB's six main libraries, or one of the several branches, which are for the most part comfortable and well-stocked at three million volumes.

Once upon a time, a large majority of UB's student body went straight into the job market after graduation, but today a third go on to graduate school. With only 2 percent of the students from out of state, the biggest contingent of homegrown New York Staters, apart from the locals, is from New York City and Long Island. As a large public university, UB has "everything from the all-American coed to the active radical." African-Americans and Hispanics combined account for 13 percent of the student body, and Asian-Americans represent another 10 percent. UB's considerable efforts in increasing awareness of diversity include a Committee on Campus Tolerance, Office of Student Multi-Cultural Affairs, and Multi-Cultural Leadership Council. More than eight hundred students receive merit scholarships ranging from $1000 to $17,809, and there are also 292 athletic scholarships available in a variety of sports.

Twenty-one percent of students live on campus; the rest commute from home or find apartments near the Main Street campus. Students warn that potential renters should shuffle off to Buffalo a couple of months early to secure a place. There is a new apartment-style residence hall for undergraduates featuring cable, computer connections, and central air-conditioning. "The dorms are comfortable and well maintained," comments one senior. Most of the on-campus dwellers are housed on the Amherst campus in modern coed dorms. The Main Street campus dorms are smaller, older, and of a more traditional collegiate design, which upperclassmen tend to prefer, and three all-freshmen dorms house extremely sociable freshmen. Security on campus is generally good. "There is a full-time police station operating on campus," says a junior. "Students feel very safe." The cafeteria food gets so-so reviews, but most dorms are equipped with kitchens for those inclined to cook for themselves.

"There is a full-time police station operating on campus. Students feel very safe."

The large number of commuters and the split campus put a damper on social life, but students seem to manage. "Buffalo is definitely a college town," says one student. Road trips are often taken to Niagara Falls, Toronto, and Cleveland. "Social life takes place off UB South campus," claims one junior. Friday-night happy hours center on beer and the chicken wings that spread the fame of Buffalo cuisine. Also popular are the Albright-Knox Art Gallery, with its world-renowned collection of modern art, and the Triple-A baseball Bisons, who play downtown. The two major pro teams, the Buffalo Bills in football and the Sabres in hockey, are both top draws. Open drinking is banned in the dorms, but that doesn't stop students from staging "progressive parties" with a different drink in each room (and we don't mean Cherry Coke and Sprite). Off-campus bars are another favorite spot for underagers.

Having a car might be a great idea, though parking is a problem on campus. Students without cars can get trapped when the intercampus bus stops running after 2:00 A.M. on weekends. The winters are cold in Buffalo. (One student claims the best thing about his school is "the tunnels that connect every building and every dorm so we can walk indoors during winter.") But the flip side is that the outlying areas of the city offer great skiing and snowshoeing—and the ski club even offers free rides to the slopes. UB supports more than five hundred other student organizations ranging from jugglers to math enthusiasts. Students can preview their honeymoons by darting over to Niagara Falls, just half an hour away, or flee the country altogether by driving to nearby Canada, where the drinking age is lower.

School spirit is sometimes generated at the Student Union and UB's impressive sports complex. "We have the fourth-largest pool in the world, as well as a ten thousand–seat arena, squash and racquetball courts, a jogging track, and weight rooms," brags one student. The men's and women's cross-country teams are among Buffalo's championship-caliber squads, as are women's basketball and men's and women's swimming. Intramural sports are popular, and earthy types appreciate the annual Oozefest—a mud-bound sports competition that is part of SpringFest.

The largest of SUNY centers, UB offers the most comprehensive education of all the New York state schools but depends on its students to come and find it. UB students sometimes lose patience with the crowds and inconvenience of two campuses. "You have to be your own advocate," advises a Spanish major. As one veteran so appropriately points out, "If you are not a go-getter, you might miss it all."

If You Apply To ➤ **SUNY–Buffalo:** Early decision: Nov. 1. Regular admissions: Nov. 1 (priority). Financial aid: Mar. 1. Housing: May 1. Campus interviews: optional, informational. No alumni interviews. SATs or ACTs: required. SAT IIs: optional. Accepts electronic applications. No essay question.

SUNY–Geneseo

1 College Circle, Geneseo, NY 14454

Geneseo is a preferred option for New Yorkers who want the feel of a private college at a public-university price. Similar in scale to William and Mary and Mary Washington in Virginia, smaller than Miami of Ohio. Offers business and education in addition to the liberal arts.

For those seeking a public alternative to small private liberal arts colleges, SUNY–Geneseo offers a comprehensive educational experience that emphasizes strong professional programs and a traditional liberal arts core. "Geneseo has a great reputation as a competitive, successful institution at a fair price," says a junior. "It has managed to keep its small size and unique atmosphere throughout the years." Students are quick to point out that faculty and staff go out of their way to ensure that each student is treated as an individual.

The campus is located in the scenic Genesee Valley, with its spectacular sunsets, in western New York State. One student defines Geneseo as special because, "There is a beautiful sunset every night and because it is spacious there are lots of fields to play in." The architectural style is a mix of Gothic and modern buildings, all nestled in a tree-lined, small community that has been designated a National Historic Landmark Community by the U.S. Department of the Interior. New student resident townhouses have been completed recently.

> **"Geneseo has a great reputation as a competitive, successful institution at a fair price."**

Geneseo operates on the semester system, and the college's offerings balance between several professional programs and the traditional liberal arts. Special education is the most popular major, followed by biology, management, psychology, and English. The John Wiley Jones School of Business boasts a strong program; 3–2 M.B.A. programs are available with Pace, SUNY–Buffalo, and Syracuse; and 3–3 programs are available with the Rochester Institute of Technology. History, English, and biology are also good, and, true to its roots as a teachers training institution, Geneseo still has an outstanding education program that offers a teaching certificate. There is also a 3–2 program in engineering. The flexible core curriculum

Website: www.geneseo.edu
Location: Small town
Total Enrollment: 5,649
Undergraduates: 5,371
Male/Female: 35/65
SAT Ranges: V 560–640
  M 570–650
ACT Range: 24–28
Financial Aid: 85%
Expense: Pub $ $
Phi Beta Kappa: No
Applicants: 7,794
Accepted: 52%
Enrolled: 27%
Grad in 6 Years: 79%
Returning Freshmen: 90%
Academics: ✍ ✍ ✍ ½
Social: ☎ ☎ ☎
Q of L: ★ ★ ★ ★
Admissions: (585) 245-5571
Email Address:
  admissions@geneseo.edu

(Continued)

Strongest Programs

Business

Communicative Disorders
and Sciences

Education

English

Natural Sciences

Music

Psychology

requires two interdisciplinary humanities courses and two courses in each of four categories: natural sciences, social sciences, fine arts, and critical reasoning; as well as one course in non-Western traditions. The general education core requirements now include Numeric and Symbolic Reasoning and Critical Writing and Reading as well as an American History requirement.

On the whole, students feel at home in Geneseo's competitive academic climate. "The courses are quite challenging," says a senior. "I think the level of competition is just right. I've been motivated to improve." The quality of teaching draws raves. "Professors are very approachable and friendly," says a psychology major. Friendly, yes. Easy, no. "They have high expectations and make the course material challenging." Students feel there is room for improvement in the way of the academic advising and the career counseling. A student claims that, "We have advisors that are helpful, but for many of them, it is their first year advising and they can't help us any more than we can help ourselves." The vast majority of classes have fifty or fewer, and upperclassmen have almost no trouble getting into courses: "Sometimes popular classes are difficult to get into. Students with more credits get priority," says a freshman.

> **"There is a beautiful sunset every night and because it is spacious there are lots of fields to play in."**

Ninety-eight percent of the students are from New York State, and 93 percent of them attended public high school. Eighty-six percent graduated in the top quarter of their high-school class. "Because the campus is relatively relaxed and conservative," one communications major says, "students with a radical view on life and issues may not be happy at Geneseo." Minority students together account for only 10 percent of the student body. One student reports that there is "no outward hostility between racial and ethnic groups; it's more of a peaceful segregation." The school offers 498 merit scholarships, ranging from $500 to $3,400.

Fifty-four percent of the students, including all freshmen, live in on-campus housing, which is guaranteed for all four years. Rooms are determined by lottery, and "many students remain on campus due to the clean, highly maintained, and safe living conditions," reports a senior. Campus security is described as "excellent" by many. Says a freshman: "I always feel safe. We have the blue-light system and S.A.F.E. cars."

The School of Business boasts a strong program; 3–2 MBA programs are available with Pace, SUNY–Buffalo, and Syracuse; and 3–3 programs are available with the Rochester Institute of Technology.

Small and idyllic, the neighboring village is considered by many students a perfect setting. "It's a typical college town," reports a senior. "There are a lot of volunteer opportunities available for students to participate in," says another student. Hiking and skiing are both nearby, and beautiful Conesus Lake is only a ten-minute drive away. As for the social life, one junior says "there is so much to do at Geneseo...that I never want to go home!" For those aching to hit the road, Rochester lies thirty miles to the north, and Buffalo sixty miles west. Twelve percent of the men and 9 percent of the women belong to fraternities and sororities, which keep life on campus from getting too humdrum. Only students over twenty-one may have alcohol in the residence halls, but that rule is "only sometimes enforced," says a freshman.

> **"I always feel safe. We have the blue-light system and S.A.F.E. cars."**

Sports are extremely popular, and Geneseo fields several excellent teams. Women's and men's basketball, cross-country, indoor/outdoor track, soccer, and men's ice hockey are very strong. Intramurals are popular, and there are nearly two hundred other student-run organizations, including a newspaper and radio and television stations.

For those seeking solid liberal arts or preprofessional training, Geneseo is worth a look. Says one student, "Geneseo offers students an excellent, quality education for a very reasonable tuition fee."

Overlaps

SUNY–Binghamton,
SUNY–Buffalo,
SUNY–Fredonia, James
Madison, University of
Rochester

If You Apply To ▷ | **SUNY–Geneseo:** Early decision: Nov. 15. Regular admissions: Feb. 1. Financial aid: Feb. 15. Housing: May 1. Does not guarantee to meet demonstrated need. Campus interviews: recommended, informational. No alumni interviews. SATs or ACTs: required. SAT IIs: optional. Essay question: write your own recommendation for admission; impact of computer technology; unpublished writing sample.

SUNY–Purchase College

735 Anderson Hill Road, Purchase, NY 10577-1400

One of the few public institutions that is also an arts specialty school. The visual and performing arts are signature programs, though Purchase has developed some liberal arts specialties in areas like environmental.

SUNY–Purchase College is a dream come true for aspiring artists of all kinds—an academic environment that provides a strong sense of community and support, yet celebrates individuals for their unique talents and contributions; it's OK to be an individual here. A senior says the best thing about Purchase is "the freedom to focus on whatever you want without feeling pressured to join anything to fit in."

Set on a five hundred–acre wooded estate in an area of Westchester's most scenic suburbia, Purchase has a campus described by one student as "sleek, modern, ominous, and brick." The college has earned a national reputation for its instruction in music, dance, visual arts, theater, and film. Almost all the faculty members in the School of the Arts are professionals who perform or exhibit regularly in the New York metropolitan area, and the spacious, dazzling facilities rank among the best in the world. Purchase College boasts of the Neuberger Museum, the sixth-largest public college museum. The four-theater Performing Arts Center is huge, and dance students, whose building contains a dozen studios, whirlpool rooms, and a "body-correction" facility, may never again work in such splendid and well-equipped surroundings. Recent campus improvements include townhouse-style student apartments that will allow more than four hundred additional students to hang their hats on campus.

Mingling with highly motivated and talented performers and artists can make some students in the liberal arts and sciences feel a little drab and out of place. "Dancers, actors, visual artists, and music students pull the most weight as far as campus life is concerned," says a student. Still, Purchase is a fine place to study humanities and the natural sciences, particularly literature, psychology, art history, environmental sciences, and biology. Most of the shaky liberal arts and sciences programs are confined to some majors in the social sciences and language and culture, where offerings are limited.

> "Dancers, actors, visual artists, and music students pull the most weight as far as campus life is concerned."

Students in the Liberal Arts and Sciences spend one-third of their time at Purchase fulfilling the general education requirements, which include ten knowledge areas. Students now take mathematics, natural sciences, social science, American history, western civilization, other world civilizations, the arts, foreign language, and basic communications. In addition to these core requirements, they also must take critical thinking and information management as skill areas, and everyone must complete a senior project. Students in the arts divisions usually have many more required courses, culminating in a senior recital or show. There are two separate sets of degree requirements, one for the Liberal Arts and Sciences and one for

Website: www.purchase.edu
Location: Suburban
Total Enrollment: 4,018
Undergraduates: 3,866
Male/Female: 43/57
SAT Ranges: V 500–610
  M 480–580
Financial Aid: 40%
Expense: Pub $ $
Phi Beta Kappa: No
Applicants: 6,427
Accepted: 33%
Enrolled: 32%
Grad in 6 Years: 35%
Returning Freshmen: 77%
Academics: ✑ ✑ ✑ ½
Social: ☎ ☎ ☎
Q of L: ★ ★ ★
Admissions: (914) 251-6300
Email Address:
  admissn@purchase.edu

Strongest Programs
  Acting
  Art History
  Dance
  Environmental Science
  Film
  Liberal Studies
  Music
  Women's Studies

the performing and visual arts. B.F.A. students in the performing and visual arts are required to sample the liberal arts; B.A. and B.S. students in the liberal arts and sciences are required to sample fine arts courses. The college also offers several certificate programs including computer science, arts management, and early child development. New majors include creative writing, journalism, dramatic writing, women's studies, and new media. A new B.F.A. program in dramatic writing was added most recently.

The atmosphere at Purchase varies between programs. "Our classes are rigorous and competitive but on a level that demands a lot from all students," reports a senior. Students tend to be very serious about their own personal achievements. Professors tend to be accessible and friendly. "My professors and advisor were more

> **"Our classes are rigorous and competitive but on a level that demands a lot from all students."**

than helpful. They were amazing," claims a senior. Eighty-two percent of the students are from New York State, most from New York City and Westchester County. Others are from Long Island, New Jersey, and Connecticut, but all are different and very political (that means very liberal). Minorities make up 22 percent of the student body. "Our student body is full of scholars and artists, most of whom are heavily driven by our politically active campus," says a women's studies/sociology major. Indeed, the largest student organization on this politically active campus is the gay and lesbian union. "We are diverse but politically we are a very liberal college," says a senior. "We believe strongly in animal rights, civil rights, women's rights, etc." In addition to need-based aid, merit scholarships are awarded each year on the basis of academic achievements, auditions, and portfolios.

> *"We are diverse but politically we are a very liberal college," says a senior. "We believe strongly in animal rights, civil rights, women's rights, etc."*

The living facilities have undergone renovations, but continue to receive mixed reviews. A sophomore says, "There is a housing shortage, which results in three people living in two-person rooms." A new residence hall should ease the burden. The two eating facilities offer decent fare, and for those who tire of institutional cuisine, there is a student-run co-op that specializes in health food. Forty-two percent of the student body commutes from nearby communities, though housing in the surrounding suburbs is expensive and hard to find.

The campus is a neighbor to the world headquarters of IBM, Texaco, AMF, General Foods, and Pepsico, but while sharing the "billion-dollar mile" with a few Fortune 500s might excite students at some other SUNY schools, "it doesn't do much for us except provide convenient antiapartheid demonstration locations," admits one Purchase activist. No college town exists per se at Purchase, so "we tend to think of our campus as our community," a senior psych major attests. "In my opinion, Purchase is not a 'college town,' however, students do participate in volunteering in the community," says another student. The Big Apple provides a regular

> **"The closest we come to Greek are the two guys from Athens who go here."**

weekend distraction that inhibits the formation of a tight campus community. Since the campus shuttle bus runs only once on the weekend, students started their own van service, which goes into Manhattan three times a day. Still, "a car is a definite must at Purchase," counsels one student. The Performing Arts Center is host to at least two student or faculty performances every weekend, and there is a constant flow of New York artists and celebrities. Notes a literature major, "Most of the social life on campus takes the form of parties thrown by apartment residents," and the over-twenty-one crowd often frequents the Pub. Fraternities and sororities are definitely out. "The closest we come to Greek are the two guys from Athens who go here," quips a staunch independent. Besides, as one artist explains, "individuality is far more important to the artist than being part of a group." Despite the unconventional aura of the place, Purchase is not without its traditions. There's an annual autumn dance, a Spring Semiformal, and an April Showers campus festival, and on Halloween there are ghost stories told at a historic graveyard on campus.

Purchase is not a member of the NCAA, and the few competitive teams include men's basketball and women's volleyball. There are plans, however, to join NCAA Division III in spring of 2002. Perhaps that is why the administration lends out the renovated gym to the NBA's New York Knicks for its practice sessions. Intramural programs and an excellent athletic facility exist, but informal Frisbee tossing remains more popular than organized sports. Says a student: "Our 'teams' are our dancers, our vocalists, our musicians, and our theater companies."

Despite a conspicuous lack of a college-town atmosphere, Purchase is a perfect place to study the arts and still be able to indulge in academics of all kinds, or vice versa. Those willing to put up with what a senior calls "an isolated campus full of ugly architecture," may find that Purchase offers the opportunity for a personalized, diverse education unique within the SUNY system.

<aside>
Overlaps

SUNY–New Paltz,
NYU, SUNY–Oneonta,
SUNY–Albany,
SUNY–Stony Brook
</aside>

<aside>
If You Apply To ➢

SUNY–Purchase College: Rolling admissions. Does not guarantee to meet demonstrated need. Campus and alumni interviews: optional, informational (required of theatre design/technology and film program applicants). SATs or ACTs: required. SAT I preferred. SAT IIs: optional. Accepts the Common Application and electronic applications. Essay question: personal or historical event of impact; personal influences; describe a time you took a leadership role. Apply to particular school or program. Auditions held for acting, dance, and music.
</aside>

SUNY–Stony Brook

118 Administration Building, Stony Brook, NY 11794-1901

Strategically located ninety minutes from New York City, Stony Brook has risen a few notches in the SUNY pecking order. The natural sciences, engineering, and health fields are the major drawing cards. Situated in the lap of Long Island luxury, Stony Brook offers easy access to beachfront play lands.

SUNY–Stony Brook boasts the best of both worlds: a small-college community with the power of a leading research institution. The public university has made a name for itself with its top-notch programs in the hard sciences. It has also become known for its highly competitive learning environment and the high quality of its professors.

The school's location on Long Island's plush North Shore (Gatsby's stomping grounds) is a wonderful drawing point. Sitting on about one thousand wooded acres just outside of the small, picturesque village of Stony Brook, and only ninety minutes from New York City and half an hour from the beaches of the South Shore, the campus architecture is a conglomeration of redbrick Federal-style buildings interspersed with several modern brick and concrete designs. Campus beautification is now a priority, and much of the uninspiring campus concrete is being replaced by grass and trees. The university recently completed phase two of the Student Activities Center and an eight thousand–seat multi-purpose outdoor stadium.

Coming of age in the high-tech era, Stony Brook quickly became widely known and respected for its science departments. Facilities are extensive, and the science faculty includes a number of internationally known researchers. The comprehensive university hospital and research center make health sciences strong, especially physical therapy. The hospital, which has been ranked among the nation's best for teaching, attracts grants to the campus and offers a lot of opportunities for various

<aside>
Website: www.stonybrook.edu
Location: City outskirts
Total Enrollment: 20,855
Undergraduates: 13,646
Male/Female: 52/48
SAT Ranges: V 500–600
M 540–648
Financial Aid: 60%
Expense: Pub $ $
Phi Beta Kappa: Yes
Applicants: 17,065
Accepted: 50%
Enrolled: 26%
Grad in 6 Years: 53%
Returning Freshmen: 85%
Academics: ✍ ✍ ✍ ✍
Social: ☎ ☎ ☎
Q of L: ★ ★
Admissions: (631) 632-6868
</aside>

(Continued)

Email Address: ugadmissions
@notes.cc.sunysb.edu

Strongest Programs
Computer science
Engineering science
English
Nursing
Geology
History
Mathematics
Physics
Biology
Music
Psychology

Stony Brook's present preprofessional student body has long since shaken off the druggie reputation its forefathers earned in the 1960s.

research programs for undergrads as well as graduate students. Students report that engineering is also strong, although it lacks civil and chemical concentrations. There are complaints that the emphasis on science overshadows the school's best social science and humanities programs, but at least efforts have been made to boost the arts with a fine arts center, complete with studios and a reference library. The center complements Stony Brook's beautiful five-theater Staller Center for the Arts. The music department faculty boasts the American pianist Gilbert Kalish. Journalism and philosophy are cited as weak.

The College of Arts and Sciences, the College of Engineering and Applied Sciences, and the Health Science Center previously had their own general education requirements, but recently the school decided to streamline the general education program. All of the schools cover writing and quantitative reasoning skills, literary and philosophic analysis, exposure to the arts, disciplinary diversity, the interrelationship of science and society, and three culminating multicultural requirements, including one course each in the European tradition, non-Western cultures, and American pluralism. Everyone in the arts and sciences must also satisfy a language requirement. Freshmen also take a one-credit course; its purpose is to provide them with knowledge about the university and give them a forum for discussing a variety of issues. The university has added majors in athletic training, environmental studies, and bioengineering, and minors in globalization and jazz music. Physical therapy is now a doctoral degree program rather than undergraduate.

> **"Counselors or advisers can help you at times. Other times they just confuse you."**

Liberal arts students are less stressed academically than their peers in the sciences, but this may change somewhat with additions of major writing-intensive courses. As professors delve into their own research projects, undergraduates must struggle for the attention of their teachers. Students who do take the considerable initiative to contact professors report that they are often met with responsive attitudes. Academic advising is described as weak. "Counselors or advisers can help you at times," says a senior. "Other times they just confuse you." Since freshmen are the last to register, they sometimes have to wait a semester or two to get into the most popular electives.

An Undergraduate Research and Creative Activities program (URECA) offers undergraduates the opportunity to work on research projects with faculty members from the time they are freshmen until they graduate. Women in Science and Engineering (WISE) is a multifaceted program for women who show promise in math, science, or engineering. There's also the Federated Learning Communities (FLC) program, in which students take a preplanned block of courses in one general area, such as The United States in Perspective, which then becomes their minor. A residential studies program links dormitories to fields of study, and interested students may live in the one of the six Living/Learning Centers: science and engineering, health and wellness, international studies, service learning, environmental studies, and interdisciplinary arts. Some students take advantage of one of Stony Brook's wonderful travel programs (France, England, Italy, Japan, and Tanzania are some possibilities), while others choose established internships in the fields of policy analysis, political science, psychology, foreign language, and social welfare. Combined B.A./M.A. or B.S./M.S. programs are available in engineering, the teaching of math, and management and policy.

> **"We have strict policies on alcohol, but if you have a roommate who is of age you do have access,"**

Stony Brook students are 94 percent in-staters, and about half commute from Long Island homes. Sixty-three percent graduated in the top quarter of their high-school class, and more than half of Stony Brook's graduates go on to graduate and professional schools. Besides the 17 percent total of African-Americans and Hispanics, Stony Brook enrolls 23 percent Asian-Americans. The university has created a Campus Relations Team, composed of University Police officers who educate the community on topics ranging from personal safety to rape prevention to drug and alcohol awareness. Students are also required to take classes focusing on different cultures. The university does not meet the demonstrated financial need of all accepted applicants. Approximately 79 percent of those who apply, however, do receive financial aid. About three hundred merit scholarships ranging from $500 to $16,000 are given out each year.

Stony Brook, which has one of the largest residential facilities in the SUNY system, has in the last several years completed a major rehabilitation, giving students access to state-of-the-art fitness centers, computing facilities, Internet access, and widescreen TV. Nearly half the student body lives in university housing. The consensus is that Mendelsohn and H quads, "very sociable and a good eye-opener for incoming students," are best for freshmen, and that the halls (as opposed to suites) are preferable because "you meet more people," as a political science major says. Commuters are given a social facility of their own, "the commuter commons." While residential freshmen must take a meal plan, upperclassmen who live on campus either opt for a flexible food-service plan or pay a nominal fee to cook for themselves. The suites come equipped with dishwashers and ranges, and each hall has a lounge and kitchen area, all of which, students say, could be kept a lot cleaner. Kosher and vegetarian food co-ops keep interested students well supplied with cheap eats. Four additional residences have also been completed and come fully furnished with full kitchens, high-speed Internet access, and cable TV.

Stony Brook's present preprofessional student body has long since shaken off the druggie reputation its forefathers earned in the 1960s. "We have strict policies on alcohol, but if you have a roommate who is of age you do have access," one senior says. Other students say that access to alcohol for underage students isn't quite so easy. The longtime ban on fraternities and sororities has been lifted, so a fledgling

"It's not much of a college town because there are so many things to do on campus."

Greek system (with no houses) is another option. Current and classic movies are screened during the week, and other entertainment is available in the form of frequent concerts, plays, and other performances. Annual festivals in the fall and spring and the football game with Hofstra are among the biggest social events of the year. Because many students go home on the weekends, Thursday is the big party night.

The students who remain on the weekends often go beachcombing on the nearby North Shore or the Atlantic Ocean shore of Long Island, or head into New York City. Cars are desirable, but many students make do with trains, and a station is conveniently located at the edge of campus. The local community is a "beautiful, wealthy area of Long Island," says a senior. "It's not much of a college town, because there are so many things to do on campus." Nearby Port Jefferson offers small shops and interesting restaurants. Sports facilities have been upgraded, and all nineteen varsity teams compete in Division I. Intramurals provide one of the school's greatest rallying points, and competition in oozeball (a mud-caked variant of volleyball) is especially fierce.

Though Stony Brook is not old enough to have ivy-covered walls, it does offer some of the best academic opportunities in the SUNY system. Students have to maneuver around lots of rough spots, including increasing class sizes and decreasing course offerings. Yet despite these budget-crisis-induced problems, students share in the promise of Stony Brook's future. In the meantime, they boast of their school's diversity and creativity as well as the feeling of hospitality that pervades campus life.

Liberal arts students are less stressed academically than their peers in the sciences, but this may change somewhat with additions of major writing-intensive courses.

Overlaps

NYU, SUNY–Binghamton, Cornell University, Columbia, Boston University

Stetson University

Campus Box 8378, DeLand, FL 32720

Stetson keeps company with the likes of Baylor and Furman among prominent Deep South institutions with historic ties to the Baptist Church. The common thread is conservatism, and business is easily the most popular program. Stetson is also strong in music and has a specialty in sport and exercise science.

Website: www.stetson.edu
Location: Suburban
Total Enrollment: 2,505
Undergraduates: 2,174
Male/Female: 43/57
SAT Ranges: V 510–610
  M 500–620
ACT Range: 21–26
Financial Aid: 57%
Expense: Pr $ $
Phi Beta Kappa: Yes
Applicants: 1,942
Accepted: 80%
Enrolled: 36%
Grad in 6 Years: 61%
Returning Freshmen: 77%
Academics: ✍ ✍ ✍
Social: ☎ ☎ ☎
Q of L: ★ ★ ★
Admissions: (386) 822-7100
Email Address:
  admissions@stetson.edu

Strongest Programs
  Accounting and Finance
  Music Performance
  Sport and Exercise Science
  Religious Studies
  Education
  Psychology

Stetson University urges students to take off their hats and stay awhile—so much the better if the hats are of the cowboy variety, since the school takes its name from the maker of the famed ten-gallon hat. Exceptional programs in music performance, accounting, and finance are highlights here, though the school also boasts comprehensive offerings in fields from Russian studies to religion, and from psychology to health sciences and sport management. The high quality of classroom instruction is augmented by Stetson's small size, says a junior: "You can make friends with professors as easily as with students. You recognize the faces, and know some by heart."

Located halfway between Walt Disney World and Daytona Beach, Stetson's 165-acre campus features mostly brick structures in architectural styles from Gothic to Moorish to Southern Colonial. A few eccentric wood buildings are also scattered about, though the theme is decidedly old-fashioned, with landscaping that relies largely on royal palms and oak trees. New structures include an addition to the duPont-Ball Library, providing space for distance learning and more books.

While undergraduates apply to Stetson as a whole, they enroll in one of three schools: music, business administration, or arts and sciences. General education requirements include two freshman English courses, and one course each in oral communications, math, civilization, fine arts, religious heritage, and contemporary culture. Students must also take one to two courses in the natural and social sciences, demonstrate

"You can make friends with professors as easily as with students."

foreign language proficiency, and—for arts and sciences majors—complete a research project. The Stetson Undergraduate Research Experience (SURE) provides stipends for students who do their research in the summer.

Business is Stetson's most popular program, with finance and accounting particularly noteworthy. Novel programs for aspiring tycoons include the Roland George Investments initiative, where would-be money managers work with an actual cash portfolio worth $2.5 million. (In 2000, the students achieved a 37 percent return.) The Prince Entrepreneurial Program offers access to successful entrepreneurs, who mentor Stetson students as they create business plans and attempt to run their own companies. The Family Business Center offers tips on how to manage a family enterprise. Stetson's music department is notable for expertise in brass instruments, organ, and voice. The digital arts program prepares students for careers in computer graphics, and teaches them how to translate music and video into multimedia content on the Internet. The College of Arts and Sciences has recently added a major in aquatic and marine biology.

Stetson's honors program allows eighty-five students to take interdisciplinary courses and create their own majors. The school offers study-abroad programs in England, Mexico, Russia, Germany, Spain, France, and Hong Kong, along with summer programs focused on language (Mexico) and business (Austria), and internship opportunities in Germany, England, and Latin America. Each year, professors also lead short off-campus study trips during semester breaks, taking students to such places as Turkey, Greece, and the Czech Republic. Stetson's education department has partnered with the Walt Disney Company and Osceola County School Board to develop a state-of-the-art school and teaching academy in the Disney-created city of Celebration, Florida. Weaker departments include theater arts and philosophy.

Stetson's Academic Quality Initiative is working to make the school more competitive, by raising admission standards. For now, though, there are three main types of people on campus, says a history major: "Very smart and motivated; rich kids who aren't as smart; and average students (the majority). Rollins College most likely has the same climate due to its price tag, but I sometimes think I'm in high school again." A psychology major disputes this assertion, calling the quality of teaching "top-notch" and insisting that the emphasis at Stetson is not (yet) on competing for grades. "The university wants students to think freely, and that's accomplished by asking questions," the junior says. "Professors keep

> **"The university wants students to think freely, and that's accomplished by asking questions."**

students' minds active and interested—this is what motivates students to work." Administrators say two-thirds of the classes taken by freshmen have twenty-five or fewer students, and the rest have fifty or less.

Three-quarters of Stetson's students are native Floridians, and the same fraction graduated from public high school. They're generally conservative and tend to lean Republican, though there isn't much interest or involvement in student government, a junior says. Historically, Stetson was affiliated with the Baptist Church, but it's now independent, so chapel worship services have been replaced by nondenominational presentations on ethics and social responsibility. African-Americans constitute nearly 4 percent of the student body, Hispanics almost 6 percent, and Asian-Americans 2 percent. The most pressing issues on campus include the role of the Greek system and how best to enforce alcohol policies, students say.

Seventy percent of Stetson students live in the dorms, which are "much better than those at state schools," says a junior. "Students higher up on the food chain, credit-wise, have a better selection of rooms," and singles are reserved for juniors and seniors. All but two of the dorms are coed, and students say the nicest options are Emily Hall, Chaudoin, Stetson, and Conrad. Still, they say more people would move off campus if the school didn't assess a financial penalty for doing so. The cafeteria has been renovated to resemble a food court, with a variety of culinary options, including stir-frying your own dish. Students may buy seven, fifteen, or twenty-one meals a week, and may also spend those tickets at the campus coffee shop, the Hat Rack.

Stetson's fraternities attract 33 percent of the men, and sororities draw 29 percent of the women. They monopolize much of the social life because alcohol is prohibited in the dorms, and the town of DeLand ("deadland") is almost as dry as the campus. DeLand "is not Tallahassee or Gainesville," sighs a junior. "It's very small,

> **"Students higher up on the food chain, credit-wise, have a better selection of rooms."**

everyone knows what goes on in your life, town residents are primarily elderly people. There's a few small bars, and one club." (One student claims the lack of distraction is actually a good thing.) For fun, then, students rely on Orlando (forty minutes away) and Daytona (twenty minutes), hitting the beach, strolling the Universal

Stetson was affiliated with the Baptist Church, but it's now independent, so chapel worship services have been replaced by nondenominational presentations on ethics and social responsibility.

When your birthday rolls around, don't forget to wear your bathing suit, because it's a tradition to be tossed into the mid-campus Holler Fountain by your peers.

Studios CityWalk, or watching the Daytona 500. Other options include Disney World, Epcot Center, and Cape Canaveral. Back on campus, the Council for Student Activities brings big-name acts to campus, such as *Saturday Night Live*'s Jimmy Fallon and the band Sister Hazel. Music majors also stage concerts, and students look forward to annual events like Homecoming, a community-service day known as Into the Streets, and Greenfeather, a week when student groups compete to raise money for charity. When your birthday rolls around, don't forget to wear your bathing suit, because it's a tradition to be tossed into the mid-campus Holler Fountain by your peers.

Stetson's varsity teams compete in Division I, though one student says the focus here is mostly academics, not athletics. Still, the school's baseball team won a conference championship in 2000, and women's softball and men's soccer did the same in 2001. Students enjoy cheering for "Mad Hatter" teams, especially in baseball, basketball, soccer, and golf, and also participate enthusiastically in the competitive intramural leagues. The new Hollis Wellness Center includes a field house, outdoor pool, game room, dance studio, and exercise room.

Stetson students know getting an education is far more important than getting a tan. They bask in the one-on-one attention freely given at this Sunshine State university. "It's very comforting, at a place away from home, to see people I know regularly," a junior says. "The small classes are also a definite plus."

If You Apply To ➤ **Stetson:** Early decision: Nov. 1. Rolling admissions and financial aid: Mar. 15. Housing: June 1. Does not guarantee to meet demonstrated need. Campus interviews: recommended, evaluative. No alumni interviews. SATs or ACTs: required. SAT IIs: optional. Accepts the Common Application and electronic applications. Essay question: significant experience or achievement with special meaning; issue of personal, local, or national concern; or influential person.

Stevens Institute of Technology

Castle Point on the Hudson, Hoboken, NJ 07030

Stevens ranks with Clarkson and Worcester Polytech among East Coast technical institutes that offer intimacy and personalized education. Youth-oriented Hoboken is a major plus and a quicker commute to Manhattan than most places in Brooklyn.

Forget the stereotypical image of the sterile engineering school devoid of wackiness and a social life. It bears no resemblance to Stevens Institute of Technology. Just across the Hudson River from Manhattan, Stevens students pursue a valuable engineering degree in an atmosphere of fun and camaraderie. Whether it's an ever-growing varsity sports scene, close teacher-student relationships, or a commitment to shaping students who can handle the high-tech world, Stevens is breaking the mold.

Stevens' fifty-five-acre parklike campus is punctuated by an eclectic mix of architecture. Many of the residence halls and administrative buildings are red brick, while classrooms and labs range from historical ivy-covered brownstones to modern glass-and-steel structures. Campus construction includes a renovation of the DeBaun playing field and full-service student center.

Stevens was the first college in the country to offer the degree of mechanical engineering, and now offers majors in the fields of business, engineering, applied sciences, computer science, and even the humanities (degrees are offered in English and American lit, history, and philosophy). But engineering, be it mechanical, biomedical, chemical, civil, electrical, environmental, or computer, is the indisputable king of the campus. New majors include computational science and science and technology. As if it would be difficult, the school tries to ensure that all students are computer fluent, not just literate, by the time they leave. Hence, all freshmen receive a new personal notebook computer.

Stevens is organized into three schools: the Charles V. Schaefer, Jr. School of Engineering, the Wesley J. Howe School of Technology Management, and the Arthur E. Imperatore School of Sciences and Arts. This organization is intended to allow Stevens to better meet the changing technological needs of business and industry by fostering collaboration across academic departments. A guiding concept at the school is Technogenesis, which encourages students to put their research and innovation into practice. For the first two years in the engineering school, students must follow a core curriculum stressing courses in the sciences and in broad areas of engineering, followed by technical electives that culminate in a senior design project. The

> **"The majority of Stevens students want to be engineers, lawyers, doctors, etc.."**

business program and the applied sciences each have their own curriculum guidelines. In addition, students must complete four semesters of calculus, eight semesters of humanities, and six semesters of physical education. But never fear, there are ways to get around this predestined courseload. For example, students not quite up to the intensity of Stevens's academic prescription may arrange for a five-year decelerated program, without extra tuition charges. Freshmen follow a core program in their chosen curriculum. Juniors can attend the school's program in Scotland, or can study abroad in one of more than fifty countries through the International Student Exchange Program. Stevens has initiated a cooperative education program, which offers all students a chance to earn on-the-job training (and earn more than $53,000 in some cases) over a five-year period. Stevens also has an active recruiting program with major corporations, entrepreneurial firms, and the government.

Students are more than pleased with their professors' teaching ability. "They have a heart for teaching and they love to see their students do well," a freshman says. All courses are taught by full professors and are usually taught in "recitations" of fewer than twenty-five students. Exams are taken under a successful student-run honor system. Given the subject matter, no one considers the workload unreasonable, and tutorial help is readily available. Students are competitive and focus heavily on their GPAs, but still, study groups abound. Stevens students have to remember to unwind after all that academic stress, or "they'll go crazy," says a computer science major.

Stevens draws half of its students from the greater New York area, and 15 percent of the students commute. Seventy percent come from public high school, and 53 percent graduated in the top tenth of their class. Minorities make up 37 percent of the student body; 22 percent are Asian-Americans, 10 percent are Hispanic, and 5 percent are African-American. Female student enrollment is 23 percent, a high percentage for a technical school. And when men and women get together here, they have no trouble finding something to talk about. "The majority of Stevens students wants to be engineers, lawyers, doctors, etc.," says one student. Admissions staffers look more closely at high-school grades, especially in math and science, than at test scores; interviews are required; and letters of recommendation from teachers, and essays are essential. Students praise the school's financial-

> **"It's a cozy extension of Manhattan. There are 150 bars and restaurants in the square-mile town of Hoboken."**

aid policy, and with 85 percent of the student body receiving some sort of aid, most speak from experience. In addition to need-based funding, Stevens also awards academic merit scholarships, ranging from $1,000 to full tuition.

Eighty-five percent of students live in the dorms, forgoing the almost impossible, very expensive housing hunt in the Hoboken area. Students say housing at

(Continued)
Academics: ✏️ ✏️ ✏️
Social: ☎ ☎
Q of L: ★ ★ ★ ★
Admissions: (201) 216-5194
Email Address:
admissions@stevens-tech.edu

Strongest Programs
Chemical Engineering
Computer Engineering
Mechanical Engineering
Electrical Engineering
Chemical Biology
Computer Science
Business

Students not quite up to the intensity of Stevens's academic prescription may arrange for a five-year decelerated program, without extra tuition charges.

Stevens is adequate and well maintained, and each room is hooked into the campus-wide wireless computer network. The seven undergraduate residence halls are conveniently located at the center of campus. As for looks, Tech Hall stands out among the crowd. An ultramodern dorm with carpets, telephones, and private bathrooms in each room, it has "all the conveniences of a modern hotel," says one student. The only difference is you can't make reservations at Stevens. Rooms are assigned by lottery or by squatter's rights. After the first year, students can, and often do, move into fraternities, old brownstones off campus, or nearby university-owned apartments. As for dining services, students report that the cafeteria food isn't anything to write home about, although there is a variety to choose from. One student dryly remarks that the variety involves "the same stuff day in and day out."

Those who don't go home can take advantage of the "extensive pleasures" of Manhattan, just across the Hudson, or kill time until the evening fraternity parties, which are the most popular of the on-campus weekend activities. About one-third of the student body go Greek, but they don't define the campus social scene. Students also benefit from the revitalization of Hoboken. "It's a cozy extension of Manhattan," says a

"Everyone gets together on ridiculously named teams and blows off steam."

science and technology major. "There are 150 bars and restaurants in the square-mile town of Hoboken." The dorms are substance-free, but the frats are nearby to quench one's thirst.

Being at a small school with a lot of engineers also gives students a chance to be editor of the college newspaper or deejay on the campus radio station without being edged out by a journalism or communications major. Fifteen minutes and a cheap PATH train ticket will land you in the middle of Manhattan's Greenwich Village. Beaches and ski slopes are within a ninety-minute drive.

Sports are popular at Stevens, especially intramurals, for which "everyone gets together on ridiculously named teams and blows off steam," in games such as floor hockey and bombardment. But Stevens is working hard on the varsity field, too. Over the past two years, teams have brought home about a dozen pennants. The women's swim, soccer, and volleyball teams are playing stronger than ever while men's lacrosse, soccer, baseball, and fencing teams are scoring high.

So there aren't many women at Stevens and the workload is pretty intense. But the end result of a stint at this small school is usually a lucrative job or a spot at a top graduate school, a close band of friends, and a sharp awareness of cutting-edge technology. When you add in a killer view of Manhattan and the myriad experiences that wonderful city has to offer, it makes a top-notch engineering education seem like icing on the cake.

Overlaps

Rensselaer Polytechnic, Cornell University, Carnegie Mellon, MIT, Cal Tech

If You Apply To ➤

Stevens: Early decision: Nov. 1. Regular admissions and financial aid: Feb. 15. Housing: May. 1. Guarantees to meet demonstrated need. Campus and alumni interviews: required, evaluative. SATs: required. SAT IIs: recommended. Accepts electronic applications. Essay question: personal statement.

Susquehanna offers welcome relief from the plodding, unimaginative education at many universities. The university's innovative core curriculum includes personal development and transition skills (e.g., computer proficiency) in addition to more conventional topics. Best-known for its business program.

"Susquewho?" That's the question many students ask when they're first introduced to this undergraduate institution. While it may not be a household name, Susquehanna University is making a reputation for itself. Challenging courses, friendly faculty, and an increasing emphasis on global community make SU a good place to expand your mind and enjoy lush scenery. "SU is gorgeous year-round," says a junior. "It's a place that makes me feel at home and puts me at ease when I'm stressed."

Susquehanna's campus is beautiful; with more than two hundred lush acres located on the banks of the Susquehanna River. Most of the fifty buildings on campus are brick, with Georgian the predominant architectural style. Selinsgrove Hall, built in 1858, and Seibert Hall, built in 1901, are on the National Register of Historic Places. The campus is compact and serene. In 2001, SU broke ground for a new $7.5 million music and art center and completed construction of a three-building complex to house nearly one hundred students.

SU's best academic programs are in business and the sciences. The Sigmund Weis School of Business is not only one of the most striking building on campus, but a prestigious accredited business program as well, which attracts the most majors on campus. The Weis School also sponsors a semester in London exclusively for its junior business majors. The business school, along with the other majors, encourages SU students to take summer internships as a crucial part of their educational search and future job search. Susquehanna is becoming increasingly recognized for its science programs, especially biology, biochemistry, and environmental science. Weaker departments at SU include classical languages and art, which are hampered by their small size and lack of funds. New minors in health studies, Jewish studies, and diversity studies have been added to the curriculum, and the urban studies minor has been dropped.

> **"SU is gorgeous year-round. It's a place that makes me feel at home and puts me at ease when I am stressed."**

Susquehanna's unusual core curriculum consists of three components: personal development (wellness/fitness and career development); transition skills (including computer proficiency, logical reasoning, and foreign languages); and world perspectives (social sciences, humanities, and sciences). All freshmen must take a writing seminar (or its honors equivalent) that involves small-group readings and discussion of a particular author. Reading centers around a common contemporary work, with the author often visiting campus to partake in the seminar. A seven-week orientation experience is offered to first-year students; topics include study skills, stress management, and interpersonal communication. Freshmen also have access to the Susquehanna Education in Leadership program, which begins with an all-day retreat and is followed by four seminars throughout the fall semester that focus on leadership styles, listening skills, time management, dealing with conflict, and team building.

For about fifty students a year, the academic experience is defined by the Susquehanna Honors Program. Unlike other programs in schools of similar size, SU's program does not separate its students from the rest of the campus. Instead, it allows students to take most of their classes in other classes with the general student body,

Website: www.susqu.edu
Location: Small town
Total Enrollment: 1,829
Undergraduates: 1,829
Male/Female: 42/58
SAT Ranges: V 520–610
    M 520–620
Financial Aid: 70%
Expense: Pr $ $
Phi Beta Kappa: No
Applicants: 2,369
Accepted: 75%
Enrolled: 28%
Grad in 6 Years: 77%
Returning Freshmen: 86%
Academics: ✐ ✐ ✐
Social: ☎ ☎ ☎
Q of L: ★ ★ ★ ★
Admissions: (800) 326-9672
    or (570) 372-4260
Email Address:
    suadmiss@susqu.edu

Strongest Programs
  Biology/Biochemistry
  Business
  Music
  Psychology
  English
  Communication
  Environmental Science

The Write Option program allows qualified applicants (those in the top fifth of their class) the option to submit two graded writing samples in place of SAT or ACT scores.

thus creating a balance between freedom of choice and a challenging education. Honors students or not, most agree that SU offers a rigorous academic climate. "Depending on the major you select, your courseload can be moderately easy to close to impossible," says a math major.

Student-faculty interaction is one of Susquehanna's strong points, and students have high praise for their professors. "The faculty is committed to Susquehanna's concept of education: student-centered, undergraduate only. They are committed to their students," says a senior. SU students may take classes at nearby Bucknell University and study abroad on almost every continent. The school also offers several study programs in Washington, D.C., as well as a 3–2 engineering program with the University of Pennsylvania. SU offers scholarships, but there are no athletic scholarships. An assistantship program for outstanding first-year students combines a $10,500 scholarship with hands-on work with a professor or staff member (ten hours per week). Past positions have included university archivist, international education, choir manager, wetlands research, and computer modeling of liquid surfaces. Families also have the option of making monthly tuition payments, available through outside vendors.

> "Depending on the major you select, our courseload can be moderately easy to close to impossible."

SU students are down-to-earth, hardworking kids. Sixty-three percent are from Pennsylvania, and 85 percent attended public high school. At a school in which 92 percent of the students are white, and which is "dominated by middle- and upper-class conservative Republicans," most agree that ethnic diversity is lacking. A communications major offers, "Diversity and multiculturalism are big issues. The university wants the student body to be more diverse."

Residence halls are described as "comfortable." A senior says, "Dorm rooms are big with great closets. All housing is pretty equal." Students must get permission to live off campus, and the 20 percent of students who have that privilege are selected by lottery. Cafeteria food is considered average, although a senior claims the "quality has declined sharply over the past three semesters." Campus security receives mixed reviews. "I feel safe because I'm on a small campus," says a student, "not because of campus security."

Favorite campus traditions include a candlelight Christmas service, a pumpkin that mysteriously appears at Halloween, and a Thanksgiving dinner at which faculty members serve traditional fare to the students.

Greeks dominate the nightlife of Susquehanna, where 26 percent of the men and 27 percent of the women belong to fraternities or sororities. Students twenty-one and over are allowed to drink on campus, but most acknowledge that underage drinking is "as easy as asking." Favorite campus traditions include a candlelight Christmas service, a pumpkin that mysteriously appears at Halloween, and a Thanksgiving dinner at which faculty members serve traditional fare to the

> "Diversity and multiculturalism are big issues. The university wants the student body to be more diverse."

students. Sports are popular among Susquehanna students, especially when the football team plays Lycoming College. Recent MAC championships were won by men's golf and baseball and women's indoor track.

Outside the university, Selinsgrove is "a small, rural, quaint town" with several restaurants and stores. A biochemistry major says, "We are not located in a 'college town.'" For those with cars, New York and Philadelphia are three hours away, and Penn State is an hour away. SU began by preparing students for the ministry and the university's commitment to the community has remained strong. Each year, two-thirds of the student population volunteer on major community-service projects.

At Susquehanna, "the professors care about their students," a biochemistry major says. A classmate adds that the "personal atmosphere, great faculty-student relationships, and beautiful campus" make Susquehanna worthwhile—and make it a name worth remembering among strong regional colleges.

Overlaps

Bucknell, Gettysburg, Dickinson, Muhlenberg, Penn State

If You Apply To ➤	**Susquehanna:** Rolling admissions: Mar. 1. Early decision: Dec. 15. Financial aid: Mar. 1 (preferred), May 1. Meets demonstrated need of 26%. Campus interviews: recommended, evaluative. Alumni interviews: optional, informational. SAT I or ACT: required; optional for students in top 20% of their class. Accepts the Common Application and electronic applications. Essay question: significant experience; issue of concern; accomplishments since high school (if applicable); or graded high-school paper.

Swarthmore College

500 College Avenue, Swarthmore, PA 19081-1397

Only at Swarthmore could the existence of a football program become a moral issue. The college finally axed it because recruiting football players skewed the atmosphere of intellectualism that the college holds dear. The college's honors program gives hardy souls a taste of graduate school, where most Swatties invariably end up.

Swarthmore College's leafy-green campus may be just eleven miles from Philadelphia, but students say they don't see much of the City of Brotherly Love. They're too busy trying to finish their work. Even for the extremely talented students who manage to get in, "misery poker is the most popular form of procrastination," quips a junior. That said, most competition in the classroom is self-motivated, a freshman reports. With no class rank and no dean's list, students push themselves for learning's sake. "There is a unique willingness to learn to view the world from different perspectives," one student explains. "Swarthmore students take each other seriously; we're always thinking, trying to figure out what we can learn from each other, and trying to share what we know."

Swarthmore's 330-acre campus is a nationally registered arboretum, distinguished by rolling wooded hills. Two-, three-, and four-story buildings with natural stone exteriors, shaped roofs, and cornices are the norm, fostering a quiet, collegiate atmosphere. The Mullan Tennis Center opened in 2000, with indoor courts, cross-training machines, and other fitness equipment. A $77 million science center will be completed in April 2004, providing

"Misery poker is the most popular form of procrastination."

students and faculty with eighty-thousand square feet of new lab space, state-of-the-art lecture halls, and flexible workstations that are more computer-friendly.

Swarthmore requires students to take three courses in each of its three divisions—Humanities, Natural Sciences and Engineering, and Social Sciences—and at least two of the three must be in different departments. Students must also complete twenty courses outside their majors, demonstrate foreign-language competency, and fulfill a physical education requirement, which includes a swimming test. Enrollment in the optional freshman seminars is kept low, to ensure close interaction with professors. In Swarthmore's unique honors program, students take four intense seminars during their last four terms, each with four to eight peers. These require extensive reading and writing, but have no final exams until the end of senior year. At that time, external examiners—faculty members from other universities—administer a series of oral and written tests in four areas of study. About a third of Swat's juniors and seniors take the honors option, after demonstrating—through their academic records—that they can handle the work.

The college has boosted the number of departments in which students may pursue honors to include studio and performing arts, as well as study abroad; Swarthmore sponsors programs in France, Japan, Poland, and Spain, and its Office of Foreign Study helps arrange programs in other countries. Cross-registration is

Website:
  www.swarthmore.edu
Location: Suburban
Total Enrollment: 1,467
Undergraduates: 1,467
Male/Female: 47/53
SAT Ranges: V 690–770
  M 670–760
Financial Aid: 49%
Expense: Pr $ $ $ $
Phi Beta Kappa: Yes
Applicants: 3,504
Accepted: 26%
Enrolled: 42%
Grad in 6 Years: 92%
Returning Freshmen: 95%
Academics: ✑ ✑ ✑ ✑ ✑
Social: ☎ ☎ ☎
Q of L: ★ ★ ★ ★
Admissions: (610) 328-8300
Email Address: admissions@
  swarthmore.edu

Strongest Programs
  Biology
  Economics
  English Literature
  Sociology/Anthropology
  History
  Political Science

also offered with nearby Haverford, Bryn Mawr, and Penn, and a semester exchange program includes Harvey Mudd, Middlebury, Mills, Pomona, Rice, and Tufts. Through the Venture Program,* students who tire of staring at the chalkboard may take time off for short-term jobs in areas of academic or professional interest.

Back on campus, the most popular majors are economics, biology, and political science, with English literature, psychology, and sociology and anthropology not

> **"Swarthmore students take each other seriously; we're always thinking, trying to figure out what we can learn from each other, and trying to share what we know."**

far behind. The school's engineering department also draws raves, unusual for an institution so focused on the liberal arts. Perhaps that's because the department believes in a "holistic" approach, requiring majors to take more than a third of their courses in disciplines other than engineering and science. Swarthmore is known for its intense academic climate, and the unofficial campus motto is "Anywhere else it would have been an A." Still, a junior says, "people come here out of a love for learning, and expect and are met with a rigorous courseload." They work in groups to bear that load, and also get help from Swarthmore's professors, who are a learned bunch. "How well they impart that knowledge onto the students may vary," says a freshman. "But I've found all my professors to have a wealth of knowledge in their fields."

A $77 million science center will be completed in April 2004, providing students and faculty with eighty thousand square feet of new lab space, state-of-the-art lecture halls, and flexible workstations that are more computer-friendly.

Aside from teaching, Swarthmore professors also serve as advisors, each helping a small group of students choose their classes each semester. Students are likewise assigned to Student Academic Mentors, who shepherd them through the transition to college and the first year on campus. The vast majority of courses have fifty students or fewer, and most have twenty-five or less, but students say it's fairly easy to get into "closed" sections—just show up to the first few sessions and speak to the professor about your interest in the subject. There are no teaching assistants, and among the more offbeat programs are Peace and Conflict Studies and Interpretation Theory. Offbeat doesn't mean easy, though. The Swarthmore library—with one million volumes, and subscriptions to more than 9,300 periodicals—is *usually* home to serious studying, except during the annual winter event known as the McCabe Mile, when students race eighteen laps amid the bookshelves in the basement. The starting gun is the slam of a book—and the winner gets a roll of toilet paper.

Students come to Swarthmore from around the country and the world; only 11 percent are Pennsylvanians. The student body is 8 percent African-American, 16 percent Asian-American, and 8 percent Hispanic; a new "Diversity Workshop" has been instituted for all first-year students in the week after Orientation. It may not be necessary, though, as Swarthmore attracts students who are socially and politically aware. "It's a very liberal campus, with a tiny Republican contingent," says a junior. Swarthmore's Quaker roots come through in the concern and respect students have for others. "Recently, there's

> **"It's such a great place to expand your horizons and discover what it is that you love to do.**

been a lot of activism to secure a living wage for the college's staff, and the college responded by increasing staff minimum pay," a freshman explains. Another example of Quaker tradition: the school's commitment to equal access means that all campus activities—dances, parties, movies, and so on—are free.

The college's twelve dorms are home to 93 percent of Swarthmore students, who are guaranteed housing for four years if they want it, says an art history major. The biggest problem lately has been rising enrollment, causing a bit of a housing crunch. All but two of the dorms are coed by room, and many have been renovated, though opinions are mixed, with a junior calling the residence halls "functional, not luxurious," and a freshman saying they are "really nice and spacious."

Freshmen are assigned to traditional double rooms, while upperclassmen enter a lottery to get singles, two-room doubles, or suites; the dorms are not separated by class year or academic interest. First-year students must buy twenty meals a week, and upperclassmen choose from fourteen- and twenty-meal plans. "The cafeteria food is actually decent," says a surprised biology major.

Most social life at Swarthmore takes place on campus, and it often begins late, since students hit the books until 10 or 11 P.M., and then head out for fun. Options range from parties, dances, and movies to performances and concerts by student troupes. There's also a student-run café, and Pub Night every Thursday. When it comes to alcohol, Swarthmore follows Pennsylvania law, which states that you must be twenty-one to drink. Monitors work the doors of every campus party, checking IDs, says a freshman. But "the unofficial policy is: act like an adult, and we'll treat you like one," says a junior. This extends to the dorms, which are stocked with condoms. Swarthmore's two fraternities attract 6 percent of the men; women are out of luck, since there are no sororities. The Greeks and other campus groups volunteer in both Philadelphia and the nearby smaller town of Chester.

The village of Swarthmore, known as the "ville," has some stores, a pizza shop, and "the usual college-town staples," but while it's "really cute," says one student, "it isn't a place for off-campus social activity." For that, students hop the commuter rail into Philadelphia, where many temptations await, including concerts, dance clubs, museums, and four different professional sports. The King of Prussia mall, with a megaplex movie theater and department stores including Nordstrom and Bloomingdale's, isn't far, either.

With Swarthmore's focus on academics, athletics aren't a high priority—the school competes in Division III, and the board of trustees recently abolished the football team, fearing that the need to give admissions preference to football players would undermine academic quality. Women's sports are the true powerhouses, with swimming, tennis, and basketball bringing home conference championships in 2001, and badminton (!) also strong. Any victory over archrival Haverford will have Swatties swelling with pride. Intramurals are also popular, with the rugby team's Dash for Cash fund-raiser a favored annual event. Players streak through the halls of the main administration building, where spectators—including faculty and administrators—hold out money for them to grab. In the Crum Regatta, student-made boats float in nearby Crum Creek—Swarthmore's answer to the America's Cup.

Swarthmore students are "intense, quirky, passionate, and activists," says a junior. The school imbues them with the sense that they can accomplish anything to which they dedicate their hearts and minds. "The people at Swarthmore just make for an incredible college experience," says a freshman. "It's such a great place to expand your horizons and discover what it is that you love to do." A biology major agrees. Swarthmore, she says, "is a place where you can get really involved with all your different interests, have an amazing education, and have fun—at the same time!"

The college has boosted the number of departments in which students may pursue honors to include studio and performing arts, as well as study abroad; Swarthmore sponsors programs in France, Japan, Poland, and Spain.

Overlaps

Yale, Harvard, Princeton, Brown, Stanford

If You Apply To ➤

Swarthmore: Early decision: Nov. 15, Jan. 1. Regular admissions: Jan. 1. Financial aid: Feb. 15. Guarantees to meet demonstrated need. Campus or alumni interviews: recommended, evaluative. SATs or ACTs: required. SAT IIs: required (writing and two others; math required for engineering students). Accepts the Common Application and electronic applications. Essay questions: why Swarthmore, activities or personal interests to which you feel particularly committed, and two-page personal statement.

Sweet Briar College

Box B, Sweet Briar, VA 24595

Sweet Briar offers the pure women's college experience—served up with plenty of tradition and gift-wrapped in one of the nation's most beautiful campuses. SBC is the country girl next to in-state rivals Randolph-Macon and Hollins. Academic standouts include English and the life sciences

Website: www.sbc.edu
Location: Rural
Total Enrollment: 738
Undergraduates: 738
Male/Female: 3/97
SAT Ranges: V 505–630
  M 490–605
ACT Range: 21–26
Financial Aid: 51%
Expense: Pr $ $
Phi Beta Kappa: Yes
Applicants: 440
Accepted: 81%
Enrolled: 44%
Grad in 6 Years: 73%
Returning Freshmen: 82%
Academics: ✍ ✍ ✍
Social: ☎ ☎
Q of L: ★ ★ ★ ★
Admissions: (434) 381-6142
  or (800) 381-6142
Email Address:
  admissions@sbc.edu

Strongest Programs
  Psychology
  Biology
  Chemistry
  Government
  English/Creative Writing
  History
  Art History
  Modern Languages and
    Literature

Indiana Fletcher Williams, who founded Sweet Briar College in 1901, envisioned a school that would educate young women "to be useful members of society." These days, the college—in the heart of beautiful, rural Virginia—produces more career women than homemakers. A few men even make an appearance as non-degree or exchange students. But this remains a place where, in the words of a popular bumper sticker, "Women are leaders and men are guests." Says a government major: "Professors and students develop intense, wonderful, special relationships, built around a solid and challenging academic experience."

Set on 3,300 acres of rolling green hills, dotted with small lakes and surrounded by the Blue Ridge Mountains, Sweet Briar's campus of early twentieth-century red-brick charmers is a picture of pastoral beauty. Sweet Briar House, now the president's residence, was the eighteenth-century home of the college's founder, and is listed on the National Register of Historic Places. The new Florence Elston Inn and Conference Center includes high-tech meeting rooms. There's also a new student center, and technology is always being upgraded.

Sweet Briar's general education program has four components: an English course called "Thought and Expression," Skills Requirements (oral and written communication, and quantitative reasoning), Experience Requirements (self-assessment, physical activity, and a major), and Knowledge Area Requirements (various courses, including Western and non-Western culture, foreign language, the arts, and economics, politics, and law). Seniors must pass a culminating exercise in their majors, which may include comprehensive exams. Students

> **"Academics are treated as top priority, making SBC a place conducive to studying, learning, and excelling."**

give high marks to Sweet Briar's programs in government, English (especially creative writing), history, and chemistry. The sciences benefit from state-of-the-art equipment such as a digital scanning electron microscope, modular laser lab, and a gas chromatograph/mass spectrograph. Psychology is the most popular major. The philosophy, religion, classical studies, German, and Italian departments have only one or two professors each, rendering them weaker, administrators say. Students may take classes in these disciplines at nearby Lynchburg College and Randolph-Macon Woman's College. A bachelor of fine arts degree was added in Fall 2002, allowing students to major in one artistic field and minor in another. Participating programs include creative writing, dance, music, studio art, and theater.

Sweet Briar's academic climate is "collegial, challenging, and vibrant," says a senior. "Academics are treated as top priority, making SBC a place conducive to studying, learning, and excelling." Most professors have terminal degrees in their fields, and the quality of teaching is exceptional, students report. "The low student-professor ratio allows teachers to know their students better, and gives students the opportunity to really enjoy the teaching," says a Spanish and business major. And with 40 percent of the faculty living on campus, "You get to know the faculty's spouses, kids, and dogs," says one woman. The Sweet Briar Honor Pledge, which states that "Sweet Briar women do not lie, cheat, steal, or violate the rights of others," makes possible self-scheduled exams and take-home tests. An honors program and self-designed majors allow some students to further challenge themselves.

Sweet Briar's Junior Year in France is the oldest and best known of its study-abroad programs. And the younger Junior Year in Spain program is gaining in popularity, as are exchanges with Germany's Heidelberg University and Oxford University in the U.K. It's also common for faculty to offer short courses abroad during semester breaks, such as a theater course in London or an antiquities course in Italy. Students can also spend time on other campuses through the Seven-College Exchange, the Tri-College Exchange, or 3–2 liberal arts and engineering programs. Classes end in early May, providing ample opportunity for internships. Sweet Briar's unusually strong alumnae network is helpful in arranging positions and housing in cities across the country.

Forty percent of Sweet Briar's student body hail from Virginia, and the school is becoming more diverse, with 4 percent African-American, 3 percent Hispanic, and 2 percent Asian-American. An increasing number of older "turning point" students also contribute a valued perspective. "We're very concerned with gay and lesbian rights, as well as racial and gender equity," says a sophomore international affairs major. "You can be 'politically different,' and you and your opinion will be respected," agrees a freshman government major. Various merit scholarships range from $500 to $15,000 each.

> **"The low student-professor ratio allows teachers to know their students better, and gives students the opportunity to really enjoy the teaching."**

Ninety-two percent of Sweet Briar's students live in the college's vintage dorms, which are more like stately antebellum homes, with sweeping wooden staircases, fireplaces, and furnished parlors. Thanks to lots of attention from the college, they have aged gracefully, with "hardwood floors and functioning ceiling fans," says a senior. "As of 2002–03, all have air-conditioning, and the rooms are spacious and light. With a few exceptions, students are required to live on campus all four years." Freshmen are advised to choose Reid, Grammer, or Randolph, though every hall has a fair share of students from all four classes. Student leaders are given the first shot at singles, and upperclassmen choose rooms in a lottery. Several dorms have twenty-four-hour male visitation, and administrators are considering the addition of newer, more independent housing for upperclassmen. All residents eat in the common dining hall.

When the weekend rolls around, the Sweet Briar Social Committee's annual fee is put to good use, covering mixers with other schools, theatrical performances, formal dances, and yearbooks. The committee's events attract men "like flies from all over," one student says—and if students don't like the ones who show up, frat parties beckon at Washington and Lee, Hampden-Sydney, and the University of Virginia (an hour away). Other popular road trips include Washington, D.C., and Virginia's beaches (three hours). Campus alcohol policies are "very strict," a sophomore says,

> **"You can be 'politically different,' and you and your opinion will be respected."**

and heavy drinking is rare—remember, these women *are* trying to preserve an image of gentility! SBC students volunteer at local schools and with Habitat for Humanity. And the Sweet Briar Outdoor Program (SWEBOP) has introduced hundreds to the joys of backpacking, canoeing, and white-water rafting with weekly expeditions. Students also lovingly nurture traditions such as Founder's Day, lantern bearing, step singing, and "tapping" for clubs. Students receive their class rings at the annual junior banquet; they are worn on the left pinkie.

SBC's Vixens compete in Division III, where the fencing team won a Virginia State Championship in 2001. Swimming, tennis, and field hockey are also popular,

Ninety-two percent of Sweet Briar's students live in the college's vintage dorms, which are more like stately antebellum homes, with sweeping wooden staircases, fireplaces, and furnished parlors. All now have air-conditioning.

The Sweet Briar Honor Pledge, which states that "Sweet Briar women do not lie, cheat, steal, or violate the rights of others," makes possible self-scheduled exams and take-home tests.

A popular Sweet Briar slogan: "Where women are athletes, and men are spectators."

having brought home Women's College Conference championships recently. And backed by the largest private indoor ring in the country, the equestrienne squad has snagged eight national championships. That's led to another Sweet Briar slogan: "Where women are athletes, and men are spectators."

Sweet Briar has transcended its reputation as a finishing school for well-bred daughters of Virginia. Women now come here for a well-balanced mix of academics, friendliness, and career preparation. While some complain about the remoteness of the school's rural location, most say the beauty of the campus and the sense of family that prevails are more than satisfactory compensation.

If You Apply To ➤

Sweet Briar: Early decision: Dec. 1. Regular admissions: Feb. 1. Financial aid: Mar. 1. Housing: May 1. Meets demonstrated need of 27%. Campus interviews: recommended, evaluative. Alumni interviews: optional, evaluative. SATs or ACTs: required. SAT IIs: recommended (three required for home-schooled students). Accepts the Common Application and electronic applications. Essay question: what you will get out of college and how Sweet Briar will help. Also, choose one or more of the following: influential course; powerful novel; what is needed to fully participate in the world community; significant historical event in which you would participate; cultural or social custom of your country, state, or region.

Syracuse University

201 Tolley Administration Bldg., Syracuse, NY 13244-1140

Syracuse has recast itself to make undergraduate education a top priority. Offerings such as the Gateway program provide small classes for first-year students. World-famous in communications, Syracuse is also strong in engineering and public affairs. Big East basketball provides solace during long winter nights.

Website: www.syracuse.edu
Location: City center
Total Enrollment: 14,421
Undergraduates: 10,702
Male/Female: 45/55
SAT Ranges: V 540–640
  M 570–660
Financial Aid: 60%
Expense: Pr $ $ $
Phi Beta Kappa: Yes
Applicants: 14,514
Accepted: 64%
Enrolled: 28%
Grad in 6 Years: 75%
Returning Freshmen: 92%
Academics: 🖋 🖋 🖋
Social: ☎ ☎ ☎
Q of L: ★ ★ ★
Admissions: (315) 443-3611
Email Address:
  orange@syr.edu

Anyone who has watched college sports is familiar with the bright orange color associated with Syracuse University. They have seen the screaming fans and the stadiums overflowing with cheering hordes. Beyond all the athletic fanfare is fanfare of another sort: Syracuse is constantly striving to meet its goal of becoming a premier student-centered research university. By fostering close relationships between students and faculty, expanding course offerings, and pouring loads of money into facility upgrades, Syracuse's reputation as an academic factory with killer sports teams is rapidly changing.

The Syracuse campus is located on a hill overlooking the town of Syracuse in central New York State. The Carrier Dome sits on the hillside like an oversized alien spacecraft. The character and mixture of architectural styles depict a continuously changing campus, which is grassy, full of trees, and bordered by residential neighborhoods. Fifteen of SU's 140 buildings are listed in the National Register of Historic Places. Many schools and colleges have restructured facilities to accommodate more faculty/student research, as well as social interaction between the two groups. All the dorms are wired with a high-speed communications network. The university is embarking on a multimillion-dollar campus-wide upgrade. There is a new $4.5 million environmental systems lab complex for engineering research and teaching; a new digital format for the broadcasting studio, plus CD and DVD burners; and state-of-the-art photography equipment and gallery space at the Menschel Center.

The academic programs are diverse. The Newhouse School of Public Communications, which has produced such media celebrities as NBC Sports announcer Bob Costas and Steve Kroft of *60 Minutes* is undoubtedly Syracuse's flagship. It offers leading programs in newspaper, magazine, and broadcast journalism, and is home to four cutting-edge computerized lab facilities for reporting and digital editing. Also well-known is the Maxwell School of Citizenship and Public Affairs, whose faculty members teach sought-after undergraduate economics, history, geography, political science, and social sciences. Teaming with NASA, the school now has a $3 million virtual aerospace engineering facility—one of three in the nation—where students have helped design a new reusable space launch vehicle. SU students

"Professors hold extensive office hours, give out home phone numbers, even arrive early to class to give students an opportunity to speak with them."

have also participated in NASA's reduced-gravity student flight programs. The College of Arts and Sciences is the largest college at Syracuse, and offers recognized programs in creative writing, philosophy, geography, and chemistry. The College of Human Services and Health Professions was recently formed. Students and the administration cite mathematics and foreign languages as weaker SU programs. The most popular majors are psychology, information management and technology, political science, marketing, and television/radio/film.

General education requirements vary, but all students are expected to take writing courses. Several schools and colleges subscribe to the Arts and Sciences core requirements, which include coursework in the sciences, math, social sciences, humanities, and contemporary issues. Entering freshmen must complete a writing seminar, and each school and college offers a small-group experience course, known as the Freshman Forum, to share common first-year experiences and stimulate discussion of academic and personal issues. The Gateway program allows freshmen to take introductory classes with senior faculty members in a small classroom setting. For upperclassmen, Syracuse offers a strong honors program based on seminars and independent research. New additions include a degree in music industry, the first

"Syracuse is incredibly diverse. Whoever you are, you can find a place to fit here."

in the nation, a dual major program combining information studies and technology with management, a B.S. in acting with an emphasis on stage management, and a minor in Latino-Latin American studies.

Despite the school's large size, students say professors are friendly and accessible. "They hold extensive office hours, give out home phone numbers, even arrive early to class to give students an opportunity to speak with them," a junior says. Career counseling is praised, but academic advising receives mixed reviews. Classes are usually small (fewer than twenty-five students) and registration can be easy. Of course, if you desperately want a class and can't get in, "if need be, beg," advises one senior.

Admissions standards differ among the various schools and are most rigorous in the professional schools, especially architecture, communications, and engineering. Forty percent of Syracuse's undergraduates come from the top 10 percent of their high-school class, and 78 percent attended public high school. African-Americans and Hispanics account for 7 and 4 percent of the student body, respectively, and Asian-Americans make up another 5 percent. "Syracuse is incredibly diverse. Whoever you are, you can find a place to fit here," says a senior. Big issues range from environmental issues to the Mideast conflict. But, as one computer science major says, "Syracuse is not a hotbed of political interest." Forty-four percent of the students are from New York State, and most of those hail from New York City and Long Island. There are about three hundred athletic scholarships in sports ranging from football and basketball to crew and lacrosse. Merit scholarships are also available, ranging from $1,000 to $12,000.

Housing on campus is clean and comfortable, and is provided all four years in modern and well-maintained halls. Seventy-three percent of the undergraduates

Teaming with NASA, the school now has a $3 million virtual aerospace engineering facility—one of three in the nation—where students have helped design a new reusable space launch vehicle. SU students have also participated in NASA's reduced-gravity student flight programs.

live in university housing. Syracuse is continually upgrading dorm facilities, and students appreciate the efforts. Freshmen and sophomores are required to live in the dorms, and should check out Brewster-Boland, Day, and Flint halls. The upper-class Skytop Apartments were recently refurbished from floor to ceiling. Living and dining in fraternity or sorority houses is another option, because 8 percent of the men and 13 percent of the women go Greek. As for campus safety, SU has a series of emergency alarms throughout the campus, and a card-key access system in all dorms. A bus service is available for students studying late at the library or in labs.

Students generally enjoy the town of Syracuse, which offers a variety of off-campus retreats. Many students are involved in the community through internships in the corporations and SU education students give more than forty thousand hours in community service in Syracuse. Downtown is within easy reach on foot or by convenient public transportation. Once there, the opportunities include an excellent art museum, a resident opera company, a symphony, and a string of movie theaters and restaurants. If you tire of the city life, several quaint country towns, complete with orchards, lakes, and waterfalls, are nearby, as are several ski resorts. The Turning Stone casino is a big draw. The six-story Carousel Mall, about ten minutes away, has an eighteen-theater cinema. Erie Boulevard is home to big chain stores, and the city's Armory Square is flanked with coffee shops, a great music store, clubs, and eateries.

The social life tends to stay on campus for freshmen and sophomores, and move off campus for upperclassmen. There are always activities available such as movies,

"Whether snowflakes are falling or students are lying on the quad soaking up the sun, SU has the perfect college feeling."

bowling, skating, and dancing. Students over twenty-one spend many an evening barhopping on Marshall Street, a lively strip near campus. For underage students, there is a campus club where student bands play and nonalcoholic drinks and snacks are free. Drama productions are frequent on the weekends, and popular road trips include Ithaca, Niagara Falls, Montreal, and Rochester.

The spacious Carrier Dome rocks every time the Orangemen take the field or the court. Football games against Miami and a basketball rivalry with Georgetown make for great fun and much enthusiasm during the year. In 2003, the men's basketball team rewarded its fans with the ultimate prize—a national Division I championship. The "painters" are famous at SU—they are the students who paint each letter of the school's name on their bare chests and run through rain, sleet, or snow to each home game in the Carrier Dome. Though the Dome seats thirty-three thousand for basketball—enough to shatter NCAA attendance records—tickets must still be parceled out by a lottery, to the disdain of some. Though receiving less attention, the men's lacrosse team has won a national championship, and the women's rowing team won a conference championship.

From special partnerships with NASA to opportunities to study abroad or help out right at home, students at Syracuse know they've got something unique. The place itself can be enough to inspire school spirit. "Whether snowflakes are falling or students are lying on the quad soaking up the sun," explains one public relations major, "SU has that perfect college feeling."

Overlaps

Boston University, NYU, Penn State— University Park, Cornell, University of Massachusetts— Amherst

University of Tennessee at Knoxville

Knoxville, TN 37996-0230

UT is in the middle of the pack among its southeastern rivals—behind UNC, U of Georgia, and Florida; ahead of Arkansas, Alabama, and Ole' Miss. As the only major public university in Tennessee, UT comes close to being all things to all students. Strong in business, engineering, and communications.

University of Tennessee students put a premium on school spirit, athletics, and academics—usually in that order. In the fall, more than one hundred thousand boisterous fans pack into one of the nation's largest on-campus football stadiums to watch the Volunteers play against national powerhouses like Florida, Alabama, and Arkansas. Also competitive are the SEC-dominating women's basketball and soccer teams and men's baseball teams. Amid this excitement, it's easy to forget that UT prides itself on having a strong academic program.

Set in the foothills of the Great Smoky Mountains, UT is in the heart of east Tennessee's urban hub and only a few miles away from Oak Ridge, Tennessee, home to the prominent Oak Ridge National Laboratory. The 511-acre campus has an array of architectural styles ranging from Gothic to Georgian to modern. Particularly noteworthy is the John C. Hodges Library—the largest one in the state—built in the shape of a ziggurat. Newest construction on campus includes a geography building and an addition to the Claxton Education Building.

Many strong academic programs are in preprofessional fields, most notably business, architecture, accounting, and engineering. On the liberal arts side, psychology and communications are popular majors. Several majors in French, German, and Spanish incorporate a concentration in international business. A cooperative arrangement with nearby Oak Ridge National Laboratory—the federal government's largest nonweapons lab—bolsters science and technology offerings, and involves more than four hundred students and faculty in majors as diverse as English and physics. The honors program at UT is a campus-wide program that offers qualified students scholarships, honors courses, seminars, and a chance to complete an original research project in collaboration with a faculty member. Students who participate in the Whittle Scholars Program are encouraged to pursue their leadership skills through campus and community organizations, and are given the opportunity to travel to a variety of different countries including Argentina, Australia, France, Mexico, and the Netherlands. The humanities, foreign languages, and philosophy programs are reportedly weak.

> **"UT has both laid-back and rigorous courses with the difficulty increasing each year."**

Competition varies, depending on the class, as does course difficulty. "UT has both laid-back and rigorous courses with the difficulty increasing each year," says a junior. UT faculty gets a mixed rating. "Most of my freshman classes were taught by teaching assistants and graduate students," said a chemistry major. Students report occasional problems with registration because preference is given to seniors, but none that would extend a four-year stay. "During the past two years, courses were difficult to get into because there were too many students attending UT," says a senior. Advising also gets mixed reviews, depending on the field of study, and students are expected to meet with their advisors each semester before registering. UT's general education requirements are fairly extensive and include two courses each in English composition, math, humanities, history, social sciences, and natural sciences, plus intermediate proficiency in a foreign language or multicultural studies.

Website: www.tennessee.edu
Location: City center
Total Enrollment: 25,890
Undergraduates: 20,009
Male/Female: 49/51
SAT Ranges: V 500–610
  M 500–620
ACT Range: 21–26
Financial Aid: 21%
Expense: Pub $ $
Phi Beta Kappa: Yes
Applicants: 10,171
Accepted: 62%
Enrolled: 61%
Grad in 6 Years: 56%
Returning Freshmen: 75%
Academics: ✍ ✍ ✍
Social: 🐿 🐿 🐿 🐿
Q of L: ★ ★ ★
Admissions: (865) 974-2184
Email Address:
  admissions@tennessee.edu

Strongest Programs
  Business
  Engineering
  Communications

Several majors in French, German, and Spanish incorporate a concentration in international business.

Business majors are immersed in a broad liberal arts program, including a foreign language requirement, during their first two years of study.

Eighty-two percent of the student body is made up of homegrown Tennesseans, and 26 percent of the undergrads graduated in the top tenth of their high-school class. Minority enrollment is low; African-Americans account for only 6 percent of the students, while Asian-Americans and Hispanics combine for 4 percent. Students also warn that the campus's size can lead to a phenomenon called the "Big Orange Screw," in which the impersonal bureaucratic system makes students' lives miserable.

"Most of my freshman classes were taught by teaching assistants and graduate stu-

Financial-aid opportunities are generous: more than three thousand merit scholarships are available, from $500 to full rides. An additional 360 athletic scholarships are awarded in sixteen sports.

Dorm rooms are average, and 67 percent of UT students live off campus. "They could be bigger, but couldn't they all?" says one psychology major. "They're better compared to most." The dorms are for the most part comfortable and well maintained, and about the only hitch is that some don't have air-conditioning (which can be brutal in August). Each of the dorms has a residence-hall association, which for a token fee provides check-out of sports equipment, games, cooking utensils, and other useful items. The university goes out of its way to ensure the security of the campus and the students. To this end, UT has installed remote alarm units that allow students to report a crime from anywhere on campus. "There are cops everywhere," a junior says. "As long as you're not stupid, you're fine."

Students warn that the campus's size can lead to the "Big Orange Screw," in which the impersonal bureaucratic system makes students' lives miserable.

Students say that the social life is "very active" both on and off-campus. The social calendar is dotted with numerous major events, including River Fest on the nearby Tennessee, Saturday Night on the Town, and the Dogwood Arts Festival. Greek life is growing more popular—14 percent of men and 18 percent of women go Greek. Alcohol flows freely, even for underage students. But nothing compares to the sea of orange that engulfs the campus on Saturday afternoons in the fall. More than one hundred thousand people jam the football stadium to see their Vols take on Southeast Conference rivals ("Alabama is a four-letter word" in these parts). Denizens liken football to religion in Knoxville, and in 1998 the Volunteers gained salvation in the form of a national championship. Coach Pat Summit's Lady Vols basketball team has won a record-breaking number of NCAA championships in recent years and enjoys tremendous crowds (drawing more fans than many NBA teams). Women's soccer enjoyed a successful 2001 season, ranking in the top twenty nationally for much of the fall.

Overlaps

Middle Tennessee State, Tennessee Tech, Auburn, Georgia, University of Memphis

The University of Tennessee is well known for its athletics, and administrators and students are hoping that it can develop the same reputation for academics. Though some may be turned off by the oft-sluggish bureaucracy, many will find the myriad of opportunities here at the "Big Orange" to be well worth the squeezing.

If You Apply To ➤ **UT:** Early action: Nov.1. Regular admissions: Jan. 15. Financial aid: March 1. Housing: Jan. 15. Campus and alumni interviews: optional, evaluative. SATs or ACTs: required, ACT preferred. Essay questions: significant experience or obstacle overcome; personally influential individual; accomplishment; personal and career objectives.

University of Texas at Austin

John Hargis Hall, Austin, TX 78712-1157

UT is on anybody's list of the top ten public universities in the nation. The Plan II liberal arts honors program is one of the nation's most renowned. Though it is also the capital of Texas, Austin ranks among the nation's best college towns.

The University of Texas at Austin has come a long way from where it began as a small school with only one building, eight teachers, two departments, and 221 students. Today, the UT campus is home to fifty thousand students and 2,580 professors. One of the most popular dorms—Jester Center—even has its own zip code. From its extensive academic programs to its powerful athletic teams to its location in one of the nation's ultimate college towns, the University of Texas has it all.

A four hundred–acre oasis near downtown Austin, replete with rolling hills, trees, creeks, and fountains, the campus features buildings ranging from "old, distinguished" limestone structures to "contemporary" Southwest architecture. Statues of famous Texans line the mall, and the fabled UT Tower is adorned with a large clock and chimes (a lifesaver for the unorganized). From the steps of the tower, one can see the verdant Austin hills. The outstanding library system at the University of Texas has more than seven million volumes located in nineteen different libraries across campus, and is the sixth-largest academic library system in the United States.

UT–Austin is one of the nation's largest single-campus universities, and some undergraduates complain that they are treated like livestock; long lines are commonplace, despite a telephone registration system. Many classes are extremely large, and smaller sections fill up quickly. Says a fine arts major, "Sometimes there is difficulty getting into classes, but it usually has to do with not getting the desired zsummer school, which offers slightly reduced class sizes, in order to graduate in four years. "A few majors actually require five years of school, but an extra year only strengthens your knowledge and

> "A few majors actually require five years of school, but an extra year only strengthens our knowledge and educates you more completely."

educates you more completely," rationalizes an architecture major. UT is a research-oriented institution, so the professors are often busy in the laboratories or the library. They do, however, have office hours. "The UT professors are intelligent and communicate well with their students," says a senior. Academic counseling draws praise.

The list of academic strengths at University of Texas is impressive for such a large school. Undergraduate offerings in accounting, architecture, botany, biology, business, foreign languages, and history are first-rate. The engineering and computer science departments are excellent and continue to expand. The English department is huge (ninety-five tenure-track professors) and students give it high marks, but say the art/photography department needs improvement. A new molecular biology building is in the works, and a new telescope is under construction for the prestigious Institute for Fusion Studies, which already boasts the world's largest telescope.

The late Pulitzer Prize–winning author James Michener was the major force behind the establishment of the Texas Center for Writers at UT, an interdisciplinary graduate program in fiction, poetry, playwriting, and screenwriting. The Plan II liberal arts honors program, a national model, is one of the oldest honors programs in the country, and one of the best academic deals anywhere. It offers qualified students a flexible curriculum, top-notch professors, small seminar courses, and individualized counseling, and provides them with all of the advantages of a large

Website: utexas.edu
Location: Urban
Total Enrollment: 49,996
Undergraduates: 38,162
Male/Female: 51/49
SAT Ranges: V 592–619 M 560–660
ACT Range: 23–28
Financial Aid: 46%
Expense: Pub $ $ $ $
Phi Beta Kappa: Yes
Applicants: 19,562
Accepted: 58%
Enrolled: 58%
Grad in 6 Years: 69%
Returning Freshmen: 90%
Academics: ✏ ✏ ✏ ✏ ½
Social: ☎ ☎ ☎ ☎
Q of L: ★ ★ ★ ★
Admissions: (512) 475-7399
Email Address:
admit@utxdp.dp.utexas.edu

Strongest Programs
Liberal Arts
Computer Science
Business
Biological Sciences
Psychology
Electrical Engineering
Applied Learning and
Development
Economics
Natural Sciences
English

university in a small-college atmosphere. Business and natural sciences honors programs are also available. Engineering majors can alternate work and study in the co-op program, while education and health majors hold term-time internships. Almost two hundred UT undergrads work for lawmakers in the Texas State House, only a twenty-minute walk from campus. A strong Reading and Study Skills Lab services students in need of remedial help. Students say the academic climate overall is competitive and rigorous. "You must keep up with your studies in order to be successful," a junior admonishes. Every freshman and transfer student must pass the Texas Academic Skills Program test, followed by courses in English composition, English literature, U.S. history and government, and Texas government. Freshmen can take University 101, which covers everything from major requirements to healthy lifestyle choices and cultural diversity. In addition, the colleges within the university have established basic requirements for all majors: four English courses, with two writing-intensive; five courses in social sciences; four courses in natural sciences and math; and one course in the fine arts or humanities.

Four out of every five UT students are Texans. Students say there is no dominant political pattern on campus—despite the fact that historically UT has been integral in the careers of big-time (conservative) Texas politicians. There definitely are monied students on campus along with "nutty granola types" and the jeans-and-sneakers crowd. Austin is the most "liberal" of Texas cities, and there is a little bit of everything both on campus and across the street along "the Drag." "Environmental earthy stuff" is one hot issue these days, and another undergrad mentions that "PC is a must on campus." Hispanics account for 12 percent of students, Asian-Americans 13 percent, and African-Americans 3 percent. Race has been a touchy issue recently due to court decisions outlawing affirmative action. The university now offers special "welcome programs" for African-American and Hispanic students, with social and educational events and peer mentoring. The university also provides thousands of merit scholarships based on academic performance (some set aside for minorities) ranging from $2,000 to $7,000, as well as athletic scholarships in a range of sports.

> "You must keep up with your studies in order to be successful."

University housing can accommodate only 6,500 students. Once in the dorms, students are guaranteed a room for four years. Accommodations range from functional to plush, and dormies have a variety of living options based on common social and educational interests. "The community showers are always clean," gushes one junior. There are a variety of dining facilities and meal plans, plus numerous fast-food joints within walking distance. Most students live off campus; apartments and condos close to campus are lovely—and very expensive. More reasonably priced digs can be found in other parts of town, a free shuttle ride away. But be forewarned: UT life requires lots of walking, especially for commuters, with 110 buildings and bus stops and parking lots scattered about. You might not even need to go to the gym!

As the state capital, Austin is not a typical college town, but it is one of the best ones. "Austin is a very student-friendly town. Student discounts are abundant and everywhere feels like a college hangout," says a senior. Nightlife centers on nearby Sixth Street, full of pubs and restaurants of all types, and a well-known music scene, with everything from jazz to rock to blues to folk. Numerous microbreweries have opened their doors in the past few years. Halloween draws an estimated eighty thousand costumed revelers to Sixth Street (and sometimes up its lampposts). Annual festivals include 40 Acres, a sprawling carnival of all the campus organizations, and Eeyore's birthday party, where students pay homage to the A. A. Milne character with food and live music. Two pep rallies get students psyched before the Longhorns play Texas A&M or Oklahoma, their biggest rivals. And Texas Independence Day provides an occasion for celebration in March.

On campus, the Texas Union sponsors movies and social events and boasts the world's only collection of orange-top pool tables. For those more interested in octaves than eight-balls, the Performing Arts Center has two concert halls that attract nationally known performers. Students hang out at the union's coffee shop or café and the on-campus pub draws top local talent to the stage (but you must be twenty-one to drink). When the weather gets too muggy (quite often in spring and summer), students head for off-campus campgrounds, lakes, and parks. The most popular road trips are to San Antonio or Dallas. For Spring Break, the students travel to Padre Island, if not New Orleans. Although only 12 percent of the men and 16 percent of the women go Greek, members of fraternities and sororities are "probably highest on the social totem pole," says one student. The chapters tend to be choosy and have high visibility, and have increased in size dramatically over the past year.

As the state capital, Austin is not a typical college town, but it is one of the best ones.

Athletics is the lifeblood of most Texans. In fact, the UT Tower is lit in Longhorn orange whenever any school team wins. The students look forward to the annual Texas–Oklahoma football game played in the Cotton Bowl in Dallas, and the Texas A&M–UT game is an incredibly noisy experience you have to see to believe. "Football games pull the student body together and give us a chance to show our school spirit," says one student. Basketball is also popular, and the men's and women's teams regularly reach their respective NCAA tournaments. The baseball program has many alumni in the major leagues, and the annual spring game between UT's baseball alumni and the current college squad is quite a contest. Other top programs nationally for men and women include swimming and diving and track and field. UT's intramural program is the largest in the nation, and offers weekend athletes access to the same great facilities that the big-time jocks use.

"Austin is a very student-friendly town. Student discounts are abundant and everywhere feels like a college hangout."

The University of Texas may seem overwhelming because of its imposing size, but students say the school spirit and sense of community found here make it feel smaller. UT also prides itself in having one of the most reasonably priced tuitions in the country, and provides the one of best all-around educational experiences a student could ask for.

Overlaps
Texas A&M, Baylor, Texas Tech, Rice, Southwest Texas State

If You Apply To > | **UT:** Rolling admissions: Feb. 1. Financial aid: Feb. 15. No campus or alumni interviews. Apply either to institution as a whole or particular program. SATs or ACTs: required. SAT IIs: recommended (for placement purposes). Essay question: an event that gives insight into your character; a fictional character who has affected you; an event that influenced your academic interest.

Texas A&M University

College Station, TX 77843-0100

Coming to A&M is like joining a fraternity with forty thousand members. In addition to fanatical school spirit, A&M offers leading programs in the national sciences, business, and engineering. To succeed in this mass of humanity, students must find the right academic niche.

Website: www.tamu.edu
Location: Small city
Total Enrollment: 44,618
Undergraduates: 36,603
Male/Female: 51/49
SAT Ranges: V 520–630
    M 550–660
ACT Range: 23–28
Financial Aid: 45%
Expense: Pub $ $
Phi Beta Kappa: No
Applicants: 16,685
Accepted: 69%
Enrolled: 59%
Grad in 6 Years: 74%
Returning Freshmen: 88%
Academics: ✑ ✑ ✑ ✑
Social: ☎ ☎ ☎
Q of L: ★ ★ ★
Admissions: (979) 845-3741
Email Address:
    admissions@tamu.edu

Strongest Programs
    Engineering
    Psychology
    Chemistry
    Business

In a state that is known for big things, Texas A&M is one of its biggest. This school of forty-three thousand students is huge; it boasts a massive endowment and more traditions than Vatican City. Since its inception as a military academy, Texas A&M has become known for its top-notch engineering program and its unsurpassed school spirit. When they're not studying for rigorous technical courses, Aggies are likely to be found at "yell practice" before each home football game or cheering for their teams at other high-energy athletic events. For the sake of their lungs, it's a good thing that A&M students have much to cheer about.

Texas A&M is now the largest university campus in the country—something that is apparent to students every time they walk to class. The A&M campus combines historic brick buildings from the turn of the century with newer structures in more modern styles, and it is pulled together by its heavy cover of live oak trees. Newer buildings include the George Bush Presidential Library and Museum Complex, featuring open lawns and a pond with bridges for pedestrians and bikers.

> "Some classes are hard, some are not, but it really depends on how much time you put into them."

Texas A&M is best known for its agriculture and engineering colleges, and for veterinary medicine, although the university is cultivating a strong liberal arts program and an even stronger business school. Aggies also stand by science programs, especially chemistry and physics. Technical programs of virtually all kinds are heartily supported at A&M, especially nuclear, space, and biotechnical research. A&M has become a sea-grant college due to its outstanding research in oceanography, and is also a "space-grant" college. Add that to the college's land-grant status, and the whole universe seems covered by A&M. Coursework sometimes takes students far from Aggieland. Participants in the Nautical Archaeology Program conduct research all over the world, delving into time periods from prehistory to the recent past. The Academy for Future International Leaders trains fifteen students per year in international business and cultural issues, followed by a summer international internship. Weaker programs include music performance, ancient languages, and religious studies.

Incoming Aggies can expect some heavy coursework in general education requirements, which consists of speech and writing, mathematics/logical reasoning, science, humanities, social science, physical education, and citizenship (political science and history). They are also expected to have at least two years of a foreign language, complete a cultural diversity requirement, and demonstrate computer literacy. Students generally agree that academics are taken seriously at A&M. "Some classes are hard, some are not, but it really all depends on how much time you put into them," says a senior marketing major. And the professors also receive rave reviews. "Every teacher I have encountered has gone above and beyond the call of duty that you would expect from a large university such as Texas A&M," a classmate reports. Because of the school's size, it's sometimes hard to enroll in a required class. "You just have to go to the professor and get forced in," one student advises.

> "Every teacher I have encountered has gone above and beyond the call of duty that you would expect from a large university such as Texas A&M."

Diversity is not a hallmark at A&M, and some students sense this: 95 percent of the student body hail from Texas, and 82 percent are white. The school's departments of Multicultural Services and Student Life offer numerous programs to enhance minority student recruitment and retention. Still, for many students, the one unifying characteristic of the A&M experience is the university spirit. "Aggies look out for other Aggies. Everyone is an Aggie," a senior history major says. To help trim the cost of earning a degree, an athlete can compete for one of hundreds

A&M boasts a massive endowment and more traditions than Vatican City.

of scholarships parceled out each year, while an academic scholar can vie for one of 8,500 merit awards, ranging from $200 to $12,000.

Thirty-eight single-sex and coed dorms range from the cheap and not-so-comfortable to the expensive and cushy (with air-conditioning and private bathrooms). "All dorms are full. In fact they are generally too full," one senior observes. "Freshmen must request a dorm as soon as they are accepted in order to get a dorm of choice or any dorm for that matter." Because of the ever-growing student population, the school's dorms provide only enough space for less than a quarter of those enrolled. Most upperclassmen end up living in the numerous apartments and houses in College Station or its twin city, Bryan. These students needn't fear being cut off from campus life, though, as the entire town is filled with fervent Aggies. Several meal plans are offered in the dining halls, and there are snack shops all over campus.

Although College Station may appear uninspiring at first glance, most of the students fall in love with it. "College Station is a model college town," a senior explains. "Every restaurant has an 'Aggie special,' the radio stations play our 'war hymn' at times throughout the day." Students are actively involved in the community, including the largest single-day service project in the nation annually, the Big Event. Although the Texas Alcohol Board is stationed in town, "those who choose to drink have no problem getting alcohol." Those with more sophisticated tastes can drive an hour and a half to either Houston or Austin or three hours to Dallas. Greeks are growing in popularity, with 7 percent of the men and 14 percent of the women in the student body joining up. In addition, there are more than seven hundred organizations available to meet whatever interests you may have.

Athletics, whether on the varsity level or for recreation, is the number-one activity on campus. Football fans rock Kyle Field with cries of "Gig 'em, Aggies," or "Hump it, Ags." After touchdowns are scored, Aggie fans kiss their dates, and the annual game against the University of Texas stirs up the Aggies and their fans all season long. Men's baseball routinely fields outstanding teams, and

> While less than 10 percent of the school belong to the Corps, it remains the single most important conservator of the spirit and tradition in Aggieland.

> "All dorms are full. In fact, they are generally too full. Freshman must request a dorm as soon as they are accepted in order to get a dorm of choice or any dorm for that matter."

the women's golf and soccer teams have brought home a few championships of their own. The well-organized and extensive intramural program includes hundreds of softball teams.

Favorite traditions include "Twelfth Man," for which all students stand for the entirety of every football game as a symbol of their loyalty and readiness to take part, and the Aggie Muster, a memorial service for A&M alumni around the world who died within the year. There's also the three hundred–plus member Fightin' Texas Aggie Band and the senior "boot line" at the end of the halftime show. The treasured Corps of Cadets, one of the largest military training programs in the country, is structured like a military unit; students lead other cadets. While less than 10 percent of the school belong to the Corps, it remains the single most important conservator of the spirit and tradition in Aggieland. Although the administration has banned the traditional on-campus bonfire before the football game against the University of Texas because of the tragic incident a few years ago, students have organized their own bonfire—albeit smaller—and now continue the tradition off campus.

Texas A&M, while extremely large, is uniquely familial. Being a student here is being a part of something seemingly so much bigger, which is what the Aggie Spirit embodies. Students get the best of two intense worlds at A&M—a large school with tons of people surrounded by a small community. A&M's no longer just a military school, it's a potpourri of varied educational opportunities worth cheering. Boasts one senior, "We have the same traditions as were created years ago and, young or old, Aggies know them all."

Overlaps

University of Texas, Baylor, Texas Tech, Southwest Texas State, Rice

Texas Christian University

TCU Box 297013, Fort Worth, TX 76129

The personalized alternative to the behemoth state universities of Texas. Tuition is about $5,000 less than that at archrival SMU. Though affiliated with the Disciples of Christ, the atmosphere at TCU goes lighter on religion than, say, Baylor. Strengths include the fine arts, business, and communications.

Website: www.tcu.edu
Location: Suburban
Total Enrollment: 8,054
Undergraduates: 6,885
Male/Female: 42/58
SAT Ranges: V 520–620
M 530–640
ACT Range: 23–28
Financial Aid: 94%
Expense: Pr $
Phi Beta Kappa: Yes
Applicants: 5,822
Accepted: 72%
Enrolled: 36%
Grad in 6 Years: 63%
Returning Freshmen: 82%
Academics: 🐸 🐸 🐸
Social: ☎ ☎ ☎
Q of L: ★ ★ ★
Admissions: (817) 257-7490
Email Address:
frogmail@tcu.edu

Strongest Programs
Business
Nursing
Communications
Fine Arts
Psychology
Premed

You know a school has spirit when its students paint themselves purple to cheer raucously for a horny frog. Texans know these folks are TCU fans cheering for the home team (known officially as the Texas Christian University Horned Frogs) at a Saturday afternoon football game. There's a true sense of solidarity and school spirit here. "Students at TCU really have a sense of community and of mutual support," says a sophomore.

The spacious 237-acre campus is kept in almost perfect condition, and features a small lake, several fountains, and a jogging track. Nearby is a lovely residential neighborhood not too far from the shops and restaurants of downtown Fort Worth. The campus features an eclectic mix of architecture, ranging from neo-Georgian to contemporary. Newer facilities include the Taylor Recreational Track and the Walsh Center for Performing Arts, a fifty-six thousand–square-foot performance hall and theater complex.

Students can choose their majors from about eighty disciplines, with the core curriculum counting for forty-seven semester hours. The core emphasizes critical thinking and is divided into three areas: foundations (writing and math); explorations (natural and social sciences, cultural heritage, language, and literature); and physical education. There are freshman seminar courses, along with a new student orientation and Frog Camp (an optional summer camp that emphasizes team building and school spirit).

TCU's stand-out programs are business, nursing, communications, psychology, and fine arts. Some business majors manage a $1.5 million investment portfolio that is one of the largest student-run investment funds in the nation. The university also offers an innovative dance program with a ballet major and a strong theater internship program. The communications program offers hands-on experience at the two fully operational TV studios, a five thousand–watt radio station, and a Center for Productive Communication.

> "TCU students are definitely concerned about academics and grades, but there is also a feeling of support and open cooperation."

The campus also features a geological center for remote sensing, a nuclear magnetic resonance facility, an observatory, and an art gallery, along with a state-of-the-art electrical engineering lab.

The academic climate at TCU is challenging but not overwhelming. "TCU students are definitely concerned about academics and grades, but there is also a feeling of support and open cooperation between students," says an English major. Professors are well liked and respected. "In my freshman year, I had three different department chairs for three different freshman level classes," enthuses one student. Academic advising received high marks, too. "My advisor is so eager to help," says a student. "I think he really enjoys giving me advice."

TCU's student body is fairly homogeneous; nearly three-quarters are from Texas, many from affluent, conservative families. TCU is affiliated with the Christian Church (Disciples of Christ), but the atmosphere is not overtly religious. This is hardly an activist campus, but it is definitely correct to be politically correct. In fact, "TCU should be called 'PCU,'" says a junior. The undergrad student body is 6 percent Hispanic, 4 percent African-American, and 2 percent Asian-American. TCU offers more than 1,300 academic merit scholarships and more than three hundred athletic scholarships for talented athletes.

Just under half the student body lives on campus, and dorm life is a good experience. Cable and free Internet access are available in all rooms. Students describe them as comfortable and clean. An escort service, Froggy 5-0, takes you wherever you want to go on campus. "There are also plenty of lights and emergency phones," one freshman says, "so students feel physically safe."

> **"My advisor is so eager to help. I think he really enjoys giving me advice."**

Many juniors and seniors move off campus, and fraternity and sorority members may live in their Greek houses after freshman year. Dorm residents must take the meal plan, which does not receive very high marks. The alcohol rules on campus are fairly strict for minors: resident advisors even perform occasional "fridge checks" looking for alcohol in students' rooms. "If you're caught you are ticketed and have to go to Alcohol Abuse meetings," one student says. "But we're all smart enough to find a way around it," another retorts.

Greek life is important at TCU; 27 percent of the men and 33 percent of the women join Greek organizations. They party in the *esprit de corps* tradition, but there's plenty of fun left in Fort Worth and on campus to keep the non-Greek frogs hopping. "Fort Worth is awesome," says a junior. "Downtown has tons of bars/clubs/theaters/comedy shows and is safe to walk around in. The stockyards let you get in touch with the inner country in you, and no one should miss a visit to Billy Bob's, the world's largest honky tonk." Dallas

> **"TCU should be called 'PCU.'"**

is only forty-five minutes to the east. Parents' Weekend, Siblings' Weekend, Homecoming, and the traditional lighting of the Christmas tree are all special events. Road trips include Austin, San Antonio, the Gulf Coast, and Shreveport, L.A.

As for athletics, the school recently joined the ranks of Conference USA. The football team's resurgence has given championship-hungry fans a reason to cheer, and big rivalries include SMU and Rice. Championship teams in the past few years include football, men's basketball, and men's and women's tennis. On-campus sports facilities feature two indoor pools, weight rooms, a track, and tennis, basketball, sand volleyball, and racquetball courts.

There's a quiet sense of accomplishment at TCU, and an appreciation for the personal attention that is given to the students. TCU provides multiple opportunities to prosper both academically and socially. "We all really love our school and what it stands for," says one student. Like the beloved Horned Frog, TCU graduates have taken a giant leap toward their futures.

TCU's stand-out programs are business, nursing, communications, psychology, and fine arts.

TCU's student body is fairly homogeneous; nearly three-quarters are from Texas, many from affluent, conservative families.

Overlaps

University of Texas, Texas A&M, Southern Methodist, Baylor, Trinity University

Texas Tech University

Lubbock, TX 79409

A child of the remote west Texas plains, Texas Tech is finally emerging from the shadow of Texas A&M. Though engineering is its specialty, Tech is a full-service university. It takes big-time sports to be on the map in Texas, and the Red Raiders are making a splash in both football and basketball.

Website: www.ttu.edu
Location: Suburban
Total Enrollment: 25,573
Undergraduates: 21,269
Male/Female: 54/46
SAT Ranges: V 490–590
 M 510–610
ACT Range: 21–26
Financial Aid: 62%
Expense: Pub $ $
Phi Beta Kappa: Yes
Applicants: 12,008
Accepted: 74%
Enrolled: 48%
Grad in 6 Years: 51%
Returning Freshmen: 81%
Academics: ✍ ✍ ✍
Social: ☎ ☎ ☎
Q of L: ★ ★ ★
Admissions: (806) 742-1480
Email Address: nrs@ttu.edu

Strongest Programs
 Agriculture Education and
  Communications
 Chemistry
 Computer Science
 Electrical Engineering
 Family Financial Planning
 Finance
 Human Development and
  Family Studies
 Technical Writing

Texas Tech University wasn't supposed to get so big. But remember, it's in Texas—where everything's bigger. For this reason, Tech has advanced far beyond the mere branch of Texas A&M that it was supposed to be—a boon to students looking for a solid education with a laid-back vibe. A comprehensive capital campaign has helped ensure that research capabilities, faculty, and facilities keep pace with Tech's Texas-sized ambitions. Though the school was founded in 1923, after other state institutions, it "has managed to grow and compete with the other Texas schools—it endures and excels," says a political science and psychology major. "We receive far less support from the state...but we have guts and endurance and personality."

After two years of governmental infighting over its status as an A&M branch, Tech finally opened its doors as an independent institution in 1925. Fewer than one thousand students came to the West Texas city of Lubbock to study liberal arts, agriculture, engineering, and home economics. Today, Tech's 1,839-acre campus hosts more than twenty-five thousand students, undergraduate programs in hundreds of disciplines, and schools of medicine and law. Expansive lawns and impressive landscaping complement red-roofed Spanish Renaissance-style buildings. "Campus is very peaceful," says an agricultural economics major. "There is a soothing breeze." A $500 million fund-raising effort helped finance the construction of a new English, philosophy, and education building, as well as new science labs. Jones Stadium and the student union are being renovated. "There is never *not* construction taking place on campus," a senior says.

Even if new money is going toward building projects, the smorgasbord of academic options hasn't been given short shrift. Tech students may still choose from more than 150 degree programs. Anything in the agriculture school is a good bet, says a senior, but stay away from math or science classes because "most professors speak little, if any, English." The accounting department and various engineering programs are also well regarded, though a senior cautions that in the popular business school, "everyone is just a number because the classes are so huge." A major in classics has replaced programs in classical humanities and Latin, though administrators admit even the revised program could be improved. Other weak spots include art history, German, and Latin American and Iberian studies, administrators say. New offerings include computer and software engineering, environmental toxicology, and systems and engineering management. There's also a women's studies department, despite Tech's conservative political slant.

> **"There is never *not* construction taking place on campus."**

Tech's general education requirements include courses in written and oral communications, math, natural science, technology and applied science, humanities, visual and performing arts, social and behavioral sciences (including U.S. history, political science, and individual or group behavior), and multiculturalism. The Tech Transition program helps ease students into college by helping them understand the philosophy and scope of higher education. Most freshman classes average less than fifty students, and the academic climate varies by program, students say. "Instructors are very supportive and want to see you succeed," says one student. Teaching is good, for the most part, says a family studies major: "I've had a few bad professors, but most have been great." An agricultural communications major says most freshmen will have three courses a semester taught by full professors.

New offerings include computer and software engineering, environmental toxicology, and systems and engineering management. There's also a women's studies department, despite Tech's conservative political slant.

Outstanding students may enroll in Tech's Honors College, where they sit on committees, help with recruiting, make decisions about course content, and evaluate faculty. They also work on research projects, either independently (with a professor's guidance), or as part of a student-faculty team. Recent study topics have included pain management, wind engineering, and sick-building syndrome. Those yearning to leave behind the hardscrabble plains of Texas may study abroad.

The Tech student body is overwhelmingly white and homegrown; only 8 percent of students hail from outside the Lone Star State. Asian-Americans account for 2 percent of the total, African-Americans 3 percent, and Hispanics 10 percent. "Tech students care about and love this university, but are not obsessed and brain-washed about it like students at Texas A&M and the University of Texas," says a senior. A majority of students are "conservative and conformist, but there are, thankfully, several who are more open and free thinkers," adds a classmate. Forget about political correctness—or even political consciousness, students say. "Most people here are only concerned with what Greek organization to join, and where the best drink specials are," one student sighs.

"Instructors are very supportive and want to see you succeed."

Twenty-six percent of students live in the residence halls, which are "well maintained, but not that comfortable," an agricultural communications major says. Freshmen are required to live on campus; upperclassmen generally flee the dorms for apartments in Lubbock (pop. 200,000), where the cost of living is low. Coed, single-sex, and quiet study dorms are available; one men's dorm lacks air-conditioning, which might be considered cruel and unusual punishment given the West Texas heat. Tech police officers—plus blue-light emergency telephones and late-night shuttle buses—help students feel safe. "You couldn't get a flea's whisker through the door most of the time," says a freshman.

Freshmen can participate in Tech Transition, a freshman seminar designed to ease high-school students into college life by educating them on the philosophy and scope of higher education.

Since three-quarters of Tech students live off campus, that's where the social life is, students say. Most bars and clubs admit anyone eighteen and over, but only those older than twenty-one may drink. Alcohol is banned on campus, though students say it's pretty easy for underage students to be served at off-campus parties. Forty-four fraternities and sororities attract 12 percent of the men and 19 percent of the women, but the Greek presence is complemented by "lots of other social, religious, and academic clubs," says a family studies major. Lubbock offers plenty of opportunities to get involved through community-service organizations or Bible study at one of many local churches. "It's a great college town, without the big-city stress," explains a business major. Still, because Lubbock is the biggest city for miles, "any road trip is a good road trip," says a senior. The best destinations? Away games played by the school's Red Raiders; the bright lights of Dallas (320 miles); or the ski slopes and hiking trails of New Mexico, a three- to four-hour drive.

"Most people here are only concerned with what Greek organization to join, and where the best drink specials are."

The Division I Red Raider teams compete in the Big 12 Conference. Tech has some intense rivalries, notably with Texas A&M and the University of Texas. Women's basketball is strong, and the Lady Raiders have won the conference championship a number of times in the past few years. The men's basketball program has gotten a lot of attention since Tech hired explosive former Indiana coach Bobby Knight who, as of press time, was still behaving himself. The football team always draws hordes of rabid fans (remember, this is the South!) to tailgate parties and games. When players take the field, the Masked Rider, replete with red and black cape and cowboy hat, motivates the crowd by galloping up and down the sidelines. Other popular sports include men's and women's golf, tennis, and track and field.

Texas Tech has a little bit of everything—or maybe a big bit, given its size—so long as you don't mind hot, dry weather, ever-present construction barricades, and taking some initiative to make friends and a name for yourself. "We have a big university, but it doesn't feel huge," says a senior. "There's lots of fun traditions and a lot of school spirit, plus lots of good programs to choose from for a major." For those seeking a dynamic education in a Southern setting, Texas Tech may be worth a look.

Trinity College

300 Summit Street, Hartford, CT 06106

While most small colleges have been treading water, Trinity has had a notable increase in applications and selectivity in recent years. Trinity is among the few small liberal arts colleges in an urban setting, and security has always been an issue. Trinity joins Lafayette, Swarthmore, and Smith among small colleges with engineering.

Though it's stuck in the middle of gritty Hartford, Connecticut, Trinity College students call their little liberal arts institution "Camp Trin-Trin." Says a senior: "In the spring, with intramural softball on the quad, Frisbee, students studying on blankets, it looks just like pictures in the college magazine—sun, smiles, and fun." Step off campus, and the picture is different, a freshman warns: "Walk to the package store, or Timothy's, a restaurant, and you are sworn at in a foreign language or yelled at by members of the community." Clearly, town-gown relations at Trinity have a ways to go. But with rising academic standards and admissions more competitive than ever, Trinity has made much progress moving from a "party school of the 1980s" to a serious intellectual institution.

Splendid Gothic-style stone buildings behind wrought-iron fences decorate Trinity's one hundred–acre campus. The large, grassy quadrangle known as the Long Walk is home to pick-up games of hackeysack and lazy relaxation on warm spring and fall afternoons. The college's $35 million Library and Information Technology Center is the newest addition to the campus.

Trinity's general education requirements include one course each in humanities, natural sciences, numerical and symbolic reasoning, and social sciences. Students must also demonstrate proficiency in writing and mathematics. The First-Year

Program includes a seminar emphasizing writing, speaking, and critical thinking; the seminar instructor serves as students' academic adviser. Freshmen may also choose one of three guided-studies programs in the humanities, natural sciences, or the history, culture, and future of cities, which a philosophy major calls "phenomenal—very challenging and rewarding."

New majors at Trinity include women, gender, and sexuality, and environmental science, which benefits from the 256-acre Field Station at Church Farm in Ashford, Connecticut. The relatively new Jewish studies program has attracted much student interest, even if it's produced only one graduate, says a freshman: "Classes have grown from fifty to 150 students, with the majority being non-Jewish." Trinity has appointed Dr. Laurel E. Baldwin-Ragaven, a family-medicine specialist and a human-rights activist, as its first Luce Professor of Health and Human Rights. In addition to teaching, she works on Trinity's Human Rights Program, community-service projects, and biennial conferences. Students also give rave reviews to Trinity's English, economics, and history departments, and say that the school's

(Continued)

Social: ☎ ☎ ☎ ☎
Q of L: ★ ★ ★
Admissions: (860) 297-2180
Email Address: admissions.
   office@trincoll.edu

Strongest Programs
   Economics
   Political Science
   History
   Biology
   Chemistry
   Engineering
   Modern Languages

> **"In the spring, with intramural softball on the quad, Frisbee, students studying on blankets, it looks like pictures in the college magazine—sun, smiles, and fun."**

small but accredited engineering program is likewise strong. That department sponsors the Fire-Fighting Home Robot Contest, the largest public robotics competition in the U.S., open to entrants of any age, ability, and experience. Through the BEACON program, biomedical engineering students can take courses at UConn, the UConn Health Center, and the University of Hartford while conducting research at three area health centers.

Faculty-student collaboration is a tradition at Trinity. Nearly 30 percent of a recent graduating class worked with professors on research and scholarly papers, and many students join their mentors to present findings at symposia. In the classroom, a laid-back vibe prevails. "The work comes in waves," says a political science major. "All of the students are bright, but the question is whether they take advantage of Trinity's opportunities." Professors get high marks, as they do the lion's share of teaching—graduate assistants only lead review sessions before exams. "Being invited to dinner at a professor's house or out to lunch in the city is common," says a psychology major. Still, there are some complaints. "Few professors have students think beyond usual social norms and the status quo," laments a sociology major.

Sixty percent of Trinity's students seek internships with businesses and government agencies in Hartford (the insurance capital of the world), and some also take terms at other schools through the Twelve-College Exchange.* The Global Sites program enables students to study with Trinity professors in seven exotic locations, from South Africa and Trinidad to Chile and Nepal; a program in China began in Spring 2003. Other enticing choices include the Mystic Seaport term* for marine biology enthusiasts, studying Italian language and art history at Trinity's campus in Rome, or learning Spanish at the University of Cordoba. In fact, nearly half of each class studies overseas. Back on campus, the Department of Theater and Dance offers an unusual integrated major, and sponsors a

> **"The work comes in waves."**

study-abroad program with LaMaMa in New York City and Europe. Administrators caution that the educational studies department offers students a richer understanding of the field, but that to get teacher certification, students must tap into the Hartford higher-education consortium.

Only 17 percent of Trinity students are Connecticut natives; many of the rest hail from Massachusetts and other nearby states. "Most students are extremely preppy and attended rigorous, well-respected boarding schools in New England," says a senior. "Trinity students are more about style than substance," a junior adds.

New majors at Trinity include women, gender, and sexuality, and environmental science, which benefits from the 256-acre Field Station at Church Farm, in Ashford, Connecticut.

The Global Sites program enables students to study with Trinity professors in seven exotic locations, from South Africa and Trinidad to Chile and Nepal; a program in China began in Spring 2003.

"Many students are more at home in a mall or at a party than in the classroom. They go to college because they're expected to." African-Americans and Asian-Americans each constitute 6 percent of the student body, and Hispanics add 5 percent. "Multiculturalism and increasing diversity are big issues," says a history major. "Students here are somewhat conservative, but we have a really active, very politically liberal group called VOID (Voices Organized in Democracy)." Trinity's three Greek groups are coed, another point of contention.

Ninety-five percent of Trinity's students live in the coed dorms. The best bets for freshmen are said to be Jones or Jarvis because of their central location on the quad. "Dorms are great compared to schools like Dickinson, where you live in a box of a room your freshman year," says a junior. After freshman year, rooms are assigned by lottery; seniors pick first, then juniors and sophomores, though everyone is guaranteed a bed. Options include singles, doubles, quads, units with kitchens, and theme houses for those interested in music, community service, wellness, art, and quiet. Freshmen must eat in Trinity's dining hall; the Bistro, an upscale but reasonable café, is another choice for students on the meal plan. Others hibernate in the Cave, which offers sandwiches and grilled fare.

When it comes to Trinity's social scene, opinions are divided. Some students praise the Trinity College Activities Council, which brings in comedians and musical performers, and organizes parties, study breaks, and community-service days. The Underground Coffeehouse and the Bistro's weekly comedy nights are also popular. A college-sponsored "culture van" takes students to downtown Hartford, to catch a show at the Busnell or visit the Wadsworth Atheneum, the nation's oldest public art museum.

> "Most students are extremely preppy and attended rigorous, well-respected boarding schools in New England."

But the action on Thursday, Friday, and Saturday nights is mostly on campus, mostly at the frats (27 percent of men and 22 percent of women join up), and mostly soaked in beer. "The social life is only good for students who like to drink alcohol and listen to loud rock music," says a sophomore. "If you want to go to a party primarily to dance and mingle, then you've gotta go off campus."

Hartford, however, is "not a college town at all," says a junior. "Its neighborhoods are unsafe, crime is high, and there's little to do." In response to these concerns (and perhaps out of self-defense), the college initiated a $175 million neighborhood revitalization campaign (including a $5.1 million grant from the W.K. Kellogg Foundation) designed to create a safe and vibrant community. The initiative draws on existing community resources and will generate $130 million in new construction. On campus, drinking is officially taboo for students under twenty-one, and at official college functions, including the frat parties, students must present two forms of ID to be served. Still, enforcement of the policy is "irrational and counterproductive," says a philosophy major. "Kids end up binge drinking in their rooms." Spring Weekend brings bands to campus for a three-day party outdoors, while the annual Tropical party finds a fraternity filling its backyard with sand to create a beach. Popular road trips include Montreal, Boston, New York City, and the beaches and mountains of Maine.

Trinity's Bantams compete in Division III, and both men's and women's squash are powerhouses, particularly when the opponent is Princeton or Harvard. (The men's squad has won the national championship for four years running, and the women's team brought home a title in 2002.) Homecoming typically brings Wesleyan or Amherst to campus for a football game that Trinity loses, but students get their revenge by burning the opposing school's letter on the quad before the game. "There is a huge competitive spirit at Trinity that cannot be matched by any school, especially when it comes to drinking games," quips a freshman.

Despite their reputation as an apathetic bunch, students at Trinity don't hesitate to express strong opinions on their home city of Hartford (love it or hate it) and their fellow students (intelligent and motivated, or preppy slackers?). A new president and honor code should help refocus the campus on academics, rather than alcohol, keeping Trinity ahead of the curve in liberal arts education. "Trinity is a beautiful campus in the middle of a city, with friendly people, great professors, and a student body that knows how to work hard and play hard," says a senior. A junior adds: "The smallness allows one to interact with all faculty and pursue individual goals."

If You Apply To ➤

Trinity College: Early decision: Nov. 15, Jan. 15. Regular admissions: Jan. 15. Financial aid: Mar. 1. Guarantees to meet demonstrated need. Campus interviews: recommended, evaluative. Alumni interviews: optional, informational. SATs or ACT: required. SAT IIs: required (writing). Accepts the Common Application and electronic applications. Essay question: topic of personal significance.

Trinity University

715 Stadium Drive, San Antonio, TX 78212-7200

The Southwest's leading liberal arts college is also one of the few in a major city. Trinity is twice as big as nearby rivals Austin and Southwestern, and offers a diverse curriculum that includes business, education, and engineering in addition to the liberal arts. Upscale and conservative.

Trinity University is a small school with big bucks. Thanks to the oil boom of the 1970s, Trinity has one of the nation's largest and fastest-growing educational endowments for a school its size. The wealth is used unashamedly to lure capable students with bargain tuition rates, and to entice talented professors with Texas-sized salaries. The result? A student body comprised of smart, ambitious men and women, and a faculty that is knowledgeable and caring. Students here enjoy challenges, but still manage a laid-back Texas attitude. "It's not 'work hard, party hard,'" says a student. "It's more like 'have fun while working.'"

Founded around the time of the Civil War, Trinity began in the tiny central Texas town of Tehuacana, moved to Waxahachie, and then, in 1942, pulled up stakes and settled on a campus on the west side of San Antonio. Ten years later, the school moved to its current location, in a residential area about three miles from downtown San Antonio, one of the most beautiful cities in the Southwest. The 117-acre campus, filled with the

> **"It's not 'work hard, party hard.' It's more like 'have fun while working.'"**

Southern architecture of O'Neill Ford, is located on what was once a rock quarry. Everything fits the school's somewhat well-to-do image, from the uniform redbrick buildings to the cobblestones in pathways that wind along gorgeous green lawns and through immaculate gardens spotted with Henry Moore sculptures. Trinity's most dominant landmark is Murchison Tower, which rises in the center of campus and is visible from numerous vantage points throughout San Antonio.

The school makes a strong effort to maintain its strict admissions standards, keeping a small enrollment, tightening the grading system, and recruiting high achievers with greater energy than is possible from larger universities. The university has set its sights on becoming the premier small liberal arts school in the Southwest. "Trinity is extremely committed to providing the best possible education for

Website: www.trinity.edu
Location: Suburban
Total Enrollment: 2,622
Undergraduates: 2,407
Male/Female: 48/52
SAT Ranges: V 580–680
 M 610–690
ACT Range: 27–30
Financial Aid: 44%
Expense: Pr $ $
Phi Beta Kappa: Yes
Applicants: 2,942
Accepted: 65%
Enrolled: 34%
Grad in 6 Years: 76%
Returning Freshmen: 86%
Academics: ✍ ✍ ✍ ½
Social: 🍷 🍷 🍷
Q of L: ★ ★ ★
Admissions: (210) 999-7207
Email Address:
 admissions@trinity.edu

Strongest Programs
 Business

(Continued)

Economics

History

English

Biology

Education

Engineering

its students," says an English and biology double major. Students report that the academics are very rigorous. "Courses are demanding, especially in the humanities," confides a student. "All of the classes require enormous amounts of study time." Forty-eight percent of students come from the top tenth of their high-school class.

The professors at Trinity are described as "knowledgeable" and "accessible." "Professors here truly care and go beyond the call of duty to make sure the students have every possible opportunity to succeed," says a religion major. Another student adds, "The professors I have experienced have been extremely qualified and enlightening, and many hold national distinctions for research in their field." Trinity has a highly praised education department, with a five-year MAT program, and a good premed program. Other strong departments include English, economics, business, and engineering. The communications department offers students hands-on training with television equipment or the chance to produce a newscast. Accounting majors are offered a chance to serve an internship with the Big Four accounting firms in San Antonio, Houston, Dallas, or Austin while earning a salary and receiving college credit. Students say the art, drama, psychology, and physical education departments are weak.

Trinity's approach to general education requirements is the Common Curriculum, an extensive list of mandatory courses including a first-year seminar dealing with a common theme, such as Justice and Human Rights or Freedom and Responsibility, and a writing seminar. Students must also take courses from five fundamental areas, called "Understandings," which include Western and one other culture, the role of values, and human social context. The common curriculum is popular with students, especially because its courses are taught by full-time faculty. As a member of the Twelve-College

"All of the classes require enormous amounts of study time."

Exchange* and the Associated Colleges of the South* programs, Trinity approves a number of study-abroad programs and encourages premed and prelaw students, as well as history and English majors, to take advantage of them. Another feature of Trinity's curriculum is an opportunity for students to participate in research projects with faculty mentors. Some students even present their findings at professional conferences or have them published in professional journals.

Almost all classes at Trinity have fifty or fewer students, and freshmen are assigned to mentor groups of ten to fifteen students for academic and guidance counseling, as well as peer tutoring from upperclassmen. "My advisors bend over backward to help me (I'm clueless as to what I want to do)," a senior chemistry major reports. Most students get the courses they want at registration and can be "pink slipped" in if a class is closed, though they may have to wait a semester or two for a common curriculum course.

Seventy percent of Trinity students are Texans. About 20 percent of the student body represent minority groups; Hispanics alone account for 10 percent, Asian-Americans another 7 percent, and African-Americans 2 percent. "Trinity students are overcommitted overachievers who are apathetic about everything but their grades," says one student. Lukewarm campus issues include gender issues, gay and lesbian rights, and abortion. Merit scholarships are available to academically gifted students, but student athletes must fend for themselves.

Seventy-seven percent of Trinity's students live on campus, but that's partly because Trinity requires students to do so through their junior year. Still, the residence halls are beautiful and spacious; most rooms are two-person suites with balconies, and maids clean the bathroom (which two suites share) and vacuum the floor once a week. Dorms are coed, with one single-sex residence hall that is off limits to freshmen; all dorms are now wired for cable and the Internet. Most seniors move off campus so that they can have single rooms. Students say San Antonio is a tourist

Students here enjoy challenges, but still manage a laid-back Texas attitude.

town, not a college town, but it boasts a Sea World, outdoor shops, and cafés at the Riverwalk, and many cultural and musical attractions. Students get involved in city life through the Trinity University Volunteer Action Center.

Weekends find students at local bars, fraternity parties, or other on-campus events. Twenty-six percent of the men and 30 percent of the women in the student body join the local fraternity and sorority organizations, but "it is not necessary to be Greek to be social," says a student. Country line-dancing is also a popular activity, and the university sponsors an excellent lecture series that brings notable politicians and public figures to campus. Alcohol may not be consumed on campus except by those of legal age in one of four "wet" dorms, but "it's easy to get away with it in your dorms if you don't draw attention to yourself," a student says. Underage students caught drinking must go before a student court, but punishments tend to be on the light side.

San Antonio's warm weather provides ample opportunities for spring fever—even in January. The Texas Hill Country, with its trees, rivers, wildflowers, and charming small towns, is an hour's drive northwest of San Antonio and is a popular destination for weekend adventures. The funky state capital of Austin is seventy miles north, and students also can roadtrip internationally—to nearby Mexico.

"People get spread too thin—so many activities, difficult classes, and not enough sleep!"

An annual event most students look forward to is Fiesta, a week-long celebration of San Antonio's mixed culture that features bands, dancing, food, and drink. They also anticipate the Tigerfest dance and parade on homecoming weekend and a Chili Cook-Off that pits Greek and other clubs against one another. The school year kicks off with a party at the school's bell tower, which students can climb to get a knockout view of San Antonio.

Trinity competes in Division III athletics as a member of the Southern Collegiate Athletic Conference, and fields eighteen varsity teams. Over the past six years, the school has won forty-six conference titles and six consecutive SCAC Presidents' Trophies, awarded to the school with the best overall athletic program. Popular sports include football, track, soccer, swimming, basketball, and tennis. But students really get a kick out of intramurals. With athletic fields and a renovated and expanded athletic facility, there's lots of room to frolic and play. In fact, a junior laments, with so many things going on, "people get spread too thin—so many activities, difficult classes, and not enough sleep!"

Trinity University offers its students a small-school atmosphere along with all the advantages of a much larger institution: challenging academics, top-notch professors, and abundant social activities all wrapped up with a hefty endowment.

Trinity has a highly praised education department, with a five-year MAT program, and a good premed program.

Overlaps
University of Texas, Texas A&M, Rice, Tulane, Vanderbilt

If You Apply To ➤

Trinity University: Early decision: Nov. 15. Early action: Dec. 15. Regular admissions: Jan. 15. Financial aid: Feb. 1. Guarantees to meet demonstrated need. Campus interviews: optional, informative. No alumni interviews. SATs or ACT: required. SAT IIs: optional. Accepts the Common Application. Essay question: describe a person, place, or event that has had a significant impact on you.

Truman State University

(formerly Northeast Missouri State University)
McClain Hall, Room 205, Kirksville, MO 63501

Truman changed its name to emphasize that it has more in common with private institutions than nondescript regional publics. Truman is looking for a public ivy niche like Miami of Ohio and William and Mary. A new residential college program will increase cocurricular learning.

Website: www.truman.edu
Location: Small town
Total Enrollment: 5,919
Undergraduates: 5,685
Male/Female: 42/58
SAT Ranges: V 560–660
  M 550–650
ACT Range: 25–30
Financial Aid: 28%
Expense: Pub $
Phi Beta Kappa: Yes
Applicants: 5,002
Accepted: 82%
Enrolled: 36%
Grad in 6 Years: 64%
Returning Freshmen: 84%
Academics: 🖉 🖉 🖉
Social: 🐨 🐨 🐨
Q of L: ★ ★ ★
Admissions: (660) 785-4114,
  (800) 892-7792
Email Address:
  admissions@truman.edu

Strongest Programs
  Accounting
  Physics
  Chemistry
  Education
  English
  Math
  Political Science
  Russian

Students expect a lot from Truman State University, Missouri's only public liberal arts and sciences institution. Happily, it delivers. Since paring down the number of majors offered from more than 140 to forty-three when it sloughed off its regional school status in 1996, Truman has focused on its strengths. The result is a thriving academic climate stuffed with high achievers who have eyes for learning, not slacking. "Although we are in the middle of small-town U.S.A., we still try to do very big things here," says a journalism major.

Truman is located in northeast Missouri, approximately two hundred miles from both Kansas City and St. Louis. The campus, which is loaded with flowers, is spread over 140 acres and includes thirty-nine buildings that reflect aesthetic details of the Georgian style. The oldest portion of the campus, which dates back to 1873, is based on Thomas Jefferson's University of Virginia. Current renovations to the Ophelia Parrish classroom building will transform it into the $20 million Truman Fine Arts Center. The Magruder Hall science building is being renovated and enlarged. The recently opened Violette Hall, the campus's largest academic facility, features state-of-the-art classrooms with laptop connections at each seat.

Although Truman is a preprofessional school, liberal arts studies form the cornerstone of its educational philosophy. The foundation consists of courses in fine arts, mathematics and science, religion, humanities, foreign language, and social science. Students must complete an interdisciplinary writing-enhanced seminar, and freshmen are required to attend an orientation program known as Freshmen Week. Strong programs include hard sciences such as chemistry and biology, and the education department. Students praise political science and business as well. More than six hundred undergrads participate in research with faculty members. The Junior Interdisciplinary Seminars are developed by faculty members and have recently included The Rock Generation and Environmental Economics. For study-abroad opportunities, nearly five hundred students attend programs in roughly fifty countries through the College Consortium for International Studies and the Council on International Educational Exchange. In keeping with the tradition of its namesake, the college also offers hands-on internships in Washington, D.C.

> **"Although we are in the middle of small-town U.S.A., we still try to do very big things here."**

Students roundly agree that the academic climate is bracing. Truman students "are accustomed to performing well and thrive in a highly competitive environment," says a sociology major. It helps that the professors are incredibly accessible. "They honestly care about their students, which can have a huge impact on a student's performance," a senior says. Many professors give out their home numbers and encourage students to drop by their offices just to chat. Academic advising, on the other hand, is "rather mediocre." Students complain that some advisors are apathetic and several professors assigned as advisors are "hard to track down." Career counseling, however, receives good marks.

Nearly three-quarters of the student body hail from Missouri and the number of freshman from out-of-state is limited to 25 percent of the incoming class. Eighty-one percent of students graduated in the top quarter of their high-school class, and 78 percent attended public school. Minority students make up 15 percent of the student body. A variety of multicultural awareness programs have been integrated into the freshman orientation week and throughout the school year, though diversity remains a big issue on campus, as does Greek life and student governance. Truman offers 3,305 merit scholarships ranging from $500 to $11,814. The school does not guarantee to meet the full demonstrated financial need of every admit, but 84 percent are offered a substantial package. Students report that they must maintain a 3.25 GPA to keep their aid. In any case, the school's annual price tag is a bargain by most standards.

Forty-six percent of Truman students live on campus and take advantage of the Residential College Program. This program creates an integrated living and learning environment within the residence halls, led by a senior faculty member called a College Rector. The dorms are comfortable and available as suites or community-style. All are are coed

"It is not uncommon to hear a student get ecstatic not over receiving high marks on a paper, but due to the latest sale at J. Crew."

except for one all-female dorm. Housing at "other campuses resembles larger versions of jail cells, but the rooms here actually look like rooms you could make a home," says a senior who remained on campus for all four years.

Students say Kirksville is not really a college town, but it "is not so small that people go crazy from having nothing to do," a sophomore says. There are tons of opportunities to get involved with the community—many students volunteer at local nursing homes and schools as tutors or mentors. While Truman is no political hotbed, student activism was instrumental in passing a state-sales-tax increase to fund a nearby highway widening project.

Social activities are plentiful both on campus and off. Greek organizations claim 30 percent of the men and 20 percent of the women and dominate the nightlife, especially since the campus is dry. But independents need not fear—the Student Activities Board gets a large budget to sponsor concerts, movies, dances, and excursions. Recent events have included the Spitfire Tour featuring Woody Harrelson and the comedy of Jimmy Fallon. Truman Day, Homecoming, and Dog Days are three annual events the students look forward to, and the a cappella group "The True Men" (get it?) draws huge crowds. The trails at Thousand Hill State Park are five miles from campus, while longer trips to Columbia, St. Louis, and Kansas City satisfy urban cravings.

Sports are popular at Truman, and the Bulldog basketball team never fails to draw a large crowd. Football does, too, but bragging rights for best squads on campus go to women's track, women's soccer, women's tennis, men's cross-country, and men's soccer, which all finished first in the MIAA Conference recently. Women's swimming recently won its second consecutive national championship, while the volleyball team finished third in the nation in 2001–2002. The oldest Division II rivalry, called the "Hickory stick game," is between Truman and Northwest Missouri.

Students at Truman are deeply engaged in their studies, but still know how to appreciate the lighter side of life. "It is not uncommon to hear a student get ecstatic not over receiving high marks on a paper, but due to the latest sale at J. Crew," a political science major says. With a state university price tag, Truman is, as its namesake would say, a fair deal.

Overlaps

University of Missouri at Columbia, Saint Louis University, Southwest Missouri State, Washington University (MO), University of Illinois

Tufts University

Bendetson Hall, Medford, MA 02155

Tufts will always be a second banana to Harvard in the Boston area, but given the Hub's runaway popularity among college students, second is not so bad. Best-known for international relations, Tufts is also strong in engineering and health-related fields. In the Experimental College, students can take off-the-wall courses for credit.

Website: www.tufts.edu
Location: Suburban
Total Enrollment: 8,876
Undergraduates: 4,791
Male/Female: 48/52
SAT Ranges: V 610–700
  M 640–720
ACT Range: 27–31
Financial Aid: 39%
Expense: Pr $ $ $ $
Phi Beta Kappa: Yes
Applicants: 12,366
Accepted: 33%
Enrolled: 30%
Grad in 6 Years: 87%
Returning Freshmen: 95%
Academics: ✍ ✍ ✍ ✍ ½
Social: ☎ ☎ ☎
Q of L: ★ ★ ★ ★
Admissions: (617) 627-3170
Email Address: uadmiss-inquiry@infonet.tufts.edu

Strongest Programs
  Engineering Technology
    Center
  Center for Environmental
    Management
  Center for Materials and
    Interfaces
  Electro-Optics Technology
    Center
  Experimental College
  International Relations

Some academic superstars used to consider Tufts University a safety school, a respectable place to go if you didn't get into Penn or Cornell. But Tufts isn't so safe anymore, at least not when it comes to admissions. Applications are up dramatically, propelling Tufts into the ranks of the most selective schools in the country. With its strong academics, high-achieving student body, and an attractive setting, some would say that not much more separates Tufts University from its illustrious neighbors, Harvard and MIT, than a few stops on the "T."

Tufts's 150-acre tree-lined, hilltop campus overlooks the heart of nearby Boston, and is a striking scene. The main campus, with its brick and stone buildings, sits on the Medford/Somerville boundary. Medford, the fifth-oldest city in the country, was a powerful shipbuilding center during the nineteenth century. Somerville, the historic Revolutionary powder house, lies adjacent to the Tufts campus, and in 1776, the first American flag was raised on its Prospect Hill. Recent construction includes a five-story parking garage and $20 million field house.

For years, Tufts has devoted resources to traditional areas of graduate strength—medicine, dentistry, law, and diplomacy—as well as new ventures, such as a Nutrition Research Center. Such additions had only a peripheral impact on the liberal arts and engineering colleges, but Tufts has made a noticeable commitment to facilities that primarily benefit undergraduates. Recent additions include the high-tech project development laboratory for student design projects, a $21 million addition to the Tisch library, which doubled its size, and the renovation of the chemistry research building, which allowed more lab space for undergraduate research. On the nonacademic but all-important quality-of-life side, Tufts renovated the Dewick/Macphie Dining Hall, which added a food court with thirteen individual prep stations, such as a noodle bar, wok station, and vegetarian grill; built a new intramural gymnasium; and hard-wired all dormitory rooms for Internet, email, and voicemail access. Tufts is conspicuously committed to self-improvement.

"Many students compete with themselves but not with each other."

Despite the recent flurry of expansion, undergraduate teaching is what attracts students. They get highly personalized attention from faculty, and they enjoy wide freedom to design their own majors, pursue independent study, and do research and internships for credit. Strong departments include international relations, political science, biology, engineering, drama, and languages, and there is an excellent child-study program. The most popular major is international relations, followed by biology, economics, English, and psychology.

While upper-level courses are reasonably sized (with an average of about twenty-five students), intro lectures can be quite large. Tufts has two popular programs in which students who need a break from being students can develop and teach courses: the thirty-one-year-old Experimental College, which annually offers more than one hundred nontraditional, full-credit courses taught by students, faculty, and outside lecturers; and the Freshman Explorations seminars, each taught by two upperclassmen and a faculty member to between ten and fifteen students. With topics ranging from media and politics to juggling, Exploration courses are a way for freshmen to get to know each other and ease into the college experience, since the teachers double as advisors.

Tufts students also get a healthy diet of traditional academic fare. Distribution requirements include a new World Civilization course in addition to art, English and foreign languages, social sciences, humanities, natural sciences, and math. Engineers only have an English requirement in addition to the standard math, science, and technically oriented curriculum, but they must complete thirty-eight credits compared to the liberal arts students' thirty-four. According to the

"Students turn out by the hundreds and watch and participate in the Naked Quad Run!"

administration, preparing students "to make the Global Village safe" is a central goal, and annually 35 to 40 percent of the junior class studies abroad. Ambitious students may enroll in five-year joint-degree programs with the university's School of the Museum of Fine Arts, the New England Conservatory of Music, and the famed Fletcher School of Law and Diplomacy, or they may pack their suitcases for engineering and liberal arts programs in England, Germany, France, Spain, and Russia. Back home, Tufts offers the Washington Semester,* the Mystic Seaport program,* an exchange with Swarthmore, and cross-registration at a number of Boston schools.

The biggest homeland of the student body is Massachusetts (21 percent). New Jersey, New York, and California are also well represented, but students hail from all fifty states and sixty-one countries. The university's reputation in international relations also attracts a substantial number of foreign students (8 percent) and Americans living abroad. Asian-Americans make up 14 percent of the population, Hispanics 6 percent, and African-Americans 5 percent. Political liberals outnumber conservatives. In general, Tufts undergraduates tend to be a little less competitive and a bit more easygoing than their counterparts at the Ivies. They are expected to do more than absorb, memorize, and regurgitate. Professors are looking for thoughtfulness, and "many students compete with themselves but not with each other," says one student. No merit or athletic scholarships are available, but several prepayment and loan options are, and in the past the school has met the full demonstrated need of all admits.

Accommodations in the Uphill and Downhill (the two quads joined by a great expanse of grass and trees) campus dorms vary from long hallways of double rooms to apartment-like suites, old houses, and co-ops. A good-natured rivalry exists between the two areas; Uphill is closer to the humanities and social sciences classrooms and supposedly a little more social, while Downhill is nearer the science facilities. Freshmen and sophomores must live on campus in the dorms, while upperclassmen compete in a lottery. Students and administration agree that the addition of South Hall makes housing available to just about anyone who wants a room. Apartments are plentiful and, according to at least one student, affordable. Still, 20 percent of the students live off campus. All but one of the dorms are coed by floor or suite or alternating rooms. Food plans for five, ten, fourteen, or twenty meals a week are offered to everyone but freshmen, who must choose one of the last two options. Kosher and vegetarian meals are available, and occasional special meals (e.g., Italian night and Mexican night) spice up standard college cuisine.

With topics ranging from media and politics to juggling, Exploration courses are a way for freshmen to get to know each other and ease into the college experience.

While suburban Medford is not very exciting for those of the college class, the "T" metro system extends to the Tufts campus, so it's easy to make a quick jaunt to "student city" (a.k.a. Boston) for work or play. Harvard Square is even nearer and provides plenty of restaurants, nightlife, and music stores. For those with valid IDs, the campus pub has become an "in" place to hang out, especially Monday through Thursday nights. Tufts, incidentally, has earned a national reputation for its programs to promote the "responsible" use of alcohol.

A small band of thirteen fraternities and three sororities provides many of the on-campus weekend parties, though only 15 percent of the men and 3 percent of the women join the Greek system, and there is talk of getting rid of it altogether. University-sponsored activities include concerts, plays (there are fifteen to twenty productions each year at Aidekman Arts Center), parties, etc., and there are $2 movies on Wednesday and weekend nights. Major campus events in the fall include Homecoming and Halloween on the Hill, the latter of which is a carnival for children in the community. At the end of finals week in December, the "students turn out by the hundreds and watch and participate in the Naked Quad Run!" confesses one student. In the spring, there is Tuftsfest, a month–long affair with festivals, an interdorm Olympics, a semiformal dance, and Spring Fling, an end-of-year hurrah. Of all student activities, the largest by far, with more than five hundred students, is the Leonard Carmichael Society, the umbrella group for all volunteer activities. The students are involved in programs of adult literacy, blood drives, elderly outreach, teaching English as a second language, hunger projects, tutoring, low-income housing construction, and active work with the homeless and battered women.

The Tufts sailing team has won the Fowle trophy for the best overall collegiate sailing team in North America numerous times, and the baseball team is strong, too. As a Division III school, Tufts is no sports powerhouse, but many of its thirty-three varsity teams are competitive on the regional level, and the school boasts an impressive number of all-American athletes. The intramural gym and athletic facility upgrades make sports more accessible to jocks of all stripes.

Tufts is in the midst of a modern-day renaissance, or what many universities know as a capital campaign. Money raised already is allowing Tufts to improve campus facilities and financial aid for students. This, along with a swelling applicant pool, makes Tufts a much hotter school than it was just a few years ago. And its proximity to Boston, an intellectual and educational Mecca, makes it even more attractive than were it in, say, Detroit. Tufts gives every indication that it's going to keep scaling the university ranks until it reaches the summit—and that's not too far from Prospect Hill.

Overlaps

Brown, Harvard, Penn, Cornell, Dartmouth

If You Apply To ➤ **Tufts:** Early decision: Nov. 15, Jan. 1. Regular admissions: Jan. 1. Financial aid: Mar. 1. Housing: June 1. No campus interviews. Alumni interviews: recommended, informational. ACTs or SATs and 3 SAT IIs: required. Guarantees to meet demonstrated need. Accepts the Common Application and electronic applications. Essay question: two Common Application essays or choose from following: how you were shaped by your environment; why have you chosen to be a leader; how have you demonstrated citizenship. Apply directly to either the College of Liberal Arts or Engineering.

6823 St. Charles Avenue, New Orleans, LA 70118

The map may say that Tulane is in the South, but Tulane has the temperament of an East Coast institution. The university is trying to shoehorn its way into the front rank of southeastern universities, though it still trails Emory and Vanderbilt. High achievers should shoot for the Tulane Scholars program.

New Orleans—a diverse metropolitan city with much excitement and a rich history, not to mention the exotic foods, soulful jazz, and lively people. And nowhere is the playful flavor of this city more evident than on the campus of Tulane University. "New Orleans is the dream college town," says an enthusiastic junior. "The students more or less own the city." Aside from its prime location, Tulane offers all the charm of the South, and all the charge of a good education.

The school's 110-acre campus is located in an attractive residential area of uptown New Orleans, about fifteen minutes from the French Quarter and the business district. Tulane's administration building, Gibson Hall, faces St. Charles Avenue, where one of the nation's last streetcar lines still clatters past mansions. Across the street is Audubon Park, a 385-acre spread where students jog, walk, study, or feed the ducks in

"The students more or less own the city."

the lagoon. The buildings of gray stone and pillared brick are modeled after the neo-collegiate/Creole mixture indigenous to Louisiana institutional-type structures. One particular point of pride is the university's thirteen Tiffany windows, one of the largest collections in existence. New buildings add modern comfort to the beauty of the traditional ones, including several residence halls, an environmental science building, and a medical center, along with multimillion-dollar renovations.

Tulane's strength lies in the natural sciences, environmental sciences, and the humanities; international studies and Latin American studies in particular are especially strong. The Stone Center for Latin American studies includes the two hundred thousand-volume Latin American Library and offers more than 150 courses taught by eighty faculty members. An interdisciplinary program in political economy (economics, political science, and philosophy) stands out among the social sciences and is very popular with prelaw students. Those undergraduates ready to focus on a career may apply to Tulane's respected schools of engineering (biomedical engineering is particularly good), architecture, and business, as well as the highly acclaimed medical and law schools. Environmental studies majors benefit from the Tulane/Xavier Center for Bioenvironmental Research, where faculty members and students work together on research projects that include hazardous-waste remediation and the ecological effects of environmental contaminants.

Tulane offers several study-abroad options, including one-semester programs to locations such as Japan to study sociology and culture, Mexico City to delve into the language, and London to study liberal arts. In addition, the Tulane/Newcomb Junior Year Abroad program is one of the country's oldest and most prestigious programs, in which the student is fully immersed in the language and culture of the particular country. For

"There is a large Northeastern constituency here who have brought their Type-A personalities and racial tolerance down to a Southern city."

students looking to go into medical or law school, approximately 66 percent of graduates are accepted. Helping freshman make the transition are several programs. One is TIDES, where students can join groups on such topics as Understanding Your

Website: www.tulane.edu
Location: Urban
Total Enrollment: 12,381
Undergraduates: 7,522
Male/Female: 49/51
SAT Ranges: V 630–710
  M 610–700
ACT Range: 28-32
Financial Aid: 73%
Expense: Pr $ $ $ $
Phi Beta Kappa: Yes
Applicants: 10,862
Accepted: 61%
Enrolled: 22%
Grad in 6 Years: 77%
Returning Freshmen: 83%
Academics: ✍ ✍ ✍ ½
Social: ☎ ☎ ☎ ☎
Q of L: ★ ★ ★
Admissions: (504) 865-5731
Email Address: undergrad. admission@tulane.edu

Strongest Programs
  Premed
  Prelaw
  Political Economy
  Biomedical Engineering
  Engineering
  Business
  Anthropology
  Latin American Studies

Classmates, World Religions, and Cultures. Another offering for freshmen is the First Year Experience, one-credit courses on such subjects as Metacognition (Thinking about Thinking), Campus Life, and Women and Leadership.

Sixty-one percent of the classes at Tulane have fewer than twenty-five students, while an additional one-fourth have fewer than fifty, making it difficult for students to get into the classes of their choice. About 60 percent of those classes are taught by full professors. Graduate instructors are most likely to teach the beginning-level classes in English, foreign languages, and math, and are rarely found in the schools of business, architecture, or engineering. Overall, students praise Tulane's faculty, and the academic atmosphere can be very intense, depending on the class.

All Tulane liberal arts majors must complete a rigorous set of general education requirements. Besides demonstrating competency in English, math, and a foreign language, these requirements mandate that students take distribution requirements in the humanities and fine arts, the social sciences, and mathematics and the sciences. In the process of satisfying the requirements, students must take at least one course in Western and non-Western civilization, as well as a writing-intensive class. Freshmen with high SATs can place out of some classes, however. Each year the university's highly acclaimed honors program invites about seven hundred outstanding students, known as Tulane Scholars, to partake in accelerated courses taught by top professors. These select scholars also have the opportunity to design their own major and spend their junior year abroad.

While Tulane has a somewhat Southern feel, it is a sophisticated and cosmopolitan institution. Says one student, "There is a large Northeastern constituency here who have brought their Type-A personalities and racial tolerance down to a Southern city. If you're a Northerner, it's impossible to escape the Southern influence of the city, and if you're a Southerner, it's impossible to escape the Northern influence that exists on campus." Eighteen percent of the students are minorities, about half of whom are African-American. Tulane awards merit scholarships, ranging from $9,000 up to full tuition, and hundreds of athletic scholarships for student athletes.

"Three years ago freshman housing was the oldest rooms on campus, now they are among the newest."

Residence halls were not always given rave reviews in the past, yet students say they are improving. A number of modern residence halls were added within the past few years, and the rooms are cheerful and efficient. "Three years ago freshman housing was the oldest rooms on campus, now they are among the newest," says a student. Except for local students, freshmen must live on campus and leave their cars at home. After freshman year, housing is by lottery, and choices include Stadium Place, a student apartment complex. Many students opt to move off campus, claiming that it's much cheaper than university housing, but others are concerned about the safety factor of living in New Orleans. Some men live in their fraternity houses, but sororities only have social halls due to an old New Orleans law that makes it illegal to have more than four unrelated women living in one house. Freshmen have to stomach the cost of Tulane's meal plan, but alternatives exist at the University Center food court.

While schoolwork is taken seriously at Tulane, so are sports. The campus-wide acclaim for men's basketball borders on hysteria. Because the basketball arena seats only 3,600, students camp out to buy tickets for big games. Tulane basketball benefits from a new arena adjacent to the Louisiana Superdome. The football team isn't as talented, but draws a loyal following nonetheless. Women's and men's tennis, women's volleyball, and men's baseball had winning teams in recent years. Club sports are big, and students can also opt for weight work, squash, or swimming among other options at the Reily Recreational Center.

Social life at Tulane goes almost without saying. "New Orleans itself never stops partying!" boasts a junior. Fraternities and sororities are a presence—19 percent of the men and 33 percent of the women join—but do not dominate the social life. Though you're supposed to be twenty-one to buy alcohol or enjoy the bar scene in the cafés and clubs that dot the French Quarter, a sophomore explains that "alcohol is accessible." Mardi Gras is such a celebration that classes are suspended for two days and students from all over the country pour in to celebrate. An annual Jazzfest in the spring also draws wide participation. Road-trip destinations include the Gulf Coast, Mississippi, Houston, Atlanta, and Memphis.

While Tulane is rich in Southern tradition, it is a forward-looking school where the possibilities seem endless. And like its hometown, it is a diverse, energetic melting pot of interests and activity. Those seeking a dynamic education in a vibrant city need look no further. *C'est si bon!*

If You Apply To ➤

Tulane: Early action: Nov. 1. Regular admissions and financial aid: Jan. 15. Housing: May 1. Meets demonstrated need of 69%. Campus and alumni interviews: optional, informational. SATs or ACTs: required. SAT IIs: recommended (home-schooled applicants only). Accepts the Common Application and electronic applications. Essay question: personal statement.

University of Tulsa

600 South College Avenue, Tulsa, OK 74104

Tulsa is a notch smaller than Texas Christian and Washington U, but bigger than most liberal arts colleges. The university has a technical orientation rooted in Oklahoma oil, but Tulsa has a much more diverse curriculum than Colorado School of Mines. Tulsa has an innovative program allowing undergraduates to do research.

The University of Tulsa has been working through some identity issues. It's a small, private, liberal arts school, but it wants to provide its students with a strong foundation on which to build a solid career. With an emphasis on undergraduate research, hands-on work experiences, and a diverse array of course offerings, TU has managed to find a balance that works.

TU's 210-acre campus is just three miles from downtown Tulsa, and there's a striking view of the city's skyline from the steps of the neo-Gothic McFarlin Library. The university's more than fifty buildings run the architectural gamut from 1930s-vintage neo-Gothic to contemporary, all variations on a theme of yellow Tennessee limestone dubbed "TU stone." New additions include the Cyber Security Classrooms and Law Clinic, which is used for practical training and community outreach. A 108-bed dorm is now refurbished, and a 432-room apartment building is open for tenants. Recently completed facilities include the eight thousand-seat Donald W. Reynolds Center, which includes a basketball arena; the TU Legal Information Center, a $10.5 million renovation and expansion of the law library; a design studio featuring computer-aided design and a virtual slide library; and high-tech computer and teaching labs in several buildings. A new state-of-the-art tennis complex, which features eighteen courts, will soon be joined by a new track and student fitness center.

> **"We have a more diverse campus than any other here in Tulsa."**

Website: www.utulsa.edu
Location: Urban
Total Enrollment: 4,119
Undergraduates: 2,769
Male/Female: 48/52
SAT Ranges: V 570–690
  M 550–680
ACT Range: 23–29
Financial Aid: 63%
Expense: Pr $
Phi Beta Kappa: Yes
Applicants: 2,235
Accepted: 67%
Enrolled: 33%
Grad in 6 Years: 61%
Returning Freshmen: 77%
Academics: ✑ ✑ ✑
Social: ☎ ☎ ☎
Q of L: ★ ★
Admissions: (918) 631-2307

(Continued)
Email Address:
  admission@utulsa.edu

Strongest Programs
  Engineering
  Finance/Accounting
  Computer Science
  Communicative Disorders
  Biological Sciences
  Anthropology
  English
  Psychology

In addition to its well-established and internationally recognized petroleum and geosciences engineering programs, TU offers solid majors in finance, accounting, and computer science. The rapidly growing English department has some impressive resources at its disposal in McFarlin Library's special collections. The collections boast original works by nineteenth- and twentieth-century American and British authors, including books, letters, manuscripts, and even a stained necktie that once belonged to James Joyce, and more than fifty thousand items representing Nobel Laureate V. S. Naipaul's life and work from the 1950s to the present. TU's Naipaul Archive is the only comprehensive collection of Naipaul manuscripts, correspondence, and family memorabilia in the world. The elementary education program has been enhanced; film studies and arts management interdisciplinary programs were recently added.

In accordance with the Tulsa Curriculum, the cornerstone of the school's emphasis on liberal arts, all undergraduates take three writing courses, at least one mathematics course, and one or two years of foreign language, depending on the degree. In addition, each student completes at least twenty-five credit hours of general curriculum classes in aesthetic inquiry and creative experience, historical and social interpretation, and scientific investigation.

> "For the most part, dorms are nice and well maintained."

All freshmen take one semester of Argumentation and Exposition, followed by Writing for the Professions (for business students and future engineers) or First Seminar (for everyone else). American Sign Language may be used to fulfill the language requirement for the College of Arts and Sciences.

Fourteen interdisciplinary programs allow the pursuit of cross-departmental interests. Honors students take exclusive seminars, complete a thesis or advanced project, and can live together in a computer-equipped house. The Tulsa Undergraduate Research Challenge, initiated in 1995, offers outstanding opportunities for cutting-edge scientific research, and has produced twenty-six Goldwater Scholarship winners, eleven National Science Foundation Graduate Fellowships, and four Fulbright Grants. About half of all engineering students and 35 percent of business undergrads do research with faculty. Another portion of students travel abroad for programs including language immersion in Spain, studio art in Italy, business integration in Germany, and environmental study in Costa Rica.

Sixty-six percent of Tulsa's students are from Oklahoma; most others are from the Midwest and Southwest, with many hailing from Dallas and St. Louis. Twelve percent of the students are foreign, coming from the Middle East, East Asia, and Scandinavia. The student body is mildly diverse, with 8 percent African-American, 2 percent Asian-American and 3 percent Hispanic. "We have a more diverse campus than any other here in Tulsa," says one junior. Rising tuition is a prominent issue on campus. Athletes can compete for 301 scholarships in sixteen sports, ranging from women's crew to men's golf. TU also offers 850 merit scholarships, ranging from $1,000 to $20,000.

At Tulsa, freshmen and sophomores are required to live on campus, but only about half of the student population use campus housing. Students have plenty of "extremely livable" options, including three mixed-sex dorms (two coed by wing and the other coed by suite), one women's dorm, one men's dorm, fraternity and sorority houses, and campus apartments. All of the dorms are equipped with free cable television, and connections to the campus mainframe and the Internet are available for a nominal charge. The single-sex dorms are quieter and more attractive to upperclassmen. Dorms get average to good reviews. "For the most part, dorms are nice and well maintained," a senior says. "It's like all college dorms—you have to personalize your own space." The school recently started a "faculty-in-residence" program in the LaFortune House and University Apartments. Faculty and their families live the facilities and interact regularly with the students.

The School of Art's Third Floor Designs, a studio that produces graphic design at cost for nonprofit organizations, allows student artists to build their portfolios.

American Sign Language may be used to fulfill the language requirement for the College of Arts and Sciences.

The social life at TU is based on the individual's motivation to participate, a trait not all students possess. "Social life at TU can be great if you take advantage of it," one student says. "Joining clubs, getting into Greek life, and hanging out in dorms allows students to meet other students." The Student Association brings top-name comedians, speakers, and entertainers to campus. Greek organizations claim 21 percent of

"Social life at TU can be great if you take advantage of it."

TU men and 23 percent of the women, and the frats host campus-wide house parties. Student-initiated policies govern drinking on campus; administrators say this self-policing has led to responsible imbibing.

Campus traditions include the ringing of the college bell in the Alumni Center cupola by each senior after his or her last class and Springfest. Other big events include Reggaefest, Homecoming, and Greek events such as the Kappa Sigma Olympics, the Sigma Chi Derby Days, and the Delta Gamma Anchor Splash. Nearby parks, lakes, and a huge recreational water park please outdoor enthusiasts. Downtown Tulsa offers symphony, ballet, opera, and an annual Oktoberfest. Popular roadtrips include Oklahoma City, or the wilds of Arkansas, New Mexico, and Colorado. Students are very active in community service.

Here in the home state of J. C. Watts and Steve Largent, pro football players turned congressmen, sports are important. Tulsa's men's basketball team and women's golf team both recently won conference championships. The school places a heavy emphasis on games against football rivals Oklahoma and Oklahoma State, and basketball games against Arkansas and OSU get students riled up.

TU is trying to do some things a differently: be a small liberal arts school in a part of the country most known for sprawling public universities, and incorporate professional preparation with an emphasis on broad intellectual challenges. It's a philosophy that serves the school well and polishes its reputation beyond the Midwestern plains.

> **Overlaps**
>
> **Texas Christian, Southern Methodist, Washington University (MO), University of Oklahoma, Oklahoma State**

> **If You Apply To ➤**
>
> **Tulsa:** Rolling admissions. Meets demonstrated need of 89%. Campus interviews: recommended, evaluative. Alumni interviews: not available. SATs or ACTs: required. SAT IIs: optional. Accepts the Common Application and electronic applications. Essay question: challenge you have faced; how you would change the world; significant life event.

Union College

807 Union Street, Schenectady, NY 12308

Union is split down the middle between liberal arts and engineering. That means its center of gravity is more toward the technical side than places like Trinity, Lafayette, and Tufts, but less so than Clarkson and Rensselaer. Schenectady is less than exciting, but there are outdoor getaways in all directions.

Union College is a study in firsts; the first in the nation to follow a formal architectural plan, the first to have Greek fraternities, and one of the first to be nondenominational, Union remains determined to stay out in front. To that end, it's deemphasizing the Greek system and implementing a House System by Fall 2004, to give every student access to a social group, and to good social and residential space. A new alcohol policy limits attendance at parties where booze is served, as well as

> **Website:** www.union.edu
> **Location:** City outskirts
> **Total Enrollment:** 2,118
> **Undergraduates:** 2,059
> **Male/Female:** 52/48

(Continued)

SAT Ranges: V 550–650
    M 580–670
Financial Aid: 51%
Expense: Pr $ $ $
Phi Beta Kappa: Yes
Applicants: 3,910
Accepted: 41%
Enrolled: 32%
Grad in 6 Years: 80%
Returning Freshmen: 92%
Academics: ✍ ✍ ✍ ✍
Social: ☎ ☎ ☎
Q of L: ★ ★ ★
Admissions: (518) 388-6112
Email Address:
    admissions@union.edu

Strongest Programs
  Mathematics
  Chemistry
  Psychology
  Political Science
  English
  Classics
  Mechanical Engineering

Each spring, Union cancels classes one afternoon for the Charles Steinmetz Symposium, where students present scholarly projects in a professional-conference atmosphere.

the amount of beer available. And the new Union Scholars Program gives entering freshmen with unusual capabilities and talents a more extensive Freshman Preceptorial Program and the chance to get involved in independent, faculty-sponsored research in the sophomore year. "The administration is increasing the emphasis on academics," says a junior. "More liberal kids are coming in—smarter kids, too," a senior agrees.

The one hundred-acre Union campus sits on a hill overlooking Schenectady. Its unified campus plan, designed in 1813 by French architect and landscaper Joseph Jacques Ramée, includes eight acres of formal gardens and woodlands. Ramée's vision took shape in brownstone and red brick, with plenty of white arches, pilasters, and lacy green trees. The sixteen-sided Nott Memorial, a National Historic Landmark, is a meeting, study, and exhibition center for students and alumni. The college has invested $10 million to revitalize an adjacent neighborhood, and many students volunteer through Big Brothers/Big Sisters and We Care About U Schenectady, which builds houses for the homeless. Also, all freshmen work on a community clean-up project during orientation.

> **"More liberal kids are coming in—smarter kids, too."**

Union's general education requirements fall into four groups. The History, Literature, and Civilization cluster includes the Freshman Preceptorial "Diversity and Dialog," plus two courses in history (ancient, European, or American), and two associated follow-up courses (two in literature, or one in literature and one in civilization). The team-taught Preceptorial focuses on critical reading, analysis, and writing, and each section is capped at sixteen students. The Social and Behavioral Science cluster requires an introductory course in anthropology, economics, political science, psychology, or sociology. The Mathematics and Natural Science cluster requires one math course and two courses in basic or applied science, one of which must have labs. The Other Languages, Other Cultures, Other Disciplines cluster includes three courses in a modern language, one term abroad, or three related courses in Africana studies, East Asian studies, or Latin American studies.

Students praise Union's programs in English, biology, political science, and psychology—all, except biology, among the five most popular majors on campus. "The chemistry, mathematics, and geology departments are superior," adds a biochemistry major. "We have state-of-the-art instrumentation, great funding to attend national and regional conferences, undergraduate research, small laboratory sections, and awesome faculty." Each spring,

> **"The chemistry, mathematics, and geology departments are superior."**

Union cancels classes one afternoon for the Charles Steinmetz Symposium, where students present scholarly projects in a professional-conference atmosphere. Last year, more than three hundred students participated.

Union's programs in engineering and computer science are legendary, especially for a liberal arts school, though they are smaller now that civil engineering has been phased out. The history department is home to Union's most esteemed lecturer, Stephen Berk, whose course on the Holocaust and Twentieth-Century Europe is a hot ticket. The Educational Studies Program allows aspiring teachers to complete courses and fieldwork required for secondary-school certification in fourteen subjects, while including a strong liberal arts grounding. Interdisciplinary majors include Russian and Eastern European studies, industrial economics, and law and public policy. Administrators say philosophy and performing arts are weaker because of lower enrollment and resources.

Union operates on a trimester system, which students call a mixed blessing. On the downside, the system means thrice-a-year exams, and a late start to summer jobs, since school doesn't finish until June. "The trimester calendar really prevents a laid-back atmosphere," says one student. On the upside, some students feel that concentrating on just three courses a term helps them learn more. More terms also mean more opportunities for independent study and internships, either in the state capital of Albany, twenty minutes away, or in Washington, D.C. About 65 percent of each class studies abroad. Some choose a summer program examining national health-care systems in England, Holland, and Hungary, while others study marine life in Bermuda, Woods Hole, or Newfoundland. A set of mini-terms abroad, during the winter and summer breaks, join engineering and liberal arts students on team projects in Brazil and Australia.

What Schenectady lacks can be found in resort-like Saratoga Springs and the Adirondacks to the north, and the Catskills to the south.

Back on campus, students give the faculty high marks. "Our professors are amazing—they are here because they want to teach, as well as do research," says a junior. "They are very concerned with our academic careers, often coming in on nights and weekends to either teach, counsel, or simply get to know us better." Sophomore and junior honors students can take interdisciplinary seminars team-taught by faculty from multiple departments, and may attend private meetings with visiting luminaries.

Forty-seven percent of Union's students come from New York State. "Students at Union are, by and large, superficial and unconcerned with their education," says a junior. "Students tend to be a little snobby," agrees a psychology and biology major. "It was hard to find a niche at first." Four percent of the student body is African-American, another 4 percent is Hispanic, and 5 percent is Asian-American. The school's Multicultural Affairs Council and the President's Commission on Diversity are working to boost these numbers, and an affirmative-action officer and community-outreach director have been

"The school spends a lot of money to keep us entertained."

hired to help with race relations. Regardless of background, a general indifference about key issues on campus and in the larger world seems to prevail. "The new alcohol policy and the administration's policy toward campus rapes are hot topics," says a biochemistry major. "However, most students are apathetic, and so little is done."

Union offers fifty-five merit scholarships of $13,500 each, as well as a complement of loans, but no athletic scholarships. The Chester Arthur Undergraduate Support for Excellence (CAUSE) award, which takes its name from the former U.S. president and most distinguished graduate, offers loans to students interested in public service, forgiven at 20 percent per year if the student pursues a service-oriented career.

Eighty-one percent of Union students live in the dorms, which are "well maintained for the most part, but some are downright cramped," says a junior. "Campus apartments are gorgeous," and reserved for upperclassmen. Underclassmen may choose from single-sex, coed, and theme houses; the new House System will bar Greek groups from offering housing. Students recommend West, which is coed by room, and thus very social, as well as Fox and Davidson, where freshmen and sophomores live in suites: four people to two bedrooms and a "huge" common room. All dorm rooms are linked to the Union computer network, and everyone eats at one of two dining halls.

Only hard-core geeks miss the Division I ice hockey games against Rensselaer Polytechnic Institute or Cornell.

Social life at Union "is like a skipping record—the same thing over and over and over again," a junior laments. "The school spends a lot of money to keep us entertained," with movies, a coffee house, dances, and guest speakers, "but it's often unsuccessful." The lack of things to do leads 22 percent of men and 19 percent of women to go Greek—significant fractions, but lower than in past years. The Greeks have actually been helped by the new alcohol policy, which restricts parties to no more than two kegs, and no more than one hundred guests, a biochemistry major reports. "The head-count limit makes it difficult for people to get in, increasing the elite status of the Greek system," the student says. The policy also hasn't stopped the underage from guzzling beer. (No hard liquor is allowed on campus, except in the president's house.) Local bars such as Van Dyck, Pinhead Susan's, and Bar One are said to be fun, but dingy. Montreal is a popular road trip.

Schenectady is an old-line industrial city that's becoming more high-tech, but it "is not a college town in the least," says a junior. What Schenectady lacks can be found in resort-like Saratoga Springs and the Adirondacks to the north, and the Catskills to the south. Fall Fest and Spring Fest feature all-campus picnics and live music; Party in the Garden is also popular, and only hard-core geeks miss the Division I ice hockey games against Rensselaer Polytechnic Institute or Cornell. Union's twenty-five other intercollegiate teams compete in Division III. Painting the Idol, a really ugly campus statue, "is something everyone does, and a great bonding experience."

Union College is a small, friendly place full of eager intellectual exchange, where students wish that the social life was as vibrant as the discussions in their labs and classrooms. "The faculty, academics, and undergraduate research opportunities are by far exceptional—for any college or university," says a junior. "We are very fortunate to obtain the well-versed and well-rounded education that we do."

Overlaps

Hamilton, Colgate, Lehigh, Bates

If You Apply To > **Union:** Early decision: Nov. 15, Jan. 15. Regular admissions and housing: Jan. 15. Financial aid: Feb. 1. Guarantees to meet demonstrated need. Campus interviews: strongly recommended, evaluative. Alumni interviews: recommended, informational. SAT I or three SAT IIs (writing and two others) or ACT: required. Accepts the Common Application and electronic applications. Essay question: significant experience, achievement, or risk you have taken; issue of personal, local, national, or international concern; influential person, fictional character, historical figure, or creative work; or a topic of your choice.

Ursinus College

Box 1000, Collegeville, PA 19426

Ursinus is the smallest of the cohort of eastern Pennsylvania liberal arts colleges that includes Franklin and Marshall, Muhlenberg, and Lafayette. The plus side is more attention from faculty and more emphasis on independent learning. Though Philly is within arm's reach, the setting is quiet.

Website: www.ursinus.edu
Location: Suburban
Total Enrollment: 1,324
Undergraduates: 1,324
Male/Female: 44/56
SAT Ranges: V 550–650
  M 550–660
ACT Range: N/A
Financial Aid: 73%
Expense: Pr $ $ $
Phi Beta Kappa: Yes
Applicants: 1,562
Accepted: 78%
Enrolled: 25%
Grad in 6 Years: 78%
Returning Freshmen: 90%
Academics:

Ursinus College was established as a school where, in the words of namesake Zacharias Ursinus, students would "examine all things and retain what is good." For many years, the college emphasized solid training in practical fields ranging from business administration to sports science, but it is now returning with a vengeance to its liberal arts roots. All new students and faculty members must now take part in a course called the Common Intellectual Experience that explores topics ranging from Plato to Buddhist scripture, and there is a requirement that each student have an Independent Learning Experience. Though Ursinus (pronounced Ur-SIGN-nus) is small, students are happy at this college in the suburbs of Philadelphia, thanks largely to close contact with professors and a cozy atmosphere where everyone knows everyone else.

Ursinus is located in Collegeville, about forty minutes west of Philadelphia, and only ten miles from the green, rolling hills of Valley Forge National Park. The 167-acre campus is mostly Pennsylvania fieldstone with a variety of restored buildings. The campus walkway includes the F.W. Olin Hall and the Berman Museum of Art. Ursinus completed a $16 million renovation and expansion of Pfahler Science Hall, which houses chemistry, computer science, mathematics, and physics. A $1 million bookstore was added to the back of the Student Center and a new, 143-bed student residence opened last year. Future construction includes a performing-arts center.

The school offers twenty-five majors and forty-seven minors, with the sciences garnering the most praise. Ursinus has cultivated a strong minor in East Asian studies, and it has a viable classics program as well as solid strength in history, English, and politics. Biology is still the most popular major, though faculty members have shifted the emphasis of instruction from premed to science. Ursinus was the first college in Pennsylvania approved by the state to certify secondary teachers of Japanese. Other language programs are popular, but the number of economics/business administration majors has declined since the economists began requiring calculus. Nearly one-quarter of the rising senior class will have paid summer academic fellowships where they work full-time with a faculty mentor. For the academically motivated who want a change from the Pennsylvania 'burbs, Ursinus offers opportunities around the globe as part of the Bradley University Consortium. The college also offers programs with its own faculty in Japan, Mexico, Spain, Italy, England, and Germany. Students can study at other U.S. universities, including Howard and American in Washington, D.C. Prospective engineers may choose 3–2 programs at Columbia University and elsewhere.

> "Ursinus has a very competitive environment, especially in the sciences."

Every freshman is issued a laptop computer, and soon all Ursinus students will be so equipped. A new graduation requirement, the Independent Learning Experience, requires every student to either complete an independent research project, become an intern, study abroad, or student teach. The newest academic offerings include majors in neuroscience, environmental studies, and biochemistry and molecular biology.

General education requirements under the Ursinus Plan revolve around the Common Intellectual Experience, which include a Freshman Seminar, English composition, two foreign language courses, two math or science courses, two courses in different social sciences, and two humanities courses. The Common Intellectual Experience for freshmen, which is taught by faculty members from all disciplines, is designed to give students a common basis for academic discussions that will spill over into the cafeteria and dorms. Honors students complete an independent research project that is evaluated by outside examiners. The library has 185,000 volumes, but the school is connected to OCLC, a consortium of more that eighteen thousand libraries, and most books are accessible within a few days. Ursinus students may also use the Penn libraries.

Ursinus students work hard for their grades. "Ursinus has a very competitive environment, especially in the sciences," a sophomore says. In fact, 40 percent of students at the school come from the top tenth of their class. Classes at the college are small and professors are outstanding. "All students are taught by professors, never graduate students. Professors get to know students and are always available outside the classroom," says one junior communications major. Academic advising also receives high marks; freshmen meet their advisors once a week during the first half of their first semester. "Advisors are there whenever you need them," one student says. Other students say Ursinus makes it easy to succeed. "Just about everyone graduates in four years, unless you are a real slacker," says a sophomore.

> "All students are taught by professors."

Sixty-one percent of the students at Ursinus are from Pennsylvania, with others hailing from New York or New Jersey. Eighty-three percent of students are white, with African-Americans making up 8 percent, Asian-Americans another 3 percent, and Hispanics 2 percent. Racial tension is minimal. The school's excellent student-life staff includes several key members who are African-American. Race relations,

(Continued)

Social: ☎ ☎ ☎
Q of L: ★ ★ ★
Admissions: (610) 409-3200
Email Address:
admissions@ursinus.edu

Strongest Programs
Biology
English
Chemistry
English
History
Politics
Psychology

Nearly one-quarter of the rising senior class will have paid summer academic fellowships where they work full-time with a faculty mentor.

Collegeville is a tiny town, only eight blocks long, and Ursinus takes up six of them.

sexual harassment, and physical safety are covered in "Ursinus in Community," which begins with freshman orientation. "Ursinus is not a politically active school at all," a sophomore says. "Too laid-back." Merit scholarships are available each year, ranging from $500 to $24,850.

Housing options at Ursinus run the gamut from typical to modern, and 97 percent of students live in the dorms, adding to the college's community feel. "Rooms are big, especially for freshmen," a student raves. Upperclassmen quickly grab the Main Street houses, a string of Victorian-era homes across the street from campus, while many first-year men take up residence in Old Men's (BWC), which has generously sized rooms. The college recently finished renovations on two of the thirty Victorian-era student residences that the college owns. The college provides three meal plans (nineteen, fourteen, or nine meals per week), and students may choose to eat in the main dining room or Zack's snack bar. The campus is very safe, one student says; the security guards are always available for anything. "If it's raining, they will bring you an umbrella. If you're locked out of your room, they will get you in."

Collegeville is a tiny town, only eight blocks long, and Ursinus takes up six of them. While the town has little that the students want, it does have some of what they need, including late-night pizza delivery. As for social life, students stick close to home. "Most parties are on campus," a student says. "Parties get crazy. Not many road trips." Campus social activities include free movies every night, lectures, and dances. Greek life draws 15 percent of the men and 30 percent of the women, but has seen a marked decline recently as students take advantage of opportunities to volunteer and attend events in nearby Phillie. In fact, Central Philadelphia is less than an hour away, and because many students have cars, they retreat to the Jersey shore during the warmer months. Finally, there are two mega-malls within a twenty-minute drive of Ursinus, including the King of Prussia complex, the second-largest mall in the country.

Students here love sports, and 60 percent of the student body play on an NCAA Division III varsity team. For women determined to pursue careers in athletics, Ursinus is a well-known stepping stone to collegiate coaching posts; more than fifty colleges have hired Ursinus alumni. The lacrosse team is recognized as a perennial contender for the national championship, and the women's field hockey team is strong. Sadly, the longest-running football rivalry in the Philadelphia area against rival Swarthmore is no more; Swarthmore dropped the sport in 2001. Among other contributions in the world of sports, Ursinus is in *The Guinness Book of World Records* for having a tree in the endzone of the football field.

Ursinus may not be in the center of some great metropolitan area, or be big enough to have a big town built around it, but to the students who attend, the college offers a solid education within a close-knit community. Says an amiable lawyer-to-be, "It is a small, comfortable atmosphere where everyone knows everyone."

Overlaps

Gettysburg, Franklin and Marshall, Villanova, St. Josephs, Muhlenberg

If You Apply To ➤ **Ursinus:** Early decision: Jan. 15. Regular admissions and housing: Feb. 15. Does not guarantee to meet demonstrated need. Campus interviews: recommended, informational. No alumni interviews. SATs: optional (required for students not in the top 10% of high-school graduating class). SAT IIs: recommended. Accepts the Common Application and electronic applications. Essay question: significant experience; personal issue; or significant person.

250 SSB, Salt Lake City, UT 84112

While the true-blue Mormons generally head for BYU, University of Utah attracts a more diverse crowd that is drawn to the region's only major city. A majority of students hail from the Salt Lake City region, and many live at home. Professional programs such as business, engineering, and communications are the most popular.

Utah may be home of the Mormons, but the University of Utah, located in Salt Lake City, is decidedly secular. In addition to being the flagship institution of the public Utah System of Higher Education, the university is a major national scientific research center. Founded in 1850, the University of Utah is unusual in its ability to offer students the advantages of living in a city while at the same time maintaining a connection with nature.

Set in the foothills of the Rocky Mountains, near the shores of the Great Salt Lake, the university enjoys a picturesque location a half-hour's drive from "the greatest snow on earth." Though not the aesthetic equal of its stunning backdrop, the Utah campus is extremely attractive. Occupying 1,500 well-landscaped acres with nearly as many different kinds of trees as undergraduates, the campus is the state's arboretum. The architectural style of the university's structures ranges from nineteenth-century, ivy-covered buildings to state-of-the-art athletic facilities. The Marriott Library renovation, a project that doubled the library's size, was completed in 1998, and a new supercomputing facility has recently been completed.

The U operates on a semester calendar with a full summer session. There is a slate of general education requirements that students must fulfill, including courses in writing, American institutions, intellectual explorations, and quantitative reasoning. Utah provides a blend of strong professional training with a solid program in liberal arts. Renowned for its research in biomedical engineering, Utah's Health Sciences Center hosted the first mechanical heart transplant. Engineering, computer science, business, and chemistry are the most popular majors. Dance programs (both ballet and modern) and physical therapy are also noteworthy. The once-troubled sociology department has been strengthened. Utah's honors program, the third-oldest in the nation, features top faculty and small classes, and routinely receives high praise. The Undergraduate Research Program gives students the chance to join faculty members in research projects and allows them to receive either academic credit or a stipend for their participation. The academic climate is competitive, but not cutthroat. "The courses are challenging but students tend to their own circumstances instead of worrying about what others are doing," says a psychology major.

> "The courses are challenging but students tend to their own circumstances instead of worrying about what others are doing."

To make it easier to sign up for classes, the school now has Web-based registration, with freshmen getting first priority. Introductory courses often enroll hundreds of students, and classes can be overcrowded. Utah's professors generally receive high marks from the students. "The professors are well versed in their subjects and eager to help their students," says one senior.

Utah's students are a middle-class, fairly homogeneous lot; out-of-staters make up 23 percent of the student body, while minority students are barely represented, with African-Americans, Hispanics, and Asian-Americans combining for less than 7 percent. Nevertheless, there seems to be little overt racial hostility. "If there is a confrontation, it's usually between the university and Mormon leaders," says one

Website: www.utah.edu
Location: City outskirts
Total Enrollment: 26,193
Undergraduates: 21,095
Male/Female: 53/46
SAT Ranges: V 460–620
  M 470–630
ACT Range: 20–27
Financial Aid: 30%
Expense: Pub $
Phi Beta Kappa: Yes
Applicants: 5,663
Accepted: 90%
Enrolled: 47%
Grad in 6 Years: 53%
Returning Freshmen: 73%
Academics: ✍ ✍ ✍
Social: ☎ ☎ ☎
Q of L: ★ ★ ★
Admissions: (801) 581-7281
Email Address: N/A

Strongest Programs
  Business
  Psychology
  Communications
  Ballet/Dance
  Chemistry
  Engineering
  Computer Science

The U recently moved from a quarter system to a semester calendar with a full summer session.

student. Many of the Mormons are of the "returned missionary" variety, older than most undergraduates and married. Despite Utah's buttoned-down image, there are at least a handful of liberals lurking around, and the Mormon influence is not as all-pervasive as at neighboring Brigham Young. Utah offers more than 1,600 scholarships for academic achievement, some reserved for state residents, along with three hundred athletic scholarships, distributed among twenty-one NCAA Division I teams.

According to one student, the U is "determined to be the largest commuter campus in the United States." Seventeen percent of students live on campus in newly built apartments and dorms. Students who live in residence halls can grab a bite at the Heritage Center or at one of the six restaurants located in the student union. As for social life, it's as good as a commuter school's can be: low-key. Still, one student states, "There's a lot of fun to be had, if you know where to look." The Outdoor Recreation Program offers excursions into nature and also has a storehouse of more than 1,500 different items to rent to students. While the university sponsors symposiums and lectures, and students do support a variety of movie houses and clubs with live acts, most socializing at this "suitcase school" takes place off campus. Road trips to Las Vegas, Seattle, or any of the nearby ski resorts (the school provides slopeside bus service) is very popular. Only 3 percent of the men and 2 percent of the women go Greek, and the city council recently clamped down on Greek growth in order to keep the system small.

> **"The professors are well versed in their subjects and eager to help their students."**

The few students who don't go home on weekends warn that "a car is requisite" to navigate the sprawling metro area surrounding the U. Adjacent to campus, the Latter-day Saints Institute of Religion sponsors dances and other social activities, though the conservative social attitudes may dampen the spirits of the party animals. The Lowell Bennion Community Service Center has received one of four national awards for community service. "The volunteer program is exceptional, very well organized, and supported," notes an economics major. "Salt Lake City offers a lot of entertainment, including restaurants, movie theaters, and all kinds of outdoor activities," says a chemistry/English major. The flourishing cultural scene is regional in scope and includes the respected Utah Symphony, several dance companies, opera, the NBA's Utah Jazz, the minor-league Utah Stingers, and, of course, the Mormon Tabernacle Choir.

> **"If there is a confrontation, it's usually between the university and Mormon leaders."**

Football and basketball are the most popular sports on campus, and both draw an enthusiastic following. The women's gymnastics team has won ten NCAA titles in the past sixteen years, and the men's basketball team is always strong. Available athletic amenities include indoor tennis, racquetball, squash courts, saunas, swimming pools, an indoor track, and weight machines. Intramurals in nearly one hundred sports, a quarter of which are coed, are an important student activity. And any match against rival BYU usually sells out. Students also rave about the three-day Mayfest, celebrated every spring, which brings the campus together for dances, plays, movies, and speakers, as well as edible delights.

If you're looking for a campus that rages with raucous parties on weekends, complemented by crowded dorms that encourage the formation of a real community, the University of Utah probably won't fulfill your expectations. On the other hand, if you are looking for solid professors, excellent academics, and a beautiful campus at a reasonable price, the U might just be the place.

Overlaps

Brigham Young, Utah State, Stanford, University of Arizona

Vanderbilt University

2305 West End Avenue, Nashville, TN 37240

More "southern" than Emory or Duke, Vandy has traditionally been a preferred choice in the Deep South suburbs of Atlanta and Birmingham. Along with Tulane, it is the only leading Southern private institution with both business and engineering (and one of the South's leading music programs to boot).

Vanderbilt University used to be a quiet, conservative school in the heart of the South. But no longer. Vanderbilt is working to diversify its student body and is gaining an impressive national reputation. Sure, football games still require dressing up and finding a date, but the flip side of that formality is a Southern ease and friendliness that make rigorous academics easier to swallow. In contrast to Duke, Emory, and Tulane, which are merely located in the South, Vanderbilt remains a bastion of Southern culture.

The 330-acre Nashville campus, named a national arboretum in the late 1980s, is park-like. Art and sculptures dot the campus, and architectural styles range from gothic to modern glass and brick. Vandy's campus also includes sixty-acre Peabody College, the central section of which is listed on the National Register of Historic Places. As it tries to preserve its roots, the campus is also growing at an incredibly fast pace. Recent construction has left little of the campus untouched and includes additions to academic buildings and the Hill Student, plus new lots and garages to ease the campus's tight parking situation. The Blair School of Music will have quadrupled in size by 2002 and includes a new auditorium. The engineering school has been overhauled, and many changes have taken place at the Sarratt Student Center, such as a new Stonehenge Café.

> "All of Vanderbilt's academic offerings are well above average."

Vanderbilt undergraduates choose from among four schools—arts and science, engineering, music, and education/human development—with all undergraduates taking their core liberal arts courses in the College of Arts and Science. Specific distribution requirements vary from school to school, but most students get a good dose of writing, math, foreign language, humanities, and natural science courses. "I've taken a wide variety of liberal arts courses and come away with the impression that all of Vanderbilt's academic offerings are well above average," a junior reports. Freshmen in the College of Arts and Science benefit from one of the best writing programs anywhere, and the university's freshman seminars offer small settings and discussion on topics ranging from Country Music in Social Context to Women and Work in the U.S.

Popular majors are engineering, psychology, education, and English. The Peabody College of education and human development—which requires its teacher licensure candidates to double major, usually in a liberal arts field—offers strong programs in elementary and special education, including the opportunity to spend a summer at England's Cambridge University and teach at a British school. Though Vandy has no undergraduate major in business administration, many students

Website: www.vanderbilt.edu
Location: City outskirts
Total Enrollment: 10,388
Undergraduates: 6,077
Male/Female: 49/51
SAT Ranges: V 600–690
    M 630–710
ACT Range: 27–31
Financial Aid: 36%
Expense: Pr $ $ $ $
Phi Beta Kappa: Yes
Applicants: 9,746
Accepted: 46%
Enrolled: 34%
Grad in 6 Years: 84%
Returning Freshmen: 94%
Academics: ✑ ✑ ✑ ✑
Social: ☎ ☎ ☎ ☎
Q of L: ★ ★ ★ ★
Admissions: (615) 322-2561
Email Address:
    admissions@vanderbilt.edu

Strongest Programs
    Musical Arts
    Education
    English
    Philosophy
    Engineering

make do as economics majors with a business minor. There is also a 3–2 program with the Owen Graduate School of Business. Newer programs include a major and an honors program in women's studies, a minor in Italian studies, a revised history major, and a concentration in collaborative arts for pianists.

Vanderbilt's popular study-abroad program features instruction in England, France, Italy, Siena, Ireland, Scotland, Mallorca, Palma de Mallorca, Germany, Spain, Balboa, Florence, China, Japan, and Australia. The optional May session allows students to spend four weeks on one concentrated project—helping some graduate with two majors in four years. Drama classes have been known to tour London theaters during the May term, while some students work at regional archeological digs. Thanks to a multiyear dorm renovation project, students in dorms are networked to the campus library computers. The state-of-the-art library also has one of the country's best videotape collections of network evening news, a special help to students majoring in history and political science.

"Professors love interacting with students."

When it comes to academic etiquette, Vanderbilt students are governed by the school's honor system, which makes unproctored exams possible. First instituted in 1875, this system governs all aspects of a student's academic conduct. Students rave about the faculty. "First rate. My experiences with professors have been extremely positive," says a biomedical engineering major. "Professors love interacting with students," adds a classmate. "I recently passed a professor in the dining room on campus and he interrupted his morning newspaper to talk to me about his fascination with Mark Twain."

While a mixture of conservative Republicans and fraternity and sorority types has set the tone at Vanderbilt in the past, students say the college is slowly becoming more liberal. "Probably the most infamous students are the affluent, socially-oriented, designer-clad types," says a student. "But another group—the probably-affluent-but-not-flaunting-it, socially conscious, intellectually minded—is probably a better representation of the student body." The changes may be due to the fact that more students are coming from outside the state of Tennessee and the suburban Birmingham-Atlanta corridor and public-school graduates now constitute about 55 percent of the student body. Still, Vandy has a much more Southern feel than Duke, the South's other leading private university.

Vanderbilt students are governed by the school's honor system, which makes possible unproctored exams. First instituted in 1875, this system governs all aspects of a student's academic conduct.

The number of minorities is increasing (Asian-Americans constitute 6 percent, African-Americans 5 percent, and Hispanics 3 percent) as is their acceptance by the student body. One student says, "Racial and gender issues are very pivotal on this campus. Political correctness is very important for many people." Vandy's need-based financial-aid program is complemented by numerous merit scholarships and more than two hundred athletic scholarships.

Eighty-three percent of Vandy's undergraduates live in the dorms. According to the students, the dorms are "typical to college" and "well maintained." Freshmen occupy singles or doubles in their own special dorms; other accommodations include ten-person town houses, six-room suites, theme dorms (wellness, environmental awareness, philosophy, foreign language), and apartments. Seniors can live off campus but report that housing is not easy to find, and that the on-campus lottery system—in which seniors get first priority—is a better bet. There are thirteen different dining facilities on campus. Freshmen are required to buy the Dinner Plan, but the quality of the food and service gets rave reviews. Upperclassmen can purchase the Dinner Plan or use other dining facilities. Fraternity houses have cooks, but sorority kitchens are used only once a week. Campus security is tight.

Fifty percent of the women and 34 percent of the men join the Greek system, which is a very active force on the campus. Interaction between the Greeks and non-Greeks is encouraged, although not always successfully, by making many functions open to the whole campus. "Fraternities have parties almost every weekend," a senior says. The Vandy Late Night Program provides free entertainment opportunities off campus from ice-skating to trips to the Grand Ol' Opry. Dating is big at Vandy; the most coveted invitation is the Accolade formal that precedes Homecoming, tickets to which are both expensive and limited. (Funds from the Accolade benefit scholarships for minority students.) Another favorite Vandy tradition is the Rites of Spring festival, a carnival and music festival that takes place on the main lawn. Though Vandy students drink as much alcohol as those at any other school, they have to work to get their hands on it. Open containers are banned in public, and kegs are taboo. "The policy is fairly effective, but underage students can find loopholes," a worldly senior says.

Vanderbilt's proximity to Music City USA provides "something for pretty much everyone": a rich supply of bluegrass, country, and rock music and an abundance of good restaurants and theaters—all within walking distance. Walk in one direction and there are fajitas and buckets of beer at the San Antonio Taco Company; walk the other way and it's CDs galore at Tower Records. For country-music fans, the wax museum in town is a must-see, and there is an ever-increasing amount of brew pubs in the city. Beyond Nashville's borders are the Smokies, state parks with picnic facilities, beautiful lakes, and skiing in the winter. The best road trips are to Memphis (home of Elvis!), New Orleans (for Mardi Gras), the Kentucky Derby, and Atlanta.

"Racial and gender issues are very pivotal on this campus."

Vanderbilt is the smallest—and the only private—institution in the competitive and football-crazy Southeastern Conference (Division IA). Among the campus sports events, basketball is the hot ticket, and both the men's and women's teams draw raves from Vanderbilt fans. The women's team won the conference championship in 2001–2002, and the men's team won the 1993 Southeastern Conference Championship and advanced to the NCAA postseason tournament's Sweet Sixteen. Women's soccer has also done quite well, winning the conference for two years straight. Rivals include Alabama, Georgia, and Tennessee, though Vanderbilt almost always comes up on the losing end against these schools in football.

Vanderbilt is quietly building a reputation for excellence that extends beyond its Southern heritage. Its talented students, who enjoy working hard and playing harder, thrive in its uniquely Southern atmosphere. It's not a cheap alternative, exemplified by one of its slogans: "Vanderbilt: It Even Sounds Expensive." But for many, it's money well spent. One student says after he had visited all the schools on his list, he felt "most at home" at Vanderbilt. It's this easygoing charm that makes the Vandy experience so appealing.

Overlaps

Duke, Emory, University of Virginia, Wake Forest, UNC–Chapel Hill

If You Apply To ➢

Vanderbilt: Early decision: Nov. 1, Jan. 15. Regular admissions: Jan. 15. Financial aid: Nov. 1 and Jan. 1 (early decision), Feb. 1. Housing: May 1. No campus or alumni interviews. SATs or ACTs: required (SAT preferred). SAT IIs: optional. Apply to particular school or program. Accepts the common application and electronic applications. Essay question: applicant's choice of topic.

Vassar College

Poughkeepsie, NY 12604

It is hard to imagine that Vassar once considered picking up and moving to Yale in the 1960s rather than become a coed institution. Thirty-five years after admitting men, still on its ancient and picturesque campus, Vassar is a thriving, highly selective, avante-garde institution with an accent on the fine arts and humanities.

Once known as the most liberal of the Seven Sisters, and still a bastion of the left, Vassar stands out among its small-college peers because of its curricular flexibility, proximity to city life, tolerance, and diversity. A Vassar diploma, whether held by a man or a woman, is well respected in the job market, and a strong Vassar GPA is highly regarded at graduate schools. But even more important is the experience behind the sheepskin and transcript.

The college's one thousand-acre campus, just outside the town of Poughkeepsie, New York, is beautifully landscaped. Daffodils circle the two lakes in springtime and foliage is inescapable in the fall. Encircled by a fieldstone wall, the campus includes an astronomical observatory with one of the largest telescopes in the Northeast, a state-of-the-art chemistry building, a farm with an ecological field station, and an art center boasting 13,500 works from Ancient Egypt to modern art. The architecture is varied, with neo-Gothic overtones, and includes buildings designed by such notables as Marcel Breuer, Eero Saarinen, and James Renwick. The most recent additions to campus include a $25 million expansion and technology upgrade of the main library and $12 million expansion of the athletic facilities, including a basketball gym and elevated running track. Work on new student townhouses and a Center for Drama and Film is underway.

There is great curricular freedom at Vassar: there is no core curriculum, which allows students to construct their own multidisciplinary area of interest. But to graduate, students are required to complete one course emphasizing oral and written expression and another requiring significant quantitative analysis, in addition to demonstrating foreign language proficiency at the first-year level.

Students agree that professors encourage group study and outside-the-classroom instruction. Vassar strikes a happy median between being a competitive or laid-back environment by keeping students sincerely motivated. "Students are responsible, respectful, and highly self-motivated," says a senior. "What sets us apart is our genuine love of education and humanity." The professors are accomplished in their fields, having written acclaimed books and edited major works, but they still make time for students—inside the classroom and beyond. "Professors are extremely approachable and available," asserts a senior. There also are team-taught courses that bring together experts in various fields (for example, in Caribbean literature and Judaism in the course Miami in the American Imagination). "The quality of teaching has overall been stellar," a senior psychology/sociology major says. English and drama are on almost everyone's list of best departments, though students also applaud history, psychology, and the sciences.

> "Classes are small and interactive, and professors make themselves readily available."

Seminars and tutorials are the rule here, even for introductory courses. Popular classes fill up quickly, but on the positive side, friendships with faculty members develop easily (80 percent of the professors live on campus). "Classes are small and interactive, and professors make themselves readily available," a history and Italian major says. Exams run on an honor system. Most people study in the Gothic-style library, with its delightful decor and twenty-four-hour study room for those all-night crams.

The biology building houses two electron microscopes, and music students are spoiled by a grand collection of Steinway pianos, sprinkled all over campus, and their own superb library of scores and books. Vassar runs the Powerhouse Summer Theater program in which apprentices are accepted from around the country to take classes, perform Shakespeare, and work in some capacities with a professional company from New York City. Also highly regarded, the Undergraduate Research Summer Institute (URSI) pays students a stipend to work one on one with faculty members on scientific-research projects, either at Vassar or at off-campus sites. The Ford Scholars program offers similar opportunities for student-faculty collaboration in the humanities and social sciences. Study abroad is popular and encouraged—one-third of students take part—with a large number of programs available under the auspices of other colleges. Vassar also sponsors programs in England, Germany, France, Spain, Morocco, Ireland, and Italy. For domestic study, Vassar has an agreement with the Bank Street College in NYC for students interested in urban education. There are programs with the other eleven members of the Twelve College Exchange* or at any of four historically black colleges, as well as opportunities to participate in a drama production at the Eugene O'Neil Theater and a maritime studies program at the Mystic Seaport,* both in Connecticut.

"Vassar students are definitely an eclectic bunch!"

Sixty-five percent of Vassar's students come from the top tenth of their class; only 27 percent are New York natives. Minorities account for a substantial subset of the student population: Asian-Americans make up 9 percent, African-Americans 6 percent, and Hispanics 6 percent. Vassar has a commitment to its ALANA Center, which supports and recognizes students of color and other ethnic and cultural groups, and students delight in the diversity found on campus. "Vassar students are definitely an eclectic bunch! However, despite some differences, students are tolerant, involved, and intelligent," a senior says. Homosexuality, free speech, women's issues, animal rights, and sweatshop labor are all hot campus issues. "Everyone does not look, dress, or think in the same way. People are very opinionated and outspoken," a senior psychology major says.

Ninety-eight percent of the students live on campus, many in singles after freshman year, and housing is guaranteed for all four years. "Vassar has beautiful dorms and the senior-year housing is amazing," one senior says. All but one of the nine dorms are coed. The word is that Lathrop is the best dorm for freshmen, but no halls are reserved strictly for first-year students. Juniors and seniors favor the college-owned townhouses (five-person suites) or the four-person Terrace Apartments, both with kitchens and living rooms, while some prefer the communal living in Ferry House. Dorm dwellers eat in relative splendor in the All-Campus Dining Center (a.k.a. ACDC) overlooking pine groves and rolling lawns.

One student suggests that, given the nature and interests of its undergraduate body, "Vassar should be located in Greenwich Village." But reality is far from this vision: Poughkeepsie is an old industrial town that leaves, as far as many of Vassar's more cosmopolitan students are concerned, much to be desired. Still, the town is the seat of Duchess County government, so internships with law

"Because there is so much taking place on the campus, students tend to focus their social life there."

firms and political offices are easy to come by, a student says. And 50 percent of Vassar students do some kind of community work in Poughkeepsie through the Step Beyond program—programs like "I Won't Grow Up Day" bring kids from the area to campus to get a taste of college life. However, most social activities—films, drama, and musical entertainment—are found on campus. Campus dances feature the latest

Considering founder Matthew Vassar was a brewer, it's no surprise that Matthew's Mug, the campus dance club/bar, is packed on weekends, as is the Aula coffeehouse for those not yet of legal age.

There is great curricular freedom at Vassar: there is no core curriculum, which allows students to construct their own multidisciplinary area of interest.

music from the East Village, and one student suggests that art is a valuable topic to be fluent in around here. Considering founder Matthew Vassar was a brewer, it's no surprise that Matthew's Mug, the campus dance club/bar, is packed on weekends, as is the Aula coffee house for those not yet of legal age. According to one Brewer, "Because there is so much taking place on the campus, students tend to focus their social life there." Vassar is not a big drinking school, but underage students can get served booze. In other words, Vassar isn't "dry," but drinking doesn't dictate what students do when classes have ceased for the week. Non-alcohol-centered activities include worthwhile jaunts to Roosevelt's Hyde Park and the Culinary Institute of America (for gourmet meals). The Bardavon Theater and Hudson Valley Philharmonic also help curb a student exodus to New York, which is easily accessible.

The annual gala formals bring high society to Vassar twice a year. There are many other social traditions, including the Founders Day carnival in May, and Serenading, a ritual in which the classes sing to one another in a competitive yet congenial way. Afternoon teatime—yes, tea—in the Rose Parlor of historic Main Building remains a popular ritual for unwinding after a day of classes.

Varsity athletics are experiencing a renaissance; tennis and volleyball are among the strongest offerings. The men's soccer and volleyball teams have won conference championships over the past few years, while the women's soccer, rugby, and volleyball squads have excelled. The up-and-coming women's crew team (ranked sixteenth nationally in Division III) works out on the Hudson River, which, at this distance from Manhattan, is still beautiful.

Vassar provides a place for curious and academic-oriented students to find out about themselves and learn from those that are different from them. Boasts one Brewer: "It's very open and diverse." Another says "It has allowed me to become my own person without dictating it to me." For those seeking a place where it's OK to color outside the lines—or erase the lines entirely—this educational oasis could be paradise found.

Overlaps

Brown, Wesleyan, Columbia, NYU, Tufts

If You Apply To ➤ **Vassar:** Early decision: Nov. 15, Jan. 1. Regular admissions and financial aid: Jan. 1. Guarantees to meet demonstrated need. No campus interviews. Alumni interviews: optional, informational. SATs or ACTs: required. SAT IIs: required (any three). Accepts the Common Application and electronic applications. Essay question: significant experience, achievement, person, or matter; also requests a graded copy of an analytical essay written in eleventh or twelfth grade; "your space" (optional).

University of Vermont

194 South Prospect Street, Burlington, VT 05401

For an out-of-stater sizing up public universities, there could hardly be a more appealing place than UVM. The size is manageable, Burlington is a fabulous college town, and Lake Champlain and the Green Mountains are on your doorstep. UVM feels like a private university, but alas, it is also priced like one.

Website: www.uvm.edu
Location: Small city
Total Enrollment: 10,081
Undergraduates: 7,472
Male/Female: 44/56

Take one part private university academics, add a commitment to scholarship and research, and season with the vitality of a liberal arts education, and you've got the formula for the University of Vermont. Nestled within New England's gorgeous scenery (its acronym doubles for *Universitas Viridis Montis*, Latin for "University of the Green Mountains"), UVM is a groovy place that inspires students to hit the books as well as the nearby ski slopes. The school's price tag, high even for Vermont natives, is offset by generous financial aid, and admissions standards are stringent. Students agree that the picturesque setting, close relationships with faculty, and the school's emphasis on undergraduate excellence create a winning recipe.

Perched on the placid shores of Lake Champlain, the UVM campus, a pleasant mix of Colonial, high Victorian Gothic, and functional modern buildings, is located in Burlington (the state's largest city and cultural Mecca, virtually on Canada's doorstep). In the heart of the campus, each building surrounding the manicured park is recognized in the National Registry of Historic Places. New additions include the Health Science Research Facility, which will add 110,000 square feet of research space, the Living/Learning Center, a cybercafe in the library, and the $4.5 million Rubenstein Ecosystem Science Laboratory at the nearby Lake Champlain Basin Center.

Like the architecture, UVM's academic atmosphere is varied. "Classes are challenging and do demand thought and time," says one student, "but there isn't a stressful competitive atmosphere." There are no university-wide general education requirements at the seven undergraduate colleges, though most students must enroll in at least thirty credits (ten courses) in the arts, humanities, social sciences, languages, literature, mathematics, and the sciences. A three-credit Race and Culture course is also required. Among the best of UVM's one hundred-plus majors are the hard sciences (particularly environmental studies), business, and physical therapy. Premeds and physical therapy students benefit from UVM's fine medical school, and learning-disabled students are supported in all majors. Weaknesses appear in a few social science areas, such as anthropology and the fine arts.

"Classes are challenging and do demand thought and time."

At UVM, you can design your own major. You can also participate in the Living and Learning Center, an imaginative residential-academic program where like-minded students live together in suites and create their own programs with a faculty advisor's help. Freshmen in Arts and Sciences may participate in the Teacher-Advisor Program (TAP), a special seminar where the professor also serves as the enrolled students' advisor. Roughly two-thirds of first-year liberal arts students enroll in a TAP seminar. The internship program is popular, and co-ops are available in engineering, business, recreation management, and agriculture. About four hundred students per year partake in UVM study-abroad programs in South America, Western Europe, and Asia and the Pacific Rim.

Students report that classes fill up quickly, which can be hard on freshmen (who register last), but graduating in four years is no problem. By junior year, most students are in classes with twenty-five or fewer students, which helps foster relationships with UVM's outstanding faculty. "Professors make the classes rigorous, but they make us feel comfortable," reports one psychology major. And the profs are more than accessible: "I've had dinner at several professors' homes," says a senior. Advisors get high marks, too. "My advisor has been key," says a nutrition major. "She helps me plan schedules, get involved in research, helps place me in jobs and internships, and writes recommendations."

"Professors make the classes rigorous, but they make us feel comfortable."

UVM students have much in common: 93 percent are white, and most are New Englanders. "Due to the high tuition cost, there are a significant number of well-to-do out-of-staters," says a student. Many complain at the relative lack of diversity on campus: Hispanic and Asian-American students make up 2 percent each, while African-Americans represent 1 percent of the student body. The campus political climate is unabashedly liberal, and recycling and other environmental concerns are big issues, say students. Nearly 1,600 merit-based scholarships are available to students who also demonstrate financial need, and UVM also offers 166 athletic scholarships.

(Continued)

SAT Ranges: V 520–620
  M 520–620
ACT Range: 22–26
Financial Aid: 49%
Expense: Pub $ $ $ $
Phi Beta Kappa: Yes
Applicants: 8,268
Accepted: 80%
Enrolled: 28%
Grad in 6 Years: 67%
Returning Freshmen: 82%
Academics: ✐ ✐ ✐ ½
Social: 🎭 🎭 🎭 🎭 🎭
Q of L: ★ ★ ★ ★ ★
Admissions: (802) 656-3370
Email Address:
  admissions@uvm.edu

Strongest Programs
  Environmental Studies
  Business
  English
  History
  Natural and Life Sciences
  Psychology
  Political Science

The Living and Learning Center is an imaginative residential-academic program where like-minded students live together in suites and create their own programs with a faculty advisor's help.

The Gund Institute for Ecological Economics has relocated to UVM from the University of Maryland. The institute develops policy and management practices to protect vital ecosystems worldwide.

There are twenty-six residence halls on campus, each with its own flavor. That's a good thing, since freshmen and sophomores are required to live on campus, and they select rooms by lottery. Dorms are situated in three residential areas separated by ten-minute walks. Other on-campus options include the Living and Learning suites, co-ops, and apartments. Redstone Campus is described as the rowdiest area, while the best freshman dorms are said to be Chittenden or Buckham, which feature tiny rooms and great atmosphere. Still, almost all juniors and seniors rent apartments in town.

A popular campus T-shirt warns: "If you want to party, come to UVM. If you want to stay, study!" While students here buckle down when they have to, they also know how to have fun when the week's studying is done. Skiing takes the prize as the most popular pastime. "Every weekend, every student goes...it is a blast," one student exclaims. College-sponsored movies, dances, bars, and coffee houses are all big draws. Only 3 percent of men and 2 percent of women join Greek organizations. One annual festival of sorts is the Primal Scream, a collective scream on campus every midnight during finals week. Underage drinking isn't tolerated, though students agree that it does happen. Students, though, are "much more aware and cautious" and less likely to throw wild parties.

> "Due to the high tuition cost, there are a significant number of well-to-do out-of-staters."

One annual festival of sorts is the Primal Scream, a collective scream on campus every midnight during finals week.

As a venue, students say Burlington is a "100 percent college town." It's stylish, with symphonies, art galleries, chic shopping, and lively bars and restaurants, as well as ample community service opportunities. "Burlington is the best college town I could imagine," says a sophomore. But as much as they love their little city, students look forward to getting out of town. The Outing Club is one of UVM's most popular student organizations, since the nearby Green Mountains, White Mountains, and Adirondacks offer prime hiking, skiing, and backpacking. The best road trips are Montreal (ninety minutes) and Boston (four hours).

The hockey team competes in the ECAC, has ranked as high as second nationally, and is the pride and joy of UVM sports. Catamount games are always sold out; students get access to tickets before the general public, and there is a lengthy waiting list for community members. Soccer draws crowds in the fall—there is no football team. Men's and women's basketball are solid programs, as are field hockey and men's and women's track, and the ski teams are NCAA powerhouses. Students love intramural sports, especially tennis and broomball (ice hockey played with brooms, on shoes instead of skates).

"Groovy UV" is a generally laid-back campus, but students are curious, intellectual, and willing to work hard. And as UVM continues blending the high points of a small liberal arts school, such as one-on-one attention, with the traits of a prime undergraduate research institution, including generous funding for student projects, the end result is sure to be sweet.

Overlaps

University of New Hampshire, University of Massachusetts, Boston University, Boston College, University of Connecticut

If You Apply To ➤

UVM: Early decision: Nov. 1. Regular admissions: Jan. 15. Financial aid: Feb. 10. Does not guarantee to meet demonstrated need. Campus and alumni interviews: optional, informational. SATs or ACTs: required. SAT IIs: optional. Apply to individual schools or programs. Accepts the Common Application and electronic applications. Essay questions: significant experience, outside interests, topic of your choice.

800 Lancaster Avenue, Villanova, PA 19085-1672

Set in upscale suburb, Villanova is Philadelphia's counterpart to Boston College. As at BC, about 80 percent of the students are Roman Catholic (compared to a figure of about 50 percent at Georgetown). The troika of business, engineering, and premed are popular at 'Nova, as is nursing.

Villanova University takes pride in its Augustinian roots, even basing its admissions essay on one of St. Augustine's teachings about "right reason." The school has all the trappings of a typical Roman Catholic university, from strong academics to deeply rooted traditions and rivalries, and students firmly dedicated to their faith. The emphasis on community creates an "inviting and friendly atmosphere," says a sophomore. "All are welcomed," adds a senior. "All feel comfortable, and all are here to enjoy college."

Villanova's lush campus, which once served as the estate of a Revolutionary War officer, occupies more than 254 acres on Philadelphia's posh Main Line. Buildings range from ivy-covered stone to modern; they're sprinkled among wide, well-kept lawns, and connected by secluded, tree-lined walkways. In 2001, Villanova completed four new apartment-style residence halls, with space for six hundred students. The school also renovated and expanded Bartley Hall, home to the College of Commerce and Finance, one of the four undergraduate schools. A new health center opened in 2002.

Aside from the College of Commerce and Finance, undergraduates may enroll in the College of Engineering, the College of Liberal Arts and Sciences, or the College of Nursing. The strong finance program is a national draw, as well as the most popular major on campus—though that may change with the addition of a new international business program. Nursing is second, followed by biology, communications, and political science. The engineering school enjoys strong regional recognition. General education requirements vary by school, but all students take the two-semester Core Humanities Seminar, team-taught by members of the English, history, philosophy, and religious studies departments. These courses stress discussion, intensive writing, readings from primary texts, and close student-faculty relationships. They also let students study a topic or theme from several perspectives, with an emphasis on Christian thought and values. There's also a four-day Freshman Orientation.

> **"All feel comfortable, and all are here to enjoy college."**

Coursework at Villanova is "rigorous," "challenging," and "very difficult," and students say they work hard outside the classroom—though they pride themselves on making time to socialize. Competitiveness varies by college, with the business school especially cut-throat. "Professors are awesome," says a computer science major, describing the quality of teaching at Villanova as "very high," and reporting that faculty members are both knowledgeable and accessible. There are few problems graduating within four years, and Villanovans register for classes online. However, those who don't log in early to choose courses may find it tough to get into popular electives. The 629,000-volume library is adequate for most needs. An honors program is available to about two hundred students, by invitation only.

A third of Villanova's students are native Pennsylvanians. Many come from upper middle-class families, and 83 percent are white, hence the nickname "Vanillanova." Boosting diversity "is becoming less and less of an issue as more types of people come," says a senior. "We want everyone to be comfortable." To that end,

Website: www.admission.villanova.edu
Location: Suburban
Total Enrollment: 10,330
Undergraduates: 7,314
Male/Female: 49/51
SAT Ranges: V 560–650
  M 590–670
ACT Range: 27–30
Financial Aid: N/A
Expense: Pr $ $ $ $
Phi Beta Kappa: Yes
Applicants: 10,293
Accepted: 49%
Enrolled: 34%
Grad in 6 Years: 85%
Returning Freshmen: 94%
Academics: ✍ ✍ ✍
Social: ☎ ☎ ☎
Q of L: ★ ★ ★
Admissions: (610) 519-4000
Email Address:
  gotovu@villanova.edu

Strongest Programs
  Accounting
  Biology
  Engineering
  Business

Many come from upper middle-class families, and 83 percent are white, hence the nickname "Vanillanova."

Villanova requires a class on diversity, whether in the U.S. or abroad. And efforts by the Multicultural Affairs office are apparently paying off, as African-Americans, Hispanics, and Asian-Americans each comprise 4 percent of the student body. Regardless of background, faith plays an important role for most students here. "We have three different masses on Sunday nights," one explains, "and each time there is barely any standing room...forget about sitting."

Two-thirds of the student body lives in Villanova's dorms, which a marketing major calls "comfortable and well maintained." Freshmen live primarily on the South Campus Circle, while upperclassmen take their chances in the lottery system, which most say works out fine. Juniors and seniors may choose rooms in one of the school-run apartment complexes. A sophomore says most seniors move off campus, despite steep rents and neighbors hostile to college types; doing so lets them skip the meal plan. About 10 percent of Villanova students are from the Philadelphia area, and they avoid the hassle entirely by commuting from home.

Even with the presence of some commuters, Villanova isn't a suitcase school. Weekend social life centers around campus events and parties, some sponsored by Greek groups, which claim 14 percent of the men and 40 percent of the women. Officially, the campus is dry, and Pennsylvania state law

"Professors are awesome."

says no one under twenty-one can drink. But "people learn to get around rules," says a political science major. Some students frequent local bars on Lancaster Avenue, although one warns these establishments card at the door. Alternatives to drinking include movies and dances, usually held in the school's multimillion-dollar Connelly Center. Community-service opportunities are plentiful, and Villanova has the largest student-run Special Olympics, in addition to Habitat for Humanity and Big Brother/Big Sister chapters. Those who tire of Villanova's suburban setting can be in Philadelphia in twelve minutes, thanks to local commuter rail. The city's cultural and social opportunities include museums and pro sports, as well as events at numerous other colleges and universities, from La Salle and Temple to St. Joseph's, Drexel, and Penn. For those with wheels, ski resorts, the Poconos, the Jersey shore, and Atlantic City are all within a two-hour drive.

When they're not out socializing, Villanova students are cheering for their Wildcats. The school's basketball team rose to national prominence in 1985, when it stunned Catholic rival Georgetown in the NCAA tournament championship game. While that victory first put Villanova's varsity sports on the national map, it's the school's women's track and field squad that brought home the

"We have three different masses on Sunday nights, and each time there is barely any standing room."

Big East title in 2000. In fact, men's track is strong, too, and both teams sometimes see their members going for Olympic gold against the best runners in the world. The football team plays to sold-out crowds in Division IAA. The school's fitness complex has a swimming center and an indoor track. For ex-high-school jocks not up to varsity status, three intramural leagues offer competition at levels ranging from serious to slapstick.

While Villanova has evolved since its 1842 founding, adding and renovating buildings and expanding its academic menu, a sophomore says the school's commitment to community, scholarship, and service hasn't changed. That focus, and the school's solid preprofessional training, keep devoted Catholics flocking here each fall. Spiritual commitments aside, most seem to think a little worldly success won't do them any everlasting harm.

Overlaps

Penn State, Boston College, University of Notre Dame, Lehigh, College of Holy Cross

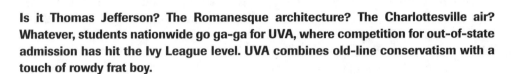

If You Apply To ➤ **Villanova:** Early action: Nov. 1. Regular admissions: Jan. 7. Financial aid: Feb. 14 (FAFSA), Mar. 7 (Villanova application). Guarantees to meet demonstrated need. No campus or alumni interviews. SATs or ACTs: required. No SAT IIs. Apply to a particular school or program. Accepts electronic applications. Essay question: a choice for change that's profoundly affected your life or the lives of others.

University of Virginia

P.O. Box 9017, Charlottesville, VA 22903

Is it Thomas Jefferson? The Romanesque architecture? The Charlottesville air? Whatever, students nationwide go ga-ga for UVA, where competition for out-of-state admission has hit the Ivy League level. UVA combines old-line conservatism with a touch of rowdy frat boy.

Easily one of the most prestigious public schools in the nation, the University of Virginia blends rich tradition with progressive attitudes. Perhaps that's a mark of its founder. UVA is known to all in Charlottesville as Mister Jefferson's University. Not just any Mister Jefferson, mind you, but *the* Mister Jefferson, author of the Declaration of Independence. Though he passed away more than 150 years ago, he is referred to here as if he ran down to the apothecary shop for a bit of snuff and will be back in a moment. Of all his accomplishments, Jefferson was arguably proudest of UVA—he even asked that his epitaph speak to his role in creating the university rather than his presidency.

Located just east of the Blue Ridge Mountains in central Virginia, UVA's campus was designed by Mister Jefferson himself, and still uses many of its original buildings today. At the core of the university is Jefferson's "academical village," with its majestic white pillars, serpentine walls, and extensive brickwork. The village is built around a rectangular terraced green—called the Lawn—that is flanked by two rows of identical one-story rooms that are reserved for undergraduate student leaders. Five pavilions, each in a different style, accent each side of the Lawn. Both the rooms and the pavilions enter into a colonnaded walkway that fronts the Lawn. Behind the rows of buildings are public gardens. The Rotunda, a half-scale model of the Roman Pantheon, overlooks the Lawn. The Cauthen House dorm is a new addition, the Health Science Library and the environmental science building are being expanded, and planning is underway for an addition to the architecture school, a special collections library, and a studio art building.

Elite among public institutions of higher education, UVA holds its own against the best of the private schools, too. Students are accepted into the four-year schools of engineering, nursing, and architecture, but the vast majority enter the liberal arts college. According to students, the best departments are history, English, religious studies, and the School of Commerce. A planning commission on the fine and performing arts is working on improving those departments, and a proposed arts precinct will include a new museum, library, and concert hall. The most popular majors are commerce, English, psychology, economics, and biology. UVA's school of education offers a five-year program that culminates in a B.A. from the College of Arts and Sciences and a Master of Teaching degree from the education school. The new International Residential College fosters close contact with faculty and special short courses.

After their second year, about three hundred Arts and Sciences students transfer into the commerce school, but competition for these spots is tough. Virginia requires

Website: www.virginia.edu
Location: Small city
Total Enrollment: 22,739
Undergraduates: 13,764
Male/Female: 46/54
SAT Ranges: V 600–700
  M 610–720
ACT Range: 25–32
Financial Aid: 23%
Expense: Pub $ $
Phi Beta Kappa: Yes
Applicants: 14,739
Accepted: 38%
Enrolled: 54%
Grad in 6 Years: 92%
Returning Freshmen: 97%
Academics: ✑ ✑ ✑ ✑ ✑
Social: ☎ ☎ ☎ ☎
Q of L: ★ ★ ★ ★ ★
Admissions: (434) 982-3200
Email Address: undergrad-admission@virginia.edu

Strongest Programs
  English
  Foreign Languages
  Physiology
  Government
  Economics
  History
  Biochemistry
  Religious Studies

Mr. Jefferson founded UVA as a place where students could come together to "drink the cup of knowledge," but today's undergraduates seem to favor a different sort of brew.

students in the College of Arts and Sciences and the commerce school to master a foreign language. Arts and Sciences students must also take courses in humanities and fine arts, social science, natural sciences and mathematics, non-Western studies, and composition. All freshmen in the College are required to take English composition. The emphasis is on top-level academic programs taught within nationally recognized departments. With more than four million volumes and one of the nation's largest collections of online materials in six digital centers, the library is more than adequate. The computer science department also has a state-of-the-art virtual reality lab.

A number of special programs are offered in addition to the regular curriculum. The most prestigious of these is the Echols Scholars program, which exempts students from distribution and major-field requirements and lets them loose to explore the academic disciplines as they see fit. The school invites up to two hundred freshmen (plan on total SATs solidly above 1400) into the program and houses them together for their first year. The Rodman Scholars Program in the engineering school selects students based on financial need, leadership qualities, and scholarship. The Distinguished Majors Program enables qualified students to pursue an independent study during their third and fourth years. Three residential colleges house approximately 1,100 students, mostly upperclassmen, with one hundred faculty members participating (a handful even living in the student housing). One focuses on international themes, with nearly one-quarter of the students hailing from other countries. Professors are said to be highly accessible and friendly. A senior says professors "have engaged me in research, hour-long discussions, and other academic pursuits." The University Seminar program features prominent faculty

"Students really do govern themselves and we are given a large amount of responsibility and opportunity."

teaching fifteen or fewer first-year students in a seminar learning environment. It also offers a number of one-credit courses called University Topics, which focus on current events. The school has added a coffee bar in the library and a fund subsidizing faculty-student lunches, both aimed at fostering informal conversations.

Virginia is noted for its honor system, which was instituted by students in 1842 after no one owned up to shooting a professor on the Lawn. "Students really do govern themselves and we are given a large amount of responsibility and opportunity," a foreign affairs major says. Don't take it lightly—the penalty for infractions is a swift dismissal from campus. A number of controversial cases recently produced a measure of reform, and discussions continue about the appropriateness of the single-sanction system and even the continued existence of the student-run honor system. But rest assured, some form of the honor code will remain a way of life here, as many students say they feel comfortable leaving backpacks and calculators unattended without worry of thieves. "Students here are kicked out if they are caught lying, cheating, or stealing, which makes for a really unique community of trust," a junior says.

One traditional local event is Foxfield, in which students dress up and host catered parties prior to attending a steeplechase horse race. Other famous traditions include streaking the Lawn, dressing up for football games, and taking in the annual visit by a hypnotist that draws more than ten thousand people.

Admission for out-of-state students—26 percent of the undergraduate body—is more competitive than for in-staters, but nearly everyone who gets in is highly qualified. Ninety-six percent of the freshmen were in the top quarter of their high-school class. Many students hail from Washington, D.C., and suburbs of northern Virginia, while most out-of-staters come from New York, New Jersey, Pennsylvania, and Maryland. The student body is somewhat diverse: 9 percent are African-American, 11 percent are Asian-American, and 3 percent are Hispanic. The consensus here is that while race relations are not overly hostile, there is a sense that African-American students "self-segregate," as one student says. Among the eighty-five merit scholarships offered at Virginia are twenty-five to thirty highly prized Jefferson Scholarships, which are awarded annually by the alumni association and are good for full tuition, as well as room and board. Up to seven out-of-state African-Americans get renewable stipends of $10,000 a year. About 450 athletes are awarded athletic scholarships in fifteen sports.

A conspicuous exception to the historic character of most of the Virginia campus is the Hereford College, a residential and dining complex that features contemporary architecture described by *The New York Times* as "proudly, almost defiantly modern." All first-year students live "on grounds," as do some top fourth-year leaders and honors students, who qualify for coveted singles in the academic village. Forty-eight percent trek off campus, but still stay involved with the university. Commuters praise the university's bus system, which is important since campus parking is extremely limited. Meal plans are required for first-year students, while many upperclassmen either cook for themselves or take meals at their Greek houses. Thirty percent each of men and women make up the Greek system, which has a fairly prominent role in campus social life.

Mr. Jefferson founded UVA as a place where students could come together to "drink the cup of knowledge," but today's undergraduates seem to favor a different sort of brew. Studious Virginians by day can metamorphose into the Rowdy Wahoos (a nickname derived from one of the college cheers about the fish that can drink twice its weight, usually shortened to Hoos) by night. As with most college students, drinking is a favorite pastime, and underage students have little problem obtaining alcohol, though the administration has been more strictly enforcing drink-

> **"Students here are kicked out if they are caught lying, cheating, or stealing, which makes for a really unique community of trust."**

ing rules. UVA has a dry rush, and guest lists are now required for all fraternity parties. The fraternities assume an obligation to provide social activities not only for their own members but for the campus at large, and the "big weekends" are still big, though far less legendary than in the early '80s. The student-run University Union and more than three hundred student organizations offer movies, concerts, social hours, and other extracurricular activities. Students also tend to immerse themselves in community-service activities. One traditional local event is Foxfield, in which students dress up and host catered parties prior to attending a steeplechase horse race. Other famous traditions include streaking the Lawn, doing the "Corner Crawl" on your twenty-first birthday, dressing up for football games (a relic from the days when UVA was all male and the games were an opportunity to meet women), and an annual visit by a hypnotist that draws more than ten thousand people. The nationally recognized Madison House is the umbrella group for a host of student volunteer groups.

Charlottesville "is the perfect college town." From a ton of amazing restaurants—Hooville is becoming famous for its gorgeous vineyards and wineries—to bars, shops, theaters, and other cultural attractions, this town is a great complement to campus. But if the city limits get old, students can road-trip two hours to Washington or Richmond. Outdoorsy folks can hike, bike, ski, and sightsee in the nearby Blue Ridge Mountains and daydream along its famous Skyline Drive. Big-time Atlantic Coast Conference basketball has long been an integral part of UVA life.

Students who attend UVA are generally thrilled with their situation: top academics, a fabulous social life, a stunning campus, and opportunities to learn with some of the best educators in the country. From its uniquely American roots and beloved legacy from Thomas Jefferson, the school has maintained its special traditions that make for "the best memories I have," says a fourth-year. And though it's unclear whether the eloquent Mister Jefferson would approve of the rather coarse tone of a popular rhetorical question on campus—"Hoo's Your Daddy?"—he wouldn't argue with the answer.

UVA has consistently placed among the top ten schools in the country, beating private schools as well as other public institutions.

Overlaps

William and Mary, Duke, Virginia Tech, University of Pennsylvania, Cornell University

Virginia Polytechnic Institute and State University

Blacksburg, VA 24061

Hokie Nation is tickled pink about the rise of its football team, which has become a consistent national power. Engineering has always been Tech's calling card; business and architecture are also popular. Blacksburg is a nice college town, but is far from the population centers near the coast.

Website: www.vt.edu
Location: Small town
Total Enrollment: 28,203
Undergraduates: 21,593
Male/Female: 58/42
SAT Ranges: V 530–630
　　M 550–660
Financial Aid: 63%
Expense: Pub $ $
Phi Beta Kappa: Yes
Applicants: 18,839
Accepted: 70%
Enrolled: 23%
Grad in 6 Years: 71%
Returning Freshmen: 88%
Academics: ✎ ✎ ✎ ✎
Social: ☎ ☎ ☎
Q of L: ★ ★ ★ ★
Admissions: (540) 231-6267
Email Address:
　vtadmiss@vt.edu

Strongest Programs
　Engineering
　Architecture and Urban
　　Studies
　Business
　Sciences
　Human Resources and
　　Education
　Mathematics
　Forestry and Wildlife
　　Resources
　Humanities / Arts

Though its full name is the Virginia Polytechnic Institute and State University, those in the know just call it Virginia Tech. Long-known for its solid engineering and architecture programs, this Southern university has recently garnered more national attention for its football team than its academics. It's no wonder students want to spend four years at the "Hokie Pokie."

Set on a plateau in the scenic Blue Ridge mountains, Tech's campus occupies three thousand acres and comes complete with a duck pond, hiking trails, and a two-hundred-year-old plantation that is a local landmark. Students enjoy unlimited outdoor recreation thanks to the proximity of the Jefferson National Forest, the Appalachian Trail, the scenic Blue Ridge Parkway, and the majestic old New River. The campus buildings are an attractive mix of gray limestone structures, Colonial-style brick, and modern cement buildings. Newer facilities include the 150,000-square-foot Advanced Communications and Information Technology Center (ACITC).

Virginia Tech is best known for its first-rate technical and professional training. For undergrads with an appetite for engineering, Tech has programs for every taste, including aerospace, ocean, biological systems, civil, chemical, computer, electrical, industrial and systems, materials, mechanical (the most popular), and mining. The Pamplin College of Business is also prominent, and the five-year architecture program is considered one of the nation's best. Though no longer Tech's centerpiece, the College of Agriculture and Life Sciences remains strong, especially in animal science. Students in the College of Natural Resources can choose from such concentrations as environmental conservation, fisheries science, forestry, and wildlife management. The College of Education merged with the College of Human Resources, where Hospitality and Tourism is the best-known program.

"Religious studies, foreign languages, and philosophy are dwindling away."

Students in the sciences reap the benefits of their high-tech environment; other disciplines do not fare so well. The humanities have been hard hit by budget cuts. In particular, "religious studies, foreign languages, and philosophy are dwindling away," says a senior. One bright spot is internationally known poet Nikki Giovanni, who teaches creative writing and advanced poetry. The university also has a tradition of excellence in the performing arts, and the school's theater group has received more awards from the American College Theater Arts Festival than any other college in the Southeast.

Introductory class size tends to be large—sometimes well into the hundreds—and the budget ax has only made matters worse. Most of the big lecture classes are taught by full-time faculty, though discussions and grading are generally handled by TAs. Nevertheless, a communications major says her professors "keep you on the edge of your seat." An accounting major adds, "Freshmen are taught by professors and grad students." All students are required to take courses in English, math, humanities, and social and natural science. There is also a foreign language requirement, though high-school coursework may cover this requirement. The 1,500 or so students who participate in the University Honors Program are guaranteed access to top faculty and research opportunities. Tech is among the nation's leaders in the integration of computers into all facets of life. All freshmen are required to own a computer. Says an engineering major, "On campus you can do anything from handing in homework to checking grades to checking out what movies are playing, all by computer."

The football team's recent appearances in postseason bowl games have cheered alumni and hiked applications by several thousand.

Each year, more than one thousand students take advantage of Tech's co-op opportunities, available in almost all majors. The nationally acclaimed Small Business Institute program enables faculty-led groups of business majors to work with local merchants, analyze their problems, and make suggestions on how to increase profits. The Corps of Cadets, a tradition once on the verge of extinction, has made a comeback. Cadets earn a minor in leadership and can choose from three tracks: military/ROTC, civic professions, or a combination of the two.

"Rooms are on the small side, but they provide all you need to live."

Students looking at pricey Northeastern technical schools will find Tech a real bargain. Not surprisingly, the admissions office is inundated with out-of-state applicants, which means stiff competition for the 25 percent of the slots available to non-Virginians. Tech's relative isolation from major cities is a drag on minority recruitment: African-Americans and Hispanics account for only 7 percent of the student body, Asian-Americans account for another 7 percent. Seventy-eight percent graduated in the top quarter of their high-school class. Students with financial need who apply for aid before the deadline receive priority consideration; those who apply later are likely to be out of luck. Tech hands out a few hundred athletic scholarships, and there are merit scholarships available to qualified students.

All students are required to take courses in English, math, humanities, and social and natural science.

Tech housing is nothing to write home about, but more than adequate to meet the needs of most students. "Rooms are on the small side, but they provide all you need to live," says a freshman. Some twenty-five undergraduate dorms serve 8,400 students; 43 percent of the student body live on campus, though only freshmen and the Corps of Cadets are required to. Most upperclassmen live off campus in nearby apartment complexes. Dietrick's Depot, the largest dining hall on campus, was recently renovated. Three specialty lines supplement the standard dining-hall fare to create an intimate, café-style atmosphere. Students who are committed to a healthy lifestyle can opt to reside

"Most students go downtown to shoot pool, dance, or go to a bar."

in the W.E.L.L. (Wellness Environment for Living and Learning), which will provide them with a substance-free atmosphere, and includes special healthy-living courses and is overseen by a specially trained wellness staff.

Leisure-time favorites include school-sponsored plays, jazz concerts, arts and crafts fairs, and dances. The nearby Cascades National Park is an especially popular retreat for lovers and camping jocks alike, and tubing down the New River is a ritual for summer students. Eleven percent of the men and 12 percent of the women join fraternities and sororities, which set the tone of the social life. If going Greek isn't for you, don't worry, as one student says, "Most students go downtown to shoot pool, dance, or go to a bar." The most important annual event is the Ring Dance (when the juniors receive their school rings), the German Club's Midwinter's Dance, and the Corps of Cadets military ball. Blacksburg offers the usual city fare and one student says the town "revolves around Tech." For real big-city action, Washington, D.C., and Richmond are four and three hours away by car, respectively.

Tech's varsity athletics program struggled for years to make the big time—and never succeeded—but the football team's recent appearances in postseason bowl games have cheered alumni and hiked applications by several thousand. The annual "big game" pits the backwoodsy Hokies against the aristocratic (snobby?) Cavaliers of the University of Virginia. (In case you're wondering, "Hokie" is taken from a nonsense lyric in the school fight song: "Hokie, Hokie, Hokie Hi—We're the Boys from V.P.I.") Tech has one of the nation's most extensive intramural programs, with everything from football to horseshoes and underwater hockey—a recent rage—and more than four hundred softball teams each spring, many of them coed. Weekend athletes benefit from the addition of a fitness center.

Anyone looking for a high-tech education garnished with Southern hospitality will find Virginia Tech just right. "I think Tech is pretty personal considering the number of students it serves," says a junior.

If You Apply To ➤

Tech: Early decision: Nov.1. Regular admissions: Jan. 15. Financial aid: Mar. 11. Does not guarantee to meet demonstrated need. Campus interviews: optional, informational. No alumni interviews. SATs: required. SAT IIs: required (writing and math I or II). Accepts electronic applications. Essay question. Level of difficulty of high-school curriculum stressed.

Wabash College

301 West Wabash, Crawfordsville, IN 47933

Wabash and Hampden-Sydney in Virginia are the last of the all-male breed. With steady enrollment and plenty of money in the bank, Wabash shows no signs of changing. Intense bonding is an important part of the Wabash experience, and few coed schools can match the loyalty of Wabash alumni.

Website: www.wabash.edu
Location: Small town
Total Enrollment: 861
Undergraduates: 861
Male/Female: 100/0
SAT Ranges: V 520–630
  M 540–650
Financial Aid: 70%
Expense: Pr $ $
Phi Beta Kappa: Yes
Applicants: 894
Accepted: 75%
Enrolled: 33%
Grad in 6 Years: 69%
Returning Freshmen: 81%
Academics:
Social: ☎ ☎
Q of L: ★ ★ ★

At all-male Wabash College, students follow the Gentleman's Rule: "Wabash men are expected to behave like gentlemen at all times. This rule encompasses alcohol, relations with women, academics, and all other areas of college life," says a history and speech major. Indeed, stepping onto the Wabash campus is much like stepping back in history to a time when men were men and the world was theirs. Wabash was founded in 1832 by transplanted Ivy Leaguers, who most certainly held a positive view of a man's future.

The Wabash campus is characterized by redbrick, white-pillared Federal-style buildings (three are originals from the 1830s). Located in the heart of tiny Crawfordsville, a small town of about fifteen thousand, Wabash is surrounded by grass and tall trees that are part of the gorgeous Fuller Arboretum. Current construction includes a 170,000-square-foot athletics and recreation center.

The Wabash educational program has certainly proved itself over the years. This small college has amassed quite an impressive list of alumni: executives of major corporations, doctors, lawyers, and a large proportion of Ph.D.s. Most Wabash alumni are faithful to their school in the form of generous donations. On a per capita basis, the school's $237 million endowment makes it one of the wealthiest in the nation. This financial security enables Wabash to refuse any federal aid, with the exception of Pell Grants, which go directly to students.

History and economics draw the most majors at Wabash, and the highest accolades go to the biology (premed) and chemistry departments, which are among the most challenging and produce many successful grads. In keeping with its reputation in the sciences, Wabash has an electron microscope and a laser spectrometer, a 180-acre biological field station, and a cell culture lab. Political science and the religion/philosophy department are also popular, but students say the speech department could be improved. A 42,600-square-foot fine arts center provides more studio space and practice rooms and is a pleasant addition to the music and art departments. The newest additions to the curriculum include international studies, gender studies, and multicultural American studies.

The academic climate at Wabash is intense, and people are serious about their studies. "The academic climate is very challenging, and you have to put in a lot of time and effort to get a good grade," says a senior. General education requirements include courses from a wide variety of fields—natural and behavioral sciences, literature and fine arts, mathematics, language studies, and a course on cultures and traditions. In addition, a freshman tutorial, which is limited to a maximum of fifteen students, is designed to improve class participation and reading and writing skills. A special writing center is available for all Wabash students who demonstrate a weakness in written communication skills. The ability to write well is definitely an asset, as many tests feature essay questions. Juniors are encouraged to study on continents throughout the world or in various domestic programs through the Great Lakes College Association.* Those who can't satisfy their high-tech interests at Wabash can opt for a 3–2 program in engineering with Columbia University or Washington University in St. Louis. Wabash also offers a tuition-free semester after graduation to train students to become teachers. Students use the words "outstanding" and "fantastic" to describe their professors. Advising is also considered excellent, and students say they have no problems getting into required courses.

> "Wabash men are expected to behave like gentlemen at all times."

Most of Wabash's students come from public high schools in Indiana, and 68 percent were in the top quarter of their high-school class. Many were active in athletics and student government and continue that tradition in college. The campus is mostly conservative, through both Republican and Democratic student organizations are strong. The administration is working with a grant to improve diversity on campus. It has expanded the freshman orientation program to include diversity and community issues, focusing on making choices and accepting the consequences. However, students agree there's still a ways to go. African-American, Hispanic, Asian-American, and foreign students combined account for 13 percent of the campus population. "There tend to be very few pressures on campus caused by diversity," one sophomore says. "All students, regardless of race, are Wabash brothers."

> "The academic climate is very challenging and you have to put in a lot of time and effort to get a good grade."

Residential life for the temporary denizens of small-town Crawfordsville revolves around the ten fraternities, each with its own house. Seventy percent of the students join up, and many end up living with their brothers. As an alternative to Greek life, there are three modern dorms, two of which have all single rooms. Dorm residents must eat in the dining hall, while fraternities have private cooks who prepare "meals that are really not that bad." Those living in the dorms (and the 9 percent who live off campus) may feel excluded from what there is of campus social life, since the fraternities "ship in" sorority members from Purdue, Indiana, DePauw, and Butler for parties. "Many people make the mistake of thinking that since Wabash has no women...we don't have good parties," says a senior history

(Continued)
Admissions: (800) 345-5385
Email Address:
admissions@wabash.edu

Strongest Programs
Religion
Premed
Prelaw
Economics
Biology

In keeping with its reputation in the sciences, Wabash has an electron microscope and a laser spectrometer, a 180-acre biological field station, and a cell culture lab.

Residential life for the temporary denizens of small-town Crawfordsville revolves around the ten fraternities, each with its own house.

major. A wise freshman, however, points out that "the absence of women on weekdays helps some to concentrate on their studies." As for drinking on campus, students agree that policies are loose. A sophomore says, "Alcohol is fairly accessible.... The big difference is that at Wabash, students behave responsibly. No one is stupid enough to drink and then decide to drive around."

Wallies are tough in athletics. The football, baseball, basketball, swimming, and the cross-country teams are very competitive. When they're not studying or partying, students are likely to be found working out in the gym or running. Most non-varsity athletes participate in intramurals, which encompass twenty-two sports, including pool and horseshoes. School spirit is abundant, especially when the opponent is long-standing rival DePauw. The annual Monon

"All students, regardless of race, are Wabash brothers."

Bell football game against the hated "Dannies" (DePauw Tigers) is "a great game, steeped in tradition." Another popular, though less sweaty, event is Chapel Sing, where all the freshmen sing the lengthy school song in unison. "Actually, we yell until we go hoarse," a participant says.

Just as it is at all-women's schools, tradition is an important part of the lives of the men at Wabash. "It is almost impossible to put into words why Wabash is special," a senior says. "You have to experience it to understand why generations of Wabash men continue to support and love the school. The traditions of Wabash have remained almost unchanged since its founding in 1832." Students here accept the workload and the social sacrifices to be part of the Wabash tradition.

Overlaps

Indiana University, Purdue, Ball State, Hanover, DePauw

If You Apply To ➤ **Wabash:** Early action: Dec. 1. Regular admissions and financial aid: March 1. Housing: June 1. Guarantees to meet demonstrated need. Campus interviews: recommended, informational. Alumni interviews: optional, informational. SATs or ACTs: required. SAT IIs: optional. Accepts the Common Application and electronic applications. Essay question: significant quotation or creative work.

Wake Forest University

Winston-Salem, NC 27109

Wake's Baptist heritage and Winston-Salem location give it a more down-home flavor than Duke or Emory. With only 4,136 undergraduates, Wake is small compared to its ACC rivals but bigger than liberal arts college. A strong Greek system dominates the social scene.

Website: www.wfu.edu
Location: City outskirts
Total Enrollment: 6,271
Undergraduates: 4,136
Male/Female: 49/51
SAT Ranges: V 610–680
 M 620–700
Financial Aid: 32%
Expense: Pr $ $ $ $
Phi Beta Kappa: Yes
Applicants: 5,271

A regional university in North Carolina might not seem a likely leader of the information technology revolution. But that's just what Wake Forest University has become. The school, which is no longer affiliated with the Baptist church, provides freshmen with laptop computers upon arrival. Students get new machines at the start of the junior year, and take these with them when they graduate. Already well-established as one of the top private schools in the Southeast, Wake Forest is working hard to transform that goodwill into a national reputation.

Located in the Piedmont region of North Carolina, the school's 340-acre campus has an air of serenity, thanks to flower gardens, wooded trails, and stately magnolias. More than forty Georgian-style buildings are constructed of old Virginia brick with granite trim. Each is connected to the campus computer network, and some also have multimedia classrooms. All of the new mortar and stone complements the school's lush surroundings, which includes the 148-acre Reynolda Gardens annex, with a formal garden, greenhouses, and a wooded area with trails. The garden features one of the first collections of Japanese cherry trees in the U.S. "We are still a large private school with a state-school feel," says a sophomore. "Not too small, but not too big—and you don't have to walk more than fifteen minutes to any class!" Just three miles south of campus is downtown Winston-Salem, a town rich in North Carolina history.

To graduate from Wake Forest, students must complete a writing seminar, a first-year seminar, one semester of foreign language literature, and two half-semesters of health and exercise science. In addition, students take three courses in history, religion, and philosophy; two in literature; one in fine arts; three in social and behavioral sciences; and three in natural sciences, mathematics, and computer science. Students must also satisfy quantitative reasoning and cultural diversity requirements. Courses at "Work Forest" are demanding.

> **"We are still a large private school with a state-school feel."**

"Many people want good GPAs for medical and law school entrance," says an economics major. "People go to the library on weekends and during sporting events." Competition is friendly, rather than cut-throat, a music major says: "It seems that one can get a B with no effort, but an A takes an absurd amount of work."

Business is Wake Forest's most popular major, followed by communication, psychology, political science, and English. Fine arts is smaller, owing to the school's location, though a religion and psychology major says Wake does have its own gallery. Graduate assistants teach labs, but full faculty members lead lectures, and students give them high marks. "The quality of teaching is very good, and professors are accessible," says a sophomore. "Most are engaging, and very welcoming—I've yet to have a professor I really don't like." Two-thirds of the courses taken by freshmen have twenty-five or fewer students, and nearly all the rest have fifty or less. A junior economics major says the quality of teaching at Wake Forest kept him from transferring to Harvard, Stanford, or Emory. The Richter Fellowships fund research collaboration between students and faculty members. And for those who feel claustrophobic in Winston-Salem, Wake Forest owns residential study centers on the Grand Canal in Venice and in London and Vienna, and more than half of the student body studies abroad. The school also offers study programs on virtually every continent aside from Antarctica.

Still, while Wake Forest students traipse around the world sampling foreign cultures, life on campus is fairly homogeneous. The student body is 88 percent white, and a junior complains that there are "lots of strict, un-open-minded, radical Christians." Only a quarter of Wake's students are native Tar Heels, though many of the rest hail from

> **"People go to the library on weekends and during sporting events."**

other Southern states. African-Americans represent 7 percent of the student body, while Hispanics, Asian-Americans, and other minorities together make up 5 percent. "Trying to extend party hours is a constant struggle, and the lack of diversity on campus is frequently discussed," says a freshman. That said, "students are for the most part respectful and accepting of differences," a chemistry major reports.

Three-quarters of Wake's students live on campus, where rooms "are small but nice," says a music major. Students are guaranteed housing for all four years, unless they move off campus and later decide to return. Campus safety isn't an issue, quips a junior: "We only fear midterms and finals." Dining options include a fairly typical cafeteria, a convenience store, the food court, and the Magnolia Room, which dishes out classier food, and thus costs more. Students use a school-issued debit card to pay for meals. Upperclassmen often choose to move off campus so that they can cook for themselves.

(Continued)
Accepted: 46%
Enrolled: 41%
Grad in 6 Years: 87%
Returning Freshmen: 93%
Academics: ✐ ✐ ✐ ✐
Social: ☎ ☎ ☎
Q of L: ★ ★ ★
Admissions: (336) 758-5201
Email Address:
  admissions@wfu.edu

Strongest Programs
  Health and Exercise Science
  Chemistry
  English
  Psychology
  Mathematics
  Economics
  Biology
  Political science
  Business

The nearby town of Winston-Salem, while not exactly a college town, has a "funky, Bohemian flavor," with a symphony, great restaurants, and a Christmastime "Moravian love feast."

Some of Wake's more wacky traditions include a midnight concert by the school orchestra every Halloween, with members in full costume, and the Lilting Banshees comedy troupe, which helps students laugh off their stressful workloads.

Fraternities and sororities dominate much of the social scene, as might be expected at a southern school; 37 percent of the men and 50 percent of the women go Greek, but the "open party" system means independents are also welcome to join the festivities. Underage students—especially women—say it's relatively easy to get alcohol at frat parties, though the school's Honor Code means that those who help facilitate illegal drinking, and those who imbibe when they shouldn't, face stiff sanctions if caught. Some of Wake's more wacky traditions include a midnight concert by the school orchestra every Halloween, with members in full costume, and the Lilting Banshees comedy troupe, which helps students laugh off their stressful workloads. "What made me love WFU so much when I came to visit was that everyone here was smart, but still normal," says a freshman. "They weren't so smart they were weird. Students here love to get involved, much more than I've noticed at other schools."

The nearby town of Winston-Salem, while not exactly a college town, has a "funky, Bohemian flavor," with a symphony, great restaurants, and a Christmas-time "Moravian love feast." In addition to the on-campus Museum of Anthropology, two art museums are within a three-mile walk of campus. The town also has a strong music scene, with Ziggy's and Freddy B's the cornerstones of the local concert circuit. "It's large enough for some exploration, but small enough to assure anxious parents," a junior reports. Students get involved in the

"Trying to extend party hours is a constant struggle, and the lack of diversity on campus is frequently discussed."

community through volunteer activities, including Project Pumpkin, a trick-or-treat night on campus for underprivileged children. For those with cars, it's four hours to Carolina's beaches, and three hours to the Great Smokey Mountains National Park.

When it comes to sports, basketball is king. Wake's Demon Deacons compete in the incredibly tough Atlantic Coast Conference, cheered on by the Screaming Demons Fan Club. Wake Forest prides itself on the ability to play with the big boys of the ACC, winning the NIT Invitational Tournament in 2000. "Athletic rivalries against Duke and Maryland make sports fun," says a freshman. "We roll the quad in toilet paper after winning, turning it into a white fairyland." The football team draws big crowds, too, especially for games against Appalachian State. And of course, virtually any contest against in-state rival UNC–Chapel Hill is guaranteed to get students excited. In 2001, Wake Forest completed the Kenneth D. Miller Center, which houses facilities for student athletes and a fitness center open to the entire university community.

Wake Forest offers an enviable combination—the championship-caliber athletics and outstanding faculty and facilities of a state school, with the competitive academics and cozy feeling of an elite private college. "It's rare to find such a small school with so much spirit," says a freshman. No wonder students' biggest complaint is that food-service employees should be more friendly!

Overlaps

Duke, UNC–Chapel Hill, University of Virginia, Davidson, Emory

If You Apply To ➤ **Wake Forest:** Early decision: Nov. 15. Regular admissions: Jan. 15. Financial aid: Feb. 1. Guarantees to meet demonstrated need. Campus interviews: optional, informational. No alumni interviews. SATs: required. SAT IIs: optional. Accepts the Common Application and electronic applications. Essay questions: What is your academic passion? Also choose one of the following: social concern that threatens community or nation; your philosophies of honor, leadership, and social responsibility; explain Wake Forest's motto of Pro Humanitate.

University of Washington

1410 N.E. Campus Parkway, Seattle, WA 98195

UDub wows visitors with its sprawling park-like campus in hugely popular Seattle. Washington is tougher than University of Oregon for out-of-state admission but not as hard as UC heavyweights Berkeley or UCLA. Location near the coast and mountains makes for strong marine and environmental studies programs.

In recent years, the University of Washington has come on strong as a solid research institution. It is a gem of a school that many in the Northwest regard as one of the best deals around. And with funds pouring in from Microsoft multi-millionaires (including head honcho Bill Gates), this public university promises to become even stronger in the future. Students on this campus understand that anonymity and size are the prices that must be paid for the wealth of opportunities that await them. Those looking for the extra, personal touch might want to investigate the school's two branch campuses in Tacoma and Bothell, where class sizes average twenty-five students. But if the Seattle campus is your focus, one senior hints, just "learn to work the system."

Washington's Seattle campus features a number of distinctive landmarks. Red Square sits atop the Central Plaza parking garage and features the Broken Obelisk, a twenty-six-foot-high steel sculpture gifted to the university by the Virginia Wright Fund.

Many of Washington's diverse undergraduate strengths correspond with its excellent graduate programs. The ultracompetitive business major, for example, benefits from the university's highly regarded business school and is the most popular undergraduate major, followed by biology, art, English, and accounting. Similarly, students majoring in public health, community medicine, pharmacy, and nursing profit from access to facilities and faculty at the medical school, an international leader in cancer and heart research, cell biology, and organ transplants. Also recommended for undergraduates are biological and life sciences (pumped up

> **"The key is to take the bull by the horns and find out which advisors are better than others."**

even more by a new physics/astronomy building), and most engineering programs, especially aero- and astronautical engineering, which are generously funded by Boeing and NASA. Reflecting the focus on natural resources in Washington's economy, the programs in fisheries and forestry are excellent, as are earth and atmospheric sciences, including oceanography. Washington has dropped its major in environmental studies and added a major in community and environmental planning.

Undergraduates in both professional and liberal arts programs must take five credits in English composition, seven credits in writing beyond composition, and one course in quantitative and symbolic reasoning. Students must also fulfill forty credits in general education requirements, including the arts, individuals and societies, and the natural world. Schools and colleges also have their own requirements that must be met. Many Washington professors are tops in their field, but students may have to be patient about seeing professors after class. As for academic advising, a student advises, "The key is to take the bull by the horns and find out which advisors are better than others." While students once complained that classes were difficult to get into, that problem seems to have been reduced, except for large 100- and 200-level courses. Ninety percent of the classes have fewer than fifty students. "It is very common to be taught by teaching assistants, but overall the quality is good in both senior-faculty and graduate-student teachers," a business major says.

Website:
www.washington.edu
Location: Urban
Total Enrollment: 35,559
Undergraduates: 25,638
Male/Female: 59/41
SAT Ranges: V 510–630
M 530–650
ACT Range: 22–27
Financial Aid: 30%
Expense: Pub $ $ $
Phi Beta Kappa: Yes
Applicants: 12,785
Accepted: 76%
Enrolled: 43%
Grad in 6 Years: 62%
Returning Freshmen: 91%
Academics: ✍ ✍ ✍ ✍ ½
Social: ☎ ☎ ☎
Q of L: ★ ★ ★
Admissions: (206) 543-9686
Email Address: askuwadm@
u.washington.edu

Strongest Programs
Business
Art
English
Psychology
Drama
Engineering
Architecture
Environmental Studies

While students once complashed that classes were difficult to get into, that problem seems to have been reduced, except for large 100- and 200- level courses. Ninety percent of the classes have fewer than fifty students.

For those interested in skirting the masses, UW sports an honors program that offers small classes on interesting subjects taught by fine professors. The academic environment at UW is "very much centered on learning. Part of that comes from the fact that this is a research institution." And if students get the itch to see some different scenery, there are sixty different study-abroad programs offered in twenty countries, including China, Denmark, and Russia. A program in experiential learning encourages students to find internships and participate in community service. This fits in with a variety of classes that give students the opportunity to volunteer as part of their coursework. A senior says, "There's simply no better way to learn than by combining challenging courses with real-world experience. When you're learning in the classroom, you can't always apply it. Experience adds to your learning, and it helps you remember it."

Part of the reason for UW's national anonymity is the fact that it turns away large numbers of out-of-state applicants, preferring to keep its focus on the home folks. Ninety percent of undergraduates are state residents, and an unusually large proportion are over the age of twenty-five. The student body is 59 percent white and 22 percent Asian-American, with Hispanics and African-Americans comprising 7 percent. Students say the school strives for diversity by offering Valuing Diversity workshops to foster increased awareness of and sensitivity to individual differences; one student calls it "the administration's way of giving lip service to issues they can't or won't deal with." The campus is very active politically, as one junior reports: "Political correctness is very big here and students find very creative ways to make their points."

"Political correctness is very big here, and students find very creative ways to make their points."

The weather is consistently temperate, and natives insist that the city's reputation for rain is undeserved.

Students say budget cuts have decreased the number of course offerings, and programs like Society and Justice. Merit scholarships are awarded to Washington residents with good high-school records and test scores. Athletic scholarships are awarded to men and women in a wide variety of sports, including swimming, women's gymnastics, golf, tennis, and track and field. Freshmen are given special attention via the Freshman Interest Group (FIG) program, which offers freshmen a chance to meet, discuss, and study with other freshmen who have similar interests. Each FIG consists of twenty to twenty-four students who share a cluster of classes (which meet graduation requirements), and includes a weekly seminar led by a junior or senior peer advisor. Also of interest to freshmen are General Studies 101, an optional two-credit course designed to help students meet the demands and expectations of college life, and Freshman Seminars, one-credit courses with ten or twelve other freshmen.

Fifty-six percent of the students live in the school's seven coed dorms. Hagget provides a comfortable setting for freshmen, and McMahon is recommended for those inclined to party. Housing is also available for married students, and the fraternity and sorority organizations are home to another 11 percent of the men and 12 percent of the women. The rest live off campus in Seattle or other parts of King County. Each dorm has its own cafeteria and fast-food line based on a debit-card system. The Husky Union Building also offers a dining hall, espresso bar, writing center, sun deck, and lounges. "Great" is how one student describes campus security, while others also report that they feel "100 percent safe" on campus.

"The dorms and fraternities seem to contain the most social activity."

Given the large number of commuters, it's no surprise that most of Washington's social life takes place away from campus, except for the Greeks (members of a combined total of forty-eight fraternities and sororities). "The dorms and fraternities seem to contain the most social activity, and what they lack is made up for by the proximity to downtown Seattle," says one student. There are also free movies and drama productions for those who must find entertainment on campus. Both dormies and Greeks are not supposed to drink if they're under twenty-one. Sooner or later most students hit the "Ave.," University Way, where shops and top restaurants await them.

And that's true of Seattle, too. A ten-minute bus ride connects students to a full array of urban offerings. The Seattle Center hosts outstanding operas, symphonies, and touring shows, while the Kingdome houses the Seahawks. But who needs pro football with Washington's Huskies around? Husky Fever breaks out on every football weekend, and the stands are always packed for UW's top-rated team. Despite some off-the-field problems among football players, the Huskies are much loved on Saturday afternoons. The team won the Rose Bowl in 2001 and is consistently on the hunt for the PAC 10 athletic crown. While students get fired up for the trip to Pasadena, they're equally excited when Washington State comes to town to vie for the coveted Apple Cup. Other strong UW teams include women's basketball, crew, cross-country, and tennis, and men's crew, baseball, soccer, and tennis.

More than anything else, the great outdoors define the University of Washington. The campus offers breathtaking views of Lake Washington and the Olympic Mountains. Outdoor pastimes for students include boating, hiking, camping, and skiing, all found nearby, and Canada is close enough for road trips to Vancouver. The weather is consistently temperate, and natives insist that the city's reputation for rain is undeserved. Then again, the sports stadium has an overhang to protect spectators from showers.

While some students won't appreciate the no-nonsense and often impersonal academic programs and the lack of a centralized social life, many students can overlook these obstacles for the big picture of the up-and-coming University of Washington—one that takes in more than just the beautiful scenery.

If You Apply To ➢ **Washington:** Regular admissions: Jan. 15. Financial aid: Feb. 28. Housing: May 1. Does not guarantee to meet demonstrated financial need. Campus interviews: optional, informational. No alumni interviews. SATs or ACTs: required. SAT IIs: optional. No essay question. Primarily committed to state residents.

Washington and Jefferson College

60 South Lincoln Street, Washington, PA 15301

Premed Central would be as good a name as any for W&J, where the proportion of students who go on to medical school is one of the nation's highest. Law school and business school are also popular destinations. The tenor of life is conservative and the Greek system is strong.

With new leadership initiating programmatic improvements and a consistent emphasis on preprofessional training, Washington and Jefferson College is becoming an attractive choice for students looking into fields ranging from medicine to theatre to literature. The quality of teaching is roundly praised as life-changing, while the preponderance of small classes means one-on-one attention is almost a given. "We are climbing at a great rate," gushes a philosophy major. "It's an exciting time to come to W&J."

The campus, like the student body, is tight-knit: just over thirty buildings residing on forty-two acres in a small town about thirty miles outside of Pittsburgh. W&J

(Continued)
ACT Range: 21–26
Financial Aid: 74%
Expense: Pr $ $
Phi Beta Kappa: Yes
Applicants: 1,110
Accepted: 85%
Enrolled: 34%
Grad in 6 Years: 70%
Returning Freshmen: 82%
Academics: ✍ ✍ ✍
Social: ☎ ☎ ☎
Q of L: ★ ★
Admissions: (724) 223-6025
Email Address:
    admission@washjeff.edu

Strongest Programs
    Premed
    Prelaw
    Business Administration
    Biology
    English

is the eleventh-oldest college in the country, and houses the eighth-oldest college building, which was built in 1793. Famous songwriter Stephen Foster was a student here until he got kicked out. The prevailing architectural style is traditional Colonial/Georgian, though modern structures have been added at a rapid pace during the past two decades. Now open for business is the Burnett Center, with new classrooms for business, language, and education majors, as well as the Vilar Technology Center. Cameron Stadium was recently expanded and renovated, and a new all-suite residence hall has opened.

W&J's formula for success starts with individual attention in small classes, three-quarters of which have twenty-five students or less. "These small group classes spark each student's intellectual curiosity," a junior says. One-third of the students ranked in the top tenth of their high-school class, but most say the academic climate is rigorous, especially for those on the premed and prelaw tracks. Tenured professors, who are eager to help them understand the requirements and assist them if they fall behind in classwork, teach most classes. "The truth is, the professors are the best point of the college," an English major says. "They don't hesitate to get students involved in their research, so we form yet another bond in

> **"We are climbing at a great rate,"**
> **gushes a philosophy major. "It's**
> **an exciting time to come to W&J."**

our field of interest." Academic advising is "help yourself," but the college's track record for graduate placement stands on its own—36 percent of recent graduates went on to professional or graduate schools and 56 percent to jobs after graduation.

New graduation requirements call for students to complete thirty-four courses and demonstrate proficiency in writing, speaking, reading, quantitative reasoning, foreign language, and use of information technology. Students must also take credits in culture and intellectual tradition, fine arts, language and literature, science and mathematics, and social sciences. A thematic major allows students to design their own course of study, while double majors produce such types as a biologist well versed in literature. Rare among liberal arts colleges are the 3–4 programs with the Pennsylvania Colleges of Optometry and Podiatry. More technically minded students can take advantage of the 3–2 engineering programs with Case Western Reserve and Washington University in St. Louis. Among the standard departments, premed or prelaw, chemistry, biology, political science, and history are popular. There are new majors in biochemistry, information technology leadership, environmental science, and a psychology

> **"These small group classes spark**
> **each student's intellectual curiosity."**

program called Mind, Brain, and Behavior. More than 90 percent of W&J graduates who apply to medical or health-related programs are accepted for admission, and the acceptance rate of W&J graduates to law schools is 90 percent.

During the January intersession, students find brief apprenticeships in prospective career areas, take a school tour abroad (marine biology trips to the Bahamas or Australia, English theater trips to London, history trips to Russia or China, and biology trips to Africa), or engage in nontraditional coursework. There is also a semester- or year-abroad option in Germany, England, Moscow, Russia, or Bogotá, Colombia. Other study abroad opportunities are also available in Australia, Europe, Asia, and Latin America.

Diversity is not a strong suit at W&J, but it is improving thanks to administrative diligence. Eighty percent of the students hail from Pennsylvania and many are from neighboring states in the Northeast. About 3 percent of students are African-American, 1 percent Hispanic, and 1 percent Asian-American. No matter what their ethnicity, excellent students get a bargain at this somewhat pricey school if they win one of the five hundred academic scholarships that range from $5,000 to a full ride. There are no athletic scholarships, and the school doesn't guarantee to meet students' full demonstrated need.

A nonalcoholic pub called
George & Tom's has become
quite a popular diversion
with comedy, musical, and
novelty/variety acts.

Students can live in either coed or single-sex dorms. Women's dorms are the newest and the nicest, according to most. Students say the older dorms are fair. "Dormitories and comfortable? That's an oxymoron at any college," says one. "I live in an older building where maintenance is always appreciated." The choices get better with academic rank, and on-campus apartments are available based on GPA, activities, and need. The administration does have plans to build new townhouses and specialty housing. In order to live off campus, students need an excuse from a parent or doctor. Students complain about the security on campus but the school is working to improve this situation.

Without a doubt, the social life at W&J centers around the Greeks, who attract 45 percent of the men and 49 percent of the women. A crackdown on alcohol and noise violations has somewhat quieted the school's tradition of enormous parties, but the Student Activity Board has begun filling the gap with more on-campus events, such as free movies, and a student-run coffee house provides another non-frat option. The school has ten national fraternities and four national sororities. "Our students put a lot of effort into Greek life and social pursuits," says one student. "However, they are also laid-back and ready to allow others to find their own niche." A nonalcoholic pub called George & Tom's has become quite a popular diversion with comedy, musical, and novelty/variety acts. During the course of the year, Carnival Weekend and Spring Concert are the most popular.

Students head home on the weekends or explore dating opportunities at nearby colleges, most notably Penn State and Pitt. One of the most popular excursions is a thirty-minute commute to Pittsburgh. Still, not all students share the administration's appreciation for "the unique characteristics of the western Pennsylvania milieu." Many complain that

> *During the January intersession, students find brief apprenticeships in prospective career areas, take a school tour abroad (marine biology trips to the Bahamas or Australia, English theater trips to London, history trips to Russia or China, and biology trips to Africa), or engage in nontraditional coursework.*

"Our students put a lot of effort into Greek life and social pursuits."

there is nothing to do in this former steel/mining town, hit by hard times. But new restaurants, such as Applebee's and TGI Friday's, are springing up. Townies tend to be a bit resentful of dressy W&J undergrads, but students try to assuage this attitude by actively volunteering in the community. "It's really a sweet, peaceful place once you get used to it," a senior says.

Just about anyone has a shot at varsity sports. Football has taken home conference championships twice in the past three years—and no wonder, the team's coach is a former Pittsburgh Steeler with three Super Bowl rings. Men's and women's swimming, golf, volleyball, and hockey all boast their own successes. For the non-varsity type, there are numerous clubs to join, everything from the cycling association to the karate club.

So many things are changing at W&J that today's complaints will likely fade and be replaced with praise for campus facilities, academic variety, and on-campus social options. In the meantime, students say the education they're getting at this "Revolutionary College" is hard to beat. Says one economics major, "I cannot express how much my life and outlook on learning have been enriched by the excellent professors at W&J."

Overlaps

Allegheny, Duquesne, Dickinson, College of Wooster, Denison

If You Apply To ➤

Washington and Jefferson: Early decision: Nov. 1. Regular admissions: Mar. 1. Financial aid: Feb. 15. Guarantees to meet demonstrated need of 35%. Campus interviews: recommended, evaluative. Alumni interviews: optional, informational. SATs: required. SAT IIs: optional. Accepts the Common Application and electronic applications. Essay question: personal statement.

Coeducation came to W&L and the pillars of the Colonade did not come tumbling down. Nearly twenty years after the coming of women, W&L is the most selective small college in the South, rivaled only by Davidson. W&L supplements the liberal arts with strong programs in business, public policy, and journalism.

Website: www.wlu.edu
Location: Small town
Total Enrollment: 2,128
Undergraduates: 1,768
Male/Female: 55/45
SAT Ranges: V 680–710
   M 640–710
ACT Range: 28–30
Financial Aid: 30%
Expense: Pr $
Phi Beta Kappa: Yes
Applicants: 2,940
Accepted: 35%
Enrolled: 48%
Grad in 6 Years: 89%
Returning Freshmen: 94%
Academics: ✏ ✏ ✏ ✏ ½
Social: ☎ ☎ ☎
Q of L: ★ ★ ★ ★
Admissions: (540) 463-8710
Email Address:
   admissions@wlu.edu

Strongest Programs
   Business
   History
   Politics
   English
   Journalism
   Economics

Washington and Lee University, which shares the town of Lexington, Virginia, with the Virginia Military Institute, is as genteel as a Southern school can be. The Fancy Dress Ball is a highlight of each year, and a "speaking tradition" results in at least casual communication between students and professors when they pass one another on the well-manicured grounds. And behind the frills and fun lies an honor system that students cite as one of their school's best features.

W&L's wooded campus sits atop a hill of lush green lawns, sweeping from one national landmark to another. Redbrick buildings feature white Doric columns and the prevailing architectural style is Greek Revival. A $23 million science center houses all science departments and facilities, and the school has completed major additions to the athletic facilities as well. The physical face is changing. A parking garage, playing fields, and sorority houses were recently completed. The school is building a new University Commons and art and music building, and renovating a gym and Reid Hall, home of the journalism and mass communications department.

Though Washington and Lee is a school steeped in tradition, it is also working hard to find the future. The number of women on campus is growing, and though they were first admitted only about a decade ago, they now account for 45 percent of the student body. Although a standard liberal arts program remains the foundation of the school's curriculum, it offers excellent preprofessional programs, particularly business, economics, public policy, and accounting through the Williams School of Commerce, Economics, and Politics. Journalism and mass communications are popular, as are biology (for premeds) and English. W&L also has bachelor's degree programs in fields as diverse as Russian studies and marine science education, which allows students to work at the Duke University Marine Laboratory for a semester. The East Asian studies program has ties to universities in Taiwan and Japan. Student can take part in the Shepherd Program for the Interdisciplinary Study of Poverty, and interdisciplinary programs were recently added in women's studies and business journalism. More and more students are spending time abroad, and the new Global Stewardship Program is designed to increase international-study opportunities.

> "Although the climate is not cut-throat, students set high academic expectations and strive to attain them."

General education requirements account for one-third of a student's courses. Distribution requirements at W&L include English composition; two literature courses; three courses in fine arts, history, philosophy, and religion; three courses in science and math; three social science courses; five terms of physical education; proficiency in swimming; and two years of a foreign language. A class on the history of Washington and Lee University is immensely popular. There are no required courses for the freshman year, but orientation-week activities are popular and some spring-term seminars are limited to freshmen and sophomores.

The academic climate ranges from intense to casual, depending on the student. "Although the climate is not cut-throat, students set high academic expectations and strive to attain them," says a senior biology major. "Courses are rigorous, requiring genuine effort and in-depth study." Classes tend to be small, and freshmen can count on getting full professors; there are no teaching assistants. "The quality of teaching is unparalleled and one of my favorite aspects of this school," says one junior. "The faculty is not only brilliant but extremely accessible." Tests and final exams are taken without faculty supervision; doors remain unlocked, calculators stay on desks, and library stacks are open twenty-four hours a day. Online registration helps quell any potential scheduling disasters. The modern library, like most W&L facilities, is superb and offers eight hundred individual study areas as well as private rooms for honors students. Well-qualified students can apply for the Robert E. Lee Undergraduate Research Program, which offers students paid fellowships for assisting professors in research or doing their own.

"Most of the rooms on campus for freshmen and sophomores are singles, which is great!"

"The majority of the W&L student body still tends to be very Southern and conservative and well-off," says a sophomore. "Even though the school takes steps to improve that, that's what is most visible." A freshman adds, "Students here are generally very bright with a lot of capability for leadership." African-Americans account for a mere 3 percent of the student body, despite the school's argument that it is strongly committed to recruiting African-American students; Hispanics and Asian-Americans, meanwhile, combine for 3 percent. Seventeen percent of students are native Virginians, but the university's geographic diversity has not prompted much other differentiation. Coeducation has been a godsend for the admissions office; applications are way up for the past several years, the median SAT scores of each freshman class are on the rise, and the acceptance rate is much lower than it was five or six years ago. The school offers a handful of merit scholarships worth up to $27,000, but no athletic awards.

Coeducation has been a godsend for the admissions office; applications are way up for the past several years, the median SAT scores of each freshman class are on the rise, and the acceptance rate is much lower than it was five or six years ago.

Students spend their first year at W&L in "quite comfortable and well maintained" coed dorms, and some freshmen may reserve singles. "Most of the rooms on campus for freshmen and sophomores are singles, which is great!" says a sophomore. Freshmen are required to buy the meal plan, and the food is reportedly good. Upperclass dorms and apartments are available, and many students move into country houses when they are juniors or seniors. Sixty-three percent of the student body reside on-campus.

"Few social options exist outside of the Greek system."

Seventy-eight percent of the men join fraternities, which, along with newly created sororities that claim 74 percent of the women, dominate the social scene. "Few social options exist outside of the Greek system," laments one senior. Underage drinking is banned in the dorms and strictly avoided because it's against the honor code, but students insist "drinking is quite prevalent" and "alcohol is easy to come by for all students."

W&L's social life focuses on Greek bashes, which often feature live bands, although the aforementioned Fancy Dress Ball, or "$100,000 prom," also draws raves. Equally well-known is W&L's mock political convention for the party out of power, held every four years, which has predicted past presidential nominees with uncanny accuracy. Aside from trips to the four women's colleges in the surrounding area and the University of Virginia, the Foxfield races near Charlottesville and the Kentucky Derby are popular road-trip destinations.

With its scenic location in the midst of the Appalachian Mountains, the university provides an abundance of activities for nature lovers, including hunting, fishing, camping, skiing, and tubing in the rivers. Washington, D.C., Richmond, and Roanoke are easily reached by car for weekend trips. Lexington, a "quiet, friendly town that has much history to offer" also offers a few bars, two movie theaters, and several restaurants. A thriving intramural program is a staple of W&L life, bringing

"The majority of the W&L student body still tends to be very Southern and conservative and well-off," says a sophomore.

fraternities and independents together in friendly rivalry. Football sparks some interest in the fall, with its attendant tailgate parties, but W&L students live for the spring and the Lee Jackson Lacrosse Classic against VMI. In general, "Athletic rivalries are not that important, but no one here likes to lose," reports a freshman. Other popular teams include men's soccer and baseball and women's soccer and tennis.

Most students are proud to look back on their college careers and point to the progress their alma mater has made in the intervening years, but not those from Washington and Lee. The culture here doesn't embrace change. "A lot of times people at W&L tend to live in a social bubble," says one European student. But those who choose Washington and Lee because of their reverence and appreciation for Southern tradition—and their desire to "work hard and play hard" while getting a solid grounding in liberal arts or business—won't be disappointed.

If You Apply To ➤

W&L: Early decision: Dec. 1. Regular admissions: Jan. 15. Does not guarantee to meet demonstrated need. Campus and alumni interviews: recommended, evaluative. ACTs or SATs: required. SAT IIs: required (writing and two nonrelated subjects). Accepts the Common Application. Essay question: significant experience or achievement with special meaning; best advice received; issue of personal, national, or local concern and its importance.

Washington University in St. Louis

Campus Box 1089, One Brookings Drive, St. Louis, MO 63130-4899

In the space of little more than a decade, Wash U has gone from Midwestern backup school to elite private university close on the heels of Northwestern. Wash U is strong in everything from art to engineering. The halo effect of the university's medical school attracts a slew of aspiring doctors.

Website:
www.admissions.wustl.edu
Location: Suburban
Total Enrollment: 12,187
Undergraduates: 6,772
Male/Female: 49/51
SAT Ranges: V 640–730
M 670–740
ACT Range: 29–32
Financial Aid: 45%
Expense: Pr $ $ $ $
Phi Beta Kappa: Yes
Applicants: 20,834
Accepted: 23%
Enrolled: 26%
Grad in 6 Years: 88%
Returning Freshmen: 96%
Academics: ✍ ✍ ✍ ✍ ½
Social: ☎ ☎ ☎
Q of L: ★ ★ ★ ★

One of higher education's rising stars, Washington University is arguably the best private school between Chicago and San Francisco. Though it's always been well-recognized regionally, Wash U is on its way to being a truly national institution—with a relaxed Midwestern feel that differentiates it from the high-strung eastern Ivies. Applications have skyrocketed, and with a hefty endowment, strong preprofessional programs, and an emphasis on research, it's not hard to see why. "Almost everyone is friendly and smiles when you see them," says a junior majoring in anthropology and accounting. "Even the food-service workers get to know you by name, and ask how your day is going."

The school's 169-acre campus adjoins Forest Park, one of the nation's three largest urban parks. Buildings are constructed in the Collegiate Gothic style, mostly in red Missouri granite and white limestone, with plenty of climbing ivy, gargoyles, and arches. The campus is continually growing, with the recent opening of new residence halls for small groups who share common interests and goals. New buildings for lab sciences and biomedical engineering were slated for completion in 2002, and the Olin Library is being renovated and expanded by seventeen thousand square feet to make room for a cybercafe and twenty-four-hour study space. Architects are working on plans for a new University Center and new space for Earth and planetary sciences.

Undergraduates enroll in one or more of Washington U's five schools—arts and sciences, architecture, art, business, or engineering. Double and interdisciplinary majors, such as environmental studies, are encouraged and easily arranged—so easily arranged, in fact, that about 60 percent of students earn either a major and minor, more than one major, and sometimes more than one degree. General education requirements vary by school and program. For liberal arts students, they include courses in quantitative reasoning, physical and life sciences, social or behavioral sciences, minority or gender studies, language or the arts, and English composition course.

Washington U's offerings in the natural sciences, especially biology and chemistry, have long been notable, especially among premeds. The outstanding medical school runs a faculty exchange program with the undergraduate biology department, which affords bio majors significant opportunities to conduct advanced laboratory research. The University Scholars Program allows students to apply for undergraduate and graduate admission before entering college. If accepted, students can begin exploring their chosen career path earlier—though they aren't obligated to follow through if their interests change.

The freshman FOCUS program helps balance the preprofessional bent of some of Washington U's best programs with the school's desire to provide a broad and deep educational experience and a smaller class size. In FOCUS, students use a weekly seminar to explore topics of contemporary significance, such as law and society. The program lets first-year students work closely with professors—including at least one Nobel Prize winner—and sample offerings from various departments. Other notable options include the two-year Hewlet Program, which allows groups of students to focus on an interdisciplinary area, such as the connection between the mind and the brain.

"Almost everyone is friendly and smiles when you see them."

As Washington U's applicant pool has gotten bigger, the admissions committee has become more selective—and classes have gotten tougher, students report. "Everyone here is the 'smart kid,'" explains a freshman. "The courses are challenging and demanding because the professors expect so much from us and the students take their studies so seriously." Those who are struggling will find plenty of help, however, from teaching assistants who conduct help sessions to study groups of their peers. "Professors really seem to care about undergraduates, and help us explore our interests," says a junior. "The quality of teaching is great."

Diversity is an issue facing most schools, and Washington University is not immune. But the school's population is relatively heterogeneous, with African-Americans comprising 8 percent, Hispanics 3 percent, and Asian-Americans 10 percent. There's also a large contingent from eastern states like New York and New Jersey, many of whom are Jewish, leading to much debate about the Arab-Israeli conflict. Organizations such as STAR (Students Together Against Racism) and ADHOC (Against Discrimination and Hatred on Campus) also help enlighten students. "Dialogue on campus is pretty open, whether the conversation is on race, social activities, or the alcohol policy," says a chemical engineering major.

Eighty percent of Wash U students live in the school's dormitories, known as residential colleges. Most are clustered in an area called South 40, a forty-acre plot next to campus. All dorms are coed and air-conditioned, and some have suites for six to eight students of the same gender. Freshmen are guaranteed rooms, and students who stay in the dorms after that are promised rooms for the following year, says a junior. It's becoming more popular to stay on campus for all four years, a psychology major reports, especially since upperclassmen may live in university-owned apartments. Some juniors and seniors do choose true off-campus digs in the nearby neighborhoods of University City and Clayton, where apartments are reasonably priced. Dorm-dwellers and others who buy the meal plan may use their credits in any of fourteen dining centers.

"Everyone here is the 'smart kid.'"

(Continued)
Admissions: (314) 935-6000
or (800) 638-0700
Email Address:
admissions@wustl.edu

Strongest Programs
Chemistry, Biology, and
Natural Sciences
Foreign Languages
English
Business
Political Science
Earth and Planetary Sciences
Art and Architecture
Computer Science
Engineering

Every spring, the whole campus turns out for the century-old Thurtene Carnival, the oldest student-run philanthropic festival in the country. Student groups—especially fraternities and sororities, which attract 25 percent of the men and 18 percent of the women—build booths, sell food, and put on plays, and profits are donated to a children's charity.

"The food is delicious—way too good to be 'college food,' but ridiculously expensive," says a psychology major.

Washington U students pride themselves on being able to balance work and play, and on weekends, movies, fraternity parties, and concerts tear them away from their books. Every spring, the whole campus turns out for the century-old Thurtene Carnival, the oldest student-run philanthropic festival in the country. Student groups—especially fraternities and sororities, which attract 25 percent of the men and 18 percent of the women—build booths, sell food, and put on plays, and profits are donated to a children's charity. Another big event is Walk-In-Lay-Down (WILD) Theater, held the first and last Fridays of the academic year. Everyone brings a blanket to the main quad, assumes a horizontal position, and listens to live bands until the wee hours. Alcohol policies emphasize responsible drinking, though students under twenty-one aren't supposed to drink at all, per Missouri law. "Students can have alcohol, and as long as they aren't hurting themselves or others, people won't step in," says an English and finance major. "The university seems to realize college is a time for experimentation."

Aside from an active campus social life, Washington U offers incredible recreational options because of its location abutting Forest Park: a golf course, an ice-skating rink, a zoo, a lake with boat rentals, art and history museums, an outdoor theater, and a science center are all within a short walk. The St. Louis Rams, Blues,

> **"The food is delicious—way too good to be 'college food,' but ridiculously expensive."**

and Cardinals attract pro football, hockey, and baseball fans, and the city is also home to the addictive Ted Drewes frozen custard. The school runs a free shuttle service to parts of St. Louis not within walking distance, and community-service programs such as "Each One Teach One," in partnership with the city's schools, attract a sizable number of students. The best road trips include Chicago; Nashville and Memphis, Tennessee; Lake of the Ozarks; and Columbia, Missouri—home of the University of Missouri.

Washington U competes in Division III, and it's a women's basketball powerhouse, bringing home national titles from 1998 through 2001. The women's softball team won a University Athletic Association title in 2000, its first year as a varsity sport. Other strong programs include women's volleyball, with seven NCAA national championships and fourteen UAA championships in its history, and football, winner of the UAA title in two of the past three years. Intramural sports range from badminton, arm wrestling, and floor hockey to pocket billiards and Ultimate Frisbee.

For too long, Washington U was a sleepy little school in a sleepy little town on the banks of the Mississippi River—not well known beyond the country's midsection. The passionate, motivated, and ambitious students who continue to flock here aim to change that misperception. "It is incredible to be in a community where people love to learn, where everyone is passionate about something, and people enjoy challenge and growth," says a junior. "The people here are extremely friendly, and the campus is gorgeous," a freshman adds. "The combination makes Wash U a great place to live and learn."

If You Apply To ➤

Washington U: Early decision I: Nov. 15. Early decision II: Jan. 1. Regular admissions: Jan. 15. Financial aid: Nov. 1 (early decision applicants), Feb. 15. Housing: May 1. Meets demonstrated need of 78%. Campus and alumni interviews: optional, evaluative. SATs or ACTs: required. SAT IIs: optional. Apply to one of five undergraduate schools. Accepts the Common Application and electronic applications. Essay question: Choose one: creative work's effect on you; how you've resolved an ethical dilemma; write and answer your own essay question.

Wellesley College

Wellesley, MA 02481

There is no better recipe for popularity than a postcard-perfect campus on the outskirts of Boston. That formula keeps Wellesley at the top of the women's college pecking order—along with superb programs in economics and the natural sciences. Nearly a quarter of the students are Asian-American, the highest proportion in the East.

Wellesley is not just the best women's college in the nation, it's one of the best colleges in the nation, period. With an alumnae roster that includes Senator Hillary Rodham Clinton, Madame Chiang Kai-shek, Madeleine Albright, and Diane Sawyer, Wellesley College should be at the top of the list for those who are seeking an all-women's education. Wellesley women excel in whatever field they choose, including traditional male bastions like economics and business. "It is a wonderful place to grow," says a senior.

Nestled in a corner of a wealthy Boston suburb, the Wellesley campus, one of the most beautiful anywhere, occupies five hundred rolling acres of cultivated and natural areas, including Lake Waban. Campus buildings range in architectural style from Gothic (with stone towers and brick quadrangles) to state-of-the-art science, arts, and sports facilities. A twenty-two-acre arboretum and botanical garden features a wide variety of trees and plants.

With its hefty endowment and top-notch facilities, Wellesley offers a top-of-the-line educational experience. The most popular majors are English, psychology, economics, political science, and international relations, though economics is known as the biggest powerhouse. In fact, Wellesley has produced virtually all of the country's high-ranking female economists. Students in molecular biology work with faculty on DNA research, and a high-tech science center houses two electron microscopes, two NMR spectrometers, ultracentrifuges, two lasers, and other such equipment. A comprehensive renovation of the social science building added videoconferencing, computer labs, and a research facility.

> **"It is a wonderful place to grow."**

In the past, Theater Studies was considered a weak department, but the school has gone to great lengths to remedy the situation by building a department students can brag about. The Ruth Nagel Jones Theater provides performance space for mainstage productions and experimental theater. The Davis Museum and Cultural Center houses eleven galleries, a cinema, and a café. The students at Wellesley will find an academic art museum to their benefit, along with more than a million volumes in the campus libraries. The five libraries sport a computerized catalog system that is accessible on- or off-campus. Anything Wellesley women find lacking in their facilities or curriculum can probably be found at MIT, where they have full cross-registration privileges. Wellesley students can also take courses at Brandeis University and Babson College, or participate in exchange programs with Spelman College in Atlanta or Mills College in Oakland, California.

Wellesley has distribution requirements that include three units drawn from language and literature and visual arts, music, theater, film, and video; one unit from social and behavioral analysis; a unit each from two of the following: epistemology and cognition, religion, ethics and moral philosophy, and historical studies; and three units from natural and physical science and mathematical modeling and problem solving. In addition, students must take a first-year writing class, a foreign language, and a course on multiculturalism. Academics are taken very seriously

---

Website: www.wellesley.edu
Location: Suburban
Total Enrollment: 2,287
Undergraduates: 2,287
Male/Female: 0/100
SAT Ranges: V 640–730
  M 630–710
ACT Range: 27–31
Financial Aid: 52%
Expense: Pr $ $ $ $
Phi Beta Kappa: Yes
Applicants: 3,047
Accepted: 43%
Enrolled: 44%
Grad in 6 Years: 90%
Returning Freshmen: 96%
Academics: ✑ ✑ ✑ ✑ ✑
Social: ☎ ☎ ☎
Q of L: ★ ★ ★ ★
Admissions: (781) 283-2270
Email Address:
  admission@wellesley.edu

Strongest Programs
  Economics
  Political Science
  Biological Sciences
  Computer Sciences
  Chinese Language

at Wellesley. "The classes can seem competitive," says a senior, "especially when the top women from high schools are placed together on the same campus." Professors are highly respected and make themselves available through email, voicemail, office hours, and by appointment. "The quality of teaching is excellent," says a senior. "All students are taught by professors and class sizes are small, so we get individual attention. Profs here are dedicated to teaching their students, and that makes a big difference."

A five-course technology studies concentration gives liberal arts students the skills necessary to understand and use technological innovations in their future studies as well as in the professional world. Grants from private foundations have allowed Wellesley to add other innovative programs, including independent research tutorials for advanced science students and fellowship funding for joint student–faculty projects.

> **"The classes can seem competitive, especially when the top women from high schools are placed together on the same campus."**

Students can participate in the Twelve-College Exchange, including the National Theater Institute, the Maritime Studies Program, or they can travel and study abroad through one of Wellesley's recently expanded international programs, including the Summer Internship Program in Washington, D.C.

Under the honor system, students may take their finals, unsupervised, at any time during exam week. Class sizes are almost always small (they average eighteen to twenty-three students per class). First-years (as they are exclusively called here) and upperclasswomen alike have faculty advisors. First-years also have a dean of first-year students to offer additional advice on courses and other academic matters. "There are good counseling resources available, but students must seek them out," explains a sophomore.

Once known as "a haven for rich white girls," Wellesley is now a picture of diversity. Twenty-three percent of Wellesley's students are Asian-American. Although the Northeast is the best-represented geographical area (though only 18 percent are from Massachusetts), students also come from every state and more than seventy-five countries. Ninety-seven percent ranked in the top quarter of their high-school class. Whatever their background, most have a fair amount of social aplomb. Issues on campus run the gamut from multiculturalism and racism to gender questions and national politics. "Political correctness is a huge issue," says a psychology and economics double major. "We have such a diverse campus racially, culturally, geographically, and religiously that the major issues address creating a supportive environment for all." There are no athletic or academic scholarships, but students don't seem to mind, rating the recently enhanced financial-aid packages as "constant and fair."

Dorm life at Wellesley is a step ahead of most institutions, to say the least. Virtually every student lives on campus, in rooms that are described as "immaculate." Dorms feature high-ceilinged living rooms, hardwood floors, fireplaces, computers and laser printers, television annexes with VCRs, walk-in closets, kitchenettes with microwaves, and even grand pianos. The dorms are renovated every five years or so and all are well maintained, students say. "Nice dorms—most of them have early-twentieth-century architecture and beautiful windows to look out on a beautiful campus," says an anthropology senior. All residence halls are smoke-free.

> **"There are good counseling resources available, but students must seek them out."**

There are no dorms specifically for first-years—all classes live on all floors. Peer tutors also live in each dorm. These students, called APT advisors, are trained to tutor in specific subjects and in study skills and time management. Juniors and seniors are granted single rooms. Two co-ops, one with a feminist bent, present an educational housing option. Meal cards are valid in every dorm, and at the campus snack bar, which is stocked with everything from milk and flour to Twinkies.

When it comes to weekend fun, Wellesley is in a prime location. Or more accurately, it's close to a prime location: Boston. Not even half an hour away, Boston is the place where Wellesley women can mingle with lots of other students—specifically male—from Harvard and MIT. Cambridge—with Harvard Square, MIT frat parties, and lots of jazz clubs—is accessible by an hourly school shuttle that runs on weekdays and weekends. There is also a trolley stop located a short walk from school. Cape Cod, Providence, and the Vermont and New Hampshire ski slopes are close by car.

The town of Wellesley is an upper-crust Boston suburb, without many amenities for students. "The town is not a college town," gripes a junior, due to "unfriendly residents and expensive stores." For campus-bound students (like many first-years, who cannot have cars on campus), dorm parties and movies are the featured attractions. "Wellesley students decide their own social lives, and there is no one way or outlet," one student notes. Wellesley is a dry town, although the school is in the process of trying to get liquor licenses for the dorms. When alcohol is served, campus police check IDs. Students enjoy going to the student-run Café Hoop, the campus coffee house, to sip tea or share a fro-yo or a chocolate croissant. The closest thing Wellesley has to sororities are societies for arts and music, literature, Shakespeare, and general lectures. These societies also sometimes hold parties.

Wellesley is chock-full of traditions, but the most endearing ones include Flower Sunday, step-singing (an all-campus sing-along on the chapel steps), the sophomore class planting a tree, a junior class variety show, Spring Weekend (with a big-name band and comedian), and a hoop-rolling contest by seniors in their graduation robes. The winner of this contest will supposedly be the first in her class to become a CEO, and she gets off to a flying start when her classmates toss her in the lake. Speaking of the lake, students mention their unofficial campus event, Lake Day, where students take breaks between (or from) classes to enjoy a festival held on the lawn near the lake.

Students balance their academic schedule with athletics to become "Healthy, Wellesley, and Wise." Lacrosse and tennis are among the top varsity sports and cross-country made the NEWMAC Conference championships for four consecutive years. Field hockey, soccer, and volleyball have also claimed championships. The sports "palace," recently renamed the Nannerl Sports Center in honor of Wellesley's eleventh president (who now runs Duke), offers an Olympic-size pool, squash, racquetball and tennis courts, dance studios,

> "I know the friendships I made here will last the rest of my life."

a weight room, and an indoor track. Harvard's Head of the Charles crew race takes honors as the most popular spectator sport of the year. The big athletic rival is Smith College, another of the Seven Sisters group of great women's colleges.

When it comes to academics, Wellesley women are no joke. Their school is competitive with all but the top three Ivies. Many of them enjoy the quaint traditions of the school and appreciate the idyllic atmosphere for contemplation, but know they are poised to dominate whatever field they enter. The graduates of this incredible school are smart, self-confident, capable, and unstoppable in their drive to the top. As one contented senior says: "It's a wonderful place to grow as individuals, as students, and as women." Another senior adds, "I know the friendships I made here will last the rest of my life."

> *When it comes to weekend fun, Wellesley is in a prime location. Or more accurately, it's close to a prime location: Boston.*

Overlaps
Harvard, Brown, Smith, Tufts, Boston University

Wells College

Aurora, NY 13026

Wells is fighting to show that a women's college with less than five hundred students can survive in rural upstate New York. A family atmosphere is the hallmark of Wells, right down to the dinner bell that calls everyone to the evening meal. Wells is big on interdisciplinary study and internships during its January term.

Website: www.wells.edu
Location: Small town
Total Enrollment: 443
Undergraduates: 443
Male/Female: 0/100
SAT Ranges: V 520–630
  M 490–590
ACT Range: 22–27
Financial Aid: 89%
Expense: Pr $
Phi Beta Kappa: Yes
Applicants: 417
Accepted: 88%
Enrolled: 28%
Grad in 6 Years: 66%
Returning Freshmen: 69%
Academics: ✎ ✎ ✎
Social: ☎ ☎
Q of L: ★ ★ ★ ★
Admissions: (800) 952-9355
Email Address:
  admissions@wells.edu

Strongest Programs
  Biological and Chemical
    Sciences
  English
  Performing Arts
  Sociology and Anthropology
  Psychology

Traditions abound at Wells College, a small, all-women's school in upstate New York. Whether it's riding to graduation in an old Wells Fargo stagecoach or showing off in a hardcore basketball game between sophomores and seniors, the history of Wells is apparent at every turn. But Wells is no throwback. It aims to educate and empower women for leadership roles in the twenty-first century while instilling in its students an appreciation for the liberal arts and an awareness of global issues. Consider a popular slogan on campus: "You can do anything because you are a Wells woman."

A few dramatic additions on campus, such as the renovation and rededication of Weld House in the Greek revival style, have maintained the classic collegiate atmosphere created by the school's massive old, ivy-covered buildings. The rolling 365-acre lakeside campus has been named to the National Register of Historic Places. With Cayuga Lake affording beautiful sunsets, boating, and fishing opportunities, students can juxtapose the rigor of their studies with relaxation in a gorgeous environment. Soon, students will be able to enjoy a $17.5 million state-of-the-art science building as well.

The liberal arts provide the basic framework for a Wells education. In addition to standard distribution requirements, all students must complete two courses in a foreign language, one course in formal reasoning, three courses in the arts and humanities, three courses in natural or social sciences, and four courses in physical education. Students are also required to do three internships and a senior thesis. Wells 101, a core course required for all freshwomen, covers the basics of college writing, speech, and analytical thinking. The most popular majors (psychology, sociology, English, biology, and math) are generally the strongest academic departments, according to students. Those who major in biology are able to use the local environment—Cayuga Lake and surrounding lands—for ecology and botany fieldwork. Accredited elementary and secondary education programs are available, and interdisciplinary minors are offered in such fields as management studies, secondary education, communications, public policy, and international studies.

"You can do anything because you are a Wells woman."

Wells also offers a variety of integrated majors, all of which require coursework across traditional disciplinary boundaries. Specialized areas include American studies; foreign languages, literature, and cultures; history; and sociology and anthropology. Qualified students may design their own majors. Wells also offers 3–2 dual degree programs in community health and business administration with the University of Rochester, in veterinary medicine with Cornell, and in engineering with Case Western Reserve, Cornell, Columbia, Clarkson, and Washington University in

St. Louis. For a change of pace, students can take one nonmajor course per semester on a pass/fail basis and cross-register to take up to four courses at nearby Cornell University.

The college operates on a semester calendar, with January being used as a time for internships, study abroad, independent study projects, or Leadership Week. In addition, Wells College sponsors a popular corporate affiliate program aimed at preparing women for the business and financial professions through special courses and lectures, portfolio management experience, and corporate internships. Foreign study is available for either a semester or a year. These programs are truly ingrained into the curriculum.

The faculty at Wells is unusually accessible and friendly, even by small-college standards. "One quality is present in every professor on campus: they are open and willing to help students outside of class anytime," says a math major. Size does matter at this small school of less than five hundred. It means all classes have fewer than twenty-five students, and can be as small as twelve students. How's that for one-on-one attention? "The classes are quite small, which means there are more class discussions and the students lead most discussions while the professor focuses the direction of the conversation," explains one student. But there

"Security knows all of us and will always approach unescorted people and ask them where they belong."

is a downside: the small classes make it "more obvious if you have been falling behind," warns a sophomore. An honor system is enforced by the student-run collegiate association, and take-home and self-scheduled tests are the rule rather than the exception.

The students pride themselves on their open-mindedness and variety of philosophies, and the school is slowly becoming more diverse. Two-thirds of the students are state residents. Asian-Americans make up 4 percent of the student body, African-Americans 5 percent, and Hispanics 4 percent. A wider range of courses with a minority focus, workshops on racial issues, and a support network for new minority students are used to educate students about diversity. Homosexual rights are a big issue on campus, and students say the gay population has increased of late. The school does not guarantee to meet the full demonstrated financial need of every admit, but 89 percent of the students receive need-based aid and there are two merit scholarships of up to $20,000 awarded each year.

All students are guaranteed housing on campus, and virtually all take advantage of this option. The dorms range from the founder's nineteenth-century mansion to a modern dorm setup with a suite system. Weld House is the newest dorm with two computer labs. Students rave about the accommodations. "The dorms are in these great old buildings with beautiful high ceilings and Stickley furniture," says one student. Upperclasswomen participate in a lottery for housing (most prefer singles), and freshwomen are usually assigned doubles. There are only five dorms on campus, and none is specifically dedicated to freshwomen. Each dorm has a lake view, and some boast bay windows and winding staircases. There is virtually no off-campus housing in Aurora, where the total population is equal to the tiny student body at Wells. Meals are served in a magnificent Tudor-style dining hall complete with two working fireplaces. The school is

"Our sisterhood shines through."

so small that "security knows all of us and will always approach unescorted people and ask them where they belong," a senior says.

The college owns a great deal of waterfront property and maintains a dock and boathouse for its students, which translates into plenty of opportunities for camping and fun in the water. Meanwhile, the ski slopes of Greek Peak are less than an hour away, and the golf course and tennis and paddle courts are usually full of lively

Wells College sponsors a popular corporate affiliate program aimed at preparing women for the business and financial professions through special courses and lectures, portfolio management experience, and corporate internships.

players. A field house provides indoor tennis courts, a pool, and other facilities. Aurora itself offers almost no entertainment. There is a market, bank, post office, flower shop, sandwich shop, and "not much else!" says a psychology major. But Ithaca to the south and Syracuse to the east provide more diversions, and a Wells van runs between the school and Ithaca several times a day. When students flee on weekends, they usually travel to nearby Cornell University or Ithaca College, where fraternity parties and mixers are the main attractions. As far as drinking is concerned, no one under twenty-one is served on campus or at the local bars, but students say it's still possible for an underage student to get alcohol. "It's easy for underage students to be served alcohol at functions and to obtain it from legal students," says a student.

The soccer and field hockey teams do fairly well, and lacrosse, tennis, swimming, and newly added softball are also popular. The college's penchant for tradition carries over into athletics in the Oddline/Evenline competition, which culminates in a basketball game between the freshwomen and the sophomores. Intramurals are available for those with the initiative, but they take a backseat to the more popular and numerous nonsports clubs.

The school is very high on traditions. Bells are rung every evening to announce dinner and when the first snow of the season falls. And alumnae may request that they be rung on the occasion of their marriage. On the first and last day of classes, professors serve the seniors a champagne breakfast; sophomores give them roses on the last day of classes and dance around the sycamore tree.

For students who choose Wells, they will find that good things come in small packages. With beautiful dorms, small classes, and a strong sense of unity on campus, "it is almost too good to be true," a math major says. "Our sisterhood shines through."

Overlaps

Cornell, NYU, SUNY-Binghamton, SUNY-Geneseo, Boston University

If You Apply To ➤ **Wells:** Early action: Dec. 15. Regular admissions: Mar. 1. Financial aid: May 15. Housing: May 1. Meets demonstrated need of 90%. Campus interviews: recommended, informational. Alumni interviews: optional, informational. SATs or ACTs: required. SAT IIs: optional. Accepts the Common Application and electronic applications. Essay question: write about a significant achievement, important issue, or a person who influenced you.

Wesleyan University

North College, Middletown, CT 06457

Often compared to Amherst or Williams, Wesleyan is really more like Swarthmore. The key difference: Wesleyan is twice as big. Wes students are progressive, politically minded, and fiercely independent. Exotic specialties like ethnomusicology and East Asian studies add spice to the scene.

Website: www.wesleyan.edu
Location: Small town
Total Enrollment: 3,158
Undergraduates: 2,705
Male/Female: 48/52
SAT Ranges: V 640–730
  M 640–720
ACT Range: N/A

One of a handful of the top small liberal arts colleges in the country by any measure, Wesleyan boasts engaging faculty members who care deeply about student performance and students who are driven by an innate desire to learn for learning's sake. Whether they're engrossed in academics, debating and demonstrating over various issues, or engaged in community service, Wes students seem to do things with a passion and intensity that helps set this school apart from tamer institutions. "Wes students take an in-your-face approach to life," says a government major.

This New England college offers more academic and extracurricular options than almost any school its size, and the Wesleyan experience means liberal learning in a climate of individual freedom. "Students work very hard, but the academic climate is not competitive," an American studies major says. "Students help each other in classes, rather than try to get ahead by inhibiting them." Another student agrees, "The courses are rigorous, but the climate is supportive and conducive to sharing ideas." The freedom at Wesleyan requires motivated students who stay on task despite the laid-back atmosphere. There are abundant opportunities open to students willing to take advantage of them, which is precisely what these doers do.

It begins with the Wesleyan campus architecture, which is as diverse as the student body. The nucleus of this stately university is a century-old row of lovely ivy-covered brownstones that look out over the football field. The rest of the buildings can be described as "eclectic" and range from mod-looking dorms of the '50s and '60s to the early nineteenth-century architecture of many academic buildings to the beautiful and modern Center for the Arts. The Wesleyan-owned student residences look freshly plucked from Main Street, U.S.A. The most recent additions to campus include classroom renovations and the initiation of a ten-year program to renovate facilities and classrooms across the campus.

Wesleyan has used its considerable wealth to attract highly rated faculty members who are expected to be scholar-teachers: academic supermen who juggle groundbreaking research, enthusiastic lectures, and personal student attention at the same time. And they seem to pull it off. "The quality of teaching is extremely high," says a junior, "but more remarkable is the

"Wes students take an in-your-face approach to life."

active interest the professors take in the students." Among Wesleyan's strongest departments are music, economics, biology, American studies, and English, which for years has been the most popular degree. But even the smaller departments attract attention. Ethnomusicology, including African drumming and dance, is a particular specialty; students can be found reclining on the wide, carpeted bleachers at the World Music Hall or watching a dozen musicians play the Indonesian gamelan. The film department is first-rate. The East Asian Studies Center has both a strong program and an authentic Japanese tea room. Even the math department, which has been a source of criticism for years, has made significant changes to emphasize problem solving in small groups rather than interminable lectures dedicated to theory.

Wesleyan's curriculum renewal program ensures the relevance of liberal arts education in the twenty-first century by adding more professors for first- and second-year students, clustering courses to help students reach their academic goals, and requiring an electronic portfolio from each student. Students are expected in their first two years to take a minimum of two courses in each of three areas—humanities and the arts, social and behavioral sciences, and natural sciences and mathematics. During their second two years, students must take one course in each of the three areas. At the end of their freshman year, Wesleyan students can apply to major in one of three competitive, interdisciplinary seminar colleges: the College of Letters (literature, politics, history with a leftist bent), the College of Social Studies (politics, economics, history with a conservative bent), and the Science in Society program (concerned with the humane use of scientific knowledge, a la Buckminster Fuller). New students can take First-Year Initiative courses designed just for

"One thing about Wesleyan, people aren't afraid to speak their minds or challenge someone else's idea."

them. The university also implements a Web-based course selection and registration system to ease the process, but a sophomore grumps, "Registration is more complicated and frustrating than it should be."

Wesleyan students are marked by an unusual commitment to debate, from political to cultural to intellectual. Chalking on the sidewalks is a cherished tradition (the

(Continued)

Financial Aid: 45%
Expense: Pr $ $ $ $
Phi Beta Kappa: Yes
Applicants: 6,862
Accepted: 27%
Enrolled: 38%
Grad in 6 Years: 88%
Returning Freshmen: 96%
Academics: 🖊 🖊 🖊 🖊 🖊
Social: ☎ ☎ ☎
Q of L: ★ ★ ★
Admissions: (860) 685-3000
Email Address:
    admissions@wesleyan.edu

Strongest Programs
East Asian Studies
English/Creative Writing
Biology
History
American Studies
Music
Film

"This is a politically aware and active campus," a history major says. "Anything and everything can be an issue."

student assembly even supplies the chalk free of charge), though not long ago the president declared a moratorium on the practice because of some negative references to specific faculty members. "One thing about Wesleyan, people aren't afraid to speak their mind or challenge someone else's idea," a student reports. "This creates an environment that is constantly debating and discussing things." It is hands-down an activist campus. One sophomore lists rallies and protests alongside parties and concerts as part of the campus social life. "This is a politically aware and active campus," a history major says. "Anything and everything can be an issue." Another student adds, "You'll have a hard time finding a more politically correct and socially active campus than Wes." But students level their smarts against topics close to home, mostly the university administration. "There's an energy on this campus, for me it's a spirit of creativity and political energy," a sophomore explains. In recent years, a significant number of Wesleyan alumni have gone on to make their mark in the entertainment industry and the high-tech world on the West Coast.

Wesleyan strives to keep its classes small and only 6 percent of the courses have fifty or more students. Some students claim they sometimes have trouble getting into the "hot" courses. "With popular classes, you have to be persistent, but you can get in," a history major says. If beseeching is not your style, studying abroad may be a temporary tonic to registration headaches. Programs are available in Israel, Germany, Africa, Japan, Latin America, France, Spain, and China. Students can also participate in the Venture Program,* study at Mystic Seaport,* or take a semester at another Twelve-College Exchange* school. Internships are popular, and students can also take advantage of 3–2 engineering programs with Columbia and Caltech.

Wesleyan likes to describe itself as "a small college with university resources." The libraries have more than a million volumes, practically unheard of at a school this size. Students claim that whenever you happen to walk past the brightly lit, glass-walled study room of Sci-Li (the science library), you're apt to see numerous students huddled over their books. Wesleyan's excellent reputation and strong recruiting network attract students from all over, ensuring the clash of viewpoints that makes it such a vital place. Of the student body, enrollment figures indicate the makeup as 9 percent African-American, 6 percent Hispanic, and 8 percent Asian-American. Students report that diversity is cherished at Wes. "Wesleyan is extremely liberal," notes a junior. "Nevertheless, it has its share of conservatives, which adds to the diversity of the student body." Another student adds, "Wes students are tolerant because there's an open dialogue both in and outside of the

> **"Wes students are tolerant because there's an open dialogue both in and outside of the classroom that creates a high level of awareness and acceptance."**

classroom that creates a high level of awareness and acceptance." Fifty-seven percent of the students graduated from public school, 37 percent from private school, and 6 percent from parochial. No academic or athletic merit scholarships are offered, but Wesleyan does guarantee to meet the financial need of all admits. Freshman orientation, which gets rave reviews, consists of a week of standard pre-registration fare, plus comedy nights, movies, and square dancing.

For housing, most freshmen are consigned to the newly renovated singles or doubles in the campus dorms. Popular opinion indicates that the Butterfield complex is the choice for quiet study, while Clark Hall is where the party people go. Ninety-three percent of undergraduates live in university housing, and housing is guaranteed for four years. Juniors and seniors enjoy numerous housing options: townhouses for four or five students, fraternities, college-owned houses and apartments, or special-interest houses organized around concerns such as ecology, feminism, or minority-student unity. Upperclass students who want to live off campus must apply for permission. Those who move off have the option of eating at home, in the school grill, or at the fraternity eating clubs. Everyone else takes meals in Mocon, the glass-walled main dining hall, or two smaller cafeterias, and complains about the mandatory meal plan.

Middletown is a small city within easy driving distance of Hartford and New Haven, but it is off the beaten track of steady public transportation. Often students contend that "it may have everything you need, but nothing you want." Still, Wes students contribute a great deal of time to community service, and help maintain a peaceful, beneficial relationship with the town. And Wesleyan's rural surroundings afford the much-appreciated opportunity to jog through the countryside, swim at nearby Wadsworth Falls, or pick apples in the local orchards. Good road trips include New York and Boston, each two hours away, and decent ski areas and beaches just under an hour away. Wesleyan sports tend to be for scholar-athletes rather than spectators. In any sport, annual encounters with "Little Three" rivals Williams and Amherst get even the most bookwormish student out of the library and into the heat of the action. The Ultimate Frisbee club (the Nietzsche Factor) almost always whips challengers, and intramurals are extremely popular. Athletics are enhanced by a complex that comes complete with a two hundred-meter indoor track, a fitness center, and a fifty-meter pool.

New students can take First-Year Initiative courses designed just for them.

Although two former fraternities have turned into coed literary societies, Greek life at the remaining three is a jock preserve. Only 4 percent of the men and 3 percent of the women go Greek. Wesleyan's enforcement of the twenty-one-year-old drinking age is moderate compared with most schools. Consistent with the university's encouragement of independence, students bear a large part of the responsibility for policing themselves. "To the University's credit, they are really stressing alcohol awareness, so to speak," says a neuroscience and behavioral studies major. Students who throw a party for seventy-five or more people must attend a workshop that stresses safe drinking. Still, most students concur that it is quite easy for the underaged to imbibe.

"There's tons going on right on campus."

"You can get alcohol if you want to," notes a sophomore. It seems, however, that drinking alcohol is a minor event when compared to the multitude of other things happening on campus. Activities abound from comedy performances to a cappella groups, films, plays, bands, lectures, parties, and events planned by the more than two hundred student groups. "There's tons going on right on campus," raves a sophomore, "so much that you feel like you're missing out if you leave." Major events on the social calendar include Spring Fling and Fall Ball—two outdoor festivals—and Uncle Duke Day and Zonker Harris Day, two similar events with a more psychedelic, 1960s flavor, in which students pay tribute to the infamous Doonesbury characters.

With so much to do and learn, students at Wesleyan take it all in stride. The key to Wesleyan's success seems to be the fostering of an intellectual milieu where independent thinking and an appreciation of differences are omnipresent. So different, in fact, that a sophomore describes the typical Wesleyan student as "sarcastic, dramatic, poetic, athletic, creative, proactive, open-minded, caring, loud, and polite." And if you're still not convinced, take it from a veteran: "We would make any liberal arts college proud, but you can only find us here."

Overlaps
Brown, Yale, Columbia, Amherst, Harvard

If You Apply To ➤

Wesleyan: Early decision: Nov. 15, Jan. 1. Regular admissions: Jan. 1. Financial aid: Feb. 15. Guarantees to meet demonstrated need. Campus and alumni interviews: recommended, evaluative. SATs and SAT IIs (writing and two others) or ACTs: required. Accepts the Common Application and electronic applications. Essay question: influential person and why; intellectual experience; and community influence.

P.O. Box 6009, Morgantown, WV 26506-6009

With the exception of a few Pennsylvanians who migrate south to Morgantown, out-of-staters find little reason to consider WVU. The honors program is a must for top students, and the university has good programs in professional fields ranging from journalism to engineering.

Website: www.wvu.edu
Location: Small city
Total Enrollment: 22,774
Undergraduates: 16,121
Male/Female: 54/46
SAT Ranges: V 460–555 M 470–570
ACT Range: 19–25
Financial Aid: 55%
Expense: Pub $ $
Phi Beta Kappa: Yes
Applicants: 8,786
Accepted: 94%
Enrolled: 44%
Grad in 6 Years: 55%
Returning Freshmen: 78%
Academics: ✍ ✍
Social: ☎ ☎ ☎ ☎
Q of L: ★ ★ ★
Admissions: (304) 293-2121
Email Address:
wvuadmissions@arc.wvu.edu

Strongest Programs
Engineering
Political Science
Allied Health
Psychology
Pharmacy

There's no denying that West Virginia University is mammoth, with more than sixteen thousand undergraduates and a total of nearly twenty-three thousand people milling about on campus. But students say the sense of community fostered by Mountaineer pride makes it feel much smaller. While WVU remains the state's flagship land-grant college, 40 percent of students now come from out of state, attracted by the reasonable price tag for its 169 degree programs, 252 student organizations, and twenty-one varsity athletic teams. Clearly, this school is no longer just for coal miners and country folks. It's become a solid choice for scholars, researchers, and athletes, too.

WVU is situated in the picturesque mountains of north-central West Virginia, a few miles from the Pennsylvania border and overlooking the Monongahela River. A driverless rail system bridges the school's two campuses, the older Morgantown and the more modern Evansdale, which are a mile and a half apart. Ten of the ivy-covered Morgantown buildings, dating mainly from the nineteenth century, are listed on the National Register of Historic Places; many of their interiors have been restored or renovated. A new five-floor, 124,000-square-foot high-tech library opened in January 2002, with 180 computers and thirty-five media-equipped workstations. The Life Sciences Building, with classrooms, labs, and a six-unit greenhouse for the psychology and biology departments, is also new.

WVU's degree programs span thirteen schools, the best of which are engineering (particularly energy-related) and the allied health sciences (medical technology, physical therapy, nursing, and occupational therapy). The most popular majors are psychology, business, and nursing; unusual options include a six-year PharmD, and a B.S. in forensic identification, developed in conjunction with the FBI. Programs in journalism, physical education, agriculture, and forestry are also solid, though students warn that math and the foreign languages are weak. Regardless of major, students must complete the liberal studies program, which helps them "acquire knowledge, make critical judgments in a logical and rational manner, and communicate their findings clearly." Graduates are expected to possess knowledge and experience in three broad clusters: arts and humanities, social and behavioral sciences, and mathematics and natural sciences, as well as to broaden their understanding of people different from themselves.

"Freedom of expression is probably the largest issue on campus."

While WVU is a big school, administrators say that about two-thirds of the classes taken by freshmen have twenty-five or fewer students. "The quality of teaching is wonderful," says a political science major. Classes are challenging, but the atmosphere is supportive. "It does not seem as competitive as the top tier of universities," says one student, "but it is certainly no blow-off." Operation Jump-Start helps students adjust to college with New Student Convocation, dorm-based Freshman Interest Groups, and Resident Faculty Leaders, who live next door to the dorms and serve as mentors and friends. A pass-fail course called "Orientation to University Life" also helps students understand the academic, social, and emotional expectations of the college experience, covering study skills, university and community support services, goal setting, and career planning. On the other end of the spectrum, an honors program offers small classes and early registration to students with a 3.5 high-school GPA and 1360 on the SAT (or a 3.8 and an 1240).

Though West Virginia attracts students from most U.S. states and nearly one hundred foreign countries, it is primarily regional. Sixty percent of students are in-staters, and a sizable contingent arrives from western Pennsylvania and southern New Jersey. African-Americans comprise 4 percent of the student body, and Hispanics and Asian-Americans are just over 1 percent each. "Freedom of expression is probably the largest issue on campus," says a senior, noting that there's been a lot of debate about so-called "free speech zones," designated areas where protest is permitted. "WVU is basically a politically conservative campus." The university offers 2,800 merit scholarships, ranging from $1,000 to $10,500, along with athletic scholarships in all twenty-one intercollegiate sports.

> "We probably have more volunteers than projects."

Twenty-one percent of WVU's undergraduates live on campus, where dorms are "very comfortable, with suites, piano lounges, and fireplaces," says a senior. Most are coed; the older ones are known for their character; the newer residential complexes on the Evansdale campus have larger rooms and luxuries like air-conditioning. Rising enrollment means that rooms are harder for upperclassmen to get, so many opt instead for nearby apartments. The 10 percent of men and 12 percent of women who go Greek may live in their chapter houses. Each dorm has its own cafeteria, and students may buy meal plans regardless of where they live. Fraternities and sororities have their own cooks.

Morgantown is a small city with a college-town feel and plenty of community-service opportunities, says a senior: "We probably have more volunteers than projects." The school has worked hard to curtail underage drinking, banning alcohol in the dorms, and limiting each frat to three social events per semester, with three hundred members and guests. Students report that it's now near impossible for those under twenty-one to be served on campus, and say off-campus bars have also cracked down. That said, social life is still centered on campus, often focused on the free food, movies, bands, and comedians offered Thursday through Saturday by the school-sponsored "Up All Night" program. Spring Fest and Fall Fest provide

> "The Mountaineer spirit is the type of pride that is unparalleled at any other school."

stress relief each semester, and Mountaineer Week showcases the customers of Appalachia. For those with cars, road trips to Columbus, Washington, D.C., or Pittsburgh are quick and easy. Football rivalries with Miami, Virginia Tech, Syracuse, Notre Dame, and Pitt (the "Backyard Brawl") take students farther afield.

Aside from Mountaineer football, which has again achieved national prominence, West Virginia fields a very competitive rifle team, and its wrestling team has recently won regular-season and conference-tournament titles. Track and field are good bets for men and women, and women's swimming and crew are also strong.

What makes WVU special? "Pride, tradition, opportunity," says a senior. "The Mountaineer spirit is the type of pride that is unparalleled at any other school," adds a classmate. "Students love the school and the state. They truly 'bleed blue and gold.'" WVU has indeed come a long way from its agricultural beginnings. For many, "Mo-town" is a great place to spend four years, even if you're not into forensic identification or livestock judging.

A new five-floor, 124,000-square-foot high-tech library opened in January 2002, with 180 computers and thirty-five media-equipped workstations.

The most popular majors are psychology, business, and nursing; unusual options include a six-year PharmD, and a B.S. in forensic identification, developed in conjunction with the FBI.

Overlaps

Marshall, Penn State, Fairmont State, Virginia Tech, University of Pittsburgh

West Virginia: Rolling admissions (priority date Mar. 1). Financial aid: Feb. 1 (for freshman scholarships), Mar. 1. Meets demonstrated need of 25%. Campus and alumni interviews: optional, informational. SATs or ACTs: required. SAT IIs: optional. Accepts the Common Application and electronic applications. No essay question.

Wheaton College

501 College Avenue, Wheaton, IL 60187

Wheaton is at the top of the heap in evangelical education, rivaled only by Pepperdine (with its Malibu digs) and traditional competitors such as Calvin and Hope. Students pledge to live a Christian life and renew the vow every semester. Wheaton's low tuition makes it a relative bargain.

Website: www.wheaton.edu
Location: Suburban
Total Enrollment: 2,680
Undergraduates: 2,346
Male/Female: 49/51
SAT Ranges: V 610–710
  M 610–710
ACT Range: 27–31
Financial Aid: 50%
Expense: Pr $
Phi Beta Kappa: No
Applicants: 1,867
Accepted: 55%
Enrolled: 56%
Grad in 6 Years: 87%
Returning Freshmen: 93%
Academics: ✍ ✍ ✍
Social: ☎ ☎ ☎
Q of L: ★ ★ ★ ★
Admissions: (630) 752-5005
  or (800) 222-2419
Email Address:
  admissions@wheaton.edu

Strongest Programs
  Literature
  Psychology
  Music
  Bible/Theology

There is no denying that Wheaton College is one dedicated place: dedicated to learning, spiritual growth, and a deep love for Jesus Christ. One of the finest evangelical schools in the country, Wheaton is also a liberal arts college that encourages its students to dip into a wide range of academic pursuits, travel the world, and help the less fortunate. Wheaties are "conservative, hard-working, and intelligent with a desire to contribute to society by serving Jesus Christ," a freshman explains.

Wheaton's eighty-acre campus is an oasis of sorts: Blanchard Hall, built in the last century, looks like a castle perched atop the front campus hill. Down the hill from the Old Main campus is the $13.5 million Billy Graham Center, a museum and library that has become a cornerstone in research on American evangelicalism.

> **"Professors are very personable and want to help you, giving you their home phones and emails."**

The mall area provides room for strolls through the wooded campus, which sits right in the middle of one of Chicago's oldest and most established suburbs. The sports and recreation center recently benefited from new basketball courts, a climbing wall, and a weight-lifting facility.

Wheaton bills itself as a "Christian, liberal arts institution that is committed to the principle that truth is revealed by God through Christ, in whom is hidden all the treasures of wisdom and knowledge." The school's deep dedication to spirituality only strengthens its commitment to education. Christian perspective is applied to disciplines across the curriculum, which is built around requirements that include studies in faith, reason, society, nature, literature, and the arts. Students are also expected to be competent in knowledge of the Bible, communications, English, foreign language, and mathematics. Eight to twelve credit hours of Bible studies and theology are required of all students, and all freshmen must take the Freshman Experience Seminar.

Students describe professors as exceptional. "Professors are very personable and want to help you, giving you their home phones and emails," says one student. "The teachers really do know what they are teaching, which makes even the hardest classes enjoyable," says a sophomore. Slacking is not part of the scripture at Wheaton. "Students really do their homework, so in-class discussions are incredible," a sophomore says.

Any fears about the gap between Christianity and science have been overcome at Wheaton, where most of the natural sciences are strong—biology and chemistry in particular. English, business/economics, elementary education, communications, and psychology are the most popular majors. In addition to major programs in the liberal arts and sciences, students can opt for the 3–2 liberal arts/nursing program or liberal arts/engineering double degree. Wheaton recently added an international relations major. Studying abroad in East Asia, England, France, Germany, Spain, Russia, Latin America, or the Holy Lands is an option for Wheaton undergraduates, as is spending a semester at one of twelve other evangelical schools in the Council for Christian Colleges and Universities. The Human Needs and Global Resources (HNGR) program coordinates studies in Third World development with six-month internships in a development project in a Third World country. "It gives students a whole new perspective on the global community," an English major gushes.

The High Road Wilderness Program provides an Outward Bound–type experience. There is also the Black Hills Science Station for summer study in botany and zoology and Honey Rock Camp for leadership training. More than a dozen other options are offered through the Council for Christian Colleges and Universities.* Students in science, math, and computer science have the opportunity to perform research at Argonne National Laboratory.

"No drinking anywhere, any time."

Christian perspective is applied to disciplines across the curriculum, which is built around requirements that include studies in faith, reason, society, nature, literature, and the arts.

Most Wheaties share a fairly similar middle-class, public-school background. Eighty-five percent graduated in the top quarter of their high-school class, a fact that adds to the academic pressures. Minorities make up 12 percent of the student body, and about one-fifth of the students are from Illinois. For the most part, people at Wheaton are educated about issues, and discussions often center on abortion, euthanasia, and genetic cloning. "The big issues tend to be more theological than political," a sophomore says, and the political bent is definitely toward the right. A large percentage of students spend their time volunteering in inner-city Chicago, tutoring, visiting nursing homes, visiting AIDS patients, and running church youth groups.

Any fears about the gap between Christianity and science have been overcome at Wheaton, where most of the natural sciences are strong— biology and chemistry in particular.

Students are pleased with their dorm rooms, which one student describes as comfortable and a decent size. "The dorms are excellent, well maintained, very clean," says one student. Many juniors and seniors live in college-owned apartments off campus, but only 12 percent of undergraduates live off campus or commute. The single-sex dorms are only open to students of the opposite gender on certain days of the week during restricted hours. Wheaton offers a beautiful dining hall with fireplaces and a variety of spaces in which to eat. Students even find room to praise the food as pretty good for institutional fare.

Two common elements of college that are noticeably absent from the Wheaton experience are Greek organizations and alcohol. Most students are committed to the pledge, which they reaffirm every semester, "to maintain a lifestyle pleasing to Christ," which includes abstaining from booze. Most students adhere to the policy. One senior says the policy works: "No drinking anywhere, any time." Wheaton's social scene is active, albeit mostly on campus. The College Union organizes activities like movies, late-night skating parties, and other activities. The school's administration has

"It is this openness of dialogue that keeps Wheaton such a dynamic place of growth."

loosened its ban on social dancing, pleasing students. Also popular are treks to the movies, and a quick half-hour train ride transports Wheaton undergrads to Chicago's Loop, which offers restaurants, blues clubs, museums, shopping, and professional sporting events. Major annual events include Fall and Spring fests, the annual Air-Jam, and the annual Christmas screening of Jimmy Stewart in *It's a Wonderful Life*.

The calm of Wheaton's mild-mannered Christian ambiance is periodically shattered by the interclass scramble for the Bench, a reinforced slab of concrete that is the subject of an ongoing and often rough-and-tumble game of keep-away. A gentler

Wheaton tradition is that engaged couples climb to the top of Blanchard Hall and ring the bell. Wheaton athletic teams, known for seventy years as the Crusaders, are now the Thunder. Critics claimed the old mascot glorified medieval Christians who killed thousands of people in the name of Jesus. The new mascot was chosen from 1,300 suggestions because it sounds strong and is one of the natural phenomena associated with God. Men's and women's soccer and football and women's basketball games are favorite events.

The school's motto, "For Christ and His Kingdom," demonstrates its deep commitment to the nurturing of one's mind and soul. "No topic is off limits" at Wheaton, a sophomore says. "It is this openness of dialogue that keeps Wheaton such a dynamic place of growth." And with an alumni roster that reads like a "Who's Who" among American Evangelical Protestants, it's clear that Wheaton's impact remains with students for the rest of their lives.

Overlaps

Taylor, Calvin, Gordon, Grove City, Northwestern

If You Apply To ➤

Wheaton: Early action: Nov. 1. Regular admissions: Jan. 15. Financial aid: Feb. 15. Campus interviews: recommended, evaluative. No alumni interviews. SATs or ACTs: required. SAT IIs: recommended. Essay question: development of your faith and its impact on your life; who would you spend an evening with (besides Jesus Christ) or describe an influential cultural experience or an influential creative work.

Wheaton College

Norton, MA 02766

Wheaton is the most recent convert to coeducation among prominent East Coast institutions, and women still outnumber men by nearly two to one. Though in Massachusetts, Wheaton is actually closer to Providence than Boston. One of the few moderately selective institutions in the area.

Website:
   www.wheatoncollege.edu
Location: Suburban
Total Enrollment: 1,551
Undergraduates: 1,551
Male/Female: 35/65
SAT Ranges: V 560–650
   M 540–640
ACT Range: 25–27
Financial Aid: 58%
Expense: Pr $ $ $ $
Phi Beta Kappa: Yes
Applicants: 3,249
Accepted: 61%
Enrolled: 25%
Grad in 6 Years: 71%
Returning Freshmen: 86%
Academics: ✍ ✍ ✍
Social: ☎ ☎ ☎
Q of L: ★ ★ ★ ★

It's been well over a decade since Wheaton College first admitted men, but the traditions and academic excellence that helped the college make its name endure. The first night of freshman year, for example, is still marked by a candlelight ceremony in the chapel. Students keep their candles until Sentimental Night, when, as seniors, they float them on Peacock Pond. And a woman who walks with a date three times around the pond may still push the hapless fellow in if he doesn't deign to kiss her. Wheaton also continues to attract students with solid programs in the social sciences, fine arts, and humanities. "It's a gorgeous campus, with unique traditions, high academic par, and the funnest and nicest students anywhere!" a sophomore enthuses.

Wheaton's rural location offers few distractions from intellectual pursuits. Its 385-acre campus blends Georgian brick buildings and modern structures, set among beautiful lawns and shade trees. The two halves of the campus are separated by the aforementioned pond, which probably qualifies as the only heated duck pond on any American campus. Wheaton has recently invested $30 million in its buildings, opening a new studio arts facility and renovating space for the art, music and theater departments. Beard Hall, the newest dorm, has twenty-five double rooms, fifty singles, and wireless Internet connections throughout.

Students say Wheaton's best programs include psychology, political science, psychology, and English. Programs in the arts are well recognized, impressive given the school's small size, and the chemistry department is also strong, producing both Wheaton's Rhodes Scholarship winner in 2000–01 and two Fulbright scholars. The major in Hispanic studies benefits from its affiliation with a study-abroad program in Cordoba, and a Mellon Foundation grant supports native speakers in Spanish and other languages. Those interested in interdisciplinary or cross-disciplinary work may design an independent major, or add classes taken at other schools in the Twelve-College Exchange Program.* Students may also take classes not offered at Wheaton at nearby Brown University. For those tired of studying on land, Wheaton offers the Maritime Studies Program.* Dual-degree programs offer motivated students the chance to earn a bachelor's degree in engineering or graduate degrees in business, communication, religion, or optometry in conjunction with schools like Dartmouth, Emerson, and Clark.

(Continued)
Admissions: (508) 286-8251
Email Address: admission@ wheatoncollege.edu

Strongest Programs
  Chemistry
  Psychology
  English
  Political Science
  Hispanic Studies (Spanish)
  Italian
  French
  Studio Art

Back on campus, Wheaton is implementing a new curriculum for the class of 2007, which will emphasize foundation courses and encourage students to explore the liberal arts through connections between and among classes. The curriculum will link experiential learning to each department and will require a capstone senior project. New requirements haven't yet been set. Currently, though, they include English 101 (writing); two courses each in a foreign language, arts and humanities, and natural sciences; and one course each in the social sciences, Western history, non-Western culture,

"Rooms are spacious, comfortable, and very homey feeling."

and diversity in the U.S. Students also choose a first-year seminar from among twenty-four sections, each focused on "Controversies" that have generated debate or heralded changes in how they experience or understand the world.

Wheaton's small classes encourage close ties between students and faculty. "I have had phenomenal professors overall, with amazing backgrounds and such a strong passion for what they teach," a sophomore says. "They are the core reason why my experience here has been so amazing." Aside from a faculty advisor, students get a staff mentor and two peer advisors, known as preceptors. Classes are demanding, but the workload is manageable, says a Hispanic studies major: "Students do not complete with each other, but rather enjoy class and learning." The Filene Center for Work and Learning gets high marks from students seeking internships—and jobs after graduation.

About a third of Wheaton's students come from Massachusetts, and nearly two-thirds went to public high schools. The student body is largely Caucasian, with African-Americans accounting for 4 percent, Hispanics 3 percent, and Asian-Americans 2 percent. "People want more diversity, and the school is working to increase numbers of students from different backgrounds," says a sophomore. Those efforts have been helped by Wheaton's decision to go coed, which sparked a dramatic increase in applications and enrollment. The administration has undertaken a massive capital campaign, using some of the proceeds to hire more minority scholars—and recruit more minority students.

When they're not hitting the books, Wheaton students love to put on their dancing shoes— whether for the Boston Bash party on a boat in Boston Harbor, for the Valentine's Dance, or for any number of events at Rosecliff, a mansion in Newport, Rhode Island.

As might be expected on this small, secluded campus, virtually everyone lives in one of Wheaton's dorms or houses (one all-women, twenty-six coed). Gebbie Hall, the all-female dorm that opened in 1992, regularly hosts panels, presentations, and colloquia on gender issues. The fifty-one residents of this self-governing hall are selected on the basis of applications that ask about their commitment to

"Our long-standing honor code reminds students about respect and community living."

gender equality. All students are guaranteed housing for four years; freshmen live in doubles, triples, or quads, and upperclassmen try their luck in the lottery system, which "bites, but how else are you doing to do it?" sighs a sophomore. "Rooms are spacious, comfortable, and very homey feeling," says a classmate. "They are very well maintained and clean." The bright and spacious dining halls offer unlimited

The first night of freshman year is still marked by a candlelight ceremony in the chapel. Students keep their candles until Sentimental Night, when, as seniors, they float them on Peacock Pond.

chow, and the biggest winners of all are the ducks, who thrive on the leftover bread students toss into Peacock Pond.

Social life at Wheaton includes dances, concerts, lectures, and parties on campus, or road trips to Boston (thirty-five miles away) and Providence (fifteen miles). The town of Norton, just outside campus, draws some students with a Big Brother/Big Sister program, hospital visits, and opportunities to tutor and mentor children, but otherwise has few redeeming qualities. "Norton is pretty much your small boring town," a sophomore explains. "There is one traffic light, some pizza shops, CVS, a bank, and mini-golf," and not a coffee shop in sight. For that, students head to the college's student center, which offers a café, dance studio, and sun deck for afternoon study breaks. There are no sororities and fraternities here, which helps cut down on underage drinking, though students say that as on most campuses, those who want to find alcohol will do so. Non-drinkers won't feel ostracized, though. "Our long-standing honor code reminds students about respect and community living," a senior says.

When they're not hitting the books, Wheaton students love to put on their dancing shoes—whether for the Boston Bash party on a boat in Boston Harbor, for the Valentine's Dance, or for any number of events at Rosecliff, a mansion in Newport, Rhode Island. Spring Weekend has the "Head of the Peacock" boat race, where

"You know a college is doing its job when you can call it home."

students build ships and race them across the pond, as well as live bands and outdoor barbecues. When it rains, students get dirty as they slide around the craters on Wheaton's lawns, an activity known as "Dimple Diving." Wheaton competes in Division III of the NCAA, and its strongest teams include men's and women's soccer, men's and women's indoor track, baseball, softball, and men's and women's lacrosse. The athletic facility boasts an eight-lane swimming pool, a field house, and an 850-seat arena for basketball or volleyball.

A classics major says Wheaton is special because it has both "an intellectual atmosphere and an involved student body." Indeed, students here take pride in their achievements inside and outside the classroom, while striving to preserve the school's friendly, small-town feel. "You know a college is doing its job when you can call it home," says a political science major. And that goes for men and women.

Overlaps

Boston University, Connecticut College, Clark, Skidmore, University of Massachusetts

If You Apply To ➤

Wheaton: Early decision: Nov. 15, Jan. 15. Regular admissions: Jan. 15. Financial aid: Feb. 1. Campus and alumni interviews: recommended, evaluative. SATs or ACTs: optional. SAT IIs: optional. Accepts the Common Application and electronic applications. Essay question: significant experience or achievement; issue of personal, local, national, or international concern; influential person; influential fictional character, historical figure, or creative work; or a topic of your choice.

Whitman College

345 Boyer Avenue, Walla Walla, WA 99362-2083

Whitman has quietly established itself as one of the West's leading liberal arts colleges. Don't sweat the umbrella: Walla Walla is in arid eastern Washington. Whitman's isolation breeds community spirit and alumni loyalty. True to its liberal arts heritage, Whitman has no business program.

Website: www.whitman.edu
Location: Small city

Going the extra mile is part of the package at Whitman College. It can be literal—students have traveled with professors in far-away lands—or a bit more figurative: the typical Whittie is probably "smart, but also an amazing skier, guitar player, and volunteer," a junior says. Somehow, in these wheat fields and vineyards of south-eastern Washington, a small school is outgrowing its confines to produce a crop of students who are engaged in the world and intently focused on the well-being of their peers. It must be something in that Blue Mountain air.

Everything important is within walking distance of campus, including the main drag of Walla Walla (a.k.a. Walla Squared), which recently won a national "Best Main Street" award. If a picturesque setting is your thing, you'll feel right at home at Whitman, with its seventy-eight-acre campus blending Colonial buildings and modern facilities, all covered in New England ivy. The campus stands in contrast to the rolling expanse of Northwestern terrain nearby, inhabited primarily by farmers and ranchers. Beyond Walla Walla (which means "many waters"), and as far as the eye can see, are scenic mountains, rivers, fields, and forests. Recent college construction includes completion of the new Reid campus center and a new science building.

Professors at Whitman are widely regarded as "brilliant, well spoken, and car-ing," a politics major says. It's not unusual for students to pop into professors' offices, regardless of their posted help hours, and just sit down for a chat (even if the professor is a relic of a past semester). Many students consider their teachers friends, not just people droning in front of a lectern. "My econ prof offered to take some friends and I snowboarding," one sophomore says. The school's small size translates into relatively limited course offerings, but students with far-flung interests can find a supportive faculty mentor

"The classes are designed to help students think and problem-solve."

and put together combination majors. The school also funds several faculty-student research teams. Seniors get first dibs at registration, but most professors allow students to enroll in full classes if students approach them.

Most students agree that academics at Whitman is challenging, but underlying that rigor is a general sense of peer support. "The classes are designed to help students think and problem-solve, but students are not out to compete with each other," a senior says. And unlike larger universities, the courses "are not designed to 'weed out' kids," the student adds. Impressive academic departments are politics, biology, chemistry, and history, and Whitman has the most active small-college theater pro-gram in the country. Recent additions to the curriculum include majors in religion, rhetoric, and film studies. The program in biochemistry, biophysics, and molecular biology offers a major at the interface of the physical and biological sciences.

All Whitman students must complete the General Studies Program, which is designed to allow for flexibility based on a student's background, interest, and apti-tude. The program is divided into the freshman core and distribution requirements. The program helps freshmen learn to read analytically and write effectively. Also, all students take at least six credits in the following areas: social sciences, humani-ties, fine arts, and science; at least one class in quantitative analysis; and two courses that fulfill the requirement in alternative voices. Seniors must also pass comprehensive written and oral exams in their major—the first college or univer-sity in the nation to require undergrads to do so.

Whitman boasts an extensive Asian art collection and expanded Asian studies and art history programs, which are supplemented by the College Summer Studies program in China. The library, with 355,000 volumes, is a great place to catch up on the latest campus news as well as to study. Whitman has 3–2 or 3–3 programs in engineering (with the University of Washington, Caltech, Columbia, Washington University, and Duke), international studies and international business (Montercy Institute of International Studies), computer science and oceanography (University of Washington), and law (Columbia). Off-campus semester programs include the Chicago Urban Studies Program, the Philadelphia Center, the Washington Semester Program, and Biosphere 2.

(Continued)
Total Enrollment: 1,439
Undergraduates: 1,439
Male/Female: 44/56
SAT Ranges: V 610–710
  M 610–6900
ACT Range: 29–31
Financial Aid: 91%
Expense: Pr $ $ $
Phi Beta Kappa: Yes
Applicants: 2,144
Accepted: 54%
Enrolled: 31%
Grad in 6 Years: 76%
Returning Freshmen: 94%
Academics: ✍ ✍ ✍ ✍
Social: ☎ ☎ ☎
Q of L: ★ ★ ★ ★
Admissions: (509) 527-5176
Email Address:
  admission@whitman.edu

Strongest Programs
  Politics
  Biology
  History
  English
  Economics

Recent additions to the curriculum include majors in religion, rhetoric, and film studies.

Whitties are "open and interesting," says a sophomore. Forty-four percent come from Washington, the rest are primarily from the suburbs of Western cities, notably San Francisco and Portland. Seven percent are Asian-American, while African-Americans and Hispanics make up only 5 percent of the students. Despite the apparent lack of diversity, the college's full-time director of multicultural student affairs is helping. The campus is pretty liberal in its political bent, and big issues range from abortion to vegetarianism, environmental issues, capital punishment, and Greek life. But Whitties are pretty open minded. "The students are willing to accept new people, things, and ideas," says one philosophy major. Whitman awards merit scholarships based on academic performance each year, ranging from $5,000 to $9,500, but there are no athletic scholarships. Ninety-one percent of students are offered aid equal to their demonstrated need.

> "The dorms are very plush and well maintained. I almost wish I still live on campus."

All freshmen and sophomores must live in campus housing, which includes some lovely old buildings with large, comfortable rooms. Prentiss Hall and Lyman House, both built in 1926, have received multimillion-dollar face-lifts. Sixty-five percent of the student body live in campus housing, and some students say it's difficult for upperclassmen to get rooms since dorm spots are in such high demand. There's also theme housing for students interested in foreign languages, fine arts, writing, community service, Asian studies, and environmental studies, as well as a multiethnic house. Overall, students seem quite pleased with housing: "The dorms are very plush and well maintained. I almost wish I still live on campus," a senior sighs. Thirty-six percent of the men belong to the four fraternities, which have their own houses. The four sororities, which claim 35 percent of the women, stake out sections in the all-female residence hall. In a break from tradition, the Bon Appetit company runs the food service featuring café and bistro styles of food.

Whitman scrapped varsity football in the late 1970s, but the "Missionaries" maintain an active interest in physical exertion—75 percent of the student body competes in the vigorous intramural club program.

Outdoor attractions are important in this area of the country, where autumn is gorgeous, winter sporadically snowy, and spring delightfully warm. Walla Walla (pop. 30,000) is located in the center of agricultural southeastern Washington near the Blue Mountains. The town has several shops and restaurants, but that's not what this part of the country is about. Go outdoors! Hiking, biking, and backpacking are minutes away, and white-water rafting and rock climbing are popular on weekends. Two ski centers and other recreational areas are within an hour's drive of campus. Seattle (260 miles) and Portland (235 miles) are a welcome change of scenery.

Whitman scrapped varsity football in the late 1970s, but the "Missionaries" maintain an active interest in physical exertion. Highly popular intramural football (both men and women participate) has filled the void nicely, and 75 percent of the student body competes in the vigorous intramural club program. "I know it sounds dorky, but I kid you not, people get into it," reports an art history major. Rock climbers can challenge themselves on two walls, one outdoor and one indoor. Men's snowboarding does very well, as does track and field, skiing, swimming, tennis, and lacrosse.

The campus is an oasis of activity. One student sums it up this way: "If you can't find something to do at Whitman, you're not looking." Students mention the very active drama department, which stages about twelve productions a year, as important to on-campus life. The lack

> "If you can't find something to do at Whitman, you're not looking."

of a football team doesn't stop Whitties from celebrating Homecoming, as well as the Ultimate Frisbee Onionfest and the Beer Mile (chug a cold one at each lap.) In the spring, Whitman shows its intellectual side with Renaissance Faire. There are also free movies and a student coffee house featuring weekly live music from various local or out-of-town bands. The alcohol policy is very loose, students say, and follows a "we don't want to see it" principle. Walla Walla supports a resident symphony, community theater, numerous art galleries, two rodeos, and a hot-air balloon festival in the spring.

Whitman is a special place because it "not only teaches classes, but teaches students how to succeed," a psychology major says. When they're not in the classroom, Whitties wax poetic about their school's warm community, with "hi's and smiles everywhere." All these positive feelings shine through when students at Whitman shout their special—and somewhat risqué—school slogan: "Missionaries! Missionaries! We're on top!"

If You Apply To ➢

Whitman: Early decision: Nov. 15, Jan. 1. Regular admissions: Jan. 15. Financial aid: April 7 (Dec. 20, Feb. 1 for early decision). Meets demonstrated need of 91%. Campus interviews: recommended, evaluative. No alumni interviews. SATs or ACT's: required. SAT IIs: recommended (English composition with essay). Accepts the Common Application and electronic applications. Essay question: significant experience; important issue; influential person; fictional/historical figure; creative work; topic of choice.

Whittier College

13406 East Philadelphia, P.O. Box 634, Whittier, CA 90608-4413

Whittier's Quaker heritage brings a touch of the east to this suburban campus on the outskirts of L.A. Less selective than Occidental and the Claremont Colleges, Whittier lures top students with an arsenal of academic scholarships. Beware the sneaky October 15 deadline for the best of them.

Founded in 1887 by members of the Society of Friends, Whittier College is fast becoming a global training ground. Whittier students can be found all around the world, studying in thirty foreign countries and even designing their entire curriculum. And when they return to the Whittier campus, they have access to caring faculty and a close-knit environment.

Located just eighteen miles away from the Los Angeles area, the college is perched on a hill overlooking the town of Whittier, California, with the San Gabriel Mountains rising up from the horizon. The seventy-three-acre campus is a pleasant mixture of modern buildings tucked between the

> **"Profs, even if I'm not in their class, know my name."**

red-roofed, white-walled Spanish traditionals. Whittier recently completed work on its landmark building (Deihl Hall) to include a digital audio/video computer lab for languages. Renovation and expansion of the Bonnie Bell Wardman Library is underway, and a new track has been completed.

Whittier officially ended its affiliation with the Quakers in the 1940s, but the prevailing spirit of community hearkens back to their traditions. Faculty wins high marks for their concern and accessibility. One freshman says, "Profs, even if I'm not in their class, know my name." Another remarks, "In my first year, I was taught by professors holding Ph.D.s from Harvard, UCLA, and UC–Berkeley." While classes are somewhat competitive, students still work together. "The school is competitive but friendly—everyone helps each other out," explains a senior.

Whittier offers its students two major programs: the liberal education program and the Whittier Scholars Program. About 80 percent of the students take the revised liberal education track, in which they fulfill distribution requirements in writing skills, mathematics, natural sciences, global perspectives, comparative knowledge,

Website: www.whittier.edu
Location: Suburban
Total Enrollment: 1,518
Undergraduates: 1,289
Male/Female: 45/55
SAT Ranges: V 480–600
  M 470–590
ACT Range: 21–26
Financial Aid: 70%
Expense: Pr $ $ $
Phi Beta Kappa: No
Applicants: 1,482
Accepted: 80%
Enrolled: 27%
Grad in 6 Years: 56%
Returning Freshmen: 75%
Academics: ✍ ✍ ✍
Social: ☎ ☎ ☎
Q of L: ★ ★ ★ ★
Admissions: (562) 907-4238
Email Address:
  admission@whittier.edu

(Continued)
Strongest Programs
English
Biology
Psychology
Political Science
Business Administration

and creative and kinesthetic performance. The emphasis of the liberal education program is on interdisciplinary focus, globalism, and critical and quantitative thinking. These liberally educated Whittierans next choose a major from among twenty-six departments, the strongest and most popular of which include English, biology, psychology, political science, and business administration, and programs that focus on teaching certification. The college added a major in environmental science.

Whittier's strongest reputation is for the Whittier Scholars Program, a path taken by 20 percent of the undergraduates, who choose to bypass the traditional liberal education program. They are relieved of most general requirements and start from square one with an "educational design" process. With the help of an academic advisor, the scholars carve their majors out of standard offerings by taking a bit of this and a bit of that. Majors have included such

"If someone searches for alcohol, they find it."

names as symbol systems, visual studies and business, and dynamics of politics and urban life. The program is highly regarded (even by those who don't elect to take it) because of the more active role it allows students to play and the freedom it affords them in pursuing their interests. All students, no matter which curriculum they choose, must fulfill a year-long freshman writing requirement. In an attempt to help freshmen develop both their critical thinking skills and their ability to communicate clearly in writing, Whittier lets students choose their preferences from a variety of seminars. They are also encouraged to take an additional writing course, mathematics, and lab science during their freshman year. First-years also must attend a series of speakers, who discuss topics relevant to student coursework and must take part in the Exploring Los Angeles series, which includes trips to museums and cultural events.

Whittier's strongest reputation is for the Whittier Scholars Program, a path taken by 20 percent of the undergraduates, who choose to bypass the traditional liberal education program and design their own study path.

Study-abroad options include programs in Denmark, India, Mexico, and Asia, and undergraduates may also take foreign-study tours during the January interim. Fifty-one percent of the students come from California, and the rest are from all over the United States and the world. Even with cultural difference, one student says, "We're all just college kids." Diversity plays a major role on this campus. While African-Americans make up only 5 percent of the students, Hispanic enrollment is an impressive 26 percent, and other minorities constitute 19 percent. One club, called Eliminating Campus Homophobia (ECHO), is quite vocal on campus, as are the Black Student Union and Hispanic Student Association. An on-campus cultural center focuses on diversity programming and resources. In addition to need-based aid, the college grants some students merit scholarships, ranging from $3,000 to $20,000.

Thirty-six percent of the students seek off-campus shelter, but the Turner Residence Hall entices many students to stay on campus and vie for a chance to get a room with a panoramic view of Los Angeles, and campus computer network access

"Whittier's best feature is that it truly is a community."

in every room. Most freshmen are assigned rooms, though Whittier Scholars, athletes, and members of Whittier's social societies tend to cluster in selected dorms and houses. All dorms are equally suited for freshmen, says one student, because each is its own little community. All campus residents must take at least ten meals at the Campus Inn dining hall, where the food is said to be typical college fare. The Spot (Whittier's popular campus coffee house) was recently expanded to include a state-of-the-art nightclub called—what else?—the Club.

Study-abroad options include programs in Denmark, India, Mexico, and Asia, and undergraduates may also take foreign-study tours during the January interim.

Nine social societies (they're not called fraternities or sororities here) attract 3 percent of the men and 4 percent of the women but don't dominate the social scene. However, their dances, which frequently feature live entertainment, are welcomed by all. For many, entertainment takes the form of road trips. "Since Whittier is only like thirty minutes from everything, we've gone to Universal CityWalk, the Block, Disneyland, Brea Mall, Costa Mesa, and Huntington/Newport Beach," says one first-year. Other common destinations include Las Vegas, Mexico, Joshua Tree, Hollywood, San Diego, and northern California.

Whittier has a fairly strict alcohol policy and underage drinking is not permitted. Students say it's difficult for underage drinkers to get served at campus events. Nevertheless, "if someone searches for alcohol, they find it." Popular annual events include a Spring Sing talent show, the football game against archrival Occidental College, and Sportsfest, which is a campus-wide competition in which dorms compete in a variety of athletic, intellectual, and wacky games and events. A favorite among students is Mona Kai, a Hawaiian party put on by the Lancer Society where tons of sand are shipped in for the event. Also favored is the Midnight Breakfast served by professors during second-semester finals. The most important campus landmark is the Rock, which sits near the front of campus and is given a fresh coat of paint by countless aspiring artists. The beach is a frequent destination, and for nightlife, Los Angeles looms large. The local community, known as Uptown Whittier, offers quaint shops, restaurants, and cobblestone sidewalks but little in the way of entertainment.

Men's lacrosse is the most successful sports team on campus. Men's football and soccer, women's soccer, softball, and track are the most popular. Facilities have gotten an upgrade, including a new football field and a fully equipped fitness center.

All in all, most students agree that Whittier is a supportive, intimate environment where people cooperate and take an active role in education. According to one student, the atmosphere is what makes Whittier unique. "Whittier's best feature is that it truly is a community," says a self-designed major. "We definitely pride ourselves on our diversity and ability to communicate across traditionally restrictive lines."

While African-Americans make up only 5 percent of the students, Hispanic enrollment is an impressive 26 percent, and other minorities constitute 19 percent.

Overlaps

Occidental, Chapman, Pitzer, Claremont McKenna, Grinnell

If You Apply To ➤ **Whittier:** Rolling admissions. Early action: Dec. 1. Regular admissions: Feb. 1. (priority). Financial aid: Feb. 15. Does not guarantee to meet demonstrated need. Campus interviews: recommended, evaluative. No alumni interviews. SATs or ACTs: required. SAT IIs: optional. Accepts the Common Application and electronic applications. Essay question: achievements in twenty-five years; high-school experience that you could change; concern or personal or broader importance; person you would like to emulate.

Willamette University

900 State Street, Salem, OR 97301

Willamette is strategically located next door to the Oregon state capitol and forty minutes from Portland. Bigger than Whitman, smaller than U of Puget Sound, and more conservative than Lewis and Clark, Willamette offers extensive study abroad enhanced by ties to Asia.

Willamette University, founded in 1842, was the first university in the Pacific Northwest. It welcomed women before most other schools—its first graduate was female—and is closely associated with the development of law and government in cities like Seattle, Portland, and Tacoma, which didn't even exist when it opened. Today, the school provides a more personal atmosphere than larger universities nearby, while boasting an endowment equal to or bigger than those of neighboring private colleges. "I love being able to walk around campus and receive hellos and hugs from friends and professors alike," says a junior sociology and Spanish major. "I also constantly feel encouraged to creatively express myself."

Website: www.willamette.edu
Location: Center city
Total Enrollment: 2,436
Undergraduates: 1,773
Male/Female: 44/56
SAT Ranges: V 570–660
M 570–650
ACT Range: 25–29

Over the next twenty years, dorms will be transformed into residential colleges. The goal is to make the campus more of a series of neighborhoods, to further build and nurture community.

Willamette has "the most aesthetically pleasing campus I've ever seen," says a junior politics and Spanish major. It's home to full trees (thanks to Oregon's omnipresent rain), small wildlife, and occasionally steelhead salmon, which splash around in the Mill Stream that runs between WU's redbrick academic buildings. New additions include the Mary Stuart Rogers Music Center and $3 million Montag Student Center, a science center and an art museum. Over the next twenty years, dorms will be transformed into residential colleges. The goal is to make the campus more of a series of neighborhoods, to further build and nurture community.

Willamette (pronounced "Will-AM-it") offers bachelor of arts and bachelor of music degrees, and most popular majors are psychology, politics, and economics, the latter two being especially strong because of the school's location in Oregon's capital. Students say other good bets include rhetoric, biology, and chemistry. All students complete the freshman World Views seminar, four writing-centered courses,

"The most aesthetically pleasing campus I've ever seen."

two courses in quantitative and analytical reasoning, study in a language other than English, and course work in six modes of inquiry—the natural world; the arts; arguments, reasons, and values; thinking historically; interpreting texts; and understanding society. Students also take capstone senior seminars, often culminating in research or thesis projects. About half of the student body participates in a robust study-abroad program, and WU also benefits from its proximity to the U.S. campus of Tokyo International University.

Classes are small; 82 percent of those taken by freshmen have twenty-five or fewer on the roster. Students work hard, but say Willamette is not cut-throat. "The pace is comfortable, yet challenging," says an art history major. Outside the classroom, the computerized card catalog and spacious study lounges in the $7.4 million Mark O. Hatfield Library (named for the former U.S. senator) makes it easier to shoulder the workload. "I've seen numerous students in the library and computer labs on Friday and Saturday evenings," says a junior. If students aren't reading or writing papers, numerous undergraduate research opportunities beckon. Support has more than doubled with the creation of the Carson Undergraduate Research Awards, the Science Collaborate Research Program, and a newly organized humanities center.

Students give Willamette's professors high marks. "Most classes are discussion-oriented, where desks are arranged in a circle, and professors are used as resources—but not there to take over the class," says a Spanish and sociology major. Six of the

"All the dorms, even the old ones, are kept up pretty well."

past eleven Oregon Professors of the Year have come from Willamette, adds a chemistry major, and the student-faculty ratio is ten to one. However, Willamette's size does result in some limitations; only minors are available in Russian, Japanese, women's studies, and earth sciences, and the music therapy program was recently dropped.

Forty percent of Willamette students are native Oregonians, and much of the remainder comes from Western states, notably California and Washington. The school is two-thirds white, with African-Americans making up 2 percent of the student body, Hispanics 5 percent, and Asian-Americans 7 percent. Foreigners and other non-Caucasian students comprise 22 percent. Women's issues, race relations, the environment, and tensions related to the Greek system spark discussion on campus. "It seems that all views are respected and honored," says a junior. Fourteen hundred merit scholarships are available, ranging from $500 to $23,150; there are no athletic awards.

Seventy-four percent of students live in campus housing, which is social and convenient to classes and parties; doing so is required for freshmen and sophomores. "All the dorms, even the old ones, are kept up pretty well," says a junior. "Some—University Apartments, especially—are pretty plush." All housing is coed, and theme wings or floors are available, focused on community service, the outdoors, wellness, or substance-free living. Twenty-eight percent of the men and twenty-two percent of the women go Greek, and some live in fraternity and sorority houses. The student-owned and -operated Bistro offers a coffeehouse atmosphere, and is a popular alternative to cafeteria fare. When it comes to crime, occasional break-ins are the biggest problem, so "campus safety recently changed their image, trying to look less like police," says one student. "The campus is totally safe, though the rest of Salem can get sketchy."

Most of Willamette's social life takes place on campus, whether it's free movies and lectures, open-mic nights at the Bistro, dance parties (salsa or swing), or performances from the music and theater departments. "When the sun is out, everyone is outside playing or studying," says a junior. "Greek and off-campus parties dominate the weekend social scene, and the Ram Brewery draws big crowds on Thursdays, college night." (Remember, this is the Pacific Northwest—coffee houses and micro-brewed beer were practically invented here.) Annual social highlights include the spring Wulapalooza, celebrating art and music, and the Hawaiian Club Luau, where students chow down on spit-roasted pig. Each fall, students from Tokyo International organize the Harvest Festival. Other wacky traditions including being "Mill-Streamed," dumped into the campus brook on your birthday. When it comes to drinking, Willamette abides by state law, which says no one under twenty-one can imbibe—but students say anyone who wants booze can find and consume it behind closed doors.

Downtown Salem is a short walk from campus, and while it isn't a college town, it does have "movies, shopping, restaurants, and more coffee houses," one student says. Also nearby are the Cascade Mountains and rugged beaches of Lincoln City and Coos Bay (an hour's drive), skiing

"When the sun is out, everyone is outside playing or studying."

and snowboarding on Mount Hood, or in the high desert town of Bend (three hours), and the cosmopolitan cities of Portland (forty minutes) and Seattle (about four hours north). San Francisco is an eight- to nine-hour drive. Willamette students remain true to the school motto, "Not unto ourselves alone are we born," when they go "Into the Streets" for a day of service each fall.

Willamette competes in Division III, and soccer, basketball, and track are strong—for both women and men. In fact, the university made history in October 1997, when junior soccer star Liz Heaston kicked her way into the record books as the first woman to play intercollegiate football. (She made the two extra points she attempted.) The annual football game against Pacific Lutheran usually has conference-championship implications, and games against Linfield are also well attended.

Willamette may be the best little school you've never heard of, especially if you're from outside the California-Oregon-Washington corridor. The school's close-knit community is strengthened by its emphasis on service, and by warm, supportive faculty members, who push students to achieve. "It is common to see President M. Lee Pelton, or the governor of the state, in Goudy Commons, the main eating area," says a film studies major. "You never have to eat alone, or be alone, if you don't want to."

The university made history in October 1997, when junior soccer star Liz Heaston kicked her way into the record books as the first woman to play intercollegiate football. (She made the two extra points she attempted.)

Overlaps

University of Oregon, University of California, Whitman, Colorado College, University of Puget Sound

If You Apply To ➤

Willamette: Early action: Dec. 1. Regular admissions and financial aid: Feb. 1. Meets demonstrated need of 53%. Campus interviews: recommended, evaluative. No alumni interviews. SATs or ACTs: required. SAT IIs: optional. Accepts the Common Application and electronic applications. Essay question: Common Application questions.

Founded in 1693, William and Mary is the original public ivy. History, government, and international studies are among the strongest departments. With 7,500 students, W&M is really a medium-sized university that is larger than University of Richmond and Mary Washington.

Website: www.wm.edu
Location: Small city
Total Enrollment: 7,530
Undergraduates: 5,585
Male/Female: 43/57
SAT Ranges: V 620–710
  M 610–700
ACT Range: 29-32
Financial Aid: 25%
Expense: Pub $
Phi Beta Kappa: Yes
Applicants: 8,129
Accepted: 41%
Enrolled: 41%
Grad in 6 Years: 89%
Returning Freshmen: 95%
Academics: 🏛 🏛 🏛 🏛
Social: ☎ ☎ ☎
Q of L: ★ ★ ★
Admissions: (757) 221-4223
Email Address:
  admiss@wm.edu

Strongest Programs
  Biology
  Business
  History
  English
  Government
  International Relations
  International Studies
  Physics

Though the physical campus might seem stuck in a time warp, students say everything about William and Mary—from the amazing faculty to the picturesque grounds—is up to date. Traditions abound, yet this historic public university—the second oldest in the nation—continues to evolve in its pursuit of academic excellence. The W&M formula of blending the old and the new has been working for more than three hundred years, and it's only getting better with age.

A profusion of azaleas and crape myrtle add splashes of color to William and Mary's finely manicured campus, located about 150 miles southeast of Washington, D.C. The campus is divided into three sections, and includes a lake and wooded wildlife preserve, which is filled with trails and widely used by the science departments. The Ancient Campus is a grouping of three Colonial structures, the oldest being Wren Hall, which has been in continuous use since 1695 and is one of the most visually pleasing buildings in American higher education. The Old Campus, where the buildings date from the '20s and '30s, is a little farther out, and next to it is New Campus, where ground was first broken in the '60s. The W&M campus boasts one of the most romantic spots of any in the nation: Crim Dell, a wooded area with a small pond spanned by an old-style wooden bridge. The ninety-five thousand-square-foot university center includes a bookstore, auditorium, game room, post office, conference rooms, and student lounge. Students say the center has enhanced campus social life by providing bands and comedians with a great performance space. A renovation of Swem Library continues and the Law School is getting an additional wing.

> **"Professors cultivate a genuine interest and students go home thinking and applying these things to our daily lives."**

William and Mary created Phi Beta Kappa in December of 1776, and the honor code demands much from the college's students. There are no "easy A" classes at the college, and the academic climate is demanding and competitive. "Everyone here was a great student in high school," says a junior, "so there is this tacit level of competitiveness that drives people in the classroom." Still, most agree that it's a healthy rivalry.

Fittingly, the history department, a joint sponsor with Colonial Williamsburg of the Institute for Early American History and Culture, is among William and Mary's best departments. Business, English, biology, psychology, and history are the most popular majors. The accounting program ranks in the top twenty nationwide, causing one government major to grumble that "accounting majors don't seek employment, employers seek them." State-mandated restructuring eliminated "master's only" programs in English, government, mathematics, and sociology, but undergraduate programs haven't yet felt the pinch. New on the academic menu are majors in biological psychology and African-American studies, and minors in biochemistry and film studies. There are summer and year-long study-abroad programs around the globe, from Europe to China, the Philippines, Australia, and Mexico, and summer field schools in archeology, including one in St. Eustatius in the Caribbean. The College's International Relations center is internationally acclaimed. About 12 percent of freshmen are designated Monroe Scholars and receive a $2,000 summer research stipend, which is typically used after their sophomore or junior year. One student used his to distribute his band's CD; another traveled to Paris to sketch and study.

Relations between students and professors are excellent. "Professors cultivate a genuine interest and students go home thinking and applying these things to our daily lives," says a student, who goes on to complain that the college "fired a few really good professors as a result of budget cuts," leading many to question the college's priorities. Sixty-five percent of freshmen classes have twenty-five or fewer students, although a few introductory lectures may have a couple hundred. Virtually every class is taught by a full professor, and TAs are used for grading or lab purposes only. The college established freshman seminars that are limited to fifteen students each that provide even closer faculty interaction. A computerized registration system has taken the headaches out of the once hellish scheduling process.

Graduation requirements are thorough and include proficiency in a foreign language, writing, computing (concentration-specific), and physical education. More specific distribution requirements include a course in mathematics and quantitative reasoning, two courses in the natural sciences, two in the social sciences, one each in literature and history of the arts and creative and performing arts, and one course in philosophical, religious, and social thought. The Center for Honors and

"It never gets dull."

Interdisciplinary Studies allows outstanding students four semesters of intensive liberal arts seminars, with lectures by top scholars from around the country, and also facilitates interdisciplinary majors like American studies, environmental science, and women's studies.

Because W&M is a state-supported university, 64 percent of its students are Virginians. Competition for the nonresident spots is stiff, with many out-of-staters from the Mid-Atlantic and farther north. Ninety-seven percent of freshmen ranked in the top quarter of their high-school class. The college has made a major effort to recruit and retain more minorities; Asian-Americans now account for 7 percent of the students, Hispanics make up 3 percent, and African-Americans contribute 5 percent. An ongoing series of programs in the residence halls addresses physical-safety issues as well as diversity and gender communication. Other major issues on campus are the "living wage" campaign to increase pay for college staff, and the controversy surrounding the school's chancellor, Henry Kissinger. W&M has its share of eagerly recruited jocks; nearly three hundred athletic scholarships are offered each year, in eighteen sports. More than 140 academic merit scholarships are awarded annually for $200 to $5200.

Seventy-seven percent of the undergraduates live on campus in mostly coed dorms that range from stately old halls with high ceilings to modern buildings equipped with air-conditioning. All freshmen are guaranteed a room on campus (with both cable and Internet connections), but after that students try their luck with the infamous lottery ("stressful but efficient"). Some students, usually sophomore men, draw the Dillard Complex—two dorms located a couple miles off campus. "The residence halls are sufficient and comfortable...far from the prison-like places I've seen at some schools," says one student. Special-interest housing is available—there are seven language houses and an International Studies House—and life in a fraternity or sorority house is also an option. Students give the three campus cafeterias mixed reviews, but all freshmen must purchase a nineteen-meal plan. Others have a variety of options, including cooking in the dorms and dinner plans open to Greeks and non-Greeks alike in sorority and fraternity houses.

W&M isn't known as a social school, but "it never gets dull," says an international relations major. "Our student are so inventive that it's a guaranteed great time." Thirty percent of the men and 30 percent of the women join Greek organizations,

William and Mary created Phi Beta Kappa in December of 1776, and the honor code demands much from the college's students.

Fittingly, the history department, a joint sponsor with Colonial Williamsburg of the Institute for Early American History and Culture, is among William and Mary's best departments.

which host most of the on-campus parties. The few local bars and delis pick up the rest. Although the college has implemented measures to prevent binge drinking and promote safety, underage drinkers still obtain alcohol. "I would be lying if I said no 'underagers' consumed alcohol," says one student. "However, because most social events take place near campus, there's never driving to events." The Student Association sponsors mixers, band and tailgate parties, and a film series. Campus security is regarded as tight, although crime is not a big issue. "Everyone feel completely safe—even in the wee hours of the night," says a senior.

Anyone who gets restless can always step across the street to Colonial Williamsburg to picnic in the restored area, walk or jog down Duke of Gloucester Street (called "Dog Street"), or study in one of the beautiful gardens. Substantial job opportunities exist for students at Colonial Williamsburg, Busch Gardens, and other tourist-oriented attractions in the area. Although the "tourons" can be trying, says one student, "We can access most of the tourist stuff for free," says an upperclassman. Volunteer opportunities abound and many students participate. Richmond and Norfolk, each an hour's drive, are top road trips; the University of Virginia, although an archrival, is also popular; and Virginia Beach, a favorite springtime Mecca, is a little farther away.

Traditions are the stuff of which William and Mary is made, and perhaps the most cherished is the annual Yule Log Ceremony in Wren Hall, where students sing carols and hear the president, dressed in a Santa Claus outfit, read the Dr. Seuss story *How the Grinch Stole Christmas.* Grand Illumination is a great Christmas fireworks display, and on Charter Day, bells chime and students celebrate the distinguished history of their three hundred-year-old institution. On Sorority Acceptance Day, the pledges must all cross the sunken garden barricaded by fraternity men, and romantics will be happy to learn that any couple who kisses at the top of Crim Dell

"Everyone feels completely safe— even in the wee hours of the night."

Bridge will be married by the end of the year. The 13 Club, a secret society of students dedicated to the college, provides students and professors with a helping hand (like missed class notes) or a pat on the back when they're feeling low—all delivered anonymously, with nothing to identify the helper but his or her number. One activity, though illegal, is always popular: jumping the wall at the Governor's Mansion at the end of Dog Street.

William and Mary isn't a football powerhouse like most southern-state schools, but the athletic program is strong nonetheless. Athletes made NCAA appearances in 2000–01 in women's and men's soccer, women's and men's cross-country, field hockey, lacrosse, men's indoor and outdoor track and field, men's tennis, and women's and men's gymnastics. Men's gymnastics have dominated the state, winning twenty-seven consecutive championships. The football team plays in Division I-AA and always stirs enthusiasm, especially on Homecoming Weekend, while basketball and soccer are other popular men's sports. Intramurals, from skydiving to Ultimate Frisbee, attract two-thirds of the student body, and a $6 million recreational athletic complex provides excellent facilities. The old gym is now the home of the graduate school of business and undergraduate student services, including admissions and career planning.

William and Mary's tradition stretches back to the dawn of this nation, and its grand old campus and stirring history makes it a distinguished and cherished part of many student's lives. And on the last day of classes, seniors return to the Wren. They climb the old stairs and reach for a cord to ring the building's bell high above. And they announce to the world, here we come!

Overlaps

University of Virginia, Georgetown, Richmond, Duke, Washington & Lee

William and Mary: Early decision: Nov. 15. Regular admissions: Jan. 5. Financial aid: March 15. Housing: May 1. Meets demonstrated need of 46%. Campus and alumni interviews: optional, informational. ACTs or SATs: required. SAT IIs: recommended (writing plus two others). Accepts electronic applications. Essay question: time in your life when you took a stand; your community; literary or film character; copy of essay you enjoyed writing for another college application.

Williams College

Williamstown, MA 01267

Running neck-in-neck with Amherst on the selectivity chart, Williams occupies a campus of surpassing beauty in the foothills of the Berkshires. Williams has shaken the preppy image, but still attracts plenty of well-toned all-around jock-intellectuals. The splendid isolation of Williamstown is either a blessing or a curse.

Whether they're hiking mountains with the deans or engaging in deep debates with professors over coffee, students at Williams College adore the close ties they nurture at this premier liberal arts school. It's a place with an abundance of school spirit, and a stunning natural backdrop of gentle mountains and wooded countryside. Williams beckons students to take in the same picturesque setting that moved Henry David Thoreau during his travels through the Massachusetts wilderness. When they're not gazing at the purple mountains' majesty, students at Williams are digging into their studies to earn the diplomas that will open doors for them after they leave this idyllic institution.

Nestled in the small village of Williamstown, the college takes full advantage of the Berkshires' rich history and natural resources. The verdant surroundings beg for the skiing, cycling, and backpacking for which Williams students are famous. Williams buildings constitute a virtual museum of architectural styles, from the elegantly simple Federal design of the original West College to contemporary designs by Charles Moore and Carlos Jimenez. Many of the buildings of brick and gray stone are arranged around loosely organized quads that provide both a sense of enclosure and of openness to nature. Students can also take advantage of MASS MoCA, a center for visual, performing, and media arts.

Williams's greatest strengths are in art history, environmental science, history, political science, economics, English, chemistry, and biology, all of which contribute directly to an acceptance rate of about 90 percent at business, law, and medical schools. Says one senior, "With one of the finest college art museums in America and one of the best impressionistic collections in the world, we have tremendous resources for an outstanding (art history) program." Students agree that the Romance languages are weak, but interdisciplinary programs in Afro-American studies, area studies, and women's studies are increasingly popular. The college recently strengthened the requirements for such majors, and is developing new team-taught courses such as "Culture, Society, and Disease." Environmental studies, based in the two thousand-acre, college-owned Hopkins Forest, makes full use of the campus's natural resources. For future engineers, 3–2 B.A./B.S. programs are offered in conjunction with Columbia and Washington universities.

The Williams curriculum places an emphasis on interdisciplinary studies and personalized teaching. Almost all classes have fewer than fifty students; two-thirds have less than twenty-five. The distribution requirements consist of three courses in each of three areas—arts and languages, social studies, and sciences and mathematics—

> **"You are in contact with experts in their fields."**

Website: www.williams.edu
Location: Small town
Total Enrollment: 2,048
Undergraduates: 1,997
Male/Female: 52/48
SAT Ranges: V 650–760
  M 660–750
ACT Range: N/A
Financial Aid: 40%
Expense: Pr $ $ $
Phi Beta Kappa: Yes
Applicants: 4,638
Accepted: 24%
Enrolled: 46%
Grad in 6 Years: 93%
Returning Freshmen: 97%
Academics: ✍ ✍ ✍ ✍ ✍
Social: ☎ ☎ ☎
Q of L: ★ ★ ★ ★
Admissions: (413) 597-2211
Email Address:
  admission@williams.edu

Strongest Programs
  Art
  Environmental Science
  History
  Political Science
  Economics
  Art History
  English
  Natural Sciences

two of which must be completed by the end of the sophomore year. Students must take at least one course on cultural pluralism, two writing-intensive classes, and one quantitative and formal reasoning course. Entering first-years have the option of taking the First-Year Residential Seminar, in which they live together in the same residential unit and take a team-taught or interdisciplinary course together.

Students must complete four winter study projects during the January intersession. There is also Free University, in which students teach one another anything from Chinese cooking to the jitterbug. In recent years, students have explored India, the Soviet Union, West Africa, and Western Europe with the college's unusual and relatively inexpensive faculty-guided tours. Opportunities for off-campus study are also available during the fall and spring. The many options include Williams at Mystic Seaport,* the Twelve-College Exchange,* and an innovative program in conjunction with Exeter College of Oxford University in England.

Williams's faculty is "far above the rest," says a freshman. "You are in contact with experts in their fields." But the profs are not just talking heads. Most professors live right in Williamstown, giving students the opportunity to see them not just in class, but at the bank, on Main Street, and even in their homes. Additionally, the college provides a stipend with which advisors sometimes take their advisees out to lunch or dinner. Academic and career counseling is comprehensive, students say. The alumni network is "amazing," a senior says, with grads offering loads of help to their undergrad kin, The computer center is impressively equipped, and Sawyer Library reportedly has ample accommodations to offer the wearied but inspired. The entire campus, including all residences, is networked, providing access from student rooms to the Internet.

> *The typical Williams student is a bright, enthusiastic, extremely energetic, well-rounded extrovert—and they're not pretentious, one student insists. "They have an uncanny ability to be involved in multiple extracurricular activities while also maintaining their academic studies," another adds.*

The typical Williams student is a bright, enthusiastic, extremely energetic, well-rounded extrovert—and they're not pretentious, one student insists. "They have an uncanny ability to be involved in multiple extracurricular activities while also maintaining their academic studies," another adds. In-state residents only account for 15 percent of the student body, while foreign and minority students make up nearly one-third. Williams clearly looks for diversity in prospective students; students who are strong in more than one area tend to stand out. "People are very open here," says a psychology major. But a classmate warns, "Sometimes it seems hard to relate to people if you aren't an athlete or a social partier." Political correct-

"People are very open here." ness does crop up on campus, where issues including gender roles and sexual identity are discussed. Nearly a third of the students are bona fide preppies; the rest just look that way. The campus uniform seems to include relatively little makeup for women and Williams sweatshirts and jeans for all. The school's mascot is a purple cow, so cows and purple naturally dominate clothes and signs. There are no athletic or merit scholarships at this expensive school, but Williams guarantees to design a financial-aid package that meets the full demonstrated need of every admit.

"Phenomenal" and "definitely above the norm" is how students describe the housing at Williams. "The dorms here are pretty and students love it," says a history major. The rooms are spacious and well maintained, and housing is guaranteed for all four years. One dormitory was once a fine old inn, with fireplaces and mahogany paneling; several others look as if they should have been. "Every dorm has lots of common space with couches, TV, VCR, fireplace, and some even have ballrooms," says an English major. Living options range from two modern complexes to the lovely row houses that were fraternities before Greek organizations were abolished in 1962. New arrivals reside in first-year-only dorms known as "entries," where the highly praised junior advisor system works to provide advice and support. Says a history major, "The minute you get here you know about

> *One dormitory was once a fine old inn, with fireplaces and mahogany paneling; several others look as if they should have been.*

twenty other people with whom to hang out." Small co-op houses are available for students who want to cook and play house. Upperclassmen, virtually ensured a single, may enter the housing lottery individually or in groups. The college permits only a handful of students to move . The best first-year dorm is said to be the quad. Beware: thin walls are a complaint. Food is another area where Williams's resident overachievers are pampered. Except for the much-feared tofu pie, the food is considered quite good for institutional fare, and nearly everyone buys the meal plan, which is usable in any of the five campus dining halls.

Williams's Berkshires setting can seem isolated at times, yet civilization—Albany, New York—is only an hour away. Even the most focused of scholars would find the peaceful Williamstown backdrop a refreshing distraction. "Williamstown has a lot of character," a biology major says. The Clark Art Institute, within walking distance of campus, possesses one of the finest collections of Renoir and Degas in the nation, as well as a great library. The modern college music center attracts top classical musicians, and the college theater is home to a renowned summer festival that often features Broadway stars. Films, lectures, and concerts abound on most weekends, as do the usual number of parties. "One of the reasons I chose Williams was because the campus social life actually exists on campus," a senior says.

Fraternities and sororities have no place at Williams, but that hasn't created a dearth of drinking opportunities. The administration has taken a tougher stance on drinking. "Our policy has recently become a lot stricter, so now it's very hard for underage students to drink at a party, and the consequences are more severe," says one senior. Still, students say it's possible to get booze "if you know the right people." Aside from imbibing, students find plenty of other things to do. The college brings in lots of cultural groups, popular concerts, and speakers, and there are always student performances or organized activities. An organization called Connections strives to distract keg-seeking students and emphasize alcohol-free alternatives, of which there are many. All parties must serve food and nonalcoholic beverages whenever alcohol is present.

Sports are more like a religion than an extracurricular activity, and Williams has become a perennial winner of the Division III Sears Cup, awarded annually to the school with the strongest overall athletic program. Everyone seems to play on some team, and any contest with archrival Amherst ensures a big crowd. After all, Amherst was founded in 1821 by a defecting Williams president and part of the student body. And the insults tend to go beyond the athletic field and consistent high

> "The minute you get here you know about twenty other people with whom to hang out."

scores. T-shirts can be seen around campus offering the following sentiment regarding its rivals in the Little Three: "The good: Williams. The bad: Wesleyan. The ugly: Amherst." The men's and women's swim teams are nationally ranked, and the men's tennis, basketball, and cross-country teams have been among the top in the nation. Women's tennis, field hockey, and lacrosse teams are also strong contenders. The men's indoor track and field team has won 122 straight Quad Cup competitions. The Taconic golf course, rated among the best collegiate facilities, has been host to several national college championships. The college helps maintain a cross-country ski trail located ten miles from town, and two alpine ski resorts within ten miles of campus are also popular. The one knock against the Williams sports program is the charge from some quarters that women's sports get less support than men's. Homecoming is always popular at Williams, as are Mountain Day, Winter Carnival, and Spring Fling. Every winter there is also a campus-wide snow sculpting contest.

When you're nestled by gorgeous purple mountains and have access to a wide range of academic options, as well as top-notch faculty, somehow the overall "smallness" of the Williams setting doesn't matter so much. For these Ephs (that's

Except for the much-feared tofu pie, the food is considered quite good for institutional fare, and nearly everyone buys the meal plan, which is usable in any of the five campus dining halls.

Overlaps
Amherst, Harvard, Dartmouth, Duke, Brown

pronounced Eefs, as in school founder Ephraim Williams) know they've got a good thing going. "Complaints are few and far between," reports a senior. "We love it!"

If You Apply To ➤

Williams: Early decision: Nov. 15. Regular admissions: Jan. 1. Financial aid: Feb. 1. Guarantees to meet demonstrated need. Campus and alumni interviews: optional, informational. SATs or ACTs: required. SAT IIs: required (any three). Accepts the Common Application and the electronic application. Essay question: experience that defined a value.

University of Wisconsin–Madison

140 Peterson Building, 750 University Avenue, Madison, WI 53706-1490

UW draws nearly 40 percent of its students from out of state, the highest proportion among leading Midwestern public universities. Why brave the cold? Reasons include top programs in an array of professional fields and several innovative living-learning programs.

Website: www.wisc.edu

Location: Center city

Total Enrollment: 40,196

Undergraduates: 27,533

Male/Female: 48/52

SAT Ranges: V 520–650
M 550–670

ACT Range: 25–29

Financial Aid: 55%

Expense: Pub $ $

Phi Beta Kappa: Yes

Applicants: 16,290

Accepted: 77%

Enrolled: 47%

Grad in 6 Years: N/A

Returning Freshmen: 95%

Academics: ✎ ✎ ✎ ✎ ½

Social: 🍷 🍷 🍷 🍷

Q of L: ★ ★ ★ ★

Admissions: (608) 262-3961

Email Address: on.wisconsin
@mail.admin.wisc.edu

Strongest Programs
Agriculture
Biological Sciences
Education
Communications
Social Studies

At the University of Wisconsin at Madison, two things are a sure bet: very cold weather and red-hot academics. On a campus where the mercury often dips below zero, you're likely to be too busy studying to notice. With nearly twenty-seven thousand undergraduates and enormous resources, Madison offers something for virtually everyone. All that's required is a desire to learn. Oh, and a very warm coat.

Described by one student as "architecturally olden with a modern touch," Madison's mainly brick campus is distinctive. It spreads out over 903 hilly, tree-covered acres and across an isthmus between two glacial lakes, Mendota and Monona, named by prehistoric Indians who once lived along their shores. From atop Bascom Hill, the center of campus, you look east past the statue of Lincoln and the liberal arts buildings, down to a library mall that was the scene of many a political demonstration during the '60s. Farther east you see rows of State Street pubs and restaurants and the bleached dome of the Wisconsin state capitol. On the other side of the hill, another campus, dedicated to the sciences, twists along Lake Mendota. But students from both sides of the hill drink beer elbow to elbow in the old student union, the Rathskeller, where political arguments and backgammon games can rage all night. Outside on the union's veranda, students can look out at the sailboats in summer or iceboats in winter. The icy wind that blows off the lakes in winter is vicious, and the academic climate is not exactly tropical either. Coursework is demanding, and in many ways akin to graduate school elsewhere. Predictably, grading is tough and inflexible and often figured on a strict curve. "There are a lot of smart people studying here," notes one student with a firm grasp of the obvious.

> **"It's easy to get lost in the crowd here, so you have to be fairly strong and confident."**

A list of first-rate academic programs at Madison would constitute a college catalog elsewhere. There are seventy programs considered in the top ten nationally. Some highlights include education, agriculture, communications, biological sciences, and social studies. The most popular majors are history, engineering, political science, psychology, and business, in that order. The math department is cited as lacking faculty, and letters and science could use better advising, according to some. Due to overcrowding, some popular fields, such as engineering and business, have had to restrict entry to their majors by requiring high GPAs. But with a smaller freshman class, students are finding it a bit easier to get into the courses of their choice. Several improvements made over the last couple of years have helped to relieve the overload. First, an automated system makes the headaches of registration a bit less severe. Second, the Grainger Hall of Business Administration, a $35-million complex, quadrupled the space in the current school of business. The biotechnology building supports research and undergraduate teaching.

Distribution requirements vary among the different schools and academic departments, but they are uniformly rigorous, with science and math courses required for B.A. students, and a foreign language for virtually everyone. All students must fulfill a two-part graduation requirement in both quantitative reasoning and communication. For students who prefer the academic road less traveled, options include the Institute for Environmental Studies and the Integrated Liberal Studies (ILS), which consists of related courses introducing the achievements of Western culture. An elite Medical Scholars program allows fifty select high-school seniors guaranteed admission to the Madison medical school after completing three years of undergraduate work. A variety of internships are available, as are study-abroad programs all over the world, including Europe, Brazil, India, Israel, and Thailand.

Professors at Madison are certainly among the nation's best, with Nobel laureates, National Academy of Science members, and Guggenheim fellows scattered liberally among the departments. The English program boasts such young, vibrant faculty as highly acclaimed writers Lorrie Moore and Debra Spark. Along with downsizing, Madison has taken a number of steps to

"Anyone can fit in, you just have to find your own niche."

strengthen the freshman experience in particular. They have emphasized more small classes, with fifteen to twenty students, to help entering freshmen adjust to college-level coursework; more comprehensive orientation and mentoring for freshmen; and more student-faculty contact. Advising has received a booster shot, too. For undergrads who find it difficult to choose one of the vast array of majors available, the university has developed a plan called Cross-College Advising System, which features a ten-member team of academic staff advisors. The idea is to help students refine their educational and career goals, so their interests, majors, and professional aspirations mesh into a complete package. Upon admission, every student is assigned an advisor to meet with at least three times in the first year.

If there is one common characteristic among the undergraduates, it is aggressiveness. "It's easy to get lost in the crowd here, so you have to be fairly strong and confident," declares one student. "No one holds your hand." The flip side is that "anyone can fit in, you just have to find your own niche." Almost two-thirds of the students are from Wisconsin. The school is a heartland of progressive politics, and Madison's reputation as a haven for liberals remains intact. "Students here are called liberal because they are eager and willing to change and are continually looking for newer and better ideas," explains an activist. The university has implemented a racial-awareness program to make the campus more hospitable to minorities. African-Americans and Hispanics currently make up 4 percent of the student body, while Asian-Americans constitute another 4 percent. CIA recruiting, women's rights, and tuition increases have all been issues recently. Thousands of academic merit scholarships ranging from $500 to $7,000 are awarded each year, and most of the sports on campus offer full scholarships to their athletes. Need-based financial-aid packages meet 100 percent of need for all in-staters, but out-of-state applicants get no guarantees. The two-day orientation program, known as SOAR, welcomes incoming freshmen in groups staggered throughout the summer.

Housing, once the bane of many a student's existence, is no longer a problem now that housing is guaranteed for all. For a school this size, that's quite an accomplishment.

"There are a lot of smart people studying here," notes one student with a firm grasp of the obvious.

If there is one common characteristic among the undergraduates, it is aggressiveness.

Dorms are either coed or single-sex and come equipped with laundry facilities, game rooms, and lounges. Most also have a cafeteria. The student union also offers two meal plans, and there are plenty of restaurants and fast-food places nearby. Campus safety is always an issue, but the school offers a variety of services for those on campus. There are escort services for those walking and those needing a ride, and a free shuttle system that operates seven days a week. Madison (a.k.a. Madtown) has been the stomping ground for many fine rock 'n' roll or blues bands on the road to fame.

There are more film clubs than anyone can follow, and everyone has a favorite bar. "This is Wisconsin, don't forget, and everybody drinks a lot of beer. If you don't drink, then you'll have to be quite comfortable with that," says one teetotaler, "because peer pressure can be quite overwhelming." About 10 percent of the men and 18 percent of the women go Greek. "Frat parties are a very popular break from the bar scene," reports one expert on both options. One old standby that is still as popular as ever is the student union, which hosts bands, shows, and so forth and provides a great atmosphere in which to hang out. Nature enthusiasts can lose themselves in the university's twelve thousand-acre nature preserve. Ski slopes are close at hand, but be prepared to confront thermometers that read twenty below zero.

> **"Frat parties are a very popular break from the bar scene."**

The students at this Big Ten school show "tons of interest" in sports, especially hockey and football, and especially when the Badgers try to rout the University of Minnesota's Gophers. Bucky Badger apparel, emblazoned with slogans ranging from the urbane to the decidedly uncouth, is ubiquitous. However, the much-acclaimed marching band known as Fifth Quarter may outdo all the teams in popularity. The Badgers are recent Big Ten champions in a number of sports, notably women's cross-country and men's basketball and indoor and outdoor track. The men's soccer team won the NCAA Division I championship recently, a feat that will undoubtedly draw attention to the school's athletic program.

All in all, Madison is a school that students sum up as "diverse, intellectual, fashionable, and moderately hedonistic." And these are the qualities that attract bright and energetic students from everywhere. "You feel you're accepted for who you are no matter what," says one student. "It's so nice to just be yourself." Perhaps one of the best and most well-rounded state schools around, Madison is truly a best buy.

Overlaps

University of Michigan, Northwestern, University of Illinois, Indiana, Boston University

If You Apply To ➤   **Wisconsin:** Rolling admissions: Feb. 1. Financial aid: Mar. 1. Guarantees to meet the demonstrated need of in-state admits. Campus interviews: recommended, informational. No alumni interviews. SATs or ACTs: required (ACTs required for Wisconsin residents). SAT IIs: optional. Essay question: personal statement. Special consideration given to students from disadvantaged backgrounds. Apply to particular school.

Wittenberg University

P.O. Box 720, Springfield, OH 45501

Wittenberg is a outpost of cozy Midwestern friendliness. Less national than Denison or Wooster, Witt has plenty of old-fashioned school spirit and powerhouse Division III athletic teams. Top students should aim for the honors and fellows programs, the latter providing a chance for undergraduate research.

Founded in 1845 by German Lutherans, Wittenberg University remains true to its faith by emphasizing strong student-faculty relationships—and making sure that students don't become too comfortable in the campus bubble. In fact, before granting their diplomas, Wittenberg requires students to complete thirty hours of community service in the surrounding town of Springfield (pop. 70,000). "There are great traditions and amazing ways to get involved here," says a junior, who adds that students' biggest complaint is that "it's over in four years!" A new president is helping the school grow and evolve, raising substantial sums of money for new academic and residential buildings, and to upgrade technological capabilities.

The Wittenberg campus is classic Midwestern collegiate, with a mixture of Gothic and 1960s-style buildings on seventy rolling acres in southwestern Ohio. The redbrick Myers residence hall, with picturesque white pillars and an open-air dome dating from the nineteenth century, stands at the center. Matthies House provides a home for the Wittenberg Honors Program, while construction of Hollenbeck Hall, a state-of-the-art learning center, was recently finished. There's also a new $15 million humanities center, and a $24 million science center.

> **"There are great traditions and amazing ways to get involved here."**

Wittenberg's general education requirements emphasize a solid liberal arts background. The school's Wittenberg Plan includes sixteen learning goals, ranging from experience with writing and research to exposure to the natural sciences and foreign languages. Students select courses from a variety of disciplines to fulfill the goals, and also must fulfill requirements in religion or philosophy, non-Western cultures, and physical education. All first-year students take the interdisciplinary Common Learning Course, focused on contemporary social issues and taught by faculty advisors. Wittenberg is also currently developing a new "First Year Experience." New additions to the curriculum include a communications major and a $2 million Freeman Grant, which will allow students pursuing East Asian studies to take a term abroad. The honors program is being upgraded; there is also a University Scholars Program for outstanding freshmen, while the Wittenberg Fellows Program provides opportunities to work on research with faculty members.

Wittenberg students give high marks to the school's education department, which a freshman calls "one of the best in the country," as well as to programs in biology, English, and business—so perhaps it's not surprising that the most popular majors on campus are management, biology, and education, in that order. Students are highly motivated, but also "very friendly and excited to meet new people—they are not judgmental and superficial," says a junior. "Competition is not so much against other students as it is against yourself," a classmate adds. "The professors continually challenge students to put forth their best work." Even so, an education major says faculty members are "more than

> **"Rooms are a decent size, with lots of space for storage."**

willing to meet with students to discuss assignments, class lectures, or assist students with problems." Administrators say weak spots include philosophy, geography, and physics.

Despite Wittenberg's small size, students say they have no trouble registering for needed courses, and graduating in four years—though a junior warns it's hard to complete requirements for an education degree if students don't choose that program freshman year, and a classmate says music majors often take longer. Still, if students declare their major on time and complete the proper coursework in the correct order, the college guarantees a degree in four years—and will pay for any additional necessary courses. Wittenberg also encourages students to take a semester or a year away from campus, either in the U.S. or abroad. Options include the International Student Exchange Program, field study in the Bahamas or Costa Rica,

Website: www.wittenberg.edu
Location: City outskirts
Total Enrollment: 2,225
Undergraduates: 2,100
Male/Female: 46/54
SAT Ranges: V 545–640
 M 535–635
ACT Range: 24–28
Financial Aid: 80%
Expense: Pr $ $
Phi Beta Kappa: Yes
Applicants: 2,610
Accepted: 83%
Enrolled: 30%
Grad in 6 Years: 72%
Returning Freshmen: 85%
Academics: ✎ ✎ ✎
Social: ☎ ☎ ☎
Q of L: ★ ★ ★
Admissions: (800) 677-7558
Email Address:
 admission@wittenberg.edu

Strongest Programs
 Biology
 Political Science
 English
 Psychology
 Chemistry
 Education
 Fine Arts
 Theater

All first-year students take the interdisciplinary Common Learning Course, focused on contemporary social issues and taught by faculty advisors.

Wittenberg is currently developing a new "First Year Experience." New additions to the curriculum include a communications major and a $2 million Freeman Grant, which will allow students pursuing East Asian studies to take a term abroad.

work with the National Institutes of Health in Washington, D.C., or a term at the United Nations in New York. Wittenberg also offers 3–2 engineering programs with Columbia, Case Western Reserve, and Washington University in St. Louis.

Fifty-eight percent of Wittenberg students are native Ohioans, and many others are from nearby states like Pennsylvania, though 3 percent are from other countries. African-Americans comprise 7 percent of the student body, and Hispanics and Asian-Americans add 2 percent each. The school's multicultural-affairs director is working to boost those numbers through changes in minority recruiting and advising. "Some of the issues on campus are gay rights, human rights and alcohol usage," says an early childhood education major. "Political correctness is very respected." Wittenberg offers an unlimited number of merit scholarships, ranging from $5,000 to full tuition, but ño athletic scholarships.

Wittenberg students are required to live on campus their first two years. After that, most chose nearby houses and apartments owned by the school. "The dorms have all been updated with Internet access, some with air-conditioning and cable TV," says a sociology and women's studies major. "Rooms are a decent size, with

"The environment allows you to be whoever you wish to be."

lots of space for storage. Sophomore students have first pick on rooms, and then the freshmen are assigned to the remaining rooms," so almost everyone gets a double when he or she first comes to campus. Greek groups draw 15 percent of the men and 35 percent of the women; members may live in chapter houses. Marriott provides the chow in Witt's dining hall, which has been rated the company's best college food service. Choices range from burgers to made-to-order breakfasts to monthly theme dinners.

When the weekend rolls around, social life centers on parties in houses, dorm rooms and apartments, on and near campus. Greek groups, the Union Board, and the Residence Hall Association also bring in guest speakers and movies, comedians, and concerts. The school's alcohol policy includes large fines and counseling for unlucky under-twenty-one-year-olds caught drinking—but that doesn't stop them from trying, says a junior. "It is more difficult as a freshman, because everyone knows that you are underage, but after that, it is pretty easy," the student says. Favorite annual events include Greek Week, Homecoming ("the alumni involvement is incredible"), and Wittfest in May, "a music festival with games, food, prizes, and socializing before finals," says an early childhood education major. "It is like a big block party—everyone goes!" adds a junior. While Springfield has movie theaters, a mall, restaurants, and a $15 million performing arts center, students with cars do like to get out of town. Popular road trips include Dayton (thirty minutes), Columbus (sixty minutes), and Cincinnati (ninety minutes), and for those with more time, Washington, D.C., New York City, and Windsor, Canada (to gamble). Nearby state parks also offer swimming, camping, and picnics in the warmer months, and skiing in the winter.

While not as well known as many of its bigger Midwestern brethren, Wittenberg's athletic teams are competitive in Division III. Recent championship teams include men's football, basketball, and track, and women's field hockey, volleyball, and basketball. Rivalries with the College of Wooster (football and basketball) and Allegheny College (football) really get students riled up. Even weekend warriors may take advantage of the Bill Edwards Athletic and Recreational Complex, which boasts a stadium and eight-lane track, football and soccer fields, twelve lighted tennis courts, and a weight room, plus a pool and racquetball courts.

Wittenberg's motto demonstrates the school's can-do spirit: "Having the light, we pass it on to others." Ambitious? Yes. Unrealistic? Students don't think so. Continuing emphasis on the personal touch has kept the close-knit feeling alive on campus, despite physical growth and an increasing emphasis on technology. "It is not uncommon for someone you have never met to greet you with a warm hello as

Overlaps

Miami University (OH), Denison, College of Wooster, Ohio Wesleyan, DePauw

you pass on the street," says an English major. "The environment allows you to be whoever you wish to be."

Wofford College

429 North Church Street, Spartanburg, SC 29303-3663

Wofford is about one-third as big as Furman and roughly the same size as Presbyterian. With more than a few gentleman jocks, Wofford is one of the smallest institutions to compete in NCAA Division I. Fraternities and sororities dominate the traditional social scene.

Wofford College is a study in contrasts. The school's average SAT score—1212—is greater than the size of its student body. It's spitting distance from both Georgia and North Carolina, but two-thirds of the students are South Carolina natives. And perhaps most unusually, Wofford offers the rigorous academics of a small liberal arts college with rough-and-tumble Division I athletics. Wofford students take pride in the Wofford Way, combining a well-rounded curriculum with career-related internships and study abroad. What makes this undiscovered gem special? "Students and faculty who are serious about studies, but never too busy to have a conversation over sweet tea," says a senior.

Wofford is near the heart of Spartanburg, a mid-size city in the northwest corner of South Carolina. Founded in 1854, it's one of fewer than two hundred existing American colleges that opened before the Civil War—and it still operates on its original 140-acre campus. Azaleas, magnolias, and dogwoods surround the distinctive, twin-towered Main Building and four original faculty homes. The Milliken Science Center has

"You don't come to Wofford, you join it."

undergone a $10 million modernization and expansion, blending a 1959 structure with 110,000 square feet of new space for the chemistry, biology, psychology, and physics departments. Spearheading the effort was Wofford's new president, Benjamin Dunlap, a Rhodes Scholar and Harvard Ph.D.

Students rave about Wofford's programs in biology and economics. About two dozen of the school's 260 graduates go on to graduate medical or dental programs within two years of graduation, and President Dunlap has recruited Dr. Warren Derrick, director of pediatrics at the University of South Carolina (and Wofford '60) to guide premeds with case-based lectures every Friday. For aspiring entrepreneurs, Wofford's alumni network has clout: more than 1,200 of its 15,000 living graduates serve as presidents or owners of corporations or organizations. Prospective engineers may apply for 3–2 programs with Clemson or New York's Columbia University. Religion, English, and foreign language, and study-abroad programs, also get high marks, especially for the one lucky junior chosen as the Presidential International Scholar. This student is sent around the world, all expenses paid, to study an issue of global importance for a year. In 2002, Kris Neely traveled seven seas and seven rivers

Website: www.wofford.edu
Location: Small city
Total Enrollment: 1,107
Undergraduates: 1,107
Male/Female: 52/48
SAT Ranges: V 550–650
M 570–660
ACT Range: 22–27
Financial Aid: 55%
Expense: Pr $ $
Phi Beta Kappa: Yes
Applicants: 1,209
Accepted: 82%
Enrolled: 25%
Grad in 6 Years: 79%
Returning Freshmen: 87%
Academics: ✐ ✐ ✐
Social: ☎ ☎
Q of L: ★ ★ ★
Admissions: (864) 597-4130
Email Address:
admissions@wofford.edu

Strongest Programs
Biology/Premed
English/Creative Writing
Finance/Accounting
Computer Science
Foreign Languages

The Greek system is a huge force in Wofford's social life, with fraternities attracting 56 percent of the men and 65 percent of the women.

to examine the spiritual, economic, sociological, historical, and political connections between peoples and waters. When he returned to campus, Neely worked with two faculty members to incorporate this theme into a freshman seminar.

Wofford's distribution requirements include six credit hours of English, three to four hours of fine arts, three to six hours of foreign languages, three hours of freshman humanities, eight hours of natural science (double that for B.S. candidates), and three credit hours each of Western civilization, philosophy, religion, and math. Also mandated are two credit hours of physical education. As Wofford uses the 4–1–4 academic calendar, students squeeze these requirements into their longer semesters, and use the January Interim to study a single topic in depth. Professors have high standards, and students feel pressure to meet them because they have personal relationships with the faculty, says a finance major. "The majority of classes are manageably difficult, with an emphasis on reading great works, written analysis of those works, and an ability to link the principles and ideals gleaned from them," explains a government and German major.

Most Wofford students (89 percent) are white, and three-quarters graduated from public high school—half in the top tenth of their class. They're generally polite, friendly, and politically conservative, says a senior, and they seek balance between studying and socializing. Most are also "Southern born and raised, from upper-middle-class families," a classmate adds. "Almost everyone is 'connected' in society." African-Americans comprise 8 percent of Wofford's total, Asian-Americans 2 percent, and Hispanics 1 percent. The school has implemented a summer program, led by a female African-American faculty member, to attract more Spartanburg County minorities and women to the sciences. The biggest political issues on campus are not boosting diversity or gay rights, but controlling underage drinking and mitigating the Greek influence.

"I can't walk to class without seeing tons of people I know."

Eighty-eight percent of Wofford's students live in the dorms, where first-year women get doubles in Greene Hall, and their male counterparts have similar digs in Marsh Hall. "Usually after freshman year, students get suites with cubes—little rooms just big enough for a desk and bed," says a junior. "However, there are some sophomores who have to live in the freshman dorms each year." Students aren't too keen on the college cafeteria—other than as a social outlet—but they praise the Canteen, a lunchtime option that serves Southern cooking. Campus safety is good—so good, in fact, that "students' dorm-room doors are always unlocked, and many feel safe walking across campus at night," says an English major.

The Greek system is a huge force in Wofford's social life, with fraternities attracting 56 percent of the men and 65 percent of the women. Each fraternity has a house, and most host parties on every Friday and Saturday—with some kicking off the weekend on Thursday. "The 'Row' is fun, but can get old," says an accounting major. "And if you are not in a fraternity, it gets old fast." The frats are a source of steady booze for most Wofford students, even those under twenty-one. "It is not hard to get alcohol underage," despite the fact that South Carolina law says you can't have it, explains a senior. "If you get caught, it is generally because you are blatantly drunk, or have alcohol on you."

The school stepped up to Division I-AA, hoping the extra revenue and exposure from playing in big-time televised games would help it recruit better athletes. The strategy has paid off, with players like kicker Darren Brown choosing Wofford over Harvard.

Off campus, Spartanburg is home to Converse College and a few other schools, but students say it's not a great college town in terms of music or the arts. For that, students head to Greenville, Atlanta, and Charlotte, "all an easy drive," says a finance major. And almost every Wofford student participates in some type of volunteer work. Terrier Play Day brings kids from the community to campus for a fair with booths and games. Bid Day, when the fraternities tap their new members, is another annual tradition, involving "lots of mud, and then a bath in the college fountain." Every year before finals, student musicians and readers perform a Festival of Nine Lessons and Carols, perhaps praying as well for luck on their exams. The Greeks clean up their acts in time for Spring Weekend, a sort of campus Olympics.

Historically, Wofford competed in the NAIA, later moving to Division II of the NCAA. By 1995, the school found itself stuck between two worlds—academics more similar to schools in Division III, but a football tradition dating back to 1889, and rivalries with powerhouses like Furman and Davidson. So the school stepped up to Division I-AA, hoping the extra revenue and exposure from playing in big-time televised games would help it recruit better athletes. The strategy has paid off, with players like kicker Darren Brown choosing Wofford over Harvard. But some things haven't changed. Wofford's biggest football rival remains the Citadel, and "every other year, practically the whole school packs up and heads to Charleston for the game weekend," says a senior. The school's golf team is also stellar, and baseball is up-and-coming, with plans underway for a new field. Women's soccer and basketball are also strong, with soccer player Jenny Nett recently winning First Team Academic All-America honors.

Wofford's chaplain has a saying: "You don't come to Wofford, you join it." And students say that's true, citing the close-knit community and intimate student-faculty relationships fostered by the school's small size. "Everyone knows everyone else, and we all work together," says an accounting major. "I can't walk to class without seeing tons of people I know," agrees an English major. "Everyone speaks to everyone, and Wofford students genuinely care about each other—and the college."

If You Apply To ➤ | **Wofford:** Early action: Nov. 15. Regular admissions: Feb. 1. Financial aid: Mar. 15. Housing: May 1. Meets demonstrated need of 90%. Campus interviews: recommended, informational. Alumni interviews: optional, informational. SATs or ACTs: required. SAT IIs: optional. Accepts the Common Application and electronic applications. Essay question: event, interest, experience, goal, or person who reveals something about you.

The College of Wooster

Wooster, OH 44691

Though not well-known to the general public, Wooster is renowned in academic circles and a number of foreign countries. Admission is not difficult, but graduating takes work. All students complete an independent study project in their last two years. More intellectually serious than competitors such as Denison.

Instead of teaching students *what* to think, the College of Wooster focuses on teaching students *how* to think. From the first courses of the freshman year seminar to the final day when seniors hand in their hard-won theses, the college paves each student's path to independence. This all happens within a tight-knit community that many students compare to a family. The one-to-one attention from faculty who really "probe and stimulate the students' minds" makes Wooster an intellectual refuge in the rural countryside of Ohio.

Located in the city of Wooster, Ohio, C.O.W.'s hilltop campus includes thirty-nine buildings spread over 240 acres, many designed in the English-Collegiate Gothic style and constructed of cream-colored brick. More recent buildings are trimmed in Indiana limestone or Ohio sandstone. The central arch and two towers of Kauke Hall, the central building in Quinby Quadrangle (the square around which the college grew), make it stand out. The Gault Library for Independent

Website: www.wooster.edu
Location: Small town
Total Enrollment: 1,823
Undergraduates: 1,823
Male/Female: 47/53
SAT Ranges: V 540–650
  M 530–640
ACT Range: 23–28
Financial Aid: 63%
Expense: Pr $ $
Phi Beta Kappa: Yes
Applicants: 2,357

(Continued)

Accepted: 72%

Enrolled: 31%

Grad in 6 Years: 73%

Returning Freshmen: 88%

Academics: ✑✑✑½

Social: ☎ ☎ ☎

Q of L: ★ ★ ★

Admissions: (330) 263-2322

E-mail Address:
  admissions@wooster.edu

Strongest Programs
  Chemistry
  Biology
  Geology
  History
  English
  Sociology/Anthropology
  Communications

Study offers a private carrel for each senior in the humanities and social sciences. The $2 million Longbrake Student Wellness Center opened in Spring 2002 and includes a student lounge.

What goes on behind the facades of Wooster's attractive buildings is more impressive than the structures themselves. Wooster is one of those colleges where "it's easy to get into, but hard to stay in," an English major says. The required first-year seminar in critical inquiry, limited to fifteen students per section, invites students to engage issues, questions, or ideas drawn from classical readings. The seminar is linked to the Wooster Forum, a series of first-semester lectures and events focused on a single, broad issue. "Classes are rigorous and there's no hiding here," says a senior. A French major says students take their studies seriously and the professors "push the minds of Wooster students."

Wooster's curriculum is built around the required Independent Study, which lets students explore subjects they're passionate about with faculty guidance. Independent Study has become such a part of C.O.W. that each year seniors celebrate I.S. Monday—the day they turn in their projects—with a campus-wide parade. "We are led around campus by the bagpipers," says a senior. "The whole campus shows up." Completion of the I.S. earns you a Tootsie Roll, to eat or keep for posterity next to your diploma. "It's a day all Wooster graduates will always remember!" a senior says. The college even awards $60,000 each year for student research, travel, materials purchases, or conference registration fees.

In addition to the critical inquiry seminar, three semesters of Independent Study, and six cross-discipline courses, Wooster mandates courses in writing, global and cultural perspectives, religious perspectives, and quantitative reasoning; foreign-language proficiency; and seven to nine courses in the major. Students praise faculty members for their devotion to teaching and mentoring; only a few introductory courses have teaching assistants, who run review sessions and offer extra help. "Professors are excellent, are always

> **"Professors are excellent, and are always available to students."**

available to students, and know each of their students personally," one student says. It's not uncommon for science majors to coauthor faculty papers, while students in the Jenny Investment Club manage a portion of the college's assets, with professors serving as advisors. Wooster's small size hasn't placed it at a technological disadvantage; WoosterNet links every academic and administrative building and residence hall, and labs and kiosks offer twenty-four-hour access to more than 150 microcomputers and terminals.

Wooster's most popular majors are English, sociology/anthropology, history, communication, and psychology, although the school also has strong programs in the sciences, including chemistry, biology, and geology. The foreign language departments are small but provide "individual attention to each student," a senior says. Recently, the college appointed its first full-time faculty member in Chinese language and added a professor in archeology. For those who tire of rural Ohio, a leadership and liberal learning program includes a seminar class and a week-long acquaintanceship, where participants shadow a prominent politician, executive, or other professional. Wooster also sponsors overseas programs on five continents, by itself and through the Great Lakes Colleges Association.*

Independent Study has become such a part of C.O.W. that each year seniors celebrate I.S. Monday—the day they turn in their projects—with a campus-wide parade. "We are led around campus by the bagpipers," says a senior. "The whole campus shows up."

Each year, Wooster's admissions office strives to assemble a diverse group of scholars each year, and as the college's reputation spreads, it's becoming more selective, with acceptance rates falling and freshman-retention rates improving. Still, diversity mainly extends to academic and extracurricular interest; 84 percent of the students are white, and 74 percent attended public school. Half are from Ohio. African-Americans constitute 5 percent of the student body, Asian-Americans and Hispanics just 1 percent each. That said, C.O.W. students aren't politically apathetic.

Gay rights, women's issues, the Middle East conflict, U.S.-Afghanistan relations, and even free-trade coffee pepper campus table talk. "You can choose to be involved in this or not," a senior says.

Ninety-five percent of students live on campus in nine coed and two single-sex dorms, where rooms are small but maid service is regular. Housing is a weak link at Wooster, where an English major delineates the dorms into three categories: nice, adequate, and crappy. Students stay connected with the community through the Wooster Volunteer Network; those seriously committed to service may apply to live in one of the college's twenty-six residential program houses, each of which is affiliated with a community group. Food in the two campus dining halls is getting better, more parking has been added, and all dorms are now wired for cable television. Given Wooster's location "in the middle of corn fields," security isn't an issue, students say, although emergency phones are strategically located just in case.

Wooster social life is campus-based, though students do travel to nearby colleges such as Denison, Oberlin, Kenyon, and Ohio State to combat cabin fever. Other popular road trips are Cleveland's Flats or warehouse district, and just across the border to Windsor, Canada, where there's legal gambling and a lower drinking age. That's important to some because "it is getting harder and harder for underage students to be served" on campus, says a senior. C.O.W. has no national Greek organizations, but local "sections" draw 9 percent of men and "clubs" attract 9 percent of women. One major weekend

"It is getting harder and harder for underage students to be served."

hangout is the Underground, a bar and dance club that hosts well-known bands, as well as the campus's bowling alley, pool hall, and game room. Wooster and about a quarter of its students are affiliated with the Presbyterian Church. The school's Scottish heritage can be seen in its band, which performs in bagpipes and kilts, and in its Scottish dancers, who trot on stage during the fall's Scot Spirit Day. Other annual traditions include the outdoor Party on the Green, a fall concert, and the formal Winter Gala, where students, faculty, and staff dance the night away to the sounds of a swing band.

Wooster fields a number of competitive Division III teams. Men's basketball is a spectator favorite—it and the men's baseball team have both come home with the North Coast Athletic Conference Championship title. Any match versus rival Wittenberg usually brings out the fan in Wooster students (you have to get the free tickets well ahead of time), and men's and women's soccer, swimming, and women's lacrosse have been strong in recent years.

Students agree that the "typical" C.O.W attendee is not really typical at all. "They are open minded, eager to learn, and overall, deep, interesting people," says a French major. Though the long, cold winters can cause even the most dedicated student to experience cabin fever at times, most agree that spending four years here is a fun, fulfilling way to earn a degree.

In addition to the critical inquiry seminar, three semesters of Independent Study, and six cross-discipline courses, Wooster curriculum requires courses in writing, global and cultural perspectives, religious perspectives, quantitative reasoning, and a foreign language.

Overlaps

Denison, Kenyon, Ohio Wesleyan, Wittenberg, Miami University (OH)

If You Apply To ➤

Wooster: Early decision: Dec. 1. Regular admissions and financial aid: Feb. 15. Housing: May 1. Meets demonstrated need of 100%. Campus interviews: recommended, informational. Alumni interviews: optional, informational. SATs or ACTs: required. SAT IIs: optional. Accepts the Common Application and electronic applications. Essay question: personal statement.

Worcester Polytechnic Institute

100 Institute Road, Worcester, MA 01609-2280

Small, innovative, and undergraduate-oriented, WPI is anything but a stodgy technical institute. The WPI Plan is hands-on and project-based. Teamwork is emphasized instead of competition. WPI is half the size of Rensselaer and a third as big as MIT.

Website: www.wpi.edu
Location: City outskirts
Total Enrollment: 3,887
Undergraduates: 2,823
Male/Female: 77/23
SAT Ranges: V 560–670
   M 630–720
Financial Aid: 67%
Expense: Pr $ $ $ $
Phi Beta Kappa: No
Applicants: 3,136
Accepted: 78%
Enrolled: 29%
Grad in 6 Years: 76%
Returning Freshmen: 93%
Academics: ✍ ✍ ✍ ½
Social: ☎ ☎ ☎
Q of L: ★ ★ ★ ★
Admissions: (508) 831-5286
Email Address:
   admissions@wpi.edu

Strongest Programs
   Computer Science
   Mechanical, Electrical, and
      Computer Engineering
   Biology/Biotechnology
   Biomedical Engineering

As a pioneer in engineering education, one might expect the Worcester Polytechnic Institute to have already claimed its highest honors. But with its ever-expanding academic curriculum, surprising devotion to music and theater, and dedication to hands-on undergraduate experiences, WPI is not content to rest on its laurels. The school continues to expect a lot from its students. They must complete several extensive projects, endure the seven-week semester program, and engage in real-world job experiences. But at the end their tenure here, the practicality of their education makes WPI students valuable commodities in the job market.

WPI is the third-oldest independent science and engineering school in the nation. Its compact eighty-acre campus is set atop one of Worcester's "seven hills" on the residential outskirts of town. Worcester is an industrial city (second largest in New England) and the home of fourteen colleges, most notably WPI, Clark University, and Holy Cross. Though WPI is less well known, one biotech major says the university is "still a small engineering school after 125 years. You are not just a number." These schools are brought together by the Colleges of Worcester Consortium, Inc.* This program is a one-stop academic and social gathering place on the World Wide Web where students can discover what is happening on each campus associated with the consortium.

The city is also a base for the rapidly growing Northeast biotechnology and biomedicine industry. The area is one of the nation's most successful high-technology regions, which supports WPI's project and research programs. WPI's campus borders two parks and the historic Highland Street District, where local merchants and students come together to form the neighborhood community. Old English stone buildings, complete with creeping ivy, dominate the architecture, but modern facilities dot the immaculately kept grounds. Recent changes include a high-speed Internet network, a student center, and extensive refurbishments in all dorms. Classrooms are constantly upgraded, with 75 percent now multimedia equipped with connections to satellite technology, videoconferencing abilities, and Internet hookups.

Worcester's WPI Plan fosters an academic atmosphere that is "intense but not overly competitive," says a physics major. Many courses are project oriented, bringing student teams and professors in close contact as problem-solving colleagues. The Interactive Qualifying Project has students apply technical knowledge to one of society's problems and the Major Qualifying Project represents a student's first chance to work on a truly professional-level problem. Courses provide the information students need to complete their projects, reemphasizing WPI's curriculum as one driven by knowledge and not credit. There are four

"I would say the best thing and the worst thing about our courses is that they are only seven (weeks) long."

terms per academic year at WPI, each lasting seven weeks, which students say changes the climate. "I would say the best thing and the worst thing about our courses is that they are only seven (weeks) long," says one student. "It makes you really focus on three courses, yet if you fall behind there is little time to play 'catch-up.'" But the setup allows them to speed through tough classes and enjoy an extended summer vacation. When students are not completing projects, they take three courses per term. It's difficult to graduate in four years in some majors, but classes are accessible.

The intent of WPI's unique grading system and educational philosophy is to polish social skills and develop teamwork abilities. The curriculum remains remarkably flexible for a high-powered engineering school. Standard course distribution requirements vary by major but include courses in engineering, math, and science. To promote cooperation and cohesiveness, the only recorded grades are A, B, C, or No Record. Failing grades do not appear on transcripts, and the school does not compute GPAs or class ranks.

The intent of WPI's unique grading system and educational philosophy is to polish social skills and develop teamwork abilities.

Technical writing, which was once seen as a somewhat anemic program, is growing swiftly. The most popular departments are, not surprisingly, computer science, electrical/computer engineering, mechanical engineering, biology/biotechnology, and civil/environmental engineering. "All departments have excellent reputations, yet the older ones are a little better established and equipped," says a physics major. There are also a number of interdisciplinary programs such as prelaw and international studies. An unusual program in biomedical engineering is offered in conjunction with the University of Massachusetts Medical School and Tufts University School of Veterinary Medicine. WPI also offers a rare Fire Protection Engineering program and a system dynamics major and minor. The theater technology major requires projects in set, lighting, or audio design, which means school shows often highlight cutting-edge production techniques. Nearly four hundred students participate in one of seventeen musical ensembles, one of the largest music programs among technological universities.

"All departments have excellent reputations."

In light of an increasingly interdependent global economy, WPI offers a Global Perspectives Program that spans five continents. Nearly 70 percent of WPI students visit locations including Germany, Ireland, Spain, Australia, Costa Rica, Hong Kong, and Switzerland. The school's residential project centers in New York, San Francisco, Washington, D.C., England, Denmark, Holland, Italy, Puerto Rico, or Thailand provide students with the opportunity to tackle current problems for a sponsor and spend their term working independently on a specific socio-technical assignment under the direction of one or more faculty members. The co-op program offers upperclassmen two eight-month work experiences and adds an extra half or full year to the degree program.

The most popular departments are, not surprisingly, computer science, electrical/computer engineering, mechanical engineering, biology/biotechnology, and civil/environmental engineering.

Eighty percent of students ranked in the top quarter of their high-school class. African-Americans and Hispanics together account for only 4 percent of the students, and Asian-Americans represent an additional 7 percent. The school offers five hundred merit scholarships, ranging from $8,000 to a full ride each year, but there are no athletic scholarships.

Only first-year students are guaranteed spots in the university residence halls; however, the room-assignment process usually allows upperclassmen their first, second, or third choice. There are six coed halls, including a spacious 230-bed residence hall that houses students in suites of four or six; on-campus apartments; and smaller houses for more home-like living. Half of students move, sometimes to nearby, "reasonably priced, close to school, off-campus" apartments that are within a mile of the college grounds. The dining halls offer multiple meal plans along with a choice of grill, healthy entrées, pizza, or wok items.

"There's always something to do on campus."

Thirty-five percent of the men join fraternities, and 25 percent of the women enter sororities. Of-age students may have alcohol, provided it is kept in their rooms, but underage students do find a way to imbibe. "Any student can get alcohol if they want it enough," says one student. BYOB is the required (and accepted) partying rule. In addition to Greek parties, there are student-organized coffee houses, concerts, poetry readings, movies, and pub shows. "There's always something to do on campus," says a biotechnology major. Nearby colleges such as Holy Cross, Assumption, and Clark University are linked to WPI through shuttle buses, which provide even more social and academic opportunities. Boston and Hartford are both an hour's drive away, as are ski resorts and beaches.

One of WPI's more notable campus traditions is the Goat's Head Rivalry, a grudge match between the freshman and sophomore classes that includes the Pennant Rush, a rope pull across Institute Pond, and a WPI trivia competition. The prize? A one hundred-year-old bronze goat's head trophy (the winning class's year is engraved on it.) There is also an annual festival of international culture and QuadFest, complete with carnival rides. Students say the new student center encourages cohesiveness across the campus and offers a viable alternative to the Greek domination of the social scene. One major gripe about WPI is its gender ratio: three to one male. "Come on, girls! What are you waiting for?" asks a still-hopeful senior. On the other hand, one female student complained that the ratio of girls to "date-able" guys is "probably one to one." Ouch.

While not particularly scenic, Worcester does offer a large number of clubs and restaurants and an art museum, as well as an upscale outlet shopping mall. A large multipurpose arena, the Centrum, is host to frequent concerts (like Phish and P. Diddy) and occasional visits from Boston's Bruins and Celtics and a minor league hockey team. On campus, an extremely large proportion of the student body takes part in the intercollegiate athletic activity. In recent years, field hockey, football, and men's soccer have qualified for NCAA postseason competition. The women's tennis and men's wrestling are titleholders, and women's soccer was added to the list of nineteen varsity sports. Crew is also popular with both sexes.

One of WPI's chants is fittingly mathematic: "E to the x, dydx, e to the xdx, cosine secant tangent sine, 3.14159, e, i, radical Pi, fight 'em fight 'em WPI!" If you know what any of that stuff means, you'll fit right in at WPI.

If You Apply To ➤

WPI: Early decision and early action: Nov. 15. Regular admissions: Feb. 1. Meets demonstrated need of 67%. Campus interviews: recommended, informational. Alumni interviews: optional, informational. ACTs or SATs and three SAT IIs (writing, math, and science): required. Accepts the Common Application and electronic applications. Essay questions: personal choice.

Xavier University of Louisiana

7325 Palmetto Street, New Orleans, LA 70125

Xavier's strategic location in New Orleans is its biggest drawing card. XU is bigger than a small college but smaller than most universities. Just more than 60 percent of the students are Catholic. Competes with other leading historically black institutions such as Spelman, Morehouse, and Howard.

Website: www.xula.edu
Location: City center
Total Enrollment: 3,912
Undergraduates: 3,096

Breaking out of the ordinary is par for the course at Xavier University of Louisiana, the nation's only historically African-American Roman Catholic college. The goal at XU is to prepare students for great careers while providing a strong foundation in the liberal arts. With its stellar reputation for graduating a wealth of scientists, the school's primary focus is much loftier: "The promotion of a more just and humane society." But it's not all math books and Mass at XU—the school's location in New Orleans promises students a variety of social and cultural options unique to the Big Easy.

Founded in 1915, Xavier is located near the heart of New Orleans in a quiet neighborhood that is dotted with bungalows. The focal point of the campus is the Library Resource, which, with its green roof and stately neo-Gothic architectural style, has become a landmark for those traveling by car from the New Orleans airport to the French Quarter. A closed campus green mutes the urban feel of the encroaching city, and yellow brick buildings have been erected among the older limestone structures. Xavier's U-shaped administration building marks the geographic center of the campus. Recently added recreation areas are popular, and a new Art Village is a welcomed addition for humanities majors.

"The departments that are important in setting the tone of the campus are biology, chemistry, and pharmacy," explains a student, "because more than half of Xavier's students major in these areas." It's true—in fact, nearly two-thirds of the student body majors in a science-related field. For the last three years, Xavier has led the nation in the number of undergraduate physical science degrees awarded to African-Americans, as well as the number of African-Americans placed into medical school. Xavier is also credited with educating 25 percent of all African-American pharmacists nationally. Forty-two percent of its alums go on to professional or grad schools. The university has built a national reputation as one of the most effective teaching institutions anywhere, and has been designated as one of only a few Model Institutions for Excellence by the National Science Foundation.

> **"The departments that are important in setting the tone of the campus are biology, chemistry, and pharmacy."**

Political science is a small but good department, and the psychology and education departments have been traditional strengths. Computer engineering is the newest major, and the school is trying to strengthen its small history and philosophy departments. Economics is no longer offered as a major, and departments constantly revise their curriculums to accommodate the evolving demands of the students. In addition to the many internships available, Xavier offers cooperative education programs in all fields and study-abroad programs throughout North, Central, and South America; Europe; Africa; and Japan. The Center for the Advancement of Teaching works to improve pedagogy across the curriculum and encourages African-American students to become teachers and researchers.

Xavier's undergraduate curriculum is centered on the liberal arts. All students are required to take a core of prescribed courses in theology and philosophy, the arts and humanities, communications, history and the social sciences, mathematics, and the natural sciences; freshmen also take a mandatory seminar titled "The Student and the University." The academic climate is competitive and challenging. "There are a lot of students here who came from private or Catholic schools, which contributes to their outstanding educational background," says a psychology major. Priests and nuns teach and help run the school, though the faculty and staff are composed mainly of multiracial laypeople. "Freshmen are rarely taught by anyone less than full professors," says a student. Another says that the "majority of teachers here are very thorough in what they teach, and they tend to follow a regular syllabus." Academic and career advising are well received, and registration doesn't present any major concerns.

For a historically African-American Catholic college, Xavier's student body is quite diverse. More than 60 percent of the students are non-Catholic and 13 percent are not African-American. Students come mostly from the Deep South; half are from parochial high schools, and a high percentage are second- or third-generation Xavierites. While school and career are priorities, social issues such as abortion,

(Continued)
Male/Female: 27/73
SAT Ranges: V 440–550
  M 430–540
ACT Range: 18–23
Financial Aid: 48%
Expense: Pr $
Phi Beta Kappa: No
Applicants: 3,670
Accepted: 93%
Enrolled: 26%
Grad in 6 Years: 56%
Returning Freshmen: 73%
Academics: ✏ ✏ ✏
Social: ☎ ☎ ☎
Q of L: ★ ★ ★
Admissions: (504) 483-7388
Email Address:
  apply@xula.edu

Strongest Programs
  Biology
  Chemistry
  Psychology
  Business Administration
  Prepharmacy
  Premed
  English

Xavier educates 25 percent of all African-American pharmacists nationally and has been designated as one of only a few Model Institutions for Excellence by the National Science Foundation.

New Orleans is home to the annual Mardi Gras bacchanal, the French Quarter, and a boundless buffet of smoky clubs and one-of-a-kind eateries.

contraception, and the environment are not forgotten. "Political correctness is a big issue here because it is a Catholic institution with moral religious values," says a sophomore. Merit scholarships are available for those who qualify, but financial aid is rated as just "okay." One student says "so many minorities go to Xavier and aid is very limited. Students are always begging for help."

Three of the four contemporary-looking residence halls are single-sex, and "housing is very limited," says a psychology major. "Many students live off campus because dorm rooms are scarce and the rules are very strict." Though the housing situation is far from perfect, students admit that dorm rooms are comfortable and well kept. New Orleans has one of the highest crime rates in the nation, so campus security is always an issue. Not everyone feels safe. "Security is abundant, but not very good," a senior gripes. A classmate adds, "The officers might be too obsessed with parking policies when spaces are limited."

When students tire of microscopes and Mass, they can trek into the Crescent City for a good time. "Students often go out for a night on the town where they can enjoy good music, fine dining, or great clubs," says a biology/premed major. New Orleans is home to Mardi Gras, the French Quarter, and a boundless buffet of smoky clubs and one-of-a-kind eateries.

> **"Students often go out for a night on the town where they can enjoy good music, fine dining, or great clubs."**

"It is a major college town," says a student. Back on campus, fraternities and sororities play a leading role in extracurricular and social life, though less than 10 percent of the student body goes Greek. Popular events include Culture Fest, Spring Fest, and Homecoming. "These events contain fashion shows, concerts, balls, dances, Greek shows, food, and rides," explains a sophomore. Xavier is "a non-alcohol, non-drug school," reports a psychology major. Underage drinkers return to the city where nearly anything goes. Basketball for men and women—the Gold Rush and Gold Nugget teams—is the only varsity sport, and the teams are enthusiastically supported, especially when the opponent is rival Dillard.

With its small size and high-caliber academics, students at Xavier "really feel like they are a part of their classes," a senior says. The school's emphasis on preprofessional training, its good reputation for turning out scientists, and its spiritual underpinnings gives this liberal arts college a unique place among its peers.

Overlaps

Spelman, Morehouse, Dillard, Howard, Southern University at Baton Rouge

If You Apply To ➢

Xavier: Early action: Jan. 15. Regular admissions: July 1. Financial aid: Jan. 1. Housing: March 1. Does not guarantee to meet demonstrated need. Campus interviews: optional, informational. No alumni interviews. Recommendations are very important. SATs or ACTs: required. SAT IIs: optional. No essay.

Yale University

38 Hillhouse Avenue, New Haven, CT 06520

Yale is the middle-sized member of the Ivy League's big three: bigger than Princeton, smaller than Harvard. Its widely imitated residential-college system helps Yale strike a balance between research university and undergraduate college. Gritty New Haven pales next to Cambridge or Morningside Heights.

Tradition is more than just a buzzword at Yale University. Founded in 1701 by Connecticut Congregationalists concerned about "backsliding" among their counterparts at a certain school in Cambridge, Massachusetts, Yale has long been recognized as one of the nation's—and maybe the world's—finest private universities, and one of the few Ivy League schools focused on undergraduates. In recent years, though, the school has been plagued by crime, strikes by university workers, unionization drives by graduate students, and the Herculean task of repairing its aging physical plant. To reverse the decline, Yale has begun the largest construction and renovation project ever undertaken at an American university. What hasn't changed are the students. Says a junior: "Absolutely everyone here is fascinating and exceptional in some way."

Yale's campus looks like the traditional archetype—magnificent courtyards, imposing quadrangles, Gothic buildings designed by James Gamble Rogers, and Harkness Tower, a 201-foot spire once washed with acid to create its aged, stately look. A massive, $2.6 billion construction and renovation project, to be completed in 2010, is slowly transforming the university's historic buildings into state-of-the-art facilities. Leaking roofs, chipping paint, and drafty corridors in Berkeley College and Branford College—two of the twelve undergraduate residential colleges—are no more, while renovations to Saybrook College continue, as part of a $300 million effort to renovate and modernize all of the colleges, some of which date to the 1930s. Yale has also invested $500 million to build and upgrade its science facilities.

Inside Yale's wrought-iron gates, academic programs are superb across the board. Arts and humanities programs are especially outstanding—just ask Meryl Streep or Jodie Foster, both School of Drama alumnae. The prominence of the arts makes for an interesting juxtaposition: while tradition is ever-present on campus, today's Yale attracts one of the most liberal and forward-thinking student bodies in the Ivy League. Still, the

"Absolutely everyone here is fascinating and exceptional in some way."

ancient Puritan work ethic remains. Graduating from Yale requires thirty-six courses, or nine courses a year, rather than the thirty-two courses required at most other colleges. "The academic climate is intense: classes are difficult, professors are demanding, and the workload may at times seem overwhelming," says a political science major. "The pressure, though, is all self-applied. Students want to learn and want to succeed, but they also take time to help each other out." Adds a biology major: "The school is so competitive that the friends you make have to be good ones. Once you make them, comfort soon follows."

The new "Selective Excellence" policy is aimed at focusing university resources on the largest and strongest departments, such as history, law, and biomedical sciences. Under the controversial plan, smaller departments such as engineering and physical sciences would seek excellence through specialization. Some are concerned that if the plan succeeds, it will be at the expense of the university's most unique and valuable programs, but most agree that change must occur to ensure continued excellence.

Although Yale has twelve graduate schools, Yale College—the undergraduate arts and sciences division—remains the university's heart. Virtually all professors teach undergraduates, and the professional schools' resources—especially architecture, fine arts, drama, and music—are available to them as well. Yale's superb history department offers the most popular undergraduate major, followed by economics, political science, English, and biology. History also has one of the most demanding programs, including a mandatory thirty- to fifty-page senior essay. The English department is routinely at the vanguard of literary theory, while an outstanding interdisciplinary humanities major includes the study of the medieval, Renaissance, and modern periods. While the sciences are excellent, "the infamously rigorous curriculum, especially

Website: www.yale.edu
Location: Urban
Total Enrollment: 11,136
Undergraduates: 5,286
Male/Female: 50/50
SAT Ranges: V 680–770
  M 680–770
ACT Range: 28-33
Financial Aid: 52%
Expense: Pr $ $ $ $
Phi Beta Kappa: Yes
Applicants: 14,809
Accepted: 14%
Enrolled: 64%
Grad in 6 Years: 94%
Returning Freshmen: 98%
Academics: ✍ ✍ ✍ ✍ ✍
Social: ☎ ☎ ☎
Q of L: ★ ★ ★
Admissions: (203) 432-9300
Email Address:
  undergraduate.admissions
  @yale.edu

Strongest Programs
  Art and Architecture
  History
  English
  Biology
  Economics
  Political Science
  Psychology
  Music
  Drama

The ancient Puritan work ethic remains. Graduating from Yale requires thirty-six credits, or nine courses a year, rather than the thirty-two courses required at most other colleges.

organic chemistry, tends to scare people away," says a junior. "The timing of the courses, which all meet in the morning, combined with the four-hour labs, don't make people run up Science Hill."

Even science majors grumble about the walk up Science Hill, where most labs and science classrooms are, but it's worth the trip. The biology department is excellent, as is a major in molecular biochemistry and biophysics. (Both fields have a high concentration of premeds.) Architecture and modern languages, especially French, are top-notch, and the school's Center for the Study of Globalization is directed by Strobe Talbott (class of '68), a former *Time* magazine reporter who served in the State Department during the Clinton administration. Elite students with a particularly strong appetite for the humanities can enroll in Directed Studies, which examines the literature, philosophy, history, and politics of Western tradition. Prospective DSers should be prepared for some serious bonding with their books—they don't call it "Directed Suicide" for nothing.

Despite its reverence for tradition, Yale doesn't require any specific courses for graduation, and it doesn't have a core curriculum. Instead, students must take three classes in each of four broad areas: language and literature (English and foreign, ancient, or modern); humanities and arts (other than literature); social sciences, including economics; and natural sciences and math. Yale also mandates intermediate-level mastery of a foreign language, though it has never been keen on study abroad because of the belief that every Yalie should spend four full years "'neath the elms" of campus. Instead of pre-registering, students spend two weeks "shopping" at the beginning of each term, sampling morsels of the various offerings before finalizing their schedules.

Introductory-level classes at Yale are usually large lectures, accompanied by small recitation and discussion sections, typically led by graduate teaching assistants. Some of the most popular courses, such as Paul Kennedy's European history class, seem more like performances, students say. Upper-level seminars are small (capped at sixteen students) and plentiful, though especially popular ones often turn away even juniors and seniors. Fortunately, says a junior, "There are no majors that a student would have difficulty completing in four years (or less!)." Faculty members are accessible and open to questions and concerns. "The professors are excellent, and have the ability to make complex processes easy to understand, in an entertaining fashion," says a psychology major. "I actually took an intro science course taught be a Nobel laureate as a freshman," adds a political science major. As for advising, "The faculty aren't always as readily available as I would like, but they are helpful once you find them," says a sophomore.

"Students want to learn and want to succeed, but they also take time to help each other out."

Yale's libraries hold more than ten million volumes, second in size only to Harvard's. Extensive renovations are underway to repair deterioration caused by age, heavy use, and environmental conditions. The flash-cube-shaped Beinecke Rare Book Library houses many extraordinary manuscripts, including a Gutenberg Bible and some music manuscripts penned by Bach, while the most frequently used books are found underground in the Cross Campus Library. Also located in CCL are rows of study carrels, "tiny beige boxes that look like phone booths with desks in them." To Yalies, these are "weenie bins," where many a tired student has dozed on an open book.

Only 9 percent of Yale students are Connecticut natives, but nearly half the student body hails from the Northeast. Yale is also consistently more popular with women than many of its rivals, most notably Princeton; the student body is evenly split along gender lines. Most traditions unique to Yale—all-male singing groups like the Whiffenpoofs, drinking at "the tables down at Mory's"—have female counterparts if they haven't gone coed. Diversity is an issue; African-Americans make up 8 percent of the students and Hispanics 6 percent, while Asian-American enrollment is fairly large at 14 percent. Yalies are more liberal than their counterparts at Harvard and Princeton, and they aren't shy about expressing their opinions. "The anti-sweatshop movement and a push to unionize grad students as teaching fellows highlight Yale students' general concern for workers'

"There are so many opportunities and things to do at Yale that many students wish they had more time."

rights," says a senior. "Yalies seem to back good causes and follow through," says a junior. The sweatshop rally "resulted in a slight but still recognizable difference."

The residential colleges that serve as dorms—and as the focal points for undergraduate social life—are "one of the greatest attractions in a Yale education," says an ethics, politics, and economics major. "The camaraderie of the residential college system makes up for its physical shortcomings," adds a psychology major. Endowed by Yale graduate Edward S. Harkness (who also began the house system at Harvard) and modeled on those at Oxford and Cambridge, Yale's colleges provide intimate living and learning communities, creating the atmosphere of a small liberal arts college within a large research university. Each college has a library, dining hall, and special facilities such as photography darkrooms or tree swings—one is even said to have an endowment used solely for whipped cream. All colleges also have their own dean and affiliated faculty members, a few of whom live in the college, who can help undergraduates struggling to adapt to the rigors of college life. College-sponsored seminars, along with plays, concerts, lectures, and other events, add to the cultural life of the university as a whole. "There are so many opportunities and things to do at Yale that many students wish they had more time," says a wistful senior.

Much of each residential college's distinctive identity comes from its architecture. Some are fashioned in a craggy, fortress-like Gothic style, while others are done in the more open Colonial style, with red brick and green shutters as the prevailing motif. All colleges have their own special nooks and crannies with cryptic inscriptions paying tribute to illustrious Yalies of generations past. Most freshmen live together in the Old Campus, the historic nineteenth-century quadrangle, before moving into their colleges as sophomores, who, along with juniors, generally live in suites of single and double rooms. Many seniors get singles. "Prospective students should realize that the quality of their freshman year will depend on how compatible they are with their roommates," says one student. "The residential colleges and an uncooperative administration make it impossible to switch rooms." Some upperclassmen move off campus, into gritty New Haven, "which gets an awful rap, mainly because of the racial makeup of the city, when juxtaposed with the makeup of the school," says one student. "In actuality, most students feel safe," because of "numerous, efficient, and friendly" campus police officers, and plenty of visible emergency phones.

In addition to identifying with their colleges, many Yale students identify strongly with extracurricular groups, clubs, and organizations, spending most of their waking hours outside class at the newspaper, radio station, or computer center. Particularly clubby are the a cappella singing groups, whose members do everything from drinking together on certain weeknights to touring together during spring break. Students whose social tastes range to the very traditional may wish to investigate Yale's mysterious secret societies, clubs such as Skull and Bones, some of which have their own mausoleum-like clubhouses.

Though studying takes the lion's share of their time, students here also find ways to unwind, though Yale doesn't have "a great social life if you thrive for one," cautions a biology major. The campus policy regarding alcohol is simple, says a junior: "Don't endanger yourself or others, and there's no problem. The emphasis is on helping you, not accusing or attacking you, if you happen to exceed your limit."

Students whose social tastes range to the very traditional may wish to investigate Yale's mysterious secret societies, clubs such as Skull and Bones, some of which have their own mausoleum-like clubhouses.

The flash-cube-shaped Beinecke Rare Book Library houses many extraordinary manuscripts, including a Gutenberg Bible and some music manuscripts penned by Bach.

Still, the drinking age of twenty-one is enforced at larger, university-sponsored bashes, pushing most socializing to private parties in the colleges or off-campus apartments. A handful of Greek organizations have yet to make their mark. For the artistically inclined, local film societies offer numerous weekend screenings, while the Yale Repertory Theater is an excellent, innovative professional company that depends heavily on graduate-school talent but always brings in a few top stage stars each season. Natural history and art museums on and near campus, especially the British Art Center, are excellent. For those who want more excitement, the typical Yalie refrain on New Haven—"It's halfway between New York and Boston"—tells it all. Metro North trains run almost hourly to New York, and visiting Boston is nearly as easy. Storrs, Connecticut, home of UConn, is also a popular road trip.

When Yale is winning the annual Yale-Harvard football extravaganza, known as "The Game," Harvard fans have been known to taunt Yalies by shouting across the stadium, "You may be winning, but you have to go back to New Haven." That's not an enticing prospect, and may be the reason Yale's applications have failed to keep pace with those of Harvard and Princeton in recent years. "New Haven is a cosmopolitan city with a lot of interesting attractions, as well as urban problems," says a junior. Revitalization is occurring, albeit slowly, with a summer jazz festival that brings thousands to the historic town green, as well as outdoor ethnic-food fairs and theatrical performances. The city's long-standing theatrical tradition—it was once the place to try out plays headed for Broadway—has been revived with the reopening of two grand old theater and concert halls a block from campus. Locals will swear that Pepe's on Wooster Street was the first (and best!) pizza parlor in the country, while Louis's Lunch was the first true hamburger joint. Relations

> **"New Haven is a cosmopolitan city with a lot of interesting attractions, as well as urban problems."**

between students and locals are improving, and more than two-thirds of Yale undergrads do volunteer work in town through Dwight Hall, the largest college community-service organization in the country.

Yale fields a full complement of athletic teams, and the gymnastics squad brought home an Ivy League title in 2001. Men's ice hockey won championships in 1999 and 2001, while women's golf and cross-country garnered titles in 2000. The football team last won an Ivy championship in 1999, the same year it won the Harvard-Yale-Princeton crown. Each year, thousands of students take part in intramural competition among the residential colleges. The Lanman Center's fifty-seven thousand-square-foot gym and an indoor track have been added to the Whitney Gym, as have eighteen squash courts. Also new are the twenty-thousand-square-foot Israel Fitness Center and the twenty-two thousand-square-foot Gilder Boathouse.

Yale is America's third-oldest institution of higher learning, preceded only by Harvard and the College of William and Mary. Students and graduates here take seriously the intonation, "For God, for country, and for Yale"—for proof, just remember that among its alumni, Yale counts the presidents or former presidents of about seventy other colleges and universities, as well as both George Bushes who've served as president of the United States. That's pretty impressive company, as well as historic levels of achievement to which current Yalies can aspire.

Overlaps
Harvard, Stanford, Princeton, Brown, Penn

If You Apply To ➢

Yale: Early action: Nov. 1. Regular admissions: Dec. 31. Financial aid: Feb. 1. Housing: June 1. Guarantees to meet demonstrated need. Campus interviews: optional, evaluative. Alumni interviews: recommended, evaluative. SATs or ACTs: required. SAT IIs: required (any three). Accepts the Common Application and electronic applications. Essay question: personal essay; the essay you would have written if you weren't trying to say just the right thing to the admissions committee.

Consortia

Students who feel that attending a small college might limit their college experiences should realize that many of these schools have banded together to offer unusual programs that they could not support on their own. Offerings range from exchange programs—trading places with a student on another campus—to a semester or two anywhere in the world on one of the seven continents or somewhere out at sea.

The following is a list of some of the largest and oldest of these programs, some sponsored by groups of colleges and others by independent agencies. An asterisk (*) after the name of a college indicates that the institution is the subject of a write-up in *The Fiske Guide*. An asterisk following the name of a program in the college write-ups means that it is described below.

The **Associated Colleges of the Midwest** (www.acm.edu) comprises fourteen institutions in five states: Beloit,* Lawrence,* and Ripon* in Wisconsin; Carleton,* Macalester,* and St. Olaf* in Minnesota; the University of Chicago,* Knox,* Lake Forest,* and Monmouth in Illinois; Coe, Cornell,* and Grinnell* in Iowa; and Colorado College.*

The consortium offers its students semester-long programs to study art in London and Florence; culture and society in Florence, the Czech Republic, and Zimbabwe; language and culture in Costa Rica and Russia; and tropical field research in Costa Rica. Year-long programs include Chinese studies in Hong Kong, India studies, and study in Japan. The Arts of London and the Florence program are the most popular with students. Language study is a component of all the ACM overseas programs. Prior language study is required for the programs in Costa Rica, Japan, and Russia. Domestic off-campus programs include Humanities at the Newberry Library (an in-depth research project) or a semester in Chicago in the arts, urban education, or urban studies. Scientists can study at the Oak Ridge National Laboratory in Tennessee, or there's a wilderness field station in northern Minnesota.

Living arrangements vary with the program and region. Students in programs in Chicago live in apartments and residential hotels; Minnesota's wilderness enthusiasts must rough it in cabins, and Oak Ridge scientists are on their own. There are no comprehensive costs for any of the ACM programs, domestic or foreign, and tuition is based on the home school's standard fees. The programs are open to sophomores, juniors, and seniors majoring in all fields. The only programs that tend to be especially strict with admissions are the Oak Ridge, Newberry, and Russian arrangements. For information, contact Associated Colleges of the Midwest, 18 South Michigan Ave., Chicago, IL 60603, (312) 263-5000.

The **Associated Colleges of the South** (www.colleges.org), incorporated in 1991, is composed of twelve southern schools (Birmingham-Southern,* Centenary, Centre,* Millsaps,* Rhodes,* University of the South,* Furman University, Hendrix College,* Morehouse College,* Southwestern University, Trinity University,* and the University of Richmond*). Established to strengthen liberal education in the South, the consortium focuses on academic program development (with attention to international programs), and faculty, staff, and student development. Overseas courses are offered year-round. Affiliated and ACS-managed programs are offered at Oxford, in Central Europe, and in Brazil. For information, contact the Associated Colleges of the South, 17 Executive Park Dr., Suite 420, Atlanta, GA 30329, (404) 636-9533.

The **Atlanta Regional Consortium for Higher Education** (www.atlantahighered.org) comprises twenty public and private colleges and universities in the Atlanta area, as well as several specialized institutions of higher education. Members are Agnes Scott College,* Atlanta College of Art, Clark Atlanta University,* Clayton College and State University, Columbia Theological Seminary, Emory University,* Georgia Institute of Technology,* Georgia State University, State University of West Georgia, Institute of Paper Science and Technology, Interdenominational Theological Center, Kennesaw State University, Mercer University, Morehouse College,* Morehouse School of Medicine, Morris Brown College,* Oglethorpe University,* Southern Polytechnic State University, Spelman College,* and the University of Georgia.*

Students from member colleges and universities may register for approved courses at any of the other institutions, including those with highly specialized courses. The consortium's interlibrary lending program uses a daily truck delivery service to put more than ten million books and other resources at students' disposal.

The **Christian College Consortium** (www.ccconsortium.org) comprises thirteen of the nation's top evangelical liberal arts schools: Asbury, Bethel (MN), George Fox, Gordon,* Greenville, Houghton,* Malone, Messiah, Seattle Pacific, Taylor, Trinity (IL), Westmont, and Wheaton (IL).*

The consortium offers a "student visitors program" whereby students can spend a semester—with little paper pushing—at any of the member schools. More than one hundred students (not including freshmen) participate each year, and the cost is strictly the home school's regular fees. Other than a reasonably good grade average, there are no special requirements. Consortium schools share a wide array of international programs on a space-available basis, and the consortium has cooperative arrangements with Daystar University College in Nairobi, Kenya, and Han Nam University in Taejon, Korea.

The **Five College Consortium** (www.fivecolleges.edu) is a nonprofit organization that comprises Amherst,* Hampshire,* Mount Holyoke,* Smith,* and the University of Massachusetts at Amherst,* and is designed to enhance the social and cultural life of the thirty thousand students attending these Connecticut Valley colleges. Legally known as Five Colleges Inc., this cooperative arrangement allows any undergraduate at the four private liberal arts colleges and UMass to take courses for credit and use the library facilities of any of the other four schools. A free bus service shuttles among the schools.

The consortium sponsors joint departments in dance and astronomy, as well as a number of interdisciplinary programs, including black studies, East Asian languages, coastal and marine sciences, Near Eastern studies, peace and world security studies, Canadian studies, and Irish studies. Certificate programs are available in African studies and Latin American studies. There are five college centers for East Asian studies, women's studies research, and foreign language resources. Students from the four smaller colleges benefit from the large number of course choices available at the university. The undergrads from UMass, in turn, take advantage of the small-college atmosphere as well as particularly strong departments such as art at Smith, sculpture at Mount Holyoke, and film and photography at Hampshire. There is also a Five College Orchestra and an open theater auditions policy that allows students to audition for parts in productions at any of the colleges. The social and cultural aspects of the Five College Consortium are more informal than the academic structure. The consortium puts out a calendar listing art shows, lectures, concerts, and films at the five schools, as well as the bus schedules. In addition, student-sponsored parties are advertised on all campuses, and there is a good deal of informal meeting of students from the various schools.

For those students taking courses on other campuses, one's home-school meal ticket is valid on any of the five member campuses for lunch. Dinners are available with special permission. Taking classes at other schools is encouraged, but not usually for first-semester freshmen. The consortium is a big drawing card for all schools involved.

The **Great Lakes Colleges Association** (www.glca.org) comprises twelve independent liberal arts institutions in three states: Antioch,* Denison,* Kenyon,* Oberlin,* Ohio Wesleyan,* and the College of Wooster* in Ohio; DePauw,* Earlham,* and Wabash* in Indiana; and Albion,* Hope,* and Kalamazoo* in Michigan. Like ACM, the Great Lakes group offers students off-campus opportunities both in the U.S. and overseas.

For adventures abroad, there are African studies programs in Sierra Leone, Senegal, and Kenya. Students can spend a year studying in Scotland or Japan, or a semester comparing socioeconomic changes in Poland, the United Kingdom, and Germany (European Academic Term). GLCA cosponsors five programs mentioned in the ACM write-up above, but these sometimes cost more: a fall or a year at a People's Republic of China university; study in Hong Kong, Russia, or the Czech Republic; and programs at the Newberry Library in Chicago and Oak Ridge National Laboratory in Tennessee. Other domestic programs include a one-semester arts internship in New York City and a liberal arts urban-study semester in Philadelphia.

Primarily juniors participate, but the programs are open to sophomores and seniors. New York and Philadelphia are the most popular domestic plans, and Scotland is the largest of those abroad. There are language requirements to meet in several of the programs, such as a year of Mandarin for China, a year of Japanese for Japan, and two years of Russian for Russia. Sometimes, however, an intensive summer language program can be substituted. Contact GLCA, 2929 Plymouth Rd., Suite 207, Ann Arbor, MI 48105-3206, (313) 761-4833.

The **Lehigh Valley Association of Independent Colleges** (www.lvaic.org) is a twenty-three-year-old cooperative effort among six colleges in the same area of Pennsylvania: Allentown College of St. Francis de Sales, Cedar Crest College, Lafayette College,* Lehigh University,* Moravian College, and Muhlenberg College.*

Approximately four hundred students each year cross-register at member campuses, although the bulk of the activity occurs between schools that are closest to each other. A Jewish studies program, headquartered at Lehigh, draws on the faculties of Lehigh, Lafayette, and Muhlenberg. Faculty members travel from college to college in order to offer students a variety of courses in this field. The association's Consortium Professors program puts faculty on two other member campuses each year to teach unusual or special-interest courses. Several members exchange courses by video conference. Special seminars are arranged at central locations for selected students, with transportation provided. The association offers a cooperative cultural program sponsoring nationally known visiting dance companies. Students at each college are eligible for reduced-rate tickets to plays and other events on campuses of association schools. But the most frequently used service of the association is its interlibrary loan program, which permits students at one institution to use the research facilities of the others. Summer study-abroad programs take students to Germany, Spain, Mexico, or Israel.

The **Maritime Studies Program** of Williams College and Mystic Seaport Museum is an interdisciplinary semester designed for twenty-two undergraduates (primarily juniors, but some second-semester sophomores and seniors) who are eager to augment liberal arts education with an in-depth study of the sea. Participants take four Williams College courses (maritime history, literature of the sea, marine policy, and oceanography or marine ecology). Classes are taught with an emphasis on independent research in the setting of the Mystic Seaport Museum. Classroom lectures are enhanced by hands-on experience in celestial navigation, boat building, sailing, blacksmithing, and other historic crafts. Students spend two weeks offshore in deep-sea oceanographic research aboard a traditionally rigged schooner highlighting the purpose of the program: to understand our relationship with the sea—past, present, and future.

Most students are drawn from twenty affiliate colleges: Amherst,* Bates,* Bowdoin,* Colby,* Colgate,* Connecticut,* Dartmouth,* Hamilton,* Middlebury,* Mount Holyoke,* Oberlin,* Smith,* Trinity,* Tufts,* Union,* Vassar,* Wellesley,* Wesleyan,* Wheaton (MA),* and Williams.* Credit is granted through Williams College, and financial aid is transferable. Students from all four-year liberal arts colleges are encouraged to apply. Write to the Maritime Studies Program, Box 6000 Mystic Seaport Museum, Mystic, CT 06355-0990, (302) 572-5359.

Sea Semester (www.sea.edu, not to be confused with Semester at Sea) is a similar venture for water lovers, but it is designed for students geared more toward the theoretical and practical applications of the subject. Five twelve-week sessions are offered each year, and there are forty-eight students in each session. One prerequisite for the program is a course in college-level lab science or the equivalent. All majors are considered as long as they're in good academic standing, submit transcripts and recommendations, and have an interview with an alumnus in their area.

Students spend the first half of the term living on Sea's campus in the Woods Hole area and immersing themselves in oceanography and maritime and nautical studies. Independent-study projects begun ashore are completed during the sea component aboard either a schooner or a brigantine, which cruises along the eastern seaboard and out into the Atlantic, North Atlantic, or Caribbean, depending on the season. Six weeks on the ocean is when theory becomes reality, and the usual mission consists of enough navigation, oceanographic data collection, and recordkeeping to keep even Columbus on the right course.

Students from affiliated colleges (Boston U,* College of Charleston,* Colgate,* Cornell,* Drexel,* Eckerd,* Franklin and Marshall,* the U. of Pennsylvania,* and Rice University*) receive a semester's worth of credit directly through their school. Students from other schools must receive credit through Boston U. Write to the Sea Education Association, P.O. Box 6, Woods Hole, MA 02543.

Semester at Sea (www.semesteratsea.com) takes qualified students from any college and whisks them around the globe on a study/cruise odyssey. Based at the University of Pittsburgh, this nonprofit group takes 450 students each term (from second-semester freshmen to grads) and puts them on a ship bound for almost everywhere. The vessel itself is a college campus in its own right. Sixty courses are taught by two dozen professors in subjects ranging from anthropology to marketing, and usually stressing the international scene as well as the sea itself. What's more, art, theater, music, and other extras can be found on board. When students aren't at sea, they're in port in any of twelve foreign countries throughout India, the Middle East, the Commonwealth of Independent States (Russia), the Far East, Africa, South America, and the Mediterranean, and it's not uncommon for leaders and diplomats to meet them along the way.

Students must be in good standing at their home colleges to be considered, which often means a GPA of 2.5 or better. Some financial aid is available in the form of the usual federal grants and loans, and thirty eligible students can use a work/study plan to pay for half the trip. Most colleges do recognize the Semester at Sea program and will provide participating students with a full term's worth of credits. Information may be obtained by writing to Semester at Sea, University of Pittsburgh, 811 William Pitt Union, Pittsburgh, PA 15260, (800) 854-0195 or (412) 648-7490.

The **Seven-College Exchange** consists of four women's colleges (Hollins,* Mary Baldwin, Randolph-Macon Woman's,* and Sweet Briar*), one men's school (Hampden-Sydney*), and two coed schools (Randolph-Macon College and Washington and Lee*). The exchange program was more popular when it began almost two decades ago and was utilized mainly for social reasons. Today the exchange program is used mainly for academic reasons and enables students to take advantage of courses offered on the other campuses. Eligibility for participation is determined by the home institution, and except for special fees, rates are those of the home institution. Designed primarily for juniors, the program also considers sophomores and seniors as applicants. Several participating members sponsor study-abroad programs.

The **Twelve-College Exchange Program** comprises a dozen selective schools in the Northeast: Amherst,* Bowdoin,* Connecticut College,* Dartmouth,* Mount Holyoke,* Smith,* Trinity,* Vassar,* Wellesley,* Wesleyan,* Wheaton (MA),* and Williams.*

The federation means that students enrolled in any of these schools can visit for a semester or two (usually the latter) with a minimum of red tape. Approximately three hundred students utilize the opportunity each year; most of them are juniors. Placement is determined mainly by available space, but students need also display good academic standing. While the home college arranges the exchange, students must meet the fees and standards of the host school. Financial-aid holders can usually carry their packages with them. Also available through this exchange is participation in the Williams College–Mystic Seaport Program in American maritime studies or study at the Eugene O'Neill National Theater Institute.

The **Venture Program** is based at Brown University, but has at various times counted many of the most prestigious East Coast and Midwestern colleges and universities in its membership. The eight current member institutions include Bates,* Brown,* Connecticut College,* Hobart and William Smith,* College of the Holy Cross,* Swarthmore College,* Vassar,* and Wesleyan.*

Venture, established in 1973, places students who want to take time off from college in short-term, full-time jobs in many fields of interest and geographic locations. Venture provides students with an opportunity to test academic, career, and personal interests on the job. There is no cost to students or employers for participation. Venture is supported by member institutions. About two hundred students apply to the program, and about half of them are eventually placed in positions. All students attending a member college are eligible to participate. Venture also works with students who want to take time off between high school and college. In 1987, the consortium initiated the Venture II program, which encourages graduating seniors from member schools to explore work opportunities in the not-for-profit sector. The consortium also operates the Urban Education Semester in collaboration with the Bank Street College of Education and Community School District Number 4 in New York City, introducing liberal arts undergraduates to issues and practice in urban education. All of Venture's programs aim to foster social awareness and responsibility among students and build connections between higher education and the community.

The **Washington Semester of American University** takes about 750 students each year from hundreds of colleges across the country (who meet minimum academic qualifications of a 2.75 GPA) and gives them unbeatable academic and political opportunities in the nation's capital. The program is the oldest of its kind in Washington.

Students take part in a semester of seminars with policymakers and lobbyists, an internship, and a choice between an elective course at the university or a self-designed, in-depth research project. Students live in dorms on the campus, and are guided by a staff of twenty American University professors.

Ninety percent of the students are drawn from 192 affiliated schools. Although admissions competition depends on the home school and how many it chooses to nominate, the average GPA hovers around a 3.3. Most who participate are juniors, but second-semester sophomores and seniors get equal consideration. The cost is either American University's tuition, room, board, and fees or that of the home school. Just over a third of the affiliated colleges are profiled in *The Fiske Guide*.

The **Worcester Consortium** is made up of ten institutions nestled in and about Worcester, Massachusetts: Anna Maria, Assumption, Becker Junior, Clark University,* Holy Cross,* Quinsigamond Community, Tufts University of Veterinary Medicine, the University of Massachusetts Medical Center, Worcester Polytechnic Institute,* and Worcester State. Member schools coordinate activities ranging from purchasing light bulbs to sharing libraries, and a bus transports scholars to the various campuses as well as public libraries. Academic cross-registration is offered, as are two special programs: a health studies option and a certificate in gerontology. The consortium calendar lists upcoming events on each campus and encourages community service with a special emphasis on college/school collaboration. The consortium also provides free academic and financial-aid counseling to low-income, first-generation students thinking about college. Write the Educational Opportunity Center, 26 Franklin St., Worcester, MA 01608.

Index

A

Agnes Scott College, 1
Alabama, University of, 3
Albertson College, 6
Albion College, 8
Alfred University, 10
Allegheny College, 12
Alma College, 15
Alverno College, 17
American University, 19
Amherst College, 21
Antioch College, 24
Arizona, University of, 27
Arizona State University, 29
Arkansas, University of, 31
Atlantic, College of the, 38
Auburn University, 41
Austin College, 43

B

Babson College, 45
Bard College, 47
Barnard College, 50
Bates College, 53
Baylor University, 55
Beloit College, 57
Bennington College, 60
Birmingham-Southern College, 62
Boston College, 64
Boston University, 66
Bowdoin College, 69
Brandeis University, 73
Brigham Young University, 74
British Columbia, University of,
115
Brown University, 77
Bryn Mawr College, 81
Bucknell University, 83

C

California colleges and universities,
87
California, University of–Berkeley, 88
California, University of–Davis, 91
California, University of–Irvine, 93
California, University of–Los
Angeles, 95

California, University of–Riverside,
98
California, University of–San Diego,
100
California, University of–Santa
Barbara, 103
California, University of–Santa
Cruz, 105
California Institute of Technology,
108
Calvin College, 111
Canadian universities, 113
Carleton College, 124
Carnegie Mellon University, 127
Case Western Reserve University, 129
Catholic University of America,
The, 132
Centre College, 135
Charleston, College of, 137
Chicago, University of, 139
Cincinnati, University of, 142
Claremont Colleges, 144
Claremont McKenna College, 146
Clark College, 34
Clark University, 157
Clarkson University, 159
Clemson University, 161
Colby College, 163
Colgate University, 166
Colorado College, 169
Colorado, University of–Boulder, 171
Colorado School of Mines, 174
Columbia College, 176
Connecticut, University of, 179
Connecticut College, 182
Cooper Union, 185
Cornell College, 187
Cornell University, 189

D

Dallas, University of, 193
Dartmouth College, 196
Davidson College, 200
Dayton, University of, 202
Deep Springs College, 205
Delaware, University of, 207
Denison University, 210

Denver, University of, 212
DePaul University, 215
DePauw University, 217
Dickinson College, 219
Drew University, 222
Drexel University, 224
Duke University, 226

E

Earlham College, 230
Eckerd College, 233
Emerson College, 235
Emory University, 237
Evergreen State College, The, 240

F

Fairfield University, 242
Florida Institute of Technology, 247
Florida, University of, 245
Florida State University, 249
Fordham University, 252
Franklin and Marshall College, 254
Furman University, 257

G

George Mason University, 259
George Washington University, 261
Georgetown University, 264
Georgia, University of, 267
Georgia Institute of Technology, 269
Gettysburg College, 272
Gordon College, 274
Goucher College, 276
Grinnell College, 278
Guilford College, 281
Gustavus Adolphus College, 284

H

Hamilton College, 286
Hampden-Sydney College, 289
Hampshire College, 291
Hartwick College, 294
Harvard University, 296
Harvey Mudd College, 148
Haverford College, 300
Hawaii, University of–Manoa, 303
Hendrix College, 305

Hiram College, 307
Hobart and William Smith
    Colleges, 310
Hollins University, 312
Holy Cross, College of the, 314
Hood College, 317
Hope College, 319
Houghton College, 322
Howard University, 324

I

Illinois, University of–Urbana-
    Champaign, 326
Illinois Institute of Technology, 329
Illinois Wesleyan University, 332
Indiana University, 334
Iowa, University of, 337
Iowa State University, 339
Ithaca College, 341

J

James Madison University, 344
Johns Hopkins University, The, 346

K

Kalamazoo College, 349
Kansas, University of, 352
Kentucky, University of, 354
Kenyon College, 357
Knox College, 360

L

Lafayette College, 362
Lake Forest College, 365
Lawrence University, 368
Lehigh University, 370
Lewis and Clark College, 373
Louisiana State University, 376
Loyola University–New Orleans, 378

M

Macalester College, 380
Maine, University of–Orono, 382
Manhattanville College, 384
Marlboro College, 386
Marquette University, 389
Maryland, University of–College
    Park, 391
Mary Washington College, 393
Massachusetts, University
    of–Amherst, 395

Massachusetts Institute of
    Technology, 398
McGill University, 117
Miami, University of, 401
Miami University (OH), 403
Michigan, University of, 405
Michigan State University, 408
Middlebury College, 411
Millsaps College, 413
Mills College, 416
Minnesota, University of–Morris, 418
Minnesota, University of–Twin
    Cities, 420
Missouri, University of–Columbia,
    422
Montana Tech of the University of
    Montana, 425
Morehouse College, 34
Morris Brown College, 34
Mount Holyoke College, 427
Muhlenberg College, 430

N

Nebraska, University of–Lincoln,
    432
New College of Florida, 435
New Hampshire, University of, 437
New Jersey, The College of, 440
New Jersey Institute of Technology,
    442
New Mexico, University of, 444
New Mexico Institute of Mining
    and Technology, 446
New School University–Eugene
    Lang College, 448
New York University, 451
North Carolina State University,
    461
North Carolina, University
    of–Asheville, 453
North Carolina, University
    of–Chapel Hill, 456
North Carolina, University
    of–Greensboro, 458
Northeastern University, 463
Northwestern University, 465
Notre Dame, University of, 468

O

Oberlin College, 471
Occidental College, 474

Oglethorpe University, 476
Ohio State University, 478
Ohio University, 481
Ohio Wesleyan University, 483
Oklahoma, University of, 485
Oregon, University of, 488
Oregon State University, 490

P

Pacific, University of the, 493
Pennsylvania, University of, 495
Pennsylvania State University, 499
Pepperdine University, 501
Pittsburgh, University of, 504
Pitzer College, 150
Pomona College, 152
Presbyterian College, 507
Prescott College, 509
Princeton University, 511
Principia College, 515
Puget Sound, University of, 517
Purdue University, 519

Q

Queen's University, 119

R

Randolph-Macon Woman's College,
    521
Redlands, University of, 524
Reed College, 527
Rensselaer Polytechnic Institute,
    529
Rhode Island, University of, 532
Rhode Island School of Design, 534
Rhodes College, 537
Rice University, 539
Richmond, University of, 542
Ripon College, 544
Rochester, University of, 547
Rochester Institute of Technology,
    549
Rollins College, 552
Rose-Hulman Institute of
    Technology, 554
Rutgers University, 556

S

St. John's College, 559
St. John's University and College of
    St. Benedict, 562

St. Lawrence University, 564
St. Mary's College of Maryland, 567
St. Olaf College, 569
Saint Louis University, 572
San Francisco, University of, 574
Santa Clara University, 576
Sarah Lawrence College, 579
Scripps College, 155
Skidmore College, 581
Smith College, 584
South, University of the (Sewanee), 587
South Carolina, University of, 589
Southern California, University of, 592
Southern Methodist University, 594
Southwestern University, 597
Spelman College, 36
Stanford University, 599
SUNY–Albany, 604
SUNY–Binghamton University, 606
SUNY–Buffalo, 609
SUNY–Geneseo, 611
SUNY–Purchase College, 613
SUNY–Stony Brook, 615
Stetson University, 618
Stevens Institute of Technology, 620
Susquehanna University, 623
Swarthmore College, 625
Sweet Briar College, 628
Syracuse University, 630

T

Tennessee, University of–Knoxville, 633
Texas, University of–Austin, 635
Texas A&M University, 637
Texas Christian University, 640
Texas Tech University, 642
Toronto, University of, 123
Trinity College, 644
Trinity University, 647
Truman State University, 650
Tufts University, 652
Tulane University, 655
Tulsa, University of, 657

U

Union College, 659
Ursinus College, 662
Utah, University of, 665

V

Vanderbilt University, 667
Vassar College, 670
Vermont, University of, 672
Villanova University, 675
Virginia, University of, 677
Virginia Polytechnic Institute and State University, 680

W

Wabash College, 682
Wake Forest University, 684

Washington, University of, 687
Washington and Jefferson College, 689
Washington and Lee University, 692
Washington University in St. Louis, 694
Wellesley College, 697
Wells College, 700
Wesleyan University, 702
West Virginia University, 706
Wheaton College (IL), 708
Wheaton College (MA), 710
Whitman College, 712
Whittier College, 715
Willamette University, 717
William and Mary, College of, 720
Williams College, 723
Wisconsin, University of–Madison, 726
Wittenberg University, 728
Wofford College, 731
Wooster, The College of, 733
Worcester Polytechnic Institute, 736

X

Xavier University of Louisiana, 738

Y

Yale University, 740

Acknowledgments

The *Fiske Guide to Colleges* Staff

Editor: Edward B. Fiske
Managing Editor: Robert Logue
Contributing Editor: Bruce G. Hammond
Production Coordinator: Julia Fiske Hogan

Writers: Jennifer Fernandez, Lisa Levenson, Samantha Levine, Terri Needham, Diane Oriel, Susan Saiter, Diane Oriel, Chrissa Shoemaker

College Counselor Advisory Group

The *Fiske Guide to Colleges* reflects the talents, energy, and ideas of many people. Chief among them are Robert Logue, the managing editor, and Julia Fiske Hogan, the production coordinator. I am also grateful for the continuing valuable contributions of Bruce G. Hammond, my coauthor on the *Fiske Guide to Getting into the Right College* and other resources in the field of college admissions. We are all grateful for the dedicated work of our intrepid team of writers, as well as the formidable editorial assistance of Todd Stocke, Peter Lynch, Laura Kuhn, Mollie Denman, and their talented colleagues at Sourcebooks. Special thanks are in order to Taylor Poole for the thoughtful and creative job he has done in translating our words into a thoughtful and effective design.

In the final analysis, the *Fiske Guide* is dependent on the contributions of the thousands of students and college administrators who took the time to answer detailed and demanding questionnaires. Their candor and cooperation are deeply appreciated; and while I, of course, accept full responsibility for the final product, the quality and usefulness of the book is a testimony to their thoughtful reflections on their colleges and universities.

Edward B. Fiske
Durham, NC
April 2003

Editorial Advisory Group

Nancy Beane, Atlanta, GA
Eileen Blattner, Shaker Heights, OH
Susan Case, Milton, MA
Angela Connor, Raleigh, NC
Anne Ferguson, Shaker Heights, OH
Carol Gill, Dobbs Ferry, NY
Marsha Irwin, San Francisco, CA
Margaret Johnson, San Antonio, TX

William Mason, Southborough, MC
Jane McClure, San Francisco, CA
Susan Moriarty Paton, New Haven, CT
Alice Purington, Andover, MA
Jan-Russell-Cebull, Danville, CA
Rod Skinner, Milton, MA
Phyllis Steinbrecher, Westport, CT

College Counselors Advisory Group

Marilyn Albarelli, Moravian Academy (PA)
Scott Anderson, Mercersburg Academy (PA)
Caroline Van Antwerp, Colorado Springs School (CO)
Christine Asmussen, St. Andrew's-Sewanee School (TN)
Bruce Bailey, Lakeside School (WA)
Greg Birk, Webb School of Knoxville (TN)
Clarice Boring, Cody H.S. (WY)
Mimi Bradley, St. Andrew's Episcopal School (MS)
Nancy Bryan, Pace Academy (GA)
Claire Cafaro, Ridgewood H.S. (NJ)
Nancy Caine, St. Augustine H.S. (CA)
Mary Calhoun, St. Cecilia Academy (TN)
Mary Chapman, St. Catherine's School (VA)
Anthony L. Clay, Carolina Friends School (NC)
Kathy Cleaver, Durham Academy (NC)
Alice Cotti, Polytechnic School (CA)
Alison Cotton, Cypress Falls H.S. (TX)
Rod Cox, St. Johns Country Day School (FL)
Carroll K. Davis, North Central H.S. (IN)
Renee C. Davis, Rocky River H.S. (OH)
Christy Dillon, Crystal Springs Uplands School (CA)
Walta Sue Dodd, Bryan H.S. (NE)
Ted de Villafranca, Peddie School (NJ)
Dan Feldhaus, Iolani School (HI)
Rafael S. Figueroa, Albuquerque Academy (NM)
Emily FitzHugh, Gunnery School (CT)
Larry Fletcher, Salesianum School (DE)
Nancy Fomby, Episcopal School of Dallas (TX)
Dan Franklin, Eaglecrest H.S. (CO)
Laura Johnson Frey, Vermont Academy (VT)
H. Scotte Gordon, Moses Brown School (RI)
Freida Gottsegen, Pace Academy (GA)
Madelyn Gray, John Burroughs H.S. (MO)
Phyllis Gill, Providence Day School (NC)
Amy Grieger, Northfield Mount Herman School (MA)
Andrea L. Hays, Lake Ridge Academy (OH)

Bruce Hunter, Rowland Hall-St. Mark's School (UT)
Rob Herald, Rockhurst H.S. (MO)
Darnell Heywood, Columbus School for Girls (OH)
John Keyes, The Catlin Gabel School (OR)
Sharon Koenings, Brookfield Academy (WI)
Joan Jacobson, Shawnee Mission South HS (KS)
Connie Jones, Okoboji H.S. (IA)
Laurie Leftwich, Brother Martin H.S. (LA)
Mary Jane London, Los Angeles Center for Enriched Studies (CA)
Martha Lyman, Deerfield Academy (MA)
Robert S. MacLellan, Jr., The Pingry School (NJ)
Margaret Man, La Pietra Hawaii School for Girls (HI)
Susan Marrs, The Seven Hills School (OH)
Karen A. Mason, Wyoming Seminary (PA)
Brad MacGowan, Newton North H.S. (MA)
Lisa Micele, University of Illinois Laboratory H.S. (IL)
Janet Miranda, Trinity Christian Academy (TX)
Richard Morey, Dwight-Englewood School (NJ)
Joyce Vining Morgan, Putney School (VT)
Daniel Murphy, The Urban School of San Francisco (CA)
Judith Nash, Highland H.S. (ID)
Arlene L. Prince, University Preparatory Academy (WA)
Julie Rollins, Episcopal H.S. (TX)
Deborah Robinson, Mandarin H.S. (FL)
Bill Rowe, Thomas Jefferson School (MO)
David Schindel, Vail Mountain School (CO)
Joe Stehno, Bishop Brady H.S. (NH)
Bruce Stempien, Weston H.S. (CT)
Audrey Threlkeld, Forest Ridge School of the Sacred Heart (WA)
Patricia Turner, Fenger Academy (IL)
Scott White, Montclair H.S. (NJ)
Maggie Young, Cherry Creek H.S. (CO)
Linda Zimring, Los Angeles Unified School District (CA)

About the Author

In 1980, when he was education editor of the *New York Times*, Edward B. Fiske sensed that college-bound students and their families needed better information on which to base their educational choices. Thus was born the *Fiske Guide to Colleges*. A graduate of Wesleyan University, Fiske did graduate work at Columbia University and assorted other bastions of higher learning. He left the *Times* in 1991 to pursue a variety of educational and journalistic interests, which included writing a book on school reform, *Smart Schools, Smart Kids*. When not visiting colleges, he can be found playing tennis, sailing, or doing research on the educational problems of South Africa and other Third World countries for UNESCO and other international organizations. Fiske lives in Durham, North Carolina, near the campus of Duke University, where his wife, Helen Ladd, is a member of the faculty. They are coauthors of *When Schools Compete: A Cautionary Tale*.

Notes

Notes

Notes

Notes

Notes